WORLDMARK ENCYCLOPEDIA *of* National Economies

Volume 4 – Europe

Sara Pendergast and Tom Pendergast, Editors

Detroit • New York • San Diego • San Francisco
Boston • New Haven, Conn. • Waterville, Maine
London • Munich

Jeffrey Lehman and Rebecca Parks, *Editors*
William Harmer, *Contributing Editor*
Brian J. Koski, Jeffrey Wilson, *Associate Editors*
Shelly Dickey, *Managing Editor*

Mary Beth Trimper, *Manager, Composition and Electronic Prepress*
Evi Seoud, *Assistant Manager, Composition Purchasing and Electronic Prepress*

Barbara J. Yarrow, *Manager, Imaging and Multimedia Content*
Randy Bassett, *Imaging Supervisor*
Pamela A. Reed, *Imaging Coordinator*
Leitha Etheridge-Sims, Mary K. Grimes, David G. Oblender, *Image Catalogers*
Robyn V. Young, *Project Manager, Imaging and Multimedia Content*
Robert Duncan, *Senior Imaging Specialist*
Christine O'Bryan, *Graphic Specialist*
Michelle DiMercurio, *Senior Art Director*
Susan Kelsch, *Indexing Manager*
Lynne Maday, *Indexing Specialist*

Library of Congress Control Number: 2001099714

Gale Group
27500 Drake Rd.
Farmington Hills, MI 48331-3535
http://www.galegroup.com
800-877-4253
248-699-4253

ISBN 0-7876-4955-4 (set)
Vol. 1 ISBN 0-7876-4956-2
Vol. 2 ISBN 0-7876-4957-0
Vol. 3 ISBN 0-7876-5629-1
Vol. 4 ISBN 0-7876-5630-5
Printed in the United States of America

TABLE OF CONTENTS

Countries are listed by most common name. Official country names are listed in the entries.

PREFACE

The *Worldmark Encyclopedia of National Economies* joins the Worldmark family of encyclopedias and attempts to provide comprehensive overviews of the economic structure and current climate of 198 countries and territories. Each signed entry provides key data and analysis on a country's economic conditions, their relationship to social and political trends, and their impact on the lives of the country's inhabitants. The goal of this set is to use plain language to offer intelligent, consistent analysis of every important economy in the world.

It is our sincere hope that this set will open the reader's mind to the fascinating world of international economics. Contained within this collection are a number of fascinating stories: of Eastern European nations struggling to adapt to capitalist economic systems in the wake of the collapse of communism; of Pacific Island nations threatened with annihilation by the slow and steady rise of ocean levels; of Asian nations channeling the vast productivity of their people into diversified economies; of the emerging power of the European Union, which dominates economic life across Europe; of Middle Eastern nations planning for the disappearance of their primary engine of economic growth, oil; and many others. To make all this information both accessible and comparable, each entry presents information in the same format, allowing readers to easily compare, for example, the balance of trade between Singapore and Hong Kong, or the political systems of North and South Korea. Economics has a language of its own, and we have **highlighted** those economic terms that may not be familiar to a general reader and provided definitions in a glossary. Other terms that are specific to a particular country but are not economic in nature are defined within parentheses in the text.

This set contains entries on every sovereign nation in the world, as well as separate entries on large territories of countries, including: French Guiana, Martinique, and Guadeloupe; Macau; Puerto Rico; and Taiwan. The larger dependencies of other countries are highlighted within the mother country's entry. For example, the entry on Denmark includes a discussion of Greenland, the United Kingdom includes information on many of its Crown territories, and the United States entry highlights the economic conditions in some of its larger territories.

ENTRY OBJECTIVES

Each entry has two objectives: one, to offer a clear picture of the economic conditions in a particular country, and two, to provide statistical information that allows for comparison between countries. To offer comparable information, we have used some common sources for the tables and graphs as well as for individual sections. Even the most exhaustive sources do not provide information for every country, however, and thus some entries either have no data available in certain areas or contain data that was obtained from an alternate source. In all entries, we tried to provide the most current data available at the time. Because collection and evaluation methods differ among international data gathering agencies such as the World Bank, United Nations, and International Monetary Fund, as well as between these agencies and the many government data collection agencies located in each country, entries sometimes provide two or more sources of information. Consequently, the text of an entry may contain more recent information from a different source than is provided in a table or graph, though the table or graph provides information that allows the easiest comparison to other entries.

No one source could provide all the information desired for this set, so some sources were substituted when the main source lacked information for specific countries. The main sources used included: the *World Factbook 2000* and *2001,* which provided the common information on the countries' gross domestic product (GDP) at purchasing power parity, the division of labor, balance of trade, chief imports, chief exports, and population, unless otherwise noted in the text; the World Bank's *World Development Indicators,* which was a valued source for information about the infrastructure and consumption patterns of many countries; the *Human Development Report,* from the United Nations, which provided GDP per capita information on many countries; and the International Monetary Fund's *International Financial Statistics Yearbook,* which provided historical records of trade balances for most countries. Each entry also contains a bibliography that lists additional sources that are specific to that entry.

ENTRY ORGANIZATION

All entries are organized under 16 specific headings to make it easy to find needed information quickly and to compare the conditions in several different countries easily. (The sole exception is the entry on the Vatican, whose unique features necessitated the removal of several sections.) The sections are as follows:

COUNTRY OVERVIEW. This section includes information about the size of all land surfaces, describing coastlines and international boundaries. It also highlights significant geographical features in the country and the location of the capital. The size of the country is compared to a U.S. state or, for smaller countries, to Washington, D.C. Also included is information on the total population, as well as other important demographic data concerning ethnicity, religion, age, and urbanization. Where relevant, this section also includes information about internal conflicts, major health problems, or significant population policies.

OVERVIEW OF ECONOMY. This overview is meant to provide an analysis of the country's overall economic conditions, mentioning those elements that are deemed most important to an understanding of the country. It provides context for the reader to understand the more specific information available in the other sections.

POLITICS, GOVERNMENT, AND TAXATION. This section identifies the structure of the government and discusses the role the government, political parties, and taxes play in the economy.

INFRASTRUCTURE, POWER, AND COMMUNICATIONS. This section offers a description of the roads, railways, harbors, and telecommunications available in the country, assesses the modernity of the systems, and provides information about the country's plans for improvements.

ECONOMIC SECTORS. This section serves as an overview for the three more specific sections that follow, providing a general description of the balance between the country's different economic sectors.

AGRICULTURE. This section discusses the agriculture, fishing, and forestry sectors of the country.

INDUSTRY. This section discusses the industrial sector of the country, including specific information on mining, manufacturing, and other major industries, where appropriate.

SERVICES. This section concentrates on major components of the diverse services sector, usually focusing on the tourism and banking or financial sectors and sometimes including descriptions of the retail sector.

INTERNATIONAL TRADE. This section focuses on the country's patterns of trade, including the commodities traded and the historical trading partners.

MONEY. This section offers a brief description of the changes in inflation and the exchange rates in the country, and the impact those may have had on the economy. It also mentions any recent changes in the currency and the nature and impact of the central banking function.

POVERTY AND WEALTH. This section paints a picture of the distribution of wealth within the country, often comparing life in the country with that in other countries in the region. It includes governmental efforts to redistribute wealth or to deal with pressing issues of poverty.

WORKING CONDITIONS. This section describes the workforce, its ability to unionize, and the effectiveness of unions within the country. It also often includes information on wages, significant changes in the workforce over time, and the existence of protections for workers.

COUNTRY HISTORY AND ECONOMIC DEVELOPMENT. This section provides a timeline of events that shaped the country and its economy. The selected events create a more cohesive picture of the nation than could be described in the entries because of their bias toward more current information.

FUTURE TRENDS. To provide readers with a view to the future, the entry ends with an analysis of how the economic conditions in the country are expected to change in the near future. It also highlights any significant challenges the country may face.

DEPENDENCIES. This section discusses any major territories or colonies and their economies.

BIBLIOGRAPHY. The bibliography at the end of the entry lists the sources used to compile the information in the entry and also includes other materials that may be of interest to readers wanting more information about the particular country. Although specific online sources are cited, many such sources are updated annually and should be expected to change.

In addition, a data box at the beginning of each entry offers helpful economic "quick facts" such as the country's capital, monetary unit, chief exports and imports, gross domestic product (GDP), and the balance of trade. The U.S. Central Intelligence Agency's *World Factbook* (2000 and 2001) was the main source of this information unless otherwise noted. Each entry also includes a map that illustrates the location of the country. Since economic conditions are often affected by geography, the map allows readers to see the location of major cities and landmarks. The map also names bordering countries to offer readers a visual aid to understand regional conflicts and trading routes.

ACKNOWLEDGMENTS

We wish to thank all those involved in this project for their efforts. This set could not have been produced without the unfailing support of the publisher and our imaginative advisory board. At the Gale Group, managing editor Shelly Dickey and Peggy Glahn in New Product Development were especially helpful. We would also like to thank Gale editor William Harmer for his work in the early stages of the project, but special thanks must go to editors Rebecca Parks and Jeffrey Lehman who brought the set to publication. Copyeditors Edward Moran, Robyn Karney, Karl Rahder, Jennifer Wallace, and Mary Sugar must also be commended for their work to polish the entries into the form you see here.

COMMENTS

We encourage you to contact us with any comments or suggestions you may have that will benefit future editions of this set. We want this set to be a meaningful addition to your search for information about the world. Please send your comments and suggestions to: The Editors, *Worldmark Encyclopedia of National Economies,* The Gale Group, 27500 Drake Road, Farmington Hills, MI 48331. Or, call toll free at 1-800-877-4253.

—Sara Pendergast and Tom Pendergast

NOTES ON CONTRIBUTORS

Abazov, Rafis. Professor, Department of Politics, LaTrobe University, Victoria, Australia. Author, *Formation of the Post-Soviet Foreign Policies in Central Asian Republics* (1999), and annual security and economic reports, *Brassey's Security Yearbook*, and Transitions Online.

Abazova, Alfia. LaTrobe University, Victoria, Australia. Reviewed for *Pacifica Review* and *Europe-Asia Studies.*

Amineh, Parvizi Mehdi, Ph.D. Department of Political Science, University of Amsterdam, the Netherlands. Author, *Towards the Control of Oil Resources in the Caspian Region* (New York: St. Martin's Press, 1999); *Die Globale Kapitalistische Expansion und Iran: Eine Studie der Iranischen Politischen Ökonomie (1500–1980)* (Hamburg-London: Lit Verlag).

Arnade, Charles W. Adviser. Distinguished Professor of International Studies, University of South Florida. Author, *The Emergence of the Republic of Bolivia.*

Audain, Linz, M.D., J.D., Ph.D. Staff physician, Greater Southeast, INOVA Fairfax and Southern Maryland hospitals; former professor of law, economics, and statistics at various universities; editor, *Foreign Trade of the United States* (2nd ed.), *Business Statistics of the United States* (6th ed.).

Benoit, Kenneth, Ph.D. Lecturer, Department of Political Science, Trinity College, University of Dublin, Ireland.

Bouillon, Markus R. Doctoral student in international relations with a regional focus on the Middle East, St. Antony's College, University of Oxford.

Burron, Neil. Graduate student in International Development, The Norman Paterson School of International Affairs, Carleton University, Ottawa.

Campling, Liam. Lecturer in International Politics and History, Seychelles Polytechnic (University of Manchester Twinning Programme). Editor, *Historical Materialism—Special Issue: Focus on Sub-Saharan Africa* (2002). Contributor to *West Africa* and *African Business* magazines.

Carper, Mark Daniel Lynn. Instructor of Geography, Central Missouri State University.

Cavatorta, Francesco. Doctoral candidate in the Department of Political Science, Trinity College, Dublin, Ireland. Author, "The Italian Political System and the Northern League," in *Contemporary Politics,* March 2001.

Chari, Raj. Lecturer, Department of Political Science, Trinity College, Dublin, Ireland. Author, "Spanish Socialists, Privatising the Right Way?" in *West European Politics,* Vol. 21, No. 4, October 1998, and "The March 2000 Spanish Election: A 'Critical Election'?" in *West European Politics,* Vol. 23, No. 3, July 2000.

Chauvin, Lucien O. Freelance journalist, Lima, Peru. President of the Foreign Press Association of Peru.

Childree, David L. Graduate student in Latin American Studies at Tulane University, specializing in politics and development.

Conteh-Morgan, Earl. Professor, Department of Government and International Affairs, University of South Florida, Tampa, Florida. Co-author, *Sierra Leone at the End of the 20th Century* (1999).

Costa, Ecio F., Ph.D. Post-doctoral associate, Center for Agribusiness and Economic Development, Department of Agricultural and Applied Economics, University of Georgia, Athens, Georgia. Author, "Brazil's New Floating Exchange Rate Regime and Competitiveness in the World Poultry Market," in *Journal of Agricultural and Applied Economics.*

Cunha, Stephen, Ph.D. Professor of Geography, Humboldt State University, Arcata, California. Consultant, USAID, World Bank, National Geographic Society.

Davoudi, Salamander. Graduate student in Middle Eastern economics, Georgetown University, Washington, D.C. Former aid at the Royal Jordanian Hashemite Court.

Deletis, Katarina. M.I.A. (Master of International Affairs), Columbia University, New York. International communications officer, Deloitte Touche Tohmatsu, New York.

Divisekera, Sarath. Ph.D., School of Applied Economics, Victoria University, Melbourne, Australia. Author, *Income Distribution, Inequality and Poverty in Sri Lanka* (1988).

Eames, Rory. Honors student, School of Resources, Environment, and Society, The Australian National University, Canberra, Australia.

Easton, Matthew. Independent consultant, Cambridge, Massachusetts. Author, *In the Name of Development: Human Rights and the World Bank in Indonesia* (1995).

Feoli, Ludovico. Graduate student in Latin American Studies, Tulane University, New Orleans, Louisiana. Publications director and academic coordinator, CIAPA, San José, Costa Rica.

Ferguson, James. Writer and researcher specializing in the Caribbean. Author, *A Traveller's History of the Caribbean* (1999).

Florkowski, Wojciech J. Associate professor, Department of Agricultural and Applied Economics, University of Georgia.

Foley, Sean. Ph.D. candidate, History, Georgetown University, Washington, D.C. Author of various articles and a chapter in *Crises and Quandaries in the Contemporary Persian Gulf* (2001).

Foroughi, Payam. Ph.D. student in International Relations, University of Utah. International development consultant, NGOs, USAID, and the United Nations, Central Asia; freelance writer.

Friesen, Wardlow. Senior lecturer, Department of Geography, The University of Auckland, New Zealand. Author, "Tangata Pasifika Aotearoa: Pacific Populations and Identity in New Zealand," in *New Zealand Population Review,* Vol. 26, No. 2, 2000; "Circulation, Urbanisation, and the Youth Boom in Melanesia," in *Espace, Populations, Sociétés,* Vol. 2, 1994; "Melanesian Economy on the Periphery: Migration and Village Economy in Choiseul," in *Pacific Viewpoint,* Vol. 34, No. 2, 1993.

Fry, Gerald W. Adviser. Professor of International/Intercultural Education, and director of Graduate Studies, Department of Educational Policy and Administration, University of Minnesota—Twin Cities; former team leader on major Asian Development Bank funded projects in Southeast Asia.

Gazis, Alexander. Commercial specialist, U.S. Embassy, N'Djamena, Chad. Author, *Country Commercial Guides* for Chad (Fiscal Year 2001 and 2002).

Genc, Emine, M.A. Budget expert, Ministry of Finance, Ankara, Turkey.

Genc, Ismail H., Ph.D. Assistant professor of Economics, University of Idaho, Moscow, Idaho.

Gleason, Gregory. Professor, University of New Mexico. Former director, USAID Rule of Law Program in Central Asia.

Guillen, April J., J.D./M.A. International Relations candidate, University of Southern California, Los Angeles, with an emphasis on International Human Rights Law.

Hadjiyski, Valentin, Ph.D. New York-based freelance author, former United Nations expert.

Hodd, Jack. Queen's College, Cambridge, researching graphical presentations of general equilibrium models.

Hodd, Michael R. V. Adviser. Professor of Economics, University of Westminster, London, and has worked as a consultant for the ILO and UNIDO. Author, *African Economic Handbook,* London, Euromonitor, 1986; *The Economies of Africa,* Aldershot, Dartmouth, 1991; with others, *Fisheries and Development in Tanzania,* London, Macmillan, 1994.

Iltanen, Suvi. Graduate of the European Studies Programme, Trinity College, Dublin, Ireland.

Jensen, Nathan. Ph.D. candidate in political science, Yale University, and visiting scholar at UCLA's International Studies and Overseas Programs. He is currently completing his dissertation titled "The Political Economy of Foreign Direct Investment."

Jugenitz, Heidi. Graduate student in Latin American Studies, Tulane University, New Orleans, Louisiana. Research assistant, Payson Center for International Development and Technology Transfer.

Kiyak, Tunga. Ph.D. candidate in marketing and international business, Michigan State University. Research assistant, Center for International Business Education and Research (MSU-CIBER). Curator, International Business Resources on the WWW.

Kuznetsova, Olga. Senior research fellow, The Manchester Metropolitan University Business School, Manchester, UK. Author, *The CIS Handbook. Regional Handbooks of Economic Development: Prospects onto the 21st Century,* edited by P. Heenan and M. Lamontagne (1999).

Lang-Tigchelaar, Amy. Graduate student in joint MBA/MA in Latin American Studies Program, Tulane University, New Orleans, Louisiana.

Lansford, Tom. Assistant professor, University of Southern Mississippi, Gulf Coast. Author, *Evolution and Devolution: The Dynamics of Sovereignty and Security in Post-Cold War Europe* (2000).

Lynch, Catherine. Doctoral candidate in political science, Dublin City University, Ireland. Areas of interest include the political economy of implementing peace agreements, the politics of peace building, the implementation of policy, and other aspects of comparative political science.

Mahoney, Lynn. M.A., University of Michigan. Associate director of development, director of communications, American University of Beirut New York Office; freelance writer.

Mann, Larisa. Graduate student of economic history, cultural studies, and legal studies, London School of Economics. Presented "Shaky Ground, Thin Air: Intellectual Property Law and the Jamaican Music Industry" at the "Rethinking Caribbean Culture" conference at the University of West Indies, Cave Hill, Barbados.

Mazor, John. Writer and journalist specializing in economic and political issues in Latin America and the Levant. Graduated from Boston University with a degree in literature and studied intelligence and national security policy at the Institute of World Politics in Washington, D.C.

Mobekk, Eirin. MacArthur postdoctoral research associate, Department of War Studies, King's College, London, United Kingdom.

Mowatt, Rosalind. Graduate student in Economics, Wits University, Johannesburg, South Africa. Former economist for National Treasury, working with Southern African Development Community (SADC) countries.

Muhutdinova-Foroughi, Raissa. M.P.A., University of Colorado at Denver. Journalist, Radio Tajikistan; consultant, United Nations, World Bank, and Eurasia Foundation, Commonwealth of Independent Nations; freelance writer.

Mukungu, Allan C. K. Graduate student, University of Westminster, London, and has done consultancy work for the World Bank.

Musakhanova, Oygul. Graduate, University of Westminster; economist, Arthur Anderson, Tashkent, Uzbekistan.

Naidu, Sujatha. LL.M. in Environment Law, University of Utah. Ph.D. student in International Relations, Department of Political Science, University of Utah; freelance writer.

Nicholls, Ana. Journalist. Assistant editor, *Business Central Europe,* The Economist Group. Author of three surveys of Romania.

Nicoleau, Michael. J.D. Cornell Law School, Ithaca, New York. Co-author, "Constitutional Governance in the Democratic Republic of the Congo: An Analysis of the Constitution Proposed by the Government of Laurent Kabila," in *Texas International Law Journal,* Spring 2000.

Nuseibeh, Reem. Graduate student in Comparative Politics/Human Rights, University of Maryland, Maryland. Middle East risk analyst, Kroll Information Services, Vienna, Virginia.

Ó Beacháin, Donnacha. Ph.D. Political Science from National University of Ireland, Dublin. Civic Education Project visiting lecturer at the Departments of International Relations and Conflict Resolution at Tbilisi State University and the Georgian Technical University, respectively, 2000–2002.

Ohaegbulam, F. Ugboaja. Professor, Government and International Affairs, University of South Florida. Author, *A Concise Introduction to American Foreign Policy* (1999), and *Nigeria and the UN Mission to the Democratic Republic of the Congo* (1982).

O'Malley, Eoin. Doctoral candidate in Political Science at Trinity College, Dublin, and visiting researcher at UNED, Madrid, Spain. Author, "Ireland" in Annual Review section of the *European Journal of Political Research* (1999, 2000, 2001).

Ozsoz, Emre. Graduate student in International Political Economy and Development, Fordham University, New York. Editorial assistant for the Middle East, The Economist Intelligence Unit, New York.

Peimani, Hooman, Ph.D. Independent consultant with international organizations in Geneva, Switzerland. Author, *The Caspian Pipeline Dilemma: Political Games and Economic Losses* (2001).

Pretes, Michael. Research scholar, Department of Human Geography, Research School of Pacific and Asian Studies, The Australian National University, Canberra, Australia.

Sabol, Steven. Ph.D., the University of North Carolina at Charlotte. Author, *Awake Kazak! Russian Colonization of Central Asia and the Genesis of Kazak National Consciousness, 1868–1920.*

Samonis, Val, Ph.D., C.P.C. Managed and/or participated in international research and advisory projects/teams sponsored by the Hudson Institute, World Bank, CASE Warsaw, Soros Foundations, the Center for European Integration Studies (ZEI Bonn), the Swedish government, and a number of other clients. Also worked with top reformers such as the Polish Deputy Prime Minister Leszek Balcerowicz, U.S. Treasury Secretary Larry Summers, the World Bank, and OECD Private Sector Advisory Group on Corporate Governance, and with the Stanford Economic Transition Group; advisor to the Czech government (Deputy Prime Minister Pavel Mertlik), the Lithuanian parliament, and several Lithuanian governments, international organizations, and multinational corporations; founding editor, *Journal of East-West Business* (The Haworth Press Inc).

Sezgin, Yuksel. Ph.D. candidate in Political Science, University of Washington. Former assistant Middle East coordinator at the Foreign Economic Relations Board of Turkey.

Schubert, Alexander. Ph.D., Cornell University.

Scott, Cleve Mc D. Ph.D. candidate and graduate assistant, Department of History, University of the West Indies, Cave Hill Campus, Barbados.

Stobwasser, Ralph. Graduate student in Middle Eastern Studies, FU Berlin, Germany. Worked in the Office of the Chief Economist Middle East and North Africa, World Bank, Washington, D.C.

Strnad, Tomas. Ph.D. student, Department of the Middle East and Africa, Charles University, Czech Republic. Chief editor of the *Arab Markets Magazine*; author of "The Kuwaiti Dilemma," "OPEC—Main Sinner or Sheer Scapegoat?," and "Globalization in the Arab and Muslim World" in *International Policy* and other magazines.

Stroschein, Sherrill. Assistant professor of Political Science, Ohio University. Frequent contributor to scholarly journals on East European topics and a former contributor to *Nations in Transit* (1995 and 1997 editions).

Thadathil, George. Associate professor of History, Paul Quinn College, Dallas, Texas. Author, "Myanmar, Agony of a People" in *History Behind Headlines*, 2000. His research interests include South and Southeast Asia, and Asian collective security.

Thapa, Rabi. Editor and environmentalist, France. Environment/development assignments in Nepal, 1998.

Tian, Robert Guang, Ph.D. Associate professor of Business Administration, Erskine College. Author, *Canadian Chinese, Chinese Canadians: Coping and Adapting in North America* (1999).

Ubarra, Maria Cecilia T. Graduate student in Public Policy and Program Administration, University of the Philippines, Quezon City, Philippines. Research fellow, Institute for Strategic and Development Studies; case writer, Asian Institute of Management, Philippines.

Vivas, Leonardo. M.Phil., Development Studies, Sussex University (UK); Ph.D., International Economics and Finance, Nanterre University (France); fellow, Weatherhead Center for International Affairs, Harvard University.

Viviers, Wilma. Program director, International Trade in School of Economics, Potchefstroom University, South Africa.

Zhang, Xingli. Ph.D. student, University of Southern California, Los Angeles. Author, "Brunei" in *East Asian Encyclopedia* (in Chinese).

INTRODUCTION

THE POWER OF ECONOMIC UNDERSTANDING

The economies of the world are becoming increasingly interconnected and interdependent, a fact dramatically illustrated on 2 July 1997 when the Thai government decided to allow its currency to "float" according to market conditions. The result was a significant drop in the value of the currency and the start of the Asian economic crisis, a contagion that spread quickly to other Asian countries such as the Republic of Korea, Indonesia, Malaysia, and the Philippines. Before long the epidemic reached Brazil and Russia.

In this way, a small economic change in one less-developed country sent economic shock waves around the world. Surprisingly, no one predicted this crisis, though economist Paul Krugman in a prominent 1994 *Foreign Affairs* article argued that there was no Asian economic miracle and the kind of growth rates attained in recent years were not sustainable over the long term. In such an interconnected global economy, it is imperative to have an understanding of other economies and economic conditions around the world. Yet that understanding is sorely lacking in the American public.

Various studies have shown that both young people and the public at large have a low level of literacy about other nations. A survey of 655 high school students in southeast Ohio indicated that students were least informed in the area of international economic concerns, and the number of economics majors at the college level is declining. The economic and geographic illiteracy has become such a national concern that the U.S. Senate recently passed a resolution calling for a national education policy that addresses Americans' lack of knowledge of other parts of the world.

The information provided by the media also frequently reflects a distorted understanding of world economies. During the Asian economic crisis, we often heard about the collapse of various Asian countries such as Korea and Thailand. They were indeed suffering a severe crisis, but usually companies, not countries, collapse. The use of the "collapse" language was therefore misleading. In another example, a distinguished journalist writing in a prominent East coast newspaper claimed that Vietnamese women paid more in transportation and food costs than they were earning while working in a factory manufacturing Nike shoes. Such a statement, while well intended in terms of genuine concern for these women workers, makes no economic sense whatsoever, and is actually not accurate. The wages of these women are indeed extremely low by U.S. standards, but such wages must be viewed in the context of another society, where the cost of living may be dramatically lower and where low salaries may be pooled. At other times, a fact—such as the fact that a minority of the Japanese workforce enjoys employment for life—is exaggerated to suggest that the Japanese economy boomed as it did in the 1980s *because* of the Japanese policy of life-long employment. Such generalizing keeps people from understanding the complexities of the Japanese economy.

"THINGS ARE NOT WHAT THEY SEEM." In defense of this lack of economic understanding, it must be said that understanding economics is not easy. Paul A. Samuelson, author of the classic textbook *Economics* (1995), once stated about economics "that things are often not what at first they seem." In Japan, for example, many young women work as office ladies in private companies as an initial job after completing school. These young ladies often stay at home with their parents and have few basic expenses. Over several years they can accumulate considerable savings, which may be used for travel, overseas study, or investing. Thus, as Samuelson noted in his textbook, actual individual economic welfare is not based on wages as such, but on the *difference* between earnings and expenditures. Wages are not the only measure of the value of labor: one must also consider purchasing power and how costs of living vary dramatically from place to place. Without taking into account purchasing power, we overestimate economic well-being in high-cost countries such as Japan and Switzerland and underestimate it in low-cost countries such as India and Cambodia.

Consider the following examples: The cost of taking an air-conditioned luxury bus from the Cambodian capital of Phnom Penh to its major port, Sihanoukville, is less than $2. The same bus trip of equal distance in Japan or the United States would cost $50 or more. Similarly, a (subsidized) lunch at a factory producing Nike shoes in Vietnam may cost the equivalent of 5 U.S. cents in 1998, while lunch at a student union on a U.S. college campus may cost $5. Thus a teaching assistant on a U.S. campus pays 100 times more for lunch than the Vietnamese factory worker. Who is more "poorly paid" in these situations? Add to this the reality that in many developing countries where extended families are common, members of the family often pool their earnings, which individually may be quite low. To look only at individual earnings can thus be rather misleading. Such cultural nuances are important to keep in mind in assessing economic conditions and welfare in other nations.

Various economic puzzles can also create confusion and misunderstanding. For example, currently the United States has the highest trade deficit in world history: it imports far more that it exports. Most countries with huge trade deficits have a weak currency, but the U.S. dollar has remained strong. Why is this the case? Actually, it is quite understandable when one knows that the balance of trade is just one of many factors that determine the value of a nation's currency. In truth, demand for the U.S. dollar has remained high. The United States is an attractive site for foreign investment because of its large and growing economic market and extremely stable politics. Second, the United States has a large tourism sector, drawing people to the country where they exchange their currency for U.S. dollars. Several years ago, for the first time ever, there were more Thais coming to the United States as tourists than those in the United States going to Thailand. Third, the United States is extremely popular among international students seeking overseas education. Economically, a German student who spends three years studying in the United States benefits the economy in the same way as a long-term tourist or conventional exports: that student invests in the U.S. economy. In the academic year 1999-2000, there were 514,723 international students in the United States spending approximately $12.3 billion. Thus, the services provided by U.S. higher education represent an important "invisible export." Fourth, 11 economies are now dollarized, which means that they use the U.S. currency as their national currency. Panama is the most well known of these economies and El Salvador became a dollarized economy on 1 January 2001. Other countries are semi-officially or partially dollarized (Cambodia and Vietnam, for example). As the result of dollarization, it is estimated by the Federal Reserve that 55 to 70 percent of all U.S. dollars are held by foreigners primarily in Latin America and former parts of the U.S.S.R. Future candidates for dollarization are Argentina, Brazil, Ecuador, Indonesia, Mexico, and even Canada. With so many countries using U.S. dollars, demand for the U.S. dollar is increased, adding to its strength. For all these reasons, the U.S. currency and economy remained strong despite the persisting large trade deficits, which in themselves, according to standard economic logic, suggest weakness.

SYSTEMS OF CLASSIFICATION. As in other fields, such as biology and botany, it is important to have a sound system of classification to understand various national economies. Unfortunately, the systems commonly used to describe various national economies are often flawed by cultural and Eurocentric biases and distortion. After the end of World War II and the start of the Cold War, it became common to speak of "developed" and "underdeveloped" countries. There were two problems with this overly simplistic distinction. First, it viewed countries only in terms of material development. Second, it implied that a nation was developed or underdeveloped across all categories. As an example, "underdeveloped" Thailand has consistently been one of the world's leading food exporters and among those countries that import the least amount of food. Similarly, in "developed" Japan there are both homeless people and institutions to house the elderly, while in "underdeveloped" Vietnam there are no homeless and the elderly are cared for by their families. Which country is more "developed"?

Later the term "Third World" became popular. This term was invented by the French demographer Alfred Sauvy and popularized by the scholar Irving Horowitz in his volume, *Three Worlds of Development.* "First World" referred to rich democracies such as the United States and the United Kingdom; "Second World" referred to communist countries such as the former U.S.S.R. and former East Germany. The term "Third World" was used to refer to the poorer nations of Africa, Latin America, and Asia (with the exception of Japan). But this distinction is also problematic, for it implies that the "First World" is superior to the "Third World." Another common term introduced was modern versus less modern nations. The Princeton sociologist Marion J. Levy made this distinction based on a technological definition: more modern nations were those that made greater use of tools and inanimate sources of power. Thus, non-Western Japan is quite modern because of its use of robots and bullet trains. Over time, however, many people criticized the modern/non-modern distinction as being culturally biased and implying that all nations had to follow the same path of progress.

More recently, economists from around the world have recognized the importance of using a variety of factors to understand the development of national economies. Each of these factors should be viewed in terms of a continuum. For example, no country is either completely industrial or completely agricultural. The entries in this volume provide the basic data to assess each national economy on several of these key criteria. One can determine, for example, the extent to which an economy is industrial by simply dividing the percentage of the economy made up by industry by the percentage made up by agriculture. Or one can determine how much energy national economies use to achieve their level of economic output and welfare. This provides an important ecological definition of efficiency, which goes beyond limited material definitions. This measure allows an estimate of how "green" versus "gray" an economy is; greener economies are those using less energy to achieve a given level of economic development. One might like to understand how international an economy is, which can be done by adding a country's exports to its imports and then dividing by GDP. This indicator reveals that economies such as the Netherlands, Malaysia, Singapore, and Hong Kong are highly international while the isolationist Democratic People's Republic of Korea (North Korea) is far less international.

Another interesting measure of an economy, particularly relevant in this age of more information-oriented economies and "the death of distance" (Cairncross 1997), is the extent to which an economy is digitalized. One measure of this factor would be the extent to which the population of a given economy has access to the Internet. Costa Rica, for example, established a national policy that all its citizens should have free access to the Internet. In other economies, such as Bhutan, Laos, and North Korea, access to the Internet is extremely limited. These differences, of course, relate to what has been termed "the digital divide." Another important factor is whether an economy is people-oriented, that is, whether it aims to provide the greatest happiness to the greatest number; economist E.F. Schumacher called this "economics as if people mattered." The King of Bhutan, for example, has candidly stated that his goal for his Buddhist nation is not Gross National Product but instead Gross National Happiness. Such goals indicate that the level of a country's economic development does not necessarily reflect its level of social welfare and quality of life.

Another important category that helps us understand economies is the degree to which they can be considered "transitional." Transitional economies are those that were once communist, state-planned economies but that are becoming or have become free-market economies. This transitional process started in China in the late 1970s when its leader Deng Xiaoping introduced his "four modernizations." Later, Soviet leader Mikhael Gorbachev introduced such reforms, called *perestroika,* in the former Soviet Union. With the dissolving of the U.S.S.R. in 1991, many new transitional economies emerged, including Belarus, Uzbekistan, Kyrgyzstan, and the Ukraine. Other countries undergoing transition were Vietnam, Laos, Cambodia, and Mongolia. These economies can be grouped into two types: full transitional and partial transitional. The full transitional economies are shifting both to free markets and to liberal democracies with free expression, multiple parties, and open elections. The partial transitional economies are changing in the economic realm, but retaining their original one-party systems. Included in the latter category are the economies of China, Vietnam, Laos, and Cuba. This volume provides valuable current information on the many new transitional economies emerging from the former Soviet world.

KEY THEMES IN THE WORLD ECONOMY. In looking at the economies of countries around the globe, a number of major common themes can be identified. There is increasing economic interdependence and interconnectivity, as stressed by Thomas Friedman in his recent controversial book about globalization titled *The Lexus and the Olive Tree: Understanding Globalization.* For example, the People's Republic of China is now highly dependent on exports to the United States. In turn, U.S. companies are dependent on the Chinese market: Boeing is dependent on China for marketing its jet airliners; the second largest market for Mastercard is now in China; and Nike is highly dependent on China and other Asian economies for manufacturing its sports products. Such deep interdependence augurs well for a peaceful century, for countries are less likely to attack the countries with whom they do a vigorous business, even if their political and social systems are radically different. In fact, new threats to peace as reflected in the tragic terrorist attack of 11 September 2001, primarily relate to long-standing *historical* conflicts and grievances.

Conventional political boundaries and borders often do not well reflect new economic realities and cultural patterns. Economic regions and region states are becoming more important. The still-emerging power of the European Union can be gauged by reading the essays of any of the countries that are currently part of the Union or hoping to become a part of it in the coming years. This volume may help readers better understand which nations are becoming more interconnected and have similar economic conditions.

The tension between equity (fairness) and efficiency is common in nearly all national economies. In some economies there is more stress on efficiency, while in others there is more stress on equity and equality. Thus, as should be expected, countries differ in the nature of the equality of their income and wealth distributions. For each entry in this volume, important data are provided on this important factor. The geographer David M. Smith has documented well both national and international inequalities in his data-rich *Where the Grass is Greener* (1979).

Invisible and informal economies—the interactions of which are outside regulated economic channels—represent a growing segment of economic interactions in some countries. In his controversial but important volume, *The Other Path* (1989), the Peruvian economist Hernando de Soto alerted us to the growing significance of the informal economy. In countries such as Peru, research has shown that in some cases individuals prefer work in the informal to the formal sector because it provides them with more control over their personal lives. The Thai economist Pasuk Phongpaichit and her colleagues have written a fascinating book on Thailand's substantial invisible economy titled *Guns, Girls, Gambling, and Ganja* (1998). Thus, official government and international statistical data reported in this volume often are unable to take into account such data from the hidden part of economies.

In an increasingly internationalized economy in which transnational corporations are highly mobile and able to move manufacturing overseas quite rapidly, it is important to distinguish between real foreign direct investment and portfolio investment. At one point during Thailand's impressive economic boom of the late 1980s and early 1990s, a new Japanese factory was coming on line every three days. This is foreign direct investment, involving actual bricks and mortar, and it creates jobs that extend beyond the actual facility being constructed. In contrast foreign portfolio investment consists of a foreign entity buying stocks, bonds, or other financial instruments in another nation. In our current wired global economy, such funds can be moved in and out of nations almost instantaneously and have little lasting effect on the economic growth of a country. Economies such as Chile and Malaysia have developed policies to try to combat uncertainty and related economic instability caused by the potential of quick withdrawal of portfolio investments.

Some argue that transnational corporations (owned by individuals all over the world), which have no national loyalties, represent the most powerful political force in the world today. Many key transnational corporations have larger revenues than the entire gross national products of many of the nations included in this volume. This means that many national economies, especially smaller ones, lack effective bargaining power in dealing with large international corporations.

Currently, it is estimated by the International Labor Office of the United Nations that one-third of the world's workforce is currently unemployed or underemployed. This means that 500 million new jobs need to be created over the next 10 years. Data on the employment situation in each economy are presented in this volume. The creation of these new jobs represents a major challenge to the world's economies.

The final and most important theme relates to the ultimate potential clash between economy and ecology. To the extent that various national economies and their peoples show a commitment to become greener and more environmentally friendly, ultimate ecological crises and catastrophes can be avoided or minimized. Paul Ray and Sherry Anderson's *The Cultural Creatives: How 50 Million People Are Changing the World* (2000) lends credence to the view that millions are changing to more environmentally conscious lifestyles.

In trying to understand the global economy, it is critically important to have good trend data. In each of the entries of this volume, there is an emphasis on providing important economic data over several decades to enable the reader to assess such patterns. Some trends will have tremendous importance for the global economy. One phenomenon with extremely important implications for population is the policy of limiting families to only one child in China's urban areas. This deliberate social engineering by the world's most populous country will have a powerful impact on the global economy of the 21st century. The global environmental implications are, of course, extremely positive. Though there is much debate about the economic, political, and socio-cultural implications of this one-child policy, overall it will probably give China a tremendous strategic advantage in terms of the key factors of human resource development and creativity.

THE POWER OF UNDERSTANDING. By enhancing our knowledge and understanding of other economies, we gain the potential for mutual learning and inspiration for continuous improvement. There is so much that we can learn from each other. Denmark, for example, is now getting seven percent of its electrical energy from wind energy. This has obvious relevance to the state of California as it faces a major energy crisis. The Netherlands and China for a long period have utilized bicycles for basic transportation. Some argue that the bicycle is the most efficient "tool" in the world in terms of output and energy inputs. Many new major highways in Vietnam are built with exclusive bike paths separated by concrete walls from the main highway. The Vietnamese have also developed electric bicycles. The efficient bullet trains of Japan and France have relevance to other areas such as coastal China and the coastal United States. Kathmandu in Nepal has experimented with non-polluting electric buses. In the tremendous biodiversity of the tropical forests of Southeast Africa, Latin America, and Africa, there may be cures for many modern diseases.

We hope to dispel the view that economics is the boring "dismal science" often written in complex, difficult language. This four-volume set presents concise, current information on all the economies of the world, including not only large well-known economies such as the United States, Germany, and Japan, but also new nations that have emerged only in recent years, and many micro-states of which we tend to be extremely uninformed. With the publication of this volume, we hope to be responsive to the following call by Professor Mark C. Schug: "The goal of economic education is to foster in students the thinking skills and substantial economic knowledge necessary to become effective and participating citizens." It is our hope that this set will enhance both economic and geographic literacy critically needed in an increasingly interconnected world.

—Gerald W. Fry, University of Minnesota

BIBLIOGRAPHY

Brown, Lester R., et al. *State of the World 2000.* New York: W. W. Norton, 2000.

Buchholz, Todd G. *From Here to Economy: A Shortcut to Economic Literacy.* New York: A Dutton Book, 1995.

Cairncross, Frances. *The Death of Distance: How the Communications Revolution Will Change Our Lives.* Boston: Harvard Business School Press, 2001.

Friedman, Thomas F. *The Lexus and the Olive Tree: Understanding Globalization.* New York: Anchor Books, 2000.

Fry, Gerald W., and Galen Martin. *The International Development Dictionary.* Oxford: ABC-Clio Press, 1991.

Hansen, Fay. "Power to the Dollar, Part One of a Series," *Business Finance* (October 1999): 17-20.

Heintz, James, Nancy Folbre, and the Center for Popular Economics. *The Ultimate Field Guide to the U.S. Economy.* New York: The New Press, 2000.

Horowitz, Irving J. *Three Worlds of Development: The Theory and Practice of International Stratification.* New York: Oxford University Press, 1966.

Jacobs, Jane. *The Nature of Economies.* New York: The Modern Library, 2000.

Korten, David C. *When Corporations Rule the World.* West Hartford, CT: Kumarian Press, 1995.

Levy, Marion J. *Modernization and the Structure of Societies.* 2 vols. New Brunswick, NJ: Transaction Publications, 1996.

Lewis, Martin W., and Kären E. Wigen. *A Critique of Metageography.* Berkeley: University of California Press, 1997.

Lohrenz, Edward. *The Essence of Chaos.* Seattle: University of Washington Press, 1993.

Ohmae, Kenichi. *The End of the Nation State: The Rise of Regional Economies.* London: HarperCollins, 1996.

Pasuk Phongpaichit, Sungsidh Priryarangsan, and Nualnoi Treerat. *Guns, Girls, Gambling, and Ganja: Thailand's Illegal Economy and Public Policy.* Chiang Mai: Silkworm Books, 1998.

Pennar, Karen. "Economics Made Too Simple." *Business Week* (20 January 1997): 32.

Ray, Paul H., and Sherry Ruth Anderson. *The Cultural Creatives: How 50 Million People Are Changing the World.* New York: Harmony Books, 2000.

Salk, Jonas, and Jonathan Salk. *World Population and Human Values: A New Reality.* New York: Harper & Row, 1981.

Samuelson, Paul A., William D. Nordhaus, with the assistance of Michael J. Mandal. *Economics.* 15th ed. New York: McGraw-Hill, 1995.

Schug, Mark C. "Introducing Children to Economic Reasoning: Some Beginning Lessons." *Social Studies* (Vol. 87, No. 3, May-June 1996): 114-118.

Schumacher, E.F. *Small is Beautiful: Economics as if People Mattered.* New York: Perennial Library, 1975.

Siegfried, John J., and Bonnie T. Meszaros. "National Voluntary Content Standards for Pre-College Economics Education." *AEA Papers and Proceedings* (Vol. 87, No. 2, May 1997): 247-253.

Smith, David. *Where the Grass Is Greener: Geographical Perspectives on Inequality.* London: Croom Helm, 1979.

Soto, Hernando de; translated by June Abbott. *The Other Path: The Invisible Revolution in the Third World.* New York: Harper & Row, 1989.

Stock, Paul A., and William D. Rader. "Level of Economic Understanding for Senior High School Students in Ohio." *The Journal of Educational Research* (Vol. 91, No. 1, September/October 1997): 60-63.

Sulloway, Frank J. *Born to Rebel: Birth Order, Family Dynamics, and Creative Lives.* New York: Pantheon Books, 1996.

Todaro, Michael P. *Economic Development.* Reading, MA: Addison Wesley, 2000.

Wentland, Daniel. "A Framework for Organizing Economic Education Teaching Methodologies." Mississippi: 2000-00-00, ERIC Document, ED 442702.

Wood, Barbara. *E.F. Schumacher: His Life and Thought.* New York: Harper & Row, 1984.

Wren, Christopher S. "World Needs to Add 500 Million Jobs in 10 Years, Report Says." *The New York Times* (25 January 2001): A13.

ALBANIA

Republic of Albania
Republika é Shqipërisë

CAPITAL: Tiranë.

MONETARY UNIT: Lek (Lk). One lek equals 100 qindarka. There are coins of 5, 10, 20, and 50 qindarka and 1 lek, and notes of 1, 3, 5, 10, 25, 50, 100, and 500 leke.

CHIEF EXPORTS: Textiles, footwear, asphalt, metals and ores, oil, fruits, tobacco, semiprocessed goods.

CHIEF IMPORTS: Machinery and equipment, foods, textiles, chemicals.

GROSS DOMESTIC PRODUCT: US$10.5 billion (2000 est.).

BALANCE OF TRADE: **Exports:** US$310 million (2000 est.). **Imports:** US$1 billion (2000 est.). [The CIA *World Factbook* estimates that exports in 1999 were US$242 million while imports were US$925 million.]

COUNTRY OVERVIEW

LOCATION AND SIZE. Albania is located in the southwestern part of the Balkan peninsula in southeastern Europe. It is bordered by the Yugoslav republics of Montenegro, Serbia, and Macedonia, and by Greece and the Adriatic and Ionian Seas. Albania has an area of 28,748 square kilometers (11,100 square miles), making it slightly smaller than Maryland. The capital, Tiranë, is situated in the west-central part of the country near the Adriatic Sea.

POPULATION. The population of Albania was 3,510,484 in July 2001, compared with 2,761,000 in 1981. Population density averaged 111 inhabitants per square kilometer (287 per square mile) but nearly two-thirds of the population were concentrated in the west, especially in the Tiranë-Durrës region. Density there reached 300 inhabitants per square kilometer (777 per square mile). In 2001, the birth rate was 19.01 per 1,000 population while the death rate equaled 6.5 per 1,000. Albania had one of the most youthful populations in Europe, with 30 percent below the age of 14 and just 7 percent older than 65. The population growth rate in 2000 was comparatively modest, at only 0.88 percent, and the **emigration** rate stood at 3.69 per 1,000. Since the collapse of **communism** in 1989, many Albanians, allowed to travel abroad for the first time, have left their impoverished country for western Europe, mostly for Italy, Greece, Switzerland, and the United States. The emigration rate has declined from a previous rate of 10.36 in 2000, however.

There are 2 major Albanian ethnic subgroups with distinct dialects: the Gegs in the north, and the Tosks in the south. The Gegs account for more than half of the population, but the Tosks have been traditionally in control. The Tosk dialect of Albanian is the official language. Albanians account for 95 percent of the population, Greeks for 3 percent, and Vlachs, Gypsies, and Bulgarians for the other 2 percent. Albania is predominantly rural, with about 59 percent of the population living in the countryside (1999). The population of the capital—Tiranë—is 312,220 (2000); other cities include Durrës, Elbasan, Shkodër, and Vlorë.

OVERVIEW OF ECONOMY

Albania is Europe's poorest country; its annual **gross domestic product (GDP) per capita** was about US$1,000 in 1997, more than 10 times lower than in neighboring Greece. Liberated from Turkish domination in 1912, the country endured periods of anarchy, autocratic rule, and foreign occupation before being taken over by communists in 1944. Until the collapse of communism in 1989, Albania was ruled in international isolation by a rigid Stalinist regime. All economic activity was **nationalized** and the production of **consumer goods** and the development of the **infrastructure** were neglected while heavy industry was stressed. Since the collapse of the Soviet Union in 1989, market reforms have taken a foothold and a **privatization** program has

been in place since 1992, when the pro-market Democratic Party formed a cabinet.

Reforms have been slow, however, and the economy shaky as a result. Particularly disastrous was the 1997 collapse of several financial **pyramid schemes**) that wiped out the life savings of half of the Albanian population, causing violent riots. The democratic government was toppled, and foreign investors fled in panic. The Kosovo refugee crisis of 1999 dealt another heavy blow. Albania has been plagued by corruption and inadequate reporting; the flow of goods crossing the frontiers has remained largely unknown, and tax collection rates have been unsatisfactory. Organized crime and the trafficking of drugs and stolen cars from western Europe are a major social problem.

The **socialist** government, in office since 1997, has curbed crime, strengthened customs inspections, improved tax collection, and carried on with privatization. Some 420 comparatively larger enterprises were put on the market after **restructuring**, including Albpetrol (oil and gas and pipelines), Albakri (copper mining), Albkromi (chrome), Telekom Shqiptar, and the Albanian Mobile Phone Company. Many state-held assets were liquidated. Stable and independent government institutions were still a dream in 2000, however, although younger **technocrats** had been involved in decision-making and a more informative economic database was created.

In 2000, the Albanian economy grew by 7 percent, although it started from a low base. The currency was stable, **inflation** was only 2 percent (in 1999), and money transfers from Albanians abroad fueled a house-building boom. The International Monetary Fund (IMF) cautiously praised the authorities for progress in structural reform and their commitment to reducing poverty. Foreign investments in 2000 reached US$143 million (up from US$43 million in 1999), a Greek-Norwegian consortium bought the first mobile-phone network, a Greek-British consortium bought the second mobile-phone license, and corruption diminished.

Poverty is still pervasive and the country is burdened by a large foreign **trade deficit** (US$690 million in 2000). Among the government's concerns are the improvement of agriculture and the obsolete road network, encouraging private enterprise, and **liberalizing** foreign trade. The opening up of **free trade zones** to attract investors is expected to be supplemented by an improved legal environment, a financial sector restructuring, and a strengthening of law and order (safety is still a big concern in Albania). Heavily dependent on foreign economic aid, in 1997 the country received US$630 million in financial support and a US$58 million poverty reduction and growth facility (loan) from the International Monetary Fund (IMF), the World Bank, and the European Union (EU). No considerable funding has yet been received from the Stability Pact for Southeastern Europe, a regional initiative backed by the EU and the United States. Albania has not yet started negotiations to become a part of the EU, which insists that more substantial reforms are needed before talks could start.

POLITICS, GOVERNMENT, AND TAXATION

Albania is a parliamentary democracy with a **unicameral** (1–house) 155-member parliament. The president is the head of state, but the prime minister is the executive head of government. The 2 major parties are the left-of-center Socialists (reformed communists) and the right-of-center Democratic Party. In the 1997 elections, the socialists won 101 seats, blaming Sali Berisha, the first post-communist president, and his democrats for the financial pyramid scams, economic chaos, rampant corruption, authoritarianism, and fraud. The socialists, whose power base lies mostly in the south, formed a coalition with the center-left social-democrats (8 seats), the small, predominantly ethnic Greek Human Rights Party (4 seats), and the smaller centrist Democratic Alliance (2 seats). They have a chance of remaining in office at the election in mid-2001. The democrats, whose power base is mainly in the north, retained 27 seats in parliament.

In early 2001, the state's role in the economy was diminishing, but the government was still highly centralized and financial resources were concentrated at the national level. In an attempt to attract foreign investors, Albania planned to create free-trade zones and companies operating in them would be exempt from import **duties** and a **value-added tax** (VAT) but not from taxes on profits. In order to curb the **budget deficit**, the government nearly doubled the VAT to 20 percent and increased **excise taxes** in 1997. The tax share of GDP was set to 22 percent in the 2001 budget, close to the norm for other economies making the transition from a communist to a market system. Albania had a **foreign debt** of US$820 million in 1998, which was not considered disproportionate.

INFRASTRUCTURE, POWER, AND COMMUNICATIONS

Albania's infrastructure is far below the standards of other European countries. There are 18,000 kilometers (11,250 miles) of roads, of which 5,400 kilometers (3,355 miles) are paved, and rapid expansion in private car ownership (prohibited in communist times) has placed a great pressure on the network. Since the Kosovo war in neighboring former Yugoslavia, NATO has rebuilt the Albanian roads it used, and western governments have offered funding for several construction projects. One of them runs north-south from the border with Montenegro via Shkodër, Durrës and Vlorë to the Greek frontier (requiring US$94.8 million for its completion). Another runs east-west from Durrës via Elbasan to the Macedonian frontier (costing US$155.9 million). Albania has received US$108 million from the European Investment Bank (EIB) for completion of the Durrës-Kukës highway and other segments.

The railroad network has 447 kilometers (277.7 miles) of single track, not connected to the railroads of any neighboring country and in poor condition. Thirty-eight kilometers (23.6 miles) of the Durrës-Tiranë line were under renovation in 2000. Two seaports are located at Durrës and Vlorë. Albania's only international airport, Rinas, is located outside Tiranë and has 1 runway and a small passenger terminal.

Albania's power system has 1,670 megawatts (MW) of installed capacity, of which 1,446 MW is in hydropower plants (the country's mountainous terrain is favorable for that type of power) and 224 MW in thermal plants. A quarter of the energy is lost due to technical inadequacies, and blackouts are still frequent. Often, electricity reaching consumers is not paid for (70 percent of the clients refused to pay their bills in 1997). A particular concern is the theft of electricity by bypassing meters. The power utility, Korporata Elektroenergjitike, is still in state hands but is scheduled for privatization in 2001. A loan of US$30 million from the World Bank, US$12 million from Exportfinans of Norway, and US$1.2 million from the Chinese government helped Albania repair its electric grid in 2000.

The telephone system is obsolete, with 42,000 main lines in 1995 (11,000 telephones in Tiranë). In 1992, rioting peasants cut the wire to about 1,000 villages and used it to build fences. There were 3,100 mobile phones

Communications

Country	Newspapers	Radios	TV Sets[a]	Cable subscribers[a]	Mobile Phones[a]	Fax Machines[a]	Personal Computers[a]	Internet Hosts[b]	Internet Users[b]
	1996	1997	1998	1998	1998	1998	1998	1999	1999
Albania	36	217	109	0.0	1	3.6	N/A	0.24	3
United States	215	2,146	847	244.3	256	78.4	458.6	1,508.77	74,100
Yugoslavia	107	297	259	N/A	23	1.9	18.8	7.65	80
Macedonia	21	200	250	N/A	15	1.5	N/A	4.40	30

[a]Data are from International Telecommunication Union, *World Telecommunication Development Report 1999* and are per 1,000 people.
[b]Data are from the Internet Software Consortium (http://www.isc.org) and are per 10,000 people.
SOURCE: World Bank. *World Development Indicators 2000.*

in 1999, with coverage limited to the main cities. In 2000, the privatization of the mobile phone company, Albanian Mobile Communications (AMC), was completed, and the sale of the fixed-line operator, Albtelekom, was set for 2001. A consortium of Vodafone (UK) and Panafon (Greece) won a mobile telephony license in early 2001 for US$38 million.

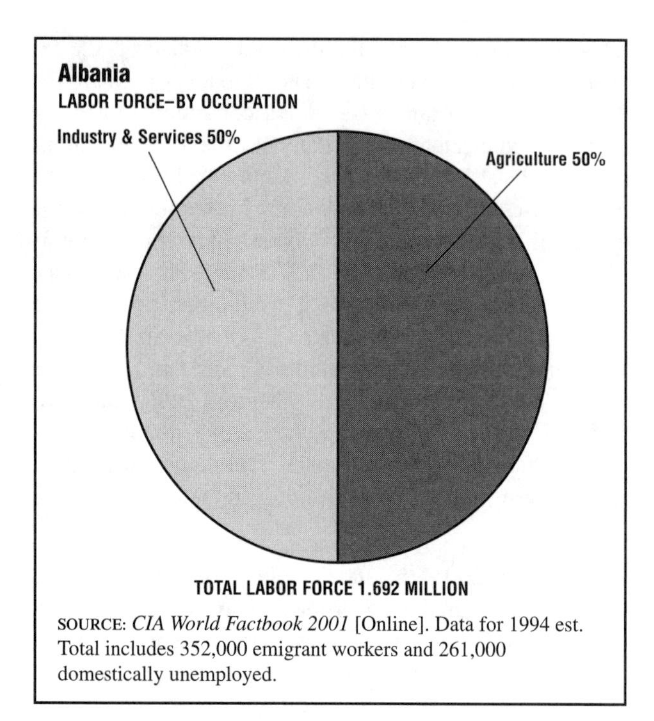

SOURCE: *CIA World Factbook 2001* [Online]. Data for 1994 est. Total includes 352,000 emigrant workers and 261,000 domestically unemployed.

ECONOMIC SECTORS

Albania's economy remains predominantly agricultural, and in 1999, the contribution of agriculture to GDP was 53 percent, up from 32.3 percent in 1989. Industry's share slipped from nearly 45 percent in 1989 to 26 percent in 1999, because of the collapse of loss-making state-run factories and the return of many workers to farming. The percentage of the population engaged in agriculture reached one-half by 1997. In 1998, 27 percent of the farms were engaged in **subsistence farming**—which means they did not sell their goods to the market—and only half used machinery. Prior to 1991, services were underdeveloped, with virturally no tourism and rudimentary banking and **retail** sectors. New service industries such as tourism and banking started to develop in the 1990s, mostly with foreign investment, but suffered in the 1997 financial collapse. The shrinking Albanian industry is based on local natural resources, notably oil, lignite, copper, chromium, limestone, bauxite, and natural gas.

AGRICULTURE

In 1992, peasants took control of formerly collectivized land and livestock. Many collective farms (farms held by the state and worked by citizens) were looted, orchards were cut down for firewood, and agricultural output collapsed by almost half. Much of the irrigation works and greenhouses of the communist regime were looted. Under private ownership, agriculture picked up and by 1995, production was above the 1990 level. Serious problems facing farmers are the lack of technology and the tiny size of land holdings. In 1999, 42 percent of farms used animal and manpower alone. Self-sufficiency, forced on farmers by the communist prohibition of private trade, is high. In 1999, 48.5 percent of farm households bought no outside food. International lenders, such as the World Bank, the EU, and the U.S. Agency for International Development (USAID), have financed repairs and drainage projects, but the consolidation of small farm plots into larger and more efficient units has been slow. Albania imports basic foods (worth Lk3.8 billion in 1999, up from Lk3.7 billion in 1998), yet agriculture provides the livelihood for the majority of the population. Crops include wheat, corn, olives, sugar beets, cotton, sunflower seeds, tobacco, potatoes, and fruits. The livestock population was estimated in the early 1990s as including some 500,000 cattle, 1 million sheep, and 170,000 pigs.

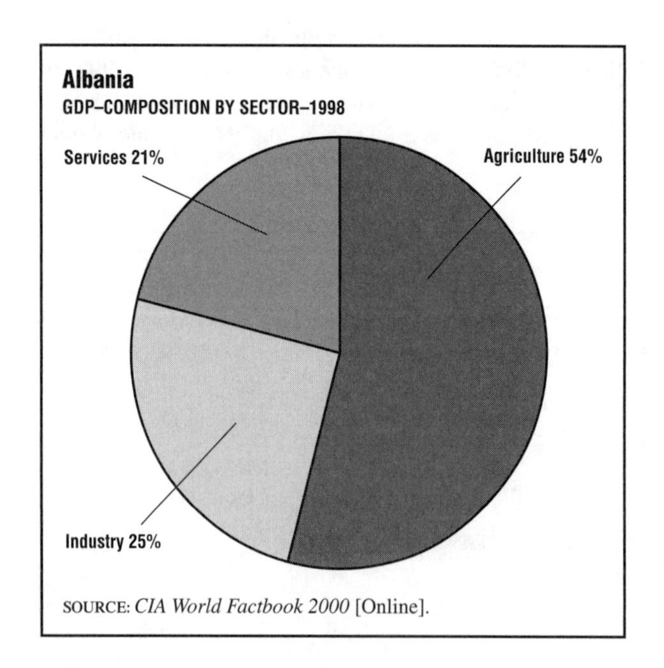

SOURCE: *CIA World Factbook 2000* [Online].

INDUSTRY

Mining, metallurgy, food processing, textiles, lumber, and cement were among the leading industries in Albania under the communist regime, when heavy industry was a priority and some factories were capable of exporting. Until 1961, most equipment was supplied by the Soviet Union and then by China until 1978. After 1989, the sector declined due to the lack of new technology and financing and the dilapidated condition of the factories.

In the 1990s, plants and equipment were destroyed and sold for scrap, or fell into disuse, unable to compete with cheaper imports that came with trade liberalization. A revival of chromium, steel, and cement industries came with the increase of foreign investments in 2000. Some new equipment was purchased in the West for a cigarette-making plant in Durrës and for a manufacture of underwear in Korçë. Construction, especially in housing, was the main factor for investment growth.

Mining is a large (but shrinking) sector of the economy, given the rich deposits of bauxite, chromium, nickel, iron, copper ores, and petroleum. The export of raw materials is crucial for foreign exchange earnings. In the 1980s, Albania ranked third worldwide in chromium ore production. Output plunged 3 times to 157,000 tons in 1997, because of the weakening of domestic demand in addition to the closing down of loss-making industries, the lack of capital, high costs, problems with the electricity supply, and the economic chaos of 1997. Albania's output of copper was reduced from 1 million tons per year in the late 1980s to 25,000 tons in 1997. Iron-nickel mining collapsed in the early 1990s with the closing down of the steel works of Elbasan, its main client, but was revived in 2000 due to Turkish involvement at the plant. Coal and petroleum output and petroleum refineries production have also declined in the 1990s due to their inadequate technology.

SERVICES

Albania's banking system under communism was state-run and underdeveloped. By the early 1990s, the 3 major state banks were cash-strapped due to irrecoverable loans to loss-making industries. Since then, almost all banks (except the largest one, the Savings Bank) have been privatized, most in the form of **joint ventures** with foreign partners, including the Italian Albanian Bank (IAB), the Arab Albanian Islamic Bank (AAIB), and the Dardania Bank (DB). The sector has been plagued by a lack of capitalization and a lack of experience and technology. Little long-term investment credit is available, and debt collection is uncertain. The 1997 financial pyramids collapse annihilated US$1 billion in savings and only US$50 million seemed recoverable by 2000. To relieve the situation, the Bank of Albania (the central bank) imposed restrictions on banks (including credit limits and minimum interest rates) that additionally contracted the credit market. Albanians became extremely cautious in depositing money in the banks, and **private sector** investment started to rely on financing through family, friends, and partners. Larger companies transferred funds abroad and Albanian banks came to rely on short-term deposits and lending to selected customers for short-term trade financing. The privatization of the remaining state-owned bank, the Savings Bank (SB), was delayed in 2000 due to improperly audited accounts and was rescheduled for June 2001.

Albania's tourist industry is in an embryonic stage. There are few foreign visitors to its picturesque Mediterranean shore because of the lack of adequate infrastructure and fears for personal safety. A few modern hotels appeared in 2000, backed by foreign investment, but revenues were weak. With the privatization of retail businesses in the early 1990s, the sector was characterized by a large number of small family retailers. The quality of service was still rather poor because of the low household income and the subsistence farming of the majority of the rural population. In 1999 and 2000, the retail and hotel industry had a modest boom due to the presence of foreign troops involved in the Kosovo war.

INTERNATIONAL TRADE

Albania depends on imports for most of its consumption. It was not able to produce enough exports to offset its large trade deficit of US$814 million in 1999, a huge sum for the size of the economy. This trade deficit may create serious problems for Albania in the near future. A major contribution to offsetting the deficit are money transfers from Albanians abroad, which grew from US$324 million in 1999 to US$531 million in 2000. Raw material exports are also crucial but gradually shrinking. Exports are declining, particularly in minerals, contributing only 8 percent of domestic exports in the last quarter of 1999, down from 45 percent in 1998. **Re-exports** of goods processed in Albania for manufacturers abroad increased mostly in textiles and footwear but also in electrical appliances, foods, and metal products. In the last quarter of 1999, they contributed 70 percent of total exports, a 29 percent increase from the last quarter of 1998. Exports by the tobacco industry were down by almost a third in 1999 from 1998, and other agricultural exports were hit by drought. The EU countries are Albania's chief trading partners, notably neighboring Italy and Greece, partly due to subcontracting for Italian and Greek manufacturers drawn by cheap local labor. Other significant trading partners include Germany, Turkey, Bulgaria, Macedonia, and the United States. Albania joined the World Trade Organization (WTO) in 2000 and is committed to trade liberalization and reducing **tariffs** on imports. In 1999, the EU promised Albania preferred trade status and reduced some tariffs on Albanian exports.

MONEY

After the economic collapse of 1997, the **monetary policy** of the Bank of Albania was tightened and the regulation of the financial sector was improved. The currency was stabilized and kept under control. The **exchange rate** of the lek shifted from 179.06 per US$1 in

Exchange rates: Albania

leke per US$1	
Dec 2000	146.08
2000	143.71
1999	137.69
1998	150.63
1997	148.93
1996	104.50

Note: Leke is the plural of lek.

SOURCE: CIA *World Factbook 2001* [ONLINE].

GDP per Capita (US$)

Country	1975	1980	1985	1990	1998
Albania	N/A	916	915	842	795
United States	19,364	21,529	23,200	25,363	29,683
Greece	8,302	9,645	10,005	10,735	12,069
Macedonia	N/A	N/A	N/A	N/A	1,349

SOURCE: United Nations. *Human Development Report 2000; Trends in human development and per capita income.*

1997 to almost 140 per dollar in 2001. New legislation included a law on bank deposit insurance and the setting up of a credit information bureau, an investment advisory office, a mediation office for commercial disputes, and an agency for the execution of bankruptcy and other related court decisions. Nevertheless, banking is not efficient, and the economy is still cash-driven. There is no formal **equities** market in the country as the Tiranë Stock Exchange (scheduled for privatization) is trading in Albanian **treasury bills** only.

POVERTY AND WEALTH

Poverty in Albania is widespread due to limited job opportunities, low income, and limited access to basic services such as education, health, water, and sewerage. Under the communist regime, employment was almost total, and the government provided some livelihood for nearly everyone. In the 1990s, the collapse of the state-run farms and industrial enterprises, unemployment, organized crime, and corruption generated widespread new poverty along with numerous illicit fortunes. Many families came to rely on transfers from family members abroad as 25 percent of working-age Albanians emigrated, only a fifth of them legally. More than 17 percent of the population lived under the poverty line in 2000, and 90 percent of the poor live in rural areas. Sixty percent of those heading poor households are self-employed in subsistence farming. The situation is worse in the north, where many rural families own less than 0.5 hectares. In Tiranë, there were about 800 street children in 2000 and child laborers numbered between 35,000–50,000 as need forced them to leave school early. Drug abuse, prostitution, trafficking in women, and child abuse have all increased with the economic hardship of the 1990s.

WORKING CONDITIONS

The Albanian **labor force** numbered 1.692 million (including 352,000 emigrants and 261,000 unemployed) in 2000. The private sector had between 900,000 and 1,000,000 workers, mostly in agriculture and small shops and enterprises. The unemployment rate was 18.2 percent in 2000, but unemployment in the rural regions, particularly in subsistence farming, was not reflected in this figure. Minimum wages are US$50 per month, insufficient to provide a decent standard of living. Many Albanians work with outdated technology and without adequate safety regulations. Workplace conditions are generally poor and often dangerous. The workweek is 48 hours, but hours are set by individual or collective agreement. Under the communist regime, unions were government-controlled and independent unions only emerged in 1991. The Independent Confederation of Trade Unions, with an estimated 127,000 members, was formed as an umbrella group for most branch unions.

Household Consumption in PPP Terms

Country	All food	Clothing and footwear	Fuel and power[a]	Health care[b]	Education[b]	Transport & Communications	Other
Albania	62	3	13	3	10	5	4
United States	13	9	9	4	6	8	51
Serbia	N/A	N/A	N/A	N/A	N/A	N/A	N/A
Macedonia	33	5	15	6	9	9	23

Data represent percentage of consumption in PPP terms.

[a]Excludes energy used for transport.

[b]Includes government and private expenditures.

SOURCE: World Bank. *World Development Indicators 2000.*

The Confederation of Trade Unions represents school, petroleum, postal, and telecommunications workers and has 80,000 members. Union membership declined after 1997 because of the expansion of the private sector (few of its workers have unions). Labor disputes have been often confrontational and passionate.

COUNTRY HISTORY AND ECONOMIC DEVELOPMENT

168 B.C. Romans take over Illyria (comprising most of present-day Albania).

1000s A.D. Illyria becomes known as Albania; feudal agriculture develops and Adriatic cities become centers of commerce.

1388. Ottoman Turks invade Albania and subdue it by the early 16th century.

1500s. The Ottomans convert many formerly Christian Albanians to Islam. The feudal economy remains unchanged into the 20th century.

1878. Albanian nationalism grows and the Prizren League is organized in the present-day Kosovo province of Serbia to work for national independence.

1912. Albania is liberated from the Ottomans. The European powers recognize its independence but leave nearly half of the ethnic Albanians outside its borders.

1919. U.S. President Woodrow Wilson vetoes the partition of Albania among its neighbors following the end of World War I.

1925. Albania is taken over by a dictatorship and gradually turns into an Italian protectorate.

1939. Italian troops occupy Albania at the start of World War II.

1944. Albanian communists take over and impose Stalinist economic rules, which last until the collapse of the Soviet Union in 1989.

1990. A multi-party system is allowed as thousands of Albanians try to escape the country by fleeing to foreign embassies in Tiranë.

1991. The first multi-party elections are won by the reformed communists, while the opposition Democratic Party wins 75 seats in the Assembly. Massive labor unrest topples the government.

1992. Elections are won by the democrats, and economic reforms and liberalization gain momentum. Elections in 1996 leave the cabinet in office but the opposition voices fraud accusations.

1997. The collapse of pyramid schemes causes violent riots. The government is toppled and the socialists (reformed communists) return to power in early elections.

1999. More than 400,000 Albanian refugees from Kosovo flood into Albania.

2000. Albania joins the World Trade Organization.

FUTURE TRENDS

With its economy reviving from the collapse of 1997, Albania remains essentially a developing country requiring heavy investment for its modernization. Without significant progress in coping with crime and weak state institutions, its internal stability is not yet guaranteed. Reforms are needed to enforce democracy and develop favorable conditions for foreign investment. Albania has strong potential for growth due to its youthful population and the large number of **guest workers**, many of whom may return with capital and know-how once domestic conditions improve. Proximity to Italy and Greece, abundant natural resources, and potential tourist attractions are additional factors that may encourage development. EU membership is not yet an issue for Albania, but with the accession of Balkan neighbors, its chances will grow.

The Socialist Party is expected to stay in power after the election in 2001 and GDP is likely to keep its growth rate of 7 percent driven by the privatization of power, the Savings Bank, hotels, and other government assets. Inflation will be low and unemployment will gradually decline, but many Albanians will continue to support their families by working abroad. Import dependency will diminish as domestic industry slowly picks up and the development of tourism and increasing money transfers may alleviate the trade deficit situation. However, Albania will remain dependent on international aid for the foreseeable future.

DEPENDENCIES

Albania has no territories or colonies.

BIBLIOGRAPHY

Economist Intelligence Unit. *Country Profile: Albania.* London: Economist Intelligence Unit, 2001.

U.S. Central Intelligence Agency. *World Factbook 2000.* <http://www.odci.gov/cia/publications/factbook/index.html>. Accessed August 2001.

U.S. Department of State. *Background Notes: Albania.* <http://www.state.gov/www/background_notes/albania_9903_bgn.html>. Accessed August 2001.

U.S. Department of State. *FY 2001 Country Commercial Guide: Albania.* <http://www.state.gov/www/about_state/business/com_guides/2001/europe/index.html>. Accessed August 2001.

Vickers, Miranda. *Albania: From Anarchy to a Balkan Identity.* New York: New York University Press, 1997.

—Valentin Hadjiyski

ANDORRA

Principality of Andorra
Principat d'Andorra

CAPITAL: Andorra la Vella.

MONETARY UNIT: No local currency; French and Spanish currencies are both used in the country. Both Spain and France, along with 9 other members of the European Union (EU), are in the process of changing over from their national currencies to the single currency of the EU, the euro, for all transactions. This transition will be completed with the introduction of euro coins and bills in January 2002.

CHIEF EXPORTS: Tobacco products, furniture.

CHIEF IMPORTS: Consumer goods, food, electricity.

GROSS DOMESTIC PRODUCT: US$1.2 billion (purchasing power parity, 1996 est.).

BALANCE OF TRADE: **Exports:** US$58 million (f.o.b., 1998 est.). **Imports:** US$1.077 billion (c.i.f., 1998 est.).

COUNTRY OVERVIEW

LOCATION AND SIZE. Andorra, a tiny landlocked principality in southwestern Europe, is situated in the eastern Pyrenees Mountains, bordered on the north and east by France and on the south and west by Spain. It comprises a region of 7 narrow valleys and the adjacent peaks reaching heights of more than 2,700 meters (about 8,860 feet) above sea level. Also named the Valleys of Andorra, the country has an area of only 468 square kilometers (181 square miles), about 2.5 times the size of Washington, D.C., or about half the size of New York City. The capital is Andorra la Vella (Andorra of the Valley), with a population of 21,985 in 1996.

POPULATION. The population of Andorra was estimated at 66,824 in July 2000, up from 64,716 in 1998. Although mountainous, the country is densely populated, with an overall density of 138 persons per square kilometer (358 per square mile). The population, however, is unevenly distributed, and is concentrated in the 7 urbanized valleys that form the country's parishes (political districts): Andorra la Vella, Canillo, Encamp, La Massana, Escaldes-Engordany, Ordino, and Sant Julia de Loria. Andorra has a slow population growth rate of 1.22 percent, fueled by a birth rate of 10.58 births per 1,000 population, a death rate of 5.27 deaths per 1,000 population, and a high net **immigration** rate of 6.9 migrants per 1,000 population

(all according to 2000 estimates). The Andorrans have a very high life expectancy at birth, standing at 83.46 years for the total population (80.56 for men and 86.56 for women). This is attributed partly to the pleasant mountainous climate, and partly to the prosperous economy and sufficient health care provisions in the country. The population is aging, as in much of the rest of Europe, with 15 percent of the Andorrans younger than 15 years, 72 percent between 15 and 64 years, and 13 percent 65 years or older.

Native Andorrans, curiously enough, represent a minority (only about 33 percent of the population) in their own country; they are Catalan in their culture and language. The official language of the principality is also Catalan, a romance language, spoken also by more than 6 million people in the regions of French and Spanish Catalonia (in southwestern France and northeastern and eastern Spain and the Balearic islands in the Mediterranean). More people of Andorran descent live outside the country (particularly in France) than in their home country, because historically, as in many similar societies with very limited land supply, land ownership has been strictly passed on to the oldest heirs while the rest often have had to seek their fortunes elsewhere. Spanish, French, and Portuguese immigrants (both working people and entrepreneurs) make up the majority of the population of the principality, and the Spanish, French, and Portuguese languages are widely spoken. Spaniards (Catalan-speaking or not) form the largest single ethnic group in the country with 43 percent; Portuguese constitute 11 percent and French 7 percent. Roman Catholicism is not only the predominant religion but also the religion of the state, unlike most European countries that strictly separate the church from the state. For example, only Roman Catholics are permitted to marry in the country, and all public records pertaining to issues such as birth, death, and family status are still kept by the church. Pilgrimages to the shrine of the Andorran patron saint, the Lady of Meritxell, are very popular among believers. The education law requires school attendance for children up to age 16 and a system of French, Spanish, and Andorran lay (secular) schools provides education up to the secondary level. Schools are built and maintained by the Andorran government but salaries for teachers are paid for the most part by France or Spain. About half of the Andorran children attend the French primary schools, and the rest attend Spanish or Andorran ones, which suggests that the role of the French language in the country's culture, communication, and business life will grow in the future.

OVERVIEW OF ECONOMY

Due to its small size and isolated mountainous location, Andorra has preserved its political independence over the years. But these factors also contributed to its economic and developmental impoverishment before World War II. The economy historically has been based on pastoral farming, the processing of tobacco and timber, and the smuggling of goods (mainly tobacco) into the neighboring regions of France and Spain. Over the last 4 or 5 decades of the 20th century, however, the principality has achieved considerable prosperity. This has been mostly due to its status as a tax-free port, the rapid development of tourism in Europe, the dramatic economic progress of its large neighbors France and Spain, and the European integration processes. Many investors and immigrants, both legal and illegal, are now attracted to its thriving economy and its lack of **income taxes**.

Tourism has been developing at a high rate since the mid-1950s and now dominates the principality's economic life. The extensive winter ski facilities, the cool summer climate, and the availability of inexpensive goods in the stores attract numerous tourists to Andorra's humming summer and winter resorts. With about 270 hotels and 400 restaurants, as well as many shops, the tourist industry provides a livelihood to a growing portion of the domestic and immigrant **labor force**.

Trade in consumer products is also very active, mostly in imported manufactured items, which, because of their **duty**-free prices, are considerably cheaper than in other European countries. Partly due to this, smuggling in the country, once a major livelihood, is still widespread. Duty-free status and the price differences between Andorra and its neighbor countries, however, are seen as a serious problem by the European Union (EU) and have had a very significant stake in the debate concerning the principality's relationship with the union. Andorra is a member of the EU customs union and is treated as an EU member for trade in manufactured goods (for which there are no **tariffs**), yet its duty-free shopping status gives it an edge over EU member states. However, the country's comparative advantage in duty-free shopping has been negatively affected as the economies of neighboring France and Spain have been **liberalized** and opened up over the 1990s, resulting in lower tariffs and a wider choice of consumer items.

Negotiations on maintaining Andorra's duty-free status and developing its trade links with the EU began in 1987, soon after neighboring Spain was admitted to the union. A difficult agreement, in effect since July 1991, has set some duty-free quotas and placed limits on certain goods such as tobacco, alcoholic beverages, and dairy products. But as of 2001, Andorra was still allowed to maintain its price differences from other EU countries, and visitors could still enjoy limited duty-free allowances. By creating a modern legal framework, however, the 1993 constitution has allowed Andorra to begin the needed shift from an economic model substantially based on duty-free shopping to one relying largely on international banking and finance.

Andorra's **gross domestic product** (GDP) for 1998 was worth US$1.2 billion, with tourism providing by far the principal component (roughly 80 percent). **GDP per capita** was a healthy US$18,000 in 1996.

POLITICS, GOVERNMENT, AND TAXATION

Independent since 1278, for more than 7 centuries Andorra has been ruled jointly by the leader (the king, later the president) of France and by Spain's Roman Catholic bishop of the diocese of Urgel, who were acknowledged as "co-princes." Andorra's government, however, had no clear-cut division of powers into executive, legislative, and judiciary, as in most other (and virtually all democratic) states, until the late 20th century. Only in 1993 did Andorran voters approve their first written constitution, transferring all power to the parliamentary principality and proclaiming a sovereign parliamentary democracy. The constitution defined for the first time the rights and obligations of the citizens and the functions and specific terms of the separate legislative, executive, and judicial branches of the government.

The co-princes remained officially Andorra's heads of state, and they serve coequally, with limited powers and without the right to a veto over government acts. Presently, the co-princes are Jacques Chirac, the president of France, and Monseigneur Juan Marti, the bishop of Urgel. Naturally, they do not participate in person in the government's deliberations but are represented by delegates. As co-princes of Andorra, the president and the bishop maintain formally their supreme authority to approve international treaties with France and Spain, as well as all those state acts that deal with important internal security, defense, Andorran territory, diplomatic representation, and judicial or penal cooperation. Although the institution of the co-princes is viewed by many liberals as a medieval anachronism, the majority of the people of Andorra still regard them as an important symbolic element of their historical traditions and a practical way to mediate and balance the influence of both France and Spain. It is also worth mentioning that, until 1993, the principality of Andorra paid every other year, as the medieval treaties stipulated, a tribute worth US$2 to the French president and US$8 to the Spanish bishop. The bishop was additionally entitled to receive a contribution consisting of 6 hams, 6 cheeses, and a dozen live chickens.

The Andorran legislature is the General Council (founded in 1419), which has 28 members, elected to 4-year terms. There is universal suffrage in Andorra, with citizens over the age of 18 having the right to vote. At least one representative from each of the 7 parishes must be present for the General Council to meet. Historically, within the General Council, 4 deputies from each of the 7 parishes have been included in the representation. This arrangement lets the smaller parishes, who have fewer than 400 voters, be represented by the same number of delegates as the larger ones that have more than 2,500 voters. To correct this imbalance, the new constitution included a provision that introduced a modification of the process of electing the Council members; under this new arrangement, half of the delegates were to be selected by the traditional system by parishes and the other half elected from nationwide lists.

The executive power is vested in the Executive Council, headed by a president (in Catalan, the *cap de govern,* or head of government) who is chosen by the General Council and then formally appointed by the co-princes. The president appoints the other executive members of the council.

In the judiciary, civil cases are heard in the first instance by *batlles* (4-judge courts), with 2 judges each appointed by a co-prince. Appeals are heard by the one-judge Court of Appeals. The highest judicial body is the 5-member Superior Council of Justice. The Tribunal of Courts in Andorra la Vella hear all criminal cases. Andorra has no standing armed forces and only a small domestic professional police brigade. All able men possessing firearms serve without compensation in the reserve army, unique in treating all its men as officers. The army's principal responsibility is to carry the Andorran flag at official ceremonies; it has not fought a battle for more than 700 years.

Andorra's young democracy is in the process of redefining its political party system. In recent years, 3 out of the 5 parties that dominated the political scene have dissolved. The former Liberal Union (UL) is reshaping itself and changing its name to the Andorran Liberal Party (PLA), intending to offer a political umbrella to small parties and groups that have not yet consolidated. The currently ruling party is the PLA, led by the *cap de govern*, Marc Forne. The Social Democratic Party (PSD) attracts groups previously aligned with **socialist** ideals, and the third major party is the National Andorran Coalition (CAN). Given the number of parties and Andorra's size, no one party controls the General Council; therefore, legislative majorities arise through coalitions.

The fundamental impetus for the recent political transformation was a recommendation by the Council of Europe in 1990 that if Andorra wished to attain full integration in the European Union (EU), it should adopt a modern constitution which guarantees the rights of those living and working there. A Tripartite Commission made up of representatives of the co-princes, the General Council, and the Executive Council drafted the 1993 constitution. Since its adoption, the government has continued to address many other long-awaited reforms. In addition to legalizing political parties and trade unions for the first time, freedom of religion and assembly also have been guaranteed.

Since its sovereignty was established with the 1993 constitution, Andorra has become an active member of the international community. In 1993, it established its first diplomatic mission to the United Nations in New York, and in 1995, it established diplomatic relations with the United States. Andorra also has expanded relations with other nations and is a full member of many international organizations, such as the United Nations (UN), the United Nations Educational, Scientific and Cultural Organization (UNESCO), the International Telecommunications Union (ITU), and the Organization for Security and Cooperation in Europe (OSCE). Since 1991, Andorra has a trade agreement with the EU.

The Andorran government collects revenue through the sale of postage stamps and a very small number of local taxes.

INFRASTRUCTURE, POWER, AND COMMUNICATIONS

Landlocked, mountainous Andorra has no railroads, harbors, or airports, but possesses a good road system and three-fourths of its nearly 270 kilometers (169 miles) of roads are paved. The country is rich in hydroelectric power and the power plant at Les Escaldes, with a capacity of 26.5 megawatts, provides 116 million kilowatt hours annually (1998), or about 40 percent of Andorra's electricity, while Spain and France provide the rest.

Andorra has a modern telecommunications system with microwave radio relay connections between the exchanges and land line circuits to France and Spain. There were 31,980 main telephone lines in use and 8,618 cellular phones in 1997. Andorra had 15 FM radio broadcast stations in 1998 but no local TV broadcasting stations, French and Spanish broadcasting and cable TV being widely available.

ECONOMIC SECTORS

Andorra's natural resources include iron and lead deposits, marble quarries, forests of pine and birch, hydropower resources, strips of fertile land in the valleys, and extensive pastures on the mountain slopes. But the economy is mostly influenced by the excellent skiing areas, the pleasant climate, and the crossroads location of the country. Nearly four-fifths of the GDP in 1998 was generated in the tourist and other related service sectors; about one-fifth was generated in industry, including construction and mining; and just about 1 percent in agriculture. The labor force was distributed by occupation as follows: agriculture, 1 percent; industry, 21 percent; services, 72 percent; and other sectors, 6 percent (1998 estimates). The most important industries included tourism (particularly skiing), cattle raising, timber, tobacco growing, banking, and **retail**. Before World War II, most families made their living off farming, tobacco and timber processing, and smuggling, but since the 1950s tourism has been the bulwark of economic progress. With the gradual dismantling of Andorra's duty-free shopping advantages in the course of EU liberalization, the economy will become gradually more dependent on banking and finance services.

AGRICULTURE

Andorra's territory is ill-suited for agriculture, comprising mostly rugged mountains traversed by narrow val-

Communications

Country	Telephones[a]	Telephones, Mobile/Cellular[a]	Radio Stations[b]	Radios[a]	TV Stations[a]	Televisions[a]	Internet Service Providers[c]	Internet Users[c]
Andorra	32,946 (1998)	14,117 (1998)	AM 0; FM 15; shortwave 0	16,000	0	27,000	1	5,000
United States	194 M	69.209 M (1998)	AM 4,762; FM 5,542; shortwave 18	575 M	1,500	219 M	7,800	148 M
France	34.86 M (1998)	11.078 M (1998)	AM 41; FM about 3,500; shortwave 2	55.3 M	584 (1995)	34.8 M	62	9 M
Spain	17.336 M (1999)	8.394 M (1999)	AM 208; FM 715; shortwave 1	13.1 M	224 (1995)	16.2 M	56	4.6 M

[a]Data is for 1997 unless otherwise noted.
[b]Data is for 1998 unless otherwise noted.
[c]Data is for 2000 unless otherwise noted.

SOURCE: CIA *World Factbook 2001* [Online].

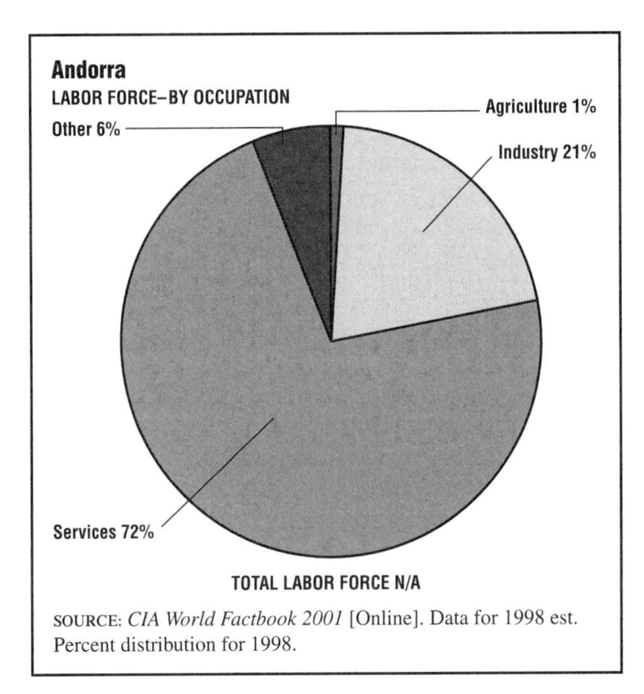

SOURCE: *CIA World Factbook 2001* [Online]. Data for 1998 est. Percent distribution for 1998.

leys with scarce arable land making up only 2–3 percent of the total area. Pasture lands suitable for sheep grazing cover about 45 percent of the territory, mostly the lower mountain slopes, and forests cover approximately 35 percent of the land. Agriculture, nevertheless, was the core of the Andorran economy until the boom in tourist activities in the 1950s. Sheep raising has usually been the principal agricultural activity, but tobacco growing, although limited, has been more lucrative, especially given the long-time Andorran tradition of smuggling tobacco products into the neighboring regions of France and Spain. Apart from the timber-related activities, agriculture products currently include small quantities of tobacco, rye, wheat, barley, oats, vegetables, and sheep products. Most food has to be imported from France and Spain.

INDUSTRY

In addition to traditional local handicrafts, manufacturing in the principality includes cigars, cigarettes, timber processing, and furniture for the domestic and export markets. Raw materials such as timber and iron and lead ore are also produced, and mining and construction are important sources of revenue and employment. However, construction is still unable to provide adequate housing at affordable prices for many of the families that migrated to Andorra over the last several decades. Given its relative size, Andorran industry is not able to play a significant role in European markets; however, it provides livelihoods for the local people, additional income for the economy, and also caters to the needs of the larger tourist and retail sectors.

SERVICES

Tourism, the powerhouse of Andorra's tiny but prosperous economy, accounts for roughly 80 percent of GDP. An estimated 9 million tourists (more than one-fifth of the number of visitors to Spain) visit the principality annually, attracted by its resorts, good ski facilities, pleasant summer climate, mineral waters, and duty-free shops. The small but vital banking sector—integrated with both the French and Spanish banking systems but maintaining its **tax haven** status—contributes substantially to the economy. In the mid- to late-1990s, the Andorran government passed a series of laws to strengthen the banking sector and deter activities such as **money laundering**. Retail trade is thriving, particularly in imported manufactured goods, notwithstanding the problems issuing from current EU liberalization and the substantial lowering of tariffs in competing neighboring countries that have diminished Andorra's advantages as a duty-free shopping area. The retail sector is comprised mostly of small privately-held stores.

INTERNATIONAL TRADE

International commerce is crucial to Andorra's otherwise isolated economy. In 1998 the country exported US$58 million worth of goods and services, while importing US$1.077 billion. This massive **trade deficit** is made up for largely by the booming tourist economy. As is to be expected given its tight integration with France and Spain, these countries are its dominant trading partners. The majority of the country's exports, 58 percent, went to Spain in 1998, while France received 34 percent. Imports in that year originated mostly from Spain (48 percent) and France (35 percent).

MONEY

Andorra has a traditional **budget surplus**, with revenues of US$385 million and expenditures of US$342 million, including capital expenditures, as estimated in

Exchange rates: Andorra

euros per US$1	
Jan 2001	1.0659
2000	1.0854
1999	0.9386
1998	N/A
1997	N/A
1996	N/A

Note: Prior to 1999 currency was in French francs and Spanish pesetas per US dollar.

SOURCE: CIA *World Factbook 2001* [ONLINE].

1997. The units of currency are both the Spanish peseta and the French franc. Both Spain and France, along with 9 other members of the EU, are in the process of changing over from their national currencies to the single currency of the EU, the euro, for all transactions. The euro started to be used in 1999, initially only for electronic bank transfers and accounting purposes. Euro coins and bills are planned to be issued in 2002, when the peseta and the franc will cease to be legal currency. The EU members have established the European Central Bank (ECB) in Frankfurt, Germany, responsible for all EU **monetary policies**. Since 1999, control over Spanish and French monetary issues, including interest rates and regulating the money supply, has been transferred to the ECB.

POVERTY AND WEALTH

Before World War II, Andorra was still living to a large extent in the ways it had known since the Middle Ages. Most of its people were rather poor and lived off small-scale farming, sheep breeding, and smuggling. Even now, many families still continue to live in the old farmhouses, and life still focuses on the family and the Roman Catholic Church. International tourism and European integration since the 1950s thoroughly modernized the country within several decades and most Andorrans have turned from agriculture to family hotels and restaurants, store-keeping, and various other tourism-related services. Currently, with an affluent service-based economy and a low **inflation rate** of 1.62 percent in 1998, Andorrans enjoy very good and comparatively equitable living standards and very high life expectancy. No extreme cases of poverty or very large private fortunes are currently known. Due to the high number of working immigrants, attracted over the past several decades mostly by jobs in the services industry, housing in Andorra is now probably the most acute social issue. Although many locals still live in their traditional family houses, housing is currently scarce; the construction sector is not yet in a position to address the challenge adequately, and the tiny real estate market in Andorra remains highly speculative.

GDP per Capita (US$)

Country	1996	1997	1998	1999	2000
Andorra	18,000	N/A	N/A	N/A	N/A
United States	28,600	30,200	31,500	33,900	36,200
France	20,900	22,700	22,600	23,300	24,400
Spain	15,300	16,400	16,500	17,300	18,000

Note: Data are estimates.

SOURCE: *Handbook of the Nations*, 17th, 18th, 19th and 20th editions for 1996, 1997, 1998 and 1999 data; CIA *World Factbook 2001* [Online] for 2000 data.

WORKING CONDITIONS

The labor force in Andorra included 30,787 salaried employees in 1998, and the unemployment rate was very close to zero. Trade unions were legalized for the first time only after 1993, and modern social institutions are still in the early phases of development. But the most significant labor-related issue recently has probably been the re-qualification for Andorran citizenship, a major challenge in a country where still only 13,000 people (20 percent of the population) are legal citizens. Citizenship issues are economically very important because the law allows non-citizens to own no more than a 33 percent share of a company, even if it is a small business. Citizenship problems generate major troubles for the enterprising immigrants forming by far the most dynamic economic group in the country. Only after residing in Andorra for 20 years are they entitled to possess full ownership of a business. A draft law aimed at reducing the required years from 20 to 10 is currently being debated. In 1995, a new, more liberal citizenship law was passed, but Andorran nationality nevertheless remains very hard to acquire. Only Andorrans can transmit it to their children, birth on Andorran soil does not confer it automatically, and dual citizenship is prohibited. Lawful permanent residents in Andorra may be naturalized only after 25 years of residency, and their children may opt for citizenship at 18 only if they have resided all of their lives in the country.

COUNTRY HISTORY AND ECONOMIC DEVELOPMENT

803. Andorra is given independence by the emperor Charlemagne, who names it a "March state," or buffer state created to keep the Muslim Moors of Spain from advancing into Christian France.

1278. Andorra comes under the joint suzerainty of France and Spain through the Catalan bishops of Urgel and of the counts of Foix of France. Throughout the Middle Ages and modern times up to World War II, Andorra remains outside the mainstream of European history, with limited ties to countries other than France and Spain. The economy is limited to small farm agriculture and forestry and is helped by smuggling.

1607. The head of the French state and the bishop of Urgel are established as the co-princes of Andorra.

1950s. International tourism starts to grow with the emergence of post-World War II western European welfare societies, the growing income and leisure time of the Europeans, and the increasing attractiveness of both neighboring France and Spain as two of the world's top tourist destinations. Tourism revenues, foreign investment, and the rapid development of tourist

infrastructure profoundly change the way of life in the course of a single generation and attract for the first time in the country's history many immigrants, lured by the opportunities for business and jobs offered by the economic boom.

1970. Women receive the right to vote.

1987. Andorra starts trade talks with the EU.

1993. Andorra adopts its first constitution and is admitted to the United Nations.

FUTURE TRENDS

The Andorran economy is now very closely related to those of France and Spain and is dependent on the overall trends in the EU. Despite positive recent changes in the economy, related to the increasing role of modern services, it is likely that Andorra will, at least over the next few years, continue to confront a number of problems arising from the large influx of foreigners and the need to develop modern social institutions.

In addition to questions of Andorran nationality and immigration, the country's priorities will include addressing housing scarcities and the tough real estate market, reinvigorating international tourism, and renegotiating its trade relationship with the EU.

The results of Andorra's polls so far have indicated that the people generally support reform initiatives and believe that the country has to integrate into the EU in order to preserve and develop its economic prosperity. It is likely that it will be successful in shifting from duty-free shopping to finance and other services as the second major economic sector and revenue source.

DEPENDENCIES

Andorra has no territories or colonies.

BIBLIOGRAPHY

Andorra. <http://www.andorra.be/eng/index.html>. Accessed July 2001.

Economist Intelligence Unit. *Country Profile: Andorra.* London: Economist Intelligence Unit, 2001.

Global Investment Business Center, Inc. staff. *Andorra: A Country Study Guide.* International Business Publications, February 2001.

U.S. Central Intelligence Agency. *World Factbook 2000.* <http://www.odci.gov/cia/publications/factbook/index.html>. Accessed August 2001.

U.S. Department of State. *U.S. Department of State Background Notes: Europe: Andorra.* <http://www.state.gov/www/background_notes/eurbgnhp.html>. Accessed January 2001.

—Valentin Hadjiyski

ARMENIA

Republic of Armenia
Hayastani Hanrapetut 'Yun

CAPITAL: Yerevan.

MONETARY UNIT: Armenian Dram (AMD). One dram equals 100 luma. Coins are in denominations of 1 dram and 50 and 20 luma. Paper currency is printed in denominations of AMD10, 25, 50, 100, 200, 1,000, and 5,000.

CHIEF EXPORTS: Diamonds, scrap metal, machinery and equipment, cognac, and copper ore.

CHIEF IMPORTS: Natural gas, petroleum, tobacco products, foodstuffs, and diamonds.

GROSS DOMESTIC PRODUCT: US$9.9 billion (purchasing power parity, 1999 est.).

BALANCE OF TRADE: **Exports:** US$240 million (1999 est.). **Imports:** US$782 million (1999 est.).

COUNTRY OVERVIEW

LOCATION AND SIZE. Armenia is located in the southwest Caucasus Region, neighboring on Georgia and Azerbaijan to the north, Iran and Turkey to the south, and a separate province of Azerbaijan in the southeast. The total area of the country is 29,800 square kilometers (11,505 square miles), making it about the size of Maryland. The nation's capital is Yerevan, with a population of 1.5 million.

POPULATION. The total population of Armenia was estimated at 3,344,336 people in July 2000. According to the United Nations' *Human Development Report*, the total population of Armenia in 1993 was estimated at 3.7 million people. Hence the population has dropped since 1993 by more than 350,000 people, or about 10 percent. This decline is the result of a low fertility rate and wide-scale **immigration** (there are 4.23 migrants per every 1,000 members of the population). Life expectancy at birth for the total population is 66.4 years (61.98 for males and 71.04 for females). The total fertility rate is 1.47 children born per woman, which is below the replacement level, with 10.97 births per 1,000 members of the population. (Replacement level is a term that refers to the number of children a couple must have to replace only themselves. Thus, a man and woman would have 2 children to achieve replacement level. If a society has an overall replacement level of 2, then it has a stable population, neither growing nor shrinking. When women in a society typically have fewer than 2 children on average, this can be a sign of a shrinking population over time.) The infant mortality rate is 41.48 deaths per 1,000 live births.

Ethnic Armenians comprise 93 percent of the population. Other ethnic groups include the Azeris at 3 percent, Russians at 2 percent, and Kurds at 2 percent. Almost 96 percent of the nation's population speak Armenian. Russian is the second most common language, although only 2 percent of the population uses it as their primary form of communication. Orthodox Christianity is the most popular religion. The population density is 137 people per square kilometer (355 per square mile). About 31 percent of the population lives in rural areas and 69 percent in urban areas.

OVERVIEW OF ECONOMY

In 1920, Armenia was incorporated into what was then the Soviet Union. While it was under Soviet control, an effort began in the 1960s to industrialize the nation. From its previous state of minimal industrial development, Armenia became a significant manufacturing center, supplying machine tools, textiles, and various manufactured goods to the other Soviet Republics. In return, Armenia received raw materials and energy from these republics. Since independence in 1991, however, many large agro-industrial complexes were divided into small-scale agricultural units. New investments and new technologies are necessary for the healthy development of the agricultural sector. The government has given a high priority to **privatization** of the industrial sector, although the speed of privatization in this sector is slower

than that in the agricultural sector. For food, Armenia relies partially on imports, and it possesses only small mineral deposits (mainly gold and bauxite).

The county experienced a severe economic decline in the beginning of the 1990s, due to a devastating 1988 earthquake, the conflict with Azerbaijan over the Nagorno-Karabakh region (see below), and the disintegration of the Soviet system. In 1994, with assistance from the International Monetary Fund (IMF), the Armenian government introduced an economic reform program which resulted in increased economic performance during the 1995–99 period. **Inflation** was reduced from a staggering 1,885 percent in 1994 to a mere 2.5 percent in 1999. In 1998, about 200 medium and large-scale enterprises and about 600 small enterprises were privatized. Thus far, 74 percent of the country's large and medium enterprises and 64 percent of the small enterprises have been privatized. As a result of economic **restructuring** and privatization, Armenia's economy has grown since 1994. In 1999, the nation's **gross domestic product** (GDP) grew by 5 percent. **GDP per capita** has also increased to US$2,900 in 1999 from only US$459 in 1994.

Armenia had no **foreign debt** when it gained independence from the Soviet Union in 1991. At that time, it signed an agreement with Russia that relieved Armenia of any obligations related to the former Soviet Union's **external debt**. In exchange, Armenia could not claim any of the Soviet Union's external assets. However, after independence the nation ran up a significant foreign debt. By 1998, Armenia's total outstanding external debt was US$827.8 million, or 53.9 percent of its GDP. The nation also has a significant **trade deficit**: in 1999, it imported US$542 million more in goods than it exported.

External factors have both harmed and helped the Armenian economy. The longstanding ethnic conflict with Azerbaijan over possession of the Nagorno-Karabakh region—an Armenian-dominated region that lies wholly within Azerbaijan—has hurt the economy in a variety of ways, creating internal instability and closing the Azerbaijani markets to Armenian goods (Azerbaijan used to be Armenia's largest trade partner). The conflict also led Turkey, which supports Azerbaijan, to impose a trade **embargo**. However, Armenia has been the recipient of substantial foreign aid. In 2000, the World Bank granted Armenia US$45 million to reduce the government's **budget deficit**. The Bank has also granted Armenia US$30 million for economic aid. The country on average has received over US$200 million per year since the mid-1990s.

POLITICS, GOVERNMENT, AND TAXATION

Armenia is a parliamentary republic. The government consists of the executive branch, a legislative branch, and a judicial branch headed by the Supreme Court. The 3 main institutions of the executive branch are the chief of state, the head of government, and the cabinet. Since March 30, 1998, the chief of state has been President Robert Kocharian, elected by popular vote for a 5-year term and winning with a vote of 59 percent. Since November 3, 1999, the head of government has been Prime Minister Aram Sarkisyan. The president appoints the prime minister (usually the leader of the largest political party in the parliament) who in turn appoints the cabinet members. The legislative branch is the **unicameral** (one-chamber) National Assembly (Azgayin Zhoghov). The Assembly consists of 131 members who are elected for 4-year terms.

In 1999, the Armenian government's revenues were US$360 million, but its expenditures were US$566 million. In an effort to reduce its deficit, the government has cut spending and received aid from the World Bank. In 1999, the government spent US$75 million on military expenditures, or about 4 percent of GDP. Payments on

Communications

Country	Newspapers	Radios	TV Sets[a]	Cable subscribers[a]	Mobile Phones[a]	Fax Machines[a]	Personal Computers[a]	Internet Hosts[b]	Internet Users[b]
	1996	1997	1998	1998	1998	1998	1998	1999	1999
Armenia	23	224	218	0.4	2	0.1	4.2	1.85	30
United States	215	2,146	847	244.3	256	78.4	458.6	1,508.77	74,100
Turkey	111	180	286	9.2	53	1.7	23.2	8.06	1,500
Georgia	N/A	555	473	2.8	11	N/A	N/A	1.59	20

[a]Data are from International Telecommunication Union, *World Telecommunication Development Report 1999* and are per 1,000 people.
[b]Data are from the Internet Software Consortium (http://www.isc.org) and are per 10,000 people.

SOURCE: World Bank. *World Development Indicators 2000.*

the debt are a major drain on the governmental resources. In 1999, the government spent US$108 million on payments on the debt.

Personal **income taxes** range from 0 to 30 percent depending on income, and corporate taxes also range up to 30 percent. Banks and insurance companies are charged a 45 percent tax rate.

In 1996, Armenia signed a trade agreement with the European Union (EU). The main benefit of this agreement has been increased foreign aid from the EU. The government has sought other trade agreements, but the ongoing conflict in Nagorno-Karabakh has created uncertainty about the Armenian economy and prevented significant foreign investment.

INFRASTRUCTURE, POWER, AND COMMUNICATIONS

Armenia's **infrastructure** needs substantial improvement. Much of the nation's roadways and railways were built during the Soviet period and are in need of repair and renovation. The length of the railway system in 1995, excluding industrial lines, was 825 kilometers (512 miles). Armenia had 15,998 kilometers (9,942 miles) of roads in 1998, of which 7,567 kilometers (4,702 miles) were expressways. All major roads were paved. Pipelines for natural gas in 1991 were 900 kilometers (560 miles) long. Armenia does not have any ports or harbors. There are 12 airports in Armenia (5 with paved runways), but only 10 are in service. Armenian Airlines, the national air carrier, operates service to a variety of international destinations including, Moscow, Paris, Athens, Amsterdam, Frankfurt, and Tehran.

In 1995, of Armenia's total production of electric energy, 60 percent was from gas-fired plants, 34 percent was hydroelectric, and 5 percent was atomic. By 1998 these rates had changed to 25 percent thermal, 49 percent hydro, and 26 percent atomic. The total production of electrical energy in that same period was 5.6 million kilowatt hours (kWh), according to the IMF.

The nation has approximately 650,000 telephones, which gives it a telephone density of 17.7 phones per 100 people. This is relatively low when compared with Western European nations. For instance, Belgium has a telephone density of 50 per 100 people. However, the German company Siemens is engaged in a US$100 million project to upgrade the nation's telephone system with fiber optic and digital telephone systems. About 90 percent of the nation's telecommunications system is now privately-owned. Mobile phone use is increasing with 20,000 mobile units in use in 1998. Use of the Internet is also on the rise with the number of Internet service providers increasing from 1 in 1999 to 7 in 2000. The United States has provided US$1 million to Armenia to supply Internet service for schools.

ECONOMIC SECTORS

Unlike most industrialized and economically developed nations where services and industry dominate the

Armenia
GDP–COMPOSITION BY SECTOR–1999 est.

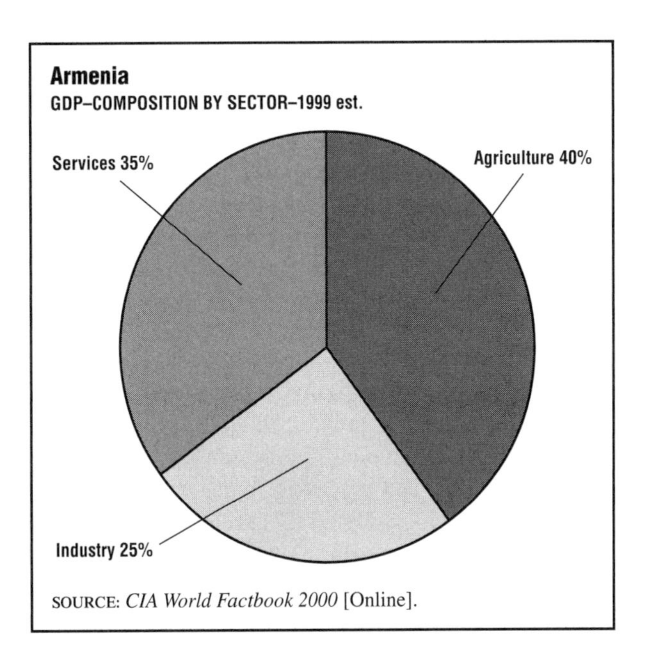

SOURCE: *CIA World Factbook 2000* [Online].

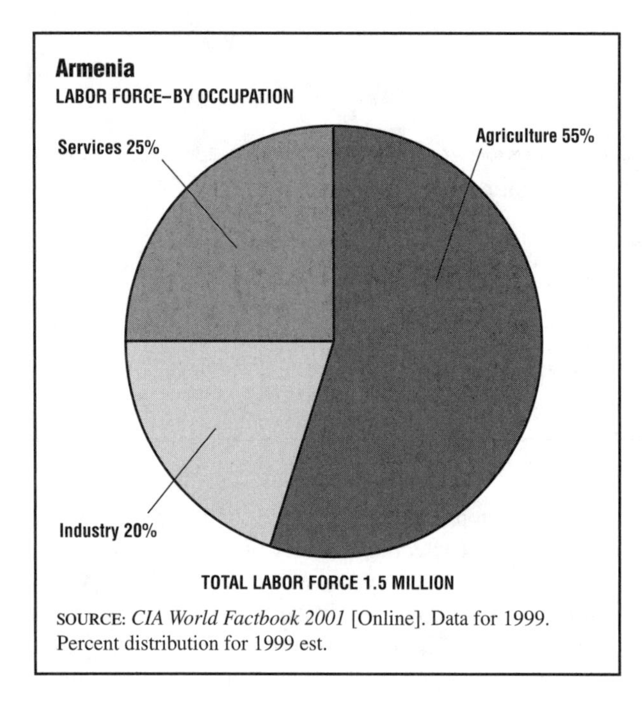

SOURCE: *CIA World Factbook 2001* [Online]. Data for 1999. Percent distribution for 1999 est.

economy, in Armenia agriculture is the main employer and largest source of GDP. According to the World Development report 2000/2001, the total **labor force** in 1999 was 1.5 million people, of which 55 percent were employed in agriculture, 25 percent in services, and 20 percent in industry. In 1999, agriculture accounted for 40 percent of GDP, industry 25 percent of GDP, and services 35 percent of GDP.

AGRICULTURE

Among the nations that made up the former Soviet Union, Armenia was the first to privatize agricultural lands. It broke up the large Soviet-style farms and reallocated the land to small, independent farmers. However, only 17 percent of the country's land is suitable for farming, which severely limits agricultural production. The nation has numerous vineyards and is a major producer of wine and cognac. In 1998 the World Bank provided US$15 million to establish a fund to furnish loans for small farmers.

Despite the limitations of this sector, agriculture provides the largest source of income for Armenia. Agricultural exports totaled US$15.4 million in 1998, or about 34 percent of all of the country's exports. The most significant exports were alcoholic beverages, various fruit juices, calf skins, and processed tomatoes. In 1998, the nation had to import US$297.7 million in agricultural products. In all, 70 percent of all food consumed in Armenia was imported in 1999. The main imports were eggs, sugar, flour, and processed foods.

A variety of crops are cultivated including barley, corn, potatoes, and wheat. In 1999, the total volume of crops produced amounted to 715,400 metric tons. This tally included 425,000 metric tons of potatoes, 220,000 metric tons of wheat, 65,000 metric tons of barley, and 5,200 metric tons of corn. The main livestock products were chicken, beef, and pork. In 1999, total agricultural production declined by 4.2 percent.

INDUSTRY

Industry in Armenia has traditionally been based on mining and the manufacture of goods such as textiles, electric motors, tires, chemicals, trucks, machine tools, and some consumer appliances (mainly washing machines). The contribution of industry to the economy fell from 46.5 percent in 1991 to 25 percent in 1999. In 1999 alone, industrial production declined by 2 percent. This decline has been the result of a lack of new investment (because of political uncertainty) and because many of the industrial markets in the former Soviet Union closed due to lack of demand.

MINING. Armenia possesses the second-largest reserves of copper in the world. Other important reserves are molybdenum, zinc, gold, silver, construction stones (mainly granite and marble), and other materials such as betonite, bauxite, perlite, zeolite, and diatomite. In the 19th century, industrial metallurgical mining started in the Alaverdy and Zangezur regions, and during Soviet times these activities increased enormously. In the 1980s, 25 percent of the Soviet molybdenum was supplied by Armenia. In 1991 the mining industry collapsed due to deteriorating conditions in the mines and declines in demand. In 1996, the mining industry started to recover, with production rising 32 percent in the period from 1996–99. From January to June 2000, it rose an additional 16 percent.

After food processing and jewelry and diamond processing, Armenia's mining sector was the third-largest industrial sector and the third-largest exporter. According to the Armenian government, exports of minerals and non-precious metals totaled roughly 23 percent of exports in 1995. Although the mining sector does relatively well, its production and export are well below its potential. The government has prepared a program to increase mining and metal production and to export more semi-finished products because of their higher **value added**. The major copper-molybdenum companies and the gold company are not yet privatized.

MANUFACTURING. Armenia was the leading chemical producer in the Caucasus in the 1970s, producing synthetic rubber, latex, acids, various glues, and special films mainly for the military sector. In the 1980s the chemical industry employed 24,200 people and accounted for 6.6

percent of the industrial production. The collapse of the Soviet Union, the energy crisis of 1992–93, and the war with Azerbaijan decreased the volume of production by more than 50 percent. In 1999, Armenia imported 6 times as many chemical products and materials as it produced itself. The main chemical export product is rubber, comprising 82 percent of total chemical exports, of which 93 percent went to states of the former Soviet Union. According to expert Jocelyne Decaye, the main weaknesses of Armenia's chemical industry are "high dependence on imported raw materials, obsolete technologies and old production lines, logistical difficulties related to Armenia's location, overstaffing and high costs for transports and electricity."

Armenia's light industry sector was well developed in the 1980s, when it had 115,000 employees and accounted for 25 percent of total industrial production. In the 1990s, however, the share of light industry in the total industrial production declined to under 2 percent. Textile and clothing production make up the most significant activities in this sector.

In 1999, the food processing industry accounted for 39 percent of total industrial output and 61 percent of total manufacturing output. In the 1980s, food processing accounted for only 18 percent of Armenia's total industrial production. The first 5 years of the 1990s saw a rise of nearly 70 percent. The major food products are wine and brandy, with such products as vegetables, fruits, tobacco, potatoes, cotton, grains, and teas making up the rest. Less than 10 percent of the total production is exported (US$16 million in 1999).

SERVICES

The value of services to the Armenian economy increased as a percentage of GDP from 31 percent in 1990 to 35 percent in 1999. The main segments of the service sector include tourism and financial services. Many common Western services do not exist in Armenia. For instance, there are no fast food or **retail** chains.

TOURISM. During the first 5 years of independence, the tourist industry declined, but since 1996, this trend has reversed itself. Since 1996, the number of tourists has more than tripled but remains low compared to the 1980s (about 21,000 visitors in 1999, including business tourism). The share of tourism as a percentage of GDP was 1.7 percent in 1999. The tourism infrastructure needs substantial development and modernization to keep this industry growing.

FINANCIAL SERVICES. During the Soviet period, the State Insurance Company provided mandatory insurance for all citizens. The responsibility to regulate the insurance market now rests in the hands of the Ministry of Finance. The Ministry of Finance provides licenses for insurance companies, and in 2001 some 65 private and state companies were registered. As of 2001, a legal framework concerning the insurance market was still being developed. Domestic and international companies are treated equally under Armenian law.

The banking system accounts for about 10 percent of GDP. In 1999, there were 31 commercial banks. The main foreign banks are Mellat Bank of Iran and Midland Bank of the United Kingdom. Only Midland Bank has established Automated Teller Machines (ATMs), and only a limited number of businesses in the major cities can accept credit cards as a form of payment. The total capital of all commercial banks in Armenia is US$60 million. The largest private bank is HSBC Armenia Bank with assets of US$9 million.

INTERNATIONAL TRADE

Armenia has maintained a trade deficit since independence in 1991. According to the *CIA World Factbook*, Armenia exported US$240 million in 1999, an increase of almost 5 percent compared to 1998. The country has also diversified its trading partners and now trades with an increasing number of Western nations. Armenia imported US$782 million in 1999, a decrease of about 6.5 percent compared to 1998, but still 3 times the amount of 1993. Until the nation's economy recovers, this deficit will continue.

Belgium is Armenia's largest export partner, importing a total value of US$84 million, followed by Russia and Iran, both of which imported US$34 million in 1999. In fourth place was the United States, importing US$16 million, and in fifth came Georgia with US$11 million. Most of the Armenian exports, US$127 million, went to industrial countries, and US$97 million went to developing countries, according to the IMF.

Armenia's main import partner was Russia, accounting for US$181 million in 1999. Second came the United States, exporting US$86 million in 1999. The

Trade (expressed in millions of US$): Armenia

	Exports	Imports
1994	215	393
1995	270	673
1996	290	855
1997	232	892
1998	223	895
1999	232	799

SOURCE: United Nations. *Monthly Bulletin of Statistics* (September 2000).

Exchange rates: Armenia

dram per US$1	
Feb 2001	554.29
2000	539.53
1999	535.06
1998	504.92
1997	490.85
1996	414.04

SOURCE: CIA *World Factbook 2001* [ONLINE].

GDP per Capita (US$)

Country	1975	1980	1985	1990	1998
Armenia	N/A	N/A	N/A	1,541	892
United States	19,364	21,529	23,200	25,363	29,683
Turkey	1,898	1,959	2,197	2,589	3,167
Georgia	1,788	2,366	2,813	2,115	703

SOURCE: United Nations. *Human Development Report 2000; Trends in human development and per capita income.*

United States was followed by Belgium, which exported US$85 million, then Iran with US$78 million, and in fifth was the United Kingdom, exporting US$67 million. Of Armenia's total imports, US$368 million came from industrial countries and US$451 million came from developing countries, according to the IMF's *Direction of Trade Statistical Yearbook 2000.*

MONEY

The value of the dram has declined significantly since the 1990s. In 1995, 405.91 drams equaled US$1. However, by 2000 it took 539.53 drams to equal US$1. This decline is the result of the continuing weaknesses in the Armenian economy.

In 1993, the Yerevan Stock Exchange (YSE) was established, which was followed by the establishment of 3 smaller exchanges. However, the total value of these 4 exchanges was only US$1.67 million in 1999.

POVERTY AND WEALTH

Officially, 45 percent of the population is considered to be poor, but unofficial estimates place the figure as high as 55 percent. Although poverty is mostly urban (59 percent), the incidence of extreme poverty is higher in rural than in urban areas. Rural poverty is expected to worsen as a result of people leaving rural areas for the cities. State expenditures on social infrastructure and product **subsidies** dropped drastically following independence from the Soviet Union in 1991, thus hurting the ability of the poor to meet basic needs. Since people make very low wages, food comprises about 67 percent of household expenditures. In 1996, the Ministry of Statistics and the World Bank found that the poor represented 55 percent of the total population, while the extremely poor constituted 28 percent. The only good news is that there has been a significant decrease in the proportion of the extremely poor, which is probably due to programs designed to help this sector.

Out of 580,000 **pensioners** (retired people receiving pensions) in Armenia, 223,000 are old age or retired pensioners, of which 186,402 are identified as needy and included in the system of family allowances. Pensions remain exceedingly low, with the average monthly pension worth US$7.5 and average family allowance at US$12. Without assistance from their families, many pensioners would face the most severe poverty.

WORKING CONDITIONS

In 1994, according to the IMF, 1,488,000 Armenians were employed and 106,000 were unemployed, resulting in an actual labor force of 1,594,000 people. The figures for 1998 give a different picture, with the number of total employed persons decreasing to 1,351,000,

Household Consumption in PPP Terms

Country	All food	Clothing and footwear	Fuel and power[a]	Health care[b]	Education[b]	Transport & Communications	Other
Armenia	52	3	18	3	15	4	5
United States	13	9	9	4	6	8	51
Turkey	45	7	18	6	5	2	16
Georgia	33	4	13	2	4	8	36

Data represent percentage of consumption in PPP terms.
[a]Excludes energy used for transport.
[b]Includes government and private expenditures.

SOURCE: World Bank. *World Development Indicators 2000.*

and a total of 139,000 unemployed, resulting in an actual labor force of 1,492,000 people. Although official figures state that the unemployment rate was 9.3 percent in 1998, unofficial estimates place the rate as high as 20 percent. In the state sector, 794,000 people had jobs in 1994, and in the **private sector** 694,000 people were employed. By 1998, 441,000 people were employed in the state sector, and 912,000 in the private sector, reflecting a major decrease in government payrolls.

According to the constitution, employees have the right to join and form trade unions and to form associations, although members of the armed forces and law enforcement agencies are forbidden to do so.

The minimum monthly wage in 1994 was AMD1,851, although by the second quarter of 1999 it had risen to AMD5,000. Forced and bonded labor is forbidden in Armenia, and for children the minimum working age is 16 years, although with the permission of a medical commission and the relevant union board, children may work from the age of 14. The standard legal work week is 41 hours, and with such a low minimum wage, most people have to take multiple jobs to support themselves and their families.

COUNTRY HISTORY AND ECONOMIC DEVELOPMENT

c. 900 B.C. A number of small kingdoms are established in what becomes Armenia.

66 B.C. Armenia is conquered by the Romans.

1080–1269. During Armenia's "Silver Age," Armenia gains independence from Byzantium and there is a flowering of Armenian culture and the arts.

1375. Armenia is conquered by the Turks.

1639. Armenia is divided between Persia and Turkey.

1828. Eastern areas of Armenia are conquered by Russia.

1902. The Tiflis-Alexandropol-Yerevan railway is completed, dramatically increasing trade.

1915. During the Armenian Genocide, an estimated 1 million Armenians were killed by the Ottoman Turks.

1918. Armenia becomes an independent nation following the collapse of the Ottoman Empire at the end of World War I (1914–1918).

1918–1920. War occurs between Armenia and Turkey.

1922. Armenia is incorporated into the Soviet Union.

1923. The predominately Armenian region of Nagorno-Karabakh is transferred to Azerbaijan.

1950s. The Soviets undertake a broad effort to industrialize Armenia.

1988. An earthquake in Armenia results in the deaths of an estimated 25,000 people.

1991. Armenia gains independence from the Soviet Union after a nation-wide referendum.

1994. Azerbaijan and Armenia go to war over Nagorno-Karabakh. Economic conditions deteriorate and inflation exceeds 1,800 percent.

1995. A new constitution is adopted.

1996. Armenia signs a trade agreement with the EU.

1999. Prime Minister Vazgen Sarkissyan and other government leaders are assassinated.

2000. Armenia's request for admission to the Council of Europe is approved.

FUTURE TRENDS

A major impediment to Armenia's economic growth is its lack of infrastructure. Antiquated equipment has not been upgraded because of a lack of funds, and as a result many sectors of the economy are neither productive nor competitive. Most privatization efforts resulted in sales to people with connections who usually lacked either the commitment or the capacity to streamline operations. Industrial output is still low, and there is a lack of foreign investment. Armenia's imports exceed its exports by a 3-to-1 margin.

Although there are objective reasons for the failure of the Armenian economy, the widespread perception of corruption at every level of society seriously hampers the government's ability to attract foreign investment. The lack of confidence in the government has also created widespread political apathy among the population.

Furthermore, the high level of unemployment and seeming lack of hope in the country's future has created an **emigration** crisis. Although reliable statistics are hard to come by, the consensus among most observers is that hundreds of thousands of people have emigrated, with no indication that the exodus will abate anytime soon.

DEPENDENCIES

Armenia has no territories or colonies.

BIBLIOGRAPHY

Bailey, H.W. "Armenian Religion." *Encyclopedia Iranica.* Vol. 2. London: Routledge & Kegan Paul, 1978.

Chetarian, Vicken. "Eurasia Insight: The Struggle to Fill the Power Vacuum in Armenia." *Eurasianet.org.* <http://www.eurasianet.org/departments/insight/articles/eav040300.shtml>. Accessed January 2001.

"Country Brief/Armenia." *World Bank Group.* <http://wbln0018.worldbank.org/eca/eca.nsf/ec6733e67523edfe852567d10012dddd/33838e84287562c6c12567e900551544?OpenDocument>. Accessed December 2000.

Decaye, Jocelyne. "Sector Profiles: Mining Industry." *Armenian European Policy and Legal Advice Centre (AEPLAC) Papers.* <http://www.aeplac.am./papers.html>. Accessed January 2001.

Economist Intelligence Unit. *Country Profile: Armenia.* London: Economist Intelligence Unit, 2001.

"Economy and Business." *Embassy of the Republic of Armenia.* <http://www.armeniaemb.org/geninfo/economy.htm>. Accessed January 2001.

"Human Development Report 2000." *United Nations Development Program.* <http://www.undp.org/hdr2000/english/HDR2000.html>. Accessed December 2000.

International Monetary Fund. *Direction of Trade Statistical Yearbook 2000.* Washington, D.C.: IMF, 2000.

Krekorian, Robert. "Armenia Under Fire." *Transitions Online.* <http://archive.tol.cz/countries/armar99.html>. Accessed January 2001.

Papazian, Dennis R. *Armenia and Armenians.* <http://www.hr-action.org/armenia/armenians.html>. Accessed August 2001.

"Poverty Assessment." *Government of the Republic of Armenia.* <http://www.gov.am/en/gov/iprsp/3.html>. Accessed July 2001.

Russel, J. R. "Armenian Religion." *Encyclopedia Iranica.* Vol. 2. London: Routledge & Kegan Paul, 1978.

"Sector Profiles." *Armenian European Policy and Legal Advice Centre (AEPLAC) Papers.* <http://www.aeplac.am./papers.html>. Accessed January 2001.

U.S. Central Intelligence Agency. *World Factbook 2000.* <http://www.odci.gov/cia/publications/factbook/index.html>. Accessed August 2001.

U.S. Department of State. *Armenia Country Report on Human Rights Practices for 1998.* <http://www.state.gov/www/global/human_rights/1998_hrp_report/armenia.html>. Accessed December 2000.

U.S. Department of State. *FY 2000 Country Commercial Guide: Ukraine.* http://www.state.gov/www/about_state/business/com_guides/2000/europe/index.html>. Accessed December 2000.

World Bank. *World Development Report 2000/2001.* Oxford: Oxford University Press, 2000.

—Mehdi Parvizi Amineh

AUSTRIA

Republic of Austria
Republik Österreich

CAPITAL: Vienna.

MONETARY UNIT: Austrian schilling (ATS). One Austrian schilling equals 100 groschen. There are 20, 50, 100, 500, 1,000, and 5,000 schilling notes, and 1, 5, 10, 20, and 50 schilling coins. There are also 10 and 50 groschen coins. In January 1999 Austria introduced the new European currency, the euro, for all electronic transactions. One euro had a fixed rate of 13.7603 Austrian schillings. It is planned that by 2002, euro bills and coins will replace the currencies in all European Union (EU) countries, including Austria.

CHIEF EXPORTS: Machinery and equipment, paper and paperboard, metal goods, chemicals, iron and steel, textiles, and foodstuffs.

CHIEF IMPORTS: Machinery and equipment, chemicals, metal goods, oil and oil products, and foodstuffs.

GROSS DOMESTIC PRODUCT: US$190.6 billion (purchasing power parity, 1999 est.).

BALANCE OF TRADE: **Exports:** US$62.9 billion (1999 est.). **Imports:** US$69.9 billion (1999 est.).

COUNTRY OVERVIEW

LOCATION AND SIZE. Austria is a landlocked country situated in southern Central Europe. Slightly smaller than Maine, it occupies a territory of approximately 84,000 square kilometers (32,000 square miles), which includes much of the mountainous territory of the eastern Alps and the Danube region. From east to west, Austria stretches to 580 kilometers (360 miles) and 294 kilometers (183 miles) from south to north. In total, the country has 2,708 kilometers (1,682 miles) of borders. It shares borders with 8 European countries: Germany (820 kilometers), the Czech Republic (469 kilometers), Italy (430 kilometers), Slovenia (330 kilometers), Hungary (354 kilometers), Switzerland (167 kilometers), Slovakia (103 kilometers), and Liechtenstein (35 kilometers).

Austria is a federal state comprised of 9 provinces: Burgenland, Carinthia, Lower Austria, Salzburg, Styria, Tyrol, Upper Austria, Vorarlberg, and Vienna. The major cities of Austria and their populations are Vienna (1.64 million), Graz (237,810), Linz (203,044), Salzburg (143,978) and Innsbruck (118,112).

Austria has always been a junction for communication, trade, and cultural exchange in Europe. The capital, Vienna, located on both banks of the Danube River, in the northeast of the country near Slovakia and Hungary, was once the political and economic center of the Austro-Hungarian Empire (1867–1918). It is now the headquarters to some of world's most important organizations, such as the International Atomic Energy Agency (IAEA) and the United Nations Industrial Development Organization (UNIDO). Other international organizations based in Vienna include the Organization for Petroleum Exporting Countries (OPEC) and its Fund for International Development and the International Institute for Applied Systems Analysis (IIASA).

POPULATION. Austria has a population of 8,139,299 (July 2000 est.). The country is highly urbanized and densely populated, with 651 people per square kilometer (251 per square mile). Nearly two-thirds of the people live in urban areas. About 4.0 million are male and 4.2 million (51.5 percent) are female. Due to improved health conditions and a low birthrate, Austria has experienced the rapid growth of its elderly population. Average life expectancy for those born in 2000 was 73.9 year for males and 80.2 years for females. About 21 percent of the population was under 18 years old. If current trends continue, by 2030, the number of children under 18 will drop to only 17 percent. The fertility rate is an estimated 9.9 per 1,000 people, and infant mortality is 6.7 per 1,000 live births. An estimated 99 percent of Austrians age 15 and

older can read and write, and there is 1 teacher for every 11 pupils.

ETHNICITY. Approximately 98 percent of the population is German. The remainder of the population is divided among a number of ethnic groups, including the Neo-Latins, Slavs, Magyars, Croats, Hungarians, Romany, Sinti, Czechs, and Slovaks. Burgenland province is home to a number of Croats and Hungarians. The majority of Austrian Slovenes live in the Gail, Rosen, and Jaun valleys of southern Carinthia and in some villages in the southern part of Styria. Romany and Sinti live mostly in Burgenland and to some extent in Vienna. Many Czechs and Slovaks also reside in Vienna and in Lower Austria, particularly in the Marchfeld and Tullnerfeld regions. The country receives refugees from a variety of nationalities, many of whom are from the former Yugoslavia.

RELIGION. Roman Catholics constitute 78 percent of the Austrian population; a further 5 percent are Protestant, and most of them belong to the Augsburg confession. About 4.5 percent of the population belongs to various other religious groups, while another 9 percent are non-denominational, and the remaining 3.5 percent of the people do not belong to any religion. Every young person over the age of 14 can freely choose his or her religion according to Austrian law. Religious education in Austrian schools is not restricted to the Roman Catholic confession, but most schools are Roman Catholic.

OVERVIEW OF ECONOMY

Austria has a small, yet open, economy with exports of goods and services accounting for 47 percent of the **gross domestic product** (GDP). In the past 2 decades Austria has enjoyed higher economic growth and lower unemployment than many European countries. The **recession** in the early 1990s led to a downward trend in annual GDP growth, from 4.2 percent in 1990 to 0.4 percent in 1994. Since 1995, however, due to positive merchandise export and investment activities brought about by membership in the European Union, the economy has experienced fairly constant growth, with annual GDP growth rates for 1998, 1999, and 2000 of 3.3 percent, 2.8 percent, and 2.7 percent respectively.

The country has a strong economic infrastructure with well developed industry, banking, transportation, services, and commercial facilities. Most of Austria's industrial and commercial enterprises are small. However, there are a number of large industrial enterprises employing thousands of people, mainly in iron and steel works and chemical plants. Overall, industry accounted for an estimated 32 percent of gross domestic product in 1998, with an average growth rate of nearly 3 percent. Though forming a relatively small component of the GDP—1.3 percent in 1998—agriculture also plays a vital role in Austria. Austrian farmers provide about 80 percent of the domestic food requirements of the country and contribute to export earnings with processed food items. Farms in Austria, like those of other mountainous European countries, are small and fragmented, with production being relatively expensive. Since Austria became a member of the EU in 1995, its agricultural sector has been undergoing reforms to comply with the EU's common agricultural policy.

Export growth was very strong during 2000. Trade with other EU countries accounts for nearly two-thirds of Austria's total imports and exports. Approximately 35 percent of the total exports went to Germany and 10 percent went to Italy. Austria's location is of immense importance for its economic growth. Vienna is one of three capitals forming a strategic Central European triangle. Slovakia's capital, Bratislava, and Hungary's capital, Budapest, are within short distances to Vienna. Expanding trade and investment in the **emerging markets** of Central and Eastern Europe continues to be a major element of Austrian economic activity. Exports to that region increased significantly since 1989, reaching an estimated 17 percent of Austrian exports by 1998. Austrian firms have sizable investments in—and continue to move labor-intensive, low-tech production to—the region. Although the Austrian government and businesses support the European Union's plans to offer membership to several East European countries, they insist that the candidates meet EU economic standards before accession. They have also favored a transition period for the free movement of labor and services to prevent severe competition in the Austrian labor market during accession.

For many years, the government and its state-owned industries played a primary role in the Austrian economy. Many of the country's largest firms were **nationalized** after World War II to protect them from Soviet takeover as war reparations. These included all oil production and refining, the largest commercial banks, and the principal companies in river and air transportation, railroad equipment, electric machinery and appliances, mining, iron, steel, and chemical manufacturing, and natural gas and electric power production. Although the government retains substantial control over the economy, many of these enterprises were **privatized** in the 1980s and 1990s. Through privatization efforts including the 1996–1998 budget consolidation programs and austerity measures, Austria brought its total **public sector** deficit down to 2.1 percent of GDP in 1999 and public debt to 63.1 percent of GDP in 1998. After the formation of a new government in February 2000, Austria promoted further economic **liberalization**, privatization, reform of the welfare system, and abolition of the system of political patronage (where those in political power protect and support certain businesses). An opinion poll published at the end of May 2000 showed that 43 percent of Austrians were in favor of these reforms, and 23 percent were against.

Membership in the EU has brought economic benefits and challenges. An influx of foreign investors, for example, have been attracted by Austria's access to the single European market. Austria also has made progress in increasing its international competitiveness. Since Austria is a member of the European Monetary Union (EMU), its economy is closely integrated with other EU member countries, especially Germany. Although economists have generally agreed that the economic effects of the EMU on Austria, such as the use of a common currency, have been and will be positive, support for the EU in late-2000 fell to an all-time low. According to a poll by the national newspaper *Die Presse*, on 27 October 2000, only 34 percent of Austrians thought that their country has benefited from EU membership; the figure was 45 percent in autumn of 1999. Some Austrians have asked for their country's complete withdrawal from the EU. It is not likely that such initiatives will get very far, however, with the Austrian chancellor having attacked the idea of withdrawal as a "betrayal of the European idea."

POLITICS, GOVERNMENT, AND TAXATION

Austria has a well-developed market economy and a federal republic form of government; the state has historically played a large role in the economy, though that role decreased dramatically at the end of the 20th century. Governed by 2 major parties, the Social Democrats (SPO) and the conservative People's Party (OVP), Austria has enjoyed political stability and economic growth since 1945. The SPO, which garnered 33 percent of the votes in the 1999 national legislative elections, traditionally draws its constituency and much of its strength from the urban and industrial areas. In the past, the SPO has advocated heavy state involvement in strategic industries, the extension of social security benefits, and a **full-employment** policy. In the mid-1980s, the party shifted more toward the advocacy of free market economics and the balancing of the federal budget. The OVP's traditional constituency has been among farmers, large and small businesses, and lay Catholic groups. Its center of strength is rural Austria. The OVP has also advocated conservative financial policies and privatization of previously nationalized industries. The OVP received 27 percent of the votes in the 1999 election.

The major opposition to both parties during the late 1990s and early 2000s elections was the populist right-of-center Freedom Movement Party, headed by the controversial Jörg Haider, characterized as an ultranationalist (one who supports the nation at any cost), and a xenophobe (one who fears foreigners). Haider made several strong remarks praising Nazi policies. The rise of the Freedom Movement Party—from 5 percent of the votes in the 1983 election to 27 percent in 1999—was credited to voters who were disappointed by the employment opportunities in Austria. A system known as Proporz, supported by the ruling parties, distributed most top jobs in state business and public service to members of those parties. After the fall of the Iron Curtain in November 1989, when the U.S.S.R. started to loosen its control on the borders of its Eastern satellites, cheap and skilled labor came into Austria from Poland, Czechoslovakia, Hungary, and Slovenia. Many Austrian workers lost their jobs to the immigrants who were willing to work for lower pay and fewer benefits. In addition, many farmers were dissatisfied over the EU agrarian policy put into place after 1995, which lowered prices for agricultural products. In addition, the lack of professional chances in the civil service and in many other state institutions due to the EU budget criteria aroused the dissatisfaction of many young people who were seeking traditionally secure government jobs. Haider's Freedom Movement Party, which was against **immigration** and interference from the European Union, won increasing support.

In February 2000 the conservative People's Party, which wanted to establish an effective and legitimate government that would enjoy the support of Parliament, formed a coalition with the Freedom Party. Nearly 54 percent of the electorate voted for the new federal government. The European Union condemned Austria's new coalition, froze diplomatic contacts, and imposed **sanctions**, accusing Haider of being a racist, xenophobe, and Nazi sympathizer. Austria criticized the European Union for interfering in a democratically elected government. Demonstrations in Austria and throughout Europe followed. Haider did not join the government, and in February 2000 he resigned from the Freedom Movement Party to concentrate on his role as governor of the Carinthia province. In September 2000, the European Union lifted sanctions against Austria. Haider was expected to wield influence from the sidelines, however.

Austria's federal structure of government involves a high degree of decentralization with the executive and legislative functions shared between the Federation (federal government) and the Länder (provinces). The Länder play a significant role in federal legislation, having independent regional legislations which cooperate with the Federation in the execution of the federal legislation. According to the constitution of 1920, the head of the country is the president, who is elected by popular vote every 6 years and who represents Austria in its international relations and serves as commander-in-chief of the armed forces. Thomas Klestil, who was elected on 8 July 1992, was elected to a second term on 19 April 1998, with 63 percent of votes. The president is limited to 2 consecutive terms or a total of 12 years in office. Presidential elections are scheduled for the spring of 2004. The president appoints the head of the government, a federal chancellor, who appoints others to the executive branch. With the chancellor's recommendation, the president appoints the ministers. The president also appoints judges. After 4 February 2000, chancellor Wolfgang Schuessel of the OVP headed Austria's government.

The constitution of Austria provides for a distinct division of power among the executive, the legislative, and the judicial branches of government. Executive authority is vested in the federal government composed of the federal chancellor, a vice-chancellor, and other ministers. Legislative authority is vested in the **bicameral** (2-chambered) Federal Assembly composed of the Nationalrat (National Council or lower chamber) and the Bundesrat (Federal Council or upper chamber). Legislative authority is concentrated in the 183 members of the Nationalrat who are elected by direct popular vote for 4-year terms according to **proportional representation**. The Bundesrat consists of 64 members elected by the legislatures of the 9 provinces for 4- or 6-year terms, also according to proportional representation, with each province guaranteed at least 3 representatives. The Bundesrat reviews legislation passed by the Nationalrat and can send legislation back for reconsideration, but the Nationalrat need only pass the legislation a second time to override a veto. Furthermore, the Bundesrat can only initiate legislation by way of the government. The 2 chambers meeting as the Federal Assembly can propose a national referendum, if needed. The highest courts of Austria's independent judiciary are the Constitutional Court, which has jurisdiction over constitutional matters; the Administrative Court, which handles bureaucratic disputes; and the Supreme Court, which deals with civil and criminal cases. All cases initiated in the Administrative and Supreme Courts can be appealed to the Constitutional Court. The president appoints justices of all 3 courts for specific terms.

The federal government is responsible for developing and implementing the domestic and foreign policies of Austria and sets economic policy in consultation with what is known as the social partnership, consisting of the representative bodies of businesses, farmers, and labor. Designed to minimize social unrest, this consensual approach has come under criticism for slowing the pace of economic reforms, particularly in inflexible labor and product markets. With an increasing number of decisions being made at the EU level, the influence of the social partnership has declined significantly. The government no longer has majority ownership in companies such as OMV (oil and gas), Voest (steel and plant engineering) and Elin (electrical machinery and equipment). **Subsidy** programs have also been scaled back to conform to EU regulations.

In 1997, the government completed an ambitious 10-year privatization program, which included the privatization of steel, aluminum, petroleum, engineering, banking, and other entities. The sale of the Postal Savings Bank and the Austrian Tobacco Company were underway in 2001. Furthermore, the federal railroads were excluded from federal budget accounts, and the newly reorganized Post und Telekom Austria (PTA) (postal and communications company) was divested as a private corporation and was required by law to list its shares on the stock market. Another focus of economic policy was employment creation. Austria has been one of the foremost supporters of the EU's national employment plans, which place strong emphasis on training and education, removal of bureaucratic hurdles, more labor flexibility, and a favorable climate for business start-ups. While some of these plans have been implemented, the government has failed to completely do away with the governing parties' special relationships with business and labor representatives.

The major source of government revenue comes from taxes. The corporate income and capital gains tax rate is 34 percent. A withholding tax of 25 percent applies to dividends, except for those paid to Austrian companies, and interest. A 20 percent tax rate applies to royalties. Only the Austrian-source income of non-resident companies is subject to taxation. When Austria joined the European Union, the government was forced to accelerate structural reforms and to liberalize its economy. Most non-**tariff** barriers to merchandise trade were removed, and cross-border capital movements were fully liberalized.

The 1996–97 economic program enabled the government to cut the federal deficit to 3.7 percent of gross domestic product in 1996, and to 2.6 percent in 1997. Because of this program, which included tax increases, the share of total taxes in gross domestic product reached a high of 44.8 percent in 1997. In 2000 the government cut taxes. The tax reform was expected to reduce the burden on taxpayers by approximately US$2.2 billion by 2003. These reforms included greater tax privileges for old age, a decrease in marginal tax rates, and an increase in the standard tax credit from US$592 to US$817 per year. These measures will ease the burden on the taxpayer by between US$268 and US$469 a year. About two-thirds of the entire reduction of the tax burden will benefit people earning monthly incomes of less than ATS23,000 (US$1,540). Through these measures, the tax burden on the majority of incomes is expected to be lowered in real terms.

Regarding the taxation of enterprises, the 2000 tax reform package contained 2 new provisions: Interest payments on personal **equity** will be taken into consideration for taxation purposes, and a tax allowance of US$335,000 will be introduced for inheritance (gift) tax in the case of enterprise transfers. Moreover, the research contribution and apprenticeship allowance will be increased. Private provision for old age will be promoted. In addition, regarding the taxation of capital gains from the disposal of securities, the retention period will be prolonged from 1 year to 2 years.

Relative to the gross domestic product, this tax reform is more comprehensive than the previous ones implemented in 1989 and 1994. The main emphasis of the reform is on easing the tax burden on private consumption. Consumer demand is expected to continue to increase by a cumulative 1.8 percent per year in real terms by 2005. Since direct incentives for investors are extremely modest, investments are not expected to grow significantly. Higher domestic demand, which also results in higher imports, is expected to only modestly contribute to the growth of GDP by 2005. The labor market is thought to be able to absorb another 9,300 employees. Price increases are expected to be insignificant at 0.2 percent.

INFRASTRUCTURE, POWER, AND COMMUNICATIONS

A distinctive feature of the Austrian energy sector is its diversified sources of supply. In 2000, the total primary energy supply included liquid fuels (38 percent), natural gas (24 percent), hydropower (13 percent), other renewable resources (13 percent) and coal (12 percent). Nuclear power is legally banned, following a referendum on the subject in 1978. The renewable resources share in Austria's energy supply increased from 16 percent in 1973 to 26 percent in 2000. The government plans to completely liberalize the electricity market by 2003. Preparations are also under way to open up the natural gas market.

For decades, the telecommunications industry was a **monopoly** in Austria, with the state-owned Post and Telecom Austria (PTA) being the only national supplier of networks and telecommunication services. Because of EU liberalization directives, the government enforced legislation to open the telecom and energy sectors to competition. The Austrian telecommunications sector now exhibits much liberalization, though high interconnection fees are still a problem. Austria has a highly developed telecommunications system with 4 million telephones, 27 radio stations, 47 television stations, and 4 satellite

Communications

Country	Newspapers	Radios	TV Sets[a]	Cable subscribers[a]	Mobile Phones[a]	Fax Machines[a]	Personal Computers[a]	Internet Hosts[b]	Internet Users[b]
	1996	1997	1998	1998	1998	1998	1998	1999	1999
Austria	296	753	516	139.1	282	N/A	233.4	252.01	1,840
United States	215	2,146	847	244.3	256	78.4	458.6	1,508.77	74,100
Germany	311	948	580	214.5	170	73.1	304.7	173.96	14,400
Hungary	186	689	437	146.5	105	17.7	58.9	93.13	600

[a]Data are from International Telecommunication Union, *World Telecommunication Development Report 1999* and are per 1,000 people.
[b]Data are from the Internet Software Consortium (http://www.isc.org) and are per 10,000 people.

SOURCE: World Bank. *World Development Indicators 2000.*

ground stations. Radio, television, telephone, and telegraph systems were all state monopolies until the broadcasting system was converted into a joint-stock company in 1957. The Austrian Broadcasting Company operates 3 radio and 2 television stations nationwide. Telephone and telegraph communications are directed by the Austrian postal and telecommunications service. More than 20 daily newspapers are published. Daily newspaper circulation averages more than 3.7 million. Influential dailies include *Die Presse* (published in Vienna) and *Salzburger Nachrichten* (published in Salzburg).

Austria has an excellent network of transportation and communication; due to its strategic location and relative political neutrality, Austria has established itself as a broker and an international place of encounter among nations. This role is exemplified by the countless summit meetings and conferences which the country hosts every year. Austria is also anticipating the increasing importance of its transport sector as an essential European communications hub. A factor of the growing importance of the transportation web is the growing European energy transit network (the transport of oil, natural gas and electricity), much of it passing through Austria.

A landlocked and mountainous country, Austria depends on roads and rail passage for a major share of its foreign trade. In the transportation segment, it has 200,000 kilometers (124,000 miles) of roads and 6,028 kilometers (3,744 miles) of railroads, of which about 5,388 kilometers (3,347 miles) are state owned and 640 kilometers (398 miles) privately owned. Furthermore, more than 350 kilometers (217 miles) of inland waterways carry approximately one-fifth of the country's total trade. The main river ports are Linz, Vienna, Salzburg, Graz, Klagenfurt, and Innsbruck. The Danube River, the only navigable waterway with barges carrying up to 1,800 tons, is an important connection between the North Sea, Germany, and the Black Sea. In terms of air connection, Austria has 55 civil airports, 20 with paved runways. The main international airport is Schwechat located in southeast Vienna. International flights are available from the airports in Graz, Innsbruck, Klagenfurt, Linz, and Salzburg.

ECONOMIC SECTORS

Austria is one of the wealthiest and most stable of the EU member countries. It has a free market economy with a strong emphasis on social factors favoring the economically less privileged and providing conditions for equitable wages and pricing. Service, industry, and agriculture are the 3 major sectors of the Austrian economy. The foremost products are foodstuffs, luxury commodities, mechanical engineering, steel, chemicals, and vehicles. Within the vehicle sector, the production of engines and transmissions is the most important, accounting for an export quota of more than 90 percent. Austria manufactures as many as 800,000 engines per year for major car manufacturers. In the electronic engineering field, Austria is known for its production of customized elec-

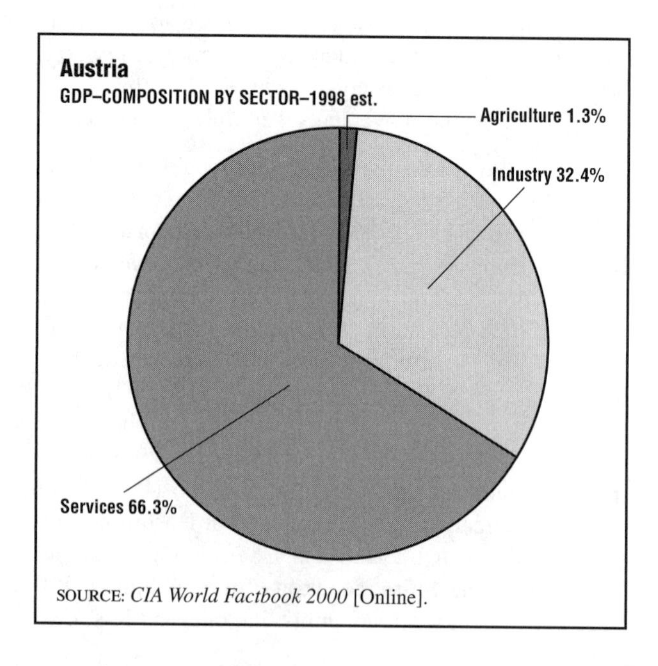

SOURCE: *CIA World Factbook 2000* [Online].

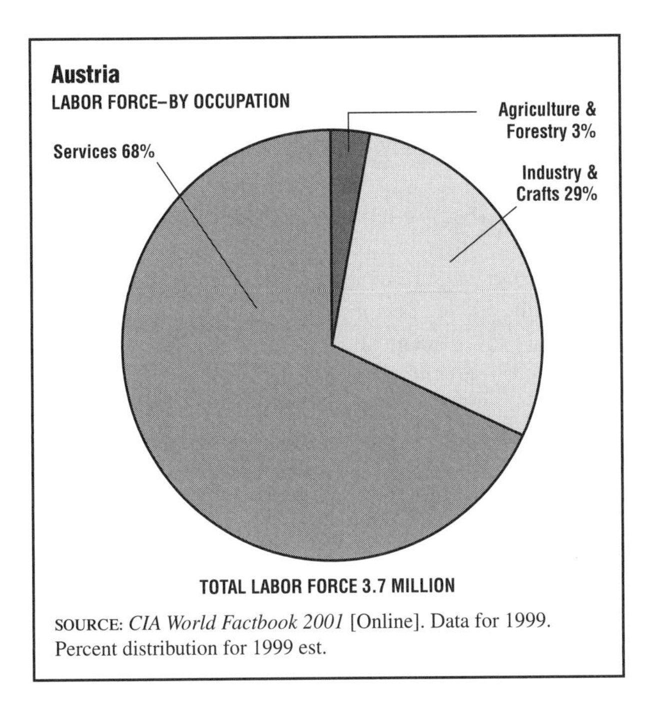

SOURCE: *CIA World Factbook 2001* [Online]. Data for 1999. Percent distribution for 1999 est.

tronics products such as microprocessors and integrated circuits for airbags, ABS braking systems, and components for Airbus airliners and for high-speed trains.

Approximately 3 percent of all Austrians work in agriculture and forestry. In 1998 that sector accounted for 1.3 percent of Austria's gross domestic product. Although about 41 percent of Austria's total area is thought to be suitable for agriculture, currently about 18 percent of the surface area is actually covered by farmland. Another 27 percent of the country's area is considered as grassland and nearly half (47 percent) is woods and forests. With its 20,000 organic farmers, Austria occupies a leading position in Europe in the branch of organic agriculture.

In 1998, Austrian industry (commodities manufacturing, energy, and mining) accounted for 32.4 percent of the GDP and employed 29 percent of the workforce. In the field of raw materials and energy generation, Austria possesses ample resources. It has major deposits of iron ore and non-ferrous metals. It also has its own resources of oil and natural gas and is the EU's number-one generator of hydroelectric power. However, the constant growth of the industrial sector necessitates a significant amount of supplementary imports. This is also true of fuels and energy and of the electricity which generates industry.

There are an unusually high number of medium-size enterprises in Austria's commercial industrial sector. Austrian industry covers practically every branch of manufacturing starting from basic goods to the labor-intensive production of finished goods. Plant construction (encompassing the planning, delivery, and assembly of industrial facilities) is among the most important industries of the country. Plant construction and electronics sectors are strongly export-oriented. Another export-oriented sector is Austria's handicrafts, famous worldwide for, among other things, costume jewelry, ceramics, and glassware.

AGRICULTURE

The agriculturally productive land of Austria covers 28.1 million hectares (69.5 million acres), or 94 percent of the total area. The provinces having the largest proportion of arable land are in the southern parts of the country. The total value of agricultural exports in 2000 was US$2.85 billion and that of imports was US$4.56 billion. A large amount of agricultural exports go to neighboring Italy.

FARMING. Austrian farms, like those of other West European mountainous countries, are small and fragmented. Their products are relatively expensive, with an emphasis on **cash crops**. Although Austrian farmers provide about 80 percent of domestic food requirements of the country, the agricultural contribution to the gross domestic product has declined since 1950. The principal agricultural products are wheat, rye, oats, barley, corn, potatoes, sugar beets, and cattle turnips. Besides these principal crops, other crops of considerable magnitude are: buckwheat, flax, tobacco, fuller's thistle, and cabbage. The principal garden products are kitchen vegetables and fruit, of which large quantities are exported. The best fruit districts are in Upper Austria and Styria. The primary meat products are beef and veal, chicken, duck, game, goose, horse, lamb, pork, rabbit, and turkey. The most valuable agricultural exports in 2000 were non-alcoholic beverages, chocolate products, beef, pastry, and processed fruit. Large quantities of wheat and maize are imported, much of it from neighboring Hungary. Important exports are barley, oats, milk, beef, and pork.

FOREST PRODUCTS. Forests occupy just over one-third of the productive area of Austria or 98,000 square kilometers (38,000 square miles). As much as 85 percent of all Austrian forests are dominated by tall timber, such as oak, pine, beech, ash, elm, and spruce, which are important in the paper and pulp industry and in building construction. In 2000 about 17 million cubic meters (590 million cubic feet) of round wood was cut. A comprehensive reforestation and conservation program has been in progress since the early 1950s to compensate for damage inflicted during WWII and for postwar overcutting of forest trees. Economic development in 1998 and the opening towards the EU market have also affected forestry. Although the number of employees and production decreased slightly, investments in forestry increased.

FISHERIES. The fisheries of Austria are very extensive. The numerous rivers of Austria swarm with a great variety of fish. The lake fisheries are largely developed and employ about 4,000 vessels and over 16,000 fishermen. Fishing for sport in the mountain streams is popular and constitutes a large source of income. However, most table fish are imported.

INDUSTRY

The essential industries in Austria are construction, machinery, vehicles and parts, food processing, chemicals, lumber and wood processing, paper and paperboard, communications equipment, energy production, and mining. Austria has favorable conditions for industrial activity, including a very well developed **infrastructure**, a rich source of raw material, and a skilled, moderately expensive **labor force**. Industrial output in 2000 (including energy production) grew by an estimated 6.8 percent over the previous year. The biggest growth rate, 11.1 percent, was recorded for **capital goods**, while production of **consumer goods** expanded by 2.6 percent.

MANUFACTURING. The Austrian manufacturing industry consists of a few large organizations, most of which operate under government control, and a great number of small and medium-size production units. Manufacturing remains focused on medium-technology sectors producing intermediate and capital goods, much of it bound as exports to neighboring Germany. Due to its well-established export markets, the manufacturing sector has a relatively low level of research and development expenditure, at 1.6 percent of gross domestic product in 1999, as compared to the EU average of 1.9 percent. The principal manufacturing products are textiles, metals, alcoholic beverages, leather, paper, sugar, glass, porcelain, earthenware, chemicals, and scientific and musical instruments. Because of the traditional popularity of Austrian wood, glass, textile, and ceramic handicrafts, many establishments produce such goods. The principal industrial products are pig iron, crude steel, rolled steel, motor vehicles, cement, fertilizers, paper, and cotton, woolen, and synthetic yarns and fabrics. Annual production of crude steel totaled about 3.95 million metric tons in 2000. The textile industry in all its branches (cotton, woolen, linen, silk, flax, and hemp) is a historic industry and is mostly concentrated in the southern part of the country.

MINING AND ENERGY. The annual production of principal minerals in 2000 included lignite coal (1.8 million metric tons), iron ore (1.6 million metric tons), crude oil (1.2 million metric tons), magnetite (1.0 million metric tons), salt (702,000 metric tons), and zinc ore (16,450 metric tons). Other substances commercially mined included copper, lead, antimony, bauxite, tungsten, and natural gas. Austria has numerous hydroelectric installations, which together produce nearly two-thirds of the country's electrical output. More than 51 billion kWh of electricity are generated each year.

SERVICES

Austria has an advanced industrial economy with a significant service sector. The service sector contributes more than 66 percent of the gross domestic product and employs 68 percent of the population. There is a substantial amount of foreign investment in the service sector. Foreign interests control most of the large computer-servicing firms, whereas tourism is in the hands of local interests. Management consultancy has also come to play a larger role in the Austrian economy, especially given Austria's role as a link between Eastern and Western Europe.

TOURISM. Because of its wealth of cultural and recreational facilities—including historical sites and winter and summer resorts in the spectacular mountains—Austria has a large tourism industry, which acts as a major earner of foreign exchange. More than 8 percent of Austrians are employed in the tourism industry. Tourism is based on the services of traditional agriculture in the Alpine region of Austria, where tourists appreciate the cultural landscape safeguarded by farmers. As many as 17,000 farmers annually rent private rooms to holiday-makers. In 1998, this category accounted for about 15 million overnight stays out of the total 111 million overnight stays in Austria. Austria's major cities are also a major attraction, for they boast some of the most impressive architecture in Europe and are known for the quality of their theatre, music, and museum art. According to the World Tourism Organization, Austria had 16.7 million visitors in 1997 and these visitors spent US$12.4 billion in the country. Increasingly, however, Austria has experienced a decline in the numbers of overnight stays due to its high prices compared to Eastern European countries.

FINANCIAL SERVICES. The contribution of the financial services sector to gross domestic product amounted to 6.3 percent in 2000. It employed some 110,000 people, or 3.6 percent of the workforce. The sector grew by 4.1 percent per year over the 1996–2000 period. Austrians' propensity to save, at about 25 percent of gross domestic product, has contributed to the success of the financial services. Austria's domestic savings to GDP ratio in 1999, according to the World Bank, was more than Germany's 23 percent or the United States' 15 percent. With about 1,000 banks, Austria has more than twice as many banks as neighboring Switzerland. Central and Eastern Europe comprise one area where Austria's banks have a competitive lead over European rivals. Raiffeisen Zentralbank has 2,500 staff and 80 branches in Central Europe and Bank Austria has 100,000 personal customers in the region. In addition to its presence in Western Europe, Austrian bank exposure abroad is also found in neighboring Hungary and the Czech Republic. Bank Austria has also been active in Russia.

RETAIL. At the turn of the 21st century Austria was undergoing a major shift in the nature of its **retail** establishments from a system based on small, locally-owned shops to one based on larger franchises and foreign-owned chains. EU membership has brought the entrance of large grocery, clothing, and household goods stores to the country, often driving family-owned businesses out of business. Small shops and boutiques once made up nearly 90 percent of the retail sector, but that number began shrinking in 1995. By 1999 large shopping centers and malls accounted for 12 percent of retail sales, and 33 new malls were in development in 2001. German retail chains represent the dominant foreign presence in the retail sector.

Franchising is a small but growing factor in the Austrian economy. Experts estimate that it accounts for about US$830 million in annual sales or just over 2 percent of total retail sales (compared to almost 50 percent in the United States). Current growth in the franchise market of Austria is around 10 percent annually. About 1 in 3 franchise systems operating in the country is of local origin. The top foreign participant in the Austrian franchising economy is Germany, with around 20 percent of the franchise systems, followed by the United States, with about 5 percent of all the systems.

INTERNATIONAL TRADE

Austria's economy is dependent on foreign trade and closely linked to the economies of other EU countries, particularly Germany. Austria trades with some 150 countries, with the European Union accounting for about two-thirds of the total. Beside a variety of goods, Austria exports money in the form of investments. It is a major investor in the former Eastern European countries, with some 40 percent of all direct foreign investments in that part of the world coming from Austria. Another important branch of Austria's foreign trade sector is transit trade for goods and services traveling east and west across Europe.

Austrian exporters sold merchandise worth US$65.6 billion in 2000, up from US$62.9 billion in 1999. In 2000, Austria's international trade continued to grow. The trade balance deficit dropped from 8.4 percent to 5.6 percent of the export volume, reaching its lowest level since 1945. The sound economic situation in Central and Eastern Europe, the booming economy in the United States, and the moderate economic development in the European Union, as well as the favorable **exchange rate** were the main contributing factors. What grew strongest was foreign trade with the Eastern European countries and the United States. Exports to Eastern Europe rose 23 percent in 2000 and imports 29 percent, while exports to North America increased by about one-third. Exports to the European Union rose 12 percent, while imports grew by 10 percent. Exports to Asia climbed by almost one-fifth in 2000, while those to Latin America showed a modest rise of 9 percent.

Trade (expressed in billions of US$): Austria

	Exports	Imports
1975	7.519	9.394
1980	17.489	24.444
1985	17.239	20.986
1990	41.265	49.146
1995	57.642	66.386
1998	62.767	68.277

SOURCE: International Monetary Fund. *International Financial Statistics Yearbook 1999.*

EU countries absorb the majority of Austrian exports and provide the majority of imports. In 1999, EU countries purchased 65 percent of Austria's exports, with Germany taking 36 percent, Italy 9 percent, and France 5 percent. Switzerland and Hungary each purchased 5 percent of Austria's exports. In 1999, 70 percent of all imports came from EU countries, with Germany providing 42 percent, Italy 8 percent, and France 5 percent. The United States is Austria's largest non-European trading partner, taking 4.5 percent of Austrian exports and providing 5 percent of its imports. Although the accession of Austria to the European Union has brought stiffer competition from European producers, U.S. exports to Austria increased considerably in the mid to late 1990s. Some U.S. exporters, particularly those in the data processing hardware and semiconductor sectors, are confronted with higher customs tariffs and regulations. Others have benefited from lower EU tariffs.

The EU ban on beef imports from cattle treated with hormones severely restricted U.S. exports of beef to Austria. Despite a World Trade Organization decision that the ban was inconsistent with the rules of international trade, the European Union did not lift the ban. Furthermore, the European Union ruled out the possibility of importing U.S. poultry or products containing poultry. The import of genetically modified food—what some Europeans call "Frankenstein food"—with the United States being the primary producer, was also banned. Austria went even further than its EU partners: Novartis corn and Monsanto BT corn, for example, which were major genetically modified foods approved by the European Commission, were banned imports in Austria.

Exchange rates: Austria

euros per US$1	
Jan 2001	1.0659
2000	1.0854
1999	0.9386
1998	12.379
1997	12.204
1996	10.587

Note: Amounts prior to 1999 are based on Austrian schillings per US dollar.

SOURCE: CIA *World Factbook 2001* [ONLINE].

GDP per Capita (US$)

Country	1975	1980	1985	1990	1998
Austria	18,857	22,200	23,828	27,261	30,869
United States	19,364	21,529	23,200	25,363	29,683
Germany	N/A	N/A	N/A	N/A	31,141
Hungary	3,581	4,199	4,637	4,857	4,920

SOURCE: United Nations. *Human Development Report 2000; Trends in human development and per capita income.*

MONEY

Austria has pursued moderate, stable, long-term **fiscal** and **monetary policies**. Throughout the decade, the money supply was constantly growing, as well as Austria's exports, imports, government revenue and spending, gross domestic product, and income. The Austrian currency, the schilling, is strong and convertible. Once called the alpine dollar, the Austrian schilling has become one of the most stable currencies in the world. The Austrian schilling depreciated against the dollar in 1996 and 1997 but was stable against most European currencies. With the decision on the European Monetary Union in place, fluctuations of the schilling against the currencies of the other 10 European Monetary Union participants were minimal during the remainder of 1998. The dollar continued to strengthen against the schilling during the first half of 1998 and 1999 parallel to its rise against the Euro.

In 1999, Austria adopted the euro, the common currency of the European Union, at a fixed conversion rate of ATS13.76 to Euro1. At the same time, Austria surrendered its sovereign power to formulate monetary policy to the European Central Bank (ECB), in line with other EU member states participating in the European Monetary Union. Austria's central bank, the Österreichische National Bank (ANB), is a full participant in the European System of Central Banks. The government successfully met all convergence criteria due to austerity measures implemented in 1996–97 and is pursuing a policy of further reducing the fiscal deficit and the public debt. The ECB's focus on maintaining price stability in formulating exchange rate and monetary policies is viewed by the ANB as a continuation of the hard schilling policy the ANB pursued since 1981. By fixing the Austrian schilling to the German mark, the government successfully kept **inflation** under control and promoted stable economic growth.

POVERTY AND WEALTH

The World Bank ranks Austria seventh in the world in terms of annual per capita income. The annual **gross domestic product per capita** is estimated to have surpassed US$30,000 by the late-1990s. Living standards are very high, and due to **socialist** policies of the federal government, the incidence of poverty is minimal. In 2000, the mean unemployment rate stood at 7.1 percent, and the mean gross monthly income was US$1,922.

There is no legally mandated minimum wage in Austria. Instead, minimum wage scales are set in annual collective bargaining agreements between employers and employee organizations. Workers whose incomes fall below the poverty line are eligible for social welfare benefits. Over half of the workforce works a maximum of about 38.5 hours per week, a result of collective bargaining agreements. The Labor Inspectorate ensures the effective protection of workers by requiring companies to meet Austria's extensive occupational health and safety standards. The Austrian system of social insurance is comprehensive, including sickness, disability, accident, old-age, and unemployment benefits; allowances for families with children; and rent aid. The program is financed by compulsory employer and employee contributions. Health insurance and some other types of insurance are voluntary for individuals who are self-employed. Health conditions and facilities in Austria are considered excellent.

Distribution of Income or Consumption by Percentage Share: Austria

Lowest 10%	4.4
Lowest 20%	10.4
Second 20%	14.8
Third 20%	18.5
Fourth 20%	22.9
Highest 20%	33.3
Highest 10%	19.3

Survey year: 1987

Note: This information refers to income shares by percentiles of the population and is ranked by per capita income.

SOURCE: *2000 World Development Indicators* [CD-ROM].

Household Consumption in PPP Terms

Country	All food	Clothing and footwear	Fuel and power[a]	Health care[b]	Education[b]	Transport & Communications	Other
Austria	20	10	11	4	9	9	38
United States	13	9	9	4	6	8	51
Germany	14	6	7	2	10	7	53
Hungary	25	5	17	6	20	12	15

Data represent percentage of consumption in PPP terms.
[a]Excludes energy used for transport.
[b]Includes government and private expenditures.

SOURCE: World Bank. *World Development Indicators 2000.*

WORKING CONDITIONS

Austria was ranked number-one in the World Competitiveness Report of 1999 for quality of life, providing high-performance infrastructure and rapidly falling telecommunications and energy costs. It also has one of the best records of price stability in the world. Corporate tax rates are one of the lowest among leading industrial nations.

There is a strong labor movement in Austria. The Austrian workforce is 3.7 million, 40 percent being females. About 45 percent of the total Austrian labor force belongs to the 14 unions that make up the Austrian Trade Union Federation. Membership in unions is voluntary, but all wage earners are required by law to join their respective chambers of labor. Guarantees in the Austrian constitution governing freedom of association cover the rights of workers to join unions and engage in union activities. The Austrian Trade Union Federation (OGB) comprises constituent unions with a total membership of about 1.5 million. Since 1945, the OGB has pursued a moderate, consensus-oriented wage policy, cooperating with industry, agriculture, and the government on a broad range of social and economic issues in what is known as Austria's social partnership.

Compared to other EU member states, Austria has the third lowest unemployment rate, with only the Netherlands and Luxembourg providing better job opportunities. (The European Union's average unemployment rate was 8.5 percent by the end of 2000.) In addition, Austria prides herself on having the lowest youth unemployment rate in Europe. In the past, both the federal government and the state governments spent billions of schillings to provide vocational training to those who left school at the end of compulsory education and to help others achieve secondary school qualifications. Now that more companies are willing to take on apprentices, the government has decided to **restructure** its vocational programs.

At a time of prosperity for the Austrian economy, however, the country received unexpectedly poor ratings from the Union of Industrial and Employers' Confederations of Europe (UNICE). It sharply criticized Austria for underfunding research and development. The organization also pointed out that Austria had far too few highly trained information technology personnel. UNICE expected a shortage of 13,000 qualified information technology workers.

COUNTRY HISTORY AND ECONOMIC DEVELOPMENT

1918. Austro-Hungarian empire collapses at the end of World War I, and the Republic of Austria is formed.

1922. Austria receives a loan from the League of Nations, pledging to remain independent for 20 years.

1930s. Dictatorship of Engelbert Dollfuss occurs.

1934. In February civil war breaks out, and the Socialist Party is outlawed.

1934. A coup d'etat by the National Socialists fails in July, and Dollfuss is assassinated by the Nazis.

1938. Austria is incorporated into Germany's Third Reich.

1945. In April Soviet troops liberate the eastern part of Austria, including Vienna. Austria is divided.

1945. Under the Potsdam agreements, the Soviets take control of German assets in their zone of occupation.

1955. All occupation forces are withdrawn, and Austria becomes free and independent.

1955. The Nationalrat enacts the Federal Constitutional Law, declaring the country's permanent neutrality. Austria becomes a member of the United Nations.

1979. Austria gains a permanent seat in the United Nations.

1972. Austria signs a free trade agreement with the European Community, abolishing all industrial tariffs.

1995. Austria becomes a full member of the European Union, together with Finland and Sweden.

1995. Austria joins NATO's Partnership for Peace program.

FUTURE TRENDS

Forecasts for economic growth in 2001 have been positive. A double-digit growth rate is expected in industrial output, retail trade has grown by 5 percent, and tourism is booming. Gross domestic product is likely to advance by 3.1 percent rather than the predicted 2.8 percent. Interest rates will rise slightly but remain low. Demand for Austrian goods is up, and this makes for full order books in the country's exporting industries. In addition to increased sales abroad, recent tax breaks are being used by private households for additional consumer spending rather than stocking up their savings accounts. Business confidence is buoyant given the competitive position of Austria's industry, strong foreign investment, and good export opportunities. Inflation is expected to remain lower than the EU average. The challenges that face the Austrian economy in the future will be securing the greatest possible congruence of its economic policy with common EU policies, most notably in the fields of trade, agriculture, regional development, taxation, and monetary policy.

On the agricultural side, Austria's organic farming and food industry may serve as an example to the world as an alternative to genetically modified food and hormone-treated cattle and poultry. With its ban on imports of genetically modified food, mostly produced in North America, and the outbreak of mad cow disease in Europe and foot-and-mouth disease worldwide, the already well-established organic farming of Austria is expected to continue to grow, generating record profits. Austria also faces social challenges of containing its right wing nationalists, as manifested by the ultranationalist Freedom Movement Party, and upholding the rights of thousands of non-ethnic Austrian and non-European immigrants who now compose an increasingly larger part of Austrian society.

DEPENDENCIES

Austria has no territories or colonies.

BIBLIOGRAPHY

Burtscher, Wolfgang. *Austria.* <http://cadmos.carlbro.be/Services/Subnat/EU_impl/Austria.htm>. Accessed February 2001.

Economist Intelligence Unit. *Austria: Country Commerce.* London: The Economist Intelligence Unit, 2000.

———. *Austria: Country Profile, 2000–2001.* London: The Economist Intelligence Unit, 2001.

———. *Austria: Country Report, January 2001.* London: The Economist Intelligence Unit, 2001.

European Union. *EuroStat.* <http://europa.eu.int/comm/eurostat/Public/datashop/print-catalogue/EN?catalogue=Eurostat>. Accessed February 2001.

Federal Ministry of Agriculture and Forestry. *Austrian Market Report 1999.* <http://www.unece.org/trade/timber/mis/market/austria.htm>. Accessed February 2001.

Federal Press Service. *Austria: Facts and Figures.* Vienna: Federal Press Service, 1993.

International Energy Agency. *Energy Policies of IEA Countries: Austria 1998 Review.* Paris: OECD, 1998.

International Monetary Fund. *World Outlook 2000.* <http://dsbb.imf.org/category.htm>. Accessed February 2001.

Pacher, Sigurd. "The Economic Development of The Second Republic." *Austrian Information.* <http://www.austria.org/sep95/austria.htm>. Accessed February 2001.

Population Reference Bureau. *2000 World Population Data Sheet.* <http://www.prb.org/pubs/wpds2000/>. Accessed February 2001.

United States Census Bureau. *International Database 2000.* <http://bized.ac.uk/dataserv/idbsum.htm>. Accessed February 2001.

University of Wuerzberg. *Austria-Constitution.* <http://www.uni-wuerzburg.de/law/au00000_.html>. Accessed February 2001.

—Payam Foroughi and Raissa Muhutdinova-Foroughi

BELARUS

Republic of Belarus
Respublika Byelarus

CAPITAL: Minsk.

MONETARY UNIT: The Belarusian ruble (BR) became the official currency in May 1992. New bank notes introduced in 2000 include 1, 5, 10, 20, 50, 100, 500, 1,000 and 5,000 ruble notes. The currency contains no coins. As of February 2001, BR1,244 equaled US$1.

CHIEF EXPORTS: Machinery, transport equipment, chemicals, metals, textiles, foodstuffs.

CHIEF IMPORTS: Fuel, natural gas, industrial raw materials, cotton fiber, sugar, foodstuffs.

GROSS DOMESTIC PRODUCT: US$55.2 billion (1999 est.).

BALANCE OF TRADE: **Exports:** US$5.95 billion (2000). **Imports:** US$6.55 billion (2000).

COUNTRY OVERVIEW

LOCATION AND SIZE. Belarus is a landlocked state in Eastern Europe bordering Poland, Lithuania, and Latvia to the west; Ukraine to the south; and Russia to the east and north. It has a total border of 3,100 kilometers (1,900 miles), with almost one-third of its border (960 kilometers, or 600 miles) touching Russia. Slightly smaller than the state of Kansas, Belarus covers an area of 208,000 square kilometers (80,000 square miles). Belarus is divided into 6 oblastsi (provinces). The cities of Minsk, Gomel, Brest, Vitsyebsk, Grodno, and Mogilev are the capital cities of these oblastsi.

Belarus is the smallest of 3 Slavic republics (with Russia and Ukraine) that were once part of the Soviet Union. These Slavic republics, along with 12 other regions, gained their independence from the Soviet Union in 1991.

POPULATION. The population of Belarus was estimated at 10.4 million in July 2000, with almost 75 percent living in urban areas. The population of the city of Minsk alone was estimated at 1.67 million in July 2000. The number of people living in Belarus peaked in 1993 and has been declining at an average annual rate of 0.5 percent. It is estimated that by 2015 the population will fall to 9.8 million. The negative population growth rate is partly due to a falling life expectancy (68 years; 62 years for males and 74 for females), a low fertility rate, and **emigration**. Belarusians are marrying at an older age and

having fewer children. Low fertility combined with increased emigration has resulted in an older population. In 1960, for example, 32 percent of the population was considered "young" and 14 percent was considered "old." The corresponding figures for 1996 were 23 percent and 21 percent.

Ethnic Belarusians make up more than 77 percent of the country's population. Russians, many of whom were migrants to Belarus while it was still part of the Soviet Union (1917–91), form the second largest ethnic group (13 percent). The remainder of the population are Poles (4 percent), Ukrainians (3 percent), and Jews (1 percent), with a small number of Latvians, Lithuanians, and Tartars (0.1 percent). Before World War II, Jews constituted the second largest ethnic group in the country.

Belarusians emigrate from their country for economic, military, political, and religious reasons. Some estimates put the number of Belarusians living abroad at between 3 to 3.5 million. The United States is one of the principal countries of Belarusian emigration. Since 1946, more than 500,000 Belarusians have emigrated to the United States, many fleeing a country devastated by World War II (1939–45).

Both Belarusian and Russian are official languages. The Belarusian language is an East Slavic language, closely related to Russian and Ukrainian. Like many of the Slavic languages, Belarusian uses the Cyrillic alphabet. Most Belarusians who profess a religion adhere to the Eastern Orthodox Church. There is, however, a sizable minority of Roman Catholics, and the Eastern-rite (Uniate) church is experiencing a revival after centuries of persecution under Eastern Orthodox-dominated Tsarist Russia and atheistic (not subscribing to any religion) Soviet rule.

OVERVIEW OF ECONOMY

The breakup of the USSR (Union of Soviet Socialist Republics) in 1991 had a negative impact on Belarus. Although the majority of the former Soviet republics quickly shifted their economies toward the free market system, Belarus was among the slowest to open up its economy. International financial institutions, such as the World Bank, International Monetary Fund (IMF), and the European Bank for Reconstruction and Development (EBRD) assisted the country with credits and special economic development projects. Although their efforts resulted in some positive outcomes, they also increased Belarus's international debt. Whereas in 1991 the country was practically debt-free, in 2000 Belarus owed nearly US$800 million to foreign banks and government bodies.

Agriculture and industry are the largest sectors of Belarus's economy, making up 13 percent and 34 percent of GDP in 2000, respectively. Wheat, rye, oats, potatoes, flax, hemp, and sugar beets are the primary agricultural products. Dairy and beef cows, pigs, and chickens are also raised. The main industrial items produced in Belarus are tractors, trucks, earth movers, metal-cutting machine tools, agricultural equipment, motorcycles, chemicals, fertilizer, textiles, and some **consumer goods**. Peat, the country's most valuable mineral resource, is used for fuel and fertilizer and in the chemical industry. Belarus also has significant deposits of clay, sand, chalk, dolomite, phosphor, and rock and potassium salt. Forests cover one-third of the country's territory and the lumber industry is economically important as a result. Having only small reserves of petroleum and natural gas of its own, Belarus imports most of its oil and gas, mainly from neighboring Russia. It also imports large quantities of grain. The main export items are machinery and household items.

The Chernobyl nuclear power plant accident that took place on 26 April 1986 in Ukraine released massive amounts of radiation, contaminating large amounts of agricultural land in Belarus. An estimated 150,000 inhabitants had to move, and many people needed medical help. Chernobyl caused the government to take more than 23 percent of the country's agricultural land and 20 percent of forest land out of production. Economic output declined for several years after the accident, but revived somewhat in the late 1990s. The economic revival was due to several factors, including improved production techniques, better relations with foreign countries, and the introduction of **privatization**.

Under the **socialist** system of the Soviet Union, Belarus's economy was merely part of the national economy of the Soviet Union. After winning independence from the Soviet Union in 1991, Belarus moved very slowly on free market reforms, keeping its basic economic reliance on Russia. Some reforms were implemented between 1991 and 1994, but they did not last long enough to make an impression. When Alexander Grigorjevich Lukashenka became president in 1994, many of these free market economic reforms were reversed. The government reintroduced **price controls** (an enforced price on an item) on at least 26 basic goods and services. Currency exchange regulations were re-imposed, and privatization was halted. The government subsidized businesses and farms. About half of all enterprises remained in state hands in 2000. Structural reform has been slower than in most other **Commonwealth of Independent States** (the CIS is made up of 12 republics of the former Soviet Union, not including the 3 Baltic countries of Latvia, Lithuania, and Estonia).

Russia remains Belarus's main trading partner, accounting for more than 50 percent of Belarus's foreign trade. Belarus has made several attempts at economic and political re-integration with Russia. Belarus seeks to use the Russian ruble as its currency by 2005, and hopes to see a common Russia-Belarus currency by 2008. Other major trading partners are Ukraine, Poland, and Germany.

POLITICS, GOVERNMENT, AND TAXATION

There are 3 governmental branches in Belarus: the executive, including the president, prime minister, and council of ministers; the legislative, consisting of parliament; and the judicial, or the Supreme Court. Belarus has a president as the head of the state, who serves a 5-year term. The president appoints the prime minister, who is the head of the government. A **bicameral** (2-house) parliament consists of the 64-seat Council of the Republic and the 110-seat Chamber of Representatives. Judicial power in Belarus is in the hands of courts. The Constitutional Court exercises control over constitutionality (determination of legal validity based on the constitution) of acts and decrees. Administratively, the country is divided into 6 oblasts (administrative divisions). Local administration and decision making are carried out primarily by the Soviets of Deputies. There are several registered political parties: the Belarusian Popular Front, Party of Popular Accord, Union of Belarusian Entrepreneurs, Belarusian Party of Communists, Belarus Peasant Party, Belarusian Socialist Party, Social Democrat Party, Agrarian Party of Belarus, and United Democratic Party of Belarus.

President Lukashenka consolidated his power through a highly controversial election held in 1994. Based on the results of this vote, the Constitutional Court lost its independence, and the democratically elected parliament was abolished and replaced by presidential appointees. President Lukashenka used his increased power to suppress the freedoms of speech, press, association, and assembly. He also eliminated the system of checks and balances over the executive branch. In 1996 Lukashenka extended his term, which should have ended in 1999, to 2001.

Taxes are the primary source of government revenue. The taxation system of Belarus includes national and local taxes as well as other types of taxes and **duties**. National taxes are collected throughout the country and transferred to the national budget and extra-budgetary state funds. Local taxes are levied only within respective administrative and territorial units and transferred to local budgets. Belarus signed international agreements on avoiding double taxation with a number of countries. The country took steps to **liberalize** taxation and customs regulations, granting some benefits to investors in the 1990s. Belarusian laws allow foreign entities to make direct private investments in the Belarusian economy through the creation of **joint ventures** with as much as 100 percent participation of foreign capital.

From 1993 to 1999, investments in Belarus totaled US$697 million, a low figure compared to other former Soviet countries. The bulk of foreign investment came from Gazprom (Russia's state-owned gas company). The Yamal pipeline project funded by Gazprom will export natural gas to Western Europe via Belarus. Western investors in Belarus include the Coca-Cola company, which has been building a US$50 million plant in the capital city of Minsk, and Ford Motor Company, which holds a 51 percent stake in a truck assembly plant outside of Minsk.

INFRASTRUCTURE, POWER, AND COMMUNICATIONS

Belarus has an extensive though aging **infrastructure**, which is badly in need of investment for repair and maintenance. A network of over 5,488 kilometers (3,409 miles) of railways and 52,131 kilometers (32,380 miles) of primary and secondary roads serve the country. About 11 percent of all roads are unpaved. The railways are used to transport both people and goods, and are in moderate use by international transit linking Western and Eastern Europe. Furthermore, the country has a large and widely used canal and river system, with 1 port at Mazyr. Nearly 5 percent of the former Soviet Union's fleet of ships are

Communications

Country	Newspapers	Radios	TV Sets[a]	Cable subscribers[a]	Mobile Phones[a]	Fax Machines[a]	Personal Computers[a]	Internet Hosts[b]	Internet Users[b]
	1996	1997	1998	1998	1998	1998	1998	1999	1999
Belarus	174	296	314	N/A	1	1.9	N/A	0.77	50
United States	215	2,146	847	244.3	256	78.4	458.6	1,508.77	74,100
Russia	105	418	420	78.5	5	0.4	40.6	13.06	2,700
Ukraine	54	884	490	15.7	2	0.0	13.8	4.56	200

[a]Data are from International Telecommunication Union, *World Telecommunication Development Report 1999* and are per 1,000 people.
[b]Data are from the Internet Software Consortium (http://www.isc.org) and are per 10,000 people.

SOURCE: World Bank. *World Development Indicators 2000.*

in Belarus. There are 118 large and small airports, few of which meet international standards. Only 36 airports have paved runways.

Belarus remains highly dependent on imported energy and has made little progress toward diversifying its exports and entering new markets. Many energy consumers, such as households, businesses, and even government offices, have not been able to pay their utility bills. Energy debt, mostly for natural gas, stood at more than US$250 million in May 2000. The government attempted to pay its debts by **bartering** and through agreements directly with Russia and Lithuania. Even though the large majority of electricity and fuel is imported, there is some domestic production of energy. In 2000 Belarus produced 25 billion kilowatts (kWh) of electric power, 1.8 million tons of gasoline, 3,500 tons of diesel fuel, and 5.6 million tons of industrial fuel oil.

Telecommunications services in Belarus are inadequate for both public and business use. Hundreds of thousands of applications from household telephones remain unsatisfied. Some investment on international connections and businesses has taken place, much of it in Minsk. There were 296 radios per 1,000 people in 1997, and 314 televisions per 1,000 people in 1998. A domestic cellular telephone system operated in Minsk, but only 1 person out of 1,000 owned a cellular phone in 1998. By 2000, the country had 9 Internet service providers. However, the number of personal computers in the country was very low.

Belarus
GDP–COMPOSITION BY SECTOR–1998 est.

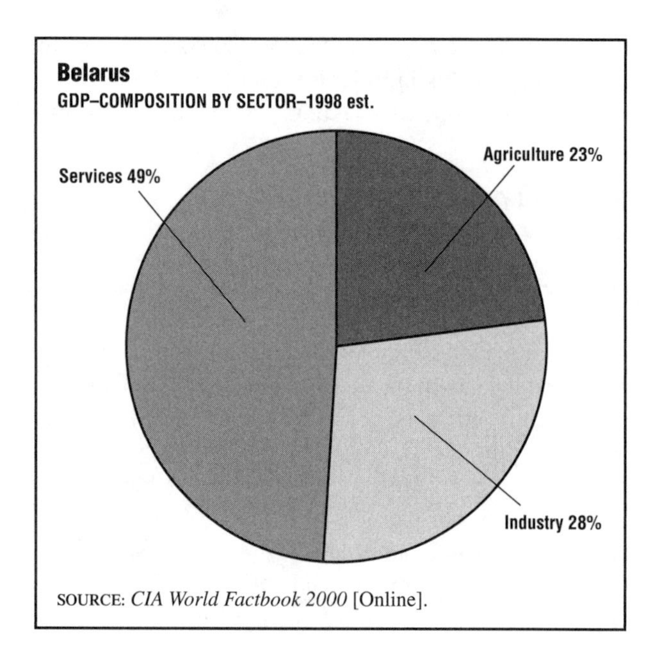

SOURCE: *CIA World Factbook 2000* [Online].

ECONOMIC SECTORS

More than half of the economy of Belarus is owned and operated by the state. The government's insistence on maintaining a centrally planned socialist economy and encouraging private and foreign investment has not been successful. Belarus's economic progress has fallen behind neighboring countries, many of which have adopted free market economic practices. Yet Belarus has a high capacity for progress. It has a relatively educated and skilled **labor force** (4.44 million in 1999) and it is situated in a strategic location of Europe. Industrial production (34 percent of GDP) dominated the economy in 1999, employing 28.9 percent of the workforce, but services employed almost half of the total workforce.

The lack of a **free market system** and human rights violations, such as the arrest of peaceful political activists and the control of radio and television stations, has discouraged substantial amounts of foreign investment. The country is short of **foreign exchange reserves** and has a relatively high **inflation rate** (more than 150 percent per year for 1998 and 1999). By March 2000, Belarus had not reached many of the economic goals through which it could receive additional International Monetary Fund aid. The government has been looking toward Russia for increased economic cooperation, such as increased trade, foreign investment, and an eventual unified currency.

AGRICULTURE

Agriculture accounted for 23 percent of the country's 1998 GDP and employed nearly 650,000 people, or more than 17 percent of the labor force in 1999. The majority of agriculture is conducted on state-owned lands and farms. Private farms, however, are much more efficient than state farms. Private farms produce an estimated 40 percent of agricultural output, even though they constitute a mere 15 percent of all agricultural lands. The primary food crops produced by Belarusian agriculture are barley, corn, potatoes, sugar beets, and wheat. Meat products include beef, veal, chicken, lamb, and pork. The most profitable agricultural exports in 2000 were butter, alcoholic beverages, condensed milk, beef, and cheese. The total value of agricultural exports in 2000 was US$377 million, while the value of agricultural imports was US$911 million.

Independence for Belarus, as in many of the former Soviet republics, brought economic hardships and food shortages. Between 1990 and 1998, total agricultural production was reduced by 29 percent, and in collective and state farms, production was reduced by 44 percent. Production of grains and pulses in 1998 was 69 percent of that of 1990, potatoes 88 percent, meat 57 percent, and milk 70 percent. Animal husbandry also saw a reduction: the average yield of milk per cow in government farms fell by 23 percent from 1990 to 1998. The nutritional value of the average daily ration shrank by 14 percent during that period. Due to the poor economic situation, the per capita annual consumption of meat decreased by 14 kg (19 percent), milk by 59 kg (19 percent), and eggs by 57 units (18 percent).

Production of grains in 1998 was 4,475,000 tons. This provided less than half of the minimal grain requirements for the country. Grain yields fell by 31 percent during the period of 1990–98. Land sown to grain also fell by 4 percent. As a result of the grain shortage, Belarus was forced to purchase and import grain from abroad. Russia was a major source of grain imports for Belarus, making up 44 percent of all grain imports in 1998. Imports of grain from Ukraine constituted another 30 percent of the whole. Ukraine was also a major provider of corn to Belarus. To encourage the domestic production of wheat, the government offered an artificially high price for wheat to farmers.

Belarus requires no less than 350,000 tons of sugar per year, but the capacity of internal sugar factories is only 150,000 tons per year. Since internal sugar beet production covers only about 44 percent of the country's needs, the rest is provided by imports. Belarus purchases the majority of its sugar from the Ukraine. During 1998 a total of 476,000 tons of sugar was both produced and imported, leading to an accumulation of sugar reserves and to the export of excess sugar to other CIS countries, mainly Russia. The sugar beet growing areas are located in the Brest, Grodno, and Minsk oblasts, where the 4 main sugar factories are located. The crop takes only 0.7 percent of total farmland in the country. In accordance with state sugar program, the development of the sugar industry aims to increase sugar beet production, increase the production capacity of the 4 sugar factories, and reduce energy and raw material expenses.

Vegetable oil is produced locally and sold to Russia, and it is imported from the Ukraine. Production capacities of the fat and oil industry meet the domestic market demand for vegetable oil, margarine, mayonnaise, and soap, as well as allow for the export of some finished products. The fields devoted to rape (a type of herb with oily seeds used to make canola oil) were increased from 88,000 hectares in 1998 to 150,000 hectares in 2000. The total sowing area under oilseeds was still 16 percent less than what it was in 1990. In order to solve the problem of domestic vegetable oil needs, to expand the growth of oilseeds and to increase the efficiency of oilseed production, the government supplied farms with quality seeds, mineral fertilizers, pesticides, and specialized harvesting machinery. Furthermore, it strengthened the material and technical base for seed processing and drying. An increase of the domestic production of vegetable oil was also induced by the rapid rise of the price for imported oils and oilseeds. In 1998 the price of vegetable oil was US$1,161 per ton as compared to US$823 per ton in 1995. The largest volume of vegetable oil export was recorded in 1998 at 11,300 tons.

INDUSTRY

Industry plays a leading role in the economy of Belarus, responsible for 34 percent of its GDP. It includes more than 100 sectors and 2,000 enterprises, many of which are fully self-supporting, and employs nearly 1 million people (26 percent of the Belarusian labor force). Before the breakup of the Soviet Union, much of Belarus's industry was geared toward making military machinery. After independence, the country faced the challenges of changing from military to peacetime production, modernizing factories, and cleaning up industrial pollution left by old factories.

MANUFACTURING. The main industrial products include metal cutting tools, trucks, earth movers, motorcycles, bicycles, television sets, radios, refrigerators, and chemical fibers. In addition, tires, timber, paper, board, textiles, and clothing are produced. Agricultural machinery is one of the specialties of Belarusian industry. Basic agricultural machinery produced in Belarus includes tractors, harvesters, fertilizers, and equipment for livestock-raising farms. Engineering and metalworking plants account for as much as 25 percent of the industrial output. The automotive industry specializes in the production of heavy-duty trucks. The Minsk tractor plant produces tractors, tractor engines, and spare parts. In 2000 alone, 26,500 tractors were produced. The electrical engineering industry produces alternating current motors, power transformers, electric bulbs, and cable products. In addition, computer-aided control systems, clocks, watches, cameras, and electrical measuring and process monitoring instruments are produced. Furthermore, road building machines, building and reclamation machines, roller bearings, passenger elevators, gas cookers, and equipment for the food industry are also produced. In 2000, exported manufactured goods included 7,800 trucks, 26,100 tractors, 3,200 metal-cutting machine tools, 505,100 refrigerators, 161,000 television sets, and 120,000 bicycles.

CHEMICAL AND PETROCHEMICALS. The chemical and petrochemical industries are well-developed. There are large complexes for the production of mineral fertilizers, tires, artificial fibers, and filament. In 2000 they produced 502,000 tons of nitrogen fertilizers, 2.8 million tons of potash fertilizers, 51.7 million tons of phosphate fertilizers, 209,000 tons of artificial fiber and filament, and 1.3 million tires for motor vehicles and farm machinery. The state dominates the chemical and petrochemical sector of industry, owning 73 percent of production. In 2000, 1 million tires, 2.6 million tons of potash fertilizers, and 161,400 tons of artificial fiber and filament were exported.

SERVICES

TOURISM. Belarus has fewer visits by tourists than its neighbors, but the numbers are increasing. In 1997, a reported 250,000 tourists visited Belarus, an increase of 36 percent from 1994. Tourists spent US$25 million in 1997. There are several reasons behind the low number of visitors to Belarus. There are few historic assets on which to build a tourist industry. Many of the country's historic buildings were destroyed during World War II. Minsk was completely flattened and is now characterized by grim Stalinist architecture (Stalin was the former dictator of the USSR) and high-rise buildings. In addition, as opposed to most Eastern European and Baltic countries that have dropped visa (government approval to enter a country) requirements for most visitors, Belarus requires visas for most tourists. The potential for increased tourism in Belarus is still favorable because it is considered a good candidate for **ecotourism**. Ecotourism could generate urgently needed revenue, create jobs, and help conserve the natural environment. The Ministry of Sports and Tourism and Ministry of Natural Resources and Environmental Protection have looked into establishing national parks and protected territories and monuments to stimulate an increase in tourism.

FINANCIAL SERVICES. After independence in 1991, the Gosbank (state bank) of the USSR was converted into the National Bank of Belarus (NBB). The specialized Soviet banks, including Sherbank, Agroprombank, Promstroibank, and Vnesheconombank, were turned into commercial banks offering corresponding specialized services. By mid-2000, Belagroprombank and Belarusbank together accounted for 51 percent of all Belarusian banking sector assets. There are 22 locally owned and joint venture banks. The largest joint venture bank was the Russian Mossbusinessbank. By mid-2000, the banking system of the republic, with a total of 28 banks, held an estimated BR1.5 trillion worth of assets (approximately US$1.6 billion). As a percentage of GDP, this made Belarus one of the lowest among the CIS countries. Assets in local currency accounted for 43 percent of total banking assets. Among the problems with the banking sector was a relatively high rate of lending to government enterprises (constituting 47 percent of all lending), considered to be economically unwise.

INTERNATIONAL TRADE

Foreign trade **turnover** totaled US$12.5 billion in 2000, nearly the same as the previous year, but down 20 percent from 1998. Exports accounted for an estimated US$5.95 billion and imports US$6.55 billion. Some 60 percent of Belarus's international trade and 85 percent of its trade with the CIS were with Russia, making that country its main trading partner. Half of the trade with Russia was in the form of barter deals. After the Russian financial crisis of August 1998, however, Belarusian exports to Russia shrank by about 17 percent and imports from Russia fell by 19 percent. Other CIS trading partners of Belarus were the Ukraine (11 percent of CIS trade), Kazakhstan (1.4 percent of CIS trade), and Moldova and Uzbekistan (1 percent each of CIS trade).

Trade (expressed in millions of US$): Belarus

	Exports	Imports
1994	2510	3066
1995	4706	5562
1996	5652	6938
1997	7300	8688
1998	7070	8548
1999	5922	6664

SOURCE: United Nations. *Monthly Bulletin of Statistics* (September 2000).

Main exports include vehicles (16 percent of total value of exports), machinery (13 percent), chemicals (13 percent), textiles (12 percent), and metal-ware (9 percent). In 1990, special priority was given to the development of bilateral links with various Russian regions. Exports to Russia in 1999 were 7 times higher than to any other country. Agricultural exports to Russia were primarily meat (12 percent of total), dairy products (21 percent), and eggs (7 percent). Nearly 90 percent of Belarusian meat and dairy exports went to Russia, in addition to 50 percent of potato, fruit, and vegetable exports. Exports to non-CIS countries decreased from 30 percent in early 1990 to less than 12 percent in 2000. Food and agricultural exports have increased, while machinery exports have decreased. Agricultural goods made up 8.2 percent of total trade in 2000 compared to 6.6 percent in 1996. Exports of meat products increased by 40 percent from 1996 to 2000, dairy products by 60 percent, eggs by more than 250 percent, and margarine by 440 percent.

Principal imports are energy (25 percent of total imports), machinery and equipment (16 percent), metals (13 percent), and food (11 percent). The main share (more than 50 percent) of food and agricultural imports comes from non-CIS countries. Another 25 to 30 percent of such products are imported from Russia. In 1997 the volume of agricultural imports was the highest it had been in years, at US$1.12 billion, and the average annual import of agricultural commodities during 1996–2000 was equivalent to US$929.3 million. The import structure changed after 1991 with some traditionally exported items such as meat, animal fats, and margarine being imported from abroad.

Belarus has had a **trade deficit** since 1995. The trade balance with Russia, however, has traditionally been positive. Exports to Russia exceeded imports by more than 200 percent in 2000. In the same year, the trade deficit with non-CIS countries amounted to US$433 million. During the 1996–2000 period, goods supplied by non-CIS countries were cheaper than items imported from Russia, except dairy products and grain. Vegetables, fruits, vegetable oil, margarine, and pasta imported from non-CIS countries were more than 200 percent cheaper; tea and candies were over 500 percent cheaper; meat products were 50 percent cheaper; fish was 30 percent cheaper; and sugar was 40 percent less expensive.

MONEY

Annual **inflation** in Belarus, as measured by changes in consumer price inflation, or CPI, has been very high during the 1990s. It stood at 294 percent by the end of 1999. There were several reasons behind the inflationary pressure on the economy. The 1998 Russian monetary crisis had a negative effect on the Belarusian ruble due to the dependence of the Belarusian economy on Russia. Government **subsidies** to several sectors of the economy (such as agriculture and housing) supported bad lending practices, poor weather conditions caused low agricultural production, and the government's periodic expansion of the money supply caused a **devaluation** of the Belarusian ruble.

In February 1993 Belarus set up the Inter-Bank Currency Exchange which is the main trading forum of the legal currency market. Trades are performed in 4 main currencies: the U.S. dollar, the German mark, the Russian ruble, and the Ukrainian grivna. The Russian financial crisis of 1998 forced the Belarusian ruble to depreciate against the Russian ruble and the U.S. dollar. In April 2000 the **exchange rate** stood at BR435 to US$1. The depreciation of the Belarusian currency continued to accelerate in the following months, reaching a whopping BR1,247 to US$1 by mid-February 2001.

Exchange rates: Belarus

Belarusian rubles per US$1	
2000	1,180
Dec 1999	730,000
Jan 1999	139,000
1998	46,080
1997	25,964
1996	15,500

Note: On January 1, 2000, the national currency was redenominated at one new ruble to 2,000 old rubles.

SOURCE: CIA *World Factbook 2001* [ONLINE].

GDP per Capita (US$)

Country	1975	1980	1985	1990	1998
Belarus	N/A	N/A	N/A	2,761	2,198
United States	19,364	21,529	23,200	25,363	29,683
Russia	2,555	3,654	3,463	3,668	2,138
Ukraine	N/A	N/A	N/A	1,979	837

SOURCE: United Nations. *Human Development Report 2000; Trends in human development and per capita income.*

POVERTY AND WEALTH

For most Belarusians, independence compromised their economic and physical welfare. Environmental problems, the loss of life savings, and the continued effects of the Chernobyl nuclear disaster undermined the health of the population. Compared to other East European and former Soviet republic nations, the income of Belarusians lagged behind. The **GDP per capita** of Belarus declined from US$2,761 in 1990 to US$2,198 in 1998, while per capita GDP in Russia and Poland increased by over US$1,000 during the decade (based on the 1995 exchange rate).

Though many of the former Soviet republics and East European countries worked to change from socialist, **centrally planned economies** to free market economies, Belarus was not anxious to follow that route; as a consequence, the economy was left behind the other former Soviet states.

The life expectancy of Belarusians, which in the mid-1970s stood at 71.5 years, was estimated at 68.0 years in 2000. The mortality rate increased from 10.7 in 1990 to 13.0 in 1998. Men had a life expectancy of only 61.8 years, while women were expected to live 74.5 years. Approximately 22 percent of the population lives below the poverty line.

Distribution of Income or Consumption by Percentage Share: Belarus

Lowest 10%	5.1
Lowest 20%	11.4
Second 20%	15.2
Third 20%	18.2
Fourth 20%	21.9
Highest 20%	33.3
Highest 10%	20.0

Survey year: 1998

Note: This information refers to expenditure shares by percentiles of the population and is ranked by per capita expenditure.

SOURCE: *2000 World Development Indicators* [CD-ROM].

Household Consumption in PPP Terms

Country	All food	Clothing and footwear	Fuel and power[a]	Health care[b]	Education[b]	Transport & Communications	Other
Belarus	36	7	15	7	10	11	14
United States	13	9	9	4	6	8	51
Russia	28	11	16	7	15	8	16
Ukraine	34	5	16	6	4	14	22

Data represent percentage of consumption in PPP terms.
[a]Excludes energy used for transport.
[b]Includes government and private expenditures.

SOURCE: World Bank. *World Development Indicators 2000.*

WORKING CONDITIONS

The official unemployment rate in the country was reported at 2.1 percent in 2000. However, the reporting of the unemployment rate in former Soviet republics is generally considered inaccurate. Many people are officially employed at state-owned enterprises, and are reported as such, yet in reality are unemployed or working part-time in the **informal sector** of the economy, selling agricultural produce in the local market or working at other small businesses.

In 2000, the Belarusian economy had 4.5 million workers, 60 percent of whom were reportedly employed in state-owned enterprises. This number may be higher, since the so-called Joint Stock companies, which were formerly state-owned and employed more than 270,000 people in 2000, were still functioning with government assistance. Less than 400,000 people, or only about 9 percent of the workforce, worked in private businesses.

A rural-urban age gap has also emerged. Many of the young job-seekers migrate to larger urban areas. This has led to a high concentration of older people in the rural areas. Older people make up as much as 35 percent of the population of rural villages. The combination of negative rural population growth, an aging society, and the state-run economy, with the emigration of many of the professionals to western countries, has led to an unhappy environment for the Belarusian worker.

COUNTRY HISTORY AND ECONOMIC DEVELOPMENT

1919. A Soviet regime is established in Belarus.

1922. Belarus becomes a member of the USSR.

1923. The forced mass collectivization of agricultural lands begins.

1944. After 4 years of occupation by Nazi Germany, Minsk is recaptured by the Soviet Army.

1986. The Chernobyl nuclear power station accident in Ukraine leaks radiation into Belarus.

1990. Belarus declares state sovereignty from the USSR.

1991. Belarus declares independence. Belarus, along with Russia and Ukraine, forms the CIS.

1994. Russia and Belarus announce a monetary union, which is abandoned by Russia a year later. Alexander Lukashenka is elected as the first president of independent Belarus.

1995. Belarus joins NATO's Partnership for Peace Program.

1995. Russia and Belarus allow the free movement of certain goods across their border.

1996. The last nuclear weapon left over from the Soviet-era is removed from Belarusian territory.

1997. Russia and Belarus sign the Act of Union, which envisions the union of the 2 countries.

FUTURE TRENDS

The parliamentary election of October 2000 showed that President Lukashenka would keep his grip on the country by making sure that his opponents remained out of power. This continued to damage the legitimacy of his administration. President Lukashenka is expected to continue to dominate the political scene in the future, and he is almost assured of re-election. The opposition will remain weak, owing to consistent pressure from the administration and a lack of media access. However, the suppression of the opposition before the presidential election would damage relations with Western countries and international lending agencies.

The Belarusian leadership has had limited vision when attempting to tackle the country's economic problems. While its neighbors to the west (Poland, Lithuania, and Latvia) have long endorsed free market programs of economic reform, with overwhelming success, Belarus has stubbornly stood by a plan of economic union with Russia at a time when Russia has been facing economic uncertainty and political instability. Some polls have indicated that a large segment of the Belarusian population believes in the supremacy of the state and continues to expect a **communist**-like state to look after their well-being. The hard grip of the former communists on power, and an aging society with an unsure attitude towards market reforms, are likely to contribute to the maintenance of the status quo in Belarus, with continuing economic hardship and political repression.

DEPENDENCIES

Belarus has no territories or colonies.

BIBLIOGRAPHY

CountryWatch.com. *Country Review: Belarus,* 2001. <http://www.countrywatch.com/files/016/cw_country.asp?vCOUNTRY=016>. Accessed April 2001.

Economist Intelligence Unit. *Country Profile: Belarus, Moldova, 2000–2001.* London: Economist Intelligence Unit, 2000.

History of Belarus (Great Litva). <http://jurix.jura.uni-sb.de/~serko/history/history.html>. Accessed February 2001.

International Monetary Fund. *Republic of Belarus: Recent Economic Developments and Selected Issues.* Washington, DC: International Monetary Fund, 2000.

Lubachko, Igor S. *Belarusia Under Soviet Rule, 1917–1957,* Lexington: University Press of Kentucky, 1972.

Marples, David R. *Belarus: A Denationalized Nation.* Australia: Hardwood Academic Publishers, 1999.

The National Academy of Sciences of Belarus. <http://www.ac.by/publications/index.html>. Accessed February 2001.

Stroev, Igor, Leonid Blyakhman, and Mikhail Krotov. *Economics of the CIS Countries on the Threshold of the New Millennium.* St. Petersburg: Nauka, 1999. <http://www.ll.georgetown.edu/cat/newbooks/jun002.html#B>. Accessed February 2001.

United Nations Development Program. *The Republic of Belarus,* 1996. <http://www.undp.org/missions/belarus/eng_pg01.htm#ECO>. Accessed April 2001.

United Nations Development Program. *Human Development Report 2000.* New York: UNDP, 2000.

Vakar, Nicholas P. *Belarusia: The Making of a Nation: A Case Study,* Cambridge, Mass.: Harvard University, 1956.

World Bank. *Country Brief: Belarus, 2000.* <http://lnweb18.worldbank.org/ECA/eca.nsf/66f872d4c0533345852567d100130887/22342855499fcbe9852567ef0053408b?OpenDocument>. Accessed February 2001.

—Payam Foroughi and Raissa Muhutdinova-Foroughi

BELGIUM

Kingdom of Belgium
Royaume de Belgique
Koninkrijk België

CAPITAL: Brussels.

MONETARY UNIT: Belgian franc (BEF). One franc is equal to 100 centimes. However, the centimes denominations are no longer used. The Belgian franc is exchangeable on an equal basis with the Luxembourg franc. In 1999, Belgium began using the euro, the common currency of the European Union. The franc is set at a fixed exchange rate of 40.3399 per euro. The euro will replace all local currencies within the EU in 2002.

CHIEF EXPORTS: Machinery and equipment, chemicals, diamonds, metals and metal products.

CHIEF IMPORTS: Machinery and equipment, chemicals, metals and metal products.

GROSS DOMESTIC PRODUCT: US$259.2 billion (purchasing power parity, 2000 est.).

BALANCE OF TRADE: **Exports:** US$181.4 billion (f.o.b., 2000). **Imports:** US$166 billion (c.i.f., 2000).

COUNTRY OVERVIEW

LOCATION AND SIZE. Belgium is a nation located in Western Europe. It is between the Netherlands to the north, Germany and Luxembourg to the east, France to the south, and the North Sea to the west. Belgium is about the size of Maryland, has an area of 30,510 square kilometers (11,780 square miles) and includes 280 square kilometers (108 square miles) of inland waterways. It has 66 kilometers (41 miles) of coastline and its borders total 1,385 kilometers (861 miles). Belgium shares 620 kilometers (385 miles) with France, 167 kilometers (103 miles) with Germany, 148 kilometers (92 miles) with Luxembourg, and 450 kilometers (280 miles) with the Netherlands. The nation also claims an exclusive fishing zone that extends 68 kilometers (42 miles) into the North Sea. Belgium is the traditional crossroads of Europe and its capital, Brussels, also serves as the capital of the European Union (EU). Brussels also serves as the headquarters of the North Atlantic Treaty Organization (NATO) and the Western European Union (WEU). Brussels is located in the middle of the country and has a population of 954,460. It is one of the largest cities in Belgium. In contrast, Antwerp, Belgium's second largest city has a population of 447,632 and is located in the northern area of the nation. Lastly, Ghent, Belgium's third largest city has a population of 224,074 and is in the northwest.

POPULATION. In July 2000, it was estimated that Belgium had a population of 10,241,506. The population growth rate is estimated at a low 0.18 percent. The fertility rate is estimated at 1.61 children born per woman and the birth rate consists of 10.91 births per 1,000 people. The death rate is 10.13 deaths per 1,000.

Like many advanced industrialized countries, Belgium's population is aging and 16 percent of the inhabitants are over the age of 65, while only 18 percent are between the ages of 0 and 14. The life expectancy for men is 74.47 years and 81.3 years for women. A majority of Belgians now live in urban areas and, as people from both the rural areas and immigrants settle in the cities, this trend is growing rapidly. The population density of Belgium is second only to the Netherlands in Europe.

The nation has 3 major ethnic communities: the Flemish, the Walloons, and the German-speakers. The Flemish make up about 58 percent of the population and speak a form of Dutch known as Flemish. The Flemish are concentrated in the northern regions of the nation. The Walloons speak French and mainly live in the southern areas of Belgium. About 31 percent of Belgians are Walloons. German-speakers are the third major group and they mainly reside in the east around the city of Liege. German-speakers comprise about 1 percent of the population. There are also numerous other ethnic minority groups in the country. Brussels alone has 19 different

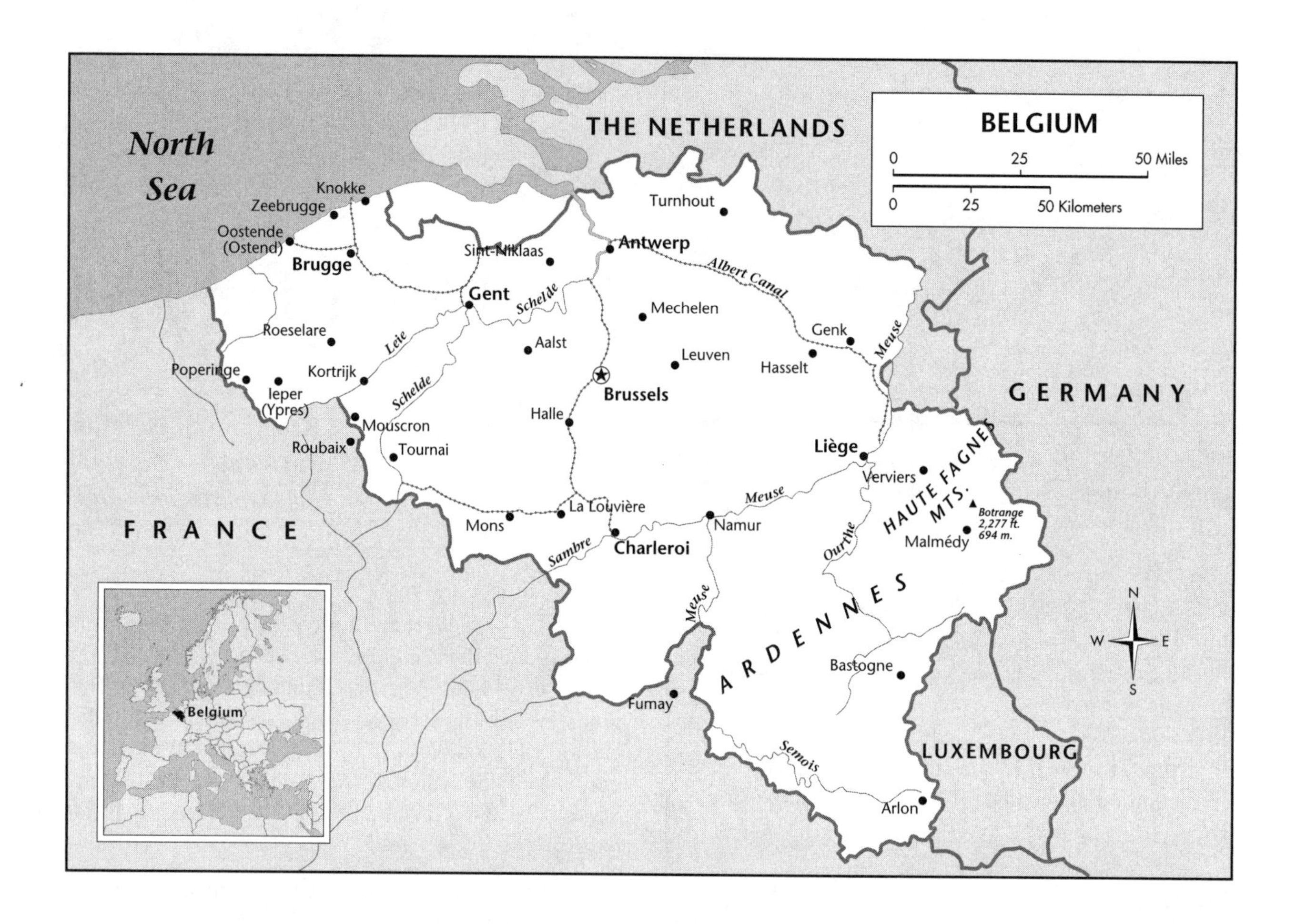

bilingual communities. Many of these other groups are from North Africa and the Middle East, particularly Turkey. There is also a significant Italian population. Since World War II, higher birth rates among the nation's foreign-born population have increased faster than that of native Belgians. The majority of new immigrants from the Mediterranean region tend to settle in the industrial areas of the Walloons—Brussels and Antwerp. There is a low migration rate of 0.98 per 1,000. Although a small number of recent Belgium immigrants return to their countries of origin each year, most emigrants go to nations within the EU or the United States.

Conflicts between the Flemish and the Walloons have traditionally divided Belgian society. Throughout most of the 19th and early 20th centuries, the French-speaking population dominated the region. However, the Flemish eventually gained reform, obtained regional autonomy, and then established Flanders as a unilingual region. The 1970 constitution created 3 autonomous political regions: Flanders, Wallonia, and Brussels. In 1984, the German community of Liege was also granted its own legislative assembly and began controlling its own educational and cultural matters. Disputes between the 2 groups continue and have led to numerous political compromises, including a new constitution in 1993, which changed Belgium from a unitary state (a country in which the central government has the most political power) to a federal system (a country in which the central government and regional governments collaboratively share power to a certain degree).

OVERVIEW OF ECONOMY

Belgium has a well-developed free market economy, based on both industrial and service sectors. It is heavily dependent on international trade and most of its economic sectors are geared toward exporting products. The nation's exports are equivalent to almost two-thirds of its GNP. On a per capita basis, Belgium exports twice as much as Germany and 5 times as much as Japan. In 1999, the nation ranked number 11 among the world's top exporters. In spite of its small size, Belgium's economy has consistently placed among the top 20 economies of the world and remains strong. The kingdom's exports have given it an account surplus that is the sixth largest among the highly developed economies of the world.

For most of its history, Belgium's economy was based on the nation's manufacturing capabilities. The country was the first in continental Europe to undergo the Industrial Revolution, and through the 19th century it was a major steel producer. Large coal deposits helped fuel the industrialization. At the same time, agriculture began to decline. This decline was even more pronounced after World War II, and by 2000, agriculture only accounted for a small percentage of the economy. Currently, agriculture is concentrated in West Flanders, Liege, and Eastern Namur. In the post-World War II era, heavy manufacturing and mining declined. However, there was significant growth in the service sector, and the country switched from heavy production to light manufacturing and began producing finished products instead of steel, textiles, and raw materials. Belgium imports basic or intermediary goods, adds value to them through advanced manufacturing and then exports the finished products. With the exception of its remaining coal resources, Belgium has no significant natural resources.

Belgium's economic strength is based on its geographic position at the crossroads of Western Europe, its highly skilled and educated workforce, and its participation in the EU. During its industrial period, Belgium developed a highly efficient and capable transportation **infrastructure** that included roads, ports, canals, and rail links. The multilingual nature of the workforce and its industriousness has made the workforce one of the most productive in the world.

The oil crisis of the 1970s and economic **restructuring** led to a series of prolonged **recessions**. The 1980–82 recession was particularly severe and resulted in massive unemployment. Personal and consumer debt soared, as did the nation's deficit. Meanwhile, the kingdom's main economic activity shifted northward into Flanders. In 1990, the government linked the Belgian franc to the German mark through interest rates. This spurred a period of economic growth. In 1992–93, another recession plagued Belgian history. During this period, the kingdom's **real GDP** declined by 1.7 percent. Foreign investments have provided new capital and funds for businesses and have consistently helped maintain the economy. Consequently, the government has consistently implemented programs to encourage foreign investment. Since Brussels is the capital of the EU, many multinational firms have relocated to the city so they can be near the bureaucracy and regional body's government seat.

There are major regional differences in the kingdom's economy. In the former industrial and agricultural areas of the countryside, unemployment rates tend to be higher. However, in the newer urban centers (where the service economy is dominant), unemployment rates are lower. For instance, in Wallonia and Brussels, unemployment rates are 2 to 3 times higher than in Flanders. Nevertheless, overall national unemployment rates continue to be lower than the EU average. In addition, wage levels are among the highest in Europe. In 1993, in an effort to give the regions greater flexibility to deal with economic problems, each region was given broad economic powers to control trade, industrial development, and environmental regulation. Each region has also endeavored to attract foreign investment, often to the detriment of other regions.

The government has also engaged in initiatives to **privatize** many companies that were formally owned by the state. Ongoing efforts are underway to privatize 2 of the largest remaining companies: Sabena (the national airline) and Belgacom (the main communications company). Since 1993, successive governments have privatized some 280 billion Belgian francs worth of business.

The kingdom has few energy sources. Consequently, it must import a substantial amount of fossil fuel (which provides 42.48 percent of Belgium's total energy needs). The country has a well-developed nuclear industry that provides more than half of Belgium's energy needs (in 1998, some 55.72 percent of total energy usage). The remaining energy needs are met by a limited number of hydroelectric and coal plants.

As the profitability of many industries declined in the post-World War II era, the government attempted to support them in order to maintain employment. Among the strategies used were subsidizing certain industries, mainly steel and textile companies. In addition, the government reduced interest rates and offered tax incentives and bonuses to attract foreign businesses. All of these measures helped maintain the economy by preventing massive unemployment, but they also led to drastic government deficits in the 1970s and 1980s. The government was then forced to borrow funds from international sources in order to maintain their imports and to continue social welfare programs. By the 1990s, successive governments diligently worked to reduce the debt. In fact, they even shifted from foreign to domestic sources in underwriting their debts. In 1999, Belgium's **external debt** was $28.3 billion or about 10 percent of the nation's total debt. Belgium is a net contributor of foreign aid. In 1997, the kingdom provided $764 million in foreign assistance.

Belgium was one of the founding members of the European Community (later the EU), and has been one of the foremost proponents of regional economic integration. In 2000, 80 percent of Belgium's trade was with other members of the EU. Membership in the EU was the culmination of longstanding national support for economic cooperation. For instance, in 1921, Belgium joined with Luxembourg to form the Belgian-Luxembourg Economic Union (BLEU). This economic union provides for an interchangeable currency and it established a joint customs union. Belgium and Luxembourg have also joined with the Netherlands to form the BENELUX customs union. This organization oversaw cross-border trade between the 3 nations. Belgium is also a member of the Organization for Economic Cooperation and Development (OECD), an organization of the world's most highly developed industrialized democracies.

Belgium has supported the main economic initiatives of the EU, including the elimination of trade barriers, such as **tariffs**, between the organization's 15 member states. The EU also coordinates the external trade of its member states. In 1999, Belgium was one of the founding members of the European Monetary Union (EMU). EMU will replace the national currencies of its members with a single currency, the euro. This is designed to further ease trade among the nations that adopt the euro by eliminating currency fluctuations.

POLITICS, GOVERNMENT, AND TAXATION

Belgium is a constitutional monarchy based on heredity. After political reforms in the 20th century, the monarch's role is now largely ceremonial and symbolic. The monarch's main political function is to appoint the prime minister following elections or the resignation of the government. In this often-divided country, the sovereign is a unifying symbol and plays an important role. The current king, Albert II, succeeded his brother Baudouin who died in 1993.

The executive branch of the Belgian government consists of the king, prime minister and cabinet. The number of cabinet ministers is limited to 15. By an unwritten rule, there is usually a rough balance between Flemish and French-speaking ministers in the cabinet. The kingdom's parliament is **bicameral** (it consists of 2 chambers). The upper house is the Senate and consists of 71 members—40 of whom are elected directly by the people; the 3 linguistic communities indirectly elect the other 31. The lower house is the Chamber of Deputies and has 150 directly elected members. Representatives in both houses serve 4-year terms. Citizens are required to vote in national elections. Elections are relatively short, usually with only a month of campaigning.

There are no national parties in Belgium. Instead the political parties are divided among the major linguistic groups. As a result, governments are usually by coalition (a government composed of members of several different political parties).

As a result of the 1993 constitutional revisions, Belgium changed from a unitary government into a federal system. There are now 3 levels of government: national, regional, and linguistic community. Including the national government in Brussels, there are now 6 different authoritative bodies. Flanders has a single 124-member assembly which represents the region and Flemish-language speakers. Wallonia has 2 assemblies, one 75-member chamber for the region and a 94-member chamber for all French-speakers. Finally, the Brussels region has a 75-member body and the German-speakers have a 25-member assembly.

The government's multi-layered structure means that each governmental body has considerable freedom over their region's economic activities. The regions and communities have jurisdiction over transportation, public works, education, housing, zoning, and industrial and economic policy. Regional governments also coordinate foreign trade with the national government. Of the total government spending, 40 percent is controlled by regional and community governments. These funds are provided through a system of revenue sharing with the national government. These governments also have the ability to levy additional taxes and borrow money.

Following the economic recessions of the 1980s and 1990s, the government attempted to stimulate the economy by implementing various programs. Initially, they tried to protect declining industries by subsidizing them. For those workers that lost their jobs because of cutbacks, generous social benefits were maintained. They also tried to attract foreign businesses and capital. However, in 1994, these efforts led to a massive **national debt** that exceeded the kingdom's GDP by over 137 percent. In 1992, the government attempted to reduce its debt by implementing various economic policies. Unfortunately, this task proved to be quite difficult because they did not meet EMU's official requirements (which called for a debt-to-GDP ratio of 60 percent). Nevertheless, Belgium was admitted in the first round of the monetary union. Its 2000 budget projected a deficit of 1.1 percent and a reduction of the national debt so that it equaled 112 percent of the kingdom's GDP.

In order to reduce this debt, the national government implemented various strategies. First, it privatized a number of industries. Since 1993, the government has privatized 280 billion Belgian francs worth of companies, and is expanding this process. For instance, in 1997, it privatized some 35 billion francs worth of assets, but in 1998, it increased its privatization campaign to 45 billion francs. Second, it has cut government spending. Some programs have been shifted to the regional governments, while others have been scaled-back. Third, the government has reformed the tax structure. The top rate on individuals is 55 percent, but companies, including foreign corporations, pay only 39 percent. However, small companies only pay between 29 and 37 percent. There are no taxes on capital gains and taxes on interest income are 15 percent. Foreign companies are attracted to special corporate tax breaks on corporate centers, such as call centers. Still, Belgium has the third highest taxes among the OECD nations.

The government utilizes various tactics to promote certain consumer behaviors and economic activities. For example, they utilize government-guaranteed mortgage loans to encourage home construction and building. They have projects that help immigrant workers build low-income housing. They have implemented special taxes, known as ecotaxes, designed to encourage consumers to purchase environmentally friendly products. In addition, they have implemented a number of programs to enhance foreign trade and also offer companies direct **subsidies**. Lastly, they provide funds for participation in trade fairs and the development of market research.

The government maintains **price controls** on products and services such as energy, rents, and pharmaceuticals. Pharmaceutical price restrictions have hurt competition and prevented foreign companies from entering the Belgian market. In addition, some U.S. firms such as Toys 'R' Us and McDonald's have had considerable problems in obtaining permits and licenses for new operations. Furthermore, the government-owned telecommunications company, Belgacom, requires new companies to pay relatively high fees in order to offer services to Belgian consumers. In spite of problems in the telecommunications sector, it is one of the fastest growing components of the Belgian economy. In order to promote the sector, the government continues to auction licenses for new mobile phone providers and to promote the use of the wireless Internet.

One of the more significant problems with the economy is that of **procurement**. Foreign companies have had difficulties competing with Belgian firms that are often given preferential treatment. Specific complaints include the failure of the government to issue public notification when it calls for bids on procurement and poor enforcement of rules.

Continuing government support for economic integration with the EU will further spur Belgian's economy. As trade barriers continue to be dismantled among members of the EU, Belgium should be able to expand its exports and enhance its role as a port of entry for goods coming into the region. Although the majority of Belgium's trade is with its EU partners, the kingdom conducts a significant amount of trade with the United States. In 1999, it was the ninth largest trading partner of the United States and imported some $11.9 billion in American services and goods.

Of special concern to the Belgian government are environmental problems. Centuries of industrialization have resulted in widespread pollution. Soil contamination and groundwater pollution exist at many former industrial sites. Steel production wastes have contaminated the Meuse River, a major source of drinking water. Other rivers are contaminated by pollution from agricultural practices, mainly fertilizers. Industrial air pollution has created significant amounts of acid rain, both within Belgium and in neighboring countries. There has been a steady increase in greenhouse gas emissions, including coal, natural gas, and petroleum emissions. From 1995 to 1999, there was a 12 percent increase in these pollutants.

INFRASTRUCTURE, POWER, AND COMMUNICATIONS

Belgium has an excellent infrastructure of roads, waterways, ports, and airports. The kingdom has 145,850 kilometers (90,631 miles) of roads that includes 117,701 kilometers (10,999 miles) of paved highways and 1,682 kilometers (1,045 miles) of expressways. In 1997, some 395,505,000 tons of goods were transported across Belgium's roads. The kingdom is the only nation in Western Europe that has an average of 50 km (31 miles) of roadways for every 1,000 square kilometers (386 miles). Brussels is the heart of a dense highway network that extends beyond the borders of the kingdom to major destinations such as Paris, Amsterdam, and London (via the tunnel under the English Channel). There are 3,437 kilometers (2,136 miles) of rail lines, the majority of which are electrified. In 1997, the railways transported approximately 60,696,000 tons of products. There are 2,043

Communications

Country	Newspapers	Radios	TV Sets[a]	Cable subscribers[a]	Mobile Phones[a]	Fax Machines[a]	Personal Computers[a]	Internet Hosts[b]	Internet Users[b]
	1996	1997	1998	1998	1998	1998	1998	1999	1999
Belgium	160	793	510	367.3	173	18.7	286.0	266.90	1,400
United States	215	2,146	847	244.3	256	78.4	458.6	1,508.77	74,100
Germany	311	948	580	214.5	170	73.1	304.7	173.96	14,400
France	218	937	601	27.5	188	47.4	207.8	110.64	5,370

[a]Data are from International Telecommunication Union, *World Telecommunication Development Report 1999* and are per 1,000 people.
[b]Data are from the Internet Software Consortium (http://www.isc.org) and are per 10,000 people.

SOURCE: World Bank. *World Development Indicators 2000.*

kilometers (1,270 miles) of waterways, of which 1,528 kilometers (950 miles) are in regular commercial use for the transport of goods. In 1997, there were some 106,978,000 tons of goods shipped across the nation's inland waterways. Finally, there is an extensive network of pipelines. There are 161 kilometers (100 miles) of crude oil pipelines, 1,167 kilometers (725 miles) of lines for petroleum products, and over 3,300 kilometers (2,051 miles) of natural gas pipelines. These pipelines transported 96,540,000 tons of fossil fuels in 1993.

Belgium's extensive transportation network and geographic position have enhanced its role as the major point of destination for goods entering Western Europe. The kingdom has 42 airports and a heliport. In 1995, 535,000 tons of goods were shipped via air. The government and the private carrier, SwissAir, jointly own Sabena, the national airline. There is also a low-cost air carrier, Citybird, which provides no-frills inexpensive fares. The international airport at Brussels has become the hub for several major U.S. air carriers. Antwerp is Europe's second largest port facility and is the center of the international diamond trade. The seaports handled some 157,413,000 tons of products in 1995. Ghent and Zeebrugge are also major seaports. Meanwhile, Brussels and Liege are major river ports. In fact, Liege is the third busiest river port in Europe. The Albert Canal can handle river barges of up to 2,000 tons, while other canals easily accommodate barges of up to 1,350 tons. The kingdom has 22 medium to large merchant marine fleets that include 7 cargo ships, 7 petroleum tankers, and 8 chemical tankers. Combined, these fleets have a combined gross tonnage of 35,075 tons.

Belgians have an average of 427 automobiles per 1,000 inhabitants. The telephone system is highly developed and advanced. There is also an extensive nationwide system of cellular phones and 3.7 million mobile phones currently in use. Mobile phone usage is increasing at a rate of 20 percent per year. The kingdom also has 3 earth satellite stations. The Internet has gained in popularity and there are 51 Internet service providers in the nation. Approximately 1 million families use the Internet and 30 percent frequently purchase goods and services online. By 2004, **e-commerce** is expected to exceed $13.8 billion per year. In relation to the telecommunications industry, the government is in the third year of a privatization plan. Currently, there are 41 telecom operators besides the national carrier, Belgacom.

Electrical power production exceeds 78.7 billion kilowatts. Nuclear plants supply the majority of power (some 55 percent). Coal provides 12 percent of the kingdom's energy needs. Most of this coal is mined within the country. The nation meets 42 percent of its electrical needs through imported fossil fuels. Some 26.7 percent of these imports are natural gas. The majority of these natural gas supplies are imported from Algeria, the Netherlands, and Norway. The government has adopted a $9 billion program to provide for the modernization and maintenance of the nation's power system. **Deregulation** is also a priority of this program. Since Electrabel controls 84 percent of the energy market, new companies face significant obstacles while trying to enter this market. Although renewable energy sources, such as solar and wind power, currently only contribute about 0.17 percent of the nation's energy needs, the government continues to promote them.

ECONOMIC SECTORS

Belgium is located in one of the most industrialized areas of the world. Its unique geographic location and port structure make it ideally suited as a point for goods to enter Western Europe. The economy remains dependent on trade and any global market disruptions impact Belgium. Nonetheless, the nation's foreign trade bolsters its economy and helps it rank among the world's top economies. Unemployment remains a problem for the economy. The nation has made significant progress in unemployment. In 1984, it declined from a high of 14.3 percent. In the 1990s, the nationwide unemployment rate averaged between 8 and 9 percent, with the lowest rate, 4 percent, in Flanders, and the highest rate, 16 percent, in Wallonia.

Since the last century, Belgium's agriculture has been in decline and currently only accounts for around 2 percent of the kingdom's GDP. Agriculture is concentrated in the northern areas of Flanders. The nation is self-sufficient in a variety of farm products, including various dairy

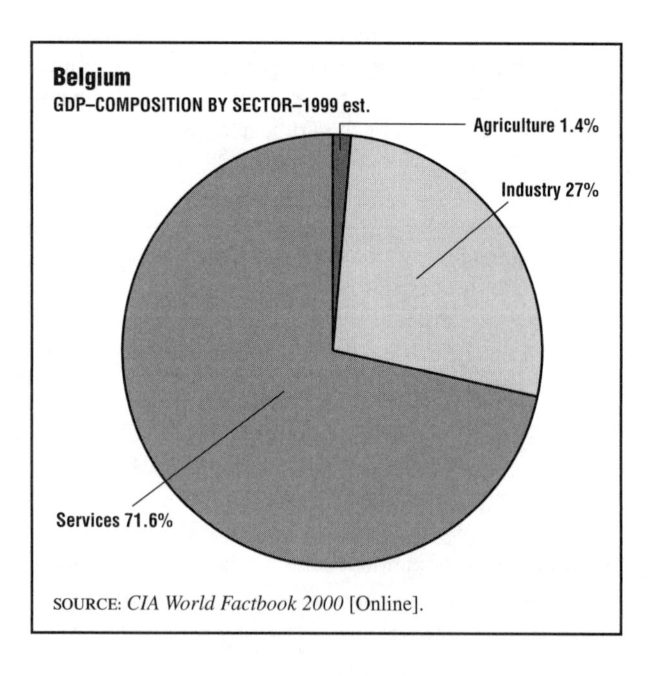

SOURCE: *CIA World Factbook 2000* [Online].

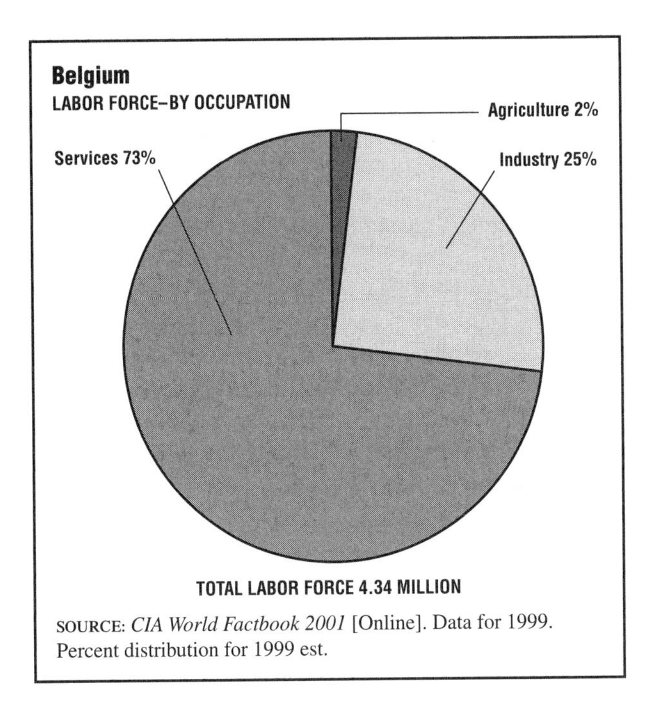

SOURCE: *CIA World Factbook 2001* [Online]. Data for 1999. Percent distribution for 1999 est.

goods, and exports some vegetables and meats. Fishing has also declined over the past decades and currently most of the catch is consumed within the kingdom.

In the post-World War II era, industry has become less important for the national economy. In contrast, the service sector continues to gain in prominence. Most of the kingdom's natural mineral resources have been exhausted. Steel and textile production have significantly declined. The remaining industry produces finished products from reprocessed materials. After the industrial transformation during the 1970s, a number of new industries emerged, including chemicals, refining, metals and machinery, food processing, and pharmaceuticals. Even newer industries such as automobile manufacturing have faced significant obstacles. Belgium has emerged as the center of the international diamond trade. Traditional manufacturing remains concentrated in Wallonia, while the newer industries tend to be located in Flanders.

As with most of the OECD nations, the service sector dominates the Belgian economy. In fact, service sector jobs now account for 73 percent of the nation's employment. In addition, the service sector is also the main area of growth for the kingdom. **Retail** businesses and tourism increasingly account for a larger percentage of the nation's GDP, while financial services continue to expand and attract foreign investment.

Belgium is the home to a number of international corporations and has outlets or subsidiaries of many multinational companies such as Ford, Volvo, and Renault. In fact, some sectors of the Belgian economy have come to be dominated by foreign firms. For instance, U.S. software manufacturers now control some 40 percent of the Belgian market while companies such as Compaq, Dell, and IBM dominate the personal computer market.

AGRICULTURE

The kingdom's agricultural sector has been declining for some time. Currently, only about 2 percent of the population is employed in agriculture and it accounts for just under the same percentage of the nation's GDP. The main areas of the country under cultivation are in the northern region of Flanders; however, small farms exist throughout Belgium. Some 39 percent of the nation's territory is used for some type of agriculture, including the production of forest products. Approximately 1 percent of the land is used for permanent crops.

There are 2 main trends in Belgian agriculture. The first is the disappearance of the small family farm. Farming is increasingly dominated by large **agribusinesses**. Over the past 3 decades, the number of small farms has decreased by 80 percent. The second major trend is the expanding output of the sector. New technologies and scientific crop research have combined to produce greater yields. Therefore, even if farmers' total acreage declines, they are still producing more. Between 1995 and 1999, crop production increased by 9 percent.

Agriculture in Belgium is mainly divided between crop production and raising livestock. The nation's main crops include barley, corn, potatoes, sugar beets, wheat, and assorted fruits and vegetables. Sugar beets, potatoes, and barley are the main staples. In 1999, the country produced 6.15 million metric tons of sugar beets, 2.7 million metric tons of potatoes, and 1.63 million tons of wheat. The country is self-sufficient in sugar, and exports certain vegetables and fruits. About 35 percent of Belgium's farms are engaged in crop production. Belgium also **re-exports** a number of fruits. For instance, bananas are imported into Belgium from the Caribbean and then exported throughout Europe. The nation also imports raw crops, processes them, and then exports them as prepared foods.

Stock farming or livestock production dominates Belgian agriculture. It accounts for 65 percent of the nation's farms. A variety of livestock is raised, including beef, veal, poultry, lamb, pork, and turkey. In 1997, there were 3.1 million head of cattle and 7.3 million pigs on Belgian farms. The beef industry is still recovering from a dioxin scare in 1999. Cattle were accidentally given feed that was contaminated with the cancer-causing chemical dioxin. This led to numerous recalls and various countries around the world banned the import of Belgian beef.

There is also a significant dairy industry and Belgium is self-sufficient in eggs, butter, and milk. In 1997, the nation produced 3.2 million tons of milk, 3.97 million eggs, and 175,000 tons of butter. Belgium also produces a variety of specialty cheeses. Currently, fishing is mainly done for domestic consumption. In 2000, the nation exported $193 million worth of fish, but it imported $833 million worth. The majority of imported fish came from the United States and included lobster, salmon, and prepared seafood meals.

While the nation is a net importer of wood products, it does have a significant timber industry. In 2000, the timber industry was worth $9.9 billion. Total exports were $991 million while imports were $3.5 billion. The United States supplied some 50 percent of Belgium's softwood and plywood needs.

INDUSTRY

Belgium's traditional industries face a number of challenges. Historically, the main industries were concentrated in the French-speaking areas of Wallonia. However, since the 1970s, the principal areas of industrial growth have been in Flanders. Newer light industries and more sophisticated technologies have replaced the older and labor-intensive manufacturing systems. Between Antwerp and Brussels, a new corridor of industries emerged. The majority of these were less labor-intensive and required more skilled workers. The principal industries that have fueled this growth have been the petrochemical and refining sectors. Nonetheless, the remaining industries tend to be highly advanced and technologically sophisticated. Light manufacturing and refining increasingly dominate the industrial sector. The entire industrial sector accounted for 26 percent of GDP in 2000.

STEEL AND PRECIOUS MINERALS. From the 1800s through the 1960s, steel making was the heart of the nation's industry. By the end of the 1960s, Belgian steel manufacturers became less competitive when foreign companies began producing steel for less by using cheap labor and less expensive resources. The twin oil crises of the 1970s further undermined the industry by reducing the worldwide demand for steel. In order to preserve jobs, the government tried to protect steel manufacturers by subsidizing the industry.

The high cost of labor continued to impair the competitiveness of these and other industries. Industry also suffers from excess capacity and continued high fuel prices. These factors have led car manufacturers such as Ford and Renault to cut production in Belgium and shift factories elsewhere. The government has also made considerable attempts to restructure its remaining industrial base. The main thrusts of these efforts have been tax incentives for both domestic and foreign companies in exchange for industry investments. It has also offered incentives for investments in new technologies and the creation of new manufacturing methods.

The steel and plastics industries continue to decline. Since 1990, steel, iron, and coke production has declined by 20 percent. Nonetheless, about 1,000 companies remain in this industry that employs 52,000 people. Belgium remains the eighteenth largest steel producer in the world. In 1999, the sector produced 11 million tons of crude steel and had revenues of 260 billion Belgian francs of which 45 percent came from exports. This was a 4 percent decline from the previous year. The primary plastic products include parts for automobile construction and for engineering projects.

Europe's largest electrolyte copper, zinc, and lead refineries are located in Belgium. The nonferrous metals industry includes: base metals such as aluminum, copper, zinc, lead, and tin; precious metals such as gold, silver, and platinum; and rare or special metals such as germanium, cobalt, and indium. The metals industry employs some 8,600 people. Its exports were worth 127 billion Belgian francs in 1999. New industrial investments totaled 2.6 billion Belgian francs in 1999 and attempted to reduce production costs. The kingdom is also a major producer of limestone, dolomite, various synthetic materials, and construction materials such as marble and concrete. There is also a significant mineral sector that is focused on the refining of imported minerals such as copper, zinc, and diamonds.

Antwerp is the center of the world's diamond trade. The diamond industry employs some 30,000 people and represents 6.4 percent of the nation's exports. In total, 9 out of 10 rough diamonds and 1 out of 2 cut diamonds pass through Antwerp. The diamond sector represents one area of industrial growth. The sector experienced an average growth rate of 6 percent in the 1990s. There are 400 companies engaged in trading rough-cut diamonds, and 700 companies engaged in trading cut diamonds. In 1998, the industry's exports were worth 369 billion Belgian francs.

Glassmaking remains a profitable and expanding industry. It employs some 12,000 people and in 1998, its output was 1.5 million tons of glass. This generated revenues of 100 billion Belgian francs. The industry's exports go mainly to other European countries (some 85 percent of glass exports). In Belgium, glass production was 3 times that of consumption and Belgian workers have among the highest levels of productivity. In 1980, Belgian glass workers produced 55 kg (lbs) of glass per hour; by 1999 that output had increased to 109 kg (lbs) per hour.

CHEMICALS. Belgium's chemical industry is highly diverse and efficient. From 1985 to 1999, the sector has grown by an average of 3.5 percent per year. It is the second largest industrial sector in the nation. The industry is geared for foreign trade and some 80 percent of its products are exported (75 percent of these exports went to EU nations). In 1999, chemicals accounted for 23.5 percent of the kingdom's total exports and were worth 1.574 trillion Belgian francs. In an effort to remain competitive, the chemical industry invested approximately 50 percent of its profits in research and the development of new products and manufacturing techniques. In 1999, there were 97,167 people employed by chemical companies, which represents an 8.4 percent increase since 1985. Chemicals and pharmaceutical products are now Belgium's top exports.

TRANSPORT. Transport equipment is one of the strongest remaining industrial sectors in Belgium. This sector includes the automotive industry, shipbuilding, railway and tram construction, bicycles, and the aeronautical and aerospace industry. Although Belgium does not have its own national automotive manufacturers, it has a large number of international companies. Ford, General Motors, Opel, Renault, Volkswagen, and Volvo have plants in Belgium. In 1999, the nation produced 1.3 million cars. It also produces specialty vehicles including vans, trucks, buses, and minibuses. Of the vehicles manufactured in Belgium, 95 percent are exported. The main markets are France, Germany, and the United Kingdom. The automotive industry also produces a variety of specialty parts for cars. The industry specializes in "just in time" (JIT) manufacturing which involves producing products to be used immediately upon receipt. This process eliminates the need to stockpile items in warehouses.

Belgium no longer builds large sea-going vessels, but its shipyards still build smaller coastal and river craft. In addition, there are a number of firms that are capable of repairing and refitting larger ships. Companies also produce a variety of specialty products for marine use. Belgium invests considerable sums in aerospace. The government works with other European nations such as France and Germany on projects such as Airbus jet aircraft and the Ariane rocket.

TEXTILES. The textile sector employs over 42,500 people in 1,320 textile factories. Belgium is now the largest carpet exporter in the world. Textile revenues accounted for 250 billion Belgian francs. Unlike many of the other traditional industries, Belgium's textile manufacturers have been able to adjust to changes in the global market. Belgium is also noted for its quality leather products. There have been widespread consolidations and advancements in manufacturing techniques. As a result, the textile sector remains one of Belgium's largest industrial employers.

ELECTRONICS. Belgium produces a wide range of electronics equipment that includes both consumer and business products. This sector of the economy employs 49,000 people in 300 companies. These businesses produced products worth more than 300 billion Belgian francs. Two-thirds of the kingdom's electronic products are exported. The majority, 75 percent, goes to other members of the EU, while the remaining exports are divided among the United States, Eastern Europe, and Asia. Medical and hospital electronics are a major part of this sector. The electronics sector is the largest investor in the economy's infrastructure and research and development. The sector annually invests some 30 billion Belgian francs of which 60 percent is in research and development.

FURNITURE. Furniture manufacturing has a long and distinguished tradition in Belgium. Adaptability and quality reputation are its keys to continued success. Increased mechanization and automation have helped contain costs and kept the industry competitive. It has strong exports to Germany and the United Kingdom and has recently enjoyed dramatic growth in the Netherlands. The sector has also aggressively targeted the markets in Eastern Europe. Belgium furniture exports have increased by 57 percent and have grown by a phenomenal 79 percent to Russia itself. In 1998, the industry had revenues of 1.89 billion euros that included 1.13 billion euros in exports.

CONSTRUCTION. The construction industry in Belgium encompasses 2 different broad areas. The majority of activity is centered on the construction of new buildings and homes. There is also a considerable market in the restoration of older dwellings. Brick is the preferred building material and most homes are custom built. On average, only 10 percent of homes built are prefabricated. In 1998, residential construction accounted for 46 percent of new contracts, business construction accounted for 41 percent, and 13 percent of new contracts were in civil engineering. In 1997, Belgium's construction companies had revenues of 1 trillion Belgian francs. Belgian companies also carried out a number of projects abroad, mainly in developing nations. In 1998, total revenues from these projects were 88 billion Belgian francs. Government plans to eliminate slums and provide housing for low-income Belgians have significantly helped the construction industry grow.

SERVICES

The service sector is the largest area of the Belgian economy, accounting for 72.6 percent of GDP in 2000. It is well developed and diversified. Because of its geographic position as the gateway to Europe and the government's efforts to attract foreign banking and financial companies, Belgium is now the eighth-largest financial center in the world. In 1999, there were 130 different banking companies in Belgium. Of these, 81 were Belgian and 39 were foreign-owned. The majority of the foreign-owned banks were from EU nations (23 of the 39). The implementation of EMU will make it even easier for foreign banks to establish a presence in Belgium as the members of the EU begin to use the common currency. The Belgian government encourages foreign banks to establish a presence in the kingdom. For instance, the government allows foreign banks to operate as either subsidiaries under Belgian law or to operate under the laws of the nation in which their parent bank is licensed.

FINANCIAL SERVICES. The financial sector has 3 main subdivisions: commercial banks, public credit institutions, and private savings banks. However, the divisions between these 3 types of institutions became less noticeable in the 1990s. There have been a substantial number of mergers across these fields. For instance, in 1999 the international banking corporation Dexia merged its Belgian and French subsidiaries to create a banking group worth $11 billion. Belgium's Banking Commission supervises private banks, finance companies, and the oversight of mutual funds. Investments in the country's financial sector ballooned from $55 billion in 1996 to $300 billion in 1999.

The 3 main trading banks in Belgium are the Fortis Bank, Brussels Bank Lambert, and KBC. Fortis has a workforce of some 40,000 and 3,000 branches. It services some 7 million customers in Belgium, Luxembourg, and the Netherlands, and is one of the leading banks in northwestern Europe. Brussels Bank Lambert has 900 traditional branches and 500 automated teller machines. It is the twelfth largest bank in Europe. KBC is the nation's third largest bank and is also one of the largest insurance companies. It has 1,500 bank employees, 500 insurance brokers, and 8,000 other brokers. This multinational bank has branches in 30 different nations. The fourth and fifth largest banks in Belgium are foreign-owned. Number-four is Dexier, a joint Belgian-French multinational, and number-five is Morgan Guaranty Trust of New York (a subsidiary of J. P. Morgan & Company). Other major international banks in Belgium are Citibank, Bank of America, and Chase Manhattan Bank.

In 2000, the EU enacted new rules that allow insurance brokers to operate in any other EU state as long as they are registered in their home nation. For instance, Belgian insurance companies will be able to set up offices in Germany or France without having to be licensed in that nation. This offers a variety of advantages to Belgian companies. For instance, 60 to 70 percent of the insurance bought by Belgian consumers was non-life (including car or home insurance). In contrast, in other EU states, non-life insurance typically accounts for some 20 percent of the market. Hence, Belgian insurance companies see these new markets as sources of great opportunities.

TOURISM. The main centers of the Belgian tourist industry are the country's coastal region and the Ardennes. The coastline has 65 resorts and numerous beaches. Most are designed for family-oriented vacations and draw tourists from France, the United Kingdom, and the Netherlands. Situated in the southeast of Belgium, the Ardennes forest is one of the few unspoiled natural areas in Western Europe. The area attracts campers and day-trippers. It is known for hiking, fishing, canoeing and kayaking, and mountaineering in the spring and summer months. In the winter, tourists engage in both downhill and cross-country skiing.

The total value of tourism in Belgium is $11.425 billion. Of this total, Belgians traveling within the country spent $4.9 billion. The United States is the number-one destination for Belgians traveling abroad. In 1999, some 257,000 Belgians visited the United States and spent $652 million.

RETAIL. Retailers in Belgium have rebounded from a period of stagnation in the early 1990s. Consumer spending has been increasing at a rate of 2.5 percent over the past few years and is expected to grow in the near future. Unlike many other markets in the EU or North America, independent companies still make up a large proportion of the retail market. For instance, although 78.5 percent of fashion merchandisers are independent, chain outlets control 16.7 percent of the market. The remaining 4.8 percent is in the hands of large department stores and supermarkets.

In 1999, there were 52,807 restaurants in Belgium. The largest chain is the Quick hamburger restaurant group that has 105 shops. The number-two chain is the U.S.-owned McDonald's. Other American chains such as Pizza Hut and Chi Chi's also hold significant market shares. Sales at foreign-owned restaurants were 10.45 billion Belgian francs while sales at locally owned stores were 7.53 billion Belgian francs.

INTERNATIONAL TRADE

Belgium's economy is dependent on international trade. From year-to-year, foreign trade accounts for approximately 70 percent of the nation's economy. This makes Belgium particularly sensitive to disruptions in global trade. Recessions or other economic problems around the world often cause reciprocal problems in Belgium's economy. Fortunately, the kingdom has a variety of trade partners so that problems in one export market are mitigated by export diversity. For instance, since companies were able to shift exports to other markets, Asia's economic problems in the late 1990s had little significant impact on Belgium.

The nation's main trade partners are in the EU. In fact, in 1998 some 76 percent of Belgium's exports went to nations in the EU. In that year, the main export market for Belgian goods was Germany (19 percent), followed closely by France (18 percent), the Netherlands (12 percent), and the United Kingdom (10 percent). Most of Belgium's imports also came from the EU that provided 71 percent of the kingdom's imported products. Germany was the main exporter to Belgium and provided 18 percent of goods, while the Netherlands provided 17 percent, France 14 percent, and the United Kingdom 9 percent. Total foreign investment in Belgium is $68.1 billion. The Netherlands is the principal source of foreign investment (21.9 percent), followed by Germany (17.1 percent), France (16 percent), and the United States (11 percent).

The United States is a major trading partner of Belgium. The kingdom is the ninth largest trading partner of the United States. In 1999, the United States exported $11.3 billion to Belgium. About half of Belgium's imports from the United States are processed and re-exported to other markets. The kingdom is home to 1,300 U.S. companies. American investment in Belgium totals $18.9 billion. The majority of this investment is concentrated manufacturing ($8.969 billion), services ($5.262 billion), and wholesaling ($2.716 billion). Belgium also has significant investments in the United States that total $6.7 billion. The majority of these investments are in manufacturing ($2.6 billion), petroleum ($1.265 billion), and retail ($882 million).

Goods and products from EU nations enter Belgium without any tariffs or **duties**. However, goods from nations outside of the EU face import duties and a **value-added tax** (VAT). Depending on the product, these taxes amount to an average of 5–6 percent of the total value of the product. Consequently, many goods from outside of the EU face a price disadvantage.

Since Belgium is home to the headquarters of the EU and over 100 international organizations, it has a unique perspective on world trade and global markets. It also has significant influence on trade. Since it joined the European Community (now EU), Belgium has supported free trade and advocated measures that lower tariffs and reduce other barriers to the free movement of goods and services, labor, and capital within Europe. Belgium and Luxembourg also continue to be economically linked through BLEU. Despite its membership in the EU and BLEU, Belgium has bilateral trade agreements with 29 different nations. It has separate investment accords with Poland and Russia. It also has treaties with Bulgaria, Cuba, Liberia, Mauritania, and Thailand. Under the auspices of BLEU, it has jointly signed with Luxembourg. Many of these agreements have yet to be fully implemented.

Besides the national trade agreements, each of the 3 regions has the authority to grant financial incentives and other inducements to attract foreign goods and services. Among the tactics used are loan or interest rebates if the project is financed, financing by the regional government, and tax breaks for foreign companies.

MONEY

Through BLEU, Belgium and Luxembourg linked their currencies in 1921. Although the Belgian franc has declined in relation to the U.S. dollar, it has maintained its value against major European currencies. In 1995, 1 U.S. dollar was equal to 29.48 francs, but by 1999, 1 dollar equaled 34.77 francs. In 1999, Belgium joined the EMU that created a single currency, the euro, for all of the EU nations. The euro is fixed at a rate of 40.3399 francs per euro. Since its introduction, the euro has been weak against the dollar. In 2000, 1 U.S. dollar equaled 0.9867 euros (when the euro was introduced it was equal to $1.1789). The euro was only used in non-cash forms (such as electronic payments and transfers) until January of 2002, when euro coins and notes were issued and national currencies were phased out.

The Belgian National Bank acts as the state bank. It prints and issues the nation's currency and acts as the lender of last resort in certain credit operations. The bank also manages **monetary policy** by controlling interest rates. The Banking Commission oversees the operations of the nation's banks while the Finance Ministry regulates credit institutions.

In September of 2000, the Brussels stock exchange merged with the exchanges of Amsterdam and the Paris Bourse exchange to form Euronext. The new stock exchange is the first truly transnational exchange that combines stock, derivative, and commodity trading. The new exchange lists 1,861 different companies and has a value of 1.1 trillion euros. The merger will streamline trading and reduce transaction costs. It will also save approximately 50 million euros per year. The exchange also increases the transparency of stocks and gives investors greater cost comparisons. The stock-trading component of Euronext is divided into 3 broad areas: blue

Exchange rates: Belgium

euros per US$1	
Jan 2001	1.0659
2000	1.0854
1999	0.9386
1998	36.229
1997	35.774
1996	30.962

Note: Amounts prior to 1999 are in Belgian francs per US dollar.

SOURCE: CIA *World Factbook 2001* [ONLINE].

GDP per Capita (US$)

Country	1975	1980	1985	1990	1998
Belgium	18,620	21,653	22,417	25,744	28,790
United States	19,364	21,529	23,200	25,363	29,683
Germany	N/A	N/A	N/A	N/A	31,141
France	18,730	21,374	22,510	25,624	27,975

SOURCE: United Nations. *Human Development Report 2000; Trends in human development and per capita income.*

Distribution of Income or Consumption by Percentage Share: Belgium

Lowest 10%	3.7
Lowest 20%	9.5
Second 20%	14.6
Third 20%	18.4
Fourth 20%	23.0
Highest 20%	34.5
Highest 10%	20.2

Survey year: 1992

Note: This information refers to income shares by percentiles of the population and is ranked by per capita income.

SOURCE: *2000 World Development Indicators* [CD-ROM].

chip traditional industrial companies, high tech stocks, and traditional securities. The new multinational exchange is actively seeking further integration and consolidation and may merge or absorb additional national exchanges.

In order to become a member of EMU, Belgium had to maintain low **inflation**. The government took steps that kept inflation low—as low as 1 percent in 1999. Low prices on imported goods are likely to aid efforts to keep inflation low for the foreseeable future.

POVERTY AND WEALTH

Belgium, like many Western European nations, enjoys a high standard of living and a high per capita income. Each year the United Nations ranks the world's countries in its *Human Development Report.* Belgium consistently ranks among the top nations in its human development index that measures the quality of life in countries. In the 2000 report, the UN ranked Belgium number-seven—just behind Switzerland and ahead of the Netherlands. Its per capita income was $28,790. Belgium ranked 8th out of 191 countries in terms of per capita income.

There are extremes of wealth and poverty in Belgium. However, the nation's generous social welfare programs prevent abject poverty. Only 3.7 percent of the population falls into the lowest 10 percent of income levels while 20.2 percent of the households are in the top 10 percentile.

The nation's social welfare programs are extensive. There are 5 main elements to the Belgian **social welfare system**: family allowance, unemployment insurance, retirement, medical benefits, and a program that provides salary in the event of illness. Employers contribute the equivalent of 35 percent of a worker's pay to the social welfare system and workers contribute 13 percent of their pay. Many companies also offer supplemental retirement and medical programs. Almost all Belgians are covered by medical insurance. Payments to medical providers were $12.97 billion in 1999. Belgium ranked thirteenth among the 24 OECD nations and fifth among the 15 EU nations. Each region has special councils that provide public assistance and aid to the poor. The National Housing Society provides low-income housing for the poor and immigrants. The Society is also in charge of eliminating slums and revitalizing urban neighborhoods.

Belgium's educational system is among the best in Europe. Freedom of education is a constitutional right in Belgium. Both public and private schools exist, but the government subsidizes private schools since the legal system abolished fees in 1958. Children must attend

Household Consumption in PPP Terms

Country	All food	Clothing and footwear	Fuel and power[a]	Health care[b]	Education[b]	Transport & Communications	Other
Belgium	17	6	8	3	1	7	57
United States	13	9	9	4	6	8	51
Germany	14	6	7	2	10	7	53
France	22	7	9	3	8	12	40

Data represent percentage of consumption in PPP terms.

[a]Excludes energy used for transport.

[b]Includes government and private expenditures.

SOURCE: World Bank. *World Development Indicators 2000.*

school between the ages of 6 and 18. The nation has 7 universities (4 that teach in French and 3 that teach in Flemish). There are also a number of specialized and technical schools.

WORKING CONDITIONS

Belgium's workforce is highly skilled, educated, and productive. Belgian workers are the most productive in the EU. The workforce is well paid and has both generous employer and government benefits. However, there are wide regional differences in wages, unemployment, and quality of life. Generally, conditions are better in Flanders and the German-speaking areas than in the French-speaking areas.

The nation's educational system is designed to prepare workers for entry into the workforce. From the age of 15 onward, children may work part-time while they attend school. In addition, industrial apprenticeship programs are available for students between the ages of 16 and 18. There is also vocational training available for both students and adults. The national government and regional governments offer a variety of incentives for retraining workers. These initiatives are designed to reduce the national social security burden.

There are laws against forced labor. The minimum age for a person to begin working is 15. Since education is mandatory until age 18, students may only work part-time during the school year. Youths may work full-time during school vacation periods. Both the national and regional governments aggressively enforce child labor laws.

In 1999, the government revised its legislation on equal opportunity in the workplace. The new laws outlawed sexual harassment, and continued the ban on gender discrimination in hiring, working conditions, wages, and termination. Equal treatment of men and women is guaranteed by the constitution. In 1999, legislation was passed requiring that women make up one-third of all candidates running for office. Economic inequities between men and women continue. For instance, the female unemployment rate was 10.9 percent in 1998, while the male unemployment rate was 6.7 percent. In addition, women only earn 84 percent of the salary that men earn in the same professions.

The constitution guarantees the right of workers to organize and to collective bargaining. Union membership is high and 63 percent of workers belong to unions. In addition, 90 percent of workers are covered by collective bargaining agreements. National laws limit wage increases to 5.9 percent per year. Special labor courts oversee disputes between workers and businesses. Although Belgian unions often have links to political parties, they are independent of the government. While there have been several significant strikes in the past decade, including those by teachers, railway workers and air traffic controllers, these disputes were settled peacefully.

National law sets a 40-hour workweek and mandates overtime pay for work beyond 40 hours per week and for more than 8 hours a day. In addition, each workweek must include a 24-hour rest period. However, many agreements between unions and companies have separate agreements that lower the workweek to either 35 or 38 hours per week. The minimum wage for workers over the age of 21 is $1,228 per month. Workers under the age of 21 are paid on a graduated scale. Workers who are 18 years old must be paid 82 percent of the minimum wage, 19 year olds must be paid 88 percent, and 20 year olds must be paid 94 percent. There are strong safety laws and many of these regulations are supplemented by collective bargaining agreements. Although companies with more than 50 employees must have health and safety committees made up of both management and workers, the Ministry of Labor oversees workplace laws.

COUNTRY HISTORY AND ECONOMIC DEVELOPMENT

500–200 B.C. The area that is now Belgium is settled by a Celtic tribe, the Belgae (who gave their name to the region).

57 B.C. Julius Caesar begins conquering Belgium. The province comes to be known as Gallia Belgae. For the next 400 years, the area prospers under Roman control.

400 A.D. As Rome declines, the Franks gain control of the territory.

431. The Franks establish the Merovingian dynasty in Belgium.

466–511. Reign of Clovis I. During his reign, the last Roman territories in Gaul are captured and the kingdom is expanded to include areas of France and Germany. The Belgian people are converted to Christianity.

751. Pepin III deposes the Merovingians and starts the Carolingian dynasty.

768. Charlemagne succeeds his father, Pepin III. Charlemagne expands the empire to include all of Western Europe, and the king is crowned Emperor of the West by the Pope in 800. During his reign, organized trade begins along Belgium's rivers. After his death, the empire declines.

843. The Treaty of Verdun divides the empire among 3 of Charlemagne's sons. The western areas of Belgium come under France's control, while the eastern territories are controlled under the Middle Kingdom of Lothair. Ultimately, Germans control the eastern territories.

867. In order to protect people from Norse raids, walled cities are created. The first of these is Ghent, followed by Bruges and Ypres.

977. Brussels is founded by Charles, the Duke of Lorraine.

1000. As the Norse raids subside, trade dramatically expands. This period is the golden age of Flanders. Merchants import wool from England that is woven into fine cloths and tapestries. Flemish cities become populous and wealthy.

1300. Because of their wealth, Ghent, Bruges, and Ypres gain virtual independence from the aristocracy. A civic culture flourishes. This independence is confirmed by the defeat of the French nobles in the Battle of the Golden Spurs.

1329. Aristocratic control is re-established and the independence of the Flemish cities is revoked.

1337–1453. There is a Hundred Years War between France and England. The English support their trade allies, the Flemish, in their continuing efforts to gain autonomy from France.

1384. Flanders comes under the control of Philip the Bold, Duke of Burgundy.

1419–1467. Philip the Good reigns. The Burgundian Empire in Belgium expands and includes the southeastern areas of Brussels, Liege, and Namur. Trade, arts, and culture expand. Prominent artists include Van Eyck, Rubens, and Van Dyck.

1490s. The canals around Bruges fill with silt and trade shifts further north to Antwerp.

1519–1713. Religious conflicts between the Protestant areas of Flanders and Catholics, led by Philip II of Spain, lead to the occupation of Belgium by Spain.

1648. The Protestant United Provinces of the North gain independence from Spain and become the Netherlands. The center of trade shifts from Antwerp and Ghent to Amsterdam. Meanwhile in order to avoid high labor costs and taxation, textile mills increasingly move from the urban areas to the countryside.

1719–1794. Austria occupies Belgium according to the terms of the Treaty of Utrecht. A revolt in 1790 leads to the establishment of the United States of Belgium, but Austrian control is soon re-established. During this period, landowners begin to mine various products, mainly coal and iron ore.

1795. France occupies Belgium and institutes a variety of civil reforms that serve as the foundation of the modern Belgian government. Encouraged by the French, industrialization begins during this period. By the turn of the century, factories with more than 100 employees become common. Ghent, home to numerous cotton mills, becomes the textile center of the country. Mining also continues to spread, especially in the French-speaking areas and in Liege.

1815. Belgium becomes part of the Netherlands by the Congress of Vienna. Dutch becomes the official language and William I of the Netherlands adopts a variety of programs to encourage industrialization in the south. However, the industrialization exacerbated the regional differences in the nation as the agrarian North sought free trade, while the industrialized South sought tariffs and other trade protections.

1831. Belgium gains independence from the Netherlands. Leopold of Saxe-Coburg becomes the Belgian king. Industrialization continues to sweep across the nation.

1835. The Banque du Belgique is founded. It provides financing for industry and serves as the model for similar banks in Germany, England, and France.

1844–46. Famine in Flanders leads to widespread economic problems and marks the final decline of the traditional linen industry. These combined problems slowed the economic development of the region well into the twentieth century.

1850. The National Bank of Belgium is formed.

1885. Congo becomes a personal possession of Leopold II.

1886. Worker unrest, which began in Liege, spreads throughout the nation. The government harshly suppresses this unrest, but it results in worker housing and wages reform.

1908. The Congo is annexed as a colony of Belgium.

1914. Germany invades Belgium at the start of World War I. During the war, some 20 percent of the nation's wealth is lost or destroyed.

1918. Universal suffrage is enacted.

1921. The Belgium-Luxembourg Economic Union (BLEU) is formed.

1930. Flanders and Wallonia become legally unilingual.

1940. During World War II, Germany invades Belgium and the Netherlands.

1944. Belgium joins the Benelux Economic Union, formed between Belgium, the Netherlands, and the Grand Duchy of Luxembourg.

1949. The nation joins NATO.

1952. Belgium joins the European Coal and Steel Community.

1957. Belgium is one of the founding members of the European Community.

1960. The Congo gains independence.

1961. Massive strikes lead to the creation of a permanent linguistic barrier between Flanders and Wallonia, while the Brussels region is officially bilingual.

1962. Rwanda and Burundi are granted independence.

1971. Flanders and Wallonia are granted cultural autonomy.

1973. The worldwide oil crisis initiates a period of deep industrial decline, which is exacerbated by the second oil crisis in 1979.

1989. A revised constitution grants greater autonomy to Flanders and Wallonia, and Brussels is granted the status of a region.

1993. King Baudouin dies and is succeeded by his brother, King Albert II.

1999. The kingdom joins EMU.

FUTURE TRENDS

Belgium is well positioned to continue its economic growth well into the 21st century. Its export-driven economy has created a **trade surplus** that will continue for the foreseeable future. In addition, Belgium's geographic position and its infrastructure indicate that the country will continuously serve as a point of entry for goods and services going into Europe. The introduction of the single European currency in 1999 will continue to make it easier for Belgian firms to trade within the EU.

While the 370 million people of the EU create one of the biggest commercial markets in the world, Belgium's dependence on intra-EU trade makes it vulnerable to economic slowdowns in the region. However, Belgium's trade with North America, namely the United States, continues to grow and may serve as a means to partially offset economic downturns in the EU.

Domestically, Belgium faces a variety of problems. Continuing tension between the Dutch- and French-speaking populations has led to the division of the nation into semi-autonomous regions that compete with one another for economic growth and investment. In addition, the unemployment rate remains stubbornly high, although it is lower than the EU average. Because of the high unemployment rate, the government is forced to maintain a high level of social welfare programs.

DEPENDENCIES

Belgium has no territories or colonies.

BIBLIOGRAPHY

Belgian Foreign Trade Board. "The Belgian Assets: An Introduction." <http://obcebdbh.be/import_en/info-center/belgium-assets/home_en.html>. Accessed September 2001.

Hermans, Theo, editor. *The Flemish Movement: A Documentary History, 1780–1990.* Atlantic Highlands, NJ: Athlone, 1992.

Organization for Economic Cooperation and Development (OECD). *OECD economic surveys: Belgium-Luxembourg, 1998/99.* Paris: OECD, 1999.

Stallaerts, Robert. *Historical Dictionary of Belgium.* Lanham, MD: Scarecrow, 1999.

U.S. Central Intelligence Agency. *World Factbook 2001.* <http://www.odci.gov/cia/publications/factbook/index.html>. Accessed September 2001.

U.S. Department of State. *Background Notes: Belgium: 1998.* <http://state.gov>. Accessed August 2001.

U.S. Department of State. *1999 Country Reports on Human Rights Practices: Belgium.* <http://state.gov>. Accessed August 2001.

U.S. Department of State. *FY 2001 Country Commercial Guide: Belgium.* <http://state.gov>. Accessed August 2001.

Van Meerhaeghe, M.A.G., editor. *Belgium and EC Membership Evaluated.* New York: St. Martin's Press, 1992.

—Tom Lansford

BOSNIA AND HERZEGOVINA

Republic of Bosnia and Herzegovina
Republika Bosnia i Herzegovina

CAPITAL: Sarajevo.

MONETARY UNIT: Marka (KM). One convertible marka equals 100 convertible pfenniga.

CHIEF EXPORTS: Manufactured goods, metals (aluminum, lead, zinc, steel), wood products, electricity, fruit and tobacco.

CHIEF IMPORTS: Fuel, machinery, transportation equipment, manufactured products, chemicals, and food.

GROSS DOMESTIC PRODUCT: US$6.5 billion (purchasing power parity, 2000 est.).

BALANCE OF TRADE: **Exports:** US$950 million (f.o.b., 2000 est.). **Imports:** US$2.45 billion (f.o.b., 2000 est.).

COUNTRY OVERVIEW

LOCATION AND SIZE. Bosnia and Herzegovina is in southeastern Europe. It is bound on the north and west by Croatia, the southwest by Croatia and the Adriatic Sea, and on the east by Yugoslavia (Serbia and Montenegro). The country has an area of 51,129 square kilometers (19,741 square miles), which is slightly smaller than West Virginia, and has a tiny coastline of 20 kilometers (13 miles). The capital, Sarajevo, is in the east-central part of the country, and other prominent cities include Zenica, Banja Luka, Mostar, and Tuzla.

POPULATION. The population of Bosnia and Herzegovina was estimated at 3,922,205 in July 2001; however, this estimation may include significant errors because of the dislocations and ethnic cleansing from the Bosnian civil war (1992–95). In contrast, the country had a population of 4,364,574, according to the 1991 census. The civil war caused hundreds of thousands of casualties and forced many others to flee. By 1998, the population had decreased by an estimated 1 million people.

With an estimated birth rate of 12.86 and death rate of 7.99 per 1,000 inhabitants, Bosnia (the shortened name for the whole country) has an estimated population growth rate of 1.38 percent. The population is young, with 20 percent below the age of 14 and just 9 percent over 65. Bosnia's population density in 1998 was estimated at 66 people per square kilometer (170 per square mile). In 1997, 42 percent of the population lived in urban areas.

Bosnia's major ethnic groups are Muslims (Bosniaks), Serbs, and Croats. The Serbs are traditionally Orthodox Christians, and the Croats are Roman Catholics. Muslims are descendants of former Christian Slavs who converted to Islam during the 15th and 16th centuries (under Ottoman rule). In 1991, the population consisted of 44 percent Muslims, 31 percent Serbs, and 17 percent Croats. In 1995, the population consisted of 40 percent Muslims, 38 percent Serbs, and 22 percent Croats. Events leading to this population change include the **immigration** of approximately 200,000 ethnic Serbs from Croatia and the deaths of about 7.4 percent of the pre-war Muslim population and 7.1 percent of the pre-war Serb population during the savage civil war. Bosnia and Herzegovina's populations of Serbs, Croats, and Muslims will likely embroil the country in struggles with its more powerful neighboring republics. Bosnian Serbs, for example, may continue to push for annexation to a "Greater Serbia."

OVERVIEW OF ECONOMY

Prior to becoming independent in 1992, Bosnia and Herzegovina was the second poorest republic in the former Socialist Federal Republic of Yugoslavia. Before the inter-ethnic war (1992–95), the economy was devoted to mining, forestry, agriculture, light and heavy manufacturing, and particularly armaments. Unlike many Eastern European countries, Bosnia and Herzegovina's farmland was never collectivized by the **communist** regime. Agriculture was insufficiently developed, and the country

heavily imported food, while its military industry was overstressed. The breakup of old Yugoslavia, the disruption of traditional markets and economic links, and the savage civil war caused industrial and agricultural output to plummet by four-fifths by 1995. Since 1996, production has recovered somewhat; however, the **gross domestic product** (GDP) remains far below its pre-war level.

By the time the civil war broke out in Bosnia and Herzegovina, the **inflation rate** was about 120 percent. During the war, **inflation** skyrocketed to over 1,000 percent. Unemployment was about 30 percent when the war began, but by 1995, it rose to 75 percent. All sectors of the economy were badly hurt, and 45 percent of industrial plants and 75 percent of the oil refineries were incapacitated.

When the war ended in 1995, the country was united under a federal government but split into 2 legal entities: the Federation of Bosnia and Herzegovina and the Republika Srpska (The Serb Republic). The end of fighting made some recovery possible, especially in construction, trade, services, and traditional light industries. The division between the Federation and the Serb Republic proved to be a significant obstacle to reconstruction. The Serb Republic included most of the agricultural land and mineral deposits. In contrast, most heavy industry and power plants were within the Federation. This division made the most basic economic functions, such as the distribution of electricity, dependent on good cooperation between the once warring entities.

Economic data on each of Bosnia's 2 units are of little use because they do not reflect the **black market**, and national-level statistics are not published. The country's **external debt** was estimated at US$3.2 billion in 2000 and US$1.2 billion of international aid is now being pledged to help the country's finances. Bosnia also receives substantial reconstruction assistance and humanitarian aid from the international community.

POLITICS, GOVERNMENT, AND TAXATION

In 1990, Bosnia and Herzegovina seceded from Yugoslavia (which further dissolved into Slovenia, Croatia, Macedonia, and a new Federal Republic of Yugoslavia comprised of Serbia and Montenegro). The newly independent Bosnia and Herzegovina could not maintain cooperation between 3 of its ethnic groups: the Serbs wanted to unite with Serbia, the Croats wanted to unite with Croatia, and the Muslims wanted Bosnia and Herzegovina to unite as an independent state. The differing opinions sparked a bloody civil war.

Between 1992 and 1995, the 2 areas of Bosnia and Herzegovina were almost devastated by inter-ethnic carnage that stunned the world. International mediation efforts helped bring about the Dayton accord, which ended the civil war in 1995 by dividing the country into 2 ethnic entities: the Federation of Bosnia and Herzegovina and the Serb Republic. The government established has been labeled an "emerging democracy."

The country has a federal government and 2 administrative divisions: the Bosniak/Croat-led Federation of Bosnia and Herzegovina and the Bosnian Serb-led Serb Republic. (There is also a self-governing administrative unit called Brcko, which is under the authority of the sovereignty of Bosnia and Herzegovina but is not a part of the Federation or the Serb Republic.)

The presidency of Bosnia and Herzegovina is held by 3 officials (1 Bosnian Muslim, 1 Croat, and 1 Serb), who are elected to a 4-year term and rotate the chairmanship of the presidency every 8 months. Both the Federation and the Serb Republic elect presidents of their own administrative entities. The country is still establishing laws for voting and terms of the legislature, which has been created as a national **bicameral** Parliamentary Assembly. The Federation also has a bicameral legislature, and the Serb Republic is served by its own National Assembly. The judiciary system is similarly split between federal and administrative jurisdiction. There is a Constitutional Court heading the federal judiciary, and the entities have their own supreme courts and a number of lower courts. (In 2000, the Constitutional Court of Bosnia and Herzegovina ruled that the new governmental structure of Bosnia and Herzegovina had undermined the country's ethnic base and should be changed to reflect the multi-ethnic character of the country.)

Bosnia's political life is still highly fragmented and organized strictly along ethnic lines. These political parties include the Croatian Democratic Union; the New Croatian Initiative; the Party of Democratic Action; the Party for Bosnia and Herzegovina; the Social Democratic Party; the Democratic Socialist Party of Republika Srpska; the Party of Democratic Progress; the Party of Independent Social Democrats; the Serb Democratic Party; the Serbian People's Alliance; the Serbian Radical Party of Republika Srpska; and the Socialist Party of Republika Srpska. In 2000, the Muslim Party of Democratic Action, the Serb Democratic Party, and the Croatian Democratic Union again won the general election. These major parties were previously influential in leading major ethnic groups in the civil war.

The government plays a large role in the economy. Although 90 percent of businesses are private, the largest conglomerates remain state-owned. Corrupt leaders often arbitrarily apply taxes and regulations, and the black market is a significant economic factor. **Privatization** legislation exists, but disposing of state assets is slow and often receives much resistance. This situation is particularly prevalent in the utilities sector that is entirely controlled by party oligarchs. In mass privatization, free company vouchers or privatization funds shares are distributed to the public. Foreign investors are attracted to cash privatization because it generates fresh foreign currency inflows and brings western technology to important companies. However, due to lack of interest, results to this tender have been modest. Between May 1999 and September 2000, more than 1,000 small enterprises were listed for privatization; however, only 200 were sold during this time.

In 2002 a comprehensive tax administration reform is expected to create a more business-friendly environment and to attract foreign investment. But foreign investment relies on continued political stability. The implementation of democratic governments in neighboring nations is expected to improve privatization efforts within Bosnia and Herzegovina and to limit the risk of renewed political instability.

INFRASTRUCTURE, POWER, AND COMMUNICATIONS

The country's **infrastructure**, including highways, railroads, and communication networks were severely

Communications

Country	Newspapers	Radios	TV Sets[a]	Cable subscribers[a]	Mobile Phones[a]	Fax Machines[a]	Personal Computers[a]	Internet Hosts[b]	Internet Users[b]
	1996	1997	1998	1998	1998	1998	1998	1999	1999
Bosnia & Herzegovina	152	248	41	N/A	7	N/A	N/A	1.38	4
United States	215	2,146	847	244.3	256	78.4	458.6	1,508.77	74,100
Yugoslavia	107	297	259	N/A	23	1.9	18.8	7.65	80
Croatia	115	336	272	N/A	41	11.2	111.6	25.94	200

[a]Data are from International Telecommunication Union, *World Telecommunication Development Report 1999* and are per 1,000 people.
[b]Data are from the Internet Software Consortium (http://www.isc.org) and are per 10,000 people.

SOURCE: World Bank. *World Development Indicators 2000.*

damaged by the war. In 1991, Bosnia had 21,168 kilometers (13,154 miles) of highways, half of which were paved. The war destroyed 35 percent of these highways and 40 percent of their bridges. The railroads had 1,000 kilometers (600 miles) of track, three-quarters electrified, and damage to the system was estimated at US$1 billion. Sarajevo's international airport was destroyed in the fighting. From 1995 to 1998, more than US$1 billion in foreign aid was provided to rebuild the infrastructure, and much is being done to reconnect the telecommunications networks. A US$20 million loan from the European Bank for Reconstruction and Development should aid in this process; however, ethnic divisions have hampered reconstruction. Guiding and implementing projects through conflicting local interests, jurisdictions, price structures, and corruption schemes is complex and often time consuming.

Electricity is produced in coal burning (32 percent) and hydroelectric (68 percent) plants. Because of the war, electricity-generating capacity declined by four-fifths. Most hydroelectric plants are in the Croat-controlled area. Therefore, close cooperation across Muslim- and Serb-held territory is essential for power distribution. Electricity prices vary substantially, with the Serb Republic subsidizing them heavily within its area. Hydropower Tyrol (Austria) is investing US$6 million in the Federation's 4 hydroelectric facilities.

ECONOMIC SECTORS

The distribution of the **labor force** and the contribution of the economy's different sectors have been difficult to estimate because of the internal conflicts in Bosnia and Herzegovina. Labor force information is limited to that estimated in 1990, when 48 percent of the labor force was employed in industry and 11 percent in agriculture. By 1996, the GDP contribution was divided as follows: 19 percent in agriculture, 23 percent in industry and utilities, and 58 percent in services. The war caused the leading industries—particularly armaments—to suffer greatly, and the disruption of economic links between the units, sanctioned by the Dayton accord, further decreased the economy's viability.

AGRICULTURE

As a part of the former Yugoslavia's **socialist** regime, agriculture was in private hands. Unlike other Eastern European countries, farms were small and inefficient. The republic has been, and still is, a net importer of food, relying on foreign supply for more than half of its food. The mountainous and rugged terrain is much less suitable for agriculture than Croatia and Serbia. Still the agriculture sector has traditionally produced wheat, corn, fruits, vegetables, tobacco, and livestock. The war and ethnic cleansing obliterated many Bosnian farms and severely affected the production of tobacco, the principal **cash crop**.

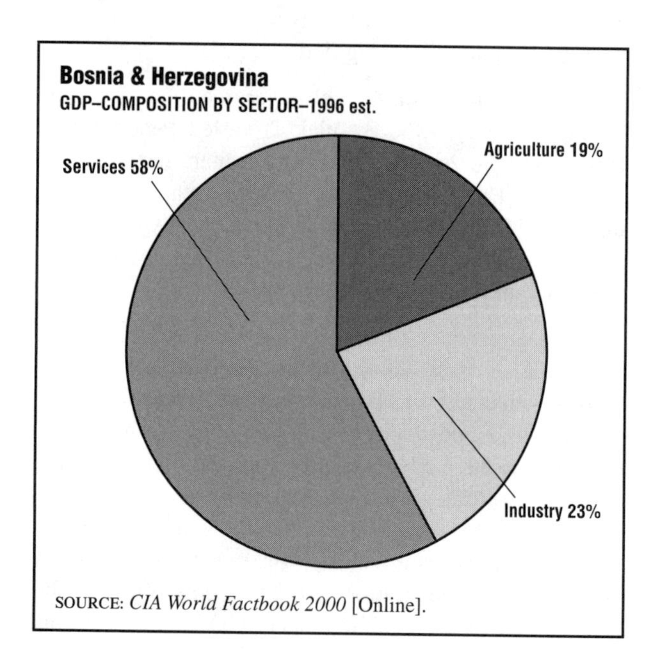

SOURCE: *CIA World Factbook 2000* [Online].

INDUSTRY

Under socialism, Bosnia specialized in mineral products; metals (steel, lead, zinc, aluminum); timber; manufactured goods (furniture, domestic appliances, and leather goods); and accounted for 40 percent of the former Yugoslavia's military production. Like Serbia and Montenegro, the industry wanted to counter unemployment and employed more workers than it really needed. Traditionally, the industrial bases were divided: heavy industry was in the Federation, and light industry was in the Serb Republic.

Most of the country's industry was damaged by the war, and in late 1995, manufacturing dropped to one-tenth of the pre-war level. Although destruction between regions varied, companies suffered because of disrupted supplier and buyer links. Given the low base, post-war industrial recovery was notable; however, it was limited to metal and wood processing, food, beverages, textiles, and clothing. Most factories are still operating at a fraction of their capacity.

In 1999, food processing accounted for 14 percent of the Federation's manufacturing production, metals for 13.4 percent, and wood processing for 5.4 percent. Recovery was much slower in engineering, chemicals, and pharmaceuticals. The Unis Vogosca company in the Federation and Germany's Volkswagen set up a **joint venture** to assemble Skoda cars, but had disappointing results. During this year, the Federation also established a consortium to manufacture tractors and other agricultural machinery. Construction grew, driven by housing reconstruction, and in 1999, Germany's Heidelberger Zement acquired a 51 percent stake in one of the cement plants, Kakanj. **Consumer goods** represent about 30 percent of total manufacturing output.

The government does not pursue a specific industrial policy. Trade is **liberalized**, there is no particular policy for protecting local companies, and domestic producers are exposed to foreign competition. Foreign investors are cautious in investing, donors favor the **private sector**, and large state-owned enterprises find it difficult to restart work because of lack of capital, technology, and extensive markets.

SERVICES

As in the former Yugoslavia, banks in the Federation and the Serb Republic are still too numerous, small, and undercapitalized. The political units have reached an agreement to allow Federation banks to operate in the Serb Republic as local ones. However, this arrangement may only add to the already over-banked sector. Although bank consolidation is needed for the gradual emergence of a sound banking system that will fuel investment and consumer spending and reinvigorate the economy, the government is more actively concerned with bank privatization.

Tourism has suffered from destruction and the general feeling of political instability. However, it has been recorded that domestic tourist visits have increased to the tiny Herzegovinian stretch of the Adriatic coast, and the number of lakeside resorts and foreign tourists has also increased. Before the war, Bosnia tourism was not as significant for the economy as in Croatia and Slovenia. However, it was given impetus as Sarajevo hosted the 1984 Winter Olympics and became internationally well known for its mountain resorts and colorful multicultural atmosphere. However, many tourist attractions were destroyed in the shelling of the city during the war.

Retail was well developed and to a large extent privatized before the war. It has since contracted because of the declining demand. The black market is still an important player in the economy. In contrast to Slovenia and Macedonia, foreign investment is limited.

INTERNATIONAL TRADE

In 1990, Bosnia imported US$1.9 billion worth of fuel, machinery, transportation equipment, manufactured products, chemicals, and food. It exported about US$2.1 billion worth of manufactured products, machinery, and raw materials. The war almost wiped out Bosnian foreign trade. As the economy was destroyed, Yugoslavia and Croatia imposed blockades and cut supply routes. In 1996, imports still totaled about US$1.9 billion, but exports were down to US$171 million. In 2000, exports grew to US$950 million, and imports remained much higher at US$2.45 billion.

From 1996 to 2000, the scope of the **trade deficit** amounted to well over US$1 billion yearly. This amount is huge for the size of the economy. Because of Bosnia's need to import vital commodities such as fuel, equipment, and food out of the limited international credit available, it is more heavily dependent on foreign aid from donor countries and international organizations than other former Yugoslav republics.

Metals and wood products were the most important components of Bosnia's exports in 2000, while electricity exports declined during and after the war. The EU accounted for 39 percent of the Federation exports in 2000 and leading trade partners included Croatia, Switzerland, Italy, and Germany (for the Federation), and Yugoslavia, Italy, Slovenia, and Hungary (for the Serb Republic).

MONEY

After the ethnic leaders failed to agree on a new currency, the UN introduced in 1998 a new currency, the

Exchange rates: Bosnia

marka per US$1	
Jan 2001	2.086
2000	2.124
1999	1.837
1998	1.760
1997	1.734
1996	0.015

SOURCE: CIA *World Factbook 2001* [ONLINE].

convertible mark. The convertible mark was fixed to the German mark. It gained acceptance, and the Central Bank of Bosnia and Herzegovina increased its reserves. Yugoslav dinars still circulate in the Serb Republic, and the Croatian kuna is used in the Croat areas of the Federation.

The government is still hoping to increase its capitalization by pressing for the privatization of the numerous small commercial banks. Raiffeisen Zentralbank Oesterreich, an Austrian bank, recently acquired many banks, including the Market Banka. The Austrian bank has also submitted privatization papers to the government bank privatization unit. It is not clear whether this will attract foreign attention, because the banking sector is weak and the economy is being reconstructed slowly.

POVERTY AND WEALTH

Before 1991, Bosnians, like most Yugoslavs, enjoyed a modestly prosperous life under the socialist governments, and Sarajevo citizens were proud hosts of the 1984 Winter Olympics. However, the war and the collapse of the economy ruined living standards. While average incomes sharply declined, prices of goods soared, particularly on the black market. Health, education, and welfare slipped into disaster. Physical survival was the only agenda for many Bosnians during the atrocities. While poverty grew, warlords, corrupt politicians, and officials made fortunes off looting and smuggling, and this caused an attitude of widespread resignation. After the war, the power of the party oligarchies remained almost unchallenged and was perpetuated by the country's highly complex ethnic-based political structure. Ethnic party elites still control much of the economy and oppose privatization in the most lucrative sectors such as energy.

GDP per Capita (US$)

Country	1996	1997	1998	1999	2000
Bosnia & Herzegovina	N/A	1,690	1,720	1,770	1,700
United States	28,600	30,200	31,500	33,900	36,200
Yugoslavia	N/A	2,280	2,300	1,800	2,300
Croatia	4,300	4,500	5,100	5,100	5,800

Note: Data are estimates.

SOURCE: *Handbook of the Nations*, 17th, 18th, 19th and 20th editions for 1996, 1997, 1998 and 1999 data; CIA *World Factbook 2001* [Online] for 2000 data.

WORKING CONDITIONS

In 1999, unemployment was estimated at 40 percent. Employees were irregularly paid their wages which provoked waves of strikes in both the Federation and the Serb Republic. When paid, the average monthly wage in the more affluent Federation was US$194 in mid-2000, up by 8.4 percent from 1999, and inflation remained low. Wages and prices varied significantly by region. In the Federation, an average net wage in March 2000 bought 52kg of butter; in January 1998, 37 kg. In the Serb Republic, the March 2000 average net wage bought 26.6 kg of butter, in December 1998, 14.5 kg.

The limited scope of recovery has resulted in modest job generation, with most growth occurring in the public administration. The World Bank (WB) announced a US$15 million program to re-deploy unemployed ex-soldiers and insists that current labor laws and regulations, a legacy from the old socialist system, are now inappropriate. The WB provides generous severance payments for employees and keeps unpaid workers on waiting lists rather than laying them off. However some believe this will burden the companies, blur unemployment numbers, and impair **labor mobility**.

COUNTRY HISTORY AND ECONOMIC DEVELOPMENT

6TH-7TH CENTURY A.D. Slavic tribes, including Serbs and Croats, settle in the present territory of Bosnia and Herzegovina.

958. The name Bosnia is used to denote the land. Most Slavic inhabitants belong to the Roman Catholic Church.

1180. Ban (a feudal title of nobility) Kulin creates an independent Bosnian state, and feudal agrarian economy develops.

1326. Ban Stephen Kotromanic unites Bosnia and Hum, which later becomes Herzegovina.

1463–83. Bosnia and Herzegovina are conquered by the Ottoman Empire, and large numbers of Christians are converted to Islam. Predominant Muslim feudal lords rule over a poor and Christian peasantry.

1878. After the European Congress at Berlin, the country is taken over by Austria-Hungary, but Muslims and Orthodox Christians resist occupation. The new regime promotes modern economic development.

1908. Austria-Hungary officially annexes Bosnia.

1914. Austria-Hungary starts World War I by declaring war on Serbia; most Bosnian Serbs, Croats, and Muslims remain loyal to Austria-Hungary.

1918. After World War I, Bosnia becomes part of the new Kingdom of Serbs, Croats, and Slovenes (renamed Yugoslavia in 1929); the economy suffers from the loss of Austro-Hungarian markets.

1941. Yugoslavia breaks up during World War II, and Nazi Germany makes Bosnia part of the Independent State of Croatia.

1945. Germany is defeated, and Bosnia joins socialist Yugoslavia as a constituent republic.

1945–80. Yugoslavia develops a socialist economy.

1980. Communist dictator Josip Broz Tito dies, and the socialist economy of Yugoslavia begins to decline. Serb nationalism begins to rise, and non-Serbs grow dissatisfied with the Federation.

1990. In a multiparty parliamentary election in Bosnia and Herzegovina, the Muslim Party of Democratic Action, led by Alija Izetbegovic, wins 34 percent of the seats; the Serbian Democratic Party, led by Radovan Karadzic, takes 30 percent; and the Croatian Democratic Union gets 18 percent. Izetbegovic becomes president of a 7-member tri-national presidency.

1991. Bosnia and Herzegovina declares independence from Yugoslavia, which is confirmed by a referendum in 1992. Bosnian Serbs, led by Karadzic and backed by neighboring Serbia and the pro-Serb Yugoslav army, start an armed offensive aimed at forming a greater Serbia and thus cause the bloody Bosnian civil war.

1994. Muslims and Croats create a Muslim-Croat Federation.

1995. In Dayton, Ohio, the warring parties sign a peace agreement, and Bosnia and Herzegovina is divided between the Federation of Bosnia and Herzegovina and a Serb Republic. A NATO-led peacekeeping force (IFOR) of 60,000 is deployed to implement the agreement, and an international high representative is appointed.

1996. A Stabilization Force (SFOR) of 19,000 (as of late 2000) troops—to prevent new inter-ethnic hostilities—succeeds IFOR.

FUTURE TRENDS

In Bosnia and Herzegovina, economic reform is at the core of the international community's strategy. Over the next few years, the government will accentuate tax reform, improve the tax administration system, aid financial sector reform and encourage privatization. Labor regulations and the pension system will also be thoroughly **restructured**. Foreign investment will be encouraged, but future support from international financial institutions will be dependent on the success of the reforms. In the long term, it is hoped that reconstruction, reform, and EU integration will bring more peace and prosperity to what is considered to be Europe's most troubled land after World War II.

DEPENDENCIES

Bosnia and Herzegovina has no territories or colonies.

BIBLIOGRAPHY

Donia, Robert J. *Bosnia and Hercegovina: A Tradition Betrayed.* New York: Columbia University Press, 1994.

Economist Intelligence Unit. *Bosnia and Herzegovina.* <http://www.eiu.com>. Accessed December 2000.

Economist Intelligence Unit. *Country Profile: Bosnia and Herzegovina.* London: Economist Intelligence Unit, 2000.

Malcolm, Noel. *Bosnia: A Short History.* New York: New York University Press, 1996.

U.S. Central Intelligence Agency. *World Factbook 2001.* <http://www.odci.gov/cia/publications/factbook/index.html>. Accessed October 2001.

U.S. Department of State. *FY 2000 Country Commercial Guide: Bosnia and Herzegovina.* <http://www.state.gov/www/about_state/business/com_guides/index.html>. Accessed December 2000.

—Valentin Hadjiyski

BULGARIA

Republic of Bulgaria
Republika Bulgaria

CAPITAL: Sofia.

MONETARY UNIT: Lev (plural Leva). One lev equals 100 stotinki. There are coins of 1, 2, 5, 10, 20 and 50 stotinki.

CHIEF EXPORTS: Machinery and equipment; metals, minerals, and fuels; chemicals and plastics; food, tobacco, and clothing.

CHIEF IMPORTS: Fuels, minerals, and raw materials; machinery and equipment; metals and ores; chemicals and plastics; food and textiles.

GROSS DOMESTIC PRODUCT: US$48 billion (purchasing power parity, 2000 est.).

BALANCE OF TRADE: **Exports:** US$4.8 billion (f.o.b., 2000 est.). **Imports:** US$5.9 billion (f.o.b., 2000 est.).

COUNTRY OVERVIEW

LOCATION AND SIZE. The Republic of Bulgaria shares its borders with 5 other countries in southeastern Europe and has a coastline on the Black Sea. Romania lies to the north, Turkey to the southeast, Greece to the south, the former Yugoslav Republic of Macedonia to the southwest, and Serbia (with Montenegro part of the Federal Republic of Yugoslavia) to the west. The eastern coastline on the Black Sea is 354 kilometers (220 miles) long, and the total area of the country is 110,910 square kilometers (42,823 square miles), making it slightly larger than the state of Tennessee. The capital, Sofia, is situated at the foot of the Balkan and Vitosha Mountains in western Bulgaria; other principal cities are Plovdiv in south-central Bulgaria, the coastal cities of Varna and Burgas, and Ruse on the Danube River.

POPULATION. The Bulgarian population recorded in the 1985 census was 8,948,649, but by July 2000, largely due to **emigration**, the population was estimated to have decreased to 7,796,694. In 2000, the birth rate stood at 8.06 and the death rate at 14.63 per 1,000 population, but this downward trend should be halted as the economy improves, emigrants return, and the country joins the European Union (EU) in 2007. By 2010, the population is projected to reach 7.26 million. Population density is about 70 persons per square kilometer (181 per square mile).

Ethnic Bulgarians account for 85 percent of the population, Turks 9 percent, and Roma (Gypsies) 3.7 percent. Other small, miscellaneous groups round out the total. Bulgarian, a Slavic language with a written tradition dating back to the 9th century, is the principal language, with other languages spoken corresponding to the ethnic breakdown. Religions include Orthodox Christian (83 percent), Muslim (13 percent), and Roman Catholic (1.5 percent), with Jewish, Protestant, and other groups making up the rest. The population of Bulgaria is aging, with 16 percent below the age of 14 and 16 percent older than 65. The median age is expected to increase from 37.5 years in 1995 to nearly 41 in 2005. A majority of the population, 69 percent, lives in urban areas, and Sofia and its suburbs are home to the largest number.

Prior to 1989, the government encouraged population growth by providing maternity benefits, free health care, affordable pre-school day care, and reasonably adequate pensions. Emigration was negligible due to government restrictions on travel. Since then, however, deteriorating living standards, the opening of the economy, and freedom to travel have generated emigration, mostly of young people, to Western Europe and North America, and of ethnic Turks to their neighboring homeland. Many of the latter, however, return or maintain households in both countries.

OVERVIEW OF ECONOMY

Until 1944, Bulgaria was a predominantly agricultural country. Under the **socialist** regime introduced after World War II, industry and **infrastructure** were **nationalized** and

operated in line with central government economic planning. Most farming was collectivized (organized into government-run units), and the development of heavy industry was made a priority. From the 1970s until 1989, Bulgaria enjoyed one of the most prosperous economies in Eastern Europe, with good health, education, and living standards. Considered by many to be the "Red Silicon Valley" (denoting its role as the **communist** equivalent of the U.S. technology breeding ground), it became the sixth nation to fly in space.

The socialist economy, however, was dependent on the imports of subsidized Soviet fuels (some **re-exported** to obtain **hard currency**) and the extensive but straightforward Soviet (and other socialist) markets for most exports of machinery, computers and peripherals, clothing, tobacco, beverages, and food. With the disintegration of the Soviet Union in 1989, the Yugoslav wars of the 1990s, economic **sanctions**, and the Persian Gulf crisis of 1990–91, Bulgaria lost many of its markets, its cheap energy sources, and hard currency revenues. As a result, living standards declined significantly in the 1990s. Bulgaria has become a poor European country and, like most its neighbors and near-neighbors, except Poland and Slovenia, it is a long way from improving on its 1989 real level of output. The Yugoslav wars interrupted both road and river (the Danube) trade routes to Western Europe and hurt the economy, but the Stability Pact, a regional initiative for economic development, democratization, and security devised in the late 1990s and backed by the United States and the EU, should facilitate future recovery.

Despite these many problems, Bulgaria earned a reputation for economic and political stability during the 1990s. The government followed a slow but sure path towards a market economy and expanded its commercial ties with Western Europe and the United States. The

European Union (EU) currently accounts for 52 percent of its exports and nearly half of its imports, and the United States is among the top foreign investors. Bulgaria aspires to join the North Atlantic Treaty Organization (NATO) in the first decade of the 21st century and is on course to join the EU.

In 1997, the government imposed tight **monetary policies** and strict financial discipline, stabilizing the banking system and cutting government spending. Triple-digit **inflation** gave way to moderate price increases, but growth and foreign investment have remained low. Ongoing market reforms include **privatization** or liquidation of state-owned enterprises and **liberalization** of agriculture and the creation of a land market. Privatization is seen as the only efficient way to **restructure** the economy, create jobs, and introduce new technology. It is also crucial for attracting foreign investment, stopping the slide in output, increasing exports, and generating cash for current needs. But the government has been criticized for relying heavily on controversial management-employee buyouts for smaller enterprises. New social policy measures include reforming social insurance and addressing the issues of crime and corruption.

The **external debt**—estimated at over $10.4 billion in 2000 and accumulated as a result of foreign **trade deficits** throughout the 1980s—is considered high but not unduly so. Although the **balance of payments** situation had stabilized by 2000, the debt has caused a negative long-term impact on economic growth and living standards. Another problem arises from the depreciation of the euro (the common currency of the EU), since most revenue is measured in euros while the debt is calculated mostly in dollars. There are attempts to encourage debt-for-**equity** swaps (transforming bank debt into **foreign direct investment**) which, along with the expected growth over the next few years, might alleviate the debt burden.

POLITICS, GOVERNMENT, AND TAXATION

In 1990, communist rule in Bulgaria gave way to a multiparty parliamentary democracy, with executive power vested in the Council of Ministers. Although political life has been active, Bulgaria has sound policies regarding minorities and is regarded as an oasis of stability in the tinderbox of the Balkans. In the 1997 parliamentary elections, the United Democratic Forces, an alliance of the reformist Union of Democratic Forces (SDS) and the People's Union, won 137 of 240 National Assembly seats. The Bulgarian Socialist Party (BSP), reformed communists, was reduced to 58 seats, which reflected the BSP responsibility for the 1996–97 financial meltdown, from which the SDS was perceived as a deliverer. The remaining seats were shared between the Movement for Rights and Freedoms (MRF); a centrist, predominantly ethnic Turkish party; the Euroleft; and the Business Block. The Bulgarian Agrarian People's Union and the Democratic Party form the People's Union coalition. The local elections in 1999 gave the BSP control over most local governments and signaled decreasing SDS popularity due to persistent economic hardship and corruption charges. All major parties currently support market reforms and membership in the EU and NATO. During the 1999 Kosovo crisis, the government cooperated fully with NATO.

The government aims to privatize all state-owned firms except for utilities, strategic railroads, natural gas, postal services, education and sciences, environmental protection, geology, and cartography. The law requires that the state retain at least a 51 percent interest in merchant shipping and passenger fleets, major ports and airports, transport, and highway construction companies. By June 1999, about 40 percent of state enterprises had been privatized, while the **public sector** accounted for 36 percent of the GDP. The **private sector** contributed 25–30 percent of the GDP in 1995; 35–40 percent in 1996; approximately 65 percent in 1997 and 1998, and 64 percent in 1999, and is expected to increase further.

Privatization processes were particularly dynamic in 1999 and 2000, with priority given to tourism, food processing, agriculture, heavy industry, engineering, textiles, and construction materials. The privatization program is being carried out through capital market offerings, mass privatization, and cash deals. The offerings on the capital market (through corporate stocks and bonds sales) are insignificant, and the local stock exchange is still in its infancy. In the mass privatization program, all citizens and company employees were made eligible to receive free vouchers for company (or privatization fund) shares. More significant for foreign investors is cash privatization, which allows investors to buy smaller enterprises from central government ministries, larger ones from the privatization agency, or municipal assets from local government. The privatization agency hires foreign consultancy firms to assess the value of important enterprises and to advise on marketing, but the process has often been described as slow and challenging. Potential investors have been frustrated by the difficulties of investing, and others are unhappy with inflexible procedures. Complex criteria for determining which buyers are eligible to invest has caused concern about corruption.

Taxes are a major source of government revenue. Personal **income tax** rates are progressive, from 20 percent to 40 percent. The profit tax rate is 20 percent for large firms and 15 percent for small firms. **Value-added tax** (VAT) is levied at a rate of 20 percent. All firms pay 10 percent on profits in municipal tax. Investors in high unemployment areas get a 10 percent reduction on government profit tax. The tax system is still perceived by many as unfriendly to business, and tax cuts are being debated within the government.

INFRASTRUCTURE, POWER, AND COMMUNICATIONS

Bulgaria's transportation infrastructure includes railroads, with 3,979 kilometers (2,472 miles) of track in use, and about 36,724 kilometers (22,819 miles) of paved roads, although some of these are unsatisfactory. There are only about 250 kilometers (160 miles) of 4-lane highway. Back in the 1980s, Somat, the state trucking company, was among the largest in Europe. However, political troubles involving Serbia made the road route to Western Europe across Serbian territory problematic. The result was greater traffic via Romania across the only existing bridge with a ferry crossing on the Danube. Bulgaria recognized the need for a second bridge, but mixed signals from Romania have held up the project. However, the reopening of traffic through Yugoslavia following the ousting of Yugoslav leader Slobodan Milosevic in 2000 may rule out bridge construction.

Bulgaria has many highway projects under construction, notably portions of the Trans-European motorway connecting Budapest, Hungary, with Athens, Greece, via Sofia, and with Istanbul, Turkey, via eastern Bulgaria. International investors and the state budget are the main sources for financing road network improvements. Completion and modernization of portions of the Trakia, Cherno More, and Hemus expressways are being given out to contractors, and there are plans for a north-south tunnel under Mount Shipka.

The Danube River is an important artery, and much of the freight traffic uses the Black Sea. There is a sizeable merchant marine fleet operated by the Navibulgar shipping company. Two major seaports and east-west transport corridor gateways, in Varna and Burgas, are planned for rehabilitation. Balkan, the national airline, serves major cities and international destinations, although it has suffered after its recent sale to the Israeli Zeevi group in a questionable privatization deal. Smaller airlines also operate, and 3 major international airports, in Sofia, Varna, and Burgas, are currently undergoing modernization. There are 129 airports with paved runways.

Bulgaria's energy sector is state-owned and derives most of its output from thermal plants burning fossil fuels, mostly coal and natural gas (52 percent), nuclear plants (41 percent), and hydroelectric facilities (7 percent). Newer units of the Kozloduy nuclear plant will be upgraded under a contract between the National Electric Company and the U.S. company, Westinghouse. Bulgaria exports energy, primarily to Turkey and Yugoslavia. The country produced 38.423 billion kilowatt hours (kWh) of energy in 1998, a slight decrease from the previous year, and electricity consumption stood at 35.493 billion kWh. Studies to determine the feasibility of oil pipelines carrying oil from the Caspian Sea through Bulgaria to the Greek Aegean Sea coast or the Albanian Adriatic Sea coast could bring future opportunities for expansion. There are extensive networks of pipelines carrying natural gas throughout the country.

Bulgaria has the highest penetration of telephone service in Eastern Europe, at 38.47 percent. The network is operated by the state-owned Bulgarian Telecommunications Company (BTC). In 1998, it replaced antiquated facilities with up-to-date equipment and connected major cities with digital exchanges, satellite ground stations, fiber-optic lines, and digital microwave networks in a $300 million project funded by international investors. Residential telephone development will reach EU standards by 2008. There is analog cellular telephone network operated by the Mobifon company, created as a **joint venture** between Cable & Wireless (49 percent), BTC (39 percent), and the Bulgarian company Radio Electronic Systems (12 percent). The Bulgarian company, Mobiltel, operates a digital cellular telephone net-

Communications

Country	Newspapers	Radios	TV Sets[a]	Cable subscribers[a]	Mobile Phones[a]	Fax Machines[a]	Personal Computers[a]	Internet Hosts[b]	Internet Users[b]
	1996	1997	1998	1998	1998	1998	1998	1999	1999
Bulgaria	257	543	398	28.8	15	N/A	N/A	11.89	235
United States	215	2,146	847	244.3	256	78.4	458.6	1,508.77	74,100
Russia	105	418	420	78.5	5	0.4	40.6	13.06	2,700
Romania	300	319	233	119.2	29	N/A	10.2	9.01	600

[a]Data are from International Telecommunication Union, *World Telecommunication Development Report 1999* and are per 1,000 people.
[b]Data are from the Internet Software Consortium (http://www.isc.org) and are per 10,000 people.

SOURCE: World Bank. *World Development Indicators 2000.*

work, and the country has many small, unregulated, Internet service providers. Privatization of 51 percent of the BTC, worth more than $500 million, will be the largest privatization deal in Bulgaria, and was being prepared in 2001, while the Greek telecommunications company, OTE, was granted a license for a second national digital cellular phone network.

ECONOMIC SECTORS

Since the late 1980s, manufacturing, mining, transport, construction, and agriculture have been declining in Bulgaria, while the service sector has been growing, particularly in **retail** business and finance. Energy, communications, and tourism have also become high-profile if turbulent industries. The *World Factbook* estimated that by 2000 agriculture accounted for 15 percent of **gross domestic product** (GDP), industry 29 percent, and services 56 percent. Estimates for the division of the **labor force** were from 1998, when 26 percent of the labor force was employed by the agriculture sector, 31 percent by the industry sector, and 43 percent by the services sector.

Much of Bulgaria's earlier economic strength lay in heavy industry powered, until the early 1990s, by subsidized energy from the Soviet Union. With the collapse of centrally planned Eastern European economies, manufacturing suffered a downturn. Major state-owned chemical, oil-refining, and metallurgical plants were targeted for privatization and examined to determine whether they could compete effectively in international markets. The largest privatization deal in heavy industry was the sale of the Sodi Devnia chemical plant to the Belgian company, Solvey, in 1999 for $160 million. Many other major assets, including oil refineries and chemical, metallurgical, and cement plants were privatized, while some were reduced to a shambles.

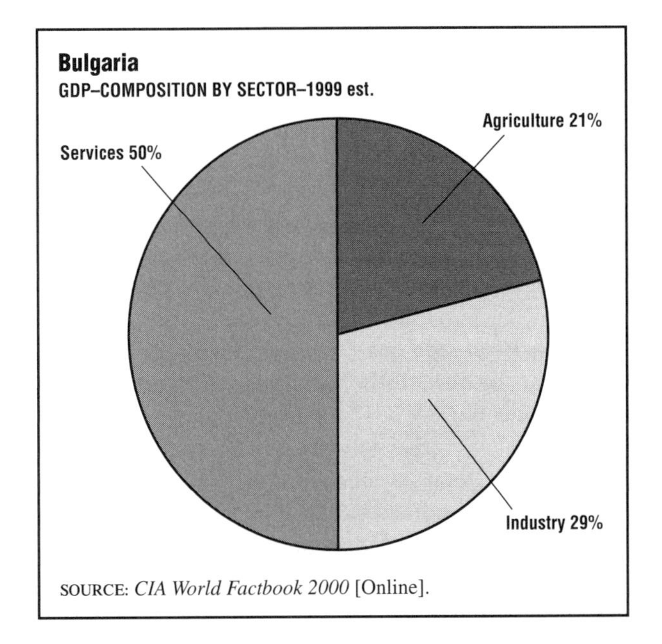

SOURCE: *CIA World Factbook 2000* [Online].

Food processing, textiles and apparel, and other **consumer goods** manufacturers have performed comparatively better, often attracting investment from renowned companies such as Kraft Jacobs Suchard or Danone. Future growth looks probable in light industry, led by electronics, textiles, and food processing. A small percentage of new private companies are involved in manufacturing. Private sector growth is greatest in the construction and food industries, maintenance and repair of electronic tools and equipment, household appliances, and automobiles.

AGRICULTURE

Bulgaria is renowned for sheep's milk cheese, oriental tobacco, wine, rose attar (used in perfumery), vegetables, fruit, medicinal herbs, and, particularly, natural yogurt. The temperate climate, abundant arable land, and soil conditions support the farming of both livestock and crops (grains, oil seeds, sugar beets, vegetables, grapes, fruit), but the country was affected by drought in the late 1990s and into 2000. Tobacco is among the most important of Bulgaria's crops, contributing nearly 20 percent to the value of agricultural goods. The principal timber areas are in the Rila, Rhodope, and Balkan Mountains. The fishing industry, which in the 1980s operated a large ocean fleet, is currently depressed. All told, the agricultural sector was estimated to account for 21 percent of the GDP in 1999 and to employ 26 percent of the workforce. Although estimations for the labor force were not available, the percentage of the GDP the sector contributed dropped slightly by 2000 to 15 percent.

Although historically a surplus food producer, Bulgarian agriculture was facing a downturn at the turn of the century. Cropland, livestock population, and yields were declining (limited use of fertilizers, however, has led to cleaner rivers and sea water). Animal feed is imported and its shortage has led to distress slaughtering, the killing of livestock in the face of a shortage of feed. The price of agricultural goods is not rising in line with inflation. Imported subsidized vegetables, fruit, dairy products, and meat from the EU adversely affect local producers. Restitution of collective farmland to private owners has been complicated and considerable collective farm assets were lost in the process. New private holdings are too small and can only be serviced with technical equipment or irrigated if their owners band together, but such efforts are proving slow to develop.

Price liberalization should encourage more output, especially as income gradually rises. Agriculture has the potential to make Bulgaria again basically self-sufficient in grains, and prospects are excellent for further increases in hard currency earnings from wine and dairy products, particularly cheese.

INDUSTRY

Before 1989, heavy industry dominated the Bulgarian economy. Metallurgy was largely dependent on iron ore imports, while locally mined copper, zinc, and lead ores were smelted in Bulgaria. The chemical industry produced fuels, plastics, rubbers, soda ash, and fertilizers. Engineering was well developed, especially in the production of electrical equipment, electric and motor trucks, heavy machinery, machine tools, electronics, and shipbuilding. Since the transition to a market economy, with a few exceptions that have attracted major foreign investment or serve sizeable international demand, the remaining heavy industry companies have struggled under management-employee privatization schemes. By 1999 industry contributed 29 percent to the GDP and employed 31 percent of the workforce. More recent labor force estimations were not available, but the percentage of GDP the sector contributed by 2000 remained the same.

Computer and software industries grew spectacularly in the 1980s, but, since then, many hi-tech players have been severely hit. DZU, a modern data storage equipment manufacturer in 1989, later leased out its production facilities to dubious firms that made Bulgaria the world's second largest producer of pirated compact discs (CDs). A government crackdown then all but ruined DZU, whose chances of survival currently lie with Hungary's Videoton, which acquired it for a nominal price. At best, it will function as a cheap assembly plant, but other companies will not even be this lucky. Bulgaria lost more than 50,000 computer programmers and engineers to developed countries over the 1990s, and this drain on a skilled workforce showed no sign of slowing down.

Textiles, the oldest industry in Bulgaria, together with apparel, leather goods, and footwear manufacturers, use largely domestic raw materials. The manufacture of building materials—cement, bricks, and glass—is well established. Pharmaceuticals and beauty products, food processing, including wine and other beverages, and tobacco processing, were once major revenue sources and show prospects for future growth.

Industries whose market prospects show promise in the 21st century include the manufacture of electrical equipment; telecommunications equipment and services; computers, software, and information technology; medical equipment; automotive parts and service equipment; agricultural equipment; building materials; chemicals; and, to some extent, metallurgy. All these enterprises, however, require massive restructuring and investment for their revitalization.

SERVICES

The service sector, generating approximately half of Bulgaria's GDP in 1999 and employing 43 percent of the workforce, continues to experience the highest growth of any sector. Most private sector activity involves some form of trade or retail, and financial services such as insurance and lending, health-care services, and tourism are well regarded by private companies.

FINANCIAL SERVICES. With the breakup of the rigid socialist banking system, the 1990s witnessed expansion of the banking and financial services sector. In 1996, however, many state-owned and some private banks collapsed under the burden of bad debts accumulated by state factories that had become obsolete and by the now infamous "credit millionaires." In 1997, the government focused on achieving stabilization and financial discipline, forcing the banks to avoid new lending and to maintain very high **liquidity** rates (a measure of how much cash is kept on hand). Bulgaria's low inflation is accompanied by low interest rates, but the level of lending is a third of that in most central European countries and is a major barrier to investment. The economy is heavily reliant on cash payments, which is detrimental to efficiency and conducive to corruption and tax evasion. Savings have been declining since 1999 due to generally low income levels.

The government is privatizing remaining state banks, and there were plans to sell in 2001 the largest, Bulbank, to a consortium made up of UniCredito (Italy) and Allianz (Germany), and the Bulgarian State Savings Bank. The large Post Bank was sold in 1998 to a consortium of Greek banks and AIG (U.S.), which also bought a stake in the United Bulgarian Bank in 1999. Most hard-won loans are now going to private companies. Consumer credit is developing, although slowly, with banks actively encouraging car and home loans to the tune of $400 million. Credit card companies have also started operations in this formerly virgin market.

TOURISM. Tourism plays a significant but not crucial role in the economy. While its competitors, Spain, Greece, and Turkey, have the advantage of aggressive and expensive marketing campaigns and decades of exposure to the market, Bulgaria has been unable to capitalize on its popular image as a land with a rich folklore tradition. The country offers extensive beach resorts along the Black Sea coast, several alpine skiing resorts in the Vitosha, Rila, Pirin, and Rhodope Mountains, and natural mineral water health spas. Nevertheless, the number of Western tourists fell by a third between 1994 and 1996, and the total revenue from the tourist industry in 1996 was $669 million. Attracted by low prices, cultural similarities, the lack of visa formalities, and a Russian-friendly population, former Soviet nationals spent 130 percent more overnight stays in Bulgaria in 1996 than in

1985, and 63 percent more than in 1993. Former East Germans are also frequent visitors. In 1996, overnight stays by Russians and Germans were around 2 million each, but the number of British and Scandinavian visitors is low. Poles, Czechs, Slovaks and Hungarians, among the top tourists to Bulgaria in the 1980s, now prefer other destinations. Foreign-acquired tourist hotels on the coast are mainly Russian-owned, while others have been leased to tour operators such as Germany's Neckermann who carry out renovation. However, it is 5-star business hotels that most attract foreign investors.

RETAIL. Growing quickly during the 1990s, the retail sector was energized by the privatization of state and municipality-owned stores, the emergence of many small private firms, and the import of cheap foreign consumer goods. Major foreign retailers, such as the German Metro, the Turkish Koc Holding, and others from Austria and France, began developing a network of large hypermarkets. The choice of goods has widened impressively, but low-income Bulgarians are generally reluctant or unable to pay more for better-looking products, often leaving consumers reliant on traditional domestic suppliers. The lower price of subsidized agricultural goods from the EU make them popular with buyers but detrimental to local producers. Direct and network marketing, which became popular in Eastern Europe after Oriflame (Sweden) made a success of it, is taking root, but only gradually, due to low levels of **disposable income**.

INTERNATIONAL TRADE

As a consequence of the **foreign debt** incurred in the late 1980s, Bulgaria suffered from declining markets and negative trade balances during the early 1990s. Although dependent on imports as heavily as ever, Bulgaria showed improvement after 1994 as the lev weakened, making exports more affordable in foreign markets; trade with former Soviet republics was revived, and trade with the EU increased. However, after 1997, the Yugoslav **embargo**, together with the government's restrictive policies aimed at financial stabilization, brought a downturn in the balance of trade. In 1998, exports of goods stood at $4.293 billion and imports at $4.609 billion, generating a current account deficit of $316 million. This trade deficit mushroomed to $1.5 billion in 1999, when Bulgaria imported $5.3 billion in goods while exporting just $3.8 billion.

Trade (expressed in billions of US$): Bulgaria

	Exports	Imports
1975	N/A	5.949
1980	N/A	N/A
1985	13.339	13.657
1990	4.822	4.710
1995	5.354	5.657
1998	4.300	4.979

SOURCE: International Monetary Fund. *International Financial Statistics Yearbook 1999.*

An accumulating trade deficit would badly affect Bulgaria's ability to meet its financial obligations in the future, but June 2000 was the tenth month in succession to see an increase in exports. Exports for that month reached $393.6 million, an increase of 21.8 percent over 1999, attributed to the recovery of EU economies in general and the rise in the international price of Bulgarian exports. Exports to the United Kingdom (UK) rose by 40 percent, due to the strong pound against the weak euro, which is linked to the lev. Export to other Organization for Economic Cooperation and Development (OECD) countries rose by almost 45 percent, with most going to Turkey. Exports to Balkan countries, mainly Serbia and Macedonia, boomed after the Kosovo war in 1999, but those to other member countries of the Central European Free Trade Agreement (CEFTA) rose by less than 6 percent and those to the former Soviet Union fell by 17 percent, with exports to Russia falling by one-third.

Imports increased by 23 percent over the previous year, to $511.2 million in June 2000. Over 50 percent of the rise was due to higher oil prices. Imports of industrial raw materials rose by more than 8 percent and imports associated with the recovering metallurgical sector grew, while those required by the food sector fell. Investment also rose in 2000, but the greatest growth, 56 percent, was in energy, mainly imported from Russia. The EU is now the main supplier of consumer and investment goods to Bulgaria. Imports from Balkan countries expanded impressively a year after the Kosovo war.

A fairly active trade-show calendar attracts firms from many countries. Major export commodities included textiles, clothing and footwear; base metals and metal products; minerals and fuels; food, beverages, and tobacco; machinery and equipment; chemicals and plastics; furniture and household appliances. Italy accounted for 14 percent of exports in 1998. Germany (10 percent), Greece (9 percent), Turkey (8 percent), and Russia (5 percent) were other major partners. Together, EU countries accounted for 52 percent of exports.

Major import commodities included fuels, minerals, and raw materials; metals and ores; textiles and apparel; machinery and equipment; automobiles; chemicals and plastics; and food. Major import partners were Russia, accounting for more than 20 percent of all imports in 1998, Germany (15 percent), Italy (9 percent), Greece (6 percent), France (5 percent), and the United States (4 percent). Together, EU countries accounted for more than 48 percent of imports.

MONEY

The Bulgarian National Bank (BNB) is the **bank of issue**. It controls government funds and state-owned enterprises. All banks were nationalized in 1947, but since 1990, private banks have been established and international banks allowed to enter the market. The banking sector has been consolidated, and complete privatization of the remaining state-owned commercial banks was expected by 2001.

The Bulgarian currency plunged dramatically in late 1996 and early 1997, reaching a low of approximately 3,000 leva per US$1. Many banks that had extended loans to failing concerns, both state-owned and private, were forced into insolvency. By early 1997, most banking institutions were bankrupt or had closed doors to depositors. The new government that took office in May of 1997 committed itself to stringent financial and structural policies for dealing with this drastic situation and received the encouragement of backing from international financial institutions.

Since July 1997, as required by the International Monetary Fund (IMF), the Bulgarian government has been operating under the control of a **currency board**. This body rules that the BNB must hold hard currency reserves in leva to cover circulation and banking reserves. Further, the currency board dictates that the BNB cannot refinance commercial banks except in an emergency and restricts the government's freedom to take on new financial liabilities or provide sovereign guarantees. The lev was tied to the German mark and later to the euro at a fixed rate, and in 1999 the currency was redenominated (new bills and coins were issued and the **exchange rate** was fixed at 1 lev to 1 German mark).

Under IMF conditions for strict financial discipline, the government was pledged to close loss-making enterprises and speed privatization, bank reform, and restructuring. It issued an isolation list of loss-making state enterprises, that is, companies denied access to commercial credit unless they privatize. These accounted for half of the public sector, but by 1999 the government succeeded in privatizing, or beginning liquidation of, all such companies. In the early 1990s, there were 30–40 virtually unregulated stock markets in Bulgaria, most of whose listed firms turned out to be dealing in **pyramid schemes**. A national stock exchange opened in October 1997, but daily **turnover** has seldom been more than $200,000, and rarely exceeded $1 million, even in 1998.

Exchange rates: Bulgaria

leva (Lv) per US$1	
Jan 2001	2.0848
2000	2.1233
1999	1.8364
1998	1,760.36
1997	1,681.88
1996	177.89

Note: On July 5, 1999, the lev was redenominated; the post-July 5, 1999 lev is equal to 1,000 of the pre-July 5, 1999 lev.

SOURCE: CIA *World Factbook 2001* [ONLINE].

POVERTY AND WEALTH

Before 1989, Bulgaria was arguably a land of economic equality. Almost no private initiative was allowed, but the vast majority of the population was employed by the state, and large government funds were allocated to free health care, free higher education, maternity and disability benefits, and pensions. Most Bulgarians owned their houses, and many had small country "villas" and motor cars. Traditionally, even the poorest Bulgarians, the ethnic Roma, held jobs, received social security payments, and enjoyed a decent standard of living, particularly in rural areas. The only exceptions to this modest yet guaranteed standard of living were the **nomenklatura** and the **informal economy** players, whose privileges inflamed discontent among the population.

The market reforms of the 1990s created both new poverty and new wealth. Unemployment, hitherto almost unknown, skyrocketed, inflation all but wiped out most social benefits, and the cooperative farms that were the livelihood of many formerly landless villagers were disbanded. Many entrepreneurs, corrupt politicians and officials, and mobsters amassed spectacular fortunes, which most people resented. Restitution of urban real estate, and particularly of farmland and woodland, was controversial and failed to generate much wealth. Mass privatization also failed in this respect.

For all its problems, Bulgaria was in 1995 still more egalitarian than neighboring Greece or the wealthy United States. The poorest 20 percent were responsible for 8.5 percent of the nation's consumption (compared to 7.5 percent in Greece and 5.2 percent in the United

GDP per Capita (US$)

Country	1975	1980	1985	1990	1998
Bulgaria	N/A	1,329	1,553	1,716	1,372
United States	19,364	21,529	23,200	25,363	29,683
Russia	2,555	3,654	3,463	3,668	2,138
Romania	1,201	1,643	1,872	1,576	1,310

SOURCE: United Nations. *Human Development Report 2000; Trends in human development and per capita income.*

Distribution of Income or Consumption by Percentage Share: Bulgaria

Lowest 10%	3.4
Lowest 20%	8.5
Second 20%	13.8
Third 20%	17.9
Fourth 20%	22.7
Highest 20%	37.0
Highest 10%	22.5

Survey year: 1995

Note: This information refers to expenditure shares by percentiles of the population and is ranked by per capita expenditure.

SOURCE: *2000 World Development Indicators* [CD-ROM].

States), while the wealthiest 20 percent consumed 37 percent (40.3 percent in Greece, 46.4 percent in the United States). Bulgaria's **Gini index**—which rates a country's level of equality with 1 representing perfect equality and 100 representing perfect inequality—was 28.3 in 1995, while Greece's was 32.7, and the United States' was 40.8. Polarization increased between 1995 and 2000, but it is believed that economic growth over the next decade and the accession to the EU will gradually increase living standards for all Bulgarians.

By 2001 most of the population was enduring hardship. The growth of wages and pensions lagged behind the index of consumer prices and unemployment is officially estimated at 15 percent, although it is believed to be much higher. The prospects for many small businesses seem bleak, due to the unavailability of loans, weak demand, crime, and corruption. Agriculture is struggling to provide a sustainable livelihood for small farmers. While many professionals and business owners make a good living, thousands of Bulgarians can afford only the bare necessities. Numerous chronically ill people suffer from an inadequate supply of life-supporting medicines, and many children, particularly those of Roma families, are unable to attend school because of the growing cost of textbooks and clothing. Many people who live in small towns and villages with high unemployment rates, as well as single parents, **pensioners**, persons in state social homes, disabled people, and others face considerable personal distress.

According to the United Nations Development Programme (UNDP), Bulgaria is currently behind Hungary and Poland, but ahead of neighboring Turkey and Romania, in terms of its human development index. In 1998, Bulgaria still had a smaller population per physician and per hospital bed than the EU average, but health-care spending per head was much lower. Food constituted 33.1 percent of household spending (but was believed to be rising), while the EU average was 14.1 percent. Cars in use per 1,000 population were 219.9 for Bulgaria and 399.7 for the EU. Houses with piped water constituted 83.4 percent of households in Bulgaria and 99 percent in the EU, and houses with flush toilets were 57.7 percent in Bulgaria against 96.3 percent in the EU.

WORKING CONDITIONS

Bulgaria is a party to all relevant major universal as well as regional legal instruments, such as the International Covenant on Economic, Social and Cultural Rights, the Convention on the Elimination of Discrimination Against Women, and the Convention on the Rights of the Child. It is also a signatory to treaties on the right to equal compensation and collective bargaining and against employment discrimination. Market reforms, though, made Bulgarians aware of unemployment and job insecurity problems. Before 1989, the economy was plagued by the sustained labor deficit for blue-collar workers, but labor disputes were virtually non-existent since the Communist Party supervised trade unions. Nevertheless, over the decades after World War II, working conditions improved in both urban and rural areas with the introduction of new technology and progressive legislation and the development of health-care and social-security systems. At the same time, safety at work and environmental protection, particularly in the mining, energy, and chemical industries, were often inadequate.

Household Consumption in PPP Terms

Country	All food	Clothing and footwear	Fuel and power[a]	Health care[b]	Education[b]	Transport & Communications	Other
Bulgaria	30	6	17	8	11	5	23
United States	13	9	9	4	6	8	51
Russia	28	11	16	7	15	8	16
Romania	36	7	9	3	20	9	16

Data represent percentage of consumption in PPP terms.

[a]Excludes energy used for transport.

[b]Includes government and private expenditures.

SOURCE: World Bank. *World Development Indicators 2000.*

Bulgaria did not develop independent labor unions as such before democratic reforms took root. The only exception was the Podkrepa Labor Confederacy, now one of the major national unions. Along with the Confederacy of Independent Syndicates of Bulgaria and other groups, the Podkrepa participates in collective bargaining, and the unions' role is growing as many Bulgarians face unemployment and deteriorating working conditions. Conditions are notably bad in clothing sweatshops set up by foreign investors in rural areas severely afflicted by unemployment. Women have traditionally participated on an equal footing in the economy but are now suffering heavily from unemployment, job-related stress, and unsafe labor conditions. Over the 1990s, hundreds of thousands of educated young Bulgarians left the country, and it is expected that the forthcoming waiver of visa requirements for most EU countries will encourage others to seek short-term employment. EU membership is likely to intensify the mobility of workers between countries until a balance is reached.

COUNTRY HISTORY AND ECONOMIC DEVELOPMENT

550 A.D. Slavs settle into present-day Bulgarian (then Byzantine) lands, comprising the ancient Roman provinces of Moesia, Thrace, and Macedonia.

681. Khan Asparuh founds the first Bulgarian state as a union between Slavs and newcomer Bulgars, militant people from the steppes of the northern Caucasus. They are to be assimilated by the Slavs but leave their name and statehood tradition to the nation.

863. Bulgaria converts to Christianity under Prince Boris I and embraces Byzantine civilization as a feudal agrarian economy takes root.

893. The Cyrillic alphabet and Old Bulgarian (Slavonic) are adopted as the official language (instead of Greek).

893–927. The territory expands under Prince (later Tsar) Simeon. A rich medieval culture spreads its influence to other Slavs in Serbia, Walachia, Kievan Rus, and later Muscovy.

927. Bulgarian rulers recognize the title of tsar (emperor); Bulgarian Orthodox Church is elevated to patriarchy.

1018. The First Bulgarian Empire is violently subdued by Byzantium.

1185. The brothers, Asen and Peter, take over an uprising to liberate the Bulgarian lands and restore the state known as the Second Bulgarian Empire.

1230. There is territorial and commercial expansion under Tsar Ivan Asen II. Bulgaria becomes a major grain supplier to Byzantium, actively trading with Venice, Genoa, and Ragusa (Dubrovnik).

1371. Commercial and cultural development accompanies political crisis under Tsar Ivan Alexander. Bulgaria is divided into several lesser kingdoms and principalities.

1396. Bulgaria is violently conquered by the rising Ottoman Empire and remains under its rule for nearly 500 years.

1762–1876. A national revival develops new Bulgarian culture and pride. Agriculture and home industries thrive, benefitting from large Ottoman markets. Merchants and industrialists emerge and benefit the economy. The national liberation movement gains momentum.

1871. An independent Bulgarian church is restored.

1876. There are mass uprisings against Ottoman rule.

1878. Bulgaria is liberated from Ottoman rule as an outcome of the 1877–78 Russo-Turkish war.

1879. The first Bulgarian constitution establishes a democracy, modeled after the Belgian constitution.

1885. North and South Bulgaria unite after being separated since 1878 by the European powers. A sizable ethnic Bulgarian population remains under the Ottoman Empire.

1887–12. Democratic statehood develops as well as a market economy that remains largely agrarian and a national culture.

1903. There are mass uprisings of Bulgarians in the Ottoman lands (Macedonia and Adrianople area).

1912–18. Bulgaria participates in the Balkan Wars and World War I, which is aimed at liberating ethnic Bulgarians outside Bulgaria's borders. The war ends in defeat and brings an influx of refugees.

1923–41. Political life is troubled by violence as democracy gives way to bitter partisanship and is finally supplanted by a pro-Nazi Germany regime. The economy grows with the influence of German investors.

1944–56. Communist rule takes over. Central economic planning is introduced, focusing on heavy industries, and farms are collectivized. Economic cooperation with the Socialist bloc develops.

1946. Bulgaria is proclaimed a people's republic.

1955. Bulgaria joins the United Nations.

1956–80. Bulgaria exhausts the extensive socialist growth model and reaches stagnation.

1985–89. Economic and political crisis occurs as *perestroika* unfolds in the Soviet Union. The Bulgarian regime desperately seeks methods of market reform, while cracking down on dissenters and the Turkish minority.

1989. Communist leader Todor Zhivkov resigns as the transition to multiparty democracy and a market economy begins. Bulgaria shifts its loyalties to the EU and NATO.

1991. A new democratic constitution of the Republic of Bulgaria is adopted, and elections bring the reformist Union of Democratic Forces (UDF) to power.

1995. Bulgaria is admitted as an associate member of the EU and applies for full membership.

1997. IMF-sponsored program for financial stabilization is implemented by the second UDF government.

1998. Effective IMF membership is established.

1999. Negotiations for full membership of the EU get underway.

FUTURE TRENDS

Bulgaria's economic policy after 2000 will be determined by the success of its preparations for EU membership. The EU opinion on its progress is favorable, but negotiations will become more difficult as they move from administrative to economic issues, such as the restructuring of the energy sector and agriculture. Bulgaria's market economy and its competitiveness within the single European market still require significant further improvement. Public expenditure will focus on investment in roads, natural gas, electricity, agriculture, and the environment. The government claims investment of some $9 billion is enough to fuel growth over the next years, but, all too optimistically, it relies on the private sector to provide most of the funds.

With Bulgarian privatization completed by the end of 2001, the IMF envisages strong annual growth of 4 percent to 5 percent over the next several years and single-digit inflation. However, slow and allegedly corrupt privatization processes are a potential obstacle to economic transformation, and corruption charges combined with insufficient growth, unemployment, poverty, and deteriorating health care and education, could bring about a change of government in 2001. This outcome would not mean any long-term changes in policy.

The end of Slobodan Milosevic's government in Serbia could prove beneficial by decreasing the risk of war on Bulgaria's borders. The reopening of land routes and river traffic on the Danube will facilitate trade with the EU, Bulgaria's largest export market, whose growth will have a positive impact on the economy.

DEPENDENCIES

Bulgaria has no territories or colonies.

BIBLIOGRAPHY

Crampton, R. J. *A Concise History of Bulgaria.* Cambridge and New York: Cambridge University Press, 1997.

Economist Intelligence Unit. *Country Report: Bulgaria.* London: 2000.

U.S. Central Intelligence Agency. *World Factbook 2001.* <http://www.odci.gov/cia/publications/factbook/index.html>. Accessed October 2001.

U.S. Department of State. *FY 2000 Country Commercial Guide: Bulgaria.* <http://www.state.gov/www/about_state/business/com_guides/2000/europe/index.html>. Accessed December 2000.

—Valentin Hadjiyski

CROATIA

Republic of Croatia
Republika Hrvatska

CAPITAL: Zagreb.

MONETARY UNIT: Croatian Kuna (HrK). One kuna equals 100 lipas. There are coins of 1, 5, 10, 20, and 50 lipas and 1, 2 and 5 kuna. There are notes of 5, 10, 20, 50, 100, 200, 500, 1000, and 2000 kunas.

CHIEF EXPORTS: Textiles, chemicals, foodstuffs, fuels.

CHIEF IMPORTS: Machinery, transport and electrical equipment, chemicals, fuels and lubricants, foodstuffs.

GROSS DOMESTIC PRODUCT: US$24.9 billion (purchasing power parity, 2000 est.).

BALANCE OF TRADE: **Exports:** US$4.3 billion (f.o.b., 1999). **Imports:** US$7.8 billion (c.i.f., 1999).

COUNTRY OVERVIEW

LOCATION AND SIZE. The Republic of Croatia is located in southeastern Europe, with a long coastline on the Adriatic Sea to the south, and borders with Slovenia and Hungary to the north, and Yugoslavia and Bosnia and Herzegovina to the east. It has an area of 56,538 square kilometers (21,829 square miles), approximately the size of West Virginia. The country's coastline stretches for 5,790 kilometers (3,598 miles), and consists of 1,778 kilometers (1,104 miles) of mainland coastline and 4,012 kilometers (2,493 miles) of island coastline. The capital, Zagreb, is located in the northwestern corner of the country. Other major cities include Osijek, Pula, Rijeka, Zadar, Split, and Dubrovnik.

POPULATION. Croatia's population has been gradually decreasing since its 1990 figure of 4,508,347 and, according to *CIA World Factbook* statistics, in July 2000 the figure stood at 4,282,216. However, the year 2000 saw a slight increase, with the birth rate, at 12.82 per 1,000, higher than the death rate (11.51 per 1,000). If this trend continues, a projected population growth rate of only 0.93 percent will not dramatically change the size of Croatia's population in the foreseeable future. By the year 2010 it is estimated to reach 4,697,548.

With 76.5 percent of its inhabitants Roman Catholics, Croatia is predominantly a Roman Catholic country. Although the majority of the population is Croatian, other ethnic groups include Serbs, Bosnian Muslims, Hungarians, Slovenians, and Czechs. Approximately 18 percent of the population is under 15, about 67 percent is aged between 15 and 64, and the remaining 18 percent is over the age of 65. According to 1997 figures, the majority of people (56.5 percent) reside in urban areas, showing a significant increase from the 1975 figure of 45.1 percent. By the year 2015, urban dwellers are expected to number 64.4 percent of the population. Although population density is only 83.5 people per square kilometer (216 per square mile), the population is not evenly dispersed. Almost a quarter of Croatians reside in the capital city of Zagreb and its suburbs, while many of the country's islands and rural areas are very sparsely populated by mostly elderly inhabitants.

Like several other European countries, Croatia is experiencing the problem of very slow population growth. The government recognizes the problem but has done very little to address it.

OVERVIEW OF ECONOMY

Prior to World War II, peasants comprised more than half of Croatia's population and the country's economy was based largely on agriculture and livestock. Croatia's northern region is rich in agricultural soil and has been exploited for those purposes since ancient times. The coastal regions are not as lush but have a perfect combination of climate and soil for growing grapes, olives, and citrus fruit. Industrialization took place after

World War II when Croatia became a part of the Socialist Federal Republic of Yugoslavia. During this time, the economy diversified, industry and trade grew rapidly, and tourism developed swiftly. Since Croatia and Slovenia were the most developed of the Yugoslavian republics, profits from their industries were used to develop poorer regions of the federation. This factor, together with hyper-**inflation** in the 1980s and austerity programs imposed by the federal government, led to both Croatia and Slovenia opting for independence from the Yugoslav federation at the beginning of the 1990s. Croatia's bid for independence was met with military force by the Yugoslavian government, unleashing a war that lasted from 1991 to 1995.

Prior to 1991, Croatia was part of a **socialist**-dominated country. Since then, it has been going through a transition from state-controlled economy to **free-market system**, but the conflict with Yugoslavia had a devastating effect on its economic **infrastructure**. During the war, parts of the country were destroyed or damaged. Many people became refugees, forced to rely on assistance from the state, while a large portion of the state budget was used for defense. The cost of material damage caused by the war was estimated at US$27 billion, more than the country's 2000 **gross domestic product** (GDP) of US$24.9 billion. The war also brought a substantial reduction in trade between Croatia and the former Yugoslav republics, and caused difficulties in competing in European markets. Croatian tourism, a very important contributor to the country's GDP, suffered disastrously, as did trade and industry.

At the end of the war, Croatia began a slow process of economic rehabilitation. The structure of the Croatian economy is currently similar to that of a developed western economy, with services accounting for 71 percent of the GDP, industry for approximately 19 percent, and agriculture for 10 percent.

The country's major economic sectors are tourism and trade. Croatia has a beautiful coastline and many national parks, which attracted hundreds of thousands of annual visitors before the war. After the war ended in 1995, tourism revenues steadily increased, approaching the pre-war levels. In terms of trade, Croatia's major export industries include chemical products, textiles, shipbuilding, food processing, and pharmaceuticals. Agricultural production does not satisfy domestic needs, and food products comprise a significant part of the country's imports. Other imports include machinery and transport equipment, chemical products, and fuel.

The total **foreign debt** of Croatia stood at US$8.3 billion in 1998. Although the debt has been growing since 1991, the rate of increase has been much slower than the increase in government revenues. In 1991 the debt accounted for 12.3 percent of the government revenue, but by 1996 this figure had fallen to 8.4 percent. More than half the debt was to private creditors such as large banks and businesses, while the balance was in outstanding loans from the International Monetary Fund (IMF), the World Bank, and the European Bank for Reconstruction and Development.

European Union countries have contributed nearly US$1 billion to reconstruction efforts in Croatia since 1991. Some of the aid went to assist over 600,000 displaced people and 250,000 Bosnian refugees. The country received co-finance for most major projects from 3 sources: the World Bank, the European Bank for Reconstruction and Development, and Hermes Kreditversicherungs, known as Hermes. Hermes is a consortium of a private insurance company and a quasi-public company which provides credit insurance on behalf of the German government. Projects financed by these sources have included post-war reconstruction of infrastructure, support for the health sector, and improvements in the financial, enterprise, and agricultural sectors.

Foreign direct investment (FDI) has played a significant role in Croatia's banking sector and its pharmaceutical industry. According to CEEBICnet Market Research, current FDI in Croatia exceeds US$3.6 billion, most of it invested in mixed ownership enterprises, those owned jointly by foreign and local entities. Major investors have come from Germany, Austria, Italy, the United States, and the Netherlands.

Although the **private sector** has grown since Croatian independence, the country still has a fairly undeveloped enterprise sector consisting of small and medium-size operations. Between 1996 and 1999 employment in these businesses remained static due to a poor business environment, high taxation, and difficulties in obtaining appropriate financing for expansion.

POLITICS, GOVERNMENT, AND TAXATION

Croatia is a parliamentary democracy consisting of executive, legislative, and judicial branches. The executive branch consists of the president and the Council of Ministers. The president, who is the head of state and commander-in-chief of the armed forces, is elected by popular vote to a 5-year term of office and may serve a maximum of 2 terms. The president appoints the prime minister and the cabinet, as well as the Council of Ministers, whose members are proposed by the prime minister. The Croatian legislature is the parliament (Sabor), which consists of a Chamber of Deputies and a Chamber of Counties (Zupanije), all of whose members are elected to a 4-year terms. The first chamber has between 100 and 160 deputies and the second 68 members.

The judicial branch of the government consists of the Constitutional and Supreme courts. The Constitutional Court makes decisions on the constitutionality of laws and has the power to repeal a law and to impeach the president. It consists of 11 judges elected for 8-year terms by the Chamber of Deputies at the proposal of the Chamber of Counties. The Supreme Court holds open hearings and makes its judgements publicly. Its judges are appointed for life.

During its first 8 years of independence Croatia was ruled by the Croatian Democratic Party (HDZ) and its president, Dr. Franjo Tudjman, who remained head of state until his death in 1999. During this time the government was preoccupied with the war and was slow to **privatize** state-owned enterprises and attract foreign investment. The ruling HDZ party has occasionally, for political purposes, supported trade legislation that has benefited certain industries and economic sectors. After the elections in 2000, a coalition of 2 parties, the Social Democratic Party (SDP) and the Croatian Social Liberal Party (HSLS), came to power. The new government—led by President Stjepan Mesic and Prime Minister Ivica Racan—is dedicated to economic and social reform but, by the end of 2001, had not been in power long enough to show significant results.

As a former socialist country, Croatia is battling against the legacy of strong state control over the economy. This control had some positive results, such as a significant post-war reconstruction effort launched by the government which, due to the lack of domestic capital, relied mainly on foreign borrowing. On the down side, however, it was very difficult for the private sector to expand or compete in a state-dominated economy; the government frequently exploited important positions in industry for political gain, which prohibited the private sector from entering the field.

Croatia generates government revenue through a wide range of taxation measures and is one of the most highly taxed countries in Central Europe. Heavy taxation has slowed the growth of the private sector and contributed to the rise of an **informal economy** whose interactions are not subject to taxation. Personal **income tax** paid on individual earnings ranges from 20 to 35 percent and **value-added tax** (VAT), paid on domestic sales and on most imports, is fixed at 22 percent. An import **duty**, levied on goods and services, is paid by the importer, while there are further taxes payable on property transactions, inheritance and gifts, tobacco and alcohol, and motor vehicles.

In 1993 the government launched a relatively successful economic program to stabilize prices and the **exchange rate**, which slowed inflation to approximately 3 percent by 1995. Since then, inflation has increased slowly by approximately 0.5 percent to 1 percent per year. At the same time, the government's continuing high rate of taxes and military expenditure to finance the war hindered the recovery process. During the first few years of the economic stabilization program, the currency remained stable, partly due to improvement in the economic climate, but largely because the central bank artificially maintained this stability.

The government established a Privatization Fund (CPF) to oversee transfer of state-owned enterprises to private hands. The privatization process used several methods, including the sale of company shares to employees at a discount, a system whereby vouchers are distributed for use in place of cash to bid for shares in companies undergoing privatization and to award compensation for property that had been taken away by the **communist** regime. These measures, however, were not very successful. They proved easy to abuse and led to many cases of corruption. Privatization of utilities and the country's main oil producer has been slow, as these are considered strategically valuable enterprises by many in the ruling party.

Croatia's ratio of **pensioners** (retired workers collecting government benefits) to workers is very high and puts a heavy burden on the economy. To ease this burden, the government, with help from the World Bank, introduced pension reforms. A 3-band pension system was approved but, by 2001, had not yet been implemented. This system will keep part of the monthly retirement contribution in government funds, while a portion will go into a privately managed fund.

The new government elected in 2000 managed to make a significant impact on speeding up privatization of the banking and telecommunications sectors, and in late November 2000, Croatia became the 139th member of the World Trade Organization.

INFRASTRUCTURE, POWER, AND COMMUNICATIONS

Judged by Eastern European standards Croatia has a comparatively developed infrastructure. In 1998, the country had 23,497 kilometers (14,601 miles) of paved highways, but only 330 kilometers (205 miles) of these were 4-lane expressways. Since the country suffered significant war damage between 1991 and 1995, it received loans from the World Bank and the European Bank for Reconstruction and Development to improve roads, railroads, the electricity and water supply network, and air-traffic control. The government is strongly committed to these efforts, and many of these projects, including the building of 1,600 kilometers (994 miles) of 4-lane highway, are under way.

There are 8 main airports in Croatia (Zagreb, Split, Zadar, Dubrovnik, Osijek, Pula, Rijeka, and Brac) ser-

Communications

Country	Newspapers	Radios	TV Sets[a]	Cable subscribers[a]	Mobile Phones[a]	Fax Machines[a]	Personal Computers[a]	Internet Hosts[b]	Internet Users[b]
	1996	1997	1998	1998	1998	1998	1998	1999	1999
Croatia	115	336	272	N/A	41	11.2	111.6	25.94	200
United States	215	2,146	847	244.3	256	78.4	458.6	1,508.77	74,100
Yugoslavia	107	297	259	N/A	23	1.9	18.8	7.65	80
Slovenia	199	406	356	150.5	84	9.8	250.9	99.34	250

[a]Data are from International Telecommunication Union, *World Telecommunication Development Report 1999* and are per 1,000 people.
[b]Data are from the Internet Software Consortium (http://www.isc.org) and are per 10,000 people.

SOURCE: World Bank. *World Development Indicators 2000.*

viced by major airline companies. Croatian seaports include Rijeka, Pula, Sibenik, Split, Ploce, and Dubrovnik, all of which are located on the Adriatic Sea. Transportation between these seaports and many islands is currently provided by only one company, Jadrolinija. The railway network extends for 2,699 kilometers (1,677 miles) but does not meet the country's needs. Plans to improve the railway system do exist, but carrying them out is not considered a priority.

Tourism is one of Croatia's main sources of revenue. Transportation facilities for tourists (a developed network of roads, railroads, and airports) plays an important role in making the tourist industry efficient. Since the majority of tourists arrive in Croatia by road, construction of highways has the highest priority. In addition, the country's odd "boomerang" shape requires excellent roads in order to link its northern, central and southern areas. If all these requirements are to be met, the country must provide a more modern and extensive highway and railroad system.

Croatia's demand for electricity is mostly satisfied by domestic production, while 10 to 20 percent is covered by imports. The country produces most of its electricity from fossil fuel and hydroelectric plants. A small portion comes from the nuclear plant Krsko, which Croatia shares with neighboring Slovenia.

Telecommunications services in Croatia are modern, although they lag behind those of Western Europe and the United States. Telephone service is provided by Croatian Telecom (HT), which has invested heavily in improving telecommunications. According to the *CIA World Factbook* there were 1.488 million telephone lines in use in 1997 and, although some domestic lines are still analog, they are being replaced by digital technology with a capacity of 2,200,000 telephone lines. The international telephone service is completely digital, and its main switch is located in Zagreb. A project is under way to install fiber-optic cables throughout the country and connect them with Slovenia. Currently there are 220,000 kilometers of fiber-optic cables connecting 4 main Croatian cities and 35 countries.

There are approximately 200,000 Internet users in the country, and, according to CEEBInet Market Research, Croatia had 5 Internet service providers in 2000. The 2000 World Development Indicators state that, in 1995, there were 272 television sets per 1000 people and 36 television broadcast stations.

ECONOMIC SECTORS

Being a small country, Croatia contributes relatively little to worldwide production in each of its 3 sectors. The country's economy is based on services, dominated by tourism and manufacturing, with international trade also an important contributor to the economy. The 5 years of war were mostly responsible for the country's poor economic performance, and post-war recovery has proceeded slowly. Other factors that limit economic growth are an inadequate legal structure and bureaucratic red tape, both of which restrict business activity; a slow privatization process; a poorly developed banking sector; and insufficient highway infrastructure. Some of these problems, such as privatization and highway construction, are being addressed, but it will take time for projects to be completed and for their effects to be felt.

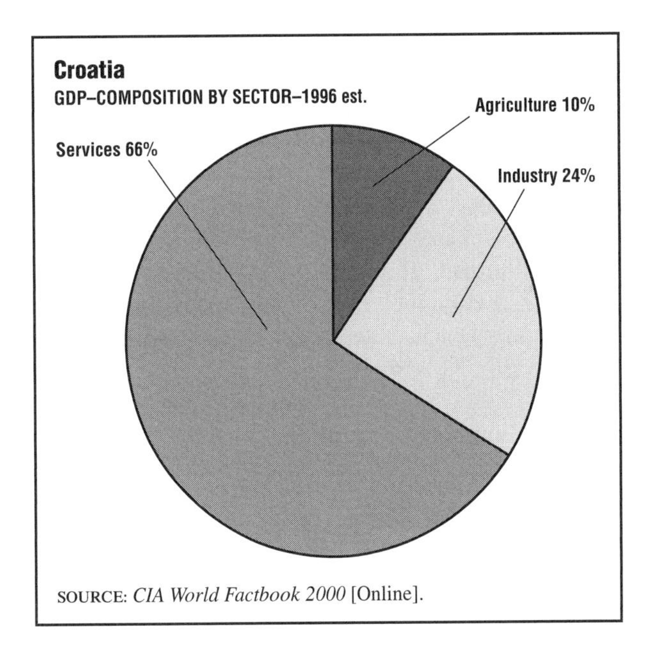

SOURCE: *CIA World Factbook 2000* [Online].

Prior to the 1990s Croatia, and especially its beautiful Dalmatian coast, was a popular vacation spot for many Europeans, but with the eruption of war in 1991, tourism was decimated. Since the end of the conflict in 1995 the sector has seen a slow but steady recovery. Tourism was an important element in the services sector and contributed 71 percent to the GDP in 1999.

Agricultural production has been in decline since 1992, averaging about 60 percent of pre-war levels. Again, the war contributed heavily to the disruption of agriculture, but 1998 brought severe heat and drought, which caused disease and further hindered crop growth. By 1999 agriculture contributed just 10 percent to the GDP.

Industrial production declined sharply during the war years. Some of the worst fighting and destruction took place in areas where industry was located. During the war, this sector produced only a half of what it had in peacetime. Since 1996, industrial production has been experiencing growth, but certain industries tend to do better than others. The most successful are those, such as the food and beverage industry and manufacturing of chemicals and chemical products, that underwent **restructuring** as a result of privatization. One of the most important companies headquartered in Croatia is the Croatian pharmaceutical giant, Pliva, whose shares are traded on the Zagreb and London stock exchanges. Major foreign companies who have a significant presence in the country are Swedish Ericsson (telecommunications), Austrian Hofmann & Pankl Bet (mineral processing), Swiss Soc. Suisse de Cim. Port. (cement production), Dutch Grassette Nederland (maritime services), Austrian Messer Griesheim (industrial gasses) and the U.S. Coca-Cola Export Corp. (beverages). All told, industry contributed 19 percent of the GDP in 1999.

AGRICULTURE

Agriculture, fishing, and forestry accounted for about 10 percent of the total GDP of Croatia in 1999, but they are nevertheless important to the overall economy. According to the Croatian Bureau of Statistics, these sectors combined to employ over 33,000 people and produce earnings of approximately US$1.4 billion per year. Croatia is fortunate not to have experienced the environmental damage from mass industrial development that characterizes its Eastern European counterparts. Environmental concerns do exist, but they do not have a heavy impact on agriculture, forestry, and fishing.

Croatia's geographical diversity led to different patterns of livelihood and culture. As a result, agriculture varies throughout the country's regions, influenced by regional climate. Agriculturally rich lowlands located in Croatia's northern part are dominated by the cultivation of wheat, corn and sunflower crops, while viticulture (the cultivation of grapes), fruit-growing, and olive-farming are popular in the coastal region, with pasture land common in the mountainous areas. Most agricultural land is privately owned, and the large cooperatives created during the communist era are being privatized and restructured. Croatian agricultural production is dominated by small farms. The *EIU Country Profile* for 2000 states that in 1991 almost 70 percent of farms were 3 hectares or less, with only 5.6 percent larger than 8 hectares.

The war had a devastating effect on Croatian agriculture, changing the country from an exporter of agricultural products to a net importer. After the war, government efforts to boost agricultural production created positive results, increasing production of wheat, improving agricultural machinery, and increasing the number of cattle. In 1999, combined earnings from agriculture, hunting, and forestry equaled US$1.39 billion. Aside from wheat, fruits, olives, and grapes, the agricultural sector also produces corn, sugar beets, seed, alfalfa, clover, livestock. and dairy products.

FORESTRY. The exploitation and management of forests in Croatia is carried out by a public company. Since one-third of the country is covered by forests, this industry is very important for the economy. In 1996 Croatia received a loan from the World Bank for replanting and protecting forests along the coast in order to stimulate tourism.

FISHING. Both war and over-fishing of the waters has had a negative impact on fishing, which is a traditional Croatian industry. The catch decreased from 40,000 metric tons in 1989 to just over 15,000 metric tons in 1995, and the sector's earnings decreased from US$32 million in 1996 to US$22 million in 1999. Current employment in the fishing industry stands at only 1,100.

INDUSTRY

MANUFACTURING. In the early 1990s total industrial output declined, partly due to the war but also because of the collapse in trade among Eastern European countries. During this time, Croatia lost a large share of its Yugoslav markets when the Yugoslav federation fell apart. After the war, industrial output began to recover, but major restructuring of industry and more investment is still necessary in order to increase efficiency. Due to a high unemployment rate of over 20 percent, the government is reluctant to worsen the situation by laying off industry workers.

Key industries in Croatia include textiles, chemicals, pharmaceuticals, and petrochemicals. The textile industry is especially well-developed and includes over 400 enterprises, the majority of which are engaged in cooperative activities with foreign manufacturers. In 1998, all of the key industries combined employed over 400,000 people and earned more than US$3 billion from exports. In the same year, the total export revenue across all sectors was approximately US$4.5 billion.

Two important heavy industries are ship building and metal products. Both were subsidized by the government during the war because of their strategic importance, but it remains unclear as to whether this **subsidy** continues. Growth of the construction sector has seen substantial expansion with the need for mass building and reconstruction caused by the war, and the government has been leading the building program and looking for international aid. The value of construction projects rose from almost US$1 billion in 1995 to over US$1.4 billion in 1997. During the same period, the number of employees in the sector rose from 23,600 to 29,500. This sector has drawn interest from international investors, such as the United Kingdom's RMC International Cement, which bought a majority stake in Croatia's largest cement producer, Dalmacijacement.

ELECTRICITY. Production in this sector has been increasing but is not able to keep up with the country's increasing demand. Currently, between 10 and 20 percent of the demand is satisfied by imports, but plans by the Croatian Electricity Board (HEP) are under way to build additional plants and renovate existing ones. The electricity sector, together with oil, gas, and water supply, employs almost 26,000 people, accounting for 2 percent of the total **workforce**.

OIL AND GAS. This sector has experienced substantial difficulties, both because of the war and the slowness in privatizing Croatia's only energy company, INA. By 1995 the production of oil and natural gas fell to 73 percent of pre-war levels. In 1999, Croatia extracted over 1.2 million metric tons of oil and over 1.5 million cubic meters of natural gas, representing a decrease in production over previous years. The country's oil and gas reserves are located southeast of Zagreb, along the border with Hungary and along the Adriatic coast. As of December 1998, Croatia's oil and natural gas reserves were estimated at 15 million metric tons and 35 million cubic meters respectively. The country's demand for extra gas supply is satisfied by imports from Russia, but projects have begun with foreign investors to develop new gas fields. These are expected to produce enough to export gas to other countries in Eastern Europe.

SERVICES

TOURISM. Tourism is of major importance in a services sector that accounts for over 70 percent of the GDP. Croatia is not only rich in natural beauty and history but enjoys a very low crime rate and a reputation as a safe destination. These factors have made it a favorite vacation spot for many Europeans and Americans, but tourism was heavily affected by the war, and the revenue it currently generates has not yet regained pre-war levels. A year after the war started, this sector earned only half a billion U.S. dollars. As the stability returned to the region, earnings from tourism gradually increased, reaching US$3.5 billion in 2000. During the 1990s, the country not only suffered from war devastation, but little was done to develop and restructure the tourism sector. This work started in 2000 when privatization of hotels and businesses was speeded up and tourism expenditure increased.

The improvement in political stability towards the end of the 1990s brought an increase in the number of tourists visiting the country. In 1998, the Croatian Bureau of Statistics recorded over 31 million overnight stays, which was 3 times as much as the 1992 figure. This number, however, still does not compare to the pre-war years, such as 1989 when more than 61 million overnight stays were registered.

Currently, Croatia has a total capacity of 725,000 beds, almost 95 percent of which are located in the coastal region. It also has 43 marinas, 17 of which are open year-round, but many of these are in dire need of reconstruction and better management.

TRANSPORT. Croatia is situated along major routes linking South Central Europe with the world, and its transport services are of major importance to the country's well-being. During the war, one-third of the country was occupied by enemy forces, causing disruption to main traffic links between different areas and a substantial increase in transportation costs. Since the war, greater regional stability has improved the situation, and the construction of a highway that will connect the country's southern region with its northern areas and the rest of Europe will greatly contribute to expansion and further improvement of service. According to the Croatian Bureau of Statistics, transport, storage, and communication employed over 83,000 people in 1999 and earned more than US$1.6 billion in the same year.

INTERNATIONAL TRADE

International trade is a significant part of the country's economy, accounting for between 6 percent and 8 percent of the GDP in the last decade. In 1999, imports totaled US$7.8 billion, against exports of US$4.3 billion. The country experienced a sharp fall in trade during the war when commerce with the country's main trading partners, namely the republics of former Yugoslavia, substantially decreased. Since then, the country reoriented the trade sector towards Western and East Central Europe. As a result, in 1999 only a quarter of Croatia's exports went to the former Yugoslav republics and only 10 percent of imports came from these countries. Due to this new trend and extensive subcontracting in the textile and leather industries, Croatia's main trading partners currently are Germany, Italy, and Slovenia. Other trading partners include Bosnia and Herzegovina, Austria, France, and Russia. Even though trade has experienced growth, revenues from Croatian exports account for less than 2 percent of total European exports and import revenues for less than 3 percent of Europe's total. At the end of the war, the trade imbalance increased as the country's

Trade (expressed in millions of US$): Croatia

	Exports	Imports
1994	4260	5229
1995	4632	7509
1996	4511	7787
1997	4170	9104
1998	4541	8383
1999	4279	7777

SOURCE: United Nations. *Monthly Bulletin of Statistics* (September 2000).

imports substantially outstripped its exports. High labor and production costs, as well as high taxes, which make Croatian products more expensive than imports, have contributed to this trend.

The largest percentage of Croatia's exports went to the following countries in 1999: Italy (18 percent), Germany (15.7), Bosnia and Herzegovina (12.8 percent), Slovenia (10.6 percent), and Austria (6.2 percent). Some of these countries are also major sources of Croatia's imports, with Germany accounting for 18.5 percent, Italy 15.9 percent, Russia 8.6 percent, Slovenia 7.9 percent, and Austria 7.1 percent. Croatia's exports include chemical products, clothing, footwear, raw materials (wood, textiles, fertilizers), fuels (petroleum and gas), food products, beverages, and tobacco. Imports include machinery, transport, and electrical equipment, chemicals, fuels and lubricants, food products, clothing, and footwear.

MONEY

The Croatian currency, established in 1991, has experienced a slight depreciation (decline in value) since it was launched. The National Bank of Croatia uses the euro as a reference currency; therefore, the recent depreciation of the euro against the U.S. dollar had the same effect on the exchange rate between the kuna and the U.S. dollar. In 1995, US$1 equaled 5.230 kuna, while at the end of 2000, the exchange rate jumped to 8.320 kuna to US$1. According to the Quarterly Economic Report of Germany's Commerzbank, this situation is likely to change by 2002 when US$1 will equal 7.88 kuna.

There are many reasons for the depreciation of the kuna, among them deficits in the pension system, the slow rate of privatization, and compensations paid to depositors of bankrupted banks. The ratio of pensioners to the employed increased from 0.65 in 1998 to 0.95 in 2000. This statistic means that for almost every retired person there is only 1 person employed in Croatia. One external factor that influenced a drop in the kuna exchange rate was the recent increase in energy prices.

Croatian **monetary policy** and supervision of the commercial banking sector is managed by the National Bank of Croatia (the central bank). Although there are over 50 banks operating in Croatia, more than 70 percent of the overall assets of the banking system belong to the 6 largest. Most of these, and some of the medium-sized banking institutions, are indirectly owned by the government, which holds large proportions of shares in these operations through government-controlled companies. There are several representative offices of foreign banks operating in Croatia.

A large portion (approximately 75 percent) of the total assets of the Croatian banking system are immobilized, which is to say they are not generating returns. Such assets consist of state bonds, public debt, ownership in companies that yield no dividends, and investments that are unlikely to produce returns. This is the main reason for high real interest rates for long term loans, which are 25 to 30 percent per year. The government is committed to restructuring the most problematic banks and has received a pledge of US$100 million from the World Bank to assist in solving this problem.

The Zagreb Stock Exchange is the only stock exchange operating in Croatia. It originated in 1918 but was abolished by the communist regime in 1945. Almost half a century later, after Croatia became independent in 1991, the stock exchange was revived by 25 banks and insurance companies as a non-governmental, non-profit-making institution. The ZST is fairly small, and there are only a few privatized firms that trade on it.

POVERTY AND WEALTH

Until 1991 Croatia was part of a socialist-governed country whose system and ideology did not allow great disparity between rich and poor. Those who benefited most from the system and were better off than the majority, were the senior functionaries of the ruling Communist Party. They lived in pleasant, state-owned apartments, drove good cars, and earned relatively high salaries. The poor generally lived in underdeveloped rural areas of the country, were badly educated, and were not politically active.

Exchange rates: Croatia

Croatian kuna per US$1	
Jan 2001	8.089
2000	8.277
1999	7.112
1998	6.362
1997	6.101
1996	5.434

SOURCE: CIA *World Factbook 2001* [ONLINE].

GDP per Capita (US$)

Country	1975	1980	1985	1990	1998
Croatia	N/A	N/A	N/A	5,432	4,846
United States	19,364	21,529	23,200	25,363	29,683
Romania	1,201	1,643	1,872	1,576	1,310
Slovenia	N/A	N/A	N/A	9,659	10,637

SOURCE: United Nations. *Human Development Report 2000; Trends in human development and per capita income.*

Distribution of Income or Consumption by Percentage Share: Croatia

Lowest 10%	4.0
Lowest 20%	9.3
Second 20%	13.8
Third 20%	17.8
Fourth 20%	22.9
Highest 20%	36.2
Highest 10%	21.6

Survey year: 1998

Note: This information refers to expenditure shares by percentiles of the population and is ranked by per capita expenditure.

SOURCE: *2000 World Development Indicators* [CD-ROM].

Since Croatian independence in 1991 and a move to the free-market system, social conditions have changed, to the benefit of some and the disadvantage of others. Inadequate progress towards privatization and the appointment of political favorites to influential positions brought corresponding wealth to the few, although the free-market system has also rewarded a number of skilled or enterprising Croatians. Those groups dependent on the government for their survival suffered as a result of the changing economic system and suffered further from the social and economic impact of the war. These disadvantaged groups include pensioners and the privileged prewar middle class who later found themselves impoverished by changes in the country.

The poor of Croatia tend to be concentrated among the uneducated and the elderly. The **United Nations Development Program**'s 1999 Human Development Report states that in 1997 the average pension was less than half of the average salary. Pension payments are often months late, and the elderly have to rely on other means for survival, such as help from relatives. Retired people represent one-fifth of the total population, and as the ratio of pensioners to workers increases, the pension system is becoming overburdened.

The Croatian education system is almost entirely state-run and is very good. Close to 100 percent of children are enrolled in primary schools, and almost 70 percent attend secondary school. As a result, literacy rates are high (99 percent for men and 96 percent for women) and similar to those of other Eastern European countries and the industrial countries. The children of both the poor and the rich attend the same elementary schools, but although the vast majority of the poor are literate as a result of primary school education, they tend to drop out of the education system early. If they do pursue secondary education, they usually attend vocational high schools and few go to college. University education is not very expensive, but the number of scholarships and stipends that would help the poor are limited, and their numbers lag behind those of other East Central European countries. Insufficient education prevents the poor from competing for jobs that would earn them a better living, thus locking them into poverty.

The state maintains the country's health care system, although a small private sector does exist. A shortage of resources for the health sector has caused problems in recent years (only 6.7 percent of GDP goes towards health expenses), including a failure in targeting the needs of the poor, but most of the population does have basic health coverage. Since the price of food and clothes is high relative to average salaries, poor people spend most or all of their income on basic necessities. They tend to have weak and monotonous diets and although the majority have housing, they often find it difficult to pay for utilities or maintenance of their homes. Those households whose monetary income falls below 350 kunas per month (approximately US$55) qualify for the social assistance program. This monetary allowance equals 15 percent of average salary and, at this level, covers only a quarter of the expenses of poor households.

Even though Croatia has experienced significant social changes in recent years, differences between the rich and poor are not as vast as in Western economies. They are, however, greater than in other Eastern European countries.

Household Consumption in PPP Terms

Country	All food	Clothing and footwear	Fuel and power[a]	Health care[b]	Education[b]	Transport & Communications	Other
Croatia	24	4	18	4	3	6	41
United States	13	9	9	4	6	8	51
Serbia	N/A	N/A	N/A	N/A	N/A	N/A	N/A
Slovenia	27	8	14	4	16	11	20

Data represent percentage of consumption in PPP terms.

[a]Excludes energy used for transport.

[b]Includes government and private expenditures.

SOURCE: World Bank. *World Development Indicators 2000.*

WORKING CONDITIONS

Croatia's transition to the free-market economy began significantly to change the structure and level of employment in the country. During the socialist era, over three-quarters of the labor force of more than 2 million was employed in the **public sector** and by large, state-run enterprises. Unemployment was kept artificially low (approximately 9 percent in 1990) by over-employment and the creation of unnecessary jobs. During this period **emigration** was encouraged, and many people left the country to work abroad, contributing to low unemployment. A small private sector did exist under socialism, employing only 13 percent of the labor force in 1990.

With the arrival of the privatization process, new businesses opened and private sector employment increased to 45 percent. At the same time, employment in state-owned firms and the public sector fell to 36 percent of the labor force. Unemployment ceased to be regulated, and privatization and competition from more efficient businesses resulted in massive layoffs and early retirements. By 1998, 17 percent of 1.6 million people in the Croatian labor force were out of work. In order to ease the effects of high unemployment, the government pursued a policy of early retirement which, in turn, strained the pension system since there were far fewer people contributing to the fund than those seeking its benefits. Many pensioners received smaller pensions than they should have and were pushed into poverty.

The country's labor laws set regulations for a 42-hour work week, a 30-minute daily break, and a minimum 24-hour rest period during the week. Eighteen days of vacation are standard and time-and-a half is required to be paid for overtime. Most unions were able to negotiate a 40-hour workweek. The average salary after deductions such as taxes and contributions in 1998 was 3039 kuna, then equivalent to US$425. Over a half of gross salary (salary before deductions) goes to the government and various funds such as health care and pensions. The highest salaries are paid by the financial sector, which employs the smallest number of people. Those working in wholesale and **retail** trade, fishing, and mining average the lowest salaries. The average net salary is not enough to provide a decent standard of living for an average family. For this reason, most people supplement their income with self-employed activities, work in the informal sectors, or earn income from property such as rents and leases, in-kind income, or help from relatives living abroad. There is also a **barter system** for the exchange of goods and services, and those who can grow fruit and vegetables on small plots or in their gardens for personal consumption. In March 1999 the government signed an agreement which established a minimum wage of 1500 kuna (approximately US$211). Unemployment benefits also exist and currently assist almost 17 percent of the unemployed.

Croatia has a much higher level of job protection than other European countries. These regulations protect workers' job stability, but are costly to employers. For example, the law on termination of employment requires an advance notice of up to 6 months and, in certain instances, the approval of the workers' council. This makes labor costs much more expensive than in other countries whose economies are in transition and prevents the creation of new jobs. The regulations slow down the process of hiring new employees and make it difficult to offer part-time work. The government also regulates health and safety standards, which are implemented by the Ministry of Health.

Child labor has not been a problem in Croatia, while discrimination against women in the labor force is common if not prevalent. On average, women still earn less than men and share a higher percentage of unemployment than men (57.3 percent of women were unemployed in 1997 compared to 43.1 percent of men). Over half of the female workforce is employed in the service sector.

A large portion of Croatia's labor force is skilled and/or highly educated. In 1999, for example, out of 320,000 (33.7 percent) unemployed, over 30 percent consisted of skilled and highly skilled workers and about 7 percent were people with college or university degrees. Unemployment is highest among the young and is rising, and poor job prospects have driven many to seek work in other countries. Since 1990, the number of unemployed people under 30 years of age increased by 25,000. Since young people are generally most mobile, they tend to be the first to emigrate. Because of demand in other countries for a high profile labor force, many skilled and educated unemployed Croatians have been filling those positions. As a result, Croatia has been experiencing a serious brain drain since the 1990s.

COUNTRY HISTORY AND ECONOMIC DEVELOPMENT

600. Croatians begin settling in the area of present-day Croatia.

679. The first international treaty is signed between Croatian Duke Borko and Pope Agathur.

810–23. Duke Ljudevit Posavski establishes a powerful state in what is present-day northern Croatia.

925. Tomislav, the unifier of the territories of Pannonia, Croatia, Dalmatia, Bosnia, and Herzegovina, is crowned the first Croatian king.

1102. After the death of Petar Svacic, the last Croatian king, Croatia enters into a union with Hungary.

1527. By the decision of the Croatian Assembly, Ferdinand of the Hapsburg dynasty is elected to the Croatian throne; massive migrations of Croatians (especially to Burhenland, Austria, and Molise, Italy) begin.

1815. After a short period under the rule of the French emperor Napoleon, almost the entire territory of present-day Croatia becomes a part of the Austrian Hapsburg monarchy.

1847. Parliament adopts Croatian as the country's official language, replacing Latin.

1848. Ban (Viceroy) Josip Jelacic defends Croatia against Hungarian attempts to occupy the country and unites all the Croatian provinces. Serfdom is abolished.

1903. Anti-Hungarian and anti-Austrian riots erupt, causing some 50,000 Croatians to leave for the United States.

1918. After the downfall of the Austro-Hungarian Empire in World War I, Croatia becomes part of the Kingdom of Serbs, Croats, and Slovenes, later proclaimed Yugoslavia.

1941. German and Italian forces occupy Yugoslavia during World War II and dismantle the country; a pro-Nazi government is installed in Croatia. The country becomes a German puppet state resisted by Croatian anti-fascists led by Josip Broz Tito.

1945. After World War II, the Federated Socialist Republic of Yugoslavia is proclaimed, consisting of 6 republics, including Croatia. Marshal Tito is made president and holds office until his death in 1980. Yugoslavia is aligned with the Soviet Union until 1990.

1990. The first multi-party elections since World War II take place in Croatia and are won by the Croatian Democratic Union. The Croatian Assembly elects Dr. Franjo Tudjman as the first president.

1991. Croatia proclaims independence from Yugoslavia. A Serbian rebellion starts in Krajina, supported by the Yugoslav National Army from Belgrade and resulting in the occupation of one-third of Croatian territory.

1992. Croatian independence is recognized by the world and the Republic of Croatia becomes a member of the United Nations.

1995. Croatia recaptures Krajina from the Serbs, and the war in Croatia officially ends.

1998. The last Serb-occupied region of Croatia, located in its eastern part which includes the city of Vukovar, is peacefully integrated into the country.

2000. Croatia becomes a member of the World Trade Organization.

FUTURE TRENDS

For Croatia the 1990s were difficult and traumatic. The country experienced war devastation, population displacement, and turbulent political change, all of which contributed to its ruined economy. As the 21st century gets under way, Croatia faces serious and urgent challenges in improving its economic situation. The country needs to make major policy reforms. Improved administration of business activity—including cutting red tape, offering tax incentives to stimulate business growth, and completing the privatization process—must be implemented. Reform is also necessary to increase the effectiveness of the health and pension systems. Improvement of the banking sector is another key factor in easing the path of such reforms. A firm commitment to these reforms would send a positive signal to foreign investors and act as an encouragement to international aid in financing reform. If these challenges are met and international investment acquired, Croatia could implement programs for sustained economic growth, thus achieving a higher standard of living for its people and full integration into the rest of Europe.

Successful restructuring is possible and realistic since the country possesses the necessary infrastructure and expertise. Its location and its promising economic opportunities are attractive to investors. What is desperately needed is decisive action by the government, which needs to grasp the necessity for economic reforms and to begin their implementation without delay; delay would serve only to burden the economy with more costly adjustments in the future. Without reform, growth will not be possible, unemployment will remain high, the banking system weak, and the economy will not recover.

DEPENDENCIES

Croatia has no territories or colonies.

BIBLIOGRAPHY

Bencic, Damjan. "Services Market Opportunities in Croatia." *CEEBICnet Market Research.* <http://www.mac.doc.gov/eebic/countryr/CROATIA/CrServices.htm>. Accessed January 2001.

Commerzbank. *Emerging Europe Economic Research: Quarterly Economic Report, 4Q00.* Frankfurt, Germany: Commerzbank, 2000.

Croatian Bureau of Statistics. <http://www.dzs.hr/Eng/ouraddress.htm>. Accessed September 2001.

Croatian Bureau of Statistics. *Statisticki ljetopis 2000: Statistical Yearbook.* Zagreb, Croatia: Croatian Bureau of Statistics, 2000.

EBRD Transition Report 1999. European Bank for Reconstruction and Development, 1999.

Economist Intelligence Unit. *Country Profile: Croatia.* London: Economist Intelligence Unit Ltd, 2001.

International Monetary Fund. "Republic of Croatia and the IMF." *International Monetary Fund.* <http://www.imf.org/external/country/HRV/index.htm>. Accessed September 2001.

U.S. Central Intelligence Agency. *World Factbook 2001.* <http://www.odci.gov/cia/publications/factbook/index.html>. Accessed September 2001.

U.S. State Department, Bureau of European Affairs. *Background Notes: Croatia.* <http://www.state.gov.www/background_notes/croatia_0001_bgn.html>. Accessed September 2001.

World Bank Group. "Croatia." *The World Bank Group.* <http://www.worldbank.org>. Accessed January 2001.

The Zagreb Stock Exchange. <http://www.zse.hr>. Accessed September 2001.

—Katarina Deletis

CZECH REPUBLIC

CAPITAL: Prague (Praha).

MONETARY UNIT: The monetary unit is the Czech crown (Èeská koruna), abbreviated as Kè. Each crown is composed of 100 hellers. There are coins of 10, 20, and 50 hellers, and 1, 2, 5, 10, 20, and 50 crowns. Czech banknotes come in denominations of 20, 50, 100, 200, 500, 1,000, 2,000, and 5,000 crowns. This monetary unit came into being with the division of Czechoslovakia into the Czech and Slovak Republics in 1993, and is now valued at a different rate than the Slovak crown.

CHIEF EXPORTS: Machinery and transport equipment, other manufactured goods, chemicals, raw materials and fuel.

CHIEF IMPORTS: Machinery and transport equipment, other manufactured goods, chemicals, raw materials and fuels, food.

GROSS DOMESTIC PRODUCT: US$120.8 billion (1999 est.).

BALANCE OF TRADE: **Exports:** US$26.34 billion (1998 est.). **Imports:** US$30.24 billion (1998 est.).

COUNTRY OVERVIEW

LOCATION AND SIZE. The Czech Republic is located in Central Europe. It is surrounded by Germany to the northwest, Poland to the northeast, Slovakia to the southeast, and Austria to the south. The total area is 78,866 square kilometers (49,007 square miles). The terrain is generally composed of rolling hills and some mountainous areas. Its 4 borders total 1,881 kilometers (1,159 miles), and it has no coastline. Its size is comparable to Mississippi (48,434 square miles) and Louisiana (51,843 square miles).

The Czech Republic features 3 primary regions: the Czech Lands to the west, Moravia to the southeast, and Silesia to the northeast. The capital, Prague, is located slightly to the country's northwest. Other important cities include Ostrava to the northeast, Brno to the southeast (in the Moravian region), and Plzen to the west.

POPULATION. In 2000 the population was estimated at 10,272,179. Approximately 1.19 million inhabitants, or 11.56 percent of the population, resided in Prague. The birth rate stood at 9.1 births per 1,000 people in 2000, while the death rate was 10.87 deaths per 1,000, resulting in a projected growth rate of -0.08 percent. The first time the population growth rate was registered as negative was in 1994. According to the Statistical Office of the Czech Republic, the projected population for 2010 was 10.24 million.

While 81.2 percent of the population is Czech, 13.2 percent is Moravian. In addition, 3.1 percent of the population is made up of ethnic Slovaks. The remainder of the population includes Roma (Gypsies), Poles, Germans, Silesians, and Hungarians. However, the Roma population is often underrepresented politically because they are a nomadic (no fixed residency) people. Approximately 40 percent of the people declare themselves to be Roman Catholic, 40 percent declare themselves to be atheist, and the remainder are primarily Protestant, Orthodox, or other religions.

OVERVIEW OF ECONOMY

The territory that is now known as the Czech Republic was part of the Austrian, or Hapsburg, portion of the Austro-Hungarian Empire until the end of World War I in 1918. It then became a part of the Czechoslovak state. During the 1930s, Czechoslovakia was an industrial powerhouse. The Czechoslovak industries, including machine and automotive manufacturing, were among the world's most developed.

After World War II, Czechoslovakia fell under the political and economic influence of the Soviet Union. The **communist** economy included state ownership of enterprises, state-led central planning of economic activities, and artificial **price controls**. After some Czechoslovak leaders attempted to introduce some political, cultural, and economic **liberalization**, the country was invaded by the troops of neighboring communist countries under the direction of the Soviet Union (1968). This intervention put a stop to liberalization, when the government attempted to

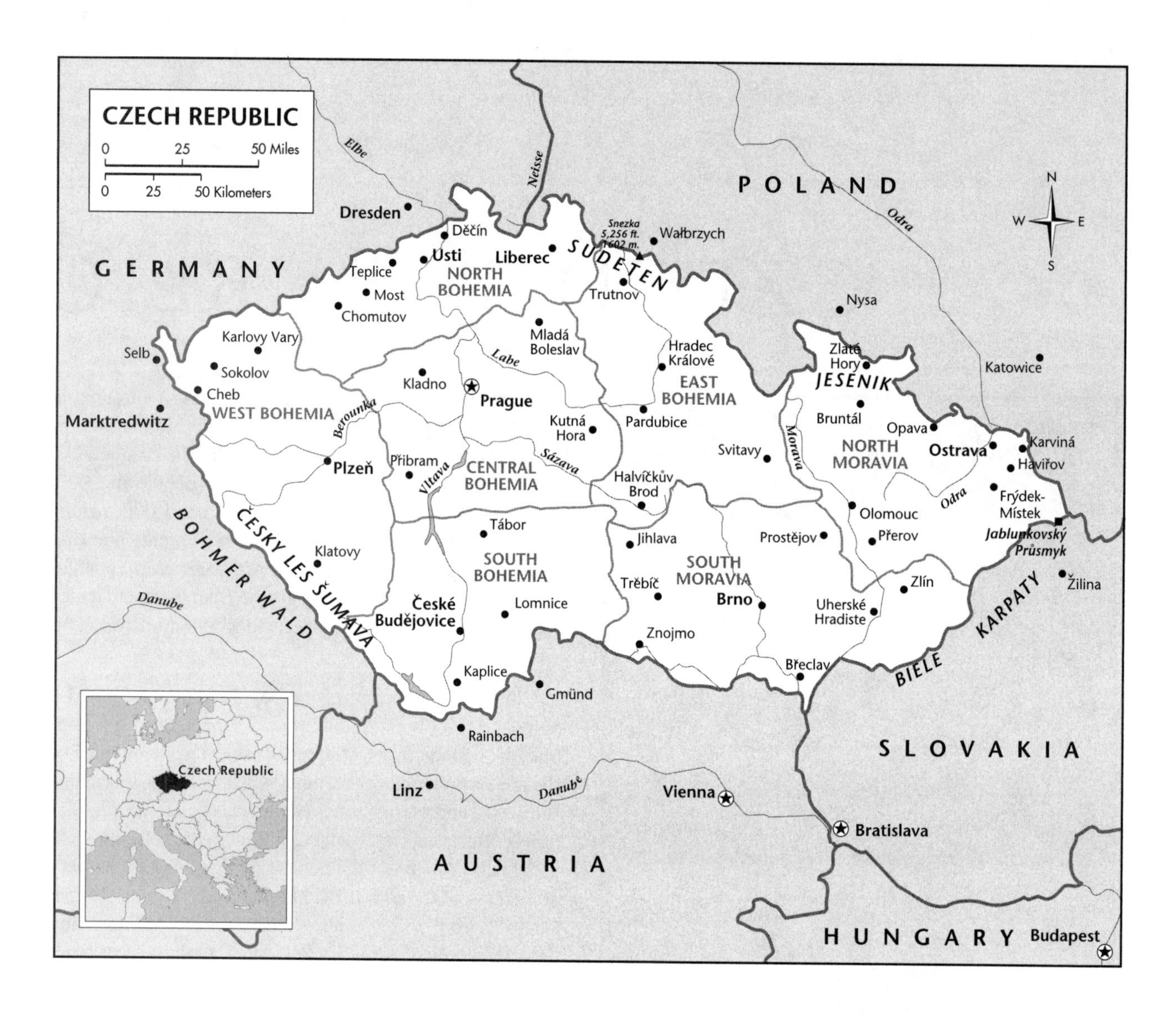

increase production of **consumer goods** in exchange for compliance among the people. In spite of the government's efforts, the economy declined, causing a crisis by the late 1980s.

A series of anti-government protests took place in the late 1980s. By 1989, the more liberal policies of the Soviet Union toward Eastern Europe, as well as the weakening of communist governments in neighboring East Germany, Hungary, and Poland, made it impossible for the Czechoslovak communists to stay in power. In November and December of 1989, the communist government stepped down. Free elections for parliament were held in 1990, and Václav Havel was elected president. The government quickly made economic reforms based on free market principles. In addition, the government began the process of **privatization**.

From 1990 to 1992, these reforms were more popular in the Czech Republic (which had a larger industrial base) than in the Slovak Republic. Under Czechoslovakia's federal structure, which gave both republics independent power, the newly-elected prime ministers of the Czech and Slovak republics negotiated the divorce of Czechoslovakia. The Czech Republic and the Slovak Republic became separate sovereign states on 1 January 1993. After an initially strong performance, the Czech Republic experienced some setbacks, most notably in 1997 when the country experienced an economic crisis and a political scandal that forced out the prime minister.

The Czech Republic's strongest economic sectors are in the areas of industry and services. Its primary industrial products include iron and steel, machinery and equipment, motor vehicles, chemicals, armaments, textiles, and glass and ceramics. In the service sector, commercial, financial, and insurance companies are important.

The Czech Republic is famous for its beers, which are exported throughout the world. Other agricultural products include potatoes, wheat, and sugarbeets. Since freeing up its international trade in 1990, the Czech Republic has imported items such as machinery, consumer goods, raw materials and chemicals, and some foods.

Along with uranium, some of the country's natural resources include coal, timber, and fuels, which remain important energy sources, though some energy must still be imported from Norway and Russia. The Czech Republic experienced a sizable amount of Western investment during the 1990s.

As a NATO member since 1999 and a prospective member of the European Union (EU), the Czech Republic has been quite successful in reorienting its trade away from the East, and towards the West. It has received aid from international organizations such as the World Bank, the International Monetary Fund (IMF), the European Bank for Reconstruction and Development, and the European Investment Bank, in the form of loans and grants. In 1994, the Czech Republic polished its world image by paying some of its IMF debts ahead of schedule. The country's estimated **external debt** for 1999 was $24.3 billion. While organized crime has a notable presence in nearly all of the countries of east-central Europe, the Czech Republic is less affected by such activities than its neighbors.

POLITICS, GOVERNMENT, AND TAXATION

The Czech Republic is a democracy with a parliamentary political system, in which the parliament elects the president. The electoral system for the Chamber of Deputies is proportional, meaning that individuals tend to vote for specific parties rather than for specific candidates. After the elections, each party receives a number of seats in parliament according to the percentage it receives of the vote, provided it receives at least 5 percent. Each party organizes a list of individuals that they will send to the parliament to fill their allotted seats. The elections for the Senate are conducted according to single member districts, in which a single candidate wins a majority vote in each of the 81 Senate districts.

The Czech president is elected by the parliament and serves a 5-year term. Václav Havel was elected in 1993 and reelected in 1998, although he was not affiliated with a particular political party. The 200 members of the Chamber of Deputies are elected for 4-year terms. The 81 Senate members are elected for 6-year terms, with one-third of the Senate elected every 2 years.

The first parliamentary elections to be held in the independent Czech Republic took place in 1996. The party that favored immediate free market reforms, the Civic Democratic Party (ODS), and the party that favored a slower pace to free market reforms, the Social Democrats (ÈSSD), emerged as the most powerful parties in the Chamber of Deputies. A political and economic crisis led to early parliamentary elections in 1998. The third most significant party in the Chamber of Deputies elections was the Communist Party (KSÈM), followed by the reformist Christian Democrats (KDU). Other significant parties include the nationalist Republicans, the free-market oriented Civic Democratic Alliance (ODA), and the conservative Freedom Union (US).

The government has directed the complex process of transforming the economy from a centrally planned communist system to a market-based system. Each reform has required the passage of new laws and the implementation of new regulations. Among other general market reforms, a Commercial Code was adopted in 1991 under the Czechoslovak state and was revised in 1996. It outlined legal protections for private property and business activities for both Czechs and foreigners. Other reforms included a Foreign Exchange Act establishing the Czech currency as convertible abroad, and a Trading Act to set conditions for trade.

Part of the economic reforms involved the privatization of assets and companies that had been the property of the state. In 1990 and 1991, under the Czechoslovak state, some property, such as farms, shops, and homes, was given back to its pre-communist owners. The privatization of small enterprises was completed through auctions by the end of 1993. The privatization of large enterprises was a more complicated process involving vouchers that allowed citizens to buy shares of some companies. It also included direct sales, auctions, and free transfer. More than 80 percent of former state assets had been privatized in 2000.

The government obtains revenues through several different taxes. There is a progressive personal **income tax** that ranges from 15 to 32 percent. The corporate income tax is 31 percent, although investment companies and pension funds are taxed at a rate of 20 percent. Some **tax holidays** are offered as part of an effort to attract foreign investment. Other taxes include property tax, road taxes for business vehicles, inheritance tax, and fees for administrative services. In addition, a **value-added tax** is imposed on all goods except necessities such as food and health care. **Excise taxes**, customs **duties**, and real property transfer taxes also bring in government revenues.

INFRASTRUCTURE, POWER, AND COMMUNICATIONS

The Czech Republic inherited an extensive network of public transportation, in the form of bus and train routes, from Czechoslovakia. Even some of the most remote locations may be reached by bus. One of the most significant changes of the post-communist era has been an increase in independent auto transportation among the population. There are 127,693 kilometers (73,348 miles) of highways, including 497 kilometers (309 miles) of expressway, all of

Communications

Country	Newspapers	Radios	TV Sets[a]	Cable subscribers[a]	Mobile Phones[a]	Fax Machines[a]	Personal Computers[a]	Internet Hosts[b]	Internet Users[b]
	1996	1997	1998	1998	1998	1998	1998	1999	1999
Czech Republic	254	803	447	77.1	94	10.4	97.3	85.58	700
United States	215	2,146	847	244.3	256	78.4	458.6	1,508.77	74,100
Germany	311	948	580	214.5	170	73.1	304.7	173.96	14,400
Slovakia	185	580	402	105.1	87	10.0	65.1	38.79	600

[a]Data are from International Telecommunication Union, *World Telecommunication Development Report 1999* and are per 1,000 people.
[b]Data are from the Internet Software Consortium (http://www.isc.org) and are per 10,000 people.

SOURCE: World Bank. *World Development Indicators 2000.*

which are paved. The country now has 9,435 kilometers (5,363 miles) of railways. Continued improvements are planned for the railway and highway systems in order to bring them more in line with EU standards.

There are 10 public international airports and 114 total airfields, 71 of which have paved runways. The largest airport is Ruzyne, in Prague, which services approximately 95 percent of the total passenger traffic. There are 677 kilometers (421 miles) of waterways in the Czech Republic, the most important being the Vltava and Elbe rivers. Tourists tend to enter the Czech Republic via the airport in Prague or by train from Austria, Germany, Hungary, Poland, or Slovakia.

Electricity production stands at 61.5 billion kilowatt hours, and the country uses a 220-volt power system. The majority of electricity is generated by fossil fuels (76 percent). While a portion of this production comes from coal, oil provides a sizable portion as well and is imported from Russia. Nuclear power contributes 20 percent of electricity production.

The Czech Republic has a rapidly-modernizing communications **infrastructure**. In the first few years after the transition from communism, the installation of telephone lines by the state company was still difficult. However, the increased entry of private telecommunication companies and the growing popularity of mobile telephones has provided a way to sidestep these difficulties, and increased competition has forced the Czech telecommunications company, STP Telecom, to improve its service. There are 94 mobile phones per 1,000 people in the Czech Republic, compared to 50 per 1,000 in neighboring Poland, and there is 1 digital cellular system and 2 global system for mobile communication (GSM) providers for cell phone service. A number of Internet service providers sprung up in the late 1990s, creating between 20 and 30 options for service. Internet cafes are readily available, and the Czech government has taken steps to promote increased public computer and Internet technologies.

ECONOMIC SECTORS

During the 1990s, the Czech Republic experienced a drastic shift away from the industry sector and towards the services sector. This change resulted partly from the Czechoslovak split, and partly from the transformation to a market-based system. The communist system created several large **monopoly** industries, particularly in large machine manufacturing. Once privatized, only some of these industries were actually competitive in a free-market environment. Moreover, while the service sector was given a low priority under the communist system, the free-market environment demonstrated a strong demand for services.

Foreign direct investment (FDI) in Czech companies has been crucial to their successful transition, and the Czech Republic has benefited from high FDI levels. Some of the most famous Czech companies that have successfully survived the transition process are the Škoda

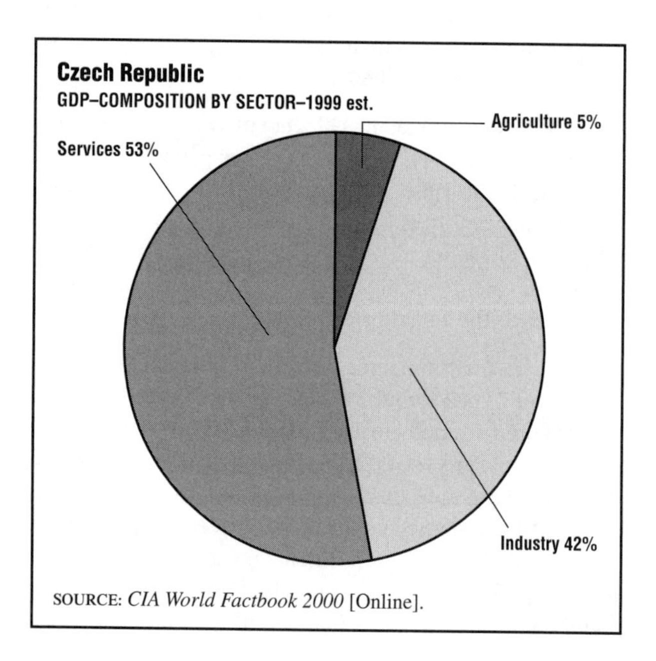

SOURCE: *CIA World Factbook 2000* [Online].

car company, the Tatra truck company, the glass production company Bohemia Glass, and several brewing companies such as Pilsner Urquell, Staropramen, and Budvar (Budweiser).

AGRICULTURE

Agriculture makes up the smallest sector in the Czech economy, contributing about 5 percent of the total GDP. In 1997 the agricultural sector employed 5.6 percent of the **labor force**, or roughly 200,000 people. This number was just 39 percent of the number of people employed in this sector under communist rule. The primary agricultural products were sugarbeets, fodder roots for animal feed, potatoes, wheat, hops, fruit, pigs, cattle, poultry, and forest products.

The Czech Republic has 3.1 million hectares of arable land, although roughly half of this land is not highly productive. Under the communist economic system, Czech agriculture was collectivized, meaning that small private farms were taken by the government in order to create state-owned cooperatives. After the end of communism in 1989, these cooperatives were transferred to private owners, often by the direct sale of the farm as a unit. However, some lands were also given back to their former owners. By 1999, 85 percent of agricultural lands were privately owned. Of this total, 40 percent are corporate farms, 34 percent are co-operatives, 24 percent are owned by individuals, and 2 percent are state owned.

Agricultural output decreased 28 percent between 1989 and 1998, with the greatest declines in livestock production. This reflects the overall decline of the agricultural sector in the Czech Republic, where more than half of all farms experience financial difficulties. Problems include the high costs of labor, machinery, fertilizer, and other agricultural inputs; the lack of modern technology; and low levels of state aid for agriculture.

INDUSTRY

Industry makes up a large but declining sector of the Czech economy, contributing 42 percent of the country's GDP in 1999, and employing 40.7 percent of the labor force in 1997. The majority of large and medium-sized enterprises have been privatized. Companies that are still run by the state are not very competitive and have sizable debts. Such companies lie primarily in the energy and mining sectors, although some of them are classified as strategic industries.

MANUFACTURING. Road vehicles are the country's most significant export, bringing in significantly more revenue than other important exports, such as electrical machinery and appliances, and industrial machinery and equipment. Other major export products include iron and steel, non-metallic mineral products, textiles, specialized machinery, transport equipment, furniture, power generation machinery, and rubber goods.

Because many of the manufacturing plants that were privatized after communism featured outdated equipment, foreign direct investment has been extremely important in determining which industries survive the transition to a market economy. The primary foreign investments have been in the area of consumer goods and tobacco, transport and communications (including equipment, commerce, and services), petrochemicals, financial and insurance affairs, mineral products, and electricity, gas, and water supply. By 1999 over 800 foreign companies had set up manufacturing subsidiaries, each employing more than 50 persons in the Czech Republic.

With increasing investments in the automotive sector, the Czech Republic is expected to become the third-largest auto manufacturer in Eastern Europe, after Russia and Poland. Other fast-growing sectors are electronics, precision engineering, environmental technologies, and software development. The government offers incentives for investment in high-tech products or machinery, and has begun a program to support the development of industrial zones throughout the republic.

The traditional Czech industries of glassmaking and beer brewing survived the economic transition in the form of the glassmaking company Bohemia Glass and the brewing companies Pilsner Urquell and Budvar/Budweiser. Companies producing transport equipment, such as Tatra Trucks, Zetor tractors, and Škoda cars, also remain visible in the current Czech economy. Other products that continued to be manufactured after communism include trams, planes, motorcycles, buses, and machines.

The most important products mined in the Czech Republic are coal and uranium. The coal is primarily used for heating purposes, while the uranium is used for the production of weapons, and a significant amount of uranium is exported. While uranium was exported almost exclusively to Soviet bloc countries before 1989, it is now exported more widely.

In the second half of the 1990s prices for commercial construction increased for small and medium enterprises, as well as for domestic non-financial corporations. The largest price increases for commercial construction were from firms employing more than 300 persons (especially for those employing more than 500), and for foreign non-financial corporations. Price increases for these types of structures indicated a higher level of demand relative to supply.

SERVICES

The service sector accounted for 53 percent of the GDP in 1999. As opposed to a negative trade balance in industry, the Czech Republic registered a positive trade balance in services between 1993 and 2000. The service sector employed 53.7 percent of the labor force in 1997.

As insurance was not provided under the communist system, there was significant growth in this area during the first decade of **capitalism**. Financial services and consulting companies experienced similar growth. Although foreign companies initiated growth in this sector, they quickly gained competition from Czech companies. The majority of commercial banks are under private ownership. Foreign banks constitute a growing proportion of this sector.

There is an ever-increasing number of Internet service providers in the Czech Republic. In addition, there has been some growth in the area of Internet software development, which began attracting foreign investment in the late 1990s.

The **retail** portion of the service sector has undergone dramatic changes since 1989. Under the communist economic system, retail operated through state-owned shops. Not only were product shortages common and the displays unattractive, but these stores were often overstaffed and employed people unsuited to the job.

Retail stores were privatized early in the transition to a free market. The retail sector consists of **restructured** stores as well as completely new stores. These stores differ greatly from their communist-era predecessors, as they have adopted capitalist marketing methods and retail decorum. Among the most popular products among consumers are foreign appliances, such as televisions, VCRs, and stereos.

Tourism has increased exponentially since the demise of communism in 1989. Nearly all tourist facilities have been privatized. Tourism contributed $3 billion to the country's net foreign currency earnings in 1999, and approximately 100 million people visit Prague, the country's capital, each year. Most tourist revenues remain in Prague, which is renowned for its architecture and history. The majority of visitors come from the Czech Republic's neighboring countries. The dramatic increase in tourism has led to an increased need for tourist services, particularly for hotels. Foreign tourists visiting Prague account for three-quarters of all hotel capacity in the Czech Republic. In addition, the city of Prague is attempting to improve its image as a potential convention site. While in the Czech Republic, tourists engage not only in sightseeing, but also in concerts, sports, and gambling.

INTERNATIONAL TRADE

The Czech Republic has had a **trade deficit** since 1975. The primary industrial commodities exported by the Czech Republic are machinery and transport equipment, as well as other manufactured goods. In 1998, these categories comprised 41 percent and 40 percent of all commodity exports, respectively. Other significant exported commodities were chemicals, which made up 8 percent, and raw materials and fuel, which were 7 percent. Aside from commodities, the Czech Republic also exports some services, and has demonstrated a positive trade balance in this sector. The primary consumers of Czech exports are Germany and Slovakia.

Trade (expressed in billions of US$): Czech Republic

	Exports	Imports
1975	N/A	N/A
1980	N/A	N/A
1985	N/A	N/A
1990	N/A	N/A
1995	21.654	26.524
1998	26.337	30.239

SOURCE: International Monetary Fund. *International Financial Statistics Yearbook 1999.*

The Czech Republic imports primarily the same type of goods as it exports. Approximately 39 percent of all imports for 1998 were classified as machinery and transport equipment. Other imports included manufactured goods, which comprised 21 percent of imports; chemicals, 12 percent; and raw materials and fuel, 10 percent. Germany and Slovakia serve as the primary sources of Czech imports.

In the first few years following 1989, the Czechoslovak state made a concentrated effort to shift trade away from the former Soviet countries, and to the European Union (EU) and the United States. The Czech government actively encouraged this shift in an effort to improve chances for entry into the EU. Czech trading patterns continue to show increased volume in trade with the EU and the United States, and decreased volume with other East European countries and the former Soviet Union. As one result of this shift, trade with the Slovak Republic has declined, in spite of a favorable customs union between the 2 countries. The Slovak Republic made up 18 percent of the Czech Republic's foreign trade **turnover** in 1993, but by 1999 it was approximately 7 percent. The EU now makes up approximately 67 percent of the foreign trade turnover of the Czech Republic.

Among the EU countries, the Czech Republic's most significant trading partner is Germany, which made up 38 percent of the Czech trade turnover in 1999. Following Slovakia (7 percent), other important European trading partners are Austria (6 percent), France, Italy, Poland, and the United Kingdom, which each make up 4 to 5 percent of the trade volume. The United States and the Russian

Federation each make up approximately 3 percent of Czech trade turnover.

MONEY

The Czech crown has been convertible to other currencies on the world market since 1995. The Czech National Bank serves as the country's central bank, and sets **monetary policy**. It is designed to be autonomous from political structures. In spite of the bank's policies to curb **inflation**, the currency began to decline in value after a political and economic crisis in 1997. In addition to this bank, there is a government-owned agency to assist companies through the bankruptcy process.

The majority of banks have been privatized, with only 2 of the largest remaining in state hands. There has been some consolidation among the private banks, and the largest 5 banks conduct the majority of operations. In addition, the number of foreign banks operating in the country has grown. This process corresponds with the country's efforts to prepare for future integration into the financial structures of the EU.

The Prague Stock Exchange registers several hundred companies for security and derivative trading. It is engaged in a process of updating its trading rules and procedures to fit EU standards. In addition, there is an off-exchange market called the RM-system, for the trade of securities.

POVERTY AND WEALTH

Four decades of communist rule (1948–89) had a strong effect on the distribution of incomes, an effect that remains visible today in the Czech Republic. The communist system resulted in a social hierarchy very different from the class system in most capitalist countries. Under communism, wages were artificially kept at similar levels, so professionals such as doctors earned wages similar to those of factory or construction workers. Because property had belonged to the state and housing was distributed through state channels, those individuals who obtained large homes often did so through political means, such as good standing with the Communist Party.

Ten years later, this system is changing. As property has become privatized, individuals with successful businesses can now afford to buy the larger homes. Political affiliation matters much less for one's living standard than it did before. However, given the fact that the privatization process has been run by the government, political affiliation and social contacts have not been irrelevant, either. In spite of the fact that the Czech Republic's transition has been one of the most transparent, some instances of corruption have allowed a few individuals to improve their economic standing through dishonest means.

Although the social structure is rapidly moving away from relatively equal income distribution to a class system, as of the late 1990s income distribution and consumption in the Czech Republic remained more equalized than in the United States. In the United States, the richest 20 percent of individuals earn and consume 46 percent of available wealth. However, in the Czech Republic, the richest 20 percent of individuals earn and consume 36 percent of available wealth. In addition, the poorest 20 percent earn and consume only 5 percent of available wealth in the United States, but in the Czech Republic the poorest 20 percent earn and consume 10 percent of available wealth.

GDP per Capita (US$)

Country	1975	1980	1985	1990	1998
Czech Republic	N/A	N/A	4,884	5,270	5,142
United States	19,364	21,529	23,200	25,363	29,683
Germany	N/A	N/A	N/A	N/A	31,141
Slovakia	N/A	N/A	3,630	3,825	3,822

SOURCE: United Nations. *Human Development Report 2000; Trends in human development and per capita income.*

Exchange rates: Czech Republic

Czech crowns per US$1	
Jan 2001	37.425
2000	38.598
1999	34.569
1998	32.281
1997	31.698
1996	27.145

SOURCE: CIA *World Factbook 2001* [ONLINE].

Distribution of Income or Consumption by Percentage Share: Czech Republic

Lowest 10%	4.3
Lowest 20%	10.3
Second 20%	14.5
Third 20%	17.7
Fourth 20%	21.7
Highest 20%	35.9
Highest 10%	22.4

Survey year: 1996

Note: This information refers to income shares by percentiles of the population and is ranked by per capita income.

SOURCE: *2000 World Development Indicators* [CD-ROM].

Household Consumption in PPP Terms

Country	All food	Clothing and footwear	Fuel and power[a]	Health care[b]	Education[b]	Transport & Communications	Other
Czech Republic	24	5	14	5	12	16	24
United States	13	9	9	4	6	8	51
Germany	14	6	7	2	10	7	53
Slovakia	26	7	16	5	12	10	24

Data represent percentage of consumption in PPP terms.
[a]Excludes energy used for transport.
[b]Includes government and private expenditures.

SOURCE: World Bank. *World Development Indicators 2000.*

Under the communist system, higher education and health care were freely provided by the state. The Czech Republic has been implementing reforms that require individuals to pay for these services. These reforms have been difficult for average individuals, because institutions such as a comprehensive student loan system or health insurance have not been developed. The state does provide social security and social assistance, such as unemployment and disability benefits.

WORKING CONDITIONS

The Czech Republic's labor force is 5.2 million, and approximately 46 percent of the total Czech population was registered as employed in 1999. In 1999, the rate of unemployment, which registers those actively looking for work, was 9 percent. Unemployment has been on an upward swing since an economic crisis in 1997, but has shown recent signs of stabilizing. Unemployment benefits are available to individuals, and slightly less than half of those registered as unemployed receive these payments.

Prague consistently maintains the lowest level of unemployment in the country. The highest levels of unemployment are in northern Bohemia and in Moravia. Wage levels reflect these differences, with the highest wages in Prague. According to estimated figures for 1997, the majority of those employed—53.7 percent—worked in the service sector. Industry employed 40.7 percent of the workforce, and the remainder—5.6 percent—worked in agriculture. Given the importance of foreign investment in the economy, those individuals who speak English and German have an advantage in the labor market.

The Czech Republic features a system of laws which prohibits employment discrimination on the basis of race, sex, language, religion, faith, political views, and sexual orientation. However, discrimination against the hiring of Roma (Gypsies) persists in practice. There are 28 weeks of maternity leave available, with a possible extension to 3 years. A woman taking maternity leave is provided some income by the social security and health insurance systems, with some contributions by employers.

Workers' unions were a fixture of the communist system. After the end of communism in 1989, the communist-affiliated unions rapidly declined in popularity. Laborers now tend to belong to non-affiliated unions, and approximately two-thirds of all workers are union members.

COUNTRY HISTORY AND ECONOMIC DEVELOPMENT

1914–17. World War I. The Austro-Hungarian Empire, which includes Czechoslovakia, disintegrates.

1918. The Czechoslovak state is founded.

1938–45. Hitler takes over Czechoslovakia during World War II.

1945. Czechoslovakia is freed from the Nazis by the Soviets in the east, and by the Allies in the west.

1948. The Communist Party takes over the Czechoslovak parliament.

1968. Attempted reforms by the Czechoslovak state are met with an invasion of tanks from Czechoslovakia's Soviet bloc neighbors.

1970s. Some political dissidents begin to visibly resist the communist leadership.

1980s. Worsening economic conditions facilitate protests against communism.

1989. The communist government is forced to step down.

1990. The first post-communist parliamentary elections are held, and Václav Havel is confirmed as Czechoslovakia's new president. The government embarks on a series of reforms to replace the communist economic system with a capitalist system.

1992. The second post-communist elections result in a disagreement between the Czech and Slovak republics. The leaders plan the country's divorce.

1993. The Czech Republic is officially founded on 1 January 1993. It establishes a separate Czech currency in February.

1997. An economic crisis and political instability cause difficulties.

1998. The Czech Republic begins accession talks with the European Union.

1999. The Czech Republic joins NATO.

FUTURE TRENDS

The Czech Republic has come a long way since its founding in 1993, through nearly a decade of transition from a communist to a capitalist economic system. It is a member of the United Nations, Organization for Security and Co-operation in Europe (OSCE), Organization for Economic Co-operation and Development (OECD), International Monetary Fund, (IMF), World Bank, European Bank for Reconstruction and Development (EBRD), and the World Trade Organization (WTO), and became a NATO member in 1999. In addition, it is an associate member of the EU and the Western European Union (WEU). The government's primary focus in recent years has been the preparation of legislative and regulatory structures for future EU membership, for which it has made a formal application. Accession talks with the EU officially began in 1998, and the Czech Republic is slated to become a full member between 2003 and 2005.

In spite of the enormous changes that the Czech Republic successfully underwent in its first few years of independence, more remains to be done. The country is expected to continue to rebound from the economic **recession** of the late 1990s, especially as it improves its trade with Western European nations. But it is the interaction with Western European nations in the EU that is expected to pose the greatest challenge to the Czech Republic in the coming decade. Restructuring the large enterprises that remain in the hands of the state, and reforming legislation to conform to EU standards will cause some economic displacement. Yet once the country moves through this difficult period, its position at the heart of Central Europe, its well-developed infrastructure, its high-quality educational institutions, and its educated populace promise a vibrant economic future.

DEPENDENCIES

Czech Republic has no territories or colonies.

BIBLIOGRAPHY

"Agency Programs" and "Key Sectors." *CzechInvest.* <http://www.czechinvest.org/ci/ci_an.nsf/?Open>. Accessed January 2001.

"Agora Elections Around the World." *Czech Republic.* <http://www.agora.stm.it/elections/election/czech.htm>. Accessed January 2001.

American Chamber of Commerce in the Czech Republic. *Czech Republic 2000.* Prague: American Chamber of Commerce, 2000.

Andrews, Edmund. "The Yoke of Capitalism." *The New York Times.* 16 January 2001.

Czech Statistical Universe. <http://www.czso.cz/eng/angl.htm>. Accessed January 2001.

Doing Business in the Czech Republic: Whatever You Need to Know. <http://www.doingbusiness.cz>. Accessed January 2001.

International Monetary Fund. *International Financial Statistics Yearbook.* Washington, DC: The International Monetary Fund, 1999.

Ministry of Finance of the Czech Republic, Department of Financial Policies. *Czech Republic Macroeconomic Forecast.* Prague, October 2000.

Ministry of Foreign Affairs. *Czech Republic.* <http://www.czech.cz>. Accessed January 2001.

O'Rourke, Breffini. "Little Hope Amid Gloom in Run-up to Czech Elections." *Radio Free Europe/Radio Liberty Newsline,* June 18, 1998. <http://www.rferl.org/newsline/1998/06/5-not/not-180698.html>. Accessed January 2001.

Shor, Boris. "Czech Republic." *Nations in Transit 1997: Civil Society, Democracy and Markets in East Central Europe and the Newly Independent States,* edited by Karatnycky, Motyl, and Shor. New York: Freedom House/Transaction Publishers, 1997.

United Nations Development Program. *Human Development Report 2000.* New York: Oxford University Press, 2000.

U.S. Central Intelligence Agency. *The World Factbook 2000.* <http://www.odci.gov/cia/publications/factbook/index.html>. Accessed January 2001.

U.S. Department of State, Bureau of European Affairs. *Background Notes: Czech Republic.* <http://www.state.gov/www/background_notes/czech_9903_bgn.html>. Accessed January 2001.

U.S. Department of State, Business Section. *FY 2001 Country Commercial Guide: Czech Republic.* <http://www.state.gov/www/about_state/business/com_guides/2001/europe/index.html>. Accessed January 2001.

World Bank. *World Development Indicators, 2000.* Washington, DC: The World Bank, 2000.

—Sherrill Stroschein

DENMARK

Kingdom of Denmark
Kongeriget Danmark

CAPITAL: Copenhagen.

MONETARY UNIT: Danish krone (DKr). 1 Danish krone is made up of 100 øre. There are coins for 20, 10, 5, 2, and 1 krone and 50 and 25 øre. Paper currency comes in denominations of DKr1,000, 500, 200, 100, and 50.

CHIEF EXPORTS: Machinery and instruments, meat and meat products, fuels, dairy products, ships, fish, and chemicals.

CHIEF IMPORTS: Machinery and equipment, petroleum, chemicals, grain and foodstuffs, textiles, and paper.

GROSS DOMESTIC PRODUCT: US$136.2 billion (purchasing power parity, 2000 est.).

BALANCE OF TRADE: **Exports:** US$50.8 billion (f.o.b., 2000). **Imports:** US$43.6 billion (f.o.b., 2000).

COUNTRY OVERVIEW

LOCATION AND SIZE. Denmark is in Northern Europe, bordered primarily by the Baltic Sea and North Sea. It consists of the peninsula of Jutland, north of Germany, and close to 406 islands, about 80 of which are inhabited. The most populated and largest of the islands is Zealand, where the country's capital can be found; Funen; and Jutland. Denmark occupies 43,094 square kilometers (16,621 square miles), a little less than twice the size of Massachusetts. Germany shares 68 kilometers (42 miles) of border with Denmark, and the other 7,314 kilometers (4,545 miles) is coastline. In 1 July 2000, the Øresund Bridge was completed, connecting Denmark and southern Sweden. The Kingdom of Denmark also includes the island of Bornholm in the Baltic Sea, and the territories of Greenland and the Faroe Islands.

POPULATION. Denmark's population in 2000 was 5,336,394, and was projected to fall to around 5,200,000 in 2025. From the late 1960s to the present, the fertility and mortality rates have been declining. Average life expectancy at birth has increased, but it is notable that life expectancy for men and for women in Denmark is still lower than all of its neighbors, especially for women (in 1999 life expectancy for women was 78.3, while in the United States it was 80.1). The overall population growth rate has been consistently low at 0.31 percent.

The Danish population is extremely homogenous. As of 2000, 97 percent are Danes (ethnic Scandinavians), and the rest are Inuit (Eskimo), Faroese, and Germans. The proportion of elderly people in the population has been increasing as well, with the result that in 2000 only 18 percent were under 14, and 15 percent were over 65.

The population is highly urbanized, with around 85 percent living in cities. However, population density is low compared to places such as the United States and European countries farther south. It is worth noting that to be classified as "urban" in Denmark, a settlement needs only 250 people (compared to Greece, where "urban" is defined as a settlement of 10,000 or more). Urbanization has slowed in the 1990s, with some Danes reversing the pattern and moving back to rural areas.

OVERVIEW OF ECONOMY

Denmark has a technologically advanced free-market economy, mainly involved in high **value-added** production such as processing and finishing products, rather than extracting and producing raw materials. Main exports are industrial products, followed by agricultural products—chiefly livestock-based products such as cheese, pork, and other meats. Denmark's reliance on export trade has meant that its economy has been sensitive to fluctuations in world demand, although its generous **welfare state** policies since the 1960s have cushioned the population from suffering much from this volatility. Because of its geographic location, Denmark is an important distribution

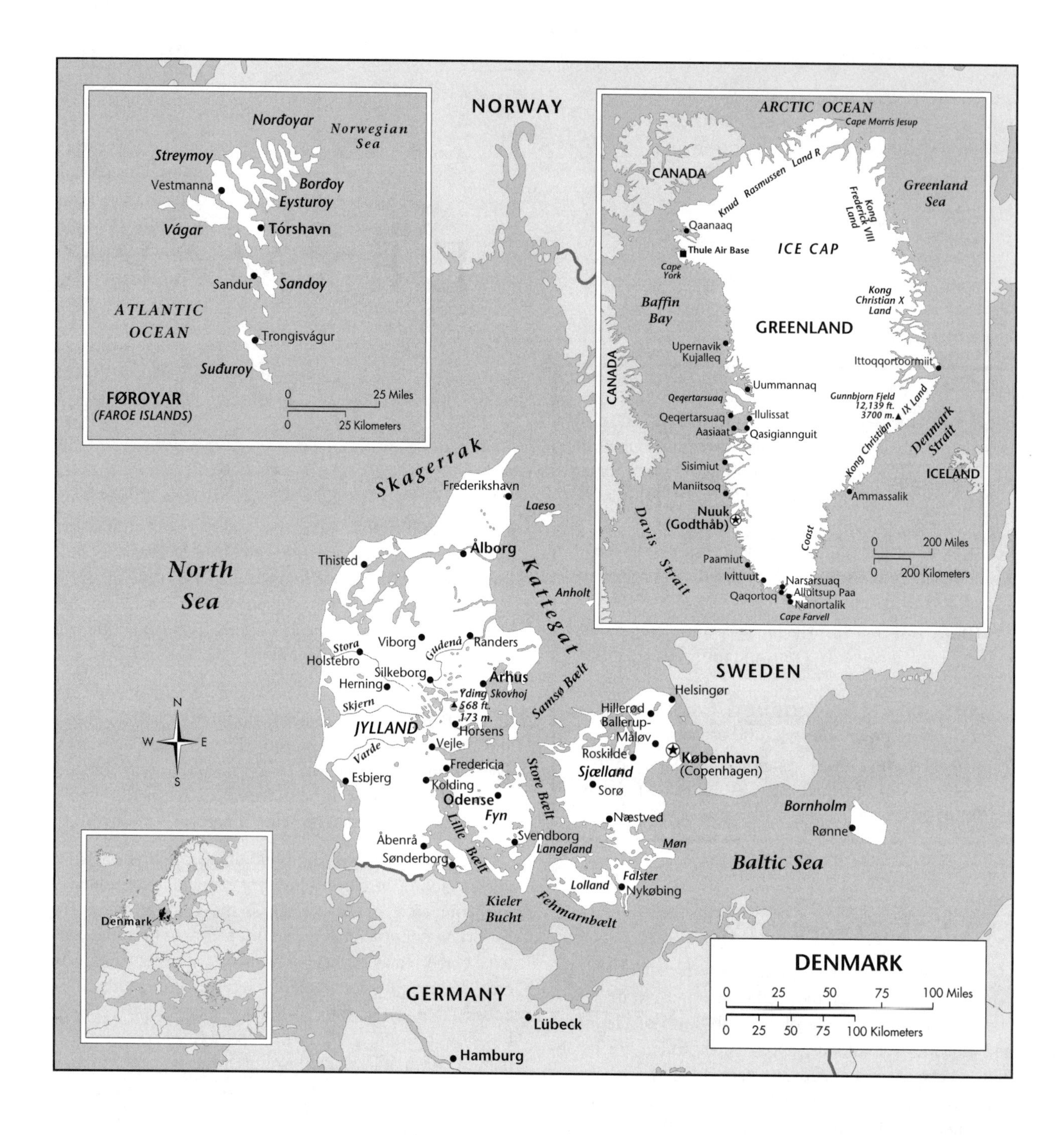

point for Eastern Europe, Scandinavia, England, and the rest of Europe.

Denmark's high-tech agricultural sector is the latest development in a long history of Danish farming. Before the late 1800s, Denmark's chief agricultural products were grains, but at the end of the 1800s an influx of cheap grains from the Americas and Russia caused prices to plummet. Danish farmers, supported by the government and the Folk High School Movement (a cultural and educational movement that encouraged knowledge-sharing, adult education, and agricultural research and reform, especially in rural areas), switched to livestock production, feeding their animals on the cheap grain. Danes developed an industry making processing machinery for its agricultural products. By the 1960s, industry had overtaken agriculture as the largest sector of the economy.

From the 1960s to the 1980s, the Danish economy followed a fairly regular cycle: increases in wages and benefits raised costs for firms, which led to price hikes and thus less ability to compete in foreign markets. This upset Denmark's **balance of trade**, as the high wages raised demands for imports, so the government would attempt to control rising consumption, usually by tightening credit and imposing a new tax. The 1970s and 1980s saw labor, political, and economic troubles as the government attempted to impose austerity measures such as harsh savings programs. Strong public opposition (including labor strikes) to various plans led to the repeated dissolution of the ruling coalition governments. After 1973, rising oil prices and the international **recession** led to high unemployment and low domestic demand.

External debt stayed high during the 1980s, consisting mainly of bonds bought by outside investors that required interest payments by the government. However, the extent of debt was not enough to discourage foreign investors, thus Danish business did not have to worry about financing drying up. While Denmark's balance of trade was positive from 1990 to 1997, that surplus was used to pay off the debt, which gradually fell from over 40 percent of GDP in 1990 to 24 percent in 1997. The **budget deficit** was not eliminated until the mid-1990s, but since then government has generally run a small surplus.

Businesses in Denmark are mainly small- and medium-sized. Over 75 percent of Danish industrial companies employ fewer than 75 people. Most farms are family-owned, a tradition that was partly supported by a law prohibiting public companies from owning farms. This prohibition was lifted in 1989. The increasing accessibility to consumers in Europe has begun to encourage Danish businesses to look at ways to supply these consumers on a larger scale, including the possibility of merging small companies together into larger ones, as well as developing networks of coordination and communication between several companies.

Across most of the political spectrum, Danes are committed to ensuring a basic level of economic equality, which has been the impetus behind the creation and maintenance of a large and generous welfare, social security, national health care, and education system. The **public sector** in 1999 employed close to 800,000 people, over 25 percent of the **labor force**. Since the 1960s, the public sector has ensured that despite economic fluctuations, everyone in Denmark has completely free access to health care and education, as well as unemployment benefits, sick leave, parental leave, and housing and childcare **subsidies**. Although unemployment has been one of Denmark's most persistent problems, in the new century it has fallen remarkably, to a current low of just under 6 percent.

In 2000, Denmark opted out of the final stage of the European Monetary Union (EMU), choosing to keep their own currency rather than join the euro. However, as the krone is closely tied with the euro, the Danish economy is not autonomous. Arguments against the EMU in Denmark mainly accentuate the need to retain political autonomy. These opponents stress that integration into the EMU could result in a threat to Denmark's commitment to economic equality and the environment, especially if Danish businesses were required to compete with those based in countries which do not require them to comply with similar environmental or labor regulations.

POLITICS, GOVERNMENT, AND TAXATION

Queen Margarethe II is officially the head of state, but actual power resides in the prime minister and his or her cabinet (called "the government" in Denmark and virtually all other parliamentary systems, and similar to a U.S. "administration") and the Folketing (the parliament). The Queen formally appoints the prime minister and the cabinet, but this appointment is always the result of behind-the-scenes maneuvering and coalition-building after a general election. The prime minister is accountable to the Folketing for his or her actions. Most ministers have their own ministries, (such as the Ministry of Finance or the Ministry of the Environment), but some individual ministers may be selected without being assigned to a specific ministry. Legislation is created cooperatively by the Folketing and the government. Proposals for laws are considered twice in the Folketing, and if approved, must then be approved by the Queen and the government. The Queen is not independent from the government in approving legislation, but rather acts under its advice.

The Folketing has 179 seats; members are elected by **proportional representation** (voters elect parties rather than individuals, that receive a number of seats in the legislature proportional to the percentage of votes received). This system encourages the proliferation of political parties that may form coalitions not only to form governments, but to pass legislation in the Folketing. The prime minister can call an election at any time in the hopes of gaining more seats for the ruling coalition. And as in virtually all parliamentary systems, new elections may be called if there is a vote of no confidence in the Folketing, although this has not happened since 1909. The minimum level of popular support necessary for a party to be represented in the Folketing is 2 percent (corresponding to 3 or 4 seats), and 2 seats each are reserved for representatives from the Faroe Islands and Greenland.

Like much of Scandinavia, Denmark has a good record on women's representation in government and politics at both the local and national levels. In the government in the year 2000, 35 percent of cabinet ministers were women, as were 37 percent of the Folketing (compared with the United States in 2000, where women were 41.4 percent of the cabinet but only 12 percent of Congress).

Since 1973, there have been 10 major political parties. Underlying all but the most extreme right wing of the parties is the Nordic emphasis on the importance of economic equality, ensured by strong social welfare programs. The issue of whether or how to join the European Community has been important to all the parties over the past 20 years, but does not divide them according to traditional "right-left" alignments.

The parties in the government in 2001 were elected in March 1998. The ruling coalition is comprised of the Social Democratic Party (65 seats), the Socialist People's Party (13 seats), the Radical Liberal Party (7 seats), and the Unity Party (5 seats); in the opposition are the Liberal Party (43 seats), the Conservative Party (17 seats), the Danish People's Party (13 seats), the Center Democratic Party (8 seats), the Christian People's Party (4 seats), and the Progress Party (4 seats).

The Social Democrats and Socialist People's Party do not wish Denmark to rely solely on market forces to organize the economy, and place a priority on equalizing income distribution and living standards. Trade unions are especially associated with the Social Democrats. The Radical Liberals (Det Radikale Venstre) are to the right of Social Democrats, and want to curb public spending, lower **income tax** rates for high earners, and reduce benefits for the unemployed. The Unity Party or Unity List is an alliance of far-leftist and environmental groups, to the left of the Social Democrats.

The Conservative Party (CP) has been generally gaining in popularity since the mid-1970s, although its peak was in the 1980s. Representing especially the interests of business and property owners, the Conservatives emphasize the rights of ownership while trying to reduce power of trade unions. While still supporting a welfare state, the CP wants to limit public spending on social programs, but increase spending on defense. The CP is fairly pro-European integration. The Liberal Party (Venstre) is close to but more extreme than the conservatives in wishing to reduce government spending and power, and are strongly pro-European integration. The Danish People's Party (DPP) is a nationalist party for ethnic Danes, against **immigration** and suspicious of refugees. They are strongly anti-European integration, although they support free trade and market-based agricultural policy. The DPP are for social welfare programs, but only for Danish citizens, and also support abolishing or greatly reducing property, inheritance, and other taxes. The Center Democratic Party wants fewer taxes, especially for individuals. They do support social welfare programs and are also pro-Europe. The Christian People's Party (CPP) was formed in response to the late-1960s legalization of abortion laws and lessening of restrictions on pornography, both of which they oppose. They want to decentralize political decisions, avoid special interests, and emphasize protecting the environment and quality of life. They have historically had a small share of popular vote, usually just above the 2 percent threshold required for representation in the Folketing. The Progress Party (PP) was founded in 1990, an extreme right-wing party with a reputation for unruliness. Their main platform is to abolish income taxes and greatly reduce government spending, and to restrict immigration. Against joining the European Union, their arguments often alienate more tolerant Danes, while some of their leaders and members have espoused more explicitly racist attitudes. Many of the other parties are reluctant to form a coalition with them.

In 1997, the public sector employed around a quarter of the workforce, and provided health care, welfare, social security, education, and administration of the government. Government-owned businesses are also still important to the economy, although there has been increasing **privatization** in recent years. Recently privatized businesses include a life insurance company (now totally private), the national telecommunications company TeleDanmark (totally private), Copenhagen Airport (now 49 percent private), and the computer services company Datacentralen, 75 percent of which was sold to the U.S.-based Computer Sciences Corp. The large Postal Service and Danish State Railroads companies have also been turned into private companies, although the government actually owns these firms. Some other public services such as sanitation, cleaning, and catering to public institutions are also being privatized.

The **value-added tax** (VAT) is the main source of government revenue, accounting for over one-quarter of total revenue in 1998. At 25 percent, it is one of the highest VAT rates in the world. Income tax is also high. In 1999, the marginal income tax rate was 40 percent for taxable incomes up to $21,500, while the highest bracket was about 60 percent for taxable incomes of more than $37,000. In 2001, 40 percent of all Danes in full-time employment were in the highest tax bracket. The Danish government, fearing an economic slowdown, is beginning to shift its tax burden somewhat away from individual incomes. "Green taxes" on pollution and to enforce environmental regulations are expected to make up some of the difference, and are already generating significant revenues; in 1995 over 8 percent of tax revenue came from environmentally-related taxes (over 2 percent of GDP). In the same year in the United States, only 4 percent of tax revenues came from environmentally-related taxes (less than 1 percent of GDP).

Even though most Danes must give almost half of their salaries to the government as income tax, they get most of it back in the form of free, high-quality health care, education, and **transfer payments**. For example, in 1996, 47 percent of the DKr386 billion collected by the national government was returned to the public in the form of transfer payments such as unemployment and sickness benefits, old-age pensions and housing subsidies. Some 60 percent of all government revenues from taxes in 1996 were spent on the health service, while transfer payments accounted for 40 percent of total public revenues (22 percent of GDP).

At 32 percent, corporate taxes are high. Denmark plans to reduce them to 26 percent by 2002. However, contrary to many economists' predictions, Denmark's high corporate tax rate has not discouraged foreign investment. In a surprising situation that suggests that there must be multiple reasons why foreign companies choose to invest, Denmark in 1997 showed an increase in foreign investment that was an amazing 308 percent—almost 10 times that of the European Union as a whole.

The Danish currency is pegged in a **fixed exchange rate** with the euro, so interest rates nearly always follow the European Central Bank. This relationship changed slightly after the referendum in 2000 when the Danes narrowly voted to reject the last stage of the EMU and keep their own separate currency. After the referendum, the Danish national bank raised its interest rates, which encouraged people to borrow less (since interest on loans was higher), and thus reduced the amount of money in circulation. As money became scarcer, its value increased, and the bank prevented the krone from **devaluation**. However, the krone has never been allowed to fluctuate beyond the level allowed by the **exchange rate mechanism** (ERM).

Denmark was the first country to establish a Ministry for the Environment, in 1972. Danes spend more per capita on environmental protection than most nations in the world. This has also inspired the development of a local industry of pollution control equipment, which is now a significant international force. This environmental focus has also affected the Danes' relation to European integration. Many have feared that joining the European Union (EU) would require them to lower their standards of environmental protection in order to remain in line with the other EU nations. Other than environmental protection laws, there are few regulatory controls on the economy.

INFRASTRUCTURE, POWER, AND COMMUNICATIONS

Denmark has a thoroughly modern and extensive **infrastructure**. Its numerous islands have encouraged the development of a network of ferry services in domestic waters with 415 kilometers (258 miles) of waterways. A well-maintained road and rail network includes 71,437 kilometers (44,388 miles) of highways (including 843 kilometers, or 524 miles, of expressways), and 2,859 kilometers (1,773 miles) of railways which serve almost every town. Some 508 kilometers (316 miles) of the railways are privately owned, while the rest are owned by the state.

In cities, environmental concerns have encouraged bicycle riding for all. Urban traffic is minimized by legislation requiring nearly all new shops be built within the existing commercial centers of cities, towns, and villages. Additionally, most new workplaces are required to be a short walking distance from a transit stop. Shops, offices, and factories must make accommodations for bicyclists and pedestrians. As a result, in 1998 less than one-third of travel within cities was via cars and trucks, and motorized traffic in the city centers had increased very little over the past 25 years.

As of 1999, Denmark had one of the world's highest density air networks, with 28 paved-runway and 90 unpaved-runway airports. Air service for Denmark, Norway, and Sweden is provided by Scandinavian Airlines Systems (SAS). Copenhagen Airport was voted "World's Best Airport of 2000" by the International Air Transport Organization, the same year that also saw the completion of the 7.8-kilometer Øresund bridge linking Denmark with Sweden.

Danes consumed 33.03 billion kilowatt-hours (kWh) of electricity in 1998, importing 2.68 billion kWh, and exporting 7.1 billion kWh. Most of the imported fuel is coal, which in 1998 amounted to 6.3 million tons. Denmark is shifting further away from coal use, as the 1998

Communications

Country	Newspapers	Radios	TV Sets[a]	Cable subscribers[a]	Mobile Phones[a]	Fax Machines[a]	Personal Computers[a]	Internet Hosts[b]	Internet Users[b]
	1996	1997	1998	1998	1998	1998	1998	1999	1999
Denmark	309	1,141	585	248.4	364	N/A	377.4	540.30	1,500
United States	215	2,146	847	244.3	256	78.4	458.6	1,508.77	74,100
Germany	311	948	580	214.5	170	73.1	304.7	173.96	14,400
Norway	588	915	579	160.1	474	50.0	373.4	754.15	2,000

[a]Data are from International Telecommunication Union, *World Telecommunication Development Report 1999* and are per 1,000 people.

[b]Data are from the Internet Software Consortium (http://www.isc.org) and are per 10,000 people.

SOURCE: World Bank. *World Development Indicators 2000.*

figure is 60 percent lower than it was just 2 years earlier. Since the discovery of oil and natural gas reserves in the 1960s, Denmark was self-sufficient in oil production by the 1980s. In 1998 oil production was 238.35 million barrels per day (bpd) with exports of 8.98 million bpd, while natural gas production was 267.68 billion cubic feet (bcf), and exports were 95.35 bcf. The state owns significant shares in both oil and natural gas extraction, although the giant Maersk/A.P. Møller Corporation is also a dominant figure. Overall, in 1998 Denmark generated 4.27 billion kWh of electricity. Fossil fuel from its own reserves accounted for 90.8 percent of this electricity, hydroelectric power for 0.07 percent, and the remaining 9.13 percent was generated by other means, including wind power. Denmark has, since 1980, banned nuclear power, and focuses much research and development on conservation and alternative energy sources.

Denmark has an excellent telecommunications system based on 3.20 million telephone lines (1995). Cellular phone ownership increased by 304 percent from 1993 to 1997, and in 1999, such telephones were owned by 49 percent of the population, including nearly every person between ages 17–25. Cell phone ownership per capita in 1997 was 190 per 1,000, as compared to the U.S. figure of 128 per 1,000. Denmark's burgeoning IT services industry is supported by high Internet connectivity; 90 percent of all businesses use some aspect of the Internet. The Danish government has strongly supported the development of personal as well as business Internet use. In January of 2001, the prime minister announced that the government intends to provide all households in Denmark with access to the Internet, while at that time nearly 50 percent of all households with a computer were already connected.

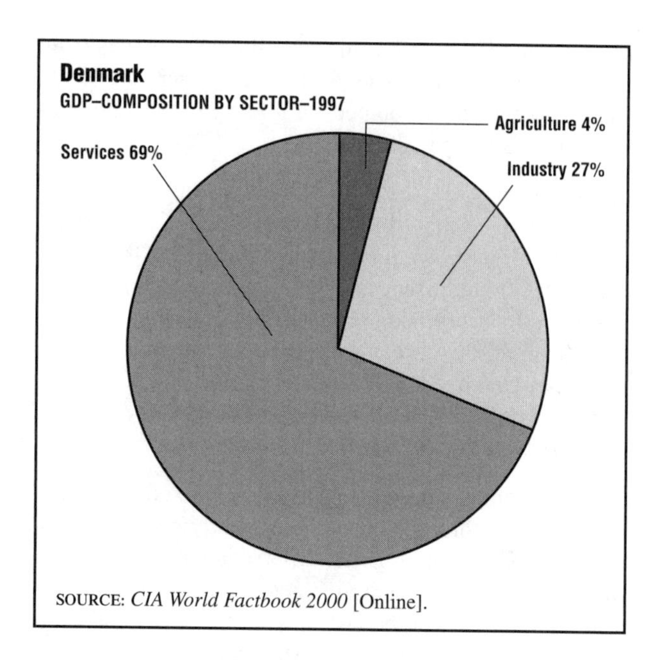

SOURCE: *CIA World Factbook 2000* [Online].

ECONOMIC SECTORS

In modern Denmark, the economic sectors of agriculture and industry are so closely linked that it is difficult to separate their influences. Both food and wood-based industries such as paper depend heavily on agriculture for raw materials while using sophisticated technology to process them. In addition, agricultural production itself is quite technologically advanced. The agricultural sector's highly technical nature means that its great productivity is generated by a small fraction of the total workforce—4 percent in 2000. In contrast, well over two-thirds of the workforce was employed in the service sector in the same year.

Agriculture in Denmark also includes forestry and fishing. The agricultural industry was Denmark's first engine of growth, especially its livestock production and forestry industry. Agriculture's economic influence relative to other sectors has basically been declining; by the 1960s, industry had surpassed it in terms of employment and percentage of GDP, and by 2000 agriculture made up 3 percent of GDP. Despite the small size of Denmark's agricultural sector today, it is comparatively highly productive, accounting for around 15 percent of exports in 1999. In 1998, Denmark was the world's seventh-largest producer of pork, while the Danish fishing industry was the second-largest in Europe.

The lack of raw materials other than agriculture (until the discovery of oil and natural gas in the 1960s), meant Denmark's industries developed as secondary production and processing concerns, usually specializing in

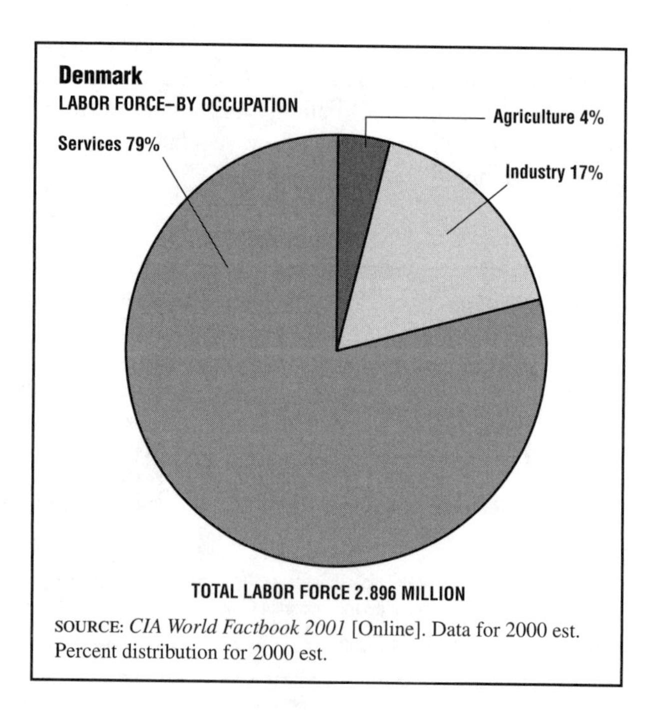

SOURCE: *CIA World Factbook 2001* [Online]. Data for 2000 est. Percent distribution for 2000 est.

narrowly-defined fields. This has led to the predominance of small- or medium-sized firms making niche products, often with a high-tech or design focus. For example, in a small design-oriented field such as furniture making, Denmark excels—in 1998 accounting for 20 percent of furniture exports by EU countries. The complexity and versatility of this organization of the industry has somewhat sheltered the Danish manufacturing industry from fluctuations in the world market. Alongside food processing and agro-industry, chemicals and engineering are important industries, and electronics are increasing in significance. Denmark's position in the North Sea has led to the development of a strong shipbuilding sector—it is currently the world's third-largest shipbuilder after Japan. The general trend in the manufacturing industry is that work- and material-intensive industries such as food processing, textiles, and metals decline or stagnate, while knowledge- and technology-based industries such as chemicals, electronics, and engineering have been expanding. Industry contributed about one-quarter of GDP in 2000. The sophisticated technology of much of Denmark's industrial sector has meant that high or increasing productivity does not always correspond with high or increasing employment. Over the past decade, the percentage of the workforce employed in manufacturing has remained fairly constant at around 25 percent.

In 2000, Denmark's services sector contributed more than two-thirds of GDP. Private services accounted for around two-thirds of productivity, and public services the remaining one-third. However, many private services are in fact subcontracted to public institutions. The majority of public services are in health, welfare, and administration. In the service sector as a whole, business services and wholesale/**retail** trade accounted for the most productivity growth. Wholesale and retail trade is the largest employer in private services, in 1997 accounting for a little over half of service sector employment. Between 1992 and 1998, the service sector saw a 12 percent increase in employment. Public services have consistently accounted for nearly one-third of employment in services (mostly in health and education) over the past decade, while telecommunications and business services have slowly increased their share of employment.

AGRICULTURE

Denmark is the only country in the Baltic region with a net export of agricultural products, producing 3 times the amount of food it needs for itself. A good percentage of arable land and moderate climate has been conducive to agriculture, but the sector's extremely advanced technology and infrastructure are what have made it so productive in recent years. Although agriculture's role in the Danish economy has steadily decreased as industrialization and economic development has progressed, it is still essential as a source of foreign currency, a direct and indirect source of jobs, and as a supply of everyday foodstuffs.

The increasing mechanization of agriculture, combined with changes in farm management and organization, plus the draw of industrial employment in the cities, has meant fewer people are required to farm ever-increasing quantities of land. Farm sizes have increased, and the number of individual farms has dropped dramatically since the 1950s. From the 1970s into the 1990s, 2,600 individual holdings disappeared every year, absorbed into larger farms. In the first half of the 20th century Denmark had around 200,000 individual farms, averaging 16 hectares in size; by 1997, there were about 60,900 farms averaging 43.6 hectares. Family-run farms are still dominant in Denmark, where even in 1997, some 91 percent of farms were family-owned and run, 7 percent company-owned, and the rest owned by the state, local authorities, and foundations. Along with increasing farm size, the typical farmer has to an increasing extent concentrated on one sole branch of farming, and specialization in animal production has led to fewer types, but larger numbers, of livestock.

In 1996, primary forestry occupied approximately 3,000 employees, while forestry formed the basis for most of the work for around 34,000 employees in the wood manufacturing industry. Denmark is Europe's primary supplier of Christmas trees. Profits from forestry have historically been invested both in modernization of the industry and in investment in other industries. The state is the largest owner of forests, with one-third of forested land under its control. The rest is owned by a multitude of private companies, individuals, and institutions.

In the early 1990s, Denmark was among the top 10 to 15 fishing nations in the world, catching 1.6 million tons in 1993. Industrial fishing (catching fish for industrial use, i.e. producing fish meal and fish oil) has been the most important branch of fishing with a total catch in 1993 of 1.2 million tons. In 1993, the export value of the fishing industry was around DKr10 billion, corresponding to some 4 to 5 percent of Denmark's total exports.

Environmental legislation has been on the increase in the past decade, some of which has directly affected productivity. For example, the greater emphasis on forests and parks has meant that some land had to be turned away from farming use. New restrictions on waste disposal and contamination have also forced some farmers to limit or end production.

INDUSTRY

MANUFACTURING. In 1996, 45 percent of the manufacturing industry's total production went to export, corresponding to 75 percent of total exports. Mechanical engineering production, especially of electronic goods, was an increasing proportion of the sector's value, and also created some 12,400 new jobs between 1980 and 1996. Nearly all Danish electronics production is exported, including products such as measuring instruments, microphones, equipment for tele- and radio communication, computer networks, power units, engine controls, and hearing aids. Food, drink, and tobacco production/processing, by contrast, has declined between 1993 and 1997 from around 30 percent to around 25 percent of production in manufacturing. The Carlsberg beer company is the most significant producer of beverages, in 1998 having a **turnover** of DKr29.3 billion and employing 20,500 workers. The largest employers in manufacturing are the makers of metal products, machinery, and equipment; the food-processing industry (bacon factories, dairies, corn mills, and breweries); the paper and graphic industries; and manufacturers of transport equipment, especially shipbuilding. A significant percentage of workers are also employed making wood and wood products.

CHEMICALS. The chemical industry has also grown through the last decade, and in 1999 accounted for 24 percent of all chemical production in the EU. Denmark, in 1996, was the world's second-largest per capita exporter of pharmaceuticals, with exports valued at almost DKr15 billion. Novo Nordisk, despite its status as one of the largest chemical companies, is still in many ways typical of Danish industrial style: a high-tech, highly-specialized firm, investing heavily in research (in this case on insulin, hormones, and enzymes), exporting 98 percent of its products.

ELECTRICITY, COAL, GAS, AND OIL. Denmark is the third-largest oil producer in Western Europe, in 1998 producing 233.35 million barrels per day (bpd) of petroleum, while in the same year natural gas reserves produced 267.69 billion cubic feet (bcf) per year. Natural gas exports at that time were over 95 bcf per year, primarily to Sweden and Germany. Danish oil and gas production in 1998 was worth just over DKr30 million. In 1999, the energy and water industries together employed 17,000 people. Maersk/A.P. Møller, the largest company (of any kind) in Denmark, is heavily involved in oil production, although it began as a shipping concern. Statoil (owned by the state of Norway), and the American-based multinational Amerada Hess are the other significant operators in this industry. At the end of the century, Denmark was still opening up new areas of the North Sea for exploration, and it is possible that new reserves will be discovered. The government retains its shares in some oil industries, and licenses the right to explore and extract.

CONSTRUCTION. The construction industry illustrates the trend of a decline in work-intensive manufacturing. Devastated in the 1970s and 1980s by a severe fall in house building, production, and employment in this construction fell considerably and stayed low through the late 1990s. The value of construction products fell from 12 percent of GDP in 1972 to 6 percent in 1996. Over that time, employment fell by 43,000. The building and construction industry is mainly made up of small companies in which independent (paid) and assisting (unpaid) spouses constitute a relatively large proportion of those employed. The rapid decline in this sector in Denmark has in the first half of the 1990s led to the industry being more export-oriented, partly through Danish firms increasing activity in Germany. Construction has shifted somewhat from mainly making new buildings (which had accounted for 47 percent of its work in 1970) to a greater focus on repairs and maintenance, which grew from 23 percent in 1970 to 38 percent of construction work in 1999. New building construction in that time frame fell to 32 percent.

SERVICES

TOURISM. In 1997, 2.2 million tourist arrivals in Denmark were recorded (a 4 percent increase from 1993). In 1999, tourism generated around DKr44 billion in revenues, an increase of 1 million from the year before. This made it the third-largest sector after industry and agriculture. The attractions most visited by tourists are Tivoli Gardens (Copenhagen), Lego Land (Billund), Hans Christian Andersen's House and Museum (Odense), and the Viking Ship Museum (Roskilde). Old manor houses and castles are also popular destinations, while Copenhagen harbor was in 2000 one of the most popular stops on European cruises.

Tourism employed over 70,000 (1999) people full-time in the facilities described above, as well as 650 hotels, 30 inns, 525 registered campsites, and over 100 youth hostels. In 1998, the Danish Ministry of Business and Industry, SAS, the Danish Tourist Council, and other tourism interest groups joined forces with local authorities to promote Denmark as a tourist destination for businesspeople and wealthy weekend tourists from the United States, Germany, Southern Europe, Sweden, and Russia. The 3-year international marketing project was estimated to cost a total of US$7.7 million, of which SAS was to pay US$4 million, the Ministry of Business and Industry US$1.3 million, and the rest will come from various municipalities.

WHOLESALE AND RETAIL TRADE. Employment in the service sector is dominated by the wholesale and retail trades, with 441,000 people in 1998. However, employment has declined since the 1970s, as the sector has seen considerable **vertical integration** (an overall integration of retail, wholesale, and in certain cases production sectors). Moreover, 1980s-era mergers within the sector (horizontal integration) have marked both areas, leaving wholesale and retail highly concentrated (with a few firms dominating the market). In 1995, 4 percent of firms accounted for about 75 percent of the total turnover. In 1998, there were 8 wholesalers operating domestically, the largest 2 of which were Maersk and the cooperative FDB, which together accounted for 61 percent of the market in 1998. Total transactions in 1998 amounted to US$10.7 billion. In retail, even though a few large players dominate the industry as a whole, there are still a large number of small shops; 3 out of 4 retail shops are one-person businesses, while the remainder are mainly small companies or cooperatives.

TELECOMMUNICATIONS. Growth in postal and telecommunications services was larger than any other business sector; from 1992 to 1998 productivity grew by 44 percent. **Deregulation** of the industry, beginning in 1986, paired with strong research and development supported by the government allowed firms to take advantage of new technologies. However, technological advances have meant that growth was not accompanied by much of a rise in employment, which in 1996 was 45,000 people, the same as in 1986. The major telecommunications companies are at least partly-owned by foreign companies. TeleDanmark, in which Ameritech (U.S.) owns a controlling interest, and Sonofon cellphones, almost half of which is owned by Bellsouth (U.S.), together account for over 75 percent of the market.

FINANCIAL SERVICES. Between 1989 and 1996 there was a one-third decline in the number of domestic bank and financial institution branches. This was mainly due to Denmark's banks being burdened by a number of bad debts in the early 1990s. Since 1994, the improvement in both Denmark's economy and the banks' lending policies has contributed to more stability in the industry, along with a number of consolidations among the country's banks. The reduction of branches of institutions coincided with a 14 percent decline in the number of employees over the same 7 years. In 1998, Denmark had 95 banks with assets of US$216 billion, while total assets of the 5 largest banks totaled US$179 billion, over 80 percent of total banking sector assets. The 2 largest banks, Den Danske Bank and Unidanmark-Gruppen, also operate as financial "supermarkets" offering a wide range of financial services, and account for 50 percent of the financial service market. Danish banks are technologically sophisticated, and have invested heavily in computers and the development of electronic transfer systems, in 1998 adopting one of the first nationwide electronic payment card systems (Dankort). Employment in business services has been increasing throughout the last decade; by 1999, 326,000 people worked in the financial services sector, with Den Danske bank employing 11,409 people, and Unidanmark-gruppen employing 9,960.

TRANSPORTATION. Road transport, both trucking/hauling and personal transport such as taxi services, dominates the domestic transportation sector. Road transport in 1996 generated just under half of the total revenues from the transport sector, while the remaining value was divided among other types of the transport: shipping (16 percent), railways (11 percent), and aviation (7 percent). The transport sector created around 9 percent of Denmark's GDP and 7 percent of total employment in 1996. Activity in the sector as a whole has risen steadily and at a faster rate than overall productivity since the 1980s. Production value in the sector rose by 74 percent between 1986–1996. In 2000, over half of Danish international trade was by road, and most of the remainder by sea. Denmark's increasing expertise in making high-tech liner and tanker ships has helped the shipping sector in recent years. Shipping accounts for most of Denmark's international freight traffic, and the country's almost 600-vessel merchant fleet is the fourth-largest in the European Union. Denmark's Maersk shipping line bought the U.S.-based Sea-Land Services in 1999 to become the largest container shipping line in the world.

INTERNATIONAL TRADE

Denmark is one of the most trade-oriented economies in the world. As a base for exporting, Denmark has many advantages. Its key location as the only Scandinavian country connected to mainland Europe, plus its position on the Baltic sea, gives it access to lucrative markets for both EU and non-EU countries. Its extensive infrastructure and well-educated, high-skilled workforce also help promote trade and foreign investment.

Germany is currently Denmark's most important export destination, followed by Sweden and the United Kingdom. Exports to these 3 countries totaled 41.7 percent of Danish exports in 1997. The United States is the largest trading partner outside the EU, and accounted for almost 5 percent of Denmark's total trade value in 1997. Over one-third of Danish industrial exports are machines and instruments, while pharmaceuticals, energy (especially oil), meat, and meat products make up the rest.

Trade (expressed in billions of US$): Denmark

	Exports	Imports
1975	8.712	10.368
1980	16.749	19.340
1985	17.090	18.245
1990	35.133	32.228
1995	49.036	43.223
1998	47.070	44.994

SOURCE: International Monetary Fund. *International Financial Statistics Yearbook 1999.*

Denmark's main imports are raw materials and unfinished products that are used in its own industrial sector. In 1997, imports for the industrial sector were about 70 percent of total imports, while the rest were consumer products, including cars. Of the services imported, computer software and management consulting are very important. Imports from Germany, Sweden, and the UK account for 42 percent of total imports.

The early 1990s were a difficult time for Danish international trade as its 3 most important markets—Germany, the UK, and Scandinavia—were all performing sluggishly. More recently trade has increased, especially due to a depreciation of the Danish krone. The krone is expected to remain stable through the next few years, which may reduce the growth in exports. However, Denmark is currently exporting more than it imports in all 3 sectors: industry, agriculture, and services.

MONEY

Since the 1980s, Denmark has pursued a fixed exchange rate linked to the German mark. On 1 January 1999, **monetary policy** was linked to the new European Central Bank. In September 2000, Denmark opted out of the European Monetary Union's (EMU) third phase (establishment of a joint EU currency and relinquishment of jurisdiction over monetary policy), although the country's economic performance exceeds the established criteria for membership. This was due to resistance on the right, especially from nationalist groups who wish to retain the Danish currency and not tie its economy so closely to that of Europe, and equal resistance on the left, where many fear that equalizing human rights and environmental regulations with the EU will chip away at the Danish welfare state and its environmentally-conscious business practices.

The National Bank of Denmark (Danmarks Nationalbanken) is the only **bank of issue** in the country and enjoys a special status as a self-governing institution under government supervision. Profits in the National Bank revert to the state treasury. Although Denmark has retained its own currency, separate from the EU, its currency is so closely tied to the euro that monetary policy often closely follows the European Central Bank. The National Bank lends to smaller banks and to the central government, and is responsible for administration of the foreign exchange policy.

The Copenhagen Stock Exchange (CSE) was established in the capital in 1861, and in 1999 had 233 listed companies. At the end of 1999 its **market capitalization** was US$105.29 billion. The CSE was a pioneer in computerized trading, being the first in the world to introduce electronic bonds and shares.

POVERTY AND WEALTH

The **Gini Index** measures the level of income inequality in a country, with 100 equal to total inequality (basically one person receiving all the income), and 1 indicating total equality (everyone having exactly the same income).

Raija Julkunen, a lecturer on social policy at the University of Jyväskylä, describes the differing U.S. and Nordic attitudes towards the role of the state: "American culture conceives citizenship and welfare as diametrically opposed, as if state-ensured welfare did not go along with a free society. In the Nordic countries, on the other hand, the notion of a welfare state has a positive ring to it. Only social rights—guaranteed minimum income, employment, education, health care—make citizens free and equal." The Nordic approach has succeeded in that there is virtually no poverty in Denmark.

Denmark's extensive **social welfare system** has existed in its current form since the 1960s, but has roots in Danish culture back to the 1930s. Because of Danes' long-standing preoccupation with economic equality, there is less of a difference between Denmark's high-income and lowest-income citizens than in the United States or many other countries. People who work in restaurants or cleaning buildings have free access to the same quality of healthcare as those who are lawyers, professors, or accountants. They have paid holidays, mater-

Exchange rates: Denmark

Danish kroner (DKr) per US$1	
Jan 2001	7.951
2000	8.083
1999	6.976
1998	6.701
1997	6.604
1996	5.799

Note: The Danes rejected the Euro in a September 28, 2000 referendum.

SOURCE: CIA *World Factbook 2001* [ONLINE].

GDP per Capita (US$)

Country	1975	1980	1985	1990	1998
Denmark	22,984	25,695	29,332	31,143	37,449
United States	19,364	21,529	23,200	25,363	29,683
Germany	N/A	N/A	N/A	N/A	31,141
Norway	19,022	23,595	27,113	28,840	36,806

SOURCE: United Nations. *Human Development Report 2000; Trends in human development and per capita income.*

Distribution of Income or Consumption by Percentage Share: Denmark

Lowest 10%	3.6
Lowest 20%	9.6
Second 20%	14.9
Third 20%	18.3
Fourth 20%	22.7
Highest 20%	34.5
Highest 10%	20.5

Survey year: 1992
Note: This information refers to income shares by percentiles of the population and is ranked by per capita income.

SOURCE: *2000 World Development Indicators* [CD-ROM].

nity and paternity leave, sick leave, and unemployment benefits.

All families with children under 18 receive, irrespective of income, family allowances consisting of a regular, tax-free amount per child, with a higher rate for children under 7 years of age. Bread-winners who are single parents or **pensioners** can receive additional allowances per child. Families with children are entitled to free home help if the person who has the responsibility for the home and the children cannot manage it on account of, for instance, illness or confinement. Among other things, families living in rented accommodation can, depending on family income and the size of the rent, receive a housing benefit (in December 1998, there were 169,000 recipients).

According to sociologists Jens Hoff and Jorgen Goul Andersen in their article "The Danish Class Structure" in *Acta Sociologica* (1989), the concept of class is difficult to compare between countries with this kind of social system and countries such as the UK, the United States, or in less-developed countries. Class in Denmark is tied less to things like income and healthcare, and more to location, profession, and the kind of work engaged in, i.e. the amount of control over one's own responsibilities. Much of the Danish labor force works without much individual control over workplace decisions, without supervising others, and without much autonomy. This might make them working class by some definitions. However, these workers' quality of life is still very high by most standards, underscoring the impression that in Denmark, there is a lack of status distinctions between those who have high-skill or low-skill jobs.

One facet of the Danish welfare model has been the belief that benefits should not be tied to the kind of job one has, or whether someone is working or not. This approach has proven problematic as the country continually struggles with its unemployment rate—especially among the young. Critics argue that there is not enough incentive for people to choose to be employed rather than collect unemployment money. However, proposals of dramatic reductions in benefits are political suicide, as Danes are wary of what they might see as the sacrifice of a commitment to equality.

WORKING CONDITIONS

In 1999, the Danish workforce numbered 2.89 million, while the unemployment rate was 5.7 percent. The labor force is shrinking in Denmark. This is partly due to the aging of the population, as more workers retire than enter the workforce each year. High income taxes combined with generous unemployment assistance also may dissuade many, especially young workers, from entering the workforce. The government is currently attempting to **restructure** its taxation system to change this picture, shifting the burden of taxation away from individual income.

The standard working week is 37 hours, with a minimum of 5 weeks mandatory vacation. Three-quarters of those in employment have a 5-day work week, while those out sick may be paid up to 90 percent of their wage (with a maximum of DKr2,556 per week).

Danish laws guarantee the right of workers to organize and all (except civil servants and essential service

Household Consumption in PPP Terms

Country	All food	Clothing and footwear	Fuel and power[a]	Health care[b]	Education[b]	Transport & Communications	Other
Denmark	16	6	11	3	17	5	43
United States	13	9	9	4	6	8	51
Germany	14	6	7	2	10	7	53
Norway	16	7	11	5	4	6	51

Data represent percentage of consumption in PPP terms.
[a]Excludes energy used for transport.
[b]Includes government and private expenditures.

SOURCE: World Bank. *World Development Indicators 2000.*

workers) have the right to strike, as well as the right to bargain collectively. The government stands behind these rights, does not interfere with unions, and prohibits anti-union discrimination by employers. More than 75 percent of all wage earners are organized in trade unions, as are about the same percentage of salaried employees, and collective bargaining is very common. Strikes are also rather common; in 1997, 101,700 workdays were lost due to labor conflict.

Mothers get extensive maternity leave—4 weeks prior to the birth of a child, and up to 24 weeks after—while fathers get paternity leave of 2 weeks after the birth. From the fifteenth week after the birth the mother can transfer all or a portion of her remaining maternity leave to the father. A tax-free benefit (known as the "children's check") is paid to the parents of all children 7 to 18 years old regardless of the household income. Denmark's child-care system enables either or both parents to work outside the home. In 1994, 80.3 percent of 3 to 6 year-olds were in childcare, (compared to 57.4 percent 10 years earlier). Women who used to be expected to care for their own children no longer face the same demand; in Denmark women's rate of participation in the workforce is very high—in 1995 89 percent that of men. In the same year women's salaries were 88.1 percent of men's.

COUNTRY HISTORY AND ECONOMIC DEVELOPMENT

1871. Denmark's **socialist** movement is officially founded, the start of a strong and diverse socialist tradition influencing Danish politics in the years to come.

1901. Change of political system to a constitutional monarchy, creating the Government (body of ministers selected by the queen) and the Folketing (representatives elected by the people).

1914–18. Denmark remains neutral during World War I.

1915. Constitutional reform; women and servants are enfranchised.

1933. Social reform movement begins, expanding the welfare and education system.

1940. Denmark occupied by Germany during World War II.

1941. United States establishes military bases in Greenland (with Danish ambassador's approval).

1945. Denmark liberated from Germany at the end of World War II.

1948. Faroe Islands, until this time part of Denmark, are granted home rule, which allows them control over domestic policy.

1949. Denmark joins North Atlantic Treaty Organization (NATO), a strategic military alliance of Western European and North American non-**communist** nations.

1960. Denmark joins European Free Trade Agreement (EFTA), which reduces or eliminates barriers to trade (such as **tariffs**) between participants.

1967. Pornographic text and photography (excluding photos of children) is legalized, a sign of Denmark's progressive/permissive social attitudes; however, response to this and the stance on abortion leads to the founding of the Danish Christian People's Party.

1973. Compulsory National Health Insurance set up (replacing sickness benefits fund).

1973. Denmark joins the European Economic Community (EEC—an organization of states that lowered barriers to trade between them).

1976. Social Assistance Act introduces a unified structure of public assistance and benefits, partly needs-based.

1979. Greenland, formerly part of Denmark, is granted home rule.

1985. Greenland leaves EEC over fears of EEC regulations' effects on its fishing industry.

1985. Denmark joins the European Union.

2000. Danes reject final stage of European Monetary Union (EMU) in a referendum.

FUTURE TRENDS

Danish manufacturing remains a strong base for growth, especially as research and development help support its further extension into high-tech industry. The Danish government's support for the growing use of Internet services for both businesses and individuals bodes well for Danish flexibility and responsiveness to global market trends. Public investment in education, particularly in relation to computers and computing, also supports prospects for growing computer-related services.

Unemployment has been reduced for the present, but the main mechanism was to shrink the size of the workforce through early-retirement plans and state-funded sabbaticals. A smaller workforce drives wages up, raising production costs for many Danish businesses, which makes them less competitive internationally. This has affected Denmark's **balance of payments**, which has even dipped into negative territory in recent years. It is not clear what effect this will have on the economy, but if the government can manage to strike a balance, keeping **inflation** and interest rates low without hurting industrial competitiveness, then a small deficit may be an acceptable price to pay.

Denmark's greatest challenge for the future is due to its aging population. Its welfare and social security system will be severely strained by the demands of the growing population of elderly people and the shrinking workforce and sources of tax revenues. If nothing is changed, Denmark will not be able to maintain the standard of benefits it currently grants to its citizens. As most Danes are fiercely supportive of state guarantees of a standard of living, any government attempting to reduce those guarantees faces hostility and resistance. The current government has made some changes in the labor market (reducing and altering some benefits and pensions), but it is unclear how much the public in the highly-unionized workforce will stand for reductions in benefits or wages. The governing coalition must tread carefully if it is to make changes without seeming to compromise its commitment to material equality.

In October of 2000, Danes voted not to join the last stage of the European Monetary Union, and to keep its own currency. Despite the urging of Prime Minister Poul Rasmussen, the Danish public did not support the euro. However, the krone is still closely tied to the euro, and Denmark's economic decisions, particularly monetary ones, will be heavily influenced by the EU. Resistance to the EMU has been made more on political grounds than economic ones. There is some fear that opting out of the EMU will hurt prospects for foreign investment, which in the previous 5 years had increased dramatically in Denmark. The current government has demonstrated its friendliness to business by lowering corporate taxes and other business taxes, which may help to counteract any possible flight of investment. It is too soon to tell if either effect has come to pass.

DEPENDENCIES

GREENLAND. Greenland (local name Kalaallit Nunaat) is the world's largest island, with an area of 2,175,590 square kilometers (840,000 square miles), slightly more than 3 times the size of Texas. Only 15 percent of the island is not covered in ice. There are no crops or trees, but there are many plants and flowers, as well as seals, fish, and reindeer. The population in 1998 was 54,100 with high birth and death rates. Greenlanders (Inuit and what the *CIA World Factbook* calls "Greenland-born whites") form the majority with 87 percent of the population, and the rest are Danish and others. Languages spoken are Greenlandic (East Inuit), Danish, and English. The 56 towns and villages on the island are mostly small; 40 have fewer than 500 people, and only 3 have more than 4,000. The administrative capital is Godthåb, called Nuuk in Greenlandic, with around 12,100 people.

Greenland was first a Danish colony in the 1300s, when Norway and Denmark were united kingdoms. In World War II, when Germany occupied Denmark, the U.S. and Danish ambassador in Washington D.C. agreed that U.S. troops could be stationed in Greenland. Some U.S. air bases remain there even now. A referendum (a nation-wide vote on a particular issue) in 1979 gave Greenland "home rule." Denmark has jurisdiction over foreign policy, defense, and justice, and there is joint authority over its oil and mineral resources. Greenland has its own legislature.

The population depends on fishing, and some also hunt seals. There is a small amount of mining, but the harsh climate and lack of transportation infrastructure have prevented much development. Greenland's economy has not been strong in the past 10 years. Since 1990, imports have outpaced exports. Following the closure of Greenland's last lead and zinc mine in 1989, the fishing industry and grants from the Danish government became the mainstay of the economy. In 1999, grants from mainland Denmark and EU payments for the right to fish in Greenland's waters made up about 50 percent of the home-rule government's revenues. As the cod is threatened with extinction, shrimp fisheries have taken over as the most important income earner.

Greenland is also looking to tourism as a sector for growth; however, the season is quite short due to the long and harsh winters. The public sector—both publicly owned businesses and municipalities—plays a dominant role in Greenland's economy. Greenland joined the European Community together with Denmark but withdrew in February of 1985 (after a referendum in 1982) due to disagreement with the EC over fishing policy.

FAROE ISLANDS. The Faroe Islands (local name Foroyar) are north of the Shetlands and northwest of Scotland, between the Norwegian Sea and the North Atlantic Ocean. There are about 30 islands, 18 of which are inhabited, with a total 2000 population of 45,296. The total land area is 1,399 square kilometers (540 square miles). The population is mostly descended from Viking settlers who landed there in the 8th century. The local language is Faroese, descended from Old Norse, although Danish is also required in schools, and adults on the island can speak it. The capital of the Faroes is Torshavn.

The Faroes have been part of the Danish Kingdom since the 14th century, but were granted home rule in 1948, although the Danish government is still responsible for defense and other aspects of administration. Denmark's Folketing (Parliament) reserves 2 seats for representatives from the Faroes.

Despite their small and remote location, the Faroes have a good domestic and international communications infrastructure, with 22,000 main telephone lines—about one for every 2 people on the island. There is also a satellite earth station and a fiber-optic submarine cable that links the Islands to Iceland and Denmark. There are 14 radio stations and 7 television stations.

The mild winters, cool summers, and rocky terrain of the Faroes are unsuitable for agriculture, and in the past, sheep farming was very important to the economy. Nowadays fish and fish products are the center of the economy, with fish products comprising 90 percent of exports. Most other food is imported. This near-total dependence on fishing means the economy is very vulnerable, both to the changes in world demand and to environmental change. Even with the fishing industry, the Faroe Islands depend significantly on grants from Denmark. Without Danish government bailouts in 1992 and 1993, the Faroese economy would have gone bankrupt. The Faroes did not join the European Community (EC) when Denmark did, because of disagreement with EC fishing policies, which, the Faroese felt, put them at a disadvantage.

BIBLIOGRAPHY

"Actions Speak Louder." *FT.com: Financial Times Survey.* <http://specials.ft.com/ln/ftsurveys/country/sc8186.htm>. Accessed February 2001.

Christensen, Donna. *Information Technology in Denmark.* <http://www.american.edu/initeb/dc4053a/denmark.htm>. Accessed July 2001.

"Denmark." *Tradeport.* <http://www.tradeport.org/ts/countries/denmark>. Accessed February 2001.

"Denmark: The Smug Debtor." *Economist.* September 3, 1988.

"Economic Indicators: Spending on the Environment." *OECD Observer.* October 1999.

Economist Information Unit. *Country Report: Denmark.* London: EIU, November 2000.

Europa World Year Book 2000. 41st edition. London: Europa Publications, 2000.

Hoff, Jens, and Jorgen Goul Andersen. "The Danish Class Structure." *Acta Sociologica.* Vol. 32, No. 1, March 1989.

International Labor Organization. <http://www.ilo.org>. Accessed February 2001.

Miller, Kenneth E. *Denmark: A Troubled Welfare State.* Boulder, Colorado: Westview Press, 1991.

Royal Danish Embassy. <http://www.denmarkemb.org>. Accessed February 2001.

Royal Danish Ministry of Foreign Affairs. *Denmark.* <http://www.um.dk/english/danmark/danmarksbog/>. Accessed February 2001.

Statistics Denmark. <http://www.dst.dk/dst/dstframesetuk.asp>. Accessed February 2001.

United Nations Development Programme. *Human Development Report 2000.* New York: Oxford University Press, 2000.

U.S. Central Intelligence Agency. *World Factbook 2000.* <http://www.odci.gov/cia/publications/factbook/indexgeo.html>. Accessed February 2001.

Walljasper, Jay. "What Works? Denmark!" *The Nation.* Vol. 266, No. 3, January 26, 1998.

—Larisa Mann

ESTONIA

Republic of Estonia
Eesti Vabariik

CAPITAL: Tallinn.

MONETARY UNIT: Estonian kroon (EEK). One kroon equals 100 sents. There are bills of 1, 2, 5, 10, 25, 50, 100, and 500 krooni, and coins of 1 and 5 krooni and 5, 10, 20, and 50 senti. The EEK is pegged to the German mark at a rate of 8:1.

CHIEF EXPORTS: Manufactured goods, machinery and transport equipment, timber, chemicals, food.

CHIEF IMPORTS: Machinery and transport equipment, manufactured goods, chemicals, fuels and lubricants, food.

GROSS DOMESTIC PRODUCT: US$7.9 billion (purchasing power parity, 1999 est.).

BALANCE OF TRADE: **Exports:** US$2.5 billion (f.o.b., 1999). **Imports:** US$3.4 billion (f.o.b., 1999).

COUNTRY OVERVIEW

LOCATION AND SIZE. Located in northeastern Europe, bordering the Baltic Sea on the west, the Gulf of Finland on the north, Latvia on the south, and Russia on the east, Estonia has an area of 45,226 square kilometers (17,500 square miles), smaller than New Hampshire and Vermont combined. The capital, Tallinn, is situated on the Gulf of Finland; other major cities include Tartu, Parnu, and Narva. Estonia is the smallest of the Baltic countries (the others being Latvia and Lithuania) that emerged as independent republics when the Soviet Union dissolved in 1991.

POPULATION. The population of Estonia was estimated at 1.43 million in July 2000, with a density of 32 persons per square kilometer (82 per square mile), one of the lowest population densities in Europe. In 2000 the birth rate was 8.45 per 1,000 population, while the death rate was 13.55 per 1,000, giving Estonia a negative population growth rate of negative .59 percent. The government may introduce tax breaks for families with 3 or more children in 2001 in an attempt to increase the population growth rate. Estonia is relatively prosperous and has not experienced any massive **emigration**, yet its net migration rate was estimated at -0.79 migrants per 1,000 population in 2000. The population is also aging, with just 18 percent below the age of 14, and approximately 14 percent older than 65 years of age. The urban population makes up about 73 percent of the total.

Ethnic Estonians, ethnically and linguistically close to the Finns, make up 64 percent of the population, and ethnic Russians (living mostly in and around Narva) form 29 percent of the population. Other minorities include Ukrainians, Belarusians, and Finns.

Ethnic Russians made up only 4 percent of the population before the Soviet Union annexed Estonia in 1940, but Russians **immigrated** in large numbers during the Soviet period of industrialization. After Estonia restored its independence in 1991, only Russians (and their descendants) who had lived in the country before 1940 were granted Estonian citizenship. All others were subject to a citizenship exam testing Estonian language proficiency. Many did not speak Estonian, and by 1998 about 22 percent of the Estonian population was considered foreign (9 percent had Russian or other foreign passports and 13 percent were stateless). In 1998, under pressure from Russia and the European Union, the government eased the citizenship provisions and amended the language law.

OVERVIEW OF ECONOMY

Until World War II, Estonia was poor and mostly agricultural. Its industrial economy was shaped during the Soviet period (1940–91) with the **nationalization** of industry and the collectivization of agricultural land into large state-run farms. Soviet central planning stressed the development of heavy industries. Prior to restoring its independence from the Soviet Union in 1991, Estonia was

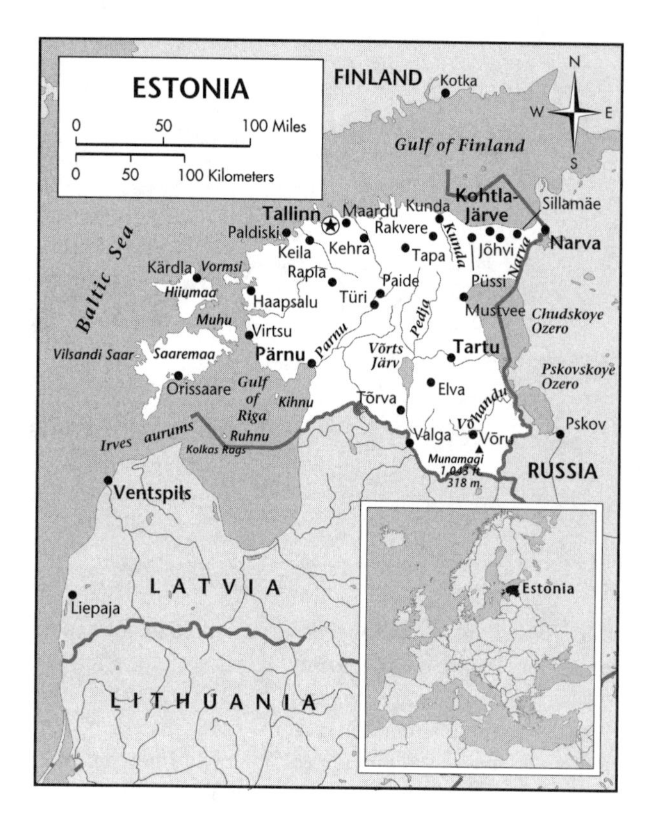

the most prosperous Soviet republic. Its policy since independence has focused on building up relations with the Nordic countries, particularly Finland and Sweden, Western Europe, and its Baltic neighbors, while weakening ties with the rest of the former Soviet countries.

Estonia's economic record is among the strongest in Eastern Europe. Although its **gross domestic product per capita** was only US$3,951 in 1998, its total **gross domestic product** grew by over 4 percent in 2000, and expectations for 2001 were for a strong 5–6 percent growth. The Estonian monetary and banking system, which suffered after independence, stabilized with the introduction of a **currency board**. The central bank holds foreign currency reserves to cover all circulation and reserves in krooni. It cannot refinance commercial banks unless there is extreme need, and the government's freedom to take on debt is restricted, as recommended by the International Monetary Fund (IMF). The Estonian kroon was pegged to the German mark at a **fixed exchange rate** of 8:1. Despite the limitations of the currency board, stable finances and economic reforms have created a predominantly free market European-style economy.

Many state-owned assets were **privatized** after independence, and the sale of public companies was still underway in the energy, telecommunications, and transportation sectors in 2000. High levels of **foreign direct investment** have supported the privatization program. Foreign investors in Estonia have been most active in communications, financial services, manufacturing, transportation, and real estate. They have acquired control of local assets relatively cheaply, while increasing the value of domestic companies through capital expenditures. Approximately 60 percent of foreign investments in Estonia are from Finland and Sweden, followed by the United States, Denmark, Norway, Liechtenstein, and the United Kingdom.

In 1998 Estonia began negotiations with the European Union for accession by the end of 2002. It is among the front-runners for membership, with a functioning market economy and the ability to cope with competitive pressure in the single European market. Estonia's **foreign debt** is estimated at a manageable US$270 million. Estonia also receives economic aid from the European Union (US$137.3 million in 1995).

POLITICS, GOVERNMENT, AND TAXATION

Estonia is a democratic republic with the legislative power vested in a Riigikogu (a 101-member **unicameral**, or single-chambered parliament) elected by universal suffrage for 4-year terms. The Riigikogu appoints the cabinet, which is led by the prime minister, who is the head of government. The president, who is elected by the Riigikogu and who appoints the prime minister, has limited executive power. Political parties include the center-right Fatherland Union (Isamaaliit), the Reform Party (RE), the Moderates, the Center Party, the left-centrist Coalition Party, the agrarian Rural Union (KMU), the Country People's Party, and the mostly ethnic Russian United People's Party (UPPE). In 1999 the opposition Coalition Party received the highest percentage of votes (23.4 percent), but the Fatherland Union, led by Prime Minister Mart Laar (16.1 percent), was able to form a coalition with the RE (15.9 percent) and the Moderates (15.2 percent) to win the elections. Particular policies may spur political feuds but the major Estonian parties are committed to economic stability, openness, and EU integration.

Economic reforms have curbed the government's role in the economy due to the currency board regime and the legal requirement of a balanced budget. The **tariff** regime was **liberalized** dramatically by removing import tariffs (excluding agricultural products from certain countries) and by restricting **excise taxes** to several goods. Yet the state exerts considerable influence with the **public sector** accounting for roughly half of gross domestic product and the public consuming over one-fifth of the total gross domestic product.

The average **income tax** burden for citizens was 26 percent in 1999 but the government was trying to reduce it by 2001. Reductions were expected in the form of tax breaks for families with a third child and an increase in the minimum taxable personal income base. Amendments sanctioning the taxation of dividends and other income earned by foreign companies in Estonia were passed in 2000.

INFRASTRUCTURE, POWER, AND COMMUNICATIONS

The transportation **infrastructure** includes 1,018 kilometers (634 miles) of railroads but only 132 kilometers (82 miles) of electrified rail lines. There are 10,935 kilometers (6,835 miles) of paved roads, including 75 kilometers (47 miles) of expressways. Estonia had 320 kilometers (200 miles) of navigable waterways and 420 kilometers (263 miles) of natural gas pipelines in 1992. All international flights use the Tallinn Airport, and there are several ports on the Baltic Sea, the port of Tallinn being the third largest in the Baltic Sea. A two-thirds stake in the state-run Eesti Raudtee railroad company was expected to be sold in a tender (possibly to RailAmerica) and the second-largest city, Tartu, was also expected to sell its public transportation company AS Liikor to a private investor in 2000.

Estonia's 2 oil-shale power plants produce twice what is consumed domestically. Under Soviet rule the country exported energy to Russia and Latvia but these markets dried up after independence. The government is forming a **joint venture** with the American NRG Energy company to renovate and operate the plants, bringing them into line with international environmental standards, and its priorities include creating an energy connection to western European electricity grids via an undersea cable.

The telecommunications market in Estonia is among the most liberalized in Eastern Europe. In 1998 a 49 percent stake in the state-held Eesti Telekom was sold to a consortium of state-controlled Telia (Sweden) and Sonera (Finland), and the government was considering selling the remainder of its stake in the company. Modern phone lines extend throughout Estonia. There are 3 mobile phone service providers: Eesti Mobiiltelefon (a subsidiary of Eesti Telekom), Radiolinja Eesti (a subsidiary of Finland's Radiolinja), and Ritabell (a joint venture between the British Millicom International and local Levicom). Estonia has the highest number of mobile phone users per capita in Central and Eastern Europe. Eesti Telefon, the fixed line division of Eesti Telekom, had a **monopoly** in domestic and international fixed line calls until 2001. In 2000, it had 521,901 subscribers (36.3 lines per 100 inhabitants), and the 3 cell phone operators had 514,000 users (35.7 per 100 inhabitants). The number of cell phones is expected to grow to 700,000 in 2003, when 1 out of every 2 Estonians is expected to own a cell phone. Estonia has one of the highest numbers of Internet subscribers in Eastern Europe, and the government intends to provide all schools with Internet access. In 2000 over 28 percent of the Estonians were online and 34 percent of them banked over the Internet.

ECONOMIC SECTORS

The economy of Estonia is service-based, with services contributing 65.7 percent of gross domestic product (GDP) in 1999, while industry is responsible for 30.7 percent, and agriculture and forestry comprise 3.6 percent of GDP. Estonia has natural deposits of shale oil, peat, phosphorite, amber, cambrian blue clay, limestone, dolomite, and timber and arable land. Services, especially transportation and tourism, are the principal growth sectors, although the manufacturing and the forest products sectors are also likely to see growth.

AGRICULTURE

Arable land covers 25 percent of the territory, permanent pastures 11 percent, and woodlands 44 percent. The foods produced include animal products, cereals, potatoes, fruits and vegetables, and fish. Agriculture was the traditional livelihood of most Estonians before

Communications

Country	Newspapers	Radios	TV Sets[a]	Cable subscribers[a]	Mobile Phones[a]	Fax Machines[a]	Personal Computers[a]	Internet Hosts[b]	Internet Users[b]
	1996	1997	1998	1998	1998	1998	1998	1999	1999
Estonia	174	693	480	15.1	170	N/A	34.4	174.65	200
United States	215	2,146	847	244.3	256	78.4	458.6	1,508.77	74,100
Russia	105	418	420	78.5	5	0.4	40.6	13.06	2,700
Latvia	247	710	492	58.0	68	N/A	N/A	50.86	105

[a]Data are from International Telecommunication Union, *World Telecommunication Development Report 1999* and are per 1,000 people.
[b]Data are from the Internet Software Consortium (http://www.isc.org) and are per 10,000 people.

SOURCE: World Bank. *World Development Indicators 2000.*

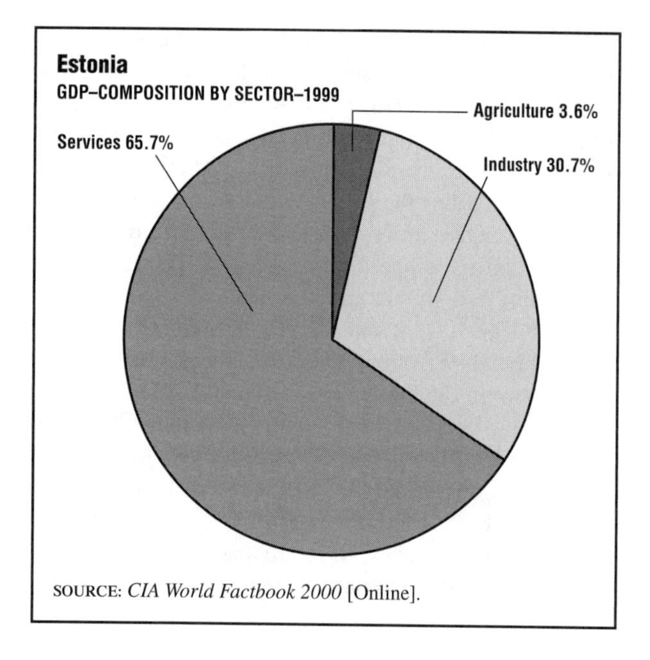

SOURCE: *CIA World Factbook 2000* [Online].

Soviet collectivization in the 1940s and there were over 100,000 family-held farms. After independence in 1991 land privatization carved thousands of new private farms out of the Soviet cooperatives. By the mid-1990s, these farms produced nearly 70 percent of the crops and 40 percent of the livestock, but most were unable to afford fertilizers, fuel, seeds, or capital investments. Competition from foreign producers put many farms out of business, and adjusting the sector to EU standards has been controversial. As a result, agricultural output decreased and almost one-fourth of the arable land was abandoned.

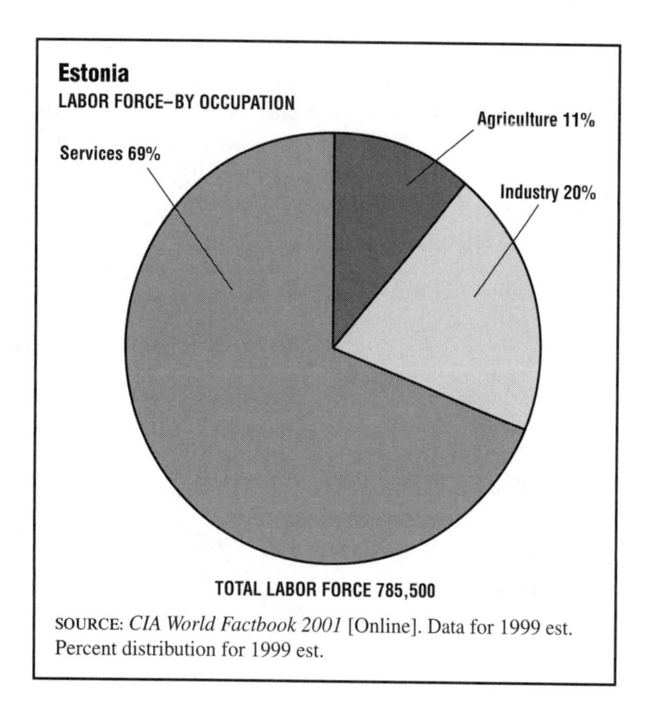

SOURCE: *CIA World Factbook 2001* [Online]. Data for 1999 est. Percent distribution for 1999 est.

INDUSTRY

Traditional Estonian industries include oil shale mining, shipbuilding, phosphates, electric motors, excavators, cement, furniture, clothing, textiles, paper, shoes, and apparel. Many of these industries stagnated after independence, deprived of their Soviet markets and sources of cheap raw materials. Yet the sector has been growing at a rate of 3 percent (1996 estimates), mostly due to the rapid privatization and the entry of foreign (mostly Scandinavian) investors in electronics, cement, chemicals, and forest products. Estonia has developed adequate assembly capacities to supply electronic components to leading Scandinavian telecommunications companies and suppliers. In addition, with its low taxes, low labor costs, and trained workforce, the country is an ideal location for electronics manufacturing. In early 2001 telecommunications giant Ericsson (Sweden), the world's leading maker of telecommunications equipment, sold its loss-making mobile handset operation, dramatically cutting its orders with Elcoteq (Finland). Elcoteq terminated the manufacture of Ericsson handsets in its Estonian subsidiary, Elcoteq Tallinn/ET, which was responsible for one-quarter of Estonian exports in 2000. But Elcoteq quickly refocused on mobile systems components for Ericsson, reflecting its long-term demand. ET continues producing handsets for Nokia (Finland), and will launch systems components production in Estonia later in 2001.

SERVICES

FINANCE. The Bank of Estonia was established in 1990, and became the central bank following its merger with the Estonian branch of Gosbank (the Soviet central bank) in 1992. The early days of independence witnessed a rapid proliferation of banks—42 were started by the end of 1992—when they encountered serious **solvency** difficulties, caused by stagnation and **bad loans** (granted to insolvent private debtors or loss-making state firms). The sector has since been consolidated through mergers and the closure of loss-makers, and in 1998 there were 11 banks. The 4 largest in 1998 were Eesti Uhispank (Union Bank of Estonia), Hansapank, Eesti Hoiupank (Estonian Savings Bank), and Tallinna Pank, and there was only 1 foreign bank branch (Merita Bank of Finland) and 5 foreign bank offices. In 2000 Hansapank and Uhispank were owned, respectively, by Swedbank and SEB (both Swedish). The financial sector is considered modern and efficient. About 10 percent of Estonians banked online in 2000, and since only a few users had credit cards, banks developed other online payment systems.

TOURISM. Boosted by crowds of Finns visiting Tallinn for shopping and pleasure, tourism has grown by 15 percent yearly since 1993. The number of visitors in 1998 was 1.5 million and the revenues US$660 million. In

1998 the number of visitors increased by one-third from the previous year due to the abolition of visa requirements for Nordic countries and the lower costs of travel to Estonia. The government-funded Estonian Tourism Board, besides attracting visitors to Tallinn and Tartu, advertises Estonia's national parks and reserves and its Baltic seaside resorts.

RETAIL. Estonia's **consumer goods** boom is based on economic growth and high consumer confidence. Estonians have a passion for household electronics and, as the absence of customs tariffs keeps imported household appliances cheaper, toasters, coffee makers, and mixers are found in the majority of Estonian homes. Finnish retailers, attracted by liberal regulations, dominate **retail** in Tallinn. Finnish tourists form a quarter of the retailers' clientele, lured by Estonia's lower **value-added tax**. Estonia's clothing is 20 percent less expensive than in Finland; and Estonian food, especially cheese and alcohol, is cheaper. In 2000 Estonia had an upper-income class of about 10,000 and a growing middle-class numbering about 60,000, both fueling domestic retail demand.

Exchange rates: Estonia

krooni (EEK) per US$1	
Jan 2001	16.663
2000	16.969
1999	14.678
1998	14.075
1997	13.882
1996	12.034

Note: Krooni are tied to the German deutsche mark at a fixed rate of 8 to 1.

SOURCE: CIA *World Factbook 2001* [ONLINE].

INTERNATIONAL TRADE

Estonia benefits from its location between prosperous Finland and Sweden and the economic potential of Russia. Estonians, both Nordic in culture and experienced in working with Russia, can provide a bridge between these growing markets. Estonia's open economy, although constrained by the currency board, is export-oriented, but still unable to reduce its foreign **trade deficit** of about 12 to 13 percent of gross domestic product. Exports in 1999 amounted to US$2.5 billion, while imports stood at US$3.4 billion. In 1999 chief exports included electronic components, machinery, and appliances (19 percent), wood products (15 percent), textiles (13 percent), food products (12 percent), metals (10 percent), and chemical products (8 percent). Estonia's leading export markets were Sweden (19.3 percent), Finland (18.8 percent), Russia (8.8 percent), Latvia (8.8 percent), Germany (7.3 percent), and the United States (2.5 percent). Chief imports included machinery and appliances (26 percent), food (15 percent), chemical products (10 percent), metal products (9 percent), and textiles (8 percent). Leading suppliers of imports were Finland (23 percent), Russia (13.2 percent), Sweden (10 percent), Germany (9.1 percent), and the United States (4.7 percent).

MONEY

The currency board and the requirement for a balanced budget has prompted Estonia to establish an offshore stabilization fund where it deposits income above its expenditures. Such revenue comes from privatization, including the initial public offering of Eesti Telekom at the Tallinn Stock Exchange in 1998. The 2 largest banks, Hansapank and Uhispank, acquired by Swedish financial institutions, opened their own brokerage houses that fueled the boom of the Tallinn Stock Exchange after 1998. Swedish SEB and Swedbank have also made Estonia a center of financial consolidation in the Baltics as they target the largest Latvian and Lithuanian banks for acquisition. **Inflation**, which had been a serious problem in the years immediately following independence, has been tamed since the mid-1990s and was estimated at 3.3 percent a year in 1999.

POVERTY AND WEALTH

Under the Soviet regime, Estonia was arguably a land of economic equality and the most affluent republic of the Soviet Union. The vast majority of the population was state-employed, no private initiative was allowed, and government funds were allocated equitably (for free health care, higher education, pensions, and other benefits). The only exceptions to this modest standard of living were the **nomenklatura** (the **Communist** Party elite) and the **informal economy** players. Market reforms in the 1990s generated new poverty and wealth, however. Unemployment, hitherto unknown, increased, although not as dramatically as elsewhere in the region. Social benefits suffered from inflation in the early 1990s. The withdrawal of the Russian military from the territory

GDP per Capita (US$)

Country	1975	1980	1985	1990	1998
Estonia	N/A	4,022	4,451	4,487	3,951
United States	19,364	21,529	23,200	25,363	29,683
Russia	2,555	3,654	3,463	3,668	2,138
Latvia	2,382	2,797	3,210	3,703	2,328

SOURCE: United Nations. *Human Development Report 2000; Trends in human development and per capita income.*

Distribution of Income or Consumption by Percentage Share: Estonia

Lowest 10%	2.2
Lowest 20%	6.2
Second 20%	12.0
Third 20%	17.0
Fourth 20%	23.1
Highest 20%	41.8
Highest 10%	26.2

Survey year: 1995

Note: This information refers to income shares by percentiles of the population and is ranked by per capita income.

SOURCE: *2000 World Development Indicators* [CD-ROM].

and the breakup of collective farms deprived many Estonians of their livelihood.

At the same time, many entrepreneurs made fortunes and a new middle class started taking shape as privatization and free initiative changed economic rules. Estonia generally avoided the surge of corruption and crime that plagued other Eastern European countries. In 1995 its **Gini index** (measuring economic equality with 0 standing for perfect equality and 100 for perfect inequality) was 35.4—more equitable than the United States, but much less equitable than most Eastern European countries and Nordic countries. Although extreme poverty in Estonia was nowhere near the size in other Eastern European countries, 6.3 percent of its population lived below the poverty line in 1994. As a country with an aging population, Estonia is struggling to maintain its pension system, and the government is formulating a much-needed pension reform.

WORKING CONDITIONS

Estonia is party to all major universal and European legal instruments on economic and social rights, the rights of the child, the right to equal compensation and collective bargaining, and the elimination of discrimination in the workplace. The Estonian **labor force** numbered 785,500 in 1999. Unemployment is around 10 percent, yet working conditions are considerably better than in many other Eastern European countries. The labor force is skilled and educated and the average salary in 1997 was US$257 a month (US$322 in the manufacturing sector), a fraction of the rate elsewhere in Scandinavia but higher than most Eastern European countries. The percentage of people working in the services industry was 69 percent, industry 20 percent, and agriculture and forestry 11 percent. Labor unions have limited influence and have a non-confrontational approach to government and employers. With a decreasing and aging population, Estonia faces serious demographic challenges. Many labor practices are inefficient and improving productivity is key for Estonia's economy.

COUNTRY HISTORY AND ECONOMIC DEVELOPMENT

1561. Estonia is subjugated by Sweden; reforms improve the economic situation of the peasants.

1721. Estonia is ceded to Russia's Peter the Great.

1816. Russian reforms abolish serfdom, and peasants obtain the right to buy land. Nationalism grows.

1905. In the wake of the first Russian revolution, nationalism is boosted by modern press and literature.

1917. The Russian tsar is toppled by the second Russian Revolution.

1918. On February 24 an independent Estonian democratic republic is proclaimed.

1920. The Tartu peace treaty between Soviet Russia and Estonia recognizes Estonia's sovereignty.

1921. The Estonian Republic is recognized by Western powers, becoming a League of Nations member.

1934. A coup establishes an authoritarian regime.

Household Consumption in PPP Terms

Country	All food	Clothing and footwear	Fuel and power[a]	Health care[b]	Education[b]	Transport & Communications	Other
Estonia	41	7	24	8	4	9	7
United States	13	9	9	4	6	8	51
Russia	28	11	16	7	15	8	16
Latvia	30	5	16	6	23	11	10

Data represent percentage of consumption in PPP terms.

[a]Excludes energy used for transport.

[b]Includes government and private expenditures.

SOURCE: World Bank. *World Development Indicators 2000.*

1939. Estonia is left in the Soviet sphere by a non-aggression pact between Germany and the USSR.

1940. The Soviets invade Estonia and on August 6 the country is incorporated into the USSR.

1941. Nazi Germany invades the USSR and occupies Estonia until it is driven out in 1944.

1945. Soviet rule is restored and the economy is reformed along Soviet lines.

1985. With the reforms of Soviet president Mikhail Gorbachev, Estonia moves towards independence.

1991. Communist rule collapses and the USSR recognizes the independence of Estonia in September.

1991. Estonia becomes a member of the United Nations and adopts reforms for democratization and privatization.

1994. Russia withdraws troops from Estonia.

1995. Estonia becomes an associated member of the European Union.

1998. Estonia starts negotiations for full membership in the European Union.

1999. Estonia joins the World Trade Organization.

FUTURE TRENDS

Estonia is a leading candidate for EU membership and hopes that its accession could be finalized as early as 2002, although internal problems in the union may postpone it. Political consensus on EU accession will generate stability throughout the transition from a communist to a free-market economy. Gross domestic product growth may accelerate slightly in 2001 due to domestic demand. Exports will grow in line with international demand but the negative foreign trade balance is not likely to be offset in the first half of the decade. The Estonian economy will become more service-based and financial services will receive more weight. Domestic manufacturing will be dependent on the high-tech sector in Sweden and Finland and is likely to grow. Privatization may be almost completed with the railroad sale in 2001. New foreign direct investments will enter Estonia and the flow will increase when the country joins the European Union. Reform of the finance services sector may lead to a further rise in credit growth. Pension reform will be key in 2001 with the government making its new pension scheme obligatory for all new employees. The living standards of the Estonians will rise gradually after the country's EU accession. Access to the development funds and the expertise of the European Union, once full membership is achieved, will be greatly beneficial for the development of the country's infrastructure, rural regions, education, social services, and virtually all aspects of economic life.

DEPENDENCIES

Estonia has no territories or colonies.

BIBLIOGRAPHY

Economist Intelligence Unit. *Country Profile: Estonia.* London: Economist Intelligence Unit, 2001.

Iwaskiw, Walter R., ed. *Estonia, Latvia and Lithuania: Country Studies.* Washington, DC: Library of Congress, 1997.

Open Estonia Foundation. *Welcome to the Estonia Country Guide.* <http://www.ciesin.ee/ESTCG>. Accessed August, 2001.

U.S. Central Intelligence Agency. *World Factbook 2000.* <http://www.odci.gov/cia/publications/factbook/index.html>. Accessed August 2001.

U.S. Department of State. *FY 2000 Country Commercial Guide: Estonia.* <http://www.state.gov/www/about_state/business/com_guides/2001/europe/index.html>. Accessed March 2001.

Welcome to the Embassy of Estonia. <http://www.estemb.org>. Accessed September 2001.

—Valentin Hadjiyski

FINLAND

Republic of Finland
Suomen Tasavalta

CAPITAL: Helsinki.

MONETARY UNIT: The markka (FMk or FIM) or finnmark. One markka equals 100 penni. Banknotes come in denominations of FMk20, 50, 100, 500, and 1000. There are 1, 5, and 10 markka coins, and 1, 10, and 50 penni coins. The markka will remain in circulation until 28 February 2002, when it will be completely replaced by the new European currency, the euro. The exchange rate for the euro is 1 euro=5.94573 markka.

CHIEF EXPORTS: Machinery and equipment, chemicals, metals, timber, paper, pulp.

CHIEF IMPORTS: Foodstuffs, petroleum and petroleum products, chemicals, transport equipment, iron and steel, machinery, textile yarn and fabrics, fodder grains.

GROSS DOMESTIC PRODUCT: US$108.6 billion (purchasing power parity, 1999 est.).

BALANCE OF TRADE: **Exports:** US$43 billion (1998 est.). **Imports:** US$30.7 billion (1998 est.).

COUNTRY OVERVIEW

LOCATION AND SIZE. Located between Sweden and Russia, Finland also borders the Baltic Sea, Gulf of Bothnia, and Gulf of Finland. Finland's area, at 337,030 square kilometers (130,127 square miles), is slightly smaller than the state of Montana. Finland shares a long border of 1,313 kilometers (816 miles) with Russia, 729 kilometers (453 miles) of border with Norway, and 586 kilometers (364 miles) of border with Sweden. The remaining 1,126 kilometers (700 miles) of its boundary is coastline, excluding islands and coastal indentations. The capital, Helsinki, is the northernmost national capital in Europe, but it is found in the south of Finland, as are the majority of its 94 towns. Finland also includes the island province of Åland, located between Sweden and Finland. The islands are locally autonomous, have their own government, and are entirely Swedish-speaking.

POPULATION. The population of Finland was estimated in July of 2000 as 5,167,486. The population growth rate is a very small 0.17 percent and generally has been small. Finland has a high proportion of elderly: only 18 percent of the population are under 14 years of age and 15 percent are over 65.

Finland is extremely homogenous. Ethnic Finns make up 93 percent of the population, ethnic Swedes 6 percent, and the rest is mainly made up of the Sami (also called Lapps), Roma, and Tatar. There are 2 official languages: Finnish (spoken by 93 percent of the population) and Swedish (by 6 percent). Due to the harsh climate in the north, population is concentrated in the lowlands in the south of Finland. Approximately 81.2 percent of Finns live in urban areas with around 1 million concentrated in the capital, Helsinki, and its metropolitan area.

Formerly a source of emigrants (people moving outwards from a country), Finland is currently becoming a destination for immigrants (people who move into a foreign country). In 1996, the number of foreigners living in Finland was 74,000, with Russians accounting for about 20 percent, followed by inhabitants with Estonian, Swedish, and Somali former citizenship.

OVERVIEW OF ECONOMY

Finland is a free market economy that is highly dependent on international trade. Around 1900, agriculture, especially forestry, was Finland's economic backbone, as trees were Finland's chief natural resource. The more arable southern provinces of Finland have always had higher population density and have dominated the agricultural economy. Finland now has a technologically advanced economy, in high-tech forest production, electronics, and other manufacturing. But the southern regions continue to dominate in population and productivity.

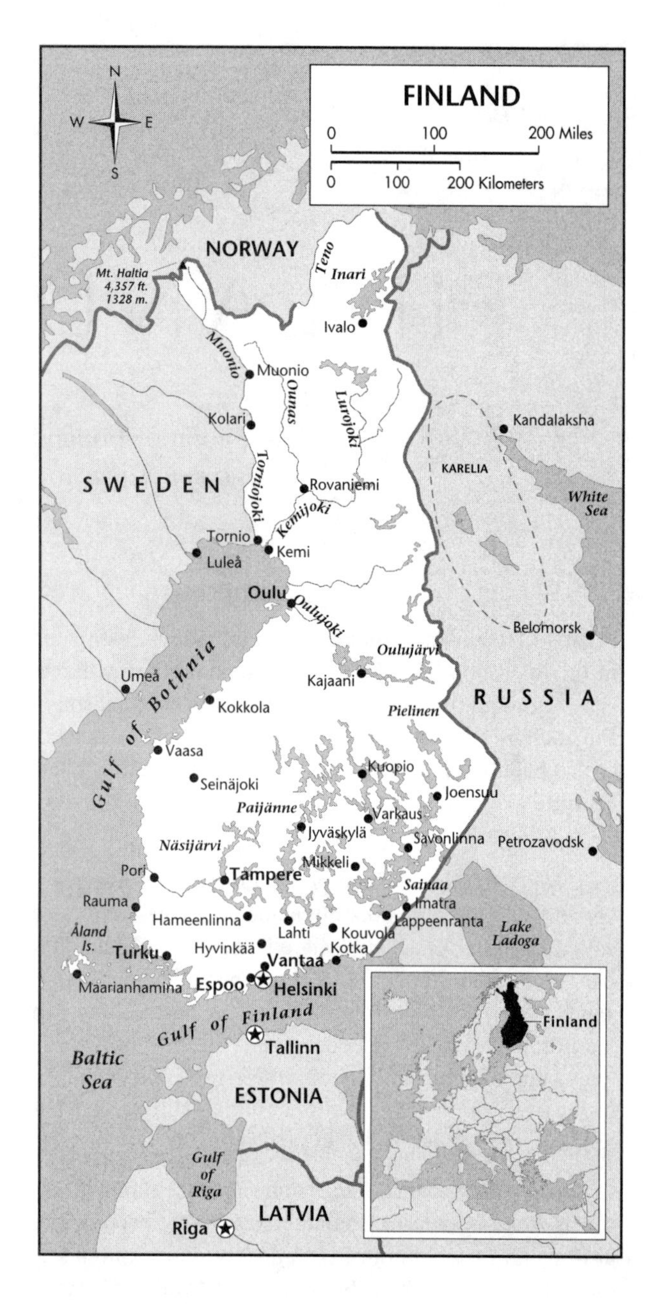

The late 19th century saw the heavily forested country first investing in sawmills and timber, followed by wood pulp and paper production. Wealth from the timber industry was used to invest in making the machinery for the pulp and paper industry. Technical know-how and growth in metalworking and engineering facilities enabled Finland to expand into metal shipbuilding after World War II. Combined with forest products, this industry led the economy until the mid-1990s. In the 1990s, high-tech electronics came to the foreground, with Finland currently the world leader in mobile-phone manufacture. Finland also produces high-tech instruments for environmental measurement and medical devices.

A strong focus on research and development (R&D) and cohesion between government, industry, and workers has helped economic development, especially in the past 50 years. The government's support and coordination of high-tech R&D began as early as 1983 when it founded the Technology Development Center (TEKES). TEKES is the principal organization in Finland for implementing technology policy. In 1984, one year after TEKES was founded, a small business called Nokia switched its focus to high-tech mobile phone production and became the largest mobile phone company in the world. Nokia's growth drove production in the manufacturing sector unlike many European economies, expanded its share of **gross domestic product** (GDP) throughout the 1990s. TEKES has also had an effect on agriculture through its support in 1997 of research into developing functional foods (foods with proven health benefits, often additives and substitutes that are less dependent on the quality of farming land than on the quality of the R&D **infrastructure**).

As in most other developed nations, the Finnish service sector has in recent years become the highest-producing sector in the economy and accounted for 63 percent of the GDP in 2000. Business services, data processing, and transportation are all key service industries, with expansion in business and financial services especially driven by new technological developments, expanding into Internet and Internet Technology (IT)-based services. Public services, primarily health care and education, are also important and employed 32 percent of the **labor force** in 2000.

A **welfare state** is made up of institutions reflecting the responsibility a government has assumed for the well-being of its citizens. In Finland, Europe, and most of the developed world, a welfare state includes health care, education, social security, and unemployment. In Finland, the extent of the welfare state is smaller than those of other Nordic countries, but it still accounts for over half of the GDP.

Finland's proximity to Russia, and formerly to the Soviet Union (USSR), has powerfully affected Finnish economic development. In the early years of the USSR, political differences prevented much trade. Yet Western European demand, especially for lumber, pulp, and paper, supported the forestry industry at that time. During World War II, Finland joined the Axis powers, partly in order to prevent partial annexation by the Soviet Union. After the war, Finland had to pay reparations to the Soviet Union, who required mainly industrial products. This requirement forced Finland to develop a substantial metal and engineering industry. After reparations were completed in 1952, trade with the USSR continued through a **barter system**, characterized by an exchange of goods for energy since Finland lacked natural fuel resources. Finland was the only free-market member of the Council of Mutual and Economic Assistance (COMECON), an economic and development cooperative association formed in 1949, which was otherwise composed of **socialist** states. Finland was able to use its good relations with socialist states as a economic buffer against downturns in the Western market. Finland did not hesitate to link itself to Western markets as well, which helped its position as a trade gateway to the USSR. Finland joined the Organization for Economic Cooperation and Development (OECD) in 1969 and the European Free Trade Agreement (EFTA), a predecessor to the European Union (EU), in 1986. However, the USSR, as Finland's closest neighbor, remained a large and influential market, and its collapse in the early 1990s worsened Finland's already severe **recession**.

Deregulation of Finnish financial markets in the 1980s led to a domestic credit boom, which collapsed in the early 1990s, leading to stock and real estate market speculation and crashes. Finnish observers called this experience "casino economics": an economy becomes dependent on speculation (first seen as a sign of growth) and speculation runs out of control. The chief casualty was productivity and employment; the GDP fell by about 15 percent in 3 years while unemployment skyrocketed to 20 percent. The recession lasted until 1993, when Finland devalued its currency. This action allowed the nation to improve its export sector, especially through growth in manufacturing high-tech electronics and expansion of its export market for paper goods into the newly-booming Asian economies.

During the recession from 1990 to 1993, the Finnish government began accumulating **external debt**, which peaked at nearly 60 percent of the GDP in 1994. There has only been a partial recovery from the recession, with high unemployment lingering and debt continuing to increase. The currency **devaluation**, however, helped economic growth rebound, and by 1996 the GDP had recovered to pre-recession levels. The flourishing high-tech industry, led by the cellular phone manufacturer Nokia, was at the center of export-led growth. In 1998, Nokia alone accounted for 1 percent of Finland's approximately 5 percent growth of the GDP. Growth was fairly steady through the second half of the 1990s, except for a slight recession in 1998 that was mainly due to the slump in many Asian economies that were importers of Finnish goods and services.

In 1999, central government debt was 45.4 percent of the GDP. Since joining the European Monetary Union (EMU) in 1999, Finland has been required to reduce its debt. Even before its membership, partial **privatization** of many state-owned businesses, such as the telecommunications provider Sonera, helped to create revenue from the sale of shares. However, public debt is still high and has been increasing, posing a continued economic challenge into the 21st century.

POLITICS, GOVERNMENT, AND TAXATION

Finland is a parliamentary republic, with a president and a prime minister. The president is elected by popular vote for a 6-year term. The prime minister and a deputy prime minister are nominated by the president after the parliamentary elections, and the Eduskunta (parliament) must approve the president's nominations. The prime minister nominates ministers for the Council of State, or Valtioneuvosto (also simply called "the Government"), which is divided into 13 ministries overseeing various aspects of government. Nominations are approved by the president, and responsible to the Eduskunta.

The Eduskunta is responsible for legislation. Members are elected popularly under a system of **proportional representation** (voters elect parties, who have a number of seats in government related to the percentage of votes they receive). The election on 15 April 1999 put 10 parties in the 200-member Eduskunta. The Social Democrats (SDP) received 25.5 percent of the votes cast, the Center Party 23.5 percent, and the National Coalition (Conservative Party) 23 percent.

Women do not participate equally in government, but Finland's showing is better than most countries in this respect. In 2000, about 35 percent of the Eduskunta and 33 percent of the Cabinet were females. The Ministers of Foreign Affairs and Defense were female, as was the Speaker of Parliament. By comparison, in the United States women held 12 percent of the Congressional seats and 41.4 percent of the Cabinet seats in 2000.

The SDP has been the largest party in the legislature in almost every election since 1907. Its main base of support is skilled laborers, lower-class white-collar workers, small farmers, and professionals. It is also the closest party to the labor unions. SDP supported Finnish membership in the EU and voted in favor of Finland's entering the EMU in 1999. The National Coalition (also called Conservative Party, Kansallinen Kokoomus or "the Kok"), mainly represents private enterprise and the business community. The Kok strongly supported EU membership, favors limited spending, deregulation, and lower taxes but is still in favor of the welfare state. The Center Party has in recent years been split on the EU question, and it opposed Finland's joining of the EMU in 1999. Many of its voters live in rural areas, and the party especially represents agricultural interests.

In 1990, a conglomeration of socialists, ex-communists, and disenchanted Social Democrats, who believed that the SDP had compromised on social issues and international human rights, formed the Left Wing Alliance. There has been pressure on the government to cut costs and spending, and it has been difficult for the Alliance to remain in government alongside the Social Democrats and

Conservatives. The long-established minority of Swedish-speaking people is represented by the Swedish People's Party (RKP), which consistently receives 5 to 6 percent of the vote and has a strong base of support in the Åland islands. The RKP generally supports center-right causes and also was in favor of EU membership. Since the party is able to compromise with both socialist and non-socialist governments, its swing vote has been used to protect Swedish-speaking community interests. As of 2000, Finland had the first Green Party in government in all of Europe. The Greens strongly oppose nuclear energy but favor a moderate approach to key economic issues such as forestry, taxation, and the welfare state. They have strong appeal to young, urban voters and to women. Of the party's 9 Eduskunta members, 6 are women.

Many other small parties in Finland also influence debate, although few make it into the Eduskunta. As in other Nordic countries, public debate in the 1990s and beyond is more likely to include a few voices from some extreme right-wing parties, some of which argue for tightening borders against immigrants and refugees, others for abolishing taxes and regulations on business.

Indirect state management of the economy is aided by regular meetings with representatives from industry and trade unions, as well as incentive programs that the government uses to promote investment in areas deemed to be in need of development. The programs include cash grants, loans, tax benefits, and investments in **equity**, guarantees, and employee training. One institution that demonstrates the Finnish government's ability to influence the economy in this way is the Technology Development Center (TEKES), founded in 1983 to fund R&D in technology. TEKES set the stage for advances and innovation in Finnish technology in the early 1980s and business in the 1990s. The government continues to invest in this direction, contributing almost one-third of the total spending on R&D in 1999. Total R&D spending in Finland is higher than in most other highly advanced economies like the United States and Japan; it was estimated at FMk22,334 million (including private investment) in 1999, or around 3 percent of the GDP. R&D expenditure had risen in real terms by almost 15 percent from the year before.

In Finland, 3 of the 10 largest companies were majority state-owned in 1998; "majority state-owned" means that the state has a majority of share-determined votes, ranging from 53.4 percent control to total control. State ownership occurs mainly in metals and mining, chemicals, and utilities. These companies do not receive **subsidies** or special treatment, and private companies are not excluded from these sectors (with the exception of Alko, the state's **monopoly** on liquor sales). Sonera, a telecommunications company, was the largest state-owned company in 1999, but it competes like any other firm in the market. In addition, the state is authorized to sell off all of its remaining shares in Sonera and is likely to do so. The state still owns significant shares in metals and mining, chemical, and utility companies, as well as Finland Post and the Finnish State Railways. Total state ownership has become rare. In November 2000, among the 15 most significant state-owned companies only Patria, a defense company; Vapo, a peat manufacturer; and Alko were 100 percent state-owned.

Until the 1970s, Finland also had a much smaller **public sector** (as a percentage of the GDP) than its neighbors. In fact, the ratio of the public sector to the GDP did not approach the rest of Scandinavia until the recession of 1990 to 1993, when the overall GDP shrank dramatically. Rather than increase spending, Finland simply did not decrease it at the rate that the other sectors had declined, so its share of the GDP overall was increased. When recovery began, the public sector grew, although still at a slower rate than other Scandinavian countries. The public sector in 1998 employed almost one-third of the population and accounted for well over half of the GDP.

The state may help to provide a new direction for Finnish agriculture, which has been challenged by EU requirements, by funding R&D for agricultural products in the "functional foods" category. The EU agricultural regime has led to falling domestic prices (as they must be on par with EU levels) and fiercer competition from EU agricultural imports. Most Finnish producers still supply the same amount of goods to the Finnish market but have thus far seen significantly lower profits.

Taxes are the government's main source of revenue. Total central government tax revenue in 1999 was FMk188,499 million, about 32 percent of which came from income and property taxes, and 32 percent from **value-added tax** (VAT). In the 1990s, Finland lowered and adjusted its VAT, especially after EU membership, since VAT rates must eventually harmonize with the EU taxation system. The standard Finnish VAT in 2000 was 22 percent, the VAT on foodstuffs and animal feed was 17 percent, and there was an 8 percent rate for entertainment events tickets, passenger transport, pharmaceuticals, and books. Personal **income taxes** are quite high; the highest bracket was officially 34.9 percent in 1999. Both the OECD and the International Monetary Fund (IMF) have urged Finland to cut its income tax to encourage employment. Corporate taxation is 29 percent, giving Finland one of the lowest rates among OECD countries, along with Sweden and Norway. To replace revenue lost from income tax and VAT reductions, the government has been imposing "green taxes," or taxes supporting environmental regulations. In 1995, over 6 percent of tax revenue came from environment-related taxes (approximately 3 percent of the GDP).

Communications

Country	Newspapers	Radios	TV Sets[a]	Cable subscribers[a]	Mobile Phones[a]	Fax Machines[a]	Personal Computers[a]	Internet Hosts[b]	Internet Users[b]
	1996	1997	1998	1998	1998	1998	1998	1999	1999
Finland	455	1,496	640	175.7	572	38.5	349.2	1,116.78	2,143
United States	215	2,146	847	244.3	256	78.4	458.6	1,508.77	74,100
Russia	105	418	420	78.5	5	0.4	40.6	13.06	2,700
Sweden	445	932	531	221.4	464	50.9	361.4	581.47	3,666

[a]Data are from International Telecommunication Union, *World Telecommunication Development Report 1999* and are per 1,000 people.
[b]Data are from the Internet Software Consortium (http://www.isc.org) and are per 10,000 people.

SOURCE: World Bank. *World Development Indicators 2000.*

INFRASTRUCTURE, POWER, AND COMMUNICATIONS

Finland has an efficient road and rail network, despite its only becoming fully developed in the mid-20th century. As late as the 1940s, difficult terrain and harsh weather had made internal communications and transport problematic. After World War II, steady improvements in infrastructure led to the current situation. By 1998, Finland had 77,895 kilometers (48,404 miles) of highways, including 473 kilometers (294 miles) of expressways. Bridges and car ferries assisted road travel in the lakeland areas and in the island archipelagoes. The gauge of Finnish railways is the same as Russia's, which enhances Finland's position as a trade gateway to the Russian region. However, Finland's 5,685-kilometer (3,533-mile) rail network is uneven, better serving the economically dominant southeast regions. Finland's sea communication and transport is extensive, with over 50 ports and loading places and 23 seaports open year round. Finland also has 157 airports and a state airline, Finnair. International air service is provided through Helsinki airport.

Finland produced 75.30 billion kilowatt hours (kWh) of electricity in 1998, of which fossil fuel comprised 41.62 percent, hydroelectric power 19.59 percent, nuclear power 27.59 percent, and other sources 11.2 percent. Total consumption was 79.28 billion kWh in the same year, or over 15,000 kWh per person, almost two-thirds higher than the average per capita consumption for the EU. This is due especially to the long Finnish winter and the high energy consumption of the paper and pulp industry. Finland relies on nuclear energy and imported hydrocarbons for almost 50 percent of its power, while imported fossil fuels make up the rest. Finland exported only 300 million kWh of electricity in 1998, while importing 9.55 billion kWh.

Finland's telecommunications system is cutting-edge and extensive, with 2.86 million main telephone lines in 1997 and 2,162,574 mobile cellular phones. The half-state-owned Sonera is the main telecommunications provider as of early 2000. Finland is famous for its quick adoption of cellular phone and wireless technology. About 60 percent of Finns had mobile phones in 1999, compared with 28 percent in the United States. Nokia, along with dominating domestic mobile phone sales, also supplies almost a quarter of the world's mobile-phone market. Internet connectivity is also very high, with more Internet service providers (ISPs) per person than any other country in the world. The telecommunications industry was fully deregulated by 1995, and subsequent laws have allowed telecom companies to share lines and have eased entry into the sector by eliminating the licensing requirement previously needed to construct a fixed telephone network. Phone **tariffs** are among the lowest in the EU.

ECONOMIC SECTORS

In 2000, the balance between Finland's economic sectors was consistent with those of most OECD nations,

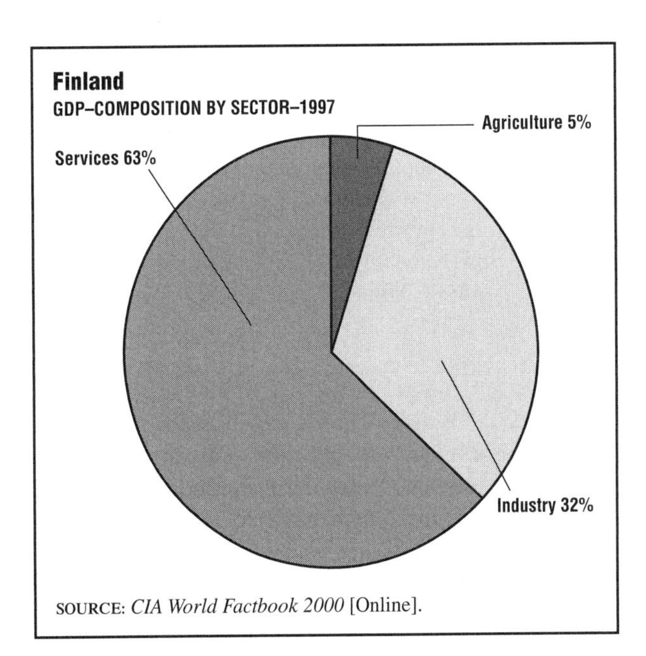

SOURCE: *CIA World Factbook 2000* [Online].

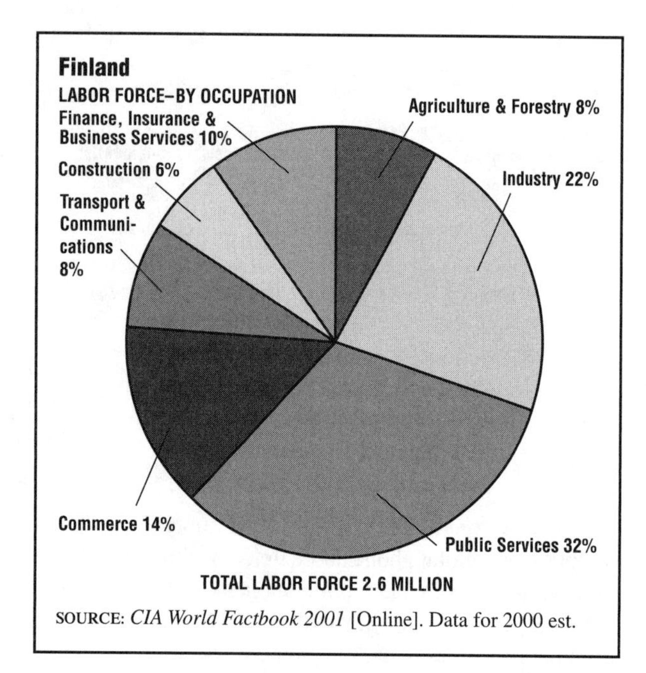

SOURCE: *CIA World Factbook 2001* [Online]. Data for 2000 est.

with agriculture contributing 5 percent to the GDP, industry 32 percent, and services 63 percent. However, until the 1960s, Finland relied much more heavily on agriculture than its neighbors. It was partly the pressure of post-World-War-II reparations to the USSR that forced Finland to build and expand its industrial base. Finland's 1999 accession to the EMU has further shifted the emphasis from agriculture and has forced the end of many subsidies to farmers. In more recent times, growth in the various sectors also has set Finland apart from its neighbors and most of the OECD countries, as manufacturing (especially high-tech products) expanded more quickly than the service sector.

The U.S. Department of Commerce identifies milk production as "the backbone of the Finnish agriculture industry." In 2000, Finland produced 2.5 million units of milk, about 0.44 percent of world milk production. Dairies and egg farms produce more than Finland needs to feed itself, while Finnish meat production roughly equals consumption. Membership in the EU has deeply affected the agriculture industry; in 1996, producer prices fell more in Finland than in any other EU country. In 1997 food prices averaged 11.2 percent lower than in 1994 (prior to EU membership). Finnish producers had to reduce prices to EU levels, especially facing competition from agricultural imports of the union's members. A new focus for agriculture is research into specific enzymes and bacilli that have health and commercial use, with the raw products of the dairy and forestry industries (milk and trees) providing some of the raw material. Finland is also basically self-sufficient in meat production.

Finland's high-tech, highly productive forestry industry overlaps and links the agriculture and industry sectors. Finland has the world's highest per capita forestry production, twice that of Sweden and 3 times that of Canada. With about 70 percent of its area covered by forests at the end of the 20th century, Finland's use of its most abundant natural resource provides the materials for Finland's industrial wood-processing industries. Finland supplies 25 percent of the world's exports of printing and writing paper and 15 percent of the world's paper and paperboard exports.

From 1993 to 1998, industry's share of the GDP rose from 31.3 percent to 33.8 percent. Manufacturing dominates this sector, with output in 1999 worth FMk504.9 billion. Nokia, the cellular phone maker, has been the main engine of Finnish industrial growth in the late 1990s. In 1998, Nokia alone contributed 1 percent to Finland's 5 percent GDP growth. However, there is some concern that Nokia holds too much responsibility for the sector and the economy. It is far and away the largest firm in manufacturing, with no other company even approaching its level of production and employment. Other branches of manufacturing in general have not seen similar growth. Unlike many other developed nations, where the service industry is often the main sector for growth in employment, Finnish industry has been the biggest job creator, especially manufacturing.

In the service sector in 1997, government services make up nearly one-third of all service sector activity. Many private services, especially business and IT services, are growing at a faster rate than public services. The production of private services increased by almost 5 percent in 1997 and has been steadily growing since the mid-1990s, with telecommunications and service to businesses marking the fastest-growing sectors. However, unlike in other OECD countries, the service sector's share of the GDP and employment has not increased as quickly as manufacturing. New jobs in the service sector are mainly created by manufacturing, which outsources many of its production-related services.

AGRICULTURE

Finland's severe winters; short, frost-interrupted growing seasons; and relatively scarce and acidic arable land has made agriculture a continually tough endeavor. Before the end of the 19th century, Finland was so isolated from the rest of the world that its farmers focused on grains to feed the local population. In the 1880s and 1890s, cheap grain from Russia and the Americas began to flood the market, while simultaneously, dairy products began to be in more demand domestically and abroad. Finnish farmers began to use the imported grain to feed dairy cattle and other livestock, a pattern that has persisted to the present. Arable land is nearly always combined with forests, which cover approximately 70 percent of Finland. Most farms have survived by a combination of farming and forestry. Farms in the more arable south and west focus less on forests than those in the more wooded north and east.

Productivity has increased and the number of farms has decreased since the 1960s. This is partly due to advances in agricultural technology, which required fewer people on the land, and partly to the expansion of the industry and services sectors, which have attracted people towards factories and the city. The traditional Nordic emphasis on family farming has meant that the image of the family farmer is a culturally heroic figure, which may have helped farmers resist the urge to set up huge impersonal **agribusinesses**. In 1999, average farm size in Finland was only 25 hectares (62 acres). The Finnish tradition of cooperative organization has meant that small farms coordinate marketing, transportation, and processing of agricultural and forestry products. Finland's desire for self-sufficiency in basic foodstuffs supported a system of subsidies for the remaining farmers, until the 1995 accession to the EU forced price equalization. Equalization meant a 50 percent or larger reduction in many producer prices. The price of a kilogram of eggs, for example, fell by over 75 percent in 1995. Finland's own budget had to try to cushion the blow, but during the first 3 years of EU membership over 10 percent of Finnish farmers gave up farming. Currently only 4 percent of the population engage in farming. Of the agricultural products exported, dairy products topped the list in 1998. Finland is a net importer of agricultural products, with a total value of agricultural exports of US$1.31 billion and imports worth US$2.3 billion in 1998.

Since the decline of other agricultural production in the past decades, forestry is now the most significant contributor to agricultural production, with a **turnover** in 2001 of around FMk10 billion. Due to improvements in management and harvest techniques, Finland's timber reserves have increased by over 25 percent since the 1970s. Much of its forest production goes to its industrial sector to make paper products, while a significant percentage goes to create wood products like furniture as well. Finland produces 5 percent of global forestry goods, and its printing and writing paper exports are 25 percent of world production.

Finland's fur industry dominates the world market for farm-raised foxes, accounting for over half of global fox pelt production in 1997 with revenues of US$2.55 million. Finnish mink furs also have a high reputation on international markets. Commercial fishing, once quite important to the economy, has gradually become less significant, currently accounting for only 0.1 percent of the GDP. The decline can be attributed to river pollution and dams built for hydroelectric works, which have adversely affected natural spawning habits.

INDUSTRY

METALS AND ENGINEERING. Metals and engineering now constitute the largest sector of Finnish industry, with motor vehicles and machinery driving much of the growth of the late 1990s. In 1999, mechanical engineering and metals manufacturing industries employed 187,175 people, and total revenues reached around FMk123 billion.

Finland holds a leading international position in the building of icebreakers, luxury liners, and other specialized ships. The are only 2 main ship building companies, Masa Yards and its rival, Finnyards, both dominated by Norwegian companies. Masa Yards was bought by the Norwegian firm Kvaerner in 1991 and Aker Maritime, another Norwegian firm, bought 60 percent of the shares in Finnyards in 1997. Both companies have specialized in niche markets in shipbuilding, which has helped them survive in an over-saturated global market. Finland's strong pollution control and other environmental laws, plus neighboring countries' environmental concerns and support from TEKES and other research organizations, has led Finnish industry to specialize in environmental technology. Finland made US$1.45 million of environmental equipment in 2000, much of it used by Finland's own pulp and paper industry.

INDUSTRIAL FORESTRY. Finland's abundance of forestry products is the historical heart of the Finnish export industry, accounting for almost 30 percent of total exports—although only 2.4 percent of the GDP—in 2001. There was record growth in nearly every aspect of forest industry in 2000. Total forest production increased by nearly 5 percent. Plywood production rose the fastest—over 8 percent compared with the previous years, with total production of about 1.2 million cubic meters. Sawnwood production rose by nearly 5 percent in 2000 to 13.3 million cubic meters. Paper and paperboard production reached 13.5 million tons, 4.3 percent higher than in 1999. Turnover in the forest industry in 2001 was worth FMk100 billion. In 1998, forest industries employed 95,886 people. Stora-Enso, the largest group in this sector, is the second largest producer of newsprint products in the world and had revenue of over FMk75 billion in 2000.

ELECTRONICS AND ELECTRO-TECHNICS. The electronics and electro-technical equipment industry employed 63,700 people and had revenues of FMk114.6 billion in 1997, while high-tech products accounted for almost 26 percent of total export value by 1999. The majority of growth in this industry can be attributed to the mobile-phone manufacturer Nokia. Nokia originated as a pulp and paper concern but began investing its profits in high-tech research in the early 1980s and is now one of the leading mobile phone manufacturers in the world. Nokia is an example of Finnish industry's emphasis on

R&D; it spent almost 9 percent of its turnover on R&D in 1999. Nokia, however, is the only high-tech company in Finland with a significant market share, unlike Sweden, which has a range of companies in competition. This means that growth in this industry is dependent on Nokia's fate, a risky situation.

CHEMICALS. The third largest industry in Finland, the chemicals industry, had a value of FMk56 billion in 1999, which was over one-tenth of the total value in Finnish manufacturing. The chemicals industry focuses on a number of core areas, including chemicals for the forest industry, agribusiness, and other industries, as well as paints, plastic products, environmental products, petrochemicals and oil products, and most recently biotechnical products. Finland's strong environmental consciousness has fuelled not only innovation in chemicals to help the environment—Finland was the world's top producer of water treatment chemicals in 2000—but also environmentally conscious business practices. In 1992 Finland joined a voluntary international program called Responsible Care, which is an environment, health, and safety initiative operating in 45 countries. Although only 12 percent of chemical firms have signed on, some of Finland's largest producers are members, meaning that over 80 percent of chemical production is covered by the initiative. Members commit themselves to continuous improvement in performance regarding environment protection, health, and safety and to open communication about activities and achievements on these issues. Some effects can be seen in the 60 percent drop in employee accident rates over the past 10 years, while emissions also fell significantly in 2000.

The recent growth of the electronics industry has spurred the production of plastic components and packaging for electronic equipment. In 1999, the chemical industry in total employed almost 39,000 people, or 9 percent of the total industrial workforce.

FOOD AND BEVERAGES. The Finnish food industry is a good example of how Finnish industry might grow throughout the 21st century. Finland has begun expansion into the niche market of "functional foods," researching and developing naturally-derived food additives which are deemed to have health benefits. One of the more well-known is xylitol, a sweetener derived from the birch wood chips of Finland's forests that has been shown to prevent tooth decay. Xylitol can be found in many chewing gums and as a sweetener in some medicines. The Finnish company Xyrofin is the market leader in producing xylitol; its predecessor Suomen Sokeri patented the industrial manufacturing method for xylitol in 1972. The more traditional sectors of the food and drink industry are also based on processing and refining raw materials and, in 1998, employed 40,700 people to produce a total output worth FMk49.3 billion. Meat processing accounts for over one-fifth of the total **value-added** sector, followed by beverages and dairy products. Russia, despite its economic troubles, is still a primary destination for food and drink exports. In 1997 Finnish food and drink industries sold Russia around 336 million euro worth of goods.

CONSTRUCTION. The construction industry faced a severe slump in the early 1990s. In 1994, commercial construction was less than 25 percent of what it had been in 1990. The decline in production reversed in 1997, partly due to government subsidies intended to rescue the industry. While a more recent economic boom has led to housing shortages in the Helsinki metropolitan area and a correspondingly high demand for house-building there, there is still little construction in other regions. In 1997, construction accounted for 5.1 percent of the GDP, employed 105,000 people, and produced FMk69 billion in revenues. Much of the construction work was exported to Russia, which in 1997 accounted for 25 percent of the construction industry's exports. The growth in construction is expected to continue, and there is some hope that it will spread outside of the city.

SERVICES

RETAIL AND WHOLESALE TRADE. Sales volumes in trade and commerce increased 5 percent in 1997, especially the purchase of vehicles, construction materials, and household appliances. **Retail**, wholesale, hotels, and restaurants accounted for a little over 12 percent of the GDP in 1998. The sales industry is very concentrated, with huge supermarkets accounting for over half of all retail outlets for everyday goods. Approximately 217,000 people were employed in retail and wholesale trade in 1998. The major Finnish wholesalers and importers are Kesko Oy, SOK-chain, and Stockmann Oy. Each company also has its own retail operation, each including several department stores and separate chain stores. Kesko, a wholesale and supermarket chain, had a turnover of FMk35.6 billion in 1998, which was 8 percent of total revenues (FMk440 billion).

TRANSPORTATION. Transportation and communications accounted for 10.2 percent of GDP in 1998. The increase of exports and industrial production in the second half of the 1990s raised demand in land, rail, and water transport and output grew by 8 percent in 1997. Road transport dominates domestically as 93 percent of passenger traffic and 67 percent of goods transport take place on the dense network of Finnish roads. The railway sector is currently state-owned, although discussions are underway to allow other companies to use the rails for moving freight. There are currently no plans to privatize the Finnish railway company, which provides long-distance passenger transport. Shipping is important for Finland's international trade; in 1998 total shipping (imports and exports) between Finland and other countries totaled 76.59 million tons. Of that, two-thirds were shipped to other EU countries, 18 percent to Germany, and 16.4 percent to Sweden. Domestic shipping totaled 12.88 million tons, up from 11.85 million tons in 1997. Due to Finland's extremely cold winters, Finnish shipbuilding and shipping is dependent on the building and use of icebreakers. Total employment in the transport sector was 154,000 and total turnover in the same year was FMk440 billion.

TELECOMMUNICATIONS. Telecommunications contributed only a little over 2 percent to the GDP in 1997; however, it is the existence of a large, inexpensive, extremely sophisticated and efficient network that has enabled almost every other industry to grow. The telecommunications sector was fully opened to competition in 1995, and the government passed a series of laws to increase the flexibility of telecommunications operators sharing and trading access to infrastructure. The government also eliminated the need for operators constructing a fixed telephone network to purchase a license, although licenses are still required for mobile phone networks. High competition in this sector has kept tariffs among the lowest in Europe. Data processing services are in great demand owing not only to the Internet but also to the turn of the millennium and the adoption of the euro. The state-owned Sonera Corporation (previously Telecom Finland) and the 45 privately owned local telephone companies operating under the Finnet Group cover the majority of the telecommunications market.

FINANCIAL SERVICES. Although accounting for only 3.5 percent of the GDP in 1998, financial services have been the source of fastest growth in the private services sector. Banks and other services have been recovering steadily since the recession of 1990 to 1993, and by 1998 net operating profits in the financial sector were FMk7.6 billion. Approximately 42,000 people were employed in the banking sector in 1999. A recent development, spurred by the advances in connectivity and other computer technology, is the rapid increase in Internet banking, which rose to around 1.5 million users in 1998. Merita Nordbanken was formed from the merger of the local Merita and the Swedish Nordbanken banks Together with the cooperative Okobank group and the state-owned Leonia. These 3 largest banking groups account for 87 percent of all domestic lending and 85.8 percent of deposits.

INTERNATIONAL TRADE

In terms of trade-orientation, Finland was almost 4 times more dependent on external trade than the United States in 1998. This outward focus of the economy rendered it quite sensitive to disturbances in external markets. The scarcity of most natural resources (except for trees) and arable land has led to reliance on imports for raw materials. The continuing abundance of trees, plus well-developed livestock farms and a technologically advanced manufacturing base, enables the processing and exporting of imported raw materials, domestic timber and wood pulp, and machinery. The majority of its forest products go to the EU and the United States.

Trade (expressed in billions of US$): Finland

	Exports	Imports
1975	5.502	7.628
1980	14.150	15.635
1985	13.617	13.232
1990	26.571	27.001
1995	39.573	28.114
1998	42.104	31.364

SOURCE: International Monetary Fund. *International Financial Statistics Yearbook 1999.*

Finland's shared border with Russia (and previously the USSR) has had a tremendous effect on its trade practices. Finnish industry was able to supply the USSR with ships and some metalwork during World War I, but the Russian military collapse and the Bolshevik Revolution in 1917 ended that relationship. After World War II, war reparations demands from the Soviets required Finland to vastly expand its industrial capacity. This necessity led to the development of a specialized Finnish industry that made icebreakers and reinforced-hull ships. After reparations were completed in 1952, Finland and the USSR continued on a barter system, with Finland mainly trading machinery and ships in exchange for oil (a resource Finland lacks).

The collapse of the USSR in the early 1990s and the Soviet-Finnish barter system was catastrophic for Finland. Trade with Russia went from 26.7 percent of Finland's external trade in 1982 to only 2.8 percent in 1992, and the number of Finnish workers supported by economic ties with Russia plunged from 230,000 in 1981 to fewer than 50,000 in 2000. Trade with Russia in 2000 was about 5 percent of external trade.

The USSR's collapse forced Finland to focus much more on exporting to the West. Demand for timber has been a somewhat risky engine of growth, but the increasing demand for high-tech goods has helped Finland to rapidly expand its high-technology sector. Finnish and general Nordic concern with environmental issues has inspired Finland to specialize in environmental pollution-monitoring equipment for domestic and exported use. In the mid-1990s, Finland also began to increase exports to

Japan and other expanding Asian economies, mostly consisting of pulp and paper products. The economic troubles of the Asian economies in the later 1990s caused a mini-recession in Finnish industry, particularly in pulp and paper exports.

Finland has been able to improve its trade situation, and has consistently run a **trade surplus** in the past few years with an estimated trade surplus of US$10.74 billion in 1998. Electronics overtook paper as the second largest export earner in 1998, generating over 25 percent of all export revenue. Germany and Sweden are the primary suppliers of imports, followed by the United States, Finland's most important non-EU trading partner. Finland's primary export markets (in descending order) are Germany, Sweden, the United Kingdom, and the United States.

MONEY

Since 1 January 1999, the Frankfurt-based European Central Bank (ECB) has been in charge of Finnish **monetary policy**. The Bank of Finland still has some responsibilities, such as holding and managing Finland's official foreign-reserve assets and contributing to supervisory credit institutions. The ECB's main **macroeconomic** goal is to keep **inflation** in the euro zone below 2 percent.

In the 1980s, Finland's economy grew faster than the European average, with stable prices and relatively low unemployment. The Finnish financial market underwent rapid change. The state's role in the money market declined, and the economy became increasingly market-oriented. Foreign banks were first allowed to operate in Finland in the early 1980s and were permitted to open branch offices there in 1991.

However, the collapse of the USSR and its loss as Finland's chief trading partner was a severe blow to the Finnish economy. Following thc banking and speculation crisis, the country fell into a severe recession. In the banking industry, nearly one-third of the employees were laid off.

Exchange rates: Finland

euros per US$1	
Jan 2001	1.0659
2000	1.0854
1999	0.9386
1998	5.3441
1997	5.1914
1996	4.5936

Note: Amounts prior to 1999 are in markkaas (FMk) per US$1.

SOURCE: CIA *World Factbook 2001* [ONLINE].

Since its devastating recession in the first 3 years of the 1990s, Finland's economy has been steadily recovering and by early 1997, GDP had returned to pre-1990 levels. Recovery was led by Finland's export sector, which was greatly aided by the Finnish currency's devaluation in 1991 and subsequently changing the markka to a **floating exchange rate**. Both actions effectively lowered the price of Finnish exports in foreign markets, which led to increased demand for them.

In 1991–92 the markka was pegged (set by the Bank of Finland in a fixed relationship) to the euro, but these limits were abandoned 2 years later, allowing the markka to float. Finland then joined the **Exchange Rate Mechanism** (ERM) of the EMU in October 1996 at the central rate of 1 euro=FMk5.8066. As of 1 January 1999, the 11 EU member countries, including Finland, joined the EMU, locking together the **exchange rates** of the 11 currencies involved. The markka was pegged to the euro at 1 euro=FMk5.9457. In 2002 Finland will adopt the euro as its paper currency.

At the beginning of the 21st century, the economy was growing, especially in the high-technology industries. Although still saddled with debt, Finland has been attempting to reduce its deficit. However, membership in the EMU has removed the Bank of Finland's ability to set an independent currency policy, which is a major tool in debt reduction. The current government is attempting to curb public spending, but with some difficulty, partly because the left-wing parties in government resist this move and have significant popular support. High unemployment (around 10 percent in 2000) is also a major problem, which many blame on a taxes-and-benefits system that makes low-wage work less attractive than collecting unemployment benefits. Inflation has been high and increasing in recent years, especially because of rising world prices of crude oil, the depreciation of the euro in relation to the dollar, high interest rates, and housing price increases.

The Helsinki Stock Exchange (HSE) is small and remote, but EMU membership is changing this situation since the HSE is the only real euro-based stock exchange in the Nordic region. Since Sweden and Denmark do not participate in the EMU, the financial focus of the area could shift towards Helsinki. Trading almost doubled from 1997 to 1998, and the value of Finland's total stock market is 3 times the GDP, the highest ratio of stock market value to the GDP in the world.

POVERTY AND WEALTH

In states with a high level of income equality and widely used welfare programs, class is difficult to identify. In Finland to some extent, it is more meaningful to look at regional or urban-rural differences. During the

GDP per Capita (US$)

Country	1975	1980	1985	1990	1998
Finland	17,608	19,925	22,347	25,957	28,075
United States	19,364	21,529	23,200	25,363	29,683
Russia	2,555	3,654	3,463	3,668	2,138
Sweden	21,157	22,283	24,168	26,397	27,705

SOURCE: United Nations. *Human Development Report 2000; Trends in human development and per capita income.*

Distribution of Income or Consumption by Percentage Share: Finland

Lowest 10%	4.2
Lowest 20%	10.0
Second 20%	14.2
Third 20%	17.6
Fourth 20%	22.3
Highest 20%	35.8
Highest 10%	21.6

Survey year: 1991

Note: This information refers to income shares by percentiles of the population and is ranked by per capita income.

SOURCE: *2000 World Development Indicators* [CD-ROM].

1960s Finland experienced one of the fastest rates of rural depopulation in the western industrialized nations. Over 10 years, 600,000 people were added to the urban population, and the urbanization rate (the rate of increase of the proportion of people living in urban areas) increased from 38.4 percent in 1960 to 50.9 percent in 1970. This uneven distribution of the population has interfered with the development of infrastructure and the provision of services, and it has made the costs of services in rural and small communities much higher.

The recession of the early 1990s led to some cutbacks in Finnish social programs. On the whole, health care and housing allowances were not diminished, but unemployment pensions, spouses' pensions, conscripts' allowances, disability benefits, refunds of medical examinations, and child-care allowances were reduced.

The poorest and most marginal members of the population tended to suffer more immediately as they had the least ability to influence those making the cutbacks. Yet in the longer term, cutbacks increasingly focused on larger programs that affected more of the population, which often made the government instituting the cutbacks less popular. Public services whose employees were numerous and well organized, such as the medical profession and trade union-dominated jobs, tended to be cut the least.

The urban-rural divide is simultaneously a regional divide, with urban areas heavily concentrated in the southern regions. In the south of Finland, overcrowding has sometimes hurt both the environment and access to social services (mostly creating waiting lists for non-emergency care), while the declining population in already sparsely inhabited areas makes it difficult to maintain even the existing economic and service facilities. However, the typical Scandinavian emphasis on social equality has ensured that nearly all inhabitants of Finland are not in a condition identifiable as poverty in terms of access to health, education, and sanitation.

WORKING CONDITIONS

For much of the post-war period, Finland had very low unemployment. The emergence of unemployment as a serious problem more or less coincides with the collapse of the USSR and the 1990s recession. Recent growth has not been able to solve the problem, especially as many of the fastest-growing businesses are in the high-technology sector and do not require as many employees as jobs of earlier eras.

The Finnish labor force was 2.53 million people in 1999, over 80 percent of whom were organized. Likewise, 80 percent of employers belong to an employers'

Household Consumption in PPP Terms

Country	All food	Clothing and footwear	Fuel and power[a]	Health care[b]	Education[b]	Transport & Communications	Other
Finland	17	4	10	4	15	7	43
United States	13	9	9	4	6	8	51
Russia	28	11	16	7	15	8	16
Sweden	17	5	12	4	14	6	41

Data represent percentage of consumption in PPP terms.
[a]Excludes energy used for transport.
[b]Includes government and private expenditures.

SOURCE: World Bank. *World Development Indicators 2000.*

association. The Finnish constitution protects the rights to organization, peaceful assembly, and strike, and these rights are adequately enforced by the state. The government, major employers' associations, and representatives from the Central Organization of Finnish Trade Unions (Suomen ammattiliittojen keskusjarjesto or SAK, an umbrella organization consisting of 25 trade unions and totaling 1.1 million members) meet at the national level and communicate to discuss economic and employment policy. However, coordination of this kind has not prevented disagreement, which has often led to strikes. There were 18 strikes in the fourth quarter of 1997 alone, including a firefighters' strike.

There is no specific minimum wage law, but employers are required to bargain with workers' organizations at the industry level (usually with government participation) over contracts that include a minimum wage, which has historically been more than adequate. This wage is extended to non-union workers, and if other wages rise (either due to general rises in the cost of living or due to improvements in the industry), that benefit must be passed on to even the minimum-wage workers, so their situation will keep pace with the higher-paid ones.

There is still wage inequality among the genders in the Finnish labor force, despite the existence of an equal rights act and a law mandating equal pay for equal work. In 1998 women's average earnings were 81 percent of those of men, and women still tend to be segregated in lower paying occupations. While women have individually attained leadership positions in the private and public sectors, there are disproportionately fewer women in top management jobs. Industry and finance, the labor movement, and some government ministries remain male dominated.

Legally, the workweek is set at 5 days with a maximum of 40 hours of work. In practice, this limit is usually understood as a minimum provision, and many workers enjoy even stronger benefits through effectively enforced collective bargaining agreements.

COUNTRY HISTORY AND ECONOMIC DEVELOPMENT

1809. Finland, a province of Sweden, is taken over by Russia.

1836–86. Finland is supposedly granted autonomous rule under the Russian tsar Alexander II, but has little real independence. Finnish joins Swedish as an official language.

1905. The Eduskunta (national parliament) is created. Universal voting rights (including women and men who hold no property) are granted.

1917–19. The Russian Empire collapses. Finland declares independence, after which civil war briefly breaks out between political factions.

1919. The Eduskunta ratifies the Finnish constitution. Finland becomes a parliamentary republic with a president as the head of state.

1932. Finland and the USSR sign a non-aggression pact.

1939. The border region of Southern Karelia is ceded to the USSR after the 15-week "Winter War."

1940. A peace treaty with the USSR ends the Winter War.

1941–44. After Germany invades Russia in 1941, Finland enters the Continuation War alongside Germany against the USSR to win back Karelia.

1944. Peace is declared, and Finland stops fighting alongside the Germans.

1944–45. Finland fights against the Germans in the Lapland War as they retreat across Finland from the Soviet front.

1946. Finland signs the Treaty of Friendship, Cooperation, and Mutual Assistance with the USSR.

1951. Self-government is granted to the Swedish-speaking Åland Islands, formerly ruled from mainland Finland.

1970. Finland adopts a 40-hour working week.

1973. Finland signs a free-trade agreement with the European Economic Community (EEC), an international body that centralizes economic decisions and organization among its member states.

1991–93. The Soviet Union collapses, worsening an already severe recession and banking/financial crisis in Finland.

1995. Finland joins the EU, a replacement of the EEC. The new union has a more explicit political and human rights agenda in addition to the economic one. The first Green Party representatives in a European government are elected to the Eduskunta.

1999. Finland joins the EMU. All EMU member nations agree to adopt a single new currency, the euro.

FUTURE TRENDS

Finland's aging population poses the greatest challenge for the future. Its extensive welfare and social security system will be strained by the shrinking workforce and increasing population of the elderly. A major difficulty the government faces is the political unpopularity of suggesting reductions in the welfare system. The guarantee of a certain standard of living is considered to be of primary importance to most Finns, but the question of where the money will come from to support this policy has no easy answer. The suggestion made by Finland's most right-wing political organizations—restricting those who are eligible for benefits based on ethnic criteria—is fortunately not popular. However, it is clear that significant re-structuring of the welfare system will be needed. The IMF, while praising Finland's strong recovery from its recession of 1991 to 1993, recommended several measures to anticipate and defuse the coming demographic crisis, including raising the effective retirement age of 59, altering individual pensions accounts, and reducing the length of time that unemployment benefit can be claimed. The Finnish government so far has focused on altering tax and wage structures and is more wary of reducing benefits.

Although steady economic growth reduced unemployment to some extent, Finland still faces an unemployment problem. National unemployment is still above 10 percent, and in areas of rural northern and eastern Finland it exceeds 30 percent. Since most export industries are highly automated and create relatively few jobs, it has been suggested that Finland is nearing its structural limit on unemployment. The state has been investing in education programs for adults and children to familiarize people with the Internet and computer programming and it is hoped to find a place for them in the new economy. However, public spending is expected to fall in 2001, and the government is trying to find a way to solve the unemployment problem without increasing government expenditure. Plans for lowering the income tax may be one way to encourage more participation in the labor force but cannot guarantee that the kind of workers required by the new economy will be available.

In 1995, the first Green Party representatives were elected to the Eduskunta, and their strong opposition to nuclear energy and fossil fuels poses a challenge to the government, which is looking for consensus on how to meet increasing energy demands. In the light of domestic and international environmental concerns about sustainability, pollution, and other risks associated with nuclear power, as well as dependence on exhaustible fossil fuels (which must be imported), Finland's energy system may need to be reexamined. It is unclear how the coalition government will deal with this challenge. Most attention has been given to research into sustainable energy sources, for which some funds have been allocated. Finnish businesses appear to be more sensitive to these issues than some of their European counterparts that may actually be better equipped to handle the task.

The importance of the timber industry to the economy may lead to future problems. Many current environmental reports describe commercial timber farming as destructive to Finland's ancient forests. The government and timber industry deny this claim, and they do not appear to distinguish between old-growth forests—which are ancient and full of a diverse range of plant, animal, and insect life—and homogenous, younger, and non-native trees that have been more recently planted. High levels of logging and clear-cutting of ancient trees and their replacement with commercially viable tree species threatens the bio-diversity of these ancient forests and poses extinction risks to local plant and animal species. Complaints by environmental groups on this issue have inspired the Finnish Ministry for the Environment to increase efforts to ease the ecological pressure on Finland's ancient forests. The timber industry, however, is highly dependent on world demand and is not as flexible in its responses as other industries. Finland's ongoing commitment to research and development in all its industries can be taken as a hopeful sign that further flexibility may come, as new industrial products are developed which can allow the industry to diversify.

Membership in the EMU has taken away Finland's ability to control the economy through interest rates and devaluation. **Fiscal policy** is now the main instrument of control. This situation could lead to problems, as the government has been running a **budget deficit**, and depends on high taxes for much of its revenue. If the EU starts to require harmonization of taxes among its members, Finland will be in great difficulty.

Although Finland has recovered well from its recessions of a decade ago, it is still in a slightly precarious position in its over-concentrated engine of growth. Specifically, Nokia alone accounts for around 65 percent of shares traded on the Helsinki Stock Exchange, and Finland is particularly sensitive to world demand of its main forest products for export. As the nation's population ages, the shift of people out of the workforce and into its pension system will strain the government's resources, which have only recently recovered from the recession. Membership in the EU gives some advantages, especially in terms of an export market but also removes some control over the economy. It is up to the Finnish state to attempt to strike a balance.

DEPENDENCIES

Finland has no territories or colonies.

BIBLIOGRAPHY

Chemical Industry Federation of Finland. <http://www.chemind.fi/english/index.html>. Accessed April 2001.

"Economic Indicators: Spending on the Environment." *OECD Observer*. October 1999.

Economist Intelligence Unit. *Country Profile: Finland*. London: Economist Intelligence Unit, 2001.

"Finland's Struggle for Prosperity in the New World Economy." *U.S. Embassy in Finland*. <http://www.usembassy.fi/usmissio/ambartic.phtml>. Accessed April 2001.

Finnish Food and Drink Industries' Federation. <http://www.etl.fi/ewww/index.htm>. Accessed April 2001.

Ministry of Agriculture and Forestry. "The Forest Industry in Finland." <http://www.mmm.fi/english/forestry/industry/>. Accessed April 2001.

Ministry of Foreign Affairs. *Virtual Finland.* <http://www.virtual.finland.fi>. Accessed April 2001.

Solsten, Eric, and Sandra W. Meditz. *Finland: A Country Study.* Area Handbook Series, Federal Research Division, Library of Congress, 1990.

Statistics Finland. "Finland in Figures." <http://tilastokeskus.fi/tk/tp/tasku/suomilukuina_en.html>. Accessed April 2001.

United Nations Development Programme. *Human Development Report.* New York: Oxford University Press, 2000.

U.S. Central Intelligence Agency. *World Factbook 2000.* <http://www.odci.gov/cia/publications/factbook/index.html>. Accessed April 2001.

U.S. Department of Commerce. *National Trade Databank.* <http://www.tradeport.org/ts/countries/finland>. Accessed April 2001.

—Larisa Mann

FRANCE

French Republic
République Française

CAPITAL: Paris.

MONETARY UNIT: French Franc (FRF). A franc equals 100 centimes. Coins are in denominations of 1, 2, 5, 10 and 20 francs, and 5, 10, 20 and 50 centimes. Paper currency is in denominations of FRF 50, 100, 200, and 500. In 1999, the European Union (EU), of which France is a member, introduced a new currency, called the euro, to be the common currency among the participating member countries. The euro is scheduled to circulate amongst the members of the European Monetary Union (EMU) by 2002. When this happens, it will be the sole currency in member states, including France. The exchange rate between the euro and franc is fixed at 6.56 francs per euro. Both the franc and euro currently **float** against all other currencies. The exchange rate for 1 U.S. dollar was 0.98 euros at the euro's inception, but it has lost substantial value since then. There are 100 cents in a euro. Coins will come in denominations of 1, 2, 5, 10, 20, and 50 cents, as well as 1 and 2 euros. Paper currency will be issued in denominations of 5, 10, 20, 50, 100, 200, and 500 euros.

CHIEF EXPORTS: Machinery and transportation equipment, chemicals, iron and steel products, agricultural products, textiles and clothing.

CHIEF IMPORTS: Crude oil, machinery and equipment, chemicals, agricultural products.

GROSS DOMESTIC PRODUCT: US$1.373 trillion (in purchasing power parity, 1999 est.).

BALANCE OF TRADE: **Exports:** US$304.7 billion (f.o.b., 1999). **Imports:** US$280.8 billion (f.o.b., 1999).

COUNTRY OVERVIEW

LOCATION AND SIZE. France has the largest land area of any Western European nation and lies between the Mediterranean Sea on the southeast and the Bay of Biscay and English Channel to the north and west. France has a total land area of 547,030 square kilometers (211,208 square miles) and a coastline of 3,427 kilometers (2,130 miles). It shares borders with Andorra, Monaco, Belgium, Luxembourg, Germany, Switzerland, Italy, and Spain. Its area is about four-fifths of the size of Texas.

Paris, the capital city, is the largest city in France and Europe (excluding Russia), and accommodates about one-sixth of the country's population. Other cities with over a million people including surrounding areas are Lyon, Marseille, and Lille.

POPULATION. France's population was estimated to be 59,329,691 in 2000, with a slow growth rate of 0.38 percent. The French population is about one-fifth of Europe's total population and ranks third in Europe and sixteenth in the world. It has about 106 inhabitants per square kilometer (or about 275 people per square mile). Roughly one-sixth of the entire population lives in the Greater Paris area. France's ethnic groups include Celtic and Latin strains, with Teutonic, Slavic, North African, Indochinese, and Basque minorities. Foreigners comprise 6.3 percent of the population.

While the majority of the population (65 percent) falls between the ages of 15 and 64, about 16 percent are older than 65 years of age. The remaining 19 percent are 14 years old and younger. At the turn of the 19th century, France was the most populous country in Europe. But by the late 19th and early 20th century, France experienced the lowest birth rate in the continent. Due to government efforts and the post-World War II baby boom, however, France reached a birth rate of 21 per 1,000 people in the post-war era. This growth declined to 18 and 13.6 per 1,000 in 1963 and 1989, respectively. Currently, France's birth rate stands at 12.27 births per 1,000 population according to 2000 estimates. (France had 9.14 deaths per 1,000 population during the same

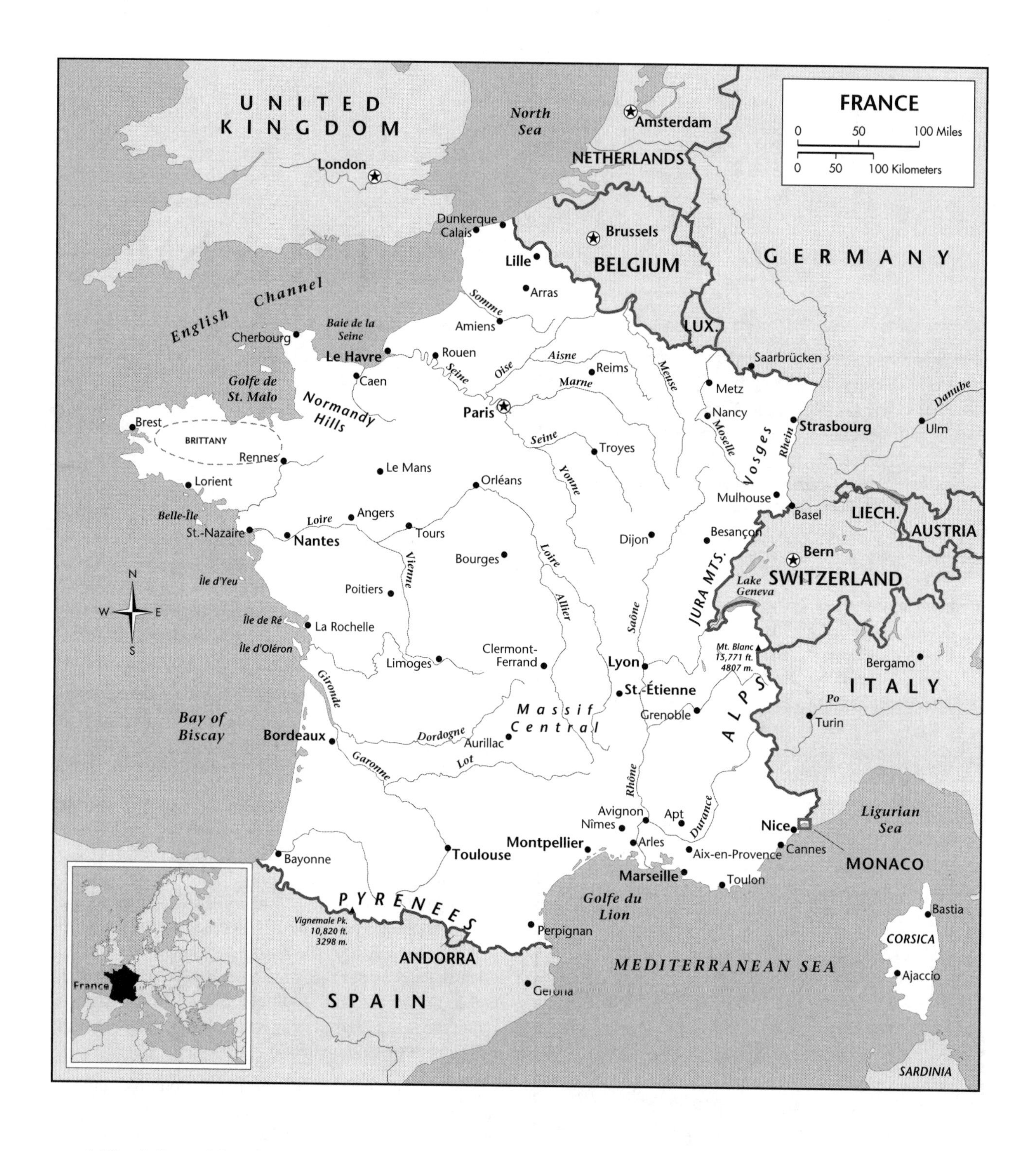

year.) The influx of immigrants into France at the last quarter of 20th century, though, has moderated the trend toward a shrinking population. It is estimated that France has received 0.66 net immigrants per 1,000 people in 2,000. The ratio between males and females is nearly one-to-one in almost all age strata of French population, with the exception of those over age 65, where there are 0.68 males per each female. This is mainly because the life expectancy for females at birth is about 83 years while it is only 75 for males. Life expectancy for the total population averages 79 years.

In 2000, France was the sixteenth most populous nation in the world. The French population is expected to decline by the year 2025 when France will rank twenty-fifth in the world. The **United Nations Development Program** (UNDP) estimates that the population will reach 61,662,000 in 2025 but drop to 59,883,000 in 2050, with 30 percent of the population over 80 years of age. (This number was 16 percent in 2000.) This means that the potential support ratio (the number of people aged 15 to 64 for each person aged 65 years or older) in 2050 will be half of its 1999 level. In other words, every 2 working people will be supporting a retired person in 2050, which doubles the burden on the society from 1999 to 2050 in providing care and benefits for the elderly.

Archaic **immigration** policies make France somewhat unattractive for foreigners who seek work or asylum, even though the need for more workers has been recognized by many. The government provides generous family and health support programs, though these have not necessarily encouraged population growth. Individuals with health problems, the unemployed, and the retired are protected from bankruptcy by the social security system. Some cities even tried to implement their own programs to encourage population growth, but they were aimed at French or European races, and thus quickly denounced as racist. Overall, the government's efforts to address the serious under-population problem of the near future have not been successful.

OVERVIEW OF ECONOMY

By the 18th century, France was one of the richest nations of the world. The potential for industrial development made France a rival to England, perhaps the most powerful country on Earth at the time. But it was its agricultural potential at the beginning of the Industrial Revolution (the period during the 18th and 19th centuries when Europe changed from agrarian, handicraft economies to the those dominated by industry and machine manufacture) which made France a world power. However, its sluggishness in moving from agrarian to industrial modes of production, together with several other factors such as a declining population, left France behind in an industrializing world in the 20th century. As this process continued, and due in part to nationalist sentiment, France largely closed its doors to foreign competition in order to protect its own industries. The **nationalization** of major industries in France took place in the late 1930s in railways, coal, natural gas, electricity, and the banking sector. Flagship companies in various transportation sectors, such as Renault and Air France, also came under the state control. Although a capitalist country, France made many **socialist** adjustments such as heavy government control over the economy, which included strict government regulation of many industries or powerful representation of the government in sectors considered essential to the national economy. As part of its statist economic policies, France implemented national economic development plans.

Despite its mixed economic system, France has also recognized since the early post-World War II era that economic integration with Europe is in its own best interests. To this end, France has been the major impetus in the formation of such bodies as the European Coal and Steel Community (in the early 1950s) and the European Economic Community. These organizations were the first steps toward both economic and political union in Europe.

Currently the government's role in the economic sphere is much less than before, especially because of the requirements of the European Union (EU). Since the early 1990s, French companies have faced competition from their European counterparts with less help from the government. In an effort to **privatize** the state-owned industries, the government is selling off its shares in France Telecom and Air France, along with companies from the insurance, banking, and defense industries.

Because of its fertile and vast land, France has become a major agricultural producer of Europe, making use of modern agricultural technology. The agricultural sector enjoys generous government support in the form of **subsidies**. This policy sometimes becomes a point of contention with France's EU counterparts. Three-fifths of the land is devoted to agricultural-related economic activities. Besides wine, France is famous for its beef, veal, poultry, and dairy products. Various types of grains also make France the leader among European nations in agricultural production. Overproduction of the world-renowned French wine and competition from foreign producers have conspired to bring about decreases in its price, although the government as of 2001 has tried to discourage overproduction in an attempt to reverse this alarming trend.

France has a long seashore, but fishing is not one of the major components of the economy, except in coastal areas such as Normandy and Brittany, the southern Atlantic coast, and the Mediterranean, where it employs a significant local **labor force**. France has few fishing ports used in shipment of fish products and ranks 20th in the world in total fish production.

Even though France has a highly-educated labor force, unemployment—which stood at 9.2 percent in December 2000, according to the International Labor Organization (ILO)—is still a major problem, mainly because of the slow growth of the economy. Employment opportunities for college graduates were especially lacking. A 35-hour work week was introduced in 1999 by the government in order to create more jobs. Small companies especially objected to the measure as burdensome, for it forced them to hire more workers. Larger firms are more comfortable with the shortened work week, arguing that participation in the European Monetary Union and a common currency have brought new flexibility into the market and hence has eliminated the costs brought by the shortened work week.

France still maintains its ties with many of its former colonies, especially those in Africa, such as Algeria, Benin, and Senegal. France provides support in the form of French francs in order to stabilize some African currencies. It also provides other types of aid to some of its former colonies, totaling US$6.3 billion in 1997.

As of the end of the 20th century, the **capital goods** sector was one of the fastest-growing sectors of the economy, followed by automobiles and services. The French government predicts continuing stable growth in the first few years of the 21st century, largely due to investments in technology and the promise of structural reforms. France's **infrastructure** is modern in all respects.

POLITICS, GOVERNMENT, AND TAXATION

A democratic republic with a constitution approved by referendum in 1958, France is both economically and politically a hybrid of many systems. Economically, it is a capitalistic country with a socialist outlook, exemplified by property rights and a capitalistic concept of private ownership on one hand and an extremely generous social security system and a socialist approach to solving the society's problems on the other. France has a presidential system combined with a more typical European parliamentary arrangement.

The president of the republic, as the head of state, is elected by direct suffrage every 7 years, and appoints the prime minister as the head of government. However, the president must choose the prime minister from a party or a group of political parties determined by the National Assembly, which is the lower house of the French Parliament. It is quite possible that the president and the prime minister may come from different, and even rival, political parties. This is known as cohabitation. Following the 1995 presidential elections, President Jacques Chirac, who represents the center-right side of the political spectrum, cohabits with a center-left government headed by Prime Minister Lionel Jospin, who was his rival in 1995 presidential elections. Prime Minister Jospin is the head of the Socialist Party, and his coalition government includes representatives from the **Communist** and Green parties.

The French parliament is **bicameral** (a representative system with 2 houses in the parliament or legislature, as in Germany or the United States). Representatives are elected to the National Assembly (the lower house of parliament) by direct universal suffrage, and senators are elected indirectly by an electoral college which is comprised of approximately 145,000 representatives of city councilmen. Representatives serve for 5 years, whereas senators are elected for 9 years. The main power brokers in the French political spectrum can be classified from right to left as National Front (FN), Rally for the Republic (RPR), Rally for France (RPF), Union for French Democracy (UDF), the Socialist Party (PS), Green Party, and the Communist Party of France (PCF). The extreme left parties support continued state control over the economy with big spending programs, while the right-wing parties want to end most forms of state support. The right-wing parties also wish to see far less immigration and more people of European origin populating the country. The high level of unemployment and rising nationalism, expressed also in the form of xenophobia (enmity against foreigners and immigrants), have fueled the popularity of the extremist National Front. President Chirac is from RPR. Both that party and the RPF are neo-Gaullist parties (parties supporting the policies and principles laid down by former French statesman Charles de Gaulle, which call for greater European and French power, prestige, and independence, especially from the United States). The UDF is relatively moderate. There are other small parties which may play roles, sometimes influential ones, at the local but not the national levels. Left-leaning parties, especially the socialists, usually advocate implementing a domestic agenda aimed at fighting unemployment and promoting social programs.

Because of pressure from the EU, more budgetary discipline has been emphasized in governmental affairs. **Protectionist policies** have been abandoned against other members of EU countries. There is strong support for the EU amongst the French people as well as from the president and prime minister. In fact, France is among the most prominent supporters of a unified Europe. Some believe the basis of this support is France's effort to counter the power of the United States in the world's economic and political affairs.

French governments changed hands between left and right in the last quarter of the 20th century, and sometimes political movements changed course. After the influential General de Gaulle's right-leaning government in 1960s, President Francois Mitterand broke with tradition when he came to power in early the 1980s. De Gaulle held the office of the president between 1959 and 1969, and Mitterand served 2 terms as president (1981–95). Catering to the demands of the powerful Communist Party, which supported Mitterand, his socialist government increased government spending by engaging in several public projects and increased taxes in order to pay for the spending. While most of the capitalist world recognized the virtues of the free market economy, the Mitterand government embarked on nationalization efforts. This policy soon led the country into economic turmoil with higher levels of **inflation** coupled with lower values for the French franc. This tendency forced the government to reverse some of its previous policy decisions, even if it meant adopting policy suggestions of political rivals. Mitterand's prime minister (Chirac) lost the presidential election in 1988 only to win it in 1995. However, the solutions to the economic problems on which Chirac based his campaigns have not yet been completely achieved. With one of the highest levels of unemployment in the EU and its president battered by corruption charges, France saw a general strike in December 1995 that brought the country to a virtual economic standstill. The French government still has a strong presence in the economy, especially in such industries as aeronautics, defense, automobiles, and telecommunications. Even though a great deal has been achieved in privatization, the government can still exert its influence on privatized companies via its large minority stakes in such companies. Nevertheless, after a policy decision of the president in 1996 to streamline defense industries, a wave of mergers and **restructuring** took place among French defense companies.

France prefers to continue with a large government budget financed mainly by taxes rather than to curtail its spending. Currently, France ranks highest in broadly defined tax categories among G8 countries (a group of the most industrialized countries of the world consists of the United States, Japan, Germany, France, Italy, Canada, Russia, and the United Kingdom). The basic corporate tax rate is 33.33 percent. The largest tax burden in France, though, is **income tax**, which in the highest income bracket runs to 54 percent. (By comparison, U.S. federal taxes range from 15 to 33 percent.) The highest tax bracket starts at only about US$40,000, so the middle and upper classes in France pay a significant portion of their salaries in taxes. This rate is one cause, some economists believe, of unemployment, because high taxation together with generous government spending programs discourages working. Incomes of less than 26,100 French francs (approximately US$3,500) a year are not taxed at all, while all income levels above US$20,000 are taxed of a rate of at least 40 percent.

INFRASTRUCTURE, POWER, AND COMMUNICATIONS

France enjoys one of the most sophisticated infrastructures in the world, developed through the government's heavy investment in the field and made possible by advanced technology. A network of various modes of transportation blankets the whole country, including air, land, and rail transportation. Transportation is also possible via rivers. The technologically advanced rail system—utilizing some of the fastest trains in the world—is operated by the French National Railways (SNCF), a state-owned company. There are a total of 31,939 kilometers (19,846 miles) of rail lines in the country. There are approximately 828,000 kilometers (514,605 miles) of roads in France, all of which are paved. About 47 per cent of the waterways are heavily used. There are a total of 474 airports in France, many of which serve international traffic. The major airline is Air France, which provides service to all corners of the globe. Many of the ports and harbors are equipped to handle the needs of freight as well as passenger ships. The major port cities are Dunkirk, Bordeaux, Marseille, Nantes, Rouen, Le Havre, Boulogne, Cherbourg, Dijon, La Pallice, Lyon, Mullhouse, Paris, Saint Nazaire, Saint Malo, and Strasbourg.

The communications infrastructure of France also ranks high among advanced countries. There were about 35 million main telephone lines in use by the end of 1998, with mobile cellular phone usage at about 35 percent of that figure. About 218 newspapers were sold in France per 1,000 people in 1996. This number slightly exceeds EMU member countries' newspaper circulation rate for the same period but falls behind the high income countries' average of 286. The number of radios per 1,000 people in 1997 was 937, which shows the same pattern with respect to the EU and high income countries' averages. Radios broadcasting in AM, FM, and short wave cater to domestic and international clienteles. Television set ownership is somewhere in the middle of EU countries. Cable TV is not as widespread in France as it is in either high-income or EU countries as a whole. France's ratio of 27.5 cable subscribers per 1,000 is a far cry from Europe's 110.3 and that of the wealthiest nations' 184. In spite of its vast mobile phone usage, France also lags behind both EU as a whole and its wealthiest countries. There are fewer Internet service providers (ISPs) in France

Communications

Country	Newspapers	Radios	TV Sets[a]	Cable subscribers[a]	Mobile Phones[a]	Fax Machines[a]	Personal Computers[a]	Internet Hosts[b]	Internet Users[b]
	1996	1997	1998	1998	1998	1998	1998	1999	1999
France	218	937	601	27.5	188	47.4	207.8	110.64	5,370
United States	215	2,146	847	244.3	256	78.4	458.6	1,508.77	74,100
Germany	311	948	580	214.5	170	73.1	304.7	173.96	14,400
Spain	100	333	506	11.8	179	17.8	144.8	76.75	4,652

[a]Data are from International Telecommunication Union, *World Telecommunication Development Report 1999* and are per 1,000 people.
[b]Data are from the Internet Software Consortium (http://www.isc.org) and are per 10,000 people.

SOURCE: World Bank. *World Development Indicators 2000.*

than in many other EU nations, but there is easy access to the Internet via both domestic and foreign ISPs. The dominant domestic telecommunications company, Minitel, is run by the government-owned France Telecom, which has a proprietary electronic commerce service. Even though it lags behind its counterparts in the developed world in some electronic communications industries such as the Internet, France is quickly catching up.

Nevertheless, France is a very conservative country, deeply committed to its own distinct national information infrastructure, which makes the country cautious in approaching innovations that do not originate within France. The government makes special efforts to prevent English, which is by far the most widely used language on the Internet, from taking over in communications. A law was even passed in the early 1990s in an attempt to bolster the use of French in the communications field, thanks to efforts of the Ministry of Culture. The French Internet industry and other communications sectors are more heavily regulated than those of Germany and Britain, and some economists maintain that this has significantly impeded developments in the Internet and related industries in the country. On the other hand, government is promoting the usage of information technology and began in 1999 to **deregulate** some aspects of the industry.

France is not rich when it comes to fuel resources, so it imports three-quarters of the fuel it needs, especially oil. The same does not hold true for electrical energy production, though. Electricity production reached over 480 billion kilowatt hours (kWh) in 1998. The biggest source of electrical power is nuclear energy, which supplies about 76 percent of the country's needs and making France the second largest supplier of nuclear energy after the United States. The next largest source of electrical power is hydroelectric, which supplies about 13 percent, which is produced by plants operating on the Isère, Durance, Rhine, Rhône, and Dordogne rivers. Additionally, a tidal power plant is located on the Rance River in Brittany. Fossil fuel represents about 11 percent of electrical power in France and supplies about 389 billion kWh of energy. France exports about 62 billion kWh of fossil fuel energy and imports 4 billion kWh more.

ECONOMIC SECTORS

The French economy is competitive on a global scale in many goods and service sectors. In 1998, about 3.3 percent of the GDP was contributed by the agricultural sector, and 26.1 percent by the industry. But the major portion of the GDP is accounted for by the service sector, which makes France a typical modern industrialized country. While most employment is provided by this sector (about 66 percent), agriculture employs only 7 percent and services 27 percent. Historically, France has been the capital of Europe with its vast expanses of farm land. French wine and cheese are famous throughout the world. For historical and cultural reasons, French farms have generally been small and family-owned, and worked with traditional tools and methods. Globalization, which involves the opening of France to the market forces of Europe, has led the country to think about modernization in agriculture, which has only partially adopted modern methods. Currently, the French economy is stronger and more competitive in world markets than before, even though many business enterprises are still smaller than their counterparts in Europe, Japan, and the United States.

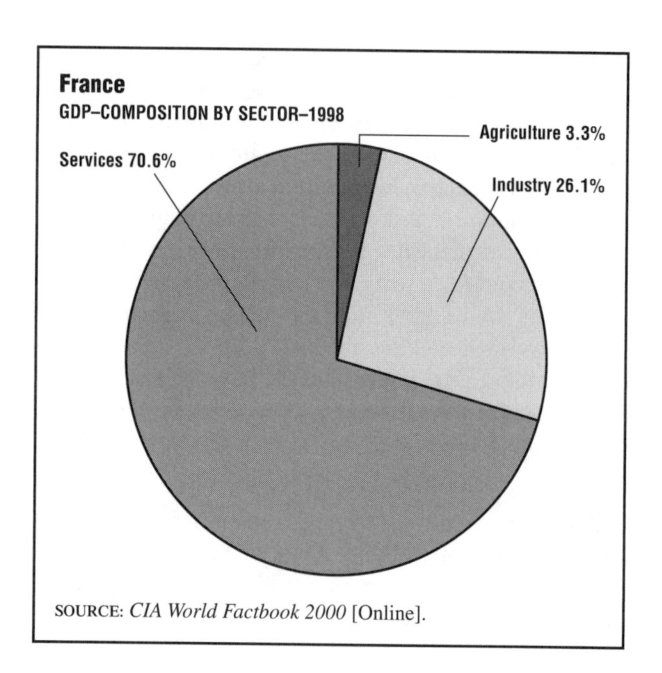

SOURCE: *CIA World Factbook 2000* [Online].

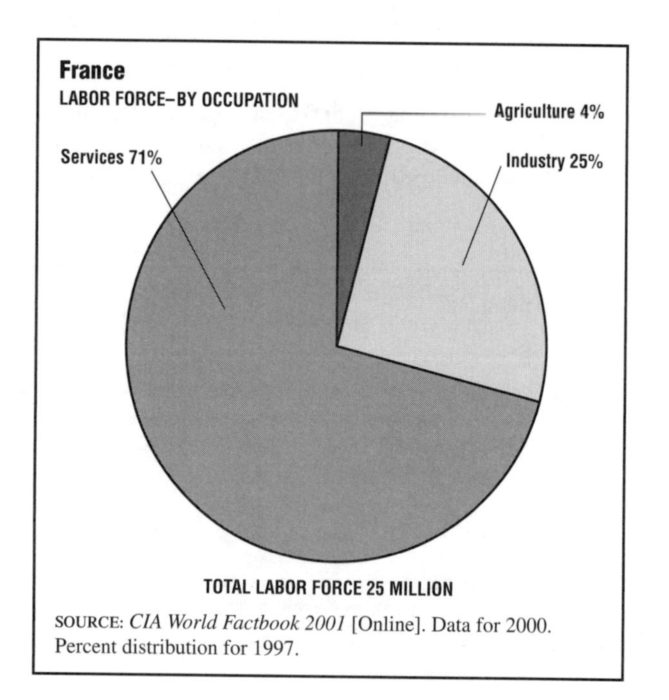

SOURCE: *CIA World Factbook 2001* [Online]. Data for 2000. Percent distribution for 1997.

The leading industries are metallurgy, mechanical and electrical engineering, chemicals, textiles, and the manufacturing of airplanes and automobiles. The auto producers, Renault and Citroen, are household names in many European countries. The French are very proud of Airbus Industrie, which is the main competitor of the Boeing Company, the leading U.S. aircraft producer. Airbus has captured a sizable portion of the commercial airplane market, a domain which had belonged exclusively to Boeing and its smaller U.S. and British competitors before the rise of Airbus in the 1970s. The world famous Mirage and Concorde are also produced by French aviation companies. The tragic July 2000 crash of a Concorde in France marred the otherwise superb reliability of Concorde airplanes, but in 2001 the sleek jet was scheduled to go back into service with Air France. France is not very rich in natural resources other than bauxite, but the country processes imported material into commercial products and resells them domestically and to the rest of the world.

France has a diverse and important services sector. Paris has the fifth largest stock market in the world. France's 4 banks rank among the biggest 25 banks in the world. The insurance industry ranks fifth in the world. France has been, for much of the last century, the world capital in fashion, setting the trends in designer clothes. Although there is a threat from countries with lower labor costs, French textile products are among the best in the world. Perfumes produced in France are synonymous with high fashion. Paris is known all over the world for its cultural attractions, architecture, and cosmopolitan lifestyle. That is why France is 1 of the 3 most-visited countries in the world, along with Spain and the United States.

AGRICULTURE

France has been one of the most dominant agricultural centers of Europe for centuries. That gave France an important role in European and, to some extent world, affairs in the pre-industrial age. Currently, France still leads Europe in agriculture, excluding the Russian Federation. With about 730,000 farms, approximately 7 percent of the workforce is employed in agriculture or similar sectors such as fishing or forestry. When all people engaged in agriculture-related activities (including the processing of agricultural goods, for example) are considered, the percentage of the population engaged in agricultural production is much larger. As of 2001, many younger people tend to look for employment outside of family farms and help out only as part-timers. This trend, however, has generated an opportunity for others looking for jobs in agriculture. According to the French Ministry of Agriculture, the share of population actively involved in farming is decreasing. Nevertheless, new creative methods of marketing and agritourism have attracted some young talent to the sector. The sheer size of the land used for farming, about three-fifths of the total, indicates the place of agriculture in the lives of French people. In the post-World War II era, government has made a significant effort to modernize French agricultural production by switching to more scientific methods and modern equipment. In 1997, about 86 percent of farms owned at least 1 tractor, and farmers increasingly upgrade equipment. The size of irrigated land in 1997 is twice that in 1979.

The major agricultural products that place France among the top producers in the world market are sugar beets, wine, milk, beef and veal, cereals, and oilseeds. Producing 29 million metric tons of sugar beets, France leads the EU. It takes second place in both the EU and the world in the production of its highly popular wine varieties, with 5.3 million metric tons. Though fifth in the world, France ranks second in the EU in milk production, totaling 23.3 million metric tons. France is the major source of meat and veal in the EU with 1,815,000 metric tons. What is commonly known as "Mad Cow Disease" (an illness first discovered in British beef that causes death if it infects humans) created a rift among European countries, especially when France prohibited British beef from entering the country. In the cereals category, which includes soft wheat and grain maze, France leads the EU. With 4.1 million metric tons of production, France also holds the leading position in oilseeds in the EU.

The biggest export items among agricultural products are various types of beverages and alcoholic drinks. According to the Ministry's numbers, the value of alcoholic exports reached 56.6 billion francs in 1999. This amount registered a 6 percent increase over the previous period. Cereals and flour exports, which increased 12 percent, totaled 36 billion francs. Meat and other animal products experienced a shrinkage of 7 percent but were still valued at 28 billion francs. All categories of prepared food brought 27 billion francs into the country in the same year. However, this reflected a decline of 10 percent from the previous year. Dairy products also suffered a loss of 2 percent in the world market share, generating 24 billion francs. Demand for French sugar and sugar refineries declined sharply in the world market by about 8 per cent in 1999. The total export revenue obtained by this category was 11 billion francs. The economic crises in world markets played a role in the declines experienced by French exporters of agricultural products. The EU and the United States are France's principal customers for agricultural products.

France is also an importer of agricultural commodities. Prepared food tops the list of imported agricultural items. Figures from 1999 indicate that France imported 19 billion francs worth of meat and other animal products. Even though it has a sizable coastline, France imports a large segment of its fish demand from abroad, which was valued at 16 billion francs in 1999. Fruits, dairy products, and various beverages cost France 14, 12 and 10 billion francs respectively in the same year. All import categories experienced moderate shrinkage between 3 and 6 per cent, except meat, animal products, and fisheries, all of which remained unchanged from 1997. France did most of its shopping from the same countries to which it sold its products.

Almost half of farm income in France is generated by livestock raising, and the other half is contributed by crops. Cattle are raised mainly in the north and west; sheep and goats primarily in the south and east, which is drier and more mountainous. Pigs and chickens are raised everywhere in France. The Paris Basin area is the source of wheat while some rice comes from irrigated fields of the Rhone delta. While Burgundy, Champagne, Bordeaux, and Alsace are well-known wine regions, wine is actually produced all over the country.

Fishing does not contribute to the French economy in comparison with the agriculture on the national scale. According to the data released by the Ministry of Agriculture, fish production in 1998 reached nearly 600,000 metric tons, a slight increase of 1.5 percent over the previous year. Because of favorable prices, though, the fish products sector exceeded 6.5 billion francs. The exports of the sector fall far behind imports, creating a **trade deficit** in fisheries which is more than double the exports. However, France still ranks twentieth in the world in total fish production. Locally, fishing plays an important role in such areas as Normandy and Brittany, the Southern Atlantic coast, and the Mediterranean. Concarneau, Boulogne-sur-Mer, Lorient, and La Rochelle are the main fishing ports of France.

France's forests are prized for both economic and ecological reasons. The National Forestry Service, founded in 1966, is responsible for managing the country's forests. From 1850 to 1900 a big reforestation campaign occurred, and as of 2001, about 27 percent of French land is covered by forests, making it the third-most forested country in the EU. Two-thirds of the forests are occupied by deciduous trees, and the rest are conifers. France's forests have grown 35 percent since 1945 and continue to grow by about 30,000 hectares each year. Close to 4 million people in France have private ownership of wooded areas. The marketed wood harvest was up in 1998 from its level in 1997 by about 1.6 percent. The rise in the wood industry is attributed to the renewal of activity in construction. As in many other countries, forests in France are utilized not only for wood production but as recreation as well. Hence, while supplying wood products and playing a role in a healthier environment, forests also contribute to the national economy by serving the tourism sector.

INDUSTRY

France is among the most industrialized countries of the world. It is a member of the G8, a group of countries which comprises the 7 largest industrial democracies, plus the Russian Federation. In 1999, the French GDP was almost identical to that of Great Britain and comfortably larger than that of Italy.

MANUFACTURING. About 19.3 per cent of the GDP was generated by manufacturing in France in 1999, compared to 17.8 percent in the United States and 18.5 percent in Britain. Manufacturing contributes roughly 20 percent of the GDP in Italy, Germany and Japan. Investment in the industrial manufacturing sector was 141 billion francs in 1999. (These figures excluded the energy and agricultural manufacturing sectors.)

Firms operating in the industrial manufacturing sector produced a variety of goods such as consumption goods , items related to the auto industry, and equipment such as electronics, machinery, and **intermediate goods**. The well-established name for French products in the fashion world helps France in the export of perfumes and even flowers. The consumption goods industry made nearly 200 billion francs from sales abroad in 1999. The contribution of the auto industry to the French exports figures in 1999 was almost 300 billion francs. France is one of the largest producers of passenger cars and commercial vehicles in the world, along with Japan, the United States, and Germany.

The principal manufacturing companies are located in Ile-de-France, Rhone-Alpes, Nord-Pas-de-Calais, and Pays de la Loire regions. New industrial areas emerged around the English Channel and Mediterranean Sea in order to save shipment costs of imported raw materials. Even though some French companies, such as Renault and Airbus, are world famous, most French firms are characterized as moderate to small-sized. But small firms tend to be ineffective in the world market because of heavy competition from companies based in countries with cheaper labor costs or higher and better production technologies. The pressure of competition was felt heavily with the unification of the European markets under the umbrella of EU, in which movement of capital and labor is not constrained. Unless smaller and relatively inefficient French firms can adapt, labor and capital may move elsewhere. With the advent of the euro, many French companies have had to restructure and form mergers.

The major European airplane producing company is Airbus, which is based in France but also supported by Germany and Britain. With more than 4,200 aircraft orders placed by international customers as of April 2001, Airbus is the world leader in aircraft production. Airbus and Boeing of the United States are in competition, and they have conflicting ideas about the future of the world air travel. The perception of future demand and air travel habits shapes the design of aircraft to be produced. Airbus believes that huge aircraft with a short flight range will shape demand in the future. Boeing, on the other hand, believes that passengers will be flying long miles in smaller aircraft. Time will show which one is on the right track.

One other field where French companies are strong is construction and civil engineering. However, a recent declining trend in enrollment in science classes in the country is a major concern of education authorities. France is the second ranked producer and the leading exporter of agri-foodstuffs (processed food such as wine, cheese, and pasta) in Europe. It is the fourth-largest exporter in the world in chemicals, rubber, and plastics; and third ranked in pharmachemicals and pharmaceuticals.

MINING. Mining is not a field in which France competes, and only a very minor fraction of the labor force (less than 1 percent) is engaged in mining. Regarding coal, 2 major fields produce most of France's coal: the Lorraine coal field near Metz and the Nord-de-Calais coal field near Lille. Most of these fields do not have economically viable reserves compared to other big producers because they lack sufficient amounts in some cases or are difficult to extract. Many coal fields have shut down since the 1950s.

France is among the biggest producers of bauxite in Europe and also plays a big role in the continent's natural gas production. France's position may be threatened, however, if some Asian companies acquire access to the European market, although the **tariff**-free regulations that EU member states enjoy put France in a strong position. France is an importer of petroleum but processes petroleum at home to produce several oil products which are sold domestically and abroad.

SERVICES

As with any other developed country, the services sector is an important component of the French economy. Out of over 2 million companies in France, roughly one-third operate in the various subsectors of the services industry. More companies are currently in the services sector in France than in any other part of the economy. The services industry (other than government) provides jobs to about 27 percent of the workforce, or 4.5 million people, and contributes 39 percent of the GDP. Investment in the industry is also significant.

FINANCIAL SERVICES. France has a developed credit market which channels savings to investors very efficiently and in large volumes. The **market capitalization** of shares listed on the Paris Stock Exchange, the fifth largest in the world, accounts for about 32 percent of the French GDP. Market capitalization at the end of 1997 reached an extraordinary 4 trillion francs. The Paris Stock Exchange is an internationally used capital market, and foreign investors hold about 35 percent of French stocks. This puts Paris in an advantageous position to attract more international capital with the help of the euro, the common currency of the EU. In an effort to adjust to the introduction of the new currency, all asset management companies in France started to offer their services in euros as of January 1999, the date the euro was introduced as the common currency of Europe. Since not all EU, let alone the European countries, decided to adopt the euro as their currency, authorities in the Paris Stock Exchange believe it has a comparative advantage over the stock markets of these nations since it can offer more opportunities via its reach to wider international audience. The Paris Stock Exchange has gone through extensive technological and legal restructuring to become more investor friendly in the international market. According to the stock exchange's data, foreign investments in the Paris Stock Exchange have tripled in monthly trading since the beginning of 1998, due in large part to the restructuring of the exchange. The exchange has trade relationships with the Chicago Mercantile Exchange and the stock exchanges of Sao Paolo, Toronto, Brussels, Lisbon, Tunis, Casablanca, Warsaw, and Amman, among others. The French bond market is among the world's leaders and ranks second after its U.S. counterpart.

The French banking system is also quite competitive in the world market. Credit Agricole, Compagnie Financiere Paribas, Groupe Caisses d'Epargne, and Banque National de Paris rank among the top 25 banks in the world. In Europe, banks are allowed to engage in activities that would normally be reserved for either commercial banks or investment banks in the United States. In a unified Europe, there will be one central bank, while national central banks will be largely autonomous.

INSURANCE. Like banking and the stock market, the French insurance sector is also a world player, ranking among the top 5 in the global insurance market. Although French insurance firms have a global presence, 60 percent of their total international activity is carried out within the borders of EU. Like other insurance industries, French insurers are institutional investors. The largest chunk of investments in the insurance industry is in the form of bonds, at 69 percent. Stocks account for only 15 percent of investment, and the rest is real estate, commercial paper and other assets. French insurers saw their overall value rise 16 percent from 1996 to 1997. The introduction of the common currency is expected to boost profits in the insurance industry.

TOURISM. Over 60 million tourists visit France every year, making it one of the largest tourist centers of the world. Visitors are attracted to its high fashion (or *haute couture*), beautiful scenery, historic heritage, and cultural activities. Paris, the center of France's tourist trade, offers attractions such as the Louvre (its famous art museum), fine restaurants, the Eiffel Tower, and the beautiful works of architecture along the Seine, its major river. With about 67 million annual tourists, France trailed behind only the United States and Spain in 1997. France has a surplus in tourism in its **balance of payments** accounts. The more than 100,000 businesses directly or indirectly involved in tourism in 1997 generated over 100 billion French francs. Investments in the sector came close to 15 billion francs in that same year. According to the Ministry of Tourism, there were about 634,640 people employed in the various categories of the tourism sector including travel agencies, restaurants, and hotels. About one-sixth of this figure is employed for less than full-time.

INTERNATIONAL TRADE

France, with its developed economy, is one of the most active participants in world trade. After World War II, the French government saw that closer ties to Germany would bring it political security and greater economic strength. Thus, the European Coal and Steel Community was formed, which brought the 2 countries and other European nations into a consultative body to discuss the production of steel and coal. The EU, which France was instrumental in creating, has helped it to diminish government intervention in economic affairs by privatizing several industries. In 1992, the Treaty of Maastricht was signed, which was the watershed event in bringing Europe into political and economic union. On a practical level, the lower trade barriers and fewer restrictions that integration has brought have opened doors to French products to be sold in many European countries and has allowed a wider freedom of movement of capital in Europe, all of which has benefitted France. The downside is that France, sharing common trade and tariff policies with the rest of the EU countries, has discussed the erection of trade barriers against non-EU companies and products. France will follow EU policy as a whole whenever the EU erects trade barriers to foreign goods and firms. The EU has made it clear that it will erect such barriers in cases involving health, safety, and environmental issues, for instance.

Trade (expressed in billions of US$): France

	Exports	Imports
1975	53.086	54.222
1980	116.030	134.866
1985	101.674	108.251
1990	216.588	234.436
1995	286.738	275.275
1998	305.384	287.687

SOURCE: International Monetary Fund. *International Financial Statistics Yearbook 1999.*

France's share of exports to the world's top ten economies was 9.3 percent in 1997, 9.8 percent in 1998, and 9.4 percent in 1999, putting it in fourth place behind the United States, Germany, and Japan. France is also the fourth largest exporter to the world, with over 5 percent of the world export market. France is the world's second largest exporter of agricultural products as well as services, including tourism and financial transactions. In the durable goods market, France ranks fourth in the world exports. The biggest trade partners of France are members of the EU, with which France enjoyed an overall trade surplus of 79 billion francs in 1999. The only EU countries with which France has a trade deficit are Germany and Italy. It also had a trade surplus with the Organization for Economic Co-operation and Development countries (OECD, a group of countries which promotes free markets and contributes to the development of members' economies through cooperation) of 66 billion francs in 1999. Its deficit with some Asian countries and Russia can be attributed to the economic crises experienced in these regions, which led to lower demand for French products.

Of over 2 million companies located in France, less than 5 percent take part in activities directly related to export, according to the Department of Foreign Trade of France. While mostly French-owned, some of these companies are **multinational corporations**. Companies such as IBM, Michelin, Hewlett Packard, and Daimler Benz are among France's top 20 exporters, with the top 3 exporters being PSA, Renault, and Airbus Industrie. The top 20 companies export mainly vehicles and such items as tires, aircraft, electricity, office products, plastic goods, industrial equipment, food items, computer products, pharmaceuticals, and chemical goods.

The 4 top exporters account for 10 percent of French exports, which is more than what the 100,000 next smaller companies bring into the country. The top 10 exporters contribute 15 percent of exports, while the first 100 make up 35 percent of it. Since some of these companies are active in more than 1 production area and usually operate under different names using subsidiaries, the real contribution of the largest 10 companies probably amounts to half of France's total exports. Hence, even though they may not appear in the list of large exporters, some conglomerates, such as Alcatel-Alsthom, are among the largest exporters.

The contribution of smaller-scale enterprises to the French export picture has been on the rise since 1990. Almost half of total exported goods and services were produced by companies having somewhere between 10 to 499 employees. These types of companies are called Small-to-Medium Enterprises (SMEs). Firms hiring fewer than 10 people are called Very Small Enterprises (VSEs). Foreigners control about 27 percent of SMEs in France and about 33 percent of VSEs. SMEs concentrate in agricultural products such as agro-foodstuffs and consumption goods such as wood and leather.

Oil tops the list of French imports. In 1997, petroleum products made up 4.64 percent of all imports. Natural gas is also a major import. Various auto parts, some from French companies located abroad, are also high in the shopping list of France.

Foreign investment in France has steadily increased since 1990. Direct foreign investment in France, in the form of expansion or start-ups, created over 31,000 new jobs in 1999, up 8 percent from its level in 1998. This trend was most likely due to France's skilled labor force combined with the government's efforts to make France attractive to foreign investors. Some 29 percent of all foreign investment-related jobs created in 1999 were due to hiring in U.S. and Canadian firms. This was followed by German investors. The information technologies and communications fields created 15 percent of new jobs. A similar pattern was observed in consultant and service sectors, including call centers and logistics, accounting for 13 percent of the jobs. France is the world's fourth largest receiver of international investments.

Realizing the importance of operating in the country where the market is, French companies have extended their presence abroad. French companies have established a sizable presence in other countries which amounted to 239.7 billion francs in 1998. France is a net exporter of direct capital investments to the rest of the world. The balance of export and import of direct capital investment almost doubled in 1997 from its 1996 value and did not change much in 1998, standing at 74.4 billion francs. This rate was due largely to the increased volume of foreign direct capital investment in France, overall, a remarkable change from the 1990 deficit of 112.3 billion francs. Emerging economies is another reason why French capital opted to take advantage of new markets abroad. But despite new investment in the developing world, two-thirds of French capital in 1998 was invested in the EU and the United States.

MONEY

The French franc is one of the reserve currencies of the world. However, its influence is nowhere close to that of the United States dollar. In 1999 France, together with certain other countries, agreed to phase out its domestic currency in favor of a common currency in Europe, which will work like the U.S. dollar among U.S. states. The euro was launched at a value slightly above the U.S. dollar, but by 2001 it had lost much of its value. The European Central Bank, with the help of the United States Federal Reserve and the Bank of Japan, undertook a salvage operation aimed at curbing further decline of the euro. The weaker euro made French products, along with other goods produced in the region that uses the euro (also known as the "Euro Zone"), cheaper with respect to the rest of the world. The sale of high-tech goods produced by U.S. firms, such as Intel and Boeing, has suffered during the process, which partly led to the U.S. central bank's participation in the joint effort to save the euro.

Exchange rates: France

euros per US$1	
Jan 2001	1.0659
2000	1.0854
1999	0.9386
1998	5.8995
1997	5.8367
1996	5.1155

Note: Amounts prior to 1999 are in French francs per US dollar.

SOURCE: CIA *World Factbook 2001* [ONLINE].

Not all EU member countries have opted to be part of the single monetary bloc. Great Britain's reluctance to join was a major blow to efforts to unite the monetary affairs of Europe. Though 10 countries initially joined, the Euro Zone now includes 12 countries (Austria, Belgium, Germany, Spain, Finland, France, Greece, Ireland, Italy, Luxembourg, Holland, and Portugal).

The euro is not yet a **hard currency**. However, it is used throughout the participating EU countries in non-currency financial transactions. Prices are quoted in both the domestic currency, such as franc, and the euro. Domestic currencies coexist with the euro in a **fixed exchange rate** regime. For example, 1 euro equals 6.56 French francs. However, the domestic currencies and the euro use market forces to determine their values on the world market in a flexible **exchange rate regime** (synonymous with a **floating exchange rate**). The transformation to the single currency will start in July 2001 when the banks begin issuing checks in the euros. A single currency is expected to ease the movement of labor and capital in Europe and generate a common market encompassing 20 percent of the world's trade.

The French monetary system is governed by the central bank of France, the Bank of France. The reserves of the Bank of France amounted to 72.19 billion euros as of January 2001. Of this amount, more than half (39 billion euros) was in foreign exchange, and 27.6 billion euros was in gold. The **Monetary Policy** Council is the decision-

GDP per Capita (US$)

Country	1975	1980	1985	1990	1998
France	18,730	21,374	22,510	25,624	27,975
United States	19,364	21,529	23,200	25,363	29,683
Germany	N/A	N/A	N/A	N/A	31,141
Spain	10,040	10,512	10,943	13,481	15,644

SOURCE: United Nations. *Human Development Report 2000; Trends in human development and per capita income.*

making arm of the Bank, similar to Federal Open Market Committee (FOMC) of the United States. The governor of the Bank and Minister of Economic Affairs and Finance cooperate in making policy decisions. However, with the common currency, a new monetary governing body will be introduced, the European System of Central Banks (ESCB), which includes the European Central Bank and the national central banks of each country.

POVERTY AND WEALTH

World War I and II, which were separated by a widespread depression, had a dramatic impact on the whole of Europe, including France. In addition to the loss of manpower, productivity, and wealth, the infrastructure of the European countries was largely destroyed. In the 1950s, only half of French families had running water in their houses, and access to television and automobiles was highly limited. Half a century later, the picture has changed drastically, at least for the larger part of society. France is an advanced industrial country in every respect, although there are pockets in French society that are still comparatively under-developed. The per capita GDP in 1995 U.S. dollars has increased from under US$20,000 in 1975 to just under US$28,000 in 1998, making France among the highest-income nations in the world. However, men tend to earn US$10,000 (1998 dollars) more than women per year. The educational system, though, is more egalitarian: 94 percent of females and 91 percent of males have attended either a primary, secondary, or tertiary educational institutions. France spends about 6 percent of the GNP on public education, slightly higher than the average for OECD countries. However, only 5 percent of the students are in science in tertiary educational institutions, which is a concern to policy makers about the country's competitiveness in information age.

Distribution of Income or Consumption by Percentage Share: France

Lowest 10%	2.8
Lowest 20%	7.2
Second 20%	12.6
Third 20%	17.2
Fourth 20%	22.8
Highest 20%	40.2
Highest 10%	25.1

Survey year: 1995

Note: This information refers to income shares by percentiles of the population and is ranked by per capita income.

SOURCE: *2000 World Development Indicators* [CD-ROM].

Standards of living are difficult to assess, and most economists group the Western European and North American countries close together at the top end of most "quality of life" scales. The United Nations Development Program ranked France as thirteenth on the "Human Development Index" in 2001, a testament to France's excellent health care, literacy, income, and life expectancy.

World Bank data show that the poorest 10 percent of the population receive only 2.8 percent of the national income in France. The poorest 20 percent receive only 7.2 per cent of the income. The highest 20 percent, on the other hand, possess 40.2 percent. Unemployment is a major problem, with a rate of 11.7 percent in 1998. Even though the unemployment rate decreased by 5 percent from 1994 to 1998, the rate is still high enough to cause concern among economists. Another related, but less apparent problem is the insecurity and low pay in

Household Consumption in PPP Terms

Country	All food	Clothing and footwear	Fuel and power[a]	Health care[b]	Education[b]	Transport & Communications	Other
France	22	7	9	33	8	12	40
United States	13	9	9	4	6	8	51
Germany	14	6	7	2	10	7	53
Spain	33	12	11	3	5	8	28

Data represent percentage of consumption in PPP terms.

[a]Excludes energy used for transport.

[b]Includes government and private expenditures.

SOURCE: World Bank. *World Development Indicators 2000.*

jobs which do not require special skills. Marginal increases in government aid programs have not alleviated the problem completely.

Worst hit by the economic inequalities in France are immigrants, who are often subjected to severe discrimination. Some authorities in certain parts of the country have tried to encourage the native population to have more children by offering child benefits while denying immigrants the same services. The EU, on the other hand, has special educational programs for minorities and immigrants.

The percentage of people living with AIDS (0.37 percent) is slightly above the OECD average (0.32 percent) according to UNDP statistics. Public expenditures on health increased from 6.6 percent of the GDP in 1990 to 7.1 percent in 1996–98.

WORKING CONDITIONS

Some 25.6 million workers were employed in France by the end of 1999. France's labor force resembles that of many advanced industrial nations and is one of the most highly-educated in Europe. The GDP per employee per hour was US$34, larger than Italy, the United States, Germany, and the United Kingdom. France ranks third in Europe in employee productivity, and fourth in labor costs.

Unionism in France has declined dramatically over time and currently stands at half the level of the United States and reached the lowest level in Europe in 1997. Traditionally, unionism is stronger in Europe than the United States, and unions fight for non-wage rights more than for issues such as job security and vacations. The major labor union in France is the Confederation Generale du Travail (CGT) with about 2.4 million members. It is controlled by communists. The independent labor union, Force Ouvriere, is estimated to have about 1 million members. Another independent union serving white-collar labor is Confederation Generale des **Cadres** with 340,000 members. Other labor unions are the Conseil National du Patronat Francais (Patronat National Council of French Employers, CNPF) and the socialist-leaning labor union Confederation Francaise Democratique du Travail (CFDT) with about 800,000 members.

The decline of unions in France has not left the labor force without protection. There are still strong laws and institutional arrangements that give workers a say in running the workplace. The labor code sets standards regarding issues ranging from the workweek to vacations. In companies with more than 10 employees, workers are represented at various decision-making levels and are free to file grievances, individually or collectively, with the courts against the employer. Worker-employer relations are peaceful overall. A total of 8.4 working days are lost per 1,000 working days in France, making it one of the lowest strike countries of Europe. The same number is well over 40 days in Spain.

Another challenge the French labor force faces is the eroding job security as a result of adjustment to the common market policies of the EU. Cheaper labor from such countries as Greece and Spain may drive unskilled French workers out of jobs. Adding to this problem is the possibility that France's skilled workers may find extended opportunities in other member countries. In 1999, the government introduced a 35-hour work week to ease the unemployment problem by creating more positions for the unemployed. (The 35-hour workweek is paid on a 39 hour basis.) Starting in the year 2000, companies gradually phased in the 35-hour workweek schedule. Businesses were vehemently opposed to the initiative, though some agreed to it after negotiations with the government. Firms that implement the rule earlier than they are required to are promised government aid based on the number of workers they employ, which is expected to be a significant burden on the national budget. The government has proposed dipping into the unemployment benefits fund to pay the costs of the new policy.

COUNTRY HISTORY AND ECONOMIC DEVELOPMENT

843. The treaty of Verdun roughly determines the borders of France. Charles the Bald becomes first monarch.

1338. The Hundred Years' War with England begins.

1643. Louis XIV's reign begins.

1789. The monarchy is overthrown by French Revolution. First Republic is founded.

1804. Napoleon Bonaparte declares himself the first emperor.

1870. France is defeated by Prussia in Franco-Prussian War.

1914. France is invaded by Germany during World War I and suffers enormous losses before winning the war, with the Allies, in 1918.

1940. France is invaded again by Germans during World War II. Allies liberate France in 1944. General Charles de Gaulle becomes head of the provisional government.

1946. France joins NATO.

1951. France plays a key role in the formation of the European Coal and Steel Community (ECSC), the first step towards the eventual formation of the European Union.

1954. France withdraws from Indochina (Vietnam) after its military defeat there.

1967. The ECSC, the European Economic Community (EEC), and Euratom all merge to form the European Community (EC).

1968. Students and workers strike in Paris in opposition to government policies regarding the poor; De Gaulle resigns after losing referendum on constitutional reform.

1974. Conservative Giscard d'Estaing becomes president.

1981. Socialist Francois Mitterand becomes president; massive nationalization campaign by the government begins.

1986. Jacques Chirac becomes the prime minister of the center-right coalition; the government embarks on privatization efforts.

1988. Francois Mitterand is elected for a second term and brings France much closer to integration with the EU.

1991. Socialist Edith Cresson becomes the first woman prime minister of France.

1992. The Treaty of Maastricht is signed, which calls for the political and economic union of European countries. A common monetary policy and legal structure is announced.

1993. France tightens immigration requirements and makes it easier to deport foreigners.

1995. Jacques Chirac wins presidency on his third try, cements relations with Germany and the European union.

1997. Socialist Lionel Jospin becomes prime minister.

1999. EU adopts the euro as the currency.

FUTURE TRENDS

France suffered twice from war in the 20th century at the hands of its neighbor Germany. The 21st century, however, looks much brighter than the preceding one. France is part of a European coalition which may create a United States of Europe in the future. Not only is France one of the leading players in this effort, it also has strong relations with Germany, once its invader, which brings it security. By joining the common currency efforts in Europe, France has secured an influential role for itself in European affairs, both economically and politically. It has already started to reap the benefits of one of the largest markets in the world by receiving a large volume of **foreign direct investment** and exporting its agricultural and other products within Europe in a tariff-free environment.

Recent **liberalization** and privatization efforts of the government, which reversed an earlier course of the 1980s, both brought confidence to markets and increased efficiency to the government, which is now much smaller than before. Its main problems lie in its relatively high unemployment rate and low population growth. The EU may provide a solution to the unemployment problem, but with a more integrated Europe comes the possibility that France may lose many of its more talented workers if they leave for better jobs. Coupled with rigid immigration policies and xenophobia, France may experience a shortage of technically capable individuals. Germany, which has many of the same racial difficulties, recently initiated a program which is similar to the U.S. green card and may encourage technologically savvy people to come to Germany. France may soon have to confront the same problem. Decreasing population growth may seem to be an answer to unemployment in the short run, but it is a fact that the burden of supporting the retired will have to be shared by fewer working people as France's demographics change. This situation may mean the need for higher spending on health care and related services, which will drain government aid funds. Perhaps this problem is the biggest challenge France has to deal with in the 21st century.

DEPENDENCIES

France has no territories or colonies.

BIBLIOGRAPHY

Airbus. <http://www1.airbus.com>. Accessed April 2001.

Aron, Raymond. "The French Economy: A Study in Paradoxes." *The Atlantic Monthly.* June 1958.

Brogna, Brunner, editor. "France." *Time Almanac 2000.* Boston, MA: Time Inc., 2000.

Discover France. <http://www.discoverfrance.net>. Accessed January 2001.

Economist Intelligence Unit. *Country Profile: France.* London: Economist Intelligence Unit, 2000.

Ministry of Economy, Finance and Industry. *Welcome to MINEFI.* <http://www.minefi.gouv.fr>. Accessed February 2001.

Ministry of Tourism. *Tourisme.* <http://www.tourisme.gouv.fr>. Accessed April 2001.

National Institute for Statistics and Economic Studies (L'Institut national de la statistique et des études économiques). *Insee.* <http://www.insee.fr/en/home/home_page.asp>. Accessed January 2001.

United Nations Development Program. *Human Development Report 2000.* New York: Oxford University Press, 2000.

United Nations Development Program. *World Population Trends.* <http://www.undp.org/popin/wdtrends>. Accessed January 2001.

U.S. Central Intelligence Agency. *World Factbook 2000.* <http://www.odci.gov/cia/publications/factbook/index.html>. Accessed July 2001.

U.S. Department of State. *FY2001 Country Commercial Guide: France.* <http://www.state.gov/www/about_state/business/com_guides/2001/europe/france_ccg2001.pdf>. Accessed November 2001.

—Ismail H. Genc and Emine U. Genc

GEORGIA

Republic of Georgia
Sakartveld Respublika

CAPITAL: T'bilisi.

MONETARY UNIT: Georgian lari (GEL). One GEL equals 100 tetri. Introduced in September 1995, the Georgian lari comes in denominations of 1, 2, 5, 10, 20, 50, 100, and 500. There are coins of 5, 10, 20, and 50 tetri.

CHIEF EXPORTS: Scrap metal, ferro-alloys, nuts, tea, and wine.

CHIEF IMPORTS: Oil, natural gas, cigarettes, electricity, and pharmaceuticals.

GROSS DOMESTIC PRODUCT: US$11.7 billion (purchasing power parity, 1999 est.).

BALANCE OF TRADE: **Exports:** US$329.9 million (2000 est.). **Imports:** US$700.2 million (2000 est.). The CIA *World Factbook* lists exports as US$372 million (2000 est.) and imports as US$898 million (2000 est.).

COUNTRY OVERVIEW

LOCATION AND SIZE. Georgia is located between Europe and Asia. East of the Black Sea, Georgia is separated from Russia by the Caucasus Mountains. It borders Turkey and Armenia to the south and Azerbaijan to the east. Georgia has a land area of 69,700 square kilometers (26,911 square miles) making it slightly smaller in size than the state of South Carolina. Approximately 75 percent of Georgia's territory is 500 or more meters above sea level. The country has a coastline of 315 kilometers (196 miles).

POPULATION. Georgia's most recent official census counted 5,400,481 in 1989. Recent state statistics, which underestimate the volume of **emigration**, keep the figure around 5.4 million. The U.S. Central Intelligence Agency (CIA) *World Factbook,* however, estimates the population in July of 2001 at 4,989,285. With estimated rates of 10.87 births and 14.52 deaths per 1,000 population and a net out-migration rate of 2.57 per 1,000 population, Georgia had an estimated growth rate of -0.62 percent in 2000.

Georgia is an ethnically diverse state. Georgians comprise only 70 percent of the population, while there are minorities of Armenians (8 percent), Azeris (6 percent), Russians (6 percent), Ossetians (3 percent), and Abkhazians (1.8 percent). These groups, while small in number, have posed problems for the T'bilisi government as they are concentrated in specific areas and some have aspirations towards independence. Georgia contains 3 autonomous republics: Abkhazia, Adjara, and South Ossetia.

OVERVIEW OF ECONOMY

It is difficult to understand the contemporary economic situation of Georgia without first understanding its tumultuous history since achieving independence from the Soviet Union (USSR) in 1991. Independence exposed the extreme reliance of the Georgian economy on the Soviet Union. At the time of independence, the vast majority of Georgia's trade was conducted within the USSR. Trade with the Newly Independent States (NIS), the name given to the states that emerged from the collapse of the USSR, was disrupted by the wars in Abkhazia and South Ossetia and by civil war. When Georgia was a part of the USSR, heavy-industrial enterprises were established throughout Georgia but fell into disuse when the country became independent. Net material product experienced an unprecedented decline in the immediate years after independence. It declined by 11.1 percent in 1990, by 20.6 percent in 1991, by 43.4 percent in 1992, and 40 percent in 1993.

Most of Georgia's recent economic problems can be attributed to the weakness of centralized authority and to an insufficiently developed civil society. The legacy

of the Soviet state is a primary cause of these problems. Georgian society was ill-prepared for independence—politically, economically, culturally, and psychologically. In particular, no social groups existed independent of the state and a democratic culture had not been established. Moreover, the de facto (existing whether lawful or not) federal administrative-political system imposed during the Soviet period weakened the power of Georgia's own government. Soviet control also fostered separatist tendencies in the region. Administratively, Georgia was a "little empire" that began to disintegrate in much the same way as the larger model of the USSR. The effective secession of Abkhazia, Adjara, and South Ossetia coincided with ineffective control over the Armenian and Azeri dominated regions. The war in Abkhazia was especially detrimental to national and civic integration as it occurred at a critical stage in the state-building process.

The economic path followed by the breakaway republics of Abkhazia, Adjara, and South Ossetia diverged considerably from that of the rest of the country. The Abkhazian victory in September 1993 led to an economic blockade by Georgia followed by a similar Russian blockade in 1996 as Moscow tried to improve relations with T'bilisi. The Russian ruble is the only currency in widespread use in Abkhazia and the region operates under Moscow time, 1 hour behind T'bilisi. Despite a flourishing unofficial trade with Russia, the Abkhazian people had to rely heavily on humanitarian handouts as a means of subsistence. The once dynamic tourism industry is in tatters. Despite maintaining the trappings of an independent state, lack of economic potential has forced South Ossetia to consider closer ties with the rest of Georgia. Adjara maintains the closest links with T'bilisi and has benefited accordingly.

Corruption has been a persistent feature of Georgian society for several decades and has been entrenched since the establishment of an independent state in 1991. The weakness of the central government is clear in its lack of control over its employees. Small and medium size businesses, which could provide a vital base for economic growth and employment are hindered by lack of resources to withstand persistent demands for bribes. Few citizens see the point in engaging in political protests as they perceive the members of the government as hopelessly corrupt and their situation as unavoidable.

For most of the 1990s, Georgia was torn between dependency on Russia and the West. Georgia relies heavily on Russia for fuel, and an estimated 800,000 Georgians who work in Russia **repatriate** a substantial sum to their families in Georgia every year. This economic lifeline was suddenly put at risk when the Russian government imposed a visa regime on Georgia. Before 5 December 2000, Georgians could travel freely to Russia but now are required to obtain permission from the Russian embassy in Georgia. An apparent punishment for alleged tolerance of Chechen guerrillas who take refuge in Georgia, the visa regime is symptomatic of a cooling of relations between Moscow and T'bilisi. Georgia has increasingly turned to the West for assistance. It has deepened relations with the European Union (EU) and declared its intention of joining the North Atlantic Treaty Organization (NATO) at some point in the future.

POLITICS, GOVERNMENT, AND TAXATION

Georgia's political system is modeled on that of the United States with a directly elected president, parliament, and judiciary. Politics in the Caucasian republic has been dominated by Eduard Shevardnadze since 1972, the year he became First Secretary of the Georgian Communist Party. Before becoming Soviet Foreign Minister under Mikhail Gorbachev in 1985, Shevardnadze gained a reputation for his anti-corruption policies and his economic initiatives. Shevardnadze entered into alliances with paramilitary forces when he felt it necessary and arrested them when he felt that he was strong enough to maintain power. He adopted an anti-Russian policy at the beginning of his administration, then sought and received Russian aid in putting down an internal rebellion. He even joined the **Commonwealth of Independent States** (CIS)—a heretical act for Georgian nationalists considering the dominant role Russia plays in that organization. When it became clear that Russian economic aid would not be forthcoming, he explained that he attained concessions for his country by such devotion. As Russia adopts a hostile position towards the small republic, some suspect that the Georgian president is now saying what the West wants to hear in order to get the loans and legitimacy necessary to retain control. Shevardnadze was elected for another—and, according to himself, final—5-year term of office in April 2000.

To consolidate his influence and further his policies, Shevardnadze founded the Citizens Union of Georgia (CUG) party in 1993. Officially dedicated to free market economics, the CUG advocates increasing the collection of taxes, fiscal rectitude, and improving social welfare provisions. The CUG emerged as the largest party after parliamentary elections in 1995 and 1999. As with society generally, politics is clannish in Georgia and many important administrative functions are handed out to family relatives and friends. Despite the more than 100 small parties in Georgia, there is little effective opposition to the Shevardnadze-led government. With the exception of the electorally insignificant **communist** faction, all political groups are committed to the free market, so alternative leaders provide a functional but not an ideological opposition to the status quo.

The "black hole" of tax collection is so great that tax revenues constituted only 10 percent of **gross domestic product** (GDP) in 1997, a year in which the Georgian economy enjoyed one of the world's fastest growth rates. Insubstantial tax revenues are partially due to the narrow tax base; most of those who do pay taxes are state employees for whom tax is automatically subtracted from salaries. While those living below the poverty line might have some ethical grounds for evading tax, many of those that have the means to pay have shown no willingness to contribute their share. The situation is aggravated by the actions of underpaid tax officials who ignore hidden income in return for pocketing a portion of the total amount due. The government has done little to develop more effective means of enforcing the law and appears resigned to the situation.

INFRASTRUCTURE, POWER, AND COMMUNICATIONS

There are 20,298 kilometers (12,613 miles) of roads in Georgia which consist of international motor roads (1,474 kilometers/916 miles), internal state motor roads (3,330 kilometers/2,069 miles), and local roads (15,494 kilometers/9,628 miles). The vast majority of roads are in poor condition. A Georgian railway network was established in 1872, which grew to 1,583 kilometers (984 miles) of track in 2000. T'bilisi is connected by rail to the capitals of Azerbaijan and Armenia, but due to unrest in Abkhazia, the route to Russia and Europe has not been in operation since the early 1990s. In 1988, during the last years of the Soviet regime, Georgian railways transported 36.2 million metric tons of cargo. The volume declined to 4.7 million metric tons in 1995, or only 13 percent of total railway production. Since that date, the volume of cargo has steadily increased, reaching 9.4 million metric tons in 1999.

The Georgian electricity power sector is in urgent need of modernization, refurbishment, and investment. The provision of electricity to Georgian citizens has declined every year since 1995 and the lack of power is an obstacle to economic growth. In 1998, a U.S.-based energy company (AES Corporation) bought Telasi, Georgia's bankrupt electricity distribution company. Government corruption, non-payment of bills, and a reliance on aging hydroelectric and thermal

Communications

Country	Newspapers	Radios	TV Sets[a]	Cable subscribers[a]	Mobile Phones[a]	Fax Machines[a]	Personal Computers[a]	Internet Hosts[b]	Internet Users[b]
	1996	1997	1998	1998	1998	1998	1998	1999	1999
Georgia	N/A	555	473	2.8	11	N/A	N/A	1.59	20
United States	215	2,146	847	244.3	256	78.4	458.6	1,508.77	74,100
Russia	105	418	420	78.5	5	0.4	40.6	13.06	2,700
Ukraine	54	884	490	15.7	2	0.0	13.8	4.56	200

[a]Data are from International Telecommunication Union, *World Telecommunication Development Report 1999* and are per 1,000 people.
[b]Data are from the Internet Software Consortium (http://www.isc.org) and are per 10,000 people.

SOURCE: World Bank. *World Development Indicators 2000.*

power stations have all contributed to the electricity shortage. During the winter of 2000–01, electricity supply to households was an average of 4 hours per day. These shortages have inflicted misery on an already disenchanted population. Widespread protests and street demonstrations during November 2000 provided a safety valve for popular frustration but aroused fears of another civil war.

The communications sector is the most stable sector of the economy and has attracted the interest of foreign investors. The modernization of ground lines is a process that will continue for some years while the mobile phone operator networks have enjoyed rapid expansion. In 1998, there were 115 telephone lines, 11 cellular phones, and 0.1 public phones per 1,000 citizens. Most of the public phones, however, were in serious disrepair. Internet service providers have also recorded increased business but access to computers remains the luxury of a privileged few (0.15 per 1,000 citizens).

ECONOMIC SECTORS

In terms of volume of goods and numbers employed, agriculture plays a key role in the Georgian economy and is crucial in reducing poverty in rural areas. The **liberalization** of prices and the **privatization** of the land were important steps taken during the 1990s to improve the agricultural sector, though lack of capital has prevented the development of modern systems of management and the attraction of new markets.

The industrial sector has enjoyed modest advances in recent years. In 2000, industrial output grew by 10.8 percent, amounting to GEL1.051 million. Industry accounted for 21.5 percent of GDP in 2000. One positive trend was the increase in the number of small businesses, which totaled 2,296 in October 2000, though they only accounted for 14.5 percent of total industrial production. There is an unequal share of production among the in-

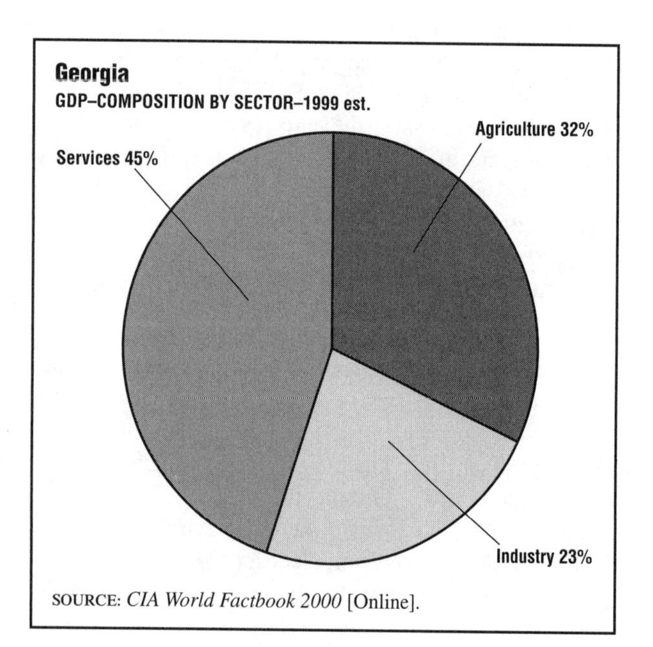

SOURCE: *CIA World Factbook 2000* [Online].

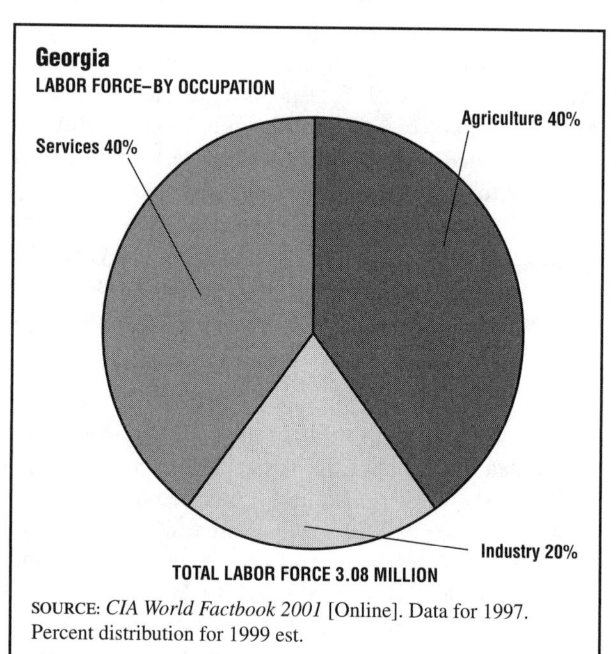

SOURCE: *CIA World Factbook 2001* [Online]. Data for 1997. Percent distribution for 1999 est.

dustries—43.8 percent of industrial production is produced by 52 of the 2,713 industrial companies—indicating a low level of diversification. In addition, the shadow industry, a legacy from Soviet times, continues to hinder growth. The volume of informal or shadow industrial production was estimated to be 177 percent of officially produced goods in 2000. Industry employed 20 percent of the workforce in 1999.

The service industry constituted 51 percent of Georgia's GDP in 2000. Trade and transport both play a major role in the service industry and each accounted for more than 10 percent of the sector, respectively, by 2000. Tourism remains one of Georgia's great unfulfilled potentials, but the loss of Abkhazia and poor **infrastructure** continue to hamper development in this area. The banking sector has consolidated greatly since 1994 but there are still too many banking groups relative to both the population and the resources of the Georgian people. Approximately 40 percent of the workforce was employed in the service industry in 1999. The remaining 5.9 percent of the GDP was accounted for by net taxes.

AGRICULTURE

During the Soviet period, agriculture and food processing were major activities in Georgia and the country continues to be a significant producer of wine, tea, fruit, and vegetables. Land use in Georgia varies with local climatic and soil patterns. The cultivation of citrus is concentrated along the Black Sea, particularly in Abkhazia and Ajara. Georgian wine has a reputation for excellence, though the industry has suffered in recent years from the manufacture of fake Georgian wine. The cultivation of nuts and tea are also of fundamental importance. Overall, agriculture, forestry, and fisheries accounted for 21.5 percent of GDP in 2000 and employed 40 percent of the workforce in 1999.

Adverse weather conditions contributed to a substantial fall in agricultural production during the year 2000. The volume of agricultural produce fell by 18.5 percent compared with 1999 and the Ministry of Agriculture and Food estimated losses at US$225 million. A prolonged drought throughout the country was particularly devastating for the agricultural heartland of eastern Georgia; almost 400,000 hectares of agricultural lands were damaged. The damage included 155,000 hectares of grain fields causing the annual grain yields to average 900–1,000 kilos per hectare, half of normal production. The effect on sunflower plantations was even greater with 58,600 hectares of the crop suffering damage and the harvest being almost entirely destroyed in some regions.

Forty-three percent of the country's territory is forested. About 97 percent are located on the slopes of the main and small Caucasus Mountain systems, the remainder are to be found in the valleys of East Georgia and the Colkheti lowlands. As a result of the energy shortage, large forest areas have been cut down, leading to soil erosion, the reduction of underground and surface water, and the formation of land and snow slides. Collectively, these processes have caused soil salination and a decrease in soil fertility in many areas. Reliance on manual labor, out-dated techniques, and poorly maintained irrigation systems also lead to decreased productivity.

INDUSTRY

MINING. Georgia used to possess one of the world's richest manganese deposits in the Tchiatura and Sachkhere regions: present-day resources are estimated at about 200 million metric tons. Significant deposits of high quality mineral and drinking water exist in Georgia. Two-thirds of estimated resources (amounting to 17–18 cubic kilometers/4–4.3 cubic miles) are located in western Georgia at 10 to 15 meters depth while the remaining third in eastern Georgia is also accessible at a depth of 250 to 300 meters. A thriving industry during the Soviet period, bottled water production declined sharply after independence and by 1993 was down to 5 percent of pre-independence levels. In recent years, however, the mineral water industry has revived with the "Borjormi" label leading the way.

MANUFACTURING. Georgia's manufacturing base is so weak that many of its most important enterprises can only operate without paying for electricity. The government, afraid of the potential redundancies, has refused to take decisive action. The metallurgy and chemical sectors are commodities of most importance to the Georgian economy, specifically manganese ore, ferromanganese, mineral fertilizers, and synthetic ammonia.

Other industrial activities include domestic processing of agricultural products, which accounted for 4.7 percent of overall GDP in 2000, and construction, which accounted for 3.5 percent. While construction has been increasing relatively rapidly (4 percent in 2000), much of this activity is part of the **shadow economy**.

SERVICES

TOURISM. Georgia was once the tourism center of the Soviet Union with 3 million visitors annually, 250,000 of whom came from outside of the USSR. As Georgia descended into civil war in the early 1990s, its tourism industry ground to a halt. According to Georgia's State Department of Tourism and Resorts, about 383,000 people visited Georgia in 1999, of which 219,000 came from the CIS and 164,000 from other countries. Many of the hotels and health resorts that had catered to tourists were used to house the thousands of internally displaced people who fled to the capital after the defeat of Georgian forces in Abkhazia. Tourism is also hindered by a cumbersome visa regime that requires letters of invitation and submission of passports to embassies prior to departure. Visas can be obtained upon arrival at the airport but only at very high prices.

The attractions for travelers in Georgia include the beautiful coastal regions along the Black Sea, though the 2 autonomous republics of Abkhazia and Adjara dominate most of the coastline. With its large mountain ranges (the highest peak is 5,150 meters/16,897 feet), Georgia is ideal for skiing, and the Bakuriani and Gudauri ski resorts were very popular among Russian tourists in the Soviet era. Revival of this tourist attraction will, however, require heavy investment and continued political stability. Though tourism could become one of the country's leading industries, hotels and restaurants contributed only 2.2 percent of GDP in 2000.

TEXTILES. The textile industry is also one that should witness significant development in the coming years. A legislative framework for investment and close proximity to EU markets complements the availability of raw materials and a cheap skilled workforce. Eighty-five percent of textile companies have been privatized, either as joint stock companies or companies with limited liability.

FINANCIAL SERVICES. The legacy of communism and the reality of corruption ensured that the creation of a strong banking system in Georgia would be troubled. The absence of an effective banking sector made it difficult for entrepreneurs to get the capital needed to invest in private enterprises, while government interference forced banks to give loans to dubious projects and individuals, further debilitating the development of financial services. Hundreds of banks were established in the early 1990s with capital of US$500 or less. Between 1998 and 2000 the number of banks fell from 294 to 33 and more closures are expected as a result of bankruptcy, closure, or merger.

INTERNATIONAL TRADE

As an integral part of the Soviet Union, Georgian trade was conducted almost exclusively within the USSR. On the eve of the country's independence, 95.7 percent of Georgia's exports and 72.3 percent of its imports were from trade with other Soviet Republics. In the decade following independence, Georgia had to seek out new trading partners because most of the former Soviet republics were poor and the new government did not wish to rely on Russia. In 1997, Russia accounted for 27.4 percent of exports and 15.2 percent of imports; 2 years later these figures had been further reduced to 12.4 percent and 7.1 percent, respectively.

Trade with the EU and Turkey has replaced much of the trade with Russia. In 2000, Georgia exported US$68.3 million to the EU and imported goods to the value of US$167.1 million. Though this meant that Georgia had a **trade deficit** of US$95.8 million, the figure represented a dramatic improvement on the 1998 figure when the trade imbalance was US$273.8 million. Germany has emerged as Georgia's largest trading partner among the EU member states. In 1999, Georgian exports to Germany amounted to US$24.5 million while it imported US$44.2 million of German produce. Despite improving the trade balance in 1999, Georgia still had a trade deficit with all EU member states except Spain.

At the beginning of 2000, Georgia had a trade deficit with 70 trading partners and enjoyed a trade surplus with 18 countries, the most significant of which were Turkey and Syria. Reducing the trade deficit is one of the key priorities of the Georgian government but its efforts are hampered by the conflict in Abkhazia and the de facto independence of South Ossetia and Adjara. The defeat of Georgian forces in Abkhazia resulted in the loss of the rail route to Russia and Europe. The independent regions are popular smuggling routes, depriving the government of revenues and hindering its regulation of trade.

MONEY

Like many former Soviet republics, Georgia used the Russian ruble as a unit of currency after achieving independence. In April 1993, however, the Georgian National Bank introduced a coupon currency to alleviate the shortage of Russian rubles, which was hampering payment of government salaries. Priced on a par with the Russian ruble, the currency was supposed to circulate with the ruble but by August 1993 it had become the sole legal tender. The value of the currency was expected to be maintained by the proceeds from privatization, but when these failed to materialize, a large quantity of unsecured credits were issued with the predictable consequence of rampant **inflation**. By 1994 US$1 was worth 2 million Georgian coupons and inflation was at 100 percent per month. Not surprisingly, most transactions were carried out in U.S. dollars or Russian rubles.

Exchange rates: Georgia

lari per US$1	
Dec 2000	1.9798
2000	1.9762
1999	2.0245
1998	1.3898
1997	1.2975
1996	1.2628

SOURCE: CIA *World Factbook 2001* [ONLINE].

The government introduced a new currency—the lari—on 25 September 1995, which became the only legal tender a week later. Coupons were exchanged at the rate of 1 million per Georgian lari (GEL). Due to the economic reforms that had already begun to take effect and the absence of war, the lari proved to be far more successful than its predecessor. Introduced at the rate of 1.23 Lari per U.S. dollar, the currency has remained relatively stable, declining to 1.35 lari by August 1998 and to 1.97 lari by September 2000. The rate of exchange dipped in the early months of 2001, reaching 2.11 by the middle of February, a decline that was attributed to economic crises in Turkey.

Only the Russian ruble is used in Abkhazia and South Ossetia. Though the lari is accepted as legal tender in the Armenian-populated region of Javaketi, the Armenian dram and the Russian ruble are the dominant currencies, the latter due to the presence of Russian troops. The relative stability of the lari since 1995 contributed to the reduction of inflation. With the ruble in circulation in 1992, inflation had stood at 913.1 percent for the year but war, the failure of economic reforms, and the introduction of the coupon saw this figure rocket to 7,380 percent in 1994. The rate of inflation dropped to 57.4 percent in 1995, 13.8 percent in 1996, 7.2 percent in 1997 and 4.6 percent in 2000.

GDP per Capita (US$)

Country	1975	1980	1985	1990	1998
Georgia	1,788	2,366	2,813	2,115	703
United States	19,364	21,529	23,200	25,363	29,683
Russia	2,555	3,654	3,463	3,668	2,138
Ukraine	N/A	N/A	N/A	1,979	837

SOURCE: United Nations. *Human Development Report 2000; Trends in human development and per capita income.*

POVERTY AND WEALTH

Before the collapse of the USSR, poverty was relatively unknown in Georgia. Since then, the standard of living has declined. In June 2000, 53 percent of the population was below the national poverty line, which meant that average spending was less than US$2 per day per person. Georgia's tradition of an extended-family support system has acted as a buffer against the worst privations of severe poverty, however.

Access to land has alleviated some of the hardships for the rural population. In 1997, the poverty gap and squared poverty gap index were 40 and 60 percent higher in urban areas, respectively, than those in rural areas. There are also significant differences in poverty rates and poverty gaps among the geographic regions, with poverty rates in the richest areas (Samegrelo/Poti, Adjara/Batumi) being half those of the poorest ones (Imereti, Guria). The people of the most impoverished region, Imereti, live in remote, mountainous areas that are almost inaccessible during winter partly due to lack of infrastructure maintenance. The former centers of Soviet heavy industry were most adversely affected while those that possessed diversified agricultural and agro-industrial sectors proved less vulnerable to the dramatic upheavals of the 1990s.

The minimum subsistence levels established by the U.S. State Department for Statistics (SDS) were GEL113.2 a month for a working man, GEL99.3 for an average consumer, and GEL197 (US$100) for a family of 4. In 2001, the country's 800,000 **pensioners** received payments of GEL14 (US$7) with GEL2 deducted for electricity. This represents only 12 percent of the SDS's suggested minimum *subsistence* income level. Pensioners, therefore, invariably rely on family, neighbors, street trading, or begging. The **dependency ratio** is 1:1.2, which is dangerously high compared to the suggested 1 dependent per 3 people. The large proportion of workers not paying taxes worsens the government's ability to introduce an adequate pension scheme. The pension system also suffers from a large number of "ghost" recipients: the 1999 registration revealed payments to 37,743

Household Consumption in PPP Terms

Country	All food	Clothing and footwear	Fuel and power[a]	Health care[b]	Education[b]	Transport & Communications	Other
Georgia	33	4	13	2	4	8	36
United States	13	9	9	4	6	8	51
Russia	28	11	16	7	15	8	16
Ukraine	34	5	16	6	4	14	22

Data represent percentage of consumption in PPP terms.
[a]Excludes energy used for transport.
[b]Includes government and private expenditures.

SOURCE: World Bank. *World Development Indicators 2000.*

deceased pensioners. This unusual situation is partially explained by the high cost of funerals, which force many people to bury their relatives without registering their deaths. Postal workers, however, earn bonuses for withholding the delivery of pensions to unreported, deceased pensioners.

While the Soviet health-care system had imperfections, it was far superior to that of independent Georgia. In 1999, government spending on health care constituted 0.59 percent of GDP, a figure that compares unfavorably with Latin America (2.6 percent), eastern Europe (3.9 percent), and high-income nations of the western world (6 percent). Georgians are expected to pay for their own health care, but surveys indicate that almost 80 percent of Georgians spend less than US$5 a month on it. Because of the strong sense of family obligation that is a fundamental part of the Georgian culture, financial support for ailing and aging citizens often becomes the responsibility of family. This family contribution is one of the factors that allows Georgians to enjoy an average life expectancy of 73 years.

The Georgian educational system was one of the few institutions that did not collapse during the wars of the early 1990s, but the standard of education has diminished since the Soviet period. The university system is notoriously corrupt. Teachers are rarely paid. There is an acute lack of resources at all levels. Once renowned for their educational achievements, Georgians face an education crisis that may ultimately undermine one of the main attractions for potential investors—an educated workforce.

WORKING CONDITIONS

As the year 2000 came to an end, government statistics indicated that Georgia had a **labor force** of 2.06 million people, 8.4 percent of whom were unemployed. Official unemployment figures are deceptively low and do not accurately reflect economic realities. Most Georgians consider their chances of securing a job by registering themselves with the authorities as low, and they are not attracted by unemployment compensation. To qualify for standard monthly unemployment benefits, an applicant must have worked in the official sector and, even then, would only be entitled to receive benefits for the first 6 months of unemployment. The payments are fixed at GEL14 for the first 2 months, GEL12 for the third and fourth months, and GEL11 for the final period. On average, 2 percent of registered unemployed workers qualify for benefits.

Government labor force survey results for the last quarter of 2000 suggested that urban unemployment stood at 24.7 percent compared to a rural unemployment rate of 4.6 percent. The capital, T'bilisi, accounted for 41 percent of the country's unemployed. While the rural rate might seem encouraging, 65 percent of those in the countryside were self-employed. Indeed, agricultural self-employment comprised 86.5 percent of those described as self-employed and most lived below the poverty line.

The role of trade unions in Georgia is exceptionally weak, largely due to the poor state of key economic sectors. Strikes and other forms of industrial protest are meaningless against a backdrop of idle and bankrupt firms that are often *unable* to pay employees. Many employees continue to work in the hope that one day their salary **arrears** will be paid, a hope that evaporates if they cease working.

While there is no official discrimination against women, Georgia is a patriarchal society and in many menial jobs women are paid as little as half of what their male counterparts earn. Mass unemployment, however, has affected males disproportionately and upset traditional gender relations. Women have proved more successful at securing high-paid jobs with international organizations, which usually require proficiency in foreign languages.

COUNTRY HISTORY AND ECONOMIC DEVELOPMENT

1099–1125. David IV (the Builder) establishes the Georgian empire. Beginning of Georgian Golden Age.

1184–1213. Georgia's favorite monarch, Queen Tamara, defeats Turks and extends Georgian rule from the Black Sea to the Caspian Sea.

1220. Georgian Golden Age ends with the invasion of the Mongols under Genghis Khan.

1553. Ottoman Turks and Persians divide Georgia between themselves.

1801. Russian annexation of Georgia.

1811. Georgian Orthodox Church is stripped of its self-governing status as part of the Russification process.

1918. Georgia gains independence.

1921. Red Army invades Georgia and drives out the democratically elected government. Georgia is annexed and becomes part of the new USSR.

1972. Eduard Shevardnadze becomes First Secretary of the Georgian Communist Party and begins anti-corruption campaign.

1989. On 9 April, Soviet troops kill 20 civilians—mainly women—who were involved in a nationalist protest outside the parliament in T'bilisi. From this point on, Soviet rule is totally discredited in Georgia.

1990. In the country's first multi-party elections, a nationalist coalition is victorious and appoints Zviad Gamsakhurdia as president.

1991. On the anniversary of the T'bilisi massacre (9 April), Georgian parliament declares Georgia independent of the Soviet Union.

1991–1992. Gamsakhurdia is elected president by popular vote in May 1991 but is deposed in a coup in January 1992. Shevardnadze is invited by coup leaders to head the transitional government.

1992–1993. Georgian armed forces are defeated in Abkhazia. Abkhazia becomes a de facto independent republic, although it remains part of Georgia's national territory under international law.

1995. Shevardnadze is elected president. His Citizens Union of Georgia party emerges as the largest parliamentary grouping.

2000. Shevardnadze is re-elected president amid many voting irregularities. On 14 June, Georgia becomes the 137th member of the World Trade Organization.

FUTURE TRENDS

Georgia is a country of great economic potential but until it regularizes the supply of power to industry and to its citizenry, economic progress will be limited. The aging Shevardnadze, despite many imperfections, has played a pivotal role in securing stability. The question of who or what will follow his departure from the political scene remains unresolved. Political institutions and civic values are not yet rooted enough in Georgian society to permit total confidence in a smooth transition to a younger generation of politicians. The country will endure great difficulties in meeting external financial obligations. The shortfall in public spending—primarily on health, education, and welfare—will continue to bear hardest on the nation's poor. Georgia's greatest potential in the short- to medium-term lies in its geographical location. The government is committed to providing a trans-Georgian transportation infrastructure connecting Europe with central Asia to cater to an anticipated oil bonanza in the coming decades. The implementation of this so-called "Silk Route" project should enhance Georgia's international credentials, but this opportunity will be squandered if the endemic corruption that has plagued Georgia for decades is not seriously addressed.

DEPENDENCIES

Georgia has no territories or colonies.

BIBLIOGRAPHY

Gachechildze, Revaz. *The New Georgia: Space, Society, Politics.* London: UCL Press, 1995.

Georgia Development Gateway. <http://georgia-gateway.org/index.php3?cid+398>. Accessed September 2001.

Georgian-European Policy and Legal Advice Centre (GEPLAC). *Georgian Economic Trends.* T'bilisi: GEPLAC, 2000.

Herzig, Edmund. *The New Caucasus.* London: The Royal Institute of International Affairs, 1999.

Rosen, Roger. *Georgia: A Sovereign Country of the Caucasus.* Hong Kong: Odyssey, 1999.

Suny, Ronald. *The Making of the Georgian Nation.* 2nd Edition. London: Indiana University Press, 1994.

U.S. Central Intelligence Agency. "World Factbook 2000." <http://www.odci.gov/cia/publications/factbook/index.html>. Accessed July 2001.

Wright, John. *The Georgians: A Handbook.* London: Curzon Press, 1998.

—Donnacha Ó Beacháin

GERMANY

Federal Republic of Germany
Bundesrepublik Deutschland

CAPITAL: Berlin.

MONETARY UNIT: Deutsche mark (DM). One deutsche mark equals 100 pfennigs. There are coins of 1, 2, 5, 10, and 50 pfennigs and 1, 2, and 5 deutsche marks, and notes of 5, 10, 20, 50, 100, 200, 500, and 1,000 deutsche marks. In January 1999 Germany switched to the new European currency unit, the euro, along with 10 other members of the European Union, as a part of the European Monetary Union (EMU) and the European System of Central Banks (ESCB). The euro was in use after 1 January 1999 for electronic transfers and accounting purposes, while euro coins and bills will be issued in 2002, and at that time the German currency will cease to be legal tender. On 1 January 1999, control over monetary policy, the setting of interest rates, and the regulation of the money supply was transferred from the German Central Bank (Bundesbank) to the European Central Bank (ECB) in Frankfurt am Main.

CHIEF EXPORTS: Machinery, vehicles, chemicals, metals and manufactures, foodstuffs, textiles.

CHIEF IMPORTS: Raw materials, machinery, vehicles, chemicals, foodstuffs, textiles, metals.

GROSS DOMESTIC PRODUCT: US$1.864 trillion (purchasing power parity, 1999 est.).

BALANCE OF TRADE: **Exports:** US$549.0 billion (1999). **Imports:** US$478.9 billion (1999). [The *CIA World Factbook* lists 1999 exports of US$610 billion and imports of US$586 billion.]

COUNTRY OVERVIEW

LOCATION AND SIZE. Located in western Central Europe, Germany has an area of 357,021 square kilometers (137,810 square miles), which makes it slightly smaller than the state of Montana. The country is bordered by the North Sea, Denmark, and the Baltic Sea to the north; Poland and the Czech Republic to the east; Austria and Switzerland to the south; and France, Luxembourg, Belgium and the Netherlands to the west. The capital city, Berlin, is located in the northeastern part of the country.

POPULATION. The population of Germany was estimated at 82.8 million in 2000, adding up to a 4.3 percent increase from 1990. The birth rate was only 9.35 births per 1,000 population and the death rate was 10.49 per 1,000, causing a decrease in the natural born population during 2000. The growth of the population during the 1990s was mainly due to **immigration**. The immigration rate was 4.01 immigrants per 1,000 population in 2000. The population of Germany has increased 21 percent over the second half of the 20th century, but it is expected to contract to 79.3 million by 2025 and 70.3 million by 2050. The birth rate is declining due to a fertility rate of 1.38 births per woman in 2000, far below the replacement threshold of 2.1 births per woman. The population, as in most of Europe, is also aging with a high life expectancy of 77.44 years for the total population (74.3 for men and 80.75 for women in 2000). In 2000, 16 percent of the population was 14 years old or younger, while an equal percentage was 65 years or older.

Germany's welfare system has supported population growth by offering social services, such as old-age pensions, health and unemployment insurance, disability benefits, subsidized housing, and **subsidies** to families raising children. However, these programs have so far failed to increase Germany's birth rate. Higher living standards and the modern economy restricted population growth during the 1990s. Germany's **labor force** is expected to shrink, particularly after 2020, and the number of **pensioners** will grow steadily. This decline in the ratio of active workers to retirees may force Germany by 2020 to bring in as many as 1.2 million immigrant workers annually (both skilled, such as computer programmers, and unskilled) to maintain its industrial output at 2000 levels. To offset these effects, the German government

has encouraged policies that sustain the life of native workers such as better health care, nutrition, and adult education. Public social security system reform is also important as the number of taxpayers decreases, causing intense financial pressures on those who still work. **Structural unemployment** has prompted the government to offer early retirement options to those who have skills and want to work yet cannot find work in their chosen fields. This has increased the pressure on the German retirement system and welfare system as a whole.

Higher living standards in Germany continuously attract many economic immigrants, mostly from eastern and southern Europe and the Middle East. The country received a considerable number of refugees from the Yugoslav wars in the early 1990s. In 2000 ethnic Germans formed 91.5 percent of the population and the most significant minority group was the ethnic Turks (2.4 percent), while Yugoslavs, Italians, Russians, Greeks, Poles, and Spaniards made up the rest. In 1998 there were about 7.3 million foreigners in the country. Some Germans blame immigrants for taking jobs from native-born people, equating unemployment with foreigners. Some occurrences of racism and ethnic hatred have been reported throughout the country but mostly in the poorer eastern states.

The population density was 233.8 people per square kilometer (605.5 per square mile) in 1995. In 1997 about 57.4 percent lived in towns and cities of 20,000 or more inhabitants. Approximately 87.3 percent of Germans lived in urban areas in 1999, mainly in the industrial region of the Ruhr in the western portion of the country. The main cities are Berlin, the capital, with a population of 3.46 million; the free port city of Hamburg on the River Elbe in the north, with 1.71 million; the Bavarian capital Munich in the south, with 1.23 million; Cologne on the Rhine in the west, with 964,000; Frankfurt am Main, a major European financial center, in west central Germany, with 648,000; and Dresden and Leipzig, historic cities and cultural centers in Saxony in the east, each with approximately 450,000 (2000 est.).

OVERVIEW OF ECONOMY

Germany has traditionally been the largest economy in Europe and a world leader in science and engineering. It had the third largest economy in the world in 2000, following the United States and Japan. In 2000 it contributed for about one-third of the **gross domestic product** (GDP) of the eurozone (the 11 member countries that joined the European Monetary Union in 1999), and was considered the economic powerhouse of the European Union (EU). Its **GDP per capita** of US$26,513 in 1999 and its living standards were among the highest in the world.

Recovering from the destruction of World War II, Germany's economy experienced a long period of strong economic growth that has been widely referred to as the "German miracle." During this period of growth, extensive and generous social services and benefits accompanied high-tech market **capitalism**. A broad cooperation among government, business, and labor complemented free market principles in economic decision-making. Companies were considered responsible not only to shareholders but also to employees, customers, suppliers, and local communities. However, this domestic capitalist model that linked business to a social conscience was challenged during the 1990s with the reunification of East and West Germany—which had been divided since 1949—and the consolidation and globalization of German businesses. The economy acquired more liberal U.S. traits in order to compete with foreign companies. European integration, including **liberalization** at the state level, the transfer to a single European market, and the adoption of the single European currency, also contributed to a more **liberal economic** landscape, which meant that market forces played a greater role in determining the shape of the economy while government decisions played a smaller role.

The integration of East Germany and West Germany after the 1989 collapse of the Berlin Wall brought the economy under significant economic strain. East Germany's large government debt and persistent unemployment—the product of years of **communist** control in that country—forced West Germany to offer an estimated US$100 billion annually to the poorer east German states. During the 1990s the shrinking number of tax-payers and the growing number of retirees, high labor costs, greater foreign competition from **emerging markets** (such as eastern Asia), and high **capital outflows** (by German banks and corporations investing abroad) also added to the economic stresses of reunification. The integration of the centrally planned East German economy was difficult, and many regions in western Germany have also been slow in **restructuring** and closing down obsolete heavy industries. Due to high labor costs and the country's image as an over-regulated economy, **foreign direct investment** in Germany was rather weak through the 1990s. The financial meltdowns in Asia, Russia, Mexico, Brazil and other emerging markets in the late 1990s also afflicted the economy, which was highly dependent on the export of manufactured, particularly capital, goods (machinery and equipment).

The government has pursued economic and social policies, such as budget cuts, tax cuts, and structural reform to encourage growth in foreign and domestic investment and job creation. In 1999 the Future Program 2000 was adopted, calling for a DM30 billion federal budget cut in 2000; radical business, family, and energy tax reforms; and a reform of the mandatory old age pension and health-care system. The government launched the Alliance for Jobs campaign with labor and business to discuss wage policies, making early retirement options more attractive for small and medium-sized firms, providing more work time flexibility, more trainee positions, and cutting overtime work. The government is working to increase the labor market flexibility (the readiness of workers to relocate to areas and industries with better growth perspectives) and to increase international competitiveness by reducing the costs of operating German businesses (by tax cuts and other measures).

POLITICS, GOVERNMENT, AND TAXATION

Following its military defeat in World War II, Germany was occupied and divided into the Federal Republic of Germany (West Germany) under western influence, and the German Democratic Republic (East Germany) within the communist bloc. On the wake of the democratic reforms in the Soviet Union initiated by President Mikhail Gorbachev in the 1980s, and the collapse of communism in eastern Europe, the German countries were reunited on October 3, 1990. The political system is based on the Basic Law (Grundgesetz, or constitution) of 1949. The country is a democratic federation of 16 states (Länder) with their own governments and local traditions. Each state has an elected legislature and government whose responsibilities include local affairs such as education and keeping a police force. The federal legislative power is vested in a **bicameral** Federal Assembly or parliament comprising the Bundestag (lower house), with 662 members (328 elected from local constituencies and 334 elected through party lists in each state for a 4-year term), and the Bundesrat (upper house) comprised of 69 members nominated by the 16 states. Each state has between 3 and 6 votes in the Bundesrat, depending on its population, and these are required to vote as a block. The role of the Bundesrat is limited, but it can veto or initiate revision of legislation passed in the Bundestag when it would affect the interests of the states. Parliamentary elections in September of 1998 brought to office the cabinet of Chancellor Gerhard Schröder of the Social Democratic Party of Germany (SPD), and elections were scheduled for 2002. The head of state is the president (a role that is largely ceremonial), elected for a maximum of 2 5-year terms by an electoral college consisting of members of the Bundestag and representatives of the state legislatures. The president in 2001 was Johannes Rau, who took office in 1999, and presidential elections were scheduled for May 2004. The federal executive power is vested in the federal government led by the chancellor (prime minister), elected by the Bundestag on the nomination of the president.

Major political parties represented in parliament in 2001 included the Socialist Party (SPD) and the environmentalist, pacifist Alliance 90/the Greens; the conservative Christian Democratic Union (CDU) and the Christian Social Union (CSU); the Free Democratic Party (FDP); and the Party of Democratic Socialism (PDS). In early 2001 the SPD (supporting social welfare) had 298 seats. The CDU and its Bavarian sister party the CSU (or CDU/CSU) had 245 seats in the Bundestag. CDU/CSU was a major party that kept office for 16 years under Chancellor Helmut Kohl until 1998. It is generally conservative on economic and social policy but was plagued by corruption scandals in the 1990s. The Alliance 90/The Greens (Buendnis 90/Die Gruenen), with 47 seats, was a junior partner in the federal coalition government. The Free Democratic Party (FDP), with a relatively market-oriented, civil libertarian platform, had 43 seats in the Bundestag and was a traditional coalition partner of the CDU/CSU. The Party of Democratic Socialism (PDS), the successor party to the Communist Party of the former East Germany, had 36 seats, maintaining its political base in the poorer eastern states.

The center-left coalition government that took office in 1998 hoped to stimulate economic growth and control the rising government debt. Total German government debt stood at DM1,500 billion, or 61 percent of the GDP in 1998, and federal **debt service** obligations reached 25 percent of federal revenues. Reducing unemployment and fostering the development of eastern Germany were also high priorities. The government worked to enhance German competitiveness by implementing tax cuts, budget spending restraints, growth incentives, and structural reforms. Pension reforms were aimed at limiting the financial pressure on the public social security system and encouraging citizens to open extra privately funded retirement accounts. Fiscal consolidation and pension reforms were expected to reduce the government debt and to allow further tax reforms, thus cutting corporate **income taxes** and reducing personal income taxes while broadening the tax base. Tax cuts were designed to provide incentives to growth, by allowing corporations to invest more easily in high technology and by supporting an increase in the export of products through a reduction in the overall tax costs of production.

By 2000 the government had implemented significant tax cuts for low-income taxpayers, a modest tax relief for businesses, and higher energy taxes in return for lower labor costs. In 1999 the corporate tax rate for local companies on profits distributed to stockholders was 30 percent and on undistributed profits it was 45 percent, but under the tax reform this split rate was reduced to a single flat rate of 25 percent applicable also to foreign companies that were once subject to a 42 percent corporate tax on total profits. Additional local taxes still pushed the total rate of taxation for individuals and companies up to around 50 percent. A **value-added tax** (VAT) applied to all sales and services, at a rate of 16 percent or at a reduced rate of 7 percent. In addition to the VAT, there were numerous excise and other taxes, mainly at the state and municipal levels, including tobacco, gasoline, oil and heating oil, alcohol, stamp **duties**, and lottery taxes. The government decided to tax energy consumption after 1 April 1999 by a **levy** on the use of gas, oil and electricity; and after 1 January 2000 further tax increases on energy consumption were implemented.

INFRASTRUCTURE, POWER, AND COMMUNICATIONS

Germany has one of the world's most developed transportation and communication infrastructures. Intensive investment since reunification in 1990 has brought the undeveloped eastern Germany in line with that of western Germany. Transport and communications utilities in Germany have been liberalized following EU requirements. A dense and efficient network of motorways, railways, and waterways connects the country with ma-

Communications

Country	Newspapers	Radios	TV Sets[a]	Cable subscribers[a]	Mobile Phones[a]	Fax Machines[a]	Personal Computers[a]	Internet Hosts[b]	Internet Users[b]
	1996	1997	1998	1998	1998	1998	1998	1999	1999
Germany	311	948	580	214.5	170	73.1	304.7	173.96	14,400
United States	215	2,146	847	244.3	256	78.4	458.6	1,508.77	74,100
France	218	937	601	27.5	188	47.4	207.8	110.64	5,370
Japan	578	955	707	114.8	374	126.8	237.2	163.75	27,060

[a]Data are from International Telecommunication Union, *World Telecommunication Development Report 1999* and are per 1,000 people.
[b]Data are from the Internet Software Consortium (http://www.isc.org) and are per 10,000 people.

SOURCE: World Bank. *World Development Indicators 2000.*

jor centers and the world. In 2000 the total length of paved highways was 650,891 kilometers (404,444 miles), including 11,400 kilometers (7,083 miles) of expressways. More than 45 million motor vehicles were on the road, causing high road usage and frequent traffic jams, but the lack of speed limits on highways helped alleviate traffic problems. However, many Germans preferred to use the extensive public transport system, or bicycles, instead of motor vehicles. In 1998 the total length of railroads was 40,826 kilometers (25,368 miles) including at least 14,253 kilometers (8,856 miles) of electrified and 14,768 kilometers (9,176 miles) of double- or multiple-tracked railroads. The national railroad carrier, Deutsche Bahn AG (DBAG), was **privatized** in 1994 but still required government subsidies.

Germany's flagship air carrier, Lufthansa, is among the world leaders in the airline industry. According to EU requirements, Lufthansa is majority owned by EU governments, while the German government has relinquished its holding in it, and the state of Bavaria has reduced its stake in the company. Since the liberalization of air transportation in the European Union in 1997, Lufthansa has fought to retain its dominant position on Germany's internal routes. In 1998 a total of 127 million passengers were carried by commercial air services in Germany. There are 320 airports, including 14 with runways over 3,047 meters (1.89 miles), with 673,300 aircraft departures registered in 1998. The busiest airport, in terms of aircraft movements, passenger departures, and freight traffic is the Rhein-Main airport outside Frankfurt am Main. Munich is the second busiest in terms of passenger traffic and Cologne-Bonn is the second busiest in terms of freight traffic. The other major passenger airports are Berlin-Tegel, Dusseldorf, and Hamburg. The federal government and cities such as Berlin and Cologne are preparing to sell their shares in major airports.

Marine transport is also developed, with major ports on the Baltic Sea, including Kiel, Rostock, and Luebeck, and on the North Sea, including Emden, Hamburg, Bremen, and Bremerhaven. Major rivers ports are at Duisburg, Cologne, Bonn, Mannheim, and Karlsruhe on the Rhine; Magdeburg and Dresden on the Elbe; and Kiel on the Kiel Canal which provides an important connection between the Baltic and North Sea. The most important port for Germany, however, is Rotterdam in the Netherlands. Hamburg is by far the largest port city in Germany, accounting for about 33 percent of all the freight. In 1998 the merchant fleet totaled 8.01 million gross registered tons, and freight traffic shipped through German ports that year totaled 210 million tons. Historically, industrial centers have grown closer to ports due to the supply of cheaper raw materials and coal. In recent decades, refinery and chemical industries have gravitated towards the 1,550 miles-long network of oil pipelines. Fuel transport by pipeline in Germany rose from 74.1 million tons in 1990 to 90.7 million tons in 1998.

The country imports most of its energy sources, including almost all of its oil. In the 1970s and 1980s it worked to reduce its dependence on imported oil by developing nuclear power and encouraging energy efficiency. In the 1990s, environmental considerations, including global warming, became a serious concern, and in 2000 a program of gradual withdrawal from nuclear power was agreed on by the SPD-Green government and electricity producers. In early 2001, a shipment of nuclear waste from France to Germany sparked massive environmental protests in the country, causing many injuries and hundreds of arrests. A total of 19 nuclear plants accounted for about 40 percent of Germany's electricity consumption in 2000. In 1998 the country produced 525.356 billion kilowatt hours of electricity and fossil fuel (coal-lignite, coal-anthracite, and natural gas) accounted for the largest portion while hydroelectricity contributed only 3.2 percent. Like all other industrialized economies, Germany has become increasingly cautious about energy consumption.

Prior to 1997 the electric sector was divided into 9 regional **monopolies**, with exclusive rights over transmission facilities within their areas. At the local level, there were hundreds of municipally controlled power distributors. City and state governments had direct financial interests in the electric sector through concession agreements and in many cases ownership of local and regional distribution organizations. Between the regional monopolies and the local distributors were about 70 middle-level distributors of electricity. Although electricity prices in Germany used to be among the highest in the European Union, they fell dramatically after the Electricity Supply Law entered into force in 1997. This law implemented the EU power market liberalization directive and went beyond its requirements to create a thorough electric market liberalization in western Germany. By 1999 electricity **tariffs** for large users fell by up to 30 percent. The local and regional monopolies were broken by permitting third-party access for both commercial and residential customers. In addition, national utilities were allowed to buy from competing power producers, and electricity purchasing pools were created. The industry has undergone deep and rapid restructuring as large regional power generators have merged and sought the integration of production and distribution by purchasing some of 900 local power distributors. The federal government participates, often as a minority shareholder, in local energy utilities and is represented on the boards of supervisory authorities.

Germany is among the world's leaders in telecommunications, served by a modern telephone system and 46.5 million main lines connected by fiber-optic cable, coaxial cable, microwave radio relay, and a domestic satellite system. The state-owned giant, Deutsche Telekom (DT), one of the leaders of the European and global telecommunications sector, became a joint-stock company in 1989, but it was not until January 1998 that it ended its monopoly in fixed lines under EU law. DT was also partially privatized: 28 percent of the company was sold in the financial markets in 1996, 25 percent was sold in 2000, and the remaining shares owned by the German government were scheduled for future sale. Liberalization brought a variety of new service providers with varying prices for services. In the first year after liberalization, DT lost 30 percent of its peak-time long-distance-call business and introduced price cuts of 60 percent in January 1999. Competition from the nearly 200 new telecommunications companies and about 1,300 companies in non-licensed sectors has fueled arguments over network access charges and rates. Growth in the areas of multimedia, mobile communications, and the Internet has also been spectacular. Germany is one of the fastest growing markets for mobile phone equipment, and Germans owned 15.318 million mobile phones in 1999. The government is considering further investments into the area because it still compares poorly with the United States by the ratio of personal computers and Internet hosts per 1,000 people.

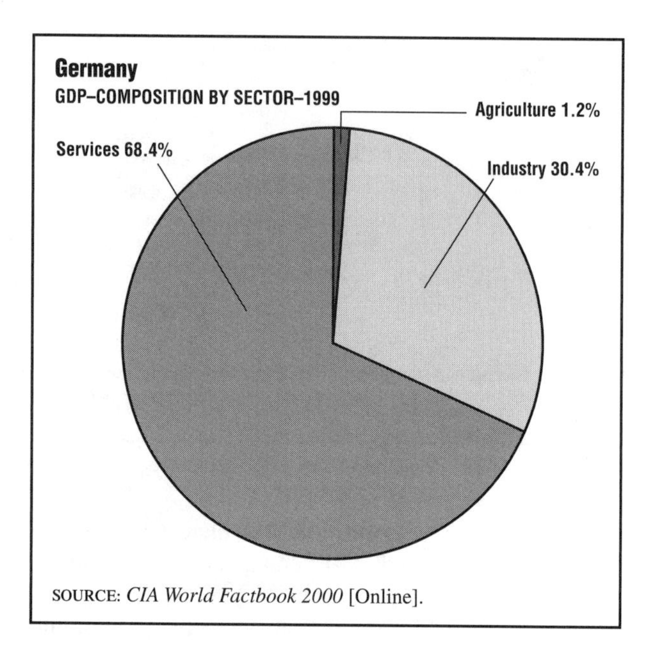

SOURCE: *CIA World Factbook 2000* [Online].

ECONOMIC SECTORS

Germany's economic structure is typical of highly industrialized economies that often have a very strong services sector. In 1999 about 68.4 percent of the GDP was contributed by services, 30.4 percent by industry, and 1.2 percent by agriculture, forestry, fishing, and hunting. Approximately 63.6 percent of the country's workforce was employed in services, 33.7 percent in industry, and 2.7 percent in agriculture. The largest industries in terms of employment in 1998 were manufacturing and mining with 8.65 million employees, miscellaneous pub-

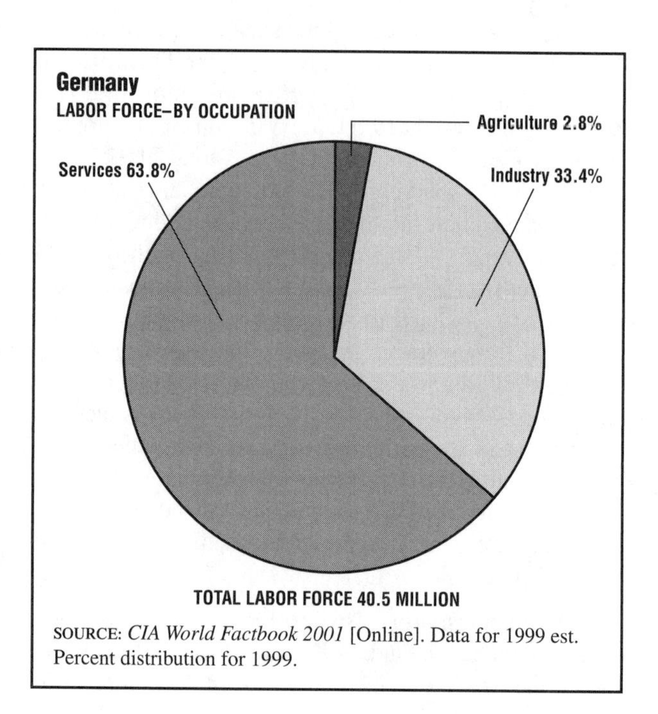

SOURCE: *CIA World Factbook 2001* [Online]. Data for 1999 est. Percent distribution for 1999.

lic and private services with 7.44 million, trade and tourism with 6.28 million, and public administration with 3.2 million. Other major employers were construction, business services and real estate, and transport and communications. Manufacturing has traditionally been the powerhouse of the economy, but its importance has declined significantly over the last third of the 20th century as a result of structural change. Manufacturing's share of the gross **value added** to the economic sector fell from 51.7 percent in 1970 to 32.8 percent in 1997. In the same period, the service sector increased its share markedly. Private services accounted for 37.3 percent of the gross value added in 1997, while commerce and transport accounted for 14.6 percent. Rapidly expanding branches, like information technology, communications, and the aerospace industry, have failed to compensate for the decline of traditional branches, such as textiles and steel, and the services sector has been unable to achieve high growth rates given that basic needs of the population are generally satisfied.

AGRICULTURE

Agriculture is important for the country's food security and also a provider of jobs. It produces about DM84 billion worth of goods annually and purchases goods for around DM52 billion. Over 80 percent of Germany's land is used for agriculture and forestry. Like other sectors of the economy, it has undergone profound structural changes in the second half of the 20th century. In the western states, the number of farms decreased dramatically between 1949 and 1997 as machines gradually replaced human workers, and productivity increased. In 1950 1 farm worker produced food for 10 people; by 1996 1 farm worker produced food for 108 people. Attracted by a better income, many farmers left agriculture for the industrial and service sectors. Family farms predominate in Germany's old western states, and in 1997, 87 percent of all farmers in western Germany worked on fewer than 124 acres. Individual farm enterprises have also gained ground in the east: in 1997 they accounted for 80 percent of agricultural output from the eastern states, while working on only slightly more than 20 percent of the agricultural land available in the east.

Chief agricultural products include milk, pork, beef, poultry, cereals, potatoes, wheat, barley, cabbages, and sugar beets. In some regions wine, fruits, and vegetables, and other horticultural products play an important role. Agricultural products vary from region to region. In the flat terrain of northern Germany and especially in the eastern portions, cereals and sugar beets are grown. Elsewhere, on more hilly terrain, and even on mountainous land, farmers produce vegetables, milk, pork, or beef. Fruit orchards and vegetable farms surround almost all large cities. River valleys in southern and western Germany along the Rhine and the Main, are covered with vineyards. German beer is world-renowned and is produced mainly, but not exclusively, in Bavaria. Germany has a high level of exports of farm products: in 1997, its exports had a total worth of DM42 billion. Agricultural imports amounted to DM72 billion, making Germany the world's largest importer of farm products.

Important areas of German agricultural policy have transferred to the European Union, particularly in market and price policy, foreign trade policy, and structural policy. EU agricultural reforms in 1992 cut market price supports, replacing artificial prices with government subsidies, and put stricter controls on output volume. Through the reduction of price supports and through additional measures, the reforms promoted more effective farming methods and more ecologically safe agricultural production. The federal and state governments, in their turn, provided financial assistance for agricultural development, land consolidation, village renewal, and construction of country roads. Special funds were available for disadvantaged areas where agriculture was an important economic and social factor. The government's requirements of good agricultural practice required that fertilization and plant protection did not exceed an established maximum, and farmers who used environmentally friendly farming methods received financial compensation in recognition of their environmental policy.

FORESTRY AND FISHING. Almost a third of Germany's total area is covered by forest and although the country has been traditionally a net importer of wood and wood products, it is a significant exporter as well. In 1994 it ranked second after the United States in imports of paper, cardboard, and goods made thereof, and first ahead of Canada, the United States, and Finland in exports. Germany's fishing policy is carried out within the European Community's Common Fisheries Policy (CFP), which is based on the principle of relative stability achieved by established quotas for member states and on exercising control over fish stocks by fixing annual total catch limits.

INDUSTRY

Manufacturing in Germany holds a declining share of the total GDP and jobs, but it remains the backbone of the economy and is highly competitive internationally. German scientific and engineering achievements fueled its phenomenal industrial growth during the 19th and 20th centuries as the country became the birthplace of television, modern airplanes, and the automobile. The creation of the gasoline motor by Gottlieb Daimler was complimented by Rudolf Diesel's invention of the engine bearing his name. From 1901 to 1930 Germans received a total of 26 Nobel prizes in physics, chemistry, and medicine. Large companies, based on the German ingenuity of the past centuries, account for just fewer than 40 percent of the industry's total revenue, while small and medium-sized companies form the vast majority of firms in the industrial sector, supplying the larger companies with parts and supplies. Many of the large German firms are known throughout the world and have branches or research facilities overseas, including the car makers, Daimler Chrysler, Volkswagen, and BMW; the chemical corporations, Hoechst, Bayer, and BASF; the energy giants, VEBA and RWE; and the machinery and equipment manufacturers, Mannesmann, Siemens, and Bosch. The ownership structure in manufacturing is predominantly private, although the federal and especially the state governments hold **equity** in a range of companies. The federal government has pursued privatization plans since the early 1980s.

MINING. Germany has a distinguished mining tradition, but the industry has taken a minor role in the 1990s and is not able to meet the country's growing needs for energy and raw materials. The chief mining products are brown coal, or lignite, with total reserves at about 43 billion tons, and 24 billion tons of hard coal, or anthracite. Lignite, inexpensive in Germany, is a principal domestic source of energy covering about 26 percent of the electricity production. The country is the world's largest lignite producer, with about 20 percent of global output. Hard coal production, on the other hand, has fallen despite subsidies. In 1950 hard coal accounted for 73 percent of the primary energy consumption in West Germany, but by 1997 its share had fallen to 14.1 percent. Germany imported 12 percent of its coal in 1998, mostly from Poland, followed by Australia, South Africa, and Colombia, and imports were expected to double by 2020, as nuclear power is phased out and hard coal domestic production is further reduced. Oil and natural gas production is mostly limited to the North German Plain and the North Sea, making Germany the third largest oil importer in the world, with primary suppliers Russia, Norway, Libya, and the United Kingdom. Natural gas is imported from Russia, the Netherlands, and Norway.

MANUFACTURING. The German manufacturing sector is large and robust, with leading branches in chemical products and pharmaceuticals, vehicles and transport equipment, metals and metal products, electrical machinery, precision instruments, paper products, and processed foods. Other products include cement and construction materials, optics, electronics, ships, and textiles. In the eastern states, chief manufacturing sectors are electrical engineering and electronics, chemicals, vehicles, glass, and ceramics. The former state-owned companies in eastern Germany, although receiving significant investments from the west after reunification, are generally more unstable, and it is unclear which of them are to survive. Large portions of the old Communist manufacturing industries in the east have been shut down since unification.

MOTOR VEHICLES. Germany is the world's third largest automobile maker after the United States and Japan, and with nearly 730,000 employees and annual revenue of almost DM340 billion in 1999, the automobile industry is a crucial economic player. The industry provides markets for many related industries like machine tools, spare parts, tires, plastics and paints, and metal processing. With all suppliers, automotive services and retailers included, a total of about 5 million workers in the country depend on the health of the automobile industry for their livelihoods. Due to the increasing automation of production and the refocusing of manufacturers on core activities, the distribution of value between manufacturers, direct suppliers, pre-suppliers, and distributors is changing, but as a whole, in 1998, the percentage of gross domestic product related to the development, manufacture, sale and use of motor vehicles amounted to almost 20 percent. Car makers, such as Daimler Chrysler, Volkswagen, Audi, and BMW, are well known throughout the world. In 2000, Daimler Chrysler, with its revenue of 162.4 billion euros, was the second largest company in the world. Of the 5.309 million vehicles manufactured in 1999, 64.6 percent were exported mainly to other EU members and to North America, and German companies also produced 3.55 million vehicles in their foreign operations. Manufacturers from western Germany have opened new plants in the eastern states and invested nearly DM7 billion with the purpose to produce 370,000 cars a year. The German automotive industry has traditionally attracted significant foreign direct investments. The car maker Opel was acquired by General Motors of the United States before World War II, and after the war Ford and other industry leaders opened operations in the country.

MACHINERY. In 1997, Germany accounted for nearly 20 percent of the world's machinery exports (Japan was responsible for 16 percent and the United States for 15.7 percent). In some products, like metallurgical plant equipment, particularly rolling mills, paper and printing machines, and woodworking machinery, German exports amounted to one-third of the world total. With almost 6,500 factories in mechanical engineering, German manufacturers have a reputation for customized machinery of high quality. Among the important products are machine tools, including manufacturing systems, power transmission engineering, air handling, refrigeration, air pollution control, vacuum and compressor equipment, and food processing and packaging technology. Only about 5.5 percent of the factories have more than 500 employees and these are the producers of large, complex machines. Some large, well known machinery manufacturers include Mannesmann Demag, a producer of plant engineering and machine tools with a total of 55,000 employees; Heidelberger Druckmaschinen, a maker of printing and paper machinery with 17,000 workers; the Bosch group, a manufacturer of packaging machines and automation technology with 7,000 employees in its machinery division; and Gildemeister, a producer of sophisticated machine tools with 2,300 employees (all figures from 1997). Over 80 percent of the companies in mechanical engineering, however, are highly specialized small- or medium-sized firms with fewer than 200 employees. In 1997 they had a workforce of 881,000 and combined revenues of DM210 billion, almost two-thirds of which were generated by exports. The German aerospace industry, which employed about 61,000 and generated a revenue of about DM21 billion by 1997, led major European technology cooperation projects, such as Airbus and Ariane.

CHEMICALS. In 1996 Germany was the largest exporter of chemical products in the world, with a share of 15.5 percent (the United States accounted for 14.4 percent and Japan for 7.5 percent). Its chemical industry, with its state-of-the-art technology, innovative products, and emphasis on research, was represented by corporate giants such as BASF, Bayer, and Hoechst, and by a multitude of small and medium-sized firms. In 1998 the industry employed 484,000 people, including 31,000 in the eastern states and generated sales of DM187 billion, while research and development expenditures reached DM11.3 billion. Nearly two-thirds of the industry output was exported, amounting to DM123.6 billion in foreign receipts. International networks of subsidiaries and branches characterized the large chemical companies, active in all major world regions. In the 1980s and 1990s, the chemical industry of western Germany underwent substantial restructuring processes and a reduction of its labor force by 45,000 people between 1991 and 1994, eliminating excess capacity and restructuring the geographical distribution of their production facilities under changing market conditions, growing international competition, new EU health and environmental regulations, and a shift in demand to environmentally friendly products.

ELECTRONICS. The electrical engineering and electronics industry, with revenue of DM242 billion and nearly 850,000 employees (1997), is also among the most research-intensive and innovative manufacturing sectors, including makers of production plant electronics, telecommunication systems, electronic components, programmable controllers, medical systems for diagnosis and therapy, household appliances, and others. The sector is dominated by a small number of large firms such as Siemens, Bosch, and IBM Germany. With annual sales of 78 billion euros in 2000 operations in 190 countries, Siemens employed 197,000 workers in Germany, and 203,000 workers abroad. Precision engineering, optical and process control technology, electromedical equipment, and timepieces generated DM52.4 billion in sales 1997, and nearly 2,000 primarily small and medium-sized firms in these industries employed more than 219,000 workers.

OTHER INDUSTRY. In 1999 Germany was the world's fifth largest producer of steel (after the United States, China, Japan, and Russia) with total production of 42.1 million metric tons, down from 44.0 million tons in 1998. With a workforce of about 830,000, the metal-producing and metal-processing industry generated sales of DM230 billion in 1997. Revenue of DM225.7 billion was reported in 1997 by the food processing industry with a labor force of 503,000. Germany has one of the highest per capita consumption rates of beer in the world and is a major producer of fine dairy products and meat delicacies. Textiles, clothing, and leather goods, some the oldest domestic industries, still play a significant role, employing 245,000 and generating a revenue of DM63 billion in 1997, but most important textile regions lost their significance during the 1980s and 1990s. With 775,000 employees and revenues of DM151 billion in 1999, construction was another important branch of German industry, and the country was considered to be Europe's largest construction market with the relocation of the federal capital from Bonn to Berlin and the eastern states' renovation following the reunification in 1990.

SERVICES

TOURISM. Although Germany is an attractive tourist destination and foreign visitors spent DM31 billion in 1999, it has a large deficit in the tourism **balance of payments**. Germans normally enjoy a 30-day paid vacation and many of them travel abroad, spending a total of DM88 billion in 1999 and bringing the negative travel balance to DM57 billion. Yet tourism is an important economic factor as approximately 2.4 million people (including part-time and seasonal help) were employed in the industry and immediately related areas such as travel, restaurants, lodging, relaxation and enjoyment, in 2000. Foreign visitors stay on average between 2 and 3 days, combining a visit to Germany with visits to neighboring countries. Approximately 11.7 million foreign guests visited Germany and about 287 million overnight stays were registered in 1997, including a total of 33.4 million overnight stays by foreign guests. About 15.2 percent of visitors came from the Netherlands, 10.9 percent from the United States, 8.9 percent from Britain, and 5.6 percent from Italy.

RETAIL. **Retail** has undergone profound structural changes over the second half of the 20th century, caused by changing consumer behavior and supply chains. Motorization and more economical bulk-buying have favored the spread of hypermarkets, self-service department stores, and discount stores, and many small retailers have gone out of business. Competition has become harder, profit margins have declined, and the retail food and beverage market is increasingly dominated by a small number of large retailers like REWE, Edeka/AVA, Aldi, Metro, Tengelmann, Spar, Karstadt, Kaufhof and Kaufhalle. The 10 largest retailers accounted in 1999 for over 80 percent of the market, up from about 56 percent in 1990. Internationalization of retail is progressing as more German firms develop operations abroad and foreign competitors like Wal Mart or the French Intermarché group enter the domestic market. Mail-order firms actively benefitted from postal services liberalization and the growth of **e-commerce**. Due to strong competition, prices are low, the product range is wide, and the leisure component of shopping has increased constantly over the 1990s. A boom of new retail facilities has followed the shortage of retail space in East Germany after unification in 1990.

In 1997 retail **turnover** represented 34.3 percent of private consumption, totaling DM715 billion, and the industry employed nearly 2.7 million people (over 45 percent of them part-time, 33 percent of the total in food, beverages, and tobacco). Additionally, 60,000 commercial agents and brokers and 55,000 motor vehicle dealerships and filling stations employed nearly 700,000 workers. A total of 294,000 firms operated in the market, most of them small: 74 percent had fewer than 5 employees, and only 2,925 enterprises had more than 50 workers. Small and medium-sized retailers have found ways to compete with large ones by catering to individual tastes, specializing in certain types of products, and offering expert advice and personalized service, and have also increasingly cooperated in purchasing, sales, and marketing.

FINANCE. No sector of the economy has grown as financial services have done over the 1990s. The turnover of the German banks has risen from DM4 trillion in 1988 to DM9.1 trillion in 1997. Savings deposits, stock and security holdings, loans, and cashless payments have all grown. Banking in Germany has traditionally been characterized by the large amount of long-term credit provided to industry and local government and by the regional or local focus of many credit institutions. In the 1990s, however, the industry was looking to foreign markets and turning to the stock exchange.

German banking is represented by private commercial banks, cooperative banks, and Sparkassen (savings banks) organized regionally and supervised and coordinated by the Landesbanken (state banks). Over half of all savings accounts are in the hands of the 563 Sparkassen, usually held by municipalities, and nearly one-third are in the about 1,800 cooperative banks. Germany's second largest fund manager, DekaBank, is owned by the Sparkassen, and the third largest one, Union Investment, by the cooperatives. As of early 2001, there were 340 commercial banks, 13 regional giro institutions, 596 savings banks, the Deutsche Genossenschaftsbank, the central institution of the cooperative Volksbanken and Raiffeisenbanken, as well as 3 regional institutions of credit cooperatives, 2,411 credit cooperatives, the Deutsche Postbank AG, 33 private and public mortgage banks, 18 credit institutions with special functions, and 34 building and loan associations. Nearly every employee in the 1990s had a salary account and more than 40 million had a Eurocheque card and used this international payment system. Credit cards have also grown in popularity: in 1980, roughly 580,000 people were using them, and in early 2001, the number was 15 million. Since 1980 it has been possible to get cash from automated teller machines (ATM), and the electronic cash system was introduced in 1990 and by 2000 was used at more than 140,000 terminals, especially in retail stores and gas stations.

Germany has 3 large commercial banks which dominated the market after World War II: Deutsche Bank, Dresdner Bank, and Commerzbank. The merger of Bayerische Vereinsbank and Bayerische Hypotheken und Wechsel Bank (Hypobank) in the late 1990s created Bayerische Hypo und Vereinsbank (BHV), which was second in size only to Deutsche Bank. In April 2000 negotiations on the proposed merger of Deutsche Bank and Dresdner Bank were suspended due to EU banking regulations and antitrust laws. Deutsche Bank and the other nationwide banks had powerful positions on the boards of some of the largest industrial and commercial companies and were estimated to own 10 percent of total shareholdings in the country. Their role as shareholders came under EU criticism in the 1990s, and banks were expected to divest themselves of many holdings. In late 1998, both Deutsche Bank and Dresdner Bank announced that they would cut their equity holdings, and Deutsche Bank shifted DM40 billion of assets into a separate company. In their move into investment banking the Landesbanken also attracted criticism from private commercial banks, resulting in investigations by the EU competition authorities into the allegedly privileged status of the Landesbanken. During the 1980s and 1990s, growing competition, declining profit margins, and pressures from shareholders to raise profitability have intensified, and banks have expanded into capital market activities in Germany and into investment and other banking activities abroad. Through Allfinanz (offering insurance, asset management, and banking activities at once), large banks have achieved minority participation in large insurance companies, while some insurers have taken over banks. In early 2001, Allianz, a giant insurer, acquired Dresdner Bank, of which it already owned more than 20 percent, creating Germany's largest company.

INTERNATIONAL TRADE

The German economy is heavily export-oriented and needs imported goods, mostly fuels and raw materials, so

Trade (expressed in billions of US$): Germany

	Exports	Imports
1975	90.176	74.930
1980	192.860	188.002
1985	183.933	158.488
1990	410.104	346.153
1995	523.802	464.271
1998	540.554	467.315

SOURCE: International Monetary Fund. *International Financial Statistics Yearbook 1999.*

with a foreign trade turnover at 48.5 percent of the GDP in 1999 (the world's second largest after the United States) international trade has traditionally played a crucial role. Germany accounted for 9.6 percent of the total world trade in 1999, and its policy of liberalization is consistent with its strong international competitiveness demonstrated by its foreign **trade surplus** of US$70.1 billion (or 3.3 percent of the GDP) in 1999. As in other major trading nations, Germany's jobs, investments, profits and standards of living have been seriously affected by disruptions of world trade and changes in the global economy.

The country's most important trading partners are the European Union and the United States. In 1999, they accounted together for 67.4 percent of exports and 61.6 percent of imports. EU integration has greatly intensified intra-European trade, and in 1999 the European Union accounted for 57.2 percent of Germany's exports and 53.4 percent of its imports. Germany's most important trading partner continues to be France, and the United States has become both the second largest market for German products, spending DM100.8 billion, and supplier of goods to Germany worth of DM71.2 billion in 1999. Other major markets for Germany are Great Britain (8.4 percent of exports), Italy (7.4 percent), the Netherlands (6.5 percent), Belgium and Luxembourg (5.5 percent), Austria (5.3 percent), Switzerland (4.5 percent), Spain (4.4 percent), and Poland (2.4 percent). After France and United States, major suppliers to Germany are the Netherlands (7.9 percent of imports), Italy (7.3 percent), Great Britain (6.8 percent), Belgium and Luxembourg (5.2 percent), Japan (4.8 percent), Austria (4.0 percent), Switzerland (3.9 percent), and Spain (3.2 percent). About 13 percent of the trade volume is exchanged with the Asia-Pacific region, and Germany's largest trade imbalance for decades has been with Japan. Germany's main exports in 1997 were motor vehicles (DM159.1 billion), machinery (DM149.3 billion), chemical products (DM130.8 billion), and electrical engineering products (DM110.3 billion). Its most important imports were raw materials and energy (25 percent), chemical products (13 percent), **consumer goods** (13 percent), electronic goods (12 percent), and motor vehicles (11 percent).

MONEY

Germany has a stable and powerful financial system, and the value of the deutsche mark has been steadily growing since the 1950s. The **exchange rate** of the deutsche mark to the U.S. dollar fell from DM4.21 in 1955 to DM2.15 in 2001 (the lowest price for US$1 was reached in 1992–1995 at DM1.43). The currencies that gained against the deutsche mark after 1950 were Japan's yen and the Swiss franc. Since 1 January 1999, in accordance with provisions of the EU Maastricht Treaty, the European Monetary Union (EMU) was established and the Deutsche Bundesbank (the central bank) became an integral part of the European System of Central Banks consisting of the European Central Bank (ECB) and the central banks of the 11 EMU member states. The euro became the currency unit but was initially used in electronic transfers and for accounting purposes only. The deutsche mark remained as legal tender until the end of the year 2001, and in 2002 the new euro will replace it completely. On 1 January 1999 the exchange rate of the euro was fixed at DM1.9558. **Monetary policy** was also transferred to the ECB, its primary objective being to ensure price stability. In 2001 the most important function of the Bundesbank was to ensure the implementation of ECB monetary policy, including banking supervision and management of national monetary reserves, acting as the house bank of the federal government, overseeing payment transactions in Germany, and controlling the issue of euro notes.

In 1997 stock exchanges in Germany reached a turnover of DM8.97 trillion, 60 percent of which related to fixed interest securities (bonds) and the rest to shares. Trading was conducted on 8 exchanges (in Berlin, Bremen, Düsseldorf, Frankfurt am Main, Hamburg, Hanover, Munich, and Stuttgart), yet the Frankfurt exchange was

Exchange rates: Germany

euros per US$1	
Jan 2001	1.0659
2000	1.0854
1999	0.9386
1998	1.7597
1997	1.7341
1996	1.5048

Note: Amounts prior to 1999 are in deutsche marks per US dollar.

SOURCE: CIA *World Factbook 2001* [ONLINE].

GDP per Capita (US$)

Country	1975	1980	1985	1990	1998
Germany	N/A	N/A	N/A	N/A	31,141
United States	19,364	21,529	23,200	25,363	29,683
France	18,730	21,374	22,510	25,624	27,975
Japan	23,296	27,672	31,588	38,713	42,081

SOURCE: United Nations. *Human Development Report 2000; Trends in human development and per capita income.*

Distribution of Income or Consumption by Percentage Share: Germany

Lowest 10%	3.3
Lowest 20%	8.2
Second 20%	13.2
Third 20%	17.5
Fourth 20%	22.7
Highest 20%	38.5
Highest 10%	23.7

Survey year: 1994

Note: This information refers to income shares by percentiles of the population and is ranked by per capita income.

SOURCE: *2000 World Development Indicators* [CD-ROM].

the largest and ranked fourth internationally (after New York, Tokyo, and London). In 1992 the Deutsche Börse AG was founded in Frankfurt am Main as a **holding company** for the Frankfurter Wertpapierbörse (Frankfurt Securities Exchange), the German part of the German-Swiss futures exchange Eurex, and the Deutsche Börse Clearing AG, responsible for securities settlement and custody. Frankfurt is also the host of many local and foreign credit institutions, including major banks and brokerages.

POVERTY AND WEALTH

After World War II Germany developed a social structure comprised predominantly of a large and prosperous middle class (about 60 percent of the population), including mid-level civil servants, most salaried employees, skilled blue-collar workers, and a shrinking number of farmers. A smaller, wealthier group is made up of the upper-middle class and the upper class; and the poorer class is made of unskilled white and blue-collar workers, and unemployed and socially disadvantaged people. Unskilled blue-collar workers perform the poorest paid and dirtiest tasks. Foreigners account for about 25 percent of this group, and German women form about 38 percent of unskilled blue-collar workers. In 1992 approximately 7.5 percent of the population in the western states and 14.8 percent in the eastern states were poor (with income less than half the national average). From 1960 to 1994, the **disposable income** of private households in the western part of the country increased 10 times, from DM188 billion to over DM1,867 billion, and in 1997 the disposable income of private households in the whole of Germany reached about DM2,355 billion. In 1997, a 4-member household in the western part of Germany disposed of about DM5,725 per month, of which DM4,293 was spent on private consumption, and only about 57 percent had to be spent on food, clothing, and housing. Spending on leisure, automobiles, education, and telephones rose markedly. In 1997, about 53 percent of the private households in the west and 30 percent in the east owned real estate.

Although living standards in the eastern states and among many foreign workers are considerably lower than among most western Germans, there are no extreme forms of poverty, and extensive social programs relieve to a large extent the economic condition of the poor. In 1992 there were 4.6 million recipients of social assistance, nearly 700,000 from the east. Households with 3 or more children, and single parents were the most likely recipients of social assistance. In terms of education, average income, and property ownership, Germany ranks among the world's leaders. In 1963, at the height of the so-called economic miracle following World War II,

Household Consumption in PPP Terms

Country	All food	Clothing and footwear	Fuel and power[a]	Health care[b]	Education[b]	Transport & Communications	Other
Germany	14	6	7	2	10	7	53
United States	13	9	9	4	6	8	51
France	22	7	9	3	8	12	40
Japan	12	7	7	2	22	13	37

Data represent percentage of consumption in PPP terms.

[a]Excludes energy used for transport.

[b]Includes government and private expenditures.

SOURCE: World Bank. *World Development Indicators 2000.*

social spending excluding education was 17.8 percent of the GDP in West Germany, compared with 13.8 percent in Sweden and 11.8 percent in the United Kingdom. Social benefits were further improved in the 1970s. In the 1990s the cost of social protection increased as a result of the aging population, rising structural unemployment, and the high rate of unemployment in the eastern states. German labor costs in the mid-1990s became the highest of most major economies, primarily as a result of high wages and non-wage social costs.

WORKING CONDITIONS

The German workforce numbered 40.5 million in 1999. Strong partnerships between labor, business, and the government after World War II contributed to the construction of a safe and responsible working environment. German companies have been held responsible for a larger array of social and community issues than is normally expected in the United States. The high environmental, health, and safety consciousness of the Germans has greatly contributed to improving general working conditions. German companies are more hierarchical than their U.S. counterparts, and employee relations are often formal. German workers have had the highest level of education in Europe, and as many as 2.5 million Germans, or almost half of the 15- to 19-year-old age group, annually receives vocational training within a range of about 400 occupational specialties, often on the basis of contracts with preselected employers. Combined on-the-job and academic training for apprentices produces many employees with the skills employers need, but the system has not kept up with the number of applicants and some say it needs to be made more flexible and responsive to the changing demands of the economy.

However, the German economy has been traditionally afflicted by a high unemployment rate (averaging a total of 10.5 percent in 1999, with 7.7 percent in western Germany, and 17.3 percent in eastern Germany), and structural unemployment is estimated at 80 percent of the total unemployment. In addition to the economic problems that contributed to high unemployment levels in 1999, the nation-wide collective bargaining system for worker representation produced wage and work time demands that failed to consider differences between regions and companies. The SDP government that took office in 1998 launched an ambitious program to cut unemployment, and more labor flexibility was reached at the company level, especially in eastern Germany. However, the rising number of companies that leave industrial organizations and negotiate contracts and wages at the company level is indicative of the growing discontent with the existing collective bargaining system. In 1998 only 48 percent of western German businesses were covered by a collective bargaining contract and about 25 percent in the east. These western German firms accounted for about 68 percent of total employees and for about 50 percent in the east. Trade union activism, however, has also been on the rise since 1998 to counter these changes in the traditional German economic model. In early 2001 a new union, ver.di, was formed as the world's largest union with 3 million members, comprising the unions of white-collar workers (DAG), the **public sector** (OTV), banking and retail (HBV), and postal workers and the media (IG Medien), with the purpose to represent labor across the growing service sector.

COUNTRY HISTORY AND ECONOMIC DEVELOPMENT

1356. Hanseatic League of northern Germany controls all trade on the Baltic Sea and in northern Europe.

1555. The Peace of Augsburg accords Protestants equal rights with those of Catholics.

1612–48. Thirty Years' War between Protestants and Catholics devastates Germany.

1700s. German states of Austria and Prussia abolish serfdom (1781 and 1773, respectively).

1806. Napoleon Bonaparte of France disbands the Holy Roman Empire and occupies Germany.

1833. Prussia organizes a customs union of 18 German states.

1867. Prussia defeats Austria, becoming the undisputed leader of the movement for the unification of the German states.

1871. The German Empire is proclaimed, with a population of over 50 million.

1900s. Germany becomes a major industrial world power and acquires colonies in Africa and the Pacific.

1918. Germany is defeated at the end of World War I (1914–18), a revolution erupts, and the country becomes a democratic republic.

1924. Germany enjoys relative economic prosperity, but millions of workers join the Nazi Party.

1933. During the Great Depression, National Socialist populist leader Adolf Hitler comes to power.

1939. With his attack on Poland, Hitler starts World War II.

1945. Germany surrenders and is divided into 4 occupation zones: British, American, Russian, and French.

1949. The Federal Republic of Germany (West Germany) is created out of the British-, American-, and French-occupied zones of Germany, while the German

Democratic Republic (East Germany) is made from the zone occupied by the USSR.

1951. West Germany is accepted into the European Coal and Steel Community and joins the North Atlantic Treaty Organization (NATO).

1961. The Berlin Wall is erected between East and West Berlin.

1968. The European Community is created to organize economic exchanges between European countries.

1970s. West Germany emerges as a leading economic power, along with the United States and Japan.

1990. East and West Germany are unified after Soviet President Mikhail Gorbachev loosens his grip.

1995. Schengen Agreement loosens border controls between Germany and bordering countries.

1998. Germany joins 10 other EU members in adopting the euro as the new single European currency.

1999. The capital of Germany moves from Bonn to Berlin.

FUTURE TRENDS

Germany will continue to be one of the world's leading economies and the powerhouse of the European Union. Its economy will be influenced mostly by European integration, the adoption of the euro, the integration and upgrading of the East German economy, the restructuring of its economic sectors, and its aging population. The ability of the government to cope successfully with these issues may result in a solution to the problems of slow economic growth, high unemployment, high government debt, high tax rates, high unit labor costs, and growing social security and non-wage labor costs. Germany has a special interest in promoting EU enlargement by the accession of eastern European countries but it is also concerned with the possible influx of immigrants and high financial transfers to new EU countries. An important priority of the federal government is fostering the development of eastern Germany, a major burden on the federal budget throughout the 1990s. Germany's responsibility as an influential member of the international community will also grow in areas such as economic assistance for developing countries, environmental protection, and cooperation in combating corruption and transnational organized crime. Future economic stability will also depend on successful European monetary policy and the performance of the other countries within the euro zone and on global economic trends as the German economy becomes more and more international.

While traditional industries such as textiles and steel are declining, growth in the services sector, particularly in finance and high-tech sectors, will be indicative of the economy's development over the first part of the 21st century. Technological advances, notably in the information and communication sectors, will fuel dramatic productivity increases and the further globalization of businesses. The determination to be among the most advanced countries in the application of new technologies forces Germany to expand its already generous investments into that area. Expected new tax reductions will allow German corporations to invest in technologies with higher productivity and to increase exports. Gloomy forecasts of an aging and declining population will foster reforms in Germany's social security system.

DEPENDENCIES

Germany has no territories or colonies.

BIBLIOGRAPHY

Behrend, Hanna, editor. *German Unification: The Destruction of an Economy.* London, and East Haven, CT: Pluto Press, 1995.

Economist Intelligence Unit. *Country Profile: Germany.* London: Economist Intelligence Unit, 2001.

Embassy of the Federal Republic of Germany, Washington, D.C. *An Overview of the Current Economic Situation in Germany.* <http://www.german-embassy.org.uk/facts_-_economics.html>. Accessed April 2001.

Federal Statistical Office Germany. <http://www.statistik-bund.de/e_home.htm>. Accessed January 2001.

Germany Online. <http://www.germany-info.org/sf_index.html>. Accessed September 2001.

Smyser, W. R. *The German Economy: Colossus at the Crossroads.* New York: St. Martin's Press, 1993.

U.S. Central Intelligence Agency. *World Factbook 2000.* <http://www.odci.gov/cia/publications/factbook/index.html>. Accessed August 2001.

U.S. Department of State. *FY 2000 Country Commercial Guide: Germany.* <http://www.state.gov/www/about_state/business/com_guides/index.html>. Accessed April 2001.

—Valentin Hadjiyski

GREECE

Hellenic Republic
Elliniki Dhimokratia

CAPITAL: Athens.

MONETARY UNIT: Drachma (Dr). 1 drachma equals 100 lepta. Coins in circulation are 1, 2, 5, 10, 20, 50 and 100 drachmae. Paper currency includes denominations of 100, 200, 500, 1,000, 5,000, and 10,000 drachmae. As a member of the European Union, Greece adopted the new currency, the euro, for non-cash transactions beginning in 2001, and will adopt the euro for cash transactions beginning in January 2002. The drachma will be replaced by the euro on February 28, 2002.

CHIEF EXPORTS: Manufactured goods, foodstuffs and beverages, fuels.

CHIEF IMPORTS: Manufactured goods, foodstuffs, fuels, chemicals.

GROSS DOMESTIC PRODUCT: $149.2 billion (1999 est.).

BALANCE OF TRADE: **Exports:** US$12.4 billion (1998 est.). **Imports:** US$27.7 billion (1998 est.).

COUNTRY OVERVIEW

LOCATION AND SIZE. Greece is located on the southernmost point of the Balkan Peninsula and is flanked by 3 large bodies of water: the Aegean Sea, the Ionian Sea, and the Mediterranean Sea. Greece is bordered to the north by Albania, the Former Yugoslav Republic of Macedonia (F.Y.R.O.M.), and Bulgaria. To the northeast and east is Turkey. The Hellenic Republic of Greece is rich with history, tradition, and archeological sites dating back thousands of years to classical ancient Greece.

With an area of 131,940 square kilometers (50,942 square miles) and a coastline of 13,676 kilometers (8,498 miles), Greece is a land of mountains and sea. Greece's mainland, the Peloponnesus Peninsula, is connected to the Isthmus of Corinth. The country also has more than 2,000 islands, of which 170 are inhabited. Greece is approximately the same size as the state of Alabama. Its cosmopolitan capital, Athens, is located on the Peloponnesus Peninsula.

Greece's position in the Aegean Sea and its access to the Turkish Straits has made it a country with a rich nautical tradition and a valued member of the North Atlantic Treaty Organization (NATO: a military alliance of certain European states, Canada, and the United States).

POPULATION. The July 2000 population of Greece was estimated at 10,601,527. The birth rate was 9.82 births per 1,000 people while the death rate was 9.64 deaths per 1,000 people. The annual population growth rate was estimated at 0.21 percent.

Nearly all of the population is of Greek descent (98 percent) with the remainder belonging to other ethnicities. However, the Greek government has claimed there are no ethnic divisions in Greece. The majority of Greek citizens are between the ages of 15 to 64 years (67 percent) with 15 percent of the population under 15 years of age and 18 percent 65 years and over.

About 98 percent of Greeks are Orthodox Christians, a religion that figures prominently in Greece's culture. Small religious minorities do exist in Greece. Muslims comprise 1.3 percent of the population and the remaining 0.7 percent includes Catholics, Jews, Old Calendar Orthodox, Jehovah's Witnesses, Mormons, Protestants, and other faiths. Most Muslims live in Thrace, and they are Greece's only officially recognized minority after receiving legal status through provisions in the Treaty of Lausanne of 1923.

The official language of Greece is Greek, which is spoken by 99 percent of the population. The Greek language has its basis in classical Greek and the language of the 21st century is quite similar to that which was spoken during the 5th century B.C.

Athens has a population of 3,096,775 and is a bustling urban center. Athens' suburban population stands at 748,110. Urbanization has been an important trend in the 20th and 21st centuries, yet more than one-third of Greek society is classified as rural. Many people moved into the cities following World War II, lured by a thriving economy that offered a better standard of living than existed in the countryside. Athens is known for its cosmopolitan lifestyle and for retaining many characteristics of village life such as the importance of family, family businesses, and the popular Greek coffeehouses.

OVERVIEW OF ECONOMY

The Greek economy grew significantly after World War II, but declined in the 1970s due to poor economic policies implemented by the government. As a result, Greece has spent much of the latter part of the 20th century and the early 21st century trying to rebuild and strengthen the economy. Thus, Greece is one of the least economically developed member countries in the European Union (EU).

While the Greek government encourages free enterprise and a capitalistic system, in some areas it still operates as a **socialist** country. For instance, in 2001 the government still controlled many sectors of the economy through state-owned banks and industries, and its **public sector** accounted for approximately half of Greece's **gross domestic product** (GDP). Limited natural resources, high debt payments, and a low level of industrialization have proved problematic for the Greek economy and have prevented high economic growth in the 1990s. Certain economic sectors are stronger and more established than others, such as shipping and tourism, which are growing and have shown promise since the 1990s.

The Greek government took measures in the late 1980s and 1990s to reduce the number of state-owned businesses and to revitalize the economy through a plan of **privatization**. This policy has received support from the Greek people and political parties of both the left and right. Despite the government's efforts, a drop in investment and the use of economic stabilization policies caused a slump in the Greek economy during the 1990s. In 2001, the Greek government fully encouraged foreign investment, particularly in its **infrastructure** projects such as highways and the Athens Metro subway system.

Soon after joining the European Union (EU), Greece became the recipient of many **subsidies** from the EU to bolster its struggling agricultural sector and to build public works projects. However, even with the European Union's financial assistance, Greece's agricultural and industrial sectors are still struggling with low productivity levels, and Greece remains behind many of its fellow EU members.

In the late 1990s, the government reformed its economic policy to be eligible to join the EU's single currency (the euro), which it became part of in January 2001. Measures included cutting Greece's **budget deficit** to below 2 percent of GDP and strengthening its **monetary policy**. As a result, **inflation** fell below 4 percent by the end of 1998—the lowest rate in 26 years—and averaged only 2.6 percent in 1999. Major challenges, including further economic **restructuring** and the unemployment reduction, still lie ahead.

The modern Greek economy began in the late 19th century with the adoption of social and industrial legislation, protective **tariffs**, and the creation of industrial enterprises. At the turn of the 20th century, industry was concentrated on food processing, shipbuilding, and the manufacturing of textile and simple consumer products. It is worth noting that, having been under direct control of the Ottoman Empire for over 400 years, Greece remained economically isolated from many of the major European intellectual movements, such as the Renaissance and the Enlightenment, as well as the beginnings of the Industrial Revolution. Therefore Greece has had to work hard to catch up to its European neighbors in industry and development.

By the late 1960s, Greece achieved high rates of economic growth due to large foreign investments. However, by the mid-1970s, Greece experienced declines in its GDP growth rate and the ratio of investment to GDP, which caused labor costs and oil prices to rise. When Greece joined the European community in 1981, protective economic barriers were removed. Hoping to get back on track financially, the Greek government pursued aggressive economic policies, which resulted in high inflation and caused debt payment problems. To stop rising public sector deficits, the government borrowed money heavily. In 1985, supported by a US$1.7 billion European Currency Unit (ECU) loan from the EU, the government began a 2-year "stabilization" program with moderate success. Inefficiency in the public sector and excessive government spending caused the government to borrow even more money. By 1992 government debt exceeded 100 percent of Greece's GDP. Greece became dependent on foreign borrowing to pay for its deficits, and by the end of 1998, public sector **external debt** was at US$32 billion, with overall government debt at US$119 billion (105.5 percent of its GDP).

By January 2001 Greece had successfully reduced its budget deficit, controlled inflation and interest rates, and stabilized **exchange rates** to gain entrance into the European Monetary Union. Greece met the economic requirements to be eligible to join the program of a single currency unit (the euro) in the EU and to have the economy governed by the European Central Bank's focused monetary policy. The Greek government now faces the challenge of structural reform and to ensure that its economic policies continue to enhance economic growth and increase Greece's standard of living.

One of the recent successes of Greece's economic policies has been the reduction of **inflation rates**. For more than 20 years, inflation remained in double digits, but a successful plan of fiscal consolidation, wage restraint, and strong drachma policies has lowered inflation, which fell to 2.0 percent by mid-1999. However, high interest rates remain troublesome despite cuts in **treasury bills** and bank rates for savings and loans institutions. Pursuing a strong **fiscal policy**, combined with public-sector borrowing and the lowering of interest rates, has been challenging for Greece. Headway was made in 1997–99 and rates are progressively declining in line with inflation.

POLITICS, GOVERNMENT, AND TAXATION

Greece is a presidential parliamentary republic. The Greek government is similar to the model found in many Western democracies, such as Germany. The prime minister and cabinet are responsible for making national and international policy. The president, whose powers are mostly ceremonial, is elected by parliament for a 5-year term and is eligible for reelection for only one additional term. His powers include declaring war and concluding agreements of peace, alliance, and representing Greece in international organizations. However, the cabinet must countersign any emergency powers exercised by the president. The constitution does not allow the president to dissolve parliament, dismiss the government, or suspend articles of the constitution.

Members of the Greek parliament are elected by secret ballot to 4-year terms; however, elections can be called before their term is up. To prevent political parties from dividing and to ensure there is always a parliamentary majority, Greece uses a complex **proportional representation** electoral system. A party must obtain at least 3 percent of the total national vote to qualify for parliamentary seats. As of 2001, there are 5 main political parties operating in Greece: the Panhellenic Socialist Movement (PASOK), New Democracy (ND), Political Spring, Communist Party of Greece (KKE), and the Coalition of the Left (SYNASPISMOS).

Greece is divided into 51 prefectures, each led by a "prefect" who is elected by direct popular vote. There are also 13 regional administrative districts (peripheries), which include a number of prefectures led by a regional governor, the periferiarch, who is appointed by the Minister of Interior. Although municipalities (a city with self-government and corporate status) and villages have elected officials, they do not have an adequate independent tax base and depend on the government for a large part of their financial needs. Accordingly, they are subject to numerous government controls.

Greece has had a rocky political experience since its independence, and has been jolted by a series of deposed (removed from power) leaders and a military coup d'etat. Soon after the civil war of 1944–49, Greece decided to align itself with the Western democracies and became a member of NATO in 1952. During the 1950s and early 1960s, Greece was ruled by a series of politically conservative parties. The Center Union Party of George Papandreou came to power in 1963 and remained in office until 1965.

Several weak coalition (multiple parties ruling together) governments ruled Greece after the Center Unionists left office. Then in 1967 a coup occurred under the leadership of Colonel George Papadopoulos. The coup introduced a dark period in Greek politics. Many civil liberties were taken away, thousands of political protesters were jailed or exiled to remote islands, and military courts replaced civil courts. University students were politically active during the coup and staged an impressive protest at the Athens Polytechnic University in 1973. The international community did not support the military-led government and called for immediate free elections.

The military junta (a small group that rules a country after a coup d'etat) lost power in 1974 when its new leader, General Dimitrios Ioannides, tried to depose the president of Cyprus, nearly causing the outbreak of war between Greece and its long-time rival Turkey. The junta fell after Ioannides lost support from his senior military officials. Order was restored that same year when former prime minister Constantine Karamanlis returned to Greece from exile in France to lead a new constitutional government. His new political party, New Democracy (ND), won the 1974 elections and he became prime minister again.

A new constitution was adopted in 1975, which restored a number of civil liberties and created the Greek presidency. The New Democracy party stayed in power until 1981. Under their leadership Greece became the tenth member of the EU in January 1981. That same year Greece elected its first socialist government headed by the Panhellenic Socialist Movement (PASOK), which was led by Andreas Papandreou.

PASOK has dominated Greek political life since the 1980s. However, in 1990 the New Democracy party gained control of the parliament but collapsed in 1993 when several party members broke off and formed their own political party, Political Spring, and new elections were held after the collapse of the government. PASOK won elections in 1996 and 2000, and under Prime Minister Constantine Simitis's leadership, the economy has been revived and relations between Greece and Turkey have improved. Perhaps one of Simitis's greatest achievements is securing Greece's entry into the European Monetary Union in January 2001.

Since the 2000 elections, the PASOK government has improved social services by creating affordable pensions, improving health services and education, and creating better jobs while moving ahead with its privatization and economic policies. However, the PASOK government has become the target of growing criticism because of its recent strict reforms to ensure economic stability. PASOK emphasized meeting the criteria for low inflation and low public debt which are necessary for participation in the "euro zone"—those countries in Europe that will use the euro as a currency. The New Democracy (ND) party has accused the government of awarding large state contracts to friends of the party and favoritism in the sale of state assets, and the government is more cautious now when awarding contracts.

The Greek government employs a taxation system for revenue in which all persons permanently or temporarily residing in Greece, regardless of nationality, are required by law to pay taxes on their income. Sources of taxable income include real estate, securities, commercial and agricultural enterprises, and salaries. Additionally, corporations, companies, foreign construction companies operating in Greece, and ship owners are taxed.

INFRASTRUCTURE, POWER, AND COMMUNICATIONS

Greece has a modern infrastructure complete with airports, railways, and paved roads and highways. There are a total of 80 airports (1999 est.), 64 of which have paved runways. There are 2,548 kilometers (1,583 miles) of railways and 117,000 kilometers (72,703 miles) of highways, 107,406 kilometers (66,742 miles) of which are paved. As expected from a historically seafaring country, Greece has 12 ports and harbors and a large merchant fleet of more than 700 ships.

Communications are also modern. The country's telephone system is adequate, with networks reaching all areas for main telephone lines and mobile cellular phones. Most telephone calls are carried by microwave radio relay. Underwater cables transmit calls to the Greek islands. In 1997 there were 5.431 million main lines in use and 328,000 mobile phone users. As of 1998 there were 26 AM radio stations, 88 FM stations, and 4 short-wave stations. In 1999, 64 television stations were operating in Greece. Computers and communications are increasing in popularity and availability. By 1999 there were 23 Internet service providers (ISPs) operating in Greece.

During the 1980s, the government dissolved its **monopoly** on radio and televisions stations. Many private television and radio stations emerged, as well as European satellite channels. By early 2001, however, the Greek government moved to shut down dozens of the popular privately-owned radio stations, saying that their proximity to the new Athens airport could cause radio interference. The announcement was widely condemned by opposition parties and media unions, as well as large numbers of loyal listeners.

The press in Greece operates much differently than it does in the United States. Journalistic objectivity, where a reporter writes the facts of a news event without his or her own political or ethical viewpoint, is often not followed. Businesspeople with extensive commercial interests in the economy own many of the media outlets and use their newspapers, magazines, and radio and television outlets to promote their commercial enterprises as well as to seek political influence.

Electrical power in Greece is supplied by lignite-fueled power stations. Lignite is a type of coal. Hydroelectric power is also used. Solar energy and wind power are being considered as alternative energy sources. Total power production in 1998 amounted to 43.677 billion kilowatt hours (kWh), while consumption in that year was 42.18 billion kWh.

Natural gas is becoming a popular alternative to coal for electricity production. The gas comes from a pipeline shared by Greece and Russia and is considered more environmentally friendly and efficient than coal. In February 2000, the Ministries of the Environment, Natural Planning, and Public Works signed an agreement to replace coal with natural gas. Natural gas is a new energy source in Athens, and many homes and businesses are beginning to use it. Another benefit is that natural gas would reduce the high smog levels in Athens.

ECONOMIC SECTORS

Greece is not a fully capitalist state as there are still many state-owned industries, but the government plans to sell many of them. Greece receives a great amount of financial assistance from the European Union, which accounts for about 4 percent of its GDP. Greece's main

Communications

Country	Newspapers	Radios	TV Sets[a]	Cable subscribers[a]	Mobile Phones[a]	Fax Machines[a]	Personal Computers[a]	Internet Hosts[b]	Internet Users[b]
	1996	1997	1998	1998	1998	1998	1998	1999	1999
Greece	153	477	466	1.2	194	3.8	51.9	59.57	750
United States	215	2,146	847	244.3	256	78.4	458.6	1,508.77	74,100
Germany	311	948	580	214.5	170	73.1	304.7	173.96	14,400
Italy	104	878	486	2.8	355	31.3	173.4	68.28	7,000

[a]Data are from International Telecommunication Union, *World Telecommunication Development Report 1999* and are per 1,000 people.
[b]Data are from the Internet Software Consortium (http://www.isc.org) and are per 10,000 people.

SOURCE: World Bank. *World Development Indicators 2000.*

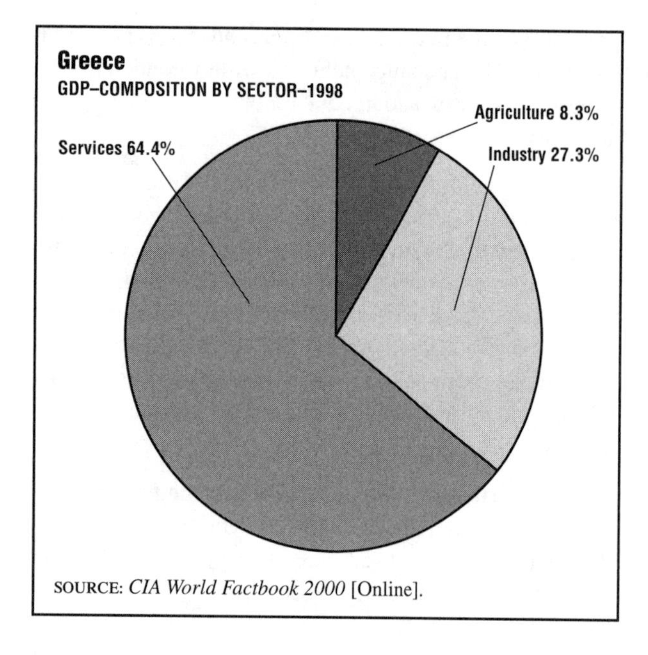

SOURCE: *CIA World Factbook 2000* [Online].

imports are industrial and **capital goods**, foodstuffs, and petroleum, and it exports manufactured goods, food and beverages, petroleum products, cement, chemicals, and pharmaceuticals.

Greece's chief sector of the economy—services—is comprised of transportation, tourism, communications, trade, banking, public administration, and defense. The service sector is the fastest-growing and largest part of the Greek economy, accounting for 64.4 percent of GDP in 1998. Tourism is the foundation of this sector. However, a poorly developed infrastructure has slowed its expansion. In 1996, more than 10 million tourists visited Greece, yet the tourist industry still faced declining revenues due in part to the drachma's weak performance. Tourism revenues exceeded US$5.2 billion in 1998, an upsurge due in part to political problems in neighboring Balkan countries and an economic recovery in the European Union.

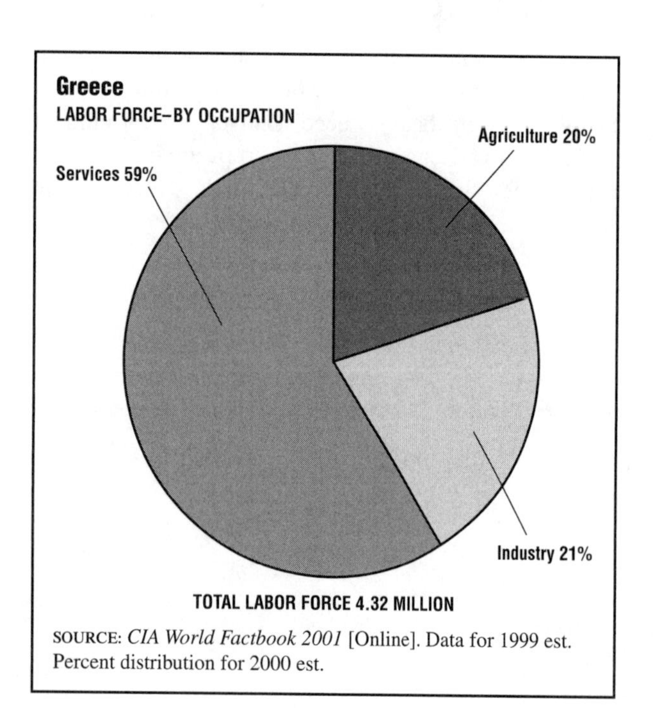

SOURCE: *CIA World Factbook 2001* [Online]. Data for 1999 est. Percent distribution for 2000 est.

The industrial sector accounts for 27.3 percent of Greece's GDP. One of the fastest growing and most profitable industries in this sector is the food industry, which has excellent export potential. High technology equipment production, especially for telecommunications, is also a fast-growing sector. Textiles, building materials, machinery, transport equipment, and electrical appliances are also a significant part of the manufacturing sector. Shipping is another industry that has shown economic promise. A nation with a great nautical tradition, Greece has built an impressive shipping industry based on its prime geographic location and the entrepreneurial skills of its owners.

AGRICULTURE

Greece's agricultural sector suffers from a lack of many natural resources. Approximately 70 percent of the land cannot be cultivated because of poor soil or because it is covered by forests. Agriculture is centered in the plains of Thessaly, Macedonia, and Thrace, where corn, wheat, barley, sugar beets, cotton, and tobacco are harvested. Greece's low rainfall, its rural land ownership system, and the **emigration** of the rural community into urban areas or abroad are factors that hold back the growth of the agricultural sector. In 1998 agriculture accounted for only 8.3 percent of GDP.

While agriculture is not a thriving economic sector, Greece is still a major EU producer of cotton and tobacco. Greece's olives—many of which are turned into olive oil—are the country's most renowned export crop. Grapes, melons, tomatoes, peaches, and oranges are also popular EU exports. Wine is an export with promise, and the government has urged vineyard owners to produce higher quality wines to increase its popularity as an international export.

Given Greece's vast coastline and its numerous islands, it is natural that a fishing industry exists. However, it is not as vital to the economy as would be expected from a country with a rich maritime history. Over-fishing has lessened the impact of fishing revenues on the economy. Pollution in the Mediterranean has also damaged the industry.

Animals and animal production constitute a significant part of Greece's agricultural output. Goat and sheep meat and milk are popular and provide about 6 percent of agricultural production, especially sheep milk, which is used for making Greece's renowned feta cheese. Hogs, cattle, chickens, rabbits, beehives, and pigeons are other important livestock.

Employment in the agricultural sector has slipped throughout the latter part of the 20th century and into the 21st. In 1981 the agricultural workforce was measured at 972,000 and had fallen to 873,000 by 1991. Women have dominated employment in the agricultural sector.

Greece adopted a system of farming cooperatives as early as 1915 to streamline farming efforts. These cooperatives are now unionized and have been supported by every government that comes to power. Under the socialist governments of the 1980s, the cooperatives were greatly enhanced, and they received a large percentage of agricultural loans.

The European Union has granted Greece a number of subsidies to bolster its agricultural sector, but it continues to perform poorly in the 21st century. To expand the market for Greek food exports, the Ministry of Agriculture established a private company, Hellagro SA, to assist Greek companies in selling their products over the Internet. Private stockholders will hold the majority share in Hellagro, and financing will come from **e-commerce**, commission (money paid for performing a given act or transaction), investment opportunities, and **joint ventures**. The government is hoping this effort will help revitalize the struggling industry.

INDUSTRY

Greece's industrial sector is weak. While it expanded during the 1960s, growth slowed from the 1970s to the 1990s. Industry has progressed to a higher level in 2000 due to large increases in mining and energy production, as well as construction, but it remains an underperforming economic sector. The shipping industry, however, is an important exception, and has performed exceptionally well. Textile production, food processing, construction, cement, and shipping are important segments of this sector. High-technology equipment production, particularly in telecommunications, is another growing and important industry.

MANUFACTURING. Manufacturing accounts for about 14 percent of the GDP. In 2000 the manufacturing sector increased modestly. During the 1990s, the most important and profitable sectors have been (in order) foodstuffs, textiles, chemicals, and nonmetallic minerals.

The economic crisis of the 1970s and 1980s, in which the Greek economy experienced declines in its GDP growth rate, rising labor and oil costs, and high inflation, hurt many manufacturing companies. The government bought many of these companies to prevent them from going out of business and help them earn a profit. Eventually, the PASOK government in the 1990s decided to embark on a continuing privatization policy in an effort to encourage foreign investment.

Prior to Greece's admittance into the EU, the government tried to bolster new manufacturing companies with tax breaks, tariff protection, and cheap loans. However, this policy was eliminated to comply with EU regulations. Today, most government assistance to manufacturing firms takes place in the form of grants and subsidies for new investment.

Foreign investment in manufacturing has not been strong, despite incentives from the Greek government as early as 1953, but it has grown since 2000. Investment by foreign companies is important, as it helps a struggling economy grow. It expands an economic sector, brings new technology into a country, increases tourism, creates new job opportunities, and accelerates growth in other sectors of the economy. Greece's EU membership helped lure some investors with the promise of working in a unified European market. In 1992, a large Italian company, Calcestruzzi, bought a substantial share of Greece's major cement company, AGET. By 1988, an estimated 18 percent of total manufacturing employment was under foreign control.

MINING. The mining industry is small but significant because of Greece's vast mineral resources. Lignite, which is used for making energy in Greece, and bauxite, the raw material needed for aluminum production, are 2 minerals that are found abundantly in Greece. Other mineral deposits include ferronickel ores, magnesite, mixed sulfurous ores, ferrochrome ores, kaolin, asbestos, and marble. Mining accounts for only 1% of the GDP. Mining of metallic ores is concentrated in the hands of a few private companies. Quarry production is divided among many small companies. In 2000 mining output rose significantly, in contrast to its negative performance of the previous 2 years.

CONSTRUCTION. Housing and building construction have always played a key role in Greece's industrial sector and have long been a major source of income. Today, construction activity accounts for approximately 7.5 percent of the GDP and is expected to rise due to new infrastructure projects financed by EU funds.

The government traditionally has seen the construction sector as a way to boost employment, income, and domestic demand. Accordingly, the housing construction industry has historically enjoyed tax advantages. However, with the fiscally conservative policies of the 1990s, increased taxation was considered.

The construction of large public works has also played a significant role in this subsector of the economy. The new international airport in Athens was a major construction project planned by the government. The first passenger flights took off in March 2001 and the government hopes the airport will become a regional hub for routes to Europe, Africa, and Asia. With its state-of-the-art facilities, the new airport is expected to boost the tourism sector and handle the tourist traffic demands of the 2004 Olympic Games, which will be held in Athens. The $1 billion construction project involved both Greek and foreign private companies and the Greek public sector. Attiki Odos, a conglomerate of Greek construction companies, constructed a high-speed toll roadway, and plans are underway to build new hotels near the airport.

The Athens Metro subway system is another construction project that is being renovated and expanded in 2000–01, as well as new roadways, railroads, and bridges. Under the terms of the EU, Greece must be open to international bidding for major projects, which provides tough competition for the Greek construction industry.

In 2000, private building activity increased. Permits for new projects, particularly in the housing industry, rose by 6.3 percent and many predict a real-estate boom in coming years. Although the residential housing market has matured, expansion seems likely in the area of home renovations and in the purchase of second homes.

SERVICES

The service industry is the most important sector of the Greek economy. In 1998, the service sector provided 64.4 percent of Greece's GDP, and accounted for nearly 60 percent of Greece's **labor force**. A variety of businesses are included in this sector: street vendors, the hotel and lodging industry, telecommunications, and public administration.

TOURISM. Greece has long been known for its warm climate, scenic Mediterranean coastlines, and classical archeological and historical sites. These attractions, together with its beautiful and quiet islands, delicious culinary offerings, and renowned hospitality have made Greece a popular tourist destination. The most popular attractions are the Acropolis of Athens, the palace of Knossos on the island of Crete, the temple of Apollo at Delphi, the Epidaurus Theater and the palace and treasure of Mycenae in the Peleponnesus, and the Acropolis of Lindos on the island of Rhodes.

The tourism industry has grown significantly since the 1960s, and is a major source of foreign exchange, but this sector has suffered from poor infrastructure and a strong drachma. European tourists visiting Greece tripled from the early 1970s to the late 1980s, and reached 11.5 million visitors in 2000. Most tourists visiting Greece hail from Great Britain and Germany; however, droves of visitors come from Italy, the former Yugoslavia, France, and the Netherlands. The number of American tourists declined during the 1990s. Lodging options have increased significantly between the 1970s and 1990s due to an expansion of hotels. In 1998, tourist revenues were high as Greece benefited from problems in neighboring countries and an economic recovery in the EU. Today Greece faces tough competition from Turkey, which has become a popular vacation destination, but improvement in the tourism sector does hold promise.

Fully understanding its importance, the government is working to improve this vital sector of the Greek economy. First, it is attempting to upgrade facilities in the country to levels found in competitors Spain and Italy. It is also looking to expand the tourist season from 6 months to year-round through sports, hosting international conferences, and cultural tourism. Developing marine tourism with activities such as cruises and sailing excursions is another priority. To accommodate more tourists, the state-controlled Hellenic Tourist Organization is planning to expand the number of marinas (docks for pleasure boats) operating in Greece.

In 2001 the PASOK government of Prime Minister Simitis launched a campaign to attract private investment in Greece's tourist industry as part of its ongoing privatization program. The Hellenic Tourist Properties (ETA), which is the asset management arm of the Hellenic Tourist Organization, is trying to attract private investors to develop its properties through long-term leases, joint operations, or **equity** operations. Some of the projects in need of investment are a theme park for Anavissos, an aquarium, and camping grounds at Voula. The city of Rhodes will build more hotels, a golf course, and athletic facilities. The government hopes these new attractions increase Greece's popularity as a tourist destination, especially with the approach of the 2004 Olympic Games, which will bring thousands of new visitors to Greece. The government is trying to ensure they will return as tourists.

TRANSPORTATION. Greece's rugged interior, its lengthy coastline, and multitude of islands have made shipping an important industry. Greece's 5 major cities—Athens, Thessaloniki, Patras, Heraklion, and Volos—are all major ports, and there are a total of 123 ports throughout the country, which are essential to transporting and importing goods to and from Europe, the Balkans, and the Middle East.

Shipping has been one of Greece's most important and profitable industries due to the business know-how of its shipowners. Its merchant fleet is one of the largest in the world totaling 3,358 ships in 1998, although many of its ships are older. However, Greek ship owners are trying to upgrade their fleets with new ships, and there were a record number of new ship-building orders placed in 2000, due to low prices offered by South Korean shipyards. Many of Greece's ships are cargo carriers to third-world countries, so the industry is sensitive to downturns in the world economy.

Road transportation saw increases in the second half of the 20th century, gaining in importance compared to rail and shipping transport. However, the closing of roads in the former Yugoslavia, traditionally Greece's route into Europe, caused sea transport to increase in importance once again.

Olympic Airways, which is partially state-owned, is Greece's exclusive airline. Olympic offers domestic flights throughout Greece's major cities and islands, as well as overseas flights to Europe, the Middle East, the United States, Japan, Singapore, Thailand, and South Africa. While passenger loads have increased, the airline has faced financial difficulty as a result of high costs. Greece has negotiated plans with the EU to restructure the airline.

Railway construction began in Greece in the 1880s and, given the rugged terrain of the country, was an extraordinary feat of engineering. Tracks cover slightly less than 2,548 kilometers (1,583 miles) of the country. The EU is providing assistance in renovating the railroad system. Since 1990, diesel locomotives have gone into service and shortened travel time.

In 2000, new registrations for automobiles increased, although many buyers have apparently postponed new purchases until Greece joins the economic and monetary union and interest rates fall to euro zone levels. Truck roads are inadequate in comparison to European standards. Greece has one of the worst automobile accident levels in Europe.

Public transportation in Athens is made up of an overcrowded and unreliable bus network and Metro subway system. Renovation and service extension of the Athens Metro finally began in 1993 after many delays. Work on the 130 year-old Athens Metro was finished in January 2000. The project faced many obstacles because of poor soil conditions, the presence of archeological remains, and contractor disputes. The Metro is expected to have a huge impact on daily life in Athens and ease passenger traffic congestion, making commuting much easier. Attiko Metro, a state-controlled company, oversaw the design, construction, and operation of the new Metro lines and U.S.-based Bechtel International acted as project manager. Further expansions are planned, particularly into lower-income neighborhoods in Athens as required in the funding package from the EU's Community Structural Fund, which provided much of the financing.

INTERNATIONAL TRADE

Member countries of the European Union have dominated international trade in Greece. Germany and Italy are Greece's main EU trading partners, with 25 and 11 percent of exports and 16 percent of imports each, respectively. Outside of the EU countries, the United States is Greece's largest trading partner, with 16 percent of exports and 11 percent of imports. Other significant partners include the United Kingdom, Central and Eastern European countries, and the former Soviet Union. In the 1990s, the biggest trade increases occurred with South Korea, Bulgaria, Egypt, Japan, and China. The former republic of Yugoslavia's internal political problems resulted in a sharp decline in its trade with Greece.

Trade (expressed in billions of US$): Greece

	Exports	Imports
1975	2.294	5.357
1980	5.153	10.548
1985	4.539	10.134
1990	8.105	19.777
1995	10.961	25.944
1998	N/A	N/A

SOURCE: International Monetary Fund. *International Financial Statistics Yearbook 1999.*

Greece's imports are machinery, transportation equipment, food, chemical products, and petroleum products. Greece's main exports are fruit, vegetables, olive oil, textiles, steel, aluminum, cement, and various manufactured items such as clothing, foodstuffs, refined petroleum and petroleum-based products. Once it joined the EU, Greece was also required to break down all trade barriers in accordance to the organization's by-laws.

Greece must keep its economy in order as a member of the EU. To do this, the government embarked on an ambitious privatization plan during the 1990s, and continues to encourage foreign investment. Greek businesspeople are getting used to competition from international firms, and the government keeps state industries, such as tourism, open to private investment. A good example of foreign investment in a state-owned industry is the operating company Athens International Airport SA, which constructed the airport and will handle its operations. The Greek government owns 55 percent of Athens International Airport SA and the remaining 45 percent belongs to the German Hochtief Group.

Membership in the European Union has been extremely beneficial for Greece. Net payments from the EU budget have significantly decreased Greece's account balance and the state budget deficit. Support packages for public works projects such as the Athens Metro, and economic and human development projects, have been especially useful in attempting to upgrade Greece's infrastructure.

Greece's **balance of trade** has traditionally been negative (see chart). In 1991–93 exports of goods fell short of imports by more than US$13 billion. By 1998 that trade imbalance had grown to US$15.3 billion on exports of US$12.4 billion and imports of US$27.7 billion. Greece's trade deficit has usually been covered by loans from the EU, **remittances** from Greeks living abroad, tourism, and shipping.

MONEY

After many years of high inflation, the Greek economy appears to have settled since 2000. Inflation is above the EU average but is under control and expected to remain that way in the near future. Reducing inflation rates has been a success of Greece's recent reformist economic measures.

Inflation, consistently above 10 percent in the past, has fallen due to government fiscal policies, wage restraints, strong monetary policies, and debt consolidation. By mid-1999 inflation fell to 2.0 percent but later rose again because of a sharp easing of Greece's monetary policy when it joined the EU's Economic and Monetary Union (EMU). Fortunately, this did not cause a huge inflation increase as had been feared.

In January 2001, Greece became a member of the EMU after 4 years of careful fiscal planning by the government of Prime Minister Costas Simitis. Greece is expected to relax its monetary policy as its short-term interest rates converge with euro zone rates. The government views the economic forecast favorably, but progress could be slowed if it remains committed to tax cuts.

Greece's banks consist of 3 kinds of institutions. The first is the Central Bank of Greece, which controls and manages the country's money supply and currency exchange rates. It does this by regulating the cash flow of other banks and by direct intervention in money markets. It also operates as a regulatory agency for commercial banks and protects the monetary system against banking catastrophes. In conformity with EU rules, the bank should be a separate entity from the state to keep the government from borrowing bank funds. A large number of Greece's banks remain under state control and in the early 1990s state-controlled banks held some 70 percent of deposits.

Commercial banks also operate in Greece and are the second type of banking institution. Both foreign and domestic commercial banks operate in Greece, and New York-based Citibank is one of the largest banks in Greece. Traditionally banks have been depositories for the people but have recently expanded their operations to include wholesale and **retail** banking services. Commercial, industrial, consumer, and mortgage loans are issued through these institutions. They can also issue credit cards and letters of credit as well as exchange foreign currency. Some banks also offer brokerage services.

Exchange rates: Greece

drachmae (Dr) per US$1	
Dec 2000	380.21
2000	365.40
1999	305.65
1998	295.53
1997	273.06
1996	240.71

SOURCE: CIA *World Factbook 2001* [ONLINE].

A third part of the Greek banking system is made up of specialized credit institutions such as investment and mortgage banks. Examples are the Agricultural Bank of Greece and the Postage Savings bank. Many of the credit institutions are directly or indirectly controlled by the state; however, legislation in the 1990s sought to limit its influence. While these banks already offer credit services, EU standards have forced them to offer a wider range of banking services so that they do not have a monopoly on one specific area. Likewise, other banks are now permitted to offer these banks' specialized services, such as entering the agricultural credit market.

Since the late 1980s, the Greek banking system has undergone a process of **liberalization**, and Greece's EU membership has pushed modernization of the banking system. Interest rates are now set by market conditions, foreign exchange and capital movements have been **deregulated**, and credit quality controls were abolished. As a result, banking in Greece has become a modern and competitive industry. Proving its capability in this new environment, the Bank of Greece successfully managed a monetary crisis, protecting the drachma by tightening its monetary policy and raising interest rates to high levels. In less than 2 months, interest rates returned back to normal.

The Athens Stock Exchange (ASE) has been modernized and revitalized since 1987. Recent changes include the formation of brokerage firms participating as members of the exchange, the introduction of an automated trading system, and the establishment of a Central Securities Depository. The early 1990s saw 118 public companies on the ASE. Traditionally, many Greeks are reluctant to invest in stocks and shares, preferring to invest their money in real estate, foreign currency, gold, and jewelry.

POVERTY AND WEALTH

Since the 19th century, upward mobility has been more common for Greeks with each generation. However, unlike most European countries, which tend to have rigid class systems, Greece's class system has been more flexible as income has been more widely distributed.

For rich and poor alike, Greek society remains somewhat traditional. The Greek people have strongly held beliefs on the importance of the family and maintaining its societal role, which extends into the economic sector. For example, most Greeks, rich and poor alike, own their own home, and real estate usually stays within families. Non-home owners are considered impoverished, and questions arise about the family's inability to take care of its children and future generations.

The family remains the basic social unit for all classes. The extended family and the obligation of family members to help each other in times of trouble are essential parts of Greek society, which remains unaltered by the expansion of the middle and upper-middle classes following World War II. It is odd for a Greek man or woman to remain single or to break ties with his or her family. Sons and daughters will often live with their parents until they marry. Parents still have influence over the choice of a child's spouse. In rural areas, a groom and his family still consider a potential bride's reputation, family, health, age, and appearance important factors before agreeing to marriage.

Paternal authority is a key part of Greek family life and in Greek society as a whole. Men can often be found smoking, drinking coffees, and discussing politics in the cafés, which are not open to women. During the 1980s, however, significant changes were made in Greek family law, which restricted the dominant role of the father in the family. Dowries for brides were outlawed and although marriage is still viewed as an economic union, civil marriages were permitted and divorce was made easier.

Greeks are noted for their strong sense of community. Despite urbanization, village life remains a strong societal influence. Village square-style meetings on topics relevant to the community are common, even in cities. Many businesses are small, family-owned and operated enterprises. This is evident in some large and more dynamic sectors of the Greek economy such as the shipping industry, which is led by a tight-knit group of Greek families. Business operations are often run on family connections and favors.

Distribution of Income or Consumption by Percentage Share: Greece

Lowest 10%	3.0
Lowest 20%	7.5
Second 20%	12.4
Third 20%	16.9
Fourth 20%	22.8
Highest 20%	40.3
Highest 10%	25.3

Survey year: 1993

Note: This information refers to income shares by percentiles of the population and is ranked by per capita income.

SOURCE: *2000 World Development Indicators* [CD-ROM].

Major strides in health care have occurred since World War II. Many diseases have been eradicated, and Greece has more doctors per person than any other EU member. However, most doctors are located in Athens, meaning many rural dwellers must travel to the city for medical care. In 1976, a government study found that the poor did not have adequate health coverage or access to services, and there was a lack of coordination between government agencies. Reform efforts took several years, but in the 1980s the PASOK government of Andreas Papandreou created a national health-care system which sought to put all medical practices under control of the state. One major goal of the plan was to provide free access to health care regardless of economic means. However, wealthier Greeks often choose to travel abroad for major operations, as they believe health-care services and doctors are more sophisticated elsewhere in Europe.

Greece's health system does provide benefits for workers. Greece has a generous maternity-leave policy for women, and when new mothers return to work they are allowed to leave work 2 hours early so that they can go home to their child. Vacation leave is generous, as it is in many European countries. Greeks take advantage of this, especially during April, the traditional month for vacationing because of the Easter holiday.

Pensions are a complex issue in Greece. Most of the working population, about 80 percent, is covered under the Social Insurance Institute and the Agricultural Insurance Organization. Workers and employers must both contribute to the pension plans for the Social Insurance Institute, which covers professionals, laborers, and craftsmen. The Agricultural Insurance Organization provides pensions for rural workers and is funded entirely by taxes.

Education has always played an important role in Greek society, dating back to its classical roots. The

GDP per Capita (US$)

Country	1975	1980	1985	1990	1998
Greece	8,302	9,645	10,005	10,735	12,069
United States	19,364	21,529	23,200	25,363	29,683
Germany	N/A	N/A	N/A	N/A	31,141
Italy	11,969	14,621	15,707	18,141	19,574

SOURCE: United Nations. *Human Development Report 2000; Trends in human development and per capita income.*

Household Consumption in PPP Terms

Country	All food	Clothing and footwear	Fuel and power[a]	Health care[b]	Education[b]	Transport & Communications	Other
Greece	32	11	14	5	14	8	16
United States	13	9	9	4	6	8	51
Germany	14	6	7	2	10	7	53
Italy	23	11	12	3	17	8	27

Data represent percentage of consumption in PPP terms.
[a]Excludes energy used for transport.
[b]Includes government and private expenditures.

SOURCE: World Bank. *World Development Indicators 2000.*

literacy rate is 93 percent. In the post-World War II period, education has been viewed as the key to upgrading one's position in society and to economic prosperity. However, Greece's education system is rigid and heavily centralized. Teaching is not a highly respected profession and as a result there are not many qualified teachers. State educational institutions are considered inadequate by the populace and, as a result, many children go for tutoring after school at private institutions called *phrontistiria.* Greek education is free and compulsory for all children to 9 years of age.

The university admissions process for students is very intense and extremely competitive, as graduating from a top university often ensures professional success. About 1 in 4 applicants are admitted. The educational system is plagued by the low social status of educators, lack of supplies and books, frequent strikes, and inadequate labs and technology. Most state universities do not have graduate-level programs, decreasing the incentive for faculty research. Currently about 100,000 students are registered at Greek universities and about 15 percent of the population hold a university degree.

Private universities are not permitted in Greece, which means that the government, and ultimately the taxpayers, must absorb the operating costs of universities and technical schools. A number of new colleges and universities were created throughout the country from the 1960s to the 1980s to meet the growing demand for higher education. However, many of these institutions are not well-equipped with books and laboratory equipment and do not offer enough openings to meet the desire for a university-level education, forcing many Greeks to study abroad. Those students who travel abroad for university tend to enroll in American universities, especially for graduate school. The Greek government evaluates all degrees from international universities to see whether graduates can work in the public sector. One concern with the increased number who study abroad, particularly with EU educational exchanges, is that a "brain drain" will occur, where Greek students will remain abroad rather than return to their home country with their new skills and education.

Following the collapse of military rule in the 1970s, the Greek government issued a number of reforms touching all levels of education such as the expansion of compulsory education and increasing technical education programs. The first PASOK government, which came to office in 1981, continued making education a priority and doubled the education budget during its first 4 years in power. Teaching methods and planning were standardized, routine educational inspections took place, and state education was placed under the Ministry of Education and Religious Affairs.

With Greece's entry into the European Union and increased urbanization, there has been an emphasis on raising educational standards to those of its fellow EU countries. In June 1999, Greece was one of 29 states to sign the Bologna Declaration. The declaration sought to standardize EU member universities and shape degree requirements around European Union needs. Once accomplished, all university degrees in the EU would be comparable with one another. The plan called for the creation of a 2-cycle educational system with a 3-year undergraduate program and a 2-year master's degree program. The goal is to reduce unemployment by allowing trained and qualified students to enter the labor market more quickly. The Greek Ministry of Education was skeptical of the program and staged a conference in January of 2000 to debate the Bologna Declaration. University officials voiced strong reservations about the plan, particularly the emphasis on professional rather than liberal arts education. The Ministry of Education opted not to adopt the 3-year undergraduate system, but will make university credit hours more similar to those of EU educational institutions.

WORKING CONDITIONS

The occupational structure of Greece has changed in the 20th century because of increased industrialization and urbanization. Since the 1960s, the number of rural workers has dropped considerably. Overall, the employment numbers reflect various sectors' contribution to the GDP, with most Greeks employed in the service sector (59.2 percent) and lesser numbers in industry (21 percent) and agriculture (19.8 percent), according to 1998 estimates in the 2000 CIA *World Factbook*. Greece's total labor force numbered 4.32 million in 1999, when unemployment was estimated at 9.9 percent.

Generally, more men work in the industry sector while women dominate the service and agriculture industries. Greek women tend to have higher unemployment rates than men and are on average paid less. For additional income many Greeks work in seasonal or nonpermanent agricultural or service industry positions. For example, a craftsman may also work at a tourist site during the summer. Public-sector employees may often take a second job in the evening. Second jobs often complicate the way employment and unemployment figures are measured within the various sectors of the Greek economy.

In the Greek workforce, labor unions have been active throughout the 20th century. But unions have been subject to legal restrictions by successive Greek governments who considered unions a threat to domestic economic stability. Organization is centered on a particular trade or craft within a community. Local chapters are generally affiliated with national federations, which in turn are organized under the umbrella of the General Confederation of Greek Workers (GSEE).

The GSEE was founded in 1918 and is one of the oldest trade unions. However, the Greek public does not hold the GSEE and the Supreme Civil Servants' Administrative Committee (ADEDI) in high regard. Public hostility is also aimed toward the white-collar Association of Greek Industrialists, although they improved their public image considerably in the 1990s.

While not popular with the Greek people or government, trade unions can yield considerable political power. For example, when the New Democracy administration was in office in 1992, labor unions staged strikes following the privatization of the Urban Transportation Company, putting the government on the defensive. However, the GSEE has been instrumental in establishing pay increases and other labor benefits, which have benefited the country as a whole.

One of the by-products of industrialization in Greece was the development of an **underground economy**, which includes unreported economic activities that are not subject to taxation. Given Greece's large service sector, there are a number of retail and small family businesses that are unregulated and untaxed by the government, and it is difficult to track the number of unpaid family members working in these businesses. Estimates of the Greek underground economy are at 50 to 60 percent of the officially reported economy, meaning that income and employment figures in Greece are actually significantly higher than the official estimates. While this unofficial sector provides employment and income to many that would otherwise be jobless, it undermines the modernization of the country's fiscal system and the development of an internationally competitive Greek economy.

COUNTRY HISTORY AND ECONOMIC DEVELOPMENT

2600 B.C. Period of early Minoan civilization in Crete, beginning more than 1,400 years of cultural development.

9TH CENTURY B.C. The poet Homer writes *The Odyssey* and *The Iliad*, the Greek classical epic poems.

8TH CENTURY B.C. Trade relations begin between Athens, Sparta, and other city-states.

450s B.C. Under the rule of Pericles, the Golden Age of Athens begins. This period is marked by achievements in architecture, sculpture, and philosophy.

336 B.C. Alexander the Great assumes power and creates the largest empire in history.

86 B.C. Rome conquers Athens. *Pax Romana* period begins in 31 B.C.

1453. Ottoman Turks capture Constantinople and Greece falls to Ottomans and remains under Ottoman control for close to 400 years.

1821–32. Inspired by the Enlightenment movement in Europe, the Greek War of Independence begins which liberates modern-day Greece. Britain and France assist Greece's efforts.

1863. New constitution establishes parliament. Prince William of Denmark named King George I of Greece.

1881. Ottomans relinquish control of Thessaly and part of Epirus to Greece following pressure from Great Powers at 1878 Congress of Berlin.

1909. Greek government is overthrown by a military coup. Eleutherios Venizelos named head of new government.

1930. World depression causes political and economic unrest in Greece.

1936–41. General Ioannis Metaxas heads dictatorship after Venizelos resigns in 1932.

1941. Nazis invade Greece. Start of 4-year occupation. National resistance movement founded.

1944. Athens is freed from German control and Greece falls under post-WWII British sphere of influence.

1946–49. Civil war erupts between government and Democratic Army of Greece.

1949. Greece receives aid for post-war rebuilding from the U.S. Marshall Plan.

1967. Military seizes the government in a coup d'etat, starting a 7-year period of international isolation. King Constantine goes into exile.

1974. Turkey invades Cyprus in response to coup attempt by Greece against Cypriot president. Greek military junta loses power and civilian government returns. Democratic institutions are restored and the monarchy is abolished by popular vote.

1975. A new constitution based on republican form of government is created. Turkish Federated State of Cyprus declared, heightening tensions between Greece and Turkey.

1981. Panhellenic Socialist Movement (PASOK) ends post-war conservative control and starts 8-year rule marked by reform program under Andreas Papandreou; Greece becomes member of European Community (EC).

1990. New government formed by Konstantinos Mitsotakis's New Democracy (ND) party, which wins control of half of assembly.

1992. The New Democracy party privatizes the mass transit system. Strikes erupt against Mitsotakis' government and its economic policies.

1993. European Union (EU) 5-year economic reform program adopted by Greece; Papandreou again elected prime minister.

1994. Greece imposes trade **embargo** against Former Yugoslav Republic of Macedonia and EU declares embargo violates international law. UN, U.S., and EU attempt to work out a solution with Greece.

1995. Government ratifies UN Convention on the Law of the Sea, causing Turkey to threaten war if treaty is applied in Aegean Sea. Greece lifts trade embargo against the Former Yugoslav Republic of Macedonia.

1996. Papandreou resigns as prime minister because of poor health and is replaced by Constantine Simitis.

2001. Greece joins European Monetary Union (EMU). New Athens International Airport opens.

FUTURE TRENDS

In the 20th century, the Greek economy has fared poorly and has been plagued with high inflation, debts, account deficits, and shaky economic policies. However, its admittance into the EU has ensured economic reform and the commitment of the government to keep Greece's economic house in order. The road ahead looks brighter and more promising for Greece's long-troubled economy. Its entrance into the European Monetary Union (EMU) demonstrates that Prime Minister Simitis's PASOK government has successfully managed the economy without causing high inflation through tough fiscal measures. All signs show that the Greek economy is likely to expand, perhaps more so than that of other EU members. Recent wage increases, tax cuts, and employment growth are likely to keep consumer spending growing.

If the Balkan region becomes more stable, Greece may have stiff competition attracting foreign investors. Likewise, receiving funds from the Community Support Framework (CSF) of the EU may prove difficult as higher implementation standards are instituted. That said, the Greek economy is far better off than it was during the second half of the 20th century. And in fact, in 2001 the government expected to achieve a small surplus in the budget.

Politically, Greece is expected to remain stable under Prime Minister Constantine Simitis, ensuring the continuation of his economic platform, although there is some resistance to his privatization policies. Improving ties with its EU neighbors will be at the forefront of his political agenda, as well as fostering better relations with Turkey, Greece's longtime adversary. Throughout 1999 and 2000, the 2 countries made significant progress toward enhancing peaceful relations in the wake of Turkey's candidacy for admission to the EU.

Greece will host the 2004 Olympics, and the country is gearing up for this historic event. The new Athens International Airport is better equipped to handle the many tourists coming in for the Games, and improvements are being made in transportation and the country's infrastructure, such as new highways and expansion of the Athens Metro. Tourism revenues should increase significantly from the influx of Olympic participants and spectators.

As Greece continues its plan to modernize its economy while retaining some socialist aspects of its government, societal changes could occur. Businesses, especially family-owned businesses, are feeling the effects of closer integration with Greece's EU partners as the country's entrepreneurs now face growing competition from their European competitors. Small family-owned businesses could crumble due to competition from large international corporations. How this all plays out in Greek society, which is marked by strong family traditions, is unknown. It is hoped that increased free enterprise and **capitalism** will not damage Greece's strong family structure, which has been a pillar of its culture and society, much like those which still hold up the Acropolis after so many centuries.

DEPENDENCIES

Greece has no territories or colonies.

BIBLIOGRAPHY

Economist Intelligence Unit. *Country Report: Greece.* London: Economist Intelligence Unit, January 2001.

Embassy of Greece. <http://www.greekembassy.org/busin-econ/tax.html>. Accessed April 2001.

Greece Now Project 2001. *Greece Now.* <http://www.greece.gr>. Accessed July 2001.

"Greece Silences Radio Stations Near Airport." *Amarillo Globe-News.* <http://www.amarillonet.com/stories/032801/usn_greece.shtml>. Accessed June 2001.

Hellenic Ministry of Agriculture. <http://www.minagric.gr/en/index.shtml>. Accessed July 2001.

Kourvetaris, Yorgos A., and Betty A. Dobratz. *A Profile of Modern Greece: In Search of Identity.* New York: Oxford University Press, 1987.

Kurtis, Glenn E., ed. *Greece: A Country Study.* Washington, D.C.: Library of Congress, 1995.

Nevradakis, Michael. "In Memory of the Athenian Free Radio." <http://www.media.net.gr>. Accessed June 2001.

U.S. Central Intelligence Agency. *World Factbook 2000.* <http://www.odci.gov/cia/publications/factbook/index.html>. Accessed July 2001.

U.S. Department of State. *Background Notes: Greece.* <http://www.state.gov/www/background_notes/greece_9910_bgn.html>. Accessed January 2001.

—Lynn Mahoney

HUNGARY

Republic of Hungary
Magyar Népköztársaság

CAPITAL: Budapest.

MONETARY UNIT: Hungarian forint (Ft). One forint equals 100 fillérs. There are coins of 10, 20, and 50 fillérs and 1, 5, 10, 20, 50, and 100 forints, and notes of 200, 500, 1,000, 2,000, 5,000, 10,000, and 20,000 forints.

CHIEF EXPORTS: Machinery and equipment, other manufactures, agriculture and food products, raw materials, fuels and electricity.

CHIEF IMPORTS: Machinery and equipment, other manufactures, fuels and electricity, agricultural and food products, raw materials.

GROSS DOMESTIC PRODUCT: US$79.4 billion (purchasing power parity, 1999 est.).

BALANCE OF TRADE: **Exports:** US$22.6 billion (f.o.b., 1999). **Imports:** US$25.1 billion (f.o.b., 1999).

COUNTRY OVERVIEW

LOCATION AND SIZE. Hungary is a landlocked country in eastern Central Europe bordered by Austria, Slovakia, the Ukraine, Romania, Serbia, Croatia, and Slovenia. Located in the Carpathian Basin, it is surrounded by the Carpathian Mountains, the Alps, and the Dinaric Alps. It has a total area of 93,030 square kilometers (35,919 square miles), 690 square kilometers (266 square miles) of which is water. Comparatively, Hungary is slightly smaller than the state of Indiana. The capital, Budapest, is located in the central northern region on the Danube river, which runs from Austria to the Croatian-Serbian border.

POPULATION. The population of Hungary was estimated at 10.04 million at the end of January 2000, a slight decrease compared to the 1990 population of 10.38 million. In 2000 the birth rate was estimated at 9.26 births per 1,000, and the death rate was 13.34 deaths per 1,000. The population growth rate estimate in 2000 was -.33 percent, making Hungary a country where population is declining. The majority religion in Hungary is Roman Catholic (67.5 percent), followed by Calvinist (20 percent), Lutheran (5 percent), and atheist and other (7.5 percent).

Some 60 percent of Hungarians live in urban areas. Compared to other European countries in population density, Hungary ranks in the middle with about 109.4 persons per square kilometer (283 per square mile). The most densely populated areas lie in the industrial axis areas, running southwest to northwest, that are rich in natural resources.

The Hungarian population is predominantly ethnic Hungarian (89.9 percent), descendants of the Finno-Ugric and Turkish tribes who merged with the Avars and Slavic tribes in the 9th century. The modern population also includes Roma (Gypsies, 4 percent), Germans (2.6 percent), Serbs (2 percent), Slovaks (0.8 percent), and Romanians (0.7 percent). An interesting feature of Hungary is that many ethnic Hungarians who identify themselves as Hungarians also live in bordering states and other countries, approximately 5 million in all. The largest Hungarian population outside Hungarian borders—approximately 2 million—lives in the Romanian region of Transylvania. Another 700,000 live in the Slovak and Czech Republics, and some 650,000 live in the former Yugoslavia.

OVERVIEW OF ECONOMY

Hungary has an advanced and diversified free-market economy. Economic growth is strong relative to other countries in Europe, and Hungary has its sights set clearly on accession to the European Union (EU) before 2010. It has been more than 10 years since the official end of state **socialism** and a semi-command economy, and over 85 percent of the economy has been **privatized**. Hungary has undergone significant economic reform since 1989 including privatization, reform of important state-supported sectors like health care, pensions, and social security, and

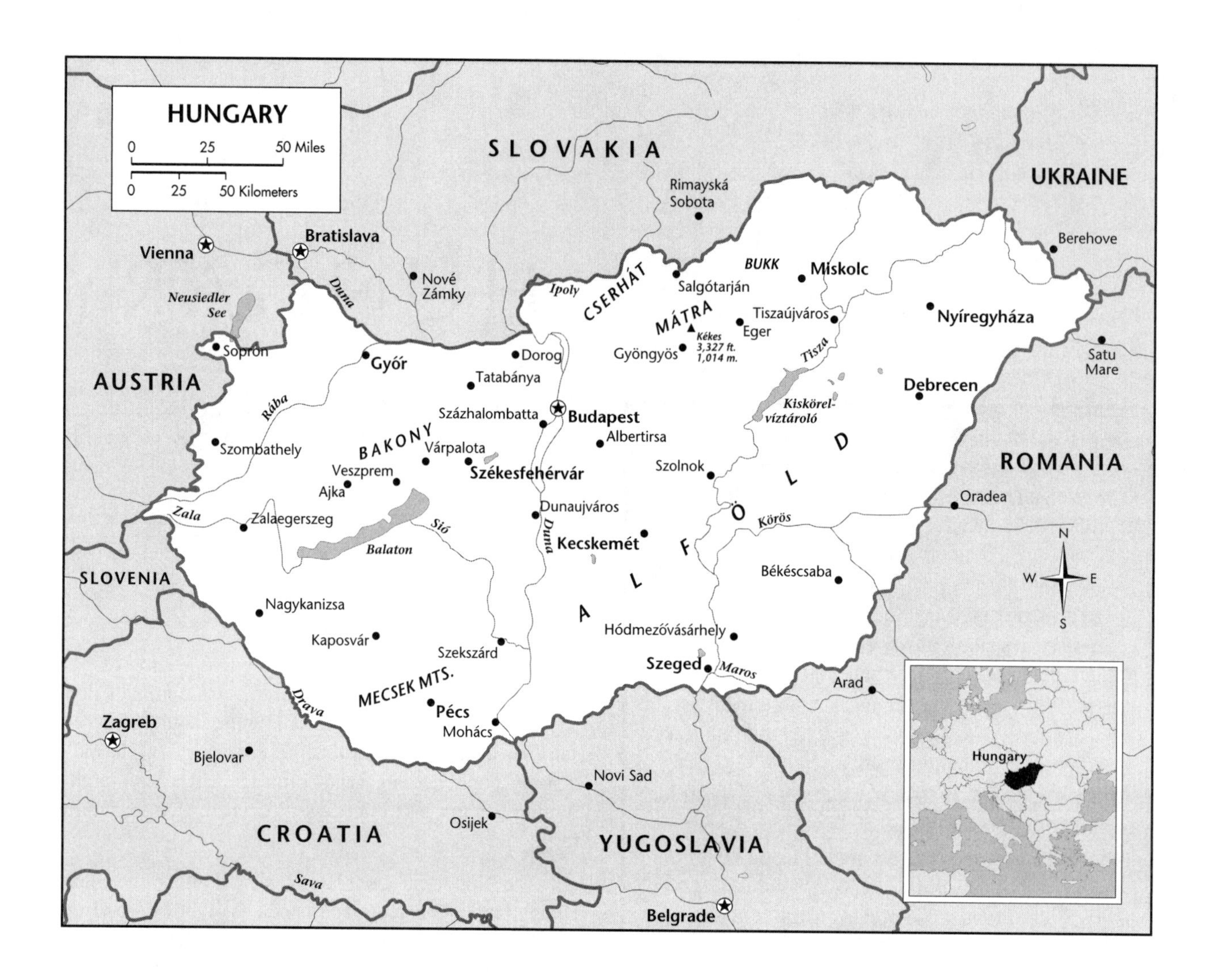

housing supports. It has also experienced significant regional development and the encouragement of both foreign and domestic investment.

Hungary's economic output has been steadily growing, yet it continues to lag behind typical western countries, including those of the European Union. Still, its growth rates have been impressive by the standards of developed countries, in recent years exceeding the EU average. Hungary's growth in the **gross domestic product** (GDP) was 5.5 percent in 2000, up from 4 percent in the previous year.

Hungary is regarded as a converging economy approaching the ranks of developed countries in general. Hungary is a member of the World Trade Organization (WTO), the International Monetary Fund (IMF), the World Bank, and the Organization for Economic Cooperation and Development (OECD). It is currently an associate member of the European Union and has been preparing for full membership since 1997.

The most significant event affecting Hungary's economy after 1950 was the experiment of state socialism. When the communists took over in 1948, the economy of Hungary was based primarily on agriculture. That emphasis shifted under **communist** rule toward industrialization, especially heavy industry and manufacturing. In the late 1950s and 1960s the government retreated on this stance somewhat, emphasizing more consumer-oriented goods. As a consequence the Hungarian standard of living rose relative to that of other Eastern European countries under communist rule, but by the 1980s the Hungarian economy began to stagnate. As a consequence, Hungary became increasingly indebted to international lenders. At the same time, its ties with foreign governments, businesses, and organizations were gradually increasing. The combination of these financial and commercial trends contributed to the shift to a multiparty system in 1989.

The introduction of multiparty competition in 1990 was quickly followed by significant free market reforms, especially in the area of privatization. The new government was also particularly aggressive at attracting foreign investment, accounting for more than half of all direct foreign investment in Eastern Europe by 1993. Since

1989 more than US$20 billion in working capital has been invested by foreign companies. About 40 of the world's top 50 multinational companies are represented in Hungary. Hungary also has the most highly capitalized stock exchange in eastern Central Europe.

The growth potential of the Hungarian economy remains strong relative to both its neighbors and to the advanced economies of the European Union. Hungarian sovereign debt now rates as investment grade (debt low enough for investors to seriously consider putting money into the country). Hungary's economic growth in 2000 exceeded 5 percent, placing it above the EU average. **Inflation**, while high at just above 10 percent, is expected to drop to single digit levels in 2001 or 2002.

Organized crime has been a problem in Hungary since its political and economic transition in 1989, especially as a consequence of its geographic location and relative economic openness. Organized crime groups have used Hungary as a transit country for smuggling drugs, people, and weapons. Hungary has passed tough laws against such activities, however, and is rated much more highly as an attractive locale for foreign investment than many other post-communist countries. As it seeks to gain accession to the European Union, Hungary is actively seeking to eradicate the further influence of organized crime.

POLITICS, GOVERNMENT, AND TAXATION

Since its transition to a multiparty system in 1989, Hungary has enjoyed a fully competitive and democratic political system. Hungary is a parliamentary democracy with the leader of the largest party as prime minister. There is also a president who acts as head of state and is elected by the legislature. The legislative branch consists of the single-chambered National Assembly, consisting of 386 representatives elected through a combination of proportional and direct representation. Elections are held every 4 years, taking place in 1990, 1994, and 1998.

The ruling coalition in 2001 consisted of the right-of-center Fidesz-Hungarian Civic Party, in concert with the Hungarian Democratic Party and the Independent Smallholders' Party. The main opposition parties were the leftist Hungarian Socialist Party and the centrist Alliance of Free Democrats. A far-right nationalist party, the Hungarian Justice and Life Party, also received 14 seats for the first time in the 1998 election. The parties differ over the emphasis and content of some key economic policy issues. The Fidesz-based coalition, for example, supports a faster pace of economic reform than does the Socialist Party, which during its period in government from 1994–98 slowed the pace of reforms. Because all major parties are committed to Hungary's joining the European Union, however, economic policy differences are muted.

Hungary's judicial branch is headed by an independent Constitutional Court, established during the regime change of 1989 by the First Act of the Constitution. By law it is the responsibility of the Constitutional Court to guarantee that the constitution is adhered to in legal and political affairs. One important duty of the Constitutional Court is to reconcile the differences between national and international law, especially important in the economic and policy sphere as Hungary prepares its laws to conform to EU standards.

The Hungarian justice system is divided into 3 areas of jurisdiction, including criminal, civil, and administrative law. Administrative law includes reviewing the legality of administrative decisions, including economic policy decision, with regard to existing regulations. Hungary has a 3-tier justice system. At the lowest level are local courts (municipal district courts), superseded by county courts (in the 19 counties and the capital Budapest), and the Supreme Court. The office of the public prosecutor also plays an important role, used to investigate criminal activity and to represent the public interest. The public prosecutor supervises investigations, enforces punishments, and oversees court proceedings.

Hungary has a large centralized tax office, known in Hungarian as APEH. APEH monitors the financial activity of citizens and businesses, processing annual returns and **value-added taxes**, currently between 12 and 25 percent in Hungary depending on the category of good. APEH has fairly sweeping powers to investigate tax non-compliance, including its own police branch. **Income tax** on individuals is progressive (meaning the proportion of tax paid increases as income increases), ranging from 25 percent to 42 percent for the highest incomes. The general tax rate on businesses is 18 percent.

INFRASTRUCTURE, POWER, AND COMMUNICATIONS

Like many former communist countries, Hungary possesses an excellent public transport system. The rail system, consisting of 7,606 kilometers (4,726 miles) of track, is state-owned and operated and connects all major cities in Hungary as well as a large number of international destinations. Hungary has 188,203 kilometers (116,944 miles) of highways, 81,680 kilometers (50,756 miles) of which are paved and 438 kilometers (272 miles) of which are expressways. Hungary also has 1,373 kilometers (853 miles) of permanently navigable waterways, including the Danube River flowing north to south through the center of the country. With its tributaries, the Danube provides a low-cost means to transport passengers and a large portion of domestic freight.

Communications

Country	Newspapers	Radios	TV Sets[a]	Cable subscribers[a]	Mobile Phones[a]	Fax Machines[a]	Personal Computers[a]	Internet Hosts[b]	Internet Users[b]
	1996	1997	1998	1998	1998	1998	1998	1999	1999
Hungary	186	689	437	146.5	105	17.7	58.9	93.13	600
United States	215	2,146	847	244.3	256	78.4	458.6	1,508.77	74,100
Germany	311	948	580	214.5	170	73.1	304.7	173.96	14,400
Austria	296	753	516	139.1	282	N/A	233.4	252.01	1,840

[a]Data are from International Telecommunication Union, *World Telecommunication Development Report 1999* and are per 1,000 people.
[b]Data are from the Internet Software Consortium (http://www.isc.org) and are per 10,000 people.

SOURCE: World Bank. *World Development Indicators 2000.*

The completion of a canal between the Main River and the Danube River in 1992 allowed for goods to be shipped from the Black Sea to the North Sea. Finally, Hungary had 43 airports in 1999, including an international airport just outside Budapest. Hungary has a national airline, Malév, serving nearly all major European cities and several destinations in North America, Asia, the Middle East, and Africa. The airline was formerly state-owned but has now been partially privatized. The Ministry of Economic Affairs approved a large-scale program, the Széchényi Plan, designed to make massive national investments in highway and property development after 2000.

Power production in Hungary relies on a combination of domestically generated energy sources and imports. In 1999 Hungarian consumption of energy was 33.317 billion kilowatt hours (kWh), while production was 35.104 billion kWh. Hungary still has artificially low subsidized energy prices, but there are plans to allow prices to rise to western European market levels. At present Hungary's energy prices are between one-third and one-half of the prices in EU countries.

Like many other former Eastern bloc countries, Hungary relies heavily on fossil fuels to meet its energy needs. Hungary's estimated sources of primary energy supplies (1996, OECD/IEA) were 16.9 percent coal, 27.1 percent oil, and 40.4 percent natural gas. Of non-fossil fuel sources, 14.6 percent came from nuclear energy, 0.1 percent from hydroelectric sources, and 0.9 percent from other sources. Nuclear energy is produced in Hungary's 1 nuclear power plant, located near the city of Paks. Nuclear energy provides 38.9 percent of Hungary's electricity production, producing 13.969 billion kWh in 1998.

Hungary's telecommunication network has until recently been underdeveloped both from a technological and a service standpoint. But partial privatization of the state telephone company Matáv in 1993 and the planned introduction of competition for land-based telephone lines in 2002 has led to many important changes. Among these has been a spectacular growth in cellular phone services and ownership, with the number of mobile phone subscribers estimated at more than 3 million in 2000. (Official data put this number at 1.62 million in 1999, and 1.034 million in 1998.) There were 3 companies providing cellular service in 2001.

Under communism the telecommunication system was underdeveloped and poorly operated. Even in the first half of the 1990s, Hungarians often had to wait more than a year to have a fixed telephone line installed. This situation has changed quickly in recent years, however. The domestic phone network is now digitized and highly automated and is able to provide almost any telecommunication service need. Trunk services are carried by fiber-optic cable and digital microwave radio relay. Subscribers have had the option of fiber-optic connections (using ISDN lines) since 1996. Hungary has fiber-optic cable connections with all neighboring countries. Total fixed-line telephones in use were 3.609 million in 1999 and estimated at over 4 million in 2000. The Hungarian state telecommunications company, Matáv, had a state-guaranteed **monopoly** on fixed-line communications, a monopoly that was scheduled to end in 2002.

Hungary has an extensive number of radio stations: 57 FM radio stations, 17 AM radio stations, and 3 shortwave radio stations in 1998. Total radio ownership in 1997 was 7.01 million. Hungary also had 39 television broadcast stations and some 4.42 million televisions in 1997. Internet activity has also grown significantly in Hungary, with 45 Internet service providers operating in 1999. Only 58.9 persons per 1,000 owned personal computers in 1998, a figure well behind the United States, although many more people use computers in school or at their workplaces. The number of Internet users in 1999 was 137,000, and estimates for 2000 put this figure at 733,000.

Since private ownership of publications was legalized in 1989, the print media in Hungary has blossomed. In 1999 there were 10 national daily newspapers, the most popular being *Népszabadság* and *Metró*, each with

207,000 copies printed per day. *Népszabadság*, meaning People's Freedom, was formerly controlled by the communist party but is now independent. Most of Hungary's daily newspapers are partially foreign owned. Hungary also has dozens of weekly and monthly magazines and papers, the largest exceeding 500,000 copies per week.

ECONOMIC SECTORS

Hungary's shift to a service-based economy, away from the agricultural and industry sectors, has been the most marked change in recent decades. Before World War II, Hungary's economy was based primarily on agriculture, and its industry was almost entirely destroyed by the war. During the communist period beginning in 1948, emphasis shifted toward the development of industry, although production goals were set unrealistically high and Hungary was not able to meet them. In the 1960s and 1970s economic reforms shifted some of the emphasis from industry and placed more focus on agriculture and **consumer goods**. More recently, services have come to dominate the economy. According to 1999 figures, services account for 65 percent of the GDP, compared to 30 percent in industry and only 5 percent in agriculture. The labor force of 4.2 million shows a similar distribution, with 65 percent employed in services, 27 percent in industry, and 8 percent in agriculture.

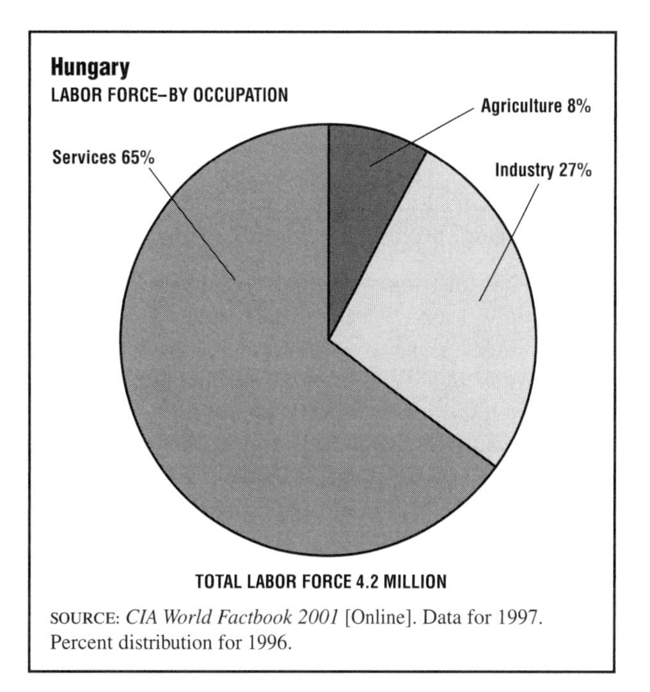

SOURCE: *CIA World Factbook 2001* [Online]. Data for 1997. Percent distribution for 1996.

AGRICULTURE

Agricultural production is important to Hungary's economy although its role in the economy has steadily declined. In 1999 agriculture provided 5 percent of the GDP and 8 percent of employment, roughly similar to proportions observable in West European countries. As a share of exports, agricultural and food products constituted 10.5 percent of Hungary's exports in 1998. Hungary has 93,000 square kilometers (35,900 square miles) of cultivated land, covering 52 percent of Hungary's total area.

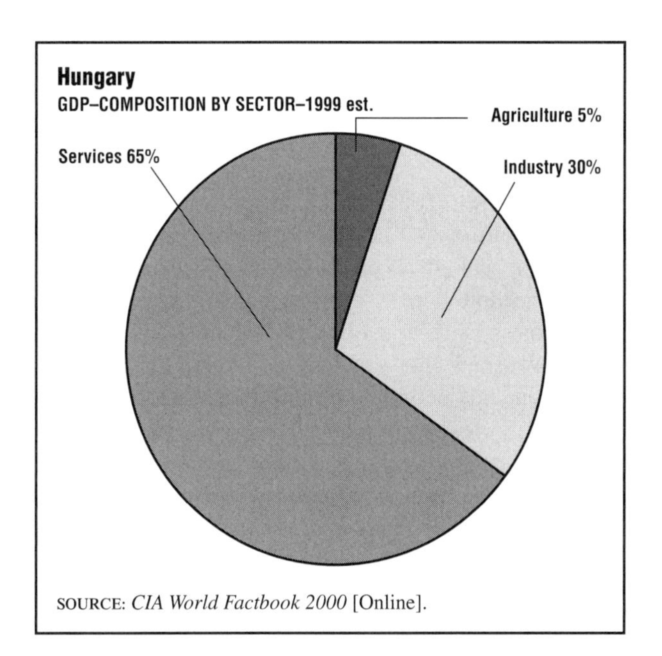

SOURCE: *CIA World Factbook 2000* [Online].

During the communist period about 90 percent of all farmland was organized into collective and state-owned farms. In collective farms, different families worked together on jointly owned land and shared the earnings from the farm's output. State farms were directly owned and managed by the government. Following the introduction of the multiparty system and the transition to a free market economy in 1990, the new government began returning farms to private hands, also introducing forms of compensation for lands that had been seized. The result is that currently about 90 percent of cultivated land in Hungary is privately owned. Severe droughts following privatization, combined with sharp drops in government **subsidies** for farming, caused a 30 percent drop in agricultural production during the past 10 years. Animal breeding has fallen by 50 percent in comparison with 1990. State subsidies for agriculture in Hungary tend to be comparatively low, an average of 5 to 7 times less per capita in Hungary than in the average European Union country.

Hungary's leading agricultural products are a combination of staple crops, famous specialty items such as wine and livestock products, and basic livestock. Hungary's most important crops include corn, wheat, sugar beets, barley, potatoes, and sunflower seeds. It also produces grapes and wine, including several famous wines such as those from the Tokaj region. Other well-known specialty items include salami, goose liver, and paprika.

Livestock production is also important in Hungary, including cattle, pigs, sheep, horses, and poultry. Important livestock products include milk, meat, butter, eggs, and wool. Finally, Hungary has some important freshwater fisheries, mostly located on the Danube and Tisza rivers, and on Lake Balaton. The commercial fish catch consists mainly of carp, pike, perch, sheatfish, and shad.

Hungary also has important forestry resources, although poor forestry management reduced Hungary's forestry resources under communism. The expansion of agriculture, a high rate of exploitation, and inadequate replanting of trees contributed to a significant decline in the period following World War II. In response, the government reduced timber cutting and launched an extensive reforestation program in the 1960s. The timber cut in 1998 was 3.88 million cubic meters (137 million cubic feet).

INDUSTRY

Once a major component of the Hungarian economy under communist rule, industrial enterprises struggled in the early 1990s to come to terms with operating in a free market. By the late 1990s, however, investments in many industries and the expertise and education of Hungarian workers contributed to a resurgence in the industrial sector. From 1999 to 2000 alone, industry expanded 18.3 percent, the third straight year of double-digit growth in this sector.

MANUFACTURING. Manufacturing forms an important component of the Hungarian economy and was responsible for 84.6 percent of Hungary's exported commodities in 1998, even though most of Hungary's industries must import the raw materials used in the manufacturing process. The engineering industry—which is dominated by automobile and automobile parts production—accounts for roughly one-third of industrial output. Other leading manufactured products include steel (both crude and rolled), cement, aluminum, textiles, paper products, and shoes. The manufacture and processing of agricultural products is also an important contributor to Hungary's manufacturing output.

CHEMICALS. The chemical industry is an important component of the Hungarian economy. The plastic base materials and plastic processing industries were major components within this sector, contributing 2.1 and 2.6 percent of total industrial output, respectively. This sector is mainly concerned with producing goods for other companies within the industrial sector, and produces some goods for export. The pharmaceutical industry contributes 2.4 percent of industrial output and is primarily oriented toward producing human and veterinary medicines, fine chemicals, pesticides and insecticides, and other pharmaceuticals.

MINING. Mining was an important component of Hungary's industry during the communist period but has declined considerably since the collapse of the communist regime in 1989. Under communism, the government owned all subsurface resources and held exclusive rights to extract and use them. The only exception was uranium ore, which was mined by an agency of the Soviet Union. In the mid-1990s Hungary's chief mineral products were hard coal, lignite, bauxite, petroleum, and natural gas.

SERVICES

TOURISM. Tourism is an important and growing contributor to Hungary's economy. Not only does it directly fuel economic activity, but it has also in the past provided an important source of foreign currency. After agriculture, Hungary's second largest net foreign exchange earning source is tourism. The capital, Budapest, is a strong attraction for many tourists, with its many museums, churches, castles, and cultural events, including an annual spring festival of music and drama. In all, Hungary maintains more than 100 public museums throughout the country. Lake Balaton is also a popular vacation spot for summer recreation activities such as boating, fishing, and swimming. In 2000, according to the Hungarian Statistical Office, 31,141 foreigners visited Hungary, generating a total balance of revenues and expenditures of 2.5 billion euros.

RETAIL. **Retail** commerce forms an important and growing part of Hungary's economy. At the end of 1999 some 103,000 economic associations and more than 150,000 retail businesses were in operation. This represents 149 retail stores for every 10,000 inhabitants. Nationwide, the most important players in the retail sector are involved in the sale of food and groceries, accounting for 35 percent of the retail trade. Leisure and other items come next at 24 percent, followed by textile and clothing retail at 17 percent. Total retail revenues have been steadily rising, at 4.3 trillion forints in 1999, compared to 3.8 trillion in 1998.

FINANCIAL SERVICES. Financial services are provided by a competitive and largely privatized banking sector. The largest bank, the National Savings Bank or OTP, has branches nationwide and provides a full range of personal and business banking services. Many other banks exist, most private and wholly or partially foreign-owned. Bank services include personal accounts, credit and debit card accounts, mortgage and personal loans, business accounts and business loans, foreign currency accounts and currency exchange, insurance services, and safety deposits. Customer service in Hungarian banks lags behind United States standards but has been steadily improving as the sector becomes more competitive. Most banks now offer Internet and mobile phone account access, and all pro-

Trade (expressed in billions of US$): Hungary

	Exports	Imports
1975	4.519	5.400
1980	8.638	9.219
1985	8.472	8.183
1990	9.550	8.621
1995	12.540	15.073
1998	N/A	N/A

SOURCE: International Monetary Fund. *International Financial Statistics Yearbook 1999.*

Exchange rates: Hungary

forints per US$1	
Jan 2001	282.240
2000	282.179
1999	237.146
1998	214.402
1997	186.789
1996	152.647

SOURCE: CIA *World Factbook 2001* [ONLINE].

vide an extensive national network of automated teller machines.

INTERNATIONAL TRADE

Hungary's international trade made an important shift following the change of regime in 1990. Under the communist system, nearly half of Hungary's annual foreign trade was with the Soviet Union and other communist nations of the Council for Mutual Economic Assistance (CMEA). Since the late 1980s and the collapse of the CMEA shortly thereafter, however, most of Hungary's international trade has taken place with western countries. Hungary's leading trade partners today are Germany, Italy, Austria, Russia, and the United States. In 1998 Hungary's exports went to Germany (37 percent), Austria (11 percent), Italy (6 percent), and the Netherlands (5 percent). The country's imports came mostly from Germany (28 percent), Austria (10 percent), Italy (8 percent), and Russia (7 percent). Exports in 1999 amounted to US$22.6 billion, and imports were valued at US$25.1 billion. Hungary's main exports are machinery and transport equipment, consumer goods, agricultural products, chemicals, apparel, textiles, iron and steel, and wine. Its main imports are machinery and transport equipment, crude petroleum, chemicals, metal ores, consumer goods, and agricultural products.

MONEY

Hungary's currency is currently linked to an **exchange rate** control mechanism known as the **crawling peg**, a mechanism used by the Hungarian National Bank to slowly devalue the currency. The objective has been to gradually make the transition between the forint, historically a non-convertible currency, to a currency that is fully convertible on world markets. Under communism, the currency was not convertible outside the communist bloc countries and an artificial exchange rate applied within Hungary, set by the government. Western currencies sold on the **black market** during this period typically fetched a much higher conversion rate than the official government rate, and such activities were difficult for the government to control. The National Bank, therefore, sets and publishes a daily rate of exchange between the forint and the world's major currencies. This rate is determined by a combination of the market value of other currencies, the **inflation rate** of the forint, and decisions by the National Bank to change the value of the forint.

As in most economies emerging from communism, inflation in Hungary has been high relative to western economies. Despite concerted efforts by the government to bring inflation into single digits, inflation in 2000 was 10.1 percent. Hungary's inflation during the post-communist transition period, however, has remained much lower than in many other Eastern European countries where rates often rose into the triple digits.

The country's central bank is the National Bank of Hungary, which issues currency and maintains checking and savings accounts. Other financial institutions include the Foreign Trade Bank, which serves businesses trading outside of Hungary, and the State Development Institution, which finances large-scale investment projects. The Budapest Stock Exchange opened in 1990 and is today the most heavily capitalized exchange in the East European region.

POVERTY AND WEALTH

Despite the official ideology of equality during the communist period, incomes in Hungary during this period were far from equal. Incomes varied according to social class and place of residence, with incomes in Budapest typically higher than in villages. The situation was much worse during the period between World War I and World War II, however, when average per capita income was very low and income inequality very high. One measure often used to measure income inequality is the ratio of the richest 10 percent of the population to the poorest 10 percent. A survey taken in 1992 suggests that the ratio of incomes of the highest to lowest 10 percent was

GDP per Capita (US$)

Country	1975	1980	1985	1990	1998
Hungary	3,581	4,199	4,637	4,857	4,920
United States	19,364	21,529	23,200	25,363	29,683
Germany	N/A	N/A	N/A	N/A	31,141
Austria	18,857	22,200	23,828	27,261	30,869

SOURCE: United Nations. *Human Development Report 2000; Trends in human development and per capita income.*

Distribution of Income or Consumption by Percentage Share: Hungary

Lowest 10%	3.9
Lowest 20%	8.8
Second 20%	12.5
Third 20%	16.6
Fourth 20%	22.3
Highest 20%	39.9
Highest 10%	24.8

Survey year: 1996

Note: This information refers to income shares by percentiles of the population and is ranked by per capita income.

SOURCE: *2000 World Development Indicators* [CD-ROM].

more than 6, making it similar to the income distribution in France and Germany. This level rose to 7.5 in 1996, according to one source, although the official figures from the World Bank place it at 6.3. The differences between social and employment categories has also widened. The social groups who were more affluent before the change in regime were able to increase their incomes in the 1990s faster than inflation, while the poorer groups had incomes that generally lagged behind inflation. In addition, the poorer segments of society were those where unemployment struck the hardest.

A large portion of Hungarian society, about 30–40 percent, suffered a loss in income after 1989. About 30–40 percent, on the other hand, were able to maintain their income, while a smaller percentage, around 10 percent, were able to increase their incomes. This small category included the managers of state and private enterprises, former government officials, and some of the intellectual elite.

Poverty is a problem in Hungary, and one which has worsened since the transition in 1989. According to estimates based on the subsistence level calculated by the Hungarian Statistical Office, in 1996 the proportion of those living under the subsistence level was at least 35 percent. Using the European definition of poverty as being 50 percent lower than the per capita average wage, then 14 percent of the population was poor in 1996.

Poverty in Hungary is disproportionately high among children, peasants and agricultural workers, housewives, and the handicapped. Geographically, poverty is higher in villages than in urban areas, with approximately 28 percent of the village population living in poverty, but only 18–19 percent of the city-based population and 5 percent of Budapest living in poverty. One social group where poverty is particularly high is the Gypsy ethnic grouping. The Gypsy population has been among the worst off in the transition to a market economy. Some 80 percent of Gypsies lived in poverty, compared to just 15 percent of non-Gypsies in 1996.

WORKING CONDITIONS

The single most significant factor affecting employment in Hungary has been the change in the early 1990s from a communist economy to a free market economy. The collapse of the communist system and the wide-scale privatization of the means of production led to a huge displacement of Hungarian workers, causing unemployment to reach 13 percent in 1993. But as the economy has continued to improve since the mid-1990s, employment has improved. Unemployment in 2000 was 6.4 percent, a respectable figure even lower than in many West

Household Consumption in PPP Terms

Country	All food	Clothing and footwear	Fuel and power[a]	Health care[b]	Education[b]	Transport & Communications	Other
Hungary	25	5	17	6	20	12	15
United States	13	9	9	4	6	8	51
Germany	14	6	7	2	10	7	53
Austria	20	10	11	4	9	9	38

Data represent percentage of consumption in PPP terms.

[a]Excludes energy used for transport.

[b]Includes government and private expenditures.

SOURCE: World Bank. *World Development Indicators 2000.*

European countries such as France or Germany. This rate is down from approximately 10 percent in 1999. Unemployment varies regionally, being the highest in the eastern and rural areas. Most Hungarian employment is in the service industry, which accounted for 65 percent in 1996. Another 27 percent was employed in industry, and some 8 percent in agriculture.

Throughout the 20th century, Hungary has seen a net migration from rural to urban areas. Urbanization in Hungary's 5 major cities accelerated this process, even though, after Budapest, the 5 major cities have populations only between 127,000 and 210,000. Currently many workers commute to urban workplaces from rural areas. In 1996, some 25 percent of the nation's workforce commuted to and from their jobs in this manner.

A labor code was passed in 1992 which recognized the collective rights of workers, including the right to organize into unions and bargain collectively. This code includes the right to strike, extended to all workers except the police and the military. Following the passage of this code the number of strikes in Hungary increased dramatically, although most lasted for only a short time. The largest union is the National Confederation of Hungarian Trade Unions, with approximately 1 million members in 1993 (from a total labor force of 4.3 million). A number of other union federations also exist.

COUNTRY HISTORY AND ECONOMIC DEVELOPMENT

1000. King Stephen of the Árpad dynasty rules the country. He is converted to Christianity and establishes Hungary as a Christian state.

1241. The Mongolian Tatars invade Hungary and occupy the territory for the year.

1526. Hungary is invaded by the Turks and the last Hungarian battle is lost in the southern town of Mohács. The Turkish occupation lasts for 150 years.

1686. Buda, the traditional seat of power on the western side of the Danube river dividing the cities of Buda and Pest, is recaptured from the Turks.

1703–11. Ferenc Rákóczi II, prince of Transylvania, leads a rebellion against the Habsburg Imperial army. The rebellion fails.

1848. A revolution against the Habsburg rule starting in Pest spreads to the whole country. Lajos Kossuth is elected governor after the Habsburg emperor is dethroned following several important Hungarian victories. The Hungarian revolutionary forces are defeated in 1849 by the Habsburgs, the ruling royal family of Austria, with the help of the Russian Army.

1867. A dual Austro-Hungarian monarchy begins following a compromise with the Habsburgs. A spectacular phase of industrial development begins.

1873. Pest, Buda, and Obuda are unified, and Budapest becomes a European metropolis, with the building of the Opera House, the National Gallery, and the Parliament. The first underground railway in continental Europe is put into operation.

1918. The Austro-Hungarian monarchy disintegrates following its defeat, along with Germany and its other allies, during World War I.

1920. The Treaty of Trianon is signed, redrawing the borders of Hungary. The new borders place one-third of Hungary's former population in other states and reduce its territory by two-thirds.

1944. The Nazis occupy Hungary in March during World War II. At the end of the war, fascists take over the country. In October, the Soviet Army liberates Hungary from fascist rule and occupies the country.

1947. The last relatively free election is followed by years of communist control, including show trials, executions, forced resettlements, forced industrial development, and a drop in living standards.

1956. Following the death of Soviet leader Joseph Stalin, a revolution against Soviet rule takes place in Hungary. The uprising is defeated by Soviet troops. János Kádár assumes power with Soviet assistance. Hundreds of Hungarians are executed, thousands more imprisoned, and about 200,000 flee the country.

1965. Cautious economic reforms are launched, causing a rise in living standards and a loosening of some of the more harsh measures of the communist system. In 1968 the New Economic Mechanism is introduced, reducing central control of the economy and allowing for greater freedom among individual business managers.

1982. Hungary becomes a member of the World Bank and the International Monetary Fund.

1988. A transition to democracy begins in Hungary, led by opposition parties demanding new institutions and the right to compete in legislative elections scheduled for 1990.

1989. The Hungarian Socialist Workers' Party agrees with opposition parties to end one-party rule and hold free elections in 1990.

1990. The Soviet Army leaves Hungary and the opposition Hungarian Democratic Forum wins the legislative elections held in March and April, ending 45 years of communist rule. Hungary also gains accession to the Council of Europe.

1991. Hungary, Poland, and Czechoslovakia sign the Visegrad Cooperation Agreement, a declaration to cooperate in preparation for accession to the European Union. Hungary also signs an agreement on cooperation with the European Union.

1992. Central European Free Trade Agreement pledging open and cooperative trade is signed by Hungary, Poland, and the Czechoslovak Customs Union.

1994. The Hungarian Socialist Party wins a legislative majority in elections held in May. Hungary joins the Partnership for Peace Program.

1996. Hungary joins the Organization for Economic Cooperation and Development (OECD).

1997. Hungary is formally invited by the European Union to begin accession talks.

1998. Hungary pays off its debts to the International Monetary Fund.The Fidesz-Hungarian Civic Party assumes power following elections held in May.

1999. Hungary becomes a full member of NATO.

FUTURE TRENDS

The future looks positive for Hungary's economy, given the trend since the end of the communist system. Growth has been steadily increasing, inflation has been declining, and unemployment has stabilized. Relative to other countries in the region, Hungary's economic conditions have proved quite favorable. The key economic event in the near future affecting Hungary will be accession to the European Union, something Hungary hopes will happen between 2004 and 2008. This event will bring about a significant **restructuring** of trade, employment, agriculture, and financial services. Hungary has already begun to introduce major fiscal and financial changes in preparation for accession, following the detailed guidelines issued by the European Union. Among other changes that accession would bring, Hungary intends to join the euro states adopting a single European currency. Doing so would link Hungary's inflation and interest rates to the European Central Bank in Frankfurt and remove the independence currently enjoyed by the Hungarian National Bank.

Hungary's main challenges for the future will be to manage its workforce, including some structural sectors where unemployment remains significantly high. There are also regions, especially in the eastern portion of the country, where unemployment and poverty remain significantly higher than the national average. In addition, Hungary in 2000 and 2001 has experienced problems with flooding that have caused significant disruption to people and to agriculture. These problems and more will have to managed in the future to enable Hungary's economy to grow and develop further.

DEPENDENCIES

Hungary has no territories or colonies.

BIBLIOGRAPHY

Economist Intelligence Unit. *Country Profile: Hungary.* London: Economist Intelligence Unit, 2001.

Hungarian Statistical Office. *Hungarian Statistical Yearbook 1999.* Budapest: Statistical Office, 2000.

Ministry of Economic Affairs. <http://www.gm.hu/kulfold/index.htm>. Accessed September 2001.

Molnár, Éva, ed. *Hungary: Essential Facts, Figures, and Pictures.* Budapest: Media Data Bank, MTI Corporation, 1997.

U.S. Central Intelligence Agency. *World Factbook 2000.* <http://www.odci.gov/cia/publications/factbook/index.html>. Accessed August 2001.

U.S. Department of State. *FY 2001 Country Commercial Guide: Hungary.* <http://www.state.gov/www/about_state/business/com_guides/2001/europe/index.html>. Accessed September 2001.

U.S. Department of Energy, Office of Fossil Energy. *An Energy Overview of the Republic of Hungary.* <http://www.fe.doe.gov/international/hungover.html>. Accessed September 2001.

Welcome to the Embassy of the Republic of Hungary. <http://www.hungaryemb.org>. Accessed September 2001.

—Kenneth Benoit

ICELAND

Republic of Iceland
Lýðveldið Ísland

CAPITAL: Reykjavík.

MONETARY UNIT: Icelandic króna (Ikr). 1 króna (Ikr1) equals 100 aurar. There are coins of 5, 10, and 50 aurar, and 1, 10, and 50 krónur. Paper notes come in denominations of 10, 50, 100, 500, 1,000, and 5,000 krónur.

CHIEF EXPORTS: Fish and fish products, animal products, aluminum, diatomite, ferrosilicon.

CHIEF IMPORTS: Machinery and equipment, petroleum products, foodstuffs, textiles.

GROSS DOMESTIC PRODUCT: US$6.42 billion (purchasing power parity, 1999 est.).

BALANCE OF TRADE: **Exports:** US$2.0 billion (1998). **Imports:** US$2.489 billion (1998).

COUNTRY OVERVIEW

LOCATION AND SIZE. A small volcanic island located between the Greenland Sea and the North Atlantic Ocean in the Arctic, Iceland is the westernmost European country. Found between Greenland and Europe, just northwest of the United Kingdom, Iceland has an area of 103,000 square kilometers (39,768 square miles) of which 100,250 square kilometers (38,707 square miles) is land and 2,750 square kilometers (1,062 square miles) is water. Its coastline is 4,988 kilometers (3,099 miles) long. Iceland is about the size of the state of Kentucky. Its capital, Reykjavík, is located on the country's southwestern coast. The climate is moderated by the North Atlantic current. In Iceland winters are mild and windy and the summers are cool. Approximately four-fifths of the country is unpopulated and uninhabitable. Glaciers cover more of the land in Iceland than in all of Europe. In addition to glaciers, the island has lakes, mountains, a lava desert, lush green areas, and natural hot springs, making Iceland a spectacle of nature.

POPULATION. The population of Iceland was estimated as 276,365 in July of 2000, with a slow growth rate of 0.57 percent. Iceland is the most sparsely populated country in Europe, with an average of 3 inhabitants per square kilometer. In 2000, the birth rate stood at 14.86 births per 1,000 population and the death rate at 6.87 deaths per 1,000 population.

The majority of Icelanders live in a narrow coastal belt in the valleys and in the southwest corner of the country. The Icelandic government reports that 99 percent of the population live in urban areas and 60 percent of the people reside in the republic's capital, Reykjavík, or in suburban areas directly outside of the city.

Iceland has a relatively young and middle-aged population—65 percent are between 15 and 64 years, 23 percent less than 14 years, and 12 percent aged 65 and older. It enjoys one of the highest life expectancy rates in the world. Life expectancy at birth was estimated in 2000 at 79.39 years (male: 77.19 years, female: 81.77 years). Iceland also possesses one of the world's highest literacy rates at 99.9 percent (1997 est.). Literature and poetry are a passion of the people and its per capita publication of books and magazines is the highest in the world.

Icelanders descended from the Norwegians and the Celts (Scottish and Irish). The national language is Icelandic, which of all the Nordic languages is the closest to the Old Norse language. The Icelandic spoken in 2001 has changed little since the 12th century. About 91 percent of the people belong to the state church, the Evangelical Lutheran Church. However, Iceland has complete religious freedom, and other Protestant and Catholic churches exist. Given Iceland's remote geographic location, its long-established culture and language, and its small population, it is a tightly-knit homogenous society.

OVERVIEW OF ECONOMY

Iceland's economy is similar to that of its Scandinavian neighbors. It is mainly capitalistic, but the republic

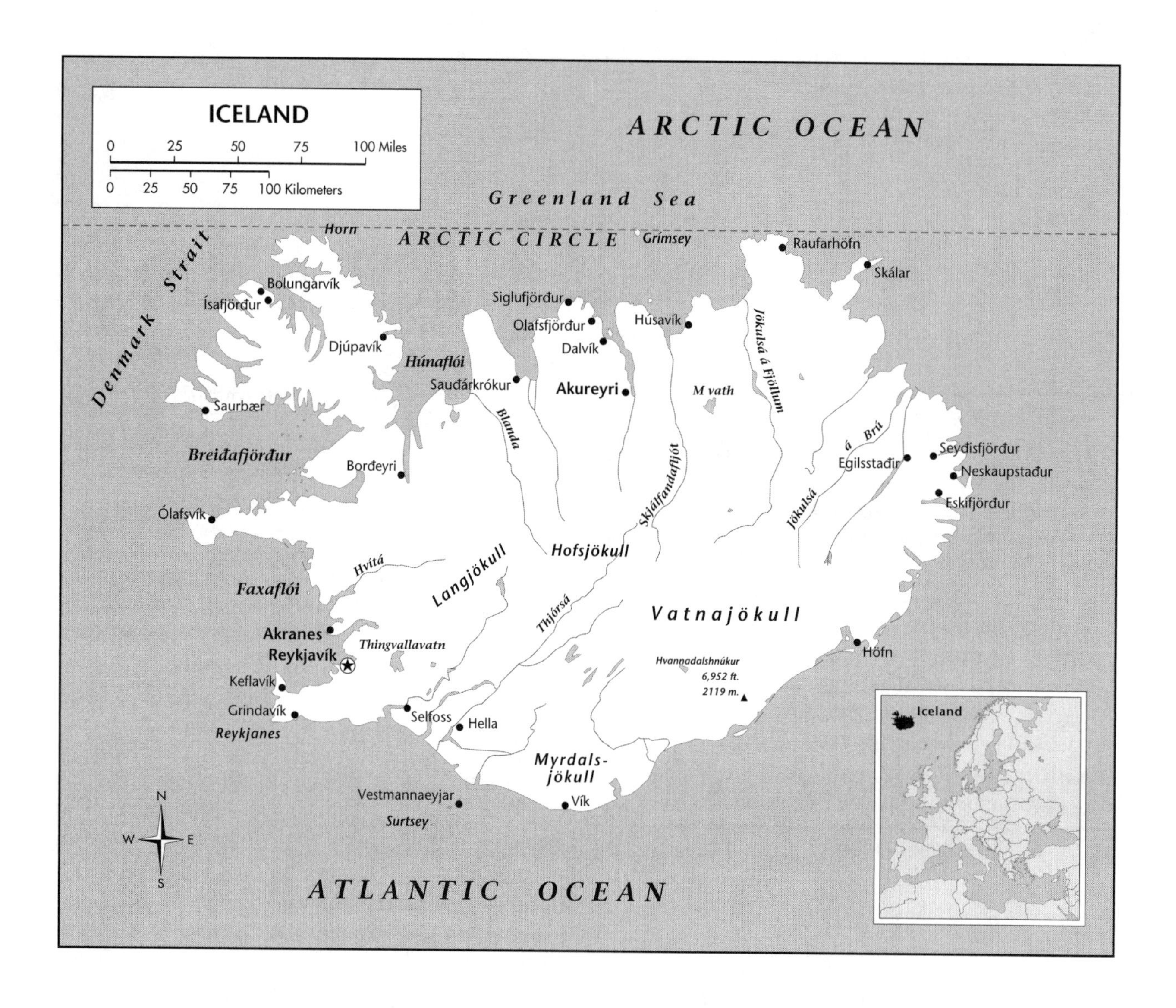

has an extensive welfare system, low to no unemployment due to labor shortages, and a wide distribution of wealth. Poverty is practically non-existent. Overall, Iceland's economy is strong and Icelanders enjoy a standard of living similar to many European countries.

Iceland's use of its natural resources has been central to its economic success. The country has achieved a high standard of living and many years of economic stability from the profits of its fish and energy resources. Given Iceland's dependence on fishing and fisheries, the economy is profoundly affected by declines in the number of fish living in its seas and in the Atlantic Ocean. The economy is also sensitive to drops in world prices for its main exports of fish and fish products, aluminum, ferrosilicon, equipment and electronic machinery for fishing and fish processing, and woolen goods.

Foreign trade also plays an important role in Iceland's economy. Exports and imports account for two-thirds of the GDP. Most of Iceland's exports go to the European Union (EU) and ETFA (European Free Trade Association) countries, the United States, and Japan.

Stability is a key aspect of the Icelandic economy, and the performance levels of the economy are not expected to change anytime soon. The policies adopted by Prime Minister Olafur Ragnar Grimsson's center-right government effectively reduced the budget and government deficits, restricted foreign borrowing, controlled rising **inflation**, and revised agricultural and fishing policies while diversifying the economy and selling state-owned industries. The economy should continue to prosper in the future.

However, one factor that remains the subject of great debate is whether Iceland should join the European Union (EU). The main reservation against EU membership is the fear of losing direct control of Iceland's fishing resources. History plays an important role in this debate, as Iceland was under Danish control for 5 centuries and only became an independent republic in 1944. Therefore it is understandable that freedom and control over their country's own natural resources is an important issue to Icelanders, and does not make EU membership very alluring.

The Icelandic economy has several strong, growing sectors outside of its economic mainstay of fishing. Since the 1990s, the economy has been branching out into the manufacturing and service industries. The financial services, biotechnology, and computer software industries are especially strong and growing. Tourism is another important industry that is increasing. The number of international visitors has risen greatly in 2000, as people are intrigued by the natural wonders of Iceland. Whale watching, visiting hot springs, and horseback riding are popular tourist activities.

Since 2000 one of the government's top priorities has been to manage and control Iceland's booming economy. To ensure stability, the government has adopted conservative **fiscal policies** and reduced its public debt. **Privatization** is another policy adopted by the government to better manage Iceland's economy. In the early 1990s, the government launched its privatization policy by selling off many state-owned industries to private buyers. In 2001, Iceland's privatization program continued with the sale of state banks and a state telecommunications company. **Monetary policy** will continue to focus on price stability and increases are expected in interest rates in order to contain accelerating inflation.

POLITICS, GOVERNMENT, AND TAXATION

Iceland is a constitutional republic that boasts the world's oldest parliament, the *Althingi*, which was established in 930 A.D. An independent country for over 300 years, Iceland was conquered by Norway in 1262. In the late 14th century, Iceland fell under the rule of Denmark when Norway and Denmark united under the Danish crown.

Abolished in 1800, the *Althingi* was reestablished in 1843 as a consultative assembly. The Act of Union, a 1918 agreement with Denmark, recognized Iceland as a fully sovereign state united with Denmark under the Danish crown. The British military briefly occupied Iceland in 1940 after Germany invaded Denmark, and then the United States became responsible for Iceland's defense in July 1942 under a U.S.-Icelandic defense agreement. In 1944, Iceland regained its independence and became a republic.

The Icelandic government consists of 3 branches. The executive branch is composed of the president who is chief of state, the prime minister who heads the government, and a cabinet of 9 ministers. The legislative branch consists of 63 members of the *Althingi*. Finally, the judicial branch has a supreme court and several district and special courts. There are 23 counties (*Syslur*) in Iceland, and there are currently 5 major active political parties: Independence (IP), Progressive (PP), Alliance (A), Left-Green Movement (LGM), and Liberal Party (LP). There is universal suffrage in Iceland and all women and men are eligible to vote once they turn 18 years old.

Iceland has a written constitution and a parliamentary form of government. The president, who is elected by direct popular vote for a 4-year term with no term limit, has limited powers and acts as a spokesperson and head of state. The prime minister and cabinet are responsible for policy-making. There are many women in the Icelandic government; 3 are heads of ministries, and 22 women have seats in the 63-member *Althingi*.

Members of the *Althingi* are elected to 4-year terms by popular vote, unless the *Althingi* is dissolved sooner. Anyone who is eligible to vote, with the exception of the president and the judges of the Icelandic Supreme Court, can run for election in parliament. Members are elected on the basis of **proportional representation** from 8 constituencies. After every election, the president gives one of the parliamentary leaders of the political parties the authority to form a cabinet, usually beginning with the leader of the largest party.

The present cabinet is a coalition government of the Independence Party (IP) and the Progressive Party (PP), which was formed in May 1999. The conservative Independence Party (IP) has dominated politics in Iceland since the 1990s. After the IP lost its majority in the *Althingi* with its former coalition partner, the liberal Social Democrat Party (SDP), the IP leader Prime Minister David Oddsson made an alliance with the more conservative Progressive Party (PP). The strategic move was a success and the IP regained its parliamentary majority with 40 *Althingi* seats. Since the 1990s, the SDP has not had much popular support because of its support of full EU membership for Iceland. The SDP are the only party to fully espouse the benefits of Iceland joining the EU, though in 2001 the PP and the Alliance party began to explore membership.

In 1996, Vigdis Finnbogadottir chose not to run for reelection as president of Iceland after serving 4 popular terms. She was the first woman elected president in the world. With a strong voter turnout, leftist party chairman Olafur Ragnar Grimsson became president by winning with a good margin against 3 other candidates.

In 2001, the center-right coalition government of the IP and PP continues to enjoy solid majority support and is expected to remain in office. However, harsh budgetary austerity measures introduced in the 2001 budget to control the rising economy could conceivably cause a decline in their popularity. The coalition partners remain in agreement on the importance of Iceland's current economic policy and have managed to avoid becoming embroiled in controversial issues, such as membership in the European Union. The largest opposition party, the left-of-center Alliance, has been preoccupied with reorganizing its **infrastructure** and is not a threat to the IP-PP coalition. The next round of parliamentary elections is scheduled for May 2003.

About 90 percent of the government revenue in 1998 came from income and wealth taxes, as well as **indirect taxes** such as those placed on corporations, payroll taxes, and **value-added taxes** on goods and services. The wealthy pay a high **income tax**, while the country's poorer citizens are exempt from taxation and receive a credit.

INFRASTRUCTURE, POWER, AND COMMUNICATIONS

Iceland enjoys an extensive infrastructure. Roads started to be built in 1900 and construction increased during the 1980s. However, there are still a number of gravel roads in Iceland. The current national road system connects most of the cities and is largely in the coastal areas. It consists of about 12,691 kilometers (7,868 miles) of roads, with 3,262 kilometers (2,022 miles) paved. There are no railroads in Iceland.

Airplanes and ships conduct travel between Reykjavík and Iceland's smaller cities. Additionally, there are daily international flights from Iceland to Europe and North America. There are 12 airports with paved runways and 74 with unpaved runways. Because of Iceland's dependence on fishing revenues, there are 9 ports and harbors. The Icelandic merchant marine has a total of 3 ships: a chemical tanker, a container ship, and a petroleum tanker.

Telecommunications are completely modern, and a high percentage of the population use cellular phones (6,746 in 1997). Icelanders enjoy adequate domestic telephone service, and international telephone systems are run by 3 satellite earth stations, one of which is shared with the other Scandinavian countries.

As of 1998, Iceland had 3 AM radio stations and about 70 FM stations. There were 14 television broadcast stations (plus 16 low-power repeaters) in 1997. In 2001, there were 2 national state radio channels and many private stations that broadcast around the clock. The first privately owned station went on the air in 1986 and others soon followed.

In the 1960s the state television station was on the air for only 2 nights a week. Later, television programming was broadcast on the other nights of the week but for years there was no television on Thursdays. Icelanders did not watch television programs in their own language until 1966. Since the 1990s less than half of television programming is in Icelandic and most programs are from the United States and Great Britain and are subtitled.

Computer use is widespread in Iceland and about 82 percent of Icelanders have Internet access at home, at school, or at work. This is reflected in the republic's ever-growing information-technology industry, with the export of software rapidly increasing.

ECONOMIC SECTORS

Iceland's economic sectors reflect the small size of the country. Natural resources are important, especially the fishing industry. For this reason, fisheries dominate Iceland's trade policies and coincide with Iceland's overriding foreign trade interests, especially free trade of fish. All told, the fishing industry contributes 13 percent of GDP. However, other sectors such as biotechnology and tourism are growing.

Communications

Country	Telephones[a]	Telephones, Mobile/Cellular[a]	Radio Stations[b]	Radios[a]	TV Stations[a]	Televisions[a]	Internet Service Providers[c]	Internet Users[c]
Iceland	168,000	65,746	AM 3; FM about 70 shortwave 1	260,000	14	98,000	7	144,000
United States	194 M	69.209 M (1998)	AM 4,762; FM 5,542; shortwave 18	575 M	1,500	219 M	7,800	148 M
United Kingdom	34.878 M	13 M (1998)	AM 219; FM 431; shortwave 3	84.5 M	228 (1995)	30.5 M	245	19.47 M
Norway	2.735 M 1998)	2,080,408 (1998)	AM 5; FM 650; shortwave 1	4.03 M	360 (1995)	2.03 M	13	2.36 M

[a]Data is for 1997 unless otherwise noted.
[b]Data is for 1998 unless otherwise noted.
[c]Data is for 2000 unless otherwise noted.

SOURCE: CIA *World Factbook 2001* [Online].

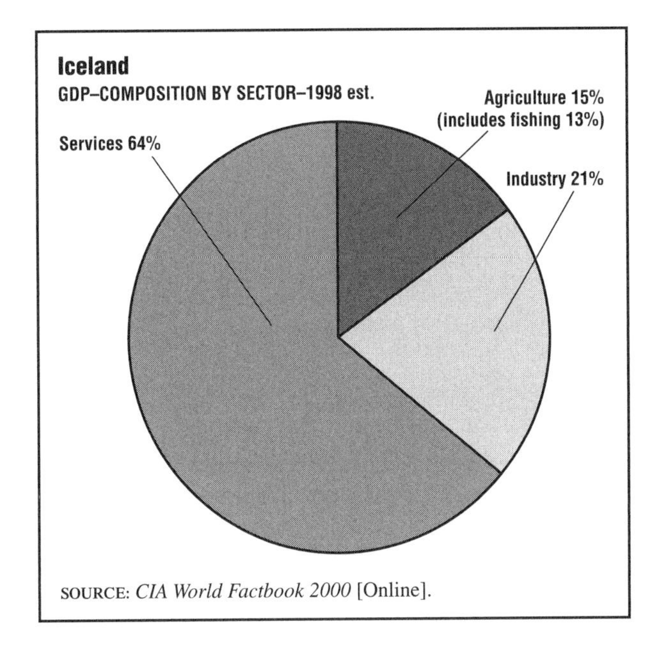

SOURCE: *CIA World Factbook 2000* [Online].

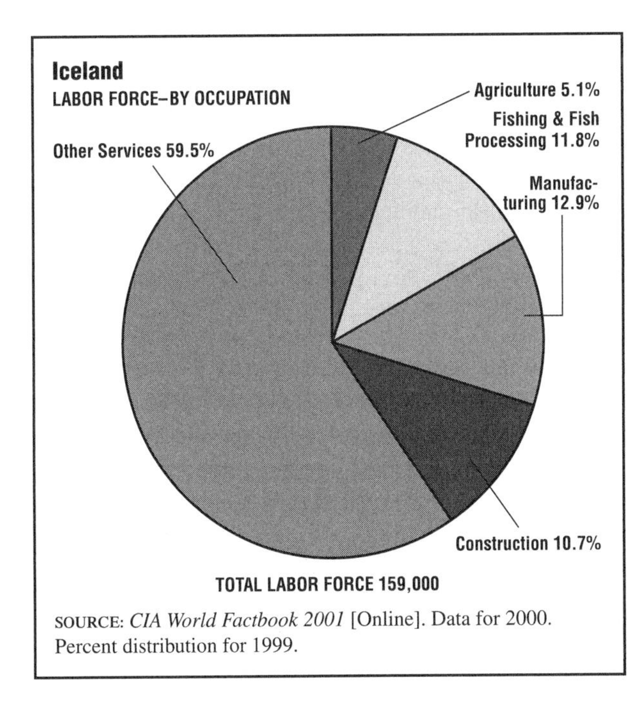

SOURCE: *CIA World Factbook 2001* [Online]. Data for 2000. Percent distribution for 1999.

AGRICULTURE

Agricultural production is a vital part of the Icelandic economy, accounting for 1 percent of its GDP (1998 est.) and employing over 16 percent of Iceland's **workforce**. Fish is the republic's main agricultural export but Iceland also produces potatoes, turnips, cattle, and sheep.

FISHING. The fishing industry has grown to symbolize Iceland's economic independence from its Scandinavian neighbors. The Icelandic Ministry of Fisheries reported that in 1999 the total catch of fish by the Icelandic fleet was 1.7 million tons. In 2000, marine products accounted for more than 70 percent of Iceland's total export earnings, making Iceland's economy vulnerable to changing world fish prices. Cod and capelin are the most abundant fish in the catch. Full free trade in fisheries products has been established not only within the European Free Trade Association (EFTA) but also in a series of free-trade agreements with countries in Central and Eastern Europe and in the Mediterranean.

Iceland recognized in the 1970s that it was in danger of depleting its fisheries, and initiated a plan involving Individual Transferable Quotas (ITQs) and Individual Vessel Quotas (IVQs). While complex, the aim of the plan is to fairly allocate fishing rights to those in the fishing industry. Some argue that the plan, because it encourages efficiency and speed, has rewarded larger vessel owners at the expense of smaller operators, thus it is still a matter of some disagreement in Iceland. But overall, most observers feel that the plan has succeeded in managing Iceland's fisheries.

Friction exists between Iceland and its European neighbors over fishing rights. Norway and Russia have complained about Iceland's herring fishing in the Barents Sea between Iceland and Norway. Canada has objected to Iceland's shrimp fishing off the coast of Newfoundland.

The European market is the most important outlet for Icelandic agricultural products. Iceland is a member of the European Economic Area (EEA), which gives it full access to the EU without requiring membership in the body. But progress in fish-processing technology and transport has opened up new trade possibilities with other countries. Exports to Japan are increasing and **emerging markets**, like China and Korea, hold promise for the future. Attempts to further open markets in the fisheries sector have given Iceland virtually **tariff**-free access for most of its exports to Europe. While EEA membership has reduced pressure for Iceland to join the EU, it risks being left on the sidelines as the European Union expands.

INDUSTRY

While a small country, Iceland has a strong industrial sector that accounts for 21 percent of its GDP. Like its 2 other main economic sectors, industry in Iceland is centered on its natural resources. Fish processing, aluminum smelting, ferrosilicon production, and geothermal power are its main industries.

ENERGY. Mineral resources are scarce in Iceland, though efforts are being made to develop deposits of diatomite (skeletal algae). Iceland has vast geothermal power sources (which develop power from the internal heat of the earth) and about 96 percent of the population enjoys geothermal heating in their homes. Geothermal energy plays an important role in Iceland's health-care system, which has shown interest in its medicinal possibilities. The Blue Lagoon, one of Iceland's most popular tourist attractions, is a good example of a combination of the traditional utilization of geothermal energy for economic reasons and its non-traditional utilization for healing. Geothermal energy is also used to generate electricity, and the effluents from power plants (extra thermal energy) can be used for many purposes in connection with spas and the tourist industry.

Iceland's abundant hydroelectric power sources are controlled by the government. The largest power station in Iceland has a capacity of 240 megawatts (mw). Other major hydroelectric stations are at Hrauneyjarfoss (210 mw) and Sigala (10 mw). Efforts are underway by the government to export hydroelectric energy to Europe by transporting it via submarine cables. The government is also investigating ways to expand its aluminum and ferrosilicon melting plants. One such venture is the Nordural aluminum plant, which accounted for a 1 percent growth rate in Iceland's 1998 GDP. Nordural is a wholly-owned $180 million investment by Columbia Ventures of the United States. As of 2001, plans were underway to build a new aluminum plant in the east of Iceland or expand existing ones. A new or expanded plant would increase investment and GDP growth.

SERVICES

Iceland's service sector accounts for approximately two-thirds of GDP, and has been rapidly increasing since the 1990s, particularly in the areas of financial services, tourism, software production, and biotechnology.

TOURISM. Tourism is a growing and important industry in Iceland. In fact, the national airline, Icelandair, is one of the country's largest employers. According to *Statistics Iceland,* by 1999 tourism accounted for 4.4 percent of GDP on net receipts of Ikr282 million, up from 3 percent just 10 years earlier. The industry is expanding with the government's promotion of the country's magnificent natural attractions such as whale-watching, hot volcanic springs, glaciers, and horseback riding throughout the country. By 1999 the country boasted 24 hotels and guesthouses. It is a promising economic growth area and its numbers increased by 16 percent in 2000.

BIOTECHNOLOGY. The sector that is showing the most rapid development is biotechnology. Iceland has unique natural resources and its position on the mid-Atlantic ridge is the source of its many hotsprings and the high-temperature areas where thermophilic bacteria (which thrive on heat) live, which can be utilized in various industries, especially pharmaceuticals. Scientists believe that thermophillic bacteria could lead to the development of better drugs and to more environmentally friendly forms of industry.

Iceland's rather limited human gene pool—due to its homogenous and cohesive population—makes it an invaluable laboratory for the study of the role of genes in the transmission of diseases. However, a fierce debate over genetics and individual rights erupted in Iceland in 1998. An Icelandic biotechnology company, deCode Genetics, wanted to include Icelanders' medical records, family trees (which are meticulously documented in Iceland; some can be traced as far back as over a thousand years ago), and genetic information into a single database. The company claimed the database would be beneficial to the health of Icelandic citizens, while critics argued such a project would simply serve the financial interests of deCode Genetics. The *Althingi* passed a bill in 1998 which allowed the Ministry of Health and Social Security to grant a license to create and operate an Icelandic Health Sector Database (IHD). In 2000, the Ministry awarded a 12-year license to Islensk erfdagreining, a subsidiary of deCode, to build and run the IHD, which has been operational since 2001.

FINANCE. Three commercial banks, with branches and savings banks, operate in Iceland. Investment credit funds, insurance companies, private pension funds, and securities firms are among Iceland's financial institutions. During the 1980s, the financial sector was **deregulated** and reformed to help bring inflation under control.

INTERNATIONAL TRADE

Historically, Iceland has been late in joining major trade agreements. It joined the General Agreement on Tariffs and Trade (GATT) in 1968 and the European Free Trade Association (EFTA) in 1970. It entered into a free trade agreement covering all industrial products with the European Economic Community (now called the EU) in 1972. In the 1990s, Iceland was the last of the EFTA countries to ratify the European Economic Area Agreement (EEA) and did so only after the longest debate in the history of the *Althingi*. It comes then as no surprise that Iceland has decided at the moment not to become a full member of the EU. Self-protection and self-preservation have characterized Iceland's foreign trade policy since its independence from Denmark.

Iceland's international treaties have strengthened foreign trade. Membership in the EEA in 1994 and the Uruguay Round agreement brought greater market access for Iceland's exports, capital, labor, and goods and services, especially seafood products. Agriculture is heavily subsidized and protected by the government, with some tariffs ranging as high as 700 percent.

Trade (expressed in billions of US$): Iceland

	Exports	Imports
1975	.306	.484
1980	.918	.999
1985	.815	.905
1990	1.592	1.680
1995	1.804	1.756
1998	2.050	2.489

SOURCE: International Monetary Fund. *International Financial Statistics Yearbook 1999.*

Exchange rates: Iceland

Icelandic kronur (IKr) per US$1	
Jan 2001	84.810
2000	78.676
1999	72.335
1998	70.958
1997	70.904
1996	66.500

SOURCE: CIA *World Factbook 2001* [ONLINE].

The question of Iceland's relationship with the EU and its possibility of becoming a member depend heavily on protection and control of its fishing industry and natural resources. The Icelandic government and the people pay close attention to the EU's resource policy, especially the Common Fisheries Policy, which is based on the premise that fisheries resources are in principle the common property of the member EU states. While this policy may not be a major obstacle to Iceland joining the EU, it could prove to be a stumbling block, calling for a creative solution in order for Icelanders to be comfortable with EU membership.

In 1999, Iceland had total exports of US$2.0 billion and imports of US$2.489 billion. Iceland's **trade deficit** widened in 2000 due to rapid import growth coinciding with a slow rise in exports. Exports did increase by 3 percent despite a slight contraction in the export of marine products. In 2000, marine exports accounted for 6 percent of total exports as compared with 68 percent in 1999. The drop in marine exports was attributed to a 31 percent growth in the value of aluminum exports—the result of increased production and favorable world prices.

In 1999, 69 percent of Iceland's exports and 66 percent of its imports came from trade with EEA countries. Germany and the United Kingdom are Iceland's most important trading partners in the EEA, with Germany accounting for 13.1 percent of Iceland's exports and 11.8 percent of its imports, and the U.K. accounting for 19.7 percent of exports and 9.2 percent of imports. The United States is the single largest trading partner outside the EEA, with 14.7 percent of exports and 10.9 percent of imports.

MONEY

In light of the recent depreciation of the króna and the threat of high inflation for 2001, the Central Bank of Iceland will likely continue its conservative fiscal policy in 2001–02 to tighten the money supply and lower domestic demand for goods and services. Inflation has eased slightly as a result, although it was recorded at a high 4.6 percent in November 2000 as Iceland's economy **overheated**. The Central Bank announced in March of 2001 that its desired inflation target was under 3 percent, and that it would take action when inflation deviated substantially from that figure.

Public finances are in good shape due to the government's conservative fiscal policies and debt consolidation, which it started in 2000. The government has implemented its program in response to the recent signals of economic troubles, which were caused by high inflation and a growing budgetary deficit.

Privatization and mergers between large private companies continued in 2001. In October of 2000, the government permitted the merger of 2 of the biggest Icelandic banks: the National Bank of Iceland and Agricultural Bank of Iceland. In May of 2000 the country's largest investment and corporate bank, Icelandic Investment Bank (FBA), merged with a leader in **retail** banking, Islandsbanki, creating IslandsbankiFBA.

POVERTY AND WEALTH

Icelanders enjoy a high quality of life, and poverty is practically nonexistent. Keeping in line with the reserved character of Icelanders, there is not much conspicuous consumption of wealth, despite the high standard of living. This contrasts to life in 18th century Iceland, which was marked by economic troubles and a drop in the population. Economic conditions improved and population numbers grew throughout the 19th and

GDP per Capita (US$)

Country	1975	1980	1985	1990	1998
Iceland	17,445	22,609	23,977	26,510	29,488
United States	19,364	21,529	23,200	25,363	29,683
United Kingdom	13,015	14,205	15,546	18,032	20,237
Norway	19,022	23,595	27,113	28,840	36,806

SOURCE: United Nations. *Human Development Report 2000; Trends in human development and per capita income.*

Household Consumption in PPP Terms

Country	All food	Clothing and footwear	Fuel and power[a]	Health care[b]	Education[b]	Transport & Communications	Other
Iceland	16	6	8	3	10	9	48
United States	13	9	9	4	6	8	51
United Kingdom	14	7	9	3	3	6	58
Norway	16	7	11	5	4	6	51

Data represent percentage of consumption in PPP terms.
[a]Excludes energy used for transport.
[b]Includes government and private expenditures.

SOURCE: World Bank. *World Development Indicators 2000.*

early 20th centuries. Following World War II, Iceland experienced an economic boom with a marked rise in its standard of living.

Icelanders, regardless of their economic circumstances, have access to the excellent health services. The social security system provides for pension insurance, occupational injury insurance, health insurance, and maternity leave. The government finances health care through taxation, and hospitalization is free. All hospital inpatient services are free and other medical services cost little. Icelanders have one of the longest life expectancies in the world.

The Icelandic government provides a number of welfare services for its citizens, including unemployment insurance, allowances for families who have children, and pensions for the elderly and disabled. Nearly all schools and universities in Iceland are free for its citizens. All students are required by law to attend school until the age of 16. Most students attend a 4-year academic college when they turn 16 and then continue their studies at the University of Iceland. A number of technical and vocational schools exist as well. Access to higher education is quite good for the young men and women of Iceland.

WORKING CONDITIONS

In the 20th century, 2 societal trends affected the Icelandic labor market: higher participation of women and changes in education. More women of all ages—many highly educated—entered the labor market. On the average, though, women still earn less money than men do.

Unemployment is extremely low in Iceland, a trend that does not seem to be changing. One of the downsides of Iceland's low unemployment is that it has created an extremely tight labor market and most Icelanders have very long workdays, some of the longest in Europe. In 2000, the unemployment rate registered at 1 percent, and in October 2000 it reached its lowest level since 1988 at 0.6 percent. Accordingly, there is a high demand for labor, especially in Reykjavík, though less so in the rest of the country. To meet labor demands, the government allowed for an increase in the number of work permits issued to foreigners. Despite the demand for labor, wage increases have been slow to rise.

About 8 percent of Icelandic workers belong to unions. The Industrial Relations Act of 1938 gives workers the right to form unions open to all persons working in a particular trade within a district. For example, carpenters are allowed to form unions in their own hometown or city to ensure their employment rights are being met and protected.

COUNTRY HISTORY AND ECONOMIC DEVELOPMENT

874. Iceland is settled by Norsemen. Ingólfur Arnarson is said to be the first settler, arriving with his family in present-day Reykjavík.

930. The ruling chiefs of Iceland establish a republican constitution and an assembly, the *Althingi,* the oldest parliament in the world.

1000. Christianity adopted in Iceland; Greenland discovered and colonized by Icelanders.

1262. Iceland enters into a treaty establishing a union with the Norwegian monarchy.

1397. Norway, Sweden, and Denmark form the Kalmar Union. Iceland falls under the sovereignty of the Danish crown but retains constitutional status.

1800. *Althingi* abolished. Iceland fully under the Danish crown.

1843. *Althingi* reestablished as a consultative assembly.

1874. Denmark grants Iceland home rule. Icelandic constitution written (revised in 1903).

1918. An agreement between Iceland and Denmark, the Act of Union, recognizes Iceland as a fully sovereign state under the Danish crown.

1940. When the German army occupies Denmark at the start of World War II, British military forces arrive to defend Iceland.

1941. The British pass responsibility for Iceland's defense to the United States under a U.S.-Icelandic defense agreement.

1944. Iceland formally becomes an independent republic.

1949. Iceland becomes a member of the North Atlantic Treaty Organization (NATO).

1968. Iceland joins the General Agreement on Tariffs and Trade (GATT).

1970. Iceland joins the European Free Trade Association (EFTA).

1972. Iceland enters a free trade agreement with the European Economic Community.

1980. Icelanders elect the world's first woman president, Vigdis Finnbogadottir; she goes on to serve 4 4-year terms.

1992. Iceland joins the Western European Union (WEU).

1994. Iceland becomes a member of the European Economic Area (EEA).

FUTURE TRENDS

Iceland has entered the 21st century on an economic high note. A tight fiscal policy, lowered inflation, exceptional social services, access to education, high literacy rates, and extremely low unemployment levels have all contributed to the good quality of life enjoyed by Icelanders.

Foreign trade and policy remain controversial areas, especially membership into the European Union, and the protection of fishing resources will remain high on Iceland's political and economic agenda. Debates over the pros and cons of EU membership will continue both inside and outside of the government, especially since the opposition leftist Alliance party is expected to adopt a pro-EU stance.

In 2001, the government looked to continue its policy of tight fiscal and budgetary restraint and the reduction of public debt. Privatization will likely continue, particularly with banks and financial companies. Interest rate increases are expected to lower any rising inflation. Economic growth is expected to slow somewhat in 2001. Overall, Iceland's economic policy and its political life appear to continue on a stable and carefully charted course.

DEPENDENCIES

Iceland has no territories or colonies.

BIBLIOGRAPHY

Central Bank of Iceland. *The Economy of Iceland (Autumn 2000).* Reykjavík, Iceland: Central Bank of Iceland, 2000.

Central Bank of Iceland: *Welcome to the Central Bank of Iceland.* <http://www.sedlabanki.is/interpro/sedlabanki/sedlabanki.nsf/pages/english-front>. Accessed June 2000.

Economist Intelligence Unit. *Country Report: Denmark and Iceland, January 2001.* London: Economist Intelligence Unit, 2001.

"Happy Family?" from "Survey: The Nordic Countries." *The Economist.* 21 January 1999.

Iceland. <http://www.iceland.org>. Accessed December 2000.

Information Centre of The Icelandic Ministry of Fisheries. *Marine Stocks: Fish, Shellfish and Crustaceans.* <http://www.fisheries.is/stocks/index.htm>. Accessed April 2001.

"Norse Code." *The Economist.* December 1998.

Statistics Iceland. *Statistics Iceland, 2000.* <http://www.statice.is>. Accessed April 2001.

U.S. Central Intelligence Agency. *World Factbook 2000.* <http://www.odci.gov/cia/publications/factbook/index.html>. Accessed July 2001.

U.S. Department of State. *Background Notes: Iceland.* <http://www.state.gov/www/background_notes/iceland_9910_bgn.html>. Accessed July 2001.

World Trade Organization. "Trade Policy Reviews: Iceland: January 2000." *World Trade Organization.* <http://www.wto.org/english/tratop_e/tpr_e/tp12_e.htm>. Accessed February 2001.

—Lynn Mahoney

IRELAND

The Republic of Ireland
Éire

CAPITAL: Dublin.

MONETARY UNIT: Irish Pound (I£). One Irish pound equals 100 pence (p). There are notes of 1, 2, 5, 10, 20, 50, and 100 pounds. There are 1, 2, 5, 10, 20, and 50 pence coins. Ireland is part of the European Monetary Union (EMU) implemented on paper in January 1999. From 1 January 2002, the pound will be phased out with the introduction of the euro. The euro has been set at 0.787564 Irish pence, with I£ equaling approximately 1.21 euros. There are 100 cents in the euro, which is denominated in notes of 5, 10, 20, 50, 100, 200, and 500 euros, and coins of 1 and 2 euros and 1, 2, 5, 10, 20, and 50 cents.

CHIEF EXPORTS: Machinery and equipment, computers (hardware and software), chemicals, pharmaceuticals, live animals, animal products.

CHIEF IMPORTS: Data processing equipment, other machinery and equipment, chemicals, petroleum and petroleum products, textiles, clothing.

GROSS DOMESTIC PRODUCT: US$83.6 billion (2000 est.).

BALANCE OF TRADE: **Exports:** US$73.8 billion (2000 est.). **Imports:** US$46.1 billion (2000 est.). [CIA *World Factbook* indicates exports to be US$66 billion (1999 est.) and imports to be US$44 billion (1999 est.).]

COUNTRY OVERVIEW

LOCATION AND SIZE. The Republic of Ireland constitutes 26 out of the 32 counties that make up the island of Ireland, with 6 northern counties under the jurisdiction of the United Kingdom. Situated in Western Europe, it is bordered on the east by the Irish Sea from the United Kingdom and bordered on the west by the North Atlantic Ocean. With a total area of 70,280 square kilometers (27,135 square miles) and a coastline measuring 1,448 kilometers (900 miles), the Republic of Ireland is slightly larger than the state of West Virginia. The capital city, Dublin, is located on the east coast.

POPULATION. The population of Ireland was estimated to be 3,797,257 in 2000. There has been a steady increase in the population since 1994 (3,586,000), marking a historic turn-about in demographic trends. This is attributed to growth in the economy, a decline in previously high levels of **emigration**, the return of former emigrants, and an increase in **immigration** to the point where net migration is inward. Despite having one of the lowest population densities in Europe, Ireland's population density has reached the highest sustained level since the foundation of the Republic in 1922.

Emigration lowered population to under 3 million in the early 1980s. Birth rates declined from a high of 17.6 per 1,000 in 1985 to a low of 13.4 in 1994, but this trend has slowly been reversed, reaching 15 per 1,000 in late 1998. If the population is to meet the demands of the labor market, further increases will be necessary. Government efforts to attract further immigration and to increase the population are marred by housing shortages and service deficiencies.

At the 1996 census, 40 percent of Ireland's population was under 25, and the Irish population is still relatively young, with only 11.33 percent over the age of 65. The people are largely concentrated in urban centers, with almost one-third of the total population living in the city of Dublin and its surrounding county. Population in the other major cities and their surrounding areas is on the increase. In the sparsely populated midlands and in the western and border counties, though, population is either stagnant or declining.

OVERVIEW OF ECONOMY

An economic policy that emphasized self-sufficiency and was characterized by huge **tariffs** on imports to

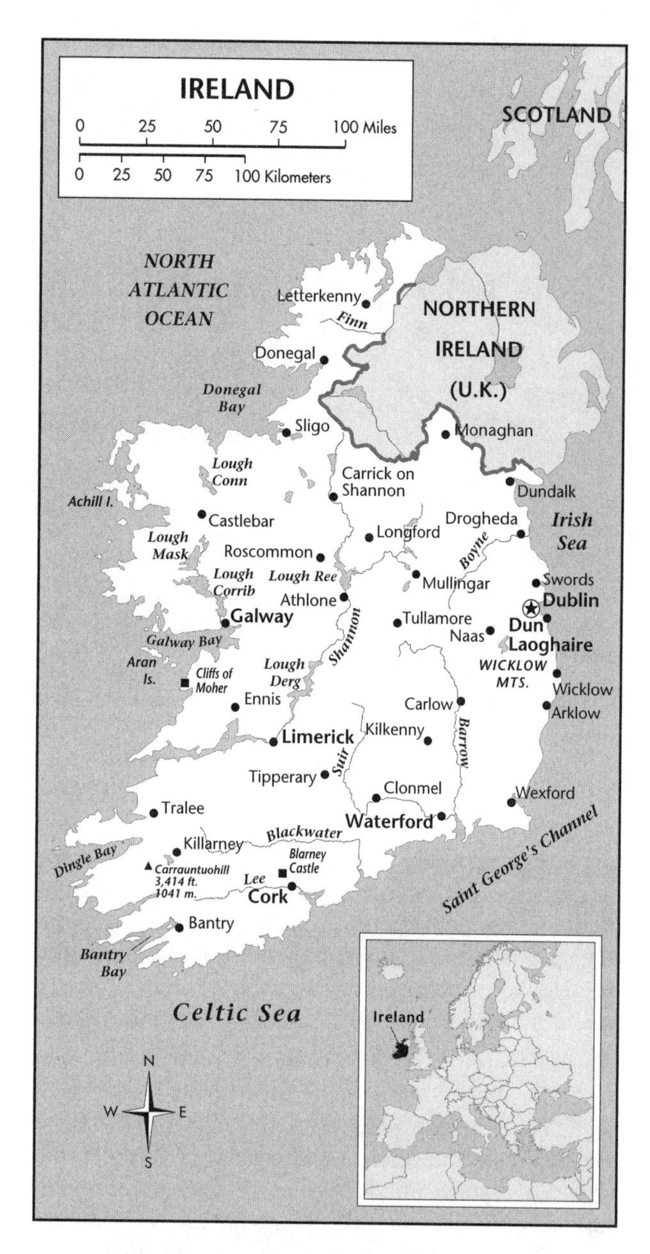

encourage indigenous growth dominated in Ireland until the late 1950s. This ideology was then abandoned in favor of a more open economic policy. Ireland's first economic boom followed this change. The failure of domestic over-spending to induce growth, along with negative global influences such as the oil crises of the 1970s, made this boom relatively short lived. The 1980s brought fast-rising **inflation** (up to 21 percent), unemployment close to 20 percent, emigration at unprecedented high levels (50,000 per year) and a soaring **national debt**.

Since the early 1990s, however, the Irish economy has produced high growth rates. It is integrated into the global trading system and, between 1994 and 1998, was the fastest growing economy in the countries of the Organization for Economic Cooperation and Development (OECD). The economy was forecast to continue expanding well in excess of any of its European Union (EU) partners during 2001 and 2002. Robust growth rates averaged 9 percent from 1995 to 1999 and some analysts predicted growth at 11 percent in 2001. Unemployment, which climbed to record levels beginning in the mid- to late 1980s, reaching 14.8 percent, fell to just 3.8 percent in 2000. Unemployment was predicted to fall below 3 percent by 2002. Living standards, measured by **gross domestic product** (GDP) per capita, were estimated to have caught up with the European average by late 1998.

This transformation can be credited to many forces, both domestic and global. Recent government policies have emphasized tight fiscal control alongside the creation of an environment highly attractive to enterprise, particularly international business. Policies based on "social consensus" and wage agreements negotiated by the government with business, farmers, trade unions and other social partners, have kept wages at moderate, business-friendly levels. A corporation tax of 10 percent, alongside grants to attract foreign business, has further contributed to the pro-business environment, as has the existence of a highly educated workforce.

EU regional policy has emphasized cash transfers to economically weaker and poorer member states. This is done to prepare these states to manage in a single market and currency. These transfers developed the Irish economy to a point where it could sustain growth. As an English-speaking country with access to the European market, Ireland is proving attractive as a base for international companies, particularly from the United States.

The reason behind the current economic boom is the high-tech manufacturing industry sector; in particular the foreign-owned multinational companies in this sector. Agriculture, while still remaining an important indigenous activity, is in decline. The industrial sector has seen growth rates higher than most industrial economies and accounts for 39 percent of GDP and about 80 percent of exports. It employs approximately 28 percent of the **labor force**. This dominance can be seen in the gap between GDP and **gross national product** (GNP), which was 15 percent lower in 1998. Although the service sector is smaller than that of other industrialized countries, it is nonetheless dominant and growing, accounting for 54.1 percent of GDP in 1998. Government remains heavily involved in the provision of health and transport services and, together with the private service sector, employs 63 percent of the workforce.

Successive Irish governments have maintained responsible **fiscal policies** over the last decade that have led to the reduction of national debt from 94.5 percent of GDP in 1993 to 56 percent of GDP in 1998. There have been concerns about the effects of current fiscal policy, with its emphasis on reducing **income tax**, on the high levels of inflation in the economy since late 1998. The government has argued that inflation is primarily due to external pressures such as the weak euro and high oil prices, which have caused increased consumer prices. Nonetheless, consumer price inflation peaked at 6.8 percent in the 12 months running up to June 2000, considerably higher than any other EU country.

POLITICS, GOVERNMENT, AND TAXATION

The Republic of Ireland is governed by a parliamentary democracy. Parliament consists of a Lower House, the Dáil (pronounced "doyl") and an upper house, the Seanad (pronounced "shinad"), or Senate. Together, the 2 houses and the president form the Oireachtas (pronounced "irrocktos"), or government. The Irish president, although directly elected, has relatively few formal powers and the government, elected by the Dáil from its membership, is led by the Taoiseach (pronounced "Teeshock"), or prime minister, who presides over a 15-member cabinet of ministers.

Fianna Fáil (pronounced "foil"), a highly organized, center-right party, dominates the party system, with popular support of between 35 and 45 percent in 2001. It leads a minority center-right coalition government (with the Progressive Democrats) that depends on the support of a number of independent TDs (member of parliament) in the Dáil for the 1997–2002 term. Fine Gael (pronounced "feena gale"), the second largest political party and commanding between 20 and 30 percent of the popular vote, also occupies the political center-right, though it has shifted more to the center and has developed a social-democratic and liberal agenda over the last 3 decades. Its support base is generally among the more affluent, but these class trends are not especially strong overall and many wealthy people, particularly from the business sector, support Fianna Fáil. Fine Gael led the 1995–97 "Rainbow" coalition government, thus referred to because of its inclusion of 3 parties and representation across the political spectrum. The Rainbow coalition included the Labor Party and the Democratic Left (a party further to the left), which has since merged with Labor.

Unlike practically all other European party systems, the Irish party system exhibits no strong left-right division. The 2 largest parties have not traditionally defined themselves in terms of ideology, but grew out of differences over the nationalist agenda at the time of independence. The Labor party, weak in comparison with its European counterparts, has consistently been the third largest party, commanding between 10 and 15 (sometimes more) percent of support nationally, and has considerable power in a system dominated by coalitions.

A number of tribunals have been in operation since 1997–98, investigating allegations of political corruption. The allegations involve unacceptable links between politicians and big business, corrupt practices in the planning process, and inept and negligent public service on sensitive health issues from the 1970s to the 1990s. The ensuing revelations are assumed to have adversely affected Fianna Fáil's popularity, but opinion polls have proved inconclusive in measuring the amount of support the party might have lost.

A number of smaller political parties are also important in Ireland. Polls conducted in 2000–01 gave the Progressive Democrats 4 to 5 percent support, the Green Party 3 to 4 percent and Sinn Féin (pronounced "shin fane"), an all-Ireland Republican party with links to the Irish Republican Army (IRA), between 2 and 6 percent. Sinn Féin's association with the provisional IRA, which is responsible for punishment beatings in Northern Ireland and vigilante activity in the Republic, could, with its increase in popular support, present larger parties with controversial questions over coalition formation.

There is currently a broad consensus among the major political parties on how to run the economy. It is unlikely that a new government coalition would significantly alter the current pro-business economic policy.

The tax system incorporates standard elements of tax on income, goods and services, capital transfers, business profits, and property, and operates a system of social insurance contributions. Income tax has been reduced substantially, to 20 percent and 40 percent, with incomes over I£17,000 subject to the higher rate (2000 budget). A controversial individualization of income tax was introduced in the 2000 budget, with the object of encouraging more women to enter the labor force. Goods bought and sold are subject to **value-added tax** (VAT) at 20 percent, which is comparatively high, while luxury goods such as alcohol, tobacco, and petrol are subject to high government **excise tax**. Capital gains tax on profits has been reduced to 20 percent, and corporation tax, levied at between 10 percent and 28 percent, is to change to 12.5 percent across the board by 2003. Both employers and employees are subject to a social insurance tax, pay-related social insurance (PSRI), and an unusual business-unfriendly measure shifted the burden of the contributions to business in the 2001 budget. In terms of social spending, a means-tested (eligibility determined by financial status) system operates, resulting in about a third of the population receiving free medical and dental treatment. However, state medical-card holders suffer from long waiting lists for treatment, as opposed to the more than 50 percent or so of the population who have private medical insurance.

In line with EU policy, recent governments stress the importance of competition. A competition authority with enhanced powers is responsible for investigating alleged breaches of competition law in all sectors. This affects overly regulated private service providers such as taxicab companies, and it is anticipated that the restrictive pub licensing laws will be tackled next.

Government control over the economy is restricted by Ireland's membership in the EU and the euro zone, as well as by its own policy that has made Ireland one of the most open economies in the world. While the European Central Bank (ECB) controls **monetary policy** and largely controls interest rates, the government does retain control over fiscal policy.

INFRASTRUCTURE, POWER, AND COMMUNICATIONS

Though vastly improved during the 1990s by grants of I£6 billion in European structural funds, the Republic of Ireland's **infrastructure** is still struggling to cope with the country's unprecedented economic growth. Long traffic delays and below average roads linking major business centers around the country are a potential threat to continued expansion. A late 1990s report commissioned by the Irish Business and Employers Association (IBEC) estimated that a further I£14 billion would have to be spent to raise the quality of the country's infrastructure to generally accepted European levels. Ireland's share of European structural funds for 2000 to 2006 has decreased to approximately I£3 billion, but increased government spending and planned joint public-private funding of projects should make up the shortfall.

Ireland has the most car-dependent transportation system in the EU, with roads carrying 86 percent of freight traffic and 97 percent of passenger traffic. Yet full inter-city motorways are not in place, making the links between Dublin and other major cities subject to heavy traffic and delays. Economic growth and increased consumer spending has pushed up car ownership levels dramatically, which, together with increased commercial traffic on the roads, has offset the considerable improvements of the 1990s. The road network is estimated to total 87,043 kilometers (54,089 miles) of paved roads and 5,457 kilometers (3,391 miles) of unpaved roads (1999).

Long rush hours and traffic gridlock occur in the major cities and gridlock in Dublin is estimated to cost the national economy around I£1.2 billion every year. Policies aiming to attract more daily users to the public transport system might take effect over the next decade. Following much debate and deliberation, the current government has commenced the implementation of a light rail system (3 lines) to cover some important routes into the capital, most importantly a link to the airport. This will add to the "Dart," Dublin's existing, relatively efficient suburban rail service, which consists of 5 lines covering 257 kilometers (160 miles) and 56 stations.

The railway linking Dublin to 2 major cities on the island, Belfast (Northern Ireland) and Cork, has been vastly improved over the last few years, but recent reports by external consultants have highlighted the poor, even dangerous, state of much of the rest of Ireland's 1,947-kilometer (1,210-mile) railway infrastructure.

Ireland has 3 international airports—at Dublin (east), Shannon (southwest), and Cork (south)—and 6 independent regional airports. Air traffic increased dramatically during the 1990s, with the number of passengers up from 6.8 million (1992) to 12.1 million (1997), while annual air freight traffic also doubled. Inevitably, these increases have led to congestion, especially at Dublin's airport, and a major capital investment program launched by the government is nearing completion, with similar projects to follow in Cork and Shannon. Cargo traffic is similar, with increases of up to 50 percent in cargo tonnage and passenger traffic passing through the main ports over the 1990s. The government recognizes that capacity must increase if major congestion is to be avoided.

Liberalization in the telecommunications sector, completed in 1998, increased the number of providers from just 1 state-owned company to 29 fully licensed telecommunications companies, operating in residential,

Communications

Country	Newspapers	Radios	TV Sets[a]	Cable subscribers[a]	Mobile Phones[a]	Fax Machines[a]	Personal Computers[a]	Internet Hosts[b]	Internet Users[b]
	1996	1997	1998	1998	1998	1998	1998	1999	1999
Ireland	150	699	403	171.1	257	27.4	271.7	156.68	679
United States	215	2,146	847	244.3	256	78.4	458.6	1,508.77	74,100
United Kingdom	329	1,436	645	45.9	252	33.9	263.0	270.60	12,500
France	218	937	601	27.5	188	47.4	207.8	110.64	5,370

[a]Data are from International Telecommunication Union, *World Telecommunication Development Report 1999* and are per 1,000 people.
[b]Data are from the Internet Software Consortium (http://www.isc.org) and are per 10,000 people.

SOURCE: World Bank. *World Development Indicators 2000.*

corporate, and specialized data services sectors. The government hopes that liberalization and the resulting competition in the market will encourage private investment and improve the state's poorly developed telecommunications infrastructure. The mobile phone market has been dominated by competition between Eircell and Esat Digiphone. Both have now been bought by the British giants, Vodaphone and British Telecom (BT), respectively, while a third mobile phone company, Meteor, has recently entered the market.

Energy consumption is, not surprisingly, on the increase. Total energy consumption rose from 8.5 million metric tons (9.35 million tons) in 1996 to 9.5 million metric tons (10.45 million tons) in 1997, with household use accounting for 3.6 million metric tons (3.6 million tons). Two-thirds of energy is supplied by imported coal and oil, with the remaining third supplied by indigenous peat (12 percent of the total) and natural gas. The distribution of gas, oil, peat, and electricity remains state dominated, though industrial users hope that recent liberalization of the gas and electricity markets will result in a lowering of prices.

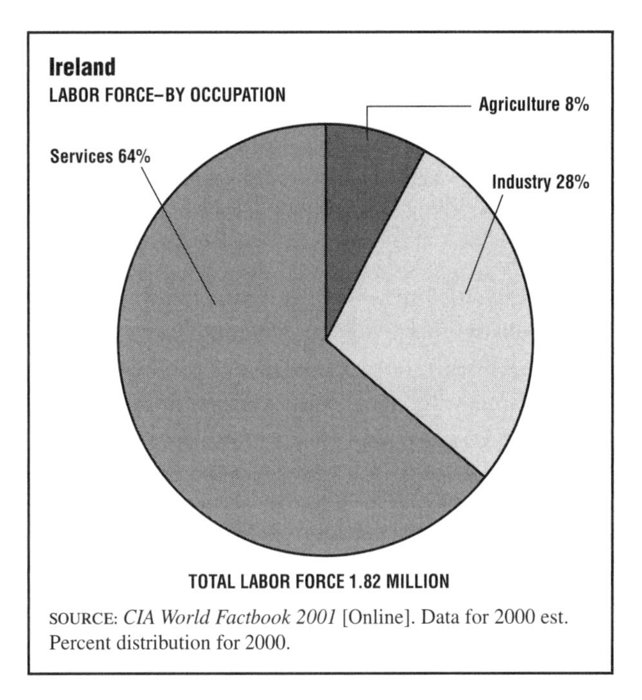

SOURCE: *CIA World Factbook 2001* [Online]. Data for 2000 est. Percent distribution for 2000.

ECONOMIC SECTORS

Strong growth (55 percent growth from 1993 to 1999) has been the recent trend in the Irish economy, but it lacks consistency across all sectors. Agriculture (forestry and fishing), as a share of total GDP, has seen a steady decline, while the fastest growth has occurred in industry, particularly high-tech industry. The expanding service sector accounted for 56 percent of GDP in 1998. Ireland's economy has remained the fastest growing economy in the EU and compares favorably with developed economies worldwide in terms of growth, output, trade volume, and employment levels.

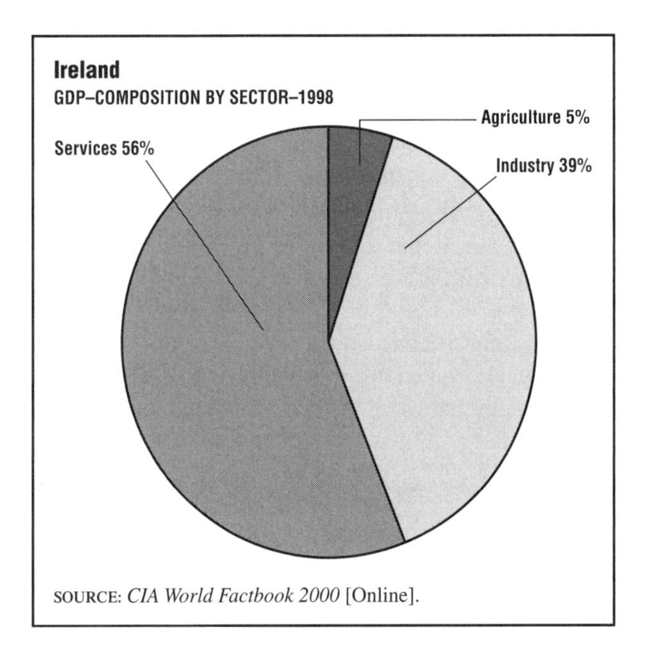

SOURCE: *CIA World Factbook 2000* [Online].

AGRICULTURE

Ireland's mild temperature, high rainfall, and fertile land offer ideal conditions for agriculture and, despite a pattern of decline over the past 2 decades, agricultural activity remains an important employer in rural and remote regions of the country.

The drop in agricultural output from 16 percent of GDP in 1975 to just 5 percent in 1998 reflects only a relative decline when measured against the steady increase in GDP driven by other sectors. While the fall in prices of agricultural products has been sharp, the volume of output has seen only a small decrease. The industry suffers from over-capacity and falling incomes and is increasingly reliant on EU **subsidies** and fixed prices. The number of small farmers remains high for an industrialized country, and many small farmers take up other employment to subsidize their income. While average farm size (29.5 hectares or 73 acres) is slowly increasing, the Irish Farmer's Association asserts that farm size remains the single biggest obstacle to generating adequate income in the agricultural sector. Adjusting to EU measures to bring prices more in line with world agricultural prices seems unlikely to help the industry, while reducing high levels of pollution in the waterways to comply with EU regulations is also not expected to aid farming profitability.

Average farming incomes fell by 6.2 percent in 1997, even though productivity per individual farmer increased significantly over the last decade. On 40 percent of all farms, the annual income was only I£5,000. On a further 25 percent of farms, it rose to between I£5,000 and I£10,000. Combined employment in agriculture, forestry, and fisheries fell from 175,000 at the beginning of the 1990s to 142,000 at the end of the decade. Figures that include related food-processing industries put employment at 176,000 in 1999, representing 12 percent of all workers in employment. Some figures estimate that agriculture generates so many service sector jobs that it indirectly accounts for 350,000 jobs (23 percent of the labor force).

BEEF AND OTHER LIVESTOCK. The most productive agricultural sector is the largely export-oriented beef and livestock industry, which accounted for 50 percent of output value in 1998. Cattle and sheep farming have, however, been hard hit by a number of crises. After EU agreements in 1999 to reduce beef prices, in February 2000, farmers were badly affected when BSE (Bovine Spongiform Encephalopathy), or "Mad Cow" disease, resulted in a 27 percent drop in beef consumption in the key European market. In February-March 2001, the unprecedentedly severe outbreak of foot and mouth disease in herds in Britain, with pockets in Northern Ireland and France also affected, brought another enormous challenge to the industry, threatening the export markets of Ireland and all the EU countries.

Overall, output decreased during the 1990s, with the annual value of livestock falling from I£1,885 million in 1993 to I£1,761 million in 1997. This represents decreases in the overall value of cattle livestock from I£1,349 million to I£1,097 million (1993 to 1997), with the value from pigs, sheep, and lambs showing small net increases in output value.

Livestock products, the most prominent of which is milk, also suffered a general, if undramatic decline in output during the mid-1990s, from I£1,132 to I£1,113 million. Crops output, with cereals and root crops dominant, also decreased marginally—from I£3,431 to I£3,315 million—during this period. Sugar beet, wheat, and barley yielded the highest commercial value (1997), with milk, eggs, and fresh vegetables also important products.

FORESTRY AND FISHING. Despite its reputation as a land of abundant greenery, Ireland has the lowest level of forest cover in Europe, with only 8 percent of the land under woodland, against a 25 percent average elsewhere. But this 8 percent is a considerable improvement from the 1 percent level of cover at the foundation of the state in 1922 and is the result of government reforestation programs. Current EU policy serves to encourage reforestation and the development of a timber-based agricultural sector. Reflecting this, timber output was expected (EIU estimate) to have reached 3 million square meters of timber by 2000. This would provide for an increase in the domestic market's share of local timber, as it previously imported 45 percent of its timber requirements.

Given Ireland's geographical position, fishing has been a naturally important economic activity, particularly in rural coastal areas where there are few other industries. The fishing industry has evolved to incorporate more diverse forms of activity such as fish farming, and employment rates have increased by 40 percent since 1980. Full and part-time workers together accounted for 16,000 jobs either directly or indirectly connected to the fishing industry in 1999. The value of exports increased from I£154 million in the early years of the 1990s to a peak of I£240 million in 1997. EU grants and government spending ensure that the industry will continue to expand.

INDUSTRY

The industrial sector has maintained its share in total economic activity at 39 percent of GDP throughout most of the 1980s and 1990s. This trend is unusual in developed countries and reflects strong growth. Although marking a slight slowdown from 1995 to 1998, growth in 1999 was high at 10.5 percent. Strong performance from both foreign-owned and indigenous Irish industry, primarily in the high-tech manufacturing sector, has driven the growth.

Significant reserves of zinc and lead ores, natural gas, and peat are to be found, and the latter 2 supply a third of domestic energy demand. Zinc and lead ores sustain one of the biggest zinc and lead mines in Europe and approximately 4,000 jobs. Ireland is a small country with limited natural resources, and a well-developed, open, and globally-integrated industrial economic policy is therefore essential to economic health.

HIGH-TECH MANUFACTURING. There are more than 1,000 foreign-owned companies operating in Ireland, mostly, though not all, in the high-tech manufacturing sector. Foreign-owned manufacturing accounts for more than half of the country's total manufacturing output. In 1998, foreign companies produced more than two-thirds of export goods and employed around 45 percent of the manufacturing sector's workforce, or 28 percent (468,800) of the total workforce. Most foreign-owned manufacturing is concentrated in high-tech sectors such as chemical production, metals, electrical engineering, and computer hardware.

Between 1993 and 1997, output in metals and engineering increased by 96 percent and employment by 49 percent. Leading metal output is the manufacture of agricultural and transport machinery. In the chemicals sector, output increased by 116 percent and employment by 38 percent. Both sectors continue to enjoy high productivity.

Performance in the indigenous high-tech sector has also been impressive. The sector's growth in volume of output increased by 37 percent from 1987 to 1995, contributing to a 113 percent increase overall (including foreign-owned). World-class manufacturing and management standards have developed, partly encouraged by the productive foreign-owned companies and by growing links between foreign-owned and indigenous sectors. An increasing percentage of inputs purchased by foreign-owned industry for production are supplied by indigenous Irish industry. Total expenditure of foreign companies in the Irish economy has reached I£6.9 billion, up from I£2.9 billion in 1990. By 1999, this economically healthy situation had brought an unprecedented 30,000 worker increase in employment by Irish-owned manufacturing firms since 1992.

Also well represented in this high-tech sector are the Industrial Development Authority (IDA)-targeted sectors of the pharmaceutical and computer software industries. The IDA is a government body charged with the task of attracting foreign investment and is part of an umbrella organization called Enterprise Ireland. The concentration of high-tech industries they have encouraged has created a clustering effect that facilitates self-sustaining growth.

TEXTILES, CLOTHING, AND FOOTWEAR. Dominated by indigenous industry, the labor-intensive textile, clothing, and footwear sectors registered no significant growth during the 1990s into the 2000s. They have suffered as a result of competition from cheaper foreign imports. Textile production in Ireland remained stagnant during the late 1990s, and employment in the sector fell by approximately 20 percent. Clothing and footwear output fell by almost 20 percent between 1993 and 1997 and has remained at that level.

FOOD, DRINK, AND TOBACCO. Food, drink, and tobacco production recorded the strongest growth in the traditional indigenous manufacturing sector, with production output, which is aimed at both domestic and export markets, increasing by 6.1 percent in 1997. Providing the backbone for the food industry is the production of beef, milk, eggs, fresh vegetables, barley, sugar-beets, and wheat.

CONSTRUCTION. A combination of increased business investment, infrastructure development and an acute housing shortage resulted in an increase in the value of construction output from I£13.7 billion in 1993 to I£16.1 billion, or 14.2 percent of GDP in 1996. In 1998, the bulk of construction was directed at residential buildings. Quarried stone exists as an important indigenous supply for the construction industry. Conditions ensured that this boom continued into 2001, but it is threatened by a shortage of labor and the accompanying effect of increasing wage demands.

The open-market economic policies adopted by successive Irish governments since the late 1980s can, in large part, explain the rapid expansion of the industrial sector, particularly the high-tech industrial sector. **Foreign direct investment** has been attracted by a number of factors, including a carefully built, business-friendly environment, a relatively inexpensive but highly skilled labor force, access to the EU market, and a range of incentives offered by the Irish government. Economic policy is currently establishing new priorities aimed at attracting industry to the poorer regions of the country, strengthening the roots of foreign-owned industry, and encouraging research and development programs.

SERVICES

Services accounted for approximately 63 percent of employment and 54.1 percent of GDP in 1999. Banking and finance and retailing and tourism dominate the private services sector, with software engineering and business consulting services growing in importance. State-owned industries dominate the provision of education, health, distribution, transport, and communication services, accounting for 18 percent of GDP in 1997. Private service providers are slowly entering these markets.

FINANCIAL SERVICES. Availability of branch banking is dominated by 4 main clearing banks—Bank of Ireland, Allied Irish Banks, Ulster Bank, and National Irish Bank. Since the early 1990s, banks and building societies have become increasingly involved in the providing of financial services, and total employment provided by these institutions increased from 25,200 in 1994 to just under 30,000 in 1998. A scheme introduced in 1987 created incentives to make Ireland an attractive base for foreign financial institutions. A particular incentive was the setting of corporation taxes at a low 10 percent. More than 300 banks, mostly North American and European, are established in the Irish Financial Services Center (IFSC) in Dublin, offering specialized services such as investment banking, fund management, capital markets, leasing, and re-insurance. The IFSC has created direct employment for between 5,000 and 7,000 people, as well as a considerable proportion of indirect employment connected with Dublin's concentration of banks.

TOURISM. The country's famously green and beautiful landscape, its fine beaches, a culture of small, atmospheric, and sociable pubs, and the friendliness of its people attract many tourists. Recent tourist expansion has largely resulted from Dublin's elevation to a very popular weekend-break destination, coupled with the government tourist board's overseas promotion programs, which highlight the country's attractions for fishing, walking, and golfing enthusiasts. Total revenue from tourism reached I£2.8 billion—more than 5.7 percent of GDP—

in 1997. This dropped slightly in 1999 (I£2.5 billion), but two-thirds of that year's revenue was generated by the arrival of more than 6 million overseas visitors. At the end of the 1990s, at least 120,000 jobs were estimated to depend on tourism. The biggest threat to the tourist industry is the poor quality of services. These are the result of a shortage of skilled labor, as well as increasing industrial unrest that periodically causes transportation disruptions and brings traffic chaos. Workers in the tourist industry have tended to be worse off than those in other sectors, but the I£4.50 per hour minimum wage introduced in 2000 stood to eradicate the worst cases of under-payment.

RETAIL. Economic expansion has facilitated increased diversification in the indigenous retailing industry. With consumer spending high, **retail** sales expanded by 53 percent in real value terms in 1997 and by 32 percent in volume terms. The surge in the growth of the retailing sector has attracted a large number of groups from the United Kingdom (UK), which have brought competition that has helped to control consumer price inflation. The volume of retail sales increased by 14 percent in the first quarter of 2000, with the purchase of new cars in the first half of that year up 42.9 percent.

INTERNATIONAL TRADE

Ireland has achieved the highest **trade surplus** relative to GDP in the EU and is in the top 20 exporting countries in the world. In 1999, the total value of the country's exports recorded a huge surplus, reaching I£44.8 billion, against imports of I£20.63 billion. The balance of trade between exports and imports continued the strong upward trend from I£13.7 billion (25 percent of GDP) in 1998 to I£24.17 billion in 1999. Figures from the first half of 2000 indicated a further increase. However, despite a robust 24 percent growth in export rates in 2000, trends indicated that import growth rates in response to high consumer demand would exceed export growth rates in 2000–01, thus threatening the surplus in the long run. The EU (including the UK) remains Ireland's most important export market. In 1998, export revenues from the EU accounted for 67 percent (I£30.27 billion) of total exports, with the UK contributing almost I£10 billion, or 22 percent of the total. Germany (14.6 percent), France, Italy, and the Netherlands are the other key European destinations, while the United States accounted for I£6.14 billion (13.7 percent) in 1998. Given the weak euro and the presence of many U.S. multi-nationals in Ireland, there are indications that the United States is set to become Ireland's biggest export market. Exports to U.S. markets increased by 54 percent to I£6.8 billion in the first 6 months of 2000. Exports to the UK, a non-euro zone, also increased by 22 percent during this period to I£6.9 billion. Ireland is a major center of computer manufacture, with U.S.-owned corporations such as Dell conducting operations there. The high-tech sectors recorded Ireland's largest export increases in 2000, with computer equipment leading the field at I£8.1 billion. The export of organic chemicals was valued at I£7.3 billion, and electronic machinery at I£2.9 billion. Chemicals, transport equipment, and machinery (including computers) accounted for 80 percent of the increase in exports between 1993 and 1997. While foreign multinationals dominate these sectors, there are positive signs of increasing domestic production in high tech manufacturing industries, such as the production of chemicals, software development, optical equipment, and electronic equipment. The production of electronic equipment and optical equipment supplied 9.2 percent of domestic exports in 1997. However, exports represented only 34 percent of domestic manufacture, while up to 90 percent of foreign-owned company output was exported. In 1997, food and livestock remained the fourth largest export commodities, with food, drink, and tobacco together accounting for an important, though declining, percentage of indigenous exports (53.9 percent, down from 61.9 percent in 1991). Fuel, lubricants, and crude materials also remain important.

Trade (expressed in billions of US$): Ireland

	Exports	Imports
1975	3.193	3.778
1980	8.398	11.153
1985	10.358	10.020
1990	23.743	20.669
1995	44.250	32.638
1998	63.959	44.355

SOURCE: International Monetary Fund. *International Financial Statistics Yearbook 1999.*

The value of imports has increased rapidly, from I£13.1 billion in 1998 to I£34.66 billion in 1999. Their value for the first 6 months of 2000 was at I£20.7 billion, recording a 25 percent increase. Once again, the high-tech sector dominated, with imports of computer equipment increasing by 28 percent and manufacturing industry inputs by 26 percent. Imports of road vehicles also increased dramatically during this period. Despite the weak euro, the UK and the United States remain Ireland's largest sources of imports, both supplying goods in the first half of 2000, showing an increase in volume of 20 percent. Machinery and transport equipment dominated the volume of imports and accounted for I£15.7 billion in 1998, with chemicals and miscellaneous manufacturing goods accounting for I£3.4 billion each. Food and live animals accounted for the next largest share in total import value at I£1.8 billion in 1998. Live animals are both imported and exported. A factor distinguishing

Exchange rates: Ireland

Irish pounds per US$1	
Jan 2001	1.0658
2000	1.0823
1999	0.9374
1998	0.7014
1997	0.6588
1996	0.6248

SOURCE: CIA *World Factbook 2001* [ONLINE].

GDP per Capita (US$)

Country	1975	1980	1985	1990	1998
Ireland	8,605	10,044	10,944	13,907	23,422
United States	19,364	21,529	23,200	25,363	29,683
United Kingdom	13,015	14,205	15,546	18,032	20,237
France	18,730	21,374	22,510	25,624	27,975

SOURCE: United Nations. *Human Development Report 2000; Trends in human development and per capita income.*

Ireland from its 10 euro-zone partners is its relatively low volume of trade within the euro zone—20 percent of imports and 45 percent of exports in 1998. Current trends do not predict a rapid change in this pattern.

MONEY

Ireland severed its links with the British pound sterling in 1979 and relinquished control over its monetary policy to the European Central Bank (ECB) in 1999. Consequently, the government is no longer free to use **exchange rates** as part of economic and trade policy. The relationship of the Irish pound to the sterling and the U.S. dollar is determined by their relationship to the euro, which itself has been consistently weak since its launch in January 1999. Higher interest rates have been introduced by the ECB to help the euro, but they would need to be considerably higher to curb Irish domestic spending and demand. A downturn in the U.S. economy could, perhaps, result in a strengthening of the euro. This would reduce the costs of imports and help curb inflation, but would at the same time decrease the value of exports. The Irish Stock Exchange (ISE) separated from the international stock exchange of the United Kingdom and the Republic of Ireland in 1995. Since then, in keeping with global trends, the ISE has grown rapidly, with **market capitalization** increasing from I£7.4 billion in 1992 to I£66.8 billion in 1998, and 81 companies listed in 2001. It appears, however, to be too small to attract significant levels of venture capital, and Irish technology companies tend to look to the NASDAQ or the EASDAQ (proposed Europe equivalent) for this reason. With this coordination of stock exchanges across Europe, investor participation in Irish stocks may increase.

POVERTY AND WEALTH

Unprecedented growth in the Irish economy during the late 1990s saw living standards in terms of per capita GDP reach the EU average for the first time in 1998. However, rapid growth does not automatically translate into a better quality of life, and Ireland is by no means immune to the risk in all industrial societies: that of creating a society where the rich get richer and the poor stay poor.

Inequality in Ireland falls generally into 2 categories. The first is essentially that of poverty traditionally created by unemployment. Despite almost **full employment**, pockets of deprivation characterized by long-term unemployment, high dropout rates from education, and a dependency culture, prevail. These disadvantaged groups, frequently plagued by social ills such as the drug-culture, suffer markedly from the considerable increase in the cost of living. To relieve deprivation of this nature requires a sustained effort at introducing more comprehensive social policies. In 2000, the Irish government spent only 16 percent of GDP on social welfare compared to the EU average of 28 percent.

The second category of poverty, arising from the disparity of income among the employed, affects a larger number of households. Comparative studies published in Brian Nolan, Chris Whelan, and P.J. O'Connell's *Bust to Boom*, reveal Ireland, along with the UK and Portugal, to have a high rate of **relative income poverty** compared to other EU member states. While there were improvements in income earned by the unskilled, skilled, highly

Distribution of Income or Consumption by Percentage Share: Ireland

Lowest 10%	2.5
Lowest 20%	6.7
Second 20%	11.6
Third 20%	16.4
Fourth 20%	22.4
Highest 20%	42.9
Highest 10%	27.4

Survey year: 1987

Note: This information refers to income shares by percentiles of the population and is ranked by per capita income.

SOURCE: *2000 World Development Indicators* [CD-ROM].

Household Consumption in PPP Terms

Country	All food	Clothing and footwear	Fuel and power[a]	Health care[b]	Education[b]	Transport & Communications	Other
Ireland	21	9	10	4	7	10	40
United States	13	9	9	4	6	8	51
United Kingdom	14	7	9	3	3	6	58
France	22	7	9	3	8	12	40

Data represent percentage of consumption in PPP terms.
[a]Excludes energy used for transport.
[b]Includes government and private expenditures.

SOURCE: World Bank. *World Development Indicators 2000.*

skilled, and educated employees alike, the overall trend from 1987 to 1997 brought more opportunities and higher wage increases for the latter 2 groups. This trend is more acute in Ireland than in other European states. The ESRI (Economic and Social Research Institute) points out that while the fortunes of wealthiest 10 percent of the employed population increased rapidly between 1987 and 1997, the top 5 percent rose even more rapidly. The only positive aspect of income distribution trends was that while the bottom, or poorest, 25 percent appeared to fall away from the average income, the bottom 10 percent did not, indicating that the very poor are not actually getting poorer. One further positive aspect is the increase in gender equality, with women moving to take advantage of increased employment opportunities. Women are establishing themselves as fundamental members of the labor force and improving their average take-home pay to 85 percent of that earned by their male counterparts.

However, trends in general income disparity are worsened by the crippling house prices. These either prevent many young people on average incomes from buying homes or leaves them with huge mortgage payments. Rents have spiraled due to shortages in the housing market. Exclusively located houses in Dublin have been sold for over I£6 million and, while this is not the norm, an adequate house with easy access to Dublin's city center costs between I£150,000 and I£500,000, having cost perhaps between I£30,000 and I£80,000 at the end of the 1980s.

The government does provide safety nets for those in need, granting free medical and dental care on the basis of means testing. Social welfare payments are available to the unemployed, but only to those who can provide an address, and there is some government-provided social, or corporation, housing. This scheme involves making low-rent housing available to the less well off, along with a tenant's long-term option of buying the government out. However, the service has suffered from the housing shortages, which show no signs of letting up (2001), and waiting lists are up to 18 months long.

WORKING CONDITIONS

The falling unemployment of the 1990s has accelerated to the extent that the key issue in 2001 is a shortage of skilled and unskilled labor. The labor force increased from 1,650,100 in early 1999 to 1,745,600 in mid-2000, with 1,670,700 in employment (mid-2000). In 1999 and 2000, surveys carried out by the Small Firms Association indicated that 91 percent of surveyed members were experiencing difficulties recruiting staff, particularly at the unskilled level. The labor market increased by 6.2 percent (96,000) in 1999, and the number of long-term unemployed decreased to just 1.7 percent of the workforce. There is a risk that this shrinkage in the volume of available labor will further fuel demands for wage increases.

Social partnership agreements over the last decade have kept wages moderate and generally lower than in other EU states. There is an increasingly widespread consensus on the part of workers, particularly in the **public sector**, that the fruits of economic growth have not been distributed, let alone distributed evenly. It is feared that demands for increased pay may undermine growth by fuelling inflation, thus pushing up the cost of living for individuals and of wages for business, both foreign and domestic owned.

The input of trade unions into economic policy-making was formalized with the introduction of national wage agreements in 1989. The umbrella body, the Irish Congress of Trade Unions, incorporates 46 unions, with a total membership of 523,700 (2000). According to the largest union, the Services, Industrial, Professional and Technical Union (SIPTU), membership increased by 60,000 to more than 200,000 in 2000. However, many multinationals do not permit union membership. Despite overall improvements in wage and employment levels, the current industrial climate is at its worst this decade. Strikes are a more regular feature across the public sector, with nurses, the Garda (police), and teachers demanding increases of up to 40 percent. The most recent wage agreement—the Programme for Prosperity and Fairness (PPF)—has proved almost impossible to implement, since the agreed annual 5 percent pay increases are no longer considered sufficient by unions; they argue that the cost of living has increased by more and, with inflation having peaked at almost 7 percent in November 2000, they appear to have a case.

Hourly rates of pay have increased significantly across all sectors. According to the government's Central Statistics Office, the average industrial wage of I£274.37 for a 40.5-hour week in 1996 rose to I£283.53 in 1997 and I£295.20 in 1998. In 1999, employees in private firms had higher average wage figures. Skilled workers earned I£461.86 for a 45.6-hour week and the unskilled and semi-skilled were paid I£346.55 for a 46.8-hour week. As indicated above, income differentials—the difference between income levels across all sectors from the highest to the lowest—are higher than in other EU countries.

COUNTRY HISTORY AND ECONOMIC DEVELOPMENT

1800. British rule over Ireland, present since the 12th century, is extended to the entire country by the 17th and 18th centuries and further centralized with the Act of Union in 1800 (whereby no parliament sat in Dublin anymore).

1870s. Strong national movement emerges in Ireland. The national political movement in favor of "home rule" succeeds in incorporating both members of the Anglo-Irish aristocracy and peasant famers who seek land reform. But resistance on the part of conservative British governments and the strong will of the Protestant population of the northern province—Ulster—to remain in the union delays home rule.

1914–18. A more radical stream of nationalism begins.

1919–21. Guerrilla-style war for independence ensues. The Unionist population of Northern Ireland remains adamant that no granting of either home rule or independence to the island should include them.

1922. The Anglo-Irish treaty gives 26 of the 32 counties of Ireland independence from the United Kingdom with some symbolic restrictions, such as the retention of the crown as head of state. The remaining 6 counties in the north of the island remain part of the UK.

1923. Those for and against the treaty fight a civil war over the spoils of government and some over the retention of symbolic links with Britain, which ends in the capitulation of the anti-treaty forces, who then form the political party Fianna Fáil in 1926.

1925. Partition of the island into Eire and Northern Island is informally made permanent.

1938. More than a decade of politically provoked and disastrous "economic war" with Britain ends.

1940. Ireland declares itself neutral in World War II.

1949. Although informally a republic since 1937, Ireland is formally declared a republic.

1950s. Emigration increases rapidly, and rural poverty becomes widespread.

1960s. The inward looking, tariff-centered economic policies are rejected in favor of an open policy, but the state still plays a huge role in the economy.

1970s. High government spending increases the national debt to unsustainable levels and sparks off high inflation. The oil crisis of 1979 also hits the country hard.

1973. Ireland joins the European Economic Community, along with Britain and Denmark.

1980s. High inflation and unemployment levels alongside income tax that reach over 65 percent.

1987. Ireland endorses the Single European Act, which establishes the common European market. The first social partnership agreements of the 1980s negotiate a plan for national economic recovery.

1990s. Tighter fiscal policies, trade and enterprise-friendly economic policies, and social partnership agreements, alongside other factors such as the long-term benefits of EU transfers, facilitate a turnaround in the economic fortunes of the country.

1991. EU countries sign the Maastricht Treaty, which formalizes the plan for European Monetary Union and agrees on the ground rules for entry into EMU.

1994–98. Following the paramilitary cease-fire in Northern Ireland and long negotiations, a peace process results in political agreements between Britain, Ireland, and Northern Ireland.

1995–96. The economy shows strong growth and a significant increase in employment opportunities.

1998. Ireland endorses the Amsterdam Treaty, which extends EU co-ordination of social and security policy and enlargement.

1999. EMU is introduced and the European Central Bank takes over monetary powers in Ireland.

FUTURE TRENDS

For most of the latter half of the 20th century, Irish policy makers focused on the challenge of how to instigate sustainable economic growth that would serve to reduce high unemployment and emigration levels and to increase standards of living to the European level. In the 21st century, the key challenge is to implement a policy mix that sustains the benefits of growth while dealing with the key interlinked threats posed by inflation and acute labor market shortages. In 2001, rising inflation has seen the cost of living increase considerably, and this, alongside more demand than supply in the labor market, puts strong upward pressure on wages.

Dealing with inflation and labor market shortages is complicated by the extent to which external forces affect Ireland's economy, which is a regional, export-oriented economy within a monetary union. For example, the health of the euro and trends in global oil prices will either help or hinder the curbing of inflation. Lower oil prices and a stronger euro would reduce the cost of imports and, thus, inflation. Another important external force is the slow-down in the U.S. economy (2001). This could decrease the United States' domestic demand for imports, at the same time decreasing multi-national companies' investment in the Irish market, thus putting trade volume, employment, and growth at risk. In turn, spiraling inflation could result as job losses cause people to struggle to pay mortgages and the high levels of credit that have been the trend throughout the 1990s and beyond.

While there are differing opinions as to which policies are most effective to curb inflation and thus reduce the upward pressure on wages, most commentators agree that a flexible fiscal policy, in particular flexible wages (using wage agreements), is vital if both are to be avoided. Flexibility is necessary because of the dual and uncertain nature of external challenges to economic success.

Different external factors call for different reactions. The immediate problem facing the government in 2001 is the threat to social partnership policy-making posed by the increasing demands of unions for higher wage agreements. Higher wages and a break in the partnership would threaten the competitiveness of the Irish labor market, which remains relatively cheap compared to the rest of Europe. But competitiveness is also at risk as a result of labor market shortages.

It is likely that moderate wage increases to maintain social consensus (partnership agreements) are required alongside policies to encourage immigration (to increase the labor market supply) and policies to encourage savings (to reduce the threat of inflation). However, different policy responses would be required should the U.S. slow-down reach the point where foreign companies pull out, thus reducing employment. Attempts have been made to prepare for this scenario; the IDA has put more emphasis on health care and **e-commerce** companies and on research and development functions to deepen the roots of foreign investment, thus lessening the risk of an exodus.

A healthy future economy largely depends on how government responds to uncertain threats, and it would appear that the adoption of a flexible approach is vital. This is in turn a prerequisite for improving the quality of life and diverting a percentage of expenditure to programs designed to narrow the disparities in individual prosperity.

DEPENDENCIES

Ireland has no territories or colonies.

BIBLIOGRAPHY

Duffy, David, John Fitzgerald, Kieran Kennedy, and Diarmaid Smyth. *ESRI Quarterly Economic Commentary.* Dublin: Economic and Social Research Institute, December 1999.

Economist Intelligence Unit. *Country Profile: Ireland.* London: Economist Intelligence Unit, 2001.

Economist Intelligence Unit. *Country Report: Ireland June 2000.* London: EIU, 2000.

Economist Intelligence Unit. *Country Report: Ireland November 2000.* London: EIU, 2000.

Irish Business and Employers Association (IBEC). "Quarterly Economic Trends." Dublin: IBEC Statements, December 2000.

Irish Business and Employers Association (IBEC). "Economy Not All Boom." Dublin: IBEC Statements, January 2001.

Irish Farmer's Association. *Structure and Competitiveness in Irish Agriculture.* Dublin: IFA, July 1999.

Nolan, Brian, P.J. O'Connell, and C. Whelan. *Bust to Boom: The Irish Experience of Growth and Inequality.* Dublin: IPA and ERSI, 2000.

Nolan, Brian, and Bertrand Maitre. "Income Inequality." *Bust to Boom: The Irish Experience of Growth and Inequality.* Dublin: IPA and ERSI, 2000.

O'Hagan. *The Economy of Ireland.* 6th edition. Dublin: IPA, 2000.

Small Firms Association. *End of Year Statement.* Dublin: SFA, 2000.

Results of Pay Survey. Dublin: SFA, January 2001.

U.S. Central Intelligence Agency. *CIA World FactBook 2000.* <http:www.odci.gov/cia/publications/factbook/index.html>. Accessed September 2001.

—Catherine Lynch and Eoin O'Malley

ITALY

Italian Republic
Repubblica Italiana

CAPITAL: Rome.

MONETARY UNIT: Italian Lira (L). One lira equals 100 centesimi. There are coins of 5, 10, 20, 50, 100, 200, 500, and 1,000 lire. There are notes of 1,000, 2,000, 5,000, 10,000, 50,000, and 100,000 lire. The lira will be replaced in January 2002 by the euro, the new unified currency of the European Union (EU). One euro will be worth 1,936.27 lira at a fixed exchange rate. All lira coins and bills will disappear, and by June 2002 only euros will be in circulation.

CHIEF EXPORTS: Engineering products, textiles, clothing, production machinery, motor vehicles, transport equipment, chemicals, food, beverages, tobacco, minerals, non-ferrous metals.

CHIEF IMPORTS: Engineering products, chemicals, transport equipment, energy products, minerals, non-ferrous metals, textiles, clothing, food, beverages, tobacco.

GROSS DOMESTIC PRODUCT: US$1.273 trillion (purchasing power parity, 2000 est.).

BALANCE OF TRADE: **Exports:** US$241.1 billion (f.o.b., 2000). **Imports:** US$231.4 billion (f.o.b., 2000).

COUNTRY OVERVIEW

LOCATION AND SIZE. Located in southern Europe, Italy is a peninsula extending into the Central Mediterranean Sea. It is shaped like a high-heeled boot kicking a "triangle"—the island of Sicily. Italy borders France to the west, Switzerland and Austria to the north, and Slovenia to the east. The country also shares a border with 2 tiny independent states, San Marino and the Vatican, both of which are entirely surrounded by Italian territory. Italy has an area of 301,230 square kilometers (116,304 square miles) and a coastline of 7,600 kilometers (4,722 miles), including the islands of Sicily and Sardinia. Comparatively, Italy is slightly larger than the state of Arizona. Rome, the capital city, is on the country's western coast at the heart of the peninsula. Other major cities include Milan, Naples, Genoa, Florence, Venice, Palermo, Bologna, and Bari.

POPULATION. In July 2000 the population of Italy was estimated at 57,634,327. In the same year the birth rate stood at 9.13 per 1,000 people while the death rate was 9.99 per 1,000 people. Thanks to the annual arrival of immigrants, the projected growth rate is 0.09 percent. The data clearly show that without the influx of foreign immigrants the Italian population would suffer a steady decline. More restrictive **immigration** policies are being adopted, and it is expected that by 2010 the population will decrease to 56,484,000.

According to 1996 statistics, just over 67 percent of Italians live in an urban setting; the rest live in the countryside. The regions with the highest density are Campania (with 426 people per square kilometer, or 1,103 per square mile, in 1998) and Lombardy (378 people per square kilometer, or 979 per square mile). The regions with the lowest density are Val d'Aosta (37 people per square kilometer, or 96 per square mile) and Basilicata (61 people per square kilometer, or 158 per square mile). The biggest city is Rome, with 2,646,000 inhabitants, followed by Milan (1,308,000), Naples (1,020,000), Turin (910,000), Palermo (687,000), and Genoa (641,000).

Ethnic Italians form 97 percent of the population, but there are small ethnic minorities such as German-Italian, French-Italian, Slovene-Italian, and Albanian-Italian, while foreign immigrants make up 1.8 percent of the population. The largest immigrant groups are Moroccans, Albanians, Filipinos, Americans, Tunisians, and Chinese. Italy—home to Vatican City, the seat of the Pope—is a predominantly Roman Catholic country, even though church attendance has been progressively falling. There are small Protestant and Jewish communities, but, as a consequence of the growing number of North

African, Bosnian, and Albanian immigrants, the second religion of Italy today is Islam. With 18 percent of people over 65 and only 14 percent below the age of 14, there is widespread concern about the rapid rate at which Italy's population is aging. With average life expectancy at 79.03 years, the government is worried about the financial costs, such as health care and pensions, associated with an aging population.

Contrary to popular perception, Italian families are no longer as large as they once were, and it is becoming common for couples to have only 1 child. Economic well-being, a high cost of living, and the entrance of women into the **workforce** have had a tremendous influence on family structure. In 1961, about 14.4 percent of families had 4 or more children, compared to 1998 when only 1.4 percent of families had 4 or more. Without the arrival of immigrants, the Italian population would have fallen over the last decade. To reverse the negative trend, the government has adopted family-friendly policies. The government encourages families to have more children through tax breaks and direct grants. The policy has not been too successful, however, because people do not consider the financial incentives to be enough.

OVERVIEW OF ECONOMY

Italy's **gross domestic product** (GDP) of US$1.273 trillion makes it the sixth richest country in the world. In income per capita, it occupies 18th place. The country's economic success is a recent accomplishment. Italy was unified in 1861 after 3 wars of independence fought against various foreign rulers who dominated different parts of the country. The driving force behind Italy's unification was Victor Emmanuel II, the king of Piedmont and Sardinia, who waged wars against foreign rule in the name of Italian independence and territorial unity. Italy had long been carved up by foreign powers, but several self-ruling cities and kingdoms also existed. With the help of committed patriots, such as Giuseppe Mazzini and Giuseppe Garibaldi, Victor Emmanuel accomplished his aim to unify the country under his rule. Despite the enthusiasm of unification, economic conditions were poor. Italy had few industries, and most people lived off agriculture. Furthermore, the difference between the more advanced northern half of the country and the poorer south was evident. The pace of industrialization was slow, and industry could not provide jobs for new generations of workers. Because of the poor standard of living and lack of work, many Italians left the country to find a better life, particularly in the United States. The first wave of mass **emigration** to the United States took place before the turn of the 20th century, followed by a second wave after World War I (1914–18). During the period of Italy's fascist rule, which lasted from 1922 until 1943, and then following the end of World War II (1939–45), many Italians migrated to European countries such as the United Kingdom, Germany, and Belgium. Before the economic boom in the late 1950s, many Italians also migrated to Australia, South Africa, Switzerland, and Latin America.

The turning point in Italian economic history was the economic prosperity of the 1960s. At the time, private and state-owned enterprises took advantage of foreign assistance from the United States under the Marshall Plan and the launch of the European Economic Community (EEC) to restore the Italian economy. Despite skepticism about the European Common Market, Italy joined and profited from the progressive integration of Western European economies. By developing strong export-related industries, the industrial triangle of Milan-Genoa-Turin led the economic boom. Italian exports became attractive, and the growth of exports led to a strong internal demand for goods and services. Small and medium enterprises began establishing themselves and prospering in Northern Italy. These companies were the force behind economic growth as they exported machinery, engineering products, textiles, and clothing. Large private companies such as FIAT and state-owned companies such as ENI and ENEL also contributed to economic growth. Meanwhile, southern Italy remained impoverished, and its inhabitants migrated north in large numbers until the late 1970s.

In the following decades, Italy was able to consolidate its economic success, even though the economy was never again as strong as it had been in the 1960s. Comparatively, the Italian economy grew faster in the 1960s than any other European country, while around the world only the Japanese economy fared better. The 1970s and 1980s saw much more uneven development. Italy is heavily dependent on Algerian gas and Arab oil supplies, so it was hit hard by the oil crises of the 1970s. Despite this trouble, Italy's economy grew over 3 percent annually during the 1970s, though it began to slow at the end of the decade. The second oil crisis in 1979 and domestic political turmoil created high unemployment and high **inflation**. Strikes, demonstrations, flight of capital, and confrontations between the trade unions and businesses plagued the country. To steer the country away from this troubled period, political parties formed a Grand Alliance to find a solution that would satisfy most of the people. A national solidarity government was formed and managed to deal with the problem of stagflation (high inflation combined with high unemployment and stagnant consumer demand), reduce civil unrest, and lay the foundations for future growth. The country began to recover about 1983 and moved toward a new period of economic expansion. Strong economic performance allowed successive governments to make improvements in the **welfare state** that provides health care, education, pensions, **infrastructure**, and benefits.

Before the 1980s, Italy was a free market economy with a strong element of state control and state ownership. Many state-owned companies had operated efficiently and contributed to economic growth. By the mid-1980s, however, the state sector was beginning to create distortions in the economy. Many Italians employed by the state lived well above their means, accumulating debts and enjoying a free ride at the public expense. By the mid-1980s, appointments to the civil service and to the management of state-owned enterprises were handed out as political favors, leading to widespread corruption. The mismanagement of public resources drained the economy. Furthermore, the high costs of the welfare system put a strain on the country's finances, thanks to widespread corruption and waste in the health care, social security, transport, and education systems. The economic slump of the early 1990s highlighted the burden of the public debt and brought about radical measures to cut costs, **privatize**, and reduce the role of government in the economy.

The state began to withdraw from its role in the economy after a first round of privatization was carried out at the end of the 1980s. Large state-owned enterprises such as the motor car manufacturing company, Alfa-Romeo, were sold to private investors. The progressive disengagement of the state from the economy created more room for private investors. With the prospect of entrance into the European Monetary Union (EMU), Italy was forced to undertake massive reforms to lower inflation, reduce the deficit, and lower interest rates. By 1992 reforms accelerated as the state disengaged from the economic sphere. The radical changes brought success in tackling the high deficit through cuts to the welfare state and measures to limit waste. Inflation was brought under control by means of restrictive **monetary policies**, and the tax system was made more efficient. Because of the initiatives, Italy succeeded in qualifying to participate in the EMU.

By 1998 and 1999, Italy experienced sustained growth after many years of high taxes, budget cuts, and high unemployment. The relative importance of the Milan-Genoa-Turin industrial triangle declined, and small and medium-sized private enterprises in the northern part of the country became the chief participants in the new boom. Recovery from the economic **recession** of the early 1990s and acceptance into the EMU was due, in part, to the social partnership pact brokered by the government. Employers and labor united to put an end to confrontation and to adopt part-time contracts, flexible hours, and lower overtime rates. Even the **public sector** embraced these changes to improve its efficiency. Investments were made in technological development, salaries were frozen for months, and the workforce increased production in exchange for job security.

The Italian economy is now much more free-market oriented than at any previous time. Several sectors have been **liberalized** and state **monopolies** disbanded. Many state-owned enterprises have been privatized over the last 8 years, with 13 percent of these sold to national private investors and another 8 percent to foreign private investors. The remaining 79 percent were sold to the public via stock offerings. Over 500,000 workers were transferred from the public to the **private sector** between 1992 and 1998. Some of the largest companies to be privatized or already privatized included: AGIP, SNAM, and Italgas (in the energy sector); ILVA, Ansaldo, Nuovo Pignone, Dalmine, and Italimpianti (in the industrial sector); Credito Italiano, Banco di Roma, and Banca Commerciale (financial sector); Telecom Italia (communication sector); and Alitalia, Tirrenia, and SEA (transportation sector).

By 2000, Italy enjoyed a healthy economy characterized by slow growth. In fact, Italy had the slowest growing economy of the 11 founding members of the EMU. With the GDP growth of 1.4 percent in 1999, Italy lagged behind the 2.9 percent annual growth rate of other countries in the EMU. But growth increased in 2000, reaching an annual rate of 2.7 percent and may be expected to continue to improve in the coming years as the country continues to adjust to the new economic scenario created by the withdrawal of the state.

Despite the relatively healthy economy, high unemployment, underdevelopment in large areas of the south, and the large presence of an often criminal, **informal economy** continue to plague Italy. Most of the unemployed live in the south. Organized crime tries to recruit those people. Unemployment has always been a problem even in times of economic growth. In 2000 unemployment stood at 11.5 percent. Although unemployment is high, it may not be reflective of reality because of the number of people employed in the nation's informal sector. Living conditions in the south of Italy are difficult, the job market is tight, and emigration is still the preferred option of many young people. The government has made a serious attempt to address this problem by granting tax breaks to companies willing to set up business and hire workers in the south. CGIL, the largest Italian trade union, calculated that between October 1997 and April 2000 over 100,000 people found work in small or medium-sized enterprises in the south.

The government has toughened laws against businesses that fail to pay their taxes and who gravitate toward the informal economy. Companies that want to move from the informal economy and legalize receive help. The re-emergence of the companies entitles workers to social benefits and helps generate revenue for the state from taxes. Most of the new enterprises are active in the clothing, footwear, agricultural, and construction sectors. Although these businesses operate on a small scale, many hire a large number of workers. It is difficult to determine precise statistics because of the informal nature of the market.

It is incorrect to treat the whole of southern Italy as a homogenous area because there are substantial differences in economic and social development in different regions. For example, Abruzzo is more prosperous and developed than Calabria. Within the same southern region, production compares favorably with the more affluent north. Although social development and the standard of living is improving, overall indicators still point, however, to a significant gap between the north and the south.

Ironically, factories in the north suffer from a shortage of labor because of recent economic growth. Despite unemployment rates below 4 percent, southerners are reluctant to move to the north. Southern objections include the high cost of living in the north and the long hours accompanied by most of the manual job opportunities. Many people from the south with higher education hold out for better job prospects. Because of job vacancies, smaller companies in the north request more visas for eastern European and African workers.

POLITICS, GOVERNMENT, AND TAXATION

Italy has been a democracy since the end of World War II, and despite its international reputation for political instability, the country has enjoyed largely consistent policies from successive governments. The country became a republic following the abdication of King Victor Emmanuel III in 1946 and the creation of a constitution in 1948. The country's president is elected by an electoral college whose members represent the popular vote. The president in turn selects a prime minister from the ruling coalition in the parliament. In elections held in 1999 Carlo Azeglio Ciampi was elected president. Following legislative elections in 2001, Silvio Berlusconi was selected as prime minister.

Italy has a **bicameral** legislature consisting of a 315-member Senate and a 630-member Chamber of Deputies. Both houses are directly elected by popular vote, and members serve 5-year terms. The judicial branch is headed by a Constitutional Court whose members are appointed in equal number by the president, the parliament, and the administrative Supreme Courts.

The major parties that have dominated politics since 1946 are: the Christian Democrats (DC), the Communist Party (PCI), and the **Socialist** Party (PSI). The Christian Democrats have been the dominant force in Italian politics, continuously leading a coalition government from 1946 until the early 1990s. Until 1963, when the Socialist Party entered parliament, the Christian Democrats' coalition partners represented 3 smaller parties, the Republican Party (PRI), the Social Democratic Party (PSDI), and the Liberal Party (PLI). The main objective of all parties was the exclusion of the communists from government, and the resulting continuity of parliamentary representation ensured that there were no major swings of policy. This government coalition presided over a long period of economic growth and a satisfied electorate opposed to any radical change. The harsh recessions of the late 1970s, mid-1980s, and early 1990s, however, undermined the popularity of the DC-PSI axis, but it was not until 1992 that the political system fell apart. In that year, a major anti-corruption investigation that implicated politicians and heads of industry in a cash-for-favors exchange shook the political and economic establishment of the country.

The corruption scandals, combined with the collapse of the USSR that ended the ideological war over **communism** in Italy, radically altered the political system. In addition, a new economic recession for which mismanagement of the national economy was largely to blame hastened the exit of an already discredited political class. Thus, traditional parties disappeared, and new parties emerged between 1991 and 1994. Electoral laws were reformed, and in a radical move, **proportional representation** was abolished. It was replaced with the first-past-the-post system, where the country is divided into constituencies, and the constituency seat goes to the winning candidate. (The congressional elections in the United States follow a comparable system.) The changes stood to give the electorate clear choices and were welcomed by many who believed that, with fewer parties in government, politicians would deal with concrete issues in non-ideological terms. Far from decreasing, however, the number of political parties has increased, and coalition government still prevails. Nevertheless, to a certain extent, expectations have been met, and the Italian electorate does face a clear choice at election time between center-right and center-left coalitions. Both sides have had periods in office since 1994.

The main parties within the center-right coalition are Forza Italia, National Alliance (AN), the Northern League (NL), and the Center Christian Democrats (CCD). The largest party is Forza Italia, led by media tycoon Silvio Berlusconi, who is also the leader of the coalition. This party believes strongly in further reducing the role of the state in the economic sphere and aims to accelerate the pace of privatization. Clearly conservative, Forza Italia also plans to cut the costs of the welfare state and introduce free-market competition in health and education, as well as cutting taxes. The Northern League shares these economic policies but also advocates increased political and fiscal autonomy for all regions by devolving responsibility to the regions for providing several fundamental services, including the provision of education, health care, transport, and law and order. Under this proposal, the regions would be empowered to raise taxes, keeping most of the revenue to spend as they decide, without central government interference. The NL represents, in electoral terms, the majority of northern voters, and its appeals for federal reforms are to be taken seriously. The National Alliance is the most right-wing party of the coalition and is mostly preoccupied with limiting foreign immigration, preserving the integrity of the national territory, and safeguarding the international credibility of Italy. It shares the broad economic approach of its partners but does not support the federal reforms advocated by the NL. The Center Christian Democrats offer a more moderate voice regarding immigration and social policies but argue for increased economic liberalization.

The center-right coalition was in power in 1994 for only 7 months and was unable to carry out their promised reforms because the Northern League withdrew from the alliance. The center-left coalition won the 1996 election. The main parties of the center-left coalition are the Democrats of the Left (DS), the People's Party (PPI), the Greens, the Democrats, and, after years in the wilderness, the Communist Party (PCI). The DS, the largest partner in the coalition, is a social-democratic party. The broad outline of its economic policy, shared by all its partners, favors liberalization, privatization, lower taxes, and job creation by means of financial incentives to employers. The PPI is one of the heirs of the old Christian Democrats (DC) and is the most socialist party of the coalition, supporting recognition of gay rights, subsidized housing for refugees, and abortion. In the economic sphere, the PPI is slightly to the left of the dominant DS and believes that the state should still play a strong role in managing the economy. One distinctive policy of the PPI is the advocacy of state aid to private schools run by the Catholic Church. The Greens subscribe to most of the economic policies advocated by the DS but are mainly concerned with the environmental aspects of those policies. In common with the Greens in the rest of Europe, they are particularly committed to limiting the use of motor cars in favor of a more environmentally friendly public transport system. Many of the economic policies of the right and left parties overlap; the difference is marked in matters of social policy, the environment, and federalism. The center-left coalition is not as keen as its opponents to introduce free-market competition in the provision of health and education, preferring a smaller, more efficient welfare state and, in principle, is not hostile to foreign immigration. Finally, the center-left supports administrative and political decentralization, but is against extensive federal reforms that would widen the already large gap between North and South.

The center-left coalition held power from 1996 to 2001, a period characterized by an economic slump and by Italian support for NATO actions in Kosovo. With the economy slumping in the runup to the 2001 legislative elections, the center-right parties, led by Silvio Berlusconi's right-wing Forza Italia, returned to power in a coalition that included some of the most right-wing parties in Europe. Since his return to power, Berlusconi has been an outspoken proponent of free trade and pro-business policies. He has promised to reduce unemployment, cut taxes, and reform education and the still-bloated state bureaucracy.

An aspect of Italian politics that should not be ignored is the growing disillusionment of the electorate. Many citizens feel that their participation in the political process makes no difference to government, and there has been a sharp decrease in party membership. Voter turnout has steadily decreased since the mid-1980s, and in the 1996 elections, 23.1 percent of voters either stayed away from the polls or spoiled their ballot papers. This is a worrying sign of disaffection, and many political parties are concerned that if this trend continues it will undermine the legitimacy of future governments.

The former leader of the Socialist Party, Giuliano Amato, launched a far-reaching privatization program in 1992, which was continued by both coalition governments. Aside from the sale of state assets, both coalitions agreed that the pension system should be reformed and its apparent generosity curtailed. The reform of the pension system was carried out in full by the center-left coalition in power from 1996 to 2001, which was able to convince the trade unions to accept a deal. Both coalitions are also in favor of increased international free trade, even though they advocate some sort of protectionist measures for so-called "cultural products" such as movies and TV programs, which promote Italian language and culture. Finally, budget cuts across the board (particularly as regards health and defense) have been welcomed by both coalitions. The general convergence of ideas on economic management should not, however, obscure the differences that still exist between left and right. These differences are highly visible when it comes to crucial social issues such as immigration, gay rights, and the environment.

Problems of corruption, including the infiltration of political institutions by organized crime, have long been a feature of Italian life. The present political system was born out of a popular reaction against the spread of corruption and crime, but the problem, though marginally worse in the 1970s and 1980s than it is as of 2001, refuses to go away. The new political structures seem only to have provided a pause in the usual pattern of "doing politics" and "doing business" in Italy.

Taxation in Italy is quite a complicated affair because there are numerous taxes that each citizen has to pay. Moreover taxation is high, representing 43.3 percent of the GDP. However, the number and quality of the public services are some justification for high taxes, and measures to simplify the tax system have been introduced since 1998. **Income tax** accounts for 34.9 percent of total tax revenues, while **value-added tax** (VAT) contributes 35.4 percent. In addition, local governments **levy** other **indirect taxes**.

The tax system is plagued by tax evasion, however. Many economists point to this problem as one of the main challenges Italy needs to resolve in the near future. The government is improving the situation, but there is still an enormous amount of work to do. Aside from the considerable sums of money that entirely escape the government due to the strength of the informal economy, there is significant income tax evasion. Employees in both the public and private sectors have their tax deducted from their paychecks and do not have to submit tax declaration forms. However, employers, self-employed professionals, and business owners must fill out tax forms and declare their profits. Huge numbers of people in these categories falsely report their earnings, thus lowering their tax bills. The state has as yet not found a method of tackling this situation. For many years tax evasion was ignored, thanks to a commonly accepted theory that it was conducive to economic development: the money would swell either consumption or investment. But tax evasion is clearly putting a strain on public finances, and its effects are particularly negative at a time of increasing cutbacks in public services. The International Monetary Fund (IMF) recognized the problem in 1998 and pointed out that far-reaching reforms had to be undertaken if tax evasion was to be reduced. The government is currently implementing certain reforms that are expected to make the system more coherent and make evasion less common.

INFRASTRUCTURE, POWER, AND COMMUNICATIONS

Italy has an efficient and modern infrastructure, even though it performs poorly compared to other Western European countries of comparable size. The whole peninsula is well connected through an extensive system of railways, expressways, national roads, airports and seaports. Most of the infrastructure was rebuilt after the ravages of World War II and is subject to constant improvement and upkeep. However, many important projects have failed to materialize, among them the subway system in Naples, and more railways in the south and east to facilitate the movement of goods. At the same time, funds were given to many useless projects, built solely to line the pockets of those whose political or economic support could thus be counted upon.

Italy has a number of important international airports and the national carrier, Alitalia, has a fleet of 166 planes which transport 25 million passengers annually and connect Italy to 60 other countries. Overall, Italy has 136 airports, the most important being Fiumicino (Rome), Malpensa and Linate (both serving Milan), Ronchi dei Legionari (Trieste), Caselle (Turin), and Marco Polo (Venice). Seaports used to be a key element of the Italian transport system; they handle a substantial percentage of cargo until the mid-1970s. Due to the development of alternative means of transportation and competition from neighboring ports, however, their traffic has declined somewhat. The ports of Trieste, Genoa, Naples, Taranto, Augusta, Gioia Tauro, and Livorno are economically important to their respective regions. Italy is a major power in container shipping in the Mediterranean. The Italian merchant fleet consists of over 2,000 ships, 1,331 of which are over 100 tons. The country also has 1,500 miles of waterways that are used for commercial purposes, but this system is relatively undeveloped.

Since most goods in Italy are transported by road, the system is constantly upgraded and improved. It provides a highly developed and efficient network of interconnected highways and lesser roads, particularly in northern regions. The main routes at the hub of the road system are Turin-Milan-Venice-Trieste, Milan-Bologna-Florence-Rome, Milan-Genoa, and Rome-Naples. There are 6,460 kilometers (4,014 miles) of expressway, mostly in the northern and central regions, and the system overall is comprised of 654,676 kilometers (406,815 miles) of paved roads. Links to the rest of Europe are excellent. However, even Italy's extensive and sophisticated road network is now barely able to cope with the steadily increasing traffic.

The country's rail system is also highly developed and traverses a distance of 19,394 kilometers (12,051 miles). Italian passenger trains are generally punctual, comfortable, and cheap compared to the rest of Europe. They are the preferred means of travel for many commuters as well as tourists, who can thus avoid congested roads and urban areas. In order to improve the system, the state-owned rail company, Ferrovie dello Stato (FS), is currently developing a project to introduce high-speed trains like the French TGV.

Infrastructure is not the same quality throughout the country. While the road and rail networks are intricate and plentiful in the north and center of the country, the southern infrastructure is poor. Northern Italy's impressive economic growth and geographical proximity to the heart of Europe made it a key commercial area, and the

Communications

Country	Newspapers	Radios	TV Sets[a]	Cable subscribers[a]	Mobile Phones[a]	Fax Machines[a]	Personal Computers[a]	Internet Hosts[b]	Internet Users[b]
	1996	1997	1998	1998	1998	1998	1998	1999	1999
Italy	104	878	486	2.8	355	31.3	173.4	68.28	7,000
United States	215	2,146	847	244.3	256	78.4	458.6	1,508.77	74,100
France	218	937	601	27.5	188	47.4	207.8	110.64	5,370
Greece	153	477	466	1.2	194	3.8	51.9	59.57	750

[a]Data are from International Telecommunication Union, *World Telecommunication Development Report 1999* and are per 1,000 people.
[b]Data are from the Internet Software Consortium (http://www.isc.org) and are per 10,000 people.

SOURCE: World Bank. *World Development Indicators 2000.*

infrastructure developed accordingly. By contrast, the geographical isolation and poor economic development of Southern Italy meant that infrastructure was never a priority except for seaports.

Italy has very few natural resources and must import most of them from neighboring countries. Crude oil comes mainly from Libya, Algeria, and countries in the Arab peninsula. Petroleum represents 4.5 percent of all Italian imports. Gas comes from Algeria, Tunisia and Russia through a number of pipelines. Furthermore, unlike Germany and France, Italy has no nuclear power capability and is completely dependent on imported energy. For this reason, Italy is one of the few Western European countries to enjoy very good relations with a number of Arab states. In 1998 and 1999, Italian prime ministers were the first Western leaders to visit countries such as Iran and Libya after many years of diplomatic isolation. In 1998, Italy consumed 266.705 billion kilowatt hours (kWh) of electricity, provided mainly by the formerly state-owned company ENEL, which was privatized in 1999. The generally reliable 220-volt power system covers the whole country.

Until recently, the state-owned company Telecom Italia provided telecommunications services in Italy, but the market recently opened to competition, thanks in part to the privatization of Telecom Italia in 1997, which remains the principal provider. There were 25 million main telephone lines in use in 1999. Like many other Western European countries, Italy is experiencing the Internet revolution, and in 1999 there were 68 Internet hosts per 10,000 people. More recent, but unconfirmed, figures claim that 10 million Italians surf the net. What distinguishes Italians from their neighbors in Western Europe is the quantity of mobile phones in circulation. They have proved particularly popular in Italy, and by 1998 there were 355 mobile phones per 1,000 people. This figure has certainly increased dramatically since then and recent figures record that 48 million cell phones have been sold in Italy since 1995.

ECONOMIC SECTORS

Like all advanced capitalist economics, Italy is quickly moving away from its traditional economic sectors to become predominantly services-oriented, although the economic importance of the industrial sector is higher than the EU average. Agriculture accounted for 2.5 percent of the GDP in 2000, while industry and services accounted, respectively, for 30.4 percent and 67.1 percent of the GDP. Italy has recovered from the economic recession of the early 1990s in part through its efforts to develop the service sector even further. Services both to commercial enterprises and private individuals have grown in importance, while the relevance of the agricultural sector continues to decline. In the south, tourism is seen as one of the principal sectors for development, one that would generate employment in the region.

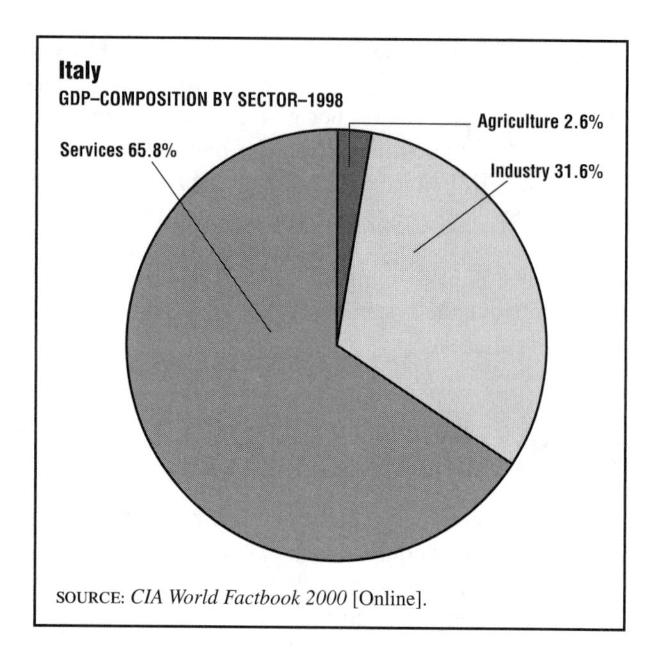

SOURCE: *CIA World Factbook 2000* [Online].

The manufacture of machinery, motor vehicles, clothing, footwear, and food processing are the main industrial sub-sectors. Many of these enterprises manufacture goods almost exclusively for foreign markets and must, therefore, monitor international economic changes very carefully. These companies are largely concentrated in the northern regions and are often small or medium in size. More often than not, they are also family run, and the business is kept within the family for generations. The

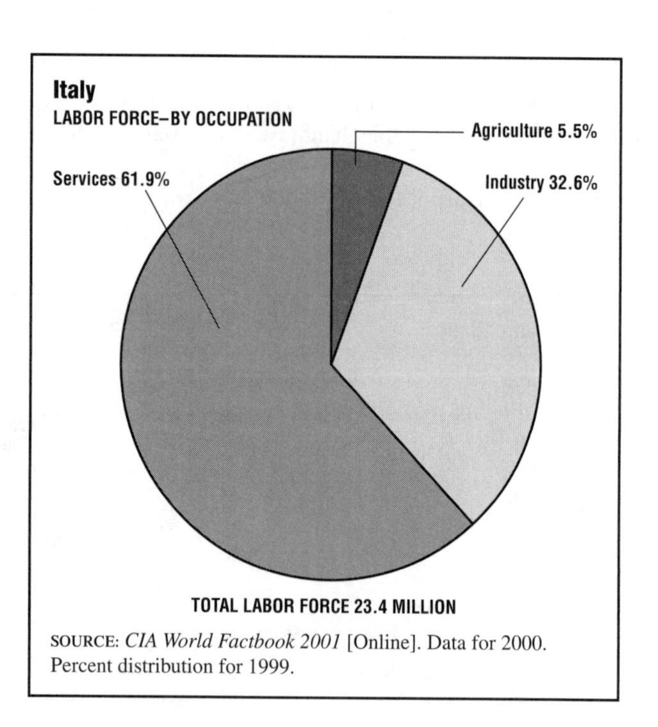

SOURCE: *CIA World Factbook 2001* [Online]. Data for 2000. Percent distribution for 1999.

large manufacturers include such internationally recognized names as FIAT, Benetton, Parmalat, Mediaset, Pirelli, and Zanussi, multinational companies which produce a wide range of products across several manufacturing sectors.

An interesting aspect of Italian economic development is the increasingly important role that small and medium enterprises have come to play. These companies are often family run and can count on a well-qualified and dedicated workforce. They receive extensive support from local government and are well integrated into their communities. These complex business networks are known as integrated industrial districts, which means that almost every company in the same geographic area makes the same products, or necessary components for those products. This pattern enables all companies in the integrated district to share a common distribution network and to take delivery of energy resources or raw materials in huge amounts in one place. The system cuts costs to business and helps them to compete in the international markets. Thus, for example, the northern area of Friuli is renowned for its furniture making factories, the region of Marche for shoemaking, and so on.

Italy's employment statistics reflect its economic trends. The agricultural labor force is steadily diminishing (down to 5.5 percent of the total workforce in 1999), and industrial employment is also shrinking due to the impact of the new economy (to 32.6 percent in 1999). The service sector employs the largest percentage, 61.9 percent, of the Italian workforce. During the 1993–95 recession, the industrial sector went through a painful period of **restructuring** and many jobs were lost. Older workers were offered the option of early retirement, while others were enrolled in retraining programs. A substantial number of jobs were saved by the introduction of the social partnership plan.

AGRICULTURE

The agricultural sector employed only 5.5 percent of the working population in 1999 and contributed only 2.5 percent of the GDP in 2000, with an output of over US$36 billion. However, in the southern regions of Basilicata, Calabria, and Molise, agriculture accounts for just over 20 percent of local employment. The decline of this sector in terms of employment and the GDP is, however, compensated for by ever-accelerating productivity. The agricultural profile is in line with all other Western European countries and is due specifically to the effects of the Common Agricultural Policy (CAP) of the European Union (EU). It is impossible to examine Italian agriculture without taking CAP into consideration since CAP is the basis for agricultural support across Western Europe. This EU policy ensures that **subsidies** and incentives are offered in order to sustain prices and guarantee a certain level of income to farmers. Thus, prices are artificially maintained, and if agriculture were to be liberalized in full, the sector would collapse throughout Europe. CAP was launched in the late 1950s to improve efficiency and as of 2001 accounts for most of EU expenditures, a staggering US$45 billion.

The CAP was not very successful in Italy in its initial stages because subsidies did not cover several traditional Mediterranean products such as olives, tomatoes, oranges, and lemons. When these were finally included, the more positive aspects of the policy emerged. First, it provided the necessary capital for mechanization, and Italy underwent rapid mechanization during the 1980s. Second, it offered an incentive to merge and thus enlarge the average farm. Through CAP, the EU buys up surplus products and, as a consequence, larger farms can be very beneficial to the economy. Finally, CAP ensures that all traditional Italian agricultural products are given some protection against cheap competition, with export traders subsidized to supply cut rates. Unfortunately, CAP seems to have favored northern farmers, but the government is attempting to correct the effects of CAP by offering grants and tax breaks to small farms in the south.

With only 5 percent of the land under cultivation, Italy is not self-sufficient in agricultural products, yet it enjoys an abundance of agricultural resources. Despite a negative **balance of trade** in agriculture, productivity is high, and the Mediterranean climate ensures that a variety of products are available both for internal consumption and external markets. Italy is a world leader in olive oil production and a major exporter of rice, tomatoes, and wine. Moreover, BSE, or "mad cow" disease, caused a major drop in beef consumption, while an increasing number of consumers turned towards organically grown produce.

The Italian government has always been a staunch defender of its national agricultural sector when it comes to negotiating production quotas with EU partners or seeking grants to defend the sector from decline. Funds to buy machinery, to compensate farmers for over-production, and to pay EU-imposed fines were constantly made available by the government. However, the Italian government was unable to stop the most recent CAP reform of 1997, which caused spending on Mediterranean products to decline in favor of increased spending for northern European dairy farmers.

In addition, Italian agriculture is suffering from changes in the climate and very poor management of the land. Large-scale farmers in the north live reasonably well, particularly in comparison to their counterparts in the south. The regional disparity is due partly to the effects of CAP and partly to organizational differences. In northern and central Italy, co-operatives has dominate. These farming co-operatives provide widespread support, both socially and economically, for their members, and help in rationalizing production and distribution. In the south, farmers have no production and distribution networks on which they can depend, and the smaller scale of their operations, combined with their isolation, curtails their ability to compete in the market.

Meat has never been a major Italian product, and most of the meat consumed in Italy is imported from other European countries, particularly Ireland and Germany. Italy is also quite weak in the dairy farming sector, although it exports a handful of distinctive cheeses such as parmesan, mozzarella, and gorgonzola. Fruit is grown almost exclusively in the south, with most of the oranges and lemons coming from Sicily. Apples grow in Trentino Alto Adige. But the real strength of Italian agriculture is the production of olives, wine, and tomatoes.

OLIVES. Olives are one of the country's most lucrative exports. In 1999 production reached a record 7.243 million quintals (a quintal is a unit of weight equal to 100 kilograms, or about 220 pounds), confirming Italy as the leading producer in the world. The hot Mediterranean climate makes the southern region of Italy well suited for olive production, with most olives produced in Puglia. The industry changed considerably during the 1990s, moving away from traditional farming methods to more intensive and mechanized production. Thus, half of the olive-producing land excludes other types of cultivation and small producers are being driven out as large companies take over processing and distribution in the olive industry. Italy's main international competitors in olive production are Greece and Spain. In 2000, due to poor weather conditions, Italy's output decreased to 4.929 million quintals and Italian olive production was outstripped by Spain.

WINE. Grapes are to be found in every Italian region. Winemaking has a very long tradition in the country, and Italy enjoys a positive trade balance in this sector. The vines yield 9,459,000 metric tons of grapes and 62,618,000 hectoliters of wine (a hectoliter is 100 liters). Until the mid-1980s, wine production was not generally of a high standard and, indeed, much table wine was cheap and of very poor quality. The industry then went through a series of reforms that introduced strict quality controls, and standards rose to a level whereby Italian wines can compete at international level with French wines. Italy's best-known wines are Chianti (produced in Tuscany), Barolo (produced in Piedmont), Soave (produced in the Veneto), and the white wines of Collio (produced in Friuli), Marsala (from Sicily), and Brunello (produced in Tuscany).

INDUSTRY

As in all other advanced Western economies, the Italian industrial sector is declining, decreasing the level of employment in industry and affecting the sector's contribution to the GDP. Industry employed 32.6 percent of the workforce in 1999, while contributing 30.4 percent to the GDP in 2000. However, manufacturing was the key to Italy's post-World War II economic boom and remains important. The steel industry in particular allowed the country to become one of the strongest economies in the world. All branches of the industrial sector grew very quickly, and Italian exports soared. Then, in the second half of the 1980s, the industrial sector went though a crisis, while the service sector expanded. With the onset of the second millennium, the loss of jobs in the industrial sector seems to have stabilized, and although facing tough international competition, Italian companies appear ready for the challenge.

MANUFACTURING. The backbone of the manufacturing sector is a few internationally known multinationals, operating in company with large numbers of small and medium enterprises. The most noteworthy manufactured products include machine tools, textiles and clothing, motorized road vehicles, domestic appliances, arms, fertilizers, and petrochemicals. Most manufacturing firms are located in the north of the country, with very few large factories in southern Italy. When Italy experienced its economic miracle in the 1950s and 1960s, the manufacturing heart of the country was the industrial triangle of Milan, Genoa, and Turin. However, this area has lost its predominant role due to the demise of the steel mills and other heavy industry. The northeast of the country, mainly the regions of Lombardy, the Veneto, and Friuli, is now the engine of the Italian economy. Certain large enterprises have relocated some of their operations to southern Italy to benefit from tax breaks and a more flexible workforce, but the region still has a very poor concentration of factories. Furthermore, large state-owned factories shut down in Taranto, Crotone, Terni, and Naples in the late 1980s, causing the loss of thousands of jobs. This action was part of a rationalization plan that required either the closure or the privatization of state-owned companies, and the public sector workforce was encouraged to seek employment in the growing service sector.

The most important, and probably best known, Italian manufacturing business is FIAT. This multinational company, headquartered in Turin and headed by the Agnelli family, has been a major force in Italian economic life since the beginning of the 20th century. FIAT is mainly involved in the production of Fiat cars and has a number of plants in Italy and abroad. It also owns Alfa-Romeo, Lancia, and Ferrari. FIAT's combined operations produce 3 million cars per year in Italy. While its export market is reasonably healthy, FIAT's large share of the Italian market allows it to compete in the European market. The Italian government is still influenced by the idea that "what is good for FIAT is good for Italy," so it lends its support to the car manufacturing company. In recent years, the government has subsidized the purchase of brand new cars (in most cases, Fiats) from car owners who want to trade in their old model. Thanks to this scheme, FIAT was able to make the Punto, one of the best-selling small cars in the company's history. Many FIAT operations are headquartered abroad, with cars and trucks made in countries such as Poland, Russia, Brazil, and Spain. Finally, the year 2000 alliance with General Motors allowed FIAT to rediscover its U.S. market, which was abandoned when Japanese car manufacturers began exporting to the United States. FIAT is also heavily involved in many other sectors of the manufacturing industry: car components, trucks, motorcycles, industrial vehicles, weapons, and engineering machinery.

TEXTILES AND CLOTHING. Another very important subsector in the manufacturing industry is textiles and clothing, which boasts some of the world's best known fashion designer labels, such as Valentino, Armani, Versace, Gianfranco Ferré, and Krizia. However, the more casual clothing market accounts for the financial success of this sector. The design, quality, and relatively inexpensive prices of its products have made textile manufacturing Italy's third largest business after engineering and construction. Almost 1 million workers are employed by the textile industry, which is a leading exporter of clothes and shoes. There are very few large enterprises in this industry; most producers have small or medium-sized factories. The real strength of the sector lies in the efficiency of its distribution networks, and in the fame they enjoy, particularly in newer markets like the United States and Asia where the top labels are status symbols.

One big name known throughout the world caters to customers of average income: Benetton. In recent years almost as well known for its controversial advertising as for its clothes, Benetton is a family-owned business located in the Veneto. In the 1980s and early 1990s, Benetton's annual sales figures passed the US$1 billion mark, with most of the income derived from export. By addressing the casual market rather than the high fashion market, Benetton was able to combine quality with affordable prices. The strategy paid off and helped other Italian manufacturers by creating a niche market from which they could all profit. However, currently, Benetton is not as strong as it was in the clothing market, and it has diversified into construction and communications. Nevertheless, the industry remains a vibrant cornerstone of Italian export.

While many of the more famous brand names are situated in northern Italy, the textile sector is reasonably strong in southern Italy, where an increasing number of producers have relocated some of their manufacturing. Fashion houses in particular tend to outsource their production to small, family-run businesses in the area of Naples or in Puglia, where workers are more flexible. They specialize in the manufacture of leather, from which clothes, handbags, wallets, and purses are made.

FOOD PROCESSING. The development of the food processing industry in Italy has been similar to that of textiles. While its contribution to the GDP is far less substantial, it is nevertheless a significant economic sector. Fragmented and small-scale until the 1980s, the sector became more competitive by the 1990s through privatization and rationalization. Very powerful food manufacturing groups such as Barilla (makers of pasta) and Parmalat (dairy products) are dominant in their respective fields, not only in Italy but also abroad. Swiss-owned Nestlé acquired Buitoni pasta and Perugina chocolate in 1987 and thus has an important presence in Italy. As well as these main players, a wide range of small firms produce traditional Italian fare such as mozzarella cheese, Parma ham, and Calabrian sausages, without much recourse to modern technology. Most of the food products are destined for local consumption, but many are also exported. The widespread network of Italian restaurants abroad contributes to the increasing reputation and popularity of Italian foods throughout the world, and processed food exports represent a major element of numerous businesses in the sector.

SERVICES

Services have become the strongest foundation on which Italy builds its economic health. With a 67.1 percent share of GDP in 2000, the sector is the largest contributor to the national economy. The enormous expansion of service industries over the last couple of decades has encouraged the government to regard as a priority further investment in the sector. Since 1991, the number of employees in the service sector of the state bureaucracy, however, has steadily decreased as part of the government's cost-cutting policy and important state-run services are being given over to the private sector.

TOURISM. Italy competes with the United States, France, and Spain as one of the most popular destinations for international tourists, who flock to it in huge numbers. Approximately 30 million tourists visited the country in 1999 and, thanks to the Catholic Jubileum (a celebration of Catholic heritage) over 40 million visited in 2000. Surprisingly, tourism was not a priority for the country until the late 1980s. Then a coherent promotion program emerged and led to general improvements in transport, hotels and other tourist accommodations, museums, and monuments. The turning point was the 1990 soccer World Cup, when tourists descended on Italy for that event and rediscovered the country's other attractions.

Italy is extraordinarily rich in history, classical art and architecture, ancient cities and villages, glorious landscapes, and a coastline well served by beaches. The vast western historical and artistic heritage draws large numbers of visitors to Rome, Venice, and Florence, while the smaller cities such as Siena, Pisa, Naples, the Isle of Capri, and Taormina in Sicily are increasingly popular. The region of Emilia-Romagna is a favorite spot for those, such as the east Europeans, on a limited budget, while Sardinia and Sicily are more upscale destinations. In 1996, receipts from tourism amounted to over US$28 billion. If those working in the transport sector were to be included in the statistics for the tourist sector, almost half of the working population would be connected with tourism. However, as with so much else in Italy, tourism is highly concentrated in the center-north, where most of the hotels and accommodations are located. In recent years, however, both central government and local administrations have begun to invest heavily in tourist services in the southern regions. Potentially, tourism can bring **hard currency** and employment to the south, encouraging development in its comparatively neglected regions of the country.

The working conditions in the tourist industry vary considerably from region to region and from business to business. Many hotels, restaurants, and bars are family owned, and extra labor is hired at a low cost during the busy months. Conditions are better for workers in state-owned museums, tourist offices, and transport. An almost unlimited supply of labor from the informal economy is available to the tourist sector, and it is needy foreign immigrants who take the lowest paid and least pleasant jobs.

RETAIL. Italy has a highly developed **retail** system. Mass outlets in the form of supermarkets, malls, and multiple stores are becoming increasingly popular, and distribution is very well organized, particularly in the northern regions. The main chains are Standa, COOP, Esselunga, Sigma, and SPAR. Nevertheless, the retail sector is largely made up small, family-owned shops, and these remain the primary sales outlets for goods and services in the south. The shop-owners' association, a very powerful lobbying group, was able to convince government to withhold licenses for supermarkets and malls for 2 years so that small shop owners could claim back some business. Working conditions are decent in family-owned shops, where employers tend to treat outside help as if they belonged to the family. Italian shop assistants, unlike those in many other countries, are professionals who are likely to stay with their jobs for life.

FINANCIAL SERVICES. Italy is a highly developed economy, and the financial and banking sector is similar to that of all other Western European countries. The Bank of Italy is the central bank, but with EMU now in place, the country's monetary policy is overseen by the European Central Bank. However, the Bank of Italy remains in charge of credit control and functions as the ultimate **guarantor** of other banks. The number of banks in Italy has always been high, with a wide range of financial institutions operating at different levels. There are national banks, both public and private, popular co-operative banks, savings banks, and chartered banks. Most of the co-operative and savings banks operate within a limited territory (provincial or regional). In general, banks are concentrated in the north. A notable exception to this is Sicily, where a large number of banks and other financial institutions are located for the less than healthy reason that organized crime requires **money-laundering** institutions under its control.

In recent years, mergers and takeovers have increased in order to strengthen and stabilize the banking system. Privatization has also helped to streamline the sector. Investment institutions, both public and private, are becoming increasingly important, with many people turning to investments to supplement their income. Since 1998, the banking system has been almost fully liberalized and most banks offer a wide range of financial services to their customers. Italian families have been traditionally very keen to save money, and, in 1999, the total deposits held in Italian banks amounted to US$450 billion. According to 1999 data, European banks use 53 percent of their available reserves to service individual loans, such as mortgages, with only 46.3 percent directed towards financing private sector businesses. Italy, however, does not conform to this pattern. Italian banks invest 66.7 percent of their resources in private enterprise, while only 18.3 percent is given to private consumers.

INTERNATIONAL TRADE

Italy recorded a trade deficit for several decades, largely due to the fact that the country lacked energy resources and was entirely dependent on imports for its supply. However, the 1990s brought a change of fortune, beginning with the **devaluation** of the lira in 1992 which allowed many businesses to compete in overseas export markets, particularly in Asia markets and the United States. The reduction of oil and gas prices in the

Trade (expressed in billions of US$): Italy

	Exports	Imports
1975	34.988	38.526
1980	78.104	100.741
1985	76.717	87.692
1990	170.304	181.968
1995	233.998	206.040
1998	242.332	215.887

SOURCE: International Monetary Fund. *International Financial Statistics Yearbook 1999.*

mid-1990s gave a further boost to small and medium-size companies, as did their aggressive promotion of their products, which enabled them to penetrate foreign markets. Today, "Made in Italy" is in many countries a well-regarded indication of quality. In 1998, Italy recorded a trade surplus, with imports totaling US$215.887 billion against exports worth US$242.332 billion. That surplus has since been trimmed, with export of US$241.1 billion in 2000 against imports of US$231.4 billion.

Italy benefits from the EU free market, which is not subject to any trade barriers or **tariffs**, and 56.8 percent of Italian exports went to other EU countries in 1999. Italy's main export destinations within Europe are Germany (16.4 percent), France (12.9 percent), the United Kingdom (7.1 percent), Spain (6.3 percent), and the Netherlands (2.9 percent). The country's biggest commercial partner outside Europe is the United States, which takes 9.5 percent of Italy's export goods. Recently, a number of Asian countries have become important buyers of Italian products, and exports, particularly of clothes and shoes, to Japan, South Korea, and China are increasing. Italy's major exports are transport equipment, electrical machinery, textiles and clothing, chemicals, and food and beverages. The single largest export is transport equipment, with FIAT the main supplier. FIAT not only exports the motor cars (including Ferraris) for which it is known worldwide, but also a number of other vehicles ranging from train carriages and metro cars to trucks and motorcycles.

The products of its EU partners also dominate Italy's imports. In 1990, over 61 percent of total imports came from EU countries: Germany (19.3 percent), France (12.6 percent), the Netherlands (6.3 percent), and Spain (4.4 percent). Outside the EU, the United States contributes 5 percent of imports. The composition of imported goods is evidence of the lack of energy resources and raw materials from which the country suffers. Thus, metal represents 9.9 percent of total imports, and petroleum represents 4.5 percent. Transport equipment also figures prominently, as do chemicals and food. All of the most important multinational businesses, across all sectors, operate in Italy, either directly or through subsidiaries. A number of them invested quite heavily in the country, particularly after the liberalization of the European market in 1987, under the auspices of the EU.

MONEY

The value of the Italian lira has been volatile over the last 30 years and is generally considered a weak currency by comparison with other major currencies. Historically, the weakness of the Italian lira has been both a curse and a blessing for the country. On the one hand, Italy had to pay for energy resources and supplies in hard currency (U.S. dollars), and imported goods were expensive. On the other hand, a weak currency contributed to making high-quality Italian exports very appealing due to their relatively low prices, and the foreign markets were duly conquered. Moreover, high production costs were offset by relatively cheap labor.

Exchange rates: Italy

euros per US$1	
Jan 2001	1.0659
2000	1.0854
1999	0.9386
1998	1,736.2
1997	1,703.1
1996	1,542.9

Note: Rates prior to 1999 are in Italian lire per US dollar.

SOURCE: CIA *World Factbook 2001* [ONLINE].

Italy's participation in the European Economic Community (EEC) failed to stem the currency's volatility, and the lira was twice forced to withdraw from the **fixed exchange rates** that had been established among the member states. Following the last withdrawal in 1992, the government devalued the currency in order to boost exports at the height of the economic recession when the lira was under tremendous speculative pressure. The calculated gamble of devaluation paid off, particularly as regards exports to the United States, where U.S. consumers were ready to enjoy their country's economic boom.

Since the launch of the euro, the lira has found a previously unknown stability. The **exchange rate** is fixed, and in January 2002, the lira will be replaced by the euro, which will become the currency that competes against the U.S. dollar, and other currencies in the global market. Public opinion in Italy, unlike that of certain other countries such as the United Kingdom, welcomes the introduction of the new currency and does not seem to mind abandoning the traditional lira.

The Italian Stock Exchange (ISE), located in Milan, was founded in 1808, but until the mid-1980s it played a comparatively insignificant role in the national economy. Many businesses were suspicious of the stock exchange and chose to remain unlisted. However, since 1998, the ISE has grown into a dynamic force as a result of privatization, a new generation of progressive managers, and the requirements of the new economy. The public, too, is increasingly interested in stocks and shares and, as in the United States and elsewhere, a greater number of people are playing the market. Consequently, the ISE has expanded, and at the end of 1998 there were 223 listed companies. During 1997 and 1998, the volume of trading increased continuously, achieving and sustaining record levels. Privatization has certainly contributed to enhancing the qualitative level of listed companies and attracted a wider public. While Milan is by no means as important as London or Paris to European share dealing, it is becoming increasingly important to the Italian economy.

POVERTY AND WEALTH

The Italian Institute of Statistics assesses the class system using 6 different categories. The first is the bourgeoisie, which includes entrepreneurs employing a minimum of 6 people, self-employed professionals, and managers, and accounts for 10 percent of the working population. The white collar middle class covers employees engaged in non-manual jobs and makes up 17 percent of the working population. The urban petit bourgeoisie comprise 14 percent of the working population, defined as small entrepreneurs with a maximum of 6 employees, shopkeepers, and self-employed artisans. The rural petit bourgeoisie, at 10 percent, own and operate small enterprises in the primary sectors of agriculture, forestry, hunting, and fishing. The urban working class is the 37 percent of the workforce that is engaged in manual labor. Finally, the rural working class, at 9 percent, are employees of the primary sector. This class breakdown, in identifying 2 categories each of the working and entrepreneurial classes, is considered to be more precise than the more common method of class division and has been used since the mid-1980s.

The situation regarding upward social, or class, mobility in Italy is quite complex. In 1998, the absolute rate of mobility—people who belong to a different social class than their parents—was 60.3 percent for men and 64.9 percent for women, the great majority of the Italian workforce. However, when one breaks down the absolute rate of mobility figures by class and analyzes them in relation to the changes in occupation structure between the current times and the 1960s, the whole picture changes. The highest mobility rate is found within the rural working class (91.1 percent), due mainly to the fact that, in the space of one generation, the occupational weight of this class has been greatly reduced. The lowest rates of mobility are found in the classes that have not been radically modified by the occupational structure: the urban working class and bourgeoisie. In these cases only half of the people are in a different class than their parents. It is, therefore, quite clear that true social mobility is perceived as being greater than it is. This conclusion is confirmed by data that give the rate of intra-generational mobility for all classes as 30.3 percent. Thus, the opportunities for social mobility still largely depend on an individual's social origins.

Despite being a wealthy country, Italy suffers from serious inequality in the distribution of wealth and resources. These dramatic statistics stand out: in 1998, 2,558,000 families (11.8 percent of the total) lived in poverty, which is equal to 7,423,000 individuals. The figure was even higher at the end of the 1980s, when families living in poverty represented 14 percent of the population. Once again, the contrast between north and south could not be clearer, with over 65 percent of impoverished families living in southern regions. The gap between the rich north and the impoverished south continues to increase, as does the depth of poverty itself. Of those classified as poor, elderly people living on a simple state pension make up 53 percent of households living in poverty. Their numbers, however, are steadily decreasing, to be overtaken by the working poor. This phenomenon, which looks likely to become a permanent feature of Italian society, affects couples with one or more children, where only one parent works, is under 40 years old, and has few qualifications and, thus, low earning power.

As a result of Italy's generous welfare state, the great majority of poor families do not live in extremes of squalor or deprivation. Essential needs provided by the state include basic health care and education, clean water supplies, and housing. Moreover, extensive family networks help those living in poverty to feel less isolated and are sometimes a source of financial help. However, it is extremely difficult for families in poverty to improve their circumstances, and over 70 percent of households classified as poor in 1994 remained poor 2 years later.

GDP per Capita (US$)

Country	1975	1980	1985	1990	1998
Italy	11,969	14,621	15,707	18,141	19,574
United States	19,364	21,529	23,200	25,363	29,683
France	18,730	21,374	22,510	25,624	27,975
Greece	8,302	9,645	10,005	10,735	12,069

SOURCE: United Nations. *Human Development Report 2000; Trends in human development and per capita income.*

Distribution of Income or Consumption by Percentage Share: Italy

Lowest 10%	3.5
Lowest 20%	8.7
Second 20%	14.0
Third 20%	18.1
Fourth 20%	22.9
Highest 20%	36.3
Highest 10%	21.8

Survey year: 1995

Note: This information refers to income shares by percentiles of the population and is ranked by per capita income.

SOURCE: *2000 World Development Indicators* [CD-ROM].

Household Consumption in PPP Terms

Country	All food	Clothing and footwear	Fuel and power[a]	Health care[b]	Education[b]	Transport & Communications	Other
Italy	23	11	12	3	17	8	27
United States	13	9	9	4	6	8	51
France	22	7	9	3	8	12	40
Greece	32	11	14	5	14	8	16

Data represent percentage of consumption in PPP terms.
[a]Excludes energy used for transport.
[b]Includes government and private expenditures.

SOURCE: World Bank. *World Development Indicators 2000.*

Necessity often forces individuals in poverty to take up low-paid and unsafe jobs in the informal economy, where they are subject to threats and blackmail. In urban areas of the south, the younger generation finds it very difficult to obtain work and poverty drives a percentage of them into the arms of organized crime. Migration to the north or leaving Italy altogether still remain ways out for many. While poverty is less visible in the wealthy north, it does exist. In particular, young couples with 2 or more children who struggle to meet the high cost of living on low salaries find themselves caught in the poverty trap.

WORKING CONDITIONS

Official 1998 figures put the Italian workforce at over 23 million, with an unemployment rate of 11.5 percent, but these statistics fail to take the informal economy into account. Unemployment is substantially higher in the south and among the younger generation. Statistically, people from the south, under age 30 and with poor qualifications stand a 50 percent chance of being unable to find employment. Thus, both geography and age are major factors in the Italian labor market.

Italy has a number of trade unions which, although formally independent, are connected to the larger political parties. The strongest union has always been the Confederazione Generale Italiana Lavoratori (CGIL), originally of communist allegiance, but now affiliated with the leftist Democrats. Italian trade unions were very strong in the past, and thanks to their efforts in the 1970s and 1980s many Italian workers currently enjoy a high level of social protection. Some of this protective network is being dismantled, but the foundations remain in place. Following mass strikes and demonstrations in 1968 and 1969, a statute of workers' rights was finally made law in 1970, thus ensuring security of employment in larger firms. Smaller firms were exempted from adopting a number of the statute's measures, but its impact has nevertheless been considerable in promoting the rights of workers. Among other significant victories for the trade union was the wage indexing system, guaranteeing that salaries would rise in line with annual inflation; common job classification, which introduced standardized salaries throughout Italy for specific categories of work; paid maternity leave; and an increase in the number of paid holidays. Despite these measures, Italian workers are among the worst paid in Europe, and higher wages for all workers is a constant demand of the trade unions, since the strong and well-organized employers' associations do not ever award substantial increases. Poor wages, though, are generally offset by a number of other social benefits, and in recent years the working week has been reduced to 37 hours (down 2.5 hours) for the same pay. Furthermore, people who are laid off can count on employment checks for a number of months and are entitled to severance pay, no matter what the grounds for dismissal.

Workers in the informal economy tend to be poorly educated, live in high unemployment areas, and are often foreign immigrants. They are unable to take advantage of the benefits enjoyed by the legally employed, and their working conditions are inadequate. Those who run the informal economy ignore safety regulations, demand working hours that far exceed the legal maximum, make no contributions to pension funds, offer no job security, and give no severance pay. The informal economy has the greatest impact on farm laborers where work is seasonal, and on construction and textile production workers employed by small firms. Wages in the informal sector tend to be at subsistence level, but it is difficult to ascertain the actual figures. Despite the efforts of the EU to curb the informal economy in Italy and enforce safety regulations, over 1,000 workers die in the work place every year.

Trade unionism in Italy has been in decline since the mid-1980s and most paid-up union members are retired workers. The influence of the unions has declined due to the reduction of the workforce in the industrial sector, the skepticism with which the trade union elite is perceived, and government policy aimed at weakening the unions. Much that was achieved by the unions has been abolished or is on the verge of being dismantled. Privatization, liberalization, and budget cuts have reduced the protection network, and businesses have a far freer hand in dealing with the workforce. Consequently, employers' contributions towards pensions are being slashed, and overtime is not as well paid. The pressure of international competition and the necessity to maintain a healthy budget mean that labor costs have to be cut in both the private and public sectors. In order to preserve jobs, the trade unions and employers entered into a pact by which workers moderate their requests and accept cuts in exchange for job security.

Women have been entering the workforce since the early 1960s. They are a significant presence in all sectors of economy and tend to continue working after marriage, and even after having children. Many, however, are still employed in sectors that have been traditionally perceived as suited to women, such as education, health care and social services. The difficulty of coping with a full time job and raising children is a real burden to many women, and they increasingly turn to part-time work, which, though becoming more common, is an underdeveloped sector in Italy.

COUNTRY HISTORY AND ECONOMIC DEVELOPMENT

1861. Italy is unified after decades of struggle against foreign occupation. The king of Piedmont becomes king of Italy.

1870. Radical land reform takes place, intended to benefit the peasant workers, but few profit from the reforms, and living conditions for farmers decline.

1880s. Prime Minister Giolitti embraces protectionism and places high tariffs on a number of agricultural and industrial products to defend the national sectors. The policy backfires, access to foreign markets collapses, and a tariff war with France ensues.

1890s. The tariff war with France ends. The economy begins to develop, but many leave the country in search of a better life. The United States and South America are the preferred destinations.

1899. Giovanni Agnelli founds FIAT in Turin.

1915. Italy joins the Allies and fights against Germany and Austro-Hungary in World War I (1914–18).

1922. In the wake of enormous postwar political and economic problems, Benito Mussolini's fascist movement comes to power. Mussolini is appointed prime minister and radically changes the country.

1925. Mussolini completes his design of transforming Italy into a fascist dictatorship. He reshapes the economy to focus on agricultural self-sufficiency, a strong industrial sector and a rapid military build-up. The economy is mixed: private companies co-exist with many state-owned companies.

1936. Italy enters the colonial race and invades Somalia, which remains an Italian colony until the end of World War II.

1939–45. Italy enters World War II as an ally of Nazi Germany in 1940. With the downfall of Mussolini in 1943, however, Italy switches its allegiance to the Allies.

1946. Following a national referendum, King Victor Emmanuel III abdicates, and Italy becomes a republic. A government of national unity is formed to tackle the country's problems.

1952. Italy becomes a founding member of the European Coal and Steel Community with Germany, France, Belgium, the Netherlands and Luxembourg.

1957. Italy becomes a founding member of the European Economic Community, the predecessor to the European Union. The Italian "economic miracle" begins through a combination of free market principles and heavy government intervention.

1963. The Socialist Party abandons its leftist stance and joins the Christian Democrat government. This coalition holds power until 1994.

1968–69. The country is shaken by a series of strikes and demonstrations. Workers and students demand the improvement of working and living conditions. The government meets many demands, and a more modern welfare state is established.

1973. The first oil crisis slows economic growth but does not stop it.

1977. The economy grinds to a sudden halt. Political crisis and stagflation lead to the formation of a government of national unity, as left- and right-wing terrorism spreads.

1980. Rationalization and privatization commence and continue throughout the decade, with private companies becoming dominant.

1984. The beginning of a new economic miracle. Low oil prices, technological innovations, and cheap labor drive the Italian economy forward. However, only the northern regions benefit from this growth.

1992. The old political class is swept away by corruption scandals. The new government embraces neo-liberal policies based on massive budgetary cuts, privatization, and the promotion of worker flexibility. The lira is devalued to boost exports. The policy succeeds, and Italy exports more than it imports. Italy signs the Maastricht Treaty, which provides for further European economic integration. Among the measures to which Italy subscribes is participation in the European Monetary Union.

1994. The center-right coalition led by media magnate Silvio Berlusconi wins the elections but remains in power only 7 months. A temporary government led by **technocrats** replaces it.

1996. The center-left coalition wins the elections and continues with economic liberalization.

1999. Italy qualifies for monetary union with 11 other EU countries and plans for the introduction of a single currency, the euro.

2001. A center-right coalition led by Silvio Berlusconi gains control of the government.

FUTURE TRENDS

The liberalizing efforts of the 1990s laid the foundations for the present growth, and Italy entered the new millennium on a high note, embracing the European Monetary Union and its new currency, the euro. The country's technological revolution is succeeding, the network of small and medium-sized enterprises is solid, international competitiveness is strong, and the balance of trade is positive. The government is consolidating the excellent results obtained by limiting expenditures and is waging a determined battle against tax evasion. Italy's economic outlook is, therefore, a positive one, particularly as the level of education is rising, and population growth is manageable. All indicators point to continued improvements in living standards. The future will see the Italian economy integrated even more into the economy of its European partners, and the European Union will eventually become a fully integrated body in all economic matters, including taxation.

There are, however, still a number of negative aspects that plague the economic and social well-being of Italy. First and foremost is the gap between the north and the south, which has widened over the past couple of decades, with government policies and EU grants proving unable to bring about any substantial improvement. Closing this gap is Italy's biggest challenge in securing a healthy future.

The weight of the informal economy also remains a major problem. While attempts have been made to reduce the impact of this sector, it remains considerable, and in escaping state control, it has a negative effect on working conditions, quality control, and fiscal revenues. While the informal economy may represent a source of income for many poorer families in the short term, in the long run it will undermine the official economy and, therefore, the country as a whole. Finally, there is the problem of persistent unemployment. Even when the economy is doing very well, the number of people out of work is higher than the European average. Unemployment stood at 11.5 percent in 2000. The government needs to address this problem as a matter of urgency.

DEPENDENCIES

Italy has no territories or colonies.

BIBLIOGRAPHY

Banca d'Italia. <http://www.bancaditalia.it>. Accessed October 2001.

Confederazione Generale Italiana Lavoratori. <http://www.cgil.it>. Accessed October 2001.

Diamanti, Ilvo. *Il Male del Nord.* Rome: Donzelli, 1996.

Economist Intelligence Unit. *Country Profile: Italy.* London: Economist Intelligence Unit, 2001.

Embassy of Italy in the United States. <http://www.italyemb.org>. Accessed October 2001.

ISTAT. *Rapporto sull'Italia.* Bologna: Il Mulino, 2000.

Permanent Mission of Italy to the United Nations. <http://www.italyun.org>. Accessed October 2001.

Randlesome, Collin. *Business Cultures in Europe.* Oxford: Butterworth-Heinemann, 1993.

Sassoon, Don. *Contemporary Italy: Economy, Society, and Politics since 1945.* London and New York: Longman, 1997.

Sechi, Salvatore, editor. *Deconstructing Italy: Italy in the Nineties.* Berkeley: University of California Press, 1995.

U.S. Central Intelligence Agency. *World Factbook 2001.* <http://www.odci.gov/cia/publications/factbook/index.html>. Accessed September 2001.

U.S. Department of State. *Background Notes: Italy, July 2000.* <http://www.state.gov/www/background_notes/italy_0007_bgn.html>. Accessed October 2001.

U.S. Department of State. *FY 2001 Country Commercial Guide: Italy.* <http://www.state.gov/www/about_state/business/com_guides/2001/europe/index.html>. Accessed October 2001.

Welcome to the Italian Trade Commission Web Site. <http://www.italtrade.com/ice/index.html>. Accessed October 2001.

—Francesco Cavatorta

LATVIA

Republic of Latvia
Latvijas Republika

CAPITAL: Riga.

MONETARY UNIT: Latvian Lat (Ls). One lat equals 100 santimis. There are coins of 1, 2, 5, 10, 20, and 50 santimi and 1 and 2 lats, and bank notes of 5, 10, 20, 50, 100, and 500 lats.

CHIEF EXPORTS: Wood and wood products, machinery and equipment, metals, textiles, foodstuffs.

CHIEF IMPORTS: Machinery and equipment, chemicals, fuels.

GROSS DOMESTIC PRODUCT: US$9.8 billion (purchasing power parity, 1999 est.).

BALANCE OF TRADE: **Exports:** US$1.9 billion (f.o.b., 1999). **Imports:** US$2.8 billion (f.o.b., 1998).

COUNTRY OVERVIEW

LOCATION AND SIZE. Located in the Baltic region of Eastern Europe, Latvia is bordered by Estonia (339 kilometers; 211 miles), Russia (217 kilometers; 135 miles), Belarus (141 kilometers; 88 miles), Lithuania (453 kilometers; 281 miles), and the Baltic Sea (531 kilometers; 330 miles). Slightly larger than the state of West Virginia, Latvia has a total area of 64,589 square kilometers (40,136 square miles). Its capital, Riga, is centrally located and lies next to its namesake, the Gulf of Riga.

POPULATION. In July of 2000 the population of Latvia was estimated at 2,404,926, a decrease of 10 percent from the 1989 population of 2,666,567. This decrease is the result of 2 factors. The first is the economic hardships that set in following the break-up of the Soviet Union in 1991—of which Latvia had been a reluctant member—and the decision of families to postpone procreation. For the first time since the 1945 flight from the advancing Red Army and the 1949 Soviet deportation of dissident Latvians to Siberia, the total number of deaths outnumbered the total number of births. The second, and more important, factor has to do with the out-migration of Slavs, primarily Russians and Ukrainians. The regained independence of Latvia in 1991 brought a shift in political power from Russian control into Latvian control. New Latvian language requirements for certain employment sectors and the sudden reality of monolingual Russian speakers living in a new "foreign" country spurred a large **emigration** movement.

In 2000 the birth rate stood at 7.8 births per 1,000 while the death rate stood at 14.88 per 1,000. With a current out migration of 1.32 per 1,000, Latvia's annual population growth rate is -0.84 percent, and the projected population for 2015 is 2.1 million and for 2030 is 2.0 million. With an official unemployment rate of 8.6 percent (unofficial estimates are close to 14 percent), there is no great demand for an immediate increase in the **labor force**. The below replacement level birth rate may factor into labor shortages should Latvia's productive economy increase significantly. Female life expectancy (74.6 years) is much greater than male life expectancy (62.4 years) and thus among older people women greatly outnumber men. The largest percentage of the population are within their working years, 20 to 64, and a great amount of economic responsibility falls upon them. The **dependency ratio** (the percentage of the population that are either above or below their productive working years) in 1997 was 49.9 percent. In this same year, the percentage of the population aged 65 and above was at 13.6 percent and is estimated to reach 16.8 percent by 2015. Despite this increase in the percentage of the aged, the dependency ratio is predicted to drop to 45.8 percent by 2015. This is due to the drop in fertility rate, from 2.0 children per mother in 1975 to 1.3 in 1997.

Language and citizenship policies that served as a reprisal against former Russian dominance fostered the out migration of that group, but criticisms from the

United Nations and the European Union for such discriminatory practices have caused the Latvian government to soften its citizenship and naturalization policies. In 1989 Latvians comprised only 52 percent of the country's population while Russians constituted 34 percent, with Belorussians, Ukrainians, Poles, and Lithuanians, in respective ranking, making up most of the remainder. Within 6 major municipalities, the Russian population grossly outnumbers the indigenous population, and the former dominance of the Russian language meant that it was impossible for a Latvian to engage in any type of economic activity without the use of Russian. Current conditions have changed and monolingual Russian speakers are faced with very difficult circumstances. In 1996 ethnic Latvians comprised 56.6 percent of the country's population, while the remaining ethnic Russians constituted 30.3 percent. However, 71 percent of the Latvian population are considered citizens while the remaining 29 percent are not, indicating that a significant portion of the ethnic Russian population has been given citizenship. This issue has been a continuing source of contention in the country's politics.

OVERVIEW OF ECONOMY

The economy of Latvia today, which is based on light industry and services, looks optimistically toward the future. But, like the other 2 Baltic States—Estonia and Lithuania—which emerged from the break-up of the Soviet Union in 1991, Latvia suffered severe economic shocks in the first decade of its transition from **communist** rule and has faced a difficult road during its transition to a market economy.

During the 1920s and 1930s, Latvia experienced a miraculous economic recovery after the ravaging of World War I (1914–18). Agrarian reform provided land for the dispossessed. Many farmsteads formed cooperatives that provided loans and export credits, the currency was stable, there was low **inflation**, unemployment was not as severe as it was in Western Europe during the Great Depression, and Latvia was able to tuck away 10.6 tons of gold in foreign banks. But this recovery was severely interrupted by World War II, and Latvia's economic processes were quickly altered by the invasion of the Red Army of the Soviet Union. As the Soviet Union took command of the economy, almost all property, including farms, was placed under state control, leading to the 1949 deportation of 40,000 mostly rural occupants. The following decades saw a continual struggle between rational communist reformers and political ideologues attached to Moscow, with the latter habitually prevailing. Though there was an attempt to reorient Latvian industry from its growing reliance on imported raw materials, by 1959 Moscow, the capital of the Soviet Union, oversaw all of Latvian industrialization and economic development. Despite such control, Latvians always remembered their previous economic successes and recognized that they would have been better off if they had remained separate from the Soviet Union.

The Soviet economic system entailed the importation of raw materials, fuel, and workers into Latvia, and the exportation of finished products. But the environment and the social welfare of Latvians suffered under this plan, as they did in all the Soviet republics. Finally, by the late 1980s, Latvia managed to gain greater control of its economy, increasing its share of control of financial activities from 17 to 42 percent by 1990. After the break-up of the Soviet Union, all the republics encountered a severe economic trauma. Rising energy prices and lack of **price controls** made Western goods too expensive for the markets of the former Soviet Union, and the quality of goods produced in Latvia was too poor to be competitive in Western markets. International trade plummeted, manufacturing slowed, and unemployment and inflation soared.

Economic reforms introduced after the declaration of independence from Russia in 1991 called for a shift in the direction of exports away from Russia and toward the West, a change and stabilization of the currency, and a shift away from heavy industry toward a more service based economy. **Privatization** —the sale or transfer of state-owned businesses to the **private sector**—has proved to be one of the most difficult aspects of transition. It was some while before a privatization agency was established. There was not enough domestic capital to successfully purchase large enterprises, and perceived political instability and the prospect of costly retrofitting obsolete production companies hindered the attraction of foreign investment, which in itself was met with resistance as Latvians feared the selling off of its assets. Honoring the claims of previous ownership proved to be a difficult task as well. Claimants feared the high cost of repairs that would be necessary for properties, and the division of collectivized farms was troubled by the unequal value of the land.

The 1998 Russian financial crises affected Latvia, which experienced no growth in **gross domestic product** (GDP) in 1999. But currently Latvia shows every sign of becoming more involved with trade with the West and the world. It has joined the World Trade Organization (WTO) and has joined talks for accession into the European Union (EU). Major foreign investment in 1999 was directed toward real estate and in the financial sector, while investment in 2000 was directed toward energy and transportation. A 5.4 percent increase in the GDP in 2000, a decline in unemployment, and the stabilization of inflation spell good news for Latvia's bid to enter the EU in 2003.

POLITICS, GOVERNMENT, AND TAXATION

In 1989 the Latvian Supreme Soviet ended the Communist Party's political **monopoly**, and there was a rise in independent political parties and the opportunities for free elections, something that had not been possible in Latvia since 1940. Results of the first free election saw only 15 of the 201 pro-Soviet deputies reelected. Approximately two-thirds of the new members belonged to the Popular Front of Latvia (LTF), a pro-independence party that formed in 1987. On 4 May 1990, the Supreme Council, or Parliament, adopted a declaration of independence, declared Soviet annexation illegal, and restored articles of the 1922 constitution. On 21 August 1991, after the Soviet coup in Moscow, Latvia declared full independence but failed to enact components of the 4 May 1990 declaration because of questions about the legitimacy of the new government and whether amendments to the 1922 constitution should be permitted. Much of the opposition was due, the critics asserted, to the fact that election had taken place while Latvia was still occupied and that members of the Soviet army had participated and had been allowed to use rules different from the rest of the voting population. It was contended that only those with Latvian citizenship prior to Soviet occupation should be allowed to decide Latvia's future. In the following election in 1993 approximately 25 percent of the permanent residents in Latvia, mostly ethnic Russians, were not allowed to vote.

In Latvia's electoral system 100 representatives are elected for a 3-year period to serve in the Saeima, which then elects a board whose chairman or deputy serves as speaker for the legislature. The Saeima elects a president who also serves for 3 years and is excluded from serving more than 2 terms. The president appoints a prime minister, who then nominates the other cabinet ministers. In their May 1994 elections—the first since independence—a majority of the representatives elected were members of the Latvian National Independence Movement or other nationalist parties. Segments of the Communist Party of Latvia, which had previously dominated, fared very poorly. A host of contending political parties emerged and their particular prominence waxed and waned as various issues became more urgent for Latvia's citizens. For example, a 1994 dispute about **tariffs** on agricultural imports prompted the Latvian Farmer's Union to withdraw from the ruling coalition and resulting in a collapse of the government. Lativia faced the critical issue of citizenship. The first bill was very restrictive for Russians and other non-Latvians, allowing only 2,000 people to naturalize per year. International as well as domestic pressure caused the Saeima to reconsider and initiate another, less restrictive policy. The revised policy was that the applicant should have lived in Latvia at least 5 years, have adequate knowledge of the country's language, history, and constitution, and have a legal source of income.

Latvia, as with the other Baltic States, has played an interesting role in the continuing geopolitical, suspicion-laden struggle between Russia and the West. Latvia's initial attempts to join with North Atlantic Treaty Organization (NATO) were unsuccessful, but efforts toward this end, as well as integration into the EU, continue. Continued strengthening of democratic policies and adherence to economic **liberalizing** policies has made Latvia's access to these groups favorable, even though Russia continues to express disfavor.

A sizable portion of the state income is derived from **value-added tax** (VAT), and this tax has been increased up to 18 percent in order to meet state expenditures. To attract foreign investment of capital and to stimulate the economy, certain conditions applied for the exemption of VAT toward foreign investment. The government also sells **treasury bills** and earns interest on loans to domestic, private, and national enterprises.

INFRASTRUCTURE, POWER, AND COMMUNICATIONS

Latvia possesses 2,406 kilometers (1,495 miles) of railroads that extend toward Russia, Belarussia, and the other Baltic States. Both they and the cars that roll across them are aging and in need of repair. A network of 59,178 kilometers (36,773 miles) of roads, roughly a third of which are paved, allows access to all regions of the country. While private car ownership has risen in that last years, railways and buses transport the majority of commuters.

Major seaports located at Riga, Ventspils, and Liepaja, which remain ice free throughout the year, are superbly linked to both rails and an extensive network of roads, allowing the domestic and international transportation of goods. Latvia, which is dependent on the importation of fuels, also serves as a transit area for outgoing supplies. The port of Ventspils is the terminus for the Volga Urals oil pipeline (which extends into Russia) and can simultaneously accommodate 3 large tankers. The port at Liepaja, the deepest port in the Baltic Sea, was formerly operated for Soviet military purposes and is in need of major modification for commercial purposes. The port at Riga, the busiest in Latvia, is responsible for the greatest movement of trade goods.

Oil and gas are imported into Latvia from Russia and help to fuel industries and the 2 thermal power plants near Riga. In addition, 3 hydroelectric dams along Latvia's largest river, the Daugava, add to the power supply, but still electricity is imported to feed this most industrialized Baltic State.

Privatization has caused a reconstruction in Latvia's telecommunications network. In 1994, 49 percent of the system was sold to a British-Finnish telecommunications consortium and international communications became available at standard international rates. The privatized telecommunications company, Lattelcom, is working toward a fully digitized network by 2012, thus alleviating the problem of unmet demand due to a shortage of lines. In 1997 there were 748,000 main telephone lines in use, and in 1999, 175,348 cellular phones in use.

ECONOMIC SECTORS

The years following World War II saw a shift in Latvia's major economic activity from agriculture and toward Soviet-style heavy industry. In 1990, agriculture

Communications

Country	Newspapers	Radios	TV Sets[a]	Cable subscribers[a]	Mobile Phones[a]	Fax Machines[a]	Personal Computers[a]	Internet Hosts[b]	Internet Users[b]
	1996	1997	1998	1998	1998	1998	1998	1999	1999
Latvia	247	710	492	58.0	68	N/A	N/A	50.86	105
United States	215	2,146	847	244.3	256	78.4	458.6	1,508.7	74,100
Russia	105	418	420	78.5	5	0.4	40.6	13.06	2,700
Lithuania	93	513	459	67.5	72	1.7	54.0	30.45	103

[a]Data are from International Telecommunication Union, *World Telecommunication Development Report 1999* and are per 1,000 people.
[b]Data are from the Internet Software Consortium (http://www.isc.org) and are per 10,000 people.

SOURCE: World Bank. *World Development Indicators 2000.*

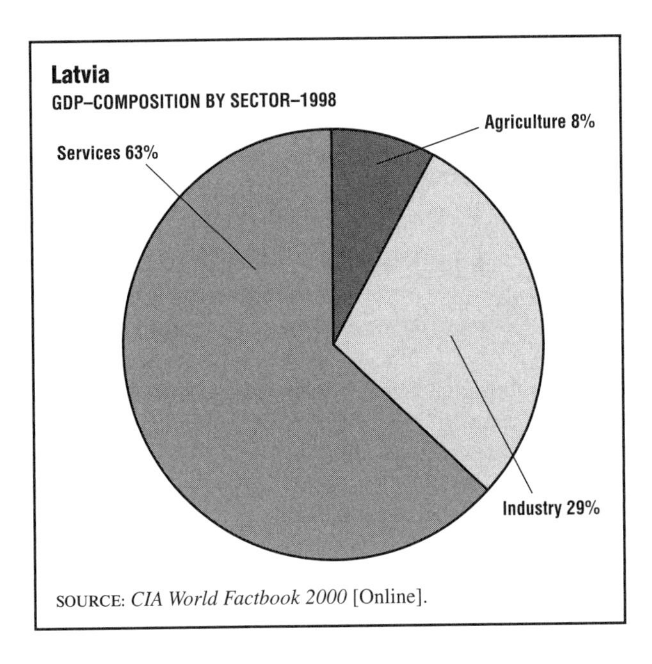

SOURCE: *CIA World Factbook 2000* [Online].

accounted for 20 percent of the GDP while industry comprised almost 43 percent and services—including transportation, communication, and construction—were around 34 percent. The transition toward a market economy, however, has created a definite shift in economic orientation toward the west. By 1998 agriculture contributed only 8 percent of the GDP, while industry contributed 29 percent and services contributed 63 percent. (Employment per sector was last recorded in 1990 at 16 percent in agriculture, 41 percent in industry, and 43 percent in services, but these numbers have likely shifted significantly over the course of the decade.)

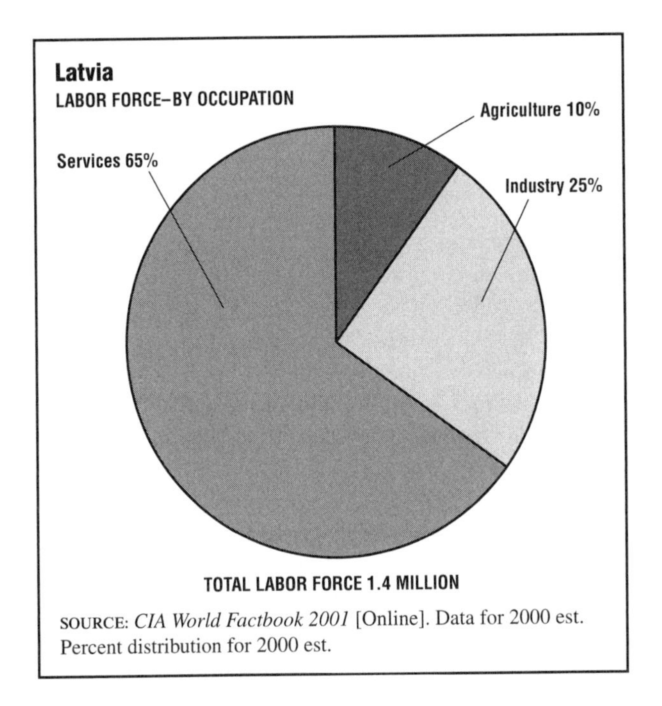

SOURCE: *CIA World Factbook 2001* [Online]. Data for 2000 est. Percent distribution for 2000 est.

In 1993, 33 percent of Latvia's exports were directed toward Western Europe while 48 percent were directed toward the republics of the former Soviet Union. By 1999, exports toward the European Union were at 63 percent while export with the former Soviet Union states was reduced to 12 percent. The export of services has experienced rapid growth—22 percent in the first three-quarters of 2000 alone. These services include information technologies and computer software, international trade banks, and cargo services. As the Latvian economy models itself on the economies of the West, such services will play an even more important role in Latvia's integration into the European Union. These exports have been of great value, providing stability at a moment when external shocks, such as a strengthened dollar and rising oil prices, have hurt the trade balance.

AGRICULTURE

Under Soviet control, once-dominant Latvian agriculture took a back seat to industry. By 1990, the amount of agricultural land in Latvia decreased 32 percent from its 1932 levels. As agriculture was brought under state control, many of the former farms were abandoned and converted to forest. Half of the arable land was used for fodder crops for the cattle and dairy industries that supplied the Soviet Union. About 40 percent of the land was used to grow grain, and the rest was for potatoes, flax, and sugar beets. Meat, dairy products, and crops were shipped to other Soviet republics in exchange for equipment, fuel, and fertilizer. Small private plots and some animal holdings were permitted by the Soviet authorities. These plots served a vital role in supplementing the poor output of the inefficient collective farms. At the end of communist rule much of the country's livestock was held on such plots. When the Soviet system fell apart, however, feed shortages and rising cost of farm equipment created a decline in agricultural production in Latvia.

From 1994 to 1998 there was a general decrease in the production of meat products. Associated with this was a drop in fodder production. The most dramatic decline in livestock was in beef production and the least dramatic was in poultry. Milk production was down slightly while egg production increased. This is likely due to the economic austerity endured and the generally higher costs associated with meat product. Eggs, being a replenishable product, are a more economic form of protein. Production of cereals and potatoes decreased, but sugar beets doubled. This shift makes sense as the resultant sugar could be easily exported and bring in much needed **hard currency**. Forest products, such as paper and timber, also added to the economy through export. Even though agriculture declined in percentage of GDP in Latvia, it still accounted for 16 percent of the labor force in 2000.

Forests cover 40 percent of Latvian territory, with the majority of them being in the northern areas, which are 50 percent wooded. Over 11 percent of forests are protected, while the remaining forests are mixed between commercial and restricted management. Forest resources are not fully exploited, and if financial resources can be found to develop the industry, the number of annual cuts could be doubled. Local and international environmental organizations, of course, oppose such increased development

INDUSTRY

MANUFACTURING. Proximity to European markets and the ease and cheapness of transport across the Baltic Sea makes Latvia well situated for delivering goods to market according to EU standards. Cheap labor, a stable currency, membership in the World Trade Organization, and future membership in the EU has made industry an important part of Latvia's development plans.

Manufacturing in Latvia is currently organized around machinery, textiles (especially woolens), food processing, and wood processing. Due to cheap labor and abundant resources, wood processing is the most dynamic sector and possesses the potential for dramatic increase. Latvia produces automobiles, electric rail cars, and **consumer goods** such as radios and appliances. Steel, cement, wood products, chemicals, and electronics are also manufactured in Latvia's major urban centers. Dependence on imported energy delivered at increased prices injured the industrial sector of Latvia, once the most industrialized of the Soviet Republics, and the service sector has increased in importance. Information technologies (IT) have recently become a rapidly developing area due to changes in the political, business, and technical **infrastructure** of the country. About 20 percent of total foreign investments is directed at manufacturing.

As of 1999, food products and beverages comprised the largest share of Latvia's manufacturing at 36.4 percent. Wood and wood products, at 17.8 percent in 1999, comprised the second largest share of Latvian manufacturing and increased 14.5 percent from the previous year. Textiles remained important at nearly 6 percent in 1999, and other significant industries in 1999 included the following: publishing and printing (4.7 percent), wear apparel (3.7 percent), chemicals (3.5 percent), metal wares (2.9 percent), and transport vehicles (2.9 percent).

SERVICES

TOURISM. Latvia is the least known of the Baltic states and does not receive much tourism. However, Riga, the largest and most vibrant city in the Baltic States, is the primary tourist destination, offering opportunities for day trips. Tourism by Russians is still present in Latvia, but Western visitors have become more numerous. Latvia's coast supports several beach resorts, but poor water quality in the Baltic Sea has discouraged bathers. In fact, the number of visitors to Latvia has decreased from 2.4 million in 1993 to just 1.7 million in 1999.

FINANCIAL SERVICES. Latvia's 2-tiered banking system began in 1988 when its first commercial banks were established. Prior to the break up of the Soviet Union, there were no private banks in any of the Baltic States. Since that time, the banking system, although suffering 2 crises, has developed well and offers a variety of services to its customers. The Central Bank of Latvia was founded in August of 1990. It is an independent bank that has the right to issue the national currency, supervise other banks and credit unions, and control the economy via **monetary policy** instruments, such as national interest rates. It is independent of the Latvian government and handles foreign currency.

The commercial banking sector is controlled by the Central Bank. The bank crises have struck Latvia since independence. Connected to a large reduction in the number of banks, the first crisis occurred in 1995. The second crisis accompanied the Russian economic collapse of 1998. Since that time, the Latvian banking system has been recovering, and a majority of the banks have ended the year with a profit.

The banking system in Latvia has been almost entirely transferred into private hands, although 70 percent of the ownership and control is with foreign institutions. There are currently 21 banks and 1 foreign bank branch in Latvia. In 12 of these banks, more than 50 percent of assets are owned by foreign shareholders. In 2000 there was a 38 percent increase in the total assets of banks as investment has increased and proved profitable. Cash and capital flow into and out of Latvia faces virtually no restrictions.

The Riga Stock Exchange (RSE), re-established in 1993, is Latvia's only licensed stock exchange. It is owned by 27 shareholders, and the Latvian Ministry of Finance regulates its activities. The shareholders include major Latvian commercial banks, brokerage companies, and the State Real Estate Fund. In June of 1997, the RSE became the first exchange in Eastern Europe to have a Dow Jones Index, meaning that the daily activities are collectively reported in a quantitative fashion to display the rise and falls in the market.

INTERNATIONAL TRADE

Latvia's geographical position has made it a strategic trading hub for generations, and this benefit continues as an increase in trade between East and West passes across its borders. There has been a significant shift in

Latvia's international trade away from the states of the former Soviet Union and toward the EU and other western markets. In 2000, about 68 percent of exports were directed toward the EU. In 1998, Germany was Latvia's single largest tracking partner, with 16 percent of exports and 17 percent of imports. The United Kingdom was the second largest source of exports from Latvia, with 14 percent, followed by Russia with 12 percent, Sweden with 10 percent, and others. Russia was the second largest importer of goods to Latvia, with 12 percent, followed by Finland with 10 percent, and Sweden with 7 percent. About 65 percent of the energy imports come from Russia, but Estonia, with its nuclear reactors and available uranium, also provides electricity to Latvia. The EU is responsible for 45 percent of the imported machinery. All told, Latvia exported US$1.9 billion of goods in 1999 and imported US$2.8 billion in goods in 1998.

GDP per Capita (US$)

Country	1975	1980	1985	1990	1998
Latvia	2,382	2,797	3,210	3,703	2,328
United States	19,364	21,529	23,200	25,363	29,683
Russia	2,555	3,654	3,463	3,668	2,138
Lithuania	N/A	N/A	N/A	3,191	2,197

SOURCE: United Nations. *Human Development Report 2000; Trends in human development and per capita income.*

MONEY

The Lat replaced the Latvian ruble in March of 1993. The **exchange rate** of the Lat has remained relatively stable, which has been crucial to Latvia's development process, for it has meant that confidence among foreign investors has remained high. Initially, following independence from the Soviet Union, Latvia experienced considerable economic difficulty as relations with their former Russian trade partner weakened and Latvian goods were not competitive in the western markets. Inflation was high and the purchasing power of the population fell and remained low. With the exception of the setback of 1998, which was tied to the Russian financial crises, Latvia's economic condition has slowly been improving. As of 2000 the purchasing power had increased 4.2 percent from the previous year. The increase in **disposable income**, at 8.1 percent, has been greater in urban areas than in rural areas, according to the Central Statistical Bureau of Latvia.

POVERTY AND WEALTH

Political changes and the reintroduction of a **free market system** in 1991 have forced people who once depended on the state to struggle independently for their economic survival. For the poorest in Latvia, life is difficult because social services, such as health care, worker's compensation, and pensions, have been dramatically cut. The percentage of Latvia's poorest is higher than well-developed nations, with 21.4 percent living below the poverty line (defined as one-half of the average income). Poverty is highest among rural residents (26 percent) and among families with 3 or more children (44.1 percent), according to a report by Petra Lantz de Bernardis.

A 1999 survey of living conditions in Latvia reported by the Central Statistical Bureau of Latvia revealed, not surprisingly, that those with the lowest degree of education had the least favorable prospects for jobs. However, an advanced education does not necessarily guarantee a high standard of living in contemporary Latvia, nor does a high standard of living necessarily indicate an advanced education. In 1999 the average wage for an individual with a high education was 156 lats while a person with a basic education received 75 lats. In comparison to state and public enterprises, private enterprises more often engage workers without a contract, put them in unfavorable work conditions, and provide no sense of job security for the worker. Of the survey respondents aged 18 and over, 7.2 percent have been robbed of personal belongings from a home or car, 3.6 percent have been threatened with violence, and 3.3 percent have been mugged.

Exchange rates: Latvia

lats (Ls) per US$1	
Jan 2001	0.614
2000	0.607
1999	0.585
1998	0.590
1997	0.581
1996	0.551

SOURCE: CIA *World Factbook 2001* [ONLINE].

Distribution of Income or Consumption by Percentage Share: Latvia

Lowest 10%	2.9
Lowest 20%	7.6
Second 20%	12.9
Third 20%	17.1
Fourth 20%	22.1
Highest 20%	40.3
Highest 10%	25.9

Survey year: 1998

Note: This information refers to income shares by percentiles of the population and is ranked by per capita income.

SOURCE: *2000 World Development Indicators* [CD-ROM].

Household Consumption in PPP Terms

Country	All food	Clothing and footwear	Fuel and power[a]	Health care[b]	Education[b]	Transport & Communications	Other
Latvia	30	5	16	6	23	11	10
United States	13	9	9	4	6	8	51
Russia	28	11	16	7	15	8	16
Lithuania	33	5	13	4	27	9	8

Data represent percentage of consumption in PPP terms.
[a]Excludes energy used for transport.
[b]Includes government and private expenditures.

SOURCE: World Bank. *World Development Indicators 2000.*

Many households cannot afford simple amenities. About 11 percent of the households cannot afford education for their children, 16 percent cannot cover emergency medical expenses, 20 percent cannot afford to eat meat or fish at least 3 times a week, 21 percent cannot afford annual dental checkups, 38 percent cannot go out for an evening at the movies or a concert, 38 percent cannot afford to entertain guests, 65 percent cannot afford new clothes, 77 percent cannot afford to replace worn furniture, and 82 percent do not have enough money for a holiday weekend abroad. While nearly half of the survey respondents reported good health, it was found that increased age was accompanied by decreased health. Also, there was a direct correlation between poor economic conditions and reports of ill health.

WORKING CONDITIONS

During Soviet rule, Latvia became the most industrialized and urbanized republic of the Soviet Union. While the importance of industry has deceased since the break-up, urbanization in Latvia remains high, hovering at around 78 percent of the population living in urban centers. The high level of pollution emitted by Latvia's factories contributes to low life expectancy, especially for males. Adding to the danger of shortened lives is a Latvian diet traditionally high in fats, a national aversion to exercise, and a male propensity toward heavy smoking. Nonetheless, the economic hardship caused by the break-up has improved the general health of Latvians and life expectancies are creeping upward.

Females live longer in Latvia but still do not experience economic equality with males. In 1998 the **real GDP** per capita for females was US$3,330 while for men it was US$4,664, a difference of almost 29 percent. There are more young women in secondary school and more in higher education. This may be due to the need for young men to begin work at an earlier age.

The dominance of service sector and light industries explains the high level of urbanization in Latvia. The city centers, which were previously most Russian, contain all of Latvia's institutions of higher education. The large percentage of Russians remaining in the city and the prohibitive cost of housing for students makes acquisition of a degree difficult for Latvians, who in 1989 were fourth in ethnic groups in Latvia to be enrolled in university.

The total workforce in Latvia in 1997 stood at 1.4 million, with an unemployment rate of 9.6 percent in 1999. As a result of economic conditions, many people are forced to work more than 40 hours per week in order to gain extra income. But simultaneously, many enterprises are unable to pay their employees a full week's wages, forcing employees to work part-time or to take unpaid leave. The legislation of Latvia regards forced holidays and a shortened business week as concealed forms of unemployment.

COUNTRY HISTORY AND ECONOMIC DEVELOPMENT

1300. Prior to this date Latvia is composed of half a dozen distinct and independent kingdoms; after 1300, German barons dominate the region and establishe a Germanic culture.

1710. A Russian elite infiltrates the bureaucracy of Latvia under the rule of Peter the Great, challenging the dominance of the Germans.

1850. First Latvian Awakening appears as resistance to Germanic and Russian influences. A Latvian elite begin to develop and push for self-determination in local affairs.

1880. Rapid industrialization of the largely landlocked Russian Empire causes it to incorporate the Baltic States in this process. The Latvian economy develops rapidly, under the direction of Russia, and the third largest port in the Russian empire is created by 1913.

1905. **Marxist** ideology spreads in the workplaces of Latvia, leading to a crackdown by authorities and the creation of a mass movement against Russian authority and German nobility.

1914. World War I (1914–18) leads to the evacuation of half the Latvian population who flee the invading German army into neighboring countries to the east. The Communist movement gains strength.

1918. Latvia claims independence on 18 November and 2 years later pro- and anti-Communist forces end their hostilities.

1921. Latvia joins the League of Nations and begins a 20 year period of economic progress, later known as the Second Awakening.

1934. Centrist politician Karlis Ulmanis gains power and ends the political instability of the multiple-party parliamentary system. He is later deported from Latvia to a prison camp in Russia by the Soviet authorities and dies in captivity in 1942.

1939. The Nazi-Soviet Nonaggression Pact between Germany and Russia puts Latvia, Estonia, and Lithuania under Soviet control.

1939. On 5 October Latvia is coerced into signing the Pact of Defense and Mutual Assistance; 30,000 Soviet troops occupy the country.

1939. In November, Soviets attack Finland, resulting in the Soviet Union being expelled from the League of Nations, along with Latvia.

1940. Soviet leader Joseph Stalin demands that the Baltic State governments be replaced with Soviet officials, leading to the creation of the Latvian Soviet Socialist Republic on 21 July.

1941. Immediately after the Soviet Union either deports or executes 35,000 Latvian dissidents, a Nazi invasion and 5 year occupation translates into an almost complete annihilation of Latvia's Gypsies and Jews.

1945. The Red Army reoccupies Latvia, and approximately 200,000 refugees flee. About 150,000 survivors settle in the West and engage in a long struggle to free their homeland from occupation.

1953. Soviet leader Joseph Stalin dies, and conditions for Latvian autonomy improve.

1957. Eduards Berklavs, a key figure in the Communist Party of Latvia (CPL), initiates de-Russification policies, i.e. restricted **immigration** from Russia, requirements that governmental functionaries know Latvian, and diversion of funds toward smaller, local activities rather than grandiose Soviet projects.

1959. Moscow purges Latvian national communists, including Berklavs and reinstitutes economic policies favoring Russia.

1985. Mikhail Gorbachev of the Soviet Union ushers in the period of perestroika, a campaign to reform the Communist Party through eased social, economic, and political mechanisms, and glasnost, the liberalization of the media and opportunity for critical discussion for the purpose of improving the system.

1987. Demonstrations for independence begin in Latvia.

1988. The Popular Front of Latvia (LTF) forms and organizes its first congress.

1989. With ever-increasing membership, the LTF becomes a de facto second government and pushes the Latvian Supreme Soviet to accept a declaration of sovereignty and economic independence.

1990. A new parliament, known as the Supreme Council, is formed and votes in favor of a transition to democracy and independence.

1991. Following a failed coup in the Soviet Union, Latvia declares independence on 21 August; Latvia joins the United Nations.

1992. Faced with high prices, problems with privatization, and hyperinflation, Latvia's economy crashes.

1993. A new currency, the Lat, is introduced and becomes the only legal tender by October.

1994. A citizenship bill, severely restricting the naturalization of Russians, is passed but later its restrictions are eased.

FUTURE TRENDS

The outlook for Latvia in the near and far future is bright. The continued stabilization of its currency, the increase in democratic activities and transparent economic activities, the growing degree of privatization, the liberalized trade policy, and the increasing skills of its workers all mean that unemployment will decline and foreign investment is likely to continue. The current downside to this situation is that poor wages prevent the average citizen from equal participation in the emerging economic system. Also, with minimal capital available to Latvian citizens, much of the country's developing assets will be foreign owned, a condition looked upon by many Latvians as unfavorable. With Latvia's accession into the EU, the situation is likely to improve even more as capital and labor will be able to move across the borders of a united Europe.

In its efforts to enter the EU, Latvia has decreased the distance between itself and the leading Eastern European countries. But Latvian officials are disappointed that a recent progress report on EU accession of Eastern European countries puts them in a lagging category. The report states that Latvia has a "functioning market" that should be able, in the medium term, to cope with the competitive pressures of the EU market. The main tasks for Latvia will be continued privatization and fiscal discipline.

The Nordic States banking group, Nordea, predicts that Latvia will experience significant growth in the near future. The country's pulp mill industry is cited as one of the key factors for this predicted growth. Nordea predicted growth in the GDP in the coming years are as follows: 5.5 percent for 2001, 6 percent for 2002, and 5.3 percent for 2003. One negative aspect mentioned in the report was the possibility of current account deficit expansion if the privatization process should slow. This has been a perceived risk because recent political support for the left-oriented Social Democrats that are threatening the incumbent coalition.

DEPENDENCIES

Latvia has no territories or colonies.

BIBLIOGRAPHY

Central Statistical Bureau of Latvia. <http://www.csb.lv/ajaunumi.html>. Accessed July 2001.

De Bernardis, Petra Lantz. "Wealth and Poverty in Transition." *UNDP: Estonia.* <http://www.undp.ee/equity>. Accessed July 2001.

Embassy of Latvia. <http://www.latvia-usa.org/economy.html>. Accessed July 2001.

International Monetary Fund. *Latvia: Selected Issues and Statistical Appendix.* <http://www.imf.org>. Accessed July 2001.

Iwaskiw, W.R. *Estonia, Latvia, and Lithuania: Country Studies.* Washington, D.C.: Federal Research Division, Library of Congress, 1996.

Latvian Development Agency. *Latvia: The Meeting Point of Two Worlds.* <http://www.lda.gov.lv>. Accessed July 2001.

Latvijas Banka. <http://www.bank.lv/englishindex.html>. Accessed July 2001.

"News from Latvia." *Central Europe Review.* <http://www.ce-review.org/00/41/latvianews41.html>. Accessed July 2001.

U.S. Central Intelligence Agency. *World Factbook 2000.* <http://www.odci.gov/cia/publications/factbook/index.html>. Accessed July 2001.

U.S. Department of State. *FY 2001 Country Commercial Guide: Latvia.* <http://www.state.gov/www/about_state/business/com_guides/2001/index.html>. Accessed July 2001.

—Mark Carper

LIECHTENSTEIN

Principality of Liechtenstein
Fürstentum Liechtenstein

CAPITAL: Vaduz.

MONETARY UNIT: Swiss Franc (SFR). One SFr equals 100 centimes or rappen. There are notes of 10, 20, 50, 100, 200, and 1,000 Swiss francs, and coins of 5, 10, 20, and 50 centimes and 1, 2, and 5 Swiss francs. The country maintains a monetary and customs union with Switzerland. The Liechtenstein monetary, fiscal, and banking systems can therefore be regarded as an extension of their Swiss counterparts.

CHIEF EXPORTS: Small specialty machinery, dental products, stamps, hardware, pottery.

CHIEF IMPORTS: Machinery, metal goods, textiles, foodstuffs, motor vehicles, fuels.

GROSS DOMESTIC PRODUCT: US$730 million (1998 est.).

BALANCE OF TRADE: **Exports:** US$2.47 billion (1996 est.). **Imports:** US$917.3 million (1996 est.).

COUNTRY OVERVIEW

LOCATION AND SIZE. The independent principality of Liechtenstein is located in central Europe and bordered on the east by Austria and on the south, west, and north by Switzerland. It is one of the smallest countries in the world, with a total area of only 160 square kilometers (62 square miles). Liechtenstein is about 25 kilometers (15.6 miles) long and 6 kilometers (3.75 miles) wide. Its total area is about 0.9 times the size of Washington, D.C. The western edge of the territory lies in the valley of the upper Rhine River and contains a narrow flat strip of arable land. The rest of the area consists of the foothills of the Alps, covered with forests and rising to several high and rugged peaks in the south. Along with Uzbekistan in Central Asia, Liechtenstein is one of the only two doubly landlocked countries in the world (bounded by other landlocked countries only). The capital and principal urban center, Vaduz, is a small town with a population of about 5,000 located in the west-central part of the country near the Rhine River.

POPULATION. The population of Liechtenstein was estimated at 32,207 in July of 2000; in 1998, it was 31,717. Although quite mountainous, Liechtenstein is densely populated, with an overall density of 198 persons per square kilometer (513 per square mile). The population is unevenly distributed and concentrated in the western, lower part of the country, along the Rhine. The principality has a population growth rate of 1.02 percent, with a birth rate of 11.83 births per 1,000 population. The death rate is 6.64 deaths per 1,000 population, and there is a high positive net migration rate of 5.03 immigrants per 1,000 population (all according to 2000 estimates).

Approximately one-third of the population are resident aliens, including Iranians, Turks, and others, while the vast majority of the Liechtenstein nationals are mostly of ethnic Germanic origin, like their neighbors in eastern Switzerland and western Austria. A south German dialect, Alemannish, is commonly spoken by some 87.5 percent of the population, while literary German is the official language of the country. In 2000, the **labor force** included 22,891 people, of which an astounding number of 13,847 were foreigners, mostly **guest workers**; 8,231 people commuted from neighboring Austrian and Swiss towns to work daily. Unlike Switzerland, however, **immigration** does not seem to be a major issue in the domestic political debates in Liechtenstein (in 2000, the Swiss electorate had to vote in a referendum on a conservative proposal to impose an 18 percent quota on the number of foreign workers in the country but decided against).

Approximately 88 percent of the population are traditionally Roman Catholic. In 1991, primary (elementary and junior high) school enrollment in the principality totaled 1,985 children, and about 1,200 attended secondary (high) schools. Primary and secondary education is free in Liechtenstein and schooling is required for 8 years. The

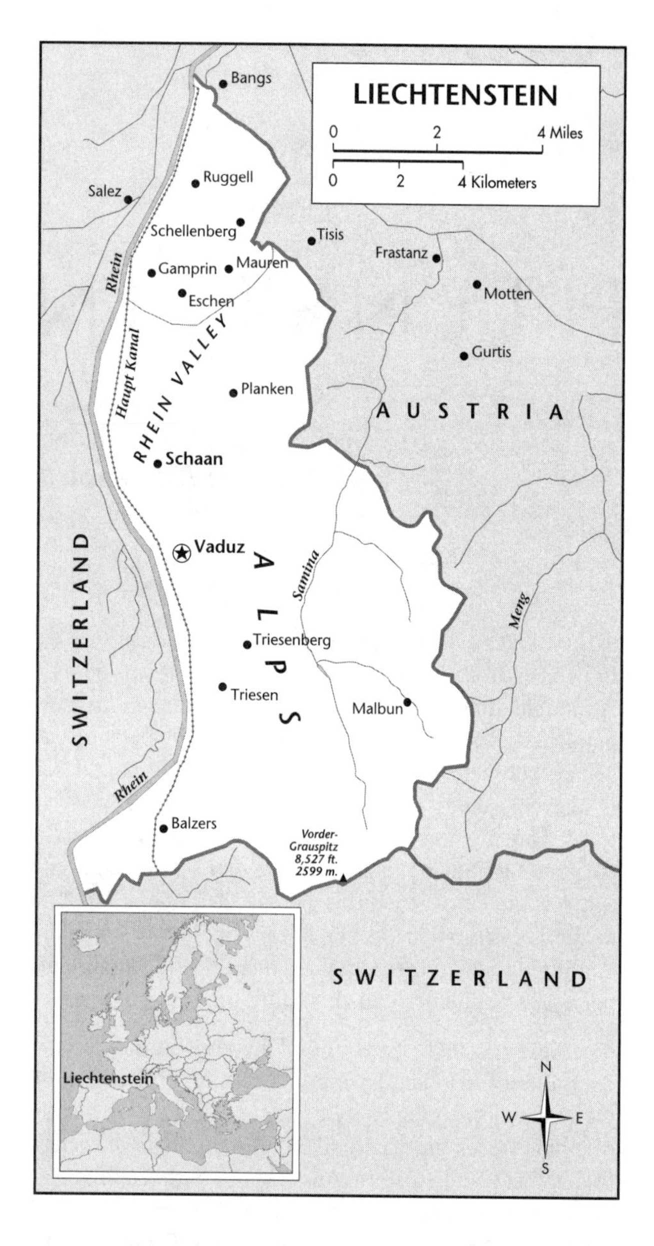

population, as elsewhere in Europe, is aging, with a high life expectancy at birth (82.47 years for women, 75.16 for men, 78.81 for the total population, all 2000 estimates). Around 18 percent of the people are 14 years of age and younger, 71 percent are between 15 and 64, and 11 percent are 65 or older. The high and stable standards of living and the declining fertility rate, combined with the limited but steady immigration flow, will contribute to a slow growth of the population and the aging of the Liechtenstein nationals, while immigrants' and guest workers' families will display a more youthful population profile.

OVERVIEW OF ECONOMY

Liechtenstein is tiny in size and has very limited natural resources, but it is nevertheless a prosperous country with a highly industrialized market economy and a robust financial services sector. Since World War II (in which the principality remained neutral), its liberal political regime and remarkably low business taxes have fueled strong economic growth and attracted many foreign companies. For over 80 years, Liechtenstein has been participating in a customs union with Switzerland; it uses the Swiss franc as its national currency, and in most aspects may be regarded as a part of the Swiss economy. Liechtenstein statistics are also included in the Swiss national statistics. Since 1919, Switzerland has represented Liechtenstein abroad diplomatically, as well. Living standards in the country are similar to those in the urban areas of neighboring Switzerland and Austria, both reckoned among the most affluent societies in the world. Its **gross domestic product (GDP) per capita** of $23,000 (1998 estimate) is also among the highest in the world.

Favorable tax treatment and extremely streamlined incorporation legislation have lured as many as 74,000 holding (or so-called "letter box") companies, operating overseas, to establish their head offices nominally in Liechtenstein, providing thus as much as 30 percent of the country's revenue basically in maintenance, administrative, and office services fees. Liechtenstein has been an active member of the European Economic Area (EEA), an organization serving as an intermediary between the European Free Trade Association (EFTA) and the European Union (EU) since May 1995. The government is working to harmonize its economic policies and legislation with those of the EU, although it is not negotiating for full membership in the union.

Some modern manufacturing industries have developed recently; notably in precision instruments, dental and optic materials, pharmaceuticals, and electronics. These industries contribute much to the country's positive trade balance. Yet much of the principality's income is also derived from tourism, banking, the sale of postage stamps and other **retail** services, and from the office expenses of the international companies maintaining their headquarters there.

POLITICS, GOVERNMENT, AND TAXATION

Liechtenstein is a constitutional monarchy governed by a hereditary prince. According to the constitution of 1921, legislative power is vested in the **unicameral** parliament (Landtag), consisting of 25 members elected by universal suffrage for 4-year terms. The Landtag members are elected in the 2 multi-seat constituencies (electoral districts): the Upper (or highland, formerly called Vaduz) and the Lower (or lowland, formerly called Schellenberg), by **proportional representation**. Although very small in size, Liechtenstein is further divided into 11 administrative units or communes (Gemeinden): Balzers, Eschen, Gamprin, Mauren, Planken, Ruggell, Schaan, Schellenberg, Triesen, Triesenberg, and Vaduz.

Elections for the Landtag held on 9 and 11 February 2001, gave 49.9 percent of the vote and 13 Landtag seats to the Progressive Citizens' Party in Liechtenstein (FBPL), a conservative group. The then ruling conservative Patriotic Union (VU) received 41.1 percent and 11 seats, and its representative, chief of government Mario Frick, resigned accordingly. An environmentalist group, Free List (FL), remained third with 8.8 percent of the vote, or just 1 seat in the House. In February 1997, the Free List (FL) had achieved the best score in its history with 11.6 percent of the vote, corresponding to 2 seats in the Landtag. Like the VU, in 2001 the FL lost some votes in favor of the FBPL and was not able to retain its former positions in the lowland constituency. Participation in the election reached 86.7 percent, just a bit less than in 1997, when 86.9 percent of the electorate voted.

The hereditary prince and the elected government constitute the executive branch of government. The ruling prince, Hans Adam II, assumed his executive powers in 1984, and his heir apparent is his son, Prince Alois von und zu Liechtenstein. On the motion of the parliament, the prince appoints a prime minister and 4 councilors to form the cabinet. Prior to the February 2001 elections, Mario Frick of the VU was the prime minister and chief of government since 15 December 1993. Following the 2001 elections, Otmar Hasler was selected as the prime minister.

Liechtenstein is a member of many international organizations such as the United Nations (it maintains a permanent mission to the UN in New York), the Council of Europe, the Organization on Security and Cooperation in Europe, the European Bank for Reconstruction and Development, the EFTA, the World Trade Organization, the International Atomic Energy Agency, and the World Intellectual Property Organization, among others.

With a maximum tax rate of 18 percent, Liechtenstein has one of the most liberal tax regimes in the world, and its banks, generally considered as members of the Swiss banking family, enjoy a stable reputation for their solidity and privacy policies. The country has a stable foreign trade balance surplus and zero **foreign debt**. But in 2000, it faced its biggest domestic and foreign political crisis since World War II as the affluent principality was shaken by allegations that it was an international **money laundering** center and by the subsequent arrests of several leading public figures ordered by a special prosecutor from Austria.

A conflict between Prince Hans Adam II and the government over the extent of the royal family's powers, reinvigorated by the money laundering allegations in 2000, almost brought about a constitutional crisis later that year. The prince and the cabinet had been at odds for quite a long time over a pending project for a constitutional reform. The prince had claimed he wanted to modernize the way Liechtenstein is run and give more power to the people, while the then prime minister Mario Frick and other critics held the opposite was true and claimed the envisaged reforms would concentrate more power in the prince's hands. The prince threatened to muster the 1,500 signatures required by law to bring about a referendum on the issue if he did not get what he wanted, and said if he was to lose the constitutional debate he would leave for Austria, the seat of his family before World War II. That might raise serious questions about how the principality would be governed in the future.

INFRASTRUCTURE, POWER, AND COMMUNICATIONS

The transportation system of Liechtenstein consists of 18.5 kilometers (11.5 miles) of railroads, all electrified, owned and operated by, and included in the statistics of

Communications

Country	Telephones[a]	Telephones, Mobile/Cellular[a]	Radio Stations[b]	Radios[a]	TV Stations[a]	Televisions[a]	Internet Service Providers[c]	Internet Users[c]
Liechtenstein	20,000	N/A	AM 0; FM 4; shortwave 0	21,000	N/A	12,000	44	N/A
United States	194 M	69.209 M (1998)	AM 4,762; FM 5,542; shortwave 18	575 M	1,500	219 M	7,800	148 M
Germany	45.2 M	15.318 M (1999)	AM 51; FM 767; shortwave 4	77.8 M	373 (1995)	51.4 M (1998)	123	18 M
Switzerland	4.82 M (1998)	1.967 M (1999)	AM 4; FM 113; shortwave 2	7.1 M	115 (1995)	3.31 M	44	2.4 M

[a]Data is for 1997 unless otherwise noted.
[b]Data is for 1998 unless otherwise noted.
[c]Data is for 2000 unless otherwise noted.

SOURCE: CIA *World Factbook 2001* [Online].

the Austrian Federal Railways. There are 323 kilometers (201 miles) of paved highways. There are no ports or harbors (the Rhine River is not yet navigable anywhere in Liechtenstein) and there are no airports in the small mountainous principality. The country is served in these respects by the extensive **infrastructure** of neighboring Switzerland and Austria. Liechtenstein is not traversed by any major international routes and road traffic in the country is 96 percent home-made while only 4 percent is accounted for by transit traffic, running mostly along the Schaanwald-Nendeln-Eschen-Bendern axis.

Electricity production in 1995 was about 150 million kilowatt hours (kWh), and Liechtenstein imported more than 90 percent of its energy from Switzerland and Austria. There is a modern telecommunications network with 19,000 main lines in use in 1995. All are linked to and operated by the Swiss telecom networks (some of the world's most technologically advanced) by cable and microwave radio relay. In 1999, 115 of the Swiss Internet service providers were offering service in Liechtenstein.

ECONOMIC SECTORS

Liechtenstein is highly industrialized, but much of its income is derived from banking, tourism, commerce, the sale of postage stamps, and from the international firms maintaining offices in the country because of more favorable tax treatment. Major manufactures include precision machinery, instruments and tools, pharmaceuticals, food products, metal goods, furniture, and pottery.

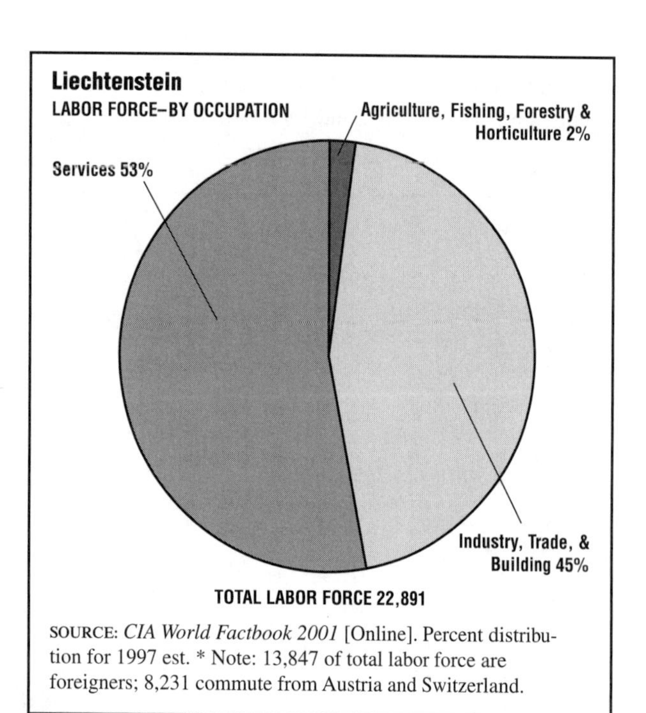

SOURCE: *CIA World Factbook 2001* [Online]. Percent distribution for 1997 est. * Note: 13,847 of total labor force are foreigners; 8,231 commute from Austria and Switzerland.

The distribution of the labor force by occupation in 1997 was estimated to be as follows: industry, trade, and building, 45 percent; services, 53 percent; and agriculture, fishing, forestry, and horticulture less than 2 percent.

AGRICULTURE

Agriculture contributes just 2 percent of GDP, although about 24 percent of Liechtenstein's territory consists of arable land, with permanent highland pastures making up 16 percent, and forests and woodland occupying 35 percent of the land. Animal husbandry and dairy farming are among the principal agricultural activities. Livestock graze in the alpine meadows during the summer. The fertile soil of the Rhine valley is used mostly for market vegetable gardening. Local agriculture products include wheat, barley, corn, potatoes, and grapes. The principality imports food, and some of it is processed and reexported.

Before World War II, almost half of the working population was occupied in agriculture. This number has continually decreased, and in 2000, about 350 persons (or 1.7 percent of the workforce) are active in agriculture, fishing, forestry, and horticulture. Despite the decline in that number, yields have been significantly increasing due to scientific rationalization and intensive machine cultivation.

INDUSTRY

About one-third of the nearly 23,000 working people of Liechtenstein are employed in industrial establishments. Due to the favorable economic conditions, an efficient, export-oriented high-tech industrial manufacturing sector developed over the last decades of the 20th century. Manufacturing, reported jointly with construction and trade, was responsible for nearly 45 percent of the jobs and the GDP by 2000 and a large percentage of the country's exports. Electronics, metal manufacturing, textiles, ceramics, pharmaceuticals, food products and beverages, and precision instruments manufacture are all well developed. The fact that Liechtenstein's economy exports so much is largely due to its high-tech manufacturing sector that accounts for the majority of its exports.

Among the most important domestic manufacturers are the Hilti Corporation, a large international supplier of rail anchors and anchor installation services to the rail transport industry, and electrical equipment; Ivoclar-Vivadent, developer and distributor of well-regarded products for prosthetic, restorative, and preventive dentistry; Balzers-Bal-Tec AG, manufacturers of electron microscopy preparation products for biological specimens; Fancoldi R.T., gem industry specialists, producing colored diamonds; and Aqualine, a major Austrian Alps mineral water bottling company.

Construction is also an important contributor to the economy, although its scope is necessarily limited. According to the building statistics, in the last quarter of 2000, 115 new buildings were granted permits. As compared to the same period of 1999, this corresponded to 39 permits less, but the construction volume increased by 5.6 percent and construction costs increased by 17.2 percent to 163.3 million Swiss francs. Building activities generally shifted from housing developments and public buildings towards industry and trade. The construction volume in that sector increased by 110.4 percent, while a decrease of 93.4 percent was registered for public buildings.

SERVICES

Liechtenstein's economy is increasingly service-based, as in most of western Europe. Services contributed to 53 percent of GDP, and about 10,000 people were employed in the sector in 2000. It particularly expanded over the last decade of the 20th century. In addition to the catering branch (made of 42 hotels and inns, and 81 restaurants and cafes), the public administration, insurance companies, and the health and educational systems, this sector is specially characterized by a vigorous presence in international commercial and financial transactions and in **fiduciary** business.

Finance in Liechtenstein is traditionally a very well-developed sector. Apart from the presence of the Swiss banks due to the monetary and customs union and the geographical and cultural proximity between the 2 states, 13 local banks exist. These include Liechtenstein-LGT Bank, an international private bank, claiming to be the largest banking operation in the country; Bank von Ernst, a financial institution providing Swiss private banking services, portfolio management, and family foundation; and Liechtenstein-VP Bank Group, a private bank founded in 1956, providing a wide range of financial services, holding assets worth some $5.5 billion, and employing about 600 people (but currently facing some serious legal troubles, as shown below), as well as the Centrum Bank AG, Liechtensteinische Landesbank AG, Neue Bank AG, Verwaltungs-und Privat-Bank AG, and Vorarlberger Volksbank AG. The largest banks in Liechtenstein belong to the Swiss Banking Association and recognize most of its rules, as do all the Swiss banks.

The Liechtenstein banks, which administer 112.5 billion Swiss francs (US$70 billion), have been known for their liberal policies and privacy, yet, following some serious money laundering allegations in 2000 described below, they intend to end anonymous accounts and carry out identity checks on their customers. Legislative changes to that effect are being pushed through parliament in hopes of averting possible **sanctions** from European Union countries and the United States following the scandals. However, bankers are reluctant to give up their judicial independence.

Tourism is also an important contributor to the economy. Despite its small size, alpine Liechtenstein is a diverse country with various communities offering a mix of attractions for all tastes. Situated between some of the most attractive tourist regions in Europe, the Swiss and Austrian Alps, the tiny principality often appears on their visitors' itineraries. Museums, banks, boutiques, dining establishments, historical sites, vineyards, and sports (particularly skiing and hiking) facilities are varied and charming. Liechtenstein is considered a microcosm of the European continent. Apart from the 42 hotels and 81 restaurants, the sale of postal stamps by the state post offices, galleries and shops offering art objects, local handicrafts, and souvenirs are also a significant source of revenue.

Retail is well-developed and targeted at serving the tourist clients as well as the local customers and commuters, but the small size of the market is still more conducive to small family-owned stores. Retail trade experienced a marked upswing over the 1990s as a result of increased specialization of stores, so that a wide range of diverse products is now available. As the Swiss retail sector is developing towards large-scale self-service and discount chain stores, Liechtenstein retailers have had to face fierce competition from the large Swiss shopping malls in the vicinity. Many of the small family-owned shops, relying basically on local customs, went out of business during the 1990s. Some 1,600 retail and wholesale trade enterprises are united in the Liechtenstein Chamber of Trade and Commerce as an umbrella organization. Trade enterprises cater mainly to the domestic market and contribute to the efficient infrastructure of the country.

Companies specializing in serving the offshore "letter box" companies' various needs in Liechtenstein include the Gestina Trust, specialists in the development and management of offshore companies, legal structures, and settlement advice; the Vazus-Syndikus Treuhandanstalt, offering financial advice and consulting in economic and legal matters, accounting, and contracts; the Vazus-Wanger Group, a law and patent firm in commercial law and asset management, and many others.

INTERNATIONAL TRADE

Due to the very small size of the country's market, Liechtenstein's industry is heavily dependent on exports. In 1996, the country exported $2.47 billion worth of goods and services, while importing $917.3 million worth. The European Economic Area (EEA) states are its most important export destinations. Liechtenstein joined the European Free Trade Association (EFTA) as an associate member in 1960 and has been a full member since

1991. In addition, it became a member of the EEA (the intermediary body between the EFTA and the EU) in 1995. Although small, the Liechtenstein economy is very open and its foreign trade balance is traditionally strikingly positive, with exports far outweighing imports, largely thanks to its high-tech manufacturing sector. Principal trade partners in 1995 were the EU and EFTA, recipients of 60.57 percent of exports, and Switzerland, recipient of 15.7 percent, and they were the origins of a comparable percentage of its imports. All trade numbers for Liechtenstein are included in the Swiss national statistics, and therefore a more clear-cut picture of its international trade is difficult to assemble.

MONEY

Liechtenstein has many advantages issuing from its use of the Swiss franc and from officially being part of the Swiss monetary system. It has a strong currency, a balanced budget with revenues of $424.2 million and expenditures of $414.1 million in 1998 (estimate), and a leading banking sector with solid private banks with a reputation for privacy, limited regulation, and the acceptance of foreign deposits with little oversight. Similarly to Switzerland in the late 1990s, however, these conditions have also led to some serious legal drawbacks.

Throughout 2000, Liechtenstein has been troubled by recurrent international allegations of domestic money laundering for transnational organized crime, an abuse of Swiss banking privacy policies. In 2000, the German press printed stunning details from a German federal intelligence agency report accusing Liechtenstein of acting as banker to Central American drug cartels and the Russian mafia. The report alleged that a former prime minister, Hans Brunhart, currently head of the Verwaltungs- und Privat-Bank (VP Bank), had been laundering drug money. The report named Liechtenstein as the only European country on an International Financial Action Task Force (FATF) list of 15 nations accused of failing to cooperate against money laundering. Finally, the Organization for Economic Cooperation and Development (OECD), in another 2000 publication, listed the principality among harmful offshore **tax havens** alongside Tonga, the Bahamas, and Barbados.

The allegations caused a storm of indignation in the country. Brunhart objected, and an independent investigator from Austria appointed by Liechtenstein did not support the case. The investigator found that Liechtenstein was not a hub of money laundering, although he criticized its preventive work against "hot money." In early 2001, the FATF confirmed that the country had made significant progress in connection with the fight against money laundering. The country was removed from the blacklist by the FATF in June of 2001.

POVERTY AND WEALTH

Liechtenstein is renowned as one of Europe's most affluent and carefree communities. With one of the highest measures of GDP per capita in the world, a low **inflation rate** (in terms of consumer prices) of 0.5 percent (1997 estimate), and the benefits of the monetary and economic union with Switzerland, the tiny principality offers its subjects one of the highest standards of living in the world, although at a very high cost of living. No data as to Liechtenstein's economic equality index (**Gini index**) are currently available, but if Switzerland's index is used for reference, economic equality in the principality is likely to be in better shape than the United States and even in the more egalitarian United Kingdom. No data as to any extreme cases of poverty are available.

WORKING CONDITIONS

Due to the number of specialized high-tech companies in Liechtenstein, there is an enormous demand for highly qualified specialists. Since the national job market, on account of its tiny size, can only partly satisfy the demand, the internationally active companies in particular are heavily recruiting in other countries, mostly Switzerland and Austria, but also elsewhere in Europe and the Middle East.

Exchange rates: Liechtenstein

Swiss francs, franken, or franchi (SFR) per US$1	
Jan 2001	1.6303
2000	1.6888
1999	1.5022
1998	1.4498
1997	1.4513
1996	1.2360

SOURCE: CIA *World Factbook 2001* [ONLINE].

GDP per Capita (US$)

Country	1996	1997	1998	1999	2000
Liechtenstein	23,000	N/A	23,000	N/A	N/A
United States	28,600	30,200	31,500	33,900	36,200
Germany	20,400	20,800	22,100	22,700	23,400
Switzerland	22,600	23,800	26,400	27,100	28,600

Note: Data are estimates.

SOURCE: *Handbook of the Nations*, 17th, 18th, 19th and 20th editions for 1996, 1997, 1998 and 1999 data; CIA *World Factbook 2001* [Online] for 2000 data.

In 2000, the labor force included 22,891 people of which 13,847 were foreigners, mostly guest workers; 8,231 people commuted from neighboring Austrian and Swiss towns to work daily. A highly skilled workforce, laws promoting labor flexibility, and agreements between trade unions and employers' associations have resulted in very little labor unrest. The late 1990s have been good for Liechtenstein workers, with salaries having increased by an average of 7 percent between 1997 and 1999. It is all the more important that it was possible at the same time to realize improvements on the job market and to lower the unemployment rate.

In 2000, the unemployment ratio fell to 1.0 percent of the domestic labor force. The number of 274 individuals registered as unemployed at the end of February 2001 represents the lowest figure since June 2000, when 260 individuals had been registered. In February 2001, 28 persons were registered as unemployed either for the first time or were re-registered. Some 51 individuals were taken out of the statistics, 32 of whom started a new job, and the rest reached retirement age or started a new business. **Full employment** is a prominent aim of domestic economic policy. It is a goal that can be reached through measures including a project for the occupation of long-time unemployed, as well as a program for the better integration of handicapped employees.

COUNTRY HISTORY AND ECONOMIC DEVELOPMENT

1719. The former domain of Schellenberg and the country of Vaduz are combined into the Principality of Liechtenstein within the Holy Roman Empire.

1806. The principality is recognized as a sovereign state. Until the end of World War I, it remains closely tied to the Austrian Empire (named the Austro-Hungarian Empire after 1867).

1918. The military defeat and the collapse of the Austro-Hungarian Empire in World War I forces Liechtenstein to conclude a customs and monetary union with its other prosperous yet neutral neighbor, Switzerland.

1938. Prince Franz Joseph II becomes sovereign; the principality remains neutral in World War II (1939–45), while neighboring Austria is annexed by Nazi Germany.

1984. Executive authority is transferred to Prince Hans Adam II (crowned in 1989); a referendum grants women the right to vote in national elections.

1990. Liechtenstein joins the United Nations.

1991. Liechtenstein joins the European Free Trade Association (EFTA).

1992. Voters approve Liechtenstein's membership in the European Economic Area (EEA).

2000. Liechtenstein is disturbed by a money-laundering scandal and a constitutional crisis between the prince and the government.

FUTURE TRENDS

The Liechtenstein economy is closely related to the Swiss one and is dependent on the latter's progress towards full integration in the EU. It is likely that, despite financial scandals and constitutional problems, the principality will preserve its sound economy and high living standards and will continue to attract foreign companies and workers in the foreseeable future.

Liechtenstein has already developed close links with the EU through its participation in the EEA, the comprehensive adjusting of its domestic economic regulations to fit the EU standards, and its close relations with the Austrian economy (Austria is a full member of the union). In the event Switzerland finally decides to join the EU, the adjustment of the monetary and banking system (and possibly some agricultural **subsidy** policies) will likely be among the serious problems facing the small principality in this regard.

As to the problems related to the 2000 banking scandal, there is reason to believe that Liechtenstein can guarantee the implementation of some effective measures to combat money laundering. The former prime minister appointed 4 new judges working at the national court, the prosecution was **restructured**, the state department for financial services was strengthened, a new Financial Intelligence Unit (FIU) was founded, and a special bank department was set up within the national police force. Some needed legislative changes are being vigorously debated. It is expected that the country's banking practices will be soon brought in line with the general EU provisions, without reducing its competitive advantages too much. The positive ruling by the FATF in June of 2001 indicated the success of these measures.

It is harder to predict the outcome of the constitutional crisis. In 2000, Hans Adam II announced that he would end the discussion around the constitution as soon as possible. But reflecting on his new constitutional proposal of 1 March 2001, the former head of the constitutional commission, Peter Wolff, noted that in the controversial points, on which parliamentary criticism focused, nothing had been changed. Whatever the decision, however, it is not likely to cause any serious political disturbance in the principality that might jeopardize social stability and economic development.

DEPENDENCIES

Liechtenstein has no territories or colonies.

BIBLIOGRAPHY

Global Investment Business Center, Inc. Staff. *Liechtenstein: A Country Study Guide.* International Business Publications, 2000.

U.S. Central Intelligence Agency. *World Factbook 2000.* <http://www.odci.gov/cia/publications/factbook/index.html>. Accessed July 2001.

U.S. Department of State. *Background Notes: Europe: Liechtenstein.* <http://www.state.gov/www/background_notes/eurbgnhp.html>. Accessed January 2001.

—Valentin Hadjiyski

LITHUANIA

Republic of Lithuania
Lietuvos Respublika

CAPITAL: Vilnius.

MONETARY UNIT: Litas (Lt). One litas equals 100 centas. There are notes in denominations of 1, 2, 5, 10, 20, 50, 100, 200, and 500 litas. There are 1, 2, and 5 litas coins, as well as 1, 2, 5, 10, 20, and 50 centas.

CHIEF EXPORTS: Food products, textiles, consumer electronics, other manufactured goods.

CHIEF IMPORTS: Oil, gas, machinery, equipment.

GROSS DOMESTIC PRODUCT: US$15.5 billion (purchasing power parity, 2000 est.). [CIA *World Factbook* estimated GDP at purchasing power parity at US$17.3 billion for 1999.]

BALANCE OF TRADE: **Exports:** US$4.033 billion (2000). **Imports:** US$5.043 billion (2000). [CIA *World Factbook* indicates exports were US$3.3 billion (f.o.b., 1999) and imports were US$4.5 billion (f.o.b., 1999).]

COUNTRY OVERVIEW

LOCATION AND SIZE. An East European country bordering on the Baltic Sea, Lithuania has an area of 65,200 square kilometers (25,174 square miles) and a total coastline of 99 kilometers (62 miles). Lithuania is a mid-size country by European standards and is about the size of West Virginia. Lithuania's border countries are: Belarus, 502 kilometers (312 miles); Latvia, 453 kilometers (282 miles); Poland, 91 kilometers (57 miles); and Russia (Kaliningrad), 227 kilometers (141 miles). Vilnius, Lithuania's capital, is located in the country's southeastern part. Vilnius is also the nation's largest city with a population of about 600,000.

POPULATION. The population of Lithuania was estimated at 3,620,800 in July of 2000 but the population is decreasing, that is the growth rate is negative (-0.29 percent). In 2000, the birth rate stood at 9.77 births per 1,000 while the death rate stood at 12.87 per 1,000, with suicide rates among the highest in the world. The nation's fertility rate is below replacement level with only 1.34 children born to each woman. In addition, Lithuania has an infant mortality rate with 14.67 deaths per 1,000 live births. The nation also loses population to **immigration**, a loss of 0.16 people per 1,000 members of the population. Life expectancy for males is 63.07 years and 75.41 years for females.

The Lithuanian population is close to 100 percent literate. The official language (Lithuanian) is related to the pre-Indo-European language Sanskrit, very archaic in its structure, and therefore studied around the world for comparative linguistic purposes. Polish and Russian are also widely spoken. Ethnic Lithuanians constitute some 80 percent of the population. The largest national minorities include Russians (9 percent), Poles (7 percent), and Belorussians (1.6 percent). Despite decades of the **communist** propaganda and persecutions, many religions survived in Lithuania, including Roman Catholicism (dominant), Lutheranism, Russian Orthodoxy, Judaism, and Islam. Reflecting average European levels of urbanization, most Lithuanians (68 percent) live in urban areas. By international standards, Lithuania's population is distributed rather evenly across the country with a population density of 56 per square kilometer (146 per square mile).

OVERVIEW OF ECONOMY

Lithuania is an economy in transition from the communist economic system to a Western-style market economy. During the years of communist control (1944–91), the economy was controlled by the government, and there were restrictions against the private ownership of property and businesses. Since the end of the communist era, Lithuania has become a regional trend-setter by aggressively pursuing economic **liberalization** programs.

Europe's largest country in the 16th century, Lithuania has a statehood tradition going as far back as the 11th

century. However, Lithuania became part of Russia in 1795 and did not regain independence until after World War I (1918). Between World War I and the onset of World War II in 1939, Lithuania made substantial economic progress despite a lack of natural resources except for land. Predominantly based on agriculture, the economy developed rather close trade relationships with the Western world, especially Germany, United Kingdom, and Scandinavia. Lithuania exported agricultural products (mainly hog and poultry products) to these countries and imported advanced machinery and other industrial products from them. Lithuania's economic development level was well below that of the United Kingdom or Germany but was considered at par with some Central European and Scandinavian countries. Even during the Depression of the 1930s, the Lithuanian currency (litas) was strongest or second strongest in Europe. World War II and the Soviet occupation which began in 1940 interrupted Lithuania's independence until it was formally restored in 1990. The Soviets forced industrialization in a heavy, distorted way to the detriment of other economic sectors, especially production of consumer products and services. In 1990, the industry was dominated by 3 major branches: first, machinery and equipment including electronics; second, light industries; and third, food industries. Combined, these produced some 70 percent of the total industry output. Even if it brought some peculiar economic growth, the communist system imposed by the USSR slowed Lithuania's comparative economic development by at least 2 decades.

Postcommunist economies like Lithuania underwent a significant transformation **recession** coupled with the outburst of corrective **inflation**. On top of these systemic changes, Lithuania suffered trade disruption caused by the collapse of the Soviet Union which was and remains its main trade partner. In combination with the usual disruption stemming from the radical **privatization** and other transformation measures, this resulted in a drop in measured output. In all, there was a 40 percent drop in the officially measured GDP that Lithuania suffered in the first half of the 1990s. That loss of GDP was recovered in part by a subsequent growth as a result of radical economic reforms. However, Lithuania suffered again as a result of the Russian financial crisis of 1998. In 2000, economic growth exceeded 3 percent and will probably accelerate to about 5 percent in the near future.

Since independence from the Soviet Union, Lithuania has been attempting to radically transform the economy. This is being done by political and economic liberalization, **macroeconomic** stabilization, and privatization as the main elements of the transition strategy. In 1997 alone, some 200 state-owned companies were sold to private industry. By 2000, an additional US$725 million in government-owned companies were sold-off. By that same year, some two-thirds of the economy was in private hands and largely working according to the rules of a competitive market economy.

By 1998, Lithuania's economy closely resembled that of most other Western European countries. Agriculture accounted for 10 percent of the GDP, industry for 32 percent, and services for 58 percent. The country's main industries are metal-cutting machine tools, electric motors, television sets, refrigerators and freezers, petroleum refining, shipbuilding, furniture making, textiles, food processing, fertilizers, agricultural machinery, optical equipment, electronic components, and computers.

Over two-thirds of its economy is dependent on foreign markets, and Lithuania has sought to increase its attractiveness to foreign investors. By 1997, foreign capitalists had invested over US$1 billion in the Lithuanian economy, and in 1998, there was an additional US$510 million in new investments. The largest single foreign investor in Lithuania is the United States which accounts for about 18 percent of all foreign investment. The low labor costs and high level of education of the workforce, when combined with the country's geographic location at the crossroads of Northern Europe, account for the attraction that foreign investors have in Lithuania. Among the major foreign companies with operations in Lithuania are Amber Consortium (Sweden-Finland), Motorola (USA), Philip Morris (USA), SEB (Sweden), Williams, Inc.(USA), Royal Dutch-Shell (the Netherlands), and Coca Cola (USA).

Following independence in 1990, the Lithuanian economy grew rapidly during the first part of the decade (with average annual growth rates which exceeded 5.0 percent). However, following an economic crisis in Russia which began in 1998, Lithuania's GDP declined by 3 percent in 1999. Unemployment rose to 10 percent in 1999. In 2000, growth in the GDP returned with a rate of 3.3 percent. Inflation remains low at 3 percent, after reaching a high of 35.6 percent in 1995.

In 1999, the European Union (EU) agreed to initiate the process to allow Lithuania to join the regional trade and political organization, beginning in 2000. By joining the EU, Lithuania will be able to trade freely with the 15 members of the organization (a market of 350 million consumers). This should increase Lithuanian exports and make imports from the EU less expensive since **tariffs** and **duties** on imports and exports would be eliminated.

POLITICS, GOVERNMENT, AND TAXATION

After regaining independence and shedding the imposed communist system (1990), Lithuania is a fully functional parliamentary democracy. The chief of state is the president, and the head of the government is the premier (who is formally appointed by the president, subject to approval by the parliament). The president is directly elected by the people and serves a 5-year term. The parliament, known as the Seimas, has 141 members who are elected for 4-year terms. Of these, 71 are directly elected by the people while 70 are elected by proportional vote.

The current president, Valdas Adamkus, had lived in the United States for 30 years after World War II. The Lithuanian political scene is dominated by 3 groups or forces: right, left, and center. Widely credited with dealing a mortal blow to the Soviet Union and restoring Lithuanian independence in 1990, the Lithuanian Independence Movement (Sajudis) was led by the Lithuanian Conservatives with Vytautas Landsbergis at its helm. Landsbergis became the nation's head of state after independence.

In the fall of 1992, Lithuania set a new trend in the post-communist world as the right-wing forces (Conservatives) lost power to the ex-communist left (Lithuanian Democratic Party of Labor, LDLP). The people's hopes for improvements in living standards were dashed by the hard reality of disastrous and development-retarding communist legacies. In another trend set for the region, the Conservatives returned to power in 1996 but were replaced by the centrist New Policy bloc by 2000; in 2001, the left-leaning government was formed with the ex-communist Algirdas Brazauskas as its leader.

Since independence, all of the Lithuanian governments and political parties have supported the transition processes to markets and democracy. The right or conservative political parties are the Homeland Union and the Conservatives who have joined together in a coalition. These parties are more pro-business and pro-Western.

The main centrist group is also a coalition of parties known as the New Policy bloc which includes the Center Union and the Democratic Party. The New Policy bloc supports policies that seek to balance business growth and social welfare programs. The left is made up of the former communist party, the LDLP, and genuine social democrats.

The LDLP is most resistant to transparent and rule-based privatization efforts, preferring the **nomenklatura privatization** instead. It has also supported increased taxation in order to expand government programs. Overall, due to privatization and other reforming efforts, the government plays a smaller and smaller role in the lives of Lithuanians. In 1997, the main privatization efforts began when the government sold the state-owned telephone company, Lithuanian Telecom. Additional privatization efforts have included the government-owned electric and utility companies. Overall, some 5,714 government-owned companies have been privatized. Still the government continues to own US$2.5 billion in property and businesses.

The government's budget in 1997 was US$1.7 billion, but it only had revenues of US$1.5 billion. The government deficit amounted to US$200 million or about 2.8 percent of the GDP. This situation marks a dramatic decline from the **budget deficit** of 9 percent of GDP in 1991. In 1999, the government spent US$181 million on defense or about 1.5 percent of the GDP. Lithuania seeks to join the North Atlantic Treaty Organization (NATO) and has worked to participate in NATO-led operations, including the peace-keeping mission in Bosnia. Lithuania receives foreign aid from a number of sources such as the EU and the United States. In 1995, foreign aid amounted to US$228.5 million.

The tax burden (mainly income and **value-added taxes**) at some one-third of the GDP is moderate by international standards and will further be reduced as the liberalization progresses. Progress has been made in strengthening and improving the tax administration. This shift will result in the removal of tax **arrears** and an increase in tax revenue. Further training of staff and improved exchange and processing of information are also needed. While the accession process to the European Union does not involve full harmonization of taxes, still the EU is assisting Lithuania in this process. Tax revenues come from a variety of sources. Goods that are imported into Lithuania face import duties that range from 10 to 100 percent (but average 15 percent on most goods). The highest tariffs are on tobacco, automobiles, jewelry, and gasoline. Corporate tax rates are officially at 24 percent, but incentives designed to draw new companies to Lithuania allow these new firms to reduce their taxes by 70 percent for a period of up to 3 years. The personal **income tax** level is 33 percent with rates of between 10 to 35 percent on supplemental income from investments or interest dividends.

In an effort to anchor itself in the West and, therefore, ensure its autonomy from Russia, Lithuania has sought to join a number of West European organizations, including NATO and the EU. It is also a member of the World Trade Organization (WTO) which has reduced trade barriers and tariffs among member states. As a small country, Lithuania sees membership in these institutions as a way to protect itself from foreign influences and enhance its economy.

INFRASTRUCTURE, POWER, AND COMMUNICATIONS

Lithuania inherited a balanced transportation system (e.g. roads, aviation, merchant marine) from the Soviet period. However, the (broad gauge) railway system was

Communications

Country	Telephones[a]	Telephones, Mobile/Cellular[a]	Radio Stations[b]	Radios[a]	TV Stations[a]	Televisions[a]	Internet Service Providers[c]	Internet Users[c]
Lithuania	1.048 M 1997)	297,500 (1998)	AM 3; FM 112; shortwave 1	1.9 M	20 (1995)	1.7 M	14	225,000
United States	194 M	69.209 M (1998)	AM 4,762; FM 5,542; shortwave 18	575 M	1,500	219 M	7,800	148 M
Russia	30 M (1998)	2.5 M (2000)	AM 420; FM 447; shortwave 56	61.5 M	7,306 (1998)	60.5 M	35	9.2 M
Latvia	748,000	77,100	AM 8; FM 56; shortwave 1	1.76 M	44 (1995)	1.22 M	42	234,000

[a]Data is for 1997 unless otherwise noted.
[b]Data is for 1998 unless otherwise noted.
[c]Data is for 2000 unless otherwise noted.

SOURCE: CIA *World Factbook 2001* [Online].

built to keep Lithuania integrated in the USSR and separated from the West. Privatization, modernization, and development of the priority transportation **infrastructure** is of particular importance for an east-west and north-south transit country like Lithuania, especially in view of the European Union accession process.

Lithuania has 71,375 kilometers (44,352 miles) of roads of which 64,951 kilometers (40,360 miles) are paved. There are 417 kilometers (259 miles) of expressways. All of the 2,002 kilometers (1,244 miles) of railways are broad gauge. Although Lithuania is a small nation, it has a substantial merchant marine fleet with 52 ships, including 23 cargo ships, 2 petroleum tankers, 3 passenger cruise ships, and 11 refrigerated cargo vessels. Lithuania has 600 kilometers (373 miles) of waterways that are navigable year-round. The nation's main ports are Kaunas and Klaipeda. Klaipeda is the largest port in the Baltics and handles 20 percent of all cargo imported to or exported from the region. In 1998, the port handled 16.1 million tons of cargo, and expansions will allow the facility to handle 30 million tons by 2004. There are 96 airports in Lithuania, but only 25 of them have paved runways. Vilnius, Kaunas, and Palanga have international airports. All told, Lithuanian Airlines carried 230,000 passengers in 1997. The United States supplied Lithuania with US$30 million to upgrade the airport at Siauliai which is now one of the largest cargo airports in Europe. Moreover, there are 105 kilometers (65 miles) of crude oil pipelines and 760 kilometers (472 miles) of natural gas pipelines.

The government is engaged in a variety of infrastructure improvement projects. By 2005, some 55 individual projects are scheduled for completion. These projects are in response to dramatic increases in land, sea, and air transport. For instance, since 1994, automobile traffic has increased by an annual rate of 15 to 20 percent per year. The nation's largest airport at Vilnius and the seaport of Klaipeda are both undergoing expansion and renovation projects. The other major project is the construction of the Via Baltica highway which will connect all the Baltic republics (Lithuania, Latvia, and Estonia). The EU would like to construct 2 major highways through Lithuania to allow the organization access to Russia and the other countries of the former Soviet Union. Although work has not begun on the road systems, the EU has already pledged aid for the projects.

Lithuania is also in the midst of constructing a power line to supply electrical exports to the West. Lithuania produced 15.58 billion kWh of electricity in 1998. Some 13 percent of this came from fossil fuels and 4.3 percent came from hydroelectric sources, but the overwhelming majority, 82.61 percent, came from nuclear power plants. The nation consumed 7.829 billion kWh of electricity in 1998 and exported 7 billion kWh while it imported 340 million kWh.

Lithuania's energy sector needs modernization as well. Post-Soviet Russia's supply network is unreliable and subject to political manipulations resulting in cuts of oil to Lithuania. The opening of the Butinge oil terminal on the Baltic Sea in 1999 allows Lithuania to diversify its supply of crude oil by sea. Currently, the nation has about 10 million barrels of proven oil reserves. Other sources of power, such as Ignalina nuclear power plant (of the Chernobyl type), are controversial for safety reasons. Electric power generation needs to be modernized and privatized, while new and profitable supply networks to Western Europe via Poland need to be established. Lithuania's power complex experiences substantial problems with generation, distribution, and sales. The capacity in the system is about 2 to 3 times higher than the national demand for power generation and gas distribution. As a result of inherited Soviet-style inefficiencies, losses amounted to about one-third of supply and were made worse by non-payment of debts by some clients, for example, in Belarus.

The telecommunications market in Lithuania is liberalized except for fixed-line telephony where Lietuvos Telekomas enjoys a **monopoly** until the end of 2002. A national fiber-optic cable system is nearing completion, and rural exchanges are being improved and expanded. By 1997, there were 1.1 million main telephone landlines in use. Mobile cellular systems are functioning and rather widely accessible. In 1997, about 297,500 mobile phones were in use. Access to the Internet is growing, and by 1999, there were 10 Internet service providers.

ECONOMIC SECTORS

After regaining independence in 1990, Lithuania underwent tremendous, regionally trend-setting changes in

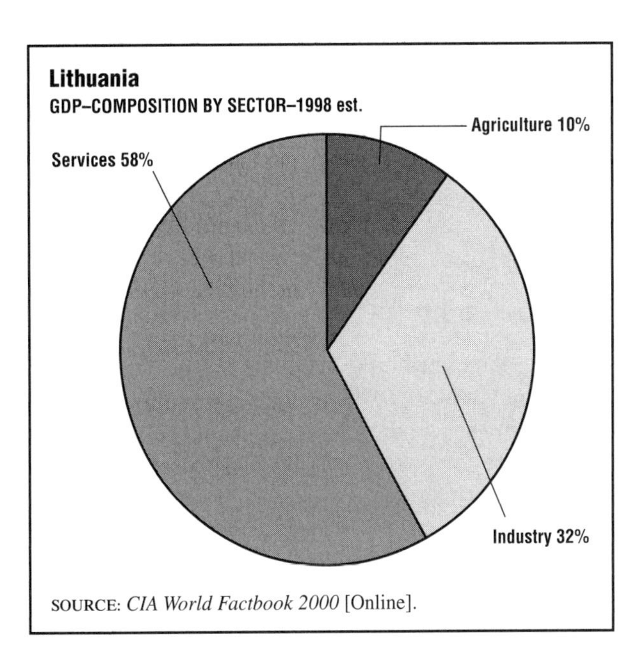

SOURCE: *CIA World Factbook 2000* [Online].

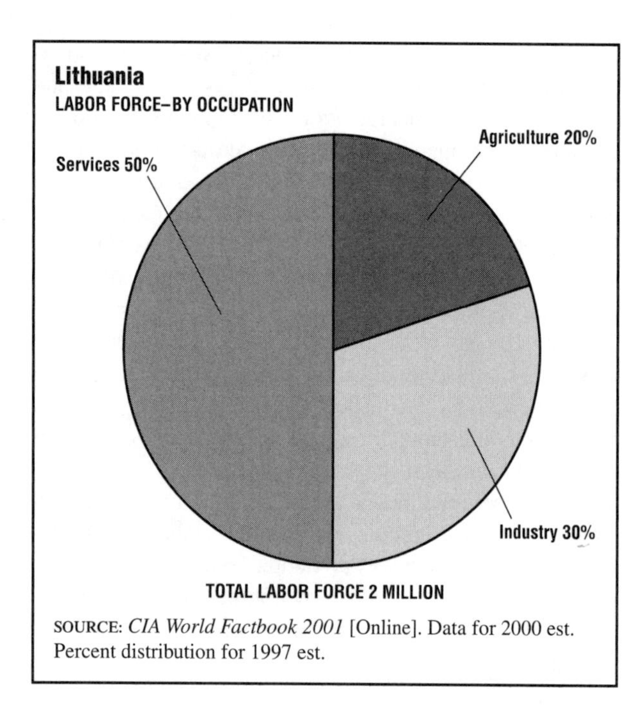

SOURCE: *CIA World Factbook 2001* [Online]. Data for 2000 est. Percent distribution for 1997 est.

the sectoral structure of its economy as measured by the percentage of the individual sectors' contribution to the GDP and/or employment. As a result of the Soviet occupation and the imposition of the communist central planning, Lithuania's economy was distorted compared to Denmark, Finland, or other comparable, free Western countries. In 1990, agriculture still occupied a special place in the Lithuanian economy, providing about a quarter of jobs and about half of the GDP. Above all, however, Lithuania was industrialized in a heavy, distorted way reflecting the communist orthodoxy and Soviet imperialistic priorities which was to the detriment of services (especially modern services) and the modern welfare-increasing economic development in general. During the independence decade (1990–2000), the normal structure of a modern economy was largely restored in Lithuania, with the services dominating (58 percent) GDP, followed by industry (32 percent) and agriculture (10 percent). About 30 percent of Lithuanian workers are employed by industry, while 20 percent work in agriculture, and 50 percent work in services.

AGRICULTURE

With three-quarters of its **labor force** employed in agriculture, Lithuania was a predominantly agricultural economy in 1940. Half a century later, agriculture still occupied a special role in the Lithuanian economy, providing about a quarter of jobs and about half the national product. By 1990, Lithuania reached roughly one-fourth of the U.S. labor productivity in agriculture. Generally, Lithuanian agricultural production costs were 2 to 3 times higher than in Western countries at the end of the communist era.

Lithuanian agriculture remains inefficient by Western standards. Most small farmers do not have the capital or resources to acquire new equipment, and few utilize new forms of fertilizer and soil-management techniques. In 1998, agricultural production decreased by 4.3 percent, and in 1999, it decreased by 13.6 percent. However, increasing competition and access to new technology have slowly increased the efficiency of some farms (mainly the larger operations). In 2000, Lithuania had 67,800 family farms and 1,244 corporate-owned farms. Since 1990, about 2,000 family farms have gone out-of-business as unprofitable operations have been unable to survive the free market economy. Currently, the nation loses about 0.03–0.04 percent of its agricultural land each year. Agricultural workers are among the lowest paid laborers in Lithuania. In 2000, on average they only earned US$177 per month while the national average monthly wage was US$267.

About 3.37 million hectares are used for agriculture, and the average farm size is 12.6 hectares. In 1998, agricultural exports had a total value of US$564.1 million while imports totaled US$697.6 million. The main exports were butter, cheese, fish, milk, and pet food. Almost 80 percent of agricultural exports go to Russia. The main imports include processed foods and fruits. The main supplier of agricultural imports is the EU with some 52 percent of imports. The largest crops were potatoes at 1.7 million metric tons, sugar beets at 890,000 metric tons, and wheat at 837,000 metric tons. The main livestock products are beef and veal, chicken, lamb, pork, and horse.

INDUSTRY

During the period of Soviet control of Lithuania, the government tried to change the economy from one based on agriculture to one based on industry. However, in the post-Soviet era, industry has declined significantly in relation to the other segments of the economy. In 1999 alone, industrial production declined by 14 percent. There have also been deep cuts in employment in industry. For instance, in 1990 there were 25,000 workers in the electronics industry, but by 1997, that number had declined to 10,000. Lithuanian industry suffers from outdated equipment and a reliance on unstable markets in the nations of the former Soviet Union.

Industrial workers on average earn less than the national average of US$267 per month. Workers in manufacturing earn an average of US$260 per month, while construction workers earn about US$242 per month. Ironically, the low wages have been somewhat helpful for Lithuanian industry. Foreign companies have relocated manufacturing plants in the country precisely because labor costs are so inexpensive. Examples of such foreign

INTRODUCTION TO WORLD CURRENCY

The following insert contains color photographs of paper currency from around the world. Where possible, the most recent issue and lowest denomination was selected to show the bank notes of the countries represented in this encyclopedia. As of the year 2002, approximately 169 countries issued their own paper money.

Bank notes are more than a measuring system for value to be used as payment for goods and services. In many instances a banknote is a graphic reflection of a country's history, politics, economy, environment, and its people. For example, many bank notes depict plant life such as flowers and trees, as well as birds and other animals native to that geographic region. The 5-lats note of Latvia has a giant oak tree on the front, while the 25-rupee note of Seychelles and the 5-guilder note of Suriname both show flowers from the homeland. Birds adorn notes from São Tomé and Príncipe, Papua New Guinea, and Zambia. Large animals such as the mountain gorillas on the 500-franc note from Rwanda, the white rhinoceros on the 10-rand note from South Africa, and the bull elephant on the 500-shilling note of Uganda are commonplace.

Famous rulers and political figures from history are prevalent. Sir Henry Parkes, a famous 19th-century statesman, graces the front of the 5-dollar note from Australia; and Canada's Sir John Alexander MacDonald, a noted Canadian prime minister from the same time period, appears on the front of the 10-dollar Canadian note. Mieszko I, a medieval prince credited with being the founder of Poland in 966, is on the 10-zloty note from that country. Bank notes also reflect the power of more contemporary rulers, as exemplified by the image of Iraq's current president, Saddam Hussein, on that country's 50-dinar note, issued in 1994. Malaysia's paramount ruler and first chief of state, Tunku Abdul Rahman, is on the front of that country's 1-ringgit note and all notes of all denominations issued since 1967.

Architectural vignettes are common on world notes. Islamic mosques with minarets can be found on the 5000-afghani note from Afghanistan, as well as the 25-piaster note from Egypt, indicating the prevalent Islamic religious influence in those 2 countries. The 5-pound 1994 regular issue note from Ireland shows the famous Mater Misericordiae Hospital in Ireland, where Sister Catherine McAuley, founder of the Sisters of Mercy religious order, served in the area of health care. The depiction of religious figures is common on European notes. Examples include St. Agnes of Bohemia on the 50-koruna note of the Czech Republic, St. John of Rila on the 1-lev note of Bulgaria, and the Archangel Gabriel on the 50-denar note of Macedonia.

Artists, authors, scientists, and musicians are also honored on many bank notes. James Ensor (1860–1949), an innovative painter and etcher, is shown on the 100-franc note from Belgium, while Baroness Karen Blixen (pen name Isak Dinesen), the famed Danish author of *Out of Africa* is found on the 50-krone note of Denmark.

Several notes commemorate the new millenium, significant local events, or anniversaries. The front of the 2000-leu commemorative note from Romania has an imaginative reproduction of the solar system as a reference to the total solar eclipse of 11 August 1999. Another example of a commemorative note is the 200-rupee note from Sri Lanka. The note was issued 4 February 1998 to commemorate the 50th anniversary of independence as a self-governing Dominion of the British Commonwealth.

As of 2002, 15 countries did not issue or use their own paper currency, but allowed the bank notes of neighboring countries as well as U.S. currency to circulate freely in their local economies. Many of these countries are relatively small in size with economies to match. Countries such as San Marino, Monaco, Liechtenstein, and Vatican City are tourist-oriented and do not see a need to issue their own homeland currency. Five of these fifteen countries—namely Marshall Islands, Micronesia, Palau, Panama, and Puerto Rico—all use the U.S. dollar as their monetary unit of exchange. As of March 2001, Ecuador and El Salvador had joined the above-mentioned countries in adopting the U.S. dollar. Countries struggling with hyperinflation (uncontrolled inflation marked by the sharp devaluation of the homeland currency) may choose to use the U.S. dollar in place of their own currencies in an attempt to stabilize their economy by linking it directly to the strength and stability of the

U.S. economy. Countries that use U.S. dollars in conjunction with sound economic policies can usually expect to control and/or minimize inflation. The complete adoption of the U.S. currency has been more successful than the practice of pegging the value of local currency to the U.S. dollar according to a fixed ratio, an approach attempted recently by Argentina to disastrous effect. Even those countries that have not completely adopted the U.S. dollar as their currency often have economies operating freely with both their own national and the U.S. currencies. The strength of the U.S. dollar has also made it the currency of choice in the global black market.

Another trend that will probably continue into the future is the joining together of several neighboring countries to form a central bank issuing a common currency. The primary objective of these economic and monetary unions is to eliminate obstacles to free trade, creating a single unified marketplace. This grouping together tends to strengthen the economy and currency of the member countries as well as providing a cost savings in currency production. While such economic partnerships have occurred throughout history, more recent examples began in the early 1950s with the union of the East Caribbean States, followed by the Central African States, French Pacific Territories, and West African States. The most recent and highly publicized example is the European Monetary Union (EMU), composed of 12 European member countries—namely Austria, Belgium, Finland, France, Germany, Greece, Ireland, Italy, Luxembourg, the Netherlands, Portugal, and Spain. On 1 January 2002, the EMU, through its newly formed central bank, replaced the participating countries' homeland currencies with a new common currency called the *euro*. An example of the 10-euro note is shown on the following currency insert pages. Those countries that had pegged their currencies to an EU member's currency prior to the euro's adoption (as several Francophone countries in Africa did with the French franc) now peg their currency to the euro.

It should be mentioned that, in contrast to this recurring trend of country unification for economic and monetary purposes, there are several countries with isolationist governments that have done just the opposite in order to limit the influence of the international community on their economies and populations. For example, Iraq and Syria have made it illegal to use or export their currency outside of their homelands. Several other nations embraced this isolationist attitude through the use of trade voucher and tourist certificates in place of currency, thus keeping their national circulating bank notes from being used or exported by visitors to their country. China, Bulgaria, and Poland are examples of countries that issued what they termed "foreign exchange certificates" for this specific purpose. However, this practice has largely been discontinued, with the exception of Cuba, which still uses a similar certificate first issued in the mid-1980s.

So what does the future have in store for the economies of the world? Trends indicate most countries in the world want free, open, and balanced trade with a strong, stable, and growing economy, free of hyperinflation. More countries are achieving this goal by unifying in regional economic partnerships such as the European Union, or by clearing the barriers to free trade through agreements such as NAFTA (North American Free Trade Agreement). As the use of the U.S. dollar increases throughout the Americas, some economists predict that this region will follow in the footsteps of Europe in terms of establishing a common currency under a central bank. The Asian and Middle-Eastern regions are also likely candidates for similar regional economic partnerships given the prevalence of established trade agreements already in existence among those countries. As the globalization of trade necessitates closer economic ties between countries, it is not inconceivable that a single central bank and common currency will eventually unite the countries of the world. While that development is still only a remote possibility at this point, there is little doubt that nations' increased dependence on international trade for economic prosperity will promote a currency policy conducive to closer trade ties and cross-border partnerships.

—Keith S. Bauman, professional numismatist
International Bank Note Society
American Numismatic Association
Professional Currency Dealers Association

Afghanistan

Albania

Algeria

Andorra
(used both Spanish and French currency until the adoption of the euro in January of 2002)

Angola

Antigua and Barbuda
(shares currency with other East Caribbean States)

Argentina

Armenia

Aruba

Australia

Austria
(adopted the euro as of January 2002)

Azerbaijan

The Bahamas

Bahrain

Bangladesh

Barbados

Belarus

Belgium
(adopted the euro as of January 2002)

Belize

Benin
(shares currency with other West African States)

Bhutan

Bolivia

Bosnia and Herzegovina

Botswana

Brazil

Brunei Darussalam

Bulgaria

Burkina Faso
(shares currency with other West African States)

Burma (Myanmar)

Burundi

Cambodia

Cameroon
(shares currency with other Central African States)

Canada

Cape Verde

Central African Republic
(shares currency with other Central African States)

Chad
(shares currency with other Central African States)

Chile

China

Colombia

Comoros

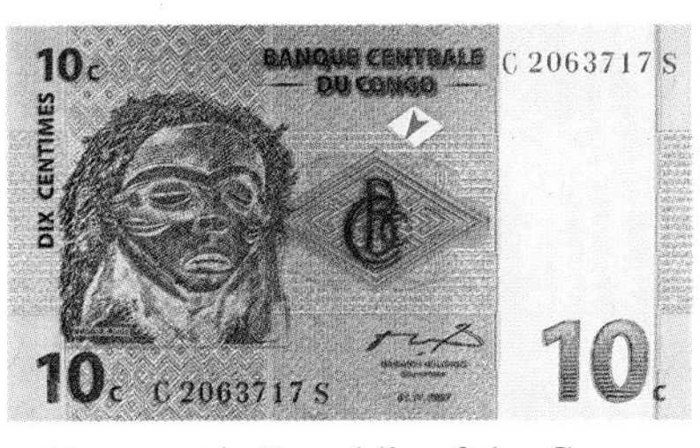

Democratic Republic of the Congo

Republic of the Congo
(shares currency with other Central African States)

Costa Rica

Côte d'Ivoire
(shares currency with other West African States)

Croatia

Cuba

Cyprus

Czech Republic

Denmark

Djibouti

Dominica
(shares currency with other East Caribbean States)

Dominican Republic

Ecuador

Egypt

El Salvador

Equatorial Guinea
(shares currency with other Central African States)

Eritrea

Estonia

Ethiopia

European Union (EU)

Fiji

Finland
(adopted the euro as of January 2002)

France
(adopted the euro as of January 2002)

French Guiana, Martinique, and Guadeloupe
(used the Fench currency until the adoption of the euro in January 2002)

French Polynesia

Gabon
(shares currency with other Central African States)

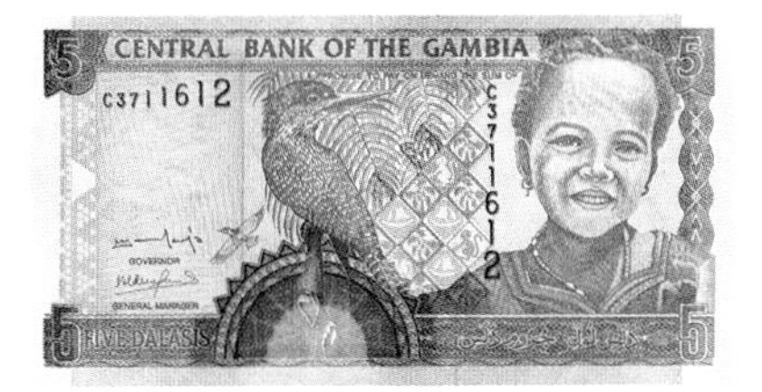

The Gambia

Georgia

Germany
(adopted the euro as of January 2002)

Ghana

Greece
(adopted the euro as of January 2002)

Grenada
(shares currency with other East Carribbean States)

Guatemala

Guinea

Guinea-Bissau
(shares currency with other West African States)

Guyana

Haiti

Honduras

Hong Kong

Hungary

Iceland

India

Indonesia

Iran

Iraq

Ireland
(adopted the euro as of January 2002)

Israel

Italy
(adopted the euro as of January 2002)

Jamaica

Japan

Jordan

Kazakhstan

Kenya

Kiribati
(uses the Australian currency)

North Korea

South Korea

Kuwait

Kyrgyzstan

Laos

Latvia

Lebanon

Lesotho

Liberia

Libya

Liechtenstein
(uses the Swiss currency)

Lithuania

Luxembourg
(adopted the euro as of January 2002)

Macau

Macedonia

Madagascar

Malawi

Malaysia

Maldives

Mali
(shares currency with other West African States)

Malta

Marshall Islands
(uses the U.S. currency)

Mauritania

Mauritius

Mexico

Micronesia
(uses the U.S. currency)

Moldova

Monaco
(used the Frency currency until the adoption of the euro in January 2002)

Mongolia

Morocco

Mozambique

Namibia

Nauru
(uses the Australian currency)

Nepal

The Netherlands
(adopted the euro as of January 2002)

Netherlands Antilles

New Zealand

Nicaragua

Niger
(shares currency with other West African States)

Nigeria

Norway

Oman

Pakistan

Palau
(uses the U.S. currency)

Panama
(uses the U.S. currency)

Papua New Guinea

Paraguay

Peru

Philippines

Poland

Portugal
(adopted the euro as of January 2002)

Puerto Rico
(uses the U.S. currency)

Qatar

Romania

Russia

Rwanda

San Marino
(used the Italian currency until the adoption of the euro in January of 2002)

São Tomé and Príncipe

Saudi Arabia

Senegal
(shares currency with other West African States)

Seychelles

Sierra Leone

Singapore

Slovakia

Slovenia

Solomon Islands

Somalia

South Africa

Spain
(adopted the euro as of January 2002)

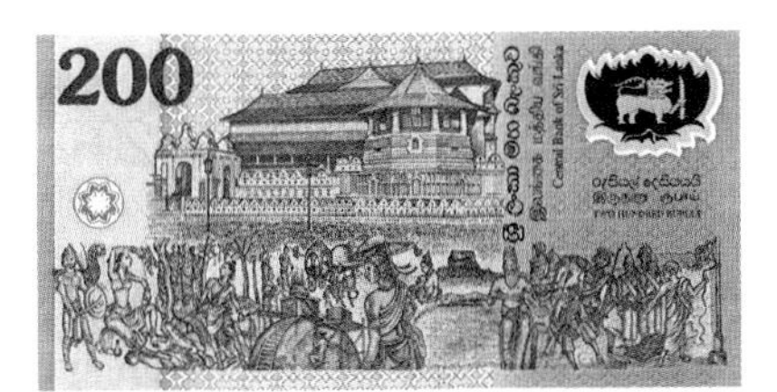

Sri Lanka

St. Kitts and Nevis
(shares currency with other East Caribbean States)

St. Lucia
(shares currency with other East Caribbean States)

St. Vincent and the Grenadines
(shares currency with other East Caribbean States)

Sudan

Suriname

Swaziland

Sweden

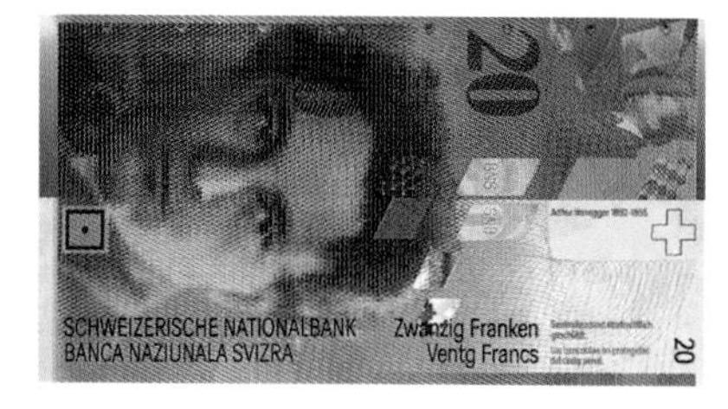

Switzerland

Syria

Taiwan

Tajikistan

Tanzania

Thailand

Togo
(shares currency with other West African States)

Tonga

Trinidad and Tobago

Tunisia

Turkey

Turkmenistan

Tuvalu
(uses Australian currency)

Uganda

Ukraine

United Arab Emirates

United Kingdom

United States

Uruguay

Uzbekistan

Vanuatu

Vatican City
(used the Italian currency until the adoption of the euro in January of 2002)

Venezuela

Vietnam

Yemen

Yugoslavia

Zambia

Zimbabwe

industrial companies include Siemens of Germany, Samsung of Korea, Farimex of Switzerland, Shell Chemical of the United Kingdom and the Netherlands, and Wilhelm Becker of Germany. Hence while most areas of industry are in decline, there are several segments that have grown.

The chemical industry remains one of Lithuania's most profitable sectors. In 1997 it accounted for almost 10 percent of all Lithuanian exports. The main elements of the chemical sector include nitrogen and phosphate fertilizers which in 1997 made-up 41 percent of chemical exports. Other segments of the industry are pharmaceuticals, cosmetics and soap, and glues, oils and resinoids. Most chemical exports (about 50 percent) go to Russia and the former communist bloc nations of Europe. The textile industry also remains profitable. The segment has attracted US$40 million in foreign investment since 1990. In 1997, textiles accounted for 3.3 percent of the GDP and employed some 60,000 people in 100 large companies and 300 medium and small companies. About 75 percent of all textiles are exported. By 2000, almost 90 percent of textile production was done by either international firms or **joint ventures** between foreign companies and Lithuanian companies. Of the exports, 65 percent go to the EU and 20 percent go to the countries of the former Soviet Union. Although the electronics sector has declined, in 1997 it was responsible for US$120 million in revenue. Among the main electronic products are televisions, electronic measurement equipment, semiconductors, and other computer equipment.

Lithuania also has a significant wood and paper processing industry. In total, Lithuanian plants processed some 3 million cubic meters of timber. These products account for about 5.4 percent of exports. Some of the main wood-based products include furniture, cardboard, and printed boxes. The main export markets are France, Germany, and Denmark. Two international companies, Ochocco Lumber of the United States and Terminal Forest Products of Canada, have established several plants in Lithuania.

The rest of the industry produces diverse goods including consumer durables, e.g. refrigerators, consumer electronics, etc. There are small but growing and technologically advanced biotechnology, computer and Internet industries. Most of the industrial production is exported to the European countries.

SERVICES

Services now account for the bulk of the Lithuanian economy. Workers in this sector are among the highest paid in the country. For instance, workers in the financial service sector earn an average of US$517 per month while workers in general business and real estate earn US$375 per month. The low pay of Lithuanian workers has constrained the **retail** sector of the economy, since most workers have little excess money to spend on consumer items. However, the renewed economic growth which began in 2000 has already caused an increase of 5 percent in the retail sector.

FINANCIAL SERVICES. The first private commercial banks in Lithuania since the period between World War I and II were established in 1989. The nation's banks underwent a period of consolidation in the mid-1990s during which several banks went out of business while others were acquired by larger banks through mergers and acquisitions. In response, the government passed a series of laws which placed additional regulations on banks in an effort to ensure their **solvency**. A number of international banks have a presence in Lithuania. These include Société Générale of France, Svedfund Financial Markets of Sweden, and DE GmbH of Germany. However, these banks only account for 3.1 percent of the banking market. About 42 percent of total banking assets were controlled by just 2 banks—both of them state-owned (although both are scheduled to be privatized by 2002). The nation's largest private bank, Vilniaus Bankas, is the largest bank among the Baltic nations. The insurance sector of Lithuania is vibrant with 31 different firms, including major multinational firms such as Lloyd's of the United Kingdom and Coris of France. From 1997 to 1998, insurance revenues increased by 40 percent.

TRAVEL AND TOURISM. Since the end of Soviet control in 1990, tourism has increased significantly in Lithuania. Since 1996, tourist revenues have increased by 50 percent to over US$420 million in 1999. That same year, Lithuania received 3.7 million visitors or more tourists than there were people in the population. In 1997, tourism accounted for 4.2 percent of the GDP. The main tourist destination was the nation's capital, Vilnius, which received 58 percent of all visitors. This has led to the construction of 15 new hotels in the capital since 1996, including ones owned by Sheraton and Radisson. The increased number of tourists has led to a doubling of restaurants, clubs, and tourist shops since 1996.

INTERNATIONAL TRADE

For smaller countries like Lithuania, international trade and economic cooperation in general is of predominant importance for economic development. The forced reorientation of Lithuania's trade after its incorporation into the USSR resulted in a complete destruction of Lithuania's economic ties with the West (mainly United Kingdom and Germany). As a result of occupation, Lithuania was forced to forego multiple benefits flowing from foreign trade in general and the cooperation with the advanced market economies in particular.

Only about 2 percent of its trade was with the West at the start of the post-Soviet independence in 1990.

With the international trade-to-GDP ratio at the level of some 90 percent, Lithuania is a strongly outward-oriented economy as of 2000. Its foreign trade is liberalized and regulated largely via market economy instruments known in the West and approved by the World Trade Organization (WTO) of which Lithuania is a member. The earlier licensing and foreign exchange surrender requirements have been repealed. Over two-thirds of the Lithuanian imports enter duty free; the rest face 5 to 15 percent duties, becoming more and more uniform as required by the WTO. By 2000, Lithuania maintained economic relations with over 160 countries. The country has bilateral trade treaties with 22 nations. However, accounting for almost one-quarter of Lithuania's trade **turnover**, Russia remains a major trade partner. Part of the Lithuanian output decline during transition was due to too slow a reorientation of trade away from the former Soviet Union (FSU) and towards the West. **Foreign direct investment** into Lithuania is still rather modest due to this and related factors having to do with instability in Russia and elsewhere in the FSU but also shortcomings of the Lithuanian reforms and some communist legacies.

From 1997 to 1999, the nation's imports increased by 27 percent, and its exports increased by 10.6 percent. Lithuania's main exports in 1998 included machinery and equipment (19 percent of exports), mineral products (19 percent), textiles and clothing (19 percent), and chemicals (10 percent). The nation's main export markets were Russia at 17.4 percent, Germany at 15.8 percent, Latvia at 12.7 percent, Denmark at 5.9 percent, and Belarus at 5.2 percent. In 1998, Lithuania's main imports were machinery and equipment at 30 percent, mineral products at 16 percent, chemicals at 9 percent, and textiles and clothing at 9 percent. In 1999, the country's major import partners were Russia with 20.4 percent of imports, Germany with 16.5 percent, Denmark with 3.8 percent, Belarus with 2.2 percent, and Latvia with 2 percent. Lithuania has consistently had a **trade deficit**. In 1996, the nation imported US$1.2 billion more than it exported, and by 1998 that deficit had increased to US$2.1 billion.

There seems to be a trend to go deeper into **external debt**. The external debt amounted to over US$2 billion at the end of 2000, balancing around the level of Lithuania's **hard currency** reserves. However, the increasing levels of foreign investment have helped offset the debt by providing inflows of capital for new investment. The Swedish-Finnish company, Amber Consortium, is the largest single investor in Lithuania with US$510 million in investments, followed by Williams International of the United States with US$150 million and Telia-Sonera, also a joint Swedish-Finnish firm, with US$66 million. By 2000, total foreign investment in Lithuania was US$2.66 billion. Investments in telecommunications accounted for 28.8 percent of total foreign investment while manufacturing accounted for 25 percent, and wholesale and retail trade accounted for 19.5 percent.

In an additional effort to attract foreign trade, in 1995, the Lithuania government established 3 **free trade zones**, located in Siauliai, Klaipeda, and Kaunas. Companies that locate themselves in these zones receive incentives of up to 30 percent of the cost of building or relocating to the areas.

The entry of Lithuania into the EU will greatly expand the nation's international trade. It will give Lithuania access to the markets of 15 countries which will also be able to use Lithuania as a gateway for entry into the markets of the former Soviet Union. Already, trade between Lithuania and the EU members has dramatically increased. Since 1997, exports to the EU have increased by 21.8 percent. Meanwhile imports from the EU increased by 13.3 percent. Lithuania is also a member of the Baltic free trade zone, a 1994 agreement between the 3 Baltic countries which abolished tariffs on all industrial goods traded among Lithuania, Latvia, and Estonia.

MONEY

As a result of Soviet legacies, Lithuania suffered rather severe price and monetary instabilities following independence in 1990. By 1995, inflation had reached 35.6 percent. In response, the Lithuanian government undertook a series of reforms that were assisted by the International Monetary Fund (IMF), an organization that lends money to governments to help them protect their national currency. By 1999, inflation had been reduced to 3 percent.

As part of the post-Soviet macroeconomic transformation, the Bank of Lithuania (B of L) was established as the main financial institution with both the currency **exchange rate** management and bank supervision functions. In 1994, Lithuania adopted a **currency board**

Exchange rates: Lithuania

litai per US$1	
2001	4.000
2000	4.000
1999	4.000
1998	4.000
1997	4.000
1996	4.000

Note: Currency has been at a fixed rate since May 1, 1994; litai is the plural of litas.

SOURCE: CIA *World Factbook 2001* [ONLINE].

which means the value of the Lithuanian litas is fixed at the level of US$0.25 or 4 litai per U.S. dollar and guarantied by Lithuania's **foreign exchange reserves**. So the value of litas travels with the value of the U.S. dollar and no exchange rate policy is currently being conducted.

The Bank of Lithuania's main function is to protect the nation's currency. However, it also regulates the private commercial banks in Lithuania and sets interest rates. It also sells government bonds and **treasury bills** which help finance the debt. Interest rates vary between 6 to 10 percent per year. High interest rate levels largely reflect higher risk and volatility in the domestic capital markets. Foreign banks must receive approval before they are allowed to purchase more than 10 percent of the shares of a local bank.

Overall, the Lithuanian banking sector is rather small but operating smoothly as of 2000. It consists of 10 commercial banks, 1 special purpose bank, and 3 foreign bank branches. The share of the **public sector** in the capital of commercial banks continues to decline, to some one-third by 2000. At the same time, the share of domestic privately owned assets rose; the role of foreign private owners increased only slightly. The stability of the nation's banking sector was such that in 1996, Lithuania became the first country of the former Soviet Union to be granted a credit rating by such international firms as Standard & Poor's and Moody's. Because the government's bonds are rated as trustworthy by these firms, these bonds are more attractive to foreign investors.

The role of non-bank financial markets is still rather weak. While a relatively large number of firms are listed on the well-organized National Stock Exchange of Lithuania (NSEL) modelled after the Paris Bourse, trading is rather low and suffers from the shortages of **liquidity**, a condition affecting most stock exchanges in the post-communist economies.

POVERTY AND WEALTH

The legacy of Soviet control in Lithuania is one of poverty and deep disparities in income. Many Lithuanians have not adjusted well to the market economy. These phenomena left most people of Lithuania quite poor at the beginning of the independence in 1990. True, **nomenklatura** lived well under the Soviets in the narrow material sense and the social security sense. But even nomenklatura were separated from the world and for that and other reasons were unable to make their lives richer in many respects.

In 1993, the wealthiest 10 percent of the population controlled 28 percent of the country's wealth, while the poorest 10 percent only controlled about 3 percent of the nation's wealth. Increases in Lithuania's unemployment rate have added to the nation's poverty. In 1996, unemployment was 6.2 percent, but by 2000, the rate had increased to 15 percent.

Those in Lithuania who earn or survive on US$28 per week or less are considered to be below the poverty line. In 1999, the poverty rate in Lithuania was 16 percent, but that wealth varies considerably. For instance, the rural poverty rate is 28 percent because of lower pay rates and higher unemployment rates among agricultural workers. Overall, some 55.1 percent of those living in poverty were aged 15 or younger.

The transition period is bringing its own opportunities and problems. An undisputed achievement of the transition period is the equilibrium on the **consumer goods** markets and the resultant wide choice of imported and domestic consumer goods available to those who can afford them. And the possession of some goods (e.g. cars, phones) increased tremendously compared to the Soviet period. As usual in a market economy, some people (younger, better educated) are able to live financially very well. Newly rich Lithuanians are not numerous but they are able to live lifestyles comparable to those of the average middle class members in the West or even better. However, some of Western ills (e.g. drugs) are making their way to Lithuania as well. Part of new wealth came from shadowy international dealings organized by the KGB (the notorious Soviet political police) and other

Distribution of Income or Consumption by Percentage Share: Lithuania

Lowest 10%	3.1
Lowest 20%	7.8
Second 20%	12.6
Third 20%	16.8
Fourth 20%	22.4
Highest 20%	40.3
Highest 10%	25.6

Survey year: 1996

Note: This information refers to expenditure shares by percentiles of the population and is ranked by per capita expenditure.

SOURCE: *2000 World Development Indicators* [CD-ROM].

GDP per Capita (US$)

Country	1975	1980	1985	1990	1998
Lithuania	N/A	N/A	N/A	3,191	2,197
United States	19,364	21,529	23,200	25,363	29,683
Russia	2,555	3,654	3,463	3,668	2,138
Latvia	2,382	2,797	3,210	3,703	2,328

SOURCE: United Nations. *Human Development Report 2000; Trends in human development and per capita income.*

Household Consumption in PPP Terms

Country	All food	Clothing and footwear	Fuel and power[a]	Health care[b]	Education[b]	Transport & Communications	Other
Lithuania	33	5	13	4	27	9	8
United States	13	9	9	4	6	8	51
Russia	28	11	16	7	15	8	16
Latvia	30	5	16	6	23	11	10

Data represent percentage of consumption in PPP terms.
[a]Excludes energy used for transport.
[b]Includes government and private expenditures.

SOURCE: World Bank. *World Development Indicators 2000.*

post-Soviet mafia. Other people (older, less educated or educated but more influenced by the communist system) suffer from higher levels of unemployment and the shortages of the social safety net. While they are able to subsist on usually rather small plots of land, most people living in rural areas are poor, old, and plagued by social ills (e.g. alcoholism) inherited from the Soviet period. They present one of the gravest problems. The Lithuanian government is trying to help people who find themselves below the poverty line, but the budgetary resources are very limited. The state provides unemployment insurance and both old age and disability pensions. It also provides limited assistance for housing. In addition, the efficiency of social assistance is low by international standards. It will take years of economic growth before the majority of the Lithuanian people are able to feel appreciable and broader-based improvements in their living standards.

WORKING CONDITIONS

There was nominally **full employment** in Soviet-occupied Lithuania except that there was some hidden unemployment and some forced "employment" characteristic of totalitarian regimes.

The Lithuanian constitution gives workers the right to establish and join unions, although there are limitations on the ability of security and law-enforcement personnel to strike. About 10 percent of businesses are unionized, and about 15 percent of workers belong to unions. Children may work at age 14 with parental consent or at age 16 with or without consent. The nation's minimum wage is US$107.50 per month. However, most workers earn more than the minimum wage, and wages vary considerably. Workers in the financial services sector earn an average monthly wage of US$517, while construction workers earn an average of US$242 per month and retail workers US$181. The standard work week is 40 hours, and there is overtime pay for hours worked in excess of 40. National laws mandate a minimum 28 days of vacation per year.

By 2000, unemployment reached 13 percent and is still growing. In 1999, the Lithuanian workforce numbered 1.8 million. About 18 percent of the workforce has a college degree, while an additional 44 percent have some specialized or technical degrees.

COUNTRY HISTORY AND ECONOMIC DEVELOPMENT

200 B.C. Baltic people settle in the area that is now Lithuania.

1200s A.D. The Lithuanian tribes become united in a loose political confederation.

1236. The Lithuanian state is founded by Duke (later king) Mindaugas.

1386–1795. Lithuania and Poland are united as a single country.

1387. Christianity is established in Lithuania.

1410. Teutonic knights are defeated by joint Lithuanian-Polish forces.

1569–1795. The Lithuanian-Polish Commonwealth (Lublin Union) occurs.

1579. The University of Vilnius (the oldest university in the Baltics) is founded.

1795–1915. Lithuania is under tsarist Russian rule.

1915–18. Lithuania is occupied by Germans during World War I.

1918. Modern Lithuania's independence is declared.

1921. Lithuania is admitted to the League of Nations.

1939. The Nazi-Soviet Pact divides Eastern Europe between Germany and the USSR.

1940. Lithuania is occupied by the USSR.

1941–44. Lithuania is occupied by Nazi Germany.

1944. Soviet occupation and re-imposition of the Soviet rule on Lithuania occurs.

1944–56. Armed resistance occurs against the Soviet occupation of Lithuania.

1957–87. Covert resistance occurs against communism with religious and secular dissent.

1990. Lithuania declares re-establishment of independence, a mortal blow to the USSR.

1991. Lithuania is admitted to the United Nations.

1993. Last Soviet troops withdraw from Lithuania.

1994. Lithuania becomes a member of NATO's Partnership-for-Peace Program; the nation becomes an associate member of the EU.

1997. The government undertakes a wide-scale privatization program.

1999. The EU agrees to initiate discussions to allow Lithuania to enter the organization.

FUTURE TRENDS

Despite a decade of determined and radical efforts at transforming the economy and society away from communism and other USSR-imposed distortions, Lithuania still faces challenges of further transformation to bring it into the European Union and NATO.

The so-called second generation reforms to be undertaken center on the modern role of the state in the European country and especially the interaction of public and **private sectors** in the process of economic development, given Lithuania's strategic economic interests and the nature of modern global economy.

Thus, further privatization of strategically important enterprises in the energy, transportation, and other infrastructure branches is required. Very important are the processes of **enterprise exit** of unviable enterprises from the Lithuanian economic system so they do not act as a burden to the state budget and release precious human and other resources for more productive uses, e.g. in the new economy. As of 2000, enterprise exit processes have been rather inefficient as about half of unviable firms in the bankruptcy stage stayed in that stage for 2 to 3 years, prolonging the negative consequences of the Soviet legacies. In the coming years, some 16,000 unviable enterprises will have to go bankrupt, hopefully using much more efficient processes. This will still be painful as some 180,000 employees need to be laid off in the process, temporarily pushing the unemployment rate even higher from its 13 percent level. These people will have to be either retired or trained for new jobs in the emerging modern economy.

The emergence of a modern economy will require liberalization of labor laws and other elements of the business environment so the new investments are attracted, especially from Western countries, and the **enterprise entry** is facilitated. In the digital age, new business models are emerging, and Lithuania badly needs to re-integrate the global economy using such modern approaches and Western investments. Further development of the Lithuanian market economy institutions (e.g. financial) is needed, especially in light of the transparency (e.g. in public **procurement**) and other requirements of the European Union. Development steps should include the improvement of the social security finances and putting them on a more sustainable basis. This and other steps will help improve the efficiency of the social safety net and help fight poverty, a big problem especially in the rural areas. Above all, Lithuania needs to put a major effort into preserving and upgrading its very considerable human resources through appropriate reforms of health care and education. Last but not least, Lithuania needs to develop a strategy for long-term development of its competitive advantages within the European and global (digital) economies.

While during 1990–2000 Lithuania made valiant trend-setting efforts to shed the legacies of communism and the Soviet occupation, the next decade will be marked by no less determined efforts to join and work within the European Union, a totally different kind of union than the USSR.

DEPENDENCIES

Lithuania has no territories or colonies.

BIBLIOGRAPHY

Samonis, V. *The Blueprint for Lithuania's Future: Main Premises.* Toronto: University of Toronto, 1997.

———. *From Dependence to Interdependence: Transforming Baltic Foreign Economic Relations.* Indianapolis: The Hudson Institute, 1991.

———. *Lietuvos Reformu Desimtmetis: Keliai, Klystkeliai, Problemos, Perspektyvos (Analize is Strategines Lyginamosios Perspektyvos).* A Study for the Parliament of Lithuania, Vilnius, 1999.

———. "Lithuania's Economic Transformation." Osteuropa-Wirtschaft (Munich: Suedost-Institut), No. 2, 1996.

———. "Road Maps to Markets: Issues in the Theory of the Post-Communist Transformation," in *Systemic Change in Post-Communist Economies,* edited by Paul G. Hare. Houndmills: Macmillan Press Ltd, 1999.

———. *State, Market and the Post-Communist Economic Transformation: A Macroanalytical Framework.* Brussels: International Institute of Administrative Sciences, 1992.

———. *Transforming Business Models in the Global Digital Economy: The Impact of the Internet.* Bonn and Toronto: The Center for European Integration Studies and SEMI Online, 2000.

———, editor. *Enterprise Restructuring and Foreign Investment in the Transforming East: The Impact of Privatization.* New York: The Haworth Press Inc., 1998.

———, editor. *Exit for Entry: Microrestructuring in Transition Economies.* Amsterdam: Kluwer Academic Publishers, forthcoming.

Shen, Raphael. *Restructuring the Baltic Economies: Disengaging Fifty Years of Integration With the USSR.* Westport: Praeger, 1994.

U.S. Central Intelligence Agency. *World Factbook 2001.* <http://www.odci.gov/cia/publications/factbook/index.html>. Accessed September 2001.

U.S. Department of State. *Background Notes: Lithuania.* <http://www.state.gov/www/background_notes/lithuania_9801_bgn.html>. Accessed September 2001.

———. *FY 2000 Country Commercial Guide: Lithuania.* <http://www.state.gov/www/about_state/business/com_guides/2000/europe/lithuania_CCG2000.pdf>. Accessed September 2001.

———. *2000 Country Reports on Human Rights Practices: Lithuania.* <http://www.state.gov/g/drl/rls/hrrpt/2000/eur/index.cfm?docid=691>. September 2001.

—Val Samonis

LUXEMBOURG

Grand Duchy of Luxembourg
Grand-Duché de Luxembourg
Grosshenzogtum Luxemburg

CAPITAL: Luxembourg.

MONETARY UNIT: Luxembourg franc (LUF). One franc equals 100 centimes. There are coins of 25 and 50 centimes and 1, 5, 10, and 20 francs. There are notes of 50 and 100 francs. Belgian currency is also legal tender in Luxembourg, and bills of 500, 1,000, and 5,000 Belgian francs also circulate. On 1 January 1999 the European Union began using the euro for non-currency financial transactions, and euro-denominated coins and notes will replace the franc as the currency in 2002.

CHIEF EXPORTS: Machinery and equipment, steel products, chemicals, rubber products, glass.

CHIEF IMPORTS: Minerals, metals, foodstuffs, quality consumer goods.

GROSS DOMESTIC PRODUCT: US$15.9 billion (purchasing power parity, 2000 est.).

BALANCE OF TRADE: **Exports:** US$7.6 billion (f.o.b., 2000). **Imports:** US$10 billion (c.i.f., 2000).

COUNTRY OVERVIEW

LOCATION AND SIZE. Luxembourg is a landlocked nation in Western Europe, at the intersection of Belgium, France, and Germany. It is one of the smallest nations in the world with an area of 2,586 square kilometers (998 square miles), which makes it slightly smaller than Rhode Island. The nation has 359 kilometers (223 miles) of borders, including 148 kilometers (92 miles) with Belgium, 73 kilometers (45 miles) with France, and 138 kilometers (86 miles) with Germany. Luxembourg, the capital, is in the southern region of the country. The nation's second and third largest cities, Esch-Alzette and Differdange, are in the southwest.

POPULATION. In July of 2000, the population of Luxembourg was estimated to be 437,389. While the overall fertility rate is below replacement levels (1.7 children per woman, or 12.45 births per 1,000 people), the population continues to grow because of **immigration**. There were 9.21 immigrants per 1,000 inhabitants in 2000. The death rate was 8.91 deaths per 1,000. In 2000, the population growth rate was 1.27 percent because of the influx of refugees and immigrant workers.

Immigration has been encouraged because of the need for workers. As much as 35 percent of the population is foreign, which gives the nation a higher proportion of foreigners than any other European country. The government has implemented different programs to integrate foreign residents into society. For instance, foreigners with resident status have the right to vote and run for office in municipal elections and may be employed in **public sector** jobs. Given the aging population, the need for workers continues. About 14 percent of Luxembourgers are over the age of 65, while 19 percent are 14 or younger. Average life expectancy is 73.8 years for males and 80.6 years for women. Besides **guest workers**, Luxembourg has also opened its borders to refugees. In 1998, there were 4,548 refugees in the nation, making up just over 1 percent of the population. Many of these refugees came from the former Yugoslavia. As the conflicts in the Balkans subside and refugees return home, population growth is expected to stabilize. However, the continuing need for workers will bring a corresponding growth in the population, which is expected to reach 700,000 by 2025.

Most Luxembourgers are descended from Celtic stock, with German and French influences. The largest minority group is the Portuguese, who account for 13 percent of the population. There are also significant numbers of Italians and other southern Europeans. Most people live in the southwest, and two-thirds of the population are urban. During the 20th century there was increasing migration from the countryside to urban areas. The population of the capital is 76,440, while 24,255 live in the

second largest city, Esch-Alzette. To maintain the declining rural population, the government has relocated some industries to the countryside. The Luxembourg language is an amalgamation of German and French, with French also used for official purposes and German—which is commonly spoken—as the language of the press. English is also widely used.

OVERVIEW OF ECONOMY

Since World War II, the economy of Luxembourg has been marked by high income levels and low unemployment. For most of this period, the iron and steel industry dominated the economy, accounting for as much as 80 percent of the nation's wealth during the 1960s. Banking and financial services are now the main considerations in the economy. In 1999, the unemployment rate was the lowest in Europe at 2.9 percent, and the **inflation rate** was only 1.1 percent. Meanwhile, the nation's GDP has grown about 5 percent per year since 1985.

Luxembourg's economic success has been due to its adaptability and the skills of its people. As the steel industry declined, the economy shifted to other enterprises, and current prosperity is based on a combination of industry, a small agricultural sector, and a growing import-export economy based on financial services. Economic diversification has resulted in the expansion of small to medium-sized companies.

The nation has one of the world's most educated **labor forces**, and the multilingual ability of most of the population is an incentive for foreign companies to invest or relocate there. While there are no 4-year universities in Luxembourg, there are 6 major universities in the region and 500 laboratories, and the government subsidizes those students who go abroad to complete their education. The nation's superb **infrastructure** also adds to its attractiveness, as do the sound relations between labor and industry.

As the steel industry declined in the 1970s, Luxembourg **restructured** its steel producers into a single entity, ARBED, a multinational group which is among the most important steelmakers in the world. Steel still accounts for 29 percent of the exports, 1.8 percent of the GDP, and 3.9 percent of employment. The government owns just under one-third of ARBED, and since 1974, it has set up reforms and modernization initiatives and assumed parts of the group's debt. The company is the second largest steel producer in Europe and one of the most productive in the world.

With the decline of the steel industry in the 1970s, the government undertook several programs to diversify the economy. A significant aspect of this diversification effort was the promotion of the financial sector. By the 1980s, the nation emerged as one of the world's premier banking centers, and by 1996 there were 222 banks in the country with 21,458 employees (9.5 percent of the workforce). Total assets exceed US$200 billion, with 81 percent of funds in foreign currencies. U.S. dollars and German marks are the primary denominations held in Luxembourg banks. Luxembourg's attractiveness as a financial center has prompted companies, such as Goodyear, Du Pont, and General Motors, to build factories there. The nation's investment fund sector is the second largest in the world (behind the United States) and accounts for 20 percent of Europe's total investments. This sector is at the forefront of new services, such as **e-commerce**. There are also more than 9,000 foreign **hold-**

ing companies in Luxembourg, and the European Investment Bank, the main financial institution of the European Union (EU), is located there.

Successive governments have enacted policies and adopted many programs to encourage foreign investment and attract foreign businesses. Examples of such policies include cuts in company tax, abolition of corporate capital gains tax, and tax credits for new products and services. Administrative reforms have reduced bureaucratic impediments to business, with relevant agencies and bureaus placed under one coordinating body. This arrangement hastens paperwork and permits, making it easier for new companies to establish themselves. The nation's banking secrecy laws also appeal to foreign investors, but problems with **money laundering** have led to efforts to compromise between privacy and the need to prevent criminal activity. The laws continue to allow Luxembourg to remain a **tax haven** for foreign investors. These government programs have been successful. For instance, outside of North America, Luxembourg has the largest U.S. **foreign direct investment** on a per capita basis.

The government has encouraged the development of audio-visual and communications sectors, and media services have become the second most significant sector in the diversification program. The government-backed company, Société Européenne des Satellites (SES), operates 5 satellites, and Radio-Television Luxembourg is 1 of the continent's leading private radio and television broadcasters.

A continuing problem for the economy of Luxembourg is energy. The nation has few sources of energy other than timber, and 95 percent of electricity is imported. The country chooses not to construct nuclear energy plants. Oil, coal, and natural gas fuels are imported. Thus, Luxembourg is dependent on foreign sources of fuel.

Luxembourg has been a strong supporter of economic integration. For 80 years, Luxembourg and Belgium have been joined under the Belgian-Luxembourg Economic Union (BLEU) which provides for an interchangeable currency and a joint customs union. Along with the Netherlands, these 2 nations also form the Benelux Economic Union which integrates cross-border trade. The most significant aspect of Luxembourg's pro-integration policies has been the nation's support for the European Union (EU). The EU has eliminated trade barriers, such as **tariffs**, among its member states (numbering 15 in 2000), and helped to coordinate external trade practices. Luxembourg also supports the European Monetary Union (EMU), which will replace the national currencies of the EU with a common currency, the euro.

Luxembourg is a net donor of foreign aid, to which it contributed US$160 million in 1999.

POLITICS, GOVERNMENT, AND TAXATION

Luxembourg is a constitutional monarchy, known formally as the Grand Duchy of Luxembourg. The nation's head of state is the grand duke, a position based on heredity. Since October 2000 the country has been led by Grand Duke Henri. The grand duke's powers are mainly formal and ceremonial, with real power resting in the hands of the prime minister, whom he appoints from among the leading party members in the elected Chamber of Deputies. The prime minister appoints a cabinet known as the Council of Ministers. There is a **unicameral** (single house) legislative body, the Chamber of Deputies, which has 60 members elected by direct popular vote every 5 years. Voting is compulsory. There is also a 21-member Council of State whose members are appointed for life and whose main purpose is to advise the Chamber of Deputies and the grand duke on issues such as judicial appointees. The nation's government is based on the constitution of 1868 and its subsequent amendments. Local government consists of 3 districts, which are subdivided into smaller cantons and communes. These bodies are responsible for public works, health care, and education.

The country is a member of the North Atlantic Treaty Organization (NATO). In 1998, the government spent US$131 million on defense. Luxembourg has an army, but no navy or air force. The 500-member military force is made up entirely of volunteers and its troops have served in NATO peacekeeping operations in the former Yugoslavia.

The Grand Duchy has been one of the most stable democracies in Europe. There are 3 main parties (the Christian Socialists, the Socialists, and the Democratic Party), and governments are usually formed from a coalition of 2 of the major parties. All parties, including the Socialists, have supported pro-business policies.

There is a close relationship between the nation's government and business and workers. Before legislation is passed, 1 of 3 advisory bodies is consulted. Labor legislation is discussed before 6 confederations, representing business, guilds, farmers, unions, and civil servants. The Social and Economic Council examines broad economic policies, and the Immigration Council advises the government on issues such as immigration or housing.

A strict fiscal and **monetary policy** has delivered a yearly **budget surplus**. In 2000 government revenues were US$4.73 billion, while expenditures were US$4.71 billion, making for a strong economy that allows Luxembourg to avoid significant debt while providing generous social policies. Luxembourgers enjoy the highest standard of living in the EU. Medical fees are low, and the national social security system covers sickness and maternity benefits, retirement pensions, family allowances, and accident and unemployment insurance. Each category of coverage is overseen by public institutions independent of the government and supervised by an elected board of representatives. There have been shortages of housing for immigrant workers, but government programs have been implemented to increase affordable homes.

Government policies are pro-business and favor tax reductions. In 1998, the total tax rate was 37.45, composed of a 30 percent corporate tax and municipal business tax. This system included a personal **income tax**, a corporate tax, a corporate capital gains tax, and municipal business taxes. Later, the government eliminated the corporate capital gains tax, decreased personal income tax by 15 percent, and plans to reduce the company tax to 35 percent by January 2002. A potential problem for Luxembourg involves EU policy that calls for the standardization of national taxes and economic policies. If adopted, these measures would force Luxembourg to **levy** corporate taxes that it previously did not impose. Furthermore, the Grand Duchy has already agreed to repeal laws on banking secrecy, which may lessen its attractiveness as an international banking center.

Conversely, continued EU integration offers advantages to Luxembourg. The country has supported the establishment of a common retirement fund for all EU member states and, because of its financial status, would be the likely beneficiary of such a policy. The government also advocates increased use of the Internet for business purposes and financial transactions. It has championed EU efforts to promote the World Wide Web, offering tax incentives for the creation of new Internet companies. Luxembourg was the first EU nation to meet the standards for adopting the euro, the common European currency that will make currency conversions unnecessary between member nations and result in less complicated financial transactions.

INFRASTRUCTURE, POWER, AND COMMUNICATIONS

Luxembourg has an excellent road system, communications network, and power supply system. The government spends a higher percentage of its GDP on infrastructure than any other European nation. There are 5,166 kilometers (3,210 miles) of paved roads, including 166 kilometers (103 miles) of expressways. The nation's railways are fully electrified, and the government is spending 12 billion francs on further improvements to the system. Railroads provide a main method to transport goods to and from Luxembourg. The Moselle River has canals which link it to the Rhine River. This waterway provides links between Luxembourg and ports on the North Sea. The Grand Duchy has a small merchant marine fleet with 56 commercial vessels. The nation's main port is the river port of Mertert, which, along with the smaller port of Bech-Kleinmacher, handled 1,868,230 tons of freight in 1994.

Findel Airport is the nation's only international airport, but it has become a major air terminal. The airport is 5 miles from the capital. The government has engaged in a continuing effort to expand the airport's capacity. Luxembourg has an open-skies agreement with the other EU members and with the United States that allows unrestricted flights between the nations. The Grand Duchy's largest airline, Cargolux, is among Europe's top 10 air cargo carriers. The state-owned airline provides 3 percent of the government's annual revenue. Luxair is the national passenger airline and transports over 1 million people annually.

Communications

Country	Telephones[a]	Telephones, Mobile/Cellular[a]	Radio Stations[b]	Radios[a]	TV Stations[a]	Televisions[a]	Internet Service Providers[c]	Internet Users[c]
Luxembourg	314,700 (1999)	215,741 (2000)	AM 2; FM 9; shortwave 2 (1999)	285,000	5 (1999)	285,000 (1998 est.)	8	86,000 (1999)
United States	194 M	69.209 M (1998)	AM 4,762; FM 5,542; shortwave 18	575 M	1,500	219 M	7,800	148 M
Germany	45.2 M	15.318 M (1999)	AM 51; FM 767; shortwave 4	77.8 M	373 (1995)	51.4 M (1998)	123	18 M
Belgium	4.769 M	974,494	FM 79; AM 7; shortwave 1	8.075 M	25	4.72 M	61	2.7 M

[a]Data is for 1997 unless otherwise noted.
[b]Data is for 1998 unless otherwise noted.
[c]Data is for 2000 unless otherwise noted.

SOURCE: CIA *World Factbook 2001* [Online].

The Grand Duchy has also engaged in a broad effort to improve its already superior communications network. This effort, known as E-Luxembourg, significantly increases the financial resources devoted to expanding Internet access and the use of information technology. Half the households have personal computers, and 1 in 3 Luxembourgers have access to the Internet. Currently, 40 percent of elementary schools and all secondary schools have Internet access. There are 5 communications satellites owned by Luxembourg and 2 more will be in orbit by 2002.

The communications infrastructure is among the best in the world which has aided the growth of the financial and banking sectors. The government is **privatizing** the telecommunications sector. The telephone system is extensive and half of Luxembourgers have mobile phones. Most of the power and telephone lines are underground, as are the nation's petroleum pipelines. Although most of the nation's electricity and power is imported, 1 percent of its energy is produced by local hydroelectric plants. The nation consumes 5.9 billion kilowatt hours (kWh) of electric power per year.

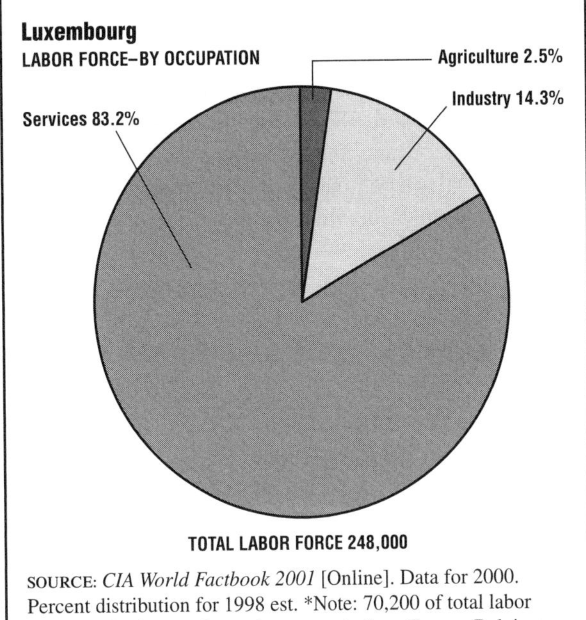

SOURCE: *CIA World Factbook 2001* [Online]. Data for 2000. Percent distribution for 1998 est. *Note: 70,200 of total labor force are foreign workers who commute from France, Belgium, and Germany.

ECONOMIC SECTORS

Since the Industrial Revolution of the 1800s, agriculture has been in decline in Luxembourg, and most farms are small, family-owned operations. Most foodstuffs consumed in Luxembourg are imported, while many of the country's agricultural products are exported. Only a small percentage of the population remains engaged in agriculture and the number of farms continues to decline. In 2000 agriculture contributed just 1 percent of the nation's GDP, and in 1998 it employed 2.5 percent of the workforce.

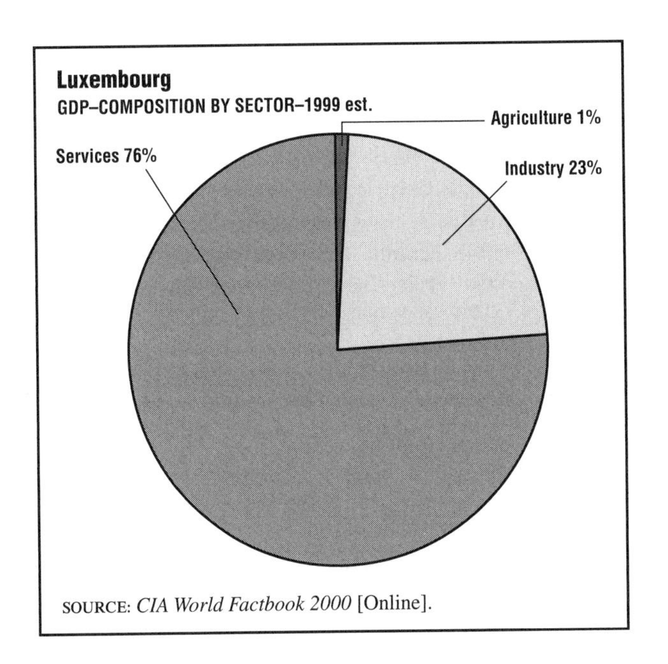

SOURCE: *CIA World Factbook 2000* [Online].

For most of the 20th century, industry provided the nation's wealth, with steel production forming the core of Luxembourg's economy. However, during the 1970s, it became difficult for local steel manufacturers to compete with companies from around the world who were producing steel more cheaply. This difficulty led to a period of restructuring and reform, during which smaller companies were consolidated into a single major steel group, ARBED, which is a highly productive steel maker. Thus, despite declining, the steel industry remains a major feature in the Grand Duchy's economy.

Efforts at diversification in industry have had some success. Major chemical and rubber manufacturing companies have built plants in Luxembourg. Significantly, these include foreign-owned companies, such as DuPont Chemicals, Goodyear Tire, and the Guardian Glass Company. Industry contributed 30 percent of the GDP in 2000 and employed 14.3 percent of the workforce in 1998.

The real growth in Luxembourg's economy has been in the services sector, especially in banking and financial services, which have experienced dramatic growth, making the nation one of Europe's top financial centers. Information services have also grown dramatically, making the nation one of the world's largest satellite service providers, while its development as a major Internet service provider continues to grow quickly. The services sector contributed 69 percent to the GDP in 2000 and employed 83.2 percent of the workforce in 1998.

AGRICULTURE

The main agricultural areas are situated around the flood plain of the Moselle River, but having suffered a marked decline, agriculture accounts for only a small percentage of the Grand Duchy's economy—just 1 percent in 2000. While the climate is conducive to several crops, poor or marginal soil limits production in many areas. The main agricultural products are barley, oats, potatoes, wheat, fruits, and grapes for wine production. Approximately 42 percent of the land is arable, with 1 percent used for permanent crops. About 10 square kilometers of the nation is irrigated, and about three-quarters of the nation's farms are smaller than 200 acres (50 hectares).

Extensive livestock production accounts for 80 percent of agricultural profits, resulting in many farmers raising crops and livestock. Meat production exceeds 15,000 tons annually. Because the nation produces 40 percent more beef than it consumes, meat is one of the few agricultural products in which Luxembourg is self-sufficient. Although farming cattle has increased in importance and profitability, sheep and pig farming have declined. About 70 percent of farms had pigs in 1970, but by 1993, this number had dropped to 15 percent. The growth of the cattle industry has led to an increase in dairy products and to the production of corn as livestock feed. The dairy industry in Luxembourg is organized differently from other agricultural enterprises, being in the hands of 2 major, and 6 minor, dairies. The dairy industry contributes approximately 55 percent of agricultural profits.

There are also 788 small vineyards along the Moselle River, covering 1 percent of agricultural land (1,200 hectares). These vineyards produce 15 million liters of wine annually. Almost four-fifths of the wine produced is consumed by Belgium and the Netherlands, with most of the remainder exported to France and Germany. Luxembourg imports 3 times as much wine as it exports. Vineyards have been the recipients of significant government aid. There are 6 independent breweries in the country, who use much of the locally grown grain in the production of their beer. There is a small tobacco firm employing 350 people, but their cigarettes are made from imported tobacco.

Forestry plays only a tiny part in the economy and accounts for 0.2 percent of the GDP. The annual production of rough timber is approximately 330,000 cubic meters. Furthermore, while wood exports amount to 980 million francs per year, imports exceed 2.8 billion francs.

INDUSTRY

From the Industrial Revolution through the 1970s, the steel industry was the backbone of the Grand Duchy's economy. In 1974 the nation produced 19 tons of steel for each inhabitant, and metal exports accounted for two-thirds of exports. However, lower demand and the energy crises of the 1970s caused a dramatic decline in the industry. By 1992, steel exports made up only one-third of Luxembourg's exports.

The government-supported conglomerate ARBED, formed to combat the steel crisis in the 1970s, shifted from producing general bulk steel to manufacturing high-quality specialized products such as galvanized metal sheet and metal wire, resulting in the replacement of older blast furnaces with sophisticated electric furnaces. In 1970, there were 30 blast furnaces; by 2000, there were none, but there were 3 electric furnaces. Reforms continue, and ARBED has set aside an 18 billion-franc investment fund for continuing modernization. Despite reductions in the industry, ARBED is the largest private employer in Luxembourg with 7,300 employees. The company remains the fourth largest producer of steel in the world and exported 22 million tons of steel products in 1999.

The Luxembourg government has aggressively tried to diversify and attract other industries. Goodyear has built several plants to produce tires and has become the second largest private employer in the nation with 3,500 employees. Many chemical companies have also built factories in Luxembourg. The Du Pont company has 1,160 workers at plants which produce polyester filaments (mylar) and another 150 workers at a plant which manufactures photographic film. Other major chemical or plastics companies in Luxembourg are Rubbermaid, T.D.K., and Recording Media Europe. The rubber, chemical, and plastics industry accounts for 10 percent of total employment in the Grand Duchy.

SERVICES

The backbone of Luxembourg's economy is the services sector. Financial services, communications, and media services form the core of this sector. Currently home to over 200 banks and 9,000 holding companies, Luxembourg has experienced the biggest growth in recent years in this sector. Employing 20,000 people, the banking sector accounts for 15 percent of the nation's GDP, while the services sector overall contributed 69 percent of the GDP in 2000.

During the 1970s, Germany and Switzerland adopted legislation that made it difficult for non-residents to deposit money in their national banks. However, Luxembourg maintained laws that encouraged foreign investment, and these led to its emergence as a banking center where foreign individuals and companies could easily deposit funds. In the 1980s, this trend accelerated as the country's banks diversified into a wide array of other financial services. By 1994, the banking sector was worth over 17.6 trillion francs. The largest banking group is Cedel, which had an operating income of US$587.6 million and returned profits of US$92.1 million in 1999.

Well into the 1980s, the insurance business in Luxembourg was concentrated on local markets, but EU economic integration opened the markets of other nations to companies in the Grand Duchy. This led to a doubling of the insurance companies by 1993. Besides life and other personal insurance, Luxembourg's companies have gained a place for themselves in maritime insurance, which now accounts for 39 percent of non-life-insurance policies. Including independent insurance brokers, there are as of 2001 approximately 6,200 people employed in insurance.

COMMUNICATIONS. With a superb communications infrastructure providing a strong platform for new information technologies, Luxembourg is a major communications center. The company, Europe-Online, was an early Internet service in Europe. The company offers multimedia services to consumers throughout Europe. The government has adopted new regulations, including rules for online shopping, to protect consumers who do business on the Internet.

With support from the government, the communications company, SES, operates ASTRA satellites. The first satellite, launched in 1991, provided television programming for 32 million homes in Europe. The launch of 8 subsequent satellites expanded the coverage to over 74 million homes, bringing a corresponding expansion of television broadcasts. The satellites also transmit 39 different radio programs. By 1999, the ASTRA satellites had captured 83.4 percent of Europe's satellite and cable market. Profits from SES exceed 4 billion francs annually.

The government began several investment incentives to promote the audiovisual sector, leading to rapid expansion in the field, which now employs 750 people in production companies. However, the real growth in this sector has been the commercial broadcasting company, CLT. From 1989 to 1994, the revenue of CLT tripled to 82 billion francs per year, and revenues have continued to increase by over 20 percent per year. The CLT group owns 12 television channels and 12 radio stations, and employs 3,089 people. A 1999 merger between CLT and the German media giant, Bertelsmann, created Europe's largest television and radio group, CLT-UFA. The combined company has also created an alliance with the Walt Disney Corporation.

RETAIL. There are 5,300 trade and **retail** sales enterprises in Luxembourg, employing 31,000 people. Retail businesses have taken advantage of the Grand Duchy's lower tax rate to attract buyers from neighboring countries. There are 2 major chain stores, Cactus and Match, and 60 other supermarkets.

TOURISM. Luxembourg has 2,350 hotels and restaurants, employing 11,000 people. Hotels declined by 70 in the 1990s, but total room numbers increased by 328 as hotel chains have built larger units. About 2 million tourists visit Luxembourg annually. But about half of these stay at campsites around the nation. The largest number of visitors come from the Netherlands, followed by Belgium, Germany, France, and the United Kingdom.

INTERNATIONAL TRADE

While Luxembourg has had a **trade deficit** since the 1980s, the strength of the financial sector has meant that the Grand Duchy maintains a surplus in earnings. Although the nation had trade deficits of 84 billion francs in 1997, 81.4 billion francs in 1998, and 106 billion francs in 1999, it had account surpluses of 86 billion francs in 1997, 84 billion francs in 1998, and 59 billion francs in 1999. The overwhelming majority of the nation's trade has been with its EU partners. The 3 main trading partners are Germany, Belgium, and France. EU nations received 75 percent of Luxembourg's exports and provided 81 percent of its imports in 1999. In 1999, Germany received 25 percent of Luxembourg's exports, France 21 percent, Belgium 12 percent, the United Kingdom 8 percent, Italy 6 percent, the Netherlands 5 percent, and 4 percent went to the United States. Meanwhile, 35 percent of Luxembourg's imports came from Belgium, 26 percent from Germany, 12 percent from France, 9 percent from the United States, and 4 percent from the Netherlands. In 2000 exports totaled US$7.6 billion while imports totaled US$10 billion.

The country has traditionally imported most of its **consumer goods** and exported industrial products (steel). The Grand Duchy continues to import manufactured consumer products, but its exports have become more diversified. Besides steel, exports now include chemical and rubber products, and finished glass, but the most profitable export is financial services. The nation remains dependent on energy imports.

While Luxembourg's economy is traditionally geared toward its immediate neighbors, the government is supportive of free trade. About 90 percent of the nation's GDP is related to foreign trade. To expand internationally, successive governments have supported regional economic integration and worldwide efforts to promote free trade. Beginning with currency integration with Belgium in 1921, Luxembourg has looked for participation in regional bodies. It was a founding member of the European Community (later the EU), and its EU membership has opened markets for itself in other member states. The population of the EU is currently 370 million, and Luxembourg hopes increasingly to market its financial services to EU citizens. The adoption of common trade rules and practices has eased the ability to conduct foreign trade. Within the EU, Luxembourg coordinates with Belgium and the Netherlands to promote their national interests and to bolster the Grand Duchy's standing within the EU. Luxembourg is also a member of the Schengen Group, which promotes the free movement of citizens within the EU. With greater freedom of movement, the government of Luxembourg hopes to continue encouraging the influx of workers necessary to maintain the economy.

GDP per Capita (US$)

Country	1975	1980	1985	1990	1998
Luxembourg	21,650	23,926	26,914	35,347	46,591
United States	19,364	21,529	23,200	25,363	29,683
Germany	N/A	N/A	N/A	N/A	31,141
Belgium	18,620	21,653	22,417	25,744	28,790

SOURCE: United Nations. *Human Development Report 2000; Trends in human development and per capita income.*

MONEY

Linking of its currency to that of Belgium in 1921 has helped Luxembourg maintain its financial stability. Despite the demand for labor, the government managed to keep **inflation** low through the 1990s. However, the Luxembourg franc has declined in relation to the U.S. dollar but has maintained its value against major European currencies. In 1995, 1 U.S. dollar was equal to 29.48 francs, but by 1999, 1 dollar equaled 34.77 francs. In 1999 Luxembourg joined the EU which created a single currency, the euro, for the EU nations. The exchange rate is fixed at a rate of 40.3399 francs per euro. Since its introduction, the euro has been weak against the dollar. In 2000, 1 U.S. dollar equaled 0.9867 euros.

Luxembourg's 200-plus national and international banks place few restrictions on operations and lend money to consumers and businesses around the world. There are no regulations on the transfer of funds or profits. Bank confidentiality, prompt payment of interest, and the Grand Duchy's political stability have combined to make Luxembourg a banking haven.

The Luxembourg Stock Market has also performed well since the 1980s. It lists over 15,000 international securities. In 1999, the total volume of trade was 1 trillion francs. By 1994, investment companies in the Grand Duchy had assets of over 100 trillion francs. Luxembourg ranks fourth in the world for asset management and second in Europe.

POVERTY AND WEALTH

Luxembourgers enjoy one of the highest standards of living in the world. The UN *Human Development Report 2000* ranks Luxembourg number 17 in the world in its human development index. Luxembourg has the world's highest per capita income of US$46,591 per person. (Figured at **purchasing power parity**, Luxembourg still led the world with a per capita income in 2000 of US$36,400.) This figure reflects the growth in the nation's economy, as the nation has overtaken the economies of Japan and Switzerland since 1990.

Low unemployment and the need for workers have prevented poverty. Generous social benefits also contribute to this healthy situation. Laws prohibit discrimination against women, ethnic minorities, and people with disabilities, and women enjoy equal rights, including property rights, with men. However, there are differences in pay because of gender, with women often earning between 9 and 25 percent less than men in comparable jobs. Companies with more than 25 employees have a quota for hiring the disabled. According to the U.S. State Department's *Country Reports on Human Rights Practices,*

Exchange rates: Luxembourg

euros per US$1	
Jan 2001	1.0659
2000	1.0854
1999	0.9386
1998	36.299
1997	35.774
1996	30.962

Note: Rates prior to 1999 are in Luxembourg francs per US$; the Luxembourg franc is at par with the Belgian franc, which circulates freely in Luxembourg.

SOURCE: CIA *World Factbook 2001* [ONLINE].

Distribution of Income or Consumption by Percentage Share: Luxembourg

Lowest 10%	4.0
Lowest 20%	9.4
Second 20%	13.8
Third 20%	17.7
Fourth 20%	22.6
Highest 20%	36.5
Highest 10%	22.0

Survey year: 1994

Note: This information refers to income shares by percentiles of the population and is ranked by per capita income.

SOURCE: *2000 World Development Indicators* [CD-ROM].

Household Consumption in PPP Terms

Country	All food	Clothing and footwear	Fuel and power[a]	Health care[b]	Education[b]	Transport & Communications	Other
Luxembourg	17	8	9	3	7	5	52
United States	13	9	9	4	6	8	51
Germany	14	6	7	2	10	7	53
Belgium	17	6	8	3	1	7	57

Data represent percentage of consumption in PPP terms.
[a]Excludes energy used for transport.
[b]Includes government and private expenditures.

SOURCE: World Bank. *World Development Indicators 2000.*

2000: Luxembourg, the government pays **subsidies** to companies that construct "disabled-friendly" buildings. The government also provides support for programs that integrate foreign residents into the mainstream of society.

Luxembourg has a first-rate education system and a literacy rate of 100 percent. School is mandatory until the age of 16, although students may continue their education in post-secondary schools (with some government financial support). The well-educated workforce of the nation has contributed to its attractiveness to foreign companies and investors.

WORKING CONDITIONS

In 1999 the unemployment rate was estimated at 2.7 percent, the lowest in Europe. Efforts to attract foreign businesses have been aided by the good labor relations in the country. Since the 1930s, there has been little labor unrest. About 57 percent of workers belong to unions, with membership highest among industrial workers. The 2 largest unions have links to political parties, but maintain their independence. Businesses with more than 15 employees must allow their workers to organize. The constitution allows employees the right to strike, except the police, army, and hospital workers. Labor negotiations are conducted cooperatively between government, business, and unions.

National laws prohibit children under the age of 16 from working, and employees under the age of 18 have special limits on overtime and the total amount of time worked. There are minimum wage laws that vary with age. For those over 18, the minimum wage is 278 francs (US$7.32) per hour. The working week is limited to 40 hours, and employers must pay special overtime rates. Most employees cannot be made to work on Sunday, except those in the steel, chemical, and glass manufacturing industries, and security personnel. Workers receive a minimum of 5 weeks of vacation.

COUNTRY HISTORY AND ECONOMIC DEVELOPMENT

450 B.C. Luxembourg is settled by 2 Belgic tribes, the Treveri and the Mediomatrici.

53 B.C. The Romans conquer the territory.

963. Luxembourg gains independence under Siegfried, the Count d'Ardennes.

1354. Luxembourg is made a duchy by the Holy Roman Emperor, Charles IV.

1555–56. The Duchy is incorporated into the Spanish Netherlands.

1618–48. During the Thirty Years War, the territory of Luxembourg is devastated by warfare, famine, and disease.

1684. France conquers Luxembourg but returns the Duchy to Spain in 1697.

1714. Luxembourg is ceded to Austria and undergoes an economic boom, especially after 1735.

1795. The Duchy is again conquered by France.

1815. At the end of the Napoleonic Wars, Luxembourg becomes a Grand Duchy under the king of the Netherlands, William I.

1830. William's heavy taxation leads the people of Luxembourg to support a Belgian revolution against his rule, and the French-speaking areas of the nation become part of Belgium.

1842. Luxembourg joins a Prussian-led customs union.

1867. Luxembourg gains full independence, with its neutrality guaranteed by the great European powers.

1879. The introduction of new methods of steel production leads to the rapid expansion of the steel industry.

1914. Germany invades Luxembourg at the start of World War I.

1919. All adults are granted the right to vote.

1922. The Belgium-Luxembourg Economic Union (BLEU) is formed.

1929. The government introduces legislation encouraging holding companies to relocate to Luxembourg.

1940. Germany occupies the Grand Duchy during World War II.

1947. Luxembourg joins the Benelux Economic Union, formed between Belgium, the Netherlands, and the Grand Duchy.

1949. The nation joins NATO.

1951. A Goodyear tire plant is built near Colmar-Berg.

1952. Luxembourg joins the European Coal and Steel Community.

1957. The Grand Duchy becomes a founding member of the European Community.

1965. Du Pont opens a chemical plant in Contern.

1974. The nation's steel industry is consolidated into a single company group, ARBED.

1986. The government-backed satellite company, SES, is created.

1991. The first ASTRA satellite is launched, marking the emergence of SES as Europe's most prominent satellite and cable television provider.

1999. Luxembourg is the first nation to meet the requirements for entry into the European Monetary Union, which it joins in January.

FUTURE TRENDS

Luxembourg is well positioned to continue its economic transformation from an industrial to a diversified economy with financial services as the base of the country's wealth. The close relationship between government and corporations and the pro-business stances of major political parties ensure that there will be little economic instability in the coming years. The continued economic integration of the EU will open new markets for the Grand Duchy's financial services, especially for pension plans.

The main danger facing the economy of Luxembourg is the possibility of labor wage inflation caused by a shortage of labor. However, the continuing momentum toward open borders and the free movement of people within the EU should ensure a steady supply of new workers. A second danger is that the harmonization of EU banking and tax laws may mean that the Grand Duchy will lose its special status as a tax haven. The concentration of banking and financial services may compensate for this trend, especially if U.S. companies and financiers continue to invest in the nation.

DEPENDENCIES

Luxembourg has no territories or colonies.

BIBLIOGRAPHY

Barteau, Harry. *Historical Dictionary of Luxembourg.* Lanham, MD: Scarecrow, 1996.

Clark, Peter. *Luxembourg.* New York: Routledge, 1994.

Economist Intelligence Unit. *Country Profile: Luxembourg.* London: Economist Intelligence Unit, 2001.

"Luxembourg: An Economic Portrait." *STATEC.* <http://www.statec.lu/html_en/statistiques/portrait_economique/index.html>. Accessed September 2001.

Organization for Economic Cooperation and Development (OECD). *OECD Economic Surveys: Belgium-Luxembourg, 1998/99.* Paris: OECD, 1999.

Permanent Mission of the Grand Duchy of Luxembourg to the United Nations. <http://www.un.int/luxembourg>. Accessed September 2001.

U.S. Central Intelligence Agency. *World Factbook 2001.* <http://www.odci.gov/cia/publications/factbook/index.html>. Accessed September 2001.

U.S. Department of State. *Background Notes: Luxembourg, July 2000.* <http://www.state.gov/www/background_notes/luxemb_0007_bgn.html>. Accessed October 2001.

U.S. Department of State. *FY 2001 Country Commercial Guide: Luxembourg.* <http://www.state.gov/www/about_state/business/com_guides/2001/europe/index.html>. Accessed October 2001.

U.S. Department of State. *1999 Country Reports on Human Rights Practices: Luxembourg.* <http://www.state.gov/www/global/human_rights/1999_hrp_report/luxembou.html>. Accessed October 2001.

—Tom Lansford

MACEDONIA

Former Yugoslav Republic of Macedonia
Republika Makedonija

CAPITAL: Skopje.

MONETARY UNIT: Macedonian Denar (MKD). One denar equals 100 deni. There are coins of 1, 2, and 3 denars and 50 denies; there are bills of 10, 50, 100, 500, 1,000, and 5,000 denars.

CHIEF EXPORTS: Food, beverages, tobacco, miscellaneous manufactures, iron, steel.

CHIEF IMPORTS: Machinery and equipment, chemicals, fuels, food products.

GROSS DOMESTIC PRODUCT: US$7.6 billion (1999 estimate).

BALANCE OF TRADE: **Exports:** US$1.317 billion (1998). **Imports:** US$1.715 billion (1998).

COUNTRY OVERVIEW

LOCATION AND SIZE. Located in southeastern Europe, the Former Yugoslav Republic of Macedonia (generally referred to as Macedonia) is a completely landlocked country, covering an area of 25,333 square kilometers (9,781 square miles). It is bounded on the north by Serbia and Montenegro (collectively the Federal Republic of Yugoslavia)—mostly by the province of Kosovo—on the east by Bulgaria, on the south by Greece, and on the west by Albania. Comparatively, the country is slightly larger than the state of Vermont. The capital, Skopje, is situated in the north-central part of the country; other cities of importance include Bitola, Kumanovo, and Tetovo.

POPULATION. According to the 1994 census, the population was 1,945,932, or 88,000 fewer than the previous census recorded in 1991. This decline resulted from the **emigration** of ethnic Serbs after the breakup of Yugoslavia, and by a boycott of the census by ethnic Albanians. By July 2000, the population had risen to 2,041,467. Its birth rate is 13.73 per 1,000 population, and the death rate is 7.69 per 1,000 population, resulting in one of the highest rates of population growth in Europe. The population is expected to reach 2.2 million by 2010. The population density is nearly 79 persons per square kilometer (205 per square mile).

Macedonian Slavs constitute two-thirds of the population, with ethnic Albanians the second largest group, accounting for 22.7 percent. Turks make up 4 percent, Roma (Gypsies) 2.2 percent, and Serbs 2.1 percent. Several other small groups round out the total. Albanians dispute census results, claiming to represent one-third of the population. While Macedonia received many Kosovar Albanian refugees during the Kosovo war of 1999, most of them have since returned to their country. The population is young, with 23.8 percent below the age of 14 and 10 percent older than 65. Over 60 percent of the population live in urban areas, 23 percent of them in the capital city Skopje, and 5 percent in its suburbs.

OVERVIEW OF ECONOMY

An agricultural economy before World War II, Macedonia was the least developed of the 6 former republics of Yugoslavia. The country inherited a poorly located state-owned industry, predominantly heavy, from the Yugoslav **socialist** period (1945–91), which is now largely seen as a deterrent to foreign investment. The breakup of Yugoslavia in 1991 deprived the country of protected markets and federal funds. In the first half of the 1990s, the economy suffered additionally from the United Nations (UN) **embargo** against Yugoslavia (Serbia and Montenegro) as all exports to Serbian markets, especially of agricultural produce, were terminated, and land corridors to western Europe through Serbia were cut. Many violations of the **sanctions** occurred, fueling organized crime and corruption, and generating some huge illicit fortunes. Worse yet, when Macedonia declared independence in 1991, Greece imposed an economic blockade that was not lifted until

1995 and badly impaired foreign trade. Finally, in 1999, the country was affected by the Kosovo war and the influx of ethnic Albanian refugees.

In 1991, the **gross domestic product (GDP) per capita** was US$1,140; between 1991 and 1994 it shrank by over 10 percent annually; by 1997 it had rebounded slightly to US$1,100 a person, signaling a period of growth. The country's isolation and underdevelopment, and the instability generated by the conflicts in neighboring Serbia, have made it unattractive to investors. Money transfers from Macedonian workers abroad and foreign aid have helped towards a recovery, and the Stability Pact—a U.S. and European Union (EU)-backed regional plan for economic development, democratization and security—may generate new investment opportunities. Most importantly, the toppling of Yugoslavia's dictator, Slobodan Milosevic, is perceived as a major advantage towards achieving stability and growth in the region.

The decision of the EU in late 2000 to open up its market to imports from southeastern Europe, including Macedonia, brought up to 95 percent the proportion of industrial and farm goods not subject to EU customs fees. To the disappointment of the Macedonian government, however, the country was still regarded as a "potential" EU member when it had expected firm guarantees that it would be considered a membership candidate like Slovenia or neighboring Bulgaria. Macedonians expect their country to be more highly favored for its record of cooperation with the international community and are unimpressed with current EU plans to spend $2.4 billion of Stability Pact funds in the region as a whole, anticipating that they would receive only a minor portion of the money.

Economic progress depends on the Macedonian government's ability to attract foreign investment, redevelop trade with its neighbors and the EU, and **liberalize** the economy by disbanding loss-making state enterprises and **privatizing** those that might be profitable in the long term. Implementation of such structural reforms is vital for economic growth and integration with the European Community.

Macedonia's **external debt** was $1.13 billion in 1997. Although quite moderate by international standards, without substantial support the cash-stripped country could not meet its short-term financial obligations. Financial aid has been forthcoming in the late 1990s and early 2000s, with $10.5 million received from Taiwan, and an EU grant of $100 million to be split with Albania. The World Bank also granted an adjustment loan worth $50 million, of which $20 million came under conditions applying to the poorest countries and is interest-free for 35 years with a 10-year grace period, and the balance—on terms for credit-worthy but poorer countries—for 17 years, with an 8-year grace period.

POLITICS, GOVERNMENT, AND TAXATION

Following its declaration of independence in 1991, Macedonia developed a consensual democratic multiparty system. Main parties include the ruling Internal Macedonian Revolutionary Organization-Democratic Party for Macedonian National Unity (VMRO-DPMNE), a moderate nationalist and reformist party with deep historic roots and liberal positions on economic and international issues; the Democratic Alternative (DA), a liberal party and former VMRO-DPMNE coalition partner; the Social Democratic Alliance of Macedonia (SDSM, reformed communists); and the 2 ethnic Albanian-dominated organizations, the Democratic Party of Albanians and the left-wing Party for Democratic Prosperity. Unlike other parts of the former Yugoslavia, Macedonian politics are not polarized along ethnic lines. Although there have been tensions between the Albanian minority and the government, the kind of ethnic violence seen elsewhere is rather unlikely, and Macedonia has occasionally compared itself with Switzerland as a land of peaceful ethnic co-existence.

The state still has considerable influence over the economy, but, since independence, the government has made progress in boosting private initiative and creating a viable **private sector** through its restitution and privatization program and by attracting **foreign direct investment**. The first step was the restitution (return) of **nationalized** property to former owners, considered a serious political gain by the VMRO-DPMNE, the first center-right reformist government since the country's independence. The privatization agency, a body overseeing both restitution and privatization, reserved a large cash fund to compensate the heirs of former property owners if restitution proved physically impossible. Out of 94 firms that were nationalized (claimed by the state) by the **communist** regime, restitution of physical assets was possible in 38 cases, and shares were distributed to the heirs in another 24 firms. Privatization of state assets is another, much more time-consuming, priority of the government, and it is being carried out through capital market offerings, mass privatization, and cash deals. The offerings on the capital market are very limited; in mass privatization, citizens and company employees are eligible to receive free vouchers for company shares; cash deals are by far the most attractive proposition for foreign direct investors. Taxes constitute 41 percent of the total government revenue, and continuing tax reform is aimed at reorienting taxation from direct towards **indirect taxes** and the **value-added tax** (VAT), which are believed to be more business-friendly.

INFRASTRUCTURE, POWER, AND COMMUNICATIONS

Macedonia's transportation **infrastructure** includes 5,540 kilometers (3,450 miles) of paved roads with 133 kilometers (83 miles) of expressways and 699 kilometers (417 miles) of railroads, with a new 56-kilometer (35-mile) railroad line under construction to the Bulgarian border in 2000. Due to the old Yugoslav policy of keeping Macedonia economically dependent on Serbia and isolated from Bulgaria, most infrastructure runs north-south, while the improvement of the east-west transport corridor connecting Italy and Albania with Bulgaria and Turkey has only been included since the introduction of EU infrastructure development programs. The government claimed US$106.9 million in compensation from NATO for the use of its infrastructure during the 1999 Kosovo crisis and is planning to spend the money on new infrastructure projects. International airports operate in Skopje and Ohrid.

Macedonia has only 10 kilometers (6 miles) of oil and gas pipelines. The energy sector is state-owned and produced 6.664 billion kilowatt-hours (kWh) of electricity in 1998 in thermal plants (85.37 percent) and hydroelectric facilities (14.63 percent). Electricity consumption was estimated at 6.198 billion kWh in 1998. Privatization is planned for ESM, the national electric utility, and in September 2000 the government began passing it into shareholder ownership. Talks have also been held with 2 potential foreign purchasers, Enron (U.S.) and RWE (Germany).

Of the international telecommunications operators interested in the privatization of the state-owned **monopoly** Makedonski Telekomunikacii (MT), the favorites are OTE (Greece), Matav (Hungary, owned by Deutsche Telekom), and Telekom Slovenije (Slovenia). A final decision on the bid was due to be made in 2001, with Matav considered the front-runner.

Growth in demand for transport and telecommunications services reflects the continuing logistical requirements of the international operations in Kosovo. The deployment of the North Atlantic Treaty Organization (NATO) peacekeepers and the UN Interim Administration Mission in Kosovo in 1999 required huge spending on transportation, energy, and telecommunications (as did the presence of the UN preventive deployment force in 1993).

Communications

Country	Newspapers	Radios	TV Sets[a]	Cable subscribers[a]	Mobile Phones[a]	Fax Machines[a]	Personal Computers[a]	Internet Hosts[b]	Internet Users[b]
	1996	1997	1998	1998	1998	1998	1998	1999	1999
Macedonia	21	200	250	N/A	15	1.5	N/A	4.40	30
United States	215	2,146	847	244.3	256	78.4	458.6	1,508.77	74,100
Yugoslavia	107	297	259	N/A	23	1.9	18.8	7.65	80
Albania	36	217	109	0.0	1	3.6	N/A	0.24	3

[a]Data are from International Telecommunication Union, *World Telecommunication Development Report 1999* and are per 1,000 people.
[b]Data are from the Internet Software Consortium (http://www.isc.org) and are per 10,000 people.

SOURCE: World Bank. *World Development Indicators 2000.*

ECONOMIC SECTORS

The largest sectors in terms of GDP contribution are services; light industry and mining; trade, tourism, and catering; agriculture, forestry and water management; transport and communications; and construction. Since independence, heavy industries have declined, while services have grown dynamically. In 1999, the economy recorded **real GDP** growth of 2.7 percent, the third consecutive year of moderate growth. In the first quarter of 2000, industrial production rose by 10.6 percent, and services (transport, communications, and **retail**) expanded, mostly due to the continuing logistical requirements of the international operation in Kosovo. In 1998, the agricultural sector contributed 13 percent to GDP, industry contributed 32 percent, and services contributed 55 percent.

AGRICULTURE

Macedonia produces a wide range of crops and other foodstuffs. Farmers grow rice, tobacco, wheat, corn, millet, cotton, sesame, mulberry leaves, citrus, and vegetables; beef, pork, poultry, mutton, and dairy products are also produced, and the country has traditionally been an exporter of sugar beets, fruits, vegetables, cheese, lamb, and tobacco. As elsewhere in the former Yugoslavia, farmland was only partly collectivized under communist rule, while in other eastern European countries such as Bulgaria, collectivization was almost complete (collectivization was the process by which communist countries coordinated production through state planning). The farming sector has, however, been hit by drought, and the wheat harvest was down by 16 percent in 2000.

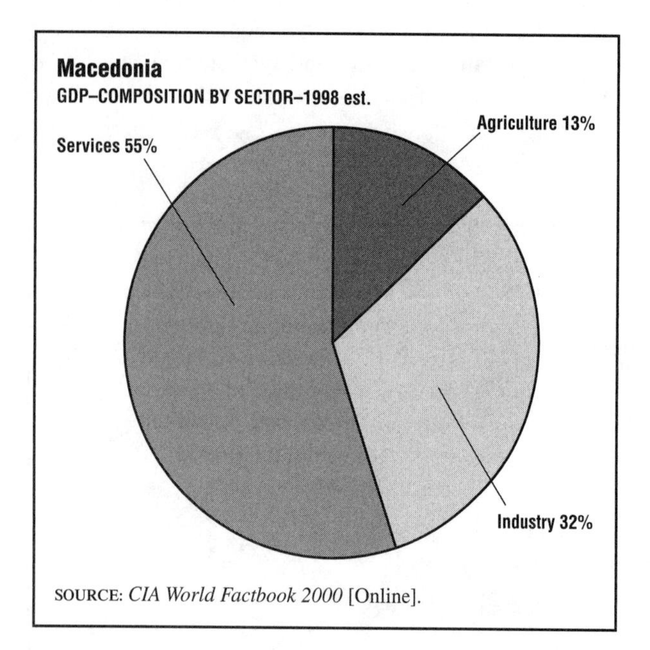

SOURCE: *CIA World Factbook 2000* [Online].

The government has come under pressure from private farmers, who have threatened to organize protests unless it pays what it owes them for the 1999 harvest and compensates them for the rising price of fuel. They have also demanded **subsidies** for their agricultural exports and a cut in the rate of the new value-added tax for agricultural products from 19 percent to 5 percent.

INDUSTRY

Industry (including mining) contributed 32 percent of GDP in 1998 and employed about 40 percent of the workforce. While the coal industry provides for the needs of the country, all other fuels, machinery, transportation equipment, and manufactured goods are imported. Manufacturing is dominated by metallurgy (iron, copper, lead, zinc, and chromium), chemicals, and textiles. Many companies have been able to keep operating despite losses and delayed payments to workers and business partners. But the VMRO-DPMNE government has planned the sale or liquidation of seriously insolvent companies by 2002. Feni, a ferro-nickel plant in Kavadarci, was sold for $2.3 million to France's Société Commerciale de Métaux et Mineraux, which will invest $36 million, while retaining all 880 employees and selling metals to Krupp Thyssen of Germany. The privatization agency is trying to support the selling of other loss-making companies, such as the Okta oil refinery, by cutting selling prices substantially.

Increased demand for post-war reconstruction in Kosovo has improved the situation in the iron and steel, construction materials, and chemicals industries, and, ironically, neighboring EU member Greece, which imposed a crippling trade embargo in the early 1990s, is now the top source of foreign cash directed to banking, fuels, brewing, tobacco processing, and construction materials.

SERVICES

The growing services sector of the Macedonian economy accounted for 55 percent of the country's GDP in 1998 and was expected to continue to grow in importance in the coming decades.

FINANCE. As in the rest of the former Yugoslavia, most banks in Macedonia were not controlled directly by the government during the communist era but by the state enterprises, their largest customers. Large firms could force banks to lend them money even when they were not credit-worthy, an ineffective and risky system. The banking sector was badly hurt in the early 1990s when many firms defaulted on their loans. To make things worse, in the wake of the Yugoslav crisis, the cash-stripped National Bank of Yugoslavia in Belgrade refused to return the Macedonian foreign exchange deposits it was holding, thereby depriving the republic of **hard currency**. Because of the high **inflation** of the denar, most people in Macedonia used to save in foreign currency and this move severely undermined confidence in the banking system. Although the Macedonian government assumed the debts, all foreign-currency deposits had to be frozen and were paid out only over time. Confidence in banks was further shaken in 1997 with the collapse of TAT, a pyramid savings firm. The authorities have since tightened regulation of the sector and have initiated projects to rebuild confidence.

TOURISM. Tourism was an important factor when the republic was part of Yugoslavia. There are several major tourist destinations—resorts and beautiful historical towns situated mainly along the Ohrid lake and in the mountains. The wars reduced tourist trade in the early 1990s, but the industry subsequently began a recovery, with income from tourism totaling $27 million in 1997. NATO troops and international staff stationed in Macedonia and Kosovo often spend their leave in Macedonia, and the number of foreign visitors to the country averaged 18,485 per month in the first half of 2000, compared with 12,060 during the same period in 1999.

RETAIL. Retail in Macedonia is predominantly private and comparatively well developed, although foreign investment is still limited. Informal retail is sizeable, and small stores prevail. Figures in 2000 showed a massive yearly increase in real terms of 57.1 percent in retail revenue. This is partly explained by the Kosovo effect (the presence of NATO and international staff), and partly by a rise in consumer spending, driven by government's payments to **pensioners**, the unfreezing of foreign-currency accounts, and payments to TAT depositors.

INTERNATIONAL TRADE

In 1998, Macedonia faced a slightly negative **balance of trade**. In that year the country exported $1.317 billion in goods and services while importing $1.715 billion. However, several issues promised to ease this trade imbalance in the future. In late 2000, EU markets were opened to Macedonian industrial and agricultural goods (but not beef and wine) as part of a new EU policy towards the region. Macedonia shipped almost 50 percent of its exports to the EU in 2000. Wine, one of the more successful export categories, was excluded from the liberalization in response to active lobbying from EU domestic winegrowers.

The greatest current rise is in exports to Yugoslavia (Serbia-Montenegro), with which Macedonia has a free-trade agreement. It is the largest single-state Macedonian export market, taking 23.7 percent of total exports in 2000. This state of affairs is likely to be reinforced by the political changes in Belgrade in 2000. In 2000, the head of the UN Interim Administration in Kosovo (UNMIK) agreed to assist in opening Kosovo further to Macedonian products. Macedonian firms secured construction contracts in Kosovo to rebuild the road between Pristina and Kosovska Mitrovica, and to a bus and truck terminal in Pristina. The contracts are worth $172 million. With the lifting of trade sanctions, Macedonia could expect to win similar contracts in Serbia proper, and to see a revival of traditional Serbian demand for their exports.

Principal Macedonian exports in 1998 included manufactured goods (34.2 percent); iron and steel (19.3 percent); drinks and tobacco (11 percent); machinery and equipment (7.5 percent); and food and livestock (5 percent). Imports in 1998 included machinery and transport equipment (19.1 percent); miscellaneous manufactured goods (14.5 percent); food products (13.4 percent); chemicals (10.6 percent); and fuels and lubricants (8.5 percent). Principal trade partners included Germany with 19.0 percent of all exports and 12.3 percent of all imports; Yugoslavia, with 23.7 percent and 8.8 percent, respectively; the United States with 15.2 percent and 3.0 percent; Greece with 5.9 percent and 7.9 percent; and Italy with 8.1 percent and 5.4 percent. Ukraine accounts for 11.7 percent of imports, and there is some trade with Russia, Slovenia, Bulgaria, and Croatia.

MONEY

As in much of Eastern Europe, the monetary and public finance sectors of Macedonia remained underdeveloped during the era of the Yugoslav communist regime. After independence, the banking sector was plagued by the collapse of the old Yugoslav finance system, the insolvency of most companies, the freezing of hard currency deposits in Belgrade (the capital of the former Yugoslavia), and the **pyramid schemes** that captured the savings of thousands of citizens. With serious reforms needed in the monetary, foreign-exchange, and banking sectors, the government launched a scheme in 1995 to **restructure** the banks by removing **bad loans** (granted to loss-making state firms or insolvent private concerns) from their balance sheets. The first step taken to regain

Exchange rates: Macedonia

denars per US$1	
Jan 2001	64.757
2000	65.904
1999	56.902
1998	54.462
1997	50.004
1996	39.981

SOURCE: CIA *World Factbook 2001* [ONLINE].

investor confidence was payment of compensation to the holders of foreign-exchange accounts frozen by the central bank, with small depositors receiving cash and larger depositors given government bonds. A new banking law is expected to be passed providing for strict supervision by the National Bank of Macedonia to ensure that banks are adequately capitalized, but legislation on foreign exchange, foreign trade, and foreign credit is also needed to introduce stringent and transparent rules to the sector.

Reforms in the public finance sector include the introduction of a value-added tax; the reduction of excessive employment in the **public sector**; the privatization of non-essential ministerial activities; the creation of a controlled treasury system; pension reform adding a private pension system to the present public one; the establishment of a **macroeconomic** and budget planning unit in the finance ministry; and a continuing movement towards indirect taxation.

The largest commercial bank, Stopanska banka, has been successfully restructured and privatized by selling a majority stake to the National Bank of Greece. The European Bank for Reconstruction and Development (EBRD) and the International Finance Corporation (IFC) also agreed to take stakes in Stopanska. The second largest bank is the privately owned Komercijalna banka, which was spun off from Stopanska under the communist regime. The EBRD has a stake in Komercijalna. Tutunska banka (Tobacco Bank), the third largest, was sold to Nova Ljubljanska banka of Slovenia.

Throughout the late 1990s and into the 21st century the denar has been declining in value compared to the U.S. dollar. In 1995, US$1 was exchanged for 37.882 denars. The rate has weakened since, with US$1 equal to 39.981 (1996), 50.004 (1997), 54.462 (1998), 56.902 (1999), and 59.773 denars (January 2000). By November 2000, the currency was trading at 71.22 denars to the dollar.

POVERTY AND WEALTH

The state provides health and social benefits, including pensions, to all citizens, but inflation and economic hardship over the 1990s have dramatically reduced most such payments. Market reforms of the 1990s created both increased poverty and new wealth. Many new entrepreneurs, corrupt politicians and other officials, and politically protected smugglers exploiting channels through Greece and Bulgaria, amassed spectacular fortunes, particularly benefiting from breaches of trade sanctions against Yugoslavia. No specific data on the distribution of consumption and income is currently available. Income levels render Macedonia a poor country with education, health, life expectancy, and consumerism low by European standards. Nevertheless, the country enjoys greater economic equality than neighboring Greece.

GDP per Capita (US$)

Country	1975	1980	1985	1990	1998
Macedonia	N/A	N/A	N/A	N/A	1,349
United States	19,364	21,529	23,200	25,363	29,683
Albania	N/A	916	915	842	795
Romania	1,201	1,643	1,872	1,576	1,310

SOURCE: United Nations. *Human Development Report 2000; Trends in human development and per capita income.*

WORKING CONDITIONS

The unemployment rate increased after independence, reaching 35 percent in 1999 and totaling 313,900 people out of work (out of a total estimated **labor force** of 890,000). The situation worsened in the first half of 2000, especially in manufacturing, due to the government's commitment to privatize or liquidate 12 large loss-making factories. Another cause of job losses was legislation requiring all employers to pay social security and pension contributions on newly hired staff, which forced many insolvent employers to lay off workers and freeze recruitment. The still weak economy does not generate new jobs fast enough to outweigh the loss of old ones.

Household Consumption in PPP Terms

Country	All food	Clothing and footwear	Fuel and power[a]	Health care[b]	Education[b]	Transport & Communications	Other
Macedonia	33	5	15	6	9	9	23
United States	13	9	9	4	6	8	51
Serbia	N/A	N/A	N/A	N/A	N/A	N/A	N/A
Albania	62	3	13	3	10	5	4

Data represent percentage of consumption in PPP terms.
[a]Excludes energy used for transport.
[b]Includes government and private expenditures.

SOURCE: World Bank. *World Development Indicators 2000.*

To counter unemployment, in 2000 the Macedonian parliament allowed the early retirement of state employees, but the Constitutional Court ruled that the law was unconstitutional in discriminating between state and private-sector employees, and treating people differently according to gender. Early retirement was stopped, and those already retired were offered the option of returning to their jobs. Teachers demanded a 20 percent pay raise that was unlikely to be granted because the court ruling upset plans to cut jobs in education. The cash-stripped government also decided to offer public employees a 40-kg (90 lb) food package worth $85 instead of annual holiday pay, but trade unions protested.

COUNTRY HISTORY AND ECONOMIC DEVELOPMENT

1912–13. Serbia occupies and annexes what is now Macedonian territory, then part of the Ottoman Empire.

1913–41. The Slav majority in Macedonia, considered ethnic Bulgarian by themselves and by the international community prior to 1913, is regarded by the Serb government as "southern Serbs" and is subjected to brutal pressure to assimilate. The economy remains agricultural and underdeveloped.

1943. Yugoslav Communist leader Josip Broz Tito's Anti-Fascist Council for People's Liberation of Yugoslavia recognizes what is now Macedonia as a distinct ethnic and political entity.

1945. A standard grammar of the new Macedonian language is compiled upon instructions by the Yugoslav government. Belgrade actively promotes Macedonian nationalism.

1946. The People's Republic (later Socialist Republic) of Macedonia is included in the Federal People's Republic (later Socialist Federal Republic) of Yugoslavia and participates in socialist economic development.

1991. Yugoslavia breaks up and Macedonians vote for independence. Serbia does not interfere and Bulgaria recognizes the new republic, but Greece refuses to acknowledge it, claiming that its name, symbol, and constitution imply territorial claims to the neighboring Greek province of Macedonia. Greece imposes a trade embargo that damages the country's economy.

1993. Macedonia is admitted to the United Nations as the "Former Yugoslav Republic of Macedonia," until a further settlement with Greece is reached. The U.N. sends 1,000 troops (including 500 U.S. soldiers) to Macedonia to prevent the Bosnian conflict from spreading.

1995. Macedonia and Greece sign an interim accord, confirming the border and establishing diplomatic relations. Greece lifts the embargo, Macedonia agrees to remove the symbol and the articles of the constitution to which Greece objects. Negotiations continue regarding the country's name. Macedonia becomes a member of the Organization for Security and Cooperation in Europe, the Council of Europe, and NATO's Partnership for Peace program.

1999. NATO begins air strikes against neighboring Serbia as Serb assaults on Kosovo force ethnic Albanians to flee to Macedonia. An international peacekeeping force is dispatched to Kosovo to help ensure the safe return of Albanian refugees from Macedonia.

2000. The EU opens its market to industrial and some agricultural goods from Macedonia, as recognition of its record in the Kosovo crisis.

FUTURE TRENDS

The Macedonian government has a long way to go before EU membership—which will fully integrate Macedonia with the developed economies of western Europe—can become a reality. However, the country has much to gain from the victory of Vojislav Kostunica at the Yugoslav presidential election in 2000 and the dismantling of the Serbian dictatorial regime. Peace in Kosovo will be particularly beneficial to the stability and, significantly, to the economy, of Macedonia. Foreign investors will be encouraged to enter the market, following the lead of the Greek investors, and, over time, traditional Yugoslavian demand for Macedonian goods and services should increase. Transit trade along the north-south corridor (connecting Serbia with Greece) and the west-east corridor (connecting Italy and Albania with Bulgaria and Turkey) should also benefit the country. Agreement may now also be reached on the Yugoslav succession—the division of the assets and liabilities of the former Socialist Federal Republic of Yugoslavia between its former republics. Finally, the expected EU membership of neighboring Bulgaria should be of major assistance to Macedonia's future efforts to join the union as a full member.

DEPENDENCIES

Macedonia has no territories or colonies.

BIBLIOGRAPHY

The Economist Intelligence Unit. "Macedonia." <http://www.eiu.com>. Accessed December 2000.

Roudometof, Victor, editor. *The Macedonian Question.* New York: Columbia University Press, 2000.

U.S. Department of State. *FY 2000 Country Commercial Guide: Macedonia.* <http://www.state.gov/www/about_state/business/com_guides/index.html>. Accessed December 2000.

—Valentin Hadjiyski

MALTA

The Republic of Malta
Repubblika Ta' Malta

CAPITAL: Valletta.

MONETARY UNIT: Maltese lira (LM). One Maltese lira equals 100 cents. Each cent is subdivided into 10 mils. There are coins of 2, 3, and 5 mils and of 1, 2, 5, 10, 25, and 50 cents. There are notes of 2, 5, 10, and 20 lira.

CHIEF EXPORTS: Machinery and transport equipment, manufactured goods.

CHIEF IMPORTS: Machinery and transport equipment, manufactured and semi-manufactured goods, food, drink, tobacco.

GROSS DOMESTIC PRODUCT: US$5.6 billion (purchasing power parity, 2000 est.).

BALANCE OF TRADE: **Exports:** US$2 billion (f.o.b., 2000). **Imports:** US$2.6 billion (f.o.b., 2000).

COUNTRY OVERVIEW

LOCATION AND SIZE. Malta consists of a series of small islands in the Mediterranean Sea, 97 kilometers (60 miles) south of the Italian territory of Sicily and 288 kilometers (179 miles) north of Africa. It is at the crossroads of Africa, Europe, and the Middle East. While Malta is an archipelago (a group of islands), only the 3 largest islands—Malta, Gozo, and Comino—are inhabited. Malta's land area is just 316 square kilometers (122 square miles), and the coastline of the Maltese islands is 140 kilometers (87 miles). Malta is about twice the size of Washington, D.C. The largest city is Valletta, which is also the nation's capital, and the second largest is Sliema.

POPULATION. The population of Malta was estimated to be 391,670 in July of 2000. The Maltese people are mainly descendants of ancient Phoenicians and Carthaginians who originally settled the islands. There are also descendants of Italians and other Mediterranean people in Malta, in addition to British influences from the colonial period. Nonetheless, the population is mainly homogeneous and overwhelmingly Roman Catholic (91 percent).

Malta's population growth rate is low (0.74 percent) and the population is aging. In 2000, 13 percent were over the age of 65, while only 20 percent were under the age of 15. The birth rate is 12.75 births per 1,000 people or 1.92 children born per woman. In 2000 the death rate was 7.7 deaths per 1,000, but the infant mortality rate was low at 5.94 deaths per 1,000 births. Life expectancy is 75.49 years for males and 80.62 for females. The Maltese **emigration** rate is low. Each year there are 2.39 migrants per 1,000 inhabitants.

The country is one of the most urban and densely populated nations in the world. The United States has 21 people per square kilometer (55 per square mile) compared to Malta's population density of 1,160 people per square kilometer (3,000 per square mile).

OVERVIEW OF ECONOMY

Malta has few natural resources. Most of its foodstuffs (almost 80 percent) must be imported, as must its energy needs. Its economy is based on the export of manufactured products and tourism. The majority of Malta's trade is with the European Union (EU). Malta has applied for membership in the EU and can expect to be among the next nations to join the trade organization in 2003–05. The government has based most of its future economic policies on EU membership. Trade between Malta and the United States rose substantially during the 1990s. For some time, Malta has had a **trade deficit**, which has increased steadily over the past decade.

Maltese wages are low when compared to other European nations. In 1998 the average annual wage was equal to US$18,620, but **inflation** has traditionally been low (1.9 percent in 1999), allowing workers to enjoy a fair to high standard of living. Unemployment has stood at about 5 percent for the past 5 years, while **gross domestic product** (GDP) rose steadily through the 1990s, increasing by 4 percent in 1999.

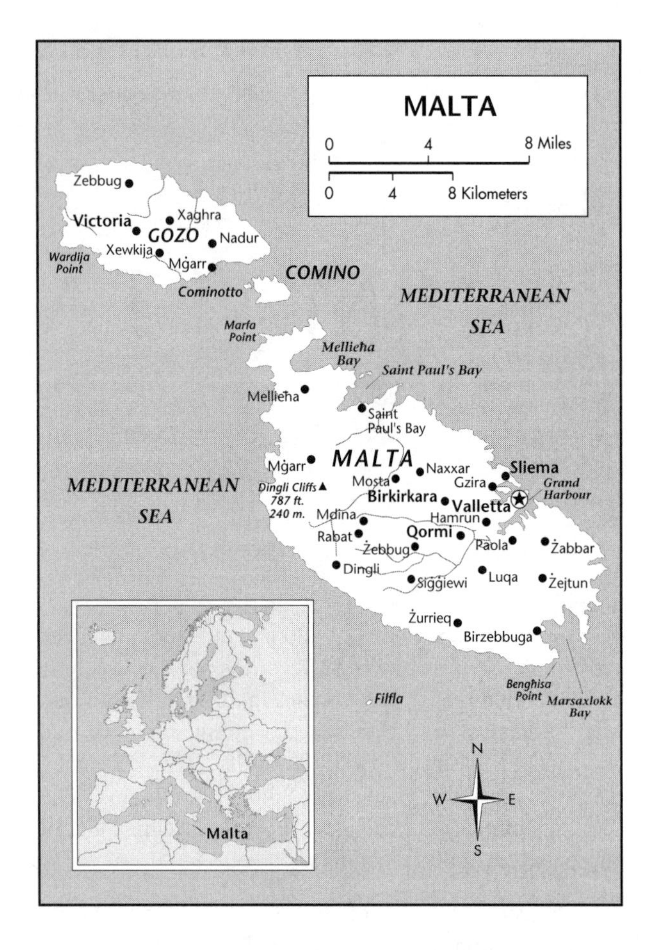

However, the nation's debt increased dramatically in the 1990s as the government began a series of large **infrastructure** programs. In 1999 debt was 56.1 percent of GDP, or US$765 million. This was an increase from 33 percent of GDP in 1994. Because of the government programs, the construction industry has become a major economic sector in Malta. Partly in an attempt to lessen the debt and partly to improve the country's competitiveness, the government has begun a large-scale program to **privatize** state-owned businesses. Now the government is responsible for about half of Malta's GDP and actively pursues outside investment, offering foreign firms full ownership of commercial enterprises. Because wages are substantially lower than those of most EU countries, foreign firms have begun relocating to the islands. This is especially true of companies that produce footwear and clothing. Foreign investment now accounts for 50 percent of all new investment in Malta.

Tourism is the mainstay of the Maltese economy, but manufacturing and financial services are the fastest growing economic segments. Ship repair and support is the country's main industrial sector, but there is also a growing electronics sector. Agriculture remains only a small fraction of the economy.

POLITICS, GOVERNMENT, AND TAXATION

Malta was a British colony from 1814 until independence in 1964. After independence, the country became a member of the British Commonwealth, with Queen Elizabeth II as the head of state. In 1974 Malta became a fully independent republic and replaced the queen with an elected president.

Malta is now a constitutional democracy, governed by the **unicameral** (one chamber) House of Representatives, whose 65 members are popularly elected to 5-year terms of office. The chief of state is the president, who also serves a 5-year term but is elected by the House of Representatives. The leader of the majority party in the legislature is appointed prime minister by the president. Because of the small size of the islands, there are no local or regional government bodies, and all police, education, and postal services are administered from the capital city of Valleta. The exception to this is the Isle of Gozo, which has a separate ministry.

Malta has 2 main political parties: the Nationalist Party and the Labor Party. The nation's political loyalty is evenly divided between the two. The Maltese people are passionate about politics and voter turnout for elections often exceeds 96 percent.

The Maltese government is deeply involved in the nation's economy. It accounts for almost half of the nation's GDP and employs 10 percent of the **workforce**. Because of several major infrastructure projects, the government has been forced to borrow to finance the resulting deficit. In 1999 Malta borrowed US$275 million. Major programs include a fiber optic telecommunications system, a new international airport, and improvements to port facilities. Loans are also used to support unprofitable government-owned businesses such as the Malta Drydocks, which cost the government US$15 million in 1999 to cover shortfalls.

The government wants to privatize several state-owned enterprises. In 1997 partial privatization of the national telecommunications company, Maltacom, began, and in 1999 the government sold 70 percent of its ownership of the Mid-Med Bank (now known as HSBC Ltd.) to a Hong Kong company for US$200 million. Plans are in place to privatize the international airport, the Public Lotto (Lottery), the Bank of Valletta, and the Malta Freeport Terminal. There are also negotiations with Tunisia over oil exploitation in the Mediterranean Sea between the 2 countries.

The armed forces are small, composed of land troops, an air squadron, and a naval squadron. In 1999 the government spent US$201 million, or 5.5. percent of the nation's GDP, on defense.

Even though Malta is on the path to membership in the EU, there is long debate over the benefits of such a move. The Labor Party froze Malta's membership efforts after taking control of the government in the 1996 elections, but the Nationalist Party restarted the application process after its return to power in 1998.

The government of Malta offers several incentives to stimulate foreign investment. Most attractive among these is a 10-year **tax holiday** to industries that export over 95 percent of their goods. **Income tax** cutbacks, **duty**-free imports of machinery and equipment, plus deduction on training, research, and development entice foreign companies. The government earns its revenue through a variety of taxes. Approximately 23 percent of revenues came from income tax, 25 percent from **social security tax**, 17 percent from consumption taxes, and the remainder from licenses, taxes, and fines; customs and excise duties; and other forms of revenue collection.

INFRASTRUCTURE, POWER, AND COMMUNICATIONS

During the 1990s, the government started several programs designed to make the infrastructure of Malta comparable to other EU nations. The centerpiece of these efforts is the new telecommunications system, and a new international airport that can handle increased passenger and cargo traffic. There are 4 Internet service providers in Malta and the islands are serviced by 1 satellite earth station and 2 undersea communication cables from Europe. There were 187,000 main phone lines in use in 1997. Significant road construction has been completed, but plans call for US$200 million in new highway improvements. The government also spent US$200 million to improve the Freeport cargo terminals, which now handle an average of 1.2 million containers per year. Much of this freight is trans-shipped from Europe to other markets globally.

Malta's energy needs are met through imported fossil fuels, mainly oil. In 1998 the nation produced 1.62 billion kilowatt-hours (kWh) of electricity and consumed 1.507 billion kWh. The country has 1,742 kilometers (1,082 miles) of roadways, of which 1,677 kilometers (1,042 miles) are paved. There are 2 major ports, in Valletta and Marsaxlokk, and a major airport. In 1999 the Maltese merchant marine included 1,484 ships. Many ships were actually owned by foreign firms from 49 different countries, notably Greece with 445 ships.

Maltacom, the nation's telecommunications company, has established GoMobile to provide cellular phone service. In 1999 there were about 15,600 mobile phones in use in Malta. Several international companies have established Internet and **e-commerce** businesses in Malta.

ECONOMIC SECTORS

Malta has few natural resources and its small population makes for a limited domestic market. Consequently, Malta is dependent on foreign trade, and the government has supported export-based companies through tax breaks and other incentives. It has also looked for foreign investment by offering similar incentives. A prolonged period of economic growth through the 1990s and continued government spending on infrastructure programs has kept unemployment low.

Malta's economy is diverse. There is a small agricultural sector, which contributed 2.8 percent of GDP in 1999, but the poor soil of the islands prevents wide-scale crop cultivation. The industrial sector experienced some growth in the 1990s, as the low cost of labor attracted light industries such as electronics, textiles, and

Communications

Country	Telephones[a]	Telephones, Mobile/Cellular[a]	Radio Stations[b]	Radios[a]	TV Stations[a]	Televisions[a]	Internet Service Providers[c]	Internet Users[c]
Malta	187,000	17,691	AM 1; FM 18; shortwave 6 (1999)	255,000	6 (2000)	280,000	2	40,000
United States	194 M	69.209 M (1998)	AM 4,762; FM 5,542; shortwave 18	575 M	1,500	219 M	7,800	148 M
Italy	25 M (1999)	20.5 M (1999)	AM 100; FM 4,600, shortwave 9	50.5 M	358 (1995)	30.3 M	93	11.6 M
Cyprus	488,162 (1998)	138,000 (1999)	AM 10; FM 71; shortwave 2	366,450	8 (1995)	300,300	6	80,000

[a]Data is for 1997 unless otherwise noted.
[b]Data is for 1998 unless otherwise noted.
[c]Data is for 2000 unless otherwise noted.

SOURCE: CIA *World Factbook 2001* [Online].

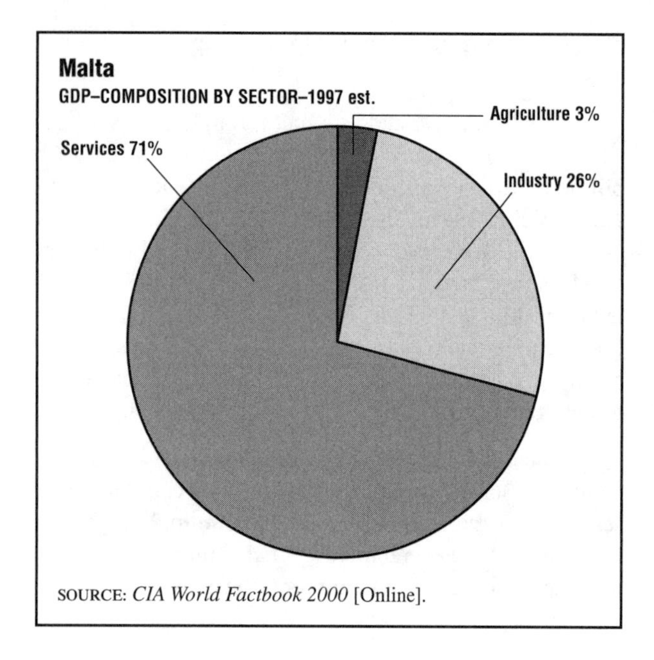

SOURCE: *CIA World Factbook 2000* [Online].

footwear. The government-owned drydocks provide the main heavy industry in the islands, and industry made up 25.5 percent of Malta's GDP in 1999. The service sector dominates the Maltese economy, accounting for 71.7 percent of the nation's GDP and providing 71 percent of employment. Tourism is one of the mainstays of the service sector.

AGRICULTURE

Malta's agricultural sector is small and only accounts for about 2.8 percent of GDP, but it is diverse. In 1999 only 5 percent of workers were employed in agriculture and there were only about 10 square kilometers (3.9 square miles) of land under irrigation. In 1998 agricultural exports totaled US$42.1 million, but imports totaled US$304 million. Since 1995 agriculture has declined annually. In 1997 the decline was 10.3 percent, and in 1998 the decline was 11.6 percent.

Most farms are small and privately owned. Most of the crops and foodstuffs produced are consumed domestically. The main crops are potatoes, cauliflower, grapes, wheat, barley, tomatoes, citrus, and green peppers. Potatoes are by far the main crop and accounted for 32,000 metric tons of the total agricultural output of 38,000 metric tons. Medigrain, a Maltese company, annually imports about 50,000 tons of wheat, which is then sold to local bakeries and restaurants. It has silo capacity to hold 86,000 metric tons of grain. The company also acts as a trans-shipment agent for the distribution of imported grain to other countries. Livestock production includes beef, chicken, lamb, pork, rabbit, and turkey. The main livestock exports are prepared meat products and fish.

INDUSTRY

Several industries have experienced growth in Malta since the early 1990s. The principal growth industries include shipbuilding and repair, construction, electronics, and textiles. Industry provides 24 percent of employment and manufactured products account for 90 percent of Malta's exports. The Malta Development Corporation (MDC) is a government venture that works to attract foreign industry to the island. The MDC also oversees the management of Malta's 12 industrial parks and provides low-interest loans for foreign companies moving to the islands. There are now about 200 foreign manufacturing firms in Malta of which the largest is SGS Thomson, a French company that employs 1,800 people in Malta and has annual sales of US$1 billion.

Malta's location along major commercial sea lanes in the Mediterranean has made it a major port area and gateway for products being shipped to Europe from Africa and the Middle East. The government has developed extensive storage facilities for goods, including grain silos and an oil terminal. Goods are shipped to Malta and then transported throughout the Mediterranean region. All aspects of marine services, including shipbuilding, repair, loading, and unloading of goods, have experienced growth in the past decade. The government has promoted the island as a major port by eliminating all taxes and **tariffs** on goods that are imported by companies licensed to trade in the Malta Freeport terminals.

New construction of homes and businesses is a steady benefit of economic growth. The construction industry has been bolstered by heavy government spending on massive road-building projects. The electronics industry has experienced dramatic growth since several computer manufacturing companies have opened plants in Malta. There are several manufacturing companies in Malta, producing everything from footwear to machine products, and automobile parts to cigarettes.

SERVICES

Services represent the fastest growing sector of the Maltese economy, employing 71 percent of Maltese workers and producing 71.7 percent of GDP in 1999. Wholesale and **retail** services account for about 11 percent of the nation's GDP, against financial services at 8 percent.

Tourism is a major component of the services sector. Each year Malta receives about 1.2 million tourists, and the tourist industry is the country's main source of foreign currency. In 1998, to attract new visitors, the government began a US$40 million project to improve the waterfront of Malta, the largest island, with new hotels and improvements to existing buildings. There is also a US$25 million project to construct a new cruise line terminal. The country's mild climate and relatively low prices are the main attractions for tourists, who also enjoy the historical sites where many castles of the Knights of Malta remain intact.

Maltacom, the nation's telecommunications company, has established GoMobile to provide cellular phone service. In 1999 there were about 15,600 mobile phones in use in Malta. Several international companies have established Internet and e-commerce businesses in Malta.

Many international firms have established franchises in Malta. North American fast-food chains such as McDonald's, Burger King, T.G.I. Fridays, and Pizza Hut have done well. In 2000 work began on a Hard Rock Café, which will be part of a local hotel. The government also chose a company from the United States to provide cable services for the nation.

The retail sector operates under some important restrictions. Shops are only open from 9:00 a.m. to 7:00 p.m., and there is a 3–4 hour break or "siesta" in the afternoon, as is customary in many Southern European countries. In addition, almost all shops are closed on Sunday.

Financial services are a big growth area in the Maltese economy. Since 1995, financial services have grown by 40 percent. Malta's banking system has assets of US$6.2 billion, and the nation has a small stock market, which lists mainly local companies. In 1999 total trades equaled 107.3 million Maltese liri.

INTERNATIONAL TRADE

Malta's economy is dependent on foreign trade and generally runs a trade deficit. In 1998 the export value of Maltese goods was US$1.8 billion, compared with imports of US$2.7 billion. Around 65 percent of the country's imports come from the EU, while 50 percent of its exports go to the EU. However, trade with the United States has increased over the past 8 years. In 1999 Maltese exports to the United States were worth US$422 million and imports from the United States totaled US$240 million.

Malta's main export markets are France, which in 2000 received 20.7 percent of Malta's goods, the United States (18.1 percent), Germany (12.6 percent), the United Kingdom (7.7 percent), and Italy (4.8 percent). In 2000 the nation's main import partners are Italy (19.3 percent), France (17.8 percent), the United Kingdom (12.4 percent), Germany (10.5 percent), and the United States (8.9 percent).

MONEY

Over the last several years the value of the Maltese lira has fallen in relation to the U.S. dollar. In 1995 1 U.S. dollar equaled 0.3529 Maltese liri, but by 2000 1 dollar equaled 0.4086 Maltese liri. Malta's entry into the EU may ultimately mean that the nation will replace the lira with the euro, the common currency of the EU.

The Maltese Central Bank issues currency and sets interest rates. It also regulates **monetary policy** and controls the nation's financial reserves. There are 2 main commercial banks in Malta: HSBC Ltd. and the Bank of Valletta, each with 40 branches in Malta. Together, the 2 banks control 80 percent of the consumer banking market. There are also 2 smaller banks: Lombard Bank and APS Bank. Local merchant banks have a difficult time competing against foreign competition despite **liberalized** lending policies in recent years.

POVERTY AND WEALTH

While wages are low in Malta, the nation's low cost of living allows workers to enjoy a comfortable lifestyle. In addition, the government provides housing **subsidies** for low-income families. Education and health care are free and available for most Maltese, though medical services are limited. With unemployment low (4.5 percent in 2000) and the standard of living relatively high, Malta is ranked 27th in the world in the United Nations *Human Development Report 2000*. The standard of living doubles every 13 years.

Trade (expressed in billions of US$): Malta

	Exports	Imports
1975	.164	.375
1980	.483	.938
1985	.400	.759
1990	1.133	1.964
1995	1.861	2.890
1998	1.820	2.686

SOURCE: International Monetary Fund. *International Financial Statistics Yearbook 1999.*

Exchange rates: Malta

Maltese liri (LM) per US$1	
Jan 2001	0.4370
2000	0.4376
1999	0.3994
1998	0.3885
1997	0.3857
1996	0.3604

SOURCE: CIA *World Factbook 2001* [ONLINE].

GDP per Capita (US$)

Country	1975	1980	1985	1990	1998
Malta	2,996	4,659	5,362	7,019	18,620
United States	19,364	21,529	23,200	25,363	29,683
Italy	11,969	14,621	15,707	18,141	19,574
Cyprus	3,619	6,334	7,818	10,405	12,857

SOURCE: United Nations. *Human Development Report 2000; Trends in human development and per capita income.*

WORKING CONDITIONS

Maltese wages are low by comparison with other European nations. The nation's minimum wage is US$2.96 per hour, or US$118.50 per week. The average wage for skilled workers is US$175 per week. There are legally enforced annual bonuses and generous vacation periods. Bonuses average US$10.58 per week and vacations average 4 weeks per year. Employers underwrite the cost of workers' health care. The standard working week is 40 hours, but some industries are allowed to operate 43 to 45 hours per week. The Maltese labor force numbers 145,590 people.

The Maltese workforce is well-educated and productive. Foreign firms are attracted to Malta because of the low labor costs and the educated workforce. Most Maltese speak English, and worker productivity compares favorably to that of most European nations. The result is that even foreign-owned businesses are usually staffed and managed by Maltese employees. Workers have the right to unionize and to strike, but the islands have one of the lowest strike rates in Europe. There are 35 registered unions in Malta, and about half of the workforce belongs to a union. National laws require unions and companies to meet each year with government officials to draft annual agreements on wages and working conditions.

Employment of children under the age of 16 is prohibited, although many children work part-time in the tourist trade during the summer. Children under the age of 17 may be paid US$108 per week, while 17-year-olds can make US$111 per week. Women are underrepresented in the workforce, especially in management positions. In addition, women are often paid less than men in similar occupations. Furthermore, the traditional nature of Maltese society leads many women to stop working after marriage.

COUNTRY HISTORY AND ECONOMIC DEVELOPMENT

4000s B.C. A religious culture develops in Malta even before that of Egypt.

218 B.C. Malta becomes part of the Roman Empire during the Second Punic War.

60 A.D. Saint Paul brings Christianity to Malta after he is shipwrecked on the island.

433. The Byzantine Empire acquires Malta.

870. Malta is conquered by the Arabs.

1090. The Arabs are driven out by Normans under Count Roger of Normandy, who had established a kingdom in Sicily. Malta remains under Sicilian control for 440 years.

1523. Malta is ceded to the Knights of St. John, a religious order of fighting monks that had participated in the Crusades, but were based in Italy after being driven out of the Middle East by the Arabs. The Knights become known as the Knights of Malta and build towns and settlements throughout the islands.

1798. Malta is conquered by France under Napoleon Bonaparte.

1800. With British support, the Maltese overthrow the French.

1814. Malta voluntarily becomes a British colony. Under the British, the islands become an important naval and trade center in the Mediterranean.

1939–45. Malta suffers an intensive air and sea assault by German and Italian forces during World War II.

1964. Malta is granted independence by Great Britain. The island joins the British Commonwealth of Nations.

1974. Malta becomes a republic and adopts a new constitution.

1979. The last British military forces depart from Malta.

1987. Tourism in Malta reaches its height, with 60 percent growth over the previous year.

1996. The Labor government halts Malta's application process for EU membership.

1998. After winning early elections, the Nationalist Party restarts the process for EU entry.

FUTURE TRENDS

Malta is well positioned to continue its economic growth over the next decade. The favorable labor situation should continue to attract foreign companies and investment, while low prices for goods and accommodations will continue to draw tourists to the islands. Because the nation is dependent on tourism and foreign trade, it is vulnerable to slowdowns in the economies of its major trading partners.

Entry into the EU will expand Malta's economic opportunities since it will cut tariffs and taxes on Maltese goods imported by EU member states. It will also make it easier for EU companies to relocate to Malta. The most important issue for Malta is the need to lessen the role of the government in the economy. Therefore, the continuing privatization efforts are crucial for long-term growth.

DEPENDENCIES

Malta has no territories or colonies.

BIBLIOGRAPHY

Boulton, Susie. *Malta and Gozo.* New York: NTC, 2000.

Department of Information Malta. <http://www.doi.gov.mt>. Accessed September 2001.

MERHBA: Welcome to the Official Website of the Maltese Government. <http://www.magnet.mt>. Accessed September 2001.

Spiteri, Edward J. *An Island in Transition: The Economic Transformation of Malta From a British Crown Colony to an Independent Democratic Republic.* Valletta, Malta: Progress Press, 1997.

U.S. Central Intelligence Agency. *World Factbook 2001.* <http://www.odci.gov/cia/publications/factbook/index.html>. Accessed September 2001.

U.S. Department of State. *FY 2001 Country Commercial Guide: Malta.* <http://www.state.gov/www/about_state/business/com_guides/2001/europe/index.html>. Accessed September 2001.

Xuereb, Peter G., editor. *Malta, the European Union and the Mediterranean: Closer Relations in the Wider Context.* Valletta, Malta: University of Malta, 1998.

—Tom Lansford

MOLDOVA

Republic of Moldova
Republica Moldoveneasca

CAPITAL: Chişinău

MONETARY UNIT: Moldovan leu (MDL; plural lei). One leu equals 100 bani. There are coins of 1, 5, 10, 25, and 50 bani, and notes of 1, 5, 10, 20, 50, 100, and 200 lei.

CHIEF EXPORTS: Foodstuffs, wine, and tobacco (66 percent); textiles and footwear, machinery.

CHIEF IMPORTS: Mineral products and fuel (31 percent); machinery and equipment, chemicals, textiles.

GROSS DOMESTIC PRODUCT: US$9.7 billion (1999 est.).

BALANCE OF TRADE: **Exports:** US$470 million (f.o.b., 1999). **Imports:** US$560 million (f.o.b., 1999).

COUNTRY OVERVIEW

LOCATION AND SIZE. Located in southeastern Europe and bordered on the west by Romania and on all other sides by Ukraine, landlocked Moldova has an area of 33,843 square kilometers (13,067 square miles), making it slightly larger than Maryland. Moldova's border totals 1,389 kilometers (864 miles). The capital, Chişinău, is situated in its central part.

The portion of the country that lays east of the Nistru River is known as the Transnistria. Populated primarily by Slavs and economically and culturally oriented toward the Ukraine, the Transnistria has been in revolt against the Moldovan majority in the country (see below).

POPULATION. The population of Moldova was 4,430,654 in 2000 and its average density was 129.1 inhabitants per square kilometer (334 per square mile) in 1994. In 2000, the birth rate was 12.86 per 1,000 population, while the death rate equaled 12.58 per 1,000. With a net migration rate of -0.31 per 1,000 and a fertility rate of 1.63 children born per woman, the population growth rate was about zero in 2000. Over the 1990s, the population declined because of net economic **emigration**.

Moldova's population is youthful by European standards, with 23 percent below the age of 14 and 10 percent older than 65. Ethnic Moldovans (Romanians) account for 64.5 percent of the population, Ukrainians for 13.8 percent, Russians for 13 percent, Gagauz (a Turkic-speaking people of Christian faith) for 3.5 percent, Bulgarians for 2 percent, Jews for 1.5 percent, and other groups for 1.7 percent, according to 1989 estimates. In the early 1990s, interethnic violence occurred between the Moldovans and the Slavic majority in the Transnistria region (east of the Nistru [Dniester] River, with a population of 750,000) and the Gagauz in the country's south. The official language is Moldovan (Romanian) but Russian is widely spoken and is the second official language in Transnistria. About 98.5 percent of the population belong to the Orthodox Church. Moldova is predominantly rural, with about 54 percent of the population living mostly in large villages in 1999. The population in the capital of Chişinău was 667,000 in 1992; other major cities include Tiraspol and Tighina (Bender) in the east, and Balti in the north.

OVERVIEW OF ECONOMY

Moldova is among Europe's poorest countries. Before Moldova gained its independence from the USSR in 1991, the Soviet regime developed some of Moldova's industries, but Moldova's favorable climate, rich farmland, and lack of mineral resources defined its role as the USSR's primary supplier of fruits, vegetables, wine, tobacco, and processed foods. Soviet planners forced Moldova to develop those economic sectors, and Moldova imported its oil, coal, and natural gas from other USSR republics. The loss of Soviet markets and cheap energy sources with independence in 1991 caused a steep economic decline, energy shortages, and unemployment. Interethnic war, the Russian crisis of 1998, the problems

of Ukraine and Romania (which, with Russia, receive 70 percent of Moldova's exports), and record droughts combined for the sharpest **gross domestic product** (GDP) decline seen in a former Soviet republic; in 1998, the economy reached only 33 percent of its size in 1989. By 1999, GDP was $2,033 per capita.

Since independence, Moldova has followed a path toward reform, introducing a convertible currency, freeing prices from state control, ending **subsidies** for state-owned enterprises, **privatizing** the formerly collectivized farmland, removing export controls, and freeing bank interest rates with assistance from the International Monetary Fund (IMF) and the World Bank. (Taken together, these corrections are called structural reform because they change the structure of the economy.) Mass privatization in 1994 transferred to the **private sector** 1,142 large and medium and 1,093 small enterprises. Cash privatizations were less successful; tenders for the Moldtelecom (the telephone company) in 1998 and the tobacco firm Tutun in 1996 were canceled, and other privatization deals were disappointing. In 1997 and 1998, 223 enterprises were sold at auctions, generating $4.45 million; **foreign direct investment** reached $7.6 million.

The country's **external debt** was estimated at $1.3 billion (December 1999) and posed a major challenge to the economy. The country handed 50 percent of its gas pipelines to Russia's gas **monopoly** Gazprom, its biggest creditor (Moldova owes it $320 million and Transnistria another $400 million). The country is dependent on economic aid, and the International Monetary Fund (IMF) and the World Bank have granted $547 million between 1992 and 1999.

POLITICS, GOVERNMENT, AND TAXATION

Independent since 1991, Moldova is a republic with a multiparty system. Moldova's **unicameral** parliament is elected by universal suffrage. In February 2001, the Communist Party of Moldova (CPM) won 71 of the 101 seats, the formerly ruling centrist Alliance got 19 seats, and the right-wing nationalist Christian Democratic Popular Party (CDPP) won 11 seats. Popularly-elected President Vladimir Voronin of the CPM appointed a cabinet led by independent ethnic Bulgarian Prime Minister Vasile Tarlev. The CPM has generally opposed privatization and independence for Transnistria, and advocated reorientation towards Russia, but it is highly unlikely that market reforms will be reversed. With its absolute majority in parliament, the CPM will be able to pursue reform without distraction. It is expected that poorer voters will more readily accept austerity policies if they come from a leftist administration such as the CPM. The CPM retained key ministers from the previous reformist cabinet to stress continuity and it maintains rigorous **inflation** and budget targets, but it focuses on restoring industrial and agricultural output through policies that may antagonize the IMF. Also on the CPM agenda are reforming the public pension system by linking contributions to benefits and raising the retirement age; **restructuring** the public health care system by partially privatizing health services; and reforming the social assistance system. The IMF expressed satisfaction with its stabilization and privatization plans.

The Democratic Convention (DCM) is a right-of-center, pro-Western bloc, and the Democratic Party of Moldova (DPM) is a centrist group that developed from the older Movement for a Democratic and Prosperous

Moldova, the Popular Democratic Party, the New Forces, and the National Youth League. There are also a variety of small and relatively insignificant parties.

The government's role in the economy is large but declining as the size of the private sector has grown considerably over the 1990s. In 1999, an estimated 60 percent of the economy was in the private sector. Industries were more than 60 percent private, agriculture 86 percent private, **retail** and services 70 percent, and construction and transport almost 44 percent. The private sector accounted for 45 percent of GDP in 1999. The tax system is considered business-unfriendly, particularly with the introduction in 1998 of **value-added tax** (VAT) of 20 percent on imported goods and services, and of **excise taxes** in 1992. The business environment, legal framework, regulation, licensing, inspection, investment climate, access to bank credits, and business **infrastructure** have been deemed unfavorable to western investment.

Moldova has faced 2 major political conflicts since gaining independence in 1991. The most pressing of these conflicts was in the Transnistria region. The Transnistria region is a narrow strip of land laying east of the Nistru River (also known as the Dniester or Dniestr River). More heavily industrialized than the rest of Moldova, and populated primarily by Slavs, the region identifies itself more closely with Ukraine than with Moldova and has sought independence. Russian forces remained east of the Nistru River after 1991, supporting the self-proclaimed Transnistria Republic, which the government in Chişinău has not recognized. Russia and Ukraine are acting as mediators between Chişinău and Transnistria; the parties have observed a cease-fire since 1992, but progress to a settlement on the status of Transnistria has been slow. The region is still used for tax and customs evasions. The government in 2001 seems more willing to accept a Russian presence in return for greater pressure on Transnistria to discard sovereignty claims. Russia's influence will likely be acknowledged, and chances of political and economic union with Russia and Belarus may grow. Less pressing is the conflict in Gagauzia, a small region in the south of the country that is populated primarily by a Christian Turkic minority known as the Gagauz. Gagauzia has been granted a great deal of autonomy, including the right to control the privatization of assets in the region and the right to determine trade relations.

INFRASTRUCTURE, POWER, AND COMMUNICATIONS

Moldova is landlocked and depends on railroad and road networks for trade. Soviet-built railroads are of decent quality and comprise 1,318 kilometers (824 miles) of tracks; 10,531 kilometers (6,582 miles) of roads account for most local transport and 80 percent of passenger travel. The major rivers—the Nistru (Dniester) and the Prut—are used for local transport. In 1995, the government established Terminal S.A., a joint Moldovan-Greek venture to build and maintain an oil terminal in Giurgiulesti on the Danube with the assistance of the European Bank for Reconstruction and Development (EBRD). The country is served also by pipelines for natural gas from Russia (310 kilometers, or 192 miles, in 1992). Air traffic is served by the state-owned carrier, Air Moldova, and by 2 smaller airlines.

Moldova's electricity production was 5.661 billion kilowatt-hours (kWh) in 1998, 93 percent of which were generated in thermal plants and 7 percent in hydropower facilities. The country imported 1.8 billion kWh in 1998. Domestic sources account for 2 percent of primary energy supply, and gas accounts for 61 percent of the imports, oil for 20 percent, and coal for 10 percent. A large gas power plant in Transnistria produces 85 percent of the electricity. Moldova remains reliant on Russian gas, and Gazprom periodically cuts off supplies due to chronic non-payment, as do Romania, Ukraine, and Transnistria for unpaid electricity. Mounting bills result from non-payment by consumers, electricity theft, and wastage. The sector has been restructured into 2 generators and 5 distributor companies, and in 2000, Moldova completed

Communications

Country	Newspapers	Radios	TV Sets[a]	Cable subscribers[a]	Mobile Phones[a]	Fax Machines[a]	Personal Computers[a]	Internet Hosts[b]	Internet Users[b]
	1996	1997	1998	1998	1998	1998	1998	1999	1999
Moldova	60	740	297	17.6	2	0.2	6.4	2.42	25
United States	215	2,146	847	244.3	256	78.4	458.6	1,508.77	74,100
Russia	105	418	420	78.5	5	0.4	40.6	13.06	2,700
Romania	300	319	233	119.2	29	N/A	10.2	9.01	600

[a]Data are from International Telecommunication Union, *World Telecommunication Development Report 1999* and are per 1,000 people.
[b]Data are from the Internet Software Consortium (http://www.isc.org) and are per 10,000 people.

SOURCE: World Bank. *World Development Indicators 2000.*

the first round of electricity privatization, selling 3 of the distributors to Union Fenosa of Spain.

Moldova has an antiquated telephone system with 15 lines per 100 inhabitants in 1997, very few pay phones, many villages without service, and a mobile phone penetration rate of just 0.3 percent in 1998. Moldtelecom, the national telecom, is currently upgrading and has signed agreements with Denmark's Great Northern Telegraph (GNT), which is investing $10 million in a digital switch system and fiber-optic technology. The government intends to sell 51 percent of Moldtelecom following a failed attempt at privatization in 1998 to a Greek company. In 1998, Voxtel, a consortium comprising 1 French, 1 Romanian, and 2 Moldovan companies, launched mobile service in the GSM standard. In 2000, Moldova awarded a second GSM license to Moldcell, a **joint venture** between Turkish Turkcell (77 percent) and Chişinău-based Accent Electronics (23 percent). In 1999, the Internet usage was 5.8 per 1,000 of the population, there were 16 Internet service providers, and Moldova leased out its "md" domain name to inhabitants of the state of Maryland in the United States.

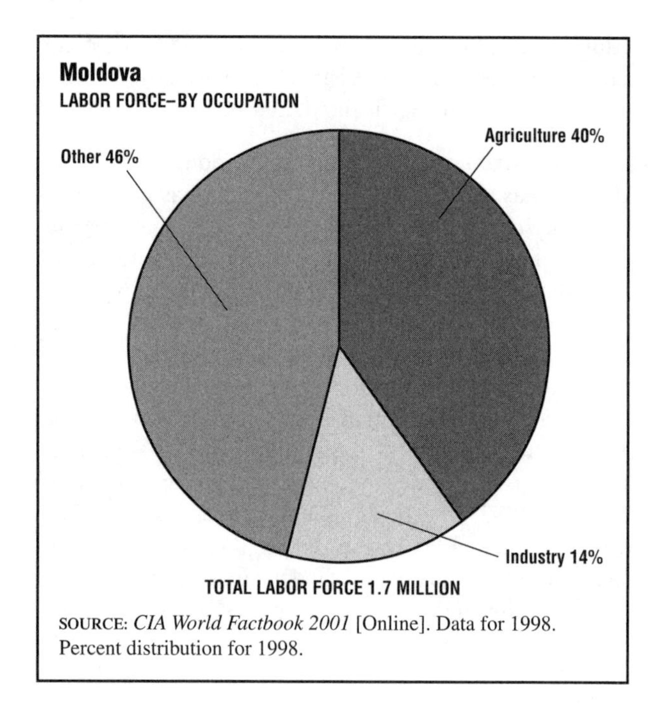

SOURCE: *CIA World Factbook 2001* [Online]. Data for 1998. Percent distribution for 1998.

ECONOMIC SECTORS

The entire economy of Moldova has been in decline since independence in 1991. In 1998, the contributions to GDP of the 3 major sectors were as follows: agriculture, 31 percent; industry, 35 percent (mostly from food processing); and services, 34 percent. Agriculture employed 40.2 percent of the **labor force**, while industry employed 14.3 percent, and other sectors employed 45.5 percent. Over the 1990s, industrial output declined 2.5 times due to the loss of markets and the drop in domestic farm production. The country has a development strategy focusing on light manufacturing (textiles, consumer electronics) and cement.

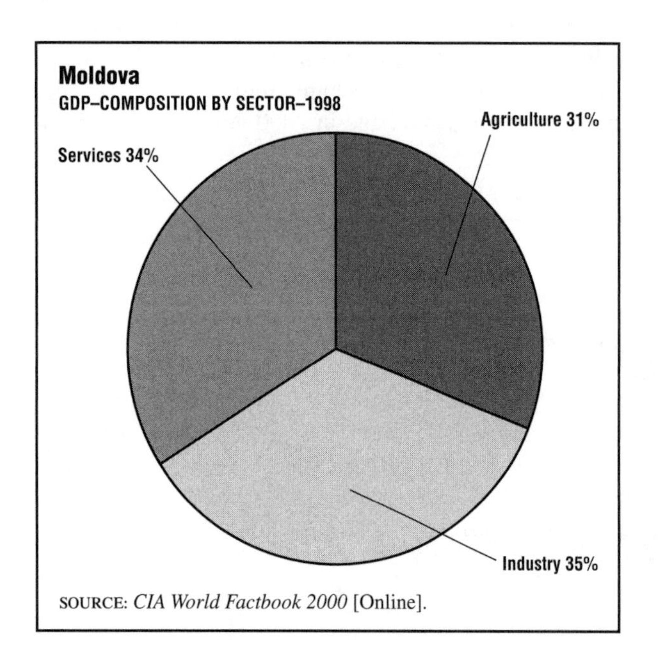

SOURCE: *CIA World Factbook 2000* [Online].

AGRICULTURE

Agriculture provides employment for over 40 percent of the population and contributes nearly a third of GDP. Some 75 percent of Moldovan territory is fertile Chernozem (black earth) and agricultural products account for 75 percent of all exports. Twenty-one percent of Moldovan agricultural land was held as individual farms, 61 percent as cooperative farms, and 18 percent by state-owned farms in 1999; in all, 85,000 private farmers were operating throughout the country. Privatization of former cooperative farms has been slow (almost nonexistent in Transnistria) and the land market has been small, not least because foreigners are not allowed to purchase land. Farm consolidation is taking root as approximately 10,000 larger farms were formed in 1998 and 1999.

Cereals, sunflowers, sugar beets, potatoes, vegetables, tobacco, fruits, and grapes are grown, but plantings of capital-intensive crops—tobacco and vegetables—have declined due to the loss of markets and limited domestic consumption. The number of livestock decreased considerably over the 1990s due to high costs and low demand. The agricultural sector has been affected over the 1990s by droughts, frosts, floods, and shortage of materials, machines, and fertilizers once supplied by the USSR. More intensive farming techniques have lowered productivity by 35 percent. The sector still receives subsidies and tax incentives, but recent command measures (such as the attempt to ban wheat exports) continue to repel potential investors.

INDUSTRY

Food processing (including sugar and vegetable oil) is the largest domestic industry, followed by power generation, engineering (mostly agricultural machinery, foundry equipment, refrigerators, freezers, and washing machines), hosiery, shoes, and textiles. Industrial production decreased by 10 percent in 1999 and the sector, which accounts for less than 15 percent of GDP, has been declining ever since independence, devastated by rising energy prices, the decline in agriculture, and the loss of markets. The conflict with Transnistria has had a significant effect on this sector since all production of electric machines, power transformers, gas containers, slate, 95 percent of the cotton fabrics, 87 percent of the electricity, and a large part of the cement industry are located there.

The food industry accounted for 58.2 percent of the manufacturing output in 1997, far ahead of energy production (18.4 percent), the second largest industry. The importance of the third largest sector, engineering and metal processing, declined from almost 18 percent in 1990 to 5.9 percent in 1997. Similarly, the importance of light industry, which was the second biggest sector after food-processing in 1990, has also declined, from 21.1 percent in 1990 to 5.8 percent in 1997. Efforts to produce exports for more stable and lucrative markets such as those in the European Union (EU) have been difficult due to the lower product quality of Moldovan firms. Wine represents a major product of Moldova's economy, with exports in a good year accounting for up to 50 percent of the total export income. The wine industry has attracted some western investment and loans from the EBRD, but in 1998 Russia still accounted for 85.6 percent of wine export sales. The tobacco processing industry remains one of the country's most important; during Soviet times, the republic produced 40 percent of the USSR's annual crop. Moldova plans to privatize Tutun, the country's largest tobacco concern. Some new industries, such as scrap metal processing, chemicals, and medical equipment, have also emerged since independence. The construction materials industry is expanding through exports of cement, gypsum, and ceramics, and through investment in civil engineering.

SERVICES

The banking system includes the independent National Bank of Moldova (NBM) and 21 commercial banks. Although small, the banking system has functioned well over the 1990s. Banking laws and accounting standards correspond to international standards, and there are no restrictions on foreign banks. There were 21 commercial banks in 2000; 3 others closed down in 1998. The largest banks, accounting for two-thirds of all assets and deposits, are Agroindbank, Petrol Bank, Banca De Economii, Moldindconbank, Banca Sociala, and Victoriabank. Victoriabank, a private commercial bank, has been most active in supporting small industry and retail. A network of savings and credit associations is being developed in villages, and insurance is becoming important, with 40 companies providing services.

Chişinău shows signs of developing a retail sector with several private Western-style shops and restaurants. Outside town, options are limited. The Green Hills is the largest of the supermarkets, while the Ninevia and the Fidesco supermarkets carry many imported supplies. High prices on imported goods make them unavailable for the majority of the population. Tourism is underdeveloped with a few Soviet-era hotels in Chişinău and no efforts to attract foreign visitors.

INTERNATIONAL TRADE

Exports amounted to $470 million in 1999 and included foodstuffs, wine, and tobacco (which accounted for 66 percent of total exports), textiles and footwear, and machinery. Most exports in 1998 were shipped to Russia (53 percent), while Romania took 10 percent, Ukraine 8 percent, Germany 5 percent, and Belarus 4 percent. Imports in 1998 were worth $560 million and included mineral products and fuel, machinery and equipment, chemicals, and textiles. The majority of imports originate from Russia (22 percent); other major importers were Ukraine (16 percent), Romania (12 percent), Belarus (9 percent), and Germany (5 percent). In 1998, the collapse in the value of the leu brought the **trade deficit** to $389.1 million from $297.3 million in 1997, due to lower exports and higher import costs.

Prospects for increased trade grew by the turn of the century. In 2000 alone Moldova's foreign trade rose 22 percent to US$1.27 billion dollars. Moreover, Moldova joined the World Trade Organization (WTO) in 2001, an action which held the promise of opening trade beyond the limited confines of former Soviet countries.

MONEY

The National Bank of Moldova (NBM) was established in 1991 and is responsible for **monetary policy** and banking supervision. The first years following independence were a difficult time for Moldovan finances. Inflation hit 2,700 percent in 1993, but prudent **fiscal policies** brought the inflation level down to 11.2 percent in 1997. The Russian crisis led to intense pressure on the Moldovan currency, and after the **devaluation** of the Russian rouble, the NBM abandoned support of the leu

Exchange rates: Moldova

lei (MDL) per US$1	
Jan 2001	12.3728
2000	12.4342
1999	10.5158
1998	5.3707
1997	4.6236
1996	4.6045

Note: Lei is the plural form of leu.

SOURCE: CIA *World Factbook 2001* [ONLINE].

Distribution of Income or Consumption by Percentage Share: Moldova

Lowest 10%	2.7
Lowest 20%	6.9
Second 20%	11.9
Third 20%	16.7
Fourth 20%	23.1
Highest 20%	41.5
Highest 10%	25.8

Survey year: 1992

Note: This information refers to income shares by percentiles of the population and is ranked by per capita income.

SOURCE: *2000 World Development Indicators* [CD-ROM].

in order to conserve its **foreign exchange reserves**, and it was devaluated at 100 percent. **Inflation rates** that peaked at 40 percent during the Russian financial crisis were expected to drop to 10 percent in 2001.

Other elements of the financial sector are less developed but include the National Commodity Exchange, established in 1991; the Moldova Interbank Currency Exchange; the Moldovan Stock Exchange, established in 1995; 15 investment funds; and 8 trust companies. The National Commission on the Securities Market supervises the market participants. The Moldovan Stock Exchange (MSE) was established in June 1995 as an electronic, screen-based, order-driven system. Only 20 companies are listed, but the trade volume increased from US$2.5 million in 1996 to US$52.6 million in 1998. The unregulated over-the-counter market accounted for 48 percent of the transactions in 1999.

POVERTY AND WEALTH

Under the Soviet regime, employment was almost total and provided modest livelihoods for nearly everyone in a relatively egalitarian society (with the exception of the more affluent groups of the communist elite and the underworld). But independence and the reforms of the 1990s generated unemployment, crime, corruption, poverty, and illicit fortunes. The population below the poverty line was estimated in 1999 at a stunning 75 percent (in Romania, it was 30 percent; in Russia and Ukraine, 25–50 percent). Moldova's **Gini index** (measuring economic equality, with 0 standing for perfect equality and 100 for perfect inequality) in 1992 was 34.4, far lower than in the United States (40.6), but considerably higher than in Bulgaria (28) and Greece (32).

GDP per Capita (US$)

Country	1975	1980	1985	1990	1998
Moldova	N/A	1,453	1,572	1,776	614
United States	19,364	21,529	23,200	25,363	29,683
Russia	2,555	3,654	3,463	3,668	2,138
Romania	1,201	1,643	1,872	1,576	1,310

SOURCE: United Nations. *Human Development Report 2000; Trends in human development and per capita income.*

The social cost of market reforms has been greater than was assumed, and the state has proved incapable of ensuring support for the poor. It failed to stimulate the private sector as a compensation for unemployment or to reorganize the social services. Mass privatization turned unworthy assets over to poor owners and funneled high-quality assets to the well connected. The reach of the **underground economy** (which was estimated at 35 percent of GDP in 1999), leads to corruption, reduced public revenues, and widening income inequality. Poverty is causing stress, particularly in rural areas, and limiting private economic initiative. To relieve poverty, the Moldovan government has relied on international aid, such as IMF's $142 million poverty reduction facility, and on plans to decentralize social services in order to boost social sector reform.

WORKING CONDITIONS

The labor force numbered 1.7 million in 1998, and the unemployment rate was about 31 percent in 2000. Economic instability, according to **United Nations Development Program** reports, makes it difficult for the government to uphold adequately the right to social insurance and protection (guaranteed by article 47 of the constitution), the right to work and labor protection (Article 43), the right to health protection (article 36), and the right to a favorable working environment (article 37). The state does not meet its commitments to protect family and orphans (article 49), the interests of mothers, children and youth (article 50), or the interests of persons with disabilities (article 51). The average monthly wage in 1999 reached $25, insufficient to provide a decent standard of living. Many workers were using outdated tech-

Household Consumption in PPP Terms

Country	All food	Clothing and footwear	Fuel and power[a]	Health care[b]	Education[b]	Transport & Communications	Other
Moldova	31	5	11	3	15	12	23
United States	13	9	9	4	6	8	51
Russia	28	11	16	7	15	8	16
Romania	36	7	9	3	20	9	16

Data represent percentage of consumption in PPP terms.
[a]Excludes energy used for transport.
[b]Includes government and private expenditures.

SOURCE: World Bank. *World Development Indicators 2000.*

nology without adequate safety regulations, and workplace conditions were poor and often dangerous. Under the Soviet regime, unions were government-controlled; independent ones began to emerge in 1991, but their influence is limited partly due to the increasing size of the private sector.

COUNTRY HISTORY AND ECONOMIC DEVELOPMENT

14TH CENTURY. The principality of Moldavia is founded by the Vlachs, inhabitants of the Carpathian Mountains and other parts of the Balkan Peninsula.

15TH CENTURY. The Ottoman Empire absorbs Moldavia and develops a feudal agricultural society.

1812. Russia annexes the eastern portion of Moldavia, historically known as Bessarabia.

1856. European powers grant Moldavia and Bessarabia independence from the Ottoman Empire and Russia, respectively, and they are united with independent Walachia in 1859, assuming the newly-minted name of Romania.

1878. Russia regains Bessarabia.

1918. After the 1917 Russian revolution, Russian Bessarabia decides in favor of unification with Romania. Western powers recognize the incorporation at the Paris Peace Conference of 1920.

1924. The Soviets establish the Moldavian Autonomous Soviet Socialist Republic (ASSR) east of the Nistru (Dniester) River within Ukraine.

1939. A German-Soviet Nonaggression Pact forces Romania to cede Bessarabia to the USSR.

1940. The Soviet government proclaims the Moldavian Soviet Socialist Republic (SSR), including the territory of the former Moldavian ASSR (Transnistria), with a capital in Chişinău.

1941. Romania, an ally of Nazi Germany, declares war on the USSR and invades Bessarabia with German assistance during World War II.

1944. The USSR reestablishes the Moldavian SSR toward the end of World War II. Over the next 50 years its economy is integrated into the Soviet system with collective and state farms on expropriated farmland. The country remains rural, although new industries appear in urban areas, and Russians become the majority in the cities.

1985. Soviet leader Mikhail Gorbachev introduces political and economic reforms in the USSR.

1989. The Popular Front of Moldova (PFM), the first opposition group, is formed.

1990. A local referendum approves autonomy for the predominantly Slavic Transnistria region, giving rise to a lasting controversy over the status of the region.

1991. The Moldavian SSR changes its name to the Republic of Moldova and declares its independence from the USSR.

1992. Moldova joins the International Monetary Fund.

1994. First multi-party elections; the first post-Soviet constitution is adopted.

2001. Moldova joins the World Trade Organization.

FUTURE TRENDS

The economic future of Moldova depends on the successful completion of its reforms, the future strength of the Russian and Ukrainian economies, and the successful accession of Romania to the European Union, since these 3 countries receive 70 percent of its exports and supply almost all its energy. Prior to elections in 2000 Moldova appeared to be heading toward greater trade relations with the international community, but the ascension to power of the Communist Party of Moldova (CMP) puts such engagement in doubt. The CMP's control of government may reduce political instability, particularly regarding the Transnistria stand-off, but any slowing of economic reforms could limit GDP growth to 3–3.5 percent a year while possible fiscal and monetary **liberalization** may cause 20 percent inflation in 2001. The more pro-Romanian and pro-European direction of centrist foreign policy may give way to closer ties and even integration with the Russian-Belarusian union.

The CPM may also run contrary to the IMF agreement with its renewed **price controls** and state monopoly over the wine and tobacco sectors; it is unlikely, however, that the general direction of reform toward a market economy will be reversed. Moldova has good long-term growth prospects in terms of geographical location, resources, and a skilled workforce, but has a long way to go before an operational market economy could create the sustainable ground for improved living standards for the majority of the people.

DEPENDENCIES

Moldova has no territories or colonies.

BIBLIOGRAPHY

Dawisha, Karen, and Bruce Parrott, eds. *Democratic Changes and Authoritarian Reactions in Russia, Ukraine, Belarus and Moldova.* Cambridge: Cambridge University Press, 1997.

Economist Intelligence Unit. *Country Profile: Moldova.* London: Economist Intelligence Unit, 2001.

Fedor, Helen, editor. *Belarus and Moldova: Country Studies.* Washington, D.C.: Library of Congress, 1996.

Republic of Moldova. <http://www.moldova.md>. Accessed August 2001.

Republic of Moldova Site. <http://www.moldova.org>. Accessed August 2001.

United Nations Development Program. *Human Development Report, Republic of Moldova.* New York, 2000.

U.S. Central Intelligence Agency. *World Factbook 2000.* <http://www.odci.gov/cia/publications/factbook/index.html>. Accessed August 2001.

U.S. Department of State. *FY 2001 Country Commercial Guide: Moldova.* <http://www.state.gov/www/about_state/business/com_guides/index.html>. Accessed August 2001.

—Valentin Hadjiyski

MONACO

Principality of Monaco
Principauté de Monaco

CAPITAL: Monaco-Ville.

MONETARY UNIT: French franc (F). One French franc equals 100 centimes. The franc comes in bank notes of 20, 50, 100, 200, and 500-franc denominations. There are coins of 1, 2, 5, 10, and 20 francs and 5, 10, 20, and 50 centimes. Monegasque coins, having the same value as the French coins, are also minted and circulated. Monaco is scheduled to switch to the new European currency, the euro, in January 2002.

CHIEF EXPORTS: Cosmetics, pharmaceuticals, glassware, precision instruments, fine processed foods, cards and postal stamps, and various re-exported commodities (estimate, no official statistics are published).

CHIEF IMPORTS: Energy, automobiles, equipment, and consumer goods (estimate, no official statistics are published).

GROSS DOMESTIC PRODUCT: US$870 million (1999 est., no official statistics are published).

BALANCE OF TRADE: **Exports:** US$415,272 (1999 est.). **Imports:** US$415,272 (1999 est.). [Estimate by Monegasque government sources; no official statistics are published.]

COUNTRY OVERVIEW

LOCATION AND SIZE. Monaco, a small independent hereditary principality in Western Europe, is located on the Mediterranean Sea along the southern coast of France, which is also known as the French Riviera or Côte d'Azur. Monaco is 18 kilometers (11 miles) east of the French city of Nice, near the border with Italy. The second smallest independent state in the world (after Vatican City), and almost entirely urban, it forms an enclave in southeastern France, surrounded on the north, east, and west by the French département (administrative division, or region) of Alpes-Maritimes. The country is only 1.95 square kilometers (0.75 square miles) in area, or about 3 times the size of the Mall in Washington, D.C. The terrain is hilly, rugged, and rocky, but very highly urbanized. The principality, a famous maritime resort, is composed of 4 quartiers (quarters): Monaco-Ville, the capital (an ancient fortified town located on a rocky promontory extending into the Mediterranean); La Condamine (the section along the port); Monte Carlo (the principal residential and resort area); and Fontvieille (a newly constructed industrial park reclaimed from the sea). The name "Monaco," derived from the ancient Greek Monoikos (meaning "of the old town"), is usually associated with the mythical hero, Hercules.

POPULATION. The population of Monaco was estimated at 31,693 in July 2000, with an average growth rate of 0.48 percent in the same year. The 2000 birth rate was estimated at 9.94 births per 1,000 population, the death rate at 13.06 deaths per 1,000 population, and the net migration rate was approximately 7.89 immigrants per 1,000 population.

With high life expectancy at birth, the Monegasque population is among the oldest populations in the world. The average life expectancy was 74.88 for men and 83 for women in 2000, indicating an overall life expectancy of 78.84. The total fertility rate in 2000 was 1.76 children born per woman. Approximately 15 percent of the population is younger than 15 years of age and 23 percent is age 65 or older. Monaco has also one of the highest population densities in the world, at 16,428 persons per square kilometer (42,549 per square mile).

Monegasques represented a mere 16 percent of the population in 2000. Other ethnic groups include the French (47 percent), Italian (16 percent), and other nationalities (21 percent). French is the official language; English, Italian, and Monegasque (a blend of French and Italian) are also widely spoken. The traditional Monegasque language is used by the older people and is taught in the schools. The economy of Monaco offers more than

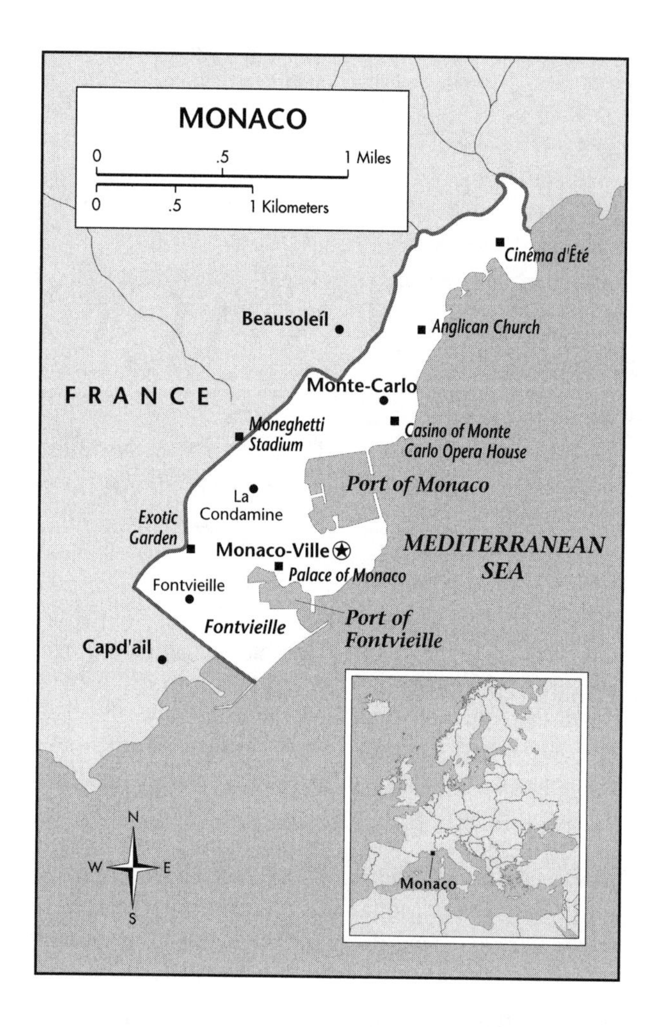

30,000 jobs. Immigrant labor, especially from France and Italy, is heavily relied upon because the number of jobs available outnumbers the number of citizens in the **labor force**. Many affluent Americans, as well as French, Britons, Swiss, Belgians, and other Europeans, live in the principality. The prevailing religion is Roman Catholicism, accounting for 95 percent of the population. Roman Catholicism also is the official religion, though freedom of religion is guaranteed by the constitution. Education is free and compulsory for children ages 6 to 16.

OVERVIEW OF ECONOMY

Renowned as a **tax haven** for the rich, Monaco is thought to have one of the most affluent and **liberal economies** in the world, though the government does not publish economic figures or other relevant statistics. A tiny territory with few natural resources—in some places stretching no more than 180 meters (600 feet) inland from the Mediterranean—the Monegasque economy is primarily geared toward tourism, modern manufacturing, finance, and commerce. From the end of the 19th century, the government of Monaco has very actively encouraged economic growth and provided the framework for the development of private enterprise. It has successfully sought to diversify into services and small, high **value-added**, nonpolluting industries.

Low corporate taxes (and no personal income or other **direct taxes**) have drawn many foreign "letter box" companies, which operate overseas but have established their head offices nominally in Monaco because of the more favorable tax treatment. These types of companies account for about 50 percent of the $586 million annual government revenue in 1997. The residential real estate market also provides some considerable income for the principality; many wealthy aliens are actively pursuing Monegasque permanent residence and/or citizenship for tax purposes and are in constant need of local property for that matter. Similarly, tourism accounts for close to 25 percent of the principality's annual income, and Monaco has been a major tourist center ever since its famed gambling casino was established in 1856. The tourist industry is still considered the economic foundation of the state. The sale of picturesque postage stamps and tobacco, the banking and insurance sectors, and the manufacture of pharmaceuticals, chemicals, electronic equipment, cosmetics, paper, textiles, and plastic goods are also of economic importance. Customs, postal services, telecommunications, and banking in Monaco are governed by the economic, monetary, and customs union with France and European Union (EU) rules. Although not an EU member, Monaco is closely associated with the economic structures of the EU. Some 1999 estimates placed the per capita **gross domestic product** (GDP) at about US$27,000, one of the highest in the world. The total **turnover** of the principality rose from the estimated 3.25 billion French francs in 1975 to 21.3 billion in 1988, 25.4 billion in 1989, 29 billion in 1990, 31 billion in 1991, 32.4 billion in 1992, and 33.2 billion in 1993.

POLITICS, GOVERNMENT, AND TAXATION

Monaco has been governed as a constitutional monarchy since 1911, with the hereditary prince (presently, Prince Rainier III) as the head of state. Unlike other European monarchies, the Monegasque sovereign is the actual, and not symbolic, head of state. In the constitution of 1962, it is clearly stated that the executive power is responsible to the supreme authority of the reigning prince. The succession to the throne passes to the direct descendants of the prince under the principle of primogeniture (inheritance of the first born), with male descendants taking precedence over female descendants of the same degree of kin. The sovereign represents Monaco in its relations with foreign powers and signs and ratifies treaties. In 1956, Rainier III married American film star Grace Kelly, who died in a car crash in 1982. They have 2 daughters and a son, who is the heir apparent to the throne.

The executive branch consists of a minister of state (head of government, presently Michel Leveque), who presides over a 4-member cabinet, the Council of Government. The minister is primarily responsible for foreign relations and is traditionally a French citizen appointed by the prince for a 3-year term from among several candidates proposed by the French government. As the prince's representative, the minister also directs the executive services, commands the police, and presides (with voting powers) over the Council of Government. The 3 other members of the Council are locals, responsible for financial and economic affairs, internal affairs, and public works and social affairs, respectively.

Monaco is a parliamentary monarchy ruled according to its 1962 constitution, which stipulates that the hereditary prince shares his power with the **unicameral** National Council. There are 18 members of this legislative body, elected by universal suffrage (by citizens over age 21) for 5-year terms. They usually meet twice annually to vote on the budget and endorse laws proposed by the prince. If the prince dissolves the National Council, new elections must be held within 3 months. Ordinances passed by the National Council are debated in the Council of Government, as are the ministerial decrees signed by the Minister of State. Once approved by the Council, the ordinances are submitted to the prince within 80 days for his approval. Once approved, the ordinances become legally valid. If no opposition is voiced on his behalf within 10 days of receipt, they become enforceable.

Legal power is also vested in the monarch, who delegates all legal procedures to the courts dispensing justice in his name. The independence of the judges, however, is guaranteed by the 1962 constitution. Monaco's legal system is closely related to the French system and is designed after the French Napoleonic Code. Local affairs—the administration of the 4 quarters—are directed by the Communal Council, which consists of 15 elected members and is presided over by a mayor. Monaco has its own local political groups that are not a part of the French political system and include the National and Democratic Union (UND), the Campora List, and the Medecin List.

The most crucial political issue in Monaco is, understandably, its bilateral relation with France. The geographical situation of Monaco as an enclave within France justifies the traditional customs and monetary union between the 2 countries, which dates back to 1861. Two major treaties in 1918 and 1919 established a reciprocal contractual basis for the relations between the 2 independent states (France recognized Monaco as a sovereign entity and undertook to build its relations on an equal footing with a limited protection over the principality). Under these arrangements, France is obligated to defend the independence and sovereignty of the principality and the integrity of Monegasque territory. In return, the government of Monaco is obligated to exercise its rights only in conformity with French interests. New bilateral agreements were signed in 1945, 1951, and 1963 with the aim of amending the earlier provisions in order to adapt them to the new economic and social conditions. Further changes and amendments arose from the development of European integration and the decision made by France in 1999 to adopt the single European currency, the euro.

Although small in size, Monaco actively participates in the United Nations (UN), which it joined in 1993, and maintains a permanent mission to the UN in New York. Monaco also is a member of many other international and intergovernmental organizations. The International Hydrographic Bureau (IHB) is headquartered in the principality. The country has 10 diplomatic missions in Europe and maintains honorary consulates in 106 cities in 45 countries. Sixty-one countries have consulates general, consulates, or honorary consulates in or accredited to Monaco.

The government's role in the economy has been traditionally one of active promotion of private enterprise and creating the necessary **infrastructure** for development. The state and the ruling Grimaldi family personally own considerable real estate assets and **equity** in the economy. Monaco's tax policies concerning its citizens are among the most liberal ones in the world, as there is no direct taxation for local residents. In 1869, land tax, personal and goods taxes, and the business tax were abolished. Since that time, Monegasque citizens or foreigners residing in the principality have not been subject to any tax on their personal income, whatever its origin. For French citizens moving to the principality after 1962, an exception was introduced in 1963 under pressure from the French government. Under the new arrangement, French nationals who moved their residence to Monaco, or who could not prove 5 years of residence in Monaco before October 1962, were subject to French taxes under the same conditions as if they had their residence in France. Since 1963, companies of any type are required to pay a corporate tax rate of 33.33 percent on profits when at least 25 percent of their turnover comes from operations outside Monegasque territory. A **value-added tax** (VAT) of 5.5 percent and a real estate added value tax of 20.6 percent were also introduced, along with some special arrangements concerning banking and financial activities and **indirect taxes**.

INFRASTRUCTURE, POWER, AND COMMUNICATIONS

Monaco, as a small, highly urbanized enclave in the French territory, is part of the well-developed French infrastructure. Electricity is provided almost entirely by France. There are 1.7 kilometers (1.1 miles) of railroads

Communications

Country	Telephones[a]	Telephones, Mobile/Cellular[a]	Radio Stations[b]	Radios[a]	TV Stations[a]	Televisions[a]	Internet Service Providers[c]	Internet Users[c]
Monaco	31,027 (1995)	N/A	AM 1; FM NA; shortwave 8	34,000	5 (1998)	25,000	2	N/A
United States	194 M	69.209 M (1998)	AM 4,762; FM 5,542; shortwave 18	575 M	1,500	219 M	7,800	148 M
France	34.86 M (1998)	11.078 M (1998)	AM 41; FM about 3,500; shortwave 2	55.3 M	584 (1995)	34.8 M	62	9 M
San Marino	18,000 (1998)	3,010 (1998)	AM 0; FM 3; shortwave 0	16,000	1	9,000	2	N/A

[a]Data is for 1997 unless otherwise noted.
[b]Data is for 1998 unless otherwise noted.
[c]Data is for 2000 unless otherwise noted.

SOURCE: CIA *World Factbook 2001* [Online].

and 50 kilometers (31 miles) of paved roads, including the highway and railroad connecting southern France with Italy along the Mediterranean. There are 2 ports, including a busy merchant harbor and several tourist marinas, although the principality has no merchant fleet of its own. There is also a helicopter shuttle line between the heliport at Fontvieille and the nearby international airport in Nice, France. Telecommunications are incorporated within the French telephone system, and there were 9 radio stations and 5 television stations in 1997, while 4 Internet service providers were offering customers their services in 1999. The access to cellular phones and to the Internet was similar in numbers and quality of service to that of French urban areas. The cable television services were comparable to the highest western European standards.

ECONOMIC SECTORS

The backbone of the Monegasque economy is formed by high-end tourism and the services related to it, construction and the real estate market, small-scale industrial and consumer products manufacturing (chemicals, food products, plastics, precision instruments, cosmetics, and ceramics), and international trade. Of the 32,691 employed, as estimated in 1999, the **private sector** was responsible for 29,311 and the **public sector** for 3,380. Approximately 46 percent of the labor force was in services (other than tourism), 7 percent in banking, 17 percent in tourism and hotels, 12 percent in **retail**, 7 percent in construction and public works, and 11 percent in industry. No official data as to the distribution of GDP were available.

AGRICULTURE

There are no arable lands or other agriculturally suited areas in the principality; virtually 100 percent of the Monaco territory is heavily urbanized. Accordingly, there is no commercial agriculture in the country. All foods are imported and some of them are further processed and exported.

INDUSTRY

Industrial activity, often little known in Monaco, is an area that has undergone considerable development over the past century. From 1906, when the state financed the construction of the first industrial platform in Fontvieille, industrial firms such as the Monaco Brewery and companies involved in flour milling and the manufacture of chocolate began to develop. Currently, the chemical-pharmaceutical-cosmetics manufacturing sector appears to be the most widespread, but companies working in the areas of plastic materials processing and the manufacture of electrical and electronic equipment are also present. Other sectors, while not on the same scale as these, are the manufactures of mechanical engineering, packaging, printing, and clothing. Since 1980, nearly 1,859 square meters (20,000 square feet) of new industrial floor-space has been built, mostly on areas reclaimed from the sea. The lack of space has led to the establishment of industrial premises in buildings that rise up to 13 floors. The government of the principality has adopted an industrial policy that operates in favor of the institution of enterprises having a high capital gain factor but that do not create any pollution. Industrial activity occupies about 4,000 members of the workforce. In 1993, they represented approximately 11.6 percent (excluding the construction and public works industry) of the total revenue in the principality.

SERVICES

The service sector has undergone spectacular growth in recent decades. It produced 49.1 percent of the total revenue of the country in 1993 and included banking, insurance, consulting agencies (technical, commercial, and financial), auxiliary services, and commercial middlemen. Banking and financial activities and business services, including those associated with the establishment of head offices and offices of non-financial companies of international size, are growing in importance in Monaco. The retail sector includes small, privately held stores, luxury boutiques, and international retail chains. Retail contributed approximately 21 percent to the principality's total revenue in 1993. The banking and retail sectors are closely integrated with the French economy through the monetary union between the 2 countries and the local branches of large French and international banks, insurance firms, and stock markets. Despite the increased competition resulting from the **liberalization** of financial services in the EU, the introduction of the single currency, and the revolution in information technology, the economic relationship between France and Monaco remains strong. Real estate activity plays a very important role in the economy, justifying the principality's extensive research and decision-making process in the field of city planning.

TOURISM. Monaco is a popular world luxury resort, attracting affluent tourists to its casino, rich cultural schedule, and pleasant climate. Situated in the heart of the Riviera—the narrow coastal strip extending along the Mediterranean from Hyeres, France, to La Spezia, Italy—it benefits from the proximity of the renowned French resorts of Saint Tropez, Antibes, Cannes, Nice, and Menton. The latter 2 cities are connected by 3 scenic highways, which run through or near the Monaco territory and its chief tourist quarter of Monte Carlo along the sheer cliffs of the Maritime Alps. Both private and business tourism are thriving in the principality, and there are about 2,500 hotel rooms, most of which are in the 4-star category or higher. In 1993, 601,111 rooms were occupied overnight, resulting in an average annual occupation rate of 48.3 percent. For several years, the government has been making considerable efforts to attract more business tourists in order to increase hotel occupation, since occupation by the private clientele is essentially seasonal. Among the points of interest in Monaco are a cathedral, a palace in the medieval and Renaissance styles, and a world-renowned oceanographic museum established in 1910. A major source of revenue is the famous gambling casino. The Monte Carlo Opera and Philharmonic Orchestra offer ballet and music events, and the museums, spas, beaches, flower gardens, marinas, fine dining spots, luxury boutiques, and vistas all contribute to the attractions of the principality. The Monaco Grand Prix and the Rally Monte Carlo are popular annual automobile-racing events. The Societe des Bains de Mer, a company partly owned by the government, operates the casino and most of the hotels, clubs, beaches, and other places of entertainment. There are also notable **foreign direct investments** in the Monaco tourist industry.

INTERNATIONAL TRADE

Monaco is a hub of international commerce, importing and exporting products and services from all over the world. It is in full customs integration with France, which collects and rebates Monegasque trade **duties**. Monaco participates in the EU market system through France. No recent trade statistics for the principality have been made available.

MONEY

As an integral part of the French monetary and banking system, the country has a balanced budget with revenues of US$518 million and expenditures of US$531 million, including capital expenditures (1995 est.).

Recent **exchange rates** for the euro per US$1 are 1.1 (February 2001), 1.20 (November 2000), 0.99 (January 2000), and 0.94 (1999). French francs (F) were exchanged at a rate of F7.22 (August 1999), 6.16 (1999 average), 5.65 (January 1999), 5.8995 (1998), 5.8367 (1997), 5.1155 (1996), and 4.9915 (1995) per US$1.

POVERTY AND WEALTH

Living standards in Monaco are high, comparable to those in the most prosperous French urban areas. Since one of the principality's priorities is to attract wealthy individuals from all over the world to acquire real estate and live and spend in the country, the government constantly uses its economic advantages to improve the quality of life and to combine work and leisure. Indeed, many of the world's rich buy property in Monaco to take advantage of Monaco's tax regime, although they seldom abide by the legal requirement to live 6 months of every year in the country, and often hire locals to maintain their

Exchange rates: Monaco

euros per US$1	
Jan 2001	1.0659
2000	1.0854
1999	0.9386
1998	5.8995
1997	5.8367
1996	5.1155

Note: Rates prior to 1999 are in French francs per US$.

SOURCE: CIA *World Factbook 2001* [ONLINE].

GDP per Capita (US$)

Country	1996	1997	1998	1999	2000
Monaco	25,000	N/A	N/A	27,000	N/A
United States	28,600	30,200	31,500	33,900	36,200
France	20,900	22,700	22,600	23,300	24,400
San Marino	N/A	20,000	N/A	N/A	32,000

Note: Data are estimates.

SOURCE: *Handbook of the Nations*, 17th, 18th, 19th and 20th editions for 1996, 1997, 1998 and 1999 data; CIA *World Factbook 2001* [Online] for 2000 data.

property instead. There are many large local private fortunes in the principality as well and extreme poverty is virtually non-existent. The number of jobs in the country (32,691 in 1999; 29,311 in the private sector) outnumbers its total population (31,693 in 2000), and the majority of the workers, particularly in the lower-paying jobs, commute daily from neighboring France and Italy. Their scale of pay and benefits are commensurable with the ones in France, and the French workforce is reckoned to be among the most privileged in the world.

WORKING CONDITIONS

Economic prosperity and the proportionally large number of jobs available, along with the government's sensitivity to safety and environmental protection, create favorable working conditions in the principality. The unemployment rate, compared to French and EU standards, is very low at 3.1 percent in 1998. No major labor unrest has been reported recently.

COUNTRY HISTORY AND ECONOMIC DEVELOPMENT

1215. Monaco is founded as a colony of the Italian trade and seafaring city, Genoa.

1297. The Grimmaldi family of Genoa and their supporters establish their rule over Monaco. A thriving economy based on trade develops.

1489. King Charles VIII of France recognizes the independence of Monaco.

1789–1814. During the French Revolution, Monaco is attached to the territory of the French Republic under the name of Fort Hercules. It becomes the chief town of the canton of Alpes-Maritimes.

1815. Monaco is made a protectorate of the Italian Kingdom of Sardinia.

1861. Monaco's sovereignty is recognized by a Franco-Monegasque Treaty.

1863. The Seabath Company is founded, which establishes a casino and several hotels in the quarter of the Spelugues, known as Monte-Carlo since 1866. Economic development is boosted in the late 19th century with a railroad link to France.

1911. Absolute monarchy gives way to the first constitution.

1918. A new treaty with France provides for limited French protection over Monaco. New agreements with France are signed in 1945, 1951, and 1963.

1962. Adoption of the current, more liberal constitution.

1993. Monaco joins the United Nations.

1999. Monaco and France both join the Euro Monetary Zone (EMZ).

FUTURE TRENDS

The Monegasque economy is closely related to that of the French, and therefore is dependent on the development trends of the EU. The liberalization of commerce, financial, and other services in the EU, the introduction of the single European currency, and the revolution in information technology will gradually increase competition, but the increasing wealth and dynamism of the EU economies will also boost demand for Monaco's unique services. Due to its size, the country is limited in its opportunities for extensive growth, but its strong ties to high-class tourism, services, and modern technology make it unlikely to endure any major negative changes in the near future. It is likely that the principality will preserve its sound economy, particularly in the areas of tourism, services, commerce, and modern manufacturing. The maintenance of its high living standards will continue to attract foreign companies, investment, and affluent tourists and residents in the foreseeable future.

DEPENDENCIES

Monaco has no territories or colonies.

BIBLIOGRAPHY

Global Investment Business Center, Inc. *Monaco: A Country Study Guide*. USA International Business Publications, February 2000.

U.S. Central Intelligence Agency. *World Factbook 2000*. <http://www.odci.gov/cia/publications/factbook/index.html>. Accessed January 2001.

U.S. Department of State. *Background Notes: Europe: Monaco*. <http://www.state.gov/www/background_notes/eurbgnhp.html>. Accessed January 2001.

—Valentin Hadjiyski

THE NETHERLANDS

Kingdom of the Netherlands
Koninkrijk der Nederlanden

CAPITAL: Amsterdam is the constitutional capital; the official seat of the government is The Hague.

MONETARY UNIT: Netherlands guilder (Dfl or Fl), also known as gulden or florin. One guilder equals 100 cents. Coins are in denominations of Dfl1, 2.5, and 5, and 5, 10, and 25 cents. Paper currency is in denominations of Dfl10, 25, 50, 100, 250, and 1,000. The euro, the currency of the European Union, replaced the guilder on 1 January 2002.

CHIEF EXPORTS: Machinery and equipment, chemicals, fuels, foodstuffs.

CHIEF IMPORTS: Machinery and transport equipment, chemicals, fuels, foodstuffs, clothing.

GROSS DOMESTIC PRODUCT: US$365.1 billion (purchasing power parity, 1999 est.).

BALANCE OF TRADE: **Exports:** US$169 billion (f.o.b., 1998 est.). **Imports:** US$152 billion (f.o.b., 1998 est.).

COUNTRY OVERVIEW

LOCATION AND SIZE. Once known as Holland, the Netherlands is located in Western Europe. It borders Belgium to the south, Germany to the east and north, and the North Sea along its western coast. The country has a total area of 41,526 square kilometers (16,485 square miles). This includes 33,889 square kilometers of land (13,084 square miles) and 7,643 square kilometers (2,950 square miles) of water. The coastline of the Netherlands is 451 kilometers (280 miles) long. Its land borders are 1,027 kilometers (638 miles) in length. The border with Germany is 577 kilometers (358 miles) long and that with Belgium is 450 kilometers (280 miles) long. The country is about the size of Maryland. The Netherlands is located at the crossroads of 3 of Europe's major rivers: the Rhine, the Meuse and the Schelde. The nation's 2 largest cities are Amsterdam, with a population of 1.1 million, and Rotterdam, also with 1.1 million people. Other major cities include The Hague (700,000 people) and Utrecht (554,000 people). Both the capital and the seat of government are located in the west-central region of the country, near the coast. The Netherlands still has 2 colonies, Aruba and the Netherlands Antilles (both are located in the Caribbean).

POPULATION. The population of the Netherlands was estimated to be 15,892,237 in July of 2000. In 2000, the nation's population growth rate was 0.57 percent. The birth rate was 12.12 births per 1,000 people. The fertility rate was 1.64 children born per woman, which is below the replacement level (this term refers to the number of children a couple must have to replace both parents, which is roughly 2 children). However, a large number of immigrants move to the Netherlands each year. Annually, there is an average of 2.3 new immigrants in the country for every 1,000 citizens. The mortality rate is 8.72 deaths per 1,000 people. The infant mortality rate is 4.42 deaths per 1,000 live births. Like many of the advanced industrialized nations, the population of the Netherlands is aging. The fastest growing segment of the population is the elderly. Those over the age of 65 make up 14 percent of the population, and this group is expected to double in size over the next 20 years. The average life expectancy for males in the Netherlands is 75.4 years and 81.28 years for females.

The majority of the people of the Netherlands are of Dutch ancestry (91 percent). The Dutch are primarily of Germanic and Gallo-Celtic origins. The remaining 9 percent of the population is split between people of Moroccan, Turkish, and Surinamese backgrounds. The society of the Netherlands is open, but in recent years there has been increasing anti-immigrant sentiment among some groups. During the 1990s, a number of new laws were passed which restricted **immigration**. The year 1998 was a peak time for political asylum seekers; some 45,217 political refugees settled in the Netherlands. Unemployment is higher among minority groups and some discrimination

exists in regard to housing, hiring, and wages. Incidents of police brutality in the 2 Dutch Caribbean colonies have led the national government to undertake a variety of reforms in the territories, including retraining of police and reforms of the prison systems.

Dutch is the official language of the nation, but English is also widely spoken. The population is highly educated and skilled. There is mandatory education through age 16 and the literacy rate is near 100 percent. The Netherlands has a relatively low rate of religious affiliation. Roman Catholics make up 34 percent of the people, Protestants 25 percent, and Muslims 3 percent. About 36 percent of the Dutch are unaffiliated with any formal religion.

The majority of people live in urban areas and the country is one of the most densely populated in the world. Its average population density is 369 per square kilometer (958 people per square mile). In comparison, the population density of Japan is 320 per square kilometer (830 per square mile), while that of the United States is 27 per square kilometer (70 per square mile). The most densely populated area of the country is known as the Randstad and includes the coastal regions of Amsterdam, Rotterdam, and Utrecht.

OVERVIEW OF ECONOMY

The Dutch have a long history as merchants and traders. From the 1600s through the 1700s, Dutch ships carried spices and other raw materials from India, Asia, and the West Indies to Europe and then carried manufactured products back to these areas. Dutch merchants were responsible for opening seaborne trade with China and Japan. Their success was based on the design of their ships which had large cargo holds and small crews. This reduced the costs of transporting goods. It was not until the late 1700s that the British displaced the Dutch as the world's main trading nation. Today that tradition continues as the nation remains dependent on foreign trade.

The Dutch economy is a private **free-market system**. The main impact of the government on the economy is through regulation and taxation. The Dutch have long been renowned as merchants and almost two-thirds of the economy is now based on foreign trade. Along with the United States, the country has consistently been one of the main proponents of international free trade and the reduction of **duties** and **tariffs** on goods and services. A member of the European Union (EU), the nation is set to replace its currency with the euro, a common currency that will be used by 11 of the 15 members of the EU. This process, known as European Monetary Union (EMU), is expected to expand the already large volume of trade between the EU member states and link the economies of these nations to a degree never seen before. The Dutch have been among the strongest supporters of EMU. The Netherlands is home to some of the world's largest corporations, including Royal Dutch Shell and Unilever. Despite its small size, the Netherlands ranks number-seven in the world in total value of its corporations.

The nation is in the midst of a long-term economic expansion that began in the 1990s. The Dutch economy grew at an average rate of 2.8 percent during the 1990s, while the rest of Europe averaged only 1.6 percent growth rates. In 2000, the kingdom's **gross domestic product** (GDP) per capita was US$25,695. The Netherlands ranks number 20 out of 191 nations in GDP and number 16 in **GDP per capita**. The Dutch workforce contains about 7 million people. The current economic expansion is based on increased foreign trade, consumer spending, and investment. By 2000, unemployment in the Netherlands was the lowest since the 1970s, and the nation's economy averaged over 4 percent growth per year. The economic growth of the past decade raised the GDP from US$299.4 billion in 1995 to US$365 billion in 1999. The success of the economy is the result of adjustments and transformations that Dutch businesses underwent in the late 1970s through the 1980s. The government cut its role in the economy by **privatizing** many public corporations, and a substantial number of Dutch companies began incorporating advanced technology and communications into their business practices. In doing so, the Dutch reformed their economy before most of their European neighbors and became far more competitive than those countries. The low level of unemployment and the rising economy have spurred **inflation**. In 2000, the kingdom's **inflation rate** was 2.6 percent and that figure is predicted to rise to 3.4 percent in 2001 (this is compared with the EU average rate of 1.6 percent).

Like many of the other industrialized European nations, the Dutch economy has been marked by the growth of the service sector and the relative decline of agriculture and industry as percentages of GDP. Despite the lessening importance of agriculture, the sector continues to be highly profitable. The modern Dutch agricultural industry is highly technological and sophisticated. Although it only employs about 4 percent of the workforce, agriculture produces enough food to feed the nation and provide a significant number of exports. The Netherlands is the world's number-three producer of agricultural goods.

Although industry has declined as a proportion of the overall economy, it remains a major factor in the Dutch economy. For centuries, the Dutch economy was based on maritime trade; however, shipping and fishing are now only minor components of trade. The main industries include chemical and metal processing. The nation is also one of the world's main producers of natural gas. The rise in global energy prices has produced high profits for Dutch energy companies. The energy company Royal Dutch Shell is the fifth-largest corporation in the world, worth US$191.3 billion in 1998, with operations throughout the globe. Other areas of industry include mining, food processing, and construction. The geographic location of the country, at the crossroads of Northern Europe, has allowed it to emerge as a major port of entry into the continent for goods and services. Many goods are shipped first to the Netherlands and then transported by land, air, or sea to other nations in Europe. Two of its ports, Rotterdam and Amsterdam, are among the busiest in the world.

Services dominate the economy and 73 percent of employees work in this sector. The primary services are transportation, the distribution of goods, and business services. There is also a strong financial sector that includes banking and insurance. The Dutch are major investors in foreign countries and foreign businesses (investment abroad is 3 times the level of foreign investment in the Netherlands). The Dutch have US$160 billion invested in other countries.

POLITICS, GOVERNMENT, AND TAXATION

The government of the Netherlands is a constitutional monarchy. The head of state is the monarch, presently Queen Beatrix, but the sovereign's powers are now mainly ceremonial. The chief of the government is the prime minister who is appointed by the queen. The prime minister is usually the leader of the majority party in the nation's parliament or the leader of the largest coalition of parties. The country also has an advisory committee, known as the Council of State, which develops and coordinates policy. Members of the council are appointed by the queen on the advice of the prime minister.

The legislative branch, or parliament, of the nation is known as the States General. The States General is a **bicameral** (2 chamber) legislative body. The 2 houses are called the First Chamber and the Second Chamber. The Second Chamber is the more influential of the 2 bodies. It initiates legislation and may amend bills that are developed by the Council of Ministers. The chamber has 150 members who are elected for 4-year terms by the general population. Unlike the American system, representatives are not elected to represent individual districts but the nation as a whole. During elections, the people do not vote for individual candidates but for a particular party. The election results are proportional so that a party that received 60 percent of the votes would have 60 percent of the seats in the Second Chamber. There are 75 members of the First Chamber. These representatives are elected by the legislatures of the nation's 12 regional governments, known as provinces.

Because of the proportional system of elections, even small parties are often able to have representation in the States General. Hence, unlike the United States, the government of the Netherlands is usually made up of a coalition of a number of small parties, and politics is not dominated by 2 major political parties. Since 1998, the government has been led by the "Purple Coalition" which is made up of 3 parties: Labor, Liberal, and Democrats '66. All of these parties support free enterprise **capitalism**, but the Labor Party and Democrats '66 tend to be more supportive of government efforts to establish social and economic equality by redistributing wealth through taxes on the wealthy and middle-class. The Liberal Party stresses individual political and economic freedom and is much more conservative on economic issues than its 2 coalition partners. The main party that opposes the coalition is the Christian Democratic Appeal or Christian Democrats. This party was initially formed from the merger of 3 religious parties and is generally one of the more conservative Dutch political groups. The party opposes most government involvement in the economy. The last major party is the Green Party which is pro-environment and advocates strict restrictions on pollution and economic activity which might harm the environment.

The government of the Netherlands does not play a major role in the nation's economy. It does not own a large number of businesses or attempt to control economic ventures. Furthermore, since the 1980s, there has been an ongoing program to turn those few government-controlled companies and businesses over to the **private sector**. An example of this would be increasing private control over telecommunications and public transport services. Public spending, including **infrastructure** projects, social spending, education, and health care amounted to 46 percent of the nation's GDP in 2000 and is expected to decline over the next decade. In 2000, the government announced tax reductions, including a cut in the **direct taxes** paid by most Dutch citizens.

The impact of the government is most significant on 3 different levels. First, there are numerous regulations and restrictions on economic activity which include the need to obtain permits for certain types of businesses and controls on product safety and advertising. Second, the government takes an active approach to managing the nation's credit supply and the value of its currency. Since the 1980s, the government has consistently pursued policies to keep inflation low. The government has also allowed the value of the currency to decline in an effort to make Dutch products less expensive and therefore more competitive in global markets. Third, and finally, the government takes an active role in managing the nation's environment. The centerpiece of Dutch environmental policy is the National Environmental Policy Plan known as the NMP. This plan seeks to cut pollution by 80 percent by 2010. Much of the nation is under sea level, and therefore prone to flooding, so the government also plays a major role in land management, including determining what types of structures can be built on different terrain.

In 1999, the government had revenues of US$163 billion and expenditures of US$170 billion, but in 2000 the government had a small surplus which equaled 0.5 percent of GDP. The government debt amounts to 63.7 percent of GDP. This is higher than the EU average of 60 percent of GDP, but the debt has declined from 67 percent of GDP in 1998.

One of the economic and foreign policy objectives of the Netherlands has been European economic and political integration. In the aftermath of World War II, the Dutch formed the Benelux Customs Union with Belgium and Luxembourg. This organization reduced tariffs between the 3 nations and set the stage for the later formation of the European Community, which itself later led to the establishment of the EU. The nation also helped develop the plans for EMU, which strives to fully integrate the economies of the EU, including replacing national currencies with the euro. Because of their experiences during World War II (when they were conquered by the Germans), the Dutch have supported political cooperation as a way to prevent new conflicts in Europe. Since the Netherlands is a small country, its government has found that the best way to achieve its foreign and economic policy goals is by cooperating with other nations in international organizations such as NATO, the EU, and the UN.

Each year the Dutch spend about US$6.9 billion on defense. The kingdom is a member of the North Atlantic Treaty Organization (NATO—a military alliance of several European nations plus the United States and Canada) and a staunch U.S. ally. For instance, Dutch military forces fought alongside American troops in both the Persian Gulf War and the military operations in Bosnia and Kosovo. The Dutch are among the world's leading providers of foreign aid. In 1999, they gave US$3.4 billion in aid, or about 1 percent of the nation's GDP. They have provided aid for victims of hurricanes in Central and South America and for refugees in places such as Africa, Bosnia, and East Timor. The Dutch are also supportive of international environmental programs.

INFRASTRUCTURE, POWER, AND COMMUNICATIONS

The Netherlands has an excellent infrastructure of ports, airports, and roadways. It also has a highly developed telecommunications system. Since the Netherlands is one of the main points of entry for goods imported into Europe, it is very important for the nation to maintain its transport system in order to move products into the interior of the continent. In order to improve the infrastructure, the government plans to launch a range of new projects over the next decade. A minimum of US$35 billion has already been budgeted to pay for a variety of projects including a high-speed rail link between Amsterdam and Brussels. There are also plans for a special rail system to connect Rotterdam and areas of Germany. Work is ongoing to improve the existing highway and rail network, and, by 2010, the government expects to spend an additional US$5.5 billion on these projects. Among these funds are US$2.4 billion to expand highways and US$500 million for improvements of regional roadways. The new work will concentrate on helping ease traffic congestion in the heavily urbanized areas of the west, including Amsterdam and Rotterdam. One of the main ongoing infrastructure projects in the Netherlands is the effort to prevent flooding. Over half of the country's territory is protected from flooding by an extensive system of dams and dikes.

In order to pay for current and future projects, the government established a special infrastructure fund. This fund is designed to provide supplemental money for infrastructure works without having too great an impact on the national budget. The fund is made up of proceeds from the sale of natural gas and any surplus tax funds. There are also plans to gain additional revenues by building toll roads and special pay lanes.

The nation has 125,757 kilometers (78,145 miles) of roads, 113,018 kilometers (70,229 miles) of which are paved. There are 2,235 kilometers (1,388 miles) of expressways that link the major cities and facilitate transportation from the coast across the country. All of the major Dutch cities have widespread and inexpensive public transportation systems. The high degree of urbanization has also led many Dutch cities to build comprehensive bicycle pathways that allow people to bike instead of using cars or other vehicles. Still, 79 percent of the Dutch use their personal cars for transportation.

The nation has 2,739 kilometers (1,702 miles) of railways. Transportation is also aided by an extensive network of waterways and canals. In total, there are 5,046 kilometers (3,135 miles) of waterways in the country, and 47 percent of these are usable by watercraft of 1,000 tons or larger. The main Dutch ports are Amsterdam, Dordecht, Groningen, Haarlem, Maastricht, Rotterdam, and Utrecht. Rotterdam is the world's largest seaport and handles more tonnage than any other harbor. Some 70 percent of all imports that go into the Netherlands come through Rotterdam. In 1996, the port set a record of 293.4

Communications

Country	Newspapers	Radios	TV Sets[a]	Cable subscribers[a]	Mobile Phones[a]	Fax Machines[a]	Personal Computers[a]	Internet Hosts[b]	Internet Users[b]
	1996	1997	1998	1998	1998	1998	1998	1999	1999
Netherlands	306	978	543	378.3	213	38.4	317.6	403.49	3,000
United States	215	2,146	847	244.3	256	78.4	458.6	1,508.77	74,100
Germany	311	948	580	214.5	170	73.1	304.7	173.96	14,400
Belgium	160	793	510	367.3	173	18.7	286.0	266.90	1,400

[a]Data are from International Telecommunication Union, *World Telecommunication Development Report 1999* and are per 1,000 people.
[b]Data are from the Internet Software Consortium (http://www.isc.org) and are per 10,000 people.

SOURCE: World Bank. *World Development Indicators 2000.*

billion tons of goods received. Because of a trench that extends into the North Sea, supertankers and other large ships with capacities of up to 350,000 tons can access the port. The Dutch merchant marine includes 563 ships of at least 1,000 tons. These ships range from cargo and petroleum tankers to passenger cruise ships. There are 28 airports in the Netherlands, 19 of which are paved. Amsterdam Airport is Europe's fifth busiest airport. The country also has 1 heliport. The kingdom's main airline, KLM Royal Dutch Airlines, is one of the largest in the world and has partnership agreements with a number of other international air carriers.

In order to provide energy resources throughout the country, the Netherlands has a well-developed pipeline system. There are 418 kilometers (260 miles) of crude oil pipelines, 965 kilometers (600 miles) of pipelines for other petroleum products, and an overwhelming 10,230 kilometers (6,356 miles) of natural gas pipelines. In 1998, the nation produced 88.7 billion kilowatt hours (kWh) of electrical power. Some 400 million kWh of electricity were exported that year, but since the nation consumed 94.3 billion kWh of power, it had to import 12.2 billion kWh of electricity. Over 91 percent of electricity is produced by fossil fuels, while atomic energy provides 4 percent. Hydroelectric plants and solar energy provide most of the rest of the nation's energy needs. The kingdom is dependent on imports of oil and coal. However, the nation is a net exporter of natural gas, and it has extensive oil and natural gas fields in the North Sea. The government is highly supportive of efforts to develop solar energy resources. By 2020, the government plans to have solar energy account for 10 percent of energy consumption (this would supply the energy needs of 400,000 homes). In theory, the Netherlands could supply all of its energy needs through solar power. It would need 800 square kilometers (308 square miles) of surface for solar panels. This area is already available on the roof surfaces of houses and buildings.

The nation's telecommunications system is also highly developed. The government began privatizing the telecommunications industry in 1989. By 1997, service for all fixed line telephones was privatized. The country has 5 underwater cables for transatlantic communications and 3 earth stations which receive satellite transmissions. The nation maintains 2 communications satellites. There is a program underway to replace the existing communications cables with fiber-optic cable. Over 90 percent of homes in the Netherlands are serviced by cable television systems. Concurrently, there have been dramatic increases in the use of mobile phones. By 2000, there were 6.8 million mobile phones in use. The Dutch are among the first people in Europe to begin using the third-generation mobile communications systems which allow mobile phone users access to high-speed data (such as e-mail and the Internet) and video communications via their phone. In 1999, there were 70 Internet service providers in the Netherlands.

ECONOMIC SECTORS

The Dutch economy is dependent on foreign trade. Like most developed nations, during the second half of the 20th century the Dutch economy underwent a transformation in which agriculture and industry declined in importance while services came to dominate the economic activity. Nonetheless, the nation's fertile soil and deposits of natural gas and oil mean that both agriculture and industry remain competitive with similar sectors in other nations.

Agriculture and fishing are highly profitable even though they account only for a small percentage of employment and of the nation's GDP. Since the 1940s, Dutch agriculture has become highly mechanized and technologically sophisticated. Dutch farmers use the latest technology to maximize crop yields and livestock production. Techniques such as scientific soil analysis and increased use of fertilizers and pesticides have been largely responsible for doubling crop yields during the century. Crops and livestock provide both exports and products which fuel the nation's domestic food-processing industries. Despite the small size of the country, the Netherlands is the world's third-largest exporter of agricultural products.

The main industries in the Netherlands are **agribusiness**, metal and engineering products, electrical machinery and equipment, chemicals, petroleum, construction, and microelectronics. The Dutch have significant oil and natural gas fields in the North Sea. This forms the basis for the nation's large energy industry. With such re-

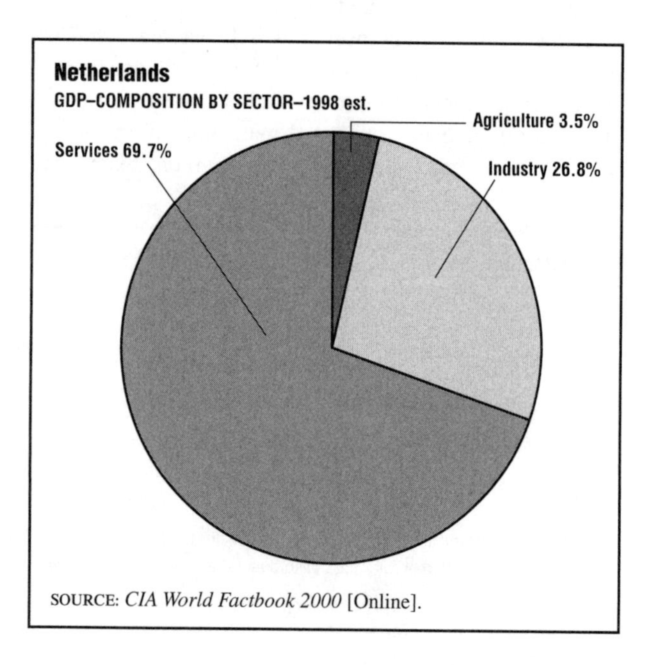

SOURCE: *CIA World Factbook 2000* [Online].

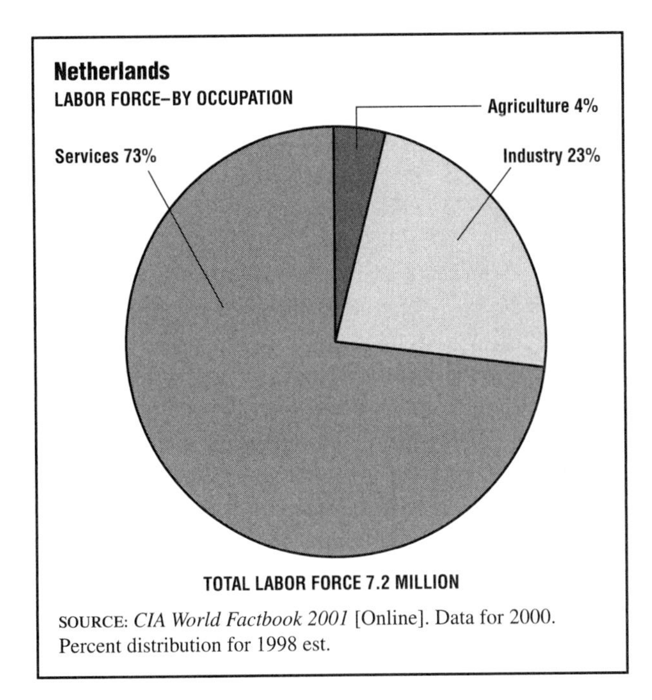

SOURCE: *CIA World Factbook 2001* [Online]. Data for 2000. Percent distribution for 1998 est.

sources, companies such as Royal Dutch Shell have gained markets around the globe. Most of the kingdom's energy resources are exported to EU countries. Other major industrial employers include the Dutch State Mines and the Royal Netherlands Blast Furnaces and Steelworks (both of which are partially-owned by the government). Construction accounts for about 6 percent of GDP and is partially propelled by government spending on infrastructure projects.

Services dominate the Dutch economy. The main segments of the service sector are transportation, goods distribution, financial services, and tourism. One of the areas of greatest growth, however, is telecommunications, especially personal communications services. Computer services are also experiencing dramatic growth. Small companies which specialize in various types of service have done the best in the nation's economy over the past decade, but there is increasing consolidation in some areas of the service sector as large corporations buy or merge with the more profitable firms.

AGRICULTURE

In 1998, agriculture accounted for 3.5 percent of the kingdom's GDP. Employment in agriculture has actually been increasing slightly over the past decade. In 1995, there were 109,000 people employed in the sector, but by 1999 that number had grown to 116,000. Much of this increase has been the result of growth in the dairy and horticulture segments of agriculture. As in many other countries, Dutch agriculture has been marked by the decline of the small, family-owned farm and the rise of large corporations that specialize in agriculture. Many Dutch agricultural firms have also become increasingly international and do a significant amount of their business overseas or in other European nations.

Dutch agriculture is divided into 3 broad areas: crop production, dairy and livestock production, and horticulture. The nation's agricultural land is also divided into 3 broad types: grasslands, farmlands, and horticultural lands. The nation's extensive waterways and network of dams and dikes allow for easy irrigation and have produced very fertile soils. On the other hand, the increased use of chemicals in agriculture has created environmental pressures and led to new ecological policies that are designed to reduce damage to the kingdom's environment. Partially because of pollution concerns and partially because of health considerations, the consumption of organic foods (crops and livestock that are raised without chemical fertilizers or pesticides) has increased. While these foods now account for 2 percent of total production, by 2010 they are expected to comprise 5–10 percent of total production.

The main food crops are barley, corn, potatoes, sugar beets, and wheat. Potatoes are the main crop by volume, and in 1999 Dutch farmers produced 8.2 million metric tons of the crop. That same year, the Dutch harvested 5.5 million metric tons of sugar beets, 1 million metric tons of wheat, 240,000 metric tons of barley, and 58,000 metric tons of corn. Despite its wheat and barley production, the nation is a major importer of wheat for animal fodder and cereal production. After suffering a significant drop in production in 1998 because of flooding and bad weather, agricultural harvests were up 23.9 percent in 1999. In 1998, the value of exports was US$18.7 billion, while in 1999 it was US$31.7 billion. The major agricultural processed product was cigarettes. The Netherlands is one of the least forested countries in the world. Over 90 percent of its forest products have to be imported.

Dairy and livestock production is highly specialized and technologically sophisticated. Extensive grasslands provide grazing for dairy cows and beef. Dutch farmers have some of the highest yields of beef and milk in the world (behind only the United States and Great Britain). The nation is self-sufficient in dairy production and most dairy goods are exported. The main dairy exports include butter, cheese, and condensed milk. The number of dairy cows has remained relatively constant in the kingdom. In 1994, there were 1.69 million dairy cows and in 1998 there were 1.61 million. In 1997, the nation produced 11 billion kiloliters of milk, about half of which was used to produce cheese.

Many of the small, independent Dutch dairy farms have been bought by large corporations. One of the largest dairy corporations in the Netherlands is Campina Melkunie. In 1999 this large, multinational company did only

36 percent of its US$5 billion business in the Netherlands, with the rest centered in various EU nations. The Dutch food and beverage company Unilever is one of the world's largest corporations. The Dutch also have a large brewing industry. Firms such as Heineken and Grolsch export beer around the world and have operations in 170 nations.

Besides dairy cows, the other main types of livestock are beef and veal, chicken, duck, lamb, pork, and turkey. Eggs and beef are the main livestock exports. Total livestock numbers have declined slightly over the past few years. For instance, in 1994 there were 7.7 million head of cattle, but by 1998 that number had declined to 4.3 million. Likewise, there has been a similar decline in the number of pigs. In 1994 there were 14.56 million pigs; however, by 1998 that number had fallen to 13.45 million.

Seafood consumption has risen substantially in the Netherlands over the past 2 decades. Dutch fishermen harvest some 407,000 metric tons of seafood each year. About half of this is consumed locally and the rest exported. The Dutch also import significant amounts of seafood, including squid, prawns, shrimp, and crab.

Horticulture, especially the growing of ornamental plants and flowers, is a major factor in Dutch agriculture. The Dutch export significant amounts of cut flowers and bulbs, and the nation is world-renowned for its tulips. About 75 percent of flowers are exported, and there has been dramatic growth in exports to the United Kingdom, Italy, and Russia. This amounts to some 9 billion flowers per year. Horticulture is conducted in both open fields and through the use of glass greenhouses. The Netherlands now contains over half of all of the greenhouses in Europe, and there is a total of 44,000 acres of flowers under cultivation. Over 3,000 companies are engaged in horticulture in the kingdom.

INDUSTRY

Although it has declined as a percentage of the nation's GDP, industry remains a viable component of the Dutch economy, contributing 26.8 percent to GDP in 1998. Dutch industry is diversified and includes a variety of businesses that range from manufacturing, mining, and energy production to construction and chemical manufacturing. The government has undertaken a variety of programs to encourage the development of new industries in the kingdom and to bring industry to areas of the country that are economically depressed. Specifically, the government has encouraged growth in the aerospace industry, biotechnology, and microelectronics.

MANUFACTURING AND CONSTRUCTION. The Dutch manufacturing sector is dominated by the production of chemicals and pharmaceuticals, metals and electronics, food processing, and tobacco. Over the past decade, the chemical industry has declined slightly (by 2 percent), while metals and electronics and food processing has expanded by 8–10 percent. In 1999, total manufacturing in the kingdom grew by 9 percent. In 1998, there were 847,591 people employed in manufacturing. The largest number, 144,645, were employed in food and tobacco processing. The number-two industry in terms of employment was metal processing with 99,753 workers, and the number-three field was machinery manufacturing with 89,688 employees.

Electronics manufacturing in the Netherlands is dominated by the **multinational corporation** Philips. The company makes lighting, consumer electronics, appliances, semiconductors, and communications systems. Philips is the ninth-largest manufacturer of semiconductors in the world. Of the 100,000 people employed in the Netherlands in the electronics field, Philips employs 44,000. Worldwide, Philips employs 265,000 people. Other major Dutch electronics firms include ASML, CMG, and Origin. The largest computer chip factory in Europe is in the Netherlands.

The most dramatic declines in employment and output were in the textile manufacturing sector and in shipbuilding and repair. Many of the manufacturing industries are based on the processing of raw materials or semi-finished materials into finished products. In other words, companies in the Netherlands import materials such as metal or chemicals and turn these items into products that consumers can use such as car parts or cleaning chemicals.

The Dutch chemical industry produces a variety of goods including synthetic rubber, plastic **consumer goods**, and polyester yarns for industrial purposes. Major Dutch chemical companies include Shell, Akzo Nobel, and DSM. Shell and Akzo Nobel are the eleventh- and twelfth-largest chemical companies in the world. DSM produces 70 percent of the polymers and rubber that the European automobile industry uses to produce new cars. Meanwhile, Dutch pharmaceutical companies have an annual output of about US$4 billion.

Ship building and repair continue to be significant factors in the Dutch economy. However, competition from countries where workers are paid less has caused drastic cutbacks in the field which is only about one-half the size it was previously. Still, the Netherlands is the world's seventh-largest producer of ships and the fourth-largest in Europe. Ship building and repair employ about 10,000 workers and are concentrated in the large ports on the western coast. The industry had revenues of US$1.66 billion in 2000, most of which were from ship building. In 2000, Dutch ship builders received orders for 88 new vessels and 45 percent of these orders were from foreign firms.

Over the past 30 years, construction has had a major impact on the Dutch economy. Because the nation is so small in geographic size and has a high population density, real estate is very valuable in the kingdom. On several occasions this has led to a bubble (a rapid increase in value that is unsustainable over many years) in the housing market. The collapse (or bursting) of the housing bubble in the 1970s led to a widespread economic **recession**. During this recession, real estate prices declined by 45 percent by 1982. Nonetheless, the construction field is aided by government spending on infrastructure projects. In 1999, there were 31,459 construction companies and 416,000 people employed in the field. During the 1990s, the sector averaged 2 percent growth per year.

MINING AND MINERAL EXTRACTION. Although there was once a vibrant coal mining industry in the Netherlands, the discovery of oil and natural gas led to the demise of the coal companies during the 1970s. By the 1990s, the only mining operations left in the kingdom were small companies that extracted salt, peat, and some sand and gravel for construction uses. In 1998, there were only about 9,000 people employed in mining. All metal ore used in manufacturing or other industries has to be imported.

The Dutch do produce a limited amount of oil. However, oil production peaked in 1986 at 66,500 barrels of oil per day. Since that time, production has declined to an average of about 60,000 barrels per day. Many of the kingdom's former oilfields in the North Sea are now in the process of being decommissioned. Energy production employed about 6,670 people in 1998, but produced considerable profits for the nation.

On the other hand, the kingdom is Western Europe's number-one supplier of natural gas. In 1958, the Geneva Convention on the Law of the Sea gave the kingdom the rights to a 56,980 square kilometer (22,000 square mile) area in the North Sea. This region contains the kingdom's main reserves of natural gas and is actually larger than the country itself. The main company in the sector is the Netherlands Natural Gas Company which is owned by Dutch and American energy firms and by the Dutch government. About half the natural gas produced is used within the country, with the rest exported to EU nations. The main export destinations are Germany, Belgium, France, Switzerland, and Italy. In 1999, the total natural gas production of the kingdom was 80 billion cubic meters. The proven reserves of natural gas exceed 2 trillion cubic meters. Government revenues from natural gas were US$1.2 billion in 2000.

SERVICES

The services sector of the economy has experienced the greatest level of growth among the major Dutch businesses over the past 2 decades. Services now account for 69.7 percent of GDP according to a 1998 estimate. The most prominent fields within the service sector are banking and financial services, telecommunications, **retail**, and tourism.

BANKING AND FINANCIAL SERVICES. The banking and financial sectors of the Dutch economy have increasingly come to be dominated by large firms. In order to compete with international banks, companies have had to merge so as to reduce costs and maximize efficiency. The 2 largest banks in the country—the General Netherlands Bank and the Amsterdam-Rotterdam Bank—merged in 1990 to become ABN Amro. ABN Amro is now one of Europe's largest banks. Recently, Postbank and the Netherlands Traders' Bank merged to create the kingdom's second-largest bank. In 1998, the Dutch insurance company Fortis merged with the large Belgian firm De Generale Bank. Financial services account for about 7.2 percent of the service sector. Other business services account for 10.5 percent of the sector.

In 1999 the banking sector of the Dutch economy was worth 1.33 trillion euros. The nation's banking sector employed 120,000 people in the Netherlands and 220,000 people worldwide. There are 115 banks in the nation. This number includes all major credit-granting institutions and foreign-owned banks. In 1999 there were 6,121 bank branches in the Netherlands, and Dutch banks had an additional 2,575 branches abroad. However, 3 large banks—ABN Amro, Rabobank and ING Bank—account for about 75 percent of lending in the kingdom.

TELECOMMUNICATIONS. In 1999, the telecommunications market in the Netherlands amounted to US$10.3 billion. Over the next 5 years, the sector is expected to grow by 5–10 percent per year. About 85 percent of the market is based on telecommunications services, and the remaining 15 percent is equipment. In 1989, the government passed legislation which privatized telecommunications services. Nonetheless, the former state-owned telecommunications company KPN Telecom continues to dominate the sector. For instance, in the field of mobile phones, KPN Telecom controls 52 percent of the market. The next largest company, Libertel, controls 32 percent, and the third-largest firm, Telfort, controls 7 percent. The government is in the process of auctioning licenses for the next generation of mobile equipment. Despite the dominance of KPN Telecom, international corporations have gained an increasing share of the telephone market. Among the major international companies that are now in the Dutch market are MCI WorldCom, Global One, and Esprit Telecom.

A growing segment of the telecommunications sector is information technology or IT (computer-based information systems and communications). In 1999, the IT market in the Netherlands was worth US$11 billion. This represented a growth rate of 15 percent from the previous year. Over the next few years, forecasts predict that the field will continue to expand at a rate of 15 to 20 percent per year. The 2 largest Dutch IT firms are Baan and Exact. The government has attempted to promote the establishment of new IT companies under a program known as "Twinning." This program provides government funds for housing, business start-up, and financial advice. Despite this and similar programs, more than 60 percent of IT products and services are imported. The United States is the main supplier of IT goods and services to the kingdom. With more than 3 million Internet users, the Dutch have the highest rate of Internet usage per person in Europe. By 2002, there will be 7.5 million Dutch Internet users. **E-commerce** (the use of the Internet to purchase goods) was worth US$325 million in 1998, but this figure grew to US$1.1 billion in 1999, and is expected to be worth US$11.5 billion by 2002. Experts rank the Netherlands as being 12–18 months behind the United States in Internet usage and e-commerce.

RETAIL. The Dutch retail sector is highly developed and diversified. In many ways it is similar to that of the United States. Supermarkets comprise 68 percent of grocery stores, while specialty stores make up 22 percent and the remainder includes food stores, local farmers' markets, department stores, and convenience stores. The Netherlands has about 12,600 clothing stores with combined sales in 1999 of US$5.3 billion. Over 60 percent of these are small retail units, and the rest are department stores or chain outlets. Employment in retail and clothing stores is 61,010. Nonetheless, as in the United States, there has been a steady trend toward larger retail units and a decline in small specialty stores.

TOURISM. In 1999, the Dutch spent US$10 billion on tourism, but US$8 billion of this was spent outside of the country. The Dutch tend to travel extensively, and 4 out of 5 have traveled on vacation at some point in their lives. In 1999, there were 30.5 million overnight vacation trips, of which 16.3 million were within the Netherlands. Tourism accounts for 5 percent of all employment in the Netherlands and includes 45,000 companies. Over 95 percent of these companies have fewer than 10 employees. In 2000, tourism was one of the 4 fastest-growing sectors of the Dutch economy, and by 2010 there will be an additional 5,000 hotel rooms built. Within tourism, short trips (those of 2 to 4 days) are becoming the most popular form of vacation. The United States is the most popular destination for Dutch tourists and accounts for about 25 percent of the total overseas tourism market. The most popular destinations for Dutch tourists are New York, Los Angeles, San Francisco, and Miami. Of those who visit tourist destinations in the Netherlands, 52 percent are Dutch and 48 percent are foreign. Germans are the main tourist group to visit the kingdom, followed by the British.

INTERNATIONAL TRADE

Almost 160 million people live within a 300-mile radius of Rotterdam. This includes more than half of the population of the EU. As a result, the Netherlands is perfectly positioned as a gateway for goods being imported into the EU. In addition, Dutch goods are easily exported throughout the region. In all, 80 percent of Dutch exports go to other nations within the EU and 70 percent of goods imported into the Netherlands come from the EU. Asia accounts for only 17 percent of the nation's exports and 7 percent of its imports. The largest individual destination for Dutch goods is Germany at 27 percent, followed by Belgium-Luxembourg at 13 percent, France at 11 percent, the United Kingdom at 10 percent, and Italy at 6 percent. Imports are divided between Germany with 20 percent of the total, Belgium-Luxembourg with 11 percent, the United Kingdom with 10 percent, the United States with 9 percent, and France with 7 percent. The Dutch are the ninth-largest trading partner with the United States and the third-largest in Europe. The United States has its largest **trade surplus** with the Netherlands, averaging US$10 billion per year.

The Netherlands leads its EU partners in issues such as trade **liberalization** and the privatization of key industries such as telecommunications and transportation. Thus, it is in a good position to continue its trade surplus. In 1999, its trade surplus in both goods and services amounted to US$18 billion. This represented a 6 percent growth rate over the previous year and accounted for 6 percent of the kingdom's GDP. Dutch exports are concentrated in products that tend to do well even during periods of recession. These exports include food and agricultural products and energy resources.

In 1998, the Dutch exported US$169 billion worth of goods and services and imported US$152 billion. This represented a 5 percent increase in exports over the previous year and continued a trend of positive growth in exports which extends back into the 1980s. Services were the fastest growing exports and increased 6.9 percent in 1998, while the export of manufactured goods increased by 3 percent.

Trade (expressed in billions of US$): Netherlands

	Exports	Imports
1975	39.939	40.854
1980	85.046	88.392
1985	78.008	73.268
1990	131.775	126.098
1995	196.276	176.874
1998	199.624	185.104

SOURCE: International Monetary Fund. *International Financial Statistics Yearbook 1999.*

Because of the importance of trade and the impact of foreign sales on the Dutch economy, the government is a staunch supporter of global free trade. The Netherlands has worked closely with the United States to open markets around the world and reduce tariffs and other impediments to international commerce. The country works through international organizations such as the World Trade Organization (WTO) and the International Monetary Fund (IMF).

The main international organization which has aided the Dutch economy has been the European Community, now known as the EU. Before the formation of this regional organization, about 40 percent of Dutch trade exports went to the nations of Europe. However, exports to Europe now account for about 80 percent of Dutch exports. The Netherlands was one of the founding members of the organization and has consistently supported increased economic integration among its members, including the establishment of a common currency, the euro. Because the use of the euro will reduce transaction costs between countries by eliminating differences in currency **exchange rates**, the implementation of the euro is expected to add US$3.5 billion in new business to the Dutch economy. It is also expected to increase foreign investment in the Netherlands by US$2.5 billion.

Since the end of the Cold War and the opening of Central and Eastern Europe to free-market capitalism, the Dutch have aggressively sought to gain access to the **emerging markets** in countries such as Poland, Hungary, and the Czech Republic. They have also supported international efforts to reform the economies in the region in order to facilitate increased trade, and they support EU expansion to bring countries in the area into the trade organization.

The geographic location of the Netherlands and its highly skilled and productive workforce has attracted numerous international companies. By 2000, there were 6,400 foreign businesses with operations in the kingdom. These companies employed 357,000 Dutch workers. In order to encourage new investment and attract foreign companies, the Dutch government established the Foreign Investment Agency. This agency has overseen the implementation of 85 different projects with a combined value of US$531 million. These projects also resulted in 5,000 new jobs. The Dutch government offers grants of up to 20 percent of the start-up costs of new companies. The bulk of foreign investment in the Netherlands is from the United States (in 2000 the U.S. accounted for 80 percent of new investment). Total American investment in the kingdom is US$106 billion. The majority of U.S. investments were in financial services and real estate. The Netherlands is the third largest recipient of U.S. investment in the world.

MONEY

The Dutch guilder or florin has fallen in value in relation to the U.S. dollar and other major European currencies. In 1995, 1 U.S. dollar was equal to 1.6057 guilders; however, in 1999, one U.S. dollar equaled 1.8904 guilders. The weakness of the Dutch currency has actually helped the nation's economy since it has made Dutch products cheaper and therefore more marketable. In 1999, the kingdom was one of the founding members of EMU. EMU created a single currency, the euro, for the EU nations which replaced national currencies in 2002. The euro is fixed at a rate of 2.20371 guilders per euro. Since its introduction, the euro has been weak against the U.S. dollar. In 2000, 1 U.S. dollar equaled 0.9867 euros (when the euro was introduced it was equal to US$1.1789). The low value of the euro is expected to continue to help Dutch exports when the nation adopts the currency.

Banks in the Netherlands manage the transfer of funds and securities and handle savings and checking accounts. They also assist companies in stock offerings. The banking system is overseen by the government-owned Dutch national bank, De Nederlandsche Bank, or DNB. The bank also oversees **monetary policy**. As a member of the European System of Central Banks, DNB coordinates with other European national banks on issues of monetary policy and national economies, as well as the implementation of EMU. Foreign-owned banks are allowed to operate in the kingdom according to the same rules and regulations as Dutch banks.

In 2002, the Amsterdam Stock Exchange will celebrate its birthday as the world's oldest stock market. The exchange has developed close ties with stock markets in Belgium and Luxembourg, and almost half of the investments in the Amsterdam Exchange come from foreign investors. The Amsterdam Exchange lists 972 different companies or investment institutions, of which 604 are Dutch and the rest foreign-owned. In 1999, the total value of the exchange was 1.497 trillion euros.

Exchange rates: Netherlands

euros per US$1	
Jan 2001	1.0659
2000	1.0854
1999	0.9386
1998	1.9837
1997	1.9513
1996	1.6859

Note: Rates prior to 1999 are in Netherlands guilders per US$.

SOURCE: CIA *World Factbook 2001* [ONLINE].

POVERTY AND WEALTH

Like most of the West European nations, the Dutch have a high standard of living. In 2000, the nation's GDP per capita was US$25,695. According to the United Nations *Human Development Report 2000,* the Netherlands ranks number-eight in the world in human development, ahead of nations such as Japan and the United Kingdom, but behind countries such as the Canada, Norway, and the United States. This report measures such features as income, literacy, and life span.

The wealthiest 10 percent of the population control 24.7 percent of the kingdom's wealth while the poorest 10 percent only control 2.9 percent. There are also regional differences in wealth and standard of living. People who live in the southern and western regions of the country tend to have higher incomes as the higher-paying industrial and new technology companies are concentrated in these regions. The northern area of the kingdom is the most rural and least prosperous area of the Netherlands.

While unemployment is low in the Netherlands, at 3.5 percent, as many as 100,000 people have simply dropped out of the **labor force**. The nation has generous social benefits and this has prevented the widespread expansion of poverty. The Dutch national drug policy continues to have an impact on poverty. The Dutch government differentiates between "hard" drugs, such as heroin or cocaine, and "soft" drugs such as marijuana. The sale and use of small quantities of soft drugs is legal, under certain guidelines. However, the use of hard drugs has risen over the past 2 decades. The government now spends about US$150 million per year on rehabilitation programs for the estimated 28,000 hard drug users in the kingdom (most of whom are unemployed and live below the nation's poverty line).

The poverty rate in the Netherlands is 4.7 percent of families. This gives the nation one of the lowest poverty rates in Europe, second only to nations such as Sweden, and well ahead of countries such as the United Kingdom, Germany, France, and the United States. However, the main reason for this low rate is generous social payments. If government aid is excluded, the poverty rate in the Netherlands rises to 18.9 percent. The highest rates of poverty are among individuals, but single-parent households account for almost 75 percent of all poor families.

GDP per Capita (US$)

Country	1975	1980	1985	1990	1998
Netherlands	18,584	20,443	21,256	24,009	28,154
United States	19,364	21,529	23,200	25,363	29,683
Germany	N/A	N/A	N/A	N/A	31,141
Belgium	18,620	21,653	22,417	25,744	28,790

SOURCE: United Nations. *Human Development Report 2000; Trends in human development and per capita income.*

Distribution of Income or Consumption by Percentage Share: Netherlands

Lowest 10%	2.8
Lowest 20%	7.3
Second 20%	12.7
Third 20%	17.2
Fourth 20%	22.8
Highest 20%	40.1
Highest 10%	25.1

Survey year: 1994

Note: This information refers to income shares by percentiles of the population and is ranked by per capita income.

SOURCE: *2000 World Development Indicators* [CD-ROM].

WORKING CONDITIONS

In 1999, the Dutch labor force numbered 7.13 million. Of this total, 4.02 million were men and 3.11 million were women. Full-time workers numbered 4.12 million, while part-time employees numbered 3.01 million. The large number of part-time workers reflects the growth of the service sector as many jobs in this segment of the economy are part-time. This is especially true of retail workers. Of the total number of employees, 805,000 had seasonal or temporary jobs. The nation had an unemployment rate of 3.5 percent in 1999. However, this figure does not truly represent those out of work in the kingdom, since an estimated 50,000 to 100,000 former or potential workers have simply dropped out of the labor force and decided to rely on the Netherlands' generous social benefits rather than try to find employment.

Dutch workers have the constitutional right to join unions. This includes all workers, even members of the military, police, and civil service. Although only about 28 percent of the workforce are active members of unions, collective bargaining agreements cover 75 percent of workers. Currently, union membership among professional workers is expanding. Organized strikes are rare in the country, and labor relations are generally regarded as harmonious. Discrimination against union members is illegal. Several major unions are presently undertaking widespread efforts to reduce the national work week to 36 hours.

Unions and private employers negotiate work contracts, known as social partnerships, which establish wage levels and benefits for workers and production targets for the companies. These contracts are renegotiated in the fall of every year and cover all workers, even those who do not belong to the union. Worker relations and union issues are

Household Consumption in PPP Terms

Country	All food	Clothing and footwear	Fuel and power[a]	Health care[b]	Education[b]	Transport & Communications	Other
Netherlands	17	7	7	2	13	8	46
United States	13	9	9	4	6	8	51
Germany	14	6	7	2	10	7	53
Belgium	17	6	8	3	1	7	57

Data represent percentage of consumption in PPP terms.
[a]Excludes energy used for transport.
[b]Includes government and private expenditures.

SOURCE: World Bank. *World Development Indicators 2000.*

overseen by the national Social and Economic Council which also advises the government on labor matters. As in many other nations, there are disparities between male and female workers in terms of hiring, salary, and promotions. Although gender discrimination is forbidden by law, women continue to earn less than their male counterparts in similar occupations. In 1999, women on average made only about 75 percent of what men earned in equal jobs.

Child labor is forbidden by law, but each year there are minor violations, especially around the Christmas holidays when children are often employed for holiday-related work. The minimum age for a person to begin work is 16 years old. But at 16, people may work only 8 hours per week. Anyone under the age of 18 may not work at night or work overtime. They are also prevented from working in hazardous occupations. Full-time employment for those 18 years old or younger is dependent upon their completion of 10 years of mandatory education. All employees must be given a 30-minute break after they complete 4.5 hours of work.

The nation's minimum wage can be changed every 6 months to adjust for inflation. However, only about 3 percent of workers earn the minimum wage, since most workers are covered by union-employer contracts. The minimum wage is US$1,172 per month. Those employees who earn minimum wage receive social security benefits and medical insurance which is paid for by the employer. These costs work out to approximately US$3,750 per worker. Employees under the age of 23 receive a percentage of the national minimum wage. This percentage ranges from 34.5 percent of the adult minimum wage for workers who are 16 years old to 85 percent of the wage for workers who are 22 years old. Labor costs in the kingdom have risen slower than inflation. In 1999 average wages rose by 2.5 percent which was only slightly higher than the inflation rate of 2.1 percent. In addition, advances in productivity offset wage increases as Dutch workers produced more goods per hour than they had the year before. This helped businesses maintain their profits and prevented an acceleration of inflation.

Under the law, the national work week is 40 hours. However, social partnership contracts have reduced the average work week for most employees to 37.5 hours per week. In addition, an increasing number of employees work non-traditional schedules. Telecommuting (working from home, using a computer or other equipment) is growing in popularity. Worker safety and working conditions are overseen by the Labor Commission. Under Dutch law, employees may refuse to work in hazardous occupations if they feel their safety is in jeopardy.

COUNTRY HISTORY AND ECONOMIC DEVELOPMENT

300 B.C. Germanic and Celtic tribes settle in the region that is now the Netherlands.

1018. Dirk III, Count of Holland, is the first to use the name Holland in his title.

1205. Amsterdam is founded.

1323. Holland gains control of Zeeland from Flanders.

1428. Holland is conquered by the Burgundians of France.

1477. The Hapsburgs gain control of Holland.

1515. Charles I incorporates Holland into the Holy Roman Empire.

1555–79. Charles I turns Holland over to his son Phillip II, King of Spain. The Dutch rise in revolt against the Catholic Spanish as Protestantism spreads throughout the region.

1581. The next 200 years is considered to be the "Golden Age" of Holland as trade flourishes and the country becomes one of the most prosperous and wealthy nations in the world. This prosperity is based on the nation's merchant fleet which transports goods around the globe.

1602. The Dutch East India Company is founded to expand trade with India and Asia. An early stock market is established.

1609. A bank is established in Amsterdam to exchange currency and to provide a safe place to deposit money.

1621. The Dutch West India Company is established to trade with North and South America. The nation again goes to war with Spain (1621–48).

1625. New Amsterdam is founded on Manhattan by the Dutch West India Company.

1648. Trade increasingly shifts away from Antwerp and Ghent to Amsterdam.

1795. The Netherlands is conquered by the French. The French establish the Batavian Republic and initiate a period of governmental and economic reforms.

1806. Louis Bonaparte is made king of Holland by his brother Napoleon Bonaparte.

1806–13. Napoleon attempts to make Holland the central economic power of the "Continental System" which was designed to cut off trade with Great Britain.

1814. After liberation from the French, the country becomes the Kingdom of the Netherlands under King William I. Under William a number of economic reforms are enacted, including a reorganization of the nation's international trade companies.

1815. Dutch troops help defeat Napoleon at the Battle of Waterloo. Belgium is made part of the Netherlands by the Treaty of Versailles. The Dutch attempt to encourage industrialization in Belgium.

1831. Following a revolt, Belgium is granted independence over a 10-year period.

1848. After liberal revolutions that sweep across Europe, the constitution is revised.

1849–90. The reign of William III. During this period, the modern system of political parties is established. Also during William's reign, revelations about harsh treatment of natives lead to reforms in the kingdom's East Indies colonies. Revolts in these colonies drain the national treasury and lead to questions over the economic value of the territories.

1870. Widespread industrialization begins in the Netherlands, much later than in the rest of Europe.

1914–18. The Dutch remain neutral during World War I. The government acts to maintain the nation's economy during the war in the face of naval blockades by both Great Britain and Germany.

1920. KLM Royal Dutch Airlines begins regular air service between Amsterdam and London.

1930s. The economy of the Netherlands is damaged by the Great Depression.

1939–45. When World War II breaks out, the Netherlands tries to maintain its neutrality but it is invaded by Germany in 1940. The Dutch colonies in Asia are conquered by the Japanese. The Allies liberate the kingdom and its colonies at the end of the war in 1945. However, after liberation the colonies in Indonesia begin a revolt and are granted independence in 1949.

1944. The Netherlands joins a customs convention with Belgium and Luxembourg. This association will evolve into the Benelux Economic Union in 1958.

1949. The kingdom is one of the founding members of NATO.

1952. The Netherlands joins the European Coal and Steel Community.

1957. The country becomes one of the founding members of the European Community. Disastrous flooding leads to the development of a comprehensive plan to control waterways and prevent future flooding.

1974. The last coal mines in the south of the kingdom close.

1980. The global recession, caused by the oil crisis of 1979, leads to a collapse of the housing market. Queen Juliana abdicates in favor of her daughter Queen Beatrix (the present monarch).

1982. The nation undergoes a severe economic recession.

1993. The Netherlands begins a period of dramatic economic growth which lasts into the next century.

1999. The Netherlands joins EMU.

FUTURE TRENDS

The most important event for the Dutch economy in the 21st century is the introduction of the euro and the subsequent discontinuation of the use of the guilder in 2002. With EMU, the Dutch will gain a number of advantages, including even lower transaction costs for importing and exporting goods with its EU partners. However, EMU will also mean that the Dutch have less control over their monetary policy, since a new European Central Bank will control most aspects of policy surrounding the euro. This might be problematic for the Dutch since the government has traditionally used monetary policy to help trade. EMU will probably mean that the Dutch will have to make a stronger effort to control inflation. This could potentially slow down the economy's rapid growth.

One potential domestic problem for the Dutch economy is that prosperity across the nation is not uniform.

The northern regions tend to be less affluent and have less industry than the southern and western regions. In light of this problem, the government has initiated a variety of programs to attract new business to the less-prosperous regions. However, these programs have not had a major impact on the regions' economy yet.

The kingdom's abundant natural gas supply and its strong agricultural sector will help the nation do well even in case of an economic recession among the EU nations. Although the Dutch economy is dependent on foreign trade, exports of energy supplies and foodstuffs tend to remain strong even during economic downturns. In addition, the presence of a number of large, multinational firms in the country means that foreign trade is likely to continue to expand as these corporations persist in opening new markets for Dutch goods and services and provide access to new or less expensive products and services for Dutch consumers.

The expanding trade between the United States and the Netherlands also bodes well for the future of the Dutch economy. The United States remains the largest single market for products and services in the world. Because of their volume of trade with the EU and the United States, the Dutch have access to both of the globe's main consumer markets. Dutch trade with Asia continues to lag, however, and efforts to improve exports to the region have not been successful because of the competitive nature of the market and the area's economic slowdown in the late 1990s.

DEPENDENCIES

The Netherlands has no territories or colonies.

BIBLIOGRAPHY

CPB Netherlands. *Challenging Neighbors: Rethinking German and Dutch Economic Institutions.* New York: Springer, 1997.

Organization for Economic Cooperation and Development (OECD). *OECD economic surveys: The Netherlands, 1998/99.* Paris: OECD, 1999.

Organization for Economic Cooperation and Development (OECD). *Regulatory Reform in the Netherlands.* Paris: OECD, 1999.

U.S. Central Intelligence Agency. *World Factbook 2000: Netherlands.* <http://www.cia.gov/cia/publications/factbook/geos/nl.html>. Accessed February 2001.

U.S. Department of State. *Background Notes: Netherlands.* <http://www.state.gov/r/pa/bgn/index.cfm?docid=3204>. Accessed February 2001.

U.S. Department of State. *FY 2001 Country Commercial Guide: Netherlands.* <http://www.state.gov/www/about_state/business/com_guides/2001/europe/index.html>. Accessed February 2001.

U.S. Department of State. "The Netherlands: Country Reports on Human Rights Practices: 1999." <http://www.state.gov/g/drl/rls/hrrpt/1999/index.cfm?docid=349>. Accessed February 2001.

Van Zanden, Jan Luiten, editor. *The Economic Development of the Netherlands Since 1870.* Brookfield, Massachusetts: Edward Elgar Publishing, 1996.

—Tom Lansford

NORWAY

Kingdom of Norway
Kongeriket Norge

CAPITAL: Oslo.

MONETARY UNIT: Norwegian krone (NOK; also known as Kr). One krone equals 100 øre. There are coins of 1, 5, 10, and 20 krone, and 50 øre, and notes of 50, 100, 200, 500, and 1,000 krone.

CHIEF EXPORTS: Petroleum and petroleum products, natural gas, raw materials, metals, chemicals, ships, fish.

CHIEF IMPORTS: Machinery and equipment, automobiles, chemicals, metals, foodstuffs.

GROSS DOMESTIC PRODUCT: US$111.3 billion (purchasing power parity, 1999 est.).

BALANCE OF TRADE: **Exports:** US$47.3 billion (f.o.b., 1999 est.). **Imports:** US$38.6 billion (f.o.b., 1999 est.).

COUNTRY OVERVIEW

LOCATION AND SIZE. Norway is situated in the western and northern parts of the Scandinavian Peninsula in northern Europe. It is bordered on the north by the Barents Sea (an arm of the Arctic Ocean), on the northeast by Finland and Russia, on the east by Sweden, on the south by Skagerrak Strait and the North Sea, and on the west by the Norwegian Sea. The Norwegian coastline extends for about 2,740 kilometers (1,700 miles) and with all its deeply cut fjords and islands it totals about 21,930 kilometers (13,620 miles) in length. These islands form an internal waterway protected from the ocean, and Norway's name, meaning "northern way," reflects the importance of that route for linking the country's large number of small isolated fjord and valley settlements separated by icy rugged mountains. Norway has a land area of 324,220 square kilometers (125,182 square miles), making it slightly larger than New Mexico. Located in the south, Oslo is Norway's capital and largest city; Bergen is the cultural center of western Norway and the second-largest city with a population of 225,439. Other important urban centers include Trondheim and Stavanger.

POPULATION. The population of Norway was estimated at 4,481,162 in 2000; in 1998 it was 4,419,955. Due to its far northern location and mountainous landscape, the country has the lowest population density in continental Europe, with only 11 persons per square kilometer (28.5 per square mile). However, the population is very unevenly distributed across the country, with over half concentrated in the southeast, in and around the capital of Oslo. In contrast, the northernmost Finnmark and other remote districts have very small populations. The migration from the countryside and the increasing urbanization of the population, despite heavy regional governmental spending, have become a source of concern in Norway in recent years. More than three-quarters of the population live within about 16 kilometers (about 10 miles) of the sea, and some 74 percent live in urban areas.

The population of Norway is growing very slowly, with an annual rate of increase of only 0.44 percent in 1998. Norway's life expectancy was among the highest in the world in that year: 79 years for all—82 years for women and 76 years for men, up from 76 years for women and 71 for men in 1965. Like much of Europe, the population is aging. One-third of the people were aged under 20 in 1971, but by 1999 the number had fallen to just over a quarter while the percentage over the age of 70 increased from 8.4 percent to 11.6 percent. In 1999, the population grew by 0.7 percent, the biggest population increase since the early 1950s. This was, however, due to a large net **immigration** of around 19,000 people, mostly Danes and Swedes, who filled in gaps in the employment market for medical professions and others. The fertility rate is currently around 1.8 children per woman, up from a low of 1.7 in 1985 but still far below the replacement level of 2.1. (Replacement levels help determine population growth. If one couple has 2 children, this is enough to "replace" themselves. So if a replacement level for a society is significantly above or below 2, then the society may be

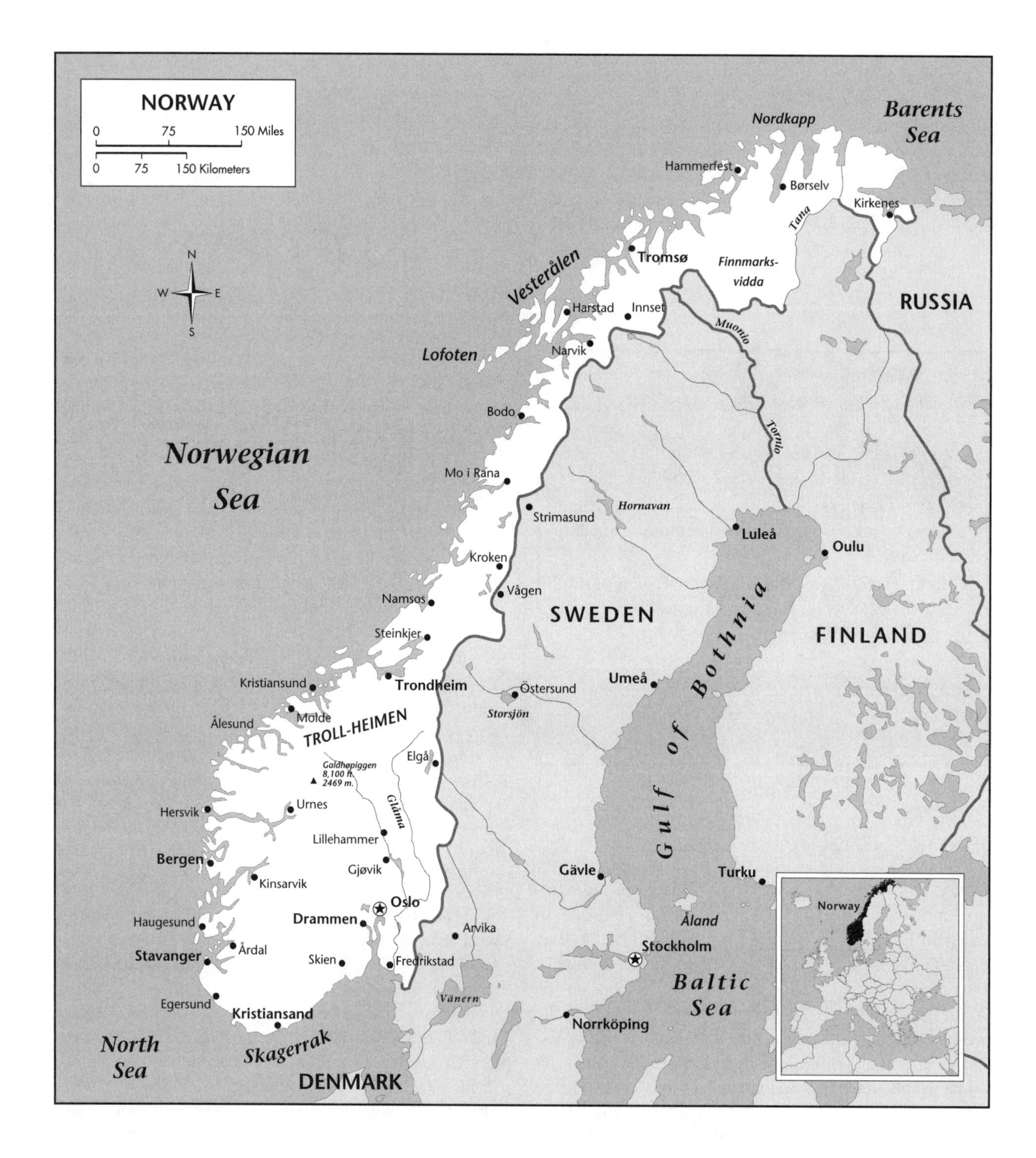

growing or shrinking in overall population.) In line with the increase in the overall population size, the **labor force** has also expanded. In 1999, it was 2.33 million, compared to 2.19 million in 1995.

Much like the other Nordic countries (Denmark, Finland, Iceland, and Sweden), the proportion of foreign citizens living in Norway is still relatively low by western European standards. The population is ethnically homogenous, and most Norwegians are Scandinavians of Germanic descent. Almost all Norwegians are fluent in English, and most of them have some cultural and family ties to the United States. Apart from about 20,000 Saami and some people of Finnish origin in the north, the country has no other significant minority groups, although there are also small numbers of Danes, Swedes, Britons, Pakistanis, Americans, Iranians, and former Yugoslavs.

At the beginning of 1999, there were 178,686 foreign citizens living in Norway (or around 4 percent of the total population), about one-third of these having come from the other Nordic states. One-sixth of all foreign citizens were registered as refugees, the largest group of them coming from Bosnia and Herzegovina's civil war in 1991–95. There were slightly more than 67,000 persons who had arrived initially with refugee status, but nearly half of them opted for Norwegian citizenship. Instances of racially and ethnically motivated violence have been growing in number in recent years despite the relatively low numbers of foreigners. Religious groups in Norway include Evangelical Lutherans, at 86 percent (state church); other Protestants and Roman Catholics, 3 percent; no religion, 10 percent; and others, 1 percent, all in 1997.

OVERVIEW OF ECONOMY

Given the country's size, Norway's economy is small by western European standards but is nevertheless considered among the healthiest in the world, largely due to its positive trade balance and lack of **foreign debt**. The country is widely hailed as an exemplary and prosperous combination of a social **welfare state**, dynamic free market activity, and active government intervention. Its **gross domestic product (GDP) per capita** is among the world's highest, at US$28,100 in 1999, or about 18 percent higher than the western European average, ranking second only to tiny Luxembourg's in western Europe.

The country is rich in natural resources, including offshore oil and natural gas fields in the North Sea, abundant hydropower in the mountains, fish, forests, and minerals. It is a major exporter of oil and natural gas, other raw materials, and semi-processed goods—all of which make it highly dependent on international oil and gas prices for its revenues. In 2000, only Saudi Arabia exported more crude oil than Norway. But other major industries are prospering too, such as information technologies, fishing, pulp and paper products, and shipbuilding. The latter industry is under increasingly heavy competition from overseas (mostly Asian) shipyards, and fishing is heavily subsidized by the state. Norway's overall trade balance is characterized by an unusually large traditional surplus (of over US$18 billion in 1999–2000), it has no foreign debt, and is a major international net creditor and donor to the developing countries. Total **foreign direct investment** in Norway was estimated at about US$22.7 billion in 1998, according to the central bank of the country. The United States is Norway's leading foreign investor, followed by neighboring Sweden and other European Union (EU) members.

For quite some time, Norway was preparing for EU membership, but, contrary to its Nordic neighbors Sweden and Denmark, Norway's citizens decisively opted to stay out of the EU in 2 referenda held in 1972 and 1994. In doing so, Norway apparently hopes to preserve in relative isolation its unique economic advantages and high living standards. Norway is still linked to the EU, however, through the European Economic Area (EEA) agreement that granted favorable access for most Norwegian non-agricultural products to the EU markets. Norway is improving its access to the European markets also by adopting internally most of the EU regulations. But its major focus at the turn of the century is rather on curbing extensive welfare spending and planning for the time when petroleum and natural gas reserves will be depleted. This is expected in less than 20 years for oil and less than 90 years for natural gas reserves at the present level of extraction and if no new fields are located.

POLITICS, GOVERNMENT, AND TAXATION

Norway, like its Nordic neighbors Sweden and Denmark, has preserved its traditional political system of a constitutional hereditary monarchy. The parliament (Storting) is elected through a proportional system every 4 years in September (the most recent parliamentary elections occurred in 2001). In recent years, there have been 3 major factions of the 165-seat Storting. First is the Labor Party, historically the largest local party, with a social democratic and internationalist character, supported by the Socialist Left Party (the 2 groups have a total 74 seats). Then there are the 3 centrist parties: the Christian Democrats, the Center Party, and the Liberals (with a total of 42 seats). Finally there are 2 right-wing parties: the Conservative Party and the Progress Party (with a total of 48 seats). The centrist parties—historically associated with particular, often contradictory, group interests and constituencies (such as the remote rural regions)—have acquired greater political clout. But Norwegian parliamentary politics has a strong tradition for consensus and continuity, and minority governments usually seek and strike legislative agreements with several different opposition parties regarding the specific political issues at stake. Because of the conflicting interests their members and supporters represent, center-right parties have generally found cooperation difficult, both in government and in opposition.

The prime minister, the head of government, is selected by the majority in the parliament and is only formally appointed by the king. The prime minister appoints his cabinet, composed of 18 ministers. The most influential ministerial offices are traditionally those for finance, industry, shipping, petroleum and energy, and foreign affairs. The administrative structure of the ministries changes frequently from one administration to the next. The fact that the Labor government of Jens Stoltenberg, the ambitious young prime minister chosen in 2000, does not have a clear parliamentary majority has contributed to its centrist political course along the lines of most previous Norwegian administrations. The son of a well-known political family, Stoltenberg is a former oil and energy minister expected to accelerate the **privatization** of state-held offshore oil and gas concerns.

In a November 1994 referendum, Norwegians decisively rejected (for the second time) EU membership simply because the net benefit of joining appeared to the majority dubious, considering Norway's petroleum wealth and strong ties with the EU through the EEA. The majority in 1994 was of the opinion that the country had more to lose than to win from a full EU membership that would, in their view, jeopardize the heavy **subsidies** for the Norwegian fishing industry, agriculture, rural regions, and welfare system. EU membership, however, is attractive for the Labor government in the long term, especially given the depletion of oil and gas fields, and the membership issue may be reviewed after the September 2001 election, particularly if the party stays in power. The population remains dramatically split, as is the Labor party itself, with the national leadership more in favor of joining the EU than the rank-and-file party members and the regional bodies. Norway has already had some negative political experiences arising from not being an EU member. As a member of NATO (a military alliance of several western European countries along with the United States and Canada), it has voiced concerns after the EU's decision taken at the summit in Nice, France, in 2000, to develop the much-debated European rapid reaction force. Norway requested to be consulted on equal terms with the rest of the EU members on the issue, fearing that it might not be properly integrated into the negotiations and troop deployment process and alienated from decision-making regarding the European force.

Norway's economy remains an essentially mixed one, with economic policies and, particularly, income distribution patterns strongly influenced by government intervention. There is still a very significant state ownership component in petroleum, telecommunications, and commercial banking. The state extensively subsidizes agriculture, fishing, some large manufacturing companies, and remote northern and mountainous regions with scarce resources. An extensive government welfare system redistributing incomes through taxes remains at the core of the Norwegian economic model. The government also heavily stresses curbing unemployment and maintaining economic opportunities in remote and undeveloped areas. The **private sector** dominates in industries such as shipping, services outside the banking sector, and small to medium-scale manufacturing facilities. In 1999, the contribution of the private sector in GDP was one of the lowest in western Europe, at just 48.5 percent, compared to an average of 56.6 percent. There is indeed some political discussion about the future reduction of **public sector** ownership, and a government privatization program has been set up.

The most significant privatization deals in Norway by 2000 were probably the sale of 21 percent of the stock of the state-owned Telenor telecommunications firm, the sale of 91 percent of the **equity** of the state-controlled Christiania Bank (Kreditkassen) to Swedish-Finnish banking operation MeritaNordbanken, and the planned partial privatization of the government-owned oil giant Statoil. The Labor Party's plan involves the privatization of about one-third of Statoil, about 10 percent via the stock markets and about 20 percent through alliances with foreign companies, most likely with large western European utilities like Ruhrgas of Germany or Gaz de France. Norway may also offer foreign investors over half of the State Direct Financial Interest fields contributing for some 40 percent of the offshore petroleum production in the country. In 1999, Statoil was roughly estimated to be worth about 120 billion Norwegian kroner but it may be more highly valued in the future if international oil prices remain higher than the level they were at in 1999. Norsk Hydro, the second large oil company in which the government also has a controlling share, is reckoned to be worth considerably less than Statoil. The government, however, seems determined to keep the most profitable oil fields under its control.

Although a social welfare economy, Norway's tax rates are generally lower than the EU average. Companies and their branches are subject to both income and capital tax. **Income tax** of 28 percent applies to all forms of income of the corporate bodies and all other entities liable to taxation. The **value-added tax** (VAT) was increased to a 24 percent rate as of 1 January 2001, and an 11 percent dividend tax for shareholders may be introduced in 2002 to support generous domestic welfare spending. Norway has no foreign debt and is a major net external creditor.

INFRASTRUCTURE, POWER, AND COMMUNICATIONS

The quality of the Norwegian transportation **infrastructure** is quite good, although its high mountains and deeply cut valleys and fjords combined with a severe northern climate make inland transportation difficult during the winter months. Railroads are located mostly in the south while most of the northern regions are accessible only by ship, car, or aircraft. The importance the government attaches to regional issues and to investments in transport and communications is significant since many tunnels, bridges, and ferryboat services are indispensable in many parts of the country.

In 1999, the road network totaled 90,741 kilometers (57,000 miles), the majority being concentrated in the more populated areas, especially in and around Oslo. The 4,023 kilometer-long railroad system is also concentrated in the south of the country, connecting Oslo with the larger towns, notably Bergen and Stavanger, and leading to neighboring Sweden. A high-speed railroad connects the new international airport at Gardemoen with down-

Communications

Country	Newspapers	Radios	TV Sets[a]	Cable subscribers[a]	Mobile Phones[a]	Fax Machines[a]	Personal Computers[a]	Internet Hosts[b]	Internet Users[b]
	1996	1997	1998	1998	1998	1998	1998	1999	1999
Norway	588	915	579	160.1	474	50.0	373.4	754.15	2,000
United States	215	2,146	847	244.3	256	78.4	458.6	1,508.77	74,100
Germany	311	948	580	214.5	170	73.1	304.7	173.96	14,400
Sweden	445	932	531	221.4	464	50.9	361.4	581.47	3,666

[a]Data are from International Telecommunication Union, *World Telecommunication Development Report 1999* and are per 1,000 people.
[b]Data are from the Internet Software Consortium (http://www.isc.org) and are per 10,000 people.

SOURCE: World Bank. *World Development Indicators 2000.*

town Oslo. The state railroad company, Norges Statsbaner, also provides local commuter services in the urbanized areas of Oslo, Bergen, and Trondheim.

Air transport is very popular and there are 58 airports in the country, 22 of which are the properties of the state. In the 1990s, sizeable public investment was invested in modernizing the larger airports, and in 1998 a new international airport opened at Gardemoen, 50 kilometers north of the capital. The new air terminal, conceived as a showcase for the country's new oil prosperity, had severe financial problems in its first year of service and the plans for a second terminal have been suspended for the time being. The government (along with Sweden and Denmark) holds a 29 percent stake in the pan-Scandinavian air company Scandinavian Airline Systems (SAS). SAS is partnering with, among others, Lufthansa (Germany), New Zealand Air, and United Airlines (U.S.) to form the Star Alliance, competing successfully in the global aviation markets. There are also a number of smaller private Norwegian airlines, the best known of which is the Braathens, serving both domestic and international destinations.

Norway relies on shipping as a vital component of its transportation system. Ports are securely built, and there are many ice-free harbors on the coastline. The west and north coasts from Bergen to the Russian border form an important international shipping route for passengers and cargo from the Atlantic into the Arctic Ocean, and many ferry lines carry automobiles from Norway to Denmark, Germany, the United Kingdom, and the Netherlands. Dependence on local ferryboat services remains very significant, including in the Oslo and Bergen urban areas.

Norway is still one of the foremost shipping nations in the world, and it offers extensive shipping and shipbuilding services, notably ship owning, brokerage, and shipyards. Norwegian merchant shipping companies own some 10 percent of the world's total fleet, and the fleet of offshore service ships is the world's second-largest in tonnage due mostly to the country's huge oil and gas industry. Norway is especially influential in the sphere of specialized and complex vessels, as Norwegian companies, among other things, control about 25 percent of the world's passenger cruise boats and close to 20 percent of all the world's chemical tankers and gas carriers.

Norway's energy production, as well as its usage per capita, ranks steadily among the highest in the world. Industry (especially the very energy-intensive aluminum and ferro-alloy industries) consumes 66 percent of all energy. Norway is one of the largest oil-producing countries in the world, yet hydropower accounts for almost all electricity generation. About 60 percent of all exploitable water resources have already been utilized. Other renewable energy sources in the country are rather limited, and there is a single atomic power plant which has not yet been used for large-scale electricity generation. The domestic energy market was **deregulated** in 1991, boosting the already significant competition for large power consumers. Power is now sold by the utilities directly to the large-scale users or is instead traded on the NordPool, a fully developed international electricity market, covering Norway, Sweden, and Finland, the first one of its kind in Europe. Domestic electricity production, however, has been insufficient to meet rising demand, forcing Norway to import energy, mostly from Denmark. Over the 1990s, Norway planned to construct 2 new gas power plants in the west, but the debate over the increased pollution from these literally brought down one of the previous governments. The cabinet in office in 2001 supports the plans but still has to offset strong public opposition. It is also considering other possibilities, however, such as recycled and renewable energy sources, and plans to sharply curb electricity consumption.

Norway's telecommunications infrastructure is one of the most developed in the world, with a complete digitization of the telephone network. The number of fast Internet connections, such as Integrated Services Digital Network (ISDN) subscriptions, is rising very rapidly, reaching around 460,000 in 1999. Norway is a world leader in the development and use of mobile phone technologies. In 1999, the number of mobile phone lines surpassed that of the fixed ones, the former amounting to 2.6 million compared with 2.3 million for the latter. This rapid development comes partly from the country's **liberalized** telecommunications market, which has been open to foreign competition since 1998. Despite this competition, the state-owned telecommunications group, Telenor, has managed to maintain a large share of the market. Attempts to merge the group with its Swedish counterpart, Telia, were aborted in late 1999, forcing the government to consider alternative plans. In 2000, the Norwegian government said it would privatize between 15 percent and 25 percent of Telenor in 2001, reducing its holding to 51 percent of the company.

Electronic commerce and use of the Internet are also on the rise and by 2000, 63 percent of the Norwegians had access to the Internet and about 340,000 customers bought goods and services online every month.

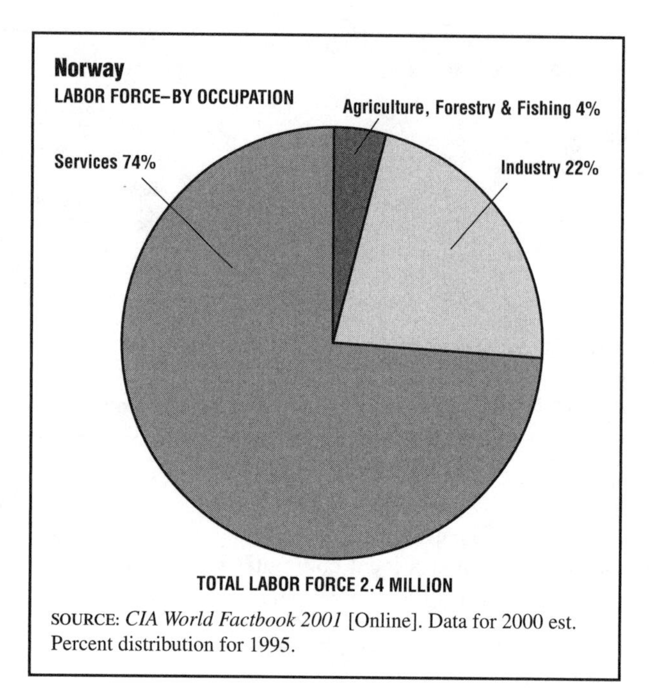

SOURCE: *CIA World Factbook 2001* [Online]. Data for 2000 est. Percent distribution for 1995.

ECONOMIC SECTORS

Like most of its Western European counterparts, the Norwegian economy has undergone significant structural changes over the last decades of the 20th century. It has become increasingly services-oriented, while the once leading sectors of agriculture, forestry, fishing, and manufacturing have gradually declined in terms of contribution to GDP. In 1999, agriculture, forestry and fishing—although still employing 4 percent of the labor force—accounted for 2.2 percent of GDP in 1998. Industry as a whole accounted for 26.3 percent of GDP while services, including those provided by the government, accounted for 71.5 percent of GDP. This distribution is much like that of other Western European countries, except that the offshore oil and gas sector is much larger in Norway.

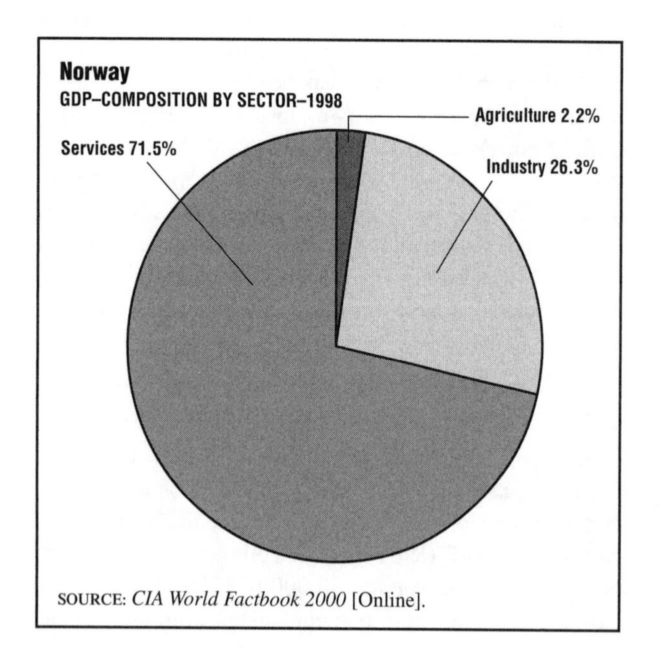

SOURCE: *CIA World Factbook 2000* [Online].

In 1995, the labor force was distributed by occupation as follows: services, 74 percent; industry, 22 percent; and agriculture, forestry, and fishing, 4 percent. The capital-intensive offshore oil sector absorbs only 3 percent of the labor force.

AGRICULTURE

Agriculture in Norway accounts for about 2 percent of annual GDP, and only 3 percent of the land is cultivated—which seems natural, given the cold climate, thin soils, and mountainous terrain. Grains are grown only in the south while western Norway has some livestock raising and dairy farming. The leading crops in 1998 were cereals—particularly barley, wheat, and oats (total output of 1.3 million metric tons)—and potatoes (400,320 tons). In 1998, there were 2.5 million sheep, 998,400 cattle, and 768,400 hogs in the country. Norway is still a major fishing nation and is self-sufficient in many agricultural products, but fruits, vegetables, and most grains are all imported. Agriculture and fishing remain heavily protected by the Norwegian government.

INDUSTRY

MINING. Mining was of relatively little importance in Norway before oil and natural gas fields were found in the North Sea and offshore drilling began in the early 1970s. In 2000, this sector accounted for about 13 percent of GDP (compared with a peak of 18.5 percent in 1984), and the percentage in any year depends mostly on world oil and gas prices. The sector is still largely state-owned, yet as a consequence of **restructuring** in the global oil industry in the late 1990s, the government has announced plans to allow some partial privatization of its assets.

Oil production started on an experimental basis in 1971, and in 1974 the first seabed pipeline was installed to bring crude oil to the United Kingdom. In 1997, annual oil output was 1.15 billion barrels and gas production was 45.3 billion cubic meters (1.6 billion cubic feet). Natural gas is now piped to Germany and Scotland. Norway also has several modern petroleum refineries. With the high world oil prices in late 2000, its external trade account remained very strong. The oil and gas sector will continue to play a leading role in the economy over the next several decades although its prominence will decline gradually with the progressive depletion of the deposits. According to the Norwegian state petroleum directorate, the remaining oil and gas resources were expected to last 19 and 87 years, respectively, from 1998 at that year's rates of extraction.

Other raw products mined and processed in Norway include iron ore, lead concentrates, titanium, iron pyrites, coal, zinc, and copper. Major iron mines are located in the far north at Sydvaranger, near the Russian border, and a large integrated iron and steel plant is situated at Mo i Rana, near the Arctic Circle. All the coal is mined in the Svalbard (Spitzbergen) archipelago beyond the Arctic Circle where a coal mining concession is also given to neighboring Russia.

MANUFACTURING. Manufacturing accounts for 1 percent of annual GDP. The electrochemical and electrometallurgical industries form the leading manufacturing sector. They need an abundance of inexpensive electrical power, which Norway can easily supply. Although all raw materials for the aluminum industry must be imported, Norway produces about 4 percent of the world's output of refined aluminum. It is also a major ferroalloy supplier.

Norway has traditionally been a major shipbuilding nation, but its share of the world's newly built tonnage was less than 1 percent in the mid-1980s. Shipbuilding declined dramatically in the late 1970s as the industry encountered financial problems and Asian competitors carved out larger market shares worldwide. Many shipyards have since shifted capacity to the manufacture of equipment for the oil and gas offshore drilling industries and to transportation. Other manufactures include confections and other food products, chemicals, pulp and paper, and machinery.

SERVICES

FINANCE. The Norges Bank (the central bank) is the executive body for monetary, credit, and exchange policies. It is also the **bank of issue**. It is a joint-stock company with the government holding all the shares. Major players in the Norwegian banking sector include some large full-service banks active in the wholesale and **retail** sectors and many small private retail institutions. Commercial banks are influential and have close relationships with trade and industry, but merchant banks have not reached the prominent position they enjoy elsewhere in Europe. There is also a wide range of savings banks with a long tradition, serving a substantial part of the local credit market. The Norwegian Post Office also keeps its own banking network. There are several specialized smaller banks serving the fisheries, agriculture, shipping, industry, house building, and export trades. The government participates in all of them to various degrees. Banking in Norway is very modern, automated, and computerized. Banking activities are regulated by several pieces of legislation such as the Commercial Banking Act, the Savings Bank Act, and the Act on Financing and Finance Institutions. The liberalization of the sector in the 1990s allowed foreign banks to operate in the country.

TOURISM. Tourism accounts for around 15 percent of total service revenues. In 1998, there were 1,176 hotels with a total capacity of over 137,000 beds, and nearly 1,000 registered campsites existed. In 1998, foreigners accounted for 32 percent of hotel guest nights, much less than in previous years. The country's main attractions are its picturesque coastline and its fjords, and it boasts a number of well-known ski resorts (Norway has hosted winter Olympic games and other major international sporting events).

RETAIL. Mainly as a result of Norway's relatively small domestic market, retailers have been unable to develop into major international players and have remained small even by the modest Nordic standards. In retail, the best-known companies include Rimi, Rema 1000, Kiwi, and ICA. Direct marketing is gaining some ground, and **e-commerce** is particularly robust as almost two-thirds of the population had access to personal computers in 2000.

INTERNATIONAL TRADE

Norway's economy is comparatively small and highly dependent on international trade and oil and gas prices, yet it seems less open than the western European average. In 1998, its exports and imports of goods and services accounted for only 38.9 percent and 33 percent of GDP, respectively. Chief export partners include the EU countries with 77 percent of exports (United Kingdom, 17 percent; Germany, 12 percent; Netherlands, 10 percent; Sweden, 10 percent; France, 8 percent), and the United States at 7 percent. Imports were shipped mostly from the EU with 69 percent (Sweden, 15 percent; Germany, 14 percent; the UK, 10 percent; Denmark, 7 percent), the United States at

Trade (expressed in billions of US$): Norway

	Exports	Imports
1975	7.232	9.705
1980	18.562	16.926
1985	19.985	15.556
1990	34.047	27.231
1995	41.992	32.968
1998	39.645	36.193

SOURCE: International Monetary Fund. *International Financial Statistics Yearbook 1999.*

7 percent, and Japan with 4 percent (1998). Norway has a strongly positive balance of trade , and its surplus increased in 1999 and 2000 due to the increase in the volume of oil exports and the higher average international oil prices. Exports in 1999 stood at US$47.3 billion while imports stood at US$38.6 billion.

Energy and raw and semi-processed goods (oil, metals, and chemicals) still account for some 80 percent of Norwegian exports. The rest consists of exports of machinery and equipment, and various manufactured goods. In 1998, petroleum accounted for some 40 percent of exports, followed by metals and metal products, chemicals, and foodstuffs (mostly fish and fish products). The bulk of imports (55 percent) consisted of machinery, automobiles, equipment, and various manufactured items, followed by industrial raw materials, notably ores for the aluminum industry (40 percent) and food and beverages (6 percent).

MONEY

Norway's financial and banking industries are following the general consolidation trend characterizing the global and the Nordic financial sector in the 1990s, yet with greater reluctance than elsewhere, largely due to its independent, somewhat insular, mindset that has kept Norway outside the EU for so long. In the late 1990s, for example, the centrist coalition government did all it could to prevent the sale of the second-largest Norwegian commercial bank, Christiania Kreditkassen, to the Scandinavian (Finnish-Swedish) conglomerate MeritaNordbanken. The government preferred a domestic Norwegian solution to the problem, potentially involving the country's largest bank, Den Norske Bank, the majority of which is state-owned.

Exchange rates: Norway

Norwegian kroner per US$1	
Jan 2001	8.7784
2000	8.8018
1999	7.7992
1998	7.5451
1997	7.0734
1996	6.4498

SOURCE: CIA *World Factbook 2001* [ONLINE].

Norway's financial system is still afflicted by a banking crisis of the early 1990s. The origin of that crisis dated back to 1984, when the dropping of lending limitations combined with very low interest rates led to a vast expansion of debt among Norwegian households and businesses. Households were not able to meet their repayments, and bankruptcies among companies increased when **macroeconomic** policies were tightened in response to rising **inflation**. In 1990 Christiania Kreditkassen and the third-largest commercial bank, Fokus Bank, were almost brought to insolvency. In 1991, to prevent a confidence crisis, the government created a bank insurance fund that provided resources for the country's largest commercial banks. As a result, the state became a major shareholder in these banks.

The Oslo Stock Exchange (OSE) is still very small by international standards, with 215 listed companies and an annual **turnover** of US$57.1 billion (1999), but it performs well mostly due to the interest in information technology and high-tech stocks in recent years. Yet the largest companies in terms of **market capitalization** still originate from the "old economy": Norsk Hydro (oil), Orkla (consumer products), and Den Norske Bank and Christiania Kreditkassen (banking). Foreign investors held 31 percent of the equity listed on the OSE in 1999, and their share has been relatively constant since 1994. Equity (stock) ownership has become popular in Norwegian society, although to a lesser degree than it is in the United States, with 7 percent of the population holding shares. The OSE is a partner in the Norex alliance, consisting of stock exchanges from Denmark and Sweden, and these 3 indexes—plus Iceland's—plan to begin trading on a new electronic system in 2001.

Government finances and external trade balance are both in surplus, and Norwegian interest rates are higher than the euro area rates. The Norwegian krone's appreciation against the euro throughout 1999 and 2000 was largely due to these factors.

POVERTY AND WEALTH

Norwegians enjoy a healthy economy with strong **socialist** traditions in equitable income distribution and generous welfare spending. Living standards are high, but so is the cost of living. Norway's **Gini index** score (which rates social equality in a country, with a score of 0 indicating perfect equality and a score of 100 indicating per-

GDP per Capita (US$)

Country	1975	1980	1985	1990	1998
Norway	19,022	23,595	27,113	28,840	36,806
United States	19,364	21,529	23,200	25,363	29,683
Germany	N/A	N/A	N/A	N/A	31,141
Sweden	21,157	22,283	24,168	26,397	27,705

SOURCE: United Nations. *Human Development Report 2000; Trends in human development and per capita income.*

Distribution of Income or Consumption by Percentage Share: Norway

Lowest 10%	4.1
Lowest 20%	9.7
Second 20%	14.3
Third 20%	17.9
Fourth 20%	22.2
Highest 20%	35.8
Highest 10%	21.8

Survey year: 1995

Note: This information refers to income shares by percentiles of the population and is ranked by per capita income.

SOURCE: *2000 World Development Indicators* [CD-ROM].

fect inequality) in 1995 was 25.8, far below those of other affluent economies such as the United States (40.8), the United Kingdom (36.1), and Switzerland (33.1), which means that there are few very large private fortunes and virtually no blatant poverty in the country. The unemployment rate was estimated at 2.9 percent in 1999, and consumer price inflation was 2.3 percent in 1998, both much lower than the western European averages. The extensive welfare system helps keep public expenditures steady at more than one-half of GDP.

Despite high per capita income and generous welfare benefits, many Norwegians worry about the time when oil and gas begin to run out in the next 2 decades. As in other Nordic countries, many young and educated Norwegians consider moving abroad partly in pursuit of greater personal challenge.

WORKING CONDITIONS

The Norwegian economy is characterized by strong socialist and labor union traditions. The annual wage growth averaged 6.3 percent in 1998, and manufacturing workers' hourly wages were 30–40 percent higher than in the United States. Safety at work and environmental protection are among the most advanced in the world, and the average working time is 37.5 hours per week. Senior executives in Norway, however, are paid considerably less than their U.S. colleagues.

In 1999, unemployment dropped to 2.9 percent (from 4.1 percent in 1997) due to the continuing economic growth. While skilled and semi-skilled labor has been traditionally available, strong economic expansion since 1992 has led to shortages of some categories of professionals (mostly medical doctors and nurses) and construction workers. The government has a practice of imposing mandatory wage mediation in the event strikes threaten to disrupt the economy seriously. In 1998, for example, the cabinet ordered striking air traffic controllers' and health workers' unions to return their members to work.

COUNTRY HISTORY AND ECONOMIC DEVELOPMENT

9TH CENTURY. King Harald I the Fairhair reigns over the first Norwegian kingdom, which is later disbanded into small feudal states. Vikings begin exploration and invasions all over Europe, settling in the late 9th century in Ireland, Britain, Iceland, the Orkney Islands, the Faeroe Islands, and the Shetland Islands.

985. King Eric the Red leads an expedition to Greenland. His son, Leif Ericson, is among the first Europeans

Household Consumption in PPP Terms

Country	All food	Clothing and footwear	Fuel and power[a]	Health care[b]	Education[b]	Transport & Communications	Other
Norway	16	7	11	5	4	6	51
United States	13	9	9	4	6	8	51
Germany	14	6	7	2	10	7	53
Sweden	17	5	12	4	14	6	41

Data represent percentage of consumption in PPP terms.
[a]Excludes energy used for transport.
[b]Includes government and private expenditures.

SOURCE: World Bank. *World Development Indicators 2000.*

to explore North America. Other Vikings settle in France, becoming ancestors of the Normans.

995. King Olaf I, a scion of Harald I, takes to Christianizing Norway and is later canonized as Norway's patron saint.

1035. Olaf's son, Magnus I, returns from Russia to the throne and unites Denmark and Norway. For 3 centuries, native kings rule Norway, which begins to emerge as a nation, enjoying a comparative prosperity due to its merchant fleet.

1397. Norway becomes a neglected part of Denmark when Denmark, Sweden, and Norway are put into a single administrative unit. Prosperity and culture decline in Norway as the plague decimates the population. For 4 centuries under the Danish rule the country remains largely stagnant.

1799–1815. Norwegian nationalism starts to rise. In 1814 Denmark cedes Norway to Sweden. The Norwegians declare independence, but European powers force them to accept Swedish rule. They are allowed in return to retain their new constitution and have autonomy with a legislature, army, navy, and customs within their boundaries.

1905. The Norwegians vote for independence from Sweden. The new liberal Norwegian government becomes one of the most advanced in Europe in the area of unemployment, insurance benefits, old-age pensions, and liberal laws on divorce and illegitimacy.

1913. Norwegian women are given the right to vote, and the government promotes equality in the workplace and other progressive policies. Women begin to play an important role in politics.

1914. Sweden, Norway, and Denmark agree to stay neutral in World War I.

1935. The Labor Party is elected to office and continues the policies of moderation and political liberalism dominating domestic politics since 1905.

1940. Norway's traditional neutrality notwithstanding, German forces invade the country in World War II, and a resistance movement in the country cooperates with the government-in-exile in London.

1945. The Labor Party takes office (after Germany surrenders) and remains in power for 20 years. Norway develops a social democratic welfare state as the government takes over the planning of the economy, reinforcing positions in international markets, redistributing wealth more equally, and introducing social welfare legislation.

1959. Norway becomes a founding member of the European Free Trade Association (EFTA).

1967. Norway starts a comprehensive social security program.

1970. Norway applies for membership in the European Community (now the EU), but in a referendum in 1972 the voters reject the government's move.

1970s. Oil and gas exploitation in the North Sea fields by a state company begins.

1981. The first woman prime minister, Gro Harlem Brundtland of the Labor party, takes office.

1994. The European Parliament endorses membership for Norway in the EU, but in a referendum, Norwegians reject joining by about 52 percent to about 48 percent, fearing that it would affect farm subsidies and fishing rights.

FUTURE TRENDS

Norway will most likely preserve its healthy economy and high living standards over the next decades, although the EU membership controversy will, no doubt, continue to be a major issue in domestic politics.

Privatization will enter the oil industry as Statoil is expected to be partly privatized in 2001. The Labor government will further sell a part of the State Direct Financial Interest in offshore oil production and will continue to invite major foreign investors to the industry. Gradual liberalization of offshore oil licensing policy will attract smaller foreign companies to the sector. Foreign trade—except in agriculture, fishing, and energy—will gradually become more and more regulated by the EU through the EEA.

Norway is seriously planning for the time when oil and gas will become depleted and is not very likely to experience significant economic disruption and social hardship once this happens. Yet a serious restructuring of the economy is expected to occur, and social welfare spending may be put to some considerable strain. The perspective of losing the oil wealth may also convince the majority of Norwegians to opt for EU membership in the long run.

DEPENDENCIES

Norway has no territories or colonies.

BIBLIOGRAPHY

Bjørnland, Hilde Christiane. *Trends, Cycles, and Measures of Persistence in the Norwegian Economy.* Oslo-Kongsvinger: Statistisk sentralbyrå, 1995.

Economist Intelligence Unit. *Country Profile: Norway.* London: Economist Intelligence Unit, 2001.

Galenson, Walter. *A Welfare State Strikes Oil: The Norwegian Experience.* Lanham, MD: University Press of America, 1986.

Norwegian Trade Council in North America. <http://www.ntcusa.org>. Accessed September 2001.

Royal Norwegian Embassy in the United States of America. *NORWAY.org.* <http://www.norway.org>. Accessed September 2001.

U.S. Central Intelligence Agency. *World Factbook 2000.* <http://www.odci.gov/cia/publications/factbook/index.html>. Accessed September 2001.

U.S. Department of State. *Background Notes: Norway.* <http://www.state.gov/www/background_notes/norway_9905_bgn.html>. Accessed January 2001.

U.S. Department of State. *FY 2000 Country Commercial Guide: Norway.* <http://www.state.gov/www/about_state/business/com_guides/index.html>. Accessed January 2001.

—Valentin Hadjiyski

POLAND

Republic of Poland
Rzeczpospolita Polska

CAPITAL: Warsaw.

MONETARY UNIT: Polish zloty (Z). One Polish zloty equals 100 groszy. There are coins of 1, 2, 5, 10, 20, and 50 groszy, and 1, 2, and 5 zlotys. There are notes of 10, 20, 50, 100, and 200 zlotys.

CHIEF EXPORTS: Machinery and transport equipment, intermediate manufactured goods, miscellaneous manufactured goods, food and live animals.

CHIEF IMPORTS: Machinery and transport equipment, intermediate manufactured goods, chemicals, miscellaneous manufactured goods.

GROSS DOMESTIC PRODUCT: US$327.5 billion (purchasing power parity, 2000 est.).

BALANCE OF TRADE: **Exports:** US$28.4 billion (f.o.b., 2000). **Imports:** US$42.7 billion (f.o.b., 2000).

COUNTRY OVERVIEW

LOCATION AND SIZE. Located in Central Europe, Poland is bordered on the west by Germany, in the north by the Baltic Sea, in the north-east by Russia and Lithuania, in the east by Belarus and Ukraine, and in the south by Slovakia and the Czech Republic. Poland covers a total area of 312,685 square kilometers (120,728 square miles), making it slightly smaller than the state of New Mexico. The capital city, Warsaw, is situated in the center of the country.

POPULATION. The population of Poland was estimated at 38,653,912 in July 2001. In 2001 the birth rate stood at 10.2 per 1,000 and the death rate at 9.98 per 1,000. After a period of uninterrupted growth that began in 1946, the population registered a slight decrease of 0.03 percent in 2001, reflecting a net migration rate of 0.49 people per 1,000. Negative population growth is expected over the next few years, before an upward turn that should see the population reach 39,065,000 in 2015. These projections could change with the arrival of immigrants of Polish descent from central Asian countries such as Kazakhstan, a law having been passed in 2000 to facilitate such **immigration**.

In 1990, Poland's population was primarily of Polish European descent (97.6 percent). Small minority groups included Germans (1.3 percent), Ukrainians (0.6 percent), and Byelorussians (0.5 percent). Prior to World War II (1939–45) the population of Poland was multiethnic, but 5 years of Nazi occupation resulted in heavy loss of life, and it is estimated that more then 6 million Polish citizens—soldiers and civilians combined—were killed. The heaviest losses were suffered by Poland's Jewish population, the vast majority of whom perished in extermination camps. Many citizens of Polish descent also died in concentration camps, labor camps, prisons, or during forced labor. The demographic profile of Poland at the end of World War II demonstrated the effect of the war on population distribution: by 1945, the number of young men and women who could have been expected to produce children was considerably diminished, although a subsequent baby boom partially improved the situation.

In 1999, approximately 19 percent of the total population was aged 14 or younger, while 12 percent were older than 64. The majority of people live in urban areas. Life expectancy for men is 69.1 years, significantly shorter than for women (77.7 years). Thus, while the genders are more or less equal in number between the ages of 14 and 64, among people aged 65 and older women outnumber men. Despite a well-organized health care service, compulsory vaccination programs against major childhood diseases, and public health information, substantial numbers of Poles die prematurely of smoking-related illnesses. Alcohol consumption has decreased in the past decade, with low alcohol beverages preferred to spirits, but the Polish diet favors red meat, dairy products, and

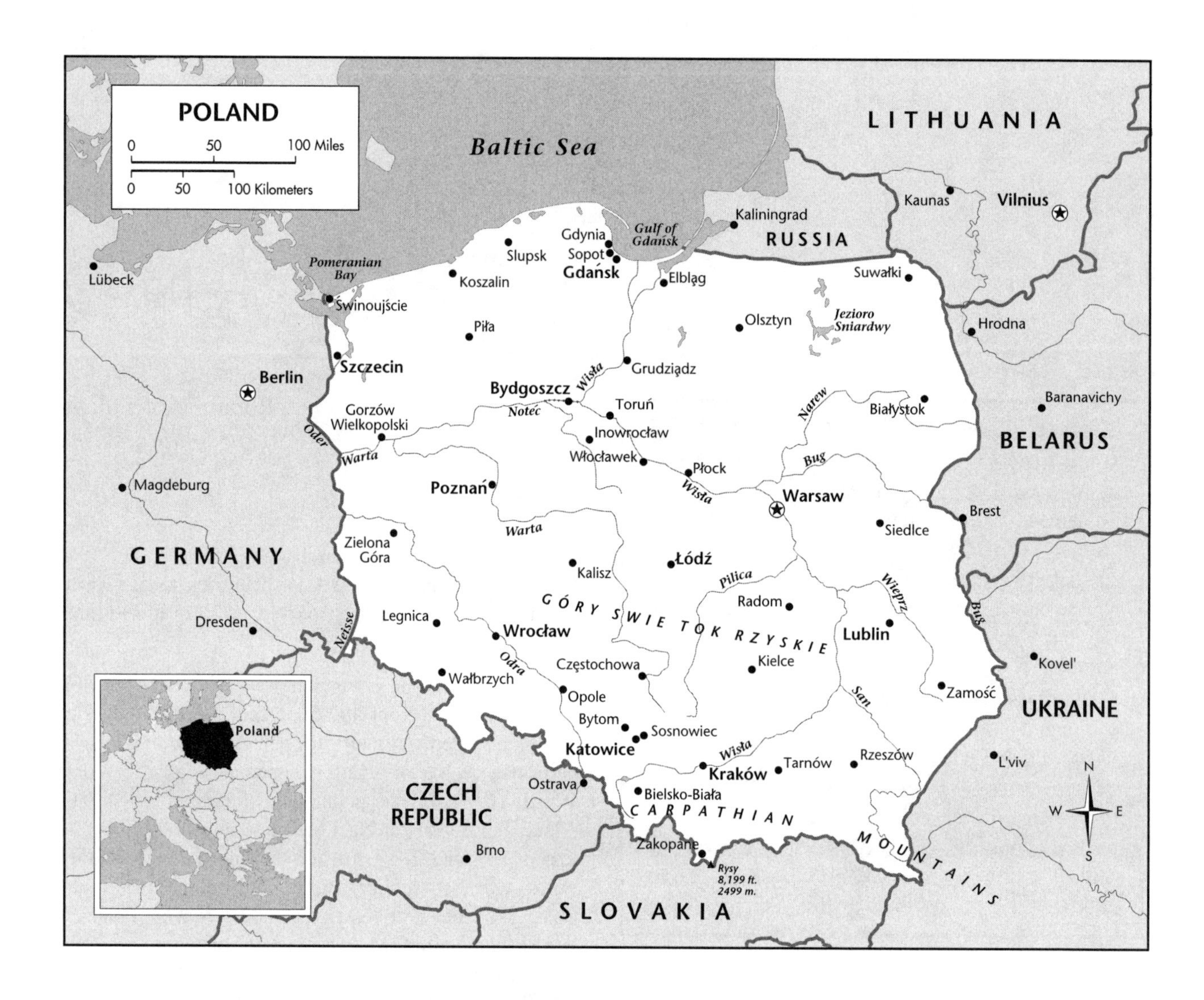

animal fats. Accordingly, Poles are subject to coronary heart disease, diabetes, and certain types of cancer, all of which are thought to relate to the nation's eating habits. In recent years, emphasis has been placed on the development of healthy eating and physical exercise as a preventive measure against such illnesses.

OVERVIEW OF ECONOMY

The main revenue-producing sector of the Polish economy is the service sector, which generated approximately 60 percent of the **gross domestic product** (GDP) in 2000. Industry, much of it connected to the mining of mineral wealth, is next in importance at nearly 37 percent of GDP. Except for the rivers traversing Poland from the mountains in the south to the Baltic Sea in the north, the country's topography is free of any major obstacles to freedom of movement and the country has provided a natural network of east-west trade links for Europe dating back to ancient Roman times. Polish cities benefitted from trade for centuries, though numerous wars and military campaigns repeatedly destroyed the **infrastructure** and depleted the country's periodically accumulated wealth. The last wave of devastation was caused by World War II (1939–45).

Traditionally, Poland has been a large agricultural producer, with the broad, open valleys of the Oder and Vistula rivers providing excellent farmland. However, in recent years, due to a combination of changing farming methods, stiff competition, and environmental hazards such as soil erosion and water pollution, agricultural activity has declined significantly and accounted for only 3.8 percent of GDP in 2000.

In the 1600s, Poland was the main grain supplier in Europe and the country prospered considerably through the grain trade. By the late 1700s, however, the country fell victim to aggressive treaties between its neighbors, Russia, Austria, and Prussia, and ceased to exist as an independent state. The country was divided into thirds, annexed by its neighbors, and absorbed into their territories. Consequently, for 123 years, until the end of World

War I in 1918, Poland was developed within separate economic and political entities. Reconstituted as an independent nation under U.S. President Woodrow Wilson's peace plan in 1918, the country had to deal with the legacy of 3 foreign economic systems and uneven levels of infrastructure.

The worldwide effects of the Great Depression of the 1930s and the devastating consequences of World War II hampered Polish economic growth in the first half of the 20th century. Freed from Nazi occupation by the spring of 1945, the country then fell into the sphere of the Soviet Union's influence. From the late 1940s until 1989, Poland's economy was again controlled by foreign dictate, which poured the country's resources into the creation of a huge industrial complex. Coal mining, steel manufacture, and other capital-intensive enterprises were built to satisfy the needs of the centrally planned system imposed by the Soviet Union on countries of Central and Eastern Europe. The Soviet program deprived other economic sectors of resources, caused environmental pollution, and lowered the quality of life in Poland. The unpopularity of the economic policies led to organized protests by the Solidarity labor movement that began in the summer of 1980 and resulted in the eventual defeat of the pro-Soviet government in 1989. Subsequent negotiations between the authoritarian regime and the democratic opposition brought political and economic change, and the non-democratic state-controlled economy gave way to the free market system.

Widely known as "shock therapy," the economic policy adopted by the newly elected democratic government early in 1990 was directed at balancing the national budget. A number of simultaneously implemented reforms **liberalized** prices and international trade, eliminated political censorship, restored private ownership, and began the **privatization** of state-owned assets. After an initial period of accelerated **inflation** in early 1990, the economy stabilized by the end of 1992. Between 1993 and 2000, Poland experienced a run of robust economic growth, offsetting the effects of economic contraction suffered in the 1980s and the early 1990s.

The **private sector** is now the country's primary job provider and, by 1999, employed 71 percent of the **labor force**, compared with 1990 when state-owned enterprises employed 52.1 percent of workers. However, the 1999 employment total of 16.069 million workers showed a drop of about 2.5 percent from 1990, although the number of self-employed people had grown by 12.8 percent to 5.6 million. Also, the number of farmers increased by about 10 percent, reflecting structural changes in the economy that reduced the labor force engaged in heavy industry and providing employment in some rural areas, particularly in southern and southeastern Poland.

In general, the Polish labor force is relatively well educated and literacy rates are high (99 percent for men and 98 percent for women). Only 15 percent of the total Polish population have had no more than a primary education, and a significant proportion of those are aged 55 and above. Among the 55–64 age group, nearly 19 percent have had a college education. In recent years, the demand for higher education has increased dramatically and about a third of those in their early twenties are enrolled in public or private colleges.

Sustained economic growth has continued despite frequent changes of government since 1989. Though governments have alternated between conservative and leftist, they have all shared a strong commitment to democracy and free market principles. Unemployment has remained relatively high, about 15 percent in 2000, largely because of the continuing structural adjustments to the economy that are necessary after decades of Soviet mismanagement. The government now attempts to focus on maximizing the use of the country's resources to assure the highest possible standard of living. For example, with the closing of a number of coal mines and a slowing down of heavy industry, with a consequent loss of jobs, new sectors such as telecommunications, banking, and insurance are developing. Growth is nonetheless steady, and this factor, combined with a large domestic market, attracts **foreign direct investment**. Recent years have witnessed rapid growth in retailing, food and hotel services, and communications.

Poland is negotiating for membership in the European Union (EU), but the question of agricultural **subsidies** is proving one of the most difficult areas on which to reach agreement. Although a date had not yet been set for joining the EU by 2001, the majority of Poles expect to become EU citizens within the first decade of the 21st century.

POLITICS, GOVERNMENT, AND TAXATION

Since the change to the political system in 1989, Poland has been governed by alternating periods of right and left-oriented governments. Tadeusz Mazowiecki became prime minister in September 1989, leading the country's first democratic government since the end of World War II. In January 2001, a minority government took power, led by Election Action Solidarity (EAS), an umbrella organization of right-wing parties and the Solidarity trade unions. Despite several changes of government since 1989, democratic, free market, and pro-Western policies have remained unchanged. The large number of political parties established around 1990 has been reduced to 4 major players. The EAS, the moderate Freedom Union (FU), the Polish Peasant Party PPP), and the Liberal-Democratic Alliance, or SLD. From 1997 until late 2000, the SLD, a conglomerate of left wing and social democratic parties, formed a coalition government with the PPP, supporting private ownership, democratic principles in political life, and freedom of expression.

The executive branch of Polish government consists of the prime minister, the cabinet, and the president of the Republic of Poland. The president signs all bills passed by parliament, participates in formulating the annual government budget, and is the commander-in-chief of the armed forces. The president serves a 5-year term and can only be elected to 2 terms of office. Presidential appointees represent the office in numerous government agencies, including the Council of Monetary Policy, an autonomous body that sets targets for the money supply and for interest rates on loans made by the central bank to commercial banks, and establishes guidelines for foreign **exchange rates**. The former Solidarity leader and Nobel Peace Prize laureate, Lech Walesa, was the first president of post-Soviet Poland.

Poland's parliament consists of a lower and an upper chamber (the Sejm and the Senate) which, together, form the National Assembly. There are 460 members of parliament in the Sejm and 100 in the Senate, all of whom are elected to serve a 4-year term. Candidates for the Senate must be at least 25 years old. The voting age is 18.

The third branch of government is the judiciary, which consists of the courts of law and a number of specially constituted bodies such as the Constitutional Tribunal. The Tribunal monitors and rules on matters alleged to be unconstitutional, protects the rights of individuals, and interprets the laws passed by the National Assembly with respect to rights defined by the Constitution. Labor disputes between employee and employer are heard by the Main Administrative Court, which was established exclusively to deal with non-criminal labor issues and deliver speedy judicial decisions. Cases considered in these courts cannot be considered in other courts.

The Criminal Code and the Civilian Code regulate the conduct of individuals and companies. The European-style legal system is strongly rooted in rules and regulations established by the National Assembly. Poland has abolished the death penalty and the longest prison sentence is 25 years, with life sentences an option only for crimes of particular gravity. However, because of public anxiety over crime, new laws were passed in 2000 approving stiffer penalties in a number of instances. The Civilian Code regulates contractual agreements and presides over divorce cases. It assigns parental custody and sets alimony payments, which are mandatory for all children up to age 18 and for those aged 18 and over who are still enrolled full-time at school. The amount of alimony is based on parental earnings.

In recent years, the Polish government has undertaken several major reforms needed to ensure both economic growth and efficient government administration. Such reforms include redrawing the boundaries of administrative districts, reducing the country's 50 provinces to 16, and the reintroduction of counties. Executive powers have been delegated from the central government to the provinces where elected legislative bodies have been established, thus reducing the number of government departments. This administrative streamlining has coincided with education reform, placing responsibility for the school system in the hands of local authorities. The Polish school system consists of grade, middle, and high schools. Important reforms in health care and social security have decreased government involvement in the provision of medical services and brought in the privatization of pension funds.

Taxes are the major source of government revenue in Poland. Businesses pay a tax of 28 percent on profits, while individuals are taxed on earned income calculated in bands of 19, 30, or 40 percent. Personal **income tax** accounted for 20.5 percent of all tax revenues in 1999. Over the past several years, tax rates have changed several times. Despite strong pressure from business-oriented leaders, including Leszek Balcerowicz who implemented the economic "shock therapy" of the early 1990s, the rates have not been lowered for some time. Parliamentary debate on this vital economic issue is expected to continue for some time. **Excise taxes**, representing 22.4 percent of all tax revenue, are collected on tobacco, alcohol, and lottery winnings, while a **value-added tax** (VAT), introduced some years ago in line with EU countries, supplies 43.3 percent of total tax revenue. The VAT is set at different rates for differing commodities.

The legislative and executive branches of government influence the economy through fiscal and monetary policies. The annual government budget is formulated by discussion of proposals put forward by the prime minister and the president, with additional policies introduced by legislators. Once approved, the budget sets short-term goals related to estimated income and expenditure and the project budgetary deficit or surplus. The economy is managed in line with these projections and, if the deficit figure is exceeded, the shortfall must be covered either through additional public borrowing or increased revenues. However, additional borrowing must have parliamentary approval, not always easily obtained, while additional taxation is limited by public opposition to increases. Consequently, the government may resort to raising excise taxes on selected goods such as alcohol, but more often obtains extra revenue by reducing or liquidating its ownership of companies owned by the Treasury. The privatization of such assets is implemented by opening the companies to bids from all interested parties. The selling off of state-owned enterprises to private companies is fiscally prudent, strengthening the private sector and reducing the necessity for government to compete directly in the financial markets.

The last Soviet troops left in 1994 and Poland, which had actively pursued membership in the North Atlantic Treaty Organization (NATO) since the restoration of democracy, became an official member in March 1999 and joined the NATO peacekeeping forces in Kosovo shortly afterwards.

INFRASTRUCTURE, POWER, AND COMMUNICATIONS

Poland has a good road and rail network, although its density varies across regions. Although the country had 251,004 kilometers (156,000 miles) of paved roads by 1999, these proved insufficient to cope with the explosion of car ownership and trucks in the country. The number of vehicles traveling on Polish roads increased to 13.2 million between 1990 and 1999, a growth of 47 percent (76 percent for passenger cars). The dated infrastructure is being modernized, but is not keeping pace with the acceleration in road traffic. Because of its location and topography Poland serves as a major route between western and eastern European countries. In recent years, trucks have become major carriers of goods from France, the Netherlands, Germany and other EU members, through Poland to Russia, Belarus, Lithuania, and Ukraine.

New multi-lane limited access highways are under construction across Poland and will increase the efficiency of the transport system. The construction of the limited access highway linking Berlin with the Polish capital, Warsaw, and extending to the border with Belarus, has been given priority. In southern Poland, a similar highway will link the western border with Germany through the city of Wroclaw in the Silesian region, and Cracow to the eastern border with Ukraine. A north-south link between Gdansk and the southern border crossings into the Czech Republic and Slovakia is also planned.

By 1999, Poland had 230,087 kilometers (143,000 miles) of well-developed railroad networks. With the increasing competition from buses and trucks, many unprofitable rail routes (12.7 percent between 1990 and 1999) have been closed. The state-owned railroad **monopoly** is being privatized, and the modernization of major railway lines undertaken in recent years has begun to reap benefits in shortened travel time. With the price of gasoline increasing, railways are once again becoming a competitive mode of passenger transport.

Poland has several well-known seaports. Starting from the northwest corner, the ports of Szczecin and Swinoujscie handle cargo, including coal exports and imports of fertilizer. The smaller ports of Kolobrzeg and Ustka mostly serve fishing fleets and coastal shipping, and handle cargo originating from, and destined for, other Baltic Sea ports. Further east, several small ports are used by fishermen and recreational sailors. Gdansk is the largest seaport. In 1999, 18.8 million tons of cargo—37 percent of all Polish cargo both incoming and outgoing—was loaded or unloaded at Gdansk. Next to Gdansk is Gdynia, Poland's youngest port, which was built as a matter of economic necessity in the 1920s. It handles various cargoes, including container shipping. East of Gdansk, the port of Elblag can only be accessed by a narrow strait belonging to Russia, and ships bound for Elblag can only pass through without delay by negotiated agreement with the Russians.

Several major rivers, including the Vistula, Oder, Warta, and Notec, are used for barge navigation. The total length of rivers and channels suitable for barge navigation was 3,813 kilometers (2,370 miles) in 1999. Through its system of channels and rivers, Poland is linked with the inland waterways of Western Europe. The economic importance of the west-east barge traffic is small because it cannot compete effectively with truck and rail shipments. However, the north-south barge traffic is competitive, plying goods between Poland's southern industrial towns and farms and the Baltic ports of Szczecin, Swinoujscie, and Gdansk.

Communications

Country	Newspapers	Radios	TV Sets[a]	Cable subscribers[a]	Mobile Phones[a]	Fax Machines[a]	Personal Computers[a]	Internet Hosts[b]	Internet Users[b]
	1996	1997	1998	1998	1998	1998	1998	1999	1999
Poland	113	523	413	83.3	50	N/A	43.9	40.86	2,100
United States	215	2,146	847	244.3	256	78.4	458.6	1,508.77	74,100
Germany	311	948	580	214.5	170	73.1	304.7	173.96	14,400
Romania	300	319	233	119.2	29	N/A	10.2	9.01	600

[a]Data are from International Telecommunication Union, *World Telecommunication Development Report 1999* and are per 1,000 people.

[b]Data are from the Internet Software Consortium (http://www.isc.org) and are per 10,000 people.

SOURCE: World Bank. *World Development Indicators 2000.*

Warsaw's Okecie airport is the largest in Poland. All major European air carriers operate services to Warsaw, while the Polish national airline, Lot, connects the capital with many cities in Europe, North America, the Middle East, and Asia. Airports in Gdansk, Poznan, and Cracow also offer international connections. Airports of domestic importance are located in Szczecin, Katowice, and Wroclaw.

About 95 percent of the country's electricity is generated by burning fossil fuels. Public opposition in the early 1990s put an end to the construction of a proposed nuclear power plant in Zarnowiec, which was converted to conventional fuels instead. Hydroelectric power is also generated, mostly in southern Poland, where the mountainous topography offers opportunities to construct dams. Since much of the country's terrain consists of open plains, there is some expectation of being able to harness wind power in the future. In 1999, Poland generated a total of 134.351 billion kilowatt-hours (kWh) of energy, enough to meet domestic needs and export demand.

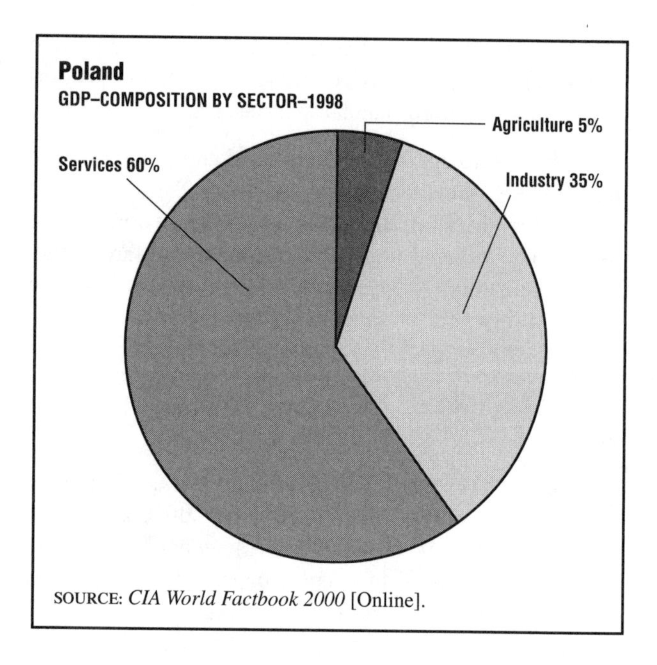

SOURCE: *CIA World Factbook 2000* [Online].

The country operates a very well-established postal service with 8,380 post offices in 1999, 58.8 percent of them located in rural areas. There is no weekend mail delivery, but many post offices in towns stay open in the evening and large cities typically have one 24-hour post office. Nearly 26,000 mailmen are employed in the daily delivery of mail. Courier services are provided by the post office and by private companies, which include branches of international couriers DHL and Federal Express.

Telecommunications services are undergoing rapid modernization. After years of neglect, new switchboards are constantly being installed and the number of telephone subscribers has increased substantially. The nation has enthusiastically adopted wireless communications and cellular phones, with the number of wire telephone subscribers exceeding 10 million in 1999 (more than treble the figure in 1990), while cellphone users increased from 75,000 in 1995 to almost 4 million in 1999.

ECONOMIC SECTORS

Agriculture is the smallest of Poland's 3 major economic sectors, contributing just 3.8 percent of GDP in 1999. The industrial sector is significant and wide-ranging and contributed 36.6 percent of GDP, but the largest and fastest-growing economic sector is services, which provided 59.6 percent of GDP in 1999.

The total labor force in Poland stood at 17.2 million at the end of 1999, an increase of 1.2 percent since 1995. Men make up 64.3 percent of the workforce as against 49.7 percent of women, and the share of the working population is slightly higher in rural areas (57.2 percent) than in urban areas (56.3 percent), reflecting some increase in the number of farmers during the 1990s. In 1999, 1.434 million women and 1.207 million men were unemployed. Overall, 44.4 percent of Poles were employed in 1998, more than in Italy (40.7 percent) or Spain (41.6 percent), but less than in Germany (48.7 percent) or the United Kingdom (49.4 percent). The majority of Poland's workers—50.4 percent—were employed in the services sector in 1999, while 27.5 percent were employed in the agricultural sector and 22.1 percent in industry.

The value of foreign direct investment (FDI) amounted to US$26 billion in 1999, a 332 percent increase since 1995. Many foreign companies operate in

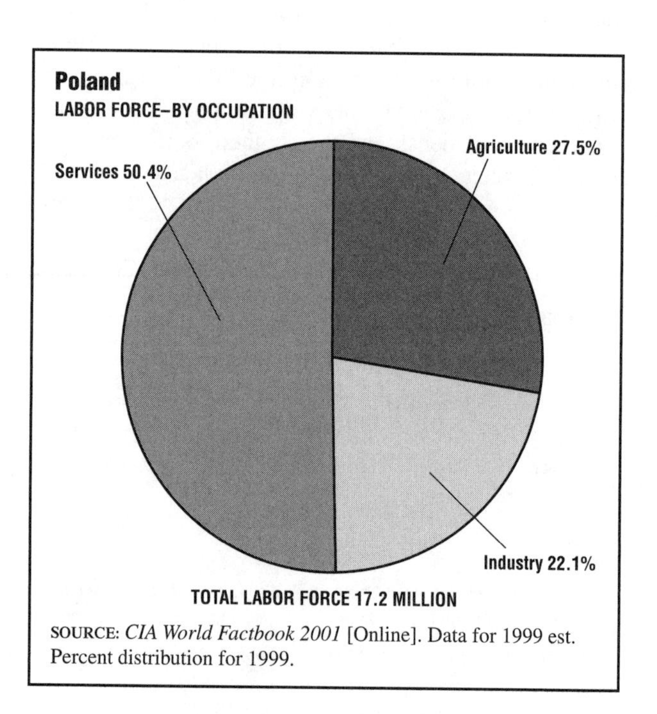

SOURCE: *CIA World Factbook 2001* [Online]. Data for 1999 est. Percent distribution for 1999.

Poland. Hormel is investing in the meat processing industry, Coca-Cola and Pepsico have expanded their operations, and fast food chains including McDonald's, Burger King, Pizza Hut, KFC, Taco Bell, and Dunkin' Donuts are now familiar names. Other major international corporations operating in Poland include GM, Daewoo, Volkswagen, and Fiat in the automotive industry. Power generation, petrochemicals, and telecommunications are other sectors that attract foreign investors since demand is high. While economic **restructuring** had already modernized a number of industries (paper and packaging, for example), foreign direct investment has led to a sizable increase in imports of technologically advanced machinery and equipment designed to speed up modernization.

AGRICULTURE

About 2 million family farms, employing approximately 27.5 percent of the labor force, supply Poland's agricultural output. As a result of land reforms in the 1940s, when the country's large estates were divided up under **communist** rule, Polish farms are generally small, averaging about 15 acres. This is changing as much bigger farms are being developed, but the majority of farmers are unable to earn sufficient income through agriculture and must take outside jobs in order to support their families. Agriculture contributed only 3.8 percent of GDP in 1999, a major change in a country that, before World War II, was primarily an agricultural economy.

Poland is among the world's leading producers of rye, potatoes, and apples, as well as pork and milk. The length of the growing season varies regionally according to climate, being much shorter in the northeast where a harsh continental climate prevails. Although the exports of certain produce (potatoes, apples and other fruits, frozen ducks and geese, and sugar) has declined over the years, Poland exports grains, sugar, pork, processed meats, and dairy products. The upwards of 150-year-old sugar industry faces stiff price competition from overseas producers and is under pressure to restructure itself as the quantities of unsold sugar mount. Similarly, the once enormous potato production has been substantially reduced by changes and improvements to the feeding of livestock. Farmers face tough competition from imported commodities and food products, and are dissatisfied by the lack of sufficient export markets. It is expected that, within a decade, there will be no more than 700,000 farms in Poland. They will be large, specialized, and commercially geared, replacing the small, diversified, but often inefficient agricultural producers. Restructuring of the farming sector is a major issue in negotiating Poland's access to the EU.

Pork and dairy farmers remain competitive. Milk and pork production have recovered from the transition from the centrally planned system of fixed prices to the market economy. Dairy plants that had been organized as co-operatives have successfully adopted modern processing and packing technologies, and planned development of dairy products has helped maintain market demand.

Even before the 20th century, deforestation occurred as a result of clearing trees in order to expand the land available for farming. This has led to problems of soil erosion caused by winds blowing across the treeless land. In recent years, the government has offered reforestation incentives to farmers, granting them exemption from land tax if they plant trees on their least productive land. Polish farmers only use pesticides in conditions of extreme necessity and the use of chemical fertilizer is also comparatively low, but there is always the threat of water pollution, mainly caused by nitrogen and phosphorus runoff in livestock production. Farmers are being educated to the dangers, and practices are changing. Local governments, too, have been using central government grants to plant trees along streams and creeks to establish a biological barrier between fields and surface water. Further progress in farming techniques will require additional investment in manure storage facilities, and the government will continue to support environmental programs relating to agriculture in order to meet EU standards.

INDUSTRY

MINING. The mining sector employed 271,000 workers in 1999, representing 2.8 percent of the workforce. Since 1995, however, the employment decreased in this sector by 27.5 percent. Mining accidents were a constant threat and resulted from gas explosions, gas poisonings, or rock collapsing on miners working underground.

Coal mining has been a traditional employer of thousands living in the regions of Upper and Lower Silesia. Poland has long produced in excess of 140 million tons of coal annually. In 1999, the country mined 112 million tons, placing it seventh among the top 10 world coal producers. New coal fields were brought into production in eastern Poland in the 1980s, but the decreasing importance of steel production and coal exports led to the reduction of the number of mines. In 2000 the government offered coal miners an incentive program encouraging early retirement and re-training because of the diminishing profitability and efforts to reduce the environmental degradation in Silesia, the primary coal mining region.

Poland is also mining lignite, used as a fossil fuel for power generation. The 1999 production was 60.8 million tons, about 10 percent lower than in 1990. Large lignite deposits have been mined in central Poland around the town of Konin and in the southwestern corner of Poland near Turoszow, where the borders of Poland, Germany, and the Czech Republic come together. Because lignite contains less energy per unit of weight than coal it is chiefly used in the immediate vicinity of the mine for power generation. Poland was the world's fourth largest lignite producer in 1999.

Sulphur mines are located in the area of Tarnobrzeg, northeast of Cracow, near the Vistula river. Poland is the third largest sulphur producer in the world and produced 1.247 million tons in 1999, roughly a quarter of what was produced in 1990. Sulphur and sulfuric acid are major exported commodities. In western Poland, around the town of Lubin, copper is mined. In 1999, the region produced 28.388 million tons of copper ore. High quality copper is smelted there as well as other ores typically found with copper such as silver. Poland was the world's eighth largest copper producer in 1999 and copper is a major export commodity, but the slowing world demand does not encourage further expansion of mines in Poland. Sodium chloride, or salt, has been mined for centuries in Poland and some of the world's oldest salt mines can be found in Wieliczka near Cracow. Today Poland continues to mine salt mostly in the central plains. In 1999, Poland produced 4.128 million tons of salt. Natural gas reserves are significant and several fields are being operated on plains in central and western regions. Oil reserves are limited and satisfy only a fraction of the domestic demand.

MANUFACTURING. The manufacturing sector has been undergoing major restructuring since 1990. Following the changes in the political and economic system, many industries were forced to compete on the market rather than having their production and prices set by the government. Many plants found it difficult to compete on the basis of quality and cost-effectiveness. After a period of attempts to adjust, many plants closed because they were using obsolete technology or because they lost their primary markets. The closings most affected the heavy industry producing machinery and equipment for the mining industry, steel mills, smelting, shipbuilding, and railroad equipment.

Steel manufacturing continues at modernized mills near Cracow and in Silesia in southern Poland. Demand for steel comes from the automotive industry and shipbuilding. Several car plants including the Italian Fiat and GM are located in Silesia. Daewoo operates a plant in Warsaw, while Volkswagen operates a new plant in Poznan. Between 1990 and 1999, car production increased by 244 percent. The shipbuilding industry, although considerably smaller than in decades past, continues to build vessels in Szczecin, Gdynia, and Gdansk located on the Baltic Sea. After a period of adjustment in the mid-1990s, the shipbuilding industry increased production in the late 1990s. The rail car industry shrunk substantially, but a plant continues to produced modernized equipment in Wroclaw. Large demand for steel is represented by the construction industry. Besides steel, Poland also produces aluminum, lead, and zinc.

Silesia is also the center for coke produced from coal and crude petroleum processing. Plock, located in central Poland, refines crude oil imported from Russia, and a refinery in Gdansk processes oil imported by sea from the Middle East and Africa. Fuel oil, gasoline, and lubricants are some of the products produced by the oil processing industry.

Fertilizers are produced at several locations. Phosphorus fertilizers are produced near Szczecin, while a plant in the town of Pulawy, southeast of Warsaw, produces nitrogen fertilizers. Another fertilizer plant is in Tarnow, east of Cracow in the southern part of the country. Fertilizer production increased in the late 1990s despite a decrease in the domestic demand for fertilizers caused by the decrease in food consumption and imports of competitively priced feed components.

The chemical industry produces a number of goods, including sulfuric acid, synthetic fibers, synthetic organic dyes, and caustic soda. The production of plastics increased by about 50 percent between 1995 and 1999, while synthetic rubber production decreased slightly. Chemical industry plants are located in Silesia and several major cities. Lacquer product production increased substantially during the 1990s. The production of tires for cars more than tripled between 1990 and 1999 in response to the increased demand resulting from increased car ownership.

The production of construction materials showed mixed trends in the 1990s. This is the result of dramatically changing technology using different materials, lighter constructions, and new insulating materials. Although the production of cement increased, plate glass production shrunk. Also, brick production decreased by nearly one-half.

Lodz and surrounding towns in central Poland have been for more than a century producing high quality yarn, fabrics, and ready-to-wear clothing. However, once **price controls** were lifted and the large market represented by the Soviet Union disappeared, the industry was forced to reduce production and employment. Many female workers were laid off because, with the outdated technology and relatively high labor costs, some textile factories were unable to compete with goods from Asia and Central America. Textiles are also produced in the city of Bialystok in the northeastern part of Poland.

The production of consumer durables is located in major cities. Poland increased the production of refrigerators, automatic washing machines, computer systems, and electronic calculating equipment and television sets in the 1990s. The increase in the production of television sets amounted to 687 percent between 1990 and 1999.

The production of furniture increased by 334 percent during the same period.

SERVICES

RETAIL. Poland's **retail** sector had been severely underdeveloped by central planners. The allocation of resources by the Soviet-backed regime gave priority to industrial development and, under the fixed-price system, made retailing a secondary concern. Furthermore, with private property ownership perceived as highly undesirable, the only companies that could operate retail stores were state-owned or cooperative enterprises. Three major organizations were virtual oligopolists (businesses which greatly affect the market by virtue of the scarcity of other businesses) in the retail sector. Two of them were transformed cooperatives: one operated grocery stores in towns and cities, and the other dominated retailing in rural areas. The government planners distributed goods according to priorities set by the government administration and in response to political influence rather than in response to the needs and actual demand.

The transition to a market-oriented economy at the end of 1989 led to the rapid re-birth of the private retail sector. Within a couple of years almost all retail trade was privatized. The old distribution system collapsed, and a new system slowly emerged. The instant effect of price liberalization and the introduction of private property was the increase in the number of retail outlets. Initially, new outlets were mostly small grocery stores, but over time specialty stores appeared, including clothing stores, shoe stores, drug stores, books and paper product outlets, stores with electronics, home furnishings, and others. The number of grocery stores continued to increase in the late 1990s, although at a decreasing rate. In 1999, the number of grocery stores was 16 percent higher than in 1995, but in 1998 the number of new stores increased by only 159, reaching a total of 147,366.

The newest trend in the retail food sector is the emergence of supermarket chains. In the first half of the 1990s, large supermarkets located in the largest cities. Although some of them were established by foreign retail corporations, others were operated by Polish entrepreneurs. Knowing the needs and preferences of Polish consumers, Polish chains located in residential neighborhoods or in areas of dense housing. The stores were medium size, offered self-service areas and serviced meat, fish, and bakery departments. In recent years, a number of large supermarkets has been constructed on the outskirts of large urban areas. They located at the intersections of major highways and depend heavily on shoppers traveling in their own vehicles. Given the rapid increase in car ownership, these new stores appeal to the new and growing middle class. Because these stores are largely operated by chains from Germany, France, Belgium, and other countries, they also brought with them the new concept of the hypermarket, which sells both groceries and non-food items ranging from cosmetics and detergent to clothing and household items.

Retail shops employed 1.35 million workers in 1999, or 13.9 percent of all employed in the economy. The employment in this sector increased by 20 percent between 1995 and 1999. However, the next few years will bring a restructuring of the food retail segment because large supermarkets operating for long hours had begun to force the closure of small shops in their area. Therefore, some jobs will be transferred from small owner-operated shops to large corporate-owned supermarkets. The process will vary across regions reflecting variability in population density and income.

CAR SERVICE INDUSTRY. The rapidly increasing number of cars in Poland led to the development of a new service sector that includes car dealerships, repair services, and gasoline stations. Car dealerships numbered 13,453 in 1999 and increased by 28.6 percent between 1995 and 1999. However, the growth rate decreased substantially over this period, reflecting the saturation of the market and the slackening demand for new cars. Although Poland's new car demand was the highest in Europe in 1998 and 1999, sales figures for 2000 were substantially lower. Increasing gasoline prices caused by higher energy prices worldwide and excise taxes made ownership less attractive. Furthermore, the increase of the short-term interest rates by the National Bank of Poland to curb inflation increased the cost of credit used by the majority of buyers to finance a purchase.

The number of gasoline stations continues to increase at a healthy pace. Between 1995 and 1999 the number increased by 42 percent. The growth in 1999 alone was almost 5 percent. With the construction of new highways and the establishment of new shopping centers on the outskirts of towns, the demand for gasoline will continue to grow. Also, the anticipated growth in cross-country transit traffic will encourage the construction of new gasoline stations in the near future. Many of the new stations are built by international corporations, e.g., Shell and BP, and include a convenience store and a fast food restaurant. McDonald's Corp. in particular joins many gasoline retailers located at major highways.

BANKING AND FINANCIAL SERVICES. The banking industry was underdeveloped at the end of the 1980s. Credit was used to finance government investment projects and was provided by state-owned banks. Credit for consumer spending was very limited. Housing cooperatives constructing and maintaining apartment complexes received government-subsidized credits. Since the change in government, the private banking industry has emerged and foreign banks opened branch offices.

The financial sector employed 287.4 thousand people at the end of 1999, 2.9 percent of the workforce and more than the mining industry. Employment grew by about one-fifth between 1995 and 1999. Revenues from operations increased for the comparable period of time by 268 percent. The gross profit rate of financial service businesses amounted to 15.5 percent in 1995 and dropped to 7.1 percent in 1999. However, the net profits were 9.9 percent in 1995, 4.2 percent in 1998, and 4.5 percent in 1999. Credit and debit card use has increased dramatically and ATMs have been installed in public access areas, facilitating customer use of their money.

In 1999 and 2000 a number of foreign banks increased their presence in Poland. Also, several major mergers were concluded strengthening the banking sector and increasing its capital. Foreign portfolio investment in Poland increased from US$9.4 billion in 1995 to US$14.2 billion in 1999. The foreign portfolio investment can choose between the bond and the stock market. In recent years, because of the growing economy, the stock market offered very good returns.

RESTAURANTS AND CAFETERIAS. This sector was particularly underdeveloped prior to 1989. The government was not interested in such investment because, under the system of controlled food prices, there was no economic incentive to operate restaurants. Instead, the government-owned companies, schools, universities, and hospitals operated cafeterias. Eating privileges were tied to employment or enrollment in the school program. The majority of cafeterias served the main meal of the day at mid-day. The food was often perceived as lacking taste, but it was convenient, saving the trouble of shopping and cooking upon returning home.

The restoration of private ownership encouraged a large number of entrepreneurs to open eating establishments. At the end of 1999, the number of restaurants was 73,099, and about 95 percent of them were privately owned. The distribution of restaurants by type indicates that the most popular among consumers and entrepreneurs were self-service restaurants, which represented 44.3 percent of all restaurants at the end of 1999. Food stands were the second most prevalent type of food service facility, representing 39.1 percent of all establishments, but their number grew very slowly between 1995 and 1999. Tablecloth restaurants represented 8.8 percent of all restaurants, but their number increased by 24.4 percent between 1995 and 1999. This growth is most visible as these restaurants locate in prime shopping or tourist areas. The fastest growth was among cafeterias, whose numbers expanded 36.4 percent between 1995 and 1999. The revenues in the food service sector as a whole doubled between 1995 and 1999. The growth was generated mostly by food sales rather than by alcohol sales.

TOURISM. Slightly over 89 million foreigners visited Poland in 1999. The growth was fully attributable to the growth in visits of citizens of neighboring countries, who represented 95.4 percent of foreign tourists. However, the short-term trends in the direction from which tourists arrive is changing. In the second half of the 1990s, the number of Ukrainian, Lithuanian, and Belarusian visitors increased, while the number of tourists from Slovakia, the Czech Republic, and Russia decreased. Czech and German tourists dominate the tourist traffic in Poland. In 1999, 53.8 million tourists came from Germany and 13.5 million tourists from the Czech Republic. The number of visiting German tourists steadily increases.

Tourists arriving from countries not bordering with Poland come mostly from the Netherlands, the United States, Sweden, Hungary, Italy, and Great Britain. Among them, the number of American tourists showed the largest gains between 1995 and 1999. Although Poland offers great tourist sites for those interested in history or nature, the climate is not conducive to all types of activities sought by tourists. The large, sandy beaches of the Baltic Sea are wonderful for walking, but sun bathing and swimming are reserved only for summer months.

The expanding hotel sector and improved quality of accommodations and service will eventually attract more tourists. The hospitality industry (hotels and restaurants) employed a total of 158.3 thousand people in 1999, or 1.6 percent of the workforce. This figure grew by more than 24 percent since 1995, showing a robust expansion of the sector. With improving access through a better highway system, faster train service, and more air connections, the tourist industry is poised for moderate growth.

INTERNATIONAL TRADE

During the last decade of the 20th century, international trade was fully liberalized. The direction of Poland's trade has changed substantially as the result of the breakup of the Soviet bloc of countries. Today, Poland's major trading partners are located mostly in Western Europe and North America and not in the for-

Trade (expressed in billions of US$): Poland

	Exports	Imports
1975	10.289	11.155
1980	14.191	16.690
1985	11.489	11.855
1990	13.627	8.413
1995	22.895	29.050
1998	N/A	N/A

SOURCE: International Monetary Fund. *International Financial Statistics Yearbook 1999.*

mer Soviet bloc states. Prior to World War II, the main trading partner in both exports and imports was Germany, receiving 31.2 percent of Polish exports and providing 27.3 percent of imports in 1928. The second and the third trading partners were the United States and Great Britain.

Following World War II and the installation of the Soviet Union-controlled regime in Poland, trade flow patterns changed. In 1950, the Soviet Union was the largest importer of Polish goods (28.8 percent) and the largest exporter to Poland (24.3 percent). Czechoslovakia and the German Democratic Republic (East Germany) were the other 2 most important trading partners. By 1990, the trade flow patterns continued to reflect the economic reorientation of Poland. The 2 main trading partners were East Germany (20.1 percent and 25.1 percent of imports and exports, respectively) and the Soviet Union (19.8 percent and 15.3 percent of imports and exports, respectively).

After 1990, however, trade patterns changed dramatically. The Soviet Union peacefully disintegrated and was replaced by Russia and 14 other independent countries. By 1999, a re-unified Germany had become the major trading partner, taking 36.1 percent of Poland's exports and providing 25.2 percent of its imports. Other major markets for Polish exports were Italy (6.5 percent), the Netherlands (5.3 percent), France (4.8 percent), the United Kingdom (4.0 percent), and the Czech Republic (3.8 percent). Major importers to Poland in 1999 include Italy (9.4 percent), France (6.8 percent), Russia (5.8 percent), the United Kingdom (4.6 percent), and the Netherlands (3.7 percent).

Poland formed together with Hungary, Slovakia, and the Czech Republic a free trade area in the early 1990s and became a member of the European Free Trade Association (EFTA). However, the main goal has been to gain access to the European Community (EC) market because of its size and the demand structure. Poland's agricultural products had particularly difficult access to EC markets because of the quota system imposed by the EU. An agreement between the 2 parties signed in September 2000 opened the trade in agricultural products and set the pace leading to full liberalization of agricultural trade between Poland and the EU within the next few years. It is expected that Poland will increase exports of milk and dairy products, pork, some fruits and vegetables, potato products, confections, and, perhaps, sugar, while increasing imports of poultry, fresh fruits and vegetables, wine, and processed foods.

Imports are associated with the rapid growth and direct foreign investment. Among some of the main types of goods imported to Poland are machinery and industrial equipment, electronics, cars and car parts, and construction materials. Oil and gas are large import items. Oil is imported from Russia and Middle Eastern countries, while gas is imported from Russia. Poland wants to import gas from Norway, but not until a pipeline link is constructed. In recent years Poland's appetite for imported goods exceeded exports. In 2000, the value of imports stood at US$42.7 billion while the value of exports stood at US$28.4 billion.

MONEY

From the end of World War II until 1990, the exchange of the Polish currency, the zloty, was suspended. The government established an elaborate system of several exchange rate regimes. The Polish zloty was valued differently against the same foreign currencies depending on the type of a transaction. For example, western tourists were forced to exchange their currency at a rate making the zloty very expensive, but foreign importers were attracted by competitively priced goods in zlotys. This system of multiple exchange rates ended in the late 1980s.

The liberalization of economic controls during the early 1990s caused the zloty to lose much of its value. By the mid-1990s, US$1 was worth in excess of 10,000 zlotys. Therefore, the National Bank of Poland decided to exchange the banknotes by introducing new coins and banknotes on 1 January 1995. The new Polish zloty was equal to 10,000 old Polish zlotys. The original exchange rate was posted at US$1:2.434 Polish zloty in January 1995. For a time, both the new and the old banknotes were in circulation. Today, old banknotes are no longer accepted for payment.

The National Bank of Poland (NBP) is the sole supplier of money in the economy. Its mission is to implement the **monetary policy** consistent with maintaining the low **inflation rate** needed for sustained economic growth. The primary tool used by the NBP was the manipulation of the short-term interest rate charged on loans made to commercial banks. The NBP is independent from the executive branch of government. Its leadership received high praise for its focused approach and has been credited with the high levels of economic activity.

With the adoption of the market economy, Poland opened its stock exchange. The Warsaw Stock Exchange

Exchange rates: Poland

zlotys per US$1	
Dec 2000	4.3126
2000	4.3461
1999	3.9671
1998	3.4754
1997	3.2793
1996	2.6961

SOURCE: CIA *World Factbook 2001* [ONLINE].

was, ironically, located in the building built specially as the headquarters of the Polish United Workers Party (a Soviet-style communist party). The increasing popularity of the stock exchange, the growing number of traded stocks, and the volume traded have forced it to move to a new, bigger facilities in recent years. Besides stocks of individual companies, several mutual funds have been established. Their popularity has increased because capital gains and dividends are tax-free in Poland.

At the end of 1999, the number of companies listed on the Warsaw Stock Exchange was 119, more than twice the number of those traded in 1995. The value of transactions more than tripled in the same time period. An average number of transactions per session on the main market was about 4,100 in 1999. The main market requires that companies exist for a minimum period of time and meet standard capital requirements. The parallel market trades shares of companies unable to meet the main market requirements, but which issue enough shares to guarantee **liquidity**. A total of 61 companies were listed on this market at the end of 1999. Finally, the free market trades shares of companies which meet similar, but less rigorous requirements than those expected from companies traded on the other 2 markets. At the end of 1999, this market listed 26 companies after 2 years in existence.

The Warsaw Stock Exchange Index (WIG) relates the current market value of companies listed on the main market to the value of companies quoted on the first session of the stock exchange on 16 April 1991. The initial level of the index was 1,000 and rose to 18,083.6 at the end of 1999.

Poland also has an active bond market. The government began issuing securities to finance the **budget deficit** in the early 1990s and gradually introduced short-, medium-, and long-term fixed rate treasury bonds. Variable rate bonds have been also introduced. Over time, the government has been issuing mostly variable rate bonds. This trend is reflected in changes in volume traded. In 1995, for example, the majority of transactions involved 5-year fixed rate bonds, but in 1999 the majority involved 3-year variable bonds. Overall, during that period, the government issued less bonds and the value of traded bonds in 1999 was roughly one-fourth of that in 1995. Traders and the public preferred trading at the stock exchange.

POVERTY AND WEALTH

Although not a poor country, the amount of wealth accumulated by Poland's citizens is limited. The loss of independence, the control by foreign powers of economic and political life, and 2 world wars brought destruction and depleted any accumulated wealth. Since the end of World War II misguided economic policies further wasted the efforts of millions of people. Only since 1990 has the country had its first real opportunity to utilize its talents and skills. It will take time, however, before the effects will be widely visible.

GDP per Capita (US$)

Country	1975	1980	1985	1990	1998
Poland	N/A	2,932	2,819	2,900	3,877
United States	19,364	21,529	23,200	25,363	29,683
Germany	N/A	N/A	N/A	N/A	31,141
Romania	1,201	1,643	1,872	1,576	1,310

SOURCE: United Nations. *Human Development Report 2000; Trends in human development and per capita income.*

The implementation of market-oriented reforms caused the whole nation to suffer during the period of transition. The previous system of widely spread subsidies for food consumption, transportation, and other areas of life could not be sustained because of the gaping hole in the government budget. Particularly hard hit by budget cuts were places of culture including museums, galleries, theaters, symphony orchestras, and other artists who had benefitted from government sponsorship. Slowly, as the economy has improved, private sponsors increased their contributions and the government budget has allocated more funds to support arts and sciences.

The new economic system offers unemployment benefits. The benefits expire after several months. However, local governments operate offices assisting the unemployed in finding jobs. In some parts of the country it is difficult to match the person with given skills to the job. Retraining programs are offered for those who lack job skills, such as high school graduates who pursued general education, or those whose skills are obsolete because of the changing economy.

Poland's health care system has been recently reformed, but everybody has access to medical services. A

Distribution of Income or Consumption by Percentage Share: Poland

Lowest 10%	3.0
Lowest 20%	7.7
Second 20%	12.6
Third 20%	16.7
Fourth 20%	22.1
Highest 20%	40.9
Highest 10%	26.3

Survey year: 1996

Note: This information refers to income shares by percentiles of the population and is ranked by per capita income.

SOURCE: *2000 World Development Indicators* [CD-ROM].

Household Consumption in PPP Terms

Country	All food	Clothing and footwear	Fuel and power[a]	Health care[b]	Education[b]	Transport & Communications	Other
Poland	28	4	19	6	1	8	34
United States	13	9	9	4	6	8	51
Germany	14	6	7	2	10	7	53
Romania	36	7	9	3	20	9	16

Data represent percentage of consumption in PPP terms.
[a]Excludes energy used for transport.
[b]Includes government and private expenditures.

SOURCE: World Bank. *World Development Indicators 2000.*

person must register with a family doctor of his or her choice. This general physician is the primary care provider. Should any additional services be required, the primary care provider directs a patient to a specialist. The health care system is organized into several regional organizations which receive government grants to finance their services. The organizations negotiate contract prices with hospitals and clinics, both private and operated by local governments. Destitute people also receive health care services and the cost of treatment is paid by grants from local or central governments. Although the system pays for psychiatric help, it does not include dental care services.

Poland has a public school system. All citizens are guaranteed education through grade 12. In recent years, private schools have been permitted, but their number remains small. Schools are operated by local governments, but the central government provides grants on a per-pupil basis. Because schools often lack funds for periodic maintenance services such as painting or decorating classrooms, parents often either collect additional funds or provide labor to complete these tasks. Fund raisers are also held to finance class trips and other special projects.

High school graduates who would like to pursue a university degree can choose from a number of private colleges and public universities. Many of these schools focus on educating students in a single area, for example, insurance, journalism, marketing, or economics and management. They offer a baccalaureate degree after 3 years of studies. Two additional years and a thesis are required to complete an MS degree. The government provides low-interest loans for students lacking funds to study at a university. Public universities do not charge tuition, but to be accepted the candidate must pass an entrance exam or graduate from high school with a high GPA.

Because economic conditions vary across regions, the government developed some programs focusing on the needs of areas lagging behind the general level of development. These areas receive additional funds for the construction of local infrastructure projects including water and sewage treatment facilities, school construction and renovation, etc. A portion of the funds is provided by the EU.

Although lifestyles between the poor and the wealthy have not yet had time to fully differentiate, some differences are visible. Besides differences in food consumption, some of the noticeable differences are in the use of vacation time. Although the number of people participating in tourist trips increased from 53 percent in 1990 to 63 percent in 1999, the percentage of those spending 5 or more days on a trip stayed roughly the same. In 1990, 34 percent spent 5 or more days on a trip, while in 1999 36 percent did so. However, the number of non-travelers decreased from 47 percent to 37 percent in the same time period. The length of a typical vacation tends to be shorter now than the standard 2 weeks prior to 1989.

The change of the economic system to one rewarding the suppliers of labor negatively affected families with a large number of small children. These families tend to spend particularly large amounts of their income on food and basic necessities, while having fewer opportunities to allocate more time to work. Government welfare programs provide additional support, but it seems that the needs of large families are increasing. Whether this situation discourages childbearing and contributes to the stagnation of the population growth has not yet been determined.

WORKING CONDITIONS

Government policy aims at sustaining economic growth as the way to solve the problem of unemployment. In 1999 an estimated 12 percent of Poland's workforce of 17.2 million were unemployed. Poland is a member of the International Labor Organization (ILO) and participates in all major world and European treaties protecting personal freedoms, rights of expression, and free association. The tradition of independent trade union organization started with Solidarity, which was a major force behind the transition to democracy and a market-oriented economy.

Workers continue to be organized in 2 major trade union organizations: Solidarity, which continues the traditions of the organization born in the summer of 1980; and the trade union organizations formed from the former government-sponsored and controlled unions that predated Solidarity. There is also a very aggressive teachers' union, which was opposed to the government-sponsored school reforms and the associated performance-based evaluation. Part of the reform included the change of the retirement age from 55 years of age to 60 years. However, none of the changes violated any domestic or international legal standard.

Disputes resulting from employment contracts are handled by special courts. These courts deal only with conflicts between employers and employees. Children under 16 years of age are not allowed to work. On farms, however, some children may help parents with regular chores or at harvest. However, no widespread use of underage children is required because many farms are small and they are relatively well equipped with machinery. Pregnant women receive special treatment. After delivery, a woman can take up to 12 months of unpaid leave, while her job is protected.

Increasingly, education influences the type of job and pay a person receives. The link between education and pay explains the increasing demand for education and the rapidly growing number of college and university students.

COUNTRY HISTORY AND ECONOMIC DEVELOPMENT

966. Poland's Duke Mieszko I is baptized and Poland accepts Christianity.

1025. Boleslaw is crowned the first king of Poland.

1385. The commonwealth of Poland and Lithuania is created through a treaty.

1683. King Jan Sobieski III defeats the army of the Ottoman Empire in the battle of Vienna.

1772. Poland is partitioned (divided) by Russia, Austria, and Prussia.

1795. Polish-American hero Tadeusz Kosciuszko leads an insurrection against Russia, one of many that occur as Poland loses all the functionings of an independent state as it is subsumed into the partitioning countries. Poland ceases to exist as an independent nation until 1918.

1918. Poland is reborn at the end of World War I; Ignacy Paderewski becomes the first prime minister.

1920. Poland fights a war with the Soviet Union and successfully defends itself against the Red Army.

1939. On 1 September Nazi Germany invades Poland signaling the beginning of World War II; on 17 September Russian leader Josef Stalin orders the Red Army to enter Poland in accordance with the secret treaty between the Soviet Union and Germany; Poland is occupied until 1945.

1940. The Polish government-in-exile formed in the United Kingdom organizes a system of military and civilian communication in occupied Poland.

1945. Warsaw is liberated and Poland is freed of Nazi occupation.

1948. The Soviet Union installs a communist government in Poland, leading to over 40 years of **centrally-planned economic** organization.

1956. In June, protests against Soviet control in the city of Poznan end with nearly 80 dead; by October, the ruling regime installs new leadership and temporarily relaxes some controls.

1970. The December protests of shipyard workers against food price increases lead to violent action by government security forces in the Baltic cities of Szczecin, Gdynia, and Gdansk.

1976. Following another wave of protests, the Polish opposition forms the Committee for Workers' Defense and begins to organize the underground publication of officially banned writers and intellectuals.

1979. Polish Cardinal Karol Wojtyla, the Roman Catholic Archbishop of Cracow, is elected Pope John Paul II.

1980. The independent trade union "Solidarity," led by Lech Walesa, is born in Gdansk.

1981. Martial law is introduced on 13 December, and there are widespread arrests of Solidarity activists.

1989. Negotiations lead to a peaceful transfer of power to the opposition; the first free elections are held in Poland since the end of World War II.

1997. A new constitution is adopted in a nationwide referendum.

1999. Poland joins the North Atlantic Treaty Organization (NATO).

FUTURE TRENDS

Poland entered the 21st century as a member of NATO and a candidate for the early accession into the European Union. The country has been firmly committed to democracy and a market economy after the implementation of economic, political, administrative, and social reforms following the collapse of communist control in 1989. The pace of changes during the 1990s moved the country from stagnation to a period of steady economic growth. The country is posed to continue its growth. Although the unemployment rate will, at least in the short run, remain relatively high, the government's **macroeconomic** policies are intended to assure long-term economic growth. The primary objective will remain the need to manage the supply of money to the economy so as to balance the need for growth with the need to assure stable prices.

In the coming years the most important economic issues facing Poland will likely include efforts to lower unemployment, while keeping inflation at bay. Furthermore, issues in regional differences in economic activity will come to the forefront. Although **labor mobility** in Poland is low because of prevailing attitudes, those who want to move to an area where the demand for labor is high face the problem of finding affordable housing.

Political stability has been achieved as governments alternate between right and left orientation, but within constitutionally defined boundaries. Although not all reforms have been popular, all of them have been necessary to assure the sustainable growth in decades to come. The transfer of many responsibilities from the central to local government strengthens the participatory democracy, allowing the people to voice their opinions and influence policies.

Within the next few years, a young, well-educated labor force will enter the labor market. Because the quality of human capital is increasingly important in today's economy, future graduates are expected to be productive and competitive contributors to further economic growth.

DEPENDENCIES

Poland has no territories or colonies.

BIBLIOGRAPHY

Economist Intelligence Unit. *Country Profile: Poland.* London: Economist Intelligence Unit, 2001.

Embassy of Poland, Washington, D.C. <http://www.polandembassy.org>. Accessed September 2001.

Holmes, Leslie T., and Wojciech Roszkowski, editors. *Changing Rules: Polish Political and Economic Transformation in Comparative Perspectives.* Warsaw: Institute of Political Studies, Polish Academy of Sciences, 1997.

National Bank of Poland. <http://www.nbp.pl/home_en.html>. Accessed September 2001.

OECD Economic Outlook. Paris: Organization for Economic Cooperation and Development, Vol. 68, December 2000.

Polish Official Statistics. <http://www.stat.gov.pl/english/index.htm>. Accessed September 2001.

U.S. Central Intelligence Agency. *World Factbook 2001.* <http://www.odci.gov/cia/publications/factbook/index.html>. Accessed September 2001.

U.S. Department of State. *FY 2001 Country Commercial Guide: Poland.* <http://www.state.gov/www/about_state/business/com_guides/2001/europe/index.html>. Accessed September 2001.

Wojtaszczyk, Konstanty Adam, editor. *Poland in Transition.* Warsaw: Dom Wydawn, ELIPSA, 1999.

—Wojciech J. Florkowski

PORTUGAL

Portuguese Republic
República Portuguesa

CAPITAL: Lisbon (Lisboa).

MONETARY UNIT: Escudo (Esc). One Portuguese escudo equals 100 centavos. There are banknotes in denominations of 10,000, 5,000, 2,000, 1,000, and 500 escudos. Coins come in denominations of 200, 100, 50, 20, 10 and 5 escudos. The escudo will remain in circulation until February 28, 2002, when it will be completely be replaced by the new European currency, the euro.

CHIEF EXPORTS: Clothing and footwear, machinery, chemicals, cork and paper products, food and beverages, and hides.

CHIEF IMPORTS: Machinery and transport equipment, chemicals, petroleum, textiles, and agricultural products.

GROSS DOMESTIC PRODUCT: US$151.4 billion (1999 est.).

BALANCE OF TRADE: **Exports:** US$25 billion (1998 est.). **Imports:** US$34.9 billion (1998 est.).

COUNTRY OVERVIEW

LOCATION AND SIZE. Located in southwestern Europe in the western part of the Iberian Peninsula, Portugal borders Spain to the north and east and the Atlantic Ocean to the south and west. The total area of the country—including the overseas territories of Azores (2,247 square kilometers/868 square miles) and the Madeira Islands (794 square kilometers/307 square miles), both autonomous regions of Portugal—is 92,345 square kilometers (35,655 square miles). The area of Portugal is thus slightly smaller than the U.S. state of Indiana. The capital and largest city is Lisbon, a major seaport situated in the west-central part of Portugal at the mouth of the Tejo (Tajo) River. Other major cities include Oporto (Porto) situated in the northwest at the mouth of the Douro (Duero) River; Coimbra, an industrial and university city on the Mondego River in central Portugal; and Faro, located in the renowned Algarve beach resort area in the south.

POPULATION. The population of Portugal numbered 10,048,232 in July 2000. The population growth rate was estimated at a rather low 0.18 percent in 2000, and the net migration rate was 0.5 immigrants per 1,000 population in the same year. The Portuguese population declined slightly in the late 1980s due to a rapid reduction of the birth rate and steady **emigration**. The figures somewhat stabilized during the 1990s, and in 1999 the population was 1 percent higher than it was in 1991. Portugal still has one of the lowest fertility rates in Western Europe with approximately 1.4 children born per woman. In 1999, the number of births rose by 2.3 percent, but this increase was still insufficient to ensure long-term population growth. According to Portuguese demographic projections (assuming a recovery in the fertility rate to 1.66 per woman in 2020), the Portuguese population is expected to peak in 2015 at 10.18 million and then again begin to decline. As in many other European countries, Portugal has an aging population with 15.2 percent over 65 years of age in 1998 (up from 13.8 percent in 1991) and only 16.8 percent aged 14 years or younger (compared with 19.4 percent in 1991). Life expectancy was 72.24 years for men and 79.49 years for women in 2000. Aging will inevitably increase the strain on Portugal's already over-stretched health-care and social security systems.

The Portuguese population has been strongly influenced by migration processes. Many nationals emigrated in the 1960s, 1970s, and to a lesser extent in the 1980s in search of higher living standards in the more affluent economies of Western Europe and elsewhere. About 4.5 million Portuguese now live abroad, or almost one-half of the domestic population, but better domestic economic conditions in recent years—particularly since the country joined the European Union (EU) in 1986—have changed this. By 2000, Portugal experienced a net **immigration**

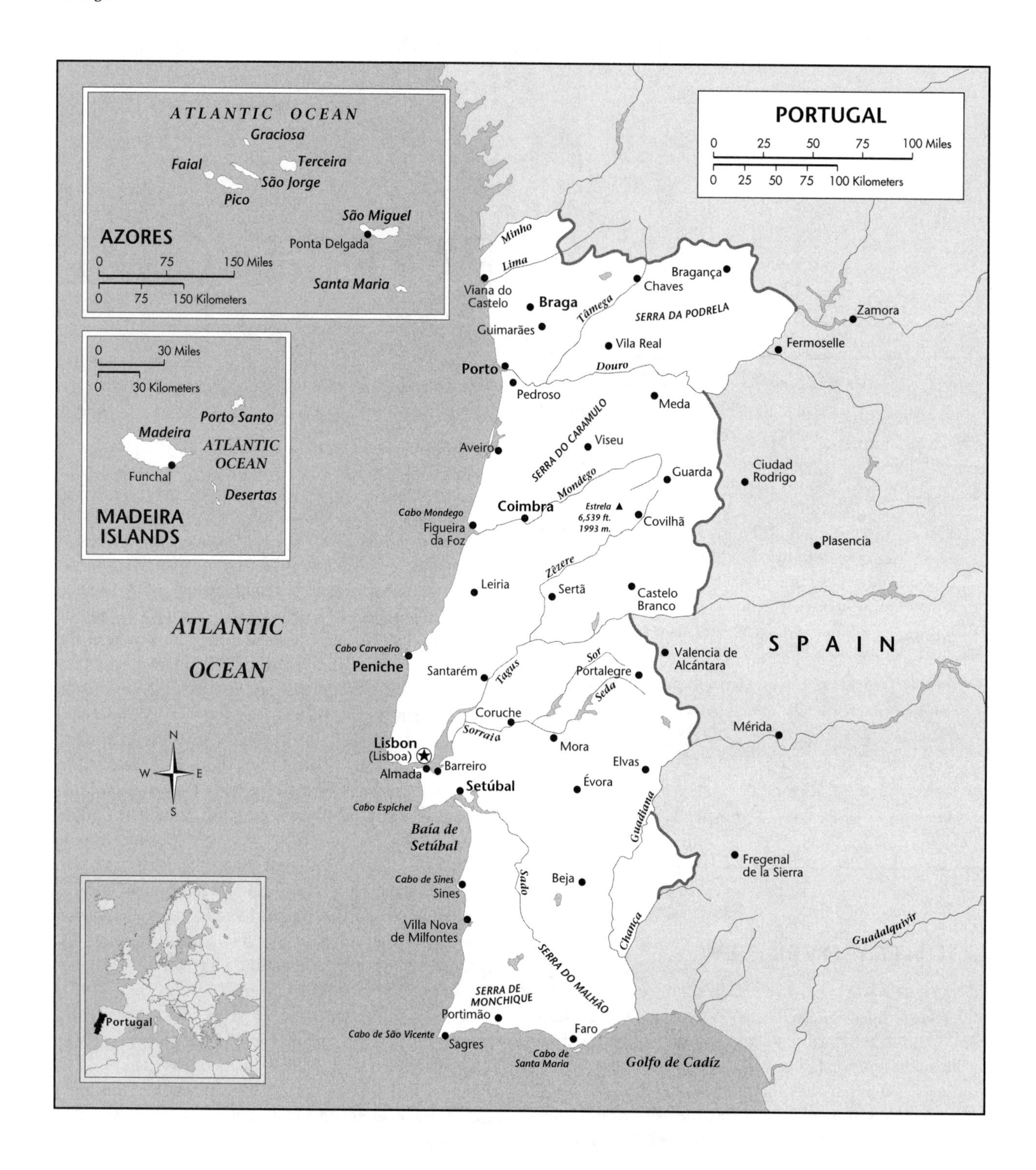

of 0.5 people per 1,000 population. In 1998, there were fewer than 178,000 immigrants legally residing in Portugal. These immigrants originated mainly from the country's former African and South American colonies and from EU countries.

The Portuguese are primarily of Mediterranean descent, as their ancestry can be traced to ancient Iberians, Romans, Visigoths, and Moors (Arabs). Black African citizens who immigrated to the mainland during the decolonization in the 1970s are fewer than 100,000 in number. Portuguese is the official language. Roman Catholicism is the religion of about 94 percent of the population, although a number of Protestants and followers of other denominations also live in the country. The main urban centers are concentrated around the Lisbon and Tejo Valley area on the Atlantic coast and in the vicinity of the city of Oporto. These 2 conurbations (zones) are home to nearly 69 percent of the population. The shift from inland rural areas to the cities was fueled by the agricultural crisis and the post-World War II industrial boom, which again gained momentum in the 1970s. The nation is still experiencing heavy migration to urban centers, along with the gradual depopulation of villages in Portugal's rural provinces.

OVERVIEW OF ECONOMY

In 2000, Portugal's economy was to a large degree modern and market-oriented, enjoying steady, although not spectacular, economic growth, decreased interest rates, comparatively low unemployment, and improved living standards. Nevertheless, it remained Western Europe's least developed country with a per capita **gross domestic product** (GDP) of US$15,975, or approximately two-thirds that of the large Western European economies. Portugal's GDP was the second lowest in the EU after that of Greece, which was estimated to have the lowest production on the basis of market **exchange rates** in late 2000. Portugal also continued to have a large trade and **balance of payments** deficit.

Following its past glory as an influential world power and the leading maritime and colonial nation in the 15th and 16th centuries, Portugal experienced economic decline, particularly after the loss of its Brazilian colony in 1822. After more than 6 decades of oppressive dictatorship, economic stagnation, and international isolation during the 20th century, Portugal was considered by many to be the laggard of Western Europe by the early 1970s. Following the country's return to democratic rule in 1974, the economy grew by an average of 5.3 percent annually during the period from 1975 to 1980.

Portugal joined the EU in 1985, and its GDP growth slowed down to less than 1 percent annually during the period of EU adjustment. After 1990, it achieved a satisfactory annual growth average of 2.1 percent, reaching 2.7 percent in 2000. In 1998, Portugal successfully qualified for the European Monetary Union (EMU) and joined with 10 other European countries in launching the European currency, the euro, on January 1, 1999. The euro will fully replace Portugal's currency unit, the escudo, in February 2002. EU and EMU membership should be considered a major success, given the condition of the Portuguese economy in the early 1970s.

EU membership has been particularly beneficial for Portugal, allowing the country access to development funds and creating favorable conditions for its economy to compete, integrate, learn from, and get closer to the advanced economies of Western Europe. The government is working to modernize the country's economic capacity and increase its competitiveness in the increasingly integrated European and world markets. Improvement in the education sector is critical to this process.

These successes notwithstanding, industrial development and **restructuring** in Portugal generally has been slower than in other EU countries. Its industrial base is still quite limited, often facing hardship from having to compete in the single European market. But driven by the pressing competition of lower-cost East and South Asian imports, some traditional Portuguese exporting industries, such as footwear, clothing, and textiles, have rapidly modernized since the 1990s. Growth has been also strong in services, especially in the financial and **retail** sectors, and in construction. Tourism has also been historically important, with its focus in the late 1990s moving from traditional mass-market beach holidays to high-end, quality, cultural tourism.

Portugal, like its EU neighbors, has developed a service-based economy, while agriculture and fishing—once major sectors—have become much less important. Although the agricultural sector represented just 3.3 percent of GDP in 1998, it still accounted for 13.5 percent of total employment, much higher than the average for EU countries. The slowness of farmers to adopt more productive agricultural technology has led to a loss of market share to the more efficient producers of Spain and France.

An important factor setting Portugal apart from the leading EU economies is its lower labor costs, with an average annual cost of US$13,084 per worker, compared, for example, with US$33,196 per worker in Germany. Cheap labor has attracted substantial foreign investment in several new industry projects, particularly in the automotive and electronics manufacturing sectors. A new technology park outside of Lisbon has attracted several high-profile computer software and hardware companies. However, alternative low-cost manufacturing locations are also growing across Central and Eastern Europe, at locations often better suited geographically to supply the main European markets. They too are becoming increasingly attractive for investors, and Portugal is aware that it can no longer rely on low wages alone to attract new investment. Preparations for EU enlargement in 2001–02 and beyond will be of crucial significance to Portugal. The country will have to strive to protect its interests in accessing the EU's development funds and protecting its market shares in competition with the new, poorer, and sometimes smaller EU members.

POLITICS, GOVERNMENT, AND TAXATION

For much of the 20th century, Portugal has been ruled by an oppressive right-wing dictatorial regime and has maintained, often by force, control of its large colonial empire. In 1974, Portuguese revolutionaries initiated broad democratic constitutional reforms. In 1975, the country granted independence to its African colonies—Angola, Mozambique, Guinea-Bissau, Cape Verde, and São Tomé and Príncipe. Its constitution was further amended several times, most notably in 1992 when the treaty that created the EU, known as the Maastricht Treaty, was ratified, reflecting the new political and economic conditions of a united Europe.

The political system that emerged from the democratic reforms in the 1970s is parliamentary, with the role of the president being largely ceremonial, although certain reserve powers are also vested in this institution. The president is directly elected for a term of 5 years by popular vote and a person can hold the office for a maximum of 2 consecutive terms. In the Portuguese executive branch, the leadership role of the prime minister is much more important. The prime minister is the head of government and is elected by parliament on a motion by the largest parliamentary party or coalition.

Legislative power is vested in the **unicameral** (one house), 250-member Assembleia da Republica (parliament). Members are elected for terms of 4 years by **proportional representation**, but elections can also be called by the president at an earlier date (the next parliamentary election is due in October of 2003). There are 20 constituencies (electoral districts) in Portugal and the electorate chooses between numerous competing party lists.

The most influential Portuguese political parties include the center-left Socialist Party (PS), the center-right Social Democratic Party (PSD), the Communist Party (PCP), and the conservative Popular Party (PP). The PS returned to power in October 1995 after 10 years in opposition and was reelected in October 1999 with 115 parliamentary seats—not a majority, but significantly more than any other party. Its major dissent on economic policy with the PSD (81 seats), the main opposition party of the PS, is the greater stress that the PS places on social welfare spending. Both parties support a market economy, **privatization**, and European integration. The PCP (17 seats, in coalition with the smaller Green Party), which used to be the most effective party in clandestine (secret) opposition to the dictatorship before 1974, is one of the few remaining hard-line leftist parties in Europe. The PCP still advocates an extensive role of the state in the economy. Its once strong base in the industrial suburbs of large cities and the rural south was weakened during the 1980s and 1990s as the economy improved and poverty diminished radically. The PP (15 seats), previously known as the Center Democrats (CDS), underwent a number of transformations in the 1990s. These were accompanied by acute internal crises, and the party finally emerged in the late 1990s as the voice of the new right, holding a populist and anti-European stance.

In January 2001, the **socialist** president, Jorge Sampaio, was reelected with 55.8 percent of the popular vote, but roughly a year into its second term, the PS government, led by socialist Prime Minister Antonio Guterres, came under controversy. The economic climate was deteriorating, GDP growth was expected to slow from 2.7 percent in 2000 to 2.3 percent in 2001, and acute budgetary disputes and depressing corruption charges plagued the government. Another major confusion was caused by the findings of the of the long-running "Camarate Affair" investigation into a 1980 plane crash that killed the then Prime Minister Francisco Sa Carneiro of the PSD, as it is now widely believed that Sa Carneiro was in fact deliberately murdered.

The government's role in the economy became very significant in the decade following the 1974 revolution. One of the chief results of the upheaval was the takeover of many important industries by the state. Following its joining of the EU in 1985, however, Portugal adopted, partly as an adjustment measure, an active privatization program aimed at making the **public sector** more limited and more profitable. As a result, the Portuguese public sector accounted for 19.7 percent of GDP and for 5.5 percent of the country's total employment in 1988, and by late 1997, the numbers had been further reduced to 8 percent and 2.6 percent, respectively.

The privatization of state companies has been generally very beneficial for the country. The approaches towards accomplishing privatization have been quite varied, including selling shares in selected companies through a public stock offering in the capital markets, private sale, or often by using both methods combined. On a number of occasions, however, the government has kept a controlling share for itself that gives it the right to overrule strategic corporate decisions in the privatized companies. From 1989 to 1998, approximately 150 sales involving the shares of nearly 100 companies generated proceeds of more than US$21 billion, and 52 percent of the revenue was used for the repayment of existing public debt.

In 1998, 58 percent of the total **market capitalization** in the Lisbon Stock Exchange (BVL) was accounted for by the market capitalization of these privatized firms. In addition to some further expected sales of the stock of state-owned companies such as the telecommunications firm, Portuguese Telecom (PT), and the electricity company, Electricidade de Portugal (EDP), there are other major state firms still in the initial stages of privatization. These include the state airline, TAP, and a new energy **holding company** that combines the government's interest in petroleum refining and natural gas transmission.

In taxation, the government is trying to bring the Portuguese system closer to those established in other EU countries. A major reform of **direct taxation** took place in 1989 to that effect, but it was widely believed that occasional gaps remained between the law and its actual enforcement practices. The 1989 tax code defined taxable income as the profits of firms involved in commerce, industry, or agriculture. All income gained by local companies abroad is taxable, but tax liability may be cancelled or decreased by various tax treaties. The income of resident corporations and branches of foreign (non-resident) companies is taxable at a rate of 32 percent. The actual tax rate in many regions of Portugal is in fact 35.2 percent because some local surcharges exist, usually at a rate of 10 percent of the base tax.

The government intends, however, to cut corporate taxes by nearly one-eighth before 2003, and companies with revenues of less than Esc100 million would be granted even more preferential treatment. The introduction of the **value-added tax** (VAT) in 1986 helped the tax authorities detect and prevent widespread tax evasion by individuals and companies who were still plaguing the economy at that time. Tax evasion has been further reduced since the government was forced to dramatically improve its tax collection efficiency and to reduce its **budget deficit** without introducing new taxes. The government was forced to do this in order to qualify for the requirements of the EMU in 1998. A 20 percent **advance tax** is applied to all payments by businesses to independent contractors and all self-employed individuals with an annual income of Esc2 million or higher.

Portugal has an **external debt** estimated at US$13.1 billion in 1997. The debt is not considered disproportionate or burdening for the economy, and Portugal handles its financial obligations properly.

INFRASTRUCTURE, POWER, AND COMMUNICATIONS

Portugal's membership in the EU was beneficial for the country's **infrastructure**. This was so not only because of the economic improvement due to European integration, but also because the country received support in financing its infrastructure projects from the union's funds. The greatest portions of these funds were raised through the European Regional Development Fund. Between 1987 and 1998, Portugal received approximately US$24 billion in development funds from the EU. Economic growth over the 1990s has been accompanied by some ambitious infrastructure improvements, most notably by the completion of an extensive system of modern highways.

Additional infrastructure projects are expected to be launched between 2001 and 2005, including additional roads, dams and ports, a new international airport (to be built at Ota, north of Lisbon), a new metro (subway) system at Oporto, modernization of the country's railroad system, and an upgrade of the natural gas pipeline system. As a result, the country has a well-developed transportation network with 59,110 kilometers (37,000 miles) of paved roads, including 797 kilometers (498 miles) of expressways, 2,850 kilometers (1,780 miles) of railroads, and some 820 kilometers (513 miles) of navigable inland waterways (of relatively little importance to the national economy). Once a great maritime nation, Portugal has many ports and harbors in Aveiro, Funchal (the Madeira Islands), Horta (the Azores), Leixoes, Lisbon, Porto, Ponta Delgada (Azores), Praia da Vitoria (Azores), Setubal, and Viana do Castelo. The country also runs a sizable merchant fleet of 151 ships totaling 1,061,267 deadweight tons (DWT). Portugal is served by nearly 40 airports and by its major national airline, TAP.

The energy industry is largely state-controlled, but energy output in Portugal is still quite low. Its dependence on foreign energy sources is thus correspondingly high. No oil or natural gas has been exploited in the country, known reserves of coal are limited (only about 30 million tons), and there are no nuclear power facilities. With financing from the EU, Portugal allocated Esc470 billion to the construction of a natural gas network to connect with the pipeline from Algeria to Europe, which opened in November 1996. The country expects the connection to the pipeline to support one-tenth of its energy

Communications

Country	Newspapers	Radios	TV Sets[a]	Cable subscribers[a]	Mobile Phones[a]	Fax Machines[a]	Personal Computers[a]	Internet Hosts[b]	Internet Users[b]
	1996	1997	1998	1998	1998	1998	1998	1999	1999
Portugal	75	304	542	59.8	309	7.0	81.3	59.40	700
United States	215	2,146	847	244.3	256	78.4	458.6	1,508.77	74,100
Spain	100	333	506	11.8	179	17.8	144.8	76.75	4,652
Greece	153	477	466	1.2	194	3.8	51.9	59.57	750

[a]Data are from International Telecommunication Union, *World Telecommunication Development Report 1999* and are per 1,000 people.
[b]Data are from the Internet Software Consortium (http://www.isc.org) and are per 10,000 people.

SOURCE: World Bank. *World Development Indicators 2000.*

needs. In 1998, electricity was generated mostly by thermal plants, using fossil fuel (63.14 percent), hydropower (33.46 percent), and other (not nuclear) sources (3.4 percent). The country is a major net importer of energy.

The Portuguese energy market in the 1990s was served by 4 government-controlled companies: the partly privatized oil company Petrogal, the partly privatized electricity utility Electricidade de Portugal (EDP), and the 2 gas companies, Transgas (operating the new natural gas pipeline) and Gas de Portugal (GdP). In 1999, the government created a new state-controlled holding company, Gas e Petroleos de Portugal (Galp) by merging Petrogal with the 2 gas companies. This process was aimed at developing an energy group that would be able to compete effectively with larger Western European utility companies in the increasingly **liberalized** market.

In telecommunications, Portugal is a small market lacking a culture that is particularly technology-oriented. Furthermore, Portugal has a relatively low saturation in terms of consumer telecom services compared with other, more developed EU countries. In 1996, 3.72 million fixed telephone lines were in use, and there were 887,216 mobile phone subscribers in 1999. For comparison, these statistics are quite lower than in Scandinavia, but still higher than in Germany. Portugal joined Finland and Venezuela as one of the only countries where, for various reasons, mobile phone penetration has overgrown the fixed phone market. About 23 percent of Portuguese homes had cable TV in 2000. Although 20 Internet service providers operated in 1999, the Portuguese still lagged well behind most other Europeans in using the Internet. Business and consumer broadband and data faster-access Internet services, popular elsewhere in Europe, are still almost non-existent.

The legacy of the decades-long Portuguese dictatorship with its nationalistic, isolationist economic policies, combined with its comparatively late entry into the EU, has resulted in Portugal's reputation as the EU's telecommunications laggard. The country started implementing the EU services directives to harmonize its telecommunications industry with the markets of its larger, more developed neighbors for the first time in the early 1990s. Portugal liberalized its basic telecommunications services in January 2000, becoming the second-to-last EU member to open its market to foreign competition, and its regulatory regime was set to manage the transition period to free competition. By early 2001, the state-run Portugal Telecom (PT) had kept its **monopoly** control on traditional segments such as fixed telephony, leased lines, and multi-channel television. The cable television market is still dominated by the PT's cable division (under the brand names of PT, Multimedia, and TV Cabo), which operates a nationwide fiber optic cable network covering nearly 95 percent of the consumer base.

However, PT faces robust competition in newer telecom services in the liberalized market environment. While PT's basic fixed line telephone market is considered rather dysfunctional, under-developed, and shrinking, its strongest competitive advantage is TMN, its mobile service operator and only serious business presence in non-traditional markets. Competition in new service segments started gaining ground when the second mobile phone operator, using the European GSM system, was launched in 1992. The liberalization of the data services market in 1994 led to several new data service entrants. Competition in non-traditional services has forced PT to reinvigorate its efforts to secure its thinning margin of leadership in market share in these segments. In January 2000, with the entry of 8 new basic services operators, competition entered the traditional market.

In 2000, the government filed for EU approval to privatize a 34 percent stake in the TAP airline, demonstrating its intention to sell it to Swissair. Other deals in the government's ambitious infrastructure privatization program include a 20 percent share in the state electricity giant EDP and the last 10 percent of state-owned stake in national telecommunications company PT, which was sold to foreign investors in 2000. In 2001, the privatization of the state's remaining 15 percent stake in the expressway operator holding, Brisa, is expected, as well as the partial privatization of the energy holding company Galp, one-third of which has already been bought by the Italian energy group ENI. However, the government's handling of the TAP, EDP, and Galp privatizations has turned highly controversial, and political and legal inquiries into the matter could delay further privatization steps.

ECONOMIC SECTORS

In 1998, the largest contributor to the Portuguese economy, as elsewhere in Western Europe, was the services industries. This sector is responsible for nearly two-thirds of the GDP, while industry, utilities, and construction together contributed more than one-third, and agriculture, forestry, and fishing contributed about 3.3 percent. By European standards, however, a disproportionately high percentage of the **labor force** was employed in agriculture. The 13.5 percent of the population that works in this industry apparently still lag behind their counterparts in other EU nations in using modern technologies and enhancing effectiveness.

AGRICULTURE

Although its contribution to GDP is very small, agriculture still employs a considerable number of Portuguese. Chief crops and production figures for 1998 include vegetables (including tomatoes, 2.2 million metric tons), fruit (including grapes and olives, 1.7 million tons),

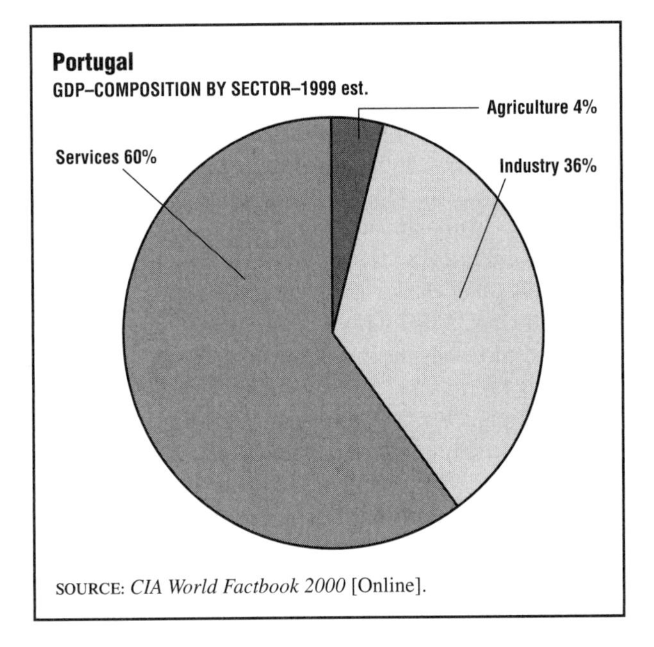

SOURCE: *CIA World Factbook 2000* [Online].

root crops (including potatoes, 1.1 million tons), and cereal grains (including corn and wheat, 1.3 million tons). Portugal is traditionally one of the world's leading producers of wine (including the world-renowned Porto and Madeira wines) and olive oil. Livestock in 1998 numbered 1.3 million cattle, 6.3 million sheep, 2.2 million pigs, and 33 million poultry. Fishing is also a major industry. Portuguese farmers and fishers—like their colleagues elsewhere in Europe—rely heavily on EU **subsidies**, but their slowness to adopt more productive technology has resulted in a loss of EU market share to competitors from Spain, France, and Italy.

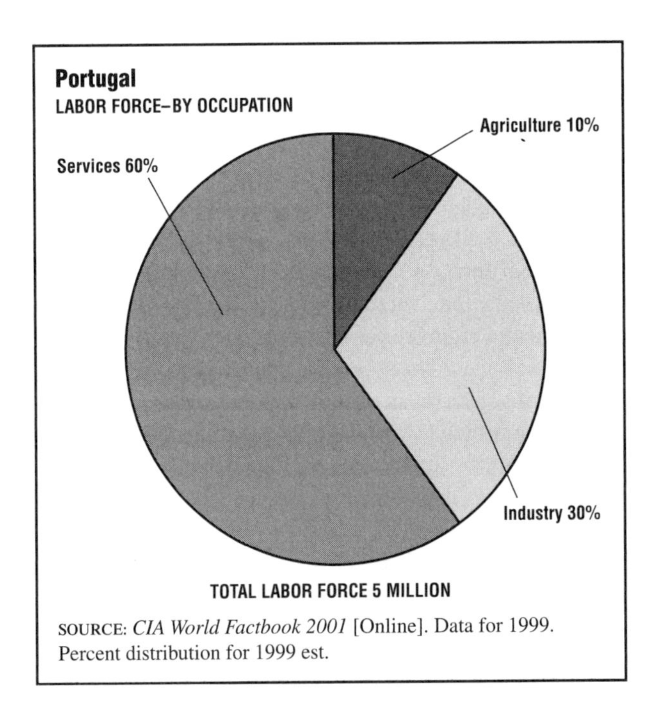

SOURCE: *CIA World Factbook 2001* [Online]. Data for 1999. Percent distribution for 1999 est.

INDUSTRY

Although the country's economy is progressively shifting its weight to the services sector, manufacturing retains significant importance in Portugal, employing (with construction and mining) more than one-third of the labor force. Major traditional manufactures include processed food, textiles, metals, machinery and ship repair, chemicals, wood (particularly cork), glass and pottery items, refined petroleum, and building materials. Annual production in the late 1980s included about 27,400 metric tons of processed sardines, 285,900 metric tons of refined sugar, 1.3 million metric tons of chemical fertilizers, and 386,900 metric tons of steel products. The products of Portuguese cottage industries, such as lace, pottery, and tiles, are world famous, and the shoe industry also performs particularly well. Some new sectors, such as automobiles and automobile components, electronics, and plastics, have also become increasingly important over the 1990s. The prosperity of the manufacturing sector generally improved during the 1990s, with output expanding by a yearly average of 3.1 percent. This was due in part to the presence of a new generation of Portuguese entrepreneurs and the appearance of major foreign investors. Industrial policy in the 1990s focused on attracting foreign capital, mostly by way of privatization, but also by offering state and EU subsidies and assistance to investors. The government intends to further privatize several manufacturing facilities, notably in power generation, chemicals, and construction materials (cement). Not all foreign investments have been successful, however, and the government has been criticized for not properly securing guarantees for the future performance of many of them. Between 1995 and 2000, for example, 2 automobile manufacturers, Ford and the French company Renault, have terminated production in Portugal.

A considerable number of Portugal's more traditional manufacturing businesses are still run by the most powerful families. Nonetheless, a new generation of family management has been successful in meeting the challenges of the European single market through technological innovations, developing export markets, and making use of the country's low wage structure. However, many of these industries face increasingly tough competition from the Asian economies, where wage levels are even lower and where currency **devaluations** in the 1990s have increased their competitive edge. Many firms have been unable to adapt to these new market realities, resulting in a decline in the production of textiles, clothing, and footwear between 1995 and 2000. Difficult economic conditions are expected to continue until 2005, as companies shift their output to more **value-added** products. Raising productivity is an important priority for Portuguese manufacturing, but its record in research and development is weak. In 1997, it spent only 0.63 percent of its GDP on research and development, less than one-third of the average amount of EU nations.

Nevertheless, the 1990s saw positive developments in the newer manufacturing sectors as well. A **joint venture** with Ford and Germany's Volkswagen (VW), Auto-Europa, was launched in April 1995 with the purpose of building multi-purpose passenger cars for export. At the time, it was Portugal's largest manufacturing operation. This US$2.6 billion investment package received the highest level ever of union subsidies in the EU at nearly US$1 billion. From the beginning, however, company executives admitted that production and employment would not meet forecasts because of weaker than expected European demand for the vehicle being produced. Ford gradually pulled out and VW acquired full ownership of the venture. Despite these setbacks, this modern plant has had a very positive impact on the economy, producing nearly 130,000 cars per year. They are almost all produced for export, generating sales of US$2.3 billion and accounting for some 12 percent of the total worth of Portuguese exports (1997 est.). The plant employs 3,000 workers and has helped to create more than 5,000 other jobs. At its full capacity, it could add as much as 15 percent to the value of Portugal's total exports and 6 to 7 percent to its import bill. The AutoEuropa plant is situated in a new industrial park outside of Lisbon in Palmela, where many of its main suppliers are located as well. Taguspark, also located outside of Lisbon in the city of Oeiras, is a science and technology park built in 1992 that housed about 100 new technology companies in 2000.

SERVICES

FINANCE. As Portugal's economy moved towards a focus on services, particularly on banking and finance, this sector gained importance in the 1990s. Following the gradual but thorough privatization of state banks begun in the late 1980s, the Caixa Geral de Depositos (CGD) remained the only state-controlled financial services firm in 2000 (the government has ruled out its privatization for the time being).

The privatization of the sector has been followed by a wave of bank mergers and acquisitions. Coping with a relatively small but increasingly crowded market as a result of the European banking liberalization policies, Portuguese banks took the opportunity to form larger and more efficient groups. In 1995, Banco Comercial Portugues (BCP) and the insurer Imperio jointly bought the country's largest private bank, Banco Portugues do Atlantico (BPA). Industrialist Antonio Champalimaud acquired half of the second largest bank, Banco Totta e Acores, and added it to his Banco Pinto e Sotto Mayor (BPSM). In 1999–2000, the banking sector underwent further consolidation when the major Spanish bank, Banco Santander Central Hispano (BSCH) tried to acquire a controlling stake in the Champalimaud group. Because it was in violation of EU legislation, the deal was banned by the government, but a compromise led to the split of the Champalimaud group and a new reorganization of the sector. BSCH acquired 2 of the splinter Champalimaud banks, Banco Totta e Acores and Credito Predial Portugues; CGD acquired the group's most valued assets, BPSM and the insurance group Mundial Confianca. This reorganization concentrated 70 percent of the country's retail banking market in 4 institutions: CGD, BCP, Banco Portuguese do Investimento (BPI), and Banco Espirito Santo (BES). BSCH of Spain controls 11 percent of the market share. Insurance firms are strongly connected to the banking groups, and 3 of them dominate the market: Mundial Confianca, acquired by CGD; Imperio, controlled by BCP; and Tranquilidade, in which BES has a major stake.

By 2000, banking services in Portugal were modern and mature. Yet as the competition from foreign banks increased with the implementation of the EU banking liberalization policies, profit margins of Portuguese banks began to shrink. Even though the Internet offered the possibilities of cost advantages such as online banking, no Portuguese bank was in a position by 2000 to use fully the Internet for significant cost savings. None had close enough ties to a major foreign bank that would have been able to provide adequate support. Decreasing lending margins in the late 1990s, on the other hand, have prompted most Portuguese retail banks to raise their commissions on customer transactions in order to stay profitable. For example, debit cards in Portugal have an annual charge of US$9.25 a year and credit cards have an even higher annual charge. As a result, commissions vary radically from bank to bank, and it is often the poorer customers who are actually bearing the burden of such dubious banking policies.

Shrinking bank profit margins, increasing bank commissions, and allegations that banks frequently gave misleading information on their charges or applied the charges after the accounts had been opened prompted the government to introduce new voluntary regulations on banking services. These regulations allowed for even the poorest citizen to have a bank account without depositing a minimum amount and to pay only low predictable charges. Only the state-owned CGD, the country's largest financial group, had previously provided a full table of its prices for any visitor to its web page to see. Several major banks adopted the new rules in 2000, but others declined for reasons of commercial secrecy.

Although Internet banking hardly exists in Portugal, its national system of automated teller machines (ATMs),

Multibanco, is a leader in Europe. The new Netpin electronic technology, compatible with the system, offers unprecedented security against fraud. Netpin's developer, the Portuguese technology-based company Grupo de Apoio a Industria Nacional (GAIN), manufactures most of the terminals distributed across the SIBS (Sociedade Interbancaria de Servitos) system, parallel to Multibanco. The Netpin system offers the services available at a regular ATM (withdrawals; balance inquiries; payment of tax, water, and energy bills; recharging of electronic "purse cards") and could serve as the basis for development of electronic commerce in Portugal. The company is considering marketing the product in foreign markets, concentrating on those where the Multibanco system already has a foothold, such as Brazil, Colombia, Spain, and Costa Rica.

Between 1994 and 1998, due to very easy and active mortgage financing, household debt (in home mortgages) rose from 28.6 percent to 60.8 percent of the **disposable income** in the country and from 21.1 percent to 44.1 percent of GDP. While the Portuguese government believes that such levels are not dangerous, the rapid growth of the debt is hardly sustainable. If household income suddenly drops, a banking crisis could be triggered by households unable to make payments. There are thus some worries that these high debt levels could worsen any future **recession**. Furthermore, household disposable income can be rapidly affected even if no recession occurs, simply due to changes in interest rates by the European Central Bank. Finally, the easy availability of home mortgage loans has contributed to an exaggerated and burdensome increase in real estate prices.

TOURISM. Tourism is one of the most important sectors of the Portuguese economy, with foreign currency earnings accounting for an estimated 4.8 percent of GDP in 1999 and employing 6 percent of the active population. Foreign exchange revenue from tourism amounted to US$2.4 billion in 1997. Nearly 25 million foreigners visit Portugal every year, and about half of them are tourists. Most of the visitors are Central and Northern Europeans attracted by the sun and beaches of the southern Algarve region and Madeira. In the mid-1990s, as mass beach tourism declined worldwide, the sector went through a sluggish period, in contrast to the tourist boom in neighboring Spain. The authorities launched a program to diversify attractions by promoting sports, culture, and conference facilities, and public investment in the late 1990s was directed into providing facilities in undeveloped areas to encourage investment by the **private sector**. The government is restoring historical and cultural assets such as castles and monasteries, with the EU meeting one-third of the costs. A renewed tourism promotional campaign helped increase revenue in 1997 and 1998. The favorable exchange rate for visitors from Britain (Portugal's most important tourist market) and the celebration of the World Fair Expo '98 in Lisbon brought in additional visitors as well. The World Fair alone contributed a 20 percent increase in foreign visitors in 1998 and a 17 percent increase in tourist revenue.

RETAIL. Portugal is slowly following general European retail trends, with a proliferation of hypermarkets and shopping malls gradually replacing small traditional retailers. These new forms of retailing thrived during the consumer boom of the late 1990s. Both foreign and domestic investors have participated in the retailing revolution, with principal domestic investors being the Oporto-based group Sonae Investimentos and Lisbon's Jeronimo Martins.

Portugal's franchise retail market, after the boom period of the 1990s, entered a phase of consolidation in 1999. At that time, 357 franchisers were already operating in the market. Of the total number of brands, 35 percent were Portuguese and 42 percent were Spanish. Banks specializing in small and medium-sized businesses, like the state-owned Banco Nacional Ultramarino, help franchises get started. Famous franchise names include Printemps and Carrefour (French supermarket chains); McDonald's, Pizza Hut and Baskin-Robbins (U.S. fast-food chains); Goody's, a Greek fast-food chain claiming to be the third largest in Europe; and Italian and French apparel stores like Massimo Dutti and Faconnable. Ready-to-wear clothes account for more than one-third of all franchised outlets. A series of new retail centers, such as the large Colombo Center in Lisbon that opened in 1997, have provided excellent opportunities for retail licensing and franchising. The company Sonae Imobiliaria, a unit of Sonae Investimentos, accounts for more than half the market for new retail centers. The next phase of retail development will most likely be the emergence of retail parks or factory outlets, and Sonae Imobiliaria, as well as its rival Mundicenter, are preparing to develop this market.

Since the late 1980s, mail order and TV sales have become popular direct marketing methods. Between 1996 and 1997, sales growth was calculated at 15 percent, and there are presently around 50 direct marketing firms. The most popular sectors are cultural, instruction and training, and amusement materials (33 percent of sales) and apparel and clothing (17 percent of sales). Other strong areas are housewares, perfumes, cosmetics, art, and collectibles. The success of direct marketing is more impressive given that Portuguese mailing expenses are considered high.

E-commerce is still lagging behind most of Europe, but several companies have emerged in the late 1990s that offer online shopping for office supplies, computer accessories, and groceries. Consumer protection regulations and laws in Portugal are considered generally adequate for online shopping, although inspections often are ineffective.

Trade (expressed in billions of US$): Portugal

	Exports	Imports
1975	1.939	3.839
1980	4.640	9.309
1985	5.685	7.652
1990	16.417	25.263
1995	22.621	32.339
1998	24.220	37.049

SOURCE: International Monetary Fund. *International Financial Statistics Yearbook 1999.*

INTERNATIONAL TRADE

In 1996, Portuguese imports totaled US$34.1 billion and exports US$23.8 billion. Principal imports typically were mineral fuels, machinery and transportation equipment, and food and livestock. Principal exports included clothing, textile yarns and fabrics, and wood and paper products. Leading purchasers of exports were Germany, Spain, France, the United Kingdom, the Netherlands, the United States, Italy, Belgium, and Sweden; chief sources for imports were Spain, Germany, France, Italy, the United Kingdom, and the Netherlands. Foreign exchange revenue from tourism, amounting to US$2.4 billion in 1997, helped to compensate for the nation's chronic **trade deficit**. The World Fair Expo '98 in Lisbon considerably enhanced the country's profile in this respect.

MONEY

Portugal and 10 other members of the EU have started changing over from their national currencies to the single European currency, the euro, for all transactions as part of their participation in the EMU. Use of the euro began in January 1999, although only for electronic bank transfers and for accounting purposes. Euro coins and bills will be issued in 2002, at which time the Portuguese escudo will cease to be legal currency. The EU members have established the European Central Bank (ECB) in Frankfurt, Germany, responsible for all EU **monetary policies**. Since 1999, the control over Portuguese monetary issues, including interest rates and the money supply regulation, has been also transferred to the ECB.

Although Portugal qualified for the initial stage of the EMU in 1998, its public finances are still considered quite unstable. In 2000, the ECB decision to hold interest rates steady was welcomed in Portugal, but financial policy challenges were still very serious. The late 1990s, years of rapid economic growth and increasing tax revenues, allowed the government to boost public spending growth in 1998 and 1999 and still meet its deficit reduction targets. But revenue growth slowed dramatically in 2000 due to the domestic economic slowdown and the government's highly controversial energy policy.

By allowing the rate of the petrol tax to fluctuate disproportionately to oil prices, the government hoped to prevent a dramatic rise in oil prices that might fuel consumer price **inflation**. That policy, however, turned into a massive drain of the public finances while budgeted revenue targets were missed by about 0.7 percent of GDP. The government, quite luckily, met its budget deficit target of 1.5 percent of GDP in 2000, as required by the EU standards, but that was only thanks to the boost of US$360 million from the sale of 4 operating licenses for third generation mobile phone operators. It was otherwise estimated that the deficit would have been almost 2 percent of GDP.

The weaknesses of Portugal's public finances were analyzed in 2000 in reports by the European Commission (the EU executive body), the International Monetary Fund (IMF), and the Organization for Economic Cooperation and Development (OECD), all of which offered a gloomy account of the situation. The government admits that, with the economy entering a period of slower growth, it has few options but to implement structural spending reforms (public spending cuts) if it is to meet future deficit reduction targets. A new public finance committee was scheduled to present proposals on spending cuts in the first half of 2001.

Financial markets in Portugal are doing considerably well by most accounts, although important pieces of legislation regarding their development are still pending in parliament. The Lisbon Stock Exchange's (Bolsa de Valores de Lisboa, or BVL) capitalization and **turnover** have grown rapidly in the late 1990s, fueled by the government's massive privatization program and by the Portuguese people's growing enthusiasm for share ownership. The privatization of a 30 percent stake in the electricity utility EDP in June of 1997 substantially increased the exchange capitalization and **liquidity**, and the number of shareholders increased from 1 percent to 6 percent of the Portuguese population. This considerable growth in activity, value, and capitalization transformed

Exchange rates: Portugal

euros per US$1	
Jan 2001	1.0659
2000	1.0854
1999	0.9386
1998	180.10
1997	175.31
1996	154.24

Note: Rates prior to 1999 are in Portuguese escudos per US$.

SOURCE: CIA *World Factbook 2001* [ONLINE].

the exchange from an **emerging market** into a developed one. The launching of a new market in Oporto in 1996, which merged with the Lisbon one in 1999, gave an additional impetus to stock market trading.

After dropping slightly in 1995, the BVL **price index** (the Portuguese counterpart for the United States' Dow Jones) increased by 32 percent in 1996, by 65 percent in 1997, by 26 percent in 1998, and by 10.2 percent in 1999. It reached its record high of 6,511 on March 3, 2000. The increase was driven by the soaring prices of a limited number of telecom, media, and Internet stocks, although concerns in Europe and the United States about overvaluation of Internet-related stock has since led to a dramatic cooling of market enthusiasm for the "new economy" stocks. The stock market also experienced a still rising tide of public offerings in this sector in 2000, including PT Multimedia and PT.com (the media and Internet subsidiaries of PT), Sonae.com (the Internet division of the other major domestic telecom operator, Sonae), and Impresa (a major media group). Nonetheless, the Portuguese stock market suffers from a lack of liquidity similar to that of other European exchanges, reflecting its disproportionate dependence on a small number of blue-chip (large and profitable company) stocks, the most influential of which, PT and EDP, are still largely controlled by the government.

The long expected New Market (Novo Mercado) for small, high-growth companies, a replica of the American Nasdaq market, failed to launch by its planned deadline of December 2000. The disappointment in Portugal was considerable as this failure was largely regarded as a sign that the BVL was lagging behind at a time of rapid transformation of European securities markets. BVL executives decided that an alliance with other exchanges would keep it from being left out of this period of European expansion. Negotiations were started for an association with the Euronext exchange group, which serves to unite stock exchanges in Amsterdam, Brussels and Paris, although there were no guarantees that the larger markets would agree to accept Portugal's much smaller exchange as an equal. In late 2000, the BVL also struck an agreement with the Spanish derivatives market, MEFF, to launch trading in financial products listed in each other's markets. The Portuguese stock market commission declared that in January 2001 the exchange would adopt several new indicators, with the current index, the BVL 30, being replaced by the Portuguese Stock Index 30. It would also be joined by other existing indexes. The indexes planned to be included in the deal are PSI 20, PSI General, PSI TMT (technology, media, and telecommunications), PSI NM (New Market, as soon as it becomes operational), and another new index for medium-sized service and industrial companies. This change has been seen largely as a cosmetic measure, however. There have been many discussions of fundamental change at the BVL, but little has been decided upon, and the market continues to suffer from large gaps between the intentions of its executives, the needed but still pending legislation, and actual achievements.

POVERTY AND WEALTH

After long decades of relative poverty for the rural and urban masses during the dictatorship, Portugal's living standards have been on the rise since the mid-1970s. Conditions particularly improved after the country joined the EU and aligned its social policies with the Union's regulations. Poverty and social exclusion, characteristic of the country earlier in the 20th century, are presently almost non-existent. Many remote, depopulated rural areas benefit vastly from EU programs on regional development. After the democratic revolution in 1974, the government implemented, under socialist and **communist** influence, a number of measures for more equitable distribution of income and land ownership.

One measure of economic inequality, the **Gini index**, gives Portugal a ranking of 35.6, lower than that of the United States (40.8) or the UK (36.1), though it is still much higher than those of Nordic EU members such as Denmark, Sweden or Finland. Yet Portugal's per capita GDP is still comparatively low by European standards, and the bank indebtedness of ordinary households is remarkably high.

Portugal's rate of inflation rose through much of 2000, exceeding the ECB price stability limit of 2 percent and the Portuguese government's original inflation target of 2 percent for the year (later revised to 2.7 percent). The actual **inflation rate** for 2000 was double the euro-zone average. The inflation rise reflected rising food prices, the effect of the euro's weakness against the U.S. dollar on 2000 import prices, and the impact of higher energy bills. Despite the government's decision to freeze the prices of retail oil products in April 2000, both producer and consumer prices continued to increase. The extremely tight labor market and rising inflation notwithstanding, average wage growth (based on collective pay agreements for non-public-sector workers) showed very

GDP per Capita (US$)

Country	1975	1980	1985	1990	1998
Portugal	6,024	7,193	7,334	9,696	11,672
United States	19,364	21,529	23,200	25,363	29,683
Spain	10,040	10,512	10,943	13,481	15,644
Greece	8,302	9,645	10,005	10,735	12,069

SOURCE: United Nations. *Human Development Report 2000; Trends in human development and per capita income.*

Distribution of Income or Consumption by Percentage Share: Portugal

Lowest 10%	3.1
Lowest 20%	7.3
Second 20%	11.6
Third 20%	15.9
Fourth 20%	21.8
Highest 20%	43.4
Highest 10%	28.4

Survey year: 1994–95

Note: This information refers to income shares by percentiles of the population and is ranked by per capita income.

SOURCE: *2000 World Development Indicators* [CD-ROM].

little increase in 2000. **Real wages** were likely to decline by the end of 2000. As a result of this, ordinary Portuguese felt rather pessimistic about their current economic prospects.

WORKING CONDITIONS

By 1997, the total labor force in Portugal was approximately 5 million. Although unemployment still averaged about 4 percent (one of the lowest in the EU), many considered Portugal to have almost achieved **full employment** and that there was little opportunity left for redirecting **underemployed** workers from agriculture to more productive sectors. The proportion of working women was already higher than in most other EU countries. Since the late 1980s, powerful syndicates (labor unions) controlled more than 55 percent of the labor force. The labor market is accordingly tight and many industries are suffering from a labor shortage.

According to the available data from the third quarter of 2000, 30,000 new jobs were created in Portugal during that period, and the rate of employment growth accelerated to 1.8 percent. New job creation was boosted mainly through the traditionally unstable construction sector, where employment rose by 11.5 percent, while service sector jobs increased by only 2.1 percent, and industrial employment fell by 3.3 percent. Growth in the number of employees reached 2.6 percent, of which fixed-term contract employees were responsible for 1 percent and permanent contracts for 0.7 percent. The tightness of the labor market was somewhat lessened by a rise in the number of persons who applied for a job for the first time. Nevertheless, the economy continued to operate in conditions of near full employment. Portugal's **participation rate** still remains well below the EU average, increasing the heavy strain on overburdened social security and health-care systems.

Although Portugal is ruled by a socialist government and enjoys friendly relations between the government and the unions, labor disputes are often quite passionate. In May 2000, after a series of nationwide railroad strikes, the government ordered 1,700 state-employed train operators back to work, claiming their actions were harming the economy and the people's lives. Legislation provides grounds for such an order as a rarely used emergency measure if key public services are at risk. The loss-making national railroad company, Caminhos de Ferro Portugueses, is Portugal's only train service provider. Once the period covered by the order expired, however, train operators decided to resume their action.

Earlier in 2000, the socialist government was shaken by the worst wave of public sector protests since it took office in 1995, when a general strike by civil service and transport unions hit services in Portugal. Schools, health centers, buses, and the Lisbon Metro were affected by the stoppages. The main communist and socialist-led union federations called upon labor opposition to push for higher wages. The strike was the latest in a series of events that had been gathering momentum since annual wage talks were aborted in March 2000, and the government fixed a 2.5 percent wage increase for public administration workers. When the government later announced an average increase of more than 11 percent in fuel prices, unions feared that real wage increases would erode. Antonio Guterres, the prime minister, warned that public sector wage increases had to be kept moderate to prevent higher inflation that could threaten Portugal's compliance with the EMU stability pact.

The dire economic forecasts in early 2001 suggest that hidden wage pressure may be still growing. Public-sector unions have demanded wage increases between 4.5 percent and 6 percent in 2001, expressing their serious concern about the fact that the government may miss the inflation target (on which wage negotiations are based) for the third consecutive year. The government, which has resisted these pressures, is still expected to agree upon an average pay raise in the public sector of about 3.7 percent for 2001 (up from 2.5 percent in 2000), which, on the other hand, may over-stretch the already very fragile public finances and fuel higher inflation.

Furthermore, with labor market conditions remaining very tight, there is a risk of even greater pressure for wage increases on the private-sector, raising the threat that even higher inflation could become inevitable. The traditional loyalty between the government and the trade union federation could, in the event that this happens, come under additional strain. Good labor relations, nonetheless, will most likely continue to be the norm. On the other hand, improvements in the quality of the workforce through education and training, which have been generously funded through EU programs, will be conducive to wage growth.

COUNTRY HISTORY AND ECONOMIC DEVELOPMENT

2ND CENTURY B.C. Present-day Portugal territory becomes a part of the Roman province of Lusitania.

5TH CENTURY A.D. The area is conquered by the Visigoths.

8TH CENTURY. The region is conquered by Muslim Moors.

997. The land between the Douro and Minho rivers is taken over by Bermudo II, the Spanish Christian king of Leon.

1064. The lands to the south of the Douro and Minho rivers, including Coimbra and including several Spanish fiefs, are united into a feudal entity by Ferdinand I, Spanish king of Castile and Leon. The northernmost of the fiefs, the Comitatus Portaculensis, situated around the old Roman seaport of Portus Cale (Oporto), later gives its name to Portugal. A feudal, agriculture-based economy develops.

1093. Henry (Henrique) of Burgundy becomes Count of Portugal.

1139. Alfonso Henriques, son of Henry of Burgundy, declares Portugal independent from the kingdom of Castile and Leon and becomes king. Aided by the Templars and other knights' orders, he extends the kingdom southward to the Tejo River.

1185. Portuguese settle in the reconquered area in self-governing municipalities. The Cistercian monks promote more efficient agricultural methods.

1248–79. The Moors are driven out of the southern province of Algarve, and the capital of Portugal is moved from Coimbra to Lisbon. The king starts governing with the help of a Cortes (a representative assembly of the nobility, clergy, and citizens).

LATE 13TH CENTURY. Diniz, "the Farmer King," encourages agriculture, founds the first university at Coimbra, develops the Portuguese navy into the strongest in all of Europe, and negotiates a commercial treaty with England.

LATE 14TH CENTURY. Under the lead of Prince Henry the Navigator, son of King John I, a century of exploration and conquest begins with exploring the African coast for a route to the Indies. Portugal later becomes a great colonial power as its navigators explore Madeira, discover the Azores Islands, and take a foothold in Africa.

MID-15TH CENTURY. Using the caravel, a tall ship adapted for Atlantic voyages, Portuguese sailors reach present-day Cape Verde, Sierra Leone, Ghana, and Angola.

1488. Bartholomeu Dias becomes the first European to sail around the southern tip of Africa, opening the sea route to the East Indies.

1494. After Christopher Columbus's voyage to America, Portugal and Spain sign the Treaty of Tordesillas, which allocates to Portugal all undiscovered lands east of a line 370 leagues west of the Cape Verde Islands.

1497–99. Vasco da Gama reaches India by the Dias route and starts a lucrative trade in spices and other luxuries. The Portuguese later conquer Goa (in present-day India), Malacca (in present-day Malaysia), the Moluccas Islands (in present-day Indonesia), and Hormuz Island in the Persian Gulf. Under pressure from Spain, Portugal expels all Jews and Muslims, depriving Portugal of much of its enterprising middle class. Trade is begun with China, and Portugal later acquires the trade colony of Macao from China.

16TH CENTURY. Portugal settles Brazil and introduces the Inquisition at home to enforce Roman Catholic loyalty. Political decline follows internal struggles for the throne, and Portugal is subdued by the Spanish Habsburgs and gradually loses its positions in the East Indies to the Dutch and the English.

1640. With help from France, Portugal restores its independence, and John IV of Braganza takes over the throne and renews ties with England. British merchants gradually come to dominate Portuguese trade, monarchy becomes more despotic, and the Cortes lose their significance.

1750–77. Chief Minister Sebastiao Jose de Carvalho e Mello encourages industry and education and ends the foreign monopoly of trade.

1807. The armies of French Emperor Napoleon threaten Portugal, and the royal family withdraws to Brazil, making Rio de Janeiro the seat of government. In 1811, Portugal is free of French influence, but the royal family remains in Brazil and makes it a separate kingdom in 1815. Brazil proclaims its independence in 1822.

1826. Pedro IV (former Pedro I of Brazil) takes over the throne in Lisbon and introduces a parliamentary regime subordinated to the monarchy. Acute internal political strife more than once requires the intervention of other European powers and popular dissatisfaction with the monarchy grows.

1910. The army and navy lead a revolution establishing a republic. A liberal constitution is then adopted, and Manuel Jose de Arriaga is elected president. Portugal is shaken by political turmoil and in 1916 begins participation in World War I fighting for the Entente.

1926. An army coup deposes the 40th successive cabinet since the founding of the republic. Antonio de

Oliveira Salazar, professor of economics, is appointed minister of finance.

1932. Salazar becomes prime minister and dictator, and Portugal becomes a incorporated state with a planned economy, called the Estado Novo (New State).

1943. Portugal remains neutral in World War II but allows the Allies to use the Azores as a naval and air base. The planned economy collapses as the fishing industry declines, refugees fill the country, and the East Indies colonies are threatened by Japan.

1945. Unemployment and poverty are rampant after the war, but opposition to the Salazar regime is suppressed.

1960s. India annexes Portuguese Goa in 1961. Uprisings start in Angola, Guinea, and Mozambique and fighting continues into the 1970s. The United Nations (UN) blames Portugal for waging colonial wars. Loans help finance domestic irrigation and construction projects and some economic growth occurs.

1974. Led by Antonio de Spinola, a 7-man junta takes power and promises democracy at home and peace in Africa.

1974–75. Guinea-Bissau, Mozambique, the Cape Verde Islands, São Tomé and Príncipe, and Angola become independent.

1975. The Movement of the Armed Forces (Movimento das Forcas Armadas, MFA) assumes a formal role in the government by establishing a single trade union confederation and starting to reform economic and social life. Heavy industry and banking are **nationalized** and large agricultural holdings are expropriated and redistributed. The Socialists win elections for a constituent assembly, but after a series of clashes between Socialists and Communists, the MFA assumes control. In the same year, Portuguese Timor is occupied by Indonesia.

1976. New parliamentary elections bring the Socialists into office and Mario Soares becomes prime minister.

1979. The Conservative Democratic Alliance wins elections and its leader, Francisco Sa Carneiro, takes office as premier but is killed in a plane crash a year later. The military Council of the Revolution is dismissed by a constitutional amendment.

1983. Socialist Soares comes back into power as prime minister. He introduces an austerity program and conducts negotiations for joining the European Community (now the EU) that are finalized in 1986.

1992. Mass student demonstrations are followed by strikes involving public employees demanding wage increases and doctors protesting plans to privatize some health services.

1996. Portugal and its former colonies of Angola, Brazil, Cape Verde, Guinea-Bissau, Mozambique, and São Tomé and Príncipe form the Commonwealth of Portuguese-Speaking Countries (CPLP), an organization seeking to preserve the language, coordinate diplomatic efforts, and improve cooperation between the countries.

FUTURE TRENDS

The Portuguese economy is very closely dependent on the overall developmental trends of the EU and its efforts to match the requirements of the single European economic space. Over the first decade of the 21st century, it will continue to progress towards more private enterprise and competition. Privatization will continue to be an important issue in telecommunications, manufacture, and the other utilities, although the government is likely to retain special rights in key companies. It will also seek international strategic partners for those companies. Incentives to attract **foreign direct investment** will receive more attention, and Portugal may attract some new additional investment from its close links with Spain and Latin America. Gradual discarding of EU quotas on imports of textiles and clothing will create conditions for increase in Portugal's exports to the union members. The possibility of further negotiations on multilateral trade liberalization within the World Trade Organization (WTO) may also contribute to the future reinvigoration of the Portuguese export sector.

Trade with non-EU countries, including its former African, Asian and Latin American colonies, should continue to increase. A major simplification of corporate taxation is expected before 2003, and the corporate tax rate might be reduced to 30 percent (although **indirect taxes** may rise). Improved investment incentives may come under further EU scrutiny while stock market liquidity and capitalization will increase, boosted by further privatization. Due to the limited size of the domestic capital markets, more medium-sized businesses will increasingly seek funding in the international markets. A further consolidation in the financial sector and the emergence of more powerful banks, able to better realize economies of scale, compete in the single European market space, and make use of the Internet revolution, is also expected.

Work on the government's ambitious road building program and the new urban rail networks in Oporto and Lisbon will continue. The main seaports will be upgraded, and Lisbon is expected to receive a new international airport.

Portugal will experience more serious problems as new Central and Eastern European members of the EU with more pressing needs start competing for development funds. Agriculture and fishing may face a corresponding decrease in subsidies. It is logical to expect that Portugal, along with Greece, would not be overzealous in the process of the new members' accession to the EU. No major dangers for the economy have been envisaged (projected) and growth is forecast to decrease only slightly below the EU average in 2001 and 2002. Yet the current high levels of household indebtedness and the recent rise in house prices suggest there could be a risk of a severe decrease in consumer spending, particularly if interest rates go higher than expected. Such developments may significantly harm retail and domestic **consumer goods** manufacturers.

DEPENDENCIES

Portugal has no territories or colonies.

BIBLIOGRAPHY

Economist Intelligence Unit. *Country Profile: Portugal.* London: EIU, 2001.

Solsten, Eric. *Portugal: A Country Study.* Washington, DC: Library of Congress, 1993.

U.S. Central Intelligence Agency. *World Factbook 2000.* <http://www.odci.gov/cia/publications/factbook/index.html>. Accessed August 2001.

U.S. Department of State. *FY 2000 Country Commercial Guide: Portugal.* <http://www.state.gov/www/about_state/business/com_guides/index.html>. Accessed January 2001.

—Valentin Hadjiyski

ROMANIA

CAPITAL: Bucharest.

MONETARY UNIT: Romania leu (L). One leu equals 100 bani, though bani are seldom used, thanks to devaluation. There are notes of 1,000, 2,000, 5,000, 10,000, 50,000, 100,000, and 500,000 lei (plural of leu), and coins of 1, 5, 10, 20, 50, 100, 500, and 1,000 lei.

CHIEF EXPORTS: Textiles and footwear, metals and metal products, machinery and equipment, minerals, fuels.

CHIEF IMPORTS: Machinery and equipment, minerals and fuels, chemicals, textiles, footwear.

GROSS DOMESTIC PRODUCT: US$36.7 billion (2000). [*CIA World Factbook 2000* reports GDP at purchasing power parity to be US$87.4 billion (1999 est.).]

BALANCE OF TRADE: **Exports:** US$10.4 billion (2000). **Imports:** US$12.0 billion (2000). [*CIA World Factbook 2000* reports exports to be US$8.4 billion (f.o.b., 1999 est.) and imports to be US$9.6 billion (f.o.b., 1999 est.).]

COUNTRY OVERVIEW

LOCATION AND SIZE. Located in southeastern Europe on the Black Sea, Romania covers an area of 238,500 square kilometers (92,085 square miles), making it slightly smaller than Oregon. It borders Hungary, Yugoslavia, Bulgaria, Moldova, and Ukraine, and has a coastline of 225 kilometers (140 miles). The capital, Bucharest, is towards the south of the country.

POPULATION. The population of Romania was estimated at 22,334,312 in July 2000, having fallen 2.6 percent since its peak in 1988. The population is expected to continue falling for the next decade thanks to net **emigration** and low birth rates, a fact that worries the government. But improved health care should slow the rate of decline as infant mortality falls from its current 19.8 deaths per 1,000 live births.

Meanwhile, the proportion of retired people is rising. By 2005, 14.6 percent of the Romanian population will be aged 65 or over, compared to 11.8 percent in 1995. For this reason, Romania has recently reformed its state pension system because rising unemployment has combined with the aging population to make the former pay-as-you-go system unaffordable. The plan is to encourage complementary private pensions, allowing younger citizens to save for their own old age while maintaining payments to those that are already **pensioners**.

Romania's population is remarkably homogenous. Almost 90 percent are ethnic Romanians, claiming descent from Latin-speaking Romans who settled among the local Dacians in 100–200 A.D. As a result, Romanian is a Romance language related to French and Italian, in contrast to the Slav languages spoken in surrounding countries. Around 70 percent of Romania's population is Romanian Orthodox.

The biggest minority group is Hungarian, which is particularly strong in the western region of Transylvania. Hungarian-Romanians have automatic rights to parliamentary representation and Hungarian-language education. There are also sizeable Roma, Turkish, and Croat populations, as well as Ukrainians, Greeks, Russians, Armenians, and Serbs. Romania used to have a Jewish population of around 300,000. Most of them survived World War II but emigrated to Israel, leaving only a few thousand now. During the 1990s, two-thirds of Romania's German population also emigrated to Germany.

OVERVIEW OF ECONOMY

Romania is well-endowed with minerals, natural fuels, and rich agricultural land, and has a good trading location on the Black Sea. But a turbulent history, culminating in the repressive **communist** regime of 1947 to 1989, have kept it from turning its natural advantages into profit. Originally settled by the Dacian tribe, the region now known as Romania fell under Roman rule in the 2nd century A.D. The Romans abandoned the area less than 2 centuries later, and Romania was split between local fiefdoms until the medieval period, when it fell under Ottoman rule.

Over the next few centuries, Hapsburg forces from Austria-Hungary took over the northwestern region of Transylvania and gradually pushed the Ottoman Empire south. But it was not until the 19th century that the Ottomans finally left Romania. Europe's other powers were anxious to stop Austria-Hungary and Russia from dominating the region, and their pressure led to Romania being declared a nation in 1878 under the German prince Carol of Hohenzollern. For the next 50 years, the country struggled to establish a liberal democracy. It cultivated links with the West, particularly France, and fought with the Allied forces in World War I. But, by 1938, it had become a dictatorship, and the country entered World War II on the side of Nazi Germany.

The country fell under full communist control at the end of 1947 after Soviet troops moved into Eastern Europe. The country's first communist leader, Gheorgiu-Dej, was originally a Stalinist but gradually loosened ties with Moscow. That process was completed by his successor, Nicolae Ceaucescu, who started to improve relations with the West. During the 1970s, he borrowed heavily abroad to build up Romania's **infrastructure** and heavy industry, often building plants without any commercial rationale. Then, in the 1980s, he adopted a policy of isolationism and self-sufficiency. Industry and infrastructure was starved of investment as Romania strove to repay all of its **foreign debts**.

Nicolae Ceaucescu was overthrown and killed in 1989 in a revolution that officially cost 689 lives. He was replaced by his former aide, Ion Iliescu, who called elections in 1990. Despite protests, these resulted in Iliescu being elected president, while his party headed the government. Since then, Romania has worked towards becoming a democratic, Western-style economy. This has involved breaking up and **privatizing** its huge industrial plants, reviving foreign trade, and allowing the growth of small businesses.

The process has been difficult, and Romania has not progressed as fast as some of its Eastern European neighbors. A decade of stop-and-go reforms meant that Romania's first post-communist **recession** was followed by another 3-year slump in the mid-1990s. By 1999, the country's GDP was just 76 percent of its 1989 level, according to the Development Ministry. Romania has struggled to maintain its infrastructure and **restructure** its outdated heavy industry. Agricultural output has fallen, largely because the land has been split up into tiny **subsistence farms**. Many of the country's largest companies are still state-owned and loss-making.

With the help of the World Bank, Romania has drawn up a list of state companies to be closed or sold in an attempt to improve the government's finances. But progress has been slow because of the job losses involved. The transition to a market economy has also put an enormous strain on the country's social support systems. Unemployment has risen rapidly and the World Bank estimates that 22 percent of the population lives in poverty.

The year 2000 may be the start of a turnaround, however. Romania's economy started growing again and is expected to continue growing for the next 2 years at least. High world commodity prices in the past 2 years have boosted exports. Meanwhile, the service sector has expanded quickly, with new private shops and trading companies springing up. Romania's tourism industry, centered around the Black Sea coast and the beautiful mountain resorts, is reviving. There has also been some limited foreign investment, notably the acquisition of the Dacia car plant by France's Renault in 1999.

Romania's main aim for the next few years is to reduce **inflation** (45.7 percent in 2000) and boost growth, partly by attracting more foreign investment. Longer-term, the country hopes to join NATO and is 1 of the 10 Eastern European countries negotiating to join the European Union (EU). Romania's own target date for EU entry is 2007, but the latest progress report from the EU Commission in October 2000 was not encouraging. It put Romania in last place out of all the current candidates, saying that the country did not yet have a functioning market economy, a prerequisite for entry. Most analysts expect it to take Romania at least another decade to pass the reforms necessary for EU entry, even if the political will is there.

POLITICS, GOVERNMENT, AND TAXATION

Since the overthrow of communist leader Nicolae Ceaucescu in 1989, Romania has been ruled by a succession of new or reformed parties, each claiming that they will be able to revive the economy. The most dominant has been the Party of Social Democracy in Romania (PDSR), a leftist party that developed out of the former Romanian Communist Party. It is headed by Ion Iliescu, a former communist who took over from Ceaucescu in 1989 in what many see as an insiders' coup.

Iliescu recognized the need to turn Romania into a democratic market economy and called elections in 1990 and 1992. These resulted in his being declared president and the PDSR becoming the main party in the governing coalition. The PDSR advocated a slow reform program and started to **liberalize** the economy, restitute land to its pre-Communist owners, and privatize smaller companies. But it kept state controls over some prices, particularly in the energy sector, and over foreign exchange markets. It also failed to break down many of the big state **monopolies**. The economy, after a recession in the early 1990s, revived on the back of government **subsidies**. But Romania's economic problems and allegations of corruption led to Iliescu and the PDSR losing the presidential and government elections in 1996.

They were succeeded by a multi-party coalition that promised more rapid reforms, including faster privatization and liberalization. Unfortunately, this new government, headed by the Democratic Coalition, proved too inexperienced and quarrelsome to push through many of the necessary measures. Others proved unexpectedly painful. Price liberalization pushed up inflation and a credit crunch boosted unemployment, while privatization was slow and scandal-ridden. The coalition went through 3 prime ministers in 3 years as politicians squabbled and the economy went into a 3-year recession.

By November 2000, when new government and presidential elections were held, the coalition government had become deeply unpopular. Romanians voted overwhelmingly for the return of Iliescu and the PDSR. However, the PDSR did not receive a majority of the votes. The ultra-nationalist Greater Romania Party received the 2nd highest percentage of votes, which generated anxiety in many national and international circles because of the party's isolationist and xenophobic rhetoric. Instead of forming a coalition with other parties to create a majority government, the PDSR formed a single-party minority government. The party claims to have changed since its previous term in office and is now presenting itself as a European-style social democratic party. It has announced its support for Romania's bids to join the EU and NATO and is trying to woo foreign investors by pushing through reforms recommended by the EU and International Monetary Fund.

In general, the elections confirmed that democracy in Romania is on a stronger footing than the economy. The European Commission says that substantial progress has been made in establishing political parties, a pluralistic media, and civilian control of the army. None of these things is yet assured, however. Parties often have similar platforms and are continually splitting, while the media is under pressure from both politicians and business lobbies. Meanwhile, corruption is widespread, according to a report published in March 2001 by the World Bank. Romania passed new anti-corruption legislation in May 2000 establishing several agencies and tightening up rules on public administration, but it will take years for the effects to show.

The trade unions, particularly in the mining industries, form a powerful and potentially disruptive lobby group. In the past decade, notably in 1991 and 1998, the miners and other unions have stepped in at moments of crisis by marching on Bucharest. Rival politicians are often accused of triggering these miners' marches for their own ends, and disagreements with the unions was one reason for the problems faced by the Democratic Coalition and its partners in government. The PDSR enjoys closer ties with the unions and is trying to use this relationship to contain wage increases. In February 2001, it struck a key social pact with the unions and employers, trying to set a framework for all 3 sides to work together.

One perennial source of political and economic problems is taxation. Weak administration and collection, the collapse of several big tax-paying firms, and widespread tax avoidance have led to a sharp decline in revenues. Some 30 to 40 percent of the real economy is probably not registered in the official figures, and the government runs a persistent deficit (7 percent of GDP in 2000) as it struggles to fund social security systems, health care, and education. In 2000, the government tried to boost its tax take partly by lowering tax rates and broadening the tax base, in a bid to lure non-payers back into the system. Despite all this, government spending still accounts for 40 percent of the economy because of slow privatization of state industry.

INFRASTRUCTURE, POWER, AND COMMUNICATIONS

Romania's infrastructure is fairly extensive, with 103,671 kilometers (64,276 miles) of road, 11,385 kilometers (7,058 miles) of rail, and 3.84 million main telephone lines. But most of it is in a poor state of repair, due to decades of underinvestment. This is a situation that successive governments are eager to rectify, though they have had difficulty finding the necessary funding. Most hopes rest on foreign aid, particularly from the EU, and on attracting foreign investment.

Since 1989, every government has instituted a road-building program, partly in an attempt to generate employment. The EU has helped, but its money has mainly gone towards improving border posts and building the major trans-European corridor routes that run through Romania. Critics say the money would be better spent on improving smaller roads, particularly in ensuring that donkeys and carts are kept off major routes. Railway services, meanwhile, are still provided by the state-owned rail company SNCFR and are loss-making, despite government subsidies. Only a third of the tracks are electrified, and speed restrictions are widespread. In March 2001, the Japanese government lent Romania US$220 million to upgrade the Bucharest-to-Constanta railway.

Romania has 6 major ports, of which Constanta is seen as the most important to the country's future. It is located where the River Danube flows into the Black Sea. The Danube itself is the country's most important trade route, but, in 1999, was blocked thanks to NATO's bombing of Serbia. It has recently reopened, but problems remain. Romania also has 3 international and 16 domestic airports. The dominant carrier is the country's national airline, Tarom. It is currently state-owned, and the government has been trying to find a strategic investor to provide financing and connect the airline into the rapidly forming global alliances. But the latest at-

Communications

Country	Newspapers	Radios	TV Sets[a]	Cable subscribers[a]	Mobile Phones[a]	Fax Machines[a]	Personal Computers[a]	Internet Hosts[b]	Internet Users[b]
	1996	1997	1998	1998	1998	1998	1998	1999	1999
Romania	300	319	233	119.2	29	N/A	10.2	9.01	600
United States	215	2,146	847	244.3	256	78.4	458.6	1,508.77	74,100
Russia	105	418	420	78.5	5	0.4	40.6	13.06	2,700
Poland	113	523	413	83.3	50	N/A	43.9	40.86	2,100

[a]Data are from International Telecommunication Union, *World Telecommunication Development Report 1999* and are per 1,000 people.
[b]Data are from the Internet Software Consortium (http://www.isc.org) and are per 10,000 people.

SOURCE: World Bank. *World Development Indicators 2000.*

tempt to sell Tarom, in late 2000, failed thanks to a lack of interest.

Investment into Romania's energy sector is also badly needed. The country currently generates 22.6 gigawatts of power from a combination of thermal, hydroelectric, and nuclear power plants. But most of the plants are over 20 years old, and about 60 percent of Romania's power capacity will have to be replaced within the next 10 years. The power market is dominated by the state monopoly Conel. To meet EU expectations and attract investment into the power market, Romania plans to liberalize the power market, break up Conel, and privatize parts of the sector. The government is also pushing for an oil and gas pipeline to be built through the country to transport fuel from the Caspian Sea region to the West. But with several countries competing to become a transit route, the outcome is uncertain.

Romania's telecommunications system is extremely outdated, with poor service. But there has been some progress in recent years. In 1998, Greece's OTE bought a 35 percent stake in the state fixed-line monopoly, Romtelecom. OTE plans substantial investment, while the government has raised US$7 to 8 billion through a 15-year telecoms program supported by the World Bank and the European Bank for Reconstruction and Development. Meanwhile, mobile telecoms have grown rapidly, led by private companies such as Mobifon and Connex. Over 1 million Romanians are now thought to have mobile phones, with 60 percent of the country covered. Internet access has been slow to develop because of poor phone lines. Internet accounts penetration is now 0.25 per 100 inhabitants, compared with 1.25 in neighboring Hungary, according to the Economist Intelligence Unit.

ECONOMIC SECTORS

Romania's economy was designed for self-sufficiency under the communist regime, and great emphasis was placed on building up manufacturing industry to supply the population's needs. This resulted in a fairly diversified economy. But the 1980s scramble to repay foreign debts led to chronic underinvestment. Then, during the 1990s, the transition to a market economy and the liberalization of foreign trade exposed many of the country's products as obsolete. Two deep recessions in the past 10 years have added to the problems afflicting many of Romania's companies.

Industry's share of GDP has fallen from 41 percent in 1990 to 28 percent in 1999. Much of the slack has been taken up by services, which were underdeveloped during the communist era. Services now account for 48 percent of GDP, largely because of a growth in trade. Agricultural production also slumped heavily during the 1990s, and the inefficient structure of farming, as well as export barriers, means it will not rise markedly in the future. Instead, Romanian growth—predicted at 3 to 4 percent in each of the next 4 years—is expected to come from reviving industry and services.

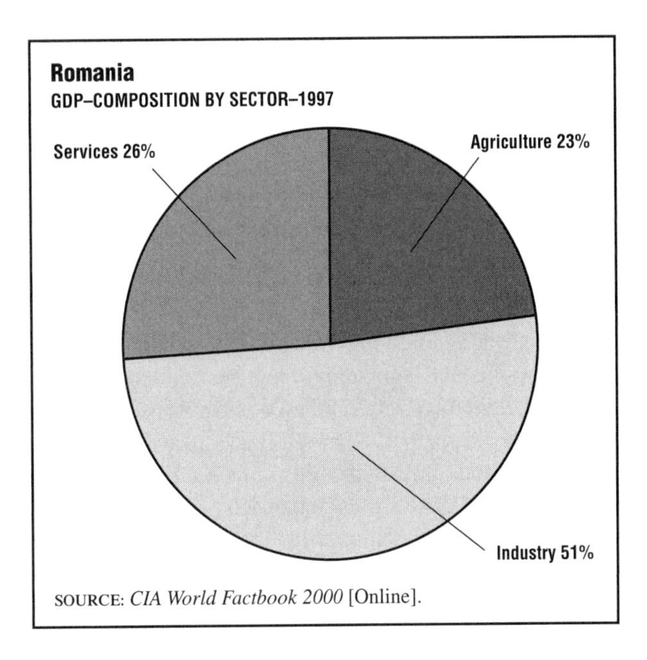

SOURCE: *CIA World Factbook 2000* [Online].

Foreign trade has developed rapidly during the 1990s, despite the disruption caused by war in former Yugoslavia, and now accounts for 64 percent of GDP. The previous Romanian government put great emphasis on encouraging exports, cutting the profit tax on exports at the start of 2000. The new government says it will continue this policy. Nevertheless, with 22 million people, the domestic market is still the main focus for most companies. It is also

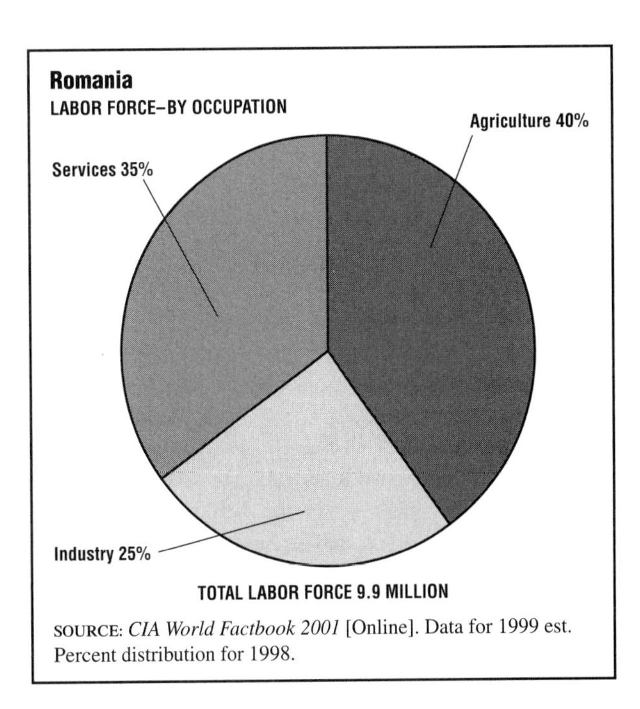

SOURCE: *CIA World Factbook 2001* [Online]. Data for 1999 est. Percent distribution for 1998.

the main reason why foreign investors such as France's Renault have moved to the country.

AGRICULTURE

Agriculture employed 42 percent of Romania's **labor force** in 1999 but generated just 16 percent of GDP. Improving this ratio is one of the biggest challenges facing Romania as it tries to raise living standards and to enter the European Union. One reason for the low productivity of farming is the agricultural reforms started in 1991, which restituted land **nationalized** under the communists to its former owners or their heirs. A limit was put on the amount of land that could be restituted, in the interests of social equality. The result is that Romania now has the most fragmented agricultural land in Eastern Europe.

The agricultural sector has 2 main components: informal and formal. On the one hand are the estimated 4 million subsistence farmers, which own 60 percent of farmland but produce mostly for their own consumption. These are deemed a social, rather than economic, problem and efforts are focused on improving their living standards, largely by persuading them to move into other jobs. The sheer number of them is a big barrier to European Union entry because, under current EU rules, they would each be entitled to income support. The formal agricultural sector consists of the large farms, which produce for domestic and export markets. Privatization of these began in 1997, though a substantial number are still state-owned.

Agricultural production fell sharply in the early 1990s, followed by a slow recovery. According to the World Bank, total production dropped 20 percent between 1989 and 1998, though gross **value-added** in the sector has only dropped 1 percent. Droughts in 2000 cut production further, but the underlying problem is the agricultural sector's inefficiency.

The small size of the plots of land makes them uneconomic to farm. In addition, Romania's self-sufficiency drive in the 1980s meant that it started producing crops like rice, which were unsuitable for local conditions. These crops disappeared as soon as agriculture was opened to market forces. Romania also suffered from the Yugoslav wars, from a drop in world commodity prices, and from export barriers imposed by the EU and its Central European neighbors.

These trade barriers have gradually been lifted throughout the 1990s, while the Yugoslav wars have calmed down and prices have risen. But, if Romania is to exploit the new opportunities, it has to increase the efficiency of its farms and of its distribution. The country should be a natural exporter of agricultural goods. It has some of the richest land in the region, with 80 percent of its territory suitable for arable farming. Yet, in 1999, agriculture accounted for just 3.4 percent of the country's exports.

INDUSTRY

MINING/NATURAL RESOURCES. Romania is well-endowed with natural resources. It has large reserves of petroleum, timber, natural gas, coal, iron ore, and salt, as well as facilities for hydropower. But lack of investment is causing the output of everything from coal to oil to fall.

The coal sector has been among the hardest-hit by the transition to a market economy. Coal production fell by 57 percent between 1989 and 1998, to 28.6 million short tons, as the economy shrank and use of other, less-polluting fuels increased. Over the past 5 years, the World Bank and the International Monetary Fund have pushed Romania to close inefficient mines, in order to stop the sector from gobbling up state subsidies. The social impact of this has been huge, with tens of thousand of miners losing their jobs, pushing unemployment in some regions to 70 percent. The current leftist government has promised that the pit closures will soon stop. It is hoping to boost electricity exports, which will mean more demand for coal.

Romania has proven oil reserves of 1.4 billion barrels, the largest in Eastern Europe. The country used to be a major oil exporter, but lack of investment has caused production to steadily fall over the last 2 decades. Romania now relies on imports to cover half its domestic needs. The government has started to attract foreign investment for oil exploration and production, both on land and in the Black Sea. There are also long-standing plans to privatize the state oil company SNP Petrom, although the attitude of the government remains unclear. Gas production has also fallen, with little money for exploration. Proven reserves of natural gas stood at 13.2 trillion cubic feet in 1998, but Romania still imports gas from Russia.

MANUFACTURING. Romania's manufacturing sector is dominated by machine-building, metals, chemicals, and textiles, all of which have had to turn from supplying the domestic market to finding export markets. Investment has been a key issue, as they try to update the outdated equipment many of them were left with when communism fell. Many of the previously state-owned firms have also been sold to private owners in an attempt to bring in money and improve management. Some of the biggest firms, seen by the government as strategic, have still to be sold, however.

The textile and footwear industries have been among the most successful in the past decade, as Western European and U.S. clothes-makers subcontract work to Romanian firms. As a result, textile exports accounted for

24.2 percent of 2000 exports, while footwear accounted for 7.6 percent. But such work depends on low wages, which is why Romania is anxious to progress from subcontracting to selling its own clothing designs. At present, the gross monthly wage in the textiles sector is just US$130 a month.

The metals sector has enjoyed a boom in the past 2 years, thanks to high world prices. The aluminum plant Alro is now Romania's biggest exporter and tripled its net profits in 2000. The country's biggest steelworks, Sidex, has also benefitted from the high prices, despite its outdated equipment and competition from stronger steel firms in Slovakia. Sidex is said to employ, directly and indirectly, over a million Romanian workers, both in and outside its home town of Galati. Both Alro and Sidex are still mainly state-owned and are expected to be sold to private owners by 2003.

During the 1990s, many of the largest firms in the machine-building sector were split up into smaller units in an attempt to boost efficiency and speed up their privatization. The disruption has been immense, and Romanian firms, long protected in an isolated market, have also found it hard to raise their production to the standard needed for export. Nevertheless, there has been some recovery in the sector. Exports rose nearly 50 percent during 2000, and it accounted for 14 percent of the total.

Romanian firms in both the metals and machine-building sectors lay great hopes on becoming subcontractors for major European manufacturers. That is why the 1999 acquisition of the Dacia car plant by France's Renault is seen as so important to Romania's future. Renault plans to use Dacia to develop, for **emerging markets**, cars selling for around US$5,000 apiece. To do that, it will have to build up a network of local, cheap suppliers such as the Sidex steelmaker. Renault's entry into Romania has also brought in other foreign investors, among them its international suppliers, such as the United States's Johnson Controls.

Romania's chemicals sector consists of both petrochemicals, based on its oil industry, and on pharmaceuticals. The pharmaceutical firms, such as Terapia, have found a niche for themselves in producing cheap versions of international drugs to sell both to Romanian hospitals and to EU countries. But they face problems as Romania moves towards EU membership because its patent laws will have to be made stricter, which will limit the drugs they can produce. Like the oil sector, the petrochemicals sector has revived in the past year due to rising world prices.

SERVICES

TOURISM. Tourism has always been an important part of Romania's economy. A combination of beautiful mountain regions, a warm sea coast, and Dracula's castles lure tourists. But the development of the industry has been hampered by a lack of money for infrastructure and tourist facilities. Service is still patchy in several parts of the country.

These factors, combined with the wars in neighboring Yugoslavia, mean that tourism numbers more than have halved since communism ended. In 1990, some 6.5 million foreigners visited the country; by 1998, that figure was down to 2.9 million. The collapse of the state tourism monopolies are partly to blame, combined with Romania's rising reputation for corruption. The number of domestic tourists has also slumped, with many Romanians no longer able to afford holidays.

Nevertheless, there are signs of a revival since the mid-1990s. Some limited foreign investment has come into the sector, particularly into Bucharest. Privatization of tourism facilities has speeded up. And the government has made development of the industry one of its prime medium-term objectives.

FINANCIAL SERVICES. The development of Romania's banking sector is seen as crucial to economic growth, because it will determine whether companies can get the loans and investment they need to become competitive. In 1990, the market was dominated by a handful of state banks. In 2000, there were 54 banks registered in the country, many of which were subsidiaries of foreign banks.

But Romanian financial services remain small in international terms. And the locally-owned banks in particular are also vulnerable to collapse because of a lack of experience in selecting borrowers, the effects of the 2 recessions, and their limited access to international capital. Several banks and funds collapsed during 2000, leaving thousands of deposit-holders demanding compensation from the government. Altogether, the government has had to spend US$3 billion in the past decade propping up the country's banks.

To overcome these problems, Romania is in the process of privatizing its remaining state banks. The aim is to find foreign strategic investors who can provide both capital and expertise and stop the banks from collapsing. The Romanian Bank for Development was sold to France's Societe Generale, while several financial investors, including America's GE Capital, have bought into Banc Post. In April 2001, Banka Agricola, the agricultural bank, was sold to the Romanian-American Enterprise Fund and Austria's Raiffeisen bank.

TRADE. Much of the growth of Romania's service sector stems from the growth of trade, both international and domestic. Trade employed 9.5 percent of Romania's workforce by 1998, compared with 5 percent in 1990. And it accounts for an estimated 90 percent of small businesses in the country, many of which operate in the **grey economy**. Many of these firms are one-person companies with a van to ship goods. Others are small shops or even street-traders.

The **retail** trade in particular was underdeveloped in the communist era when all shops were state-owned. Now a multitude of small shops have sprung up and are increasingly having to compete with the new supermarkets. Some of the investment has come from foreign countries, with retailers such as Austria's Billa, Germany's Metro, and France's Carrefour building supermarkets and hypermarkets in the major towns. The investors seem unconcerned by the low purchasing power of Romanians. They see fast growth for the sector because it is so underdeveloped, and are keen to establish their position.

INTERNATIONAL TRADE

Foreign trade has grown rapidly during the 1990s, as Romania has quickly liberalized its trade regime. The country joined the World Trade Organization in 1995 and the Central European Free Trade Area in 1997. It also enjoys special trading rights with the European Union as a precursor to membership. Some 63.8 percent of exports go to EU countries, making Romania's economy dependent on that of major markets, particularly Italy. Great hopes are placed on the ending of the wars in the former Yugoslavia, the successor countries to which are natural trading partners for Romania.

Romanian companies have found it hard to take advantage of the new export opportunities, however. Meanwhile, imports have risen by 42 percent in dollar terms since 1990, as Romanians take advantage of their new access to **consumer goods** and as companies import investment goods such as computers. As a result, the country runs a persistent **trade deficit**.

Fortunately, export growth has accelerated in the past 2 years, thanks in part to high world commodity prices for Romanian exports such as steel, aluminum, and refined oil products. Nevertheless, 2000 exports rose 21.9 percent in dollar terms compared to the previous year, while imports rose 25.6 percent, according to the national statistics office. And the trade gap is expected to remain large for at least the next 4 years.

MONEY

The value of the Romanian leu has slowly declined on the world market for the past 10 years. In 1990, there were 24 lei to the U.S. dollar. By 2000, the average **exchange rate** was 21,693. The government and national bank have attempted to control this **devaluation** by defending the currency within a controlled band. Inflation averaged 45.7 percent in 2000, and, though the trend appears to be gradually downwards, the government's finances are still strained. There remains a slight risk of a return to the high inflation of the early 1990s (256 percent in 1993). For this reason, international rating agencies do not yet define Romania as an investment grade country.

Romania has 2 stock exchanges: the Bucharest Stock Exchange, which handles the biggest companies; and the Rasdaq, intended for smaller companies. Both exchanges peaked during the mini-boom of 1997, but confidence and **turnover** is now low. The Bucharest Stock Exchange is capitalized at US$11.5 billion, while the Rasdaq is capitalized at US$826 million.

POVERTY AND WEALTH

Under communism, Romania was a comparatively egalitarian society, and this has remained the case. Nevertheless, inequality has increased in the past 10 years. In 1989, the top 10 percent of the population earned around 2.1 times more than the bottom 10 percent. By 1998, the ratio was 3.0, around Western European levels.

At the same time, the rapid rise of inflation during the 1990s and the collapsing power of the Romanian currency have left many in poverty. Cornelia Tesliuc, in a study for the World Bank, estimates that poverty has risen

Trade (expressed in billions of US$): Romania

	Exports	Imports
1975	5.341	5.769
1980	11.209	13.843
1985	12.167	11.267
1990	5.775	9.843
1995	7.910	10.278
1998	8.300	11.821

SOURCE: International Monetary Fund. *International Financial Statistics Yearbook 1999.*

Exchange rates: Romania

lei (L) per US$1	
Jan 2001	26,243.0
2000	21,708.7
1999	15,332.8
1998	8,875.6
1997	7,167.9
1996	3,084.2

Note: Lei is the plural form of leu.

SOURCE: CIA *World Factbook 2001* [ONLINE].

GDP per Capita (US$)

Country	1975	1980	1985	1990	1998
Romania	1,201	1,643	1,872	1,576	1,310
United States	19,364	21,529	23,200	25,363	29,683
Russia	2,555	3,654	3,463	3,668	2,138
Poland	N/A	2,932	2,819	2,900	3,877

SOURCE: United Nations. *Human Development Report 2000; Trends in human development and per capita income.*

Distribution of Income or Consumption by Percentage Share: Romania

Lowest 10%	3.7
Lowest 20%	8.9
Second 20%	13.6
Third 20%	17.6
Fourth 20%	22.6
Highest 20%	37.3
Highest 10%	22.7

Survey year: 1994

Note: This information refers to income shares by percentiles of the population and is ranked by per capita income.

SOURCE: *2000 World Development Indicators* [CD-ROM].

six-fold since 1989. That has left some two-thirds of the population (14.7 million people) living on the international equivalent of less than US$4 a day. Yet nearly all these people can still afford a basic food basket, and malnutrition is still rare.

Poverty is far greater in rural areas than in the towns. The northeastern regions, near the border with Moldova, have suffered most, thanks to the collapse of badly located industrial plants placed in these regions in the 1970s. Southern regions, near the Bulgarian border, are also poor. Meanwhile, the wealthiest regions are around Bucharest and in the western regions around Timisoara. But even in wealthier regions, pockets of poverty remain.

One major reason was the break-up and restitution of agricultural land, which left many people living on small subsistence farms. Unemployment has risen to over 10 percent from zero in communist times, thanks to struggling industry. A comprehensive government safety net is in place, providing a wide range of payments to pensioners, the unemployed, and large families. But strained government finances means the social payments have become tiny in real terms. Meanwhile, the average gross salary was just US$136.60 a month in January 2001.

As yet, the growing inequality has not had a noticeable effect on education levels. As in other ex-communist countries, Romania's literacy rate is relatively high, at 97 percent for women and 98 percent for men. The government accepts that it is vital to maintain these standards if Romania is to overcome poverty in the future. Unemployment is already affecting the less well-educated disproportionately. And there are worrying, if unsubstantiated, reports that school attendance is falling rapidly in some of the poorest rural areas and particularly among the Roma minority.

Maintaining health standards is also important. Romania's health-care system provides for universal access to care, funded from a state insurance fund. But it has proved difficult to maintain standards in the face of rising health-care costs. Many patients report that they have to make unofficial payments to doctors and nurses in order to get treatment, which makes access difficult for the poor. Health-care workers argue that low wages force them to accept such tips.

One of the key problems facing Romania is its orphanages. Abortion and contraception were made illegal in 1966, in an attempt to build up a communist workforce. The result was thousands of unwanted births. Some 150,000 children now live in orphanages, and though Westerners' attempts to adopt some of these children or donate money have helped, they have also brought new problems. A system of illegal adoption agencies has

Household Consumption in PPP Terms

Country	All food	Clothing and footwear	Fuel and power[a]	Health care[b]	Education[b]	Transport & Communications	Other
Romania	36	7	9	3	20	9	16
United States	13	9	9	4	6	8	51
Russia	28	11	16	7	15	8	16
Poland	28	4	19	6	1	8	34

Data represent percentage of consumption in PPP terms.

[a]Excludes energy used for transport.

[b]Includes government and private expenditures.

SOURCE: World Bank. *World Development Indicators 2000.*

grown up around the orphanages, and the foreign aid has encouraged corruption. In 1999, the European Union told Romania that it would have to stamp out this corruption and improve conditions in the orphanages before it could be admitted to EU membership.

A poor family in Romania is likely to be one with 6 or more members, including 4 or more children. It will probably be headed by a woman (particularly an elderly woman), with only primary education. The head of the household will be either unemployed, self-employed, or a subsistence farmer with less than 2 hectares of land. The family is also likely to be a Roma family—Roma are 3.5 times more likely to be poor than other Romanians.

A wealthy family in Romania is likely to be an urban couple with no children and high education. They are likely to be young and employed in a high-paying sector such as financial services.

WORKING CONDITIONS

Between 1994 and 1998, Romania's labor force has fallen from 10 million to 8.8 million. Part of the drop came from growing unemployment. But even more people simply fell out of the labor force by taking early retirement or invalid benefits. Agriculture has also soaked up a huge proportion of the spare labor force as industrial firms collapsed and land was restored to its owners. In 1990, agriculture used to account for 28 percent of the workforce. It now accounts for 42 percent.

Working conditions are regulated by various laws, most importantly the Labor Code of 1991. It sets a working week of 40 hours per week, and paid holidays of 18–24 days a year. It also stipulates redundancy payments and higher pay for workers in dangerous sectors. Nevertheless, workers still complain that working conditions are worsening in Romania. Wages have been slow to recover from a slump in 1997, when they fell 22.6 percent in real terms. And accidents at work are still one of the biggest causes of death for men aged 30 to 50.

The bargaining power of Romanian workers is limited in most sectors, thanks to the weak economy. The huge unions of the communist era have collapsed as the country turned to democracy, and their successors are far weaker. Unions and strikes are both allowed under the 1991 law, but workers complain that there are restrictions on their activity. Politicized sectors, like the miners, have frequently held large street protests. But these have often had political aims rather than pushing for improvements to working conditions.

The current leftist government views relations with the unions as key to its ability to govern the country. That is why it formed a social pact with unions and employers in February 2001. The unions have agreed that wage increases should keep pace with productivity in order to make the country's exports competitive. In return, the government has promised to keep unemployment below 10 percent, improve workplace safety, reduce the grey economy, and stop appointing political managers to state-owned firms.

COUNTRY HISTORY AND ECONOMIC DEVELOPMENT

106 A.D. Roman troops defeat the local Dacians, and Dacia becomes a province of the Roman empire.

271. Goth attacks force the Romans to withdraw.

4TH CENTURY. Christianity arrives in the region and is adopted by the Latin-speaking Daco-Romans. The area gradually coalesces into 3 regions: Wallachia, Moldavia and Transylvania.

1415. The ruler of Wallachia is forced to recognize the suzerainty of the Ottomans, who go on to conquer and unite all 3 regions.

1686. Hapsburg forces from Austria-Hungary take over Transylvania and annex parts of Moldavia over the next 200 years.

1859. After the Turko-Russian war, Wallachia and Moldavia are united and become independent.

1878. Romanian independence is recognized by the UK, France, and Germany. The country later chooses Carol I of Prussia as its first king.

1916. Romania declares war on Hungary and invades Transylvania, which it eventually wins.

1919. The Treaty of Versailles, which ends the First World War, sees Romania double in size, taking over Bukovina and parts of Bessarabia as well as Transylvania. Even now, this Greater Romania is still seen as the country's rightful territory by some politicians, e.g. those in the Greater Romania Party.

1938. King Carol II declares a royal dictatorship to stem a wave of fascist terror sweeping through the country. At the onset of the Second World War, Romania loses many of its northern territories under the Molotov-Ribbentrop pact between Germany and Russia. Carol II steps down.

1941. Under General Ion Antonescu, Romania forms a pact with Nazi Germany and fights to regain its territories. Thousands of Jews are deported.

1944. A royal coup topples Antonescu, and Romania fights the rest of the war on the Allied side.

1947. Romania is declared a People's Republic after communists gain 80 percent of the vote in rigged elections the previous year. Russia takes over northern Bukovina and Bessarabia.

1965. The country's first communist leader, Gheorghe Gheorghiu-Dej, dies. His successor, Nicolae Ceaucescu, continues to draw Romania away from Russian influence and towards the West.

1980s. Romania adopts a policy of isolationism and scrambles to pay off its US$10 billion in foreign debts. The clampdown on trade results in widespread shortages of goods, including gasoline. The debt is repaid by 1989.

1989. Nicolae Ceaucescu is overthrown and is shot, together with his wife, Elena. The National Salvation Front (NSF), headed by former Ceaucescu aide Ion Iliescu, takes over the government.

1990. Parliamentary elections are held, resulting in an overwhelming victory for the NSF. Iliescu becomes president. But he has to bus hundreds of miners into Bucharest to quell public demonstrations against the NSF.

1992. Parliamentary elections are won by Iliescu's National Democratic Salvation Front, an offshoot of the NSF. This later becomes the Party of Social Democracy of Romania (PDSR).

1993–95. Romania joins the Council of Europe and the World Trade Organization, and becomes an associated member of the European Union and a member of NATO's Partnership for Peace.

1996. Centrist opposition parties win a majority in parliamentary elections and come to power promising faster economic reforms. But the economy subsequently goes into a 3-year recession.

1997. Romania joins the Central European Free Trade Area.

1999. The European Union officially invites Romania, together with 6 other candidates, to negotiate for membership.

2000. The PDSR regains power and promises to continue Romania's progress towards EU and NATO membership.

FUTURE TRENDS

As Romania enters the 21st century under a new government, its immediate troubles seem to be behind it. The recession is over and growth is predicted for the next 4 years. This is partly for unhealthy reasons, with the government trying to stimulate the economy. But it is also for more healthy reasons. The country's exports are rising as Romanian firms learn to compete in international markets, and more foreign investment is coming into the country.

But for the long term, a lot depends on whether Romania progresses towards membership in the European Union. Even now, the goal of EU membership forces the government to tackle some of the uncomfortable reforms still needed if the economy is to thrive, such as closing down uneconomic factories and rooting out corruption. It also encourages much-needed investment in the country. Meanwhile, the EU itself is contributing billions of dollars in aid to help Romania repair its infrastructure.

These benefits can only increase if Romania achieves its goal and joins the EU within the next decade. EU aid should increase, along with the investment. And trade will be eased, raising living standards. It is the country's best chance for economic security and of achieving some kind of political security. NATO membership would be an added boon, bringing military security.

But there are plenty of risks along the way. One is that Romania's governments will fail to do the work they need to do to persuade the EU and NATO to let them join. Existing EU and NATO members could block Romania's entry to both organizations if the potential problems seem too big. Worst of all, Romania's attempts to establish democracy could fail if there is a backlash against some of the job cuts and austerity measures needed to revive the economy.

DEPENDENCIES

Romania has no territories or colonies.

BIBLIOGRAPHY

Business Central Europe. <http://www.bcemag.com>. Accessed April 2001.

Economist Intelligence Unit. <http://www.eiu.com> (subscription necessary to access all reports). Accessed April 2001.

Economist Intelligence Unit. *Country Profile: Romania.* London: Economist Intelligence Unit, 2001.

"Enlargement." *Europa. European Commission.* <http://www.europa.eu.int/comm/enlargement/romania/index.htm>. Accessed April 2001.

National Bank of Romania. <http://www.bnro.ro/def_en.htm>. Accessed April 2001.

"Report on Romanian Energy." *Energy Information Administration.* <http://www.eia.doe.gov/emeu/cabs/romania2.html>. Accessed April 2001.

"Romania." *World Bank.* <http://www.worldbank.org/ro>. Accessed April 2001.

Romania In Your Pocket. <http://www.inyourpocket.com/Romania/index.shtml>. Accessed April 2001.

Romanian National Commission for Statistics. <http://www.cns.ro/indexe.htm>. Accessed April 2001.

"A Survey of Romania, November 2000." *Business Central Europe.* <http://www.bcemag.com/servlets/bce.application.issue?cid=1284&parent_cid=1268>. Accessed April 2001.

U.S. Central Intelligence Agency. *World Factbook 2000: Romania.* <http://www.cia.gov/cia/publications/factbook/geos/ro.html>. Accessed April 2001.

Vienna Institute of Comparative Economic Studies (WIIW). <http://www.wiiw.ac.at>. (Subscription necessary to access all reports.) Accessed April 2001.

—Ana Nicholls

RUSSIA

Russian Federation
Rossiyskaya Federatsiya

CAPITAL: Moscow.

MONETARY UNIT: Ruble (R). R1 equals 100 kopeks. Coins are in denominations of R1, 2, and 5. Paper currency is in denominations of R10, 50, 100, and 500.

CHIEF EXPORTS: Petroleum and petroleum products, natural gas, wood and wood products, metals, chemicals, and a wide variety of civilian and military manufactures.

CHIEF IMPORTS: Machinery and equipment, consumer goods, medicines, meat, grain, sugar, semi-finished metal products.

GROSS DOMESTIC PRODUCT: US$1.12 trillion (purchasing power parity, 2000 est.).

BALANCE OF TRADE: **Exports:** US$105.1 billion (2000 est.). **Imports:** US$44.2 billion (2000 est.).

COUNTRY OVERVIEW

LOCATION AND SIZE. In terms of territory, Russia is the world's largest country. With a total area of 17,075,200 kilometers (6,592,735 square miles), Russia covers about one-eighth of the world's land surface. Russia is 60 percent larger than the world's second-largest country, Canada. But, like Canada, much of Russia's territory is located above the 50th parallel, where subarctic and arctic weather conditions are prevalent. Until the disintegration of the Union of Soviet Socialist Republics (USSR or "Soviet Union") in 1991, the Russian Soviet Federated Socialist Republic was the largest and dominant administrative component of the Soviet Union. In August 1991, the Russian Republic was one of the 15 countries that declared independence from the Soviet Union.

Russia stretches from its westernmost point in the city of Kaliningrad, just north of Warsaw, Poland, to its easternmost point at Big Diomede Island in the Bering Strait. Within eyesight is Little Diomede Island, belonging to the United States just off the coast of Alaska's Seward Peninsula. Russia's great breadth of territory includes many different geographical regions. These include areas of permafrost (areas of eternal ice) in Siberia and the Far North as well as taiga and steppes (vast grassland). Much of Russia's northern and eastern coastline is hemmed in by ice for much of the year, complicating navigation. However, Russia has year-round warm water seaports at Murmansk on its northwestern coastline of the Barents Sea and at Vladivostok at the far eastern coast on the Sea of Japan.

POPULATION. The population of Russia was estimated at 146,001,176 (July 2000 est.) by official U.S. government sources. According to official figures, the Russian population growth rate is negative, declining at a rate of 3 percent a year. The birth rate was at 9 births per 1,000 persons per year in 2000. The death rate was at 13.8 deaths per population per year. The declining population in Russia is taking place in the presence of a net in-flow of migrants. Migration to Russia averaged 1.38 migrants per year per 1,000 persons during 2000. The migration into Russia is composed heavily of migrants from the 14 countries of the former USSR that adjoin Russia but became independent states in late 1991.

Roughly 80 percent of Russia's population is ethnic Russian. The remaining 20 percent is made up of a wide variety of ethnic groups including Tatar, Ukrainian, Belarussian, Moldavian, Kazakh, and many others. About three-fourths of the population of Russia is urban. Moscow, Russia's capital and largest city, is home to some 9 million people. Russia has a well-educated population with near universal literacy.

Previously Russia was the world's sixth most populous country, following China, India, the United States, Indonesia, and Brazil. The Population Reference Bureau, one of the world's leading professional demographic organizations, differs with the official U.S. government

estimates regarding the size of Russia's population, and estimated Russia's population in July 2000 to be 145,231,000. At the same time, the bureau estimated Pakistan's population to be 150,648,000. This differs with the U.S. Central Intelligence Agency's (CIA) *World Factbook,* which estimated Russia's population to be 146,001,176 and Pakistan's to be 141,553,775. Despite the difficulties in measuring population accurately, it is clear that Russia's population is declining and Pakistan's is growing rapidly. If the estimates of the Population Reference Bureau are accurate, Pakistan has already overtaken Russia. This would mean that Russia, previously the world's sixth most populous country, has fallen to seventh place behind Pakistan. Even if the figures are not exactly accurate, the population trends suggest that this transition is not far away.

The USSR was a multinational country with a population of 289 million people. The country was made up of more than 100 ethnic or "national" groups. Today's Russian Federation (or simply "Russia") emerged from the USSR with roughly one-half of the USSR's population. In the aftermath of the Soviet breakup, millions of people relocated from the parts of the USSR in which they lived to new homes in the 15 countries that resulted. This migration involved many of the citizens of the USSR relocating to their native homelands. Even after these population adjustments, however, Russia is still a large and varied country. Dozens of different language groups and ethnic groups occupy Russia today.

Many of the minority groups within Russia have asserted their right to greater cultural autonomy and, sometimes, political autonomy. A minority area within Russia inhabited largely by the Chechen people proclaimed independence from Russia in 1994. Russian troops crushed the separatist movement. Russia proclaimed victory over the breakaway area of Chechnya in 1996, but the war erupted again in 1997. The brutal Chechen war has left much of this corner of Russia in ruins and has contributed to an ethnic terrorist campaign against Russia. Chechnya lies in one of Russia's most economically strategic regions, across which passes oil and gas pipelines carrying energy resources to European and world markets. Independence in Chechnya would result in these pipelines falling under the control of Chechnya rather than Russia.

OVERVIEW OF ECONOMY

Russia today has a diversified economy, but its most important sector is the sale of raw materials and **primary commodities** such as oil, timber, and gold. Russia is well-endowed with natural resources and raw materials. Russia ranks among the world's leading producers of petroleum and gas, copper, manganese, bauxite, graphite, uranium, titanium, gold, silver, and platinum. The former Soviet Union was a leading international producer of manufactured items such as chemicals, weapons, and military and aerospace equipment. Much of the industrial base of these manufacturing sectors was located within the Russian Republic itself. However, the disintegration of the USSR led to significant interruptions in commercial relationships.

During its 73 years of existence, the USSR grew to be a great military superpower. Measured in terms of crude output, the USSR created the foundation for massive production possibilities. The USSR became one of the world's largest producers of numerous processed materials and manufactured items, ranging from foodstuffs to nuclear warheads. But efficiency of production—that is the ratio of inputs to outputs for any given product—was not a major objective of the Soviet economic system. Great emphasis was put on outputs. Accordingly, the USSR developed an economic system that was focused almost exclusively on the achievement of production targets. The system proved to be extremely bureaucratic and highly resistant to technological change. The Soviet economic system was not capable of meeting the requirements of the dynamic international markets of the 21st century. Even before the Soviet Union broke up, the Russian government began initiating reforms to move the economy from a centrally-planned to a market-based **liberal economy**. This process of change has come to be known as the transition to a market economy.

Soon after independence, the Russian government announced a much more ambitious program of political and economic reform. The program included a transformation of the economy from the principles of state planning and administrative direction to market-based economics. **Price controls** were lifted. Government **subsidies** were eliminated or reduced. The government budget was organized along new lines so that it could be balanced through bringing tax revenues into line with government spending. A restrictive **monetary policy** was adopted. Foreign trade was **liberalized** through the lifting of export and import controls. The Russian currency, the ruble, was allowed to devalue to bring it into line with market rates. **Privatization** and **restructuring** of state **monopolies** was undertaken. Efforts were commenced to establish the legal and regulatory structure for a market environment. New legislation was passed to establish laws and procedures for the banking industry, capital markets, civil and contract law, adjudication of commercial disputes, and the development of a social safety net to cushion the social impact of economic structural transformation.

But the first years of transition proved very difficult for Russia. In its first decade as a market-oriented economy, the Russian economy suffered a contraction of nearly 60 percent over pre-independence levels as measured by GDP. Sharp declines in production in key industries and exports led to a continuously contracting economy between 1990 and 1997 as industrial production went into a "free fall," dropping more than 50 percent during the decade of the 1990s. The Soviet military-industrial complex, suppliers of goods to the state sector, and light industry were the hardest hit by the structural adjustment to a market-oriented economy and the withdrawal from superpower status.

In 1997 the economy began to show the first signs of post-transition recovery, posting a growth rate of slightly less than 1 percent. Despite the "shock therapy" of a rapid transition and the decline in industrial production, increase in poverty and unemployment, and the weakening of the social service **infrastructure**, Russia was beginning to show signs of an economic turnaround. **Inflation**, which skyrocketed in 1993 and 1994, finally had been brought under control. The ruble was stabilized. An ambitious privatization program had transferred thousands of enterprises to private ownership. Important market-oriented laws had also been passed, including a commercial code governing business relations and the establishment of an arbitration court for resolving economic disputes.

However, in the summer of 1998, a powerful wave of financial instability that originated in the Asian financial crisis of 1997 swept through the Russian financial community. The Russian economy has undergone tremendous stress as it has moved from a **centrally-planned economy** toward a **free market system**. Difficulties in implementing fiscal reforms aimed at raising government revenues and a dependence on short-term borrowing to finance government **budget deficits** led to a serious financial crisis in 1998. Lower prices for Russia's major export earners (oil and minerals) and a loss of investor confidence due to the Asian financial crisis exacerbated financial problems. The result was a rapid decline in the value of the ruble, flight of foreign investment, delayed payments on government and private debts, a breakdown of commercial transactions through the banking system, and the threat of runaway inflation. In August 1998 the Russian government allowed the ruble to fall precipitously and postponed payment on US$40 billion in treasury bonds. In the wake of the financial crisis, billions of dollars of **foreign direct investment** were swept out of the country, investor confidence fell, and Russia moved into a sharp economic contraction.

The 1998 financial crisis produced a steep and sudden decline in personal incomes, as **GDP per capita** in Russia dropped from US$3,056 in 1997 to US$1,867 in 1998. The sharp decline in per capita income and contraction of the financial markets also had some benign effects, however. In some economic sectors, Russian economic performance improved as higher world prices for fuels—world oil prices nearly tripled in 1999—and some metals facilitated improvement in exports. The Russian ruble was devalued in connection with the financial crisis. The devalued ruble rendered Russian-made products relatively cheaper than imports. This contributed to increased purchases of domestically produced goods and services as well as facilitating exports.

In 1999 output increased for only the second time since 1991, by an officially estimated 3.2 percent, regaining much of the ground lost during the 4.6 percent drop of 1998. The 1999 increase was achieved despite a year of potential turmoil that included the ousting of 3 premiers and culminated in the New Year's Eve resignation of President Boris Yeltsin. Of great help was the tripling of international oil prices in the second half of 1999, raising the export surplus to US$29 billion. On the negative side, inflation rose to an average 86 percent in 1999, compared with a 28 percent average in 1998. Average citizens found their **real wages** fall by roughly 30 percent and their pensions by 45 percent. The new Russian government, under the leadership of Vladimir Putin, gave high priority to supplementing low incomes by paying back wage and pension IOUs. However, many investors, both domestic and international, remained on the sidelines, scared off by Russia's long-standing problems with **capital flight**, widespread corruption, and newspaper articles on organized crime and the Russian mafia. The international press gave sensational coverage to investigations of **money laundering** schemes designed to move ill-gotten gains into safe havens out of Russia.

The rebound continued in 2000 as the Russian economy grew briskly throughout the year, far exceeding expectations. Buoyed by the **devaluation** of the ruble and a sharp increase in average oil export prices over 1999 levels, **real GDP** surpassed its pre-1998 crisis level, growing by over 8 percent in 2000. Growth in industrial output, which reached 8 percent in 1999, further increased in 2000. The increase in industrial production led to a reduction in the unemployment rate, with recorded unemployment falling to just over 10 percent by the end of 2000.

On the negative side, it must be noted that Russia's economic growth was still largely concentrated in a few sectors. Nor were the benefits of growth widely distributed throughout the society. More than one-third of the population of the Russian Federation continued to live below the poverty line. The social assistance provided by the government was not sufficient and was not successfully targeted to the poor and those most in need. In sum, the general quality of the government's services has deteriorated since 1991. The poor and the most vulnerable were the most directly affected by this deterioration.

The declines in industrial production have taken place simultaneously with a modest but steady growth in the trade and service sectors. These sectors were underdeveloped during the years of the USSR's central planning. The majority of Russian manufacturing enterprises remain uncompetitive if judged by world standards. Output has continued to fall at medium and large Russian enterprises, while many small companies and **joint ventures** have grown in output and efficiency. Overall, services have grown to account for more than 50 percent of GDP, with manufacturing contributing just slightly less than 40 percent and agriculture accounting for just under 10 percent. Overall trends indicate that the portion of GDP accounted for by services and taxes was increasing while industrial production and manufacturing were decreasing in importance as contributors to GDP. In December 2000, the Russian parliament (the Federal Assembly) passed Russia's first post-Soviet balanced budget.

POLITICS, GOVERNMENT, AND TAXATION

Until 1991 Russia was the largest republic in the Union of Soviet Socialist Republics, born out of the Russian Revolution that took place in 1917–18. Russia was ruled by a monarchy headed by a tsar until 1917 when, following Russia's disastrous participation in the First World War, the tsar abdicated the throne, leaving a provisional government in power. In the harsh Russian winter of 1917 a band of **Marxist** revolutionaries seized power. The Marxists called themselves the *Bolsheviks* (*bolshe* in the Russian language means "larger," and this group of Marxists claimed to be in the majority, hence "Bolsheviks").

The Bolshevik Revolution introduced a new form of government and economics to the world. The Bolsheviks promised that they would create a humanitarian Marxist form of economics. The Bolsheviks championed the labor theory of value, claiming that all value was derived from the importance of the human effort that went into creating a good or service. They promised to create a new economic system that would eliminate economic exploitation of people, would substitute cooperative production for boom and bust cycles of production under **capitalism**, and would free people to take only what they needed from society and contribute whatever they could. The Soviet government followed this economic policy throughout its 73-year rule.

Political and economic discord brought the USSR to a critical juncture in the 1980s, when a new and dynamic political leader, Mikhail Gorbachev, introduced plans for economic restructuring and political reform. Gorbachev announced major political changes at the 19th Conference of the Communist Party of the Soviet Union (CPSU) in June and July 1988. Gorbachev invited the leaders from the 15 Soviet Socialist Republics of the USSR to announce that free elections and economic reform were on the country's agenda.

There were those who thought that the reform efforts would allow the system to release some steam. In reality, once the lid was off, the situation quickly boiled over into a massive change of political and economic systems. A group of high party leaders from 11 of the 15 Soviet republics met in December 1991 in Alma-Ata, Kazakhstan, to pass an agreement that declared the "Union of Soviet Socialist Republics shall henceforth cease to exist." The leading countries in the world rapidly acknowledged this declaration. The Alma-Ata Declaration sealed the fate of the Soviet Union and created a successor, the **Commonwealth of Independent States** (CIS). The CIS—a loose affiliation of the former Soviet states—has not proved to be a viable political entity, and today exists largely in form. Without a popular referendum or mandate, without parliamentary advice or consent, and without judicial review, the Soviet state simply was declared a thing of the past. USSR President Mikhail Gorbachev, acknowledging the inevitable, resigned on 25 December 1991. The Soviet flag ceased to fly over the Kremlin.

Today, the Russian Federation is a constitutional democracy with 3 branches: executive, legislative, and judicial. The Russian Constitution, which came into effect on 12 December 1993, recognizes a separation of powers. The constitution describes the purposes of government, outlines the rights and responsibilities of citizens, and defines the structure of public institutions in the Russian Federation. The legal framework is based on a civil law system, and there is judicial review of legislation.

Despite the separation of powers, in terms of process, the Russian Federation functions as a presidential style of government, which concentrates most authority in the president as the head of state. The first president of the Russian Federation was Boris Nikolaevich Yeltsin, who was succeeded by Vladimir Putin. The Russian president is elected for a 4-year term. There is no vice-president. In the event of the incapacity of the president to carry out the constitutional mandate, the prime minister succeeds the president. The legislative branch consists of the Federal Assembly, made up of an upper house—the Council of Federation, made up of 1 representative from each of Russia's 89 federal constituent units—and a lower house—the State Duma, made of up 450 seats.

The executive branch includes: 1) the Presidential Administration, which drafts presidential decrees and provides staff and policy support to the entire executive branch; 2) the Security Council, which was established as a presidential advisory body in June 1991 and restructured in March 1992, when it was given responsibility for managing state security; 3) the Cabinet, which includes the ministers—the heads of the government ministries, who are appointed by the president; 4) the Council of Heads of Republics, which includes the leaders of the 21 ethnic-based republics; and 5) the Council of Heads of Administrations, which includes the leaders of the 66 autonomous territories and regions, as well as the mayors of Moscow and St. Petersburg.

Since 1991 the Russian government has frequently tried to minimize its budget deficits by failing to pay for wages and pensions. Weak tax administration, a cumbersome tax system with high rates that invite tax evasion, falling industrial output, the use of **barter** in the economy, and blunt refusal to pay by large, politically powerful firms has weakened the government's ability to meet its obligations. Under the new leadership of President Vladimir Putin, overcoming the travail of the collapse of the financial markets in Russia in August 1998 is high on the government's agenda. A comprehensive program to transform the Russian economy was approved on 26 July 2000. The Putin government has sought to establish a prudent **fiscal policy** in part by collecting significantly higher tax revenues than anticipated under the state budget and managing to restrain spending. The government placed considerable emphasis on reforms of the tax code.

But there are other weaknesses in the structure of the government. The Russian state bureaucracy is still at an early stage of its adjustment to the needs of a modern market-oriented economy. The objectives, functions, and competencies of the different governance structures are poorly defined, leaving substantial space open for discretionary action by bureaucrats. Civil servants are underpaid and inadequately monitored, which creates a strong incentive for the use of public office for private gain. Government decisions, privileges, and regulatory exemptions in Russia are routinely and quite openly influenced by bribes to public officials. While there are many civil servants who maintain high professional standards, the institutions within which they serve are poorly equipped to regulate a market-oriented economy.

Fair and impartial adjudication of disputes is a key to an effectively functioning market economy. Russia's judiciary and justice system remain weak. Numerous matters that are dealt with by administrative authority in European countries remain subject to political influence in Russia. The 1993 constitution empowers the courts to arbitrate disputes between the executive and legislative branches and between Moscow and the regional and local governments. The court also is authorized to rule on violations of constitutional rights, to examine appeals from various bodies, and to participate in impeachment proceedings against the president. The July 1994 Law on the Constitutional Court prohibits the court from examining cases on its own initiative and limits the scope of issues the court can hear. President Yeltsin reconvened the Constitutional Court in March 1995 following its suspension in October 1993. The Russian government has begun to reform the criminal justice system and judicial institutions, including the reintroduction of jury trials in certain criminal cases. Despite these efforts, judges are only beginning to assert their constitutionally-mandated independence from other branches of government.

Public accountability is complicated by the existence of a substantial **informal sector**. One of its features is the practice of barter arrangements. Many enterprises, being unable to meet their commercial or their tax obligations, turn to barter transactions. Because these barters are not always denominated in currency, their true value for purposes of taxation is often obscure. Moreover, many local and regional governments have been willing in the past to sometimes accept barter payments or "in-kind" payments in lieu of taxes from enterprises that could not pay but had an important social role as a major employer in the community.

When Russia liberalized its economy, explicit budgetary subsidies for enterprises were drastically curtailed. However, industrial enterprises have continued to be supported by "implicit subsidies" channeled largely through the energy sector and lax tax enforcement. These implicit subsidies have taken the form of non-cash settlements for energy and tax payments. Sometimes these non-cash settlements were "payments-in-kind," such as when a factory could not pay its tax bill in rubles because it was not selling its goods. It would then agree with the local tax authorities to pay in production of the goods it makes. This might mean that a tire factory, for instance, would pay its local tax bill in the form of tires supplied to the local tax authority. The tires, in turn, would be used or traded by the tax authorities. These forms of payment were also used to pay energy companies for electricity and gas, which are critical for the operation of factories.

INFRASTRUCTURE, POWER, AND COMMUNICATIONS

The transportation infrastructure in Russia is underdeveloped. The transport system is heavily Moscow-centered, with virtually all transportation channels of economic significance emanating from Moscow. Commercial transportation relies heavily on rail. Roughly 90 percent of commercial haulage is rail-based and insufficiently integrated into world transport systems. The Russian trucking industry is only minimally developed, and roads are not designed to carry heavy and long-distance truck traffic.

The Russian railway system includes a total of 150,000 kilometers (93,210 miles) of broad gauge rail, making it one of the most extensive railway systems in the world. However, of this total only 87,000 kilometers (54,061 miles) is in "common carrier" service. The remaining 63,000 kilometers (39,148 miles) serve specific industries or are dedicated railways lines and are not available for common carrier use. Following decades of insufficient investment in maintenance and capital improvement, the railway infrastructure has badly deteriorated. About 30 percent of freight cars, 40 percent of passenger cars, and nearly half the locomotives are of such poor quality that they should be replaced immediately.

The Russian highway system includes a total of 948,000 kilometers (589,087 miles) of road including 416,000 kilometers (258,502 miles) that serve specific industries or farms and are not maintained by governmental highway maintenance departments. Of the total road system, only 336,000 kilometers (208,790 miles) are paved. Russia's great territorial expanses and rugged terrain have hindered the development of a nation-wide high-

Communications

Country	Newspapers	Radios	TV Sets[a]	Cable subscribers[a]	Mobile Phones[a]	Fax Machines[a]	Personal Computers[a]	Internet Hosts[b]	Internet Users[b]
	1996	1997	1998	1998	1998	1998	1998	1999	1999
Russia	105	418	420	78.5	5	0.4	40.6	13.06	2,700
United States	215	2,146	847	244.3	256	78.4	458.6	1,508.77	74,100
China	N/A	333	272	40.0	19	1.6	8.9	0.50	8,900
Germany	311	948	580	214.5	170	73.1	304.7	173.96	14,400

[a]Data are from International Telecommunication Union, *World Telecommunication Development Report 1999* and are per 1,000 people.
[b]Data are from the Internet Software Consortium (http://www.isc.org) and are per 10,000 people.

SOURCE: World Bank. *World Development Indicators 2000.*

way system. The European parts of the country are much better served than the areas east of the Ural mountains.

The Russian waterways system is an important component of the transportation infrastructure. Total navigable routes in general use by the Russian River Fleet amount to 101,000 kilometers (62,761 miles). Among Russia's most important ports are Arkhangelsk, Kaliningrad, Kazan, Krasnoyarsk, Moscow, Murmansk, Novorossiysk, St. Petersburg, Rostov, Sochi, Vladivostok, Volgograd, and Vyborg. The Russian merchant marine includes some 700 ocean-going vessels, but its fleet is twice as old as the global average.

Russia has some 630 improved airport facilities, 50 of which are capable of accommodating international flights. The country also has an extensive oil and gas pipeline system, with some 48,000 kilometers (29,827 miles) of pipelines for crude petroleum, 15,000 kilometers (9,321 miles) designed for shipment of refined petroleum products, and 140,000 kilometers (86,996 miles) designed for shipment of natural gas.

There are serious capital and operating inefficiencies and poor financial performance in what should be cost-recovery sectors, that is, sectors that should be able to pay their own way through user fees rather than through central government subsidies or direct administration. These include public utilities (called "natural monopolies" in Russia) such as public transportation, water, gas, and electricity, as well as some commercial transportation systems such as river and lake navigation. Transportation **tariffs** (user fees) have not kept pace with inflation.

Russia's overall electricity production (1998) was 771.94 billion kilowatt hours (kWh). Of this amount, some 69 percent was produced through burning fossil fuel, 20 percent resulted from hydroelectric generation, and roughly 13 percent was produced at commercial atomic generating stations. Electricity consumption amounted to 702.71 billion kWh, while 21 billion kWh was exported and 5.8 billion kWh was imported.

Effective wholesale gas and electricity tariffs have been at only around one-tenth of the Western European level for the past decade, with the ratio even worse in distribution to households. The problem has been exacerbated by low rates of cash collection. In the power sector, cash collection rates stood at less than 20 percent in 2000. Due to its financial unattractiveness but also due to the lack of an appropriate legal and regulatory framework to facilitate **private sector** participation, infrastructure services are generally provided by state and local government-owned entities. Progress in the corporatization (turning utility systems into corporate entities) and commercialization of infrastructure has been poor. There has been some separation of publicly-owned service providers from government, transforming them into legally autonomous corporate entities. However, there continues to be a high degree of government (federal, regional, and local) interference in their management and financial operations.

Russia's telecommunications system is in the midst of the global telecommunications revolution. The country's phone system has undergone significant changes since the breakup of the state phone monopoly in 1990. By 2000, there were over 1,000 companies licensed to offer communication services. During this period access to digital lines has improved, particularly in urban centers. Internet and e-mail services are now widespread and rapidly improving. In a few short years, Russia made significant progress toward building the telecommunications infrastructure necessary for a market economy. Cross-country digital trunk lines run from Saint Petersburg in the northwest to Khabarovsk in the Russian Far East and from Moscow in the country's European center to Novorossiysk in the south. The telephone systems in over 60 regional capitals had installed modern digital infrastructures by 2000. Cellular services, both analog and digital, expanded rapidly in 2000 and 2001. Three undersea fiber-optic cables connect Russia to the international phone system. Digital switches in several cities provide more than 50,000 lines for international calls. Satellite earth stations provide access to Intelsat, Intersputnik, Eutelsat, Inmarsat, and Orbita.

ECONOMIC SECTORS

The chief sectors of the Russian economy are natural resources, industry, and agriculture. The natural resources sector includes petroleum, natural gas, timber, furs, and precious and nonferrous metals. The agriculture

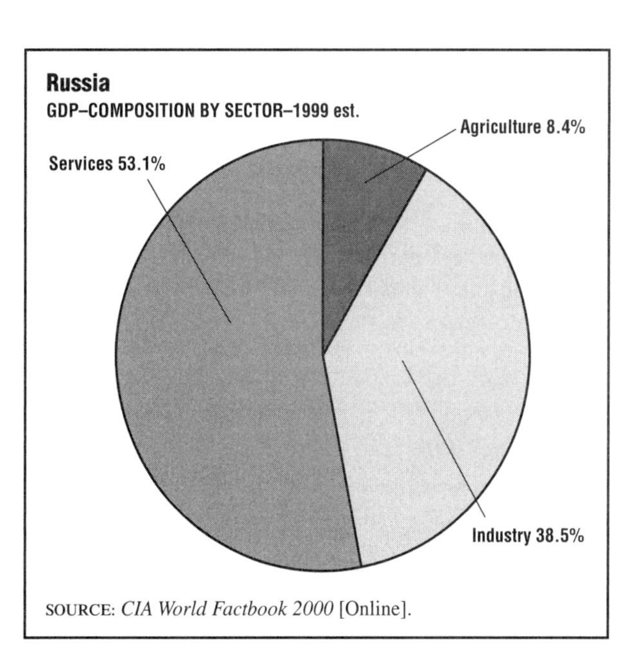

SOURCE: *CIA World Factbook 2000* [Online].

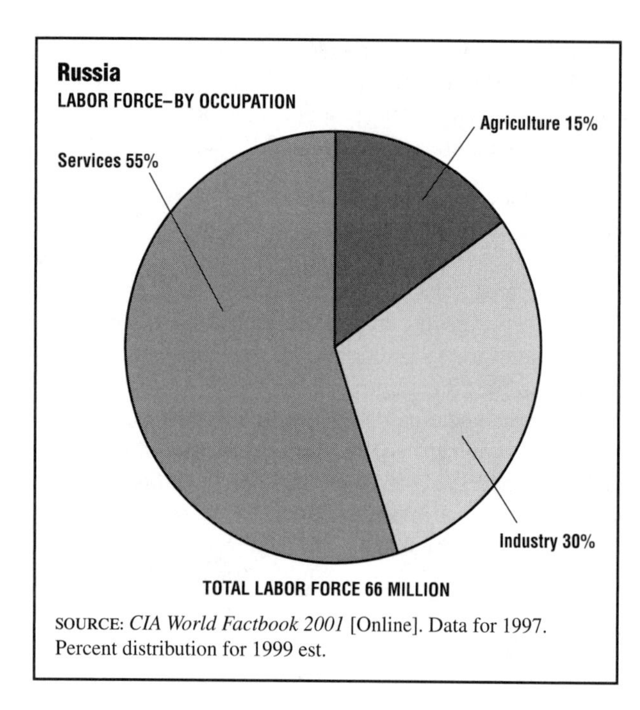

SOURCE: *CIA World Factbook 2001* [Online]. Data for 1997. Percent distribution for 1999 est.

sector includes grain, sugar beets, sunflower seeds, meat, and dairy products. Manufacturing and industry includes a complete range of manufactures, notably automobiles, trucks, trains, agricultural equipment, advanced aircraft, aerospace, machine and equipment products, mining and extractive industry, medical and scientific instruments, and construction equipment. Trade exports emphasize petroleum and petroleum products, natural gas, woods and wood products, metals, and chemicals. Major markets include the countries of the European Union, the other former Soviet countries, China, and Japan, as well as countries of the Middle East. Imports include machinery and equipment, chemicals, **consumer goods**, medicines, meat, sugar, and semi-finished metal products. The trading partners for imports are the same as those for exports.

The Soviet economy created distorting policies and reduced the interest of firms and individuals to use natural resources carefully. The costly and destructive environmental legacy of the Soviet economy is still very much evident in Russia. There is a high risk of environmental accidents and emergencies. Environmental policy at both the federal and regional levels is not always consistent or clear. Enforcement of regulations to protect the environment is often left to the discretion of the firms that create the problems. The merging of the independent environmental agency into the Ministry of Natural Resources in 1999 created a further cause for concern given the potential conflicts of interest of the institutions involved.

Russia is the most industrialized of the former Soviet Republics. However, much of its industry is antiquated and highly inefficient. Besides its resource-based industries, it has developed large manufacturing capacities, notably in machinery. Russia inherited most of the defense industrial base of the Soviet Union. Efforts have been made with little significant success over the past few years to convert defense industries to civilian use.

Most major industry sectors showed an increase in output in 1999 over 1998. However, this was not true of **agribusiness** and the power and fuel sectors, which showed improvements over 1998, but declines compared to 1997. The sub-sectors showing declines in output in 1999 over 1998 include heating oil, machine tools, television, and sausage production. Some sub-sectors that fared poorly in the mid- and late 1990s, such as light industry and the pulp/paper, chemical, and building materials sector, showed increased output in 1999 over 1998. Sectors that fared the worst in 1998 included light industry, metallurgy, chemicals, and agribusiness. Despite across-the-board improvements in recent years, many Russian enterprises remain uncompetitive. In addition, output through 2000 continued to decline at medium and large Russian enterprises, while small companies and joint ventures were responsible for increased output. The CIA *World Factbook* estimated that agriculture accounted for 7 percent of GDP, industry 34 percent, and services 59 percent in 1999.

AGRICULTURE

Employment in agriculture and forestry remained relatively constant in recent years. Agriculture and forestry employment accounted for about 14 percent of total employment in 1999, about the same level as a decade earlier. Russia comprises roughly three-quarters of the territory of the former Soviet Union, but only a small amount of this vast area is suited for agriculture because of its arid climate and inconsistent rainfall. Nevertheless, with 133 million hectares of arable land, a large agrarian **workforce** (14 percent of the total), and 146 million inhabitants to feed, Russia is a major regional and global agricultural producer and consumer. The Russian fishing industry is the world's fourth-largest, behind Japan, the United States, and China. Russia accounts for one-quarter of the world's production of fresh and frozen fish and about one-third of world output of canned fish. Russia has a major forestry industry, possessing one-quarter of the world's forests.

Northern areas concentrate mainly on livestock and the southern parts and western Siberia produce grain. Restructuring of former state farms has been an extremely slow process, partially due to the lack of a land code allowing for the free sale, purchase, and mortgage of agricultural land. Private farms and garden plots of individuals account for more than one-half of all agricultural production. Much of the agricultural sector has been almost unaffected by the transition to the free market. Accordingly, the output performance of agriculture has been very weak. This has tended to strengthen the arguments of those who oppose economic reform in favor of a return to the state-managed economy of the past.

Primary agriculture in Russia continues to be dominated by inefficient, Soviet-type collective farms with outdated technologies and management skills and strong political connections, especially at the regional level. Household plots and small private farms comprising only 3 percent of the agricultural land account for over 40 percent of the country's food production. The business infrastructure for the agriculture sector is especially underdeveloped including support services, transportation, distribution networks, and financial services. For agriculture in Russia to go through the transformation to a modern system, the key step will be establishing and enforcing farmers' rights to use land. The first step in this process is to develop an efficient system of issuing and protecting title to land rights. This will also require a more reliable and enforceable framework for secured financial transactions so that farmers can buy and sell their land or use the land as collateral for obtaining loans.

The economic reform that began in Russia in the early 1990s reduced Russia's livestock sector. The downsizing of the livestock sector ended the need for imports of feed grain, soybeans, and meal. At the same time, imports of meat and other high-value products such as processed foods, fruit, and beverages grew considerably. The 1998 economic crisis reduced Russia's ability to import food. After plunging to extremely low levels in late 1998, agricultural imports rebounded in 1999. Imports of most agricultural and food products grew to roughly 60 percent of the level of the pre-crisis period. Imports dropped because the crisis reduced consumer incomes, thereby decreasing demand for food in general, and the severe crisis-induced depreciation of the ruble made imported food more expensive compared to Russian domestic output.

The large former state and collective farms control most land. Farm workers can branch off as private farmers by obtaining a grant of land from their parent farm, though they lack full ownership rights. The land code proposed by the Russian legislature (the Duma) does not change existing law—that is, it does not allow the free purchase and sale of land for agricultural use. Rather, it would allow land to be bought and sold solely for economically insignificant purposes, such as building a summer cottage, a *dacha.*

INDUSTRY

Russia has a range of mining and extractive industries. These include coal, oil, and gas extraction as well as the chemicals and metals industries. Russian enterprises take part in all forms of machine building from rolling mills to high-performance aircraft and space vehicles. Russian enterprises are involved in shipbuilding, manufacturing of road and rail transportation equipment, communications equipment, agricultural machinery, tractors, and construction equipment. Russian firms produce electric power generating and transmitting equipment, medical and scientific instruments, consumer durables, textiles, foodstuffs, processed food products, and handicrafts.

Russia is a leading producer and exporter of minerals, gold, and all major fuels. Oil and gas exports continue to be the main source of **hard currency**. Russia has vast reserves of oil, gas, and timber. Siberia and the Russian Far East are particularly rich in natural resources. However, most deposits of resources are located in remote areas with challenging climate conditions.

The most important export sector is energy. Russia is the world leader in natural gas production, third in oil, and fourth in coal. Gazprom, the large natural gas monopoly, inherited from the former USSR a massive network of production and distribution facilities that was built over a period of decades. The energy industry is significant also in its intricate ties with political elites. Energy monopolies are thus able to enjoy special privileges such as subsidies of various kinds. However, much of the physical infrastructure is in a state of disrepair. Gazprom will require billions of dollars to upgrade its physical systems. Declining energy prices hit Russia hard in the mid-1990s. The rebound in energy prices in the late 1990s was a great benefit to Russia's foreign trade account.

The oil sector has undergone substantial liberalization and now is primarily restructured and privately held. The oil industry, unlike gas and electricity, was broken up into a dozen companies as it was privatized. Oil prices have therefore moved very quickly toward world prices. Oil export tariffs were phased out entirely in July 1996. Simultaneously, however, oil production **excise taxes** were increased.

Russia has an estimated 49 to 55 billion barrels of oil in proven reserves, but aging equipment and poorly developed fields are making it difficult to develop these reserves. The depletion of existing oilfields, deterioration in transport infrastructure, and an acute shortage of investment—aggravated by the country's August 1998 financial crisis—may lead to further declines in oil production unless these trends can be reversed.

Natural gas is the predominant fuel in Russia, accounting for nearly half of the country's domestic consumption. With 1.7 quadrillion cubic feet (TCF) in proven gas reserves, Russia has more than enough for itself, allowing it to export significant amounts of gas. In fact, Russia is the world's largest gas exporter. Europe is a major consumer. Although the country's natural gas production has dipped only slightly (8 percent from 1992 to 1999) during the transition to democracy, low investment has raised concerns about future production levels. Gas production in the established West Siberian fields that account for 76 percent of Russian gas output is declining. At the same time, the planned development of new fields continues to be delayed as a result of lack of investment resources.

SERVICES

Russia's previously underdeveloped services sector has played an important role in containing the social calamity of the collapse of the USSR, manufacturing and industrial sectors. The service sector employed 55 percent of the workforce and contributed 59 percent of GDP in 1999, according to the CIA *World Factbook.* Important service industries include financial services; advertising, marketing, and sales; tourism; and **retail** trade.

TOURISM. Foreign and domestic tourism was centrally managed during the Soviet Union. In 1991 the tourism industry was reorganized and today is one of the most important branches of the service sector, both in terms of total revenue and numbers of employees. The number of tourist companies has grown from several state tourist organizations in 1991 to several hundred in the larger Russian cities today. Most tourist firms are small, employing fewer than 15 people, and function as both operators and agencies. Operators are those firms that develop their own tourist routes. Tourist agencies market the existing routes established by operators. Most travel transactions involve the domestic market, offering travel services within Russia either for foreigners or for domestic travelers. Providing services for Russians traveling abroad is a smaller but more lucrative market.

The August 1998 financial crisis in Russia had a major impact upon the tourist industry. The number of Russian tourists traveling to foreign countries dropped off sharply and the number of foreign tourists visiting Russia also declined. According to the Russian Statistical Committee, the number of Russians visiting the United States in 1999 fell by nearly half between 1998 (175,660) and 1999 (95,280). The number of Americans visiting Russia also fell considerably between 1998 (216,976) and 1999 (177,120).

In the old USSR domestic tourism was one of the largest industries. There were many resorts, recreational centers, tourist bases, and summer camps for children. Large enterprise and labor unions provided people with inexpensive package tours. During the first years after the breakup of the Soviet Union, domestic tourism declined sharply, but has regained ground since then. Russian tourists travel abroad to Europe, the countries of the Mediterranean, and the United States—a popular tourist destination for young people. Local foreign language schools often offer English language training in the United States to teenagers and young people. Obtaining visas to travel to the United States, however, involves complicated regulations and is often a hindrance.

Russia is a popular destination for foreign tourists, primarily because of its cultural attractions. Over 80 percent of foreign tourists come to Russia with the intention of visiting Moscow and/or St. Petersburg. However, in recent years the country's natural environment has attracted a growing proportion of foreign travelers. Russia may one day become a popular destination for eco-travel, attracting adventure travelers and tourists looking for something out of the ordinary. Travel to Russia is particularly well-represented by travelers from Germany, China, the United States, Japan, Italy, Poland, Turkey, and Israel.

A legacy of Soviet-era infrastructure neglect, oppressive paperwork, high costs, and lack of local marketing know-how have limited attractiveness of travel to Russia for many foreigners. Despite improvements in the first decade since the Soviet breakup, the Russian travel industry continues to be hindered by the lack of accommodations and travel-related services that are in accordance with international standards. Recent years have witnessed improvements in the quality of services. In addition, new programs have been instituted that provide training in hotel and restaurant management services. At the same time, new hotel, restaurant, and recreational equipment and expertise have become more widely available.

FINANCIAL SERVICES. The Russian government has put considerable emphasis in recent years on restructuring and stabilizing the banking system and the financial services industry. A legal framework was adopted, establishing procedures for forming statutory capital, specifying procedures for starting and terminating commercial bank activities, procedures of issuing and recalling licenses for bank audits, establishing procedures for bank bankruptcies, and establishing procedures for the operation of non-banking financial organizations that offer financial services and were licensed and regulated by the National Bank.

But the Russian banking system is still in a state of transition. Banks do not have the resources, capability, or the population's trust to attract substantial savings and channel them to productive investments. While ruble lending doubled in the 2 years following the August 1998 financial crisis, loans remained at the pre-crisis level of 30 percent of total bank assets. The Russian Central Bank reduced its refinancing rate 3 times in 2000, to 33 percent, signaling an attempt to lower lending rates. However, banks still perceived commercial lending as risky, and some banks were inexperienced at assessing credit risk. The Russian Central Bank announced that it was developing a procedure to finance banks for promissary notes, rights of claim under credit agreements, and mortgages.

INTERNATIONAL TRADE

Russia's foreign trade consisted of US$75 billion in exports and imports of US$48.2 billion in 1999 and then to US$105.1 billion in exports and US$44.2 billion in imports by 2000. Russia sells a broad range of commodities and manufactures including petroleum and petroleum products, natural gas, wood and wood products, metals, chemicals, and a wide variety of civilian and military manufactures. Russia's largest trading partners for exports are Ukraine, Germany, United States, Belarus, the Netherlands, and China. Russia imports machinery and equipment, consumer goods, medicines, meat, grain, sugar, and semi-finished metal products. Russia's largest trading partners for imports are Germany, Belarus, Ukraine, the United States, Kazakhstan, and Italy.

Real GDP growth in Russia in 1999 was over 3 percent. The main contributing factors were the devaluation of the ruble, which made Russian products competitive abroad and at home; high commodity prices on international markets, particularly oil (while domestic costs were substantially lower); low inflation and a consensus that inflation must be controlled; and a relatively healthy fiscal situation based on strict government budget discipline. The major contributor to growth was trade performance. Exports rose to US$74.3 billion while imports slumped by 30 percent to US$41.1 billion. As a result, net exports ballooned to US$33.2 billion, more than double the previous year's level. Higher oil prices had a major effect on export performance, particularly in the latter half of the year. Even though volumes of crude oil exports (to non-CIS countries) were down by 3 percent, prices jumped 46 percent. Fuels and energy comprise 42 percent of Russian exports. Other exports performed better in 1999; fertilizer exports were up 16.7 percent, forestry products up 38 percent, copper up 17.6 percent, and aluminum up 10 percent.

Trade (expressed in billions of US$): Russia

	Exports	Imports
1975	N/A	N/A
1980	N/A	N/A
1985	N/A	N/A
1990	N/A	N/A
1995	81.096	60.945
1998	74.160	58.996

SOURCE: International Monetary Fund. *International Financial Statistics Yearbook 1999.*

Trade with other former Soviet states is overwhelmingly in energy and industrial products, and in many instances has been, until quite recently, conducted by barter. Russia's **trade surpluses** eroded over the course of 1998. Imports to Russia grew by 10–15 percent per year between 1995 and 1997, as consumers benefited from an appreciating ruble and rising average wages. At the same time, export revenues were falling, due in particular to sharply lower prices for oil and gas (accounting for 43 percent of merchandise exports in 1997). Moreover, Russia's manufactured exports compete poorly on the world market, especially since Asian goods have become less expensive following steep currency devaluations. The devaluation of the ruble and difficulties in completing transactions through the Russian banking system reduced imports substantially. Frequent changes in customs regulations also have created problems for foreign and domestic traders and investors.

Russian oil companies have been rushing to export their oil (resulting in a windfall of hard currency coming into the country) to such an extent that Russian officials have set export quotas in order to maintain an adequate domestic supply of oil. In 2000, Russian net oil exports totaled 4.3 million metric barrels a day (MMBD). In addition to export quotas and higher taxes levied on oil exports, a serious problem facing exporters is the lack of export routes. Russia is maneuvering to become a major player in the exploration, development, and export of oil from the Caspian Sea. Transneft is the **parastatal** responsible for Russia's extensive oil pipeline system. Many of these pipelines are in a poor state of repair. The Russian Fuel and Energy Ministry notes that almost 5 percent of crude oil produced in Russia is lost through pipeline leaks. Transneft lacks the funding to repair or upgrade many of these malfunctioning pipes. The company's focus has been on building new pipelines rather than repairing the old. In addition to those in the Caspian Sea Region, Russia has a number of new oil and gas pipelines planned or already under construction.

MONEY

At the start of the economic transition, key reform-oriented policy makers in the Russian government sought to get market price mechanisms working as quickly as possible. These reformists argued that price liberalization and policies designed to bring about **macroeconomic** stabilization could be expected to impose some economic hardship for a period of time, but that it was better to live with temporary difficulties than to be burdened by distorted prices and unsound policies that might endure for years or even decades. This pro-reform perspective became known as "shock therapy." The reformists took their inspiration in large measure from Western monetarist doctrines that maintained that

Exchange rates: Russia

rubles per US$1	
Jan 2001	28.3592
2000	28.1292
1999	24.6199
1998	9.7051
1997	5,785
1996	5,121

Note: The post-January 1, 1998 ruble is equal to 1,000 of the pre-January 1, 1998 rubles.

SOURCE: CIA *World Factbook 2001* [ONLINE].

sound monetary policy should be the basis of a government's economic programs.

The Russian post-**communist** economic transition thus started with prices being rapidly liberated from artificially low levels. This led to a rapid rise in prices for many basic commodities. It also led quickly to an immediate burst of inflation. The pent-up demand for consumer goods that had been suppressed during the period of Soviet central planning gave additional impetus to inflation as consumers rushed to buy previously unavailable goods, thereby bidding up prices. Early in the transition, inflation averaged over 1,000 percent per year in Russia. As inflation ate away at the value of the ruble, the amount of money necessary to buy a loaf of bread, for instance, appeared to grow inordinately large. While the size of the numbers on a country's currency should be arbitrary—that is, no one should care if the cost of a loaf of bread is 1 ruble or 1,000 rubles—what matters is what proportion this represents of a person's income. The fact that it had become necessary in Russia to hand over large amounts of rubles to buy simple, everyday necessities was psychologically unnerving for the public. To address this problem, on 1 January 1998 Russia "redenominated" its ruble, introducing new bills with 3 fewer zeros than pre-1998 rubles.

Redenomination is a process by which a country's money is reissued but assigned a different number. The Russian bank authorities simply decided to remove the "excess" 3 zeroes after the numbers on the face of the currency. For instance, a 1,000 ruble note was reissued as a 1 ruble note. At the same time, Russia re-introduced the traditional coin, the kopek, valued at 1/100th of a ruble.

These redenomination measures were primarily for convenience. They were designed to have no technical effect on the value of the currency. However, they did have an effect on the public. These measures tended to contribute to the erosion in public confidence in the currency and an increase in the use of foreign currencies, particularly the dollar, as an alternative to saving.

Russia has undertaken a number of different approaches to **exchange rate** policy. These included establishing a "currency corridor" in 1995 and a "crawling band" mechanism from 1995 to 1997. For the most part, these measures were viewed as part of an effort to establish a more "natural" ruble-to-foreign currency rate. From 1994 until 1998, falling inflation, slow money supply growth, and the effective functioning of Russia's ruble-dollar mechanisms contributed to a period of relative ruble stability. In January 1998, with the ruble trading at just over 6 to the dollar, Russia replaced the crawling band mechanism with a more freely floating but still semi-managed ruble. The exchange rate policy allowed the ruble to fluctuate within 15 percent around a central exchange rate, which Russia intended to maintain at between 6.1 and 6.2 rubles to the U.S. dollar between 1998 and 2000. In July 1998, the ruble was trading at R6.2 to the U.S. dollar. In August of 1998, Russia widened the band within which the ruble was allowed to fluctuate, resulting in an unofficial but real devaluation of the ruble. In total, the ruble lost 71 percent of its value in 1998, closing the year at R20.65 to the dollar. The ruble fell to R25 and lower to the dollar in April 1999, mildly appreciated in value through early summer, but began to decline again at the height of summer. The ruble ended 1999 at R27 to the dollar.

The monetary authority in the former Soviet Union was the Soviet Central Bank. The Soviet Central Bank functioned as an investment mechanism to achieve social objectives, not as a bank in the Western sense of provider of specific financial services. Soviet practice emphasized financial stability and the assignment of prices not on the basis of relationships of scarcity (that is, supply and demand) but on the basis of social criteria. Prices were established at levels that the government thought would achieve the most social good. Typically, necessities such as bread and housing were extraordinarily cheap to the consumer while luxuries, such as cars and foreign vacations were extremely high or unavailable altogether. Prices of foreign goods were established indirectly through the exchange rate that was stipulated by the Central Bank for foreign currencies. When the transition started, price liberalization implied that buyers and sellers should be able to establish their own agreed-upon prices. New laws were passed to allow the functioning of private banks, but initially these banks did not have provisions for inter-bank settlement of accounts. Consequently, the private banks begin to function less as banks and more as investment funds.

Spurred on by the potential gains of the initial waves of privatization of state enterprises between 1993 and 1995, these private banks in fact offered few financial services but served mainly as **holding companies** for large investors and conglomerates. The unevenness of supply and demand in the transitional markets created opportunities for great profit-taking and great risk-taking. This led to a serious problem of capital flight. As investors and speculators captured gains from buying and selling, they sought to park their earnings in stable investments. For the most part, this meant foreign currencies, particularly the American dollar. For a period of time in 1992 and 1993, Western currencies were in popular use in Russia and were preferred to the ruble. Massive amounts of money moved out of the Russian economy to Europe and America. To address this problem of capital flight, the government imposed a series of frequently changing regulations on the financial services industry between 1993 and 1994. In 1994, the Central Bank imposed new currency controls, requiring all exchanges of foreign currency to go through licensed currency traders who were closely regulated by the government.

After the financial markets collapsed in 1998, the Russian central bank, aided by increased technical assistance from the international financial institutions and Western countries, developed a considerable amount of autonomy from the Russian government. This allowed the central banking authorities to resist the attempts of the government to call upon the bank's assets to solve short-term problems or address the demands of important political constituencies. Gradually, the role of the Russian Central Bank came to resemble that of most market economies, a role in which the bank functions as a neutral and independent manager of financial functions, not as a personal banker to the government or government officials.

POVERTY AND WEALTH

The transition from communism to a market-based economy did not create poverty in Russia, but it certainly made life more difficult for many groups of people. Poverty became widespread in 1992 and grew in 1993, widening from not more than about 10 percent of the population in the 1980s to nearly 30 percent by 1993. Poverty, often associated with family size, was concentrated increasingly in families with children, as well as in families with unemployed or handicapped persons. Poverty grew especially quickly in the rural areas. Certain geographical regions of Russia were disproportionately affected by poverty, reflecting increasing disparities in wages. The Russian Far North and Far East were hard hit. Poverty was strongly associated with single-parent status, and the majority of such households were female-headed.

GDP per Capita (US$)

Country	1975	1980	1985	1990	1998
Russia	2,555	3,654	3,463	3,668	2,138
United States	19,364	21,529	23,200	25,363	29,683
China	138	168	261	349	727
Germany	N/A	N/A	N/A	N/A	31,141

SOURCE: United Nations. *Human Development Report 2000; Trends in human development and per capita income.*

Distribution of Income or Consumption by Percentage Share: Russia

Lowest 10%	1.7
Lowest 20%	4.4
Second 20%	8.6
Third 20%	13.3
Fourth 20%	20.1
Highest 20%	53.7
Highest 10%	38.7

Survey year: 1998

Note: This information refers to expenditure shares by percentiles of the population and is ranked by per capita expenditure.

SOURCE: *2000 World Development Indicators* [CD-ROM].

Measuring poverty is difficult. Nevertheless, it is undisputed that a large share of the Russian population lives below the poverty line. The social assistance provided by the Russian government has not been sufficiently targeted to the poor. According to surveys of the standard of living, the share of eligible households who did not receive social benefits increased from 60 to 80 percent. Further, the share of the households that were legally entitled to public benefits and received them has decreased dramatically as local governments have "postponed" payments. Measures of public satisfaction indicate the quality of government services has generally deteriorated since 1991, and the poor, particularly the elderly poor, have been the most directly affected.

The economic transition also witnessed the "feminization" of poverty. Single-mother families and single elderly women make up a group with the highest poverty risk. In the case of single-mother families, poverty factors include the low individual income of the mother. Added to this is the insufficient amount of private and public transfers designed to partly offset the absence of other income sources such as alimony after divorce or pensions for the benefit of children after the death of their father.

The elderly also suffer from insufficient pensions, of which 90 percent go to women, according to a World Bank report. The average pension allowance is two-thirds of a retiree's cost of living. This means that pensions cannot meet even the most basic necessities of the elderly population. The problem for women retirees is compounded by the fact that pensions, which for this age group is largely the only source of income, are higher for men of retirement age than for women.

Household Consumption in PPP Terms

Country	All food	Clothing and footwear	Fuel and power[a]	Health care[b]	Education[b]	Transport & Communications	Other
Russia	28	11	16	7	15	8	16
United States	13	9	9	4	6	8	51
China	N/A	N/A	N/A	N/A	N/A	N/A	N/A
Germany	14	6	7	2	10	7	53

Data represent percentage of consumption in PPP terms.
[a]Excludes energy used for transport.
[b]Includes government and private expenditures.

SOURCE: World Bank. *World Development Indicators 2000.*

WORKING CONDITIONS

Russia has paid a high social price for its rapid progress in the transition from communism. Under communism, economic growth was restrained but there was a very low level of inequality. Most workers made roughly the same income. Extremes of high and low incomes were rare. Since embarking on a market economy, Russia's rapid macroeconomic and political reforms created anxiety among the citizens who came to expect a modest but dependable lifestyle. Russia's abandonment of subsidies for Soviet-era industries permitted a steep industrial decline, throwing millions of citizens out of work. Today the Russian labor force is undergoing tremendous change. Although well-educated and skilled, it is mismatched to the rapidly changing needs of the Russian economy. Millions of Russian workers are **underemployed**. Unemployment is highest among women and young people. Many Russian workers compensate by working other part-time jobs.

Russia's financial crisis had a severe effect on wages in the country. Many employees were helpless as ruble devaluation and price increases drastically eroded the buying power of their salaries. Meanwhile, both foreign and Russian companies, faced with their own challenges stemming from the crisis, resorted to pay cuts in order to maintain what staff they felt able to keep. As a result of the financial crisis, although nominal wages in Russia continued to climb, real wages in the country continued to fall. The average nominal monthly wage in January 1999 was approximately 1,200 rubles. In January 2000, the nominal wage was roughly 1,575 rubles, or about US$58 at the prevailing exchange rate at the time. According to official figures, real wages and real **disposable income** had fallen roughly 30 percent by the end of 1999 compared to 1997.

According to a minimum wage law signed by President Putin in June 2000, the minimum wage increased to 300 rubles per month by mid-2001. In December 1999, the average monthly subsistence minimum was 943 rubles, or approximately US$36 at the prevailing exchange rate. Therefore, approximately one-third of Russia's population is living below the subsistence level. As of 1 February 2000, Russian pensions increased 20 percent. The minimum Russian pension is 410 rubles per month. The average pension is 650 rubles per month, which is still below the subsistence minimum.

Although the Russian government has been using International Labor Organization (an arm of the United Nations) statistical methods to determine unemployment, officially reported unemployment levels in Russia, as with other official statistics, have often been lower than figures determined by the international community. Russia reported several years of very slowly growing unemployment, which temporarily peaked at 9.6 percent in the spring of 1997 before dropping to a low of 9 percent at the end of 1997. During this time, alternative estimates of unemployment suggested a combined unemployment and underemployment rate of between 12 and 15 percent. In 1998 unemployment levels resumed their climb. In the wake of Russia's financial crisis, both Russian and foreign companies resorted to layoffs and salary cuts. In November 1998, when the official unemployment rate was 11.6 percent, the Russian Ministry of Economy predicted that unemployment would grow 70 percent by 2001. In early June 1999 the Russian government reported that unemployment had reached 14.2 percent of the country's workforce, or 10.4 million people, the highest level ever officially reported by Russia. For much of 1999 the unemployment rate hovered at 12.4 percent, or 9.12 million people. Russia closed 1999 with an official unemployment level of 11.7 percent.

Russia's well-educated but relatively inexpensive labor force has been a leading attraction for foreign firms. While in the early 1990s many Western firms initially found it challenging to find employees educated in Western business concepts and practices, there is a growing pool in Russia of individuals with Western business exposure, education, and experience. Russian law requires that wages be paid in rubles.

COUNTRY HISTORY AND ECONOMIC DEVELOPMENT

945. Treaty of Igor with Byzantium (Constantinople) establishes first claim to government in the many lands of Russia, known as the many "Russias."

1237. Mongol tribesmen, invading from the East, conquer Russia and impose foreign rule for over 240 years.

1565–72. Ivan the Terrible's "reign of terror" establishes a precedent of strong, unaccountable central government.

1802. Formation of the first government ministries, establishing a strong principle of government control of the private economy.

1864–85. Conquest of Central Asia.

1891. Beginning of the Trans-Siberian railway.

1906. First Duma (parliament) established; first written constitution adopted.

1914. World War I begins.

1917. Russia pulls out of World War I; Bolsheviks take power and begin communist era.

1918. The period of "war communism" with emphasis on administrative direction of the economy is introduced.

1921. Retreating from tight control of the economy, the government introduces the "New Economic Policy" (NEP). The policy favors market-based economic relations in lieu of administrative measures.

1928. Return to communism and top-down direction of the economy as the first "Five-Year Plan" is adopted. Joseph Stalin (Iosef Dhugashvili) assumes control of the communist party organization. Agriculture is collectivized. A massive industrialization campaign begins.

1932–33. A severe famine in Ukraine is testimony to the effects of the agricultural collectivization program.

1937–41. The Stalin-era purges of political opponents take place.

1941. German invasion of USSR (June 22) and Second World War.

1957. First Soviet "Sputnik" (satellite) is launched. The "space race" begins.

1973. United States and the USSR embrace "Détente," a policy of relaxation of tensions, and adopt a new bilateral trade agreement, but implementation is not successful.

1979. In December, Soviets invade Afghanistan. This futile war drains Soviet resources and creates negative sentiment toward communist party rule. This eventually plays an important role in the collapse of communism.

1985. Mikhail Gorbachev becomes communist party leader, calling for economic reforms (*perestroika*) and greater openness (*glasnost*).

1986. 26 April disaster at Chernobyl nuclear generating station debunks myth of Soviet technological superiority.

1989. Political reforms begin in Central Europe; Berlin Wall comes down.

1991. On 19 August, a group of Communist Party hardliners announces takeover of the Soviet government. The takeover fails. Boris Yeltsin emerges as the most popular politician.

1991. On 21 December, 11 high leaders of USSR meet in Alma-Ata, Kazakhstan, to sign the "Alma-Ata Declaration" ending the USSR and establishing the "Commonwealth of Independent States" (CIS).

1992. On 2 January, Russian prime minister frees prices; ruble value plummets; prices skyrocket.

1992. On 1 October, **voucher privatization** begins in Russia.

1993. On 21 September President Yeltsin dissolves the parliament. On 22 September a breakaway parliament appoints Vice President Alexander Rutskoi as president. On 4 October, government forces loyal to Yeltsin storm the parliament building and arrest Rutskoi and the disloyal parliament.

1998. Following a massive sell-off of Russian bonds, securities, and rubles, the prime minister announces a ruble devaluation; financial markets are paralyzed by **liquidity** shortages, and share prices plunge. Unable to pay its creditors, Russia defaults on foreign loans.

1998. Yeltsin fires the prime minister and the entire government cabinet. He appoints Victor Chernomyrdin as interim prime minister, but parliament refuses to confirm him.

1999. After months of political turmoil, Yeltsin appoints Vladimir Putin as prime minister.

2000. On 31 December, Yeltsin resigns the presidency (with a full pardon), leaving Vladimir Putin as head of state.

2000. Vladimir Putin is elected president.

FUTURE TRENDS

The Russian economy faces serious challenges. Russian industry is not likely to regain an important role in a global economy that demands peak efficiency. Consequently, the export of primary commodities and raw materials is likely to remain the bulwark of economic development. Primary commodity markets are relatively more susceptible to fluctuations than are industrial markets.

Russia is likely to continue to be influenced by economic trends that it cannot control. International investors, including the major investment banks, commercial investors, and companies interested in expanding their businesses in world markets have remained on the sidelines, scared off by Russia's long-standing problems with capital flight, reliance on barter transactions, corruption of government officials, and fears of organized crime.

The Russian government and leading economists in the country have developed a consensus on the need for various kinds of administrative changes. Failures such as corruption are not moral failures, but a failure of administrative structure. There is a consensus that the country needs to strengthen the institutional and legal underpinnings of a market economy. Improving the legal and regulatory structure would provide a reliable framework for improving governance, strengthening the rule of law, reducing corruption, and attracting the long-term capital needed for deep restructuring and sustained growth. The country also needs to improve its tax system to encourage greater tax compliance and a realistic appreciation in the population that the people must pay for the costs of a modern society. The government must avoid pressures to use central bank money to finance its budget deficit. Further reforms are needed in the banking sector, including a legal framework to make it easier to close down troubled banks.

Any measures aiming to reduce poverty levels among workers are primarily associated with the increase in the official wages drawn by the lower paid workers, the majority of which are women, and also with the identification and taxation of income in Russia's informal sector.

A positive sign was that in mid-year 2000, the Russian government adopted an official development strategy for the period 2000–10. The strategy identified economic policy directed at ensuring equal conditions of market competition, protecting ownership rights, eliminating administrative barriers to entrepreneurship, making the economy more open, and carrying out tax reform. The strategy identified the creation of an effective state performing the function of a **guarantor** of external and internal security and also of social, political, and economic stability. The strategy spoke of a "new social contract" between the more active sections of Russian society and the reformed government.

Russia's economy remains very vulnerable to external shocks and has not yet been able to develop a stable base for continued growth and poverty reduction. While the data are not yet sufficient to carefully assess the impact of the economic recovery on the enterprise sector, it appears that the rebound in the non-oil/gas traded goods sector has so far been driven by the real depreciation of the ruble and the greater availability of capital. Furthermore, there are indications that industrial growth is beginning to slow. Therefore, maintaining a realistic exchange rate, while controlling inflation, must remain a policy priority for sustaining the recovery and future growth of the real economy. Strong fiscal discipline needs to be maintained. A large swing factor is, of course, the level of capital flight, the reduction of which depends on progressive improvement in the investment climate in Russia. Finally, over the longer-term, Russia's deteriorating infrastructure is a matter of concern. Russia's basic public infrastructure—including roads, bridges, railways, ports, housing, and public facilities such as schools and hospitals—was built during the Soviet period. After independence, investment in maintenance and new construction of public infrastructure has fallen dramatically. Russia's aging physical plant is likely to become an increasing constraint to growth unless an improved investment climate can ensure substantially higher levels of investments than is presently the case.

DEPENDENCIES

Russia has no territories or colonies.

BIBLIOGRAPHY

Economist Intelligence Unit. *Country Profile: Russia.* London: Economist Intelligence Unit, 2001.

Embassy of the Russian Federation. <http://www.russianembassy.org>. Accessed October 2001.

Fedorov, Boris. "Killing with Kindness: No More 'Help' for Russia, Please." *Asian Wall Street Journal.* 12 June 2000.

Fischer, Stanley, and Alan Gelb. "Issues in Socialist Economy Reform." *Journal of Economic Perspectives.* Vol. 5, No. 4, Fall 1991.

Government of the Russian Federation. <http://www.pravitelstvo.gov.ru/english/>. Accessed June 2001.

Kornai, Janos. "Making the Transition to Private Ownership." *Finance and Development.* Vol. 37, No. 3, September 2000.

Lane, David Stuart. *The Political Economy of Russian Oil.* New York: Rowman & Littlefield, 1999.

Ledeneva, Alena C. *Russia's Economy of Favours: Blat, Networking and Informal Exchanges.* Cambridge: Cambridge University Press, 1998.

Loungani, Prakash, and Nathan Sheets. "Central Bank Independence, Inflation and Growth in Transition Economies." *Journal of Money, Credit and Banking.* Vol. 29, No. 3, August 1997.

Oleh, Havrylyshyn, and John Odling-Smee. "Political Economy of Stalled Reforms." *Finance & Development.* Vol. 37, No. 3, September 2000.

Population Reference Bureau. "2000 World Population Data Sheet." <http://www.prb.org/Content/NavigationMenu/Other_reports/2000–2002/2001_World_Population_Data_Sheet.htm>. Accessed June 2001.

Stuart, Robert C., and Paul R. Gregory. *The Russian Economy: Past, Present, and Future.* New York: Addison-Wesley, 1995.

Varese, Federico. *The Russian Mafia: Private Protection in a New Market Economy.* Oxford: Oxford University Press, 2001.

World Bank Group. "Summary: Feminization of Poverty in Russia." <http://www.worldbank.org.ru/eng/statistics/femine1/femine1_4.htm>. October 2001.

World Bank Group. "Whither Reform? Ten Years of the Transition." <http://www.worldbank.org/research/abcde/stiglitz.html>. Accessed June 2001.

—Gregory Gleason

SAN MARINO

Republic of San Marino
Repubblica di San Marino

CAPITAL: San Marino.

MONETARY UNIT: Italian lira (plural is lire). One Italian lira (L) equals 100 centesimi. There are notes of L1,000, 2,000, 5,000, 10,000, 50,000, and 100,000, and coins of L50, 100, 200, and 500. San Marino also mints its own coins, having the same value as the Italian ones. San Marino has a customs union with Italy, and it switched to the new European unit, the euro, along with Italy and other members of the European Union (EU) in 1999 for all forms of "written money"—checks, bank transactions, and credit cards. In January 2002, the euro will be issued as coins and notes, and the lira will be phased out.

CHIEF EXPORTS: Building stone, lime, wood, chestnuts, wheat, wine, baked goods, hides, ceramics, furnishings, textiles, apparel.

CHIEF IMPORTS: Energy, automobiles, equipment, a wide variety of consumer manufactures, clothing, food.

GROSS DOMESTIC PRODUCT: $860 million (purchasing power parity, 2000 estimate).

BALANCE OF TRADE: All San Marino foreign trade data are included with the statistics for Italy and no separate statistics are available.

COUNTRY OVERVIEW

LOCATION AND SIZE. San Marino is an enclave lying wholly within northern Italy. It surrounds the 3-peaked Mount Titano (739 meters/2,425 feet) in the central Apennine Mountains, east of the city of Florence, Italy, and southwest of the city of Rimini, Italy, near the Adriatic Sea. With a total area of only 61.2 square kilometers (23.6 square miles), or about one-third the size of Washington, D.C., San Marino is one of the smallest countries in the world. The republic is also arguably the oldest in the world. It is named for its legendary founder, the 4th-century, Christian stonecutter and Catholic Saint Marinus. The capital is San Marino, a small town on the slopes of Mount Titano with a population of 4,498 (1996 estimate). Other population centers include Borgo Maggiore, Serravalle, and Domagnano.

POPULATION. The population of San Marino was estimated at 27,336 in July 2001; it was less than 25,000 two years earlier. The growth rate was estimated at 1.49 percent in the same year, with a birth rate of 10.88 births per 1,000 population, exceeding the death rate of 7.65 per 1,000 population, all estimated in 2000. There is a high migration rate of 11.62 per 1,000 population (2000), mostly of people from adjacent Italian towns and villages. The population is somewhat less elderly than other European countries, and the percent of people under 15 years of age, 16 percent, is equal to that of people 65 or older. San Marino has a very high life expectancy at birth—81.14 years for the total population, 85.02 years for women and 77.57 years for men. The fertility rate is estimated at 1.3 children per woman, which is comparable to Italy's rate. The **workforce** in 1999 included about 15,600 persons. The people of San Marino are distinctively Italian in their language, appearance, and culture; they use the Italian currency, and are mostly Roman Catholic, but are very proud of their independent political heritage. In addition to the native Sammarinese, there are also Italian immigrants.

OVERVIEW OF ECONOMY

The economy of San Marino is tiny but, nevertheless, it is stable and quite prosperous, particularly when compared to other Southern European countries. More than half of the country's **gross domestic product**'s (GDP) total worth of about $860 million has been traditionally produced in the tourism industry. On the average, close to 3.5 million visitors travel to San Marino annually, a huge number compared to the country's population of about 27,000.

Interestingly, one of the most reliable sources of income within tourism, apart from hotels, restaurants, shops, and other facilities, is the sale of collectibles and souvenirs such as historic coins and the world famous Sammarinese picturesque postage stamps, which are produced by the government. San Marino issued its first commemorative stamps in 1894 and, since then, these have become part of a notable and sustainable source of income. All 10 of the post office branches in San Marino sell such stamps and collectable coins, including some legal gold tender coins (lawful money).

Besides the tourism industry, San Marino makes most of its income from the manufacture and export of ceramics, tiles, building material, furniture, clothing, fabrics, paints, and some quality brands of spirits and wines. San Marino's bank system forms an integral part of the Italian banking system. Other key sectors are electronics and Internet-related activities.

Traditional economic activity in San Marino in the past relied mostly on stone quarrying, agriculture, sheep breeding, and wine and cheese making. Most Sammarinese families historically made their living as farmers and/or stone cutters. Building stone is the most important of the natural resources, as in much of Italy. Today's tiny agriculture sector focuses mostly on grains, grapes, and other fruits, as well as on animal husbandry, mostly cattle and pigs.

The per capita level of output and standard of living in San Marino are reasonably high and comparable to those of surrounding Italy, with a **GDP per capita** of about $32,000 (2000 estimate). GDP growth for the same year was 8 percent. San Marino is closely associated with the economic structures of the EU through the Italian economy and monetary and customs systems, with which it is closely integrated. San Marino also receives payments from the Italian government in exchange for permitting its **monopolies** on tobacco and other commodities on its territory.

POLITICS, GOVERNMENT, AND TAXATION

San Marino is a republic that has preserved some very ancient traditions that additionally attract tourists to the country. Although it has been greatly influenced by modern political developments in surrounding Italy, it also has been spared some of the turbulent moments in its larger neighbor's contemporary history. It is democratic and neutral, and even more sensitive than ever to the importance of liberty. San Marino is governed according to a constitution adopted on 8 October 1600. A newer electoral law of 1926 and a "Manuscript of Rights" of 1974 also serve some of the functions of a constitution. San Marino claims to be the world's oldest surviving republic, founded by Saint Marinus in 301 A.D. Its foreign policy is aligned with that of Italy, and the social trends in the republic also follow closely with those of its neighbor.

The executive authority comprises the 2 Captains Regent, the traditional co-heads of state, who are both members of the parliament and elected by that body; a Congress of State (cabinet), also elected by the parliament; and a senior Secretary of State for foreign and political affairs, who acts as the traditional head of government. In their tenure, the Captains Regent preside over the deliberations of the executive body, the Congress of State. Every 6 months, the Sammarinese parliament elects new Captains Regent—traditionally from opposing parties to provide checks and balances. Their investiture (inauguration ceremony) takes place on 1 April and 1 October of every year and is accompanied by a centuries-old ceremony. Once their term is over, Sammarinese citizens have 3 days in which to file any complaints about the in-office activities and behavior of out-going Captains Regent. If so warranted, judicial proceedings against the ex-heads of state may be initiated.

The legislative power is vested in a **unicameral** (having 1 chamber) parliament, a 60-member house named the Grand and General Council that is elected by universal suffrage for a term of 5 years. The electoral body once comprised the heads of the Sammarinese families exclusively, but it was gradually extended to include all citizens over 18 years of age.

Italian magistrates, for both historical and social reasons of impartiality, have staffed the judicial system. The only native Sammarinese judges are the several Justices of the Peace, who may handle only civil cases in which disputed sums do not exceed 25 million lire (about $15,000). The traditional local Council of the Twelve serves as the highest court of appeals. It is elected by the Grand and General Council for the duration of the legislature.

The political parties in San Marino are traditionally very close to those in Italy, particularly the Christian Democrats, Socialists, and Communists. In the 1990s, however, among a series of disruptive political scandals, the Italian post-war political system was discredited and finally collapsed. A more complex and diversified system of new parties and alliances emerged from its debris. The centrist Christian Democratic Party, part of all ruling coalitions after 1948, dissolved and its members formed 2 new organizations, the Popular Party and the Christian Democratic Center. The new Democratic Party of the Left became the major left-wing party, including the majority of the reformed communists and many socialists. A smaller leftist group, the Communist Refoundation, retained some of the traditional **Marxist** policies, characteristic of the old communist party. The numerous Sammarinese political groups of the late 1990s accordingly included the conservative Democratic Christian Party (PDCS), the Progressive Democratic Party (PPDS), the Popular Democratic Party (APDS), the left-of-center Socialist Party (PSS), and the Communist Refoundation (RC), plus several other smaller groups, such as the Democratic Movement, the Popular Alliance, and the Socialists for Reform. Due to the small size of San Marino's population and electorate, no party has gained an absolute majority, so the government is usually run by a coalition. The parties sharing power currently are the Democratic Christian Party and the Socialist Party, but for several decades after World War II, San Marino was the only European country outside the Soviet sphere of influence ruled by a **communist-socialist** coalition. The elections held on 31 May 1998 (the next elections are to be held in May 2003) gave PDCS 40.8 percent of the popular vote, PSS received 23.3 percent, and PPDS had 18.6 percent. The composition of the current parliament and the Captains Regent reflects the stable economic situation in San Marino arising from having one of the lowest unemployment rates in Europe, a stable **budget surplus**, and zero **national debt**.

The role of the government in the economy is significant, although San Marino has developed a mature market economy. In the late 1980s, annual government revenue and expenditure were balanced at about $183 million, and since then the budget has accumulated a surplus. The state executive congress (cabinet), composed of 3 secretaries and 7 ministries, oversees the most vital economic activities, including those of the state-run Philatelic and Numismatic Office (stamps and coins). The government relies not only on tourism, taxes, and customs for revenue, but also on the sale of coins and stamps to collectors from throughout the world. In addition, the Italian government pays San Marino an annual budget **subsidy** provided under the terms of its basic treaty with Italy. The main issues facing the current government include economic and administrative problems related to San Marino's status as a close financial and trading partner with Italy while at the same time remaining officially separated from the EU.

Despite the tiny size of San Marino, it is an active player in the international community, with diplomatic ties to more than 70 countries. San Marino is a full member of the United Nations (UN), the International Court of Justice, the UN Educational, Scientific and Cultural Organization (UNESCO), the International Monetary Fund (IMF), the World Health Organization (WHO), the World Tourism Organization (WTO), the Council of Europe, the International Red Cross Organization, and the International Institution for the Unification of Private Law (UNIDROIT), among others. It also cooperates with the UN Children's Fund (UNICEF) and the UN High Commissioner for Refugees, and has official relations with the European Union. From May to November 1990, San Marino held the rotating presidency of the European Council of Ministers.

INFRASTRUCTURE, POWER, AND COMMUNICATIONS

Italy supplies virtually all of San Marino's electricity, and the domestic automatic telephone system is completely integrated into the Italian telecommunications system. Main (fixed) phone lines (nearly 20,000) and cellular phones are ubiquitous, yet in 1999 there was only 1 local Internet service provider. The country has its own local television station and 3 local FM radio stations, although Italian broadcasting and cable TV is available everywhere. The republic has only a 1.5-kilometer (1 mile) cable railway, which connects the city of San Marino to the community of Borgo Maggiore. Virtually all of the 220 kilometers (138 miles) of roads in San Marino are paved. The country has no naval ports or airports, relying instead on Italy's extensive and advanced transportation facilities.

ECONOMIC SECTORS

The traditional foundation of San Marino's economy was agriculture and stone quarrying, while tourism and

Communications

Country	Telephones[a]	Telephones, Mobile/Cellular[a]	Radio Stations[b]	Radios[a]	TV Stations[a]	Televisions[a]	Internet Service Providers[c]	Internet Users[c]
San Marino	18,000 (1998)	3,010 (1998)	AM 0; FM 3; shortwave 0	16,000	1	9,000	2	N/A
United States	194 M	69.209 M (1998)	AM 4,762; FM 5,542; shortwave 18	575 M	1,500	219 M	7,800	148 M
Italy	25 M (1999)	20.5 M (1999)	AM 100; FM 4,600; shortwave 9	50.5 M	358 (1995)	30.3 M	93	11.6 M
Monaco	31,027 (1995)	N/A	AM 1; FM N/A; shortwave 8	34,000	5 (1998)	25,000	2	N/A

[a]Data is for 1997 unless otherwise noted.
[b]Data is for 1998 unless otherwise noted.
[c]Data is for 2000 unless otherwise noted.

SOURCE: CIA *World Factbook 2001* [Online].

light industry have grown in importance. Wheat, barley, maize, olives, wine, and livestock and dairy products dominate agricultural output. Some building stone is still quarried. Manufactures include textiles, cement and building materials, leather goods, synthetic rubber products, and ceramics. Other important sources of income are the sale of postage stamps and collectible coins. In 1998, 60 percent of the labor force worked in the services sector, 38 percent in industry, and 2 percent in agriculture. In terms of industries, most workers were employed in tourism, banking, textiles, electronics, ceramics, cement, and wine production. No exact figures for sales of any industry are available, as the figures for San Marino are recorded as part of Italy's output.

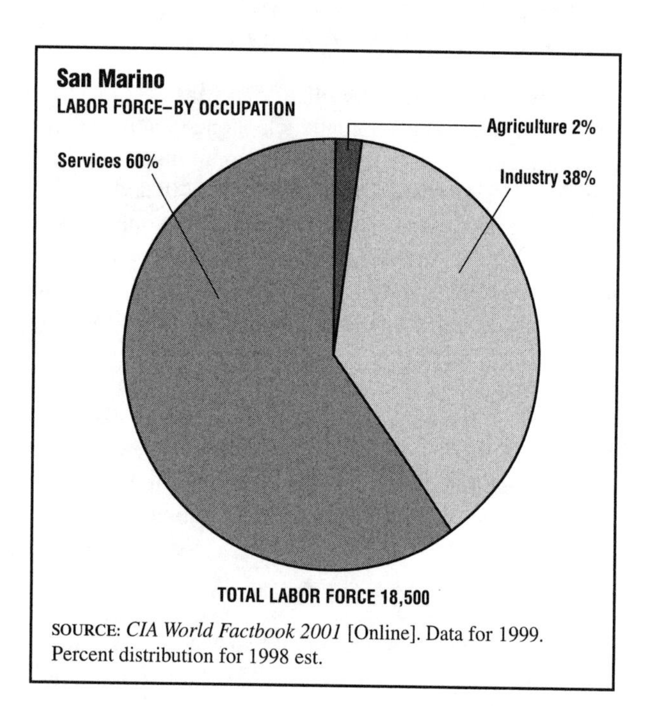

SOURCE: *CIA World Factbook 2001* [Online]. Data for 1999. Percent distribution for 1998 est.

AGRICULTURE

Arable land comprises some 17 percent of San Marino's rugged territory, and agricultural products include wheat, grapes, corn, olives, cattle, pigs, horses, beef, cheese, and hides. Italy supplies much of the republic's food, while main export products are wine and cheeses, renowned in Italy and abroad. Woods also cover a part of the land.

INDUSTRY

The government has a sound policy of promoting local producers. Electronics and Internet related activities have been added to the traditional Sammarinese construction materials manufacture, which includes building-stone quarrying, cement, ceramics, and tiles fabrication. Wood processing and fine furniture manufacturing are also well developed. Minting of coins and medals, printing of stamps and cards, and fine local handicrafts are the largest contributors to the economy in terms of revenue. Construction and the real estate market are another important source of income and occupation. Chemical industries, textiles, and apparel manufacturing also contribute to the country's exports.

SERVICES

The tourist sector is estimated to contribute over 50 percent of San Marino's GDP. In 1997, San Marino's rich history, charming mountain views, fine dining, and shopping attracted 3.4 million tourists. The republic's proximity to major maritime tourist resorts on the Adriatic Sea at Rimini and and to world centers of sophisticated tourism such as the museum cities of Florence and Venice also stimulated tourism. In finance, apart from the major Italian banks and insurance firms, there is only 1 local credit institution, the Istituto di Credito Sammarinese, which performs the functions of a central bank. Among other duties, this institution coordinates the country's banking system and performs treasury and tax collection services. Given the small size of the **retail** market, small, family-owned stores prevail. The Sammarinese also shop in larger retail establishments in Italy, however.

INTERNATIONAL TRADE

International trade is light in volume. About 85 percent of exports and imports are shipped to, or come from, Italy. Energy, automobiles, equipment, and most manufactured goods and food are imported. Besides Italy, primary trade partners include some EU members, eastern European and South America countries, China, and Taiwan.

MONEY

The Sammarinese economy is closely integrated with the Italian monetary and banking system. The Banking Act in Italy of 1990 introduced major changes as a part of the EU policy for free capital movement within the member states and a currency union, creating conditions for the reduction of public ownership of banks and **liberalizing** the regulations on foreign capital. In 1999, Italy and 10 other members of the EU switched from their national currencies to the single currency of the euro, as a part of the European System of Central Banks (ESCB). The euro has been in use since 1 January 1999, initially for electronic transfers and accounting purposes only, while euro coins and bills will be issued in 2002. At that time the Italian currency will cease to be legal tender. On 1 January 1999, control over Italian **monetary policy**, including the issues of setting the interest rates and regulating the money supply, was transferred to the European Central Bank (ECB). The need to adjust to the centralized European monetary and banking system requirements without being officially a member of the EU will be a serious challenge for the Sammarinese government in the near future. The benefits from the single European economic space, however, are expected to outweigh the drawbacks.

POVERTY AND WEALTH

With a high measure of GDP per capita, a low **inflation rate** (in terms of consumer prices) of 2 percent (1997 estimate), and the benefits of the monetary and economic union with Italy, the tiny republic offers its citizens a high standard of living. No data as to San Marino's economic equality index (**Gini index**) are available, but if Italy's index is used, the degree of economic equality in the republic should be characterized as outstanding compared with that of the United States and the United Kingdom. The size of the republic and its economic activity render little space for the accumulation of large private fortunes, but extreme poverty is not an issue in the country either. This is no wonder given the influence of socialist politics in the country's history. In this and other ways, San Marino more closely resembles the above-average economic and social structures of industrialized northern Italy

WORKING CONDITIONS

The small but affluent Sammarinese economy, the close popular scrutiny over the government's deliberations, the long tradition of socialist control, and one of the lowest unemployment rates in Europe almost rule out labor unrest in the republic. The new, more environmentally friendly industries that are gradually supplanting traditional stone quarrying are also more conducive to enhancing safety at work. Of a workforce of some 18,500, only 3 percent were unemployed in 1999.

COUNTRY HISTORY AND ECONOMIC DEVELOPMENT

301 A.D. According to legend, San Marino was founded by the Christian stonecutter Marinus who sought refuge on Mount Titano from religious persecution.

Exchange rates: San Marino

euros per US$1	
Jan 2001	1.06594
2000	1.08540
1999	0.93863
1998	1,736.2
1997	1,703.1
1996	1,542.9

Note: Rates prior to 1999 are in Italian lire per US$.

SOURCE: CIA *World Factbook 2001* [ONLINE].

GDP per Capita (US$)

Country	1996	1997	1998	1999	2000
San Marino	N/A	20,000	N/A	N/A	32,000
United States	28,600	30,200	31,500	33,900	36,200
Italy	19,600	21,500	20,800	21,400	22,100
Monaco	25,000	N/A	N/A	27,000	N/A

Note: Data are estimates.

SOURCE: *Handbook of the Nations*, 17th, 18th, 19th and 20th editions for 1996, 1997, 1998 and 1999 data; CIA *World Factbook 2001* [Online] for 2000 data.

4TH TO 13TH CENTURIES. San Marino retains its independence despite the ambitions of the neighboring rulers and as new political entities develop and disappear throughout the land. The economy is based on agriculture and stonecutting.

1291. Roman Pope Nicholas IV officially recognizes San Marino's independence.

1503. Italian general Cesare Borgia briefly occupies the republic until his death several months later.

1739. Italian Roman Catholic Cardinal Alberoni uses military force to occupy San Marino, but civil disobedience against the invader and letters of protest to the Pope are answered by renewed papal recognition of San Marino's rights and restoration of independence.

1797. French leader Napoleon Bonaparte offers to expand the territory of San Marino as a gift and as a sign of friendship with the republic, but the Sammarinese authorities refuse.

1849. San Marino offers refuge to Italian revolutionary leader Giuseppe Garibaldi.

1862. San Marino signs a treaty of friendship (revised several times since) with Italy.

1943–45. During World War II, neutral San Marino hosts about 100,000 refugees from the embattled neighboring zones of Italy.

1945. A coalition of Communists and Socialists wins elections and rules for 12 years, creating the base of the **welfare state** and modern economic development.

1957. The Christian Democratic Party, aided by Communist dissidents, takes control of the government.

1978. A Communist coalition regains power and retains it for 14 years.

1992. San Marino becomes a member of the United Nations, while the Christian Democrats form a coalition government with the Socialists, a regime that continues to govern after the 1993 general elections.

1999. Control over the Italian monetary and banking system, used in San Marino, is transferred to the European Central Bank (ECB).

FUTURE TRENDS

The Sammarinese economy is closely related to Italy's and is highly dependent on the developmental trends of the EU. It is likely that the country will preserve its economy—particularly in the areas of tourism, services, and modern manufacturing—maintain its high living standards, and continue to attract tourists and collectors for the foreseeable future. The number of foreign visitors may even increase as the movement of people, particularly from Central Europe, becomes easier with their gradual integration in the EU and the positive changes concerning the wealth and leisure of their people.

The government's desire to maintain the republic's autonomy and independence may be challenged, however, by the advance of European integration, the increasing competition following the liberalization of commerce and services, and notably by the coming of the single European monetary system. The benefits of the unified European economic space, however, will almost definitely outweigh the problems and possible drawbacks. It is not likely that Sammarinese bank revenues will significantly decline without the exchange fees they charged before San Marino adopted the euro: the monetary union with Italy and the location of the republic as an enclave in Italian territory never generated a large foreign exchange **turnover** even before the European monetary union took effect.

DEPENDENCIES

San Marino has no territories or colonies.

BIBLIOGRAPHY

Global Investment Business Center, Inc. staff. *San Marino: A Country Study Guide.* International Business Publications, February 2001.

Repubblica di San Marino. <http://www.sanita.segreteria.sm>. Accessed August 2001.

U.S. Central Intelligence Agency. *World Factbook 2000.* <http://www.odci.gov/cia/publications/factbook/index.html>. Accessed August 2001.

U.S. Department of State. *U.S. Department of State Background Notes: San Marino, November 1998.* <http://www.state.gov/www/background_notes/sanmarino_9811-bgn.html>. Accessed January 2001.

—Valentin Hadjiyski

SLOVAKIA

Slovak Republic
Slovenska Republika

CAPITAL: Bratislava.

MONETARY UNIT: Slovenská koruna (Sk). One koruna equals 100 hellers. There are coins of 10, 20, and 50 hellers, and 1, 2, 5, and 10 korunas. There are notes of 20, 50, 100, 500, 1,000, and 5,000 korunas. The koruna came into being with the division of Czechoslovakia into the Czech and Slovak Republics in 1993 and is now valued at a different rate than the Czech currency.

CHIEF EXPORTS: Machinery and transport equipment, intermediate manufactured goods, chemicals, raw materials.

CHIEF IMPORTS: Machinery and transport equipment, intermediate manufactured goods, fuels, chemicals.

GROSS DOMESTIC PRODUCT: US$45.9 billion (purchasing power parity, 1999 est.).

BALANCE OF TRADE: **Exports:** US$10.1 billion (f.o.b., 1999 est.). **Imports:** US$11.2 billion (f.o.b., 1999 est.).

COUNTRY OVERVIEW

LOCATION AND SIZE. The Slovak Republic is a landlocked nation in the eastern portion of Central Europe, with access to the Black Sea via the Danube River. Its neighbors are the Czech Republic to the northwest, Poland to the north, Ukraine to the east, Hungary to the south, and Austria to the west. The country's total area is 48,845 square kilometers (18,859 square miles). Much of its northern and central terrain is composed of striking mountains, similar to the American Rockies. Terrain in southern Slovakia consists of plains in the west and rolling hills. Slovakia is about the size of South Carolina, and it does not border a sea. The capital, Bratislava, is located near the country's western border and is not far from Vienna, Austria. Other major cities include Košice in the east and Banská Bystrica in the center of the country.

POPULATION. The population of Slovakia was estimated to be 5,407,956 in July 2000, an increase of 3.25 percent over the 1980 population of approximately 4,996,000. The birth rate stood at 10 per 1,000 in 2000, and the death rate was 9.29 per 1,000, resulting in a growth rate of .12 percent for 2000. Following this trend, the population for 2010 is projected at 5,473,203. The population has become increasingly urbanized, with 56.7 percent of Slovaks living in cities in 1999, up from 49.2 percent in 1980 and 32.8 percent in 1960.

Several ethnic groups make up the population. About 85.7 percent of the people are Slovak, and 10.6 percent are ethnic Hungarians. Although the census data registers 1.6 percent of the population as Romany (Gypsy), this figure is believed to be an underrepresentation, with some experts estimating as many as 500,000 Romany living in Slovakia. There are also small numbers of Czechs, Moravians, Silesians, Ruthenians, Ukrainians, and Poles. Approximately 60 percent of the population is Roman Catholic, about 10 percent is atheist, 8 percent is Protestant, 4 percent is Orthodox, and 17.5 percent list their religion as "other."

OVERVIEW OF ECONOMY

The nation that is now known as Slovakia was part of the Hungarian portion of the Austro-Hungarian Empire until the end of World War I in 1918. It then became a part of the new nation of Czechoslovakia. During the 1930s, Czechoslovakia was an industrial powerhouse in Europe. After World War II, Czechoslovakia fell under the political and economic influence of the Soviet Union, and Czechoslovak economic performance began to stagnate under **communist** rule, which mandated state ownership of enterprises, state-led central planning of economic activities, and artificial **price controls**. In 1968, after some Czechoslovak leaders attempted to introduce some political, cultural, and economic **liberalization**, the country was invaded by the Warsaw Pact troops of neighboring

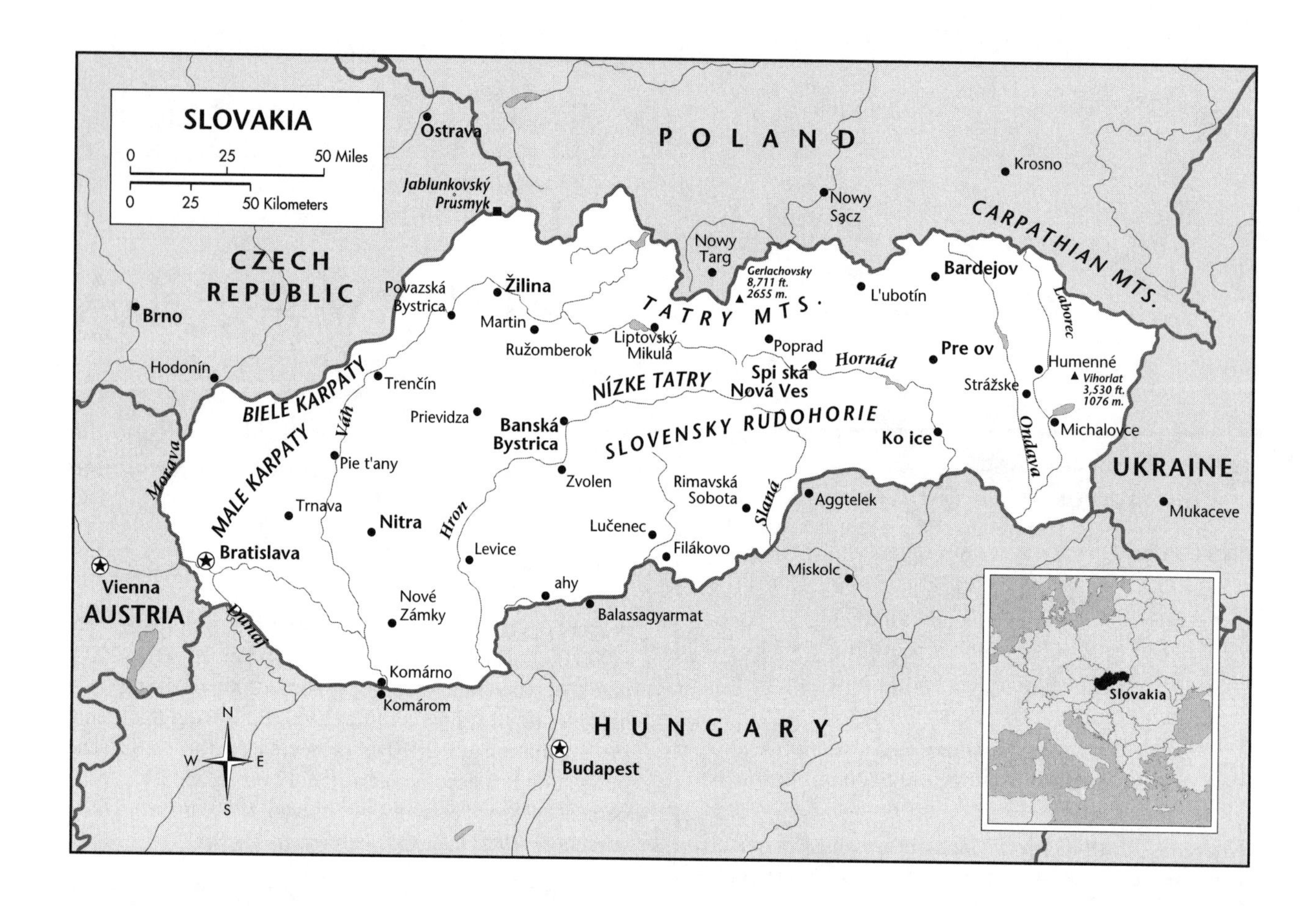

communist countries under the direction of the Soviet Union. This intervention put a stop to liberalization and introduced a period of "normalization" in which the government attempted to increase production of **consumer goods** in exchange for political compliance by the people. In spite of these efforts, the economy continued to decline, culminating in an economic crisis by the late 1980s that sparked more popular protests.

By late 1989, the more liberal policies of the Soviet Union toward Eastern Europe, as well as the weakening of communist governments in neighboring East Germany, Hungary, and Poland, made it harder for the Czechoslovak communists to retain power. In November and December of 1989, the communist government stepped down. Free elections for parliament were held in 1990, and Václav Havel was elected president. The government quickly embarked on a series of economic reforms aimed to reorient the economy towards free market principles. These reforms included economic **restructuring** and the elimination of government price controls. In addition, the government began the process of **privatization**.

From 1990 to 1992, these reforms were more popular in what is now the Czech Republic, which had a larger industrial base, than in what is now Slovakia, where several factories that had produced arms during the Cold War had been shut down. Under the country's federal structure, which gave each republic a measure of independent powers, the 1992 elections resulted in a governmental deadlock, and the newly-elected prime ministers of the Czech and Slovak republics began to negotiate the separation of Czechoslovakia into 2 independent states. The Czech Republic and the Slovak Republic became separate sovereign states on January 1, 1993.

Compared to the pre-1993 economic reforms in Czechoslovakia, the economic reforms that took place in Slovakia between 1993 and 1998 occurred at a slower pace. While the country registered continued growth in GDP during this time, international investment did not reach desired levels. In 1998, a more reformist government was elected and began to accelerate the pace of economic reforms. For example, as part of the privatization process, property was now being sold to qualified individuals at regular prices, putting a halt to the previous government's attempts to sell off property to unqualified friends of government officials at artificially low prices. Reforms also improved conditions for foreign investment in Slovakia, paving the way for increased employment and for future accession to the European Union.

Slovakia's strongest economic sectors are industry and services. Its primary industrial products include iron and steel, machinery and equipment, motor vehicles, manufactured goods, plastics, chemicals, and armaments. The country's primary agricultural products are wheat, potatoes, barley, sugar beets, and grapes for wine-making. The Slovak Republic's primary mineral products include copper, iron, lead, lignite, manganese, and zinc. The vast majority of the country's energy is imported from outside sources, although there is some hydroelectric and nuclear power.

The Slovak Republic has applied for membership in the North Atlantic Treaty Organization (NATO) and is a prospective member of the European Union (EU). Its largest trading partners are the EU and the Czech Republic. It has received some aid, in the form of grants and loans, from international organizations such as the European Investment Bank, the European Bank for Reconstruction and Development, the International Monetary Fund (IMF), and the World Bank. Slovakia's **external debt** for 1999 was US$10.6 billion. Organized crime has been a negative factor in the development of the economy, as occasional violence between organized crime factions, such as car bombings, have deterred potential foreign investors. These gangs, composed of Slovaks and immigrants from the former Soviet Union, have in some cases also extorted payments from some small business owners.

POLITICS, GOVERNMENT, AND TAXATION

Slovakia is a parliamentary democracy with a directly-elected president. A **unicameral** (one-house) National Council of 150 members is elected via a proportional system in which voters indicate a preference for parties rather than for specific candidates. Each party that receives at least 5 percent of the vote is assigned a number of seats in parliament according to the percentage of ballots it receives. Terms are for 4 years. Judicial power is vested in a Supreme Court, elected by the National Council and a Constitutional Court appointed by the president from nominees approved by the National Council.

Although the president was initially elected by the parliament, the office of president has been chosen by direct election since 1999. The 1st president to be chosen by direct election, Rudolf Schuster, was elected in 1999 for a 5-year term. He succeeded Michal Kovac, who served as the 1st president after being elected by the parliament in 1993.

The 1st elections in the independent Republic of Slovakia took place in 1994. At that time, the Movement for a Democratic Slovakia (HZDS) emerged as a clear victor, as it had in 1992. This party, which is a weak supporter of free-market reforms, formed a governing coalition with the xenophobic (anti-foreign involvement) Slovak Nationalists (SNS) and the Slovak Workers (ZRS). In spite of a very slight victory for the HZDS in the 1998 elections, the party's inability to form a governing coalition gave power to a broad-based coalition that included the free-market reformist Slovak Democratic Coalition (SDK). Other significant political parties include the Slovak Communist Party (KSS) and the reformist Democratic Union (DU). There is also a new, centrist party called Smer (Direction).

The government has played a significant role in the economy during the process of changing from a centrally planned communist system to a market-based system. The HZDS-SNS government in power from 1994 to 1998 not only slowed economic reforms but also did some damage to the privatization process by selling direct shares of state industries instead of distributing shares through a voucher process (in which all citizens obtained vouchers to purchase shares in formerly state-run industries), as had been initiated under the Czechoslovak state. It had originally been intended that these sales would take place via public auction, but the HZDS-SNS government made the transfers independently of public discussion or knowledge. There have been allegations that the transfer of many of these enterprises occurred under dubious circumstances, especially between 1996 and 1998.

In spite of these setbacks, the economy is currently dominated by private activity, and the vast majority of economic activity originates in the **private sector**. The reformist government that took power in 1998 has actively attempted to implement numerous reforms at a rapid pace, with the goal of having Slovakia enter the European Union in the near future.

The Slovak Republic adopted the Commercial Code that was initially formulated in 1991 under the Czechoslovak state. It outlines legal protections for private property and business activities for both Slovaks and foreign persons. Government reforms have also stabilized the Slovak currency and made it convertible to other currencies on the world market. The government has effectively reoriented trade towards Western partners in an attempt to integrate with EU markets.

The government obtains revenue through several different forms of taxes. There is a progressive personal **income tax** with 7 rates that ranges from 12 to 42 percent. The corporate income tax is 29 percent, although **tax holidays** or specific tax breaks for some businesses are offered as part of an effort to attract foreign investment. Other taxes include property taxes, road taxes for business vehicles, inheritance tax, and fees for administrative services. There is also a **value-added tax** on goods; **excise taxes** on alcohol, tobacco, and some fuels; customs **duties**; and real-property transfer taxes. The court system enforces the commercial code, but as it is often overloaded, plaintiffs may experience significant delays. The military has little or no role in controlling economic development, except for the armaments industry.

Communications

Country	Newspapers	Radios	TV Sets[a]	Cable subscribers[a]	Mobile Phones[a]	Fax Machines[a]	Personal Computers[a]	Internet Hosts[b]	Internet Users[b]
	1996	1997	1998	1998	1998	1998	1998	1999	1999
Slovakia	185	580	402	105.1	87	10.0	65.1	38.79	600
United States	215	2,146	847	244.3	256	78.4	458.6	1,508.77	74,100
Germany	311	948	580	214.5	170	73.1	304.7	173.96	14,400
Czech Republic	254	803	447	77.1	94	10.4	97.3	85.58	700

[a]Data are from International Telecommunication Union, *World Telecommunication Development Report 1999* and are per 1,000 people.
[b]Data are from the Internet Software Consortium (http://www.isc.org) and are per 10,000 people.

SOURCE: World Bank. *World Development Indicators 2000.*

INFRASTRUCTURE, POWER, AND COMMUNICATIONS

Given the former communist emphasis on public goods, Slovakia inherited an extensive network of public transportation, in the form of bus and train routes, from Czechoslovakia. Even some of the most remote locations may be reached by bus. One of the most significant changes of the post-communist era has been an increase in independent auto ownership. There are 17,710 kilometers (11,005 miles) of highways, including 288 kilometers (179 miles) of expressway, with only 177 kilometers (110 miles) remaining unpaved. A large-scale improvement is planned for the highway system with a cross-country expressway slated for construction. Continued improvements are planned for the railway system in order to bring it more in line with EU standards. The country now has 3,660 kilometers (2,274 miles) of railways.

There are 18 airports in the country. The largest public airports are in Bratislava and in Košice, the second-largest city. Many visitors also enter Slovakia via the Vienna airport, which is only 25 miles away from Bratislava. The 172 kilometers (107 miles) of waterway are provided by the Danube River, which gives Slovakia access to the Black Sea via ports in Austria, Hungary, the former Yugoslavia, and Romania. The 2 port cities are Bratislava and Komárno, both of which host shipping companies.

Electricity production stands at 20 billion kilowatt hours (kWh), and the country relies on a 220-volt power system. Most electricity is generated by nuclear power (56 percent), followed by imported fossil fuels (24 percent) and hydroelectric power (20 percent). One of the 2 nuclear plants was being upgraded as of 2000, and the construction of an additional hydroelectric power plant on the Danube has been delayed by a dispute with Hungary.

Slovakia's communications **infrastructure** is rapidly modernizing. In 2000, Slovak Telecom, the former state-owned communications **monopoly**, was largely privatized, and access to telephone service is easier. The increased entry of private telecommunications providers and the growing popularity of mobile telephones now provide more competition in this industry. There are 87 mobile phones per 1,000 people in the Slovak Republic, compared to 50 per 1,000 in neighboring Poland, and there are 2 providers of cellular phone service and 5 large Internet service providers. Internet cafes are readily available, which make up for the fact that relatively few Slovak households contain computers (65.1 per 1000 people in Slovakia, compared to 97.3 per 1,000 in the Czech Republic and 457 per 1,000 in the United States). Slovakia also lags behind the Czech Republic in the proportion of radios and televisions but is on a rough par with Poland in these categories.

ECONOMIC SECTORS

Since the 1990s, Slovakia has experienced a drastic production shift away from the industrial sector and to-

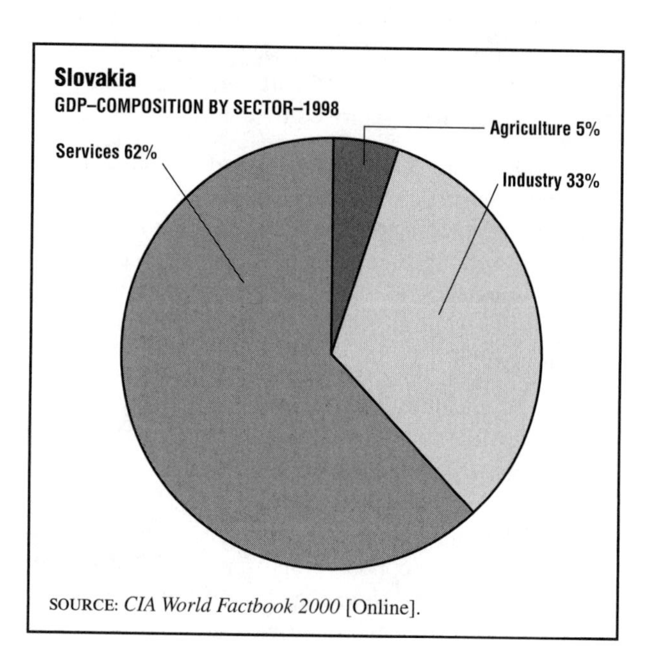

SOURCE: *CIA World Factbook 2000* [Online].

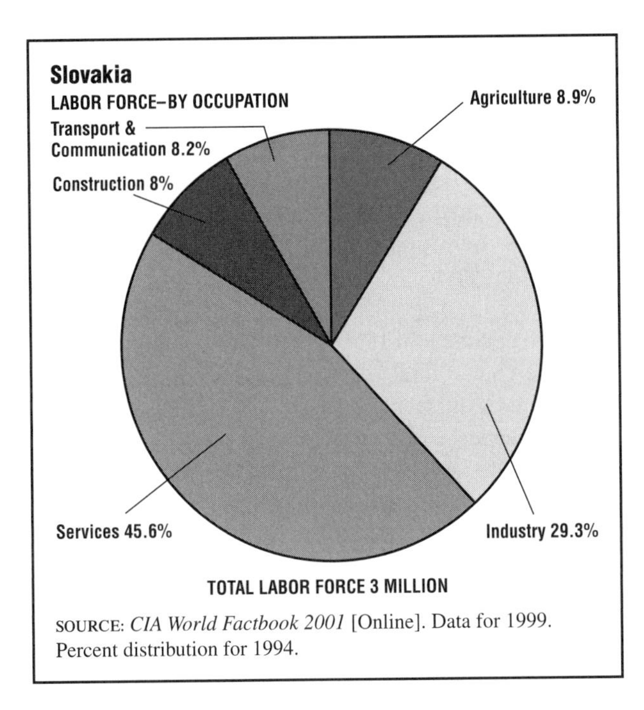

SOURCE: *CIA World Factbook 2001* [Online]. Data for 1999. Percent distribution for 1994.

wards the services sector. In 1998, the proportion of contributions to GDP from services, industry, and agriculture were 62 percent, 33 percent, and 5 percent, respectively. This change has not merely resulted from the 1993 separation of Czechoslovakia, since the Czech Republic has been experiencing similar dramatic shifts. Rather, it is a side effect of the transformation from the central planning of the communist system to a market-based system. The communist system created several large monopoly industries in specific sectors, such as pharmaceuticals and machine production. Once privatized, only some of these industries have been competitive in a free-market environment. While the service sector was given a low priority under the communist system, the free-market environment has demonstrated a strong demand for growth in this sector.

GDP showed generally continuous growth during the 1st decade of the transition. However, some irregularities in the privatization process were among the factors that prevented Slovakia from attaining levels of **foreign direct investment** (FDI) comparable to that of its neighbors. A restructuring of the government and economic policies in 1998 has brought renewed investor interest in Slovakia. The most famous Slovak industry to survive the transition process is the VSŽ Steel company in Košice, now a partnership with U.S. Steel. Volkswagen also set up operations in Slovakia in the late 1990s.

Under the communist system in Czechoslovakia, Slovakia produced 80 percent of the state's armaments, many of which were exported to eastern-bloc allies. With the end of the Cold War, these factories were shut down. This sector had at one time contributed 5 percent of total industrial production and 12 percent of exports, employing 80,000 people. The closing of the factories was highly unpopular in Slovakia, and played a contributing role to the eventual breakup of the Czechoslovak state. Some Slovak arms production has now been resumed.

The sectors that are projected to have particular growth potential are pharmaceuticals, infrastructure, information technology, equipment and equipment services, business services, and tourism.

AGRICULTURE

The agricultural sector is the smallest in the Slovak economy, making up approximately 5 percent of the GDP, although some sources argue that this proportion is higher. According to 1994 figures, the agricultural sector employs 8.9 percent of the **labor force**, or 295,480 people. More than one-third of Slovakia's territory is cultivated, and the primary agricultural products are sugar beets, potatoes, wheat, barley, fruit, forest products, corn, pigs, cattle, poultry, and sheep. Grapes for wine production are grown in some hilly areas, and tobacco is cultivated in valleys. Animal products, including oils, represent over 80 percent of all agricultural receipts.

Under the communist economic system, much of Slovakia's agriculture, particularly on the plains, was collectivized, meaning that small private farms were taken by the government in order to create state-owned cooperatives. Under this setup, individuals who lived in a village would be employed by the nearby collective farm. After the collapse of communism in 1989, these cooperatives were transferred to private owners, often by the direct sale of the farm as a unit, though some lands were also restored to their former owners. The government has embarked upon a long-term agricultural policy in an effort to modernize this sector for the world market.

Food consumption has diversified with the introduction of the **free market system**, and food items that are not produced domestically, such as tropical fruits, are easily imported. These items were more difficult for individuals to obtain under the communist economic system.

INDUSTRY

Industry is a large but declining sector of the economy of Slovakia. According to 1998 data, industrial production made up 33 percent of the country's GDP and employed 37 percent of the labor force, or 1,238,360 people, in 1994. Slovakia is experiencing a long-term decline of industrial production as fewer unnecessary products are being produced under **capitalism** as were produced under communism. There has also been a reduction of heavy and light industry and a move toward services. In the first decade of the free-market economy, employment in the industrial sector shrank, with the most significant job losses in the areas of construction, machinery and equipment, metals and fabricated metal products, and mining and quarrying. The only increase came in the area of textile production. In spite of this decline, industry continues to produce a significant portion of exports from Slovakia to other countries.

While the majority of large and medium-sized enterprises have been privatized, some companies remained in government hands until as late as 1999 and 2000. Some of these companies had significant debts, making their privatization politically unpopular because of potential job losses. Other companies were initially categorized as strategic enterprises and were left out of the first efforts of privatization. In 1998, Slovak Telecom and SPP, the Slovak gas company, were privatized.

MANUFACTURING. Many of the remaining manufacturing plants that were privatized after communism included outdated equipment. Thus, foreign direct investment has been extremely important in determining which industries survive the transition to a market economy. Foreign investment was particularly helpful in the areas of transport machines, auto production, and steel production. The most sizable investments were made by the German company Volkswagen and by U.S. Steel, which purchased the large East Slovakia VSŽ Steel plant in the late 1990s. Automobiles and steel are among Slovakia's most successful exports. Chemical production has recently averaged approximately 18 percent of total industrial output and includes chemical fibers and plastics. Other important sectors are the production of textiles, clothing, and leather products such as footwear, fuel and power production, and construction.

The late 1990s saw some decreases in the production of manufactured products, as well as in chemicals, while exports of crude materials remained at steady levels. According to employment figures for 1999, employment trends in various manufacturing sectors varied widely. There have been significant declines in employment in the areas of basic metals and fabricated metal products, machinery and equipment, and construction. The following manufacturing areas registered positive increases between 1998 and 1999: textiles, electrical and optical equipment, pulp and paper products, leather products, and transport equipment.

MINING. Approximately 4.6 million tons of coal are mined in Slovakia each year. Other significant minerals include iron, copper, lead, manganese, zinc, mercury, and lignite. Employment in the mining sector declined during the 1990s.

CONSTRUCTION. Construction levels initially increased dramatically after 1989, and building materials represent over 3 percent of industrial output. However, at the end of the 1990s, construction began to experience some fluctuations in employment.

SERVICES

As part of the general transformation of the economy in the transition from a communist to a capitalist system, the service sector in Slovakia has experienced sizable growth while the industrial and agricultural sectors have declined. In 1998, the services sector accounted for 62 percent of total GDP, and, as of 1994, it employed 54 percent of the labor force, or 1,786,160 workers. Significant increases in employment in the late 1990s were located in the service sector, in the areas of wholesale and **retail** trade, repairs, and hotels and restaurants.

FINANCE, BANKING, AND INSURANCE. As insurance was not provided under the communist system, there was significant growth in this area during the 1990s. Financial services and consulting companies experienced similar growth. Although foreign companies initiated growth in this sector, they now have some domestic competitors. An increasing number of commercial banks are under private and/or foreign ownership.

RETAIL. The retail portion of the service sector has undergone dramatic changes since 1989. Under the communist economic system, retail was limited to state-owned shops where product shortages were common and the displays unattractive. In an effort to promote **full employment**, these stores maintained a complicated point-of-purchase system that required several steps with different clerks at each level (selecting the product, paying for it, and receiving it). Retail stores were privatized as part of the process that took place under the Czechoslovak state before 1993. The current retail sector consists of privatized, restructured stores as well as completely new stores that have adopted capitalist marketing methods. Among the most popular products for consumer consumption are automobiles and foreign-produced appliances, such as televisions, VCRs, and stereos. The repair sector is also growing.

TOURISM. Tourism has increased significantly since 1989, and it is targeted as a primary sector of growth. Slovakia's chief urban attractions are its largest cities, the capital city of Bratislava and Košice. The country's best known feature is the striking High Tatra mountains, comparable to the American Rockies, which offer numerous opportunities for outdoor tourism such as skiing, hiking, mountain climbing, and cave exploration. Visitors are also attracted by the region's historic spas and castles. Slovakia hopes to make a bid to be a site for a future Winter Olympics.

The number of tourists visiting Slovakia steadily increased after 1989, with the majority of visitors coming from Western Europe and neighboring countries. The dramatic increase in tourism has led to an increased need for tourist services, particularly hotels, and hotel accommodation income increased from 1.1 billion korunas in 1993 to 1.8 billion korunas in 1995. In 2000, some 2.8 million tourists spent US$431 million in Slovakia. Unlike the situation under the communist system, which featured a state-run, monopolistic tourist bureau, the majority of tourist facilities have now been privatized.

INTERNATIONAL TRADE

Since it became an independent state in 1993, Slovakia has had a **trade deficit**, meaning that it imports more than it exports. The former Czechoslovak state also consistently registered a negative trade balance between 1975 and its separation into the Czech and Slovak Republics. In 1999, it exported US$11.2 billion worth of goods and services while importing US$10.1 billion.

Slovakia's primary industrial exports are various manufactured goods, among them metal products and wood products, such as paper, as well as machinery and transport equipment. In 1998, these categories comprised 43 percent and 37 percent of all commodity exports, respectively. Other significant exported commodities were chemicals, which made up 9 percent, and raw materials, which amounted to 4 percent. Of the EU countries, Germany and Austria are the primary consumers of Slovak exports (at 29 and 7 percent of exports, respectively), but the Czech Republic (with 20 percent) also consumes a significant volume of Slovak products.

Some 40 percent of all of Slovakia's imports for 1998 were classified as machinery and transport equipment. Other imports included intermediate and miscellaneous manufactured goods, which comprised 28 percent of imports, chemicals (11 percent), and fuels (11 percent), although increasing fuel demand makes this a rapidly-growing import sector. The primary sources of imports from EU countries are Germany (26 percent) and Italy (6 percent), with the Czech Republic (18 percent) and Russia (10 percent) also serving as important importers.

In the early 1990s, the Czechoslovak state made a concentrated effort to shift trade away from the former Soviet Union and former Soviet Bloc countries and to the European Union and the United States. In contrast to the previous Slovakian government, the government elected in 1998 began to actively encourage this shift in an effort to improve the country's chances for entry into the European Union. Trading patterns now show increased volume in trade with the European Union and the United States and decreased volume with other eastern European countries and the former Soviet Union. As one result of this shift, trade with the Czech Republic has been in decline, in spite of a favorable customs union between the 2 countries. The Czech Republic made up 39 percent of Slovakia's foreign trade **turnover** in 1993, but, by 1999, it was about half that (18 percent). Both countries have instead been registering increased trade with the European Union, which now accounts for approximately 56 percent of Slovakia's foreign trade.

MONEY

Since 1995, the Slovakian koruna has been generally convertible to other currencies on the world market for trading purposes. In January 2000, it was being exchanged at the rate of 42.059 korunas to the U.S. dollar, up from 29.713 in 1995. The Slovak National Bank serves as the country's central bank and sets **monetary policy**. It is designed to be autonomous from political structures. In spite of the bank's generally responsible policies to curb **inflation**, the currency has been in a slow state of decline for several years. As a result, imported products are becoming increasingly harder for Slovaks to afford. In addition to the central bank, there are 2 agencies to assist banks and companies through the bankruptcy process.

The privatization of banks in Slovakia has been a complicated process, and the state retained shares in the 3 strongest banks as of 1999. In that year, the government began a program to reduce the amount of state ownership in the banking sector (a holdover from the communist system) and to increase the amount of private ownership of banking. This restructuring is understood as a crucial step in the transition to a market economic system. There is also a growing amount of foreign investment and ownership in the banking sector. This process corresponds with the country's efforts to prepare for future integration into the financial structures of the European Union.

The Bratislava Stock Exchange is the seat of much of the securities trading in the Slovak Republic. There is also an electronic exchange market called the RM-system, also for the trade of securities. A database of all listed companies is maintained by the Center of Securities of the Slovak Republic, a joint-stock company.

Exchange rates: Slovakia

koruny (Sk) per US$1	
Mar 2001	48.09
2000	46.395
1999	41.363
1998	35.233
1997	33.616
1996	30.654

SOURCE: CIA *World Factbook 2001* [ONLINE].

GDP per Capita (US$)

Country	1975	1980	1985	1990	1998
Slovakia	N/A	N/A	3,630	3,825	3,822
United States	19,364	21,529	23,200	25,363	29,683
Germany	N/A	N/A	N/A	N/A	31,141
Czech Republic	N/A	N/A	4,884	5,270	5,142

SOURCE: United Nations. *Human Development Report 2000; Trends in human development and per capita income.*

Distribution of Income or Consumption by Percentage Share: Slovakia

Lowest 10%	5.1
Lowest 20%	11.9
Second 20%	15.8
Third 20%	18.8
Fourth 20%	22.2
Highest 20%	31.4
Highest 10%	18.2

Survey year: 1992

Note: This information refers to income shares by percentiles of the population and is ranked by per capita income.

SOURCE: *2000 World Development Indicators* [CD-ROM].

POVERTY AND WEALTH

In 1998, **GDP per capita** was US$3,822 in Slovakia, as compared to $5,142 in the Czech Republic, US$2,900 in Poland, and US$23,200 in the United States. Four decades of communist rule in Czechoslovakia (1948 to 1989) had a strong and enduring effect on the distribution of incomes in Slovakia. Under communism, wages were artificially kept at similar levels, so professionals such as doctors earned wages similar to those of factory or construction workers. Because property had belonged to the state and housing was distributed through state channels, those individuals who obtained large homes often did so through political means, such as good standing with the Communist Party.

By 2000, with the privatization of property, home ownership is increasingly becoming a privilege of financial success. However, the Slovakian government that administered the privatization process throughout most of the 1990s did so in a non-transparent (secretive) way, making it clear that political affiliation mattered for the acquisition of property at reduced rates. Such instances of corruption have allowed a few individuals to improve their economic standing through dubious means.

Although the social structure is rapidly moving toward a hierarchical class system, as of the late 1990s, income distribution and consumption in Slovakia remained more equalized than in the United States. In the United States, the richest 20 percent of people earn and consume 46 percent of available wealth, as compared with Slovakia, where the richest 20 percent earn and consume only 31 percent of available wealth. In the United States, the poorest 20 percent earn and consume only 5 percent of available wealth, but in the Slovakia, the poorest 20 percent earn and consume nearly 12 percent.

Under the communist system, higher education and health care were freely provided by the state. Slovakia has been implementing reforms that require individuals to pay for these services. These reforms have been difficult for average individuals because institutions such as a comprehensive student loan system or health insurance have not yet been fully developed. The state does provide a social security system and some social assistance.

WORKING CONDITIONS

Slovakia's labor force is 3.32 million. Because the previous communist system required women to work outside the home, many are now choosing to remain at home when they have children, in contrast to trends in the United States. In 1999 and early 2000, the rate of unemployment, which registers those actively looking for work, reached

Household Consumption in PPP Terms

Country	All food	Clothing and footwear	Fuel and power[a]	Health care[b]	Education[b]	Transport & Communications	Other
Slovakia	26	7	16	5	12	10	24
United States	13	9	9	4	6	8	51
Germany	14	6	7	2	10	7	53
Czech Republic	24	5	14	5	12	16	24

Data represent percentage of consumption in PPP terms.

[a]Excludes energy used for transport.

[b]Includes government and private expenditures.

SOURCE: World Bank. *World Development Indicators 2000.*

nearly 20 percent. It now appears to be declining, with unemployment for late 2000 at 16–17 percent. Many experts believe that high levels of unemployment are difficult to avoid in the ongoing transition period. The government has focused its energies on improving foreign investment and business possibilities in an effort to promote new jobs, and unemployment benefits are available, as well as progressive provisions for paid maternity leave.

Unemployment is at the lowest level in the capital of Bratislava, where wages are at the highest level in the country, and in the eastern region of Košice. In 1994, the majority of those employed, 53.8 percent, worked in the service sector. Industry employed 37.3 percent of the workforce, and the remaining 8.9 percent worked in agriculture. Given the importance of foreign investment in the economy, those workers who speak English and German have an advantage in the labor market.

There is an active confederation of trade unions, with the largest single union being the Engineering and Metal Union. The majority of all workers are union members. Slovakia has instituted a system of laws that prohibits employment discrimination on the basis of race, sex, language, religion, faith, and political views. However, discrimination against the hiring of Romany people (Gypsies) persists in practice.

COUNTRY HISTORY AND ECONOMIC DEVELOPMENT

500 A.D. First Slavonic tribes appear in region.

830–900. Period of the Great Moravian Empire.

863. Christianity enters the region, brought by the monks Cyril and Methodius.

907. The Moravian Empire is overthrown by the Hungarians (Magyars), leading to rule by various Hungarian kings.

1526. The defeat of Hungarians by the Turks in a battle moves the administrative seat of Hungary northward, to what is now Slovakia. This situation lasts until the late 1600s.

MID-1800s. Increasing Slovak national identity is particularly centered around language.

1867. The Austro-Hungarian Empire is divided into 2 parts. The Slovaks remain under the rule of the Hungarians, based in Budapest, while the Czechs are under Hapsburg rule.

1918. The Austro-Hungarian Empire disintegrates at the end of World War I and Czechoslovakia becomes an independent nation.

1938. Adolf Hitler's Germany is given a piece of Czechoslovakia by the Munich Agreement.

1939. Germany attacks Czechoslovakia at the start of World War II. Czechoslovakia is dissolved and Slovakia becomes a puppet state allied with Hitler's Germany. Many Jews perish in camps during the war.

1944. Approximately 60,000 Slovak troops engage in the Slovak National Uprising against German rule, a resistance that is put down by the Nazis.

1948. The Communist Party takes over Czechoslovakia's parliament. A communist political and economic system dominates for the next 4 decades.

1968. The Soviet Union and Eastern Bloc nations invade Czechoslovakia to counter reform attempts during the "Prague Spring" of Premier Alexander Dub ek.

1970s. Strict repression and control of the population by the Communist Party.

1977. Some political dissidents, emboldened by principles of human rights, begin to visibly resist the communist leadership.

1980s. Worsening economic conditions lead to increasing numbers of protests against communism.

1990. The first post-communist parliamentary elections are held in Czechoslovakia, and the new government embarks on a series of reforms to replace the communist economic system with a capitalist system.

1992. The second post-communist elections result in a leadership stalemate between the Czech and Slovak republics under the federal Czechoslovak state.

1993. The Republic of Slovakia is constituted on January 1. In February, it establishes a separate Slovakian currency.

2000. Slovakia is invited to begin accession talks with the European Union, of which it is already an associate member.

FUTURE TRENDS

Slovakia has come a long way since its founding in 1993 and its first decade of transition from a communist to a capitalist economic system. It is a member of several international organizations, including the United Nations, the IMF, the World Bank, and the World Trade Organization (WTO). It is also an associate member of the European Union. It aspires to become a member of NATO and is working to update its military infrastructure for this purpose. The government's primary focus in recent years has been the preparation of legislative and regulatory structures for future EU membership, for which it has made a formal application.

In spite of the enormous changes that Slovakia has successfully undergone in its first few years of independence, and particularly since 1998, more remains to be done. Some areas for improvement include: some restructuring of the enterprise sector after the negative results of corrupt "insider" privatization by the first Slovak government, increased foreign investment, a reduction of high unemployment levels, and further reforms of legislation to incorporate EU standards. Although the Slovak economy faces many difficulties, the EU has responded favorably to the economic reforms initiated by the reformist government. Whether the country is able to complete its reform process and attain membership in the EU will depend largely upon the fate of the reformist government in the next elections.

DEPENDENCIES

Slovakia has no territories or colonies.

BIBLIOGRAPHY

"Elections in Slovakia." <http://www.electionworld.org/election/slovakia.htm>. Accessed January 2001.

Foreign Trade Support Fund. <http://www.fpzo.sk/indexlEuk.htm>. Accessed August 2001.

International Monetary Fund. *International Financial Statistics Yearbook.* Washington: The International Monetary Fund, 1999.

Kirschbaum, Stanislav. *A History of Slovakia: The Struggle for Survival.* New York: St. Martin's Griffin, 1995.

Ministry of Agriculture of the Slovak Republic. <http://www.mpsr.sk/english>. Accessed August 2001.

National Bank of Slovakia. <http://www.nbs.sk/mena/bezmin/indexa.htm>. Accessed August 2001.

Organization for Economic Cooperation and Development. *OECD Interim Economic Assessment, Slovak Republic, 2000.* Paris: OECD, May 2000.

Ratjar, Jozef. "Customs Union between the Czech and Slovak Republics." *Doing Business.CZ.* <http://www.doingbusiness.cz/article.asp?ArticleID=40>. Accessed January 2001.

Slovakia.org: The Guide to the Slovak Republic. <http://www.slovakia.org>. Accessed January 2001.

Statistical Office of the Slovak Republic. <http://www.statistics.sk/webdata/english/index2_a.htm>. Accessed August 2001.

Stroschein, Sherrill. "Slovakia." In *Nations in Transit 1997: Civil Society, Democracy and Markets in East Central Europe and the Newly Independent States,* edited by Motyl and Shor Karatnycky. New York: Freedom House/Transaction Publishers, 1997.

United Nations Development Program. *Human Development Report 2000.* New York: Oxford University Press, 2000.

U.S. Central Intelligence Agency. *World Factbook 2000.* <http://www.odci.gov/cia/publications/factbook/index.html>. Accessed August 2001.

U.S. Department of State. *Background Notes: Slovakia.* <http://www.state.gov/www/background_notes/slovakia_9908_bgn.html>. Accessed January 2001.

U.S. Department of State. *FY 2001 Country Commercial Guide: Slovakia.* <http://www.state.gov/www/about_state/business/com_guides/2001/europe/index.html>. Accessed January 2001.

—Sherrill Stroschein

SLOVENIA

Republic of Slovenia
Republika Slovenije

CAPITAL: Ljubljana.

MONETARY UNIT: Slovene tolar (SIT). One tolar (SIT) equals 100 stotins. There are coins of 50 stotins, and 1, 2, and 5 tolars, and notes of 10, 20, 50, 100, 200, 500, 1,000, 5,000, and 10,000 tolars.

CHIEF EXPORTS: Manufactured goods, machinery and transport equipment, chemicals, food.

CHIEF IMPORTS: Machinery and transport equipment, manufactured goods, chemicals, fuels and lubricants, food.

GROSS DOMESTIC PRODUCT: US$22.9 billion (2000 est.).

BALANCE OF TRADE: **Exports:** US$8.9 billion (f.o.b., 2000). **Imports:** US$9.9 billion (f.o.b., 2000).

COUNTRY OVERVIEW

LOCATION AND SIZE. Located in southeastern Europe, bounded on the north by Austria, on the northeast by Hungary, on the southeast and south by Croatia, and on the west by Italy and the Adriatic Sea, Slovenia has an area of 20,253 square kilometers (7,820 square miles), slightly smaller comparatively than New Jersey, and a coastline of 46.6 kilometers (29 miles). The capital city, Ljubljana, is situated on the Sava River in the central part of the country; the second major city is Maribor on the Drava River in the northeast.

POPULATION. The population of Slovenia was estimated at 1,930,132 in July 2001. At the 1991 census, it was 1,962,606, giving it an overall population density of 97 persons per square kilometers (252 per square miles). In 2001, the birth rate was estimated at 9.32 per 1,000 population, while the death rate stood at 9.98 per 1,000, giving Slovenia a negative rate of natural increase. In 2001, however, a positive population growth rate was estimated, partly due to **immigration** from other former Yugoslav republics. Unlike many Eastern European countries, Slovenia has not been seriously affected by economic **emigration** in the 1990s.

Slovenes, a Slavic ethnic group, constitute about 88 percent of the republic's population; ethnic Croats (about 3 percent), ethnic Serbs (about 2 percent), and several other ethnic groups (about 7 percent) constitute the remainder. Slovenian culture has been strongly influenced by Austrian and German culture. Languages include Slovenian and others, corresponding to the ethnic breakdown. Most Slovenes (about 69 percent) are Roman Catholics, with smaller numbers of Lutherans and others. In the mid-1990s, Slovenia was home to some 20,000 refugees from the war in Bosnia and Herzegovina. About 52 percent of the population lives in urban areas, particularly in Ljubljana. The population is aging, with 16 percent below the age of 14 and 19 percent older than 60.

The aging of the population was spectacularly illustrated by the success of the Democratic Party of Slovene Pensioners (Desus) in the late 1990s. Having entered parliament in 1996, this retiree party achieved a record 5.2 percent share of the popular vote in 2000, pledging to put off pension reform. The Slovenian government has been consistent in its commitment to supporting families and youth, yet unable to reverse the aging trend, characteristic of Europe as a whole.

OVERVIEW OF ECONOMY

Slovenia had been a part of Austria for many centuries before joining the former Yugoslavia as its most prosperous part in 1918. After the breakup of Yugoslavia in 1991, newly independent Slovenia was the richest (although the smallest) country in central-eastern Europe; it is also considered one of the easiest to be absorbed in the enlarged European Union (EU), made up of, as of early 2001, 15 European countries joining together to form a more competitive economic and political force in the region and the world. Slovenia's foreign policy since independence has focused on strengthening relations with

western Europe while weakening its ties with the rest of the former Yugoslavia, which, through much of the 1990s, suffered from the devastation brought by war.

Slovenia's economic record is among the best in Eastern Europe; the budget is under control, the currency is stable, and the economy has been growing for 10 years. In 1989 (the last year in which Slovenia was part of **communist** Yugoslavia), its **gross domestic product (GDP) per capita** was US$11,510, putting it considerably ahead of smaller EU members such as Portugal and Greece, and in 1999, after a good performance in the 1990s, it had risen to US$13,283, which came just under 60 percent of the EU average. In 1999, **real GDP** rose by 4.9 percent, making Slovenia the fastest growing country in central-eastern Europe. In the second half of the 1990s, however, its average growth rate was 4.2 percent, leaving it behind Poland, Slovakia, and Croatia during the same period, largely because Slovenia, unlike its neighbors, experienced only a limited decline at the beginning of the decade and had a somewhat slow approach to **privatization**.

The real output level in Slovenia in 1999 was 9.3 percent above 1989, while most countries in Eastern Europe are still far below their 1989 level, and only Poland's 1999 output of 21.8 percent was higher than Slovenia's. Slovenia's openness to trade, with total trade equivalent to about 115 percent of GDP, has been instrumental in sustaining economic growth, and maintaining export competitiveness has consistently been the focus of government attention. Slovenia's dependence on Eastern European markets before 1989 was also small compared to that of most of its neighbors.

Slovenia competes with Hungary for 1st place in the line of formerly communist countries wanting to join the EU, which will make it a more attractive venue for foreign investment than most other ex-Yugoslav republics. Although the government was criticized in the mid-1990s for slow structural reforms and a comparatively rigid economy, it has fulfilled the EU entry criteria of developing a functioning market economy and is getting closer to meeting the second requirement of being capable to withstand competitive pressure in the single European market.

Yet the EU complains that large banks and utilities are still in state hands, which means that Slovenia has one of the lowest shares of **private-sector** activity in GDP among the EU applicant countries. Moreover, the EU believes that the Slovenian economy in general, and labor markets in particular, are over regulated and leave little ground for new investment and innovation. Consequently, much work remains yet to be done in the areas of privatization and capital market reform. Privatization is expected in banking, telecommunications, and public utility sectors. Government and corporate restrictions on foreign investment are slowly being discarded, and direct investment is expected to increase in the 21st century.

Although Slovenia's **external debt** rose from $4 billion in 1996 to $6.1 billion in 2000 (estimate), the increase is considered proportionate to the GDP; a **trade deficit** has contributed to its accumulation as imports steadily outgrow exports. The strong banking sector and the steady growth of GDP, however, are generally offsetting any possible negative effects on the economy and living standards.

POLITICS, GOVERNMENT, AND TAXATION

Slovenia emerged from the former communist Yugoslavia in 1991 as a parliamentary republic with a multiparty democratic system, remarkably moderate and consensus-oriented. The center-left Liberal Democracy of Slovenia (LDS) won the parliamentary election in October 2000, securing 34 seats in the 90-member National Assembly, which gave it a wide edge over the largest center-right group, the Social Democratic Party (SDS), which took 14 seats. The left-of-center United List of Social Democrats (ZLSD) won 11 seats, while the Democratic Party of Slovene Pensioners (Desus) and the Slovene National Party (SNS), 2 other left-of-center formations, made their way back into the Assembly. The election ended in defeat for the 3 main center-right parties of the Slovene Spring movement—the SDS, the Slovene People's Party, and the New Slovenia-Christian People's Party, which together got only 31 seats, one-third down from the 45 deputies that they had after the 1996 election—a result that destroyed their ambitions of reviving the coalition government that they formed in June 2000. All major parties (with the possible exception of SNS) firmly support EU membership and (with the possible exception of ZLSD) entrance into the North Atlantic Treaty Organization (NATO), both of which are expected in the 1st decade of the 21st century.

The LDS positioned itself as a party equipped to guide Slovenia through the challenges likely to be encountered on the path to EU membership and globalization. It demonstrated its commitment to modernization, along with its **liberal economic** agenda, including plans to privatize banking, insurance, and the energy sector. The electorate swung to the LDS primarily because of its record for competence. This party in fact ran the country from early 1992 until April 2000, playing the leading role in 3 coalition governments, all of which were headed by the party leader, Janez Drnovsek. Convincing evidence has not backed up innuendoes from the right that the LDS has grown corrupt. The LDS government is expected to fulfill its pledges for privatization of state assets, **deregulation**, reducing the time needed to set up a company, technology development, and boosting the GDP growth rate to 5 percent. Also expected is expansion of post-graduate study programs, computerization of schools, increased social assistance to the poor by 60 percent, cutting of unemployment by 20 percent, and an active social housing policy.

The state still has considerable influence in the economy, with the **public sector** accounting for roughly 50 percent of the output and public consumption over 20 percent of the total. The continued dominance of the financial sector by state-owned banks is said to hold back development and competition. The slow progress on privatization and somewhat rigid business conditions are keeping **foreign direct investment** at a low level. Progress in improving the economic climate, combined with a full and timely completion of privatization, structural reforms, and market **liberalization**, would attract more foreign investors and provide better conditions for sustained future growth. Privatization deals in Slovenia, however, have been largely a success, unlike the ones in Bulgaria, where many enterprises went to management-employee ventures in deals largely seen as politically motivated, ineffective, and even corrupt.

Public accounts show that the overall tax burden in 1998 stood at 40.5 percent of GDP. **Income taxes** are progressive, and a **value-added tax** was recently introduced at a standard rate of 19 percent and a lower rate of 8 percent. Parliament passed a law in 1998 taxing motor vehicles, which had frequently been discussed but never adopted. The new tax rate depends on the price, varying from 1 to 13 percent. A new law governing taxation of the insurance business was also recently passed, providing for premiums to be taxed at a rate of 6.5 percent. No tax will be paid on certain insurance products, including mandatory pension and health insurance.

INFRASTRUCTURE, POWER, AND COMMUNICATIONS

Slovenia's **infrastructure** is relatively developed, and the government is investing ever more in it to take advantage of its geographic, trade, and cultural potential. There is a good transportation network, containing 19,586 kilometers (12,143 miles) of roads (1998), including good quality expressways. Construction of highways is a priority, with US$4 billion in funding for 700 kilometers (435 miles) of highways to be completed by 2000. There are 3 major airports. Upgrading rail links will cost US$2.5 billion by the year 2005, with priority given to the east-west and northwest-southeast corridors. The Adriatic port of Koper, near Trieste in Italy, serves as a principle port for Austrian and Hungarian exports and is essential for Czech and Slovak exports.

Communications

Country	Newspapers	Radios	TV Sets[a]	Cable subscribers[a]	Mobile Phones[a]	Fax Machines[a]	Personal Computers[a]	Internet Hosts[b]	Internet Users[b]
	1996	1997	1998	1998	1998	1998	1998	1999	1999
Slovenia	199	406	356	150.5	84	9.8	250.9	99.34	250
United States	215	2,146	847	244.3	256	78.4	458.6	1,508.77	74,100
Yugoslavia	107	297	259	N/A	23	1.9	18.8	7.65	80
Hungary	186	689	437	145.5	105	17.7	58.9	93.13	600

[a]Data are from International Telecommunication Union, *World Telecommunication Development Report 1999* and are per 1,000 people.
[b]Data are from the Internet Software Consortium (http://www.isc.org) and are per 10,000 people.

SOURCE: World Bank. *World Development Indicators 2000.*

Slovenia's energy sector is state-owned and derives most of its output from nuclear plants (38.2 percent), thermal plants burning fossil fuels (37.1 percent), and hydroelectric facilities (24.7 percent). Electricity production was 13.18 billion kilowatt hours (kWh) and consumption stood at 10.661 billion kWh in 1998. Slovenia also exports some energy. The German Siemens and the French engineering group Framatome have won a $38 million contract to replace 2 steam generators at the Krsko nuclear power plant, jointly owned by the Slovenian and Croatian electricity companies. American-owned Westinghouse has also announced its contracts to supply fuel assemblies to the plant.

In communications, Slovenia has been at the leading edge of the Internet revolution, with the highest concentration in Eastern Europe of Internet connections per inhabitant (and per server), and it offers a promising ground for emerging electronic commerce players. It has a well-developed modern telecommunications infrastructure and ranks second in Eastern Europe, after Hungary, in terms of cellular telephone penetration (4.5 percent) and telephone density is 36 percent. A second cellular service provider, Simobil, a **joint venture** between Telia of Sweden (25 percent) and 8 Slovene companies, including Intereuropa (15 percent) and switching manufacturer Iskratel (15 percent), that is using the pan-European Global System for Mobile Communication (GSM) standard, has recently joined the leading cellular company, Mobitel. At the end of 1997, Mobitel had a total of 100,000 cellular subscribers, out of which approximately 60 percent were GSM users. In traditional telecommunications, the national **monopoly**, Telekom Slovenije (ST), will invest about $700 million to expand and modernize in preparation for its full privatization. ST will retain its fixed-line monopoly until 2000. Slovenia's ambition is to become a transit area for Balkan communications connections and talks are under way with several countries in the region. Competition in this area, however, may come from Hungary.

ECONOMIC SECTORS

Most major sectors reported growth in 1999. Industry constituted 35 percent of GDP in 1998. Agriculture accounted for a modest 4 percent, although its contribution to the market value of products rose by 2.2 percent, and services were by far the largest sector in the economy with 61 percent of GDP and almost half of the **value added** to all commercial companies.

AGRICULTURE

Given the mountainous terrain of the country, with forests accounting for more than 50 percent of the territory, agriculture accounted for just about 4 percent of GDP in 1998, with dairy farming and livestock (cattle, sheep, and poultry) dominating this sector. Major crops include cereals such as corn and wheat, potatoes, sugar beets, and fruits (particularly grapes). Agriculture in

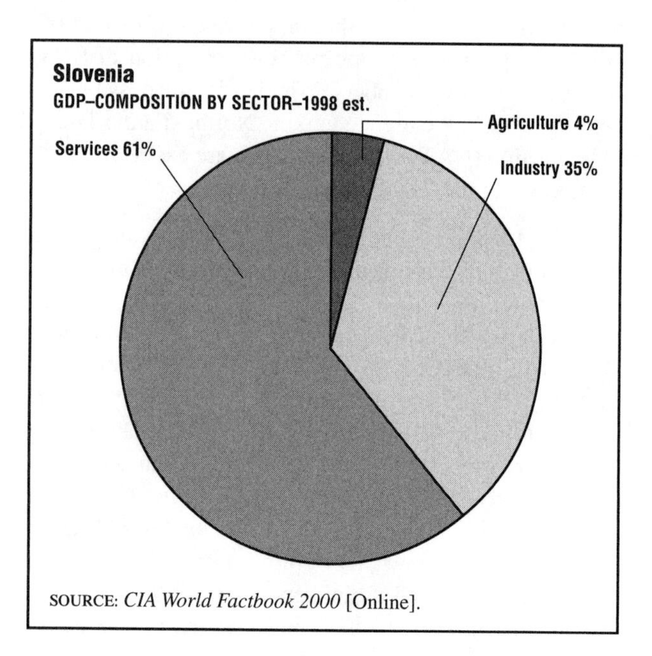

SOURCE: *CIA World Factbook 2000* [Online].

Slovenia was much less collectivized (state-owned) than in other Eastern European countries, and consequently did not suffer greatly from market reforms. The country exports some beverages, particularly wine, and food, mainly to EU markets.

INDUSTRY

Chief Slovene industries produce electrical equipment, electronics, trucks, chemicals, processed food, textiles, paper and paper products, and wood products. Ferrous metallurgy and rolling mill products, aluminum reduction and rolled products, and lead and zinc smelting are also developed. In the third quarter of 2000, industrial production grew by 6.2 percent, although there was a slowdown in the largely loss-making coal-mining sector and in power output. Net profits in manufacturing, however, have soared from SIT 2 billion in 1997 to SIT 28.7 billion in 1998, all due to an increase in production, as opposed to previous years in which job cuts had played the primary role in boosting productivity.

Foreign strategic investors are allowed under Slovene law to acquire stakes of up to 60 percent in the formerly government-owned entities being sold. The state fund retains 20 percent stakes, while the remaining 20 percent are sold in **voucher privatization** or used to pay wage **arrears** (unpaid and overdue wages) to workers. Several major foreign companies have recently acquired stakes in Slovene manufacturing firms. Tire manufacturer Goodyear (U.S.) invested US$120 million in a 60 percent stake in Sava tire unit and 75 percent in its engineered rubber division. The government plans to sell the entire steel industry by accepting bids for its 3 main steel producers, Store, Ravne, and Jesenice. Inexa (Sweden) has recently expressed an interest in Store. Renault (France), BASF, Hoechst and Siemens (Germany) are among the top foreign investors.

Slovene homes abound with consumer durables such as electrical household appliances, due in part to the strong position of the local manufacturer Gorenje. The company holds about a 40 percent market share in refrigerators, kitchen ranges, washing machines, and related items, and output rose by 9.8 percent in 1999. Its products are cheaper and compete well in terms of quality with popular Italian imports like Candy. In addition, the company has started moving into more expensive high-end household products that have captured part of the market once reserved for German and Austrian brands.

SERVICES

TOURISM. Tourism is a significant source of foreign currency, accounting for US$1.22 billion in revenue in 1996, a record for independent Slovenia, but still far behind the results before 1991, when many more foreign tourists visited its famous mountain resorts (around Lake Bled) and coastal areas. The authorities have been somewhat slow in recognizing the earning potential of that sector. Even now, opinions are divided on this activity whose fortunes depend sometimes on circumstances beyond the country's control. More recently the view has prevailed that tourism deserves more support, given the potential in a country combining an Alpine setting and a Mediterranean coast within a short distance, as well as numerous places of historical and architectural interest and broadly acclaimed health spas located in resort towns along the coast.

Germans (782,128), Italians (537,412), Austrians (483,472), Croats (212,676), Dutch (151,470) and British (135,269) made most overnight stays in 1999. The government plan is to achieve some 9 million overnight stays of foreign guests by 2005 in order to surpass the level of nearly 8 million in 1990, but few in Slovenia are relying on a return to mass-market tourism—which is rather unlikely, given the overall decline of the industry in Europe and the country's relatively high labor costs. Casinos, which bring in 30 percent of all tourism earnings, will also be encouraged. But foreign involvement in this sector has been limited so far, and some foreign tour operators sometimes get a hostile reception by domestic firms.

FINANCIAL SERVICES. With 25 banks, 6 savings institutions, and 70 commercial credit houses at the end of 1999, Slovenia is considered to be rather over-banked. The role played by financial institutions in the economy is in line with other leading Eastern European transition economies but still lags below levels found in Western Europe. The 3 largest banks, Nova Ljubljanska Banka, SKB banka, and Nova Kreditna Banka Maribor, hold more than half of the total banking assets, but are still state-owned despite long-standing privatization plans. The Slovene banking sector has avoided the calamities that have plagued other east-central European countries. Slovene banks tend to be more profitable and efficient than their counterparts there, but they are still behind those in the EU, owing to a large extent to the lack of competition. Credit card companies have been active throughout the 1990s, and their market is steadily growing.

RETAIL. Slovenia's retailers, especially the chains with near monopolies in their regions, have been growing throughout the 1990s. Mercator, the largest Slovene retailer, presently accounts for some 40 percent of the entire **retail** sector, the structure of which is now much closer to that in Austria or Switzerland than to Croatia or Hungary. There are also about 11,000 small stores, with an average size less than one-third of the European average. About half of them have less than 5 employees, and sales per vendor are less than 50 percent of the European average number. The sector is considered ripe for consolidation and for heavy foreign investment. The arrival of heavyweight western-European retailers such as Interspar (Austria) and Leclerc (France) has helped focus interest on higher-volume and lower-margin sales. Competition from such large chains, building hypermarkets (large supermarkets) with western European standards of layout and service, will likely drive many of the smaller retailers out of business.

In Slovenia, direct marketing is quite a serious business as many large direct sales companies, including Amway, Avon, Tupperware, Golden Neo-Life Diamite, Stanhome, Kirby (of the United States), and AMC (of Switzerland), have established their presence. Some, such as Amway and Golden Neo-Life Diamite, have direct representation in the Slovenian market while others, like Avon and Tupperware, use independent agents. Direct marketers complain, however, that their business is made unnecessarily difficult by the many restrictive regulations. A reason for this is the occurrence of many fraudulent **pyramid schemes** in the early 1990s, which has led to the annihilation of millions of dollars in personal savings and has generated broad government skepticism about direct sales, particularly multi-level marketing ventures.

INTERNATIONAL TRADE

Slovenia's total trade equivalent is estimated at about 115 percent of the country's GDP, and both imports and exports are currently growing, thanks to the improved foreign demand and the rise in domestic manufacturing production. In 2000, according to the CIA World Factbook, exports stood at US$8.9 billion and imports at US$9.9 billion. Robust exports growth has more than offset weaknesses in domestic demand. The EU is the leading market for Slovenia's trade, with an over 65 percent share of exports and almost 70 percent of imports. Slovenia's top trading partners include Germany (31 percent of exports and 21 percent of imports), Italy (14 percent of exports and 17 percent of imports), France (6 percent of exports and 11 percent of imports), and Austria (7 percent of exports and 8 percent of imports).

Apart from the EU countries, the other important market for export growth has come from Eastern European markets, especially from countries belonging to the Central European Free Trade Agreement (CEFTA). There has also been a continuing revival of exports to former Yugoslav neighbors Croatia, Bosnia and Herzegovina, and Macedonia—which amounted to US$1.2 billion in 1999, or 14 percent of total revenues—while exports to Russia, although also growing, remain low in absolute terms.

Although Slovene exports to Yugoslavia (Serbia-Montenegro) totaled just $85 million in 1999, they have risen quickly after the Kosovo war, reaching $92 million in the first 8 months of 2000. Although the low level of Yugoslav living standards, compounded by the poor state of the Yugoslav banking system, will present serious barriers to foreign trade, Slovene exports to that country will probably continue to expand relatively rapidly. There is likely to be strong growth in exports of **consumer goods** by companies such as Tobacna Tovarna (cigarettes), Gorenje (household appliances), Mura (clothes), and Droga Portoroz (teas and spices). Serbia was an important market for these companies before the break-up of Yugoslavia, and their brand names are still well known. They should also be in a good position to compete in what will definitely be an even more price-sensitive market.

Slovene exports include electrical machinery, road vehicles, chemicals and chemical products, footwear, furniture, food, cigarettes, and components and semi-finished goods. Tourism is also a major source of revenue. Exports of services have also exhibited relatively solid growth, reflecting a mixture of strong growth in transport services and other services. The expansion of the latter category has been propelled by the information technology sector, which has displayed strong growth in sales to the rest of the former Yugoslavia.

Imports include machinery and transport equipment, manufactured goods, chemicals, fuels and lubricants, and food. The strongest growing category of imports has been that of **intermediate goods**, partly because the strength of export growth has spurred demands for imported components and raw materials. Rising oil prices, coupled with the weakness of the euro, have been the main reasons for the increase in imports of mineral fuels and lubricants.

MONEY

The Bank of Slovenia (BS, the central bank) is the bank that issues money and handles government funds. In October 1991, it released its own currency, the tolar, to replace the former Yugoslav dinar. Despite its consistently tight **monetary policy**, banks in Slovenia are relatively strong because of a decrease in consumer lending and also because many banks have received strong foreign currency inflows. This has been a reason for the growth in

Exchange rates: Slovenia

tolars (SIT) per US$1	
Jan 2001	225.93
2000	222.66
1999	181.77
1998	166.13
1997	159.69
1996	135.36

SOURCE: CIA *World Factbook 2001* [ONLINE].

corporate lending. The tightening of monetary policy has a significant impact on keeping interest rates low.

Slovenia's stability and high per-capita GDP make its stock market an attractive ground for foreign institutional investors. Brokerages hold that Slovene voucher-privatization funds offer one of the most attractive investment opportunities in the region. But tight restrictions on foreign capital have sent many investors looking elsewhere, and even the recent relaxation of the rules is not certain to bring them back. Foreign investors in Slovenia must choose between 2 types of investment accounts. The first one allows the player to participate in local trading and transact with local entities, but requires a fee that is in fact a foreign currency forward. The second type is fee-free, but there is a holding period of 7 years during which any such shares could be traded among foreign investors, but not sold to the local market. This scheme was aimed at creating a parallel foreign market, but trading volumes at first failed to generate the amount of cash needed. As restrictions took effect, money inflows decreased dramatically, and the main index of the Ljubljana Stock Exchange fell by 20 percent. But soon after the scheme was put to this test, it started working as intended. Slovenia welcomed this as a victory over the changeable nature of international capital flows. However, it is expected that the restrictions could become an obstacle in Slovenia's negotiations to join the EU.

GDP per Capita (US$)

Country	1975	1980	1985	1990	1998
Slovenia	N/A	N/A	N/A	9,659	10,637
United States	19,364	21,529	23,200	25,363	29,683
Germany	N/A	N/A	N/A	N/A	31,141
Hungary	3,581	4,199	4,637	4,857	4,920

SOURCE: United Nations. *Human Development Report 2000; Trends in human development and per capita income.*

Distribution of Income or Consumption by Percentage Share: Slovenia

Lowest 10%	3.2
Lowest 20%	8.4
Second 20%	14.3
Third 20%	18.5
Fourth 20%	23.4
Highest 20%	35.4
Highest 10%	20.7

Survey year: 1995

Note: This information refers to income shares by percentiles of the population and is ranked by per capita income.

SOURCE: *2000 World Development Indicators* [CD-ROM].

POVERTY AND WEALTH

Before 1991, Slovenia was the most prosperous of the former Yugoslav republics and, arguably, of all Eastern European countries. Since independence, it has stayed away from political and economic disturbances that have plagued the region and has been cautious in its reform policies, displaying continuity as well as an affinity to consensus. Although unemployment is still an issue, the new government has pledged to cut it by 20 percent, while increasing social assistance by 60 percent and pursuing an active social housing policy. Pension funds have generally run a balanced budget, as any shortfalls in revenue (mostly derived from payroll contributions) have been covered by government transfers. Privatization, although slow, has been more transparent than elsewhere in the Balkans and has not led to serious charges of corruption and illicit fortunes. The rule of law has kept crime on lower levels, thus contributing to social stability and justice. Slovenia has avoided poverty of the proportions of other economies in Eastern Europe.

The structure of consumption in Slovenia is closer to central European models than to its Balkan neighbors, and private consumption per capita is more than twice the level in Bulgaria. Due to its **socialist** legacy, in 1995,

Household Consumption in PPP Terms

Country	All food	Clothing and footwear	Fuel and power[a]	Health care[b]	Education[b]	Transport & Communications	Other
Slovenia	27	8	14	4	16	11	20
United States	13	9	9	4	6	8	51
Serbia	N/A	N/A	N/A	N/A	N/A	N/A	N/A
Hungary	25	5	17	6	20	12	15

Data represent percentage of consumption in PPP terms.

[a]Excludes energy used for transport.

[b]Includes government and private expenditures.

SOURCE: World Bank. *World Development Indicators 2000.*

Slovenia was still considerably more egalitarian than Greece or the United States. The poorest 20 percent controlled 8.4 percent of the nation's consumption (compared to 7.5 percent in Greece and 5.2 percent in the U.S.) while the wealthiest 20 percent consumed 35.4 percent (40.3 percent in Greece and 46.4 percent in the U.S.). Slovenia's **Gini index** in 1995 was 26.8, while Greece's was 32.7, and the United States' was 40.8. Economic growth over the next decade and the accession to the European Union will further increase living standards for the Slovenes.

According to the United Nations Development Programme, Slovenia is a leader among Eastern European countries measured by its human development index, almost equaling those of the poorer members of the EU.

WORKING CONDITIONS

Working conditions are considerably better in Slovenia than in many other Eastern European countries. The rate of registered unemployment decreased from 14.5 percent in 1998 to 11.7 percent in 2000, its lowest level for 8 years. The official figures may overstate the level of unemployment since periodic surveys, conducted according to the International Labor Office methodologies, have reported lower estimates, and Slovenia may in fact be approaching **full employment**. Of greater concern to the government, however, in the light of EU employment directives, is **structural unemployment**. An impediment to job creation is the apparent lack of **labor mobility**, which has prevented workers from moving from rural higher-unemployment areas in the poorer east of the country to areas such as Ljubljana, where full employment has in effect already been attained. This is one of the reasons for the high number of vacancies, at around 11,500 in July 2000, compared to the number of the unemployed.

A minimum wage agreement reached in 1999 between the government, employers, and trade unions linked rises in base wages to the pace of **inflation** as of the December 1999 level. Once prices reach at least 4 percent above that level, base wages will rise by 85 percent of the price rise. If prices rise 5 percent above that level, base wages would be fully reindexed in line with inflation. Public-sector wages are strongly correlated with base wages, but manufacturing wages are less responsive to their changes. In September 2000, the government granted doctors' wage demands that may prompt other public-sector employees to demand increases. Inflation has also convinced the government to tie pensions to the base wages and raise them accordingly over time. The EU has been concerned about the "inflexibility" of the Slovenian labor market, which allegedly will impair the ability of the country to compete in the single European market. However, the government has been extremely careful not to jeopardize the existing consensual support for market reforms by putting too much strain on workers and **pensioners**.

Slovenia has signed all major universal and regional legal instruments regarding labor, including as the International Covenant on Economic, Social, and Cultural Rights, the Convention on the Elimination of Discrimination Against Women, the Convention on the Rights of the Child, as well as treaties on the right to equal compensation and collective bargaining and against employment discrimination.

COUNTRY HISTORY AND ECONOMIC DEVELOPMENT

6TH CENTURY A.D. Slavs settle in present Slovene lands, comprising parts of the ancient Roman provinces of Pannonia and Noricum, driving out Avar tribesmen. Bavarian domination brings most of the population into Roman Catholicism.

623. Chieftain Franko Samo creates the first independent Slavic state, stretching from Lake Balaton (now in Hungary) to the Adriatic Sea, but it later disintegrates.

8TH CENTURY. The region is taken over by the Frankish Empire, and a feudal agrarian economy takes root.

10TH CENTURY. The Duchy of Carantania is formed in the region, which is included in the Holy Roman Empire.

1335–1918. Slovenes are governed by the Habsburgs of the Austrian (later Austro-Hungarian) Empire. The majority of them live in parts of the Austrian crown lands of Carinthia, Carniola, and Styria. A minority of Slovenes along the coast of the Adriatic Sea remain in the republic of Venice, which later, too, is incorporated into the Habsburg Empire.

1918. Austria-Hungary collapses at the close of World War I, and the Kingdom of the Serbs, Croats, and Slovenes (later Yugoslavia) is formed with much enthusiasm, but soon many Slovenes find themselves disenchanted with the new regime.

1918–1929. Dissatisfaction with the Serb-dominated centralist policy of the kingdom grows as a political crisis brings about a dictatorial Serbian monarchist regime and the abolishment of the traditional provinces. The country is renamed the Kingdom of Yugoslavia in 1929.

1941. Yugoslavia collapses in World War II, and Germany (which has annexed Austria in 1938), Italy, and Hungary divide the territory of Slovenia and force the transfers of population.

1945. Slovenia is liberated and Josip Broz Tito's communist government proclaims the Federal People's Republic of Yugoslavia. The Slovenian republic is then created as a member of the new federation and included in Yugoslavia's socialist economy. Heavy industry develops, but, since the late 1950s, economic control is decentralized, and some private initiative is allowed. Slovenes enjoy more affluent lives and more freedom of travel and communication than other Eastern European nations.

1947. Slovenia acquires Slovenian-speaking districts on the Adriatic Sea in Istria from Italy.

1980–1990. Slovenia's dissatisfaction with the Yugoslav federation after Tito's death increases sentiment for greater autonomy and later for independence. The economy opens further to neighboring Italy and Austria.

1990. Communist power collapses throughout Eastern Europe, and Slovenia holds the first multiparty elections in Yugoslavia since World War II in April, and votes for independence in a December referendum.

1991. Slovenia declares independence from Yugoslavia in June. The Serb-dominated Yugoslav People's Army (JNA) sends forces in an attempt to secure Yugoslavia's borders. In a 10-day war, Slovene forces defeat the JNA, allowing Slovenia to quickly secure independence and international recognition. It later displays a steady pattern of political and economic continuity, almost unseen in other parts of Eastern Europe.

1991. The new democratic constitution is adopted.

1992. The European Union and the United States acknowledge the independence of Slovenia, and it joins the United Nations and the Council of Europe. Milan Kucan, president of the republic since 1990, is reelected to the office by 64 percent of the vote. The center-left Liberal Democracy of Slovenia (LDS), headed by Janez Drnovsek, wins a plurality of seats in parliament.

1993. Slovenia joins the International Monetary Fund.

1996. Slovenia signs the association agreement and applies for membership to the European Union.

1997. President Kucan reelected to a third term; Slovenia is invited to EU accession.

FUTURE TRENDS

Slovenia's economic policy after 2000 will be mostly determined by government negotiations for full EU membership. Slovenia will be included in the first wave of the EU enlargement, along with Hungary, Poland, the Czech Republic, and Estonia. But the government will have to speed up structural reforms in order to maintain the momentum of its drive for accession. It will probably focus initially on the long-delayed privatization of the banking sector. The 2 largest state-owned banks, Nova Ljubljanska Banka and Nova Kreditna Banka Maribor, may be sold in the second half of 2001. The government may also come under pressure from the EU to deregulate more actively. However, the principal immediate challenge facing the new government will be to take control of the budget, following some excesses in spending in 2000. The Bank of Slovenia will have no serious problems in maintaining its tight monetary policy in order to oppose concerns fueled by the rise of inflation in 2000 and the risk of a possible wage hike.

The relative strength of the global economy and particularly of the EU will boost Slovenia's growth prospects over the next several years. Its trade deficit may remain large but will imply a decrease relative to GDP, reflecting a gradual improvement in the terms of trade, as fuel prices fall and the euro recovers. The current-account deficit may still rise because of the gradual deterioration in the services balance as Slovene businesses become more dependent on foreign services, as well as in the income balance in response to its rising **debt-service** costs. This will pose no serious threats to Slovenia's economic stability and living standards.

Although Slovenia's foreign policy since independence has focused on building up relations with Western Europe, the country stands to benefit if, as seems possible, Vojislav Kostunica's victory in the Yugoslav presidential election of 2000 leads to peace in the Balkans. Slovenia's political risks will certainly decrease as the probability of a resumption of fighting in Bosnia and Herzegovina will be further reduced. Kostunica's victory also increases the chances of a final agreement being reached on the issue of Yugoslav succession. But Slovenia's main benefits are likely to come through increased trade and **equity** investments in the rest of former Yugoslavia. Many local companies, ranging from retailer Mercator to brewery Pivovarna Lasko, have invested primarily in Bosnia and Herzegovina, Croatia, and, to a much lesser extent, in Macedonia. Some Slovene companies, such as SKB Banka, have negotiated to go into Montenegro as well. Most of the deals have so far been relatively small, but, with the larger reconstruction efforts in the framework of the regional Stability Pact, new investment opportunities may occur.

DEPENDENCIES

Slovenia has no territories or colonies.

BIBLIOGRAPHY

Hafner, Danica Fink, and John R. Robbins, eds. *Making a New Nation: The Formation of Slovenia.* Hanover, New Hampshire: Dartmouth University Press, 1997.

The Economist Intelligence Unit. *Slovenia.* <http://www.eiu.com>. Accessed December 2000.

United States Central Intelligence Agency. *World Factbook 2000.* <http://www.odci.gov/cia/publications/factbook/index.html>. Accessed November 2001.

United States Department of State. *FY 2000 Country Commercial Guide: Slovenia.* Online, 2000. <http://www.state.gov>. Accessed December 2000.

—Valentin Hadjiyski

SPAIN

Kingdom of Spain
España

CAPITAL: Madrid.

MONETARY UNIT: Peseta (Pta). There are coins of 1, 5, 10, 25, 50, 100, and 500 pesetas and bills of 1,000, 2,000, 5,000, and 10,000 pesetas. Similar to other Western European countries which comply with the European Union's Economic and Monetary Union (EMU), the Spanish currency will no longer circulate after January 2002 when it will be replaced by the euro, the new unified currency of 12 European Union member states. The fixed exchange rate is 1 euro will be worth 166.667 pesetas. Since January 2000, transactions on the Spanish stock market have already been done in the new currency.

CHIEF EXPORTS: Production machinery, motor vehicles, transport equipment, foodstuffs, leather products, and minerals.

CHIEF IMPORTS: Machinery and heavy equipment, fuels, chemicals, semi-finished goods, foodstuffs, and consumer goods.

GROSS DOMESTIC PRODUCT: US$677.5 billion (purchasing power parity, 1999 est.).

BALANCE OF TRADE: **Exports:** US$112.3 billion (f.o.b., 1999 est.). **Imports:** US$137.5 billion (f.o.b., 1999 est.).

COUNTRY OVERVIEW

LOCATION AND SIZE. Spain is located in southwestern Europe. It is bordered by the Atlantic Ocean and the Bay of Biscay in the northwest and by the Mediterranean Sea in the east and the south. It has a 1,214 kilometer (754 mile) land border with Portugal in the west and a 623 kilometer (387 mile) border with France and a 63.7 kilometer (39.5 mile) border with the tiny city-state of Andorra in the northeast, characterized by the Pyrenean Mountains. In the south it has a 1.2 kilometer (.75 mile) border with Gibraltar (which legally belongs to the United Kingdom) and a 96 kilometer (59.6 mile) border with Morocco (Ceuta, Melilla). All together Spain's 504,782 square kilometer (194,896 square mile) territory, including the Balearic Islands in the Mediterranean, the Canary Islands in the Atlantic, Ceuta, and Melilla, has 1,917.8 kilometers (1,191.7 miles) of land boundaries and 4,964 kilometers (3,084.6 miles) of coastline. Spain is slightly bigger than twice the size of Oregon. Its capital, Madrid (with 2,866,850 inhabitants), is situated on the Central Plateau, and Barcelona (with 1,508,805 inhabitants), another major city, is in the northeast by the Balearic Sea (Western Mediterranean). Madrid and Barcelona are the only Spanish cities with a population over a million.

POPULATION. The population of Spain was 39,996,671 in July 2000. This compares to 37.7 million in 1981 and 38.7 million in 1984. Population growth was encouraged by the totalitarian regime of General Francisco Franco (1939–1975) through different state-sponsored programs that financially rewarded families with more than 5 children. Moreover, Spain experienced an urban boom in the 1960s and as a consequence over half the population lived in towns of at least 50,000 inhabitants by 1970. This boom was primarily a consequence of the "economic miracle" of the late 1950s and early 1960s spurred on by the stabilization plans led by the International Monetary Fund (IMF) and the Organization for Economic Co-operation and Development (OECD). There was rapid industrialization, agriculture was transformed, the industry and service sector came to dominate, and subsequently, there were major migratory shifts from rural to urban centers.

During the Spanish transition to democracy that followed Franco's death in November 1975 and after the establishment of the Spanish constitution in 1978, population growth decreased. The population growth was a meager 0.11 percent in 2000. According to the last census (1998), the population density is 201.3 per square kilometer (521.4 per square mile). Similar to other western European nations, this lack of growth can be attributed to

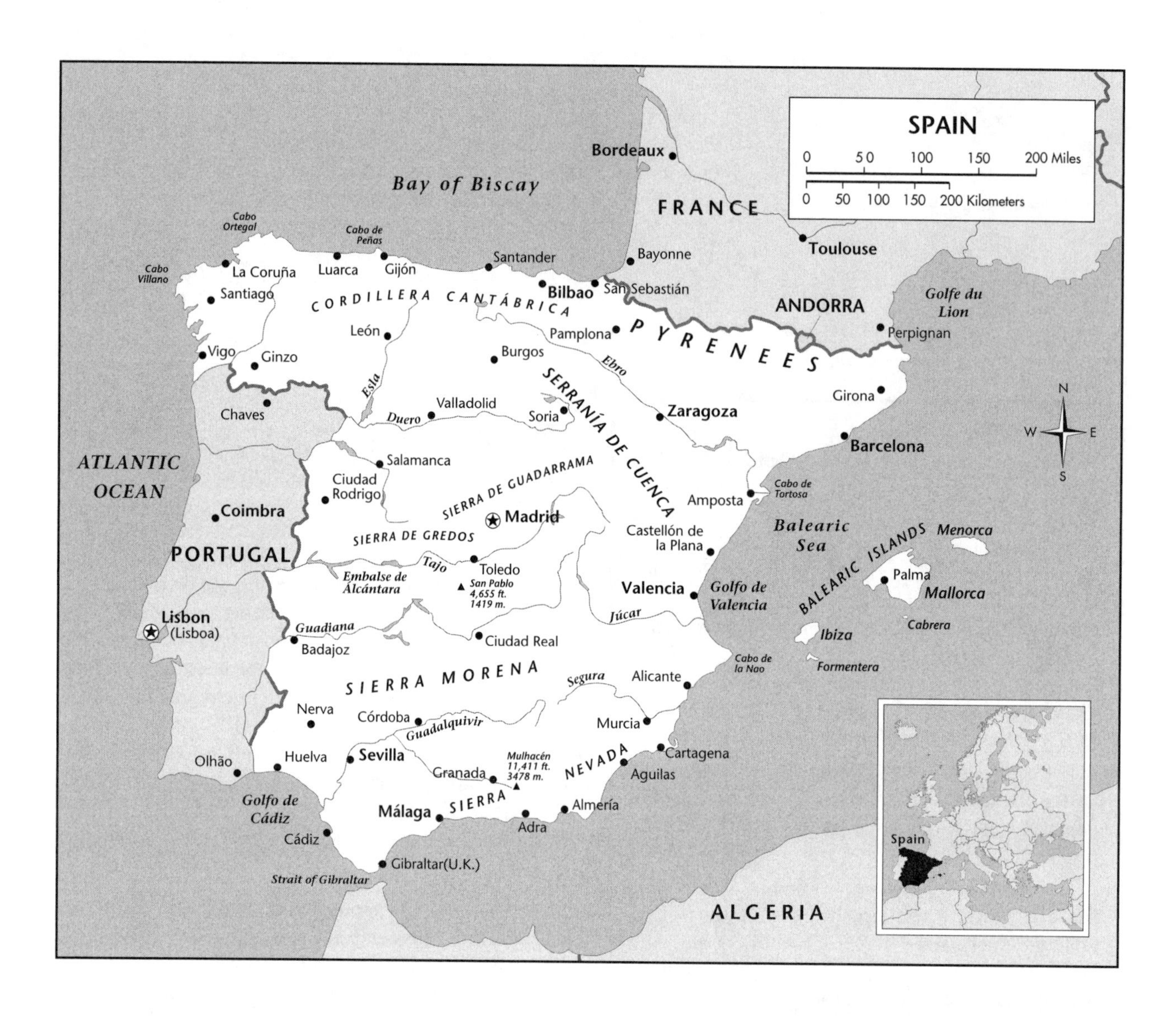

the increase in the cost of living, increasing housing prices, and the incorporation of women into the workforce. The main growth centers today are Madrid, Barcelona, Bilbao, Valencia, Sevilla, Zaragoza, Malaga, and Murcia. This reflects the importance of the Spanish "sub-cultures," in particular the importance of the Catalans and the Basques. Despite the fact that church attendance has been progressively waning, the population of Spain is predominantly Roman Catholic.

The projected population for 2010 is 39,917,000. Like other Western European nations Spain will have to face the challenge of a decrease in the proportion of active population due to the aging of the nation. Moreover, it remains to be seen how tighter **immigration** laws can be reconciled with the fact that the projections show that without the influx of foreign immigrants, the population of Spain will in fact decline much more significantly. This immigrant population, which has increasingly entered Spain since the mid-1980s, is concentrated from Northern Africa (Morocco) and South America (Colombia, El Salvador, and Argentina).

OVERVIEW OF ECONOMY

Spain's economy in the latter half of the twentieth century developed under the shadow of General Franco's authoritarian regime, which had ascended to power at the end of the Civil War in 1939. However, unlike the self-enclosed, state-dominated economies of other authoritarian governments, Franco integrated Spain's economy into the western capitalist framework through a series of **liberalization** initiatives. Begun in 1957, these initiatives included the **devaluation** of the peseta, the introduction of a single **exchange rate**, a program of monetary and fiscal restraint, and a liberalization of **price controls** and trade restrictions. As a result, Spain's economy underwent a rapid industrialization that affected every segment of society. The ascension of the industry and service sectors resulted in migratory shifts from rural to urban centers as people sought jobs, and also opened the borders to foreign interests. Foreign machinery boosted Spain's modernization process, and foreign products competed with Spain's domestic offerings. Franco also permitted investors and banks from other countries to work within Spain's borders. In 1970, a preferential agreement with the European Community further boosted trade liberalization.

It is important to note that Franco's liberal approach to the economy was not duplicated in his approach to labor issues. Franco's policies enforced hierarchy, military obedience, strong centralism, and police-state suppression of human rights which resulted in the imprisonment and execution of thousands of dissident citizens over the course of Franco's rule. Workers agitating for political freedom to complement Spain's economic freedom were quickly suppressed.

By the mid-1970s, Spain enjoyed a strong, modern capitalist economy. Spain's annual growth rate in the first half of the 1970s held steady at 6 percent, ranking it eighth in the world in terms of GDP measured at current prices and current exchange rates, according to the Organization for Economic Co-operation and Development (OECD). Only the United States, Japan, West Germany, France, the United Kingdom, Canada, and Italy placed ahead of Spain in 1975. Of all the OECD capitalist countries with strong economies, Spain was the only one without a democratic government. The existence of free-market **capitalism** without democratic legitimacy made Spain an anomaly (a deviation from the common rule) in a world where the economic transition from command to free-market economy was expected to take place only after the political transition from authoritarian to democratic rule.

King Juan Carlos, Franco's successor, inherited Spain's robust economy and fascist legacy after Franco's death in 1975. He began moving the country towards democracy shortly after ascending to power. The appointment of Adolfo Suárez as president in late 1976 was one of his first transition moves, followed by general elections the next year. Spain's newfound freedom on the political front opened up further opportunities for labor and business, including the legalization of trade unions in 1977. One of the key initiatives of this transition period was the formulation of the Moncloa Pacts that same year. The Moncloa Pacts endeavored to bring Spain fully into the **free-market system** through the moderation of wages and the elimination of favoritism between the government and specific businesses. The Pacts favored the consolidation of a market economy and recognized that business activities should be pursued within the free-market framework. They also laid the framework for a more comprehensive policy on unemployment and pension benefits, previously lacking under Franco. These political and economic reforms—which included the creation of a Constitution in 1978, as well as various other legislative agreements guaranteeing the functioning of democratic institutions—placed Spain squarely on footing with other Western European capitalist states by 1980.

The Spanish Socialist Workers Party (PSOE) came to power in 1982. Contrary to generally-accepted socialist economic policies, the Party worked to increase **privatization** and competition within Spanish markets during its 14-year rule. The time period is oftentimes referred to as the post-consolidation period of Spanish politics. Economic policies pursued by PSOE included privatization of state companies which belonged to the National Industry Institute in 1986 and the passing of legislation to end the state telecommunications **monopoly** in 1987. PSOE accomplished the latter by abolishing Telefónica's right to supply customer apparatuses and allowing other firms to run such systems. The Party also liberalized the energy sector by allowing Repsol's pipeline network to be used by competing suppliers wishing to transport gas in 1987. In late 1986, PSOE introduced the IVA (Impuestos sobre Valor Añadido) which is a 6 percent **value-added tax**; by late 1991, the party announced decreasing employers' tax payments by roughly 8 percent as a means to increase competitiveness and profits in Spanish business.

In the 1990s, the PSOE moved even further from **socialist** policy through a series of budget cuts aimed at decreasing the role of government in health and human services. In 1987 and in 1992 cuts to the pension system were made by decreasing payments to both contributory and non-contributory programs; by 1993, the average maximum allowable payment from a public pension (measured in constant pesetas) was approximately 10 percent less than the value in 1986. Based on 1992 reforms to the education service, several secondary schools with falling enrollments were closed between 1992 and 1996; the percentage of the yearly budget devoted towards education fell from almost 9 percent in 1991 to approximately 5 percent by 1996. In 1994, PSOE pursued health reform, and the closing of several urban and rural hospitals resulted in a shortage of hospital beds. The PSOE mandated that users of the National Health Service (Insalud) pay for prescription costs (referred to as the medicamentazo), as well as some aspects of non-emergency treatment.

The PSOE instituted similar cuts and **deregulation** in its approach to labor issues. In early 1993, the PSOE decreed that minimum wages would fall by almost 5 percent in real terms from the year before. In 1994, the PSOE sought almost full deregulation of the labor market by passing legislation rescinding many of the rights, benefits, and guarantees of the Workers' Statute. As a result, less expensive contract types were introduced in the labor market, rules governing salaries of all workers were modified, workers could be more easily unilaterally fired without state interference, indemnity benefits were decreased, a worker was no longer guaranteed basic working conditions such as a 40-hour work week, fewer workers became eligible for unemployment insurance benefits, and basic functional and geographical mobility rights were rescinded. This overall policy pursued by the Socialists has been followed more recently by further liberalization, deregulation, and privatization by the Partido Popular (Popular Party, or PP) that has ruled since 1996. Some neo-liberal critics suggest that more liberalization, including that of deregulating the labor market, is still required in order to make the economy competitive.

The reasons behind Spain's **liberal economic** policies are most clearly rooted in its membership in the European Union (EU). Spain joined the EU in 1986, when it was still known as the European Community (EC). While membership opened up a host of opportunities in the greater European markets, it also came with strict regulations that required significant adjustments of member countries to ensure standardization with EU's Economic and Monetary Union (EMU). The problems associated with the introduction of a common currency among the member countries (known as the euro, slated for circulation in 2002) were especially formidable. The Maastricht Treaty of 1992 established strict objectives concerning decreasing **inflation** and interest rates, as well as decreasing **budget deficits** and government debts which were necessary for EMU entrance. In effect, domestic strategies had to be pursued in order to qualify for the EMU club, ultimately allowing for the single European currency to be used in Spain. The country successfully qualified for EMU entrance in 1998. Spain also receives funding from the EU to finance varied programs, reducing the current account deficit and improving infrastructures.

Industrial production continues to be the driving force of the Spanish economy, although in recent years the service sector has gained importance. Metalworking, shipbuilding, and data-processing equipment are particularly important in the industrial sector, while automobiles remain the main export item. Private consumption, investment, increased agricultural exports, and construction are spurring growth. At the same time, virtually all service sectors—especially tourism and finance—are expanding. With regard to the latter, Spanish banks have some of the highest capitalization of all banks in Europe, thanks to a series of mergers permitted in the late 1980s and early 1990s. The 2 main banks today in Spain are BBVA (Banco Bilbao Vizcaya Argentaria) and BCHS (Banco Central Hispano Santander). Spanish mining is among the most important in Europe. Wine production—about 30 to 40 percent of which is destined to export markets—is also among the largest worldwide. Spain's abundant arable land and long coastline make agriculture, maritime transport, and fisheries all important industries. Spain possesses hardly any petroleum and only limited amounts of natural gas. This problem has been tackled with a large-scale nuclear energy program, the realization of which has, however, been delayed because of an accident in the Vandellos nuclear power plant in 1989.

Spanish industries were small in scale until the liberalization of the economy in the late 1950s and early 1960s when foreign investment and large multinational companies arrived on Spanish soil. Although almost two-thirds of the workforce is still estimated to work for what are defined as small- and medium-sized enterprises, more workers are increasingly working for large multinationals which have roots in Western Europe, including those such as VW (Germany), Fiat (Italy), and Correfour (France). Spain is an attractive location for foreign companies for 2 reasons. First, Spanish workers' salaries are some of the lowest in Western Europe, higher only than those in Greece and Portugal. From a Western European business perspective, therefore, the cheap Spanish labor market keeps costs of production low. Second, Spain's geographical location is strategic in marketing products to Southern European states such as Portugal, France, and Italy.

The Spanish government debt of US$90 billion in 1993 has declined in absolute terms since the late 1990s. The declining debt is a function of the tight economic policy pursued by Rodrigo Rato, the Minister of Economy and Finance under the center-right PP government since 1999. Rato pursued cuts to the health and welfare program. This, along with a foreseeable cut in interest rates, makes it likely that the downward trends will continue.

There are 3 main structural problems that the Spanish economy faces, despite recent liberalizing and modernizing efforts. The first is illegal immigration, which makes a particularly large impact on the agricultural labor market of southern Spain. The second problem is high unemployment compared to the rest of Europe. During the mid-1990s the official unemployment rate was at over 20 percent. Governmental reforms have sought to make the labor market more flexible for less-skilled workers, thereby decreasing the unemployment rate by almost 4 percent by 2001. Nevertheless, this is still high compared to most other western industrialized states. Many economists fear that the high rate has only contributed to the **black market** in labor, although there are no firm and credible estimates of what percentage of the economy this actually constitutes. The third main problem is terrorism that has a disturbing impact on the economy. In particular, the Basque terrorist organization, ETA, which seeks independence for the Basque region located in Spain and France, has claimed responsibility for hundreds of deaths over the last 20 years, including killings of military officials, politicians, and citizens caught in the crossfire. The terrorism has particularly stifled some business leaders' plans for future investment in the Basque region and, more generally, made citizens throughout Spain fearful and cautious.

POLITICS, GOVERNMENT, AND TAXATION

Spain has been a parliamentary democracy since the celebration of the first general election in 1977, following the death of Franco in 1975. In addition to the multiparty system, Spanish government supports the royal family of Spain, headed by King Juan Carlos. Much like the Queen of England, the King of Spain is a figurehead who holds virtually no political power, but who nevertheless serves as a symbol for Spain.

There are 2 main legislative bodies, both of which are elected usually every 4 to 5 years. The first is the lower house, officially called the Cortes. The second is the upper house, referred to as the Senado. There are 350 members in the Cortes and 208 in the Senado. The party holding the majority in the lower house controls the government. In the absence of a majority, the party with a plurality of seats will govern in minority, either in coalition government (which has yet to happen in contemporary Spain) or, as occurred in 1993 and 1996, with the legislative support (apoyo legislativo) of another party. A coalition government is made up of ministers from 2 or more parties. In a legislative support government only the plurality party has ministers in government while all of its bills are passed with the support of smaller parties in the house (who have potentially gained adoption of some of their own policies in return). The leader of the government is first chosen in a leadership selection contest of the party in which card-holding members vote. The winning party's leader is the president of the state and the leading political figure in Spain. From this perspective, the Cortes remains the more important of the 2 houses. The method of election used is the D'Hondt method of election (based on the concept of **proportional representation**, where seats attained by a political party are proportional to the votes received). At the judicial level, the highest court of the land is the Constitutional Tribunal, which is independent. Judges on the Tribunal are nominated by the president of the government and appointments must be approved by the Senado. Judges remain on the Tribunal for life.

There have been 3 main political parties in contemporary Spanish politics: the Centre Democratic Union (UCD), the Spanish Socialists (PSOE), and the Popular Party (PP). In the first 2 general elections, Adolfo Suárez's UCD won minority government. However, due to internal fighting within the party's coalition of 14 smaller parties, it disbanded in the early 1980s.

The Spanish Socialist Workers Party (PSOE) won the 1982, 1986, 1989, and 1993 elections under the leadership of Felipe Gonzalez. Though originally committed to socialist policies, the PSOE pursued policies aimed at liberalizing the Spanish economy, much to the chagrin of its working-class electoral base. The PSOE had traditionally been affiliated with one of Spain's major trade unions, the UGT, but its efforts to improve Spain's international competitiveness in preparation for full European economic integration resulted in the distancing of trade unions from the party. The PSOE closed unprofitable state corporations which were in the state **holding company** INI (The National Industry Institute), downsizing most notably the coal, iron, and steel industries. It also reduced public spending in order to tackle the budget deficit. The PSOE abandoned socialist policies in its battle against inflation and for the modernization of the industry through support of a capitalist market economy. Spain's entrance to the European Community (EC) in 1986 was seen as a triumph of PSOE's policies. Not only had PSOE tied Spain to the influence of the greater European community, it had implemented the single market policies found in the Single European Act (1986) and the domestic-level policies consistent with the Maastricht Treaty EMU criteria (that is, reduction of deficits, debts, interest, and **inflation rates**), to do so.

However, the harsh budget and social-welfare cuts, along with the erosion of labor's trust, helped unseat the PSOE in the 1996 elections. The more conservative Popular Party assumed control that year as a minority government under the leadership of Jose Maria Aznar. Although the 2 parties were polar opposites on the political spectrum (with the PSOE on the left and the PP on the right), Spain's economic policy did not shift radically with the new government. The PP continued to pursue PSOE's policies of deregulation and liberalization, with the goal of a complete privatization of state-owned enterprises. To this end, Aznar and the PP liberalized the energy sector (electricity, gas, fuels), national telecommunications, and television broadcasting. In order to ensure the success of these liberalizations, the new Free Competition Tribunal (Anti-Trust regulators) was set up and strengthened in order to restrict monopolistic practices and to increase judicial oversight of leasing, factoring, and franchising contracts. Nevertheless, observers highlight that it remains to be seen if the Tribunal will be effective.

There are some factors which stand in the way of the PP's economic goals. While new legislation generally allows for foreign investment without limitations, inflexible labor laws and restrictive legislation on intellectual property rights both still present problems in attracting new foreign business. The high unemployment rate (which hovered around 20 percent throughout the mid-to-late 1990s and is presently at 16 percent) is another major issue for the government. Hiring practices have been liberalized, but the government has criticized dismissal costs as too high and welfare benefits as too generous. The 1997 labor market reforms increased the number of temporary contracts by limiting the state's ability to interfere in business contracts. The PP government has attempted to deregulate the economy as much as possible in the belief that the less state involvement there is, and the more prevention of anti-competitive practices, the more efficient the economic system will be.

In the immediate future, the PP government hopes to eliminate the budget deficit by 2001 through the privatization of unprofitable state-owned companies. Aznar's government also encourages small enterprise by facilitating access to corporate finance and Spanish investment abroad as a way to diversify the economy. Investment in developing countries is supported by means of tied-aid credit and development assistance programs, but Spanish presence in the global economy is still modest. From this perspective, Spain attempts to promote investment and assistance in developing nations as a partner in initiatives taken along with other EU states.

The only party that has clearly distinguished itself from the PP and the PSOE is the United Left (IU). The IU is a coalition of several "left wing" parties and its main organizational party is the Spanish Communist Party (PCE). It was originally affiliated with the other main Spanish trade union, the CCOO (the Worker's Commission). Despite high expectations that the party would do well since its legalization in 1976 after 40 years of underground work, it has performed very poorly, at best gaining a little more than 10 percent of the popular vote.

Other parties which are of importance are the regional-based ones in Catalonia and the Basque Country: Convergence and Union (CiU) and Basque Nationalist Party (PNV). The CiU is a center-right and nationalist party (i.e. fights for the independence of Catalonia from Spain) that has been governing at the state (autonomous community) level in Catalonia since 1978. It came to importance at the national level after both the 1993 and 1996 general elections; although it did not participate in coalitions with the minority governing PSOE (1993) and PP (1996) governments, the CiU did offer its legislative support to both minority governments, basically allowing them to formulate policies unilaterally and easily pass them in the legislature. The PNV is a Christian democratic regionalist party seeking Basque independence. Its Basque middle-class support base has kept it in power at the regional level, either in majority position or as coalition partner, over the last 20 years. It is important to note that PNV is not associated with the terrorist organization ETA; whereas the PNV is a center-right party that uses peaceful means to pursue Basque independence, ETA is a terrorist organization (whose political wing is called Herri Batasuna, or HB) that prefers more violent and revolutionary means for independence.

Almost half of the Spanish government's tax income (46.8 percent) derives from **direct taxation**, 38.9 percent from **indirect taxation**, and 24.1 percent of which is accounted for by value-added tax (VAT). Other taxes on production constitute 14.3 percent of the tax income. Tax evasion is a major problem in Spain with the self-employed and black market workers (such as construction contractors) most often the guilty party. Because self-employed professionals (or, autonomous workers, as they are referred to in Spain, such as taxi drivers and free-lance writers) all have to make tax declarations themselves, there is no firm system by which revenue officials can verify or falsify their statements. It is therefore relatively easy to falsify tax declarations, a problem rampant in the 1990s. Although the Ministry of Economy and Finance led by Rodrigo Rato under the PP has attempted to clamp down on this practice in the last 2 years, the likelihood of evasion remains high and represents a potential drain of revenue that would otherwise be used for the **social-welfare system**.

INFRASTRUCTURE, POWER, AND COMMUNICATIONS

The most developed part of Spain's **infrastructure** is the train system, which is one of the best in Western Europe. The National Network of Spanish Railroads (Renfe) operates the best part of Spain's 15,430 kilometers (9,588 miles, 1999) of railroads which originate from Madrid as the center point. Several lines were eliminated in the 1980s after the company experienced losses. However, in 1990 an ambitious long-term investment program was initiated with the goal of introducing super-speed trains on several lines. Similar to the TGV in France, Spain's AVE started high-speed train operations between Madrid and Seville. As a result, a trip that would otherwise last approximately 5 hours by car could be completed in almost 2 hours. A similar high-speed line linking Madrid and Barcelona is presently under construction and is expected to be completed by 2003. At the regional level, the Cercanias is a rail system that links smaller communities (or suburban areas) to the closest major city, being most fully operative in major urban centers such as Madrid, Barcelona, Bilbao, and Seville. For example, Madrid Cercanias links the southern part of Madrid (Getafe, which is about 20 kilometers south of Madrid) with the north (Tres Cantos, approximately 30 kilometers north), with trains running approximately every 10–15 minutes and generally always on schedule. At the urban level, all major cities have a metro (subway) system, which allows for quick travel within the city. Madrid has the most extensive metro at present with 10 lines operating.

With regard to roads, Spain's 343,389 kilometers (213,382 miles, 1999) of paved highway are similarly ra-

Communications

Country	Newspapers	Radios	TV Sets[a]	Cable subscribers[a]	Mobile Phones[a]	Fax Machines[a]	Personal Computers[a]	Internet Hosts[b]	Internet Users[b]
	1996	1997	1998	1998	1998	1998	1998	1999	1999
Spain	100	333	506	11.8	179	17.8	144.8	76.75	4,652
United States	215	2,146	847	244.3	256	78.4	458.6	1,508.77	74,100
France	218	937	601	27.5	188	47.4	207.8	110.64	5,370
Portugal	75	304	542	59.8	309	7.0	81.3	59.40	700

[a]Data are from International Telecommunication Union, *World Telecommunication Development Report 1999* and are per 1,000 people.
[b]Data are from the Internet Software Consortium (http://www.isc.org) and are per 10,000 people.

SOURCE: World Bank. *World Development Indicators 2000.*

dial in design and 9,063 kilometers (5,632 miles) of it is expressway (1997). Most of the road network has only been constructed in the second half of the 20th century, primarily due to the efforts of the Spanish Socialists in the early 1980s. Nevertheless, despite the major **restructuring** of roads over the last 30 years, many complain that it is not sufficient for the greatly increased traffic, which is very heavy both on the highways and in cities. Examples of the former can be seen in the over-congested highways between Barcelona and Madrid and Bilbao and Madrid. Congestion is especially problematic in larger urban centers such as Madrid and Barcelona where a 20-minute journey by car usually translates into 1.5 hours during rush hour.

With respect to airports, there are 99 usable airports in Spain and 42 of them receive commercial traffic. The busiest is Madrid's Barajas airport, which has been recently expanded with the addition of the infamous "third runway" that took several years to plan and finally complete. The second busiest is Prats Airport in Barcelona, and the third is the international airport in Palma de Mallorca, which is a popular tourist spot. Both Barajas and Prats enjoy daily flights from all EU capitals as well as the United States. The major carrier operating out of them is the national airline Iberia, which up until recently was state-owned; it was fully privatized (sold to private investors) in 2001. Although Iberia's fleet seems less modern than some other European carriers, a recent major purchase of several A-320s from Airbus will help in its drive to full modernization.

Due to its long coastline, Spain depends heavily on maritime transport for the import and export of goods to both European states as well as those outside of Western Europe. Its merchant marine and fishing fleet is among the largest and most important in the world. Traffic is heavily concentrated in the ports of Bilbao, Algeciras, Tarragona, and Barcelona.

Although Spain's infrastructure is similar to the rest of Western Europe, there is nevertheless an ongoing process of upgrading roads, airports, seaports, and railroads through public, private, and joint investment. The continuation of investment is necessary primarily because the government has made commitments to improving the infrastructure through EU funding conditions. In particular, part of the Maastricht Treaty earmarked funds towards the development of Spain's infrastructure through what are referred to as Cohesion Funds. Similarly, the European Commission's White Book on Growth Competitiveness and Employment stressed infrastructure development in order to make the economy more competitive.

Almost half of Spanish electricity is based on fossil fuels (48.23 percent), 31.23 percent on nuclear power, 19.16 percent on hydroelectricity, and 1.38 percent by other means (1998). In 1998 Spain produced 179.468 billion kWh of electricity and of that consumed only 170.306 billion kWh. National shortage of petroleum and gas is compensated with nuclear energy. The main electricity companies in Spain are Endesa and Iberdrola. Both are national companies, although full liberalization of the electricity sector has taken place in principle. Nevertheless, because both major operators have approximately 80 percent of the market, foreign investors are more seriously considering the strategy of buying parts of these 2 companies in order to enter into the Spanish market (as has been the case of German electricity companies seeking to buy Iberdrola).

Spanish telecommunications facilities are generally modern and are experiencing dramatic economic growth. The main operator in Spain is Telefónica. At present, the mobile telephone business is flourishing. In 1999 there were 17.336 million main telephone lines and 8.396 million cellular phones. The popularity of mobile phones has risen with the aggressive marketing strategies of new telephone companies such as Airtel and Amena, which have sought to enter the communications market previously dominated by Telefónica. The number of Internet service providers (49 in 1999) was expected to grow beyond saturation point, after which competition is expected to root out the weaker companies. Because local calls in Spain are not free, there is a push to establish an industry-wide regulation aimed at eliminating the price of calls associated with Internet connection time. Such efforts to promote Internet use would increase the number of personal computers in Spain, which is one of the lowest in the European Community.

Almost all Spanish homes have a television (99.7 percent) and 91 percent of Spaniards watch television every day. There is a comparable decline in newspapers: 10 to 15 percent of the population frequently buys and reads newspapers, a majority of which are actually sports newspapers (such as *Marca y As*) as opposed to those predominately concerned with current events (such as *El Pais, El Mundo, Diario 16,* and *ABC*). Most Spaniards receive the daily news from the television as opposed to the paper, with radio as their second choice; almost 60 percent listen to the radio daily, where talk shows are the leading radio programs. Until 1990 the Spanish only had the 2 channels provided by the state-run Television Española (TVE) and regional stations run by the autonomous governments (such as Telemadrid for the community of Madrid). Commercial television was authorized in 1989 and broadcasting fully liberalized in 1998. As a result, there are 4 main channels that can be freely viewed at the national level: La 1 (the main state station from RTE), La 2 (the second state channel which is dedicated to more cultural programming), Antena 3, and Telecinco. There are also 6 regional and over 75 local stations. TVE still runs large budget deficits and is accused by the opposition of favoring the government party in its news coverage. It has recently been absorbed into the state holding company, SEPI, in order to deal with its financial problems and help in its management. La 2 has the highest acclaimed nightly newscast. Two additional channels, Canal Plus and Via Digital, offer newly released movies as well as some major sporting events for a monthly fee by cable and satellite. Yet, only 10 percent of Spanish homes have either satellite or cable television. By 2010, it is estimated that all Spaniards should have access to Terrestrial Digital TV, and significant growth is predicted, especially for cable television.

ECONOMIC SECTORS

Over a 25 year span, the sector evolution of Spain's economy is similar to that of western liberal democratic states. Agriculture production has declined significantly (from contributing 16.7 percent of the GDP in 1974 to 3.2 percent in 1999), service has expanded (from 48.8 percent in 1974 to 63.2 percent in 1999), and industry has remained somewhat constant (hovering around 34 percent). Although these overall trends are similar to those found in western industrialized states, industrial production is comparatively higher in Spain.

Spain

GDP–COMPOSITION BY SECTOR–1998 est.

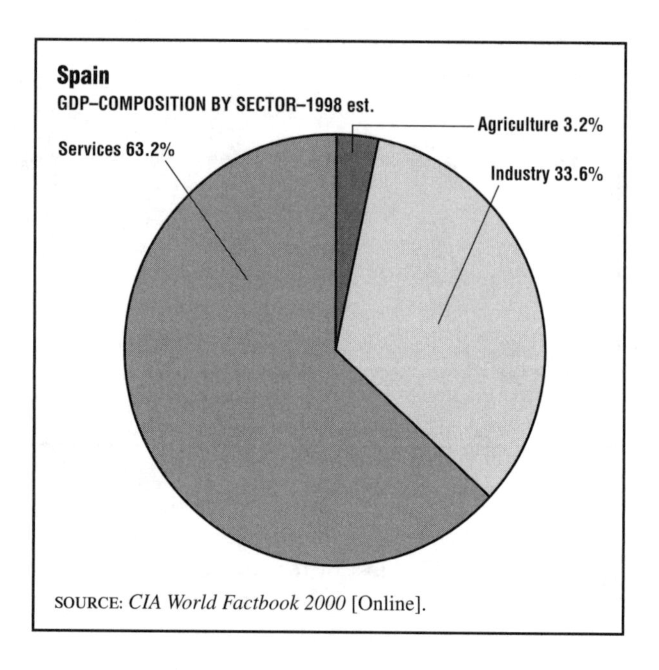

SOURCE: *CIA World Factbook 2000* [Online].

The decline of agriculture is rooted in several different factors. Spain aligned itself with the Common Agriculture Policy (CAP) as part of its membership with the EU, which placed limits on Spanish agricultural production. A drought in the 1990s—particularly in the South—further limited the growth of the industry. These factors, combined with the modernization of farming techniques, caused a significant drop-off in the number of agricultural laborers. In 2000 much-needed rainfall increased agricultural output but also lowered prices as the larger food supply lowered demand. The outlook for Spanish agriculture is not entirely grim, however. Spain's position as the most varied agricultural producer in the EU promises the sector increased growth in the greater European market.

The industry sector constitutes a large part of the GDP due to the strength of mining, manufacturing, and metalworking, which have been important to the economy since the 1960s. At present, Spanish industry has been recovering from the **recession** of the early 1990s, largely due to growth in the metalworking sector, which includes data-processing equipment and other transportation equipment. While Spain has continued involvement in traditional industries such as mining, it has also focused more on capital-intensive industries such as high technological equipment, which are also attractive for foreign investors.

The service sector is expanding in almost all areas, particularly finance, tourism, and telecommunications. Spanish banks, which constitute some of the largest and most powerful in Europe, have a dual-pronged strategy to enter into other sectors of the economy (such as telecoms) and to expand into foreign markets in both the EU

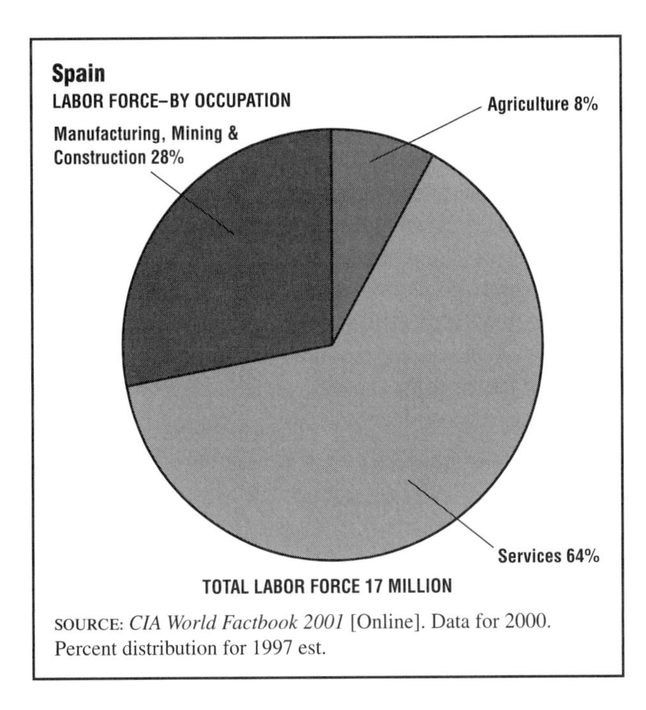

SOURCE: *CIA World Factbook 2001* [Online]. Data for 2000. Percent distribution for 1997 est.

and South America. Tourism—particularly in both Catalonia as well as the South of Spain—increasingly attracts tourists from the EU as travel costs to Spain decrease. The telecom market has also seen great expansion, especially with the onset of liberalizing legislation in the sector and the complementary popularity of mobile phones.

AGRICULTURE

Spanish agriculture has traditionally been most affected by the level of rainfall, since drought is always a threat. However, in recent years a much more decisive factor has been the Spanish membership in the EC/EU. While encouraging production in some agricultural sectors, the EU has discouraged it in others. Small farms have been closed down, with grape growers and dairy farmers the hardest hit. In 1999 a EU reform of the Common Agricultural Policy was approved as part of the "Agenda2000." The reform mandated that at least 10 percent of land be set aside until 2006 in order to avoid overproduction. In spite of this limitation, the abundance of Spain's agricultural resources guarantees overall growth.

LIVESTOCK, DAIRY, AND POULTRY. This sector has traditionally been financially the most important sector, accounting for 39 percent of overall agricultural output in 1999. However, the sector has suffered from increased competition from other EU countries, and the "Agenda2000" will gradually cut the beef support prices by 20 percent. Although economists predicted that livestock production would increase slightly in 2000 with improved pasture conditions and more rain, outbreaks of "mad cow disease" prevented such increase. BSE (bovine spongiform encephalopathy), which is also referred to as "mad cow disease," is a highly contagious, lethal disease of the central nervous system in cattle. There have been several cases, particularly in Britain in the 1990s, of people who have died after eating meat from cows infected with BSE. In Spain, the first cases of mad cow disease were detected in September 2000 in Galicia, with subsequent cases arising in other provinces in Spain. The cases in Spain can be traced back to Britain; the same feed that was given to cows that developed BSE in the UK was transported and used in other western European farms. Although there have been no human fatalities reported in Spain as a result of the contamination, consumer confidence in beef plummeted. By February 2001, consumption of beef had fallen by an estimated 80 percent. More consumers turned to other meats, including fish, pork, poultry, and lamb, in spite of the subsequent rise in prices. The price of beef, in the meantime, continues to slide, which leaves the future of Spain's beef industry in doubt.

HORTICULTURAL CROPS. This sector—which includes citrus, deciduous fruit, olives and olive oil, nuts, wine, and vegetables—is gaining importance to the point that its value of production now equals that of livestock, dairy, and poultry at 39 percent. This sector has greatly benefitted from access to EU markets and accounts for 70 percent of overall agricultural exports. Both Spanish olive oil and wine production were initially subject to the tough restrictions imposed by the Common Agriculture Policy during the 1990s. However, recent policy changes have allowed for Spain's quota for olive oil production to reflect the actual production capacity. Spain's vineyards have also benefitted from policy changes; previous programs which uprooted vineyards are now replaced with new programs that concentrate on restructuring vineyards to make the Spanish wine industry more competitive. Spain produces some of the best red wines in world, with the most famous being those from the Rioja region. More than 30 percent of such wines are destined to the EU, North American, and Latin American markets. Other regions producing fine wines include Catalonia, Ribera del Duero, Navarra, and La Mancha. These wines are generally made from the Tempranillo variety of grapes and offer a distinct taste to those from France, for example, which use the Merlot variety.

FIELD CROPS. This sector includes grain, tobacco, cotton, forage, sugar beets, and oil seeds. It covers a larger area than the horticultural crops, but accounted for only 15 percent of the total value of production in 1999. The most important sector of field crops is cereals, especially wheat and barley. However, Spanish cereal production has suffered from competition from the EU, and, under the "Agenda2000," support prices for all grains will be reduced by 15 percent. The most plentifully produced field crop is alfalfa, used for animal fodder. The "Agenda2000" will also reduce area payments for oilseeds to the same level with grains, which is expected to reduce the production of the sunflower seed crop significantly.

FISHING. Even though the total catch declined in the 1980s, the fishing industry is still important in Spain. The main fishing ports are Vigo and La Coruna in the Northwest. Despite Spain's vast fishing waters, Spanish fishermen have several times been arrested for fishing illegally in Canadian and Moroccan waters. The most visible conflict of late has been the so-called "Turbot War" with Canada in 1995 when Canadian authorities fired on Spanish fisherman for trespassing in Canadian waters. Legal experts argue that the Canadian government clearly violated international law by firing upon a vessel which was, in fact, in international waters. Although there was a peaceful resolution to the conflict, the incident highlights concerns voiced by other countries in the past, such as Ireland and Morocco, about Spanish fishermen.

INDUSTRY

Ever since liberalization became a goal in the late 1950s, Spanish industry has been growing and becoming more diversified. This is particularly the case in mining, manufacturing, and metalworking. As a result, companies have grown bigger, and foreign investment has become more significant.

MINING. Spain has one of Europe's most important and diversified mining sectors. Over half the production is coal, while other major products are iron, pyrites, copper, lead, zinc, tungsten, uranium, mercury, potash, and chloride. Despite its strength, Spanish mining is not sufficient to satisfy domestic demand and, therefore, Spain continues to be a large-scale importer of minerals. Due to competition from other EU countries, the Spanish mining industry has been subject to restructuring and closures, especially in the Asturian coal industry, which has led to miners' protests. The mining sector remains stagnant but is expected to recover when Spain increases its gold production.

METALWORKING. The iron, steel, and shipbuilding of Asturias and the Basque Country experienced downsizing in the 1980s. However, the sector has been recovering strongly since 1996, thanks to increased production in shipbuilding, data-processing equipment, and transportation equipment.

MANUFACTURING. In the automobile industry, Spain's top exporters—Opel, SEAT, Volkswagen, Citroen, and Renault—set records in 1996 and 1999. The fact that all car producers in Spain are foreign multinationals is reflective of their strength in the economy. The German car company Volkswagen, for example, actually received large amounts of **subsidies** from the Spanish governments of the 1980s and 1990s to take over the (then) only native Spanish car manufacturer, SEAT.

In other manufacturing activities, however, foreign multinationals play less of a role. For example, the cotton, woollen textiles, and clothing industries have maintained their importance in the economy. Predominantly located in the Catalan area since the 19th century, they are characterized as being small- and medium-sized enterprises that are family-owned. Spain also manufactures toys, shoes, electrical appliances (televisions, refrigerators, and washing machines), and foodstuffs. Toys and shoes, in particular, have a reputation for high quality and constitute a main export for the manufacturing sector.

SERVICES

TOURISM. Spain overtook the United States recently as the world's second most important tourist resort. The tourist industry employs 12.5 percent of the Spanish **workforce** and accounts for 10 percent of GDP, with a 9 percent annual growth rate. The success of the industry stems from a variety of factors. It generally costs less to travel and vacation in Spain compared to many places in the world. Spain's already high-quality resorts are improving as aging accommodations are restored. The warm weather is another draw for tourists, especially in southern Spain. The main tourist areas are Mallorca, the Canary Islands, and the Costa Brava. The total number of tourists in 1999 was 58,588,944, and the total number of available accommodations in the country was 1,282,013. This booming industry's role in the Spanish economy does have a downside, however; some analysts worry that the seasonal nature of the tourist industry may add to the precariousness of the Spanish labor market.

FINANCIAL SERVICES. The largest Spanish bank is the BBVA (Banco Bilbao Vizcaya Argentaria), and the second largest is the BSCH (Banco Santander Central Hispano), both the fruit of mergers in 1999. BBVA is the product of the merger of the Banco de Bilbao (founded in 1857), Banco de Vizcaya (1901), and Argentaria (1983); the BSCH comes from the merger of Banco de Santander (1857), Banco Hispano-Americano (1900), and Banco Central (1919). Other important banks in Spain include Banco Urquijo, the Grupo March, la Caixa, and Caja de Madrid. The concentration of native Spanish banks in the sector stems from the *Ley de Ordenación Bancaria* of 1921 that disallowed foreign banks from operating in Spain for several years. Although foreign banks were allowed to enter into Spain in the early 1960s, the stronghold obtained by main Spanish players effectively prevented outside competition. In fact, when many of the foreign banks entered the Spanish market in the late 1960s and early 1970s—such as Deutsche Bank, Barclays, and Manufacturer's Hanover Trust—they did so only with the cooperation of big Spanish financial players such as Banco Bilbao, Vizcaya, and Santander. Cooperation included the sharing of staff with members of Spanish financial institutions—especially important given the fact that many foreigners cannot speak Spanish. Despite liberalization of the financial sector, Spanish financial capital maintained its dominance.

Today, Spain's financial services are diversified and fully integrated in the international financial markets. The EU single market in banking and insurance services has intensified competition, brought down interest rates, and encouraged mergers. Spanish banks are well capitalized. Beyond the main players mentioned above (BBVA, BSCH), there are 103 domestic private banks—mostly headquartered in Madrid—and 53 foreign ones—34 of which are headquartered in the EU. There are also 50 confederated savings banks and 12 regional savings bank federations that are, in principle, non-profit making. They concentrate on private savings and loans and financing public and private projects. To this day, Spanish investment and brokerage entities have increased in number and in the volume of their investments. The credit market is structured around private banks.

TELECOMMUNICATIONS. The sector is registering spectacular increases. The main operator of telecommunications is Telefónica, but, given recent liberalization initiatives, other operators such as Airtel and Amena have gained significant market strength in a short period of time. The mobile telephone market increased from 14 million to 19 million users during the first half of 1999. Growth is also expected in the cable television sector, even though only 10 percent of the population subscribes to these services. Although the number of PCs per household is low in Spain compared to other industrialized states, it is projected that falling PC prices and cuts to prices on local calls will allow for PC consumption to triple within 5 years.

AVIATION. The EU liberalized the aviation sector due to increased demand for air transport services. As a result, many new local airlines are in competition with the main national airline, Iberia. Two major new competitors, Spanair and Air Europa, have daily flights between major cities in Spain as well as the rest of Continental Europe and the United Kingdom.

INTERNATIONAL TRADE

The EU accounts for 72 percent of Spain's exports and 67 percent of imports, the most important trading partners being France and Germany (1998). The share of EU states involved in Spanish trade has grown in importance since Spain joined the EC/EU in 1986, reflective of the goals of the EC's Single European Act of 1986, which stressed completion of the internal market and decreasing trade barriers between member states. Spanish trade with Latin America (7 percent of exports, 4 percent of imports) is explainable through the historical connections between the countries. Imports from OPEC (5 percent) reflect Spain's dependence on imported petroleum. Fifty years ago Spain exported agricultural products and minerals and imported industrial goods. The fact that the exports today are dominated by **consumer goods** and imports by machinery and equipment, fuels, chemicals, and semi-finished goods reveals how fundamentally the pattern has changed.

Trade (expressed in billions of US$): Spain

	Exports	Imports
1975	7.690	16.265
1980	20.720	34.078
1985	24.247	29.963
1990	55.642	87.715
1995	91.716	115.019
1998	109.228	133.149

SOURCE: International Monetary Fund. *International Financial Statistics Yearbook 1999.*

The Spanish **balance of trade** has long been negative; despite rapid growth in trade in the 1980s, imports continue to outweigh exports. Due to increased petroleum prices, the weakness of the Euro, and loss of competitiveness, the Spanish trade deficit increased significantly in 1999. The dependence on imported petroleum makes Spain vulnerable to developments in the Middle East.

MONEY

Since the early 1990s, the Central Bank of Spain has pursued a **monetary policy** independent from the national government, similar to most other western European states. However, Spain's membership in the Economic and Monetary Union (EMU) means its rates are set by the European Central Bank (ECB). While submission to the ECB is required of all EMU states, some have argued that such a move detracts from the state's right to pursue autonomous monetary policy. Indeed, implicit in being an EMU state is that domestic-level actors cannot easily pursue macro-economic stabilization initiatives as they see fit. For example, as was the case during the 1980s for states that belonged to the EMS/ERM (the European Monetary System/**Exchange Rate Mechanism**, which was a fixed but adjustable parameter within which European currencies could fluctuate), states could not devalue their currency in order to boost their economies by promoting export-led growth. When the ECB sets long-term interest rates for all the EMU countries, states lose the ability to modify those rates in such

Exchange rates: Spain

euros per US$1	
Jan 2001	1.0659
2000	1.0854
1999	0.9386
1998	149.40
1997	146.41
1996	126.66

Note: Rates prior to 1999 are in pesetas per US$.

SOURCE: CIA *World Factbook 2001* [ONLINE].

GDP per Capita (US$)

Country	1975	1980	1985	1990	1998
Spain	10,040	10,512	10,943	13,481	15,644
United States	19,364	21,529	23,200	25,363	29,683
France	18,730	21,374	22,510	25,624	27,975
Portugal	6,024	7,193	7,334	9,696	11,672

SOURCE: United Nations. *Human Development Report 2000; Trends in human development and per capita income.*

a way as to control inflation. Spain's traditionally high inflation in comparison with the rest of western Europe makes this a special concern for the country. Certainly, based on the attempt to achieve convergence criteria which stressed that inflation rates be reduced, in 1999 inflation was low at 2.3 percent. Although it was expected to decrease to 2.0 percent in 2000, structural problems in the past, such as wage-push inflation that is partly driven by union demands for higher wages, may result in price increases in the next few years. In such a scenario, the country's powerlessness in controlling interest rates may make it difficult to counter the rise.

Between 1995 and 1999 the peseta weakened from 124.69 pesetas to US$1 down to 149.40 pesetas to US$1. Since 1 January 1999 the exchange rate of the peseta is fixed to the euro, which has been decreasing in value since it was launched. This is same for all currencies of the EU (save most especially the British Pound Sterling) that are tied to the euro. Even though the fall in the peseta/Euro may boost the export market to non-euro countries, it will be offset with increase in import prices (of goods from outside EMU states) and inflationary tendencies are thus likely to follow. In such a scenario, pressure to increase long-term interest rates will likely ensue.

There are 4 stock exchanges in the Spanish stock market; the major ones are in Madrid (Bolsa de Madrid, The Madrid Stock Exchange) and Barcelona (Bolsa de Barcelona, The Barcelona Stock Exchange). Major stocks are listed in what is referred to as the Ibex-35, and the most heavily traded recently include Telefónica, Terra, Endesa, and Iberdrola. Due to recent reforms, the Spanish stock markets have become safer and more transparent, and their ways of operating and types of financial assets more varied.

POVERTY AND WEALTH

Until the 1950s there was only a small industrial working class in Catalonia and the Basque Country, a traditional agricultural working class in the rest of the country, and a small middle class. Industrialization came relatively late to Spain and was concentrated in few areas. The social structure was polarized between a small upper class, consisting fundamentally of large landowners (latifundia) and a large rural proletariat (jornaleros). In the South agricultural day laborers were employed on a seasonal basis by the large landowners; in the North ownership was more evenly distributed and there were many small family farms. In 1957 1 percent of the population belonged to the upper class, 38.8 percent to the middle class, and 60.2 percent to the lower class.

By 1988 the figures were 4.8 percent, 59.4 percent, and 32.9 percent, respectively. The growth of the middle class had begun by 1970. The numbers of agricultural workers fell, eroding the power of the large landowners and the rural bourgeoisie and diminishing the problem of the rural workers' social conditions. Today, professional, technical, managerial, and administrative groups have increased significantly as levels of education and qualifications have improved. The service sector has grown while manufacturing and construction declined. The urbanization, modernization, and economic development of the country can be seen in the social structure of the 1990s.

Earnings differential have increased in recent years. In 1981 a blue-collar worker in manufacturing or service earned 67.7 percent of a white-collar worker's salary in

Distribution of Income or Consumption by Percentage Share: Spain

Lowest 10%	2.8
Lowest 20%	7.5
Second 20%	12.6
Third 20%	17.0
Fourth 20%	22.6
Highest 20%	40.3
Highest 10%	25.2

Survey year: 1990

Note: This information refers to income shares by percentiles of the population and is ranked by per capita income.

SOURCE: *2000 World Development Indicators* [CD-ROM].

Household Consumption in PPP Terms

Country	All food	Clothing and footwear	Fuel and power[a]	Health care[b]	Education[b]	Transport & Communications	Other
Spain	33	12	11	3	5	8	28
United States	13	9	9	4	6	8	51
France	22	7	9	3	8	12	40
Portugal	29	8	7	2	19	6	29

Data represent percentage of consumption in PPP terms.
[a]Excludes energy used for transport.
[b]Includes government and private expenditures.

SOURCE: World Bank. *World Development Indicators 2000.*

the same sector; in 1992 the figure was only 62.5 percent. The earnings ratio between an unskilled laborer and a university graduate in 1988 was 100 to 371. In 1991 the poorer half of the households received 27.42 percent of total income and the richer half 72.58 percent.

The standards of living have risen significantly due to the improvement of the education, health, and other social welfare programs over the last 25 years. Education is compulsory until the age of 16, and university education is no longer the privilege of a small elite; by 1990 almost half the university students had parents with only elementary education. Twenty-nine of the 33 universities are public and access is merit-based. In cases where the regional government has responsibility over education, regional languages such as Catalan and Basque are obligatory. There is a free, universal health-care service for all citizens. There are both contributory and non-contributory unemployment benefits and pension provisions. It should be noted, though, that in the drive to decrease public spending, it is harder to qualify for unemployment benefits (for example, those holding temporary contracts are not eligible for unemployment payments). The amount given to those receiving non-contributory pensions (such as what is called the SOVI) received almost 10 percent less in real terms than 5 years ago. Vulnerable groups—the disabled, elderly, abandoned children, single mothers, battered wives, families without income, and the homeless—receive special attention through different state-sponsored funding programs. Nevertheless, these services were only properly organized in the 1980s and the 1990s and Spain still spends a smaller share of the GDP on them than the EU average. Interestingly, Spain has one of the highest life expectancies in the world. While some have argued that this is a benefit of the social welfare system that attempts to universally cover all, others argue that long life expectancy is a consequence of the generally healthier Mediterranean diet, characterized by olive oil, fruits, vegetables, and legumes.

Despite the apparent strength of the policies of redistribution (such as education, health, and other social welfare programs), regional differences in wealth persist. The 3 richest autonomous communities are Madrid, Barcelona, and the Basque Country, which are representative of the financial and industrial strongholds of the country. The poorer regions in the country remain in the North and South, where the larger part of the economy remains agriculturally-based. These include Galicia, Castilla la Mancha, and Extremadura.

WORKING CONDITIONS

With regard to working conditions, the Spanish government's emphasis is on increasing flexibility, deregulation, and training programs. Compared to American standards, some say that the labor law is inflexible and discourages new hiring. Also, many consider the severance payments to be very high. Compared to the rest of the EU, the Spanish labor market is one of the lowest-paying and precarious. More than 35 percent of the workforce is actually on temporary contracts which are generally low-paying and can be canceled unilaterally any time by employers.

The government pursued 2 major Labor Market Reforms to achieve this flexibility. The first was in 1994 under the socialists and the second in 1997 by the Popular Party. Both reforms rescinded the rights and guarantees enjoyed by workers as originally framed within the Workers' Statute (ET) of the early 1980s. The reforms to the ET included allowing temporary contracts, opening space for private companies (agencies) to place temporary workers, introducing low-paying apprenticeship contracts, scrapping concepts such as extra pay for overtime work or a 40-hour work week, decreasing severance costs, and allowing employers to move workers between different functions and geographic locations.

The government pursued these reforms with the participation of the main business organization, CEOE (Confederación Española de Organizaciones Empresariales, the Spanish Employers Organization), which reflects the increasingly marginalized role of trade unions. Trade unions of the early 1980s actively participated in the formulation of the Workers' Statute. Originally the UGT was affiliated with the socialists and CCOO to the communists, but both unions distanced themselves from the parties. Although they have been cooperating with each other more closely since, membership in both unions is low (estimated to be around 15 percent of active workers) and their role in collective bargaining has diminished, especially since the labor market reforms of the 1990s. As a result unions are hampered by organizational and financial weakness, which reduces their ability to negotiate.

With unemployment at 16 percent today, it is one of the highest in the industrialized world. It is therefore not surprising that this issue continues to dominate the government agenda. Unemployment is highest in Andalucia, Extremadura, Ceuta, and Melilla. Catalonia and Madrid enjoy the highest employment figures. The reasons behind the high unemployment rate are the decline in agricultural employment, inadequate skills of the labor force, small companies' difficulties in an increasingly competitive environment, and previously high inflation. Some economists estimate that the black market actually employs some 10 percent of the active population, mostly younger workers with few qualifications to enter the regular labor market.

The presence of women in the Spanish labor market is below European average even after increases in the 1980s and the 1990s. In rural areas women always participated in agricultural work and in urban context they are concentrated in manufacturing (textiles, leather, footwear) and services (retailing, hotels, restaurants, catering, public administration, education, health services, domestic and personal services). The presence of married and older women in the labor market is increasing, and legislation to prevent discrimination is among the most progressive in western Europe. Since 1989 women are offered 16 weeks paid maternity leave. Despite legislation, inequalities remain; women's unemployment in 1996 was 30.4 percent and women's work contracts tend to be either part-time or temporary. An average woman earns 72 percent of the average man, and women are underrepresented in the higher status occupations. A significant exception to this trend remains the fact that many scientists in Spain, especially in natural science, are female. The state's Council for Scientific Investigation has a slight female majority.

COUNTRY HISTORY AND ECONOMIC DEVELOPMENT

1492. On 12 October, Christopher Columbus discovers America.

1516. Carlos I of Spain and V of Germany assumes the Spanish Crown, following the death of Fernando of Aragon. Carlos I effectively unites the Spanish kingdoms of Castilla and Aragon, as well as the European and Italian dominions of the Habsburgs.

1700–14. The War of the Spanish Succession breaks out in 1700 (involving France, England and Austria) and ends in 1714. The French victors place Felipe V, who is the grandson of Louis XIV, as king of Spain.

1808–13. The War of Independence—Spanish citizens rise against French domination (1808) and help defeat Napoleon.

1898. Spain loses the last of its remaining overseas colonies in Cuba, Puerto Rico, and the Philippines. This officially marks the end of the Spanish empire.

1931–36. Second Republic. After the dictatorship of Primo de Rivera in the 1920s, the Second Republic is established in 1931. The Second Republic provided a democratic and stable system of governance whereby there were free elections (where women had the right to vote as well) and guaranteed rights and freedoms for all citizens for the first time in Spanish history.

1936–39. Civil War between the Republicans (backed by the workers, socialists, and communists), and the Nationalists (led by General Francisco Franco, with the support of economic elites, Hitler, and Mussolini). Upon victory, General Francisco Franco leads Spain's government as a fascist dictator until his death in 1975.

1957–59. Stabilization Plan is proposed by the OECD and the IMF. Economy is liberalized and foreign investment enters, opening up Spain to international markets in order to save the state's economy from collapse after the policy of self-sufficiency. Followed by economic boom in 1960s and 1970s, known as the "economic miracle."

1975. King Juan Carlos assumes control in November, after Franco's death.

1977–82. First General Elections held (1977), won by UCD (Center Democratic Union); signing of Moncloa Pacts which aim to moderate wages, and strengthen the social welfare system (1977). UCD second victory in 1979.

1978. Democratic constitution, which guarantees rights and freedoms and basic liberal democratic principles for Spain, is approved by referendum.

1982–96. Socialist Party in power in Spain for 14 consecutive years. The first Socialist victory was one of the largest majorities in contemporary western Europe (1982); Spain joins NATO (1986). Despite strengthening the **welfare state**, Spanish Socialists strongly pursue neo-liberal economic policies, including privatization, deregulation, and labor market reform, especially between 1986–1996.

1986. Spain joins the European Community. Adoption of Single European Act solidifies Spanish commitment to the European Single Market Program (which highlights free movement of goods, persons, capital, and services). Unprecedented economic growth in Spain yields an annual increase in GDP of over 4 percent, 1986–1991.

1992. Spain agrees to Maastricht Treaty, which outlines criteria to be achieved by late 1990 for those EU states wanting to join the European single currency (Economic and Monetary Union, EMU). Spain therefore commits itself to deficit and debt reduction. Heavy cuts to the health, education, and pension systems ensue.

1996-PRESENT. Popular Party (Christian Democrats) comes to power for the first time in contemporary Spain. Commitment to deficit and debt reduction as well as controlling interest and inflation rates is reinforced. Second PP election victory, March 2000.

1999. Spain qualifies for EMU.

FUTURE TRENDS

Spain is likely to experience further liberalization of markets and privatization in the sectors of telecommunications, defense, energy, transportation, and aerospace. In order to attract more foreign investors, the government will likely institute more labor law reform with the aim of increasing the flexibility of the labor market. Such reforms would result in lower salaries and more precarious forms of employment, which may also have negative social repercussions. Given increased economic and monetary integration in the European Union, it is likely that Spain will benefit in terms of its growth. In fact, economists project growth in telecommunication equipment, service markets, environmental services, and equipment and agriculture. Moreover, linguistic and historical links to Central and South America could increase the influence of Spanish firms in these geographical areas, with reciprocal investment by Latin American business leaders in Spain. Spanish representatives in the European Commission will play a key role in negotiating trade agreements between the EU and Latin America.

There are 3 main challenges that Spain faces in the next decade: 2 are at the domestic level and one at the EU level. First, illegal immigration and the high unemployment rate will continue to offer serious problems. Illegal immigration from Northern Africa to the South of Spain has become an increased focus of attention, especially considering that many die in their attempt to come to Spain. This, coupled with the fact that many illegal immigrants work in the black market, will continue to increase social tensions in a country that already has one of the highest unemployment rates in the industrialized world.

The second main challenge deals with eradicating the Basque terrorist group ETA. The group's activities are not contained to the Basque Country, which means that businesses in targeted metropolitan areas like Madrid, Seville, and Barcelona, are significantly and negatively affected. The threat of terrorist activity may likewise discourage foreign investors from locating their business in Spain. Although the Interior Ministry has made recent attempts to crack-down on ETA's activities, the terrorists' strong infrastructure and continued activities make it doubtful that an indefinite ceasefire is on the horizon.

The third main challenge facing Spain relates to its compliance with future EU initiatives. Spain has generally accepted EU deregulatory policies (that is, policies which attempt to discourage barriers to trade and prevent anti-competitive practices in the free-market) and economic and monetary policies (that is, Economic and Monetary Union and the Single Currency). However, EU policies which attempt to replace national legislation in areas such as the environment may continue to offer challenges. Further, policies which attempt to increase the size of the Union may be met with caution by Spain; enlargement may mean a slow down in structural funds flowing into Spain and movement of foreign investors presently in Spain to other low-paying, better educated, labor markets in Eastern Europe. Notwithstanding these potential challenges, Spain will continue to be one of the engines behind deeper integration and, along with Germany and France, will attempt to ensure that the EU remains an important player in the world economy.

DEPENDENCIES

Spain has no territories or colonies.

BIBLIOGRAPHY

Chari, R. "The March 2000 Spanish Election: A 'Critical Election'?" *West European Politics,* Vol. 23, No. 3, July 2000.

Heywood, P. *The Government and Politics of Spain. Comparative Government and Politics Series*, edited by V. Wright. Oxford: Oxford University Press, 1995.

Holman, O. *Integrating Southern Europe: EC Expansion and the Transnationalization of Spain.* London: Routledge, 1996.

Instituto Nacional de Estadística (INE) *Anuario de Estadística.* Madrid: INE, 1996–2000.

Lawlor, Teresa, and Mike Rigby. *Contemporary Spain.* New York, 1998.

Share, D. *The Making of Spanish Democracy.* New York: Praeger, 1986.

U.S. Central Intelligence Agency. *World Factbook 2000.* <http://www.odci.gov/cia/publications/factbook/index.html>. Accessed August 2001.

U.S. Department of the State. *FY 2001 Country Commercial Guide: Spain.* <http://www.state.gov/www/about_state/business/com_guides/index.html>. Accessed August 2001.

—Raj S. Chari and Suvi Iltanen

SWEDEN

Kingdom of Sweden
Konungariket Sverige

CAPITAL: Stockholm.

MONETARY UNIT: Swedish krona (SKr, plural is kronor). One krona is comprised of 100 öre. There are coins of 50 öre and 1, 5, and 10 kronor, and notes of 20, 50, 100, 500, 1,000, and 10,000 kronor.

CHIEF EXPORTS: Machinery, motor vehicles, electronics, paper products, pulp and wood, iron and steel products, and chemicals.

CHIEF IMPORTS: Machinery, petroleum and petroleum products, chemicals, motor vehicles, iron and steel, foodstuffs, and clothing.

GROSS DOMESTIC PRODUCT: US$184 billion (1999 est.).

BALANCE OF TRADE: Exports: US$85.7 billion (1999). **Imports:** US$67.9 billion (1999).

COUNTRY OVERVIEW

LOCATION AND SIZE. Located in northern Europe, in the eastern part of the Scandinavian peninsula, Sweden is bordered on the west and northwest by Norway, on the northeast by Finland, on the east by the Baltic Sea and its arm, the Gulf of Bothnia, On the southwest, Sweden is separated from Denmark by the Skagerrak, Kattegat, and Ôresund straits that connect the Baltic and the North Seas. The fourth largest country in Europe, Sweden has an area of 449,964 square kilometers (173,731 square miles), slightly larger than California. The area also includes 39,030 square kilometers (15,070 square miles) of inland water pools, mostly lakes. The capital city of Stockholm is situated in the southeast, on waterways and islands between Lake Malaren and the Baltic Sea. Other major cities include Göteborg in the southwest; Malmö in the south, and Uppsala, Linköping, Ôrebro, and Norrköping in the southeast.

POPULATION. The population of Sweden was estimated at 8,873,052 in July 2000 with an annual growth rate of 0.02 percent. The **immigration** rate is 0.86 per 1,000 population. Population density is one of the lowest in Europe, with about 20 persons per square kilometer (52 per square mile). Due to the cold northern climate, the great majority of the population lives in the south, especially in the central lowlands and the coastal areas. Large parts of the north and the mountains are very sparsely inhabited. Some 83 percent of Sweden's population is urban. The population, as in most of Europe, is aging, and with a high life expectancy of 79.58 years at birth (76.95 for men and 82.37 for women). The median age increased to 41 years in 1999 from 38.4 five years earlier. Some 17.2 percent of the population is 14 years old and younger, and 18.7 percent are 65 or older. The fertility rate was 1.53 children per woman, far below the replacement threshold of 2.1. In 1999, polls showed that more young and educated Swedes were prone to leave their country and settle elsewhere than were their counterparts in most of western Europe.

Like the other Nordic countries (Denmark, Finland, Iceland, and Norway), Sweden is still ethnically homogenous (similar). Its population is Scandinavian of Germanic descent. Most Swedes speak English and have cultural and family ties to the United States. Minorities include a small number of ethnic Finns and about 17,000 semi-nomadic Lapps (Saami) in the north; there are also more than half a million first generation immigrants, including Finns, Norwegians, Danes, former Yugoslavs, Greeks, Turks, Iranians, Chileans, and others. In the 1990s, Sweden received a large number of refugees from the war in Bosnia and Herzegovina and Kosovo (the former Yugoslavia), and since the mid-1980s, it also has received numerous ethnic Kurdish immigrants from the Middle East. Some 87 percent of Swedes are Lutherans, and there are small numbers of Roman Catholics, Orthodox Christians, Baptists, Muslims, Jews, and Buddhists.

Historically, Sweden's **social welfare system** has been extensive, insuring that all citizens receive old-age pensions, health and unemployment insurance, and

disability benefits. Special provisions include generous **subsidies** to families raising children, such as parental benefits, and subsidized low-rent housing. Higher living standards, as elsewhere, have restricted population growth over the 1990s.

OVERVIEW OF ECONOMY

Sweden is among the leading economies of the world. Once a major European military power, the Nordic country has not waged any wars for more than 180 years. Instead, while enjoying the fruits of peace and neutrality, it has achieved impressive economic and social results under a unique mixed system of high-technology **capitalism** and extensive social-welfare benefits. With an educated and highly efficient **labor force**, Sweden has developed a world-class manufacturing sector with advanced communications. The country provides excellent conditions for scientific innovation, and the size of its investments in research and development is about 4 percent of its **gross domestic product** (GDP), or more than twice the average in western Europe. Sweden is a world leader in terms of the number of patents it holds and of the relative weight of the technology sector in its economy. Timber, hydropower, and rich iron ore, with which Sweden is abundantly endowed, make up the traditional resource base of an economy that has been predominantly export-oriented. For a long time after World War II, the country has been considered as a perfect example of an economically prosperous democratic society with an equitable distribution of wealth, generous social benefits, and an enviable living standard for the majority of the population. Although the country encountered some economic difficulties in the early 1990s, by 1995 it was still second only to Switzerland in terms of its **GDP per capita**, and by the end of the decade it was growing faster than most of western Europe.

During the 1990s, this extraordinarily successful economy was somewhat disturbed by budgetary problems, a bank crisis, and rising **inflation** and unemployment, combined with high personal taxes and a gradual decline of its competitiveness in international markets. The lack of venture capital (money needed to start a business) to support new business ideas and the high tax rate on individual entrepreneurs are thought to have diluted Sweden's full capacity for economic innovation before the late 1990s. Also, low **labor mobility** (the willingness of the workers to relocate to areas with higher demands for labor) has been considered as an impediment to effectively combating unemployment. The government is trying to address these problems. Analyzing Sweden's economic problems in the late 1990s, the International Monetary Fund (IMF) and the Organization on Economic Cooperation and Development (OECD) have commended the country's overall economic management, its budget consolidation, and its **monetary policy**, but pointed out that structural reforms will still be needed particularly to increase labor market flexibility and to lower individual taxes.

After Sweden joined the European Union (EU) in 1995, its efforts to meet the group's rigorous standards caused some additional economic strains. Some political indecision over the country's role in the political and economic integration of Europe had prevented it from joining the EU at an earlier stage and from becoming a charter member of the European economic and monetary union (EMU) in 1999. Sweden has not yet decided to switch to the single euro currency and transfer control over its monetary issues to the European Central Bank (ECB) as 11 other EU members did in 1999. It has harmonized, however, its economic policies and regulations with those of the EU, and Sweden's government plans to hold a referendum in the future on whether the country should join the EMU.

Sweden is one of the world's most attractive countries for foreign investors. Apart from offering a favorable business climate, a strong domestic market, an advanced high-tech sector, a qualified labor force, optimal management skills, and generous "**welfare-state**" benefits, it also offers the second lowest corporate tax rate in Europe. **Foreign direct investment** in the 1990s has increased more than elsewhere in Europe. Between 1990 and 1997, the number of foreign companies active in Sweden has increased by almost one-half. In 1997, foreign-owned firms (mostly from Finland and the United States) employed more than 14 percent of the labor force. Although Sweden's economy is relative small, in 1998 it had 29 out of the 500 largest companies in Europe—by far the highest number per capita in the continent. Swedish managers are also reckoned among the world's leaders in terms of their international experience and their language skills.

POLITICS, GOVERNMENT, AND TAXATION

Like its Nordic neighbors Norway and Denmark, Sweden is a constitutional monarchy. It is essentially a mature, multi-party parliamentary democracy, governed under a 1975 constitution that removed the last vestiges of royal power, included an extensive bill of rights, and declared that all power emanated from the people. Executive power is vested in the Cabinet, elected by parliament and consisting of the prime minister, the head of government, and 20 cabinet ministers. The monarch remains officially the head of state, an exclusively ceremonial post, but is no longer the commander-in-chief of the armed forces and does not chair the cabinet meetings. Succession to the throne was opened to women in 1980. Legislative power is vested in a **unicameral** parliament (Riksdag) with 349 seats whose members are elected for 4-year terms on a proportional basis by universal suffrage. After elections in September 1998, the seats were distributed as follows: Social Democrats (131), Moderates (82), the Left Party (43), Christian Democrats (42), the Center Party (18), the Liberal Party (17), and the Greens (16).

The Social Democratic Party, which had been Sweden's ruling party since World War II, regained office in the 1994 elections. With its traditional ties to the trade-union movement, it has made reducing unemployment a top priority, and stands for a strong **public sector**. Blue-collar workers and public-sector employees form its base. The conservative Moderate Party demands minimum involvement by the government, lower taxes, public assistance for private industry and business, and a strong defense. The Left Party has **socialist** and **communist** traditions and normally supports the Social Democratic government, but it opposes EU membership fearing that European integration and regulations would jeopardize benefits for Swedish workers. The Christian Democratic Party supports a traditional values-based government, is strongly anti-abortion, and pleads for greater support for families in order to fight youth problems, alcoholism, and crime. It demands more aid to developing countries and a more liberal immigration policy.

An important priority for Social Democratic prime minister Goran Persson and his party in 2000 was convincing the Swedish population of the benefits of the EMU. The party had officially adopted a pro-membership policy, but its argument that Sweden had to join the single currency on purely economic grounds sounded less convincing in late 2000, as the country's economy was growing faster than those who had joined the EMU in 1999. Other factors also discouraged a national consensus in favor of the EMU: Sweden's tradition of restricting alcohol use by administrative means conflicted with the EU's trade **liberalization** rules, and the EU's unhappiness with the intended merger between the 2 large Swedish truck makers, Volvo and Scania.

Denmark's decision to stay out of the EMU membership also weakened popular support for a similar move in Sweden. Many ordinary Swedes are suspicious about further European integration and worry about its impact on their generally healthy economy and its traditional welfare programs, as are the Danes. Businesspeople in Sweden, on the other hand, are unified in support of EMU membership, citing the benefits of a stable **exchange rate** for their trade with the euro zone (countries that have adopted the euro currency), which accounts for more than half of Swedish trade. They fear EMU would also force Sweden to harmonize its legislation, putting national business on an equal footing with its EU competitors.

Labor market regulations remain of particular concern for the government in the EMU debate. The current wage bargaining system sets the wages for a fixed period of 2 years. Consequently, a large part of the Swedish companies are bound by rigid wage costs over that period. In the event of an international economic slowdown and decreasing foreign sales, the export-driven Swedish industry would suffer from these high fixed wage costs. In similar situations in the past, its price competitiveness abroad has been restored by a depreciation of the krona. If Sweden joins EMU, however, such depreciation would be ruled out (all monetary issues will be decided upon by the European Central Bank), and a more flexible system of wage fixing would be needed to avoid massive layoffs in times of low foreign demand. But Sweden's traditional commitment to wage stability and solidarity and its opposition to layoffs form the heart of the country's economic model. EMU membership is supported by trade-union leadership, but less so by its rank-and-file members (typical workers).

The government's role in the Swedish economy is larger than in other industrialized countries such as the United States. The state owns shares in an array of important industries, such as commercial banks, credit institutions, telecommunications, information technology, broadcasting, postal services, nuclear and hydroelectric power production, air transport, railroads, mining companies, drug chains, pharmaceuticals, and the defense industry. It provides also extensive educational, health, old-age, disability, unemployment, and other social services. The Swedish government is planning a new program aimed at establishing more market discipline and improving the performance of state-owned firms by publishing their quarterly reports as a manifestation of accountability.

Sweden's corporate tax rate is 28 percent, levied on the company's worldwide income. **Value-added tax** (VAT) applies to the sale of goods and most services; its basic rate is 25 percent of the pre-tax price for all goods (12 percent on food items since 1996). Although corporate taxes are low by western European standards, individual ones, although progressive, are reckoned quite high and the IMF advocates lowering them if the country is to continue its steady growth.

Sweden has an **external debt** of US$66.5 billion (1994) which is considered proportionate, and is a major economic aid donor with US$1.7 billion in direct aid (1997). The country has a significant foreign **trade surplus** (more than US$17 billion in 1999) due to its large and robust export sector.

INFRASTRUCTURE, POWER, AND COMMUNICATIONS

Sweden possesses a modern transportation network, regarded as a vital component of equitable wealth distribution. The country's railroads have 12,821 kilometers (7,967 miles) of track, about a third of them privately owned. A rapid railroad link connects Stockholm's main airport, Arlanda, with the city center, and there is a 16-kilometer (10-mile) long bridge and tunnel across the strait of Ôresund from Malmö in Sweden to Denmark's capital, Copenhagen, opened in 2000. There are 163,453 kilometers (101,570 miles) of paved highways, including 1,439 kilometers (894 miles) of expressways. Sweden has 2,052 kilometers (1,275 miles) of navigable waterways and 84 kilometers (52 miles) of natural-gas pipelines. Major ports and harbors, all equipped with modern terminals, including container handling, include Gaevle, Göteborg, Halmstad, Helsingborg, Hudiksvall, Kalmar, Karlshamn, Malmö, Solvesborg, Stockholm, and Sundsvall, The Swedish merchant fleet comprises 165 modern ships. The Swedish marine carrier Stena Bulk AB has recently partnered with OceanConnect.com, an independent online marketplace, for the sale of marine products and services, but mostly to help buyers and sellers complete fuel transactions.

Since the **deregulation** of the domestic air market in 1991, several Swedish airlines, such as the Scandinavian Airlines System (SAS), Malmö Aviation, and Transwede, have been competing for passengers and cargo. The largest player is SAS, collectively owned by Sweden, Denmark, and Norway. Sweden holds a three-sevenths stake in it, of which the government owns half. SAS is a champion of air-transport liberalization (the "open skies" policy) and has struck many strategic partnerships. In 1998, there were 14 million international departures from the Stockholm airports alone. In 2000, the Swedish government was in the process of **privatizing** several enterprises in its transportation sector. Norway's Schoyen Gruppen and U.S. investment bank Goldman, Sachs ac-

Communications

Country	Newspapers	Radios	TV Sets[a]	Cable subscribers[a]	Mobile Phones[a]	Fax Machines[a]	Personal Computers[a]	Internet Hosts[b]	Internet Users[b]
	1996	1997	1998	1998	1998	1998	1998	1999	1999
Sweden	445	932	531	221.4	464	50.9	361.4	581.47	3,666
United States	215	2,146	847	244.3	256	78.4	458.6	1,508.77	74,100
Germany	311	948	580	214.5	170	73.1	304.7	173.96	14,400
Norway	588	915	579	160.1	474	50.0	373.4	754.15	2,000

[a]Data are from International Telecommunication Union, *World Telecommunication Development Report 1999* and are per 1,000 people.
[b]Data are from the Internet Software Consortium (http://www.isc.org) and are per 10,000 people.

SOURCE: World Bank. *World Development Indicators 2000.*

quired the public transit company Swebus, including its bus operations in Finland, in 1999. Swebus serves about 30 percent of the market in Sweden with its 3,400 buses and 5,200 employees. In another similar privatization deal, the French company CGEA Transport bought 60 percent of the **equity** of the Stockholm subway system from the city of Stockholm.

Sweden's energy sector is strong, with energy production and usage per capita being among the highest in Europe. State-run Svenska Kraftnat runs the national electricity grid. The country is rich in water resources, and 46.5 percent of total power is generated by hydroelectricity; nuclear energy supplies 45.1 percent, and thermal plants provide the rest. In 1980, Swedes voted in a referendum to decommission its nuclear plants by 2010, but the law that was needed to enable the decision is still pending in the Riksdag. The parliamentary opposition has undertaken to reverse the law, alleging that there has been a change in public opinion. Sydkraft, a private company that owns a nuclear power plant, is threatening to contest its scheduled closure in the European Court of Justice. Deregulation of Sweden's electricity market began by 2000 with the intent of giving all households the freedom to choose among energy suppliers.

Sweden is among the world's leaders in information technology, computer hardware, software, and services. It has the highest number of phone lines (combined fixed and mobile) per capita, as well as the highest percentage of Internet users in the world. Some 74 percent of Swedish companies and 45 percent of households had Internet access in early 2000. In 2000, the phone **infrastructure** had 68 fixed lines per 100 inhabitants, and mobile phone penetration was approximately 48 percent. Sweden is also a leader in the implementation of new wireless phone and Internet technology. In 1993, the Swedish telecommunications market was one of the first in Europe to deregulate, and telecom investments in 2000 amounted to more than 6 percent of GDP. Virtually no restrictions protect domestic interests or restrict foreign operations from establishing themselves locally.

The Swedish government emphasizes electronic commerce, both in the consumer and business sectors, encourages state-owned companies to use electronic purchasing as a means for cost-cutting, and is committed to creating a national broadband network aimed at bringing high-speed Internet access to every household, even in the remotest parts of the country. Although the system will be open to all Internet providers, some municipalities have decided not to wait for the national system, expected to be completed in 2005, and have begun building their own networks. Much of the Swedish **e-commerce** revolution is also driven by the utilities. Faced with falling electricity prices in the deregulated market, they are trying to sell other services with higher profit margins to their existing customers and use their electricity grids more effectively.

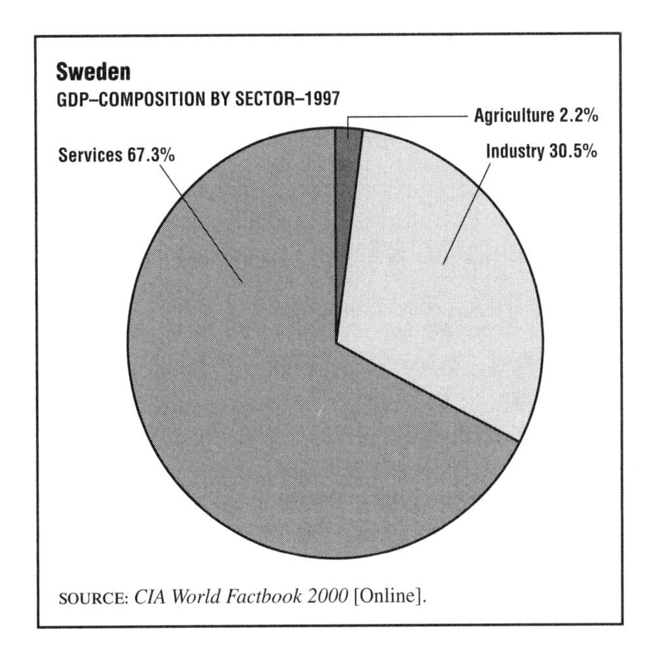

SOURCE: *CIA World Factbook 2000* [Online].

ECONOMIC SECTORS

As in much of western Europe, the Swedish economy after World War II has gradually become service-oriented, and by 1997, the service sector accounted for 67.3 percent of GDP. Manufacturing contributes 30.5 percent to GDP, and agriculture 2 percent. Private companies account for about 90 percent of manufacturing output, of which the engineering sector accounts for half of

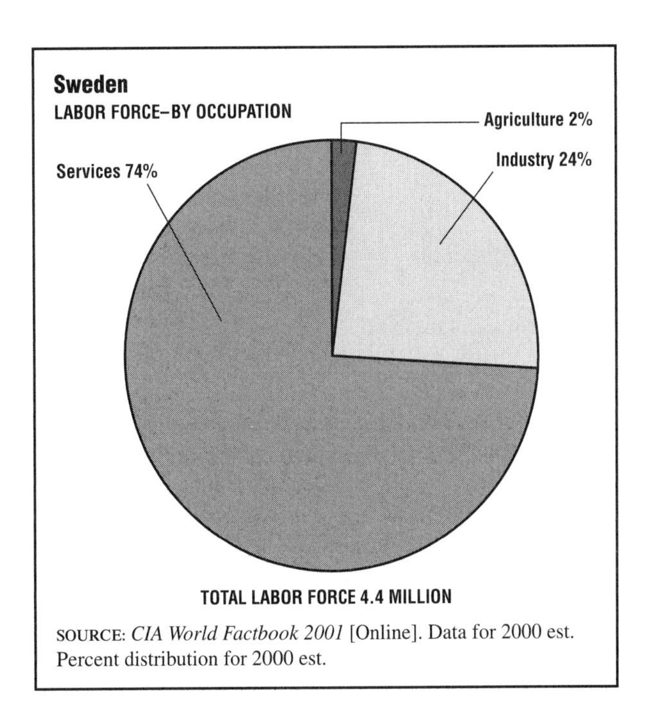

SOURCE: *CIA World Factbook 2001* [Online]. Data for 2000 est. Percent distribution for 2000 est.

both output and exports. Among the healthiest sectors of the Swedish economy are traditional export-oriented industries like automobiles and construction equipment, as well as services, information technology, and telecommunications.

AGRICULTURE

Sweden is almost self-sufficient in many agricultural products, although the sector employs no more than 2 percent of the labor force and contributes 2 percent of GDP. About 7 percent of Sweden's land is cultivated, mostly in the southern plains. Modern farming, including fertilization and mechanization, make high yields possible although soils are generally poor and the cold climate renders the growing season much shorter than elsewhere in Europe. Farms vary in size from large to small ones, many of which combine into various larger units and cooperatives. Traditionally important sectors such as dairies have declined in the 1990s compared to grain and vegetable production, but livestock and animal products remain among the main commodity items. Other crops include wheat, barley, oats, rye, potatoes, and sugar beets. In 1997, livestock included 1.8 million cattle, 2.4 million pigs, 470,000 sheep, and 11.2 million poultry. The country also exports some fur pelts, notably mink.

INDUSTRY

Sweden's world-class domestic industries originated in the 17th century from its vast natural resources of forests, rich iron ore and waterpower. Over the course of the 20th century, Swedish industry has evolved from traditional sectors with lower added value, such as wood and iron ore processing, to modern industries with a higher degree of skill and technology input, such as automobiles and precision and specialized engineering. The change of priorities became even more evident in the 1990s, with the emergence of new research-intensive industries, such as information technology and pharmaceuticals, which replaced the more traditional engineering industries as the driving force of growth and business activity.

During this transition, some sectors, like textiles and iron, contracted considerably while others, such as shipbuilding, have all but disappeared, but Swedish **restructuring** has been smooth in terms of economic and social stability. By 2000, major industries included information technology (telephone, radio, and computer equipment), communications, pharmaceuticals, precision equipment (bearings and armaments), high-quality steel, automobiles, electrical motors and other electrical equipment, printed and published goods (including software and popular music), home and office furnishings, and processed foods. Most of the manufacturing plants are private and small, though Sweden also accounts for 29 of the 500 largest companies in Europe, perhaps the highest number per capita in the world). Several of the world's most sophisticated and diversified engineering companies bear Swedish names, although many of them are now foreign-owned or in multinational cooperation. They include, among others, Volvo, Saab, Scania, Electrolux, SKF, and ABB. The most dynamic sector by the late 1990s was telecommunications and information technology, with Ericsson being the most outstanding company in that field.

The automotive sector, one of the most important industries, has lived through major changes in the 1990s due to global restructuring and consolidation. General Motors acquired a 50 percent equity stake in Saab in 1989, and GM acquired the remaining stake in 1999. In 1999, Volvo sold its car division to the Ford Motor Company. Volvo shifted gears to concentrate on commercial transport equipment, and in 1999 acquired 75 percent of Scania, the second major Swedish truck maker. Volvo thus became one of the world's largest manufacturers of heavy vehicles. Sweden also is a major manufacturer of pharmaceuticals; its Pharmacia company merged in 1995 with the U.S. group Upjohn, while Astra merged in 1998 with British Zeneca, to form AstraZeneca.

During the 1990s, the information technology industry has been by far the fastest-growing sector in Sweden. In 1999, the country had more than 250 information technology companies (including foreign-owned ones) with an annual revenue of more than US$10 million, and a huge number of smaller ones. By far the largest of them was Ericsson, with net sales of US$26 billion in 1999. Telia was its second largest company, in net sales and employees. Many important international information technology companies, including Intel, Microsoft, Hewlett-Packard and Nortel, have chosen Sweden as the base for their European operations or for advanced research and development.

SERVICES

As in most of the industrialized world, the Swedish economy is becoming increasingly service-based, with more than two-thirds of GDP formed in that sector, and the role of finance and banking dramatically increasing. **Retail** is a traditionally strong industry, and tourism is also gaining ground with the increasing affluence of the Swedes and the growing interest of foreign visitors in traveling in the country.

BANKING AND FINANCIAL SERVICES. Financial institutions in Sweden, both banking and capital-market ones, are well developed and stable. In addition to Riksbanken, the central bank, there are 2 types of banks, joint stock (commercial) and savings banks. Several "member-banks," formed as economic associations, also operate, but generally all banks are entitled to activity in all areas of the industry. In 1986, Sweden opened its borders to 12 foreign commercial banks, allowing them to open branches offices in the country, and they have since focused on business services. In 1990, all restrictions concerning foreign ownership of Swedish bank stock were abolished, though the banks' activities are subject to close supervision to insure that all necessary standards are met. According to the law, financial statements are audited only by internationally recognized auditors. The largest banks in the mid-1990s were Nordbanken, Skandinaviska Enskilda Banken, Svenska Handelsbanken and Foreningssparbanken (Savings Bank Foundation). American institutions Citibank and GE Capital Bank were also in operation.

Many Swedish banks suffered losses in the early 1990s due to **recession**, the increased competition generated by deregulation of the sector, sharply expanded lending, especially for real estate (mortgages), plus high inflation in the second half of the 1980s. In 1992, the government guaranteed all commitments of banks and mortgage lenders to their depositors and investors, establishing a Bank Support Council to manage a bank assistance program. Following EU directives, the government guarantee was replaced in 1996 (after Sweden's accession to the EU) by a bank deposit guarantee.

Since the mid-1990s, following global consolidation trends, the number of banks in Sweden was reduced through mergers. The largest merger was the 1998 deal between Nordbanken and Finland's Merita that formed the huge MeritaNordbanken Group. The deregulation of financial markets encouraged many foreign banks to enter Sweden. Credit Lyonnais of France was one of the leaders, although competition in Swedish retail banking forced it to sell its operation to the Trygg-Hansa insurance group in 1997. There were 32 commercial banks doing business in 1999, 15 of which were foreign subsidiaries. Smaller "niche banks" have also emerged (like "dial-in" banks for services by telephone), and all major banks are offering virtual services through the Internet. In 1999, 3 out of the top 4 Internet banks were Swedish. All major banks offer online services, and almost 40 percent of the Swedes conducted their financial transactions at least partly online in 2000, making the country, along with its Nordic neighbors, a leader in Internet banking. Swedbank's Internet system was named the best in Europe in 1999 and proved so convenient that Swedbank was also able to sell it to Norway's Sparbank 1.

Four of Sweden's major commercial banks plan to start a joint system for electronic stock trading in the hope of taking some customers away from the well-established OM Stockholm Stock Exchange by offering trading services on weekends, and eventually, around the clock.

Long considered underdeveloped, the Swedish venture-capital sector finally began to grow dramatically in late 1998 and 1999 thanks to the Internet and high-tech stock boom. It was badly hit by the meltdown in information-technology stocks in late 2000. Probably one-fifth of the 140 venture capital firms existing in late 2000 will either merge, close down, or leave the country. The remaining venture-capital firms will shift resources, possibly meaning that less capital will be available for new startups and expansions in 2001–2002.

RETAIL. The Swedish retail sector has been traditionally strong. It is following European retail trends, with large stores and shopping malls replacing the small traditional retailers, although to a lesser extent than in Continental Europe, given the smaller size of the market. New forms of retailing have benefited vastly from improvements in consumer confidence, a rise in earnings, and an expansion of employment. Furthermore, the reduction in value-added tax (VAT) on food since 1995, and Sweden's entry into the EU the same year, led to a fall in many prices. In 1998 and 1999, consumer demand for cars and audiovisual and computer equipment boosted the volume of retail trade to nearly 6 percent higher than in the previous year. By far the best known name worldwide in Swedish retail is IKEA, the furnishing retailer that registers 53 percent of its sales and 26 percent of its purchasing in the euro zone. IKEA also has a very strong presence in the U.S. Another strong retailer is Apoteksbolaget, a state-owned chain of pharmacies with a **monopoly** on the sale of all prescription and non-prescription medication.

E-commerce is already widely established, and online revenue as a share of total retail revenue is the second highest in the world after the United States. A growing number of Sweden's online retailers, including Boxman, Europe's largest online CD music and video retailer, have expanded even beyond the domestic market and built up a presence in other countries in Europe. Direct marketing is also expanding, and well-established mail-order firms have emerged in the areas of beauty products (such as Oriflame), clothing, sporting goods and hardware. Telemarketing is still relatively rare, but the use of cable TV sales channels is increasing.

For decades, Sweden has had a tradition of government policy aimed at restricting alcohol consumption through a state liquor monopoly and high taxes at more than twice the British and more than 10 times the French and German rates. When Sweden joined the EU in 1995, the state import monopoly was discarded, but the distribution and retail market remained under government control and the Swedish government negotiated a temporary exemption from the EU regulations, restricting the amount of alcohol individuals can import into the country. The European Commission has objected to future extension of this exemption, and Swedes take advantage of short trips to Denmark and Germany to import large quantities of alcohol for domestic consumption, especially after the bridge and tunnel link to Denmark opened in 2000.

TOURISM. Tourism is not a traditionally important sector in Sweden, but it has been growing throughout the 1980s and 1990s, with most foreign visitors coming from Germany, Britain, and the United States. The tourist season has traditionally been confined to the summer months, but winter skiing holidays began to attract foreign visitors during the 1990s. The first direct charter flight between Swedish ski resorts and Britain was launched in 1997. Still, about 80 percent of the guests were Swedes and about 6 percent were other Nordic nationals. Most Swedes continue to prefer traveling abroad during the obligatory 5 weeks of vacation and the increasing number of special holidays. The Norwegian hotel chain Norlandia plans to build up to 5 new hotel and conference centers in Sweden to add to the 6 it now has in the country.

INTERNATIONAL TRADE

Sweden has had a traditionally strong export sector and has recorded large surpluses on its trade since the mid-1990s (more than US$7 billion in 1999). The trade surplus is likely to increase in 2001, driven by an expected fall in oil prices. Principal exported commodities include machinery and equipment (35 percent), motor vehicles, paper products, pulp and wood, iron and steel products, and chemicals. Leading export markets in 1998 were the European Union (57 percent), Germany (11 percent), the United Kingdom, Norway, and the United States (9 percent each), Denmark (6 percent), and Finland (5 percent). Imported commodities include machinery, petroleum and petroleum products, chemicals, motor vehicles, iron and steel, foodstuffs, and clothing. Chief import partners in 1998 were the European Union (68 percent), Germany (19 percent), the United Kingdom (10 percent), Norway (10 percent), and Denmark, France, and the United States (6 percent each). Swedish export brands such as Ericsson, Volvo, Saab, Electrolux, IKEA, and Oriflame, are among the best known in the world.

In 2000, the increase in the imports of mineral fuels, lubricants and related products amounted to SKr18.7 billion, but this was easily offset by the growth in the value of Swedish exports. Electrical machinery was one of the rapidly growing export categories, and revenue increased also in wood pulp, iron and steel, while in manufacturing they remained flat. In 2000, the U.S. economy alone absorbed SKr47.7 billion of Swedish exports, or an increase of 20.6 percent, and Swedish deliveries to Japan also rose sharply. The price of Swedish imports remained relatively stable, although high oil prices produced a sharp increase in the value of Norwegian imports (Norway is the major exporter of oil and natural gas for many countries in the region).

Trade (expressed in billions of US$): Sweden

	Exports	Imports
1975	17.383	17.450
1980	30.906	33.438
1985	30.461	28.547
1990	57.540	54.264
1995	79.801	64.645
1998	84.730	68.413

SOURCE: International Monetary Fund. *International Financial Statistics Yearbook 1999.*

MONEY

In 2000, the exchange rate for Swedish kronor stood at SKr8.4831 to US$1; it stood at SKr7.1333 in 1995 and SKr6.7060 in 1996. In the late 1990s, the Swedish government's budget balance improved dramatically. After a deficit of more than 12 percent of GDP in 1993, there was a surplus by 1998, and large surpluses are expected every year through 2002. Credibility improved with the introduction of new strict budget regulations with spending ceilings, and the establishment of a truly independent central bank, the Riksbanken. The government still has a high consolidated debt, although it declined from a peak of 79 percent of GDP in 1994 to 67.6 percent in 1999 and 62.2 percent in 2000. The Swedish Financial Supervisory Authority has established a close monitoring of household borrowing, fearing that rapid expansion in lending could lead to credit losses. Riksbanken is expected to be successful in meeting its EU-mandated 2 percent annual inflation target in the longer term. The government and the Social Democratic party remain split over whether Sweden should join the European Monetary Union, concerned that Swedish exports could be hurt, although local businesses are eager to join EMU. Many believe it will take another 2 to 3 years for Sweden to adopt the euro even if a decision to join EMU is made.

The respected though insignificant Stockholm Stock Exchange (SSE), formed in 1863, became the world's first for-profit exchange in 1992. In 1995, it merged with the OM Derivative Exchange (formed in 1985 to offer options trading) to form the new OM Stockholm Exchange; it maintains an investment exchange in London. The OM Stockholm Exchange has been one of the most successful in western Europe in the 1990s, and it ended 1999 with its SX General Index at a record high of 5,382, or 66.4 percent higher than in 1998. The dramatic rise in the share index and in the **market capitalization** were

Exchange rates: Sweden

Swedish kronor (SKr) per US$1	
Jan 2001	9.4669
2000	9.1622
1999	8.2624
1998	7.9499
1997	7.6349
1996	6.7060

SOURCE: CIA *World Factbook 2001* [ONLINE].

GDP per Capita (US$)

Country	1975	1980	1985	1990	1998
Sweden	21,157	22,283	24,168	26,397	27,705
United States	19,364	21,529	23,200	25,363	29,683
Germany	N/A	N/A	N/A	N/A	31,141
Norway	19,022	23,595	27,113	28,840	36,806

SOURCE: United Nations. *Human Development Report 2000; Trends in human development and per capita income.*

mainly due to the high-tech boom of the late 1990s, and the **turnover** in Ericsson's and Nokia's shares contributed to almost half of the total figure. Since 1999, the OM Stockholm and the Copenhagen stock exchanges have been part of the Norex alliance, in which all shares listed on both exchanges are traded on a joint electronic system. In late 1999, the Oslo stock exchange also joined Norex, and the stock exchanges of the Baltic states (Estonia, Latvia, and Lithuania) and Iceland have expressed interest in joining. The joint stock exchanges, along with several newly-opened Swedish online brokerages, help broaden the pool of capital available to businesses and make raising capital easier and cheaper while the economy becomes more dynamic, effective, and flexible.

As the OM was facing volatile stock prices and the Internet meltdown was plaguing world markets in late 2000, a number of Swedish companies, mostly from the information technology sector, started fundraising by targeting new share offerings directly to interested institutions, mostly to save time and money, but also to avoid the risk that their public offerings might not be successful, given the growing skepticism about information-technology stocks. Another advantage of direct offering was that it helped companies avoid the large price fluctuations of a new public offering and the administrative costs associated with it.

By 2000, the Swedish government was also considering a legal amendment aimed at making it easier for banks and other financial institutions to securitize (replace non-marketable bank loans with negotiable securities) some of their own assets. These would include mortgages, to be securitized by selling them to security brokerage firms who would issue them securities (bonds) against the loans, that, in turn, may be used as investment capital. Securitization is essentially a method of freeing up capital from long-term loans.

POVERTY AND WEALTH

Sweden is well-known for its system that combines a strong market-based economy with extensive social-welfare services. Central and local authorities play a dominant role in providing a wide variety of social services, such as education, health, old age, disability, and unemployment benefits. The governing Social Democratic Party has a platform that includes **full employment**, wage solidarity, and the maintenance of current living standards among its basic goals.

Swedes enjoy a traditionally high and stable standard of living, although at a high cost to individual taxpayers. Sweden is among the most equitable societies in the world, with a 1995 **Gini index** (an index that measuring economic equality in which 0 stands for perfect equality and 100 for perfect inequality) of 25. By comparison, the United States had a Gini rating of 40.8, the United Kingdom had a 36.1, and Switzerland had a 33.1). This means that there are no extremes of wealth and poverty in the country. Progressive personal **income taxes** and comparatively lower executive compensation (compared to that in the U.S.) contribute to maintaining equal social opportunity. Sweden's excellent distribution and transportation system, along with generous regional subsidies, work to prevent inequalities in living standards between urban and rural areas.

Social security programs are exceptionally comprehensive and are subsidized by the government, although some are administered by the trade unions. In response

Distribution of Income or Consumption by Percentage Share: Sweden

Lowest 10%	3.7
Lowest 20%	9.6
Second 20%	14.5
Third 20%	18.1
Fourth 20%	23.2
Highest 20%	34.5
Highest 10%	20.1

Survey year: 1992

Note: This information refers to income shares by percentiles of the population and is ranked by per capita income.

SOURCE: *2000 World Development Indicators* [CD-ROM].

Household Consumption in PPP Terms

Country	All food	Clothing and footwear	Fuel and power[a]	Health care[b]	Education[b]	Transport & Communications	Other
Sweden	17	5	12	4	14	6	41
United States	13	9	9	4	6	8	51
Germany	14	6	7	2	10	7	53
Norway	16	7	11	5	4	6	51

Data represent percentage of consumption in PPP terms.
[a]Excludes energy used for transport.
[b]Includes government and private expenditures.

SOURCE: World Bank. *World Development Indicators 2000.*

to the recession of the early 1990s, the government started reductions in the level and range of social programs. Still, some surveys have found that 62 percent of all young and educated Swedes have considered moving abroad, partly in pursuit of greater personal challenge.

WORKING CONDITIONS

Working conditions in Sweden are among the best in the world, thanks to sophisticated environmental and worker-safety regulations. Its labor force of some 4.3 million is disciplined, educated, and experienced in most modern technologies. About 87 percent of Swedish workers belong to a labor union, arguably the world's highest rate, and unions are active partners with businesses in implementing more efficient programs. Swedish legislation provides for labor representation on the boards of directors of large corporations and requires management to negotiate with the unions prior to implementing major changes. Management-labor cooperation is traditionally non-confrontational. There is no fixed minimum wage, and all wages are set by collective bargaining. Since 1991, **real wage** increases have exceeded those of most EU countries. As the EMU debate gains momentum, labor unions are calling for buffer funds, similar to those created in Finland, as a "cushion" for pension savings and other worker benefits during the transition period to the euro, in the event that there are any large currency fluctuations.

Many pro-business observers, including those from the International Monetary Fund (IMF), have recommended some fundamental labor market reforms, including wage differentiation (to reduce labor costs for low-skilled jobs), introducing an incentive to increase individual competence, strict eligibility requirements and limitations on unemployment benefits, the reduction of income taxes and non-wage labor costs, making the unions and their members bear the costs of the unemployment insurance system, and liberalizing employment protection legislation. Such measures are believed to increase efficiency and competitiveness, but labor representatives complain that they would place more burdens on workers.

Sweden's primary labor-related problem remains its level of unemployment. During a very short period in the early 1990s, the unemployment rate rose from levels among the lowest in the industrialized world to the average EU levels, where it remained until the business cycle improved in 1998–99. By 2000, the unemployment rate was less than 5 percent, but was 8.7 percent for those employees involved in training programs. Sweden's government plans to reduce the unemployment rate to 4 percent and to assure that 80 percent of the working-age population have a full-time job by 2004.

COUNTRY HISTORY AND ECONOMIC DEVELOPMENT

700s. The present-day territory of Sweden is inhabited by Suiones and Gothones, Germanic tribes at war with each other.

800. Swedish Vikings start exploring the seas, establishing colonies in western Russia and eastern Europe and developing commercial ties with Byzantium, the Khazar Khaganate, and the Arab Caliphate.

9TH CENTURY. Frankish Christian missionaries penetrate Sweden, which is slowly Christianized.

1150–1160. Under king Erik IX, Sweden invades Finland and forces Christianity on the conquered Finns. A feudal economy based on agriculture and trade develops.

1397. The Union of Kalmar unites the 3 Scandinavian kingdoms of Denmark, Norway, and Sweden under a single (Danish) monarch but constant wars follow between the Danes and Swedes.

1521. A rebellion of Swedes led by Gustav Vasa, later king Gustav I Vasa, overthrows Danish influence in most of Sweden, which becomes a hereditary monarchy that establishes Lutheranism as the state religion.

MID-1500s. Sweden enters a century-long period of military expansion, waging wars against Poland and Russia, and acquiring many territories around the Baltic, including Estonia, Karelia, Ingria, and Livonia.

1630. King Gustav II Adolph (Gustavus Adolphus II), considered the greatest Swedish king and a champion of Protestantism, leads Sweden in the Thirty Years' War.

1648. By the Peace of Westphalia ending the Thirty Years' War, Sweden acquires a large part of Pomerania, the island of Ruegen, Wismar, the sees (bishoprics) of Bremen and Verden, and other German lands. Sweden participates in German affairs and makes an alliance with France but is defeated by the Prussians in 1675.

1700–1721. In the Great Northern War, king Charles XII invades northwestern Russia and defeats the Poles, but the Swedes are finally routed and replaced by Russia as the dominant power in the region. Sweden loses much of its German territory and cedes Livonia, Estonia, Ingria, part of Karelia, and several important Baltic islands to Russia.

1718. A new constitution is adopted, rejecting absolute monarchy and vesting the legislative power in a parliament (Riksdag) composed of 4 estates (nobles, clergy, burghers, and peasants). The executive power becomes the domain of a "secret committee" of the first 3 estates.

1805. King Gustav IV Adolph joins the European coalition of Britain, Russia, and Austria against France, but Russia later unites with France's Napoleon and attacks Sweden, which is forced to cede Finland and the Aland Islands.

1810. To appease Napoleon, the Riksdag chooses Marshal Jean Bernadotte, one of Napoleon's generals, as crown prince, heir to Sweden's childless king. Bernadotte fights against Napoleon in 1813–14 and Denmark is forced to yield Norway to Sweden in exchange for the Swedish lands in Pomerania. In 1815, the union of Norway with Sweden is recognized by the European powers.

1818. Bernadotte succeeds to the throne as Charles XIV John, and Sweden makes considerable progress materially, politically, and culturally under his reign. An early capitalist economy develops.

1867–86. Nearly 500,000 Swedes **emigrate** to America because of rising unemployment.

1905. Norway secedes from Sweden, without opposition from the Riksdag.

EARLY 1900s. Sweden adopts much progressive social legislation, notably in factory laws, accident insurance, and pension funds for workers, and limitation of working hours for women and children. Major developments in industry turn Sweden into a technologically advanced economy.

1914. Sweden declares neutrality in World War I and joins an agreement to protect the common economic interests of the 3 Scandinavian countries.

1920. Sweden joins the League of Nations.

1920s-1930s. The Social Democratic Party becomes the leading force in Swedish politics. Socialist governments in the 1920s and 1930s enact significant social reforms.

1945. Having been neutral throughout World War II, Sweden joins the United Nations and maintains its neutral stance during the Cold War, refusing to join NATO in 1949 but trying to upgrade its armed forces adequately.

1950s-1970s. Postwar Social Democratic governments vastly expand the welfare state while developing a strong export-oriented market economy based on engineering and research.

1972. Swedish opposition to the Vietnam war voiced by popular Social Democratic prime minister Olof Palme arouses indignation in the U.S. as many young American war resisters are given political asylum in Sweden.

1991. Social Democrats decline in authority, although they remain the largest parliamentary party. Carl Bildt of the Moderate Party forms a coalition cabinet with the Center, Liberal, and Christian Democratic parties, stressing deregulation of the economy, privatization of state companies, cuts in government spending, including welfare, and removing restrictions on foreign companies in Sweden.

1994. Social Democrats return to power.

1995. Sweden enters the European Union as a full member.

FUTURE TRENDS

Sweden is expected to preserve its healthy economy and high living standards into the foreseeable future, although the EMU membership controversy will continue to considerably influence domestic politics. In January 2001, Sweden took over the 6-month rotating EU presidency, but opinion polls showed that only half of the electorate wanted the country to remain in the European Union. Economic growth is likely to slow from 4 percent in 2000 to 3.5 percent in 2001 and 3.2 percent in 2002; inflation is projected to remain moderate and under control, while the unemployment rate will likely continue to fall. The Swedish trade surplus is likely to increase in 2001 due to the expected decline in oil prices and continued growth in exports. A decrease in the U.S. consumer spending may reduce Swedish exports to that major market in 2001, but exports to the EU will continue to grow steadily.

In the longer run, the restructuring of the Swedish economy will give further priority to information technology and other high-tech industries and, increasingly, financial services at the expense of traditional engineering industries. The living standards of the Swedes will continue to rise, although more slowly than in the late 1990s, and the government will put major efforts in planning for its eventual entry into the EMU in order to avoid negative effects on employment and welfare. Sweden will also continue to provide an important economic and social model, especially for the new EU members.

DEPENDENCIES

Sweden has no territories or colonies.

BIBLIOGRAPHY

Economist Intelligence Unit. *Country Profile: Sweden.* <http://www.eiu.com>. Accessed January 2001.

Pontusson, Jonas. *The Limits of Social Democracy: Investment Politics in Sweden.* Ithaca, New York: Cornell University Press, 1992.

U.S. Central Intelligence Agency. *The World Factbook, 2000.* <http://www.cia.gov/cia/publications/factbook>. Accessed May 2001.

U.S. Department of State. *FY 2000 Country Commercial Guide: Sweden.* <http://www.state.gov/www/about_state/business/com_guides/index.html>. Accessed May 2001.

—Valentin Hadjiyski

SWITZERLAND

Swiss Confederation
Confédération Suisse
Schweizerische Eidgenossenschaft

CAPITAL: Bern.

MONETARY UNIT: Swiss franc (SwFr). One Swiss franc equals 100 centimes, or rappen. There are coins of 1, 5, 10, 20, and 50 centimes and 1, 2, and 5 francs, and notes of 10, 20, 50, 100, 500, and 1,000 francs.

CHIEF EXPORTS: Machinery, electronics, chemicals, pharmaceuticals, metals, watches agricultural products, textiles, and handicrafts.

CHIEF IMPORTS: Raw materials, machinery, chemicals, vehicles, metals, agricultural products, textiles.

GROSS DOMESTIC PRODUCT: US$197 billion (1999 est.).

BALANCE OF TRADE: **Exports:** US$98.5 billion (1999 est.). **Imports:** US$99 billion (1999 est.).

COUNTRY OVERVIEW

LOCATION AND SIZE. Located in west central Europe, bordered on the north by France and Germany, on the east by Austria and Liechtenstein, on the south by Italy, and on the west and south-west by France, this landlocked alpine country has an area of 41,290 square kilometers (15,942 square mi), making it slightly less than twice the size of New Jersey. The capital, Bern, is situated on the Aare River in the north-western part of the country; the largest city is Zürich in the north; other major cities include Geneva and Lausanne in the south-west, Basel in the north, and Lugano in the south.

POPULATION. The population of Switzerland was estimated at 7,262,372 in July 2000; the population growth rate in that year was 0.3 percent, and the **immigration** rate was 1.38 per 1,000 population. Population density was among the highest in Europe, at about 176 persons per square kilometer (455 per square mile). The population is aging, and it has a high life expectancy—79.6 years for the total population (76.73 for men, and 82.63 for women). Consequently, the median age increased to 42.6 years in 1999 from 37.2 five years earlier. Some 15.4 percent of the population are 14 years old and younger, and 16.7 percent are 65 and older.

The majority of the population, about 62 percent, lives in urban areas, and with the exception of Zürich, Geneva, Basel, and Lausanne, mostly in small towns. Most of Switzerland is mountainous and the population is unevenly distributed, concentrated in the valleys and the plains.

Switzerland's ethnic composition is complex and includes 3 major traditional language communities: German (about 64 percent of Swiss citizens), French (about 19 percent), and Italian (about 10 percent), along with the traditional Romansch (Rhaeto-Roman) language community (about 1 percent). Other ethnic groups include Spaniards, Portuguese, Turks, Albanians, former Yugoslavs, and others. Religious groups include Roman Catholics (46 percent), Protestants (40 percent), others (7 percent), and no religious faith is reported by 7 percent. The very slow population growth and the sizeable surplus of jobs in the economy (particularly in the services sector) have brought in many foreign **guest workers** from Italy, Spain, Portugal, the former Yugoslavia, and elsewhere. Guest workers are now estimated, with their families, to constitute nearly one-fifth of the entire population.

Switzerland has been the destination for many economic immigrants and asylum seekers, which has led to growing internal tensions. The fear of being overrun by foreigners has been a persistent Swiss topic in domestic political debate for decades. There have been many attempts to limit the number of foreigners by legislative means. In 2000, the Swiss electorate voted on a referendum to impose an 18 percent quota on the number of foreign workers in the country. They decided against the

measure, although the supporters of the quota argued that the influx of foreigners in the 1990s was equal to the population of the 6 smallest (and politically most conservative) Swiss cantons (confederate units).

OVERVIEW OF ECONOMY

Switzerland, by all accounts one of the most prosperous and stable market economies in the world, has a **gross domestic product (GDP) per capita** of $27,100, roughly one-fifth higher than the average of the large Western European countries. Its per capita income remains the highest in Europe, even after a decade of comparative stagnation in the 1990s. Switzerland is traditionally considered a safe haven for foreign investors, because it has maintained political neutrality, an elaborate banking system with a high degree of bank secrecy, and it has maintained its currency's value through the instabilities of surrounding Europe's wars and crises. Switzerland is pursuing European Union (EU) membership only in the long run—over a ten-year period—because of the widely-held suspicions of many Swiss that effective involvement with the rest of Europe could jeopardize their unique economic stability. Yet the EU is by far its largest trading partner and Switzerland has signed several agreements to **liberalize** trade ties with the union. Switzerland has also brought its economy largely into conformity with EU regulations to improve its international competitiveness.

Swiss industries, notably engineering and machinery, electronics, metals, chemicals, and pharmaceuticals, are renowned for their precision and quality and contribute to more than half of the country's export revenues. In agriculture, Switzerland is self-sufficient for almost two-thirds of its food and exports several world-famous delicacies, yet it also imports about $6 billion worth of agricultural commodities annually. Its mostly small-scale farmers are among the most highly protected and subsidized producers in the world. Tourism, banking, and insurance are traditionally leading sectors in the economy. Swiss trading companies have good expertise in many parts of the world, such as eastern Europe, the Far East, Africa, and the Middle East. Switzerland has a well-developed tourist **infrastructure** and the Swiss themselves are keen travelers. The country is the seat of many international inter-governmental and private organizations, from the United Nations (UN) and its associated organizations, to CERN, the European Laboratory for Particle Physics (which gave birth to the World Wide Web), to the International Red Cross, and is also host to numerous **multinational corporations**.

In the late 1990s, the Swiss economy emerged from several years without growth caused primarily by the strong Swiss franc, which made its exports too expensive abroad. The overall slowdown in Europe, which also hurt tourism, was another barrier to exports. Following the depreciation of the franc in 1997 and the stronger economic conditions in Europe since, Swiss growth reached 2.3 percent in 1998, fell off to 1.54 percent in 1999, and then hit 3.43 percent in 2000. Unemployment peaked at 5.2 percent in 1997 and was reduced to less than 2 percent by 2000. Domestic consumer spending is an important factor keeping the economy in good shape, and competitive pressures in the European markets are supporting extensive domestic capital spending.

After Swiss voters, doubtful of the benefits of more intimate ties with their neighbors, rejected the framework European Economic Area (EEA, providing for closer cooperation as a possible introduction to EU membership) in a referendum in 1992, the Swiss federal government started negotiating separate bilateral sectoral agreements with the EU. An agreement covering several sectors (including land and air transport and agriculture) was signed in 1998. The federal government has declared its commitment to EU membership as a long-term goal, although it is opposed by many citizens who fear such results as harm to heavily subsidized Swiss agriculture by letting in cheaper EU foods, increases in unemployment by flooding the country with more guest workers, and damage to the environment from heavier truck traffic through Swiss territory.

Yet a substantial majority of 67.2 percent in 2000 backed, in a referendum pushed through by anti-European nationalist groups, a new package of bilateral agreements with the EU. Only 2 of the 26 cantons, Ticino and Schwyz, voted against the package. The Italian-speaking Ticino was concerned about the influx of workers from neighboring Italy, and Schwyz, a German-speaking conservative stronghold, had stood in the way of every pro-European initiative. The agreements, which include the introduction of free movement of people between the EU and Switzerland and the removal of existing administrative barriers to EU trucking through Swiss territory, are designed to compensate for the country's non-membership in the EEA, with which it conducts over two-thirds of its trade. The prudent Swiss have negotiated a number of opt-out clauses in case the inflow of EU citizens and trucks gets higher than expected.

POLITICS, GOVERNMENT, AND TAXATION

Switzerland has developed a unique federal system with a weak collective federal government, local autonomy, and a strong, largely self-regulating civil society. Many powers are delegated to the 26 cantonal (confederate units) governments and the smaller communes (counties). For instance, it is the communes (and the population itself by referendums) that grant applying individuals Swiss citizenship.

The **bicameral** legislature, called the Federal Assembly, consists of a 46-member Council of States, or Standerat, whose members are elected in cantonal elections, and a 200-member National Council, or Nationalrat, whose members are elected by popular vote on the basis of **proportional representation** every 4 years. The members of the Federal Assembly select the 7 members of the Federal Council (cabinet), who lead the federal ministries for finance, foreign affairs, justice, economics, interior, transportation (with energy and environment), and defense (with sports). The mostly ceremonial position of president of the council (head of government) is rotated annually according to the seniority of the member councilors. Members sometimes exchange their responsibilities as new members are appointed, or new appointees may take over the portfolios of outgoing councilors. The council strives to present a collegial image and rule by consensus but its deliberations are private. Issues on which no consensus can be reached are determined by a secret cabinet vote and its results are not reported. The composition of the council parallels the traditional 4-party coalition that has ruled Switzerland since the late 1950s.

The 4 political groups, usually receiving 70–75 percent of the total popular vote at parliamentary elections, fill the seats on the council. These elections are held once every 4 years. These include the Free Democrats (FDP), the Christian People's Party (CVP), and the Swiss People's Party (SVP), all center-right parties, and the Social Democrats (SP), a left-of-center formation. The 3 largest parties by their popular vote, FDP, CVP, and SP, receive 2 seats each on the Federal Council; and the SVP gets one. In addition, there are at least 2 seats on the council reserved for French-speaking members from any party. This consensual combination of left and right wings and ethnic elements has allowed the coalition to maintain political, ethnic, and social peace, although it has been criticized by supporters of more radical moves.

Since the 1990s, the need for a more streamlined executive branch has led to the consideration of some revisions to the Swiss constitution that may eventually result in a strengthening of the president's powers. Any revision of the legislation, however, is slow and is subject to a referendum challenge before coming into force. Treaties and agreements approved by the 200-seat Nationalrat (parliament) are also subject to challenge by popular vote in the unique Swiss system of people's initiative and referendum. Virtually every major decision in the country may be put to vote by all the citizens. Only 100,000 signatures are required by law for a people's initiative (petition) to be put to a referendum. The system allows strong popular involvement in the federal and local government and keeps both branches under a close and constant civic scrutiny.

The approval of the bilateral agreements with the European Union (EU) and the rejection of the initiative to limit the proportion of foreigners at the 2 referendums in 2000 were welcomed with relief by the federal government. Given the fresh controversy over the treatment of Holocaust victims by Swiss banks during and after World War II (1939–45), a vote in favor of foreigners' restriction and against the EU agreements would have presented a serious embarrassment for the government and would gravely damage the country's reputation abroad.

European integration policy remains an important focus of political debates, as the government remains convinced that strategic national interests would be best protected by a complete integration into the EU. Switzerland is not economically disadvantaged by staying outside the EU. In the late 1990s, it has been doing better than EU leaders Germany or Italy, growing at a rate unseen since the 1980s, when Switzerland was regarded as Europe's economic model. It also has an uniquely massive balance of foreign payments surplus equal to more than 8 percent of its GDP.

Switzerland lies in the center of Europe, and almost two-thirds of its exports are shipped to EU members, and four-fifths of its imports come from the union. Consequently, Switzerland's future prosperity is definitely related to the development of the EU. Many Swiss feel that their country is becoming isolated in Europe. The fact that Switzerland submitted 16 proposals for negotiation to the EU headquarters in Brussels and had to be satisfied with finalizing only 7 of them might indicate that it needs the EU more than vice versa.

Some feel Switzerland is also losing its position in international financial circles. In 1983, the world's leading industrial countries invited Switzerland, as an exception, to share membership in the Group of Ten—with the world's largest economies—but when the leading finance ministers decided in 1999 to form the Group of 20 of the "systemically most important countries," Switzerland's name was missing. Thus the Swiss no longer have a reserved seat at the top table of the world's economic deliberations. Furthermore, Switzerland, along with small countries like the Vatican and Tuvalu, has so far refused to join the United Nations (UN), although it is a big financial contributor to the organization and hosts the UN office in Geneva plus many other international organizations. It also refuses to be drawn into peacekeeping and peacemaking operations on the grounds that this would jeopardize its neutrality. Still, Switzerland's influence in the world is far higher than its size and even its economic capacity might suggest.

Switzerland has long since developed a market economy based on free initiative, and government participation in the economy is rather moderate. Freedom of trade and industry are guaranteed by the federal and the cantonal constitutions; state intervention is limited, primarily aimed at providing a favorable economic framework, stable currency and prices, efficient infrastructures, and training the workers. In most areas, the federal government legislates and supervises, but the 26 cantonal governments implement the decisions and enforce the laws. The cantons enjoy a high degree of administrative authority, and their own constitutions and laws. The communes (counties), over 3,000 in number, also have independence, control over all local issues, and collect their own taxes. All levels of government have little involvement in manufacturing and services, but their role is considerable in agriculture protection and in trade regulation. Indirect involvement is particularly reflected in the large number of government regulations, especially at the local level. Rules concerning labor laws, business hours, zoning rules, building codes, environmental and noise codes, and administered prices may seem quite pervasive opposed to the United States or even the EU. Obligatory health insurance is another example of the local approach to state involvement in the economy: insurance and health care are provided privately, but the law requires employees to have the insurance. The government subsidizes those who cannot afford it. In the area of competition, unlike the United States and the EU, legislation is loose and cartels in Switzerland have been openly permitted and only broken up when the government has been able to prove that they are socially and economically harmful, which has seldom been the case. In 1996, a new law strengthened the government's antitrust position in mergers, shifting the burden of proof from the court to corporations engaged in anti-competitive activities. Even by EU standards, the new law was relatively weak.

Swiss tax revenues accounted for 35 percent of GDP in 1998, far below the EU average of 41.5 percent and the

Organization for Economic Cooperation and Development (OECD) average of 37.2 percent. The level of taxation has risen somewhat during the 1990s, reflecting higher social security and medical insurance costs, as well as a lack of economic growth. But the Swiss tax system is widely known in the world business circles for its fairness and is characterized by moderate local and foreign operating **income taxation** and tax exemption of **holding-company** income. For this reason, many foreign companies have set up holdings or mixed Swiss subsidiaries to conduct international operations from Switzerland in order to take advantage of lower taxes on their foreign income. Branches of foreign corporations are liberally taxed at the same rate as domestic corporations, unlike many other nations more protective of their national capital. Switzerland has undertaken to make itself even more fiscally attractive for corporate investors, and a corporate tax reform at the federal level removed the annual federal tax on capital in 1998, setting a fixed federal tax on profits at a rate of 8.5 percent.

INFRASTRUCTURE, POWER, AND COMMUNICATIONS

Switzerland has a dense and efficient rail network and an extensive high-class road system with many tunnels to compensate for the mountainous terrain. Overall there are 4,492 kilometers (2,791 miles) of rail lines and 71,059 kilometers (44,156 miles) of roadways. There are 2 large international airports (at Zürich and Geneva) and a few smaller airports with international connections. Landlocked Switzerland also has a modern marine network with some 30 ocean-going vessels based abroad, and carries out river cargo services with connections to the North Sea via the Rhine river. The port of Basel on the Rhine is a major trading hub with efficient connections between rail, road, and water routes. Switzerland is located on strategic crossroads connecting some of the fastest-growing areas of the EU in France, Germany, and Italy.

The agreements with the EU, approved by the referendum in 2000, included the areas of air transport (providing for improved access for Swiss carriers in Europe and similar rights for EU carriers in Switzerland) and road transport (in return for better access to the EU's road haulage market, Switzerland's 28-metric ton truck weight limit will be relaxed in 2001, with full access for the EU's larger 40-metric ton trucks by 2004). Under the new system of taxing heavy trucks by weight, distance traveled, and pollution caused, big trucks will be required to pay a toll of up to US$200 to cross the country. The opening to bigger trucks prompts Swiss authorities to reexamine road infrastructure, and they have started installing electronic devices on trucks to record the mileage traveled in the country, so that tolls could be calculated correctly. In 2001, a 34-metric ton truck meeting the environmental standards is expected to pay about US$95 to travel from Basel on the German border to Chiasso on the Italian border (in 1999, the toll was about US$24).

Airlines also benefited after Swiss voters approved closer economic ties with the EU in 2000. SAirGroup, the holding company of the Swissair airline, got the opportunity to buy a controlling stake in Sabena Belgian Airlines. That will expand its scope of cooperation with foreign partners like American Airlines and boost its presence in France, where it also bought a 49 percent stake in a US$1.4 billion umbrella company that included 3 smaller domestic carriers (Air Liberte, Air Littoral, and AOM) that will have a 30 percent share of the domestic market and will be able to challenge the local giant Air France.

Switzerland has large resources of hydroelectric power in the mighty alpine rivers flowing down from glaciers; they are almost fully exploited. In 1996, hydroelectric plants supplied 54 percent of the Swiss electricity production of 55.1 billion kilowatt-hours (kWh), the lowest proportion for decades, while the country's 5 modern nuclear power stations provided 43 percent. Conventional thermal plants, burning fossil fuels, contributed for only

Communications

Country	Newspapers	Radios	TV Sets[a]	Cable subscribers[a]	Mobile Phones[a]	Fax Machines[a]	Personal Computers[a]	Internet Hosts[b]	Internet Users[b]
	1996	1997	1998	1998	1998	1998	1998	1999	1999
Switzerland	337	1,000	535	352.7	235	29.2	421.8	371.37	1,427
United States	215	2,146	847	244.3	256	78.4	458.6	1,508.77	74,100
Germany	311	948	580	214.5	170	73.1	304.7	173.96	14,400
Sweden	445	932	531	221.4	464	50.9	361.4	581.47	3,666

[a]Data are from International Telecommunication Union, *World Telecommunication Development Report 1999* and are per 1,000 people.
[b]Data are from the Internet Software Consortium (http://www.isc.org) and are per 10,000 people.

SOURCE: World Bank. *World Development Indicators 2000.*

3 percent of the electricity. Switzerland usually exports and sometimes imports some electricity when in need, mostly from French nuclear power plants across the border from Geneva. During the 1990s, energy consumption declined slightly, relative to the population. This was possibly because of newer energy saving technologies. The government's 1991 "Energy 2000" program aims to stabilize overall energy consumption, following a referendum in 1990 in which the Swiss voted for a ten-year moratorium on the construction of nuclear power plants, but against abandoning nuclear power altogether.

In 2000, the government proposed the liberalizing of the electricity market (allowing many competing utilities to sell power directly to businesses and households), after an earlier reform version had been disapproved. The new plan envisaged a gradual liberalization of the sector starting in 2001, with complete liberalization 6 years later, at a faster pace than required by the EU rules. In the first 3 years of the reform, only the 110 largest Swiss electricity users (all large companies) will have a free choice of supplier, followed by smaller enterprises, and finally by individual consumers. The government holds that a single company must run the national electricity grid. However, critics of the reform, more suspicious of energy liberalization after the California blackouts in early 2001, stress that the new proposals do not provide remedies for the amortization (pay back) of existing sizeable investments in plant and equipment that may be made unprofitable by liberalization. The revenues from a new energy tax, the introduction of which is under consideration and has not yet been approved by parliament, however, may fund some of the required investments. Others may be funded by a surcharge on electricity bills for domestic consumers who are unable to change their suppliers and will be required to pay for the right to remain with their providers. Swiss industry captains pushed for a quick transition. This would cut their electricity bills, which are the highest in Europe, by as much as 25 to 30 percent. The liberalization program, nevertheless, makes a referendum challenge likely, given the political clout of the liberalization critics. The country has some 1,200-electricity producers, most of which are likely to go out of business when liberalization occurs. Many are small companies owned by mountain communes and still enjoy considerable political influence. In anticipation of liberalization, the electricity sector is already undergoing **restructuring**. In 2000, 3 electricity companies in western Switzerland struck a strategic alliance aimed mainly at providing electricity services to customers, including buying electricity for them in the European markets.

The Swiss telecommunications market was fully liberalized in 1998, in line with the EU telecom regulations. The state-owned telecommunications company, Swisscom, was split off from the postal service and partly **privatized** through stock market offerings in 1998. Private companies such as Diax and Sunrise compete with Swisscom in the full range of telecom services, though in early 1998 they were still arguing over the very high charges demanded by Swisscom to allow them to use its network. Rival private operators are not allowed to build competing networks for connection to private homes, and therefore the interconnection rates charged by Swisscom are crucial for them. By cutting rates for international long-distance calls, Sunrise has already begun to attract customers from Swisscom, which faces additional competition from numerous mobile phone operators.

There is still a growing demand for telecom services, but they are subject to an already very competitive environment as more than 40 local and international carriers are competing in all areas of telecommunication services. Swisscom tries to keep its grip on the most profitable sectors of growth, such as mobile communications, voice transmission, closed user groups, and particularly large business accounts, **value-added** services, including private virtual networks, and design and operation (with its partners Cisco, Siemens, Alcatel, Ascom/Ericsson) of asynchronous transfer mode (ATM) computer networks. Foreign investment in the Swiss telecom sector is heavy, as many international carriers, such as the American MCI/Worldcom and Sprint-Global One, have established themselves locally, followed by other large players like British Telecom, France Telecom, and Tele Denmark. Vodafone, the British wireless giant, is expected to invest about 5 billion euros in Swiss mobile phone operators. Vodafone has agreed to acquire a 25 percent stake in Swisscom's mobile division but is waiting for final approval from the government, which still has a 65.5 percent stake in the company; the deal will be worth up to 4 billion euros. France Telecom has increased its stake in the Swiss operator Orange Communications by buying (for approximately 1 billion euros) 42.5 percent of Orange's stock from Eon, a German energy group. Massive foreign investment is not only beneficial for customers, but also helps Swiss companies keep up with the latest trends in the market. The introduction of telephone cards by AT&T, MCI, and Sprint-Global One, for example, prompted Swiss companies to introduce their own telecom cards to Swiss subscribers and international travelers.

The International Telecommunication Union, based in Geneva, is an important facilitator in world telecommunications, issuing standard recommendations and organizing important conferences and trade events, such as the quadrennial Telecom exhibition, which is a forum for multinational debates.

Switzerland has high computer usage rates and a large percentage of the population uses computers on a regular basis. 57 percent of the Swiss households owned personal computers and 38 percent had access to the Internet by 2000. This was less than Sweden's 53.5 percent but more than Germany, France, or Italy, where only around 18.1 percent of the population had Internet access. There are more than 150 Internet service providers (ISPs) in Switzerland. Some of the major firms include Blue Window, Iprolink, Infomaniak, Compuserve, and AOL Switzerland. There are also many smaller free services. **E-commerce** is also increasing rapidly, but the cautious and conservative approach of European consumers has meant that growth will be slower than in the United States in 1998–1999, particularly after the U.S. and European dotcom meltdown in late 2000.

ECONOMIC SECTORS

As a country deprived of large natural resources but abounding in skilled labor, Switzerland has concentrated on the financial services sector and on research-intensive engineering, world-famous for precision and quality. Both sectors together account for more than half of export revenues. In agriculture, Switzerland is about 65 percent self-sufficient and imports about US$6 billion of agricultural products annually. Swiss farmers, since World War II among the most heavily subsidized groups of producers in the world, are challenged as EU pressure mounts on Switzerland to liberalize food imports. Tourism is also a traditionally major economic powerhouse. International trade is a large contributor to the economy. In 1995, 2.8 percent of GDP was created in agriculture, 31.1 percent in industry, and 66.1 percent in services.

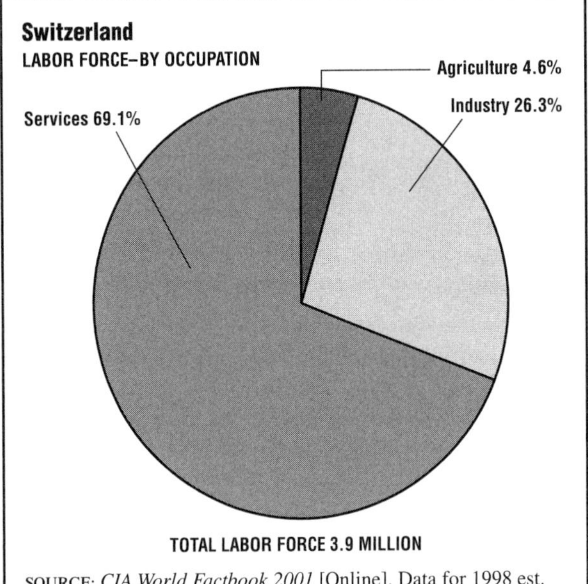

SOURCE: *CIA World Factbook 2001* [Online]. Data for 1998 est. Percent distribution for 1998 est. *Note: 964,000 of total labor force are foreign workers, mostly Italian.

AGRICULTURE

The Swiss soils, terrain, and climate do not favor agriculture particularly and farms are usually family enterprises, mostly small in size. They produce cereals such as wheat and barley, root crops such as sugar beets and potatoes, and fruits such as apples and grapes. About 124 million liters (33 million gallons) of wine, at subsidized prices, are produced annually. Dairy products, such as cow's milk and world-renowned Swiss cheeses, make up a significant portion of the agricultural revenue. Livestock include cattle, pigs, sheep, horses, and poultry. After World War II, agriculture has lost its relative weight in the economy (though not its traditional clout in society or politics), and its preservation as a sector has been due largely to governmental intervention and support. To protect farmers and serve the national security goal to remain largely self-sufficient in food, the federal government has developed a complex system of protections effectively restricting imports of agricultural products, notably dairy and grains. High import **tariffs** and tariff rate quotas (limiting the merchandise quantities that can be imported from a certain country or generally) are maintained for most products which are domestically produced. Producers, particularly those in alpine and other difficult zones, are especially actively supported. Approximately 80 percent of gross farm income can be attributed to government intervention. Milk price supports are one of the principal staples of protectionism and that product's prices remain significantly higher than in the EU markets.

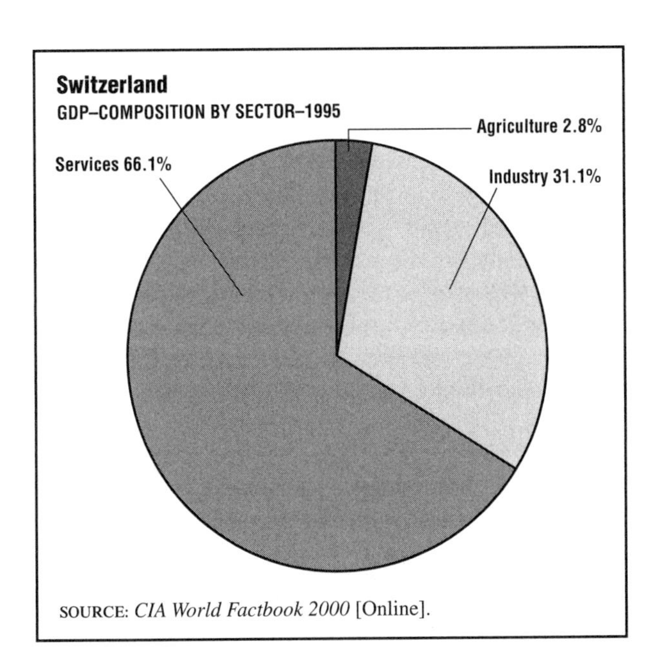

SOURCE: *CIA World Factbook 2000* [Online].

Since 1993, the Swiss system for protecting farmers has slowly begun a fundamental reform, due to the need to reduce costs for the budget and to the pressure from consumers and trading partners. Trade liberalization agreements require Switzerland to eliminate import barriers, reduce export **subsidies**, revise agricultural tariffs, and cut domestic support. Consequently, the Swiss agricultural sector will become less protected and more open to market forces and increasingly accessible to foreign goods. The government's position is that Swiss agricultural policy and regulations will be adjusted to be more in line with EU policies leading to reductions in administered prices. The process of agricultural policy reform started in 1993 when the prices of the politically sensitive dairy sector were first slightly reduced. The reform culminated in 1998, when the Parliament approved a new package of agricultural policy measures. According to the package, administrated prices will continue to decline and direct payments to farms will be gradually linked to their of use environmental production methods such as organic agriculture. On the other hand, trade agreements with the EU that lowered tariffs and other barriers to trade in agricultural goods will boost both exports of Swiss cheese and other delicacies and the imports of a range of EU-produced fruit, vegetables, and beverages into Switzerland.

INDUSTRY

Although raw materials are very limited in Switzerland, the country has a world-class manufacturing economy fabricating raw material imports into high-value added exports. The engineering industry, together with metals and electronics, employs about 9 percent of the country's workforce and contributes around 40 percent to Swiss export revenues. Leading areas in the sector include precision engineering, in particular the world-renowned Swiss clocks and watches (accounting for 8 percent of export revenues in the early 1990s); scientific instruments; heavy engineering and machine building, including specialized, custom-built equipment such as generators and turbines; food products, particularly specialized luxury goods such as chocolate and cheese; textiles; chemicals; quality pharmaceuticals; and fine handicrafts.

Moderate GDP growth, both domestically and in Europe, has been keeping manufacturing growth down over much of the early and mid-1990s, but restructuring efforts carried out over the late 1990s have left the sector in a better and more competitive position. The strong tradition for creativity and innovation demonstrated by the Swiss industry in the past continues to thrive, particularly in new materials technology, micromechanics, and microelectronics, and other research and development-based products. Environmental technologies are expected to have a very good growth potential. The entering into force of multilateral trade liberalization accords signed in the 1990s (under the former General Agreement on Tariffs and Trade, which was succeeded by the World Trade Organization, and also with the EU) will be very important for the Swiss machinery sector. Export-oriented engineering manufacturers will benefit from lower tariffs and the liberalization of public **procurement** procedures within the EU. They will also improve conditions for Swiss direct investments abroad, and bring better protection for Swiss patents and technical know-how in the international markets.

The chemical industry (including the valued Swiss pharmaceuticals) was one of the sectors in the Swiss economy that performed very well in spite of the 1991–1997 **recession**. As with the engineering sector, chemicals will also benefit from liberalization; the positive effects may be of even greater magnitude. Within the chemical branch, pharmaceuticals offer the biggest growth potential and they will benefit most from better patent protection abroad. Agreements with the EU on the elimination of technical obstacles to trade by mutual recognition of trademarks, technical regulations, other rules and procedures for the testing and certification of industrial goods, will also boost Swiss trade with the union.

SERVICES

FINANCE. Long regarded as the country of the bankers, Switzerland has a robust finance services sector and its most vibrant components are banking and insurance. Within the banking sector, commercial and private banks have the largest influence and growth potential. Swiss banks have been historically renowned for their stability, strictly enforced secrecy policies, privacy, personalized service, and reliability. The increase in world trade and industrial activity after World War II brought more business to commercial banks, particularly to their global operations. With the merger of the Union Bank of Switzerland and Swiss Bank Corporation in 1998, the new United Bank of Switzerland (UBS) is now Europe's second largest bank by total assets. Mutual funds and institutional investors have also vastly gained in importance, and represent very good growth prospects for commercial and private banks. The insurance industry is equally important for Switzerland, and the Swiss are by all measures the most heavily insured people in the world. There are over 100 insurance companies, approximately 10 percent of which specialize solely in the reinsurance business; of the latter, Rueckversicherung is the world's second-largest reinsurance company. Swiss insurance companies have been consistently very strong performers with steadily growing earnings.

TOURISM. A country of scenic landscapes and enterprising people, Switzerland has one of the most robust tourist industries in the world, with extensive facilities and centuries-old traditions, a sector that is one of the leading sources of foreign exchange and employment in the economy. Although the country is a humming crossroads between some of the fastest-growing regions in the

EU, foreign visitors usually enjoy lengthy stays instead of simply transiting through. Foreign tourists spent US$11.355 billion in 1998 and over 69 million overnight stays were recorded in the sector offering slightly more than 1 million hotel, chalet, campsite, and youth hostel beds. Foreign tourist positive credit balance reached US$1.046 billion in 1998, and revenue from domestic tourists exceeded US$9 billion. Expenditures in the foreign tourist sector, including investments, surpassed US$10 billion. The country attracted the widest possible range of guests, from affluent elderly people visiting the spas to low-budget young backpackers trekking or "canyoneering" across its numerous mountains. Switzerland has a long list of world-renowned alpine (skiing and hiking) and lakeside tourist resorts, spas, and casinos; world-class cultural events; and many important international organizations and conferences, drawing huge numbers of participants, activists, and observers.

RETAIL. The structure of **retail** trade in Switzerland has been changing since the 1980s. Independent retailers are decreasing in number, giving way to self-service and discount stores and supermarkets, and a tendency toward specialization in food distribution has been particularly noticeable. Department and chain stores, consumer cooperatives, discount stores, and supermarkets account for a large part of local trade. The tendency in those companies is to deal in a wide range of products and services. Their centralized buying gives them a competitive advantage over independent retailers (they are given a discount by suppliers due to the vast scale of their purchases). Retail traders continue to streamline their operations in order to counter their stiff competition. Scanner cash registers for bar-coded articles are ubiquitous, and the use of electronic cards to ease payment transactions is growing (cards are issued, among others, by the Swiss Post, where numerous Swiss have bank accounts, and are becoming increasingly popular). In 1987, Swiss retail groups united to form an Electronic Payment System Association.

Yet, faced with the competition of large retail establishments with nationwide coverage, individual retailers also set up organizations to provide wholesale purchasing, importing, and other services. Functioning as cooperatives, most of these small retailers' buying groups and associations operate in the foodstuffs business but also in textiles, leather goods, sports articles, pharmaceuticals, toys, and hardware. Home shopping, or the direct sale from a private location, is becoming increasingly popular and has recorded enormous growth. The **turnover** for direct sales companies has doubled after 1995. The home-shopping boom has reached a record high and products sold range from Tupperware to lingerie to new recipes and cleansing agents. More than 5,700 salespeople are members of the Swiss Association of Direct Marketing Companies (VDF), mail order companies not included. They can count more than 1 million client-contacts yearly, generating a turnover of US$195 million (in 1998). Most of the products sold at "Home Shopping Parties" are top quality and innovative and cannot be found at retail stores. The advantages of home shopping are the advice offered by the sales persons, the relaxed and friendly atmosphere of the private location, the combined shopping and meeting friends experience, and the possibility of testing the products on the spot.

INTERNATIONAL TRADE

International trade has long been the key to prosperity in Switzerland. Traditionally, its merchandise **trade deficit** has been generously compensated by a surplus trade in services. This surplus amounted in 1999 to US$18.7 billion or 7.5 percent of GDP. The country is heavily dependent on export markets to maintain its large export sector, supply raw materials for the domestic manufacturers, and diversify the array of goods and services available locally. Switzerland has traditionally very liberal trade and investment policies, its commercial law and legal system are highly developed, and foreign investments are protected by solid domestic policies. The Swiss franc is one of the strongest currencies in the world and the country is known for the soundness of its banking industry, so it has all the major factors benefiting international trade.

Chief Swiss exports include machinery, chemicals, metals, watches, textiles, agricultural products, and imports include raw materials, machinery, chemicals, vehicles, metals, agricultural products, and textiles. Principal economic partners in 1998 included the EU, 80 percent (Germany, 33 percent; France, 12 percent; Italy, 10 percent; the Netherlands, 5 percent; Britain, 5 percent); the United States, 6 percent; and Japan, 3 percent. Trade with the EU in 2000 fell below average by 9.9 percent, while exports to the U.S. went up by 15.9 percent and to Japan by 16.4 percent. Export growth was also impressive to the **Commonwealth of Independent States** (CIS, the former USSR), South Korea, China, and Turkey, each

Trade (expressed in billions of US$): Switzerland

	Exports	Imports
1975	12.958	13.305
1980	29.632	36.341
1985	27.433	30.696
1990	63.784	69.681
1995	78.040	76.985
1998	75.431	73.877

SOURCE: International Monetary Fund. *International Financial Statistics Yearbook 1999.*

with growth of more than 40 percent, although from a low base in 1999. Irrespective of the fluctuations, the EU remained the crucial economic partner for Switzerland. The strong and flexible Swiss economy reacts to international market fluctuations with an elaborate precision, keeping itself competitive.

Contrary to its traditionally positive foreign trade balance, Switzerland accumulated a trade deficit of nearly US$554 million in the first 9 months of 2000, compared to more than a US$1 billion surplus for the same period of 1998. Such negative trade balance is typical, however, in periods of strong economic growth—like the one Switzerland went through between 1998 and 2000—when higher local incomes boost domestic consumption and imports consequently outgrow exports. The 2000 imbalance, however, was caused by foreign price changes rather than by the strong domestic demand. It is almost certain that if international crude oil prices had remained unchanged over that period, the Swiss trade balance would have accumulated probably a surplus of more than US$500 million. Import growth during the same period was 13.2 percent and the value of imports of energy rose by 87 percent also largely due to increasing oil prices. Export growth was driven by the expansion of the EU and other foreign markets, and strong export growth product categories included precision instruments, watches, and metals. The traditional Swiss watch industry in late 1990s was very successful in exporting mostly watch parts, while exports of ready-made watches were somewhat shrinking. Exports of food (notably cheese and chocolate) were rather weak, as were the international sales of the troubled Swiss textile industry.

Exchange rates: Switzerland

Swiss francs, franken, or franchi (SwFR) per US$1	
Jan 2001	1.6303
2000	1.6888
1999	1.5022
1998	1.4498
1997	1.4513
1996	1.2360

SOURCE: CIA *World Factbook 2001* [ONLINE].

MONEY

The Swiss National Bank, the central bank and the institution which issues currency, has been successful in maintaining the arguably most stable currency in the world but also very skeptical of the benefits of integrating Switzerland with the EU or with its euro currency. With its private banks and insurance companies active globally and rated among the world's best, the Swiss financial services industry is traditionally one of the largest employers and an important export revenue source. Swiss banks, with their firm reputation for financial solidity and respect for privacy, are leaders in global asset management. More than one-half of the US$1.76 trillion in assets managed by Swiss banks are thought to be of foreign origin (according to the Swiss National Bank).

The local banking scene, however, has undergone some serious structural changes in the 1990s, following global consolidation trends. Many small local banks closed or merged and many large ones streamlined their Swiss retail networks while expanding their overseas operations. The total number of banks dropped from 495 in 1990 to 403 in 1996 and the number of regional banks was cut by more than one-third. In 1990, the Swiss banks had also, under pressure from the federal government, to abandon a series of price-fixing arrangements they were indulging in, increasing competition for customers and funds. The domestic recession between 1991 and 1997 and the cuts in spending and borrowing it initiated helped send out of business a number of regional banks with limited deposit bases relying heavily on mortgage lending and loans for local businesses. All these developments have increased the concentration of the Swiss banking sector where the 4 largest banks, including the merged Union Bank of Switzerland (UBS) and Swiss Bank Corporation (SBC), account for half the total combined balance sheet. Nevertheless, Switzerland maintains a high bank density, with 1 branch for every 1,400 inhabitants (compared with 2,000 in Germany or 4,700 in the United States), although bank employment decreased from 127,626 in 1990 to 119,771 in 1996. In the long run, the Swiss Bankers' Association fears, up to one-third of the 1996 bank employment could be lost due to consolidation and the use of new technologies in the sector.

Zürich has traditionally been a major international banking center and its equivalent to the New York's Wall Street is the renowned Bahnhofstrasse where the headquarters of the UBS and the Credit Suisse, 2 of Europe's leading banks, as well as many smaller private banks, are located. Although the majority of the UBS staff is based in Switzerland, almost one-third of it is located internationally throughout the world; its global investment banking operations are in London, and its fund management head office is based in Chicago. Credit Suisse has an equally strong presence in both the United States and Europe. But the robust growth and restructuring of Zürich's 2 big banks has generated new opportunities for smaller competitors as well. For example, seasoned bankers that were laid off in the UBS's 1998 merger with SBC have helped the management teams of smaller banks build up their skills. Furthermore, Zuercher Kantonalbank (ZKB), the third-biggest bank in Zürich that subscribed 75,000 new customers in 1999, holds that over 30 percent of those new customers were due to the effects of the merger. And many of the even smaller banks have performed at an even better rate. Julius Baer, for instance, the biggest independent private bank in Zürich, attracted the same amount of new funds in 1998 as did UBS, more than 16 times larger. Vontobel, Zürich's second-largest private bank, increased its profits almost 2 times in 1999 and its return on **equity** was over 30 percent. The numbers of bank employees, previously decreasing, have stabilized, the leading banks have enlarged their international market share, and a large number of small fund management and corporate finance boutique firms have flourished.

But, in the longer term, there still may be serious threats as Switzerland's big banks and insurance companies have long since outgrown the size of their country, and Zürich's relative importance as an international financial center has decreased as business has moved to major international centers like London, Frankfurt, and New York. A united Europe, with the emergence of the single European currency, the euro, also contributes to the country's increasing financial isolation. But it is still the world's top **offshore banking** center for private customers, attracting many offshore affiliates of major international firms that use Switzerland as a **tax haven**. Its success, however, receives the attention of European officials who believe that Switzerland's bank secrecy laws and loose tax rules give it an unfair competitive advantage in attracting offshore capital and also that it is harboring major tax evaders from other countries.

Money laundering allegations and related banking scandals have disturbed the Swiss public opinion throughout the 1990s. To combat transnational organized crime, abusing the liberal Swiss banking system, and partly responding to international pressures, Switzerland gradually relaxed its banking secrecy policies and allowed foreign investigators access to bank records in cases where illegal acquisition or use of funds were suspected. In 1998, new strict money laundering laws were introduced and a significant number of high-profile international money laundering cases were investigated by magistrates in many cantons, particularly in Geneva. In the late 1990s, Swiss prosecutors investigated some serious allegations of money laundering by former top Russian officials through the Swiss company Mabetex. In January 2001, Pavel Borodin, former head of Russian President Boris Yeltsin's administration, was detained by U.S. authorities in New York on request of the prosecution and may be turned over to the Swiss judiciary. Following the Mabetex scandal, the Swiss government launched a political campaign abroad over Switzerland's reputation as a financial center, defending banking secrecy yet emphasizing its willingness to join international efforts to fight transnational organized crime. The government has even quietly encouraged the new government of Nigeria to take legal action in Switzerland to recover national assets allegedly siphoned off by the previous government. It is not certain, however, how the Swiss government will react to pressures from the EU to fight tax evasion that is not a criminal offence in Switzerland. Although unwilling to change its tax and secrecy laws, it is reassuring to many that Swiss laws on fraud and money laundering are so extensive that they effectively cover cases of major tax evasion as well.

In the mid-1990s, the Swiss Banking Association, under pressure from world Jewish organizations, agreed to search its vaults for unclaimed bank deposits allegedly containing assets belonging to Jewish victims of the Holocaust during the World War II. In 1997, the Swiss government endorsed a proposal by several leading banks and businesses to establish a memorial fund for compensating Holocaust survivors and their descendants, although many individuals and groups claimed Switzerland was not doing enough to aid the victims and their descendants. In 1998, class action suits and potential U.S. **sanctions** against Swiss banks prompted 3 large private banks to agree to participate in a global settlement of all claims and suits against them. The banks agreed to a settlement of US$1.25 billion, allowing Holocaust survivors and their descendants to receive compensation.

The Swiss Exchange was 1 of the 8 European exchanges to sign a memorandum of understanding, formally confirming a commitment to work towards a pan-European equity market with one single electronic trading platform for blue-chip stocks (of large and creditworthy companies renowned for the quality and wide acceptance of their products or services, and for their ability to make money), with common rules and regulations. In addition, the exchange is strengthening ties to London, Europe's leading financial center. In 1999, the exchange granted remote membership for the first time to an institution based in Britain. From its London office, the American securities firm Donaldson, Lufkin & Jenrette (DLJ) International Securities became a remote member that can participate in trading on the Swiss electronic exchange from outside the country. DLJ's remote membership followed the admission of Germany's Mees Pierson and Hull Trading. The exchange is trying to make its membership more attractive and to promote the country as a trading area, lowering its admission fee for new members to SwFr25,000 (from SwFr350,000) as the old fee was prohibitive for many brokers. The high fees were intended to pay off the expenses for installing an electronic exchange system in the 1990s.

The Swiss government sees eventual membership into the EU as a core foreign policy target over the next 10 years. However, the SNB has been skeptical of the rewards of integrating with the euro currency. Many Swiss believe that such a move would result in Switzerland

GDP per Capita (US$)

Country	1975	1980	1985	1990	1998
Switzerland	36,154	39,841	41,718	45,951	44,908
United States	19,364	21,529	23,200	25,363	29,683
Germany	N/A	N/A	N/A	N/A	31,141
Luxembourg	21,650	23,926	26,914	35,347	46,591

SOURCE: United Nations. *Human Development Report 2000; Trends in human development and per capita income.*

importing the risk of instability associated with the eastward enlargement of the EU. Others hold that linking the Swiss franc to the euro would be risky. If the Swiss franc remained independent, they suggest, it would gain in importance as a diversification currency for international investors.

POVERTY AND WEALTH

The Swiss traditionally enjoy one of the highest living standards in the world although they also have an exceptionally high cost of living. Although there are many large private fortunes of local and foreign persons, Switzerland's **Gini index** score (which measures economic equality, with 0 standing for perfect equality and 100 for perfect inequality) of 33.1 is quite a bit lower than that of the United States (40.8) or the United Kingdom (36.1). The structure of consumption and the quality of life are also among the world's most advanced, according to UN studies. Switzerland's government is working hard to improve its environmental policies and to fight organized crime, reducing the impact of these 2 threats to modern life everywhere in the world.

But there is also some growing sense of insecurity in Switzerland, manifesting itself in a rising concern about immigration, unemployment, and the higher levels of foreign ownership of Swiss property and firms, although such concerns are largely overstated. An in other

Distribution of Income or Consumption by Percentage Share: Switzerland

Lowest 10%	2.6
Lowest 20%	6.9
Second 20%	12.7
Third 20%	17.3
Fourth 20%	22.9
Highest 20%	40.3
Highest 10%	25.2

Survey year: 1992

Note: This information refers to income shares by percentiles of the population and is ranked by per capita income.

SOURCE: *2000 World Development Indicators* [CD-ROM].

affluent countries in which unemployment is very low (less than 2 percent), the perception of job insecurity is much greater than unemployment itself. The average period employees remain in a job hasn't changed since 1980, and moreover, labor shortages, rather than high unemployment, are likely to be more prevalent in Switzerland, at least over the next 5 years. Likewise, the concern about the influx of refugees is grossly exaggerated. Eastern European countries remain the main source of potential refugees, but as they narrow the GDP per head gap with western Europe, the already quite low levels of migration are likely to be decreased further. The political processes in the former Yugoslavia after the toppling of Slobodan Milosevic in late 2000 may also contribute to a more stable condition and less immigrants from the Balkans region.

Recent takeovers of Swiss firms by large foreign companies have also led to misplaced concerns. As firms denationalize, becoming increasingly international and global in character, the competitiveness of the business environment as a location for firms becomes more important. With Switzerland's highly educated workforce and other positive assets, the result may rather be a long period of high value industrial development and there is little reason to believe that foreign ownership will lead

Household Consumption in PPP Terms

Country	All food	Clothing and footwear	Fuel and power[a]	Health care[b]	Education[b]	Transport & Communications	Other
Switzerland	19	6	9	3	18	8	36
United States	13	9	9	4	6	8	51
Germany	14	6	7	2	10	7	53
Luxembourg	17	8	9	3	7	5	52

Data represent percentage of consumption in PPP terms.

[a]Excludes energy used for transport.

[b]Includes government and private expenditures.

SOURCE: World Bank. *World Development Indicators 2000.*

to money flight from the country. If feelings of economic insecurity grow, there may be further calls for protection for Swiss industry in order to preserve domestic employment. Also, there may almost certainly be further tightening of legislation to curb immigration, with the potential for a backlash against government's plans to integrate the Swiss and EU labor markets.

WORKING CONDITIONS

The educated and skilled Swiss workforce, the elaborated laws promoting labor flexibility and safety, and the agreements between the influential trade unions and employers' associations have protected Switzerland from significant labor unrest. The unemployment rate dropped to 1.7 percent in September 2000 and the rate is likely to stabilize, as the principal component of unemployment was caused by the disparity between the required and offered qualifications and mostly unskilled workers continued to have problems in finding jobs. This rate of unemployment was the lowest one since December 1991 and substantially below levels prevalent in EU countries (the most favored of which, Luxembourg, had a rate of 2.2 percent in July 2000, while the preliminary EU rate for August was 8.3 percent).

The economic stagnation from 1991 to 1997 had a major impact on the labor market. Over this period, 255,000 jobs (in full-time job equivalents) were lost. Surprisingly, however, the unemployment situation improved dramatically from a rate of 5.7 percent in February 1997 (the highest in decades) to the low level found in 2000. Indeed, statistics tend to underestimate the real level of unemployment, and if the number of persons in active labor market programs, retraining schemes, and temporary jobs are added, that would raise the underlying rate of unemployment by probably 1 percentage point. Rising employment has also enabled the government to almost halve the number of publicly sponsored jobs, to 7,106 in August 2000 from 13,095 just a year earlier. The ratio of long-term unemployed among all unemployed remained relatively high at 20.9 percent in August 2000, and this number did not include those who fell out of the statistics after reaching the end of the benefit entitlement period (a total of 1,078 persons).

Mutual recognition of academic degrees, diplomas, professional certifications, and social security entitlements was an important element of the recent agreements with the EU aimed at increasing **labor mobility**. The government envisages the scrapping, over a 6-year period, of the Swiss quota system for work permits for EU and European Free-Trade Association (EFTA) citizens, although limits may be introduced again if inflows of immigrants are stronger than expected. After 7 years, Switzerland can opt out of the pact or continue with it for another 7 years. At this point, freedom of movement for EU and EFTA citizens will become permanent.

COUNTRY HISTORY AND ECONOMIC DEVELOPMENT

4TH CENTURY A.D. Germanic tribes conquer ancient Roman Helvetia, the site of present-day Switzerland.

9TH CENTURY. Most of Switzerland joins the Duchy of Alemannia (Swabia), one of the feudal units of the German kingdom; the southwestern part of the area is taken over by the feudal kingdom of Transjurane Bourgogne.

1033. The Bourguignon part of Switzerland is taken over by Emperor Conrad II and becomes a part of the Holy Roman Empire of the German Nation, consisting of small feudal states ruled by lords, bishops, and abbots, and many independent city-states, which later become cantonal commonwealths.

1276. Emperor Rudolf I Habsburg of the Holy Roman Empire attempts to assert his feudal rights in a threat to the traditional liberties of the Swiss. Three forest cantons—Schwyz, Uri, and Unterwalden—based around the Lake of Lucerne form a league for mutual defense in 1291. During the 14th century, the cantons of Zürich, Glarus, Bern, Lucerne, and Zug join the league, and in the 15th century Fribourg and Solothurn follow suit.

1474. The Habsburgs, unable to tame the militant Swiss mountaineers, abandon their attempts to acquire their territory, and their confederation becomes directly dependent on the empire.

1499. Emperor Maximilian I attempts to abrogate various Swiss rights; he is later defeated, and, by the Treaty of Basel of the same year, recognizes the virtual independence of the Swiss.

1513. The cantons of Appenzell, Schaffhausen, and Basel enter the confederation and send 2 delegates each to the federal assembly. Swiss mercenaries gradually become famous throughout Europe (and still constitute the papal guard in the Vatican City). Swiss troops annex Italian towns that now form the canton of Ticino in the south of Switzerland. In 1536, Bernese Swiss take Lausanne on the Lake Geneva and various other territories from the duchy of Savoy.

1515. Swiss troops are defeated by the French in 1515 and Switzerland's neutrality policy is then adopted.

1648. Swiss cantons preserve their neutrality in the Thirty Years' War of 1618 to 1648 and achieve formal recognition as a completely independent state by the Peace of Westphalia in 1648. The union of the cantons is still quite weak, but a modern market economy develops as Swiss craftsmen win reputation across Europe for quality and skill, and financial services develop.

1798. French-backed revolutionaries occupy Swiss territory. Napoleon Bonaparte, the future emperor of France, unifies the country under the name Helvetic Republic and imposes a written constitution, which, like the French military occupation, is bitterly resented by most of the Swiss.

1803. Napoleon withdraws French troops and by the Act of Mediation grants a new constitution with Swiss approval.

1815. The Congress at Vienna recognizes the perpetual neutrality of Switzerland, and Swiss territory is expanded to include 22 cantons (Geneva is ceded by France), acquiring its modern form.

1847. Political struggles between autocratic and democratic elements and between Roman Catholic and Protestant areas culminate in a civil war between the Sonderbund, a Catholic league, and the federal government, which takes the upper hand. The new constitution of 1848 greatly increases federal power.

1874. A new constitution is passed, which, with modifications, is still in force; it completes the development of Switzerland from a group of cantons to a unified federal state.

1940s-1950s. Switzerland develops its powerful modern economy and, although maintaining its neutrality, becomes a member of the General Agreement on Tariffs and Trade (GATT), the international trade organization replaced in 1995 by the World Trade Organization (WTO), headquartered in Geneva. Also joins the Organization for European Economic Cooperation (1948), the European Free Trade Association (1959), and the Council of Europe (1963).

1971. Switzerland grants women the right to vote in federal elections and to hold federal office.

1992. Switzerland joins the International Bank for Reconstruction and Development (World Bank) and the International Monetary Fund (IMF). However, Swiss voters reject joining the European Economic Area, a **free-trade zone** linking many Western European countries.

1994. A referendum declares racial discrimination, racist propaganda, and denial of the Nazi Holocaust illegal.

1995. Under international pressures, Switzerland begins to relax its banking secrecy policies to help fight organized transnational crime.

1997. The Swiss government endorses a proposal to establish a memorial fund to compensate Holocaust survivors and their relatives for funds allegedly retained by Swiss banks.

1998. In December, the parliament elects Social Democrat and former labor union leader Ruth Dreifuss as Switzerland's first woman and first Jewish president.

2000. The Swiss voters approve by referendum a bilateral agreement with the EU and turn down a proposal to limit the quota of foreigners allowed in the country to 18 percent.

FUTURE TRENDS

By all accounts, Switzerland is likely to maintain and develop its stable and prosperous economy in the foreseeable future but its role in the changing world is likely to be strongly dependent on its gradual integration with the EU. The debates between Euro-skeptics and Euro-enthusiasts will most likely dominate domestic policies, along with the foreign workers controversy. The Swiss economy and society will be trying hard to reformulate their unique identity in the globalizing world.

EU integration will benefit the leading Swiss industries, particularly in manufacturing, but offshore banking and agricultural firms may suffer, which, given their strong political clout, may further disturb the integration process. The participation of the Swiss in the European political process may generate new domestic controversies over time. But in the long run, the benefits of the single European market of goods, capitals, persons, and ideas will outweigh the drawbacks for Switzerland.

The Swiss financial industry will overcome the scandals that have been plaguing in throughout the 1990s, and although a radical change in the tax laws is not likely, will cooperate with the EU and other countries in combating organized transnational crime and tax evasion. The Swiss will preserve their unique system of self-governing and their high standard of living with rising level of employment but the fear of unemployment and of being "overrun" by foreigners will continue to influence the domestic political debate and will often raise the issue of solidarity with the people of less fortunate countries.

DEPENDENCIES

Switzerland has no territories or colonies.

BIBLIOGRAPHY

Confoederatio Helvetica. <http://www.admin.ch/ch/index.en.html>. Accessed August 2001.

Economist Intelligence Unit. *Country Profile: Switzerland.* London: Economist Intelligence Unit, 2001.

Embassy of Switzerland in the United States. <http://www.swissemb.org>. Accessed August 2001.

Enright, Michael J., and Rolf Weder, editors. *Studies in Swiss Competitive Advantage.* Bern and New York: P. Lang, 1995.

New, Mitya. *Switzerland Unwrapped: Exposing the Myths.* London and New York: I.B. Tauris, 1997.

U.S. Central Intelligence Agency. *World Factbook 2000.* <http://www.odci.gov/cia/publications/factbook/index.html>. Accessed August 2001.

U.S. Department of State. *FY 2000 Country Commercial Guide: Switzerland.* <http://www.state.gov/www/about_state/business/com_guides/index.html>. Accessed January 2001.

—Valentin Hadjiyski

UKRAINE

CAPITAL: Kiev.

MONETARY UNIT: Hryvnya. One hryvnya (UAH) equals 100 kopiyok. There are coins of 1, 5, 10, 25 and 50 kopiyok, and notes of 1, 2, 5, 10, 20, 50, and 100 hryvnya.

CHIEF EXPORTS: Ferrous and non-ferrous metals, fuel and petroleum products, machinery and transport equipment, and food products.

CHIEF IMPORTS: Oil and gas, machinery and parts, transportation equipment, and chemicals.

GROSS DOMESTIC PRODUCT: US$189.4 billion (2000 est.).

BALANCE OF TRADE: **Exports:** US$14.6 billion (2000 est.). **Imports:** US$15 billion (2000 est.).

COUNTRY OVERVIEW

LOCATION AND SIZE. Ukraine is situated in Eastern Europe. It shares borders with Hungary, Slovakia, and Poland to the west; Belarus to the north; Russia to the north and east; and Romania and Moldova to the south. It also has a coastline of 2,782 kilometers (1,729 miles) on the Black Sea and the Sea of Azov. The total border length of Ukraine is 4,558 kilometers (2,832 miles) in length. The country's total area is 603,700 square kilometers (233,000 square miles), making Ukraine about the size of Texas. The capital of Ukraine is Kiev, which is located in the north-central region of the country and is also the largest city in Ukraine with a population of 2.6 million.

POPULATION. The total population of Ukraine was estimated at 48,760,474 in July 2001. The most notable recent demographic trend has been the decline in population. According to the Human Development Report (HDR) of 1996, the total population of Ukraine in 1994 was estimated at 51.7 million people. Hence, since 1994, the population has dropped by more than 3 million people, or more than 5 percent. According to estimates of July 2001, the population growth rate is -0.78 percent, the birth rate is 9.31 birth per 1,000 people, and there is a high mortality rate of 16.43 deaths per 1,000 people.

In 2001, 17.3 percent of the population was younger than 15 years, 68.57 percent was between the age of 15 years and 65 years, and 14.13 percent were over 65. The life expectancy at birth of the total population is 66 years—for males it is 60.62 years, and for females it is 71.96 years. The total fertility rate is 1.29 (which is below replacement level), and the infant mortality rate is 21.4 (per 1,000 children born). The leading factors of the country's low fertility are environmental pollution, poor diet, widespread smoking and alcoholism, and deteriorating medical care.

The ethnic distribution among the Ukrainian population is 73 percent Ukrainian; 22 percent Russian; 1 percent Jewish; and 4 percent are of other ethnic groups. The major religious groups are the Ukrainian Orthodox under the Moscow Patriarchate, the Ukrainian Orthodox under the Kiev Patriarchate, the Ukrainian Autocephalous Orthodox, the Ukrainian Catholic (Uniate), Protestant, and Jewish. The official state language of the Ukraine is Ukrainian, but in 1991, the Law on National Minorities gave individual citizens the right to use their ethnic language, and ethnic groups may establish their own schools. Other languages spoken in the Ukraine are Russian, Romanian, Polish, and Hungarian. However, potential students have to pass a Ukrainian language test, which is seen as a form of discrimination by the Russians.

OVERVIEW OF ECONOMY

As a former member of the Union of Soviet Socialist Republics (USSR), Ukraine was once deeply integrated into the former Soviet economy, particularly in the agricultural and military industries. Ukraine's fertile black soil accounted for an estimated one-quarter of Soviet agricultural output. Its farms provided substantial quantities of meat, milk, grain, and vegetables to other republics. Similarly, Ukraine's diversified heavy industry supplied equipment and raw materials to industrial and mining sites in other republics of the former USSR.

Ukraine was the second most important economic component in the former Soviet Union.

Since gaining independence in 1991, Ukraine's economy has contracted substantially. The **gross domestic product** (GDP) has fallen steadily over the past decade, and only recently has it begun to rebound. Overall, Ukraine's GDP fell more than 60 percent since it declared independence from the Soviet Union in August 1991. However, these official figures overstate the fall in output, since the **informal economy** has been expanding beyond the reach of government regulations and taxes. Estimates for the informal sector or **black market** (whose economic activities are unregulated and untaxed) economy range as high as 60 percent of the total GDP.

As in the Soviet days, the government remains the dominant player in the economy. It still pays **subsidies** to the agricultural, transport, telecommunications, and housing sectors. These subsidies are paid to keep **full employment**, and the slow speed of **privatization** allocates substantial resources to state-owned enterprises, which are still quite prevalent in the economy. In 1999, government expenditures were $8.8 billion.

The year 1998 saw moderate economic growth of 0.2 percent in the first half of the year. However, financial crises in both Asia and Russia had a strong influence on Ukraine's economy, and the GDP decreased by 1.9 percent by the end of 1998 and then by 0.4 percent in 1999. Buoyed by a significant real **devaluation** of the hryvnya in the wake of the Russian crisis, Ukraine's economy started to show signs of a new recovery in late 1999. In 2000, GDP grew 6.0 percent from 1999, with the highest growth rates achieved in **import-substituting** (textiles and food) and export-oriented industries (metallurgy and chemicals).

The nation's major industries are coal and electric power, ferrous and nonferrous metals, machinery and transport equipment, chemicals, and food-processing. Ukraine also has considerable agricultural exports. These include grains, sugar beets, sunflower seeds, vegetables, beef, and milk.

Over the past several years, **inflation** has been low, prices **liberalized**, and the currency, the hryvnya, relatively stable. The country's continual decline in industrial production has slowed down in recent years. The greatest economic achievement of the government has been to bring inflation down progressively from the hyperinflation of 1993—when inflation rose to 10,000 percent (making the currency essentially worthless)—to 10 percent in 1997. Inflation was even lower during the first half of 1998, but prices rose sharply in late 1998 after the steep drop in the Russian ruble led to a significant (though more modest) depreciation of the Ukrainian hryvnya. Total inflation for 1999 was 20 percent, and for 2000, 25.8 percent. In February 2000, the **exchange rate** was about 5.59 hryvnya per U.S. dollar.

The first 3 years of privatization, from January 1995 to January 1998, resulted in the selling off of 45,000 small businesses and 8,000 larger enterprises. By 2000, more than 67,000 enterprises had been privatized, including more than 7,000 medium-and large-scale industrial enterprises. For small-scale enterprises, privatization is virtually complete. The sale of larger enterprises has been slowed by a lack of supporting legislation for privatization, resistance from some local authorities and the management of large enterprises, and extensive parliamentary opposition. The main opposition to further privatization is the belief that such programs will result in higher unemployment.

Corruption is one of the biggest problems plaguing Ukraine's economy. According to the U.S. State Department, corruption is present in much of Ukraine's government, judiciary, and law enforcement, with no meaningful work being done to eradicate it. Such problems have been a major impediment to increased foreign investment.

POLITICS, GOVERNMENT, AND TAXATION

On August 24, 1991, after the collapse of the Soviet Union, Ukraine declared its independence, and the political system underwent rapid changes. Ukraine became a member of the **Commonwealth of Independent States** (CIS), a loose confederation of countries that were formerly states of the Soviet Union. In 1991, the first democratically elected President of Ukraine was the former chairman of the **Communist** Party, Leonid M. Kravchuk. He stayed in office until July 1994, when he lost the election to former Prime Minister Leonid Kuchma.

Ukraine has a parliamentary democratic government with separate executive, judicial, and legislative branches. The head of state is the president, who nominates the prime minister. The president is elected for a 5-year term. The prime minister must be confirmed by the parliament. The 450-member parliament initiates legislation, ratifies international agreements, and approves the budget. Its members are elected to 4-year terms. On June 28, 1996, Ukraine adopted a new constitution. The Constitution adopted a multi-party system, and legislative guarantees of civil and political rights for national minorities.

There are 8 major organized political forces in Ukraine. First, there is the Communist Party of Ukraine or Komunistychna Partiya Ukraine (KPU). The KPU is the strongest organized political force. It opposed the Ukrainian Constitution of 1996 and most economic reforms. They are supporters of closer ties with Russia. The second major group is the Popular Rukh of Ukraine or Narodny Rukh Ukraine (Rukh), established in 1989, which draws its support from the intelligentsia (the intellectual and professional class) and some political elites. Third, there is the Socialist Party (SP), which was established in 1991. The SP advocates for more state control of the key economic sectors and closer ties with Russia and the CIS. The SP formed a faction with the leftist Peasant Party, which was established in 1992.

The fourth main party is the Green Party (GP). Formed in the early 1990s, the Green Party supports environmentally-friendly policies, an overhauling of Ukraine's tax system to better accommodate business and consumer interests, and Ukrainian neutrality in most foreign policy matters. The People's Democratic Party (PDP) is the fifth major political group. The PDP advocates economic reform, including a reformed tax system, an improved climate for investment, integration into the world economy, and privatization and land reforms. They favor strong relationships with both Russia and the West. Hromada, established in 1993 by a group of former Communists is the sixth main group. They strongly oppose economic reforms.

The seventh significant political group is the Progressive Socialist Party (PSP), who split with the SP in 1997. They are anti-reform and are among the hard left of the political spectrum. The PSP want to rebuild a Soviet Socialist Ukraine, abolish the presidency, and establish closer ties with Russia and Belarus. They also oppose cooperation with NATO and international financial institutions like the International Monetary Fund (IMF) and the World Bank. The eighth and final faction is the Social Democratic Party (United) or SDP(U). The SDP(U) supports a "socially-oriented market economy," using market economics to generate resources for better social protection, the state-supervised sale of land, and closer ties with both Russia and the West.

The level of taxation is moderate when compared with that of the nations of Western Europe and slightly higher than tax rates in the United States. The maximum personal **income tax** rate is 30 percent. Corporate taxes range from 20 to 30 percent depending upon the size of the company's profits. Employers also must pay **social**

security taxes for their employees. These include the Social Insurance Fund, Pension Fund, and Employment Fund. These social security taxes are equal to an estimated 47.5 percent of wages and dramatically increase labor costs. For instance, for each worker earning $10 per hour, an employer would have to pay $10 in wages and $4.75 in taxes or $14.75 per hour. In addition to taxes on wages, Ukrainians must pay high taxes on the purchase of goods and services. This tax is known as the **value-added tax** (VAT) and the standard VAT rate is 20 percent. The VAT is charged on the majority of goods and services except insurance, reinsurance, and education. Ukraine also has high taxes on imported goods. These import **duties** range from 5 to 200 percent and there are **excise taxes** that range from 10 to 300 percent.

Ukraine's **foreign debt** stood at $12.6 billion in 2000. The largest amount is owed to Russia and Turkmenistan, primarily for past trade credits of gas deliveries, which have been rescheduled into long-term state credits. Ukraine owed approximately $5.07 billion to international financial institutions and bilateral export credit agencies.

Ukraine is a net recipient of foreign aid. In 1998, the IMF provided $2.2 billion to Ukraine. Since the mid-1990s, Ukraine has received an average of $500 million annually in aid. The European Union (EU) and the United States are the main providers of aid. The nation's large **external debt** ($12.6 billion in 2000) and continuing deficit are a drain on the Ukrainian economy. In proportion to GDP, Ukraine's debt is about twice that of comparable countries in Europe. In 2000, the deficit was 5 percent of GDP and required 3.5 percent of total GDP to make payments on the debt.

In 1999, the nation spent $500 million in defense outlays. Overall, military spending accounts for 1.4 percent of GDP. The Ukrainian military numbers approximately 500,000. In its effort to establish closer ties with the West, Ukraine joined NATO's Partnership-for-Peace Program. Ukrainian troops have joined in joint exercises with NATO and contributed troops to NATO's peacekeeping mission in Bosnia.

INFRASTRUCTURE, POWER, AND COMMUNICATIONS

Ukraine enjoys an extensive though aging **infrastructure** that has received much government attention in the 1990s. The transport network of Ukraine is dominated by railways, which total 23,350 kilometers (14,510 miles). It also has 273,700 kilometers (170,077 miles) of highways, 86 percent of which are paved. In 1990, the total length of navigable waterways was 4,499 kilometers. (2,796 miles).

There is a comparably well-developed air transport communication system in Ukraine. In 2000, there were 718 airports, 114 of which had paved runways. The main international airport is at Kiev and the nation's main airline is Air Ukraine. In 1997, about 1.8 million people either landed at or departed from airports in Ukraine.

Ukraine has a powerful merchant and passenger fleet, operating in the basins of the Black Sea and Sea of Asov, and on the navigable rivers. In 1999, the merchant marine included 156 ships that were larger than 1,000 tons. This included 105 general cargo ships, 14 rail carrier vessels, and 11 passenger ships. The nation's main ports are Kerch, Kiev, Odessa, Sevastopol, and Reni.

An expanding array of tele- and radio communications are increasingly available and constantly improving, and new **joint-venture** companies provide modern technology development in this sphere. According to an estimate by the World Bank (2000–01), Ukraine has 54 daily newspapers (1996), 884 radios (1997), 490 televisions (1998), 191 telephone mainlines (1998), 2 mobile telephones (1998), and 13.8 personal computers (1998) per 1000 people. There are also 5.39 Internet hosts per 10,000 people (January 2000), or a total of 35 Internet service providers

Communications

Country	Newspapers	Radios	TV Sets[a]	Cable subscribers[a]	Mobile Phones[a]	Fax Machines[a]	Personal Computers[a]	Internet Hosts[b]	Internet Users[b]
	1996	1997	1998	1998	1998	1998	1998	1999	1999
Ukraine	54	884	490	15.7	2	0.0	13.8	4.56	200
United States	215	2,146	847	244.3	256	78.4	458.6	1,508.77	74,100
Russia	105	418	420	78.5	5	0.4	40.6	13.06	2,700
Poland	113	523	413	83.3	50	N/A	43.9	40.86	2,100

[a]Data are from International Telecommunication Union, *World Telecommunication Development Report 1999* and are per 1,000 people.
[b]Data are from the Internet Software Consortium (http://www.isc.org) and are per 10,000 people.

SOURCE: World Bank. *World Development Indicators 2000.*

In the Soviet period, Ukraine was a net exporter of electricity both to former Soviet states, and to Eastern Europe. After independence it became a net energy importer. Overall, Ukraine generated about 158 billion kilowatt-hours (kWh) of electricity in 1999, a 25 percent decline from 212 billion kWh in 1994. According to the World Bank, the electrical power consumption per capita in Ukraine has also drastically declined, from 4,308 kWh in 1990 to 2,449 kWh in 1997. With about 60 percent of Ukraine's electricity generated by fossil fuels (the remaining 40 percent being produced by nuclear and hydroelectric plants), this production decline has been exacerbated by problems in obtaining natural gas, oil, and coal supplies, mostly imported from Russia, who also provides Ukraine with nuclear fuel, for which Ukraine currently owes Russia $800 million. In 1998, Ukraine imported an estimated 344,000 barrels of oil per day and almost 2 trillion cubic feet of natural gas.

Ukraine's 5 nuclear power plants, with a capacity of 12.8 giga-watts (nearly one-quarter of the country's total capacity), generate around 70 billion kWh of energy (more than 40 percent of the country's power output). The construction of 2 new reactors (capacity 2 giga-watts) is in its final phase. In June 2000, Ukraine's nuclear power plants generated more than half of the nation's total electricity output, the first time that has happened since 1996, despite the fact that 5 of the nation's 14 nuclear reactors, with 24 percent of national capacity, were inactive in June. The 1986 Chernobyl nuclear accident cast serious doubts about the safety of nuclear reactors in Ukraine and their ability to meet the long-term power needs of the nation.

Another factor which has harmed the nation's electrical sector, next to import and capacity problems, has been the growing number of defaulting electricity consumers. A report in mid-1996 stated that 40,000 businesses owed the electric companies some $1 billion in energy bills, representing 30 percent of the electricity consumed in the country. Also, about 35 percent of Ukrainian families receive their electricity free by law. Largely as a result of this situation, the Ukrainian Ministry of Power Engineering and Electrification has described itself as bankrupt.

ECONOMIC SECTORS

Ukraine's economic sectors are diverse, but in need of new capital and investments to compete with sectors in the West. Due to the country's rich soil, agriculture accounts for a large percentage of GDP. Ukraine was once the breadbasket of the Soviet Union. Agriculture, including forestry and fishing, accounted for 14 percent of the total GDP in 1999. Industry, including mining, manufacturing and construction, accounted for 34 percent in the same period. Meanwhile, trade and other services accounted for 51 percent. The country's **labor force** in 1999 totaled 25 million people. The share of the labor force in industry, agriculture, and services in 1996 was 32 percent, 24 percent, and 44 percent, respectively.

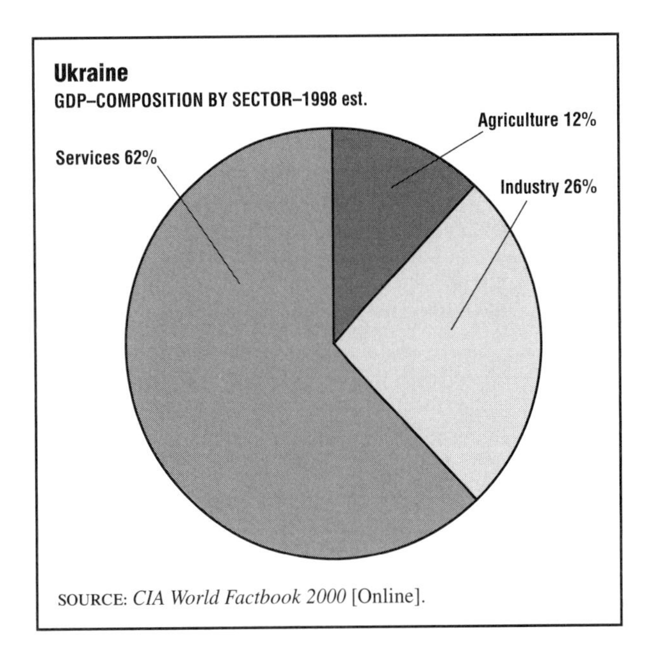

SOURCE: *CIA World Factbook 2000* [Online].

AGRICULTURE

Ukraine is blessed with rich farming and forestry resources. According to the *Statistical Year Book of Ukraine* (1996), about 71 percent of the country's surface (41 million hectares) was used for agricultural activities.

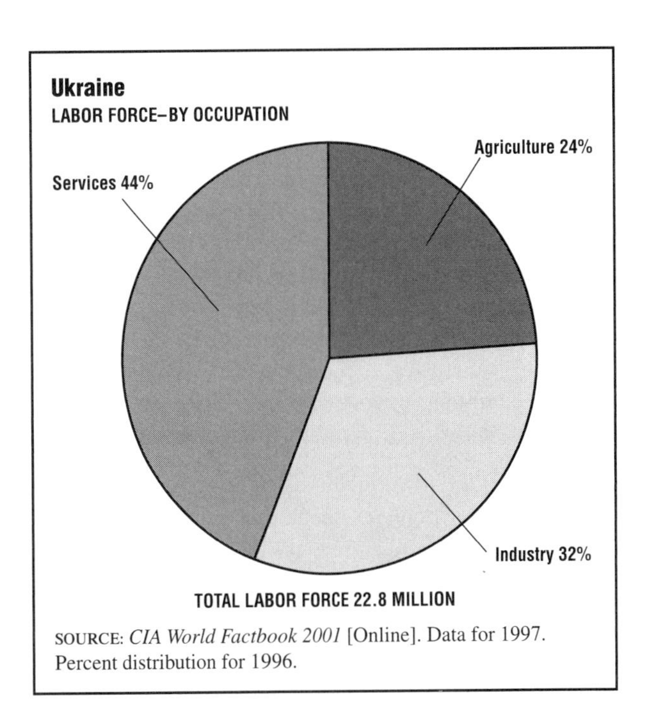

SOURCE: *CIA World Factbook 2001* [Online]. Data for 1997. Percent distribution for 1996.

About 80 percent of the agricultural area is arable land, two-thirds of it the agriculturally rich "black soil" (chernozem). The primary food harvest products are barley, maize, potatoes, rice, soybeans, sugar beets, and wheat. The primary meat products are beef and veal, lamb, pork, chicken, horse, and rabbit. In terms of value, the largest agricultural exports in 1998 were refined sugar, raw sugar, beef and veal, sunflower seed, and fish. The total value of agricultural exports in 1998 estimated $1.898 billion. The total value of agricultural imports in 1998 was $999 million. The largest single crop produced in 1999 was potatoes at 15.4 million metric tons. The number-two crop was sugar beets at 13.89 million metric tons, followed by wheat at 13.47 million metric tons. The main livestock product was beef and veal with 786,000 metric tons, followed by swine with 668,000 tons, and chicken with 194,500 tons.

In recent years, agricultural production has declined drastically because of a decrease in the number of tractors and combine harvesters in working order and to the lack of fertilizers and pesticides. According to official data, between 1991 and 1997, the number of tractors in use decreased from 497,300 to 361,000. (In order to operate efficiently, it is estimated that the country would need 515,000 tractors in use.) Similar shortfalls exist for harvesting combines. Between 1990 and 1997, the consumption of pesticides and fertilizers per hectare declined about 78 percent. From 1995 to 1999, crop production declined by an average of almost 10 percent per year, while livestock production declined by an average of 9 percent per year. These shortfalls in agricultural inputs reflect declining investment in agriculture, and feed directly into declining production.

Under communism, agricultural lands were held by the government and worked by the people, who owned no land. Privatization planned to shift most such land into the hands of individuals and farming collectives (jointly held farming cooperatives). By August 1995, the transfer of lands into private hands had begun. Over 8 million hectares of land had been privatized, with plots averaging 5 hectares. By 1996, most of the agricultural land in Ukraine was in collective and private hands, although 40 percent was still owned by the government. Household plots and private farms accounted for about 15 percent of the Ukrainian territory and they filled an important role in the delivery of products to the marketplace.

In general, the agricultural sector is experiencing serious internal difficulties, due to the transitional nature of the economy. A new policy and direction for Ukraine's agricultural sector is necessary. Agriculture poses the greatest challenge to the survival of Ukraine's political leaders, because almost half of the Ukraine's population live in rural areas.

INDUSTRY

Under the Soviet economic system, the Ukrainian industrial infrastructure was based around its rich mineral endowments. Heavy industry and the defense industry were predominant in Ukraine (Ukraine produced almost 25 percent of all Soviet military goods). Sizeable production of steel and pig iron was based on generous supplies of coal and iron ore. Other important heavy industrial products included ferro-alloys, non-ferrous metals, cement, mineral fertilizers, and building materials. Ukraine remains a significant producer of non-ferrous metals, automobiles, and machine tools. With the disappearance of the central command system, the former links between the economic sectors has diminished. The old distribution system has gone and industry cannot rely on regular state subsidies anymore. The Soviet military industrial complex has come to a practical standstill (but is recovering), and links with other former Soviet Republics have diminished. All these factors contributed to a lack of cash in the industrial sector, resulting in a depreciation of the national currency and price inflation.

MINING. Ukraine is rich in mineral deposits, including iron ore (of which it once produced 50 percent of the entire Soviet output), manganese ore (of which it produced 40 percent of world output during the Soviet era), mercury, titanium, and nickel.

Ukraine is one of the world's most important mineral producing countries, in terms of both the range and size of its reserves. There are nearly 8,000 separate deposits, harboring some 90 different minerals, of which about 20 are economically significant. About half of all the known deposits are under exploitation. Coal reserves in Ukraine amount to 47.1 billion tons. The annual domestic demand for coal as fuel is about 100 million tons, of which 85 percent can be satisfied by domestic production. Ukraine has oil and gas fields that meet 10 percent of her oil and 20 percent of her gas consumption, respectively. Ukraine contains natural gas reserves of 39.6 trillion cubic feet, but only about 20 percent of the country's demand is met by domestic production. Deposits of iron ore (estimated at 28 billion tons), manganese ore (3 billion tons), chalk and limestone (1.5 billion tons) are also large in Ukraine. The domestic industrial sector suffers from constant energy shortages and energy supply payment debts totaling about $792 million at the end of 1995.

MANUFACTURING. Following independence, Ukraine's manufacturing sector has steadily declined, from 36 percent of the GDP in 1990 to 29 percent of the GDP in 1999. In 1994, the output of light manufacturing decreased by about 34 percent and engineering by 28 percent. Primary production and semi-manufactured goods registered lower output falls in 1995. One of the main results of this has been a move towards primary production in the Ukraine's industrial sector in recent years. Primary production consists of electricity, oil, gas, coal, and steel. This kind of production accounted for 53 percent of total industrial production in 1995, compared to 38 percent in 1990. Ukraine's manufactured goods have suffered greatly through the loss of former Soviet markets. Locally, their generally low quality has made them vulnerable to imports from the EU; at the same time, this low quality diminishes their viability as exports.

Since 1994, Ukraine has significantly increased its arms exports, from $20 million in 1994, to more than $100 million in 1995, to over $1 billion by the end of 1996. Ukraine merged 3 major arms export firms into a single company, Ukrspetsexport, in order to increase competitiveness in what is now its fastest-growing source of foreign exchange. The growth in the arms trade has been the result of the far lower costs of Ukrainian weapons than Western European or American arms.

The underperforming manufacturing sector is thought to be ripe for foreign investment. Growing domestic need for **consumer goods**, durable goods (appliances, etc.), and machinery, especially agricultural machinery, has encouraged investment across these sectors.

SERVICES

Contrary to the decline of the industrial and agricultural production, the contribution of services to GDP increased from 30 percent in 1990 to 51 percent in 1999. The most prominent segments of the service sector are tourism and financial services. The following services can be classified as relatively developed branches of service sectors in Ukraine: telecommunications services, banking services, advertising and public relations services, legal services, audit and accounting services, and tourism services. But the following service sectors are still quite underdeveloped: engineering, insurance, private health care, and security.

Transportation is another important sector of the services economy. Russia is highly dependent on Ukraine for its transport of gas to Europe. Ukraine has made several proposals in an effort to be included into the energy transport network for Caspian Sea energy resources. The dominant method of transporting goods in Ukraine is by trucks, though deteriorating roads and high fuel costs make trucking expensive.

TOURISM. Since independence in 1991, Ukraine has emerged as the most stable and peaceful country among the former states of the Soviet Union despite all her economic and political crises. Policy makers actively welcomed foreign investors, business people, and tourists. Ukraine is developing as one of the most active and diverse tourist countries in the former Soviet region. The nation offers a broad range and rich tapestry of high level cultural, historical, national-folklore, and environmental tourism. Strategically, Ukraine is situated in immediate proximity to the great tourist centers of Europe and the Mediterranean and is opportunely connected to them by air, railroad and sea transportation routes. The most popular tourist destinations in Ukraine are Kiev, the capital city; the Crimea, which is popular for its warm climate and many spas; and the Carpathian mountains, with their alpine sports, and historic and ethnic cultural sites.

According to the U.S. State Department, nearly 11 million people visited Ukraine in 1999 (down from 12 million in 1998 and 14.6 million in 1997). Ukraine received over 6.2 million foreign tourists, placing Ukraine in the top 25 most visited countries of the world. The share of the tourism sector to GDP was estimated at 8.6 percent ($3.8 billion) in 1998. In Crimea alone, proceeds from tourism make up to 40 percent of the Crimean government budget.

Ukraine's tourist industry has great potential to develop into a major source of foreign exchange generation by the 2000s. In view of Ukraine's critical need to develop viable **hard currency** in the economic sectors, the government and tourist industry are seeking to upgrade hotel and resort facilities to high international standards, in order to maximize the long-term potential of the industry and sufficiently harness the nation's diversified tourist market and to try to attract foreign investors.

The high number of tourists has not led to a high level of tourist services, however. As of 2001, Ukraine still lacks a major international hotel. Most tourist services lay in the hands of owners connected to local political bosses, who have sought to keep control of this sector by excluding outside investment. Of all visitors, 75 percent arrive from Russia. Russians' low service expectations have kept Ukraine insulated from the relatively higher expectations of Western tourists.

FINANCIAL SERVICES. The financial sector is relatively undeveloped in Ukraine. According to the report of the U.S. Embassy in Kiev, there are a variety of problems in this sector: setting up service projects requires legal endorsement; there is rampant corruption in the licensing and administrative approval process; the payments system is antiquated, with most Ukrainians having neither bank accounts or credit cards; and legal recourse in collecting on unpaid services is almost non-existent.

The Ukrainian banking system includes the central bank—the National Bank of Ukraine (NBU)—and an assortment of commercial banks. NBU responsibilities consist of monetary circulation, registration and oversight of commercial banks, and intervening in the currency market. As of January, 203 banks were registered in Ukraine, of which 165 banks are in actual operation, including 30 backed by foreign capital, and 9 with 100 percent foreign capital. With the exception of 2 state-owned banks,

Trade (expressed in millions of US$): Ukraine

	Exports	Imports
1994	10304	10748
1995	13316	16052
1996	14440	18639
1997	14232	17113
1998	12636	14675
1999	11581	11846

SOURCE: United Nations. *Monthly Bulletin of Statistics* (September 2000).

Oshchadbank and Ukreximbank, the banks are joint-stock companies or limited liability companies.

INTERNATIONAL TRADE

Ukraine's trade is still heavily oriented towards the CIS and especially to Russia. Its major trading partners are CIS countries, the EU nations, Central Europe, China, and the United States. Most imports of oil and gas are from Russia and Turkmenistan, while imports of technologies are mainly from Western countries. Exports, which are minimal for a developed country, consist mainly of raw materials and agricultural goods.

In 2000, exports totaled $14.6 billion and imports totaled $15 billion. Ukraine's main export markets are in Russia (24 percent), the European Union (30 percent), and the United States (5 percent). Its main importers are Russia (42 percent), the European Union (29 percent), and the United States (3 percent).

Ukraine remains interested in bilateral trade and economic cooperation with Russia and the CIS, but is careful to pass up any larger political or security relationship. As an Associate Member of the CIS, Ukraine has rejected all attempts to transform the CIS into a supra-national organization. As a result, Ukraine has refrained from joining the Russia-Belarus Union, the CIS Customs Union, and the Payments Union. However, mindful of the preference for bilateral relations with the CIS countries, in March 1998, Ukraine and Russia concluded an Interstate Economic Treaty.

Under the trade provisions of the PCA (EU-Ukraine Partnership and Co-operation Agreement), trade between Ukraine and the EU is in theory free of most restrictions. In practice, trade in steel and textiles are subject to special taxation schemes, and Ukraine is subject to actual or prospective EU anti-dumping measures for a variety of products, including silicon, carbide, and magnesium. (Anti-dumping measures keep a country from flooding the market with a product that it can produce much more cheaply than its competitors.)

Progress on an EU-Ukraine **free trade zone** most likely will not get underway until Ukraine is admitted to the World Trade Organization (WTO). Ukraine is continuing negotiations with the WTO on the basis of its initial offer and revised service offer. The EU supports Ukraine's eventual entry into the WTO, but does not believe that Ukraine yet meets the conditions for membership. WTO membership is an issue on which the United States and the EU consult and co-operate, as affirmed in the Joint Statement on Ukraine released at the December 1997 U.S.-EU summit.

MONEY

In 1996, Ukraine introduced the hryvnya (UAH) as a new national currency. The greatest success in regards to the economy has been the stabilization of the national currency. The hyperinflation (10,000 percent) of the early 1990s has been reduced to less than 20 percent. However, the hryvnya continues to depreciate in value. This is caused by the Asian and Russian financial crises of the late 1990s on the one hand, and Ukraine's current financial uncertainties and instability on the other. The value of the currency stood at UAH1.8295:$1 in 1996, but by February 2000, the value had slipped to UAH5.59:$1. The hryvnya lost 75 percent of its value to the dollar in 1999 alone. The hryvnya was badly affected by a fuel crisis in July 1999, when gasoline prices doubled over 1 week after imports from Russia declined. Price inflation reached about 25 percent by the end of 1999. The country's currency reserves diminished, as a result of trying to prop up the hryvnya. In early 1999, reserves stood at $2.34 billion, and by mid-1999 were reduced to $860 million. In order to shore up the hryvnya, in September of the same year the government decreed that Ukrainian banks had to keep at least 75 percent of their currency holdings in the national currency. After protests, the government relented and decreased the amount to 50 percent.

In 1991, legislation was enacted that created the nation's first stock market. By 1999, the market, known as the PFTS (the Ukrainian Broker/Dealer Association and Over-the-Counter Trading System), had 125 companies

Exchange rates: Ukraine

hryvnia per US$1	
Jan 2001	5.4331
2000	5.4402
1999	4.1304
1998	2.4495
1997	1.8617
1996	1.8295

SOURCE: CIA *World Factbook 2001* [ONLINE].

GDP per Capita (US$)

Country	1975	1980	1985	1990	1998
Ukraine	N/A	N/A	N/A	1,979	837
United States	19,364	21,529	23,200	25,363	29,683
Russia	2,555	3,654	3,463	3,668	2,138
Poland	N/A	2,932	2,819	2,900	3,877

SOURCE: United Nations. *Human Development Report 2000; Trends in human development and per capita income.*

Distribution of Income or Consumption by Percentage Share: Ukraine

Lowest 10%	3.9
Lowest 20%	8.6
Second 20%	12.0
Third 20%	16.2
Fourth 20%	22.0
Highest 20%	41.2
Highest 10%	26.4

Survey year: 1996

Note: This information refers to expenditure shares by percentiles of the population and is ranked by per capita expenditure.

SOURCE: *2000 World Development Indicators* [CD-ROM].

listed with a market value of $1.121 billion. The PFTS has an electronic trading system that is responsible for about 95 percent of all trades and investments. The PFTS is constrained by widespread public suspicion and mistrust and by inadequate trading and regulatory laws.

POVERTY AND WEALTH

For the majority of people, the standard of living has deteriorated since independence. According to the World Bank (2000–01), as much as 31.7 percent of the population was below the poverty level in 1995. However, by 1999, the CIA estimated that 50 percent of the population lived below the poverty level, which is based on an income of $50 per month. The average wage is 60 to 80 dollars per month, and for most, payment is delayed for several months. Wage **arrears** are an all too common feature of daily life. Because companies have seen their output in 1999 decrease to less than 40 percent of the 1991 level, they often have a difficult time paying their employees on time. Ukraine's **GDP per capita** has declined from $1,979 in 1990 to $837 in 1998. It is similar to the former Soviet States of central Asia and Caucasus and to many African and Middle Eastern countries.

For the majority of the population, the transition from the Soviet period has meant a catastrophic decline in living standards. According to the official government statistics, the cumulative decline measured in national income was about 60 percent between 1991 and 1999. Hence, someone earning the equivalent of $1,800 in 1990 only earned a salary comparable to $600 in 1999. In the same period, the average standards of living declined by about 80 percent. **Pensioners** and retirees were the most affected by these declines.

At the same time, several indicators show that the health status of the Ukrainian population has deteriorated in the years after the independence. Life expectancy at birth has decreased from 70 years to 67.7 years, with a greater fall in males (who reached 62 years) than in females (73 years). Life expectancy is 10 years shorter than the population of the EU. In addition, infant mortality has increased since 1989 and in 1998 was 17 per 1,000 live births. The lack of clean water is a big problem in Ukraine, resulting in disease and early deaths. Contagious diseases in Ukraine are cholera, dysentery, typhoid, hepatitis, and AIDS. Radiation from the now-closed Chernobyl nuclear power plant is also posing serious difficulties to the Ukrainian population.

WORKING CONDITIONS

The country's labor force in 1999 totaled 25 million people. The official unemployment rate in 1999 was 4.3

Household Consumption in PPP Terms

Country	All food	Clothing and footwear	Fuel and power[a]	Health care[b]	Education[b]	Transport & Communications	Other
Ukraine	34	5	16	6	4	14	22
United States	13	9	9	4	6	8	51
Russia	28	11	16	7	15	8	16
Poland	28	4	19	6	1	8	34

Data represent percentage of consumption in PPP terms.

[a]Excludes energy used for transport.

[b]Includes government and private expenditures.

SOURCE: World Bank. *World Development Indicators 2000.*

percent, though this number is thought to significantly underestimate a large number of unregistered or unemployed workers. The minimum wage is $21.70 and the minimum pension for retirees and those on public assistance is only $4.70. The average wage is $41.60 per month. The very low wages paid in the country mean that many Ukrainians must work second or third jobs. Because many such jobs are in the informal sector, the wages and production earned there are not accounted for in government statistics. Some estimates conclude that the informal economy may be as large as 70 percent of the formal economy.

The Labor Code (the body of laws which govern labor standards, working conditions and wages) provides for a maximum 40-hour work-week, one 24-hour day of rest per week, and at least 24 days of paid vacation per year. The minimum employment age is 17 years. In certain non-hazardous industries, however, enterprises may negotiate with the government to hire employees between 14 and 17 years of age, with the consent of one parent.

Ukrainian law contains occupational safety and health standards, but these are frequently ignored in practice since there is little enforcement of the laws. Because of limited funding, there are few officials to inspect workplaces and the labor laws only provide minor punishments for violations (therefore many employers find it more affordable to pay the fines rather than upgrade working areas to meet government standards). In 1999, 913 people were killed and over 47,000 injured in accidents at work. Under the law, workers have a legal right to remove themselves from dangerous work situations without jeopardizing continued employment. However, many workers fear that if they leave their job they will not be able to find another.

Ukrainian workers have the right of association, and the right to organize and bargain collectively. Although officially they have these rights, the government is actively trying to stop the workers of some economic sectors from using these rights, such as in the nuclear industry. Forced or compulsory labor is prohibited by the Ukrainian constitution, however, there are some forms of compulsory labor. For example, the common use of army conscripts and youths in the alternative service for refurbishing and building private houses for army and government officials; also, students, whose studies have been paid for by the government, have to work in the **public sector** at government-designated jobs for 3 years or more to repay fully the cost of their education.

COUNTRY HISTORY AND ECONOMIC DEVELOPMENT

700s A.D. The Kievan Rus state is created by Norse traders seeking commercial routes to the Middle East.

988. Prince Volodymyr accepts Christianity and begins the process of converting the Kievan state to his religion.

1237–1241. Conquest of Kiev by the Tatars.

1300s. Foundation of the Galician-Volynian principality. which included much of the territory of the former Kievan Rus. Lithuania, Poland, and Turkey begin to occupy regions of Kievan Rus.

1569. Treaty of Lublin between Lithuania and Poland allows further Polish expansion into what is now Ukraine.

1667. Ukraine is partitioned between Poland and Russia.

1793. Ukraine is reunited as part of the Russian Empire.

1917–18. During the Russian Revolution, Communists seize power in Ukraine. Three separate Ukrainian republics declare their independence.

1921. Poland absorbs the western Ukrainian republic, while the Soviet Union absorbs the remainder of Ukraine, making it a Soviet Republic.

1929. In an effort to suppress Ukrainian nationalism, the Soviets undertake a broad campaign which results in the arrests and murder of thousands of intellectuals, and political and church leaders.

1932–1933. In an effort to abolish private farms and force industrialization, the Soviets collectivize farms and force millions to leave their farms and settle on government-owned farms. A famine results and causes the death of an estimated 8 million rural Ukrainians.

1941–1944. Ukraine is occupied by German forces during World War II (1939–45), but returns to Soviet control after the war.

1950s. Forced industrialization reaches its peak as the Soviets try to transform the economy from an agrarian one to one based on manufacturing.

1954. The Crimea region is transferred to Ukraine by Soviet premier Nikita Khrushchev.

1972. New rounds of Soviet suppression result in the arrests of hundreds of Ukrainian nationalists.

1986. Chernobyl nuclear accident kills 30 and results in an estimated 1,800 cases of cancer caused by radiation exposure.

1990. The Ukrainian government declares national sovereignty.

1991. On August 24, Ukraine declares independence and becomes a founding member of the Commonwealth of Independent States (CIS).

1994. Ukraine joins NATO's Partnership-for-Peace Program.

1996. The United States and Ukraine agree to a joint investment treaty designed to protect U.S. investors in Ukraine.

1997. Russia and Ukraine agree to a treaty which divides the Black Sea fleet and its bases between the 2 nations. Romania and Ukraine sign a treaty on oil exploration in the Black Sea.

FUTURE TRENDS

During the 1990s, Ukraine achieved little economic growth, thanks largely to economic mismanagement and inherited structural problems. Some years after the government's "Program of Radical Reforms" in 1994, very little real structural transformation has taken place. The serious economic problems confronting Ukraine are of a deep structural nature and include modest industrial **restructuring**, inefficient privatization, a heavy state machinery, a narrow tax base, the rise of powerful criminals, controlling parts of the economy, and economic dependence on Russia. These factors have caused a large part of the economy to operate in the informal sector.

While foreign assistance is crucial in the transitional economic process, official flows of assistance in the longer term should be dwarfed by private capital flows if Ukraine creates a more favorable environment for the development of the **private sector**. Ukraine requires technology, management expertise, and access to international markets that only private businesses can provide. Although Ukraine is taking steps in adapting its trade regime to conform to the World Trade Organization's (WTO) membership requirements, progress is slow and difficult.

Ukraine's history and geography tie it to Russia, but its economic future lies with Western Europe. In order to ensure its integration into Western organizations such as the WTO and the EU, Ukraine has to implement a number of economic reforms. The most pressing of these reforms is continuing privatization and improvements in regulatory laws. Meanwhile, Ukrainian industry must transform itself from the production of primary materials such as steel and energy resources, materials in which Ukraine cannot compete with lower priced manufacturers, to refined or processed materials.

DEPENDENCIES

Ukraine has no territories or colonies.

BIBLIOGRAPHY

Economist Intelligence Unit. *Country Profile: Ukraine.* London: Economist Intelligence Unit, 2001.

The Embassy of Ukraine, Washington, D.C. <http://www.ukremb.com>. Accessed September 2001.

Kuzio, Taras, editor. *Dynamics of Post-Soviet Transformation: Contemporary Ukraine.* Armonk, NY, and London: M.E. Sharpe, 1998.

Murphy, Richard W., William Green Miller, et al. *Collected Papers: Ukraine in Europe.* Centre for Strategic & International Studies: Occasional Report in European Studies, September 1999.

Statistical Yearbook. Kiev: Ministry of Statistics, 1996.

U.S. Central Intelligence Agency. *World Factbook 2000.* <http://www.odci.gov/cia/publications/factbook/index.html>. Accessed August 2001.

U.S. Department of Energy. "Ukraine." *Energy Information Administration.* <http://www.eia.doe.gov/emeu/cabs/ukraine.html> Accessed September 2001.

U.S. Department of State. *Background Notes: Ukraine.* <http://www.state.gov/www/background_notes/ukraine_0005_bgn.html#history>. Accessed September 2001.

U.S. Department of State. *FY 2000 Country Commercial Guide: Ukraine.* <http://www.state.gov/www/about_state/business/com_guides/2001/europe/index.html>. Accessed September 2001.

World Bank. *Land Reform in Ukraine: The First Five Years.* Washington, D.C.: World Bank, 1997.

World Bank. *World Development Report 2000/2001.* New York and London: Oxford University Press. 2000.

—Mehdi Parvizi Amineh

UNITED KINGDOM

United Kingdom of Great Britain and
Northern Ireland

CAPITAL: London.

MONETARY UNIT: Pound sterling (£). One pound equals 100 pence. Coins are in denominations of £2 and 1, as well as 50, 20, 10, 5, 2, and 1 pence. Currency comes in denominations of £50, 20, 10, and 5.

CHIEF EXPORTS: Manufactured goods, fuels, chemicals, food, beverages, and tobacco.

CHIEF IMPORTS: Manufactured goods, machinery, fuels, and foodstuffs.

GROSS DOMESTIC PRODUCT: US$1.36 trillion (2000 est.).

BALANCE OF TRADE: **Exports:** US$282 billion (2000 est.). **Imports:** US$324 billion (2000 est.).

COUNTRY OVERVIEW

LOCATION AND SIZE. The United Kingdom consists of a collection of islands which are located off the northwestern coast of Europe between the Atlantic Ocean and the North Sea. Its total area of 244,820 square kilometers (94,525 square miles) is shared by 4 main territories. The largest is England, with an area of 130,373 square kilometers (50,337 square miles). To the west of England is Wales, with 20,767 square kilometers (8,018 square miles), and to England's north is Scotland, with an area of 78,775 square kilometers (30,415 square miles). Northern Ireland occupies 14,120 square kilometers (5,452 square miles) on the island of Ireland. England, Wales, and Scotland are collectively and commonly known as Great Britain. The United Kingdom also includes numerous small islands. These include the Orkney Islands, the Shetland Islands, the Outer Hebrides, Skye, Mull, Arran, the Isle of Man, the Isles of Scilly, and the Channel Islands. From the southern coast of England to the north of Scotland is a distance of some 1,000 kilometers (622 miles) and the widest part of Great Britain is under 500 kilometers (311 miles). The total boundary length of 8,352 kilometers (5,190 miles) includes a coastline of 7,918 kilometers (4,920 miles) and a land boundary with the Irish Republic of 434 kilometers (270 miles). London is the capital and it is located in southeastern England. London has a population of some 7,000,000, including its suburbs. Birmingham is the United Kingdom's second-largest city, with 934,000 people.

POPULATION. In July of 2001, the population of the United Kingdom was estimated to be 59,647,790. The nation has the third-largest population in Europe and the eighteenth-largest in the world. Currently, the population growth rate is 0.23 percent. A low birth rate and **emigration** will cause the population to decrease to under 57 million by 2030. The birth rate has remained low since the early 1970s. The current rate is 11.76 births per 1,000 people and the fertility rate is 1.76 children born for each woman. The infant mortality rate is 5.63 deaths per 1,000 live births. The overall mortality rate is 10.38 deaths per 1,000. About 75 percent of the population lives in urban areas and about 40 percent lives in the southeast region of the country. Many regions of Northern Ireland and areas of Scotland remain essentially rural. The United Kingdom has a large elderly population (nearly 16 percent of the total population is over age 65). The elderly are the fastest growing segment of the British population. Over time, this will put additional strains on the kingdom's social security and medical systems. The life expectancy for males is 74.97 years and 80.49 years for females.

The English make up 81.5 percent of the population, followed by the Scots at 9.6 percent, the Irish at 2.4 percent, the Welsh at 1.9 percent, and the Ulster Irish at 1.8 percent. Since the demise of the British Empire in the mid-1900s, many former colonial citizens have **immigrated** to the United Kingdom. There is a sizable community of immigrants and descendants of immigrants who combine to account for 2.8 percent of the population. The largest ethnic minority groups are Indian, West

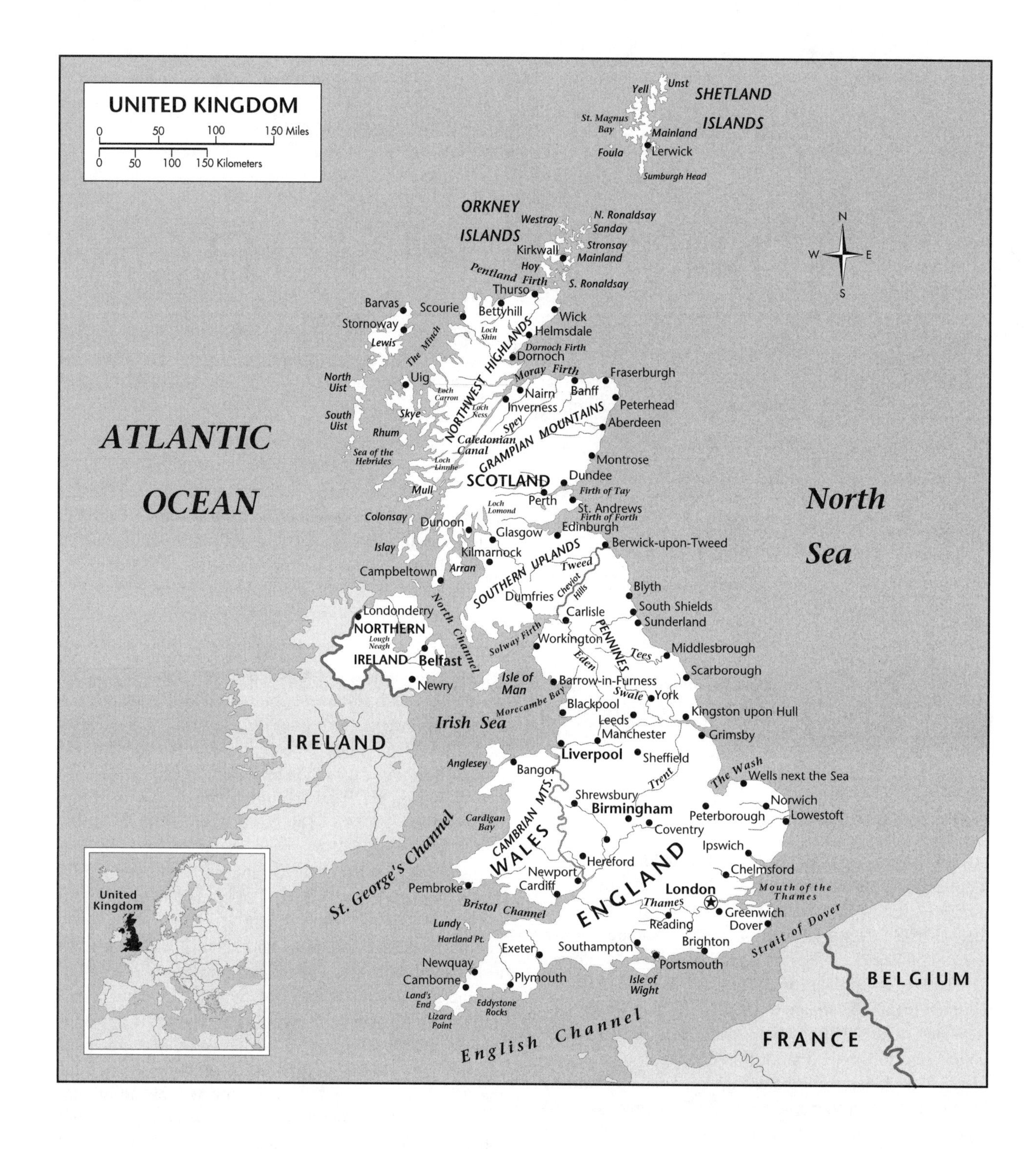

Indian, Pakistani, and Bangladeshi. About 40 percent of the ethnic community were born in the United Kingdom, and some 74 percent are of mixed ethnicity. One of the most significant differences between the English and minority communities is age. About 42 percent of the British and Irish population is under 30, while 60 percent of the West Indian population and 70 percent of those from the Indian subcontinent are under 30. Ethnic minorities are also geographically concentrated in the greater London area. Both Scotland and Northern Ireland have very small ethnic minorities (less than 0.8 percent of the total population). English is the official language of the United Kingdom. About 26 percent of the people of Wales speak Welsh and about 60,000 Scots, mainly in western Scotland, still speak the Scottish dialect of Gaelic. A small number of the Northern Irish continue to speak the Irish form of Gaelic.

Christianity is the dominant religion of the United Kingdom. Anglicans and Roman Catholics are largest Christian groups. There are 27 million Anglicans, 9 million Roman Catholics, 800,000 Presbyterians and 760,000 Methodists. Immigration has resulted in a large non-Christian community. The Muslim community now numbers more than 1 million. In addition, there are some 400,000 Sikhs in the nation and 350,000 Hindus. The Jewish population is approximately 300,000. The United Kingdom has a history of religious strife between the Protestants and Catholics and while religious toleration is now widespread, conflict between the 2 groups continues in Northern Ireland.

OVERVIEW OF ECONOMY

During the 16th and 17th centuries, Great Britain became one of the world's foremost trading nations. The kingdom established colonies in India, Asia, the Caribbean, and North America. These colonies supplied raw materials to Great Britain, which then turned those resources into manufactured goods. These goods were then exported to markets in the colonies and around the world. As a result of this trading system, the United Kingdom was one of the first nations in the world to undergo an industrial revolution (a period of rapid industrial growth and a corresponding decline in agriculture). By the 1800s, the British industrial sector was the largest in the world. Economic expansion in Great Britain was fueled by the kingdom's empire, which at its height included one-quarter of the world's territory and almost one-third of its population. By 1900, rival economic powers such as Germany and the United States began to challenge British commercial advantages. The effects of World War I and World War II and the subsequent period of de-colonization in the 1950s and 1960s led to an erosion of British economic superiority. After decades of economic decline, the British economy began to rebound in the 1980s.

The British economy is currently one of the largest and most diversified in the world. In 1999, its GDP ranked seventh in the world. Its **GDP per capita** was US$21,800, which ranked twentieth in the world. When foreign investments are included, the British economy is the fourth-largest in the world and the second-largest in Europe. Its capital, London, ranks alongside New York as one of the globe's main financial centers. As such, the kingdom is one of the world's leading trading nations. The United Kingdom is also home to some of the largest international companies, including the oil company BP-Amoco (worth US$116 billion), British Telecommunications (US$92.58 billion), the telecommunications company Vodafone Airtouch (US$91.68 billion), HSBC Bank (US$69.56 billion) and the pharmaceutical company Glaxo Wellcome (US$61.53 billion). In addition to its economic advantages, the country has a variety of natural resources including oil, natural gas, coal, tin, limestone, iron ore, salt, clay, chalk, gypsum, lead, and silicia.

The robustness of the British economy has led to considerable foreign investment and prompted many foreign companies to relocate to the kingdom. It has also led a number of large multinational companies to merge with or acquire British companies. In 2000, there were 560 international mergers and acquisitions in the United Kingdom. These had a value of US$86 billion and represented 42 percent of all multinational mergers and acquisitions in the European Union (EU).

The British economy has experienced a period of prolonged growth since the early 1990s. For instance, from 1995 to 1999 the economy of the United Kingdom grew by a total of 10.6 percent. Growth rates have averaged more than 2.7 percent per year. GDP per capita increased during this period from US$18,714 to US$21,800. In 2000, the economy grew by 2.8 percent, although the economic slowdown in the United States has produced a slower rate of growth than economic analysts predicted. The subsequent economic recovery of the country has not proceeded evenly. Most of the recent growth has occurred in southern England. Areas of Scotland and Wales remain economically depressed, as does the region of Northern Ireland. While the United Kingdom as a whole receives significant amounts of foreign investment, religious strife in Northern Ireland has led most foreign firms to avoid the area. That region consequently has the highest unemployment rate in the United Kingdom.

Like many of the world's leading economies, the United Kingdom's economy is marked by a growing service sector and a declining industrial base. The kingdom is one of the few nations in the world that has the capability to compete with the United States in some of the leading high-tech sectors, including **e-commerce** (business and services bought and sold through the Internet) and telecommunications. The United Kingdom is also home to some of the world's largest banking and financial service firms. Agriculture in the United Kingdom remains a strong, but small component of the economy. British farmers are among the most productive in Europe, but recent problems with hoof and mouth disease and mad-cow disease have caused widespread declines in agricultural production. While the industrial sector is declining in relation to other areas, it is a diversified and productive component of the kingdom's economy. For instance, British Steel is the largest steel manufacturer in Europe and the third-largest producer in the world. Other major industries include aerospace, chemicals, clothing, communications equipment, the production of machine tools and electric power tools, railroad equipment, shipbuilding, textiles, and paper and paper products. The most productive industry in the United Kingdom is the energy sector, which contributes 10 percent of the kingdom's

GDP. The British produce coal, natural gas, and oil for both domestic use and export.

The British economy has 3 major problems that may limit future growth and long-term stability. First, British workers do not have the same levels of productivity as their American, European, or Japanese counterparts. This means that during a given period of time, British workers produce less of a product than workers in these other markets. Reasons for this include lower education rates for the British and less investment in new technology and manufacturing methods. Currently, wages are lower in the United Kingdom than these other areas. In addition to preventing **inflation**, the lower wages also continue to attract foreign investment, since investors pay less for labor. Second, the aging population will lead to a shortage of new workers beginning in the next decade. Immigration will alleviate some of this problem. However, the aging population's additional tax burden on the social security and health system will require increases in taxes or other government revenues. Third, and finally, the nation has had a **trade deficit** for some time. On average, the kingdom's trade deficit is 1.5 percent of GDP. In 1998, the trade deficit totaled US$35 billion. The strength of the British currency in relation to the euro (the new currency of the European Union) and the money of other nations has meant that imports into the kingdom are relatively inexpensive, while British exports are expensive.

POLITICS, GOVERNMENT, AND TAXATION

The United Kingdom is a democratic, constitutional monarchy. Queen Elizabeth II is the nation's monarch, and she serves as the head of state. Along with New Zealand and Israel, the United Kingdom is unique among the nations of the world in that it does not have a single formal written constitution. Instead, its constitution is based on a series of historical documents and traditional legal and political practices that are collectively known as English Common Law. The principal constitutional documents include the Magna Carta (1215), the Petition of Right (1628), the Bill of Rights (1689), and the Act of Settlement (1701). This gives the constitution great flexibility since, unlike the United States, there is no formal amendment process needed to change it. The Parliament can simply enact legislation that changes the nature of a particular area of the constitution. An example of an unwritten component of the constitution is the practice that the prime minister must be a member of the Parliament (which is not recorded as a law).

There are 2 main principles behind the unwritten constitution. These are the rule of law and parliamentary sovereignty. The rule of law is based on the principle that the government is not above the law and can only do what it has the legal power to do. Parliamentary sovereignty means that the Parliament can legally pass any law it wishes, and no person or institution can override it. Any law can be repealed or changed by Parliament. This makes the government more powerful than its counterparts in Western Europe or the United States.

While the monarch has a lot of power in principle, custom has dictated that such power is only used sparingly. The role of the monarch is now mainly ceremonial. The Queen also serves as the head of state for many former British colonies such as Antigua and Barbuda, Australia, the Bahamas, Belize, Canada, Jamaica, Mauritius, New Zealand, Papua New Guinea, St. Lucia, the Solomon Islands, and Tuvalu.

The government is led by the prime minister, who is appointed by the Queen. The prime minister is usually the leader of the largest political party in Parliament. Parliament itself is **bicameral** (it consists of 2 chambers). The upper chamber is known as the House of Lords and the lower chamber is known as the House of Commons. Parliament can pass laws for the United Kingdom as a whole or for any of its constituent parts, including the dependencies such as the Channel Islands.

The House of Lords is comprised of nobles, senior bishops, and senior judges known as law lords. The 1999 House of Lords Act reduced the number of hereditary peers to 92. (A peer is a lord. Hereditary peers pass their status to their heirs, and in turn, their heirs become lords. "Life peers" do not have hereditary titles, thus their heirs cannot inherit their status.) This reduced the size of the House of Lords from 1,200 seats in 1997 to 670 in 2000. There are no elections for the House of Lords, and with the exception of bishops who retire, members serve for life. The most substantial legislative power of the chamber is its delaying capability. The Lords may reject a motion from the Commons. The lower house must then wait a year to resubmit it. The House of Commons consists of 659 members who are elected by universal adult suffrage. Of the members, 529 are from England, 40 from Wales, 72 from Scotland and 18 from Northern Ireland. Each is elected from single-member districts for a 5-year period, although new elections can be called early at the discretion of the prime minister. (In single-member districts, 1 person is elected to serve the entire district. This is the system in the United Kingdom and the United States. Some countries use proportional districts, in which several representatives are elected. This guarantees some minority-party representation in all districts.)

One of the major goals of the government has been to give the regions of the United Kingdom more political power. By 1999, Scotland, Wales, and Northern Ireland had all been granted some degree of self-government and each area had a national legislative body. The kingdom's Parliament retains control over defense, foreign policy, and social security systems. The regional assemblies have a high degree of control over education, the environment, and culture.

There are 2 main political parties in the United Kingdom, the Conservative Party and the Labour Party. The Conservatives, known popularly as the Tories, are a center-right party that supports lower taxes and a smaller role for government in the economy. The Labour Party is center-left. It has traditionally supported unions and government control of major industries, but has recently moved closer to the Tory position on a number of economic issues, including trade and state-ownership of industries. The United Kingdom also has a number of minor or regional parties, including the Liberal Democrats, Ulster Unionists, Sinn Fein, Scottish National Party, and Plaid Cymru (Welsh National Party).

Among the nations of Europe, the government of the United Kingdom has traditionally been the most supportive of free trade and free enterprise in the domestic market. Nonetheless, the influence of the government runs deeper than that of nations such as the United States. Since the late 1970s, the government has been engaged in a program to sell off state-owned companies. Examples of companies that have already been **privatized** include British Airways, British Aerospace, British Gas, British Steel, and British Telecom. One continuing problem for the British government is the ongoing effort to reform the National Health System (NHS) which provides health care for Britons. The popularity of NHS has made it difficult for the government to carry out reforms that are needed to keep the program **solvent**. The aging of the British population has placed new pressures on the NHS, and the Conservative Party has called for the privatization of the system in order to prevent a potential economic crisis in the future.

In 1999, the British government had revenues of US$541 billion and expenditures of US$507.5 billion. Government spending accounted for 36.3 percent of GDP in 1998, down from more than 40 percent just 2 years prior. From 1995 to 1998, the government had **budget deficits**, but in 1998, the government had a surplus of 1.6 percent, and it has had surpluses since then. About 11.3 percent of the workforce is employed by government at some level, whether it be the national, regional or local governments. Government revenues are augmented by the kingdom's considerable energy resources in the North Sea. Although most companies in the energy sector are privately owned, they pay licensing fees to the government in exchange for the right to produce oil and natural gas. Corporate tax rates in the United Kingdom are designed to encourage the growth of small businesses. The tax rate for large corporations is 31 percent. Smaller companies, those with revenues of less than £300,000, have a corporate rate of 21 percent. The United Kingdom and Luxembourg have the lowest corporate tax levels in the EU. Personal tax brackets range from 20 percent to 40 percent, depending on income levels. When personal and corporate taxes are combined, the kingdom has the lowest tax levels in the EU.

The United Kingdom is a net contributor of foreign aid. In 1997, it donated US$3.4 billion in aid. Military expenditures hover around 2.7 percent of the GDP. In 1998, this amounted to US$36.9 billion. In 1999, the British military numbered 209,000 personnel, with 110,000 in the army, 44,000 in the Royal Navy and 55,000 in the Royal Air Force (RAF). The United Kingdom is a member of the North Atlantic Treaty Organization (NATO, a military alliance of many western European countries plus the United States and Canada). Britain is one of the few nations in the world to possess nuclear weapons, although it has cut back on its total number of nuclear warheads since the end of the Cold War in 1991.

The United Kingdom is the closest military and economic ally of the United States. The 2 nations have a long history of security cooperation that includes being allies in both World Wars as well as the Cold War. The United Kingdom has also cooperated closely with the United States in the United Nations and in various international economic organizations. The kingdom is a member of the World Trade Organization (WTO), the Organization of Economically Developed Countries (OECD) and the Group of Eight Industrialized Nations. One area in which the United States and the United Kingdom are currently collaborating on is the development of a transatlantic free-trade area that would eliminate **tariffs** and **duties** on goods and services between the United States and Europe.

A deep debate within the government and British public is over adoption of the euro as a common currency. The United Kingdom is a member of the European Union, but when other members of the EU decided to replace their national currencies with the euro in 1999, the British opted out of the agreement. Those who support replacing the pound sterling with the euro argue that this would make trade with other EU nations easier and less expensive. Those who oppose the euro maintain that loss of the pound sterling would also mean loss of control over **monetary policy** and make the United Kingdom vulnerable to economic problems from the European continent.

Government policy continues to emphasize low inflation. In 1999, the kingdom's **inflation rate** was 2.3 percent, down a full percentage point from 1996. However, many economists contend that the official inflation rate is actually about one point lower than it should be. The government has also worked to lower unemployment, which stood at 6 percent in 1999. There are few restrictions on foreign companies in the United Kingdom, and the government has adopted a variety of programs to attract foreign investment and foreign businesses. One result of these efforts is that the United Kingdom and the United States are the largest foreign investors in each other's markets. The only significant restrictions on foreign ownership of businesses are those firms in the broadcasting, air and maritime transport, fishing, and defense sectors. For instance, foreign ownership of a British airline is limited to 49 percent.

INFRASTRUCTURE, POWER, AND COMMUNICATIONS

The United Kingdom has one of the most developed and extensive **infrastructure** systems in the world. Increasingly, many aspects of the infrastructure, including roads, railways and the communication systems, are aging and in need of repair. Because of constraints on the government's budget, London has endeavored to transfer responsibility for the maintenance and construction of new roads to local and regional governments. There are also increasing efforts to transfer control of infrastructure projects to private industry. To achieve these transfers, the government has 2 main programs, Public-Private Partnerships (PPP) and Private Finance Initiatives (PFI). The 2 programs use public funds to establish private corporations that then engage in infrastructure projects. PPP and PFI programs mean that the private companies take any risks in these projects, but also retain any profits. The government has also initiated privatization programs in the kingdom's infrastructure. Telecommunications, utilities (including electricity), gas and water supply, and passenger rail service have all been privatized.

The United Kingdom has 371,603 kilometers (230,914 miles) of roadways. This includes 3,303 kilometers (2,052 miles) of expressways. There are few roads that are not paved in some fashion. The kingdom also has 16,878 kilometers (10,488 miles) of railways. The majority of this track is standard gauge and one-quarter of it is electrified. Northern Ireland has 342 kilometers (212 miles) of older 1.6 meter gauge track. The extensive road and railway networks facilitate the movement of goods throughout the kingdom. The large oil and natural gas fields in the North Sea have led to the construction of lengthy pipelines to transport energy resources from the fields to refineries in the kingdom. There are 933 kilometers (580 miles) of crude oil pipelines, 2,993 kilometers (1,860 miles) of pipelines for other types of petroleum products, and 12,800 kilometers (7,954 miles) of natural gas pipelines. There is also an extensive network of canals and waterways which total 3,200 kilometers (1,988 miles).

Since the United Kingdom is an island, it is dependent on the maritime and air transport of goods. The nation has some of the world's busiest ports such as London, Glasgow, Manchester, and Portsmouth. Other major ports include Aberdeen, Belfast, Cardiff, Dover, Falmouth, Hull, Leith, Liverpool, Peterhead, Scapa Flow, Tees, and Tyne. These ports handled some 4.08 million tons of cargo per year. The kingdom has a large merchant marine, which totaled 173 ships in 2000. Of these, 50 ships were petroleum tankers, 39 were container vessels, 33 were general cargo ships, and 10 were passenger cruise ships. The British account for 6 percent of the world's maritime trade. The United Kingdom has 498 airports, of which 357 have paved runways. There are also 12 heliports. The nation's largest national airline is British Air. In 1997, the British air market totaled 130 million passengers and 17.9 million tons of cargo. By 2015, that market is expected to total 300 million passengers.

One of the most significant infrastructure projects in the history of the kingdom was the completion in 1994 of the Channel Tunnel, popularly known as the "Chunnel." This 35-kilometer (22-mile) tunnel under the English Channel connects England and France. For the first time in its history, the United Kingdom had a direct, if limited, land route for the transport of goods and people to and from the continent. Since its opening, the amount of goods that are transported through the Chunnel has grown by almost 20 percent per year.

Communications

Country	Newspapers	Radios	TV Sets[a]	Cable subscribers[a]	Mobile Phones[a]	Fax Machines[a]	Personal Computers[a]	Internet Hosts[b]	Internet Users[b]
	1996	1997	1998	1998	1998	1998	1998	1999	1999
United Kingdom	329	1,436	645	45.9	252	33.9	263.0	270.60	12,500
United States	215	2,146	847	244.3	256	78.4	458.6	1,508.77	74,100
Germany	311	948	580	214.5	170	73.1	304.7	173.96	14,400
France	218	937	601	27.5	188	47.4	207.8	110.64	5,370

[a]Data are from International Telecommunication Union, *World Telecommunication Development Report 1999* and are per 1,000 people.
[b]Data are from the Internet Software Consortium (http://www.isc.org) and are per 10,000 people.

SOURCE: World Bank. *World Development Indicators 2000.*

The kingdom's communication systems are technologically advanced and sophisticated. The system has a mixture of underground cables, microwave relay systems, and fiber-optic links. The islands have 40 undersea cables that provide communications links with Europe and the Western Hemisphere. There is also an extensive satellite system that is supported by 10 earth relay stations. Mobile phone use has increased dramatically. Between 1993 and 1997, the number of cellular phone users increased by 294 percent. By 1998, there were 13 million mobile phones in use, but by 1999, that number had increased to 21.8 million. Internet usage has also increased substantially. In 1999, there were 364 Internet service providers. Approximately 8.6 million homes in the United Kingdom have Internet access (about 35 percent of all homes). This is 4 times the number of homes with Internet access from the previous 2 years. Two government-owned corporations, the British Broadcast Corporation (BBC) and the Independent Broadcasting Authority (IBA), provide television and radio service throughout the kingdom. The BBC also provides a world radio service with broadcasts in many languages. Increasingly, consumers are using satellite and cable television in order to access programming from other nations, particularly the United States.

Consumption of electricity in the United Kingdom was 333.012 billion kilowatt hours (kWh) in 1999. Domestic production of electricity that same year was 342.771 billion kWh. Electrical production was dominated by fossil fuels at 69.38 percent, followed by atomic power with 26.68 percent and hydroelectric generation at 1.55 percent. Renewable energy sources accounted for only 1.79 percent of production.

ECONOMIC SECTORS

The economic sectors of the United Kingdom follow the pattern of most economically developed nations. The economy is dominated by the service sector, while industry and agriculture continue to decline in overall importance. Services are dominated by the financial sector and telecommunications. British firms have done especially well in overseas markets. During the last half of the 1900s, industrial decline was greatest. While many nations around the world invested in new technology and built new manufacturing plants, British firms were handicapped by a heavy tax burden and high labor costs. By the 1970s, few British firms were able to compete. However, during the 1980s, government privatization programs and legislation that reduced taxes and **liberalized** corporate law helped strengthen British industry. Corporations in specific industries, including the aerospace, energy, and steel sectors, are competitive and include some of the world's largest international firms. British agriculture is highly productive and is able to meet most of the kingdom's domestic needs.

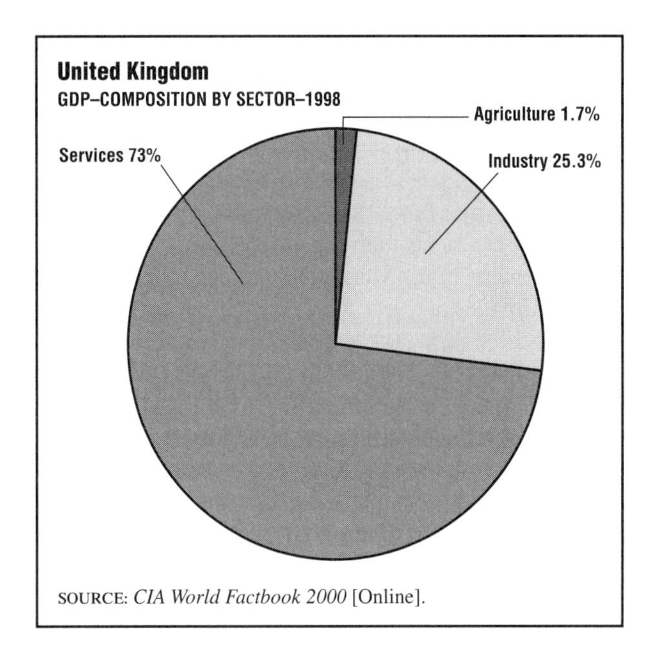

SOURCE: *CIA World Factbook 2000* [Online].

The agricultural sector declined significantly during the 1900s. It now accounts for only a small percentage of the nation's workforce and GDP. In 1999, agriculture and fishing accounted for 2 percent of employment and 1.7 percent of GDP. The industrial sector has also declined in recent years. In 1999, industry employed 22.1 percent of the workforce and contributed 25.3 percent of the kingdom's GDP. Throughout the 1990s industrial production, with the exception of the energy sector, declined. In 1999 industrial production decreased by 0.3 percent. In the

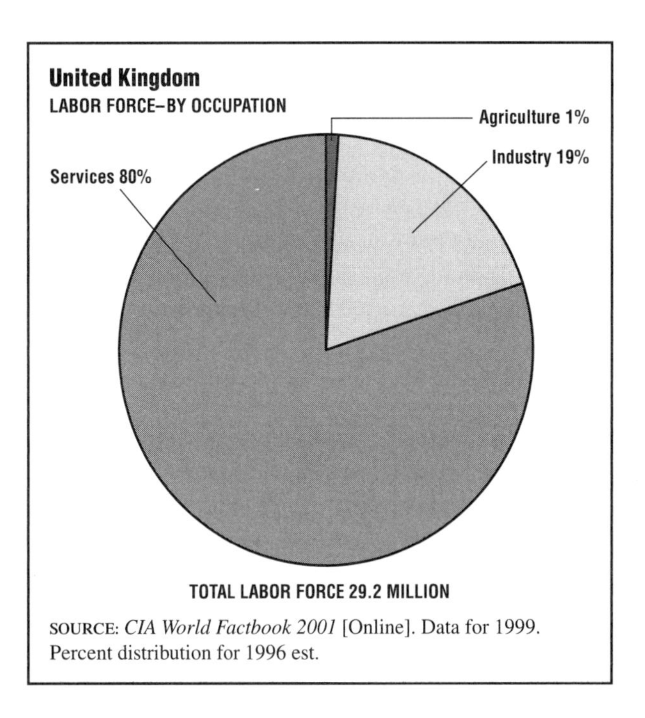

SOURCE: *CIA World Factbook 2001* [Online]. Data for 1999. Percent distribution for 1996 est.

same year, the service sector accounted for nearly 76 percent of employment and 73 percent of GDP.

AGRICULTURE

British agriculture is highly mechanized and productive. It is among the most efficient in Europe. With only 2 percent of the workforce, British agriculture and fishing provides 60 percent of the kingdom's food needs. In 1999, there were 500,000 tractors in use in the United Kingdom, 157,000 milking machines, and 47,000 harvesters. Large-scale agriculture is concentrated in the fertile soils of the southeast region of England. Diseases such as hoof and mouth disease and mad cow disease have led to declines in the livestock sector. In 1999, production in the sector declined by 3.78 percent. Concerns over the potential spread of these diseases have led to broad bans on the importation of British beef and veal by a variety of nations, including the EU countries and the United States.

In 1998, the total value of British agricultural exports was US$17.89 billion. Agricultural imports totaled US$30.76 billion. Approximately 18.5 million hectares are devoted to agriculture in the United Kingdom. Of this total, about 5 million hectares are used for crops and the rest for grazing livestock. In 1998, there were about 615,000 Britons engaged in agriculture for a living, of which approximately 80,000 were seasonal workers.

The primary crops include cereals, oilseeds, potatoes, and vegetables. Primary crop production in 1999 was 38.81 million metric tons. In 1996, production grew by some 15.43 percent, but there were declines of 1.14 percent in 1997 and 6.18 percent in 1998. These declines were stopped by a rise in production of 0.74 percent in 1999. Wheat is the largest individual crop. In 1999 total production of wheat amounted to 14.87 million metric tons. This marked a decline from previous years, including a recent high point of 16.1 million metric tons in 1996. Declines in wheat production have been driven by lower demand. The second largest crop is sugar beets. Production in 1999 was 10.33 million metric tons. That same year, potato production was 7.1 million metric tons and barley production was 6.5 million metric tons.

The primary livestock products include beef, veal, chicken, duck, goose, lamb, swine, and turkey. During the 1990s British beef and sheep farmers suffered from the outbreak of Bovine Spongiform Encephalopathy (BSE), commonly known as "mad cow" disease. The disease affects the nervous system of cattle and a similar disease, known as scrapie, affects sheep. Both are incurable. Ultimately, about 160,000 head of cattle were found to have BSE. No sooner had BSE been brought under control than a viral infection known as hoof and mouth or foot and mouth disease reached epidemic proportions. The disease is one of the most contagious in the world. By 2000, 408,000 cattle and sheep had been destroyed because of the disease and as many as 500,000 more faced future destruction. In an effort to prevent the spread of hoof and mouth disease, the government has ordered the inoculation of 200,000 cattle and the vaccination of an equal number of sheep. Concerns over the spread of foot and mouth disease have led most countries, including the EU nations and the United States, to ban imports of British livestock products.

In 1999, total livestock production was 3.59 million metric tons. Restrictions on the import of British beef and veal and the culling of herds in order to contain the spread of hoof and mouth disease have caused beef production to decline by one-third since 1995. Total beef production in 1999 was 678,000 metric tons. Lamb production has also declined since 1995 (by 20 percent) and production in 1999 was 361,000 metric tons. While there have been declines in these sectors, output of other livestock products has increased. Chicken production increased from 1.07 million metric tons in 1995 to 1.19 million tons in 1999, while swine output increased slightly from 1.01 million metric tons in 1995 to 1.04 million metric tons in 1999. The production of duck meat increased from 30,000 metric tons in 1995 to 41,000 metric tons in 1999. In 1998, there were 11.52 million head of cattle, 8.1 million pigs, 44.5 million sheep, and 61.4 million chickens and other fowl.

Fishing production in the United Kingdom increased from approximately 936,000 metric tons in 1993 to more than 1.1 million metric tons in 1999. In 1999, the total value of fish exports was US$1.3 billion. The main fish catches are cod, haddock, whiting, mackerel, herring, and shellfish. In 1998 haddock was the largest catch at 82,800 tons, followed by cod at 72,700 tons, and mackerel at 54,400 tons. Total shellfish catches exceeded 124,000 tons. The British fishing fleet numbered 7,639 ships in 1998, down from 11,189 in 1990. That same year there were about 18,000 people employed in the fishing sector. Exports of fish and shellfish amounted to £743.7 million.

For most of the 1900s, there was little significant production of forest products in the United Kingdom. Most of the land had either already been cleared or was owned by private or state entities. However, during the 1990s, production of forest products began to increase as the various species of trees on timber farms began to reach maturity. Production of forest products, mainly timber, increased from 7,093 metric tons to 10,094 metric tons in 1999.

INDUSTRY

British industry is a combination of publicly- and privately-owned companies. Since the 1980s, successive governments have worked to privatize most state-owned industries, but concerns over unemployment and public opposition to further privatization has slowed future plans. Examples of industries that remain owned by the government include railways, ship building, and some steel companies. Major segments of British industry include energy, mining, manufacturing, and construction.

One of the strongest components of the British economy is the energy sector. The United Kingdom is a net exporter of energy. In addition to oil, the kingdom has abundant reserves of natural gas, coal, and atomic power. Most of the kingdom's energy resources are concentrated in the North Sea. Currently there are more than 100 active oil and natural gas fields. In addition to the British companies operating in the area, there are a number of international firms, including Texaco, Philips Petroleum, and Chevron. The main energy resource is oil. The kingdom's proven reserves of oil exceed 5 billion barrels. In 1999, oil production reached it highest level at an average of 2.95 million barrels per day at 15 major oil refineries. Continued international demand for oil will lead companies to maintain these high levels of output. One distinguishing characteristic of the British energy industry has been consolidation. Many medium- and small-sized companies have merged or been bought out. The natural gas industry has been marked by increasing liberalization following the 1986 privatization of the state-**monopoly** British Gas. This was followed by the 1994 privatization of the nation's coal industry. The coal sector has undergone a dramatic decline. Coal production fell from 119 million short tons in 1986 to 46 million short tons in 1999.

The mining of minerals has declined over the past thirty years as the stocks of various minerals have been depleted. However, because British companies have substantial refining capabilities, many have switched to the processing of imported minerals. The main minerals still being mined are lead and tin. There is also significant production of refined metals such as aluminum and steel. The United Kingdom has substantial production of minerals used for construction. These include clay, kaolin, and gypsum. Britain is a major cement producer. About 75 percent of the market is controlled by 2 companies, Blue Circle Cement and Castle Cement. Blue Circle also controls about 25 percent of the Canadian market. British Steel is Europe's largest steel producer with revenues of US$12 billion. In the United Kingdom, British Steel produces about 13 million metric tons of steel per year. However, competition from foreign companies has led to plans by the manufacturer for significant reductions in the number of workers over the next 5 years.

MANUFACTURING. The manufacturing sector in the United Kingdom is diverse and includes industries that range from aerospace to automobiles to chemicals. In 2000, there were 4.14 million Britons employed in manufacturing. There are 1,500 aerospace companies in the United Kingdom. British Aerospace manufacturers had revenues of US$12.8 billion, including exports of US$9.2 billion. About half of the British aerospace industry is geared toward the production of military aircraft and parts. Several British defense manufacturers, including British Aerospace (Bae), are the among the largest arms firms in the world. In 2000, the United Kingdom was the world's fourth-largest arms exporter. British weapons sales included missiles, ships, tanks, and aircraft. Most of the sales were concentrated to countries in the Middle East such as Kuwait, Saudi Arabia, and the United Arab Emirates.

The United Kingdom is also one of the foremost publishing centers in the world, publishing more than 50,000 book titles per year. Several major British publishers, including Pearson and Palgrave, have moved into the American market by purchasing U.S. firms. Automobile manufacturers have a long and productive history in the United Kingdom. However, many British firms have recently been purchased by foreign companies. For example, Jaguar and Aston Martin are now owned by Ford, while Rover is owned by BMW. The world-renowned Bentley is now owned by the German firm Volkswagen, and after 2003, BMW will own Rolls Royce automobiles. Japanese automobile manufacturers such as Nissan, Honda, and Toyota have plants in the United Kingdom, and produce a combined 700,000 cars per year. Automobile manufacturers and car part makers employ some 850,000 British workers. In 2000, UK firms produced 1.629 million cars. Of this number, 1.138 million were exported. British manufacturers also produced 185,905 commercial vehicles, mainly trucks. Unlike cars, most commercial vehicles are made for the domestic market (only 74,922 were exported in 2000).

The British chemical industry has averaged 5 percent annual growth since the early 1990s. Most of this growth has been concentrated in the pharmaceutical sector, where demand for new medical products has risen dramatically. The increased demand for prescription and over-the-counter drugs has led to a drug store market that includes some 12,000 pharmacies. The chemical sector was worth US$56 billion, of which US$12.6 billion was pharmaceuticals.

After several years of decline, the construction industry rebounded in 1999 because of dramatic increases in the housing market. After several years of strong economic growth and increases in wages, many workers began to purchase new homes, or add expansions to their existing homes in 1999. Government spending on new projects, including hospitals, public housing, and government buildings, has also helped stabilize the market. In 2000 there were 1.8 million Britons employed in construction.

SERVICES

The service sector dominates the British economy. Business and financial services alone provide jobs for 5.23 million Britons, and in overall terms, services provide employment for 21.36 million Britons. Much like this segment in the United States, the British service sector is highly diversified and marked by high levels of competition. This provides consumers with wide choices over products and keeps prices in check. One trend in some segments of the service sector has been the emergence of large companies and the disappearance of smaller firms. This is especially true in the **retail** and food sectors. Like their American counterparts, British consumers tend to prefer "one-stop" shopping at stores where they can find a variety of products that range from groceries to hardware to apparel. The result has been the decline of traditional supermarkets and department stores and the emergence of hyper-markets (large chain stores that combine the different products and services of a grocery store, pharmacy, hardware or automotive store, and a department store) such as Wal-Mart. The main elements of the service sector include telecommunications, financial services, retail, and tourism.

TELECOMMUNICATIONS. The British telecommunications sector is currently worth US$34 billion. This equates to 2 percent of GDP and 1.7 percent of consumer spending. About 96 percent of British homes have a telephone, and there is an increasing demand for second telephone lines for computer or fax access. The market is adding about 500,000 new telephone land-lines per year. British Telecom is no longer a state monopoly, but it still dominates the British telecommunications sector with about 80 percent of the business market and 64 percent of the consumer market. Many U.S. companies have had success in the United Kingdom's long distance market, including Sprint, MCI, and AT&T. There are 4 companies with licenses to offer cellular service. These include the British Telecom-owned BT Cellnet, Vodafone, One-2-One and Orange.

The United Kingdom has an expanding e-commerce market. In 1999, the market was worth US$3 billion. There are about 9,000 companies primarily involved in e-commerce, and 72,000 that do some business over the Internet. E-commerce companies range from booksellers to food delivery services. Meanwhile, the computer software market was worth US$10.3 billion. Personal computer use is expected to increase by 15 percent over the next few years. Computer software sales and supplies totaled US$39 billion in 2000.

FINANCIAL SERVICES. British insurance firms dominate the maritime insurance market and provide insurance for about 25 percent of the world's merchant ships. London is a major international center for buying and selling currencies from around the world; almost one-third of all foreign exchange transactions in the world take place in London. In addition, 25 percent of all banking assets in the EU are located in the United Kingdom and the kingdom's banks accounted for 21 percent of all cross-border lending. The prominence of the United Kingdom as an international financial center is reflected by the number of banks and financial institutions in the country. There are 420 different banks in the United Kingdom. Of these, 190 are incorporated in the kingdom, 103 are banks from the EU, and 127 are from other countries in the world. The British banking sector is worth £2.66 trillion. Banking employs 415,000 people, or about 1.7 percent of the workforce. The British banking sector is dominated by banking groups or consortia of several different individual banks. The largest of these is Lloyds TSB. Lloyds TSB is made up of 8 banks with 2,529 branches. The second largest bank group is Barclays, with 1,899 branches in the United Kingdom. There are 37 different American banks with branches in the United Kingdom, including branches of Citibank, Bank of America, American Express, and Bank Boston.

RETAIL. Franchises account for a significant share (one-third) of the British retail sector. This includes about 40 American franchises that employ about 30,000 workers in 3,000 stores and have revenues of US$1.65 billion. American specialty clothing stores such as The Gap, Calvin Klein, and Tommy Hilfiger have done especially well in the US$40 billion United Kingdom clothing and apparel market. Retail food sales in the kingdom in 1998 were US$81.5 billion. Five major supermarkets control about 70 percent of the retail food market. These 5 companies are Tesco, Sainsbury, Asda/Wal-Mart, Safeway, and Somerfield. Restaurant sales in 2000 were US$25 billion and bar sales (which include food since many British citizens eat at pubs that serve both food and alcohol) were US$30 billion. There are 12 American restaurant franchisers in the United Kingdom, ranging from Denny's to Subway to Kentucky Fried Chicken (KFC). McDonald's alone operates 750 restaurants in the United Kingdom.

TOURISM. The hotel industry in the United Kingdom is worth US$10 billion alone. There are 22,000 economy hotels in the country and 10,000 medium to high-class hotels. One demonstration of the strength of the hotel sector is the fact that occupancy rates average 80 percent nationwide. Travel Inn and Travelodge account for 75 percent of the low-budget hotels in the kingdom while international firms such as Holiday Inn and Sheraton constitute a significant percentage of the upper scale lodgings. In 1997, about 25.5 million tourists visited the United Kingdom. This represented a 28 percent increase since 1993. In 1997, tourist revenues amounted to US$20 billion.

Trade (expressed in billions of US$): United Kingdom

	Exports	Imports
1975	43.423	53.343
1980	110.134	115.545
1985	101.252	108.957
1990	185.172	222.977
1995	242.042	263.719
1998	271.865	314.106

SOURCE: International Monetary Fund. *International Financial Statistics Yearbook 1999.*

INTERNATIONAL TRADE

The United Kingdom's economy is dependent on foreign trade. The government supports free and unrestricted trade and has championed international trade organizations such as the World Trade Organization and the EU. Because of its dependency on trade, the British have few restrictions on foreign trade and investment. Of the kingdom's 500 largest corporations, 60 are American. The United Kingdom's main trade partner is the EU. Some 58 percent of the kingdom's exports go to EU nations. Its main EU partners are Germany, which accounts for 12 percent of exports; France, with 12 percent; and the Netherlands with 8 percent. The United Kingdom's largest single market is the United States, which accounts for 13 percent of its exports. The United States also provides 14 percent of the kingdom's imports. As a combined group, the EU provides 53 percent of British imports. Germany provides 13 percent, France 9 percent, the Netherlands 7 percent, and Italy 5 percent. The United Kingdom has trade treaties with 90 different nations.

The strength of the British pound and the state of the economy has made the United Kingdom an attractive investment area for foreign investors. The kingdom is the world's second-largest destination for investment. About 30 percent of all foreign investment going into the EU is directed at the United Kingdom. The British also invest heavily in other nations. In 1998, the United Kingdom had US$120 billion invested abroad. The United States is the largest single investor in the United Kingdom and accounts for 44 percent of all foreign investment in the United Kingdom. In 1997, U.S. investment in the United Kingdom amounted to US$138.8 billion. The total U.S. investment in the United Kingdom is more than the total American investment in Germany, France, Italy, and the Netherlands combined. In overall terms, foreign investment accounted for 5 percent of GDP.

For several decades, the United Kingdom has had a trade deficit, as it has imported more goods and services than it has exported. In 1998, the trade deficit amounted to US$35 billion or 1.5 percent of GDP. However, because of the attractiveness of the kingdom to foreign investors, new investment capital continues to allow the British to fund this deficit because the new investment monies exceed the money the kingdom loses through its trade deficit.

Foreign companies provide 40 percent of British exports and they have a significant presence in the manufacturing sector. About 20 percent of manufacturing companies are foreign-owned and 16 percent of employment in the sector is tied to foreign firms. In 1998 there were 25,800 foreign companies in the United Kingdom. Among the major international companies in the United Kingdom are Dupont, with sales in 1998 of US$2.7 billion, the Swiss chemical company Ciba, with sales of US$2.3 billion, and Coca-Cola, with sales of US$2.1 billion.

In order to attract foreign businesses and foreign investment, the British government has adopted a variety of programs. For instance, the Parliament allows local and regional governments to establish enterprise zones. In these zones, companies receive exemptions from property taxes and reimbursement for costs involved in the construction of new factories or business locations. These inducements may be extended for up to 10 years. There are also programs that provide incentives for companies to locate in economically depressed urban areas that are known as "Assisted Areas." In 1998, the total value of these programs was US$315 million. There are 7 **free trade zones** in the United Kingdom (Birmingham, Humberside, Liverpool, Prestwick, Sheerness, Southampton, and Tilbury). These zones allow goods to be stored for shipment without tariffs or import duties.

MONEY

The British pound sterling has traditionally been one of the world's strongest currencies. In fact, the recent increase in value of the pound relative to other currencies such as the yen or the dollar has meant that goods imported are worth less than similar goods manufactured in the United Kingdom. It has also meant that British exports are more expensive than similar goods from other nations. In 1995, 1 U.S. dollar was equal to 0.6335 pounds. By 2000, 1 U.S. dollar was only equal to 0.6092 pounds.

London is one of the world's leading financial centers. The London Stock Exchange is the nation's largest stock exchange. In 1999, there were 1,945 companies listed on British stock markets. Total stock value in 1999 was US$2.93 trillion. While the British market is generally free and open, there are restrictions on foreign stock ownership of companies that the government still partially owns. In the case of state-owned companies, foreign ownership is limited to 49 percent of stock.

Exchange rates: United Kingdom

British pounds per US$1	
Jan 2001	0.6764
2000	0.6596
1999	0.6180
1998	0.6037
1997	0.6106
1996	0.6403

SOURCE: CIA *World Factbook 2001* [ONLINE].

GDP per Capita (US$)

Country	1975	1980	1985	1990	1998
United Kingdom	13,015	14,205	15,546	18,032	20,237
United States	19,364	21,529	23,200	25,363	29,683
Germany	N/A	N/A	N/A	N/A	31,141
France	18,730	21,374	22,510	25,624	27,975

SOURCE: United Nations. *Human Development Report 2000; Trends in human development and per capita income.*

In 1997, the government gave the Bank of England independence in currency matters. This means that the bank, not the government, is now responsible for monetary policy in the United Kingdom. The Bank sets the interest rates in the country and controls the amount of currency in circulation. One of the main policy goals of the bank is to keep inflation low, with a target of maintaining inflation at 2.3 percent. The bank has allowed the **foreign exchange reserves** of the United Kingdom to decline from US$42 billion in 1995 to US$32 billion in 1998 and US$29.8 billion in 1999. The reason for this decline has been the effort of the Bank of England to increase the amount of money in circulation (since 1995, the bank has increased the amount of currency by 7 percent per year). Partially because of these increases, inflation remains low—1.6 percent by government estimates in 2000.

POVERTY AND WEALTH

The United Kingdom has traditionally had deep divisions between the wealthy and poor. Unlike the United States, the middle class of the United Kingdom is smaller and there continues to be a more formal class system in the country. The United Kingdom has the highest degree of income inequality of any of the EU nations. The wealthiest 10 percent of the population controls 24.7 percent of the kingdom's wealth, while the poorest 10 percent controls only about 2.4 percent of wealth. Most significantly, since 1990 the poorest segment of the British population has seen a decline in income of about 8 percent, while the richest sector of the population has seen an increase in income of almost 68 percent. About 17 percent of the British population is considered to live in poverty. However, it should be noted that unlike most other developed nations, the United Kingdom does not have an official definition of poverty. Nonetheless, a government survey estimated that 22 percent of Britons were underpaid (paid at a rate that would not support the housing, food, and transportation needs of an individual).

The poor in the United Kingdom suffer from a variety of impediments that make it difficult to advance economically or socially. For instance, 20 percent of all Britons do not have a bank account. In addition, the infant mortality rate for the poor was 8.9 deaths per 1,000 births, while the rate for the middle class was 5.3 deaths per 1,000 live births, and only 4 deaths per 1,000 live births for the wealthiest families. Finally, the middle and upper classes have an average life expectancy that is 7 years longer than that of the poor. Poverty in the United Kingdom is partially alleviated by several social security programs. The most significant of these is the national health care system, or NHS. This provides essentially free health care to all Britons. However, recent economic problems with NHS has led to efforts to economize and some reduction in services. Studies continue to show that the more affluent parts of society have better health care since they can afford some private medical services.

The country's first minimum wage law did not go into effect until 1999. Since that time, government agencies have collected US$4 million for employees who were still paid less than the minimum wage of US$5.50 per hour. While poverty rates increased in the United Kingdom during the 1990s, the unemployment rate decreased. In 2000, unemployment stood at its lowest level since the 1970s at 6 percent. However, unemployment rates are higher among several groups including minorities, Catholics in Northern Ireland, and the country's

Distribution of Income or Consumption by Percentage Share: United Kingdom

Lowest 10%	2.6
Lowest 20%	6.6
Second 20%	11.5
Third 20%	16.3
Fourth 20%	22.7
Highest 20%	43.0
Highest 10%	27.3

Survey year: 1991

Note: This information refers to income shares by percentiles of the population and is ranked by per capita income.

SOURCE: *2000 World Development Indicators* [CD-ROM].

Household Consumption in PPP Terms

Country	All food	Clothing and footwear	Fuel and power[a]	Health care[b]	Education[b]	Transport & Communications	Other
United Kingdom	14	7	9	3	3	6	58
United States	13	9	9	4	6	8	51
Germany	14	6	7	2	10	7	53
France	22	7	9	3	8	12	40

Data represent percentage of consumption in PPP terms.
[a]Excludes energy used for transport.
[b]Includes government and private expenditures.

SOURCE: World Bank. *World Development Indicators 2000.*

youth. In order to help families who only earn minimum wage, the working families tax credit was established in 1999 to provide all families with a minimum weekly income of US$320. About 1.5 million British families receive some government assistance.

Poverty rates are highest among ethnic minorities. For instance, the poverty rate and unemployment is twice as high for people of African descent than it is for white Britons. Minorities receive only about 90 percent of the pay of their white counterparts in similar occupations. Although ethnic minorities make up only 2.8 percent of the population, they make up 12 percent of the poor. Women face even greater degrees of economic discrimination than do minorities, especially in hiring, promotion, and pay. On average, women receive only about 84 percent of the pay of their male counterparts who are working in the same jobs. A recent government report predicted that it would be the year 2040 before women gained **equity** in pay. About 44 percent of all women work, but women also have the highest rate of part-time work (45 percent of all women have only part-time jobs).

WORKING CONDITIONS

Under British law, all workers have the right to establish unions except those in law enforcement and the military. The 1999 Employment Relations Act reformed the regulations concerning unions and workers' rights. The law formalizes a worker's right to strike. In addition, the law mandates that all companies with 20 or more employees must allow unionization. About 30 percent of the British workforce is unionized. Union membership is highest in the construction and manufacturing sectors. The number of strikes in the United Kingdom has decreased by 43 percent since 1990. Among the 15 members of the EU, the United Kingdom had the sixth-lowest strike rate. On average, British companies lost 12 days per year per 1,000 workers due to strikes.

Forced labor is illegal, and children under the age of 16 are not allowed to be employed as industrial workers. The national minimum wage is US$5.50 per hour, but youths under the age of 18 may be paid a lower rate of US$4.75 per hour. Currently about 1.5 million British workers earn the minimum wage. New labor legislation enacted in 1999 established a 48-hour maximum work week. However, the average work week for most workers is between 37.5 and 40 hours. People employed in the financial sector tend to have shorter hours, while those employed in construction and other forms of manual labor have longer work weeks. Workers also receive mandatory rest periods after 4 hours of work each day and at least one day's rest per week (most Britons work a 5-day work week). Laws mandate additional pay for overtime work. In addition, national laws require that full-time workers receive a minimum of 4 weeks paid vacation per year.

Flexible work schedules (allowing workers to choose when to work their hours during the week) are becoming popular among both employers and employees. In 2000, 24 percent of all British workers reported some flexibility in their schedules. Workers who telecommute (use a computer to work from their home) make up 1 percent of the workforce.

One major problem that continues to affect British workers is a lack of mobility. British workers seldom change geographic location, even if they are unemployed. British workers are traditionally reluctant to change jobs and have one of the lowest rates of job transfer in the EU. In order to overcome this social phenomenon, the government has enacted a variety of worker retraining programs. Worker retraining in the United Kingdom increased by 8 percent from 1995 to 2000.

COUNTRY HISTORY AND ECONOMIC DEVELOPMENT

600s B.C. Celts begin to settle the British Isles.

55–44 B.C. Under Julius Caesar, Rome invades and ultimately conquers Britain.

901. The West Saxons, under Alfred the Great, conquer most of England.

1066. The French duke William the Conqueror defeats the Saxon forces under Harold Godwin and establishes a Norman dynasty.

1154–1189. Henry II establishes the Angevin dynasty and consolidates royal power through a series of political and legal reforms. The nation also begins a period of economic growth.

1215. The Magna Carta is signed. The document gives increased political power to the kingdom's nobles while it reduces the power of the king. The Magna Carta forms one of the components of the kingdom's contemporary constitution.

1337. The Hundred Years' War with France begins.

1415. Scottish forces under Robert the Bruce win the Battle of Bannockburn, which guarantees Scottish independence for several centuries.

1509–1547. Henry VIII breaks with the Catholic Church and establishes Anglicanism as the official religion.

1588. Under Elizabeth I, the British become a global power and defeat the Spanish Armada. British merchants begin trading with India and North America.

1600s. Numerous colonies are established in North America and the Caribbean. Trade patterns develop in which Great Britain imports raw materials from its colonies which are converted into manufactured goods and sold back to the colonies.

1642–1649. Civil War between the Royalists—who support the Catholic King Charles I—and the Puritans results in the beheading of the king.

1660. The monarchy is restored under Charles II.

1688. The Stuarts are overthrown during the "Glorious Revolution." The English Bill of Rights is adopted and William and Mary of the House of Orange ascend to the throne.

1707. The Treaty for the Union of Scotland and England creates a single monarchy for the 2 countries.

1760–1820. The reign of George III witnesses the loss of colonies in North America, but the general expansion of the empire. The British lead the coalition that defeats Napoleon in 1815.

1800s. Wide expansion of the empire and industrialization takes place. There is significant emigration from the British Isles to North America and other colonial areas such as Australia.

1832. Slavery is abolished in the empire.

1890s. Nations such as Germany and the United States overtake Great Britain as the dominant industrial powers in the world.

1914–1918. World War I deals major blow to British imperial supremacy.

1922. The 26 counties of southern Ireland are granted independence and form the Irish Free State (later the Irish Republic).

1939–1945. World War II. Alone among the major Western European powers, the British hold out against the Axis and are one of the 3 main powers, along with the United States and the USSR, in the wartime coalition that defeats the Axis.

1945. Widespread economic **recession** extends throughout the United Kingdom and its empire.

1947. India and Pakistan are granted independence.

1948. The National Health System (NHS) is created. Independence is granted to Burma and Ceylon (now Sri Lanka).

1952. George VI dies and is succeeded by his daughter, who is crowned Elizabeth II.

1970. Oil is discovered in the North Sea.

1972. As unrest escalates into violence in Northern Ireland, direct rule is imposed by London.

1973. The United Kingdom joins the European Community (now the EU). The Bahamas gains independence.

1975. Full production of offshore oil in the North Sea begins.

1979. Conservatives return to power with a substantial majority under Margaret Thatcher, Western Europe's first female prime minister. Thatcher implements a number of economic reforms which privatize industries and cut corporate taxes.

1982. Argentine military forces invade the Falkland Islands. These forces are defeated by the British during the Falkland Islands War.

1986. The natural gas industry is privatized.

1987. Thatcher wins a third term and ultimately becomes the longest-serving prime minister since Lord Liverpool in the 19th century.

1990. Economic problems and the proposal for an unpopular poll tax cause John Major to replace Margaret Thatcher as prime minister. The United Kingdom participates in the coalition that defeats Iraq in the Persian Gulf War.

1994. The "Chunnel" inaugurates direct transportation between the United Kingdom and France via a tunnel under the English Channel. The outbreak of "mad cow" disease (BSE) significantly harms British agriculture. The coal industry is privatized.

1997. Discontent over the economy leads the Labour Party to win a general election and Tony Blair becomes prime minister. The colony of Hong Kong is returned to China. The Bank of England is granted full autonomy in monetary matters.

1998. Scotland and Wales are granted limited self-government. The Good Friday Peace Accords in Northern Ireland establish a regional assembly.

1999. The House of Lords is reformed and reduced in size. The kingdom declines to join the European Monetary Union. The United Kingdom participates in the NATO-led military campaign against Serbia during the Kosovo Crisis.

2000. Unemployment reaches its lowest level since the 1970s (6 percent). Foot and mouth disease affects almost 50 percent of British livestock, devastating the beef and sheep sectors.

FUTURE TRENDS

The British economy is sound and the country is poised for future growth. As a member of the European Union, the kingdom is able to export goods and services to the 14 other major economies of Western Europe without paying significant tariffs or duties. EU membership and the country's low tax burden have made it attractive to foreign companies. The United Kingdom continues to lead the EU in direct foreign investment with US$274 billion, or 22.95 percent, of the EU total (the number-two country is France with US$174 billion, or 14.57 percent). The availability of inexpensive labor and the well-developed infrastructure of the kingdom will also sustain the investment of new capital and new companies.

Since English is the primary language of the Internet, software development, telecommunications, and pharmaceuticals, the United Kingdom will draw high-tech industries well into the next century. The linguistic and cultural ties between the United States and the United Kingdom mean that tourism will continue to be a strong component of the economy. The kingdom's energy sector will further propel the economy since world energy prices will remain high for the foreseeable future.

There are, however, a number of issues that continue to create doubt about the British economy. Questions over the United Kingdom's relationship to the EU have created uncertainty in the economy. The government has indicated that it would develop criteria that might ultimately lead to the United Kingdom joining the European Monetary Union and adopting the euro as the country's currency. However, there is deep public sentiment against adopting the euro. During the 1990s, the EU implemented a ban on British beef because of mad cow disease. Although the rest of the EU ended the ban in 1996, France continues to enforce restrictions on British imports. These actions have created a backlash among the public against the EU and increased economic cooperation with EU members such as France. In addition, the euro has declined in value by 20 percent when compared with the British pound. These factors continue to constrain the ability of the government to adopt the euro.

One of the main political problems facing the United Kingdom is the status of Northern Ireland. For centuries, there has been an ongoing conflict in Ireland between the Protestants and the Catholics. When Ireland became independent in 1921, the 6 northern, mostly Protestant, counties remained part of the United Kingdom and became known as Northern Ireland. Since then, the pro-Catholic Irish Republican Army (IRA) has waged a terrorist campaign to reunite the 2 areas of Ireland. After years of difficult negotiations, in 1999 the "Good Friday Agreement" brought together both Catholics and Protestants in a regional assembly led by an elected executive committee. Problems arising over the implementations of the Agreement have delayed the ability of the executive committee to become the government of the region. Continued uncertainty over the future of Northern Ireland has significantly constrained the region's economy, as few firms are willing to invest in the area. Unemployment in Northern Ireland is the highest in the United Kingdom at approximately 10 percent.

The final major problem confronting the United Kingdom is the aging of the workforce. As the elderly population of the country continues to expand, the need for younger workers will become acute. The aging population will place strains on the country's already overburdened social security system. The most pressing problem for the social security is the National Health System (NHS).

DEPENDENCIES

THE CHANNEL ISLANDS AND THE ISLE OF MAN. The United Kingdom has a number of territories that are known as British Crown Dependencies. These areas were once directly owned by the British monarch. The main Crown Dependencies include the Isle of Man and the islands of Jersey and Guernsey (which are known as the Channel Islands). These regions are part of the United Kingdom, but they enjoy a significant amount of political and economic freedom. The Queen is the head of state of these dependencies and appoints the head of the government. The Channel Islands each have an appointed lieutenant-governor, while the Isle of Man is led by a chief minister chosen by the Queen. Each dependency has its own elected assembly, which may enact legislation that does not conflict with the laws of the United Kingdom. These laws are subject to approval by the head of government. The kingdom has responsibility for the defense and foreign policy of the dependency, and judges are appointed by the Lord Chancellor of England (who is the chief justice of both England and Wales). In the Channel Islands, the Queen also appoints the bailiff, who is the chief law-enforcement officer.

The Isle of Man has a total area of 572 square kilometers (221 square miles). It is located in the Irish Sea, between Great Britain and Ireland. It is 3 times the size of Washington, D.C. In 2001, the population of the Isle of Man was 73,489. The Channel Islands are located in the English Channel between France and the United Kingdom. Jersey is a single island with a size of 116 square kilometers (45 square miles) and a population of 89,361. Guernsey consists of 4 main islands and a number of smaller islands. It has an area of 194 square kilometers (75 square miles) and a population of 64,342. On the Isle of Man, the Manx dialect of the Celtic language is spoken alongside English. In the Channel Islands, some people still use a Norman French dialect, while French is still used in Jersey for official ceremonies.

Because of their degree of independence in local economic matters, each of the dependencies has enacted legislation which has made the particular territory attractive to international banking and financial firms. Incorporation fees are low, as are corporate taxes. Individual taxation is also lower, mainly in the case of **estate taxes**. This has led many Britons to transfer funds to bank accounts in the dependencies.

In 1998, the GDP of the Isle of Man was US$1.2 billion. The GDP per capita was US$16,000. Agriculture accounts for 1 percent of GDP and employs 3 percent of the population. Industry comprises 10 percent of the GDP and 21 percent of the workforce. Services account for 89 percent of GDP and 76 percent of workers. The dominant forces in the economy are **offshore banking** and tourism. The main exports are clothing, herring, shellfish and livestock. The island has an astoundingly low unemployment rate of 0.7 percent. The currency of the Island is the Manx pound, which is fixed at a one-for-one **exchange rate** with the British pound. The dependency's main trade partner is the United Kingdom

The GDP of Jersey in 1999 was US$2.2 billion. Its GDP per capita was US$24,800. Agriculture makes up 5 percent of GDP, while industry accounts for 2 percent and services make up 93 percent. The service sector also dominates employment with over 90 percent of the workforce. Financial services account for 60 percent of GDP, while tourism accounts for 24 percent. Dairy production is also significant. Exports include dairy products, electrical goods, foodstuffs and textiles. Jersey's unemployment rate is also extremely low at 0.7 percent. The Jersey pound is the currency of the island, with an exchange rate of one-to-one with the British pound. The area's main trade partners are the EU and the United Kingdom

In 1999, Guernsey's GDP was US$1.3 billion. Guernsey's GDP per capita was US$20,000. Financial services tower over other sectors of the economy and provide about 53 percent of GDP. In overall terms, agriculture accounts for 3 percent of the economy, industry 10 percent, and services 87 percent. The islands have **full employment** with an unemployment rate of only 0.5 percent. The main exports of the islands include tomatoes, flowers and ferns, sweet peppers, eggplants, and fruit. The Guernsey pound is the currency of the islands. It is fixed to the British pound at a one-to-one exchange rate. The main trading partners of Guernsey are the EU and the United Kingdom.

BERMUDA AND THE CARIBBEAN TERRITORIES. At its height in the early 1900s, the British Empire controlled one-fourth of the world's territory and one-third of its people. Following World War II, most of the British colonies became independent. Some of the few remaining colonial possessions are in the Caribbean and North Atlantic. These areas are known as Overseas Territories and include Bermuda, the British Virgin Islands, the Cayman Islands, and the Turks and Caicos Islands. In each of the Territories, the Queen is the head of state and she appoints a governor-general to represent her. In turn, the governor general appoints the head of the government from the largest political party or group in the area's elected assembly. The Territories have a high degree of independence on local matters, but the United Kingdom remains responsible for foreign policy and defense matters. The United Kingdom also provides economic assistance to the territories, mainly in the form of aid for infrastructure projects such as roads and ports. This political connection between the Territories and the United Kingdom has proven to be very popular. In 1995, the residents of Bermuda soundly rejected a referendum that would have granted the islands independence. After signing an agreement for independence that was supposed to go into effect in 1982, the government of the Turks and Caicos Islands worked out an arrangement to remain a Territory and forego independence.

Tourism is the mainstay of the economies of all of the islands, although in recent years, several Territories have developed significant financial sectors by adopting very liberal banking laws. These rules imposed low incorporation fees and low taxes on financial gains and allowed citizens of other countries to keep large accounts in international banks with little scrutiny.

Bermuda consists of a series of small islands in the Atlantic Ocean, east of North Carolina. It has an area of just 58 square kilometers (22 square miles) and is about

0.3 the size of Washington, D.C. In 2001, the islands had a population of 63,503. Its 2000 GDP was US$2.1 billion. This gives Bermuda one of the highest per capita GDPs in the world (US$33,000). Bermuda's economy is concentrated on tourism and international banking. Each year, Bermuda receives about 360,000 tourists and that sector accounts for about 28 percent of GDP. Financial services account for 45 percent of GDP. About 1 percent of GDP is based on agriculture, 10 percent on industry, and 89 percent on services. The Territories' main trade partners are the United Kingdom, the United States, and Mexico. In 1995, Bermuda received US$27.9 million in foreign aid, most of it from the United States and the United Kingdom. The currency is the Bermudan dollar which is fixed to the U.S. dollar at a one-for-one exchange rate.

The British Virgin Islands are located in the Caribbean, just east of Puerto Rico. The islands are 150 square kilometers (58 square miles) in size and had a population of 20,812 in 2001. The GDP of the Territory was US$311 million in 2000, and its GDP per capita was US$16,000. The economy is dependent on tourism, which contributed 45 percent of GDP in 1999. About 350,000 tourists, mostly Americans, visit the islands each year. Reforms enacted in 1997 have made the region a haven for international insurance companies, and some 200,000 insurance companies are registered in the islands because of their low incorporation fees and liberal insurance regulations. Agriculture accounts for 1.8 percent of GDP, while industry, mainly construction, accounts for 6.2 percent, and services account for 92 percent. The nation uses the American dollar as its official currency and its main trade partners are Puerto Rico, the U.S. Virgin Islands, and the United States. The nation receives about US$3 million per year in economic aid, mainly from the United Kingdom.

The Cayman Islands were part of Jamaica until 1962. When Jamaica became independent, the Cayman Islands decided to remain part of the United Kingdom. The Islands are located in the Caribbean between Cuba and Central America. There are 3 main islands that have a total area of 259 square kilometers (100 square miles). Unlike the other territories, the Cayman Islands have an appointed governor who acts as the head of government. The islands have no **direct taxation** and, as a result, have become a major center for international companies and banks. In 1999, the islands had 600 international banks and over 44,000 corporations. Nonetheless, tourism provides 70 percent of GDP. Total GDP in 1997 was US$930 million and per capita GDP was US$24,500. The Cayman's main trading partners are the United States, the United Kingdom, and Japan. The territory has its own currency, the Caymanian dollar, which in 1999 had an exchange rate of 1 Caymanian dollar to 0.89 U.S. dollars.

The Turks and Caicos Islands were under the jurisdiction of Jamaica until that colony became independent in 1962. The islands were then administered by the British governor of the Bahamas. Full independence for the Turks and Caicos was set for 1982, but popular pressure led to the Territories remaining part of the United Kingdom. The Territory consists of 30 small islands with a total area of 430 square kilometers (166 square miles). In 2001, their population was 18,122. The Turks and Caicos had a GDP of US$128 million in 1999. Its GDP per capita was US$7,300. Tourism is the dominant factor in the economy, although government employs about one-third of the population. In 1998, 93,000 tourists visited the islands. Most of these were Americans. The Territory uses the American dollar as its currency and the United States and the United Kingdom are its main trade partners. The Turks and Caicos receive about US$6 million annually in foreign aid, most of it from the United Kingdom.

BIBLIOGRAPHY

Darian-Smith, Eve. *Bridging Divides: The Channel Tunnel and English Legal Identity in the New Europe.* Berkeley: University of California, 1999.

Holden, Ken, Kent Mathews, and John Thompson. *The UK Economy Today.* Manchester: Manchester University Press, 1995.

Gowland, David, and Arthur Turner. *Reluctant Europeans: Britain and European Integration, 1945–1998.* New York: St. Martin's Press, 2000.

Lowe, Rodney. *The Welfare State in Britain Since 1945.* New York: St. Martin's Press, 1999.

Middleton, Roger. *The British Economy Since 1945: Engaging With the Debate.* New York: St. Martin's Press, 2000.

U.S. Central Intelligence Agency. *World Factbook 2000: United Kingdom.* <http://www.cia.gov/cia/publications/factbook/geos/uk.html>. Accessed February 2001.

U.S. Department of State. *Background Notes: United Kingdom.* <http://www.state.gov/r/pa/bgn/index.cfm?docid=3846>. Accessed February 2001.

U.S. Department of State. *FY 2000 Country Commercial Guide: United Kingdom.* <http://www.state.gov/www/about_state/business/com_guides/2000/europe/index.html>. Accessed February 2001.

U.S. Department of State. *The United Kingdom: Country Reports on Human Rights Practices 1999.* <http://www.state.gov/g/drl/rls/hrrpt/1999/index.cfm?docid=368>. Accessed February 2001.

—Tom Lansford

VATICAN CITY

The Holy See
Santa Sede

MONETARY UNIT: Vatican lira. One lira equals 100 centesimi. There are coins of 10, 20, 50, 100, and 500 lire. The Vatican lira is at par with the Italian lira, which also circulates as valid currency within the Holy See. Conversely, Vatican coins—similar in value, size and denomination to those of Italy, but carrying an image of the head of the Pope—are legal tender in Italy, and in San Marino, another tiny city-state in Italian territory. Despite this reciprocal arrangement between Italy and the Holy See, their monetary systems are separate.

GROSS DOMESTIC PRODUCT: Despite having no balance of trade figures, the Holy See registers a gross domestic product (GDP), which was estimated at US$21 million for 1999. The singular nature of the Holy See's economic structure has yielded considerable sums of money. In 1997, the CIA *World Factbook* recorded state revenues of US$209.6 million, against expenditures (including capital outlays) of US$198.5 million, thus registering an impressive budget surplus of US$11.1 million.

BALANCE OF TRADE: The Holy See imports almost all agricultural produce and other foodstuffs and all manufactured goods from Italy, which supplies all its water, gas, and electricity. It has no agricultural or industrial sectors and exports nothing. It therefore has no balance of trade statistics.

COUNTRY OVERVIEW

LOCATION AND SIZE. A Southern European state, the Holy See, or State of the Vatican City, is a landlocked urban enclave, situated entirely within the Italian capital city of Rome, which forms its only borders. With an area of only 0.44 square kilometers (0.17 square miles), it is approximately 0.7 times the size of The Mall in Washington, D.C. Outside the Vatican's walls, in Rome itself, is the Pope's summer residence, Castel Gandolfo, together with 13 other buildings that belong to Vatican City and fall under its jurisdiction. The length of the country's border, formed by medieval and renaissance walls except for St. Peter's Square in the southeast, is 3.2 kilometers (2.0 miles). The state, city, and capital are one and the same.

POPULATION. In July 2001, the population of Vatican City was estimated at 890, with an estimated growth rate of 1.15 percent. The birth rate is extremely low by the very nature of the Holy See, which exists primarily as the center of authority over the Roman Catholic Church throughout the world. Its citizenry is, therefore, largely ecclesiastical (relating to the Church), supplemented by (often elderly) officers and servants of the Church. However, other dignitaries, as well as priests, nuns, guards, and some 3,000 lay workers actually reside outside the Vatican. There is no such thing as Vatican nationality, although rights of citizenship are conferred on non-Italians, such as members of the Swiss Papal Guard who are the traditional sentries at the city gates. Passports, issued by the Holy See rather than the Vatican state, are for diplomatic purposes only, and possession of a Holy See diplomatic passport does not automatically entitle the holder to rights of entry, residency, or citizenship.

The official language of the state is Italian; the Papal Guard's language, which is made up of Swiss nationals, is German. Several other languages are spoken, and the official acts of the Holy See are documented in Latin.

OVERVIEW OF ECONOMY

The Holy See, often referred to as Vatican City or simply the Vatican, is the seat of the Roman Catholic Church and its ruler, the Supreme Pontiff or Pope. The Holy See is not only the world's smallest independent state, but the workings of its government and financial affairs are unique, as are its non-commercially based economic structures, which do not conform to any conventional

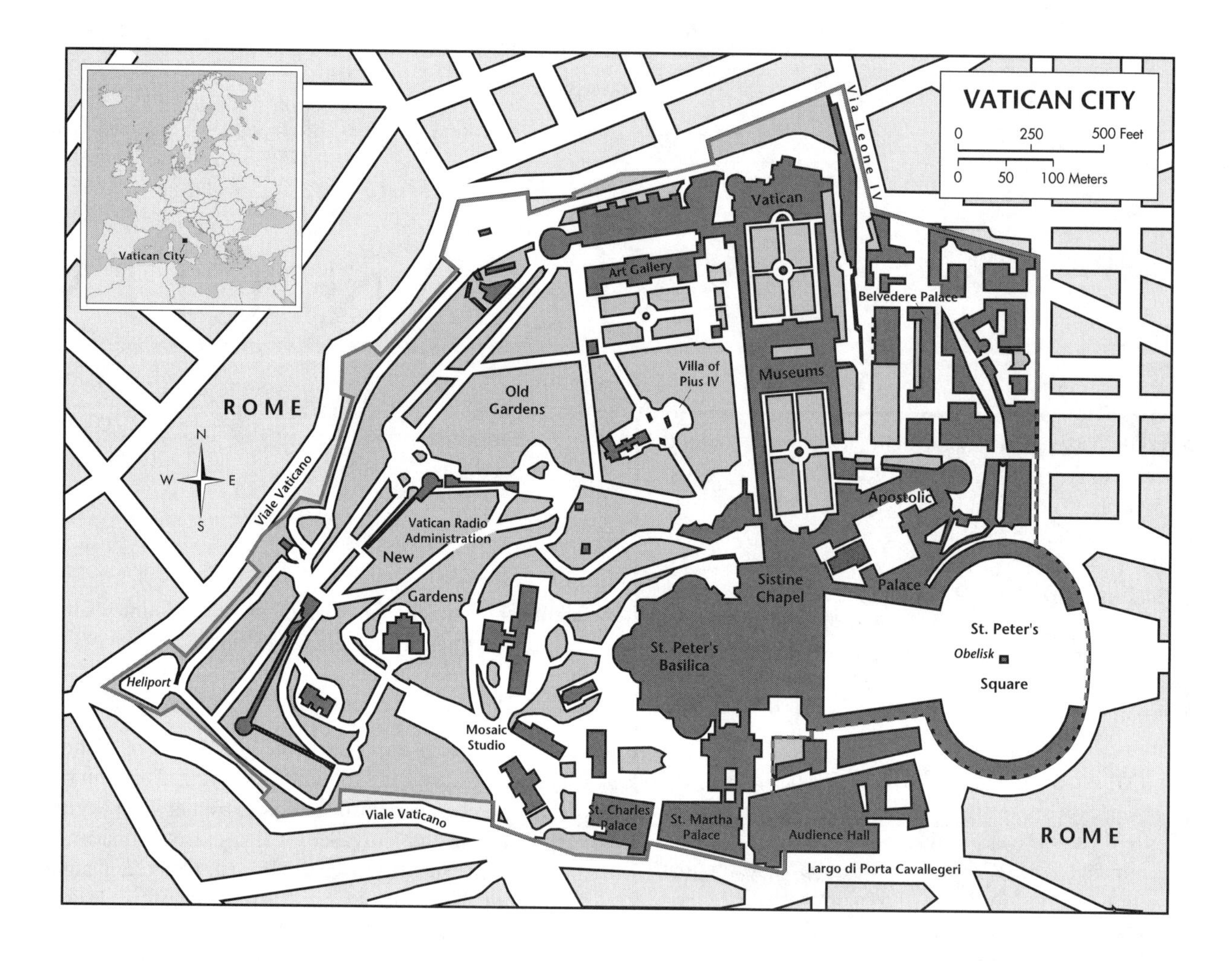

pattern. It is therefore not possible to examine or analyze the economy in terms of the usual sectors.

There is much confusion regarding the country's names, the Holy See and Vatican City. According to the country's permanent mission to the United Nations, the term Vatican City refers "to the physical or territorial base of the Holy See, almost a pedestal upon which is posed a much larger and unique independent and sovereign power: that of the Universal [Catholic] Church. . . . The State of Vatican City itself . . . possessed a personality under international law and, because of such, enters into international agreements. However, it is the Holy See which internationally represents Vatican City State." Since 1957, most agreements have been entered into by the Holy See as the supreme authority of the Catholic Church. The Holy See, then, refers to the governing bodies of the nation, while the term Vatican City refers to the physical nation.

The Holy See generates its substantial wealth through worldwide donations to the Church. These voluntary contributions are made by individuals of the Roman Catholic faith, and are known as Peter's Pence. The term dates back to the 8th century, when the custom of collecting money for the Church originated in the early English kingdom of Wessex, which imposed an annual tax of 1 penny (or pence) on each family to send to Rome. The custom spread, and nowadays, the largest sums are given by Catholics in the United States.

The Holy See has a special department to administer the funds that arrive annually and to distribute them according to the needs of organizations, charities, and individuals. However, because there are no rules governing when, how, or how much money is sent—or spent—it is not possible to give an accurate assessment of this income.

Additional revenues flow in from the massive number of tourists who visit the Vatican, and from international banking and financial activities that yield interest from substantial investments worldwide. A handful of small light-manufacturing enterprises within the state cater to particular domestic requirements such as printing of church publications, the production of uniforms for Vatican staff, the manufacture of religious mementos and mosaics for the tourist market, collectible items such as stamps and coins, and Vatican telephone cards.

Although the Vatican has never developed or promoted an organized tourist industry, tourism contributes significantly to the economy of the tiny state. The Vatican is one of Europe's outstanding tourist attractions. The city is rich in history and priceless cultural treasures, and its unique geographical location makes for its effortless inclusion in the itinerary of any visitor to Rome. Aside from the Basilica of St. Peter's, visitors flock to the Sistine Chapel, whose magnificent ceiling frescoes by the Renaissance artist Michelangelo have been restored, and to the extensive Vatican museums and libraries. Substantial sums come from tourists' purchases of souvenirs (most of them religious in nature), postage stamps, coin issues, and publications, and from admission charges to the Vatican museums, which can accommodate 20,000 visitors daily.

The sale of stamps, in particular the sale of special series to stamp dealers and collectors, has turned into a sizable enterprise since these have great appeal and increase in value within weeks of their issue. A limited number of each series is sold to private dealers and collectors who place advance orders, and the rest to religious orders and other church institutions, which, in turn, sell them on to dealers at a handsome profit. Thus, both the Holy See and the Church as a whole derive considerable gain from the trade in stamps.

State expenditure relates to the maintenance of buildings and **infrastructure**, the financing of foreign visits made by the Pope or his emissaries, the running costs of diplomatic missions and overseas offices, financing of charities, and the publication of the state's newspaper, *L'Osservatore Romano*.

POLITICS, GOVERNMENT, AND TAXATION

The Holy See is a monarchical-sacerdotal state, which is to say that it operates as a monarchy in which the Pope is the "king" (monarchical), with senior members of the church hierarchy, appointed by the Pope, as the governing body (sacerdotal). The Pope himself is elected from candidates worldwide by 120 members of the College of Cardinals and is the chief of state as well as head of the Church. Appointed to office for life (the Polish cardinal, Karol Wojtila, became Pope John Paul II in 1978 and was still on the throne in 2001), the Pope has supreme executive, legislative, and judicial power over both the State of the Vatican City and the universal Roman Catholic Church. Given the wide scope of the Pontiff's authority, an intricate and complex structure of official agencies has been established to administer power within carefully designed categories. This structure is commonly known as the Roman Curia and its members are appointed and granted authority by the Pope.

The Holy See is recognized under international law and enters into certain international agreements, but, strictly speaking, it is not a civil state operating under civil laws, but an absolute monarchy in control of the Roman Catholic Church, ruling according to the Apostolic Constitution of 1967. It is as the Holy See rather than the State of the Vatican that the country sends and receives diplomatic representatives to and from around the world. The head of government, generally a cardinal or archbishop whose appointment and authority is conferred by the Pope, is the secretary of state. He presides over the Pontifical Commission, or cabinet. The legal system governing church matters is founded in canon, or ecclesiastical, law but judicial matters outside the Church are dealt with by the Italian judiciary in Rome.

There are no political parties in the country, but all cardinals under the age of 80 have the vote in electoral issues within the Church. Internally, the Swiss Guard has been responsible for the personal safety of the Pope since 1506, but in reality, its function is ceremonial and policing of the state is left to the Civil Guard. There is no military arm, and Italy takes responsibility for defense.

There are no taxes, no restrictions on the import or export of funds, and no customs or excise **duties** payable in the Vatican City. Employees of the Vatican pay no **income tax** and no customs duty on gasoline or goods that they buy in the Vatican. Non-Italians enjoy allowances on their monthly salaries.

The Holy See is a member of numerous international organizations and institutions, such as the International Telecommunications Satellite Organization (Intelsat), the Organization for Security and Co-operation in Europe (OSCE), and the United Nations High Commission for Refugees (UNHCR), although its status is sometimes that of an observer only. The Holy See is especially active within the framework of the United Nations (UN) and has permanent observer status at the UN's New York headquarters and Geneva offices. This also includes specialized UN branches such as the Food and Agriculture Organization in Rome, and the Educational, Scientific, and Cultural Organization in Paris. The Holy See has a member delegate attached to the International Atomic Energy Agency and the UN Industrial Development Organization in Vienna, and engages in diplomatic relations with the European Union (EU) in Brussels.

INFRASTRUCTURE, POWER, AND COMMUNICATIONS

Vatican City has a heliport connecting to the Rome airport for the convenience of foreign visitors, and an 862-meter (about half a mile) rail track that connects to the Italian network at Rome's Saint Peter's station. This is used solely for carrying freight.

Regular telephone services within the Vatican began after it gained independence in 1929, when a number of telephones were installed via Rome's urban network to link various Vatican offices and residences. The state's first central telephone exchange, donated by American Catholics, was installed in 1930 and provided telephone service to approximately 360 end users. In 1960, this exchange was replaced by a new exchange with a capacity of 1,500 numbers, later expanding to 3,000. In June 1992, the Vatican's third central exchange was inaugurated, providing the city with a highly advanced state-of-the-art network, connecting 5,120 terminals, via optic fiber, to TelecomItalia's network and a radio link to extra-territorial zones.

The Vatican has its own post office, pharmacy, publishing house, influential radio station (Radio Vatican broadcasting throughout Europe), an Internet web site, an important observatory that hosts international astronomers' conferences, and a unique banking system that is central to the finances of the state.

SERVICES

There is no conventional service sector in the Holy See although, quite obviously, public service is provided by **retail** sales people, museum attendants, and other workers necessary to the smooth operation of the city. Financial services provide the most significant economic component of the sector, but again, they operate primarily to generate wealth for Church and state, benefitting only a few handpicked individuals outside of this. No opportunities for private business organizations or enterprises to operate independently are provided within the Vatican's confines.

The Administration of the Patrimony of the Holy See (APSA) manages the Holy See's cash and investments, including its patrimony and pension fund. There is a growing demand for public financial reporting, and Pope John Paul II has partly met this demand. A report, *Consolidated Financial Statements of the Holy See,* is prepared by the president of the Prefecture for the Economic Affairs of the Holy See, who acts as the Pope's treasurer. This report, however, only reveals details of the financial administration in the Holy See, a partial disclosure that conceals details of other accounts such as the Vatican Bank and the Vatican City State. It is known, though, that about half the income of the Vatican City State is used to help finance the Holy See.

The heart of the Vatican's finances is the Vatican Bank. The bank's official designation is that of The Institute for Works of Religion (IOR), a title that reveals its original purpose as a body charged with the financing of religious works. However, the Vatican Bank has evolved into a major financial institution, responsible for the investment and administration of all state funds, as well as dealing with the banking requirements of church officials, diplomats, and other servants of the state. The bank is not open to any individuals or corporations outside Vatican City.

The Holy See engages in substantial investments worldwide, which yield huge revenues in interest payments. Details of the state's financial activities tend to be shrouded in secrecy, but it is known that the main avenues of investment are banking, insurance, real estate, utilities, and building. The Holy See also has financial interests in the lucrative production of flour and spaghetti. Investment is largely directed towards companies that cater to basic human needs and are thus fundamentally sound, which contributes to the state's reputation as a prudent investor.

Apart from shares in private enterprise, the Holy See holds a large amount of government bonds and debentures (*titoli* and *obbligazioni*), and derives a percentage of its income from the rentals of apartments and shops. It owns several thousand hectares of land including some valuable building sites, particularly in the vicinity of Rome, and has gold reserves in Fort Knox.

POVERTY AND WEALTH

While it is not known how much personal wealth Vatican citizens have, the state is free of poverty. Although it is the smallest of all countries in terms of population, its estimated **GDP per capita** of $21,198 makes Vatican City the 18th wealthiest nation in the world per capita. Health and pension provisions are good, and average incomes and living standards of lay workers are generally comparable to—and in some cases, better than—those enjoyed by employees in Rome. No individual, whether or not they are a citizen of the Vatican, may own land within the borders of the state because it is the private domain of the Holy See.

Several hundred lay persons are engaged in secretarial, domestic, trade, and service jobs in the Vatican. The working week is reasonable, although high officials of the Secretariat of State keep longer hours then many senior business executives in other countries. Workers in the Vatican benefit from the numerous religious holidays, and Italians who work in the Holy See are exempt from military service. Swiss Guards are paid a relatively low salary, but are usually young men with private incomes. Civil Guards have higher salaries plus family allowances.

The most highly paid Vatican officials are the cardinals of the Curia. Immediately after appointment to the Curia, a cardinal has two-thirds of his first month's plate (as his salary is known, from the days when he was paid with gold and silver coins presented on a silver plate) deducted and kept aside for his funeral expenses.

COUNTRY HISTORY AND ECONOMIC DEVELOPMENT

The papacy has a very long and complex history, dating back to medieval times. Over the centuries, successive popes came to rule in Papal States across Europe (notably in France) as well as taking control of much of Italy in a secular as well as religious capacity for 1000 years. The present-day Italian capital of Rome was the capital of the Italian Papal State. In the 5th century, the Emperor Constantine I built the Basilica of St. Peter's. After this, Pope Symmachus built a palace nearby, but this did not become the Papal residence—the Vatican Palace—until 1377 when the papacy returned from its period of exile in Avignon, France.

It was from this time that a succession of popes—most notable among them Sixtus IV, Innocent VIII, Alexander VI, Leo X, and Clement VII—proved to be committed patrons of the arts, and were variously responsible for building and stocking the magnificent libraries and museums that can be seen today. From the 17th to the 19th centuries, the Papal residence was transferred to the Quirinal Palace, later Italy's royal palace, and now the official residence of the Italian president.

Papal rule ended with the Unification of Italy in 1870, when Victor Emmanuel became king of Italy, and the Papal territories, including Rome, were incorporated into the newly formed Italian state. The papacy retreated to the Vatican, where a succession of popes disputed their position with the Italian government.

In 1929, the Italian government and the Holy See finally reached agreement and signed a treaty recognizing the independence of the Holy See and creating the sovereign State of the Vatican City. Under this agreement, known as the Lateran Accords, the Italian government also awarded the Vatican 750 million lire in cash and 1 billion lire in government bonds as partial compensation for the papal territories annexed by Italy during the process of unification.

In 1984, a major reshuffle of offices in the Roman Curia resulted in the delegation of the routine administration of Vatican City to a pontifically appointed commission of 5 cardinals headed by the Secretariat of State.

FUTURE TRENDS

Despite the importance of the papacy to the Catholic Church and its role in international affairs, the Holy See's internal workings are little known to Catholics, to world leaders, or to the public at large. The Vatican Bank was the focus of several major financial scandals during the late 1970s and early 1980s, and while much effort has gone into repairing the damage to its reputation, the Vatican may well have to address public disquiet at its secrecy.

The question of who succeeds Pope John Paul II must, as with any papal succession, lend uncertainty to the Vatican since each successive pope rules according to his own principles. Perhaps the major cause for concern, therefore, is whether the papacy learns to adapt far more radically than it has done in the past to the huge changes in society at large. Increasingly, modern-day Catholics are finding the Church stance on issues such as birth control repressive, and if the Church is to retain the loyalty of its billion followers, it will have to modernize certain of its practices.

DEPENDENCIES

Vatican City has no territories or colonies.

BIBLIOGRAPHY

Bull, George. *Inside Vatican.* London: Hutchinson & Co. Ltd., 1982.

Coppa, Frank J. *Encyclopaedia of the Vatican and Papacy.* London: Aldwych Press; Westport, CT: Greenwood Press, 1999.

The Holy Father. <http://www.vatican.va/phome_en.htm>. Accessed October 2001.

Holy See Mission: The Permanent Observer Mission of the Holy See to the United Nations. <http://www.holyseemission.org>. Accessed October 2001.

Hutchinson, Robert. *When in Rome: An Authorized Guide to the Vatican.* London: HarperCollins, 1999.

Pallenberg, Corrado. *Vatican Finances.* London: Peter Owen, 1971.

Tully, S. "The Vatican's Finances." *Fortune.* 21 December 1987.

U.S. Central Intelligence Agency. *World Factbook 2001.* <http://www.odci.gov/cia/publications/factbook/index.html>. Accessed September 2001.

U.S. Department of State. *Background Notes: The Holy See, July 2000.* <http://www.state.gov/www/background_notes/holysee_0007_bgn.html>. Accessed October 2001.

—Olga Kuznetsova

YUGOSLAVIA

Federal Republic of Yugoslavia
Federativna Republika Jugoslavijá

CAPITAL: Belgrade.

MONETARY UNIT: Yugoslav dinar. 1 New Dinar (YD) equals 100 pari (in Serbia). Montenegro made the German mark (DM equals 100 pfennige) legal currency alongside the YD in 1999.

CHIEF EXPORTS: Manufactured goods, food (grain) and live animals, raw materials, and metals.

CHIEF IMPORTS: Machinery and transport equipment, fuels and lubricants, manufactured goods, chemicals, food and live animals, and raw materials.

GROSS DOMESTIC PRODUCT: US$24.2 billion (2000 est.).

BALANCE OF TRADE: **Exports:** US$1.5 billion (1999 est.). **Imports:** US$3.3 billion (1999 est.).

COUNTRY OVERVIEW

LOCATION AND SIZE. Although the country is recognized by others, the United States does not officially recognize the federation consisting of Serbia and Montenegro as Yugoslavia; it calls the country "Serbia and Montenegro."

Located in southeastern Europe, bounded on the north by Hungary, on the northeast by Romania, on the southeast by Bulgaria, on the south by Albania and Macedonia, on the southwest by the Adriatic Sea, and on the west by Croatia, Bosnia, and Herzegovina, Yugoslavia has an area of 102,350 square kilometers (39,518 square miles). Serbia, including the province of Kosovo, accounts for 88,412 square kilometers (34,136 square miles) while Montenegro accounts for 13,938 square kilometers (5,382 square miles), 199 kilometers (124 miles) of which is coastline. The total area is slightly smaller than Kentucky (Serbia is slightly larger than Maine, Montenegro is slightly smaller than Connecticut). The capital, Belgrade, is situated on the Danube and Sava rivers in north-central Serbia. Until the early 1990s, Yugoslavia incorporated the republics of Serbia, Montenegro, Macedonia, Slovenia, Croatia, and Bosnia and Herzegovina. The territory has yet to resolve all the territorial disputes between the former Yugoslav republics.

POPULATION. The population was estimated to be 10,662,087 (Serbia—9,981,929; Montenegro—680,158) in July 2000. By 2001, the *World Factbook* estimated that the population had grown to 10,677,290. The numbers are not exact, however, because of the dislocations caused by the devastating Yugoslav wars and the ethnic cleansing (killing carried out on ethnic minorities by a majority group) that had raged from 1991 to 1999. In 1998, the population was estimated at 11,206,039, including a significant number of Serb refugees from Croatia and Bosnia. In 1999, a mass exodus of ethnic Albanians from the Serbian province of Kosovo into adjacent Albania and Macedonia occurred; most have since returned. The population growth rate in Serbia is positive, with a birth rate of 12.2 and a death rate of 11.08 per 1,000 population (estimated in 2000). In Montenegro, **emigration** caused a decline in the population, although in 2000 the estimated birth rate stood at 14.9 and the death rate at 7.9 per 1,000.

The ethnic composition before the recent wars included Serbs, 62.6 percent; Albanians, 16.5 percent; Montenegrins (close to Serbs), 5 percent; Hungarians, 3.3 percent; Muslims (or Bosniaks), 3 percent; along with Roma (Gypsies), Bulgarians, Croats, and other groups. Religions include Orthodox Christian (65 percent), Muslim (19 percent), Roman Catholic (4 percent), Protestant (1 percent), and others (11 percent). The population in Montenegro, and to some extent in Serbia, is young, with 22.05 percent below the age of 14 and 11.79 percent older than 65; in Serbia, 19.95 percent are below the age of 14 and 14.83 percent are older than 65. In 1997, 58 percent of the population lived in urban areas.

OVERVIEW OF ECONOMY

The Yugoslav economy is severely damaged due to more than 10 years of internal fighting and fighting among some republics that were formerly part of the federation. Prior to 1991, Serbia and Montenegro were 2 of 7 constituent republics of the Socialist Federal Republic of Yugoslavia (FRY). The disintegration of the federation in 1991–1992 and the secession (withdrawal from an organization in order to gain independence) of 4 republics, including the most prosperous ones, Slovenia and Croatia, were an economic disaster for the newly formed FRY (Serbia and Montenegro).

The republics struggled for control of the area and some, especially Serbia, mounted genocidal attacks on neighboring Kosovo. The conflicts led to market disruption, and international **sanctions**. Corrupt economic policies led to devastation, high **inflation**, and the reversal of market reforms that had started in the 1980s. Industry was almost ruined, production was cut by more than 50 percent, the **gross domestic product (GDP) per capita** in 2000 was half of the 1989 level, and unemployment was up by 50 percent. Liquidity, large trade and fiscal deficits, and politically based economic inefficiencies threaten economic stability.

Serbian president Slobodan Milosevic led much of the area's troubles. The international community enforced strict sanctions against the area to try to stop the fighting and, finally, in 1999, NATO began a bombing campaign to end the internal fighting.

The international community welcomed the ouster of Milosevic in October 2000, and radical institutional and economic reforms were expected in 2001. The European Union (EU) opened up its market to imports of Yugoslav industrial and agricultural goods, and sanctions were lifted as the West accepted that the only way to stabilize the country was to help reintegrate it with the rest of Europe. Before the new government turns to reforms, however, companies and institutions must first be made operational. The almost continuous conflicts in the area have destroyed much of the country's **infrastructure**.

POLITICS, GOVERNMENT, AND TAXATION

Slavic republics had been separated for much of history by larger national powers, such as the Austro-Hungarian Empire in the 19th century. After World War II, Slovenia, Croatia, Serbia, Macedonia, and Montenegro, and Bosnia and Herzegovina were united. But the federation of these republics was far from easy. Although mostly Slavic republics, the populations in the republics were a blend of people with strong, differing cultural affinities that did not match territorial boundaries. By the 1990s, tensions between the republics led to the dissolution of Yugoslavia. The break was not clean, however, because people within the republics struggled to redraw the territorial boundaries along cultural lines. Ethnic Serbs in Bosnia and Herzegovina, for example, wished to join with Serbia. War between many of the republics led to severe political and economic disruption in the area.

In 1992, Serbia and Montenegro adopted a new constitution that set up a parliamentary government with a **bicameral** (2 house) legislature. Despite the new government, President Milosevic headed a dictatorial regime from 1987 to 2000. Milosevic's regime is responsible for much of the devastation caused by years of war from 1991 to 1999.

Following the presidential elections in September 2000, a popular uprising toppled Milosevic. The new president, Vojislav Kostunica, pledged a return to democracy and the rule of law. He promised to begin much needed reforms and to seek full reintegration into Europe. Furthermore, he secured Yugoslavia's return to the United Nations (UN) and admission to the International Monetary Fund (IMF).

Parliamentary elections in December 2000 brought to power the Democratic Coalition of Serbia (DOS), a reformist union of 18 parties and a trade union, led by Zoran Djindjic of the Democratic party, with 64 percent of the vote. Milosevic's Socialist Party of Serbia that ruled along with the ultra-nationalist Serbian Radical Party and the Yugoslav United Left garnered only 14 percent of the vote.

Recovery is expected to be long and painstaking. The DOS favors swift change, but Kostunica holds that it would jeopardize stability before a new legal framework is instituted. But the squabbles between the former Yugoslav republics are far from over. The UN Interim Administration Mission in Kosovo (UNMIK), established after the 1999 war, is now the authority in what was the former Autonomous Province of Kosovo and Metohija, and Albanian separatists are wreaking havoc in south Serbia, adjacent to Kosovo. Montenegro, which boycotted federal elections, continues its push toward independence. Bosnia and Herzegovina and Serbia, Serbia and Montenegro and Croatia, and Serbia and Montenegro and Macedonia have yet to resolve respective territorial issues.

The government's role in the economy is significant, as state enterprises owned more than 80 percent of the capital, and the **private sector** accounted for only 37 percent of GDP in 1996. Federal and republic governments have retained many formal and informal levers of authority over the economy, export and import licenses, credit, and jobs. The Montenegrin government has been more reform-oriented, and its law establishes tax exemptions, tax relief, and other privileges for foreign business activity.

INFRASTRUCTURE, POWER, AND COMMUNICATIONS

Serbia enjoys a central location in the Balkans, but the loss of markets and economic sanctions and NATO's (North Atlantic Treaty Organization) bombardment in 1999 devastated the transportation and communications sector; billions of dollars are needed for repair and modernization.

In 1997, the road network included 50,414 kilometers (31,326 miles) of roads (55 percent paved), with 380 kilometers (237 miles) of expressways, and 171 kilometers (106 miles) of semi-expressways. There were 4,031 kilometers (2,505 miles) of railroad tracks. Harbors on Montenegro's coast and at Belgrade serve as shipping centers, and plans to clear debris from the Danube left

Communications

Country	Newspapers	Radios	TV Sets[a]	Cable subscribers[a]	Mobile Phones[a]	Fax Machines[a]	Personal Computers[a]	Internet Hosts[b]	Internet Users[b]
	1996	1997	1998	1998	1998	1998	1998	1999	1999
Yugoslavia	107	297	259	N/A	23	1.9	18.8	7.65	80
United States	215	2,146	847	244.3	256	78.4	458.6	1,508.77	74,100
Russia	105	418	420	78.5	5	0.4	40.6	13.06	2,700
Romania	300	319	233	119.2	29	N/A	10.2	9.01	600

[a]Data are from International Telecommunication Union, *World Telecommunication Development Report 1999* and are per 1,000 people.
[b]Data are from the Internet Software Consortium (http://www.isc.org) and are per 10,000 people.

SOURCE: World Bank. *World Development Indicators 2000.*

by the bombing campaign will make trade along the river active again. The national airline, JAT, operates out of international airports in Belgrade and Podgorica, but under the 1992–1995 **embargo**, flights to Yugoslavia were banned, and the bombing of 1999 caused damage to civilian airports.

Before 1999, the country was self-sufficient in electricity from coal and hydropower. The sector is dominated by the state-owned **monopolies** of Serbia and Montenegro. The bombing in 1999 destroyed or damaged 14 power stations and 2 major oil refineries.

In 1997, the purchase of a 49 percent share of the Serbian Telecommunications Company PTT by the Italian company Stet and Greece's OTE pumped nearly US$1 billion into the budget. War and sanctions delayed modernization, but this has led to fast mobile telephone growth. Access to the Internet was introduced in 1997, and there are about 100,000 registered users and 150,000 personal computers.

ECONOMIC SECTORS

The sanctions of the 1990s hurt the economic sectors of Yugoslavia, especially industry. Unable to reach export markets or to import needed materials, many companies had to cease operations. Formerly one of the chief sources of copper in Europe, Serbia's mining industry also suffered during the 1990s, and many factories in the manufacturing sector became idle. But as sanctions were lifted, the industrial sector soon started up again. By 1998, the contributions of industry to the GDP were as follows: manufacturing and mining accounted for 33.9 percent; construction, 5.6 percent; agriculture, forestry, and fishing, 19.9 percent; trade, tourism, and catering, 18.7 percent; crafts, 9.9 percent; and transport and communications, 12 percent. Agriculture was estimated to account for 20 percent of GDP, industry 50 percent, and services 30 percent by 1998. The government hoped to encourage exports in agricultural goods, food processing, textiles, furniture, pharmaceuticals, metallic ores, and to boost tourism, particularly in Montenegro, in order to earn foreign exchange.

AGRICULTURE

Chief agricultural products include corn, sugar beets, wheat, potatoes, grapes, plums, cattle, pigs, and sheep. Vojvodina, in northern Serbia, contains the most fertile land. Cooperative farms in Yugoslavia did not take root under the **socialist** regime, but the government of Milosevic exported wheat and corn heavily (contributing 25 percent of Serbia's **hard currency**) and **bartered** grain for oil and gas from Iraq, Libya, Syria, and the Ukraine. This practice exploited farmers by paying them below-market prices and limiting their access to the free market. Farmers had no alternatives but to sell to state mills as most did not have storage facilities and permits to trade. Police harassed them, and if caught selling outside

Yugoslavia
GDP–COMPOSITION BY SECTOR–1998 est.

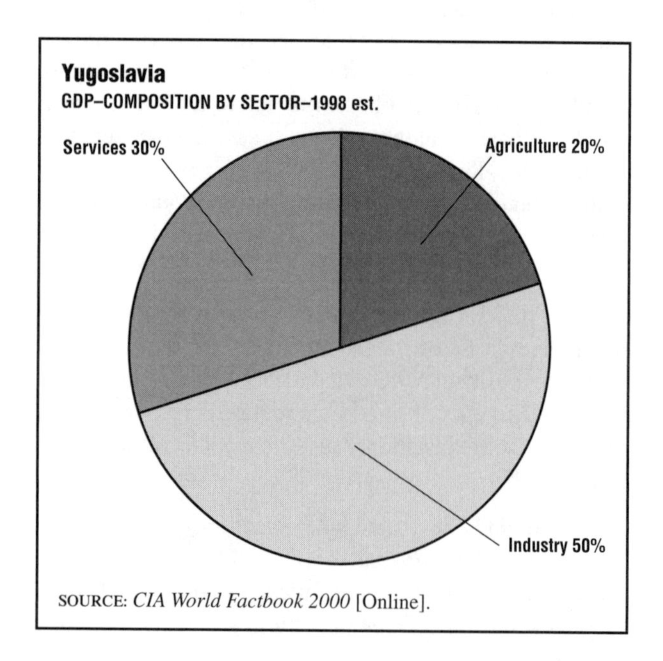

SOURCE: *CIA World Factbook 2000* [Online].

state outlets, they were fined US$2,000. The drought in the summer of 2000 was considered the worst in 7 decades and food shortages threatened throughout the winter of 2000–2001, with the corn harvest about 50 percent lower compared to 1999. Sunflower seeds were also down by 60–70 percent, soya by 40–50 percent, and fodder crops by 40–50 percent. International humanitarian aid pledged by the European Union and other donors following Milosevic's removal in October 2000 may compensate for the shortages.

INDUSTRY

Unlike other former socialist countries with inappropriate concentration of heavy industry, Yugoslavia inherited a diversity of industries. Before the disintegration of the federation there were thriving metallurgy, chemicals, textiles, automobile, furniture, and food-processing sectors. Industrial output plunged by 70 percent over the 1990s. Although industry wasn't literally "wiped out," it became less commercial than in **communist** times. During the 1980s, the communist regime set up **joint ventures** with foreign companies. Then, during the wars, strategic firms were re-**nationalized**, most other companies remained in social ownership, and less than a third were private. By the end of 2000, there were indications that much of what had already been **privatized** by Milosevic might be re-nationalized.

Industry is considered about 50 percent over-staffed, and most firms are bankrupt. In 1996, overdue inter-company debt was nearly US$2 billion (roughly 30 percent of the sector's contribution to GDP). The biggest loss-makers were 30 large state and socially owned companies, responsible for more than 60 percent of all losses. The complex system of workers' ownership of companies, a legacy from the socialist past, confuses shareholder issues. Although Montenegro was affected by the same problems, its active privatization policy transferred all state-owned capital to government funds to attract foreign investment.

Among the industrial enterprises that have ties with foreign investors, but were bombed in 1999, were the Zastava factory in Kragujevac, maker of the Yugo automobiles, the Sloboda domestic appliances factory at Cacak, and the 14 Oktobar factory in Krusevac, the largest heavy machinery plant in the Balkans.

Copper, zinc, and lead mining were an important contributor to industry. The Trepca complex near Mitrovica in Kosovo was the main mining area. In 2000, it was taken over by the U.N. administration in Kosovo because of environmental and health hazards, provoking protest from Belgrade, which accused the U.N. of confiscating the mine. Negative environmental impact from mining in Serbia is considerable, but no serious measures were taken by the Milosevic regime to counter it. Additionally, rivers and soils throughout Serbia, and particularly in Kosovo, were heavily polluted by oil spills from destroyed refineries and radioactive, depleted uranium shell debris from the 1999 bombing campaign. Serious concerns arose in the Balkans and Western Europe about the health of the population and the international peacekeeping troops based in the region. Sizeable international assistance could help to improve the situation, but most likely only in a long-term scenario. Sustained recovery in Yugoslav industrial performance will require, apart from ending the isolation and instituting trade preferences, considerable foreign investment and new technologies to be brought into the country.

SERVICES

FINANCE. Yugoslavia has about 100 small commercial banks with **bad loans** amounting to more than US$4 billion. Under-capitalization (insufficient funds) is rampant and, according to official data, the assets of the 10 largest banks in Yugoslavia now total about US$3.5 billion, or 60 percent of all bank assets. Some experts estimate that even this modest number is overstated by approximately 25 percent, because the banking system is not sound. Around 50 percent of assets are of low quality (dubious receivables), while another 40 percent are non-performing (frozen). Confidence in banks was destroyed after the sequestration (seizure) by the state of the population's hard currency savings of US$3.4 billion for its war efforts in 1991–92 and the collapse of a series of **pyramid schemes** in the early 1990s. The repayment of the savings to depositors in dinars started in 2000, but most preferred to wait for future payments in hard currency. Many banks did not have hard currency and offered gold coins instead. The commercial banks put the blame on the National Bank of Yugoslavia (NBY, the central bank) for its failure to provide funds for the reimbursement.

TOURISM. Tourism is the most promising sector in Montenegro, given the short but beautiful stretch of Adriatic coastline, adjacent to Croatian Dalmatia, with numerous resorts and picturesque small towns. The sector was well developed before the wars, but is now in shambles. Some limited foreign investment, primarily from Slovenian companies, may be expected in the short run, but it will take longer to restore the one-time attractiveness of Montenegro for Western tourists. In Serbia, the importance of the sector was lower and is now negligible.

RETAIL. This sector was well developed and a major portion of it was privatized before the wars, but it contracted with the economic collapse of the 1990s. By 2000, some small **retail** stores were reopened and some experts hoped the success of small shops, such as gas stations and other

Trade (expressed in billions of US$): Yugoslavia

	Exports	Imports
1975	4.072	7.697
1980	8.978	15.076
1985	10.700	12.207
1990	14.308	18.871
1995	N/A	N/A
1998	N/A	N/A

SOURCE: International Monetary Fund. *International Financial Statistics Yearbook 1999.*

Exchange rates: Yugoslavia

Yugoslav New Dinars (YD) per US$1	
2000	N/A
1999	N/A
Dec 1998	10.0
Dec 1997	5.85
Sep 1996	5.02
early 1995	1.5

Note: Rates in table are official; black market rate: 14.5 (Dec 1998), 8.9 (Dec 1997), 2 to 3 (early 1995).

SOURCE: CIA *World Factbook 2001* [ONLINE].

retail stores, would support growth of medium and large retail companies.

INTERNATIONAL TRADE

International sanctions on Yugoslavia were implemented in 1991 with weapons embargoes. As the conflict in the area escalated, more sanctions were enforced and full trade was blocked from 1992 until 1994. Embargoes against weapons sales were again imposed between 1998 and 2001.

The sanctions had a dramatic effect on trade. Trade with the United States, for example, went from US$38.7 million worth of imports and US$5.9 million worth of exports in 1992 to US$1.7 million in exports and no imports in 1993. Trade with the United States improved as the sanctions were lifted in the late 1990s. In 1996, the United States exported US$46 million to Yugoslavia and imported US$8.2 million worth of goods. Yugoslavia's total trade in 1996 reached US$1.8 billion for exports and imports rose to US$4.1 billion. The trade numbers for 1999 were US$1.5 billion for exports and US$3.3 billion for imports.

The imbalance between exports and imports reflected the weakness of the economy and the export-oriented sectors. The lack of international recognition of the FRY made receiving loans, foreign investment, and trade credit difficult and, in turn, did nothing to help develop trade relations with other countries.

MONEY

Banking remains weak as many businesses owe large sums and show little inclination to pay them back to the banks, which are now largely insolvent. Over the first half of 2000, the 28 largest banks made a loss of US$190 million at the **black market exchange rate**, and most are unable to observe their own national banking regulations. Small banks were more cost-efficient and less vulnerable to political and business pressure. Some small steps towards reform and consolidation of the fragmented sector were taken in 1997, when 16 small banks and 4 large ones—Beogradska Banka, Investbanka, Agrobanka and Beobanka—were consolidated. The 20 banks together controlled about 75 percent of the market, and in 2000, the Montenegrin government passed a bill seeking stringent safeguards in the banking system. Radical **restructuring** of the banking sector is more likely now as Yugoslavia is restoring its membership in international financial institutions.

Capital markets are underdeveloped. The Belgrade Stock Exchange was established in 1989 and the Podgorica Stock Exchange in 1996. Given the current state of privatization, trading in securities is very limited and both exchanges operate primarily in short-term (30 days or less) commercial paper (notes) issued by large Yugoslav corporations.

In November 2000, Montenegro made the German mark legal tender. All payments between the 2 republics will be conducted in marks. The dinar was tied to the German mark in 1995 (at a fixed rate of 3.3 dinars per mark). The street exchange rate in mid-2000 was at about 3.5 dinars per mark (5.7 dinars per US$1), but analysts believe the dinar was overvalued by 30–50 percent. The black market in foreign currencies was robust, and inflation lowered the real income of salaried workers.

POVERTY AND WEALTH

Before 1991, Serbs and Montenegrins enjoyed a comparatively prosperous life, and their access to information, travel, and work abroad was easier than in most Eastern European countries. As a socialist economy, old Yugoslavia was generally more egalitarian than Western European countries. During the 1990s, as the economy collapsed, the majority of Serbs grew desperately poor. Average salaries in Serbia hit the bottom at US$40 per month in 2000. Payments to employees on state payrolls—health workers, teachers, soldiers, police, and **pen-**

GDP per Capita (US$)

Country	1996	1997	1998	1999	2000
Yugoslavia	N/A	2,280	2,300	1,800	2,300
United States	28,600	30,200	31,500	33,900	36,200
Russia	5,200	4,700	4,000	4,200	7,700
Romania	5,200	5,300	4,050	3,900	5,900

Note: Data are estimates.

SOURCE: *Handbook of the Nations*, 17th, 18th, 19th and 20th editions for 1996, 1997, 1998 and 1999 data; CIA *World Factbook 2001* [Online] for 2000 data.

sioners—were months overdue. The 1999 bombing of major cities led to many casualties and devastation. Health, education, and welfare were also seriously jeopardized, and energy shortages plagued the people. Widespread indignation fueled the mass protests of 1996 and the popular uprising that finally toppled Milosevic in October 2000.

At the same time, many members of Milosevic's inner circle amassed—through nepotism, corruption, and smuggling—largely illegitimate fortunes that the new government will work to recover from foreign bank accounts. The dictator's notorious playboy son, Marko, was particularly resented, and as soon as his father was out of office, many assets of his self-styled business empire were looted and burned by angry crowds.

WORKING CONDITIONS

About a quarter of Serbs are officially unemployed, but the number rises to 50 percent if people in insolvent companies are included. Over-staffing and underpayment in most remaining firms mean that few workers have real jobs. The way to provide people with sustainable livelihoods is to revive the companies with capacity to provide new jobs. These companies must end their isolation and become able to export. Labor activism was instrumental in ousting Milosevic and could hardly be underestimated as an economic factor in a country with largely socialist traditions. Unions will influence economic decisions, as workers, having taken control of their companies from Milosevic's managers, are pushing for reversal of the privatization schemes that benefited Milosevic's cronies. Revisions of these privatization deals seem more likely than elsewhere in Eastern Europe.

By late 1999, about 2 million people were employed in the state sector, about a million and a half in industry and agriculture, and the rest in education, government, and services. Slightly more than 300,000 were employed in private sector trade and services, and 560,000 were independent farmers, while up to 1 million, including most Serb refugees from Croatia, Bosnia, and Kosovo, engaged in subsistence agriculture and lived in deep poverty.

COUNTRY HISTORY AND ECONOMIC DEVELOPMENT

600s. Slavs settle in parts of the present Serbian and Montenegrin lands, comprising portions of the ancient Roman province of Illyricum, then ruled by Byzantium, from which the Slavs accept Orthodox Christianity.

1168. King Stefan Nemanja establishes the first kingdom of Serbia.

1331–55. Under King Stefan Dusan, Serbia acquires new lands as the feudal economy develops and gives way to decentralization.

1389. Ottomans rout a Christian army including Serbs under King Lazar at Kosovo Polje.

1459. Serbia is violently conquered by the Ottoman Empire and remains under its rule for nearly 4 centuries, while Montenegro, the one-time Serbian province of Zeta, remains virtually independent.

1815. A revolt frees most of Serbia from Ottoman domination; a Serbian national revival thrives. Serb nationalists aim at uniting all South Slavs under the Serbian state.

1912–13. In the Balkan Wars, Serbia annexes extensive territories, including the Sandjak, Kosovo, and the present-day Republic of Macedonia.

1914. Austria-Hungary starts World War I, occupying Serbia by 1915. The Serbian army and government flee.

1918. The Kingdom of the Serbs, Croats, and Slovenes (Kingdom of Yugoslavia from 1929) is proclaimed (it includes Montenegro).

1941. In World War II, Yugoslavia breaks up as Nazi Germany occupies Serbia. Serb nationalist Chetniks compete with Partisans led by Croatian communist Josip Broz Tito in resisting the Germans.

1945. Tito's communists proclaim the Federal People's Republic of Yugoslavia. Serbia and Montenegro become constituent socialist republics. In 1946, the regions of Kosovo and Metohija and Vojvodina become autonomous provinces.

1945–80. Yugoslavia's socialist economy develops, and heavy industry is stressed, but since the late 1950s economic control is decentralized, and some private initiative is allowed.

1987. Dissatisfaction with the federation grows among constituent republics after Tito's death. Serbia, led by President Milosevic, tries to impose control over them and revokes the autonomy of Kosovo (the 90 percent ethnic Albanian province) and Vojvodina (where a sizeable ethnic Hungarian minority lives).

1991. Slovenia, Croatia, and Macedonia declare their independence, and Bosnia joins them in 1992. Serbia and Montenegro subsequently declare themselves the Federal Republic of Yugoslavia, which is not recognized by the international community. Its U.N. membership is suspended.

1991–95. The Milosevic regime plays an active role in the civil wars in Bosnia and Croatia and is severely criticized by the international community for military atrocities and the brutal oppression of domestic opposition and minorities.

1995. The Dayton peace accord puts an end to the war in Croatia and Bosnia.

1996. Mass demonstrations, led by the united democratic opposition against the Milosevic regime, begin.

1999. Mass expulsion of ethnic Albanians from Kosovo, to counter the underground insurgent Kosovo Liberation Army (UCK), provokes an international response, including bombing and the stationing of NATO and Russian peacekeepers in Kosovo while Montenegro declares the German mark official currency.

2000. Milosevic is defeated in presidential elections and democrat Vojislav Kostunica takes over. Montenegro aspires for independence, and Albanian separatists strike in southern Serbia. Readmission to the U.N. is approved; membership in the European Bank for Reconstruction and Development and in the IMF is expected. The Democratic Coalition of Serbia wins parliamentary elections in December, led by reformist Zoran Djindjic.

FUTURE TRENDS

Yugoslavia's economic problems will not disappear simply because it now has a democratically elected president. The new government faces the challenge of reconstruction, and the legacy of 10 years of war, sanctions, and corrupt officials' looting will take a considerable amount of time to reverse and will not occur without a substantial inflow of foreign capital. Trade relations can be normalized quickly and co-operation with the West can be energized with the swift resolution of pending political issues.

The government's tasks will include stabilization and economic reform, imposing law and order, and helping vulnerable sectors of society. They will be trying their best to attract **foreign direct investment** and to unfreeze the assets of the former Yugoslavia by reaching agreement with the other successor republics. The frozen private bank accounts in the names of Milosevic and his associates in Switzerland and elsewhere may be transferred back to the country, and immediate aid of US$172 million was pledged by the EU in late 2000 for medicine, heating, and food through the winter. The Stability Pact for South-eastern Europe, a regional development plan backed by the EU and the United States, the IMF, the World Bank, and regional banks will contribute to the reconstruction and reform process. The prosperity of Serbia and Montenegro will be crucial for establishing lasting peace in the Balkans.

DEPENDENCIES

Yugoslavia has no territories or colonies.

BIBLIOGRAPHY

Curtis, Glenn E. *Yugoslavia: A Country Study*. Library of Congress, 1992.

Economist Intelligence Unit. *Country Profile: Yugoslavia*. London: Economist Intelligence Unit, 2000.

Stokes, Gale. *Three Eras of Political Change in Eastern Europe*. Oxford: Oxford University Press, 1996.

U.S. Central Intelligence Agency. *World Factbook 2001*. <http://www.odci.gov/cia/publications/factbook/index.html>. Accessed October 2001.

U.S. Department of State. *FY 2000 Country Commercial Guide: Serbia and Montenegro*. <http://www.state.gov/www/about_state/business/com_guides/index.html>. Accessed December 2000.

"U.S. Trade Balance with Yugoslavia." *U.S. Census Bureau*. <http://www.census.gov/foreign-trade/balance/c4799.html>. Accessed October 2001.

—Valentin Hadjiyski

GLOSSARY

Advance Tax: A percentage of the previous year's tax bill which is paid at the beginning of the new fiscal year and later credited back at its end.

Agribusiness: Agricultural and livestock production on a large scale, often engaged in by large, multinational companies; also used to refer to the companies themselves.

Arrear: Usually plural, **arrears**. Unpaid, overdue debt.

Bad Loan: An unrecoverable loan; the amount cannot be reclaimed by the lender.

Balance of Payments: The measure of all the money coming into a country and all the money leaving the country in a given period, usually a year. The balance of payments includes merchandise exports and imports, the measure of which is called the **balance of trade**, as well as several other factors.

Balance of Trade: A measure of the value of exports and imports, not including services. When imports exceed exports, there is a trade deficit. When exports exceed imports, there is a trade surplus.

Bank of Issue: The bank that is given the right to issue and circulate currency in a country.

Barter System: An exchange of goods and/or services for other goods and/or services, rather than for money.

Bear Market: A sustained period of negative growth in the stock market.

Bicameral: A legislative body consisting of two houses or chambers.

Black Market: An informal market in which buyers and sellers can negotiate and exchange prohibited or illegal goods (such as exchanging local money for foreign currency). Black markets often exist to avoid government controls. *See also* **Informal Sector.**

Budget Deficit: A government budget deficit occurs when a government spends more money on government programs than it generates in revenues. Governments must borrow money or print currency to pay for this excess spending, thus creating potential financial difficulties. *See also* **Budget Surplus.**

Budget Surplus: A government budget surplus occurs when a government generates more revenues than it spends on government programs. Governments can adjust to surpluses by lowering tax rates, paying down the national debt, or stockpiling the money. *See also* **Budget Deficit.**

Cadre: A group of important and influential members of political parties who direct the actions of that party.

Capital Adequacy: The state of a bank having enough capital to maintain its loans and operating costs.

Capital Flight; also called **Capital Outflow:** Money sent abroad because investors fear that economic conditions within a country are too risky.

Capital Good: A manufactured good used in the production of other goods. For example, factories or machinery used to produce goods are considered capital goods.

Capitalism: An economic system based on the private ownership of the means of production and on an open system of competitive markets. It is assumed that producers in a capitalist system can use their skills and capital in the pursuit of profit.

Capital Outflow: *See* **Capital Flight.**

Cash Crop: An agricultural good produced for direct sale on the market.

Centrally-planned Economy: An economy in which the government exerts a great deal of control over economic planning, including the control of production, the allocation of goods, distribution, and prices. Common in **socialist** countries.

c.i.f.: Abbreviation of **cost, insurance, and freight**; a method of determining the value of imports or exports that includes cost, insurance, and freight in determining the total amount.

Commonwealth of Independent States (CIS): A loose union of 12 of the former republics of the Soviet Union, excluding Estonia, Latvia, and Lithuania.

Communism: An economic system in which the means of production and distribution are held in common by all members of the society, and in which the rewards are distributed based on need. In actual communist countries, the state usually controls all the capital and land, and the economy is centrally planned. *See also* **Centrally-planned Economy.**

Consumer Good: A product sold directly to the end user, or consumer, such as food and clothing.

Crawling Peg: A fixed **exchange rate** between two currencies which is adjusted incrementally based on the movement of an economic indicator such as inflation.

Currency Board: An arrangement whereby a currency's value is fixed in some proportion to a strong foreign currency and such an exchange rate is guaranteed by the country's foreign exchange reserves.

Current Account Balance: The portion of the **balance of payments** that includes merchandise imports and exports (known as the **balance of trade**) plus imports and exports of services.

Debt Relief: Partial or full forgiveness of debts, offered to impoverished countries by lenders, usually after it becomes clear that continued payment on such debt is likely to ruin the country's economy.

Debt Service: Payment of interest on a loan or other debt. Debt servicing can be very expensive and debilitating for developing countries.

Deflation: Falling prices across an economy, expressed as a percentage per year. *See also* **Inflation.**

Dependency Ratio: The ratio of **pensioners** to the number of people employed.

Deregulation: A lessening of government restrictions on the economy.

Desertification: The progressive drying of the land.

Devaluation: An act by the government or central bank which decreases the official price of a nation's currency. When a currency is devalued, it can result in the country's exports becoming cheaper and more attractive.

Direct Tax: A tax levied directly on individuals or companies, such as income and property taxes. *See also* **Indirect Tax.**

Disposable Income: Those parts of a household income not needed for essentials such as food, healthcare, or housing costs. Disposable income may be saved, invested, or spent on non-essential goods.

Duty: A tax imposed on imported goods. *See also* **Indirect Tax.**

E-commerce: Economic activity conducted on the Internet.

Ecotourism: Tourism to natural and cultural areas which tries to minimize environmental impacts.

Embargo: A prohibition by a government against some or all trade with a foreign nation. *See also* **Sanctions.**

Emerging Market: A country with still evolving economic, social, and political structures that shows evidence of moving toward an open market system.

Emigration: To leave one's country to live elsewhere.

Enterprise Entry: The creation of new, predominantly small and medium size enterprises.

Enterprise Exit: The removal of businesses from an economy, either through bankruptcy or downsizing.

Equity: The value of all the shares in a company.

Estate Tax: A tax on inherited property and wealth.

Exchange Rate: The rate at which one country's currency is exchanged for that of another country.

Exchange Rate Mechanism (ERM): A mechanism set up in 1978 to handle fluctuations in the **exchange rates** of various European currencies. Each currency in the ERM may fluctuate only within agreed limits against any other currency.

Exchange Rate Regime: The mode of determining the **exchange rate** between the national currency and other major foreign currencies. In a fixed exchange rate regime, a currency is fixed or "pegged" to the currency of another, usually very stable currency, such as that of the United States. In a **floating** or flexible exchange rate regime, governments allow the value of their currency to be determined by supply and demand in the foreign exchange market.

Excise Tax: A tax on the sale or use of certain products or transactions, sometimes luxury or non-essential items.

Exclusive Economic Zone (EEZ): The area extending from a country's coastline over which that country has exclusive control of its resources.

External Debt: The total amount of money in a country's economy owed to enterprises and financial institutions outside the country.

Fiduciary: Related to a trust or trusteeship.

Fiscal Policy: The programs of a national government relating to spending on goods, services, **transfer payments**, and the tax system.

Fiscal Year: Any period of 12 consecutive months for which a company or a government calculates earnings, profits, and losses.

Fixed Exchange Rate: *See* **Exchange Rate Regime.**

Floating Exchange Rate: *See* **Exchange Rate Regime.**

Floor Price: The minimum price for a good or service which normally cannot be further reduced due to political, economic, or trade considerations.

f.o.b.: Abbreviation of **Free on board**; a method of determining the value of exports or imports that considers the value of goods excluding the cost of insurance and freight charges.

Foreign Debt: *See* **External Debt.**

Foreign Direct Investment (FDI): The total value of investment by foreign entities in a country, usually expressed on an annual or cumulative basis.

Foreign Exchange Reserves: The amount of money a country has in its treasury consisting of currency from foreign countries.

Free Market System: An economic system based on little government intervention and the freedom of private association and control of goods. *See also* **Capitalism.**

Free Trade Zone: Also called **Free Zone.** An industrial area where foreign companies may import, store, and sometimes export goods without paying taxes.

Full Employment: The level of employment at which a minimal amount of involuntary unemployment exists. It is considered the maximum level of employment in an economy.

Fully Convertible Currency: A currency that can be freely traded in international foreign exchanges for units of another currency.

GDP per Capita: **Gross domestic product** divided by the number of people in a country. GDP per capita is a convenient way to measure comparative international wealth.

Gini Index: An index used to measure the extent to which the distribution of income within an economy deviates from perfectly equal distribution. A score of 0 would mean perfect equality (with everyone having the same level of wealth) and 100 would signify perfect inequality (with a few extraordinarily wealthy people and the large majority living in dire poverty).

Glut: An excess of goods in a particular market, which typically causes the price of that good to fall.

Grey Economy: Economic activity that takes place in both the formal and **informal economy,** meaning that some but not all economic activity is reported to authorities such as tax collectors.

Gross Domestic Product (GDP): The total market value of all goods and services produced inside a country in a given year, which excludes money made by citizens or companies working abroad.

Gross National Product (GNP): The total market value of all goods and services produced in a year by a nation, including those goods produced by citizens or companies working abroad.

Guarantor: An institution or individual that guarantees to pay the debts of another institution or individual in the case of bankruptcy.

Guest Worker: Persons from a foreign country who are allowed to live in a host country so long as they are employed. Many guest workers send **remittances** to their native country.

Hard Currency: Money that can be exchanged on the foreign market and is stable enough to purchase goods from other countries.

Hawking: Selling wares, often pirated goods, in the **informal sector.**

Holding Company: A company that owns or controls several other companies.

Immigration: To move into a country that is not one's native country.

Import Substitution: A policy which calls for the local production of goods that have traditionally been imported. The goal of import substitution is to lessen a country's dependence on foreign suppliers.

Income Tax: A **direct tax** on an individual's earned income.

Indirect Tax: A tax which is not paid directly, but is passed on as part of the cost of an item or service. For instance, **tariffs** and **value-added taxes** are passed on to the consumer and included in the final price of the product. *See also* **Direct Tax.**

Inflation: A persistent increase in the average price of goods in an economy, usually accompanied by declining purchasing power of the national currency.

Inflation Rate: The rate at which prices rise from one period to the next.

Informal Sector: Also called **Informal Economy**. The part of an economy that lies outside government regulations and tax systems. It usually consists of small-scale and usually labor-intensive activities; it often includes illegal activities. *See also* **Black Market.**

Infrastructure: The system of public facilities, services, and resources in a country, including roads, railways, airports, power generation, and communication systems.

Intermediate Good: A good used as an ingredient or component in the production of other goods. For instance, wood pulp is used to produce paper.

Internally Displaced Person: A person fleeing danger (such as war or persecution) who has not crossed international boundaries. Those who relocate to another country are called "refugees."

Joint Sector: An economic sector in which private enterprise and the government invest jointly.

Joint Venture: A special economic initiative or company formed by a foreign firm and a domestic company, usually in a developing state. The domestic partner often holds a majority interest, thus allowing the host country to control the amount and kind of foreign economic activity. Can also be a simple joint operation by two or more companies.

Labor Force: Also called **Workforce**. The total number of people employed in a country plus the number of people unemployed and looking for a job.

Labor Mobility: The ability and readiness of workers to move to regions or sectors of higher growth within a country or economy.

Levy: A tax based on the assessed value of personal property and/or income.

Liberal Economy: An economy in which markets operate with minimal government interference and in which individual choice and private ownership are the guiding forces.

Liberalization: The opening of an economy to free competition and a self-regulating market, with minimal government-imposed regulations or limitations.

Liquidity: Generally, the amount of money on hand. When related to government, it refers to the amount of money in circulation.

Macroeconomics: Economic issues large enough to impact the nation as a whole.

Market Capitalization: The total market value of a company, expressed by multiplying the value of a company's outstanding shares by the current price of the stock.

Marxism: A set of economic and political theories based on the work of 19th century theorists Karl Marx and Friedrich Engels that holds that human history is a struggle between classes, especially those who own property and those who do not (the workers). Marxism provided the theoretical basis for the economic systems of modern **communism** and **socialism.**

Microcredit: The lending of small amounts of startup capital to the very poor as a way of helping them out of poverty. The World Bank and other aid agencies often make mircrocredit loans to small-scale entrepreneurs in the developing world.

Monetary Policy: A government policy designed to regulate the money supply and interest rates in an economy. These policies are usually determined by the central bank or treasury in order to react to or to anticipate inflationary trends and other factors that affect an economy. They are said to be "tight" when interest rates are raised and other measures are implemented in an effort to control inflation and stabilize currency values.

Monetized Economy: An economy based on money as opposed to barter.

Money Laundering: A method used by criminal organizations to hide income gained from illicit activities, such as drug smuggling, by manipulating banks to provide a legitimate explanation for the source of money.

Monopoly: A company or corporation that has exclusive control over the distribution and availability of a product or service.

Multinational Corporation (MNC): A corporation which has economic ties to or operations in two or more countries.

National Debt: The amount of money owed to lenders by a government. The debt occurs when a government spends more each year than it has raised through taxes. Thus, to spend more than it has, the government must borrow money from banks or through the issuance of bonds.

Nationalization: The movement of privately-owned (and usually foreign-owned) companies into government ownership. Companies have often been nationalized by the developing countries whose government argued that the foreign firms involved did not pay their fair share of the profits to the host country and unfairly exploited it in other ways.

Nomenklatura: The elite members of the Communist Party in communist nations, who were often given privileges not extended to ordinary citizens.

Nomenklatura Privatization: A system of **privatization** in communist nations that openly or covertly transferred ownership of state assets to the **nomenklatura.**

Non-performing Loan: A delinquent loan or one in danger of going into default.

Offshore Banking: Banking operations that offer financial services to people and companies from other countries, usually with associated tax benefits. Offshore banking operations are often suspected as a cover for **money laundering** or other illegal financial activities.

Overheated Economy: An economy that is growing at a very high annual rate, which leads to low interest rates, a high borrowing rate, and an abundance of money in the economy—all of which can lead to **inflation.**

Parastatal: A partly or wholly government-owned enterprise.

Participation Rate: The ratio between the labor force and the total population, which indicates how many people are either working or actively seeking work.

Pensioner: A retired person who lives off a government pension.

Price Control: Artificial limitation on the prices of goods set by the government, usually in a **centrally-planned economy.**

Price Index: An index that shows how the average price of a commodity or bundle of goods has changed over a period of time, usually by comparing their value in constant dollars.

Primary Commodity: A commodity, such as a particular crop or mineral, which is a natural rather than manufactured resource.

Private Sector: The part of an economy that is not directly controlled by the government, including businesses and households.

Privatization: The transition of a company or companies from state ownership or control to private ownership. Privatization often takes place in societies that are making a transition from a **socialist** or mixed-socialist economy to a **capitalist** economy.

Procurement: The purchase of goods or services by the government.

Progressive Taxation: An income taxation system in which tax rates rise in accordance with income levels. Thus, a person making a large salary will be taxed at a higher rate than someone who makes less money.

Proportional Representation: An electoral system whereby the number of legislative seats allocated to a particular political party is decided in proportion to the number of votes that party won in an election.

Protectionist Policy: A government policy used to protect local producers from competition from imported foreign goods. Countries may erect various trade barriers such as **tariffs** or quotas in an effort to protect domestic firms or products.

Public Sector: The part of the economy that is owned and operated by the government.

Purchasing Power Parity (PPP): The purchasing power parity method attempts to determine that relative purchasing power of different currencies over equivalent goods and services. For example, if it costs someone in the United States US$300 to buy a month's worth of groceries, but it costs someone in Ghana only US$100 to buy the same amount of groceries, then the person in Ghana can purchase three times as much for the same amount of money. This means that though the average citizen of Ghana may earn less money than the average citizen of the United States, that money buys more because goods and services cost less in Ghana. The PPP calculation attempts to account for these differences in prices and is used to calculate **GDP** and **GDP per capita** figures that are comparable across nations. Note: GDP figured at purchasing power parity may be three or more times as large as GDP figured at **exchange rate** parity.

Pyramid Scheme: Fraudulent investment strategy involving a series of buying and selling transactions that generate a paper profit, which, in turn, is used to buy more stocks. They were prevalent in Eastern Europe following the fall of the Soviet Union, and preyed on the average citizen's lack of understanding of **free-market** investment transactions.

Real GDP: The **gross domestic product** of a country expressed in constant prices which are determined by a baseline year. Real GDP thus ignores the effects of inflation and deflation and allows for comparisons over time.

Real Wage: Income measured in constant dollars, and thus corrected to account for the effects of inflation.

Recession: A period of negative growth in an economy, usually defined as two consecutive quarters of negative **GDP** growth. A recession is characterized by factors such as low consumer spending, low output, and high unemployment.

Re-export: An imported good that does not undergo any changes (e.g., not turned into a new product) before being exported.

Relative Income Poverty: This is a measure of the overall equality in income among employed workers. Relative income poverty is high when a high percentage of the sum of total income is concentrated in the hands of a small percentage of the working population, and it is low when income is more equally spread among all workers.

Remittance: Money that is sent back to people, usually relatives, living in the home country of a national working abroad.

Repatriation: Taking money out of a foreign country in which it had been invested and reinvesting it in the country where it originated.

Reserve Ratio: The percentage of a bank's assets in reserve against the possibility of customers withdrawing their deposited funds. Some governments impose a minimum percentage, usually enforced by a central bank in proportion to the total amount of currency in circulation.

Restructuring: A catch-all phrase for turning around a company, involving cutting costs, restoring finances, and improving products.

Retail: The sale of goods and services to individuals in small amounts.

Sanction: A penalty, often in the form of a trade restriction, placed on one country by one or several other countries as a penalty for an action by the country under sanctions. Sanctions are designed to force the country experiencing them to change a policy, such as its human rights practices.

Shadow Economy: Economic interactions that are invisible to standard accounting and taxing procedures. See **Informal Economy.**

Sharecropper: A farmer who works someone else's land in exchange for a share of the crops they produce.

Smallholder: A farmer who has only a very small farm or plot of land.

Social Security Tax: A **direct tax** levied partly on the worker and partly on the employer in order to provide funds for a nation's **social welfare system.**

Social Welfare System: A set of government programs that provides for the needs of the unemployed, aged, disabled, or other groups deemed in need of government assistance.

Socialism: An economic system in which means of production and distribution are owned by the community, and profits are shared among the community. Countries with socialist economies put a premium on centralized control over an economy rather than allowing market forces to operate, and tend to have a relatively equal distribution of income.

Solvency: Financial stability.

Statist Economic Policy: A policy in **capitalist** or quasi-capitalist countries that favor state control or guidance of companies or sectors of the economy that are thought to be vital.

Strategic Industry: An industry considered extremely important to the well being of a country.

Structural Adjustment Program (SAP): A set of economic programs and policies aimed at stabilizing the overall structure of a troubled economy. Structural adjustment programs are often required by international lending agencies such as the World Bank and the International Monetary Fund. These programs often involve devaluing the currency, reducing government spending, and increasing exports.

Structural Unemployment: Unemployment caused by a mismatch between the needs of employers and the skills and training of the labor force.

Subsidy: A payment made by a government to an individual or company that produces a specific good or commodity. Some countries subsidize the production of certain agricultural crops, while others may subsidize mass transit or public art.

Subsistence Farming: Farming which generates only enough produce to feed the farmer's family, with little or nothing left over to sell.

Tariff: An **indirect tax** that is applied to an imported product or class of products.

Tax Haven: A place where investors shield their money from the national taxes of their own country. *See also* **Offshore Banking.**

Tax Holiday: A period of time in which businesses or investors enjoy exemptions from paying taxes. Tax holidays are offered as a lure to investment or business development.

Technocrat: Government official who is expert in specialized—usually technological—areas.

Trade Deficit: *See* **Balance of Trade.**

Trade Surplus: *See* **Balance of Trade.**

Transfer Payment: Cash paid directly to individuals by a government, usually as part of a **social welfare system.**

Transfer Pricing: A method used by foreign firms to overprice their overseas costs and thereby reduce their local tax liabilities.

Treasury Bill: Also called a **T-bill**. A guaranteed government investment bond sold to the public. They usually reach maturity after short periods, for example, three months or six months.

Trickle Down: An economic theory that contends that tax relief and other governmental incentives should be given primarily to the highest income earners in a society, on the assumption that their increased economic investment and other activity will provide benefits that "trickle down" to the lower- and middle-income wage-earners.

Turnover: The measure of trade activity in terms of the aggregated prices of all goods and services sold in the country during a year.

Two-tier Economy: An economy where skilled or educated workers enjoy a high standard of living, but unskilled workers are trapped in poverty.

Underemployment: A situation in which people are not reaching their economic potential because they are employed in low-paying or part-time jobs. For example, an engineer who is working in a fast food restaurant would be said to be experiencing underemployment.

Underground Economy: Economic transactions that are not reported to government, and therefore not taxable. **Informal sectors** and **black markets** are examples of underground economic activity.

Unicameral: A legislative body consisting of a single house or chamber.

United Nations Development Program (UNDP): The United Nations' principal provider of development advice, advocacy, and grant support.

Value Added: The increase in the value of a good at each stage in the production process. When a company adds value to its products it is able to gain a higher price for them, but it may be liable for a **value-added tax.**

Value-added Tax (VAT): A tax levied on the amount of **value added** to a total product at each stage of its manufacture.

Vertical Integration: Control over all stages of the production and distribution of a certain product. For example, if one company owns the mines, the steel plant, the transportation network, the factories, and the dealerships involved in making and selling automobiles, it is vertically integrated.

Voucher Privatization: A system for selling off state-owned companies in which citizens are given "vouchers" which they may invest in such companies. This system was devised to allow all citizens the opportunity to invest in formerly state-owned businesses; however, in practice many citizens invest their vouchers in voucher funds, which are professionally managed investment groups who amass vouchers in order to exert control over the direction of companies.

Welfare State: A government that assumes the responsibility for the well-being of its citizens by providing institutions and organizations that contribute to their care. *See also* **Social Welfare System.**

Workforce: *See* **Labor Force.**

INDEX

Page numbers appearing in boldface indicate major treatment of entries. A page number accompanied by an italicized "t" indicates that there is a table on that page, while a page number accompanied by an italicized "f" indicates there is a figure on that page.

A

B

D

E

G

H

I

M

N

O

U

X

Y

Z